THE NATION'S NEWSPAPER

USA TODAY

NO. 1 IN THE USA

Baseball Weekly

1996 Almanac

The All-In-One Baseball Resource

EDITED BY:

Editor / Baseball Weekly, Paul White

With contributions from the staffs of Baseball Weekly
and USA TODAY Sports

A Balliett & Fitzgerald Book

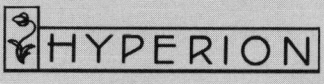

HYPERION

New York

ISBN 0-7868-8113-5

FIFTH EDITION
10 9 8 7 6 5 4 3 2 1

Balliett & Fitzgerald, Inc.
Project editor: Liz Barrett
Managing editor: Duncan Bock
Production editor: Sue Canavan
Copyeditor: John Shostrom
Proofreaders: Jerilyn Famighetti, Roger Mooney
Page artist: Iain McDonald
Assistant editor: Maria Fernandez
Editorial assistant: Erin Dowding

Acknowledgments
Our continued thanks to Managing Editor/Sports at USA TODAY, Gene
Policinski, without whom this book would not be possible.
We are also grateful to Susan Bokern and Betty George at Gannett New Media for
their support. Also, much appreciation to everyone at Hyperion, especially Bob Miller,
Leslie Wells, and Jennifer Lang.

Major league statistics provided by Elias Sports Bureau.
Minor league statistics provided by Howe SportsData International.
Record book and historical statistics provided by Pete Palmer.
Disabled list information provided by The Baseball Workshop.
Photographs of Major League Baseball are used with the permission of
Major League Baseball.

Contents

*L*eading off

▶ We had the Braves, the Indians and Cal

▶ Free agents

▶ Television deals and *Game of the Week*

▶ *and more . . .*

USA SNAPSHOTS®

A look at statistics that shape the sports world

Still in the dugout

1995 major league managers with most years as a manager:

Years	Manager (teams)
	Sparky Anderson (Tigers, Reds)
	Tommy Lasorda (Dodgers)
	Tony LaRussa (A's, White Sox)

Source: Baseball Register   By Scott Boeck and Julie Stacey, USA TODAY

We had the Braves, the Indians & Cal

The off-season we never got a year ago—the real off-season of speculation, anticipation and hot-stove debates—officially began Nov. 13 with the deadline for free-agent filings. The shopping list was back.

It had 137 names. That number would roughly double by mid-December as teams decided not to exercise options on players who could not choose to enter their own market.

Most fans and teams were looking longingly at names like Roberto Alomar, Craig Biggio, Jack McDowell and Fred McGriff. Where would those guys end up? What teams would they bring more talent and more hope to?

But who would take the time to consider Kevin Bass and Frank Viola, Howard Johnson and Rob Dibble? Hardly Hall of Famers, but guys who have had some pretty decent years. Hey, you want Hall of Fame? Stick Dave Winfield on the list.

Take a longer look at the free agents every year. It could be your last chance to say good-bye to some familiar names. It happens more and more these days. No retirement announcements. No warm sendoffs. Simply, no takers.

For me, this is an anniversary of sorts, 10 winters since these disappearances really sunk in. That's when Rod Carew came off a 443 at-bat, .280 season and was next seen at his Cooperstown induction. The California Angels had to make room for a kid named Wally Joyner that winter. Tough to argue with what that kid did: He drove in 100 runs and, at .290, was the Angels' only every-day player to top Carew's 1985 average.

Sometimes we get lucky. I remember watching Jim Palmer pitch rather ineffectively in relief in May '84 against Oakland. Certainly it wasn't vintage Palmer, but when he retired before the week was out, there was the feeling of a proper farewell.

During 1995, Dave Stewart and Kirk Gibson got the opportunity to say farewell on their terms during the season. They admitted the years and the game had done the inevitable, overtaken them. It was time to step aside gracefully.

For us fans, these were at least defining moments when we could think back on the special memories they had given us:
▶Stewart's glare in oh-so-many playoff games
▶Gibson's movie-script home run to end a World Series game
▶Even John Kruk slapped one last line drive in '95 before heading for the hills, literally. He singled one Sunday afternoon in Baltimore, asked for the ball as a souvenir and, after the game, got in his truck and went home to West Virginia.

But does anybody remember the last hit for Lonnie Smith, Tom Brunansky, Kevin McReynolds or Sid Bream? They were on that free-agent list a year ago. We never saw them during the '95 season.

Nevertheless, 1995 was good, if for no other reason than that Atlanta finally got its World Series victory, Cleveland got back to a World Series and, of course, there was Cal. Even before that historic September night when he passed Lou Gehrig's "unbreakable" record, the Baltimore shortstop named Ripken was simply Cal.

What better tribute can there be? First-name basis with the world. It's special. It's rare. The Babe. Willie. The Mick. Even a guy with another unbreakable record had to settle for being Joe D.

How does that happen? It's performance, for sure. But it's also persona.

As the 1995 season ended, we knew Albert and Randy and Edgar and Hideo. Their names might not transcend the ages but, for now, they're dominating peformers. Yet the most dominant player of the decade, with four Cy Young Awards, hadn't graduated from Maddux to Greg.

Maybe it's not just about bringing us good things. As the months rolled on without a labor agreement, a sign of the times was that we had to admit we were just as familiar with Bud.

—by Paul White, editor

Help wanted: 1996 free agent list

American League

▶**Baltimore Orioles (6):** Harold Baines, dh; Kevin Bass, of; Kevin Brown, rhp; Mark Eichhorn, rhp; Doug Jones, rhp; Jamie Moyer, lhp.

▶**Boston Red Sox (7):** Rick Aguilera, rhp; Jose Canseco, of; Erik Hanson, rhp; Mike Macfarlane, c; Mike Maddux, rhp; Willie McGee, of; Zane Smith, lhp.

▶**California Angels (13):** Jim Abbott, lhp; Mike Aldrete, 1b; Mike Bielecki, rhp; Chuck Finley, lhp; Dave Gallagher, of; Rene Gonzales, 3b; John Habyan, rhp; Greg Myers, c; Spike Owen, ss; Bob Patterson, lhp; Tony Phillips, of; Scott Sanderson, rhp; Dick Schofield, ss.

▶**Chicago White Sox (3):** Lance Johnson, of; Dave Martinez, of; Dave Righetti, lhp.

▶**Cleveland Indians (8):** Alvaro Espinoza, ss; John Farrell, rhp; Orel Hershiser, rhp; Ken Hill, rhp; Eddie Murray, 1b; Tony Pena, c; Bill Ripken, 2b; Dave Winfield, of.

▶**Detroit (3):** Scott Fletcher, 2b; Franklin Stubbs, 1b; Lou Whitaker, 2b.

▶**Kansas City (8):** Tom Browning, lhp; Gary Gaetti, 3b; Greg Gagne, ss; Tom Gordon, rhp; Mark Gubicza, rhp; Jeff Montgomery, rhp; Gregg Olson, rhp; Juan Samuel, 2b.

▶**Milwaukee (6):** Rob Dibble, rhp; Darryl Hamilton, of; Joe Oliver, c; Kevin Seitzer, 3b; B.J. Surhoff, of; Bill Wegman, rhp.

▶**New York Yankees (9):** Wade Boggs, 3b; David Cone, rhp; Rick Honeycutt, lhp; Steve Howe, lhp; Dion James, of; Don Mattingly, 1b; Jack McDowell, rhp; Mike Stanley, c; Randy Velarde, ss.

▶**Oakland Athletics (5):** Mike Gallego, ss; Brian Harper, inf; Rickey Henderson, of; Stan Javier, of; Steve Ontiveros, rhp.

▶**Seattle Mariners (4):** Tim Belcher, rhp; Andy Benes, rhp; Vince Coleman, of; Lee Guetterman, lhp.

▶**Texas Rangers (10):** Danny Darwin, rhp; Candy Maldonado, of; Roger McDowell, rhp; Otis Nixon, of; Mike Pagliarulo, 3b; Kenny Rogers, lhp; Jeff Russell, rhp; Mickey Tettleton, c; Bob Tewksbury, rhp; Bobby Witt, rhp.

▶**Toronto Blue Jays (7):** Roberto Alomar, 2b; Danny Cox, rhp; Al Leiter, lhp; Paul Molitor, dh; Lance Parrish, c; Duane Ward, rhp; Devon White, of.

National League

▶**Atlanta Braves (6):** Mike Devereaux, of; Fred McGriff, 1b; Charlie O'Brien, c; Alejandro Pena, rhp; Luis Polonia, of; Dwight Smith, of.

▶**Chicago Cubs (6):** Shawon Dunston, ss; Mark Grace, 1b; Howard Johnson, of; Randy Myers, lhp; Jaime Navarro, rhp; Mark Parent, c.

▶**Cincinnati Reds (6):** Mariano Duncan, 2b; Ron Gant, of; Mike Jackson, rhp; Hal Morris, 1b; Benito Santiago, c; Frank Viola, lhp.

▶**Colorado Rockies (2):** Mike Kingery, of; Walt Weiss, ss.

▶**Florida Marlins (3):** Jerry Browne, of; Andre Dawson, of; Bryan Harvey, rhp.

▶**Houston Astros (6):** Craig Biggio, 2b; Pat Borders, c; John Cangelosi, of; Mike Henneman, rhp; Dave Magadan, 3b; Milt Thompson, of.

▶**Los Angeles Dodgers (4):** Tom Candiotti, rhp; Roberto Kelly, of; Ramon Martinez, rhp; Tim Wallach, 3b.

▶**New York Mets (2):** Joe Orsulak, of; Bill Spiers, 2b.

▶**Philadelphia Phillies (4):** Jim Eisenreich, of; Sid Fernandez, lhp; Charlie Hayes, 3b; Andy Van Slyke, of.

▶**Pittsburgh Pirates (1):** Don Slaught, c.

▶**St. Louis Cardinals (4):** Tom Henke, rhp; Mike Morgan, rhp; Jeff Parrett, rhp; Jose Oquendo, 2b.

▶**San Diego Padres (2):** Jody Reed, 2b; Fernando Valenzuela, lhp.

▶**San Francisco Giants (3):** Terry Mulholland, lhp; Jeff Reed, c; Trevor Wilson, lhp.

1996 AL managers

Baltimore, Davey Johnson; Boston, Kevin Kennedy; California, Marcel Lachemann; Chicago, Terry Bevington; Cleveland, Mike Hargrove; Detroit, Buddy Bell; Kansas City, Bob Boone; Milwaukee, Phil Garner; Minnesota, Tom Kelly; New York, Joe Torre; Oakland, Art Howe; Seattle, Lou Piniella; Texas, Johnny Oates; Toronto, Cito Gaston.

1996 NL managers

Atlanta, Bobby Cox; Chicago, Jim Riggleman; Cincinnati, Ray Knight; Colorado, Don Baylor; Florida, Rene Lachemann; Houston, Terry Collins; Los Angeles, Tommy Lasorda; Montreal, Felipe Alou; New York, Dallas Green; Philadelphia, Jim Fregosi; Pittsburgh, Jim Leyland; St. Louis, Tony LaRussa; San Diego, Bruce Bochy; San Francisco, Dusty Baker.

New TV deal to air *Game of the Week*, all playoffs

After the worst postseason television coverage in history, Major League Baseball announced a new five-year, $1.7 billion national TV deal that promises to air all playoff games coast-to-coast and to bring back the traditional Saturday-afternoon *Game of the Week* after a self-imposed two-year exile.

The deal involves the Fox Network, NBC, ESPN, and Prime Liberty Media Cable. Highlights:

▶Fox will air the World Series in 1996, 1998 and 2000, as well as the All-Star Game in 1997 and 1999. Fox will also telecast one of the League Championship Series (second round) games each year. Four of the Division Series (first round) games will be in prime time, the other on Saturday afternoon. Fox will also resurrect the *Game of the Week* on Saturday afternoons, although that package will not start until Memorial Day 1996. The *Game of the Week* package will consist of four games each Saturday, to be televised regionally. The *Game of the Week* will be preceded by an hour-long pregame show, including a half-hour "dedicated to children," according to acting commissioner Bud Selig.

▶NBC will broadcast the World Series in 1997 and 1999, as well as the All-Star Game in 1996, 1998 and 2000. NBC also gets the other League Championship Series in its entirety, as well as three prime-time Division Series games each year. The two League Championship Series will alternate between Fox and NBC each year.

▶ESPN will extend its regular-season package of Wednesday- and Sunday-night baseball through the year 2000 and will add all the Division Series games not shown on Fox or NBC. It's the first time postseason games will be broadcast on cable. ESPN's playoff games will be in the afternoon and the late-night time slots. ESPN will also add a Sunday-night game on the next-to-last week of the season and will continue to air its daily *Baseball Tonight* show. Additionally, ESPN will air the annual Hall of Fame induction ceremony and other specials.

▶Prime Liberty will come aboard in 1997, when it will air regular-season games two nights per week on Monday, Tuesday, Thursday or Friday. The games will be shown on a nonexclusive basis, which means teams may telecast their own games locally.

Owners were cautious, salaries dropped

Roberto Alomar took the biggest swing of his splendid career—a request to the Yankees for a record $25 million, three-year deal. You can still hear the whoooosh as his uppercut missed contact.

Once the undisputed crown jewel of this free-agent class, Alomar seemed to initially price himself too high, unwittingly creating a wider market for another all-star second baseman and free agent, Craig Biggio.

Yes, it was the return after a one-year hiatus of the annual winter rite of free agency.

Teams coast to coast coveted Alomar or Biggio but no one fell over themselves to hand either one of them a blank check.

Pat Gillick, the new Baltimore general manager, says Alomar's request to him—a "bargain" $23 million— left him speechless.

To see how much baseball has changed in two years, return to November 1993, when free agent Will Clark was on sale. The cross-country marketing of Clark had all the trappings of a college-recruit tour.

In Dallas, TV cameras were waiting at the airport. In Baltimore, a uniform with his name was hanging in a locker and a mock lineup posted on the Camden Yards scoreboard included his name—a couple of tricks right out of the late Jim Valvano's playbook. There were dinners in four-star restaurants at every stop.

Clark eventually signed with the Texas Rangers for $30 million over five years.

Several days later, Rafael Palmeiro—the man he dislodged in Texas—signed a similar five-year, $30.35 million deal with Baltimore.

There was no such frivolity this offseason. With a record crop of players available, teams could pick and choose.

Unlike last April, when the sudden end of the players' strike forced teams to assemble their personnel quickly, the players waited this time.

"The pace of the free-agent market has gotten slower," says agent Jeff Moorad, who helped Clark get that windfall two years ago. "Teams spend more time evaluating their options and, as a result, it becomes harder to gauge where the market will end up."

But Alomar's initial demands created a torrent of criticism directed at one of the game's brightest stars.

"For the money he's talking, you expect more than what he puts on the field," Blue Jays general manager Gord Ash says. "You expect him to take on a leadership role. He's got to realize that he's a veteran player now."

Did Alomar show that leadership last year?

"Absolutely not," Ash says.

Alomar lost credibility when he sat out the final three games of the 1995 season against the Yankees. Some critics accused him of sitting out to preserve a .300 batting average rather than to protect a sore lower back.

Teams were signing players but dire predictions of a growing dichotomy between rich and poor clubs were coming true.

Here's how the 1995 playoff teams approached the offseason:

▶**Atlanta:** The world champions were set for '96, with young players and Fred McGriff, Marquis Grissom as the core. The Braves didn't keep their bench intact because buying one in the crowded marketplace was cheaper.

▶**Cleveland:** The guys who got them there will be back in '96. Charles Nagy, Orel Hershiser, Eddie Murray, Tony Pena and Alvaro Espinoza were re-signed and the Indians added .300-hitting Julio Franco. Only Ken Hill's starting pitching slot was vacated.

The American League champions, with every seat at Jacobs Field for 1996 sold out before Christmas (read: $45 million in the bank) spent about $34 million in three days to line up those players.

▶**Cincinnati:** Keeping Hal Morris softened the sting of the payroll cuts. But Ron Gant was out of the Reds' price range and Benito Santiago couldn't be kept. The available money was needed to maintain some semblance of the strong pitching staff.

Morris took a pay cut of more than 50% next season to remain with the Reds. "My loyalties are to Cincinnati and (manager) Ray Knight," he said after signing a two-year, $5 million deal. "The money was never a driving force behind anything."

▶**Seattle:** The magic might have been used up in '95. Hard work in the front office will be key to '96. Subtracted were Mike Blowers, Tino Martinez, Andy Benes, Tim Belcher and Vince Coleman. The Martinez trade brought budding stars Sterling Hitchcock and Russ Davis.

▶**Boston:** The Red Sox kept their punch by re-signing DH Jose Canseco for two years but were forced to reassess the bullpen situation when Rick Aguilera left.

The deal appeared to be good for both sides—the Sox needed their DH back and Canseco was limited in his options.

The deal includes an option for a third year, has a $9 million guarantee and could max out at about $15 million.

Some of the incentives are based on the number of times the DH plays in the field, something the Sox have talked about.

"They gave me the terms of the contract and I was extremely happy with it," said Canseco, who made $5.1 million in 1995 and took a cut in guaranteed pay. "It turned out great. Those were the numbers I was working for. One of the incentives—games played—will be easy for me to get. That would put me close to last year's salary."

▶**Colorado:** The Rockies opted to keep Dante Bichette's bat and Walt Weiss' leadership but had to deal with losing catcher Joe Girardi to the Yankees.

▶**New York Yankees:** Tino Martinez and Joe Girardi will have their hands full trying to replace Don Mattingly and Mike Stanley. New GM Bob Watson had his hands full, too ... with money like he never saw during his days with the Astros.

He paid $20.25 million for just one guy, locking up first baseman Tino Martinez for five years after getting him in a trade with Seattle. That was two days after the Yankees re-signed third-baseman Wade Boggs, 37, to a two-year, $4 million contract. That enabled them to include prospect Russ Davis in the Martinez deal.

They also signed utility man Mariano Duncan to fill the vacancy created when Randy Velarde signed with California.

▶**Los Angeles:** The Dodgers' major moves were re-signing pitcher Ramon Martinez and getting a new left side of the infield in Greg Gagne and Mike Blowers.

Meanwhile, other teams were trying to catch up.

The Florida Marlins spent nearly $10 million on outfielder Devon White and another $1.275 million on outfielder Joe Orsulak before turning their attention to pitching.

Things bottomed out last season for the Minnesota Twins, who at 56-88 tied Toronto for the worst record in baseball. Yet they signed free agent Paul Molitor to a $2 million, one-year contract, then regained the services of Rick Aguilera for $9 million over three years.

No one reflects the new baseball economics better than Lance Johnson.

At 32, the fleet-footed outfielder had his best season in 1995 with the Chicago White Sox, leading the American League with 186 hits and compiling career highs in home runs (10) and RBI (57). He had 12 triples and 40 stolen bases while earning $2.67 million.

He was replaced by slick-fielding, lighter-hitting but cheaper Darren Lewis.

"I know what the owner has lost in the last two years," White Sox GM Ron Schuelker said. "If I give it all to Lance, we're not a better ballclub. We had salary slots and I knew exactly where he fit in."

The average major league salary went down last season for the first time in 30 years. The median salary has dropped nearly one-third in just two years. That trend will probably continue.

—by Paul White

Around the league

▶ **1995 highlights and lowlights**

▶ **AL and NL award winners**

▶ **Hall of Fame inductees**

▶ *and more . . .*

USA SNAPSHOTS®

A look at statistics that shape the sports world

Baseball's haves, have nots

Metro-area population per seat in their ballparks:

AMERICAN LEAGUE

Most		Fewest	

342.4 — New York Yankees

233.0 — California Angels

30.6 — Milwaukee Brewers

39.8 — Kansas City Royals

Source: Baseball Weekly Almanac, Statistical Abstract of the U.S.

By Scott Boeck and Gary Visgaitis, USA TODAY

Ripken, Murray bring magic back to baseball

June 30: Eddie Murray gets his 3,000th hit

Eddie Murray's teammates weren't going to let the moment pass without a little celebration. As soon as the ball skidded through the hole between first and second—Murray's 3,000th career hit—the Indians spilled onto the field. The first one there was the only other active player with 3,000 hits—Dave Winfield. He gave Murray a high five before the rest of the Indians piled on. Murray and Winfield are the first teammates with 3,000 hits since Ty Cobb, Tris Speaker and Eddie Collins all played for the 1928 Philadelphia Athletics. Murray joined Pete Rose, the career hit leader with 4,256, as switch-hitters to get 3,000. Murray ranked his 3,000th hit as the second-biggest accomplishment of his 18-year career. The biggest came in 1987 when he hit home runs from both sides of the plate on consecutive days against Chicago in old Comiskey Park.

July 14: Dodgers' Ramon Martinez throws no-hitter

Ramon Martinez's eyes filled with tears the moment the ball left Quilvio Veras's bat July 14. He squinted, watched it drop softly into left fielder Roberto Kelly's glove, and turned around, waiting for catcher Mike Piazza to reach the mound. He jumped into Piazza's arms to celebrate the most glorious night of his baseball career—the 27-year-old Dodger became the only pitcher of 1995 to throw a no-hitter, shutting out the Florida Marlins 7-0 and coming within one batter of pitching a perfect game.

"I have pride and I wanted to let people know that I can still pitch," said Martinez. "I think people had forgotten about me."

When Cal Ripken broke Lou Gehrig's consecutive-game record, fans fell in love with baseball again.

By Russell Beeker, Baseball Weekly

Sept. 6: Cal Ripken made magic as well as history

Three-quarters of a century ago, a Baltimore native—Babe Ruth—saved baseball after one of its darkest hours, the Black Sox scandal. It was only fitting that another Baltimore legend—Cal Ripken Jr.—should not only shatter Ruth's teammate Lou Gehrig's record, but also engender a sorely needed outpouring of affection for the game when it was at its lowest ebb in years. President Clinton had predicted that Ripken's feat would "do a lot to help America fall in love with baseball."

Cal Ripken played his 2,131st consecutive game Sept. 6 before a jubilant home crowd (46,272) at Camden Yards. It was a moment captured on television and shared with some of baseball's greatest legends, including Gehrig's teammate Joe DiMaggio, but for Ripken, the central focus was his family. Just after the game became official in the fifth inning, he walked to the stands and literally gave the shirt off his back, along with his cap, to his two children.

When DiMaggio told Ripken he was sure that, "wherever Lou Gehrig is today, he's tipping his hat to you," Ripken responded with typical propriety: "I'm truly humbled to have our names mentioned in the same breath."

1995 Hall of Fame inductees

Mike Schmidt made an emotional speech to the huge crowd at Cooperstown when he was inducted to the Hall of Fame.

Schmidt, Ashburn: From Philly to Fame

In his 18 big-league seasons, Mike Schmidt's only uniform was that of the Philadelphia Phillies. Richie Ashburn spent 12 of 15 seasons with Philadelphia and broadcast Phillies' games for 33 years. Now they're both in Cooperstown together—in the Hall of Fame.

Schmidt is considered by many to be the game's finest third baseman ever. He won 10 Gold Gloves, eight home run titles, four RBI titles and three National League MVP awards. His mantle also includes awards for World Series MVP and player of the decade.

Ashburn was the prototypical leadoff man, leading the league in on-base percentage four times, hits three times and batting average two times. He played center field during the Golden Age at his position and held his own—except in the power categories—against counterparts

named Willie, Mickey and the Duke.

Both played their hearts out for the Phillies, but Schmidt was openly critical of fans and the club at various points in his career, which didn't endear him to either group. He made peace with the fans at his induction ceremony, but he chastised players and owners for continuing to alienate their national audience. He also pushed for the reinstatement of his pal, Pete Rose, so he might join Schmidt in the hallowed shrine.

"I join millions of baseball fans around the country in hoping that some day soon, some day real soon, Pete will be standing right here," said Schmidt, who wore a No. 14 lapel pin to honor his former teammate.

That drew a tremendous roar from the record throng—estimated between 25,000 and 28,000.

"See," Schmidt deadpanned, "the Philadelphia fans and I can agree on something."

Other inductees

▶**Leon Day:** Former Negro leagues superstar who died in Baltimore six days after his March 7 election. The Baltimore Orioles donated $3,000 to send his family and friends to Cooperstown. He was a pitcher, outfielder and second baseman for the Newark Eagles. He is the first Negro leagues star elected since 1987.

▶**Vic Willis:** Pitcher who compiled a 249-205 record and 2.63 ERA with Boston (NL), Pittsburgh and St. Louis (NL) between 1898 and 1910. He had 388 complete games, including 45 in 1902.

▶**William Hulbert:** National League founder and second president (1877-82). He made strides to rid the game of gambling.

▶**Bob Wolff:** Winner of the Ford C. Frick Award. He had been in broadcasting for 57 years when he was inducted.

1995: Best of the American League

By Porter Binks, USA TODAY

Lou Piniella's calmer style fired up the Mariners.

Manager of the Year: Seattle's Lou Piniella

Lou Piniella, who guided the Seattle Mariners to an American League West title and a berth in the AL Championship Series, was voted 1995 AL Manager of the Year. He was named first on nine of the 28 ballots cast by members of the Baseball Writers Association of America.

"The players deserve all the credit for getting the job done on the field, and my staff for getting them ready to play," Piniella said.

Cy Young Award winner: Seattle's Randy Johnson

After winning his first AL Cy Young Award, Randy Johnson paid tribute to his National League counterpart: "The greatest compliment I got was from Greg Maddux, saying that I was more of a pitcher [than I used to be]." Johnson's 100-mph fastball, along with his slider, changeup and improved control were so wicked that batters hit a league-low .201 against him. Lefties hit just .129. He ended 13 Seattle losing streaks and gave up just 65 walks while setting a major league record by averaging 12.35 strikeouts per nine innings. The old record: Nolan Ryan's 11.48 with Houston in '87.

Most Valuable Player: Boston's Mo Vaughn

Mo Vaughn, who hit .300 with 39 home runs and 126 RBI to lead the Red Sox to a division title, was voted AL Most Valuable Player in one of the closest votes in the history of the award. Vaughn, a personable, popular player, edged out Cleveland's Albert Belle (first player ever to hit 50 home runs and 50 doubles in a season) by one first-place vote and eight points. Belle was at odds with reporters, many of whom vote for the award. Cleveland manager Mike Hargrove said he hoped politics had nothing to do with it, emphasizing that both players were deserving. Vaughn has led the Red Sox in homers, RBI, extra-base hits and intentional walks for three consecutive seasons.

By Russell Beeker, USA TODAY

Mo Vaughn has led the Red Sox in home runs, RBI, extra-base hits and intentional walks for three years.

Rookie of the Year: Twins' Marty Cordova

Minnesota's Marty Cordova was voted American League's Rookie of the Year He hit .277 with 24 home runs, 84 RBI and 20 steals for the Twins. He said the steals were easier than the home runs, because he gave himself a little help by borrowing Kirby Puckett's bats all season.

1995: Best of the National League

Manager of the Year: Colorado's Don Baylor

Three years ago, Don Baylor was a managerial candidate with no managerial experience. Now, he is National League Manager of the Year. After guiding the Rockies to the playoffs in only their third season, he said being the club's first and only manager has worked to his advantage: "I wanted to set [my] own mark." The Rockies finished 77-67 to win the NL wild-card spot by one game over the Houston Astros, marking the quickest rise to the playoffs by an expansion team.

Barry Larkin was the Reds' spark plug, leading the team both on and off the field.

Most Valuable Player: Cincinnati's Barry Larkin

Barry Larkin became the first shortstop in 33 years to be voted National League Most Valuable Player. He hit .319 with 15 home runs, 66 RBI, 51 stolen bases and stellar defense, but it was his role as team leader that helped guide the Reds to a division title. He edged out Colorado's Dante Bichette (.340, 40 homers, 128 RBI) and Atlanta's Greg Maddux (19-2, 1.63 ERA) in the MVP voting by 30 and 32 votes, respectively.

Don Baylor never allowed the Rockies to be just another expansion team—they made the playoffs in three years.

Cy Young winner: Greg Maddux, fourth in a row

As good as he is, Greg Maddux expects he can be better: "There's always room for improvement," he said after becoming the first pitcher in history to win four consecutive Cy Young awards. "I do think I can become a better pitcher—my breaking pitches might get better one day, who knows?" He led the NL at 19-2 with a 1.63 ERA and is the first pitcher since Hall of Famer Walter Johnson (1918-19) to post consecutive seasons with a sub-1.80 ERA.

Rookie of the Year: Dodgers' Hideo Nomo

Los Angeles Dodgers right-hander Hideo Nomo needs an interpreter to translate his words into English, but his pitching speaks universally. "I am very, very proud of Hideo," manager Tommy Lasorda said after Nomo was named 1995 National League Rookie of the Year. "He had a tough, tough assignment coming into a league he knew absolutely nothing about and with everybody watching him. It was a tremendous strain to accomplish what he did. I really admire him." Nomo led the NL with 236 strikeouts in 191 innings. He posted a 13-6 record and a 2.54 ERA.

Despite his legendary career, Mickey Mantle urged others not to follow in his drinking footsteps.

Mickey Mantle 1931-1995: Lifetime of a legend

▶**Oct. 20, 1931**: Born in Spavinaw, Okla.; named after Philadephia Athletics catcher Mickey Cochrane.

▶**1949 season:** Signs Class D contract with Yankees ($1,150 bonus, $140 a month).

▶**April 17, 1951:** Makes major league debut against Chicago White Sox.

▶**May 16, 1951:** Hits first Yankee Stadium HR.

▶**Oct. 5, 1951:** Spikes catch on an outfield sprinkler in the second game of the World Series; first of four knee operations.

▶**July 8, 1952:** First of 16 All-Star Games (elected, did not play).

▶**Oct. 7, 1952:** Snaps 2-2 tie in seventh World Series game against Brooklyn with sixth-inning homer; adds RBI single for 4-2 victory and World Championship.

▶**April 17, 1953:** Hits 565-foot homer against Washington Senators at Griffith Stadium.

▶**Oct. 4, 1953:** After striking out five consecutive times against the Dodgers in the World Series, hits grand slam in Game Five at Ebbets Field. Yanks win 11-7 and go on to win the world championship the next day.

▶**May 13, 1955:** Hits homer from each side of the plate in the same game—the first of 10 times he would do that.

▶**May 30, 1956:** Homer hits the facade hanging from the right-field roof in New York, misses leaving the park by only 18 inches.

▶**Oct. 8, 1956:** Makes a running, one-handed grab of Gil Hodges' line drive to left-center to preserve Don Larsen's perfect game against the Brooklyn Dodgers in Game 5 of the World Series.

▶**1956 season:** Wins Triple Crown (.353, 52 HR, 130 RBI); is unanimous choice for his first MVP Award.

1957 season: Earns second consecutive MVP (.365, 34 HR, 94 RBI).

1961 season: Hits 54 homers to finish second behind Maris, who had 61.

1962 season: Wins third MVP (.321, 30 HR, 89 RBI).

May 22, 1963: Another homer hits the facade in right field, misses leaving the park by three feet, but is still rising when it hits facade.

June 5, 1963: Fractures bone in left foot and injures left knee; misses 61 games.

Sept. 17, 1964: Gets 2,000th career hit and 450th homer.

Oct. 10, 1964: Hits leadoff homer in ninth inning of his final World Series to win Game 3 and break Babe Ruth's record for lifetime Series home runs (it was his 16th; he went on to hit two more).

April 9, 1965: Hits the first home run in the Houston Astrodome.

Sept. 18, 1965: Plays his 2,000th game (he finished with 2,401 in pinstripes).

March 1, 1969: Announces his retirement in spring training.

June 8, 1969: His No. 7 is retired on Mickey Mantle Day at Yankee Stadium.

Jan. 16, 1974: Gets elected to the Hall of Fame—seventh player to make it on his first try.

Feb. 8, 1983: Ordered by Commissioner Bowie Kuhn to sever ties with baseball for relations with casinos.

March 18, 1985: Reinstated by Commissioner Peter Ueberroth.

Jan. 6, 1994: Checks into Betty Ford Center for treatment for alcohol abuse.

June 8, 1995: Undergoes 7½-hour liver transplant for liver cancer.

Aug. 13, 1995: Mickey Mantle dies.

Quotes from The Mick

On hitting: During my 18 years I came to bat almost 10,000 times. I struck out about 1,700 times and walked maybe 1,800 times. You figure a ballplayer will average 500 at-bats a season. That means I played seven years without ever hitting the ball.

On being a Yankees executive: I'm a vice president in charge of special marketing. That means I play golf and go to cocktail parties. I'm pretty good at my job.

On owners in the '90s: When I played, the players were dumb. Now the owners are.

On his drinking: God gave me the ability to play baseball. God gave me everything. For the kids out there . . . don't be like me.

Quotes about The Mick

Casey Stengel: He was the best one-legged player I ever saw play the game.

Waite Hoyt: Everybody who roomed with Mickey said he took five years off their careers.

Bob Costas on why he carries two Mantle baseball cards in his wallet: I believe everyone should carry some type of religious artifact on his or her person at all times.

Yankees manager Buck Showalter: As Little Leaguers, we all wanted to wear No. 7. Once I got to the Yankees, No. 7 didn't seem to be available in the minor leagues.

Career highlights

Won AL Triple Crown: 1956.

AL MVP: 1956, 1957, 1962.

Led AL in home runs: 1955, 1956, 1958, 1960.

Career home runs: 536 (eighth place).

Most games played for the Yankees: 2,401.

Most at-bats for the Yankees: 8,102.

Career grand slams: 9.

Pinch-hit home runs: 7.

Three home runs in one game: May 13, 1955.

All-Star Team: 1952-1968; both games, 1959-1962.

Gold Glove: 1962.

Elected to Baseball Hall of Fame: 1974.

1995 Obituaries: Former major leaguers

Bob Allison: April 9, Rio Verde, Ariz.; Senators, Twins, 1958-70.

Stan Andrews: June 10, Bradenton, Fla.; Braves, Dodgers, Phillies, 1939-45.

Dick Bartell: Aug. 4, Alameda, Calif.; Pirates, Phillies, Giants, Cubs, Tigers, 1927-46.

Russ Bainers: Jan. 21, Hines, Ill.; Pirates, Cubs, Browns, 1936-50.

Ollie Bejma: Jan. 3, South Bend, Ind.; Browns, White Sox, 1934-39.

Gus Bell: May 7, Montgomery, Ohio; Pirates, Reds, Mets, Braves, 1950-64.

Norm Brown: May 31, Bennettsville, S.C.; Athletics, 1943-46.

Elmer Burkart: Feb. 6, Baltimore; Phillies, 1936-39.

Glenn Burke: May 30, San Leandro, Calif.; Dodgers, Athletics, 1976-79.

Bruce Campbell: June 17, unknown; White Sox, Browns, Indians, Tigers, Senators, 1930-42.

John Campbell: April 24, Daytona Beach, Fla.; Senators, 1933.

Harry Craft: Aug. 3, Conroe, Texas; Reds, 1937-42.

Tony Cuccinello: Sept. 21, Tampa; Reds, Dodgers, Braves, Giants, White Sox, 1930-45.

Peaches Davis: April 28, Duncan, Okla.; Reds, 1936-39.

Don Elston: Jan. 2, Evanston, Ill.; Cubs, Dodgers, 1953-64.

Rick Ferrell: July 27, Bloomfield Hills, Mich.; Browns, Red Sox, Senators, 1929-47.

Marc Filley: Jan. 20, Yarmouth, Maine; Senators, 1934.

Ed Gill: Oct. 10, Brockton, Mass.; Senators, 1919.

Harry Gumbert: Jan. 4, Wimberley, Texas; Giants, Cardinals, Reds, Pirates, 1935-50.

Mickey Haefner: Jan. 3, New Athens, Ill.; Senators, White Sox, Braves, 1943-50.

John Hall: Jan. 17, Midwest City, Calif.; Dodgers, 1948.

Herb Hippauf: July 17, Santa Clara, Calif.; Braves, 1966.

Herm Holshouser: July 26, Concord, N.C.; Browns, 1930.

Roy Hughes: March 5, Asheville, N.C.; Indians, Browns, Phillies, Cubs, 1935-46.

Nippy Jones: Oct. 3, Sacramento; Cardinals, Phillies, Braves, 1946-57.

Bill Kennedy: Aug. 20, Alexandria, Va.; Senators, 1942-47.

Jack Kramer: May 18, Metairie, La.; Browns, Red Sox, Giants, Yankees, 1939-51.

Eddie Lake: June 7, Castro Valley, Calif.; Red Sox, 1944.

Charlie Letchas: March 14, Tampa; Phillies, Senators, 1939-46.

Mickey Mantle: Aug. 13, Dallas; Yankees, 1951-68

Von McDaniel: Aug. 20, Lawton, Okla.; Cardinals, 1957-58.

Catfish Metkovich: May 17, Costa Mesa, Calif.; Red Sox, Indians, Pirates, Cubs, Braves, 1943-54.

Wally Millies: Feb. 28, Oak Lawn, Ill.; Dodgers, Senators, Phillies, 1934-41.

Ray Moore: March 2, Clinton, Md.; Dodgers, Orioles, White Sox, Senators, Twins, 1952-63.

Terry Moore: March 29, Collinsville, Ill.; Cardinals, 1937–48.

Chet Nichols Jr.: March 27, Lincoln, R.I.; Braves, Red Sox, Reds, 1951-64.

Ralph Onis: Jan. 4, Tampa; Dodgers, 1935.

Al Papai: Sept. 7, Springfield, Ill.; Cardinals, Browns, Red Sox, White Sox, 1948-55.

Hal Peck: April 13, Milwaukee; Dodgers, Athletics, Indians, 1943-49.

Kent Peterson: April 27, Orem, Utah; Reds, Phillies, 1944-53.

Vada Pinson: Oct. 21, Oakland; Reds, Cardinals, Indians, Royals, 1958-75.

Gus Polidor: April 28, Caracas, Venezuela; Angels, Brewers, Marlins, 1985-93.

Ray Prim: April 29, Monte Rio, Calif.; Senators, Phillies, Cubs, 1933-46.

Nap Reyes: Sept. 15, Miami; Giants, 1943-50.

Saul Rogovin: Jan. 23, New York; Tigers, White Sox, Orioles, Phillies; 1949-57.

Frank Secory: April 7, Port Huron, Mich.; Tigers, Reds, Cubs, 1940-46.

Dick Tettelbach: Jan. 26, East Harwich, Mass.; Yankees, Senators, 1955-57.

Kite Thomas: Jan. 7, Rocky Mount, N.C.; Athletics, Senators, 1952-53.

Jim Tyack: Jan. 3, Bakersfield, Calif.; Athletics, 1943.

Jimmy Uchrinscko: March 17, Mount Pleasant, Pa.; Senators, 1926.

Al Unser: July 5, Decatur, Ill.; Tigers, Reds, 1942-45.

Cecil Upshaw: Feb. 7, Lawrenceville, Ga.; Braves, Astros, Indians, Yankees, White Sox, 1966-75.

Zoilo Versalles: June 9, Bloomington, Minn.; Senators, Twins, Dodgers, Indians, Braves, 1959-71.

Woody Williams: Feb. 24, Appomattox, Va.; Dodgers, Reds, 1938-45.

Jack Wilson: April 19, Edmonds, Wash.; Athletics, Red Sox, Senators, Tigers, 1934-42.

—compiled by Bill Carle (through Nov. 1)

NL/AL beat

- ▶ 1995 division-by-division wrap-ups
- ▶ 1995 All-Star Game
- ▶ League batting and pitching leaders

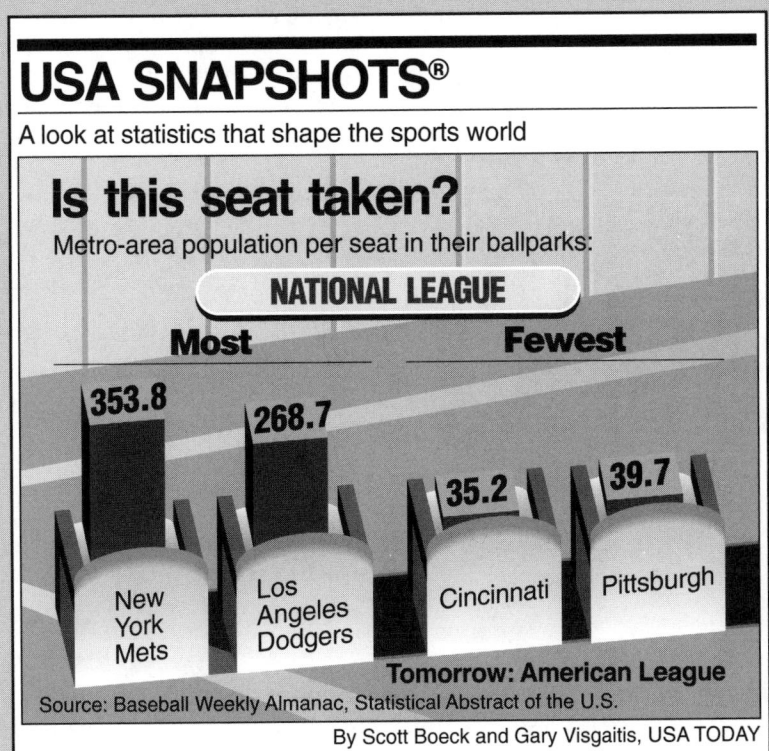

USA SNAPSHOTS®

A look at statistics that shape the sports world

Is this seat taken?

Metro-area population per seat in their ballparks:

NATIONAL LEAGUE

Most — Fewest

353.8 — New York Mets
268.7 — Los Angeles Dodgers
35.2 — Cincinnati
39.7 — Pittsburgh

Tomorrow: American League

Source: Baseball Weekly Almanac, Statistical Abstract of the U.S.

By Scott Boeck and Gary Visgaitis, USA TODAY

AL East 1995: Boston led the whole way

The Boston Red Sox got a new general manager, a new manager, a new approach, and a big surprise—the American League East title. They took over first place May 13 and led the rest of the way. The biggest surprise was knuckleballer Tim Wakefield—signed as a free agent after his release by Pittsburgh—who finished 16-8. At one point, he won 10 consecutive games, the most by a Boston pitcher since Roger Clemens in 1986. Mo Vaughn led the pack at .300 with 39 home runs and 126 RBI, but veteran outfielder Mike Greenwell, shortstop John Valentin, third baseman Tim Naehring, designated hitter Jose Canseco and pitcher Erik Hanson also had outstanding years.

Meanwhile, the New York Yankees earned the first American League wild-card spot with a torrid 26-7 stretch run. It was the first postseason appearance for first baseman Don Mattingly, ending a 13-year drought—he played 1,785 regular-season games before getting his first postseason shot—the longest streak ever by a Yankee. David Cone, Jack McDowell and Andy Pettitte carried the Yankees into contention. Starting Aug. 29, Pettitte was 6-1, McDowell 4-0 and Cone 4-1. Cone was 9-2 after he was acquired July 28 from Toronto, giving him an overall mark of 18-8. Third baseman Wade Boggs hit .324 and picked up his 2,500th hit.

STANDINGS THROUGH JULY 11

Team	W	L	Pct.	GB
Boston	39	29	.574	—
Detroit	37	33	.529	3
Baltimore	33	35	.485	6
New York	30	36	.455	8
Toronto	27	40	.403	11.5

The Baltimore Orioles were baseball's most disappointing team, although they provided the game with its most magical moment of the season on Sept. 6, when shortstop Cal Ripken Jr. played in his 2,131st consecutive game, eclipsing Lou Gehrig's "unbreakable" record. His ovation lasted over 22 minutes. It was one of the O's few highlights. After moving within 4½ games of Boston on July 31, they dropped 14 of their next 18 games to fall by the wayside. First baseman Rafael Palmeiro had a spectacular season (.310, 39 homers, 104 RBI). Pitcher Mike Mussina (19-9, 3.29) finished off with 26 consecutive scoreless innings. In fact, the Orioles finished the season with five consecutive shutouts to tie the club and league records.

The 1995 season marked the end of an era in Detroit—manager Sparky Anderson, shortstop Alan Trammell and second baseman Lou Whitaker said good-bye. Anderson had 2,194 victories—the third highest total of all time—at the end of his 23rd major league season. Trammell and Whitaker—who came up in 1977 and played 19 years together—both collected their 2,300rd hits, and their 1,918 games together broke the league record for teammates.

Toronto finished last at 56-88—its most losses since 1980. Juan Guzman, slowed by shoulder and control problems, was just 4-14 with a 6.32 ERA. Pat Hentgen slipped to 10-14 with a 5.11 ERA. Three pitchers from Class AAA Syracuse—Edwin Hurtado, Paul Menhart and Giovanni Carrara—moved into the rotation. Veteran Paul Molitor began the year as a .307 career hitter and got two hits the final day to keep alive his streak of never hitting below .270 for a full season. Second baseman Roberto Alomar and center fielder Devon White became coveted free agents after the season.

FINAL STANDINGS

Team	W	L	Pct.	GB
Boston	86	58	.597	—
New York	79	65	.549	7
Baltimore	71	73	.493	15
Detroit	60	84	.417	26
Toronto	56	88	.389	30

—by Bill Koenig

AL Central 1995: No one neared the Indians

The American League Central Division was supposed to be a fierce battle between the Cleveland Indians and Chicago White Sox, but it turned out to be the great race that wasn't.

Cleveland won 100 of 144 games—30 ahead of second-place Kansas City for baseball's largest lead ever—and made it to the postseason for the first time since 1954. Their offense was the best in baseball, leading the AL in average, on-base and slugging percentages, runs, hits, total bases, home runs and steals. The pitching was almost as good. Dennis Martinez and Orel Hershiser teamed with Charles Nagy for a league-best 3.83 ERA, and the bullpen led at 3.05 with 50 saves (46 by Jose Mesa) and 32 wins. Albert Belle became the first player to hit at least 50 doubles and 50 homers in the same season.

STANDING THROUGH JULY 11				
Team	W	L	Pct.	GB
Cleveland	46	21	.687	—
Kansas City	33	32	.508	12
Milwaukee	32	35	.478	14½
Chicago	28	38	.424	17½
Minnesota	22	46	.324	24½

Rookie manager Bob Boone and the feisty Kansas City Royals managed to finish second, four games under .500, despite scoring the fewest runs in the league. Bob Hamelin hit just .168—Gary Gaetti's career-high 35 homers and Wally Joyner's .310 average couldn't compensate for Hamelin's tailspin. The Royals had problems on the mound as well. Kevin Appier was 11-2 at the All-Star break but finished 15-10. There were encouraging signs from some of the youngsters, including Johnny Damon—who jumped from Class AA and hit .282—and Tommy Goodwin, whose 50 steals nearly ended the four-year reign of Indian Kenny Lofton (54).

Chicago's Frank Thomas notched his usual spectacular numbers for the White Sox—the first player ever to hit .300 with 20 homers, 100 walks, 100 RBI and 100 runs in five consecutive seasons—and belted his 40th homer on the final day. But the Sox finished eight games under .500. The most glaring weakness was starting pitching. Wilson Alvarez, Alex Fernandez and Jason Bere finished at 28-34—but only after Fernandez won his last seven decisions. Manager Gene Lamont and pitching coach Jackie Brown lost their jobs as a result of Chicago's 11-20 start, with Terry Bevington and Don Cooper named as replacements.

Replacements were all the rage in Milwaukee. There were three former "replacement" players on the Brewers' pitching staff at one point, plus eight rookies, including four starters. But the Brewers were one of the league's surprise teams in the first half, as manager Phil Garner kept them competitive despite baseball's second lowest payroll. They were within a half-game of the wild-card lead on Aug. 27 but lost 25 of their final 32 games—a spiral that coincided with the loss of second-year shortstop Jose Valentin, who anchored a defense that led the AL in double plays before he broke a finger Aug. 31.

Inexperience led to Minnesota's tying for the worst record in baseball (56-88). The Twins used more players (46) and more rookies (19) than in any other year in franchise history. Of 33 players on the final day, 18 were rookies. Highlights: rookie Marty Cordova had 24 homers, 20 stolen bases and 84 RBI, and Chuck Knoblauch hit .333 with 11 homers, 63 RBI, and 46 steals—all career bests. Kirby Puckett hit .314 with 23 homers and 99 RBI.

FINAL STANDINGS				
Team	W	L	Pct.	GB
Cleveland	100	44	.694	—
Kansas City	70	74	.486	30
Chicago	68	76	.472	32
Milwaukee	65	79	.451	35
Minnesota	56	88	.389	44

AL West 1995: The end was hell for Angels

The 1995 American League West will be remembered for the California Angels' letting the title slip through their fingers and the Mariners' giving their fans a strong argument to keep baseball in Seattle.

For much of the year, the Angels looked like the best team in the game. Hitting instructor Rod Carew turned his young players into .300 hitters and pitching coach turned manager Marcel Lachemann worked magic with Chuck Finley, Mark Langston and a bunch of castaways. The Angels had been playing for a postseason berth because of the emergence of a talented group of young players—center fielder Jim Edmonds (.290, 33 home runs, 107 RBI) was a leading contender for MVP honors until a September slump; J.T. Snow (.289, 24, 102) solidified himself as the team's first baseman; and Garrett Anderson hit .321 (16 home runs, 69 RBI in 106 games) to emerge as the front-runner for Rookie of the Year. But the team's late-season swoon coincided with the Mariners' surge, and after the teams tied the Angels lost the division's one-game playoff to the nearly unhittable Randy Johnson.

STANDINGS THROUGH JULY 11				
Team	W	L	Pct.	GB
California	39	30	.565	—
Texas	39	30	.565	—
Oakland	36	35	.507	4
Seattle	34	35	.493	5

When Ken Griffey Jr. suffered a broken wrist early in the season, the Mariners' playoff hopes seemingly followed him onto the disabled list. Remarkably, the team made up for his absence—DH Edgar Martinez captured his second batting title in four years, hitting .356 to go with career highs in home runs (29) and RBI (113); first baseman Tino Martinez hit .293 (31 home runs, 111 RBI); and right fielder Jay Buhner hit 40 home runs (121 RBI). With Griffey's return and the addition of pitcher Andy Benes and left fielder Vince Coleman before the trading deadline, the team was nearly unbeatable down the stretch. Johnson completed his transformation into the most imposing pitcher in the game, finishing 18-2 with 294 strikeouts and just 65 walks in 214 innings.

Expanded playoffs made wild-card contenders out of sub-.500 teams, so the Texas Rangers and Oakland A's kept their postseason hopes alive well into September. New manager Johnny Oates kept the Rangers (74-70) in contention despite long absences by Juan Gonzalez, Dean Palmer and Bob Tewksbury. Steady Will Clark hit .302 with 92 RBI, while ageless Otis Nixon stole 50 bases. Ironically, the club's MVP might have been Mickey Tettleton (32 home runs), whom new general manager Bob Melvin signed off the Homestead, Fla., free-agent camp for $500,000.

Oakland manager Tony La Russa left after the season to become the St. Louis Cardinals' new skipper in 1996, but the A's sent him off with a memorable year. Leadoff hitter Rickey Henderson led the team in batting at .300 (despite a subpar year in base stealing), and Mark McGwire had 39 home runs and 90 RBI in just 317 at-bats but continued to battle ankle injuries. Todd Stottlemyre (14-7, 205 strikeouts) came into his own under the tutelage of pitching coach Dave Duncan (also gone to St. Louis for 1996), and rookie Doug Johns went 5-3 after a late-season callup, but the rest of the pitching staff was lackluster.

FINAL STANDINGS				
Team	W	L	Pct.	GB
Seattle	79	66	.545	—
California	78	67	.538	1
Texas	74	70	.514	4½
Oakland	67	77	.465	11½

NL East 1995: Maddux took Atlanta to top

There were two seasons in the National League East. The surprising Philadelphia Phillies got out of the gate 37-18 and led the division throughout May and June. Then their magic ran out, and the cream rose to the top. The Atlanta Braves, fueled by Greg Maddux, passed the Phils on July 5 and never looked back.

The Braves surged from five games behind Philadelphia to six games ahead during a three-week stretch. As for Maddux, he finished the season 19-2 with a 1.63 earned run average. His .905 winning percentage was the best in major league history for a pitcher who made at least 20 starts. And he became the first pitcher since Walter Johnson in 1918 and 1919 to have an ERA under 2.00 in consecutive seasons. Maddux had a perfect sidekick in Tom Glavine, who finished 16-7 with a 3.08 ERA. Left fielder Ryan Klesko hit .310 with 23 home runs and 70 RBI. The Braves managed their divisional romp despite finishing just 13th in the league in batting average.

STANDINGS THROUGH JULY 11

Team	W	L	Pct.	GB
Atlanta	43	54	.625	—
Philadelphia	39	29	.574	4
Montreal	32	37	.464	11½
Florida	24	42	.364	18
New York	25	44	.362	18½

Meanwhile, the Phillies put together the greatest swan dive in the NL since the advent of divisional play in 1969. After their fast start, they lost 29 of their next 40 games. Injuries robbed them of starters Bobby Munoz (elbow), Tommy Greene (shoulder), Curt Schilling (shoulder) and David West (shoulder). Outfielder Len Dykstra left the lineup for good in late July with a knee injury. Catcher Darren Daulton, who probably leads the planet in stitches, had his sixth knee operation on Sept. 1.

The New York Mets downloaded big salaries and upgraded their future. Four high-priced players—David Segui, Bobby Bonilla, Bret Saberhagen and Brett Butler—left the team over the course of the season, cutting the payroll in half. But the Mets future looks bright with pitchers Jason Isringhausen, Bill Pulsipher, Bobby Jones, Pete Harnisch (who had shoulder surgery Aug. 18), Robert Person, Dave Mlicki and minor-leaguer Paul Wilson; also promising are outfielders Jay Payton, Ryan Thompson, Carl Everett, Damon Buford and Alex Ochoa. The Mets tied for second.

The Florida Marlins finished fourth and set a club record with 67 wins. Jeff Conine hit .302 with 25 home runs and 105 RBI, leading the team in all three categories. Pat Rapp and John Burkett each won 14 games. Second baseman Quilvio Veras became the second Marlin rookie to win the NL stolen base title, joining Chuck Carr. Veras had a major-league-high 56 steals.

Take away Larry Walker, Marquis Grissom, Ken Hill and John Wetteland, and what have you got? A Montreal team that went from first to worst. The Expos' 74-40 record was best in the majors in the strike-shortened 1994 season, but the team dropped to 66-78 after cutting their budget and cleaning house. David Segui, obtained from the Mets on June 8 for pitcher Reid Cornelius, was a bright spot. He hit .309 with 12 home runs and 68 RBI. Pedro Martinez won 14 games, while Butch Henry had a 2.84 ERA before going down with Tommy John elbow surgery. General manager Kevin Malone resigned after the season.

FINAL STANDINGS

Team	W	L	Pct.	GB
Atlanta	90	54	.625	—
Philadelphia	69	75	.479	21
New York	69	75	.479	21
Florida	67	76	.469	22½
Montreal	66	78	.458	24

—by Bill Koenig

NL Central 1995: Reds knew they had it

The Cincinnati Reds said they never doubted themselves in the season's early weeks, even though they stumbled out of the gate at 0-6. By the end of the race, they were nine lengths ahead of second-place Houston. Shortstop Barry Larkin, right fielder Reggie Sanders and left fielder Ron Gant gave Cincinnati a threesome as impressive as any in the league. Gant hit 29 homers and drove in 88 runs, Sanders put together a career year (.306, 28 homers, 99 RBI and 36 steals), and Larkin (.319, 51 steals) was the unquestioned team leader on and off the field. On the mound, Pete Schourek, a reclamation project from the Mets, was the team's best pitcher. General manager Jim Bowden continued to make good deals, strengthening his staff with Mark Portugal and Dave Burba (in the Deion Sanders trade) and left-hander David Wells.

STANDINGS THROUGH JULY 11

Team	W	L	Pct.	GB
Cincinnati	43	25	.632	—
Houston	38	30	.559	4
Chicago	37	32	.536	6½
Pittsburgh	28	37	.431	13½
St. Louis	30	40	.429	14

Houston played well enough to be firmly entrenched in the wild-card race late into the season, when an 11-game losing streak changed everything, and Colorado won the playoff berth on the final day of the season. Much of the fall was due to crippling injuries and a bullpen that went flat down the stretch. Derek Bell (.334) led the team in hitting all year but was lost for the season on Aug. 22 (leg surgery); center fielder Brian Hunter missed 18 games (broken hand); and Jeff Bagwell lost all of August (broken hand). With Bagwell out of the lineup, the Astros had losing streaks of six and 11 games. Craig Biggio kept the team together through it all, batting .302 with 22 homers, 77 RBI and 33 steals.

Nothing was disappointing about the early-season Cubs, who got off to a great start before suffering their traditional June swoon. They recovered around Labor Day and were back in the thick of things before nose-diving again. They made one last run down the stretch, winning eight consecutive games to put the heat on Colorado in the wild-card race and to serve notice that they were legitimate contenders. The players credited the new brain trust—president Andy MacPhail, general manager Ed Lynch and manager Jim Riggleman.

The Cardinals believed they would be in the wild-card hunt, but they were so weak after 47 games that manager Joe Torre was fired. Mike Jorgenson did slightly better—a .438 winning percentage (42-54) compared with Torre's .426 (20-27). St. Louis suffered one blow after another. Danny Jackson had problems after thyroid-cancer surgery and finished a dismal 2-12, and Ken Hill went 6-7 with an ERA over 5.00 before being shipped to Cleveland. But Tom Henke had 36 saves in 38 chances with a 1.82 ERA. He and Tony Fossas gave St. Louis the NL's best bullpen.

Pittsburgh had the league's worst record. The few recognizable names from their 1990-92 division championship teams—Jay Bell, Orlando Merced, Don Slaught, Jeff King—all had respectable seasons. Merced hit .300 and had a career-high 83 RBI, and King hit .265 with 18 homers and 87 RBI. Bell hit .262 but was exceptional defensively. The rest of the lineup was patchwork, and the pitching abysmal.

FINAL STANDINGS

Team	W	L	Pct.	GB
Cincinnati	85	59	.590	—
Houston	76	68	.528	9
Chicago	73	71	.507	12
St. Louis	62	81	.434	22½
Pittsburgh	58	86	.403	27

—by Deron Snyder

NL West 1995: The Rockies almost made it

The Los Angeles Dodgers and the upstart Colorado Rockies battled for the division crown until the last weekend of the season, with the Dodgers (78-66) winning by one game and the Rockies (77-67) becoming the first NL wild-card team. It was no easy journey for the atrocious Dodger defense—they led the league with 130 errors. But their rotation of Ramon Martinez (17-7), Ismael Valdes (13-11), Hideo Nomo (13-6), Tom Candiotti (7-14) and Pedro Astacio (7-8) was second to the Atlanta Braves' in ERA. Martinez had a Cy Young-caliber season that included a no-hitter, but it was Japanese star Nomo and his herky-jerky delivery that brought excitement not seen since Mexican pitcher Fernando Valenzuela stormed onto the scene with the Dodgers in 1981. An entourage of Japanese reporters followed wherever he went, chronicling "Nomomania." He dominated the league the first half of the season and finished the year with a league-high 236 strikeouts.

STANDINGS THROUGH JULY 11

Team	W	L	Pct.	GB
Colorado	39	67	.565	—
Los Angeles	34	35	.493	5
San Diego	33	36	.478	6
San Francisco	33	36	.478	6

The Rockies became the only team other than the 1977 Dodgers to have four players—Dante Bichette, Vinny Castilla, Andres Galarraga, and Larry Walker—hit at least 30 home runs each. As a team, they hit .282 with 200 home runs and 785 RBI—all league highs. General manager Bob Gebhard had inked Walker and pitcher Bill Swift to multiyear deals in spring training and acquired Bret Saberhagen from the Mets for the stretch run. Still, manager Don Baylor's struggling staff had a league-high 4.97 ERA. Swift and Saberhagen missed large chunks of the season with injuries. David Nied pitched only four innings after suffering a mysterious elbow injury in spring training. The team's most effective starter was Kevin Ritz (11-11, 4.21 ERA).

The San Diego Padres entered spring training optimistic for the first time since 1993. When computer software magnate John Moores purchased the team during the strike from Tom Werner's "Gang of 13," he pledged to bring excitement back to the "New Padres." General manager Randy Smith pulled off a blockbuster deal with the Houston Astros that brought third baseman Ken Caminiti (.302, 26 home runs, 94 RBI) and center fielder Steve Finley to San Diego. Tony Gwynn again won the NL batting title and provided a career-high 90 RBI. The development of young pitchers Andy Ashby and Joey Hamilton allowed Smith to deal Andy Benes to Seattle moments before the trading deadline for prospects Ron Villone and Marc Newfield. The Padres remained in wild-card contention until late in September. That was not enough to keep the 32-year-old Smith, who had clashed frequently with new president Larry Lucchino, from resigning.

With pitchers John Burkett and Bill Swift lost to free agency, the San Francisco Giants were a skeleton of their 1993 team. Barry Bonds was his normal MVP-caliber self (33 home runs, 104 RBI) and journeyman outfielder Glenallen Hill was a pleasant surprise (24 homers, 86 RBI), but infielders Matt Williams and Robby Thompson missed much of the year with injuries, and only the Rockies had a team ERA higher than the Giants' 4.86.

FINAL STANDINGS

Team	W	L	Pct.	GB
Los Angeles	78	66	.542	—
x-Colorado	77	67	.535	1
San Diego	70	74	.486	8
San Francisco	67	77	.465	11
x-wild card				

—by Pete Williams

All-Star Game: NL box score

National	000 001 11 0	3
American	000 200 00 0	2

Batter	ab	r	h	bi	bb	so	lo	avg
Dykstra cf	2	0	0	0	1	0	0	.000
Sosa cf	1	0	0	0	0	0	0	.000
Gwynn rf	2	0	0	0	0	0	1	.000
RSanders rf	1	0	0	0	0	1	0	.000
Mondesi rf	1	0	0	0	0	0	0	.000
Bonds lf	3	0	0	0	0	1	0	.000
Bichette lf	1	0	0	0	0	1	0	.000
Piazza c	3	1	1	1	0	0	0	.333
Daulton c	0	0	0	0	0	0	0	—
McGriff 1b	3	0	0	0	0	2	0	.000
Grace 1b	0	0	0	0	0	0	0	—
Gant dh	2	0	0	0	0	1	0	.000
a-Conine ph	1	1	1	1	0	0	0	1.000
Larkin ss	3	0	0	0	0	0	0	.000
Offerman ss	0	0	0	0	0	0	0	—
Castilla 3b	2	0	0	0	0	1	0	.000
Bonilla 3b	1	0	0	0	0	1	0	.000
Biggio 2b	2	1	1	1	0	0	0	.500
Morandini 2b	1	0	0	0	0	1	0	.000
Totals	**29**	**3**	**3**	**3**	**1**	**9**	**1**	

a-homered for Gant in the 8th.

Pitcher	ip	h	r	er	bb	so	era
Nomo	2	1	0	0	0	3	0.00
Smiley	2	2	2	2	0	0	9.00
Green	1	2	0	0	0	1	0.00
Neagle	1	1	0	0	0	1	0.00
Perez	.1	1	0	0	1	0	0.00
Slocumb (W)	1	1	0	0	0	2	0.00
Henke (H)	.2	0	0	0	0	1	0.00
Myers (S)	1	0	0	0	1	0	0.00

▶**Batting**—HR: Biggio (6th inning off DMartinez, 0 on, 2 out); Piazza (7th inning off Rogers, 0 on, 2 out); Conine (8th inning off Ontiveros, 0 on, 0 out).
▶**RBI**—Biggio, Piazza, Conine. 2-out RBI: Biggio, Piazza. Team LOB: 0.
▶**Baserunning**—CS: Dykstra (2nd base by Johnson/Rodriguez).
▶**Umpires**—HP: Durwood Merrill. 1B: Charlie Williams. 2B: Al Clark. 3B: Mike Winters. LF: Ted Hendry. RF: Ed Rapuano.

By Robert Hanashiro, USA TODAY

Jeff Conine's game-winning homer made him the All-Star Game MVP.

Conine's first at-bat sparks All-Star win for Nationals

It was an All-Star Game of New Age heroes, from Jeff Conine to Craig Biggio to Heathcliff Slocumb. Baseball needed a fresh start, and fresh faces would lead the way. Take Conine, the lone Florida Marlin in town. When he finally got his first All-Star at-bat in the eighth inning, his solo homer gave the National League a 3-2 victory.

"That rush of adrenaline was hard to describe," Conine said. "You don't want to get into an All-Star Game and embarrass yourself. I put a good swing on it."

The pitching was solid all night long, disturbed only by an occasional blast. Conine's homer was the third NL hit of the game—all were homers (Craig Biggio and Mike Piazza hit the other two). There were four home runs in all—the most in an All-Star Game in 14 years—accounting for all five runs. The NL's only baserunner was leadoff hitter Lenny Dykstra, who walked and then was caught stealing.

"You see a lot of strange things happen in this game, and that was definitely one of them," Biggio said of the hit drought/home-run parade.

The pitchers ruled much of the game, as 17 strikeouts would suggest. The thermometer was at 9 degrees when the game began, and more heat came from strikeout leaders Randy Johnson and Hideo Nomo. Each worked two shutout innings. Each faced six batters and fanned three.

Neither team put a man past first base until Frank Thomas—the previous day's home-run contest champ—blew a two-run shot past the left-field foul pole in the fourth off John Smiley for a 2-0 lead.

"I just wanted to get some entertainment going," said Thomas, who became the first Chicago White Sox player in history to hit an All-Star home run.

The National League did not have a hit for 5 ⅔ innings—an All-Star record—and of its first 17 at-bats against Randy Johnson, Kevin Appier and Dennis Martinez, only two balls left the infield. Then Craig Biggio homered off Martinez in the sixth to make it 2-1. The second NL hit was a Mike Piazza homer in the seventh off Arlington home-crowd favorite Kenny Rogers, tying it up 2-2.

There it stayed until Conine knocked out Steve Ontiveros's 1-0 pitch in the eighth. Ontiveros called the fateful pitch "a cut fastball over the middle of the plate that did nothing. It was one of those pitches where you say, 'Don't swing at it, take ball two.'"

It was the last swing Conine would take with that bat, which he reluctantly turned over to a Hall of Fame representative after the game to become part of the permanent All-Star Game display in Cooperstown. Conine was the 10th player in All-Star history to homer in his first at-bat, the first since Bo Jackson in 1989. The homer also was the 16th in All-Star history by a pinch hitter, as he led off the eighth hitting for designated hitter Ron Gant of Cincinnati.

—by Mike Lopresti and Rob Rains

Behind the scenes

▶**Letterman's advice made it to the locker room:** Novelty shop proprietors Mujibur and Sirajul from Late Show with David Letterman made the rounds before the game. They had individual messages from the talk show host for many of the All-Stars. Among the favorites: to Wade Boggs, "Dave says to keep your eye on the ball," and to Kevin Seitzer, "The key for you is 110%." Kirby Puckett tried to avoid the duo, but they caught up to him in the American League clubhouse. When Ken Griffey asked who Puckett's visitors were, the Twins outfielder replied, "I got to get my jock on. David Letterman's buddies are here." As Mujibur and Sirajul departed, Puckett told them, "I'm in New York on Thursday. Don't bother me."
▶**Busted:** A sting operation to catch those scalping tickets for the All-Star Game landed Texas Rangers reliever Ed Vosberg. Vosberg faced a $500 fine for allegedly trying to sell his complimentary tickets. He was cited outside The Ballpark in Arlington by undercover officers enforcing a new city ordinance that

All-Star Game: AL box score

National	000 001 110—3	
American	000 200 000—2	

Batter	ab	r	h	bi	bb	so	lo	avg
Lofton cf	3	0	0	0	0	1	2	.000
c-Edmnds ph-f	1	0	0	0	0	1	2	.000
Baerga 2b	3	1	3	0	0	0	0	1.000
Alomar pr-2b	1	0	0	0	0	0	0	.000
EMartinez dh	3	0	0	0	0	1	2	.000
d-TMrtnz ph	1	0	1	0	0	0	0	1.000
Thomas 1b	2	1	1	2	0	0	0	.500
Vaughn 1b	2	0	0	0	0	2	2	.000
Belle lf	3	0	0	0	0	1	1	.000
O'Neill lf	1	0	0	0	0	0	1	.000
Ripken ss	3	0	2	0	0	0	0	.667
DiSrcnpr-ss	1	0	0	0	0	0	0	.000
Boggs 3b	2	0	1	0	0	0	0	.500
a-Stzr ph-3b	2	0	0	0	0	0	1	.000
Puckett rf	2	0	0	0	0	1	2	.000
b-Rmrz ph-rf	0	0	0	0	2	0	0	.000
Rodriguez c	3	0	0	0	0	1	4	.000
Stanley c	1	0	0	0	0	0	1	.000
Totals	34	2	8	2	2	8	18	

a-flied to right for Boggs in the 7th; b-walked for Puckett in the 7th; c-struck out for Lofton in the 7th; d-singled for EMartinez in the 8th.

Pitcher	ip	h	r	er	bb	so	era
Johnson	2	0	0	0	1	3	0.00
Appier	2	0	0	0	0	1	0.00
DMartinez	2	1	1	1	0	0	4.50
Rogers (BS)	1	1	1	1	0	2	9.00
Ontiveros (L)	.2	1	1	1	1	0	13.50
Wells	.1	0	0	0	0	1	0.00
Mesa	1	0	0	0	0	1	0.00

▶**Batting**—2B: Baerga (Neagle). HR: Thomas (4th inning off Smiley, 1 on, 2 out).
▶**RBI**—Thomas 2. 2-out RBI: Thomas 2. Runners left in scoring position, 2 out: Lofton 1, Belle 1, Edmonds 1. Team LOB: 7.
▶**Baserunning**—SB: Alomar (3rd base off Neagle/Piazza). CS: Baerga (2nd base by Nomo/Piazza).
▶**Game data**—T: 2:40. Att: 50,920. Weather: 101 degrees, clear. Wind: 10 mph, in from center.

American League

▸**C:** 1, Ivan Rodriguez, Tex., 1,151,708. 2, Sandy Alomar, Cle., 958,853. 3, Terry Steinbach, Oak., 467,853.

▸**1B:** 1, Frank Thomas, Chi., 895,576. 2, Eddie Murray, Cle., 729,027. 3, Will Clark, Tex., 505,103.

▸**2B:** 1, Carlos Baerga, Cle., 1,152,652. 2, Roberto Alomar, Tor., 1,003,550. 3, Chuck Knoblauch, Min., 583,195.

▸**3B:** 1, Wade Boggs, N.Y., 884,651. 2, Jim Thome, Cle., 753,092. 3, Robin Ventura, Chi., 468,334.

▸**SS:** 1, Cal Ripken Jr., Bal., 1,698,524. 2, Benji Gil, Tex., 675,963. 3, Omar Vizquel, Cle., 666,506.

▸**OF:** 1, Ken Griffey Jr., Sea., 1,204,748. 2, Albert Belle, Cle., 1,056,134. 3, Kirby Puckett, Min., 997,623. 4, Kenny Lofton, Cle., 975,801. 5, Manny Ramirez, Cle., 863,890. 6, Rickey Henderson, Oak., 702,257. 7, Joe Carter, Tor., 418,611. 8, Jose Canseco, Bos., 404,758. 9, Paul Molitor, Tor., 387,060.

National League

▸**C:** 1, Mike Piazza, L.A., 1,195,136. 2, Darren Daulton, Phi., 780,126. 3, Joe Girardi, Col., 473,210.

▸**1B:** 1. Fred McGriff, Atl., 871,904. 2, Andres Galarraga, Col., 802,672. 3, Jeff Bagwell, Hou., 717,663.

▸**2B:** 1, Craig Biggio, Hou., 825,062. 2, Mickey Morandini, Phi., 737,270. 3, Delino DeShields, L.A., 438,235.

▸**3B:** 1, Matt Williams, S.F., 1,029,519. 2, Scott Cooper, St. Louis, 899,505. 3, Vinny Castilla, Col., 604,823.

▸**SS:** 1, Ozzie Smith, St. Louis, 1,367,518. 2, Barry Larkin, Cin., 948,945. 3, Wil Cordero, Mon., 634,885.

▸**OF:** 1, Barry Bonds, S.F., 1,392,130. 2, Lenny Dykstra, Phi., 903,952. 3, Tony Gwynn, S.D., 898,951. 4, David Justice, Atl., 851,644. 5, Dante Bichette, Col., 706,249. 6, Larry Walker, Col., 579,722. 7, Deion Sanders, Cin., 564,231. 8, Ron Gant, Cin., 532,814. 9, Raul Mondesi, L.A., 446,119.

makes it a misdemeanor to sell tickets for more than face value, KXAS-TV reported.

▸**Fehr's souvenir:** Even the All-Star Game couldn't escape the Major League Baseball Players Association. Frank Thomas's fourth-inning homer off John Smiley wound up in the hands of 9-year-old Alex Fehr, the nephew of union head Donald Fehr. The drive went into the last suite in left field—rented by the players' association. "It's symbolic," said Eugene Orza, the union's No. 2 official. "The first home run hit in the All-Star Game goes to the players' association.... It's definitely got poetic significance." The ball bounced in the aisle behind the two rows of outdoor seats. Ebony Bernazard, the 17-year-old son of former major leaguer Tony Bernazard—now a union official—picked it up and gave it to Alex Fehr, the son of Donald's brother Steve.

▸**A touching moment:** Glenn Sherlock, this game was for you. At least that's what Yankees catcher Mike Stanley and a couple of his coaches signaled to a national TV audience in pre-game introductions. When their names were called, Stanley and Yankees coaches Brian Butterfield and Willie Randolph raised an index finger to their chins in a silent tribute to Sherlock. The reason: Sherlock was the only Yankees coach who wasn't invited to the game.

▸**A blast from the past:** One by one, many of the All-Stars visited the dugouts during the Legends of the Game contest, part of the annual festivities on Monday's All-Star workout day. They came to renew old friendships, and, more important, to gaze again upon the ballplayers who had proceeded them. "This is always a good time," said Cleveland Indians pitcher Dennis Martinez, the oldest of this year's All-Star crew at age 40. "This is one of the highlights." Out on the field, the stars of yesterday were doing their best to hold up under temperatures that soared into the triple digits. "I don't think I could have lasted another inning," said former Rangers catcher Jim Sundberg. "That was some kind of heat out there." For the record, the American League old-timers topped the National League 1-0 on Willie Randolph's RBI double. Former Ranger Bert Campaneris scored the game's only run, and Ferguson Jenkins, another ex-Ranger, got the victory. J.R. Richard, who had been homeless for much of the past two years, pitched two-thirds of an inning for the NL.

—Contributing: Pat Coleman

American League Leaders: 1995 statistics

Batting

BATTING AVERAGE*	G	AB	R	H	PCT
E.Martinz, Sea	145	511	121	182	.356
Knoblauch, Min	136	538	107	179	.333
Salmon, Cal	143	537	111	177	.330
Boggs, NY	126	460	76	149	.324
Murray, Clev	113	436	68	141	.323
Surhoff, Mil	117	415	72	133	.320
Davis, Cal	119	424	81	135	.318
Belle, Clev	143	546	121	173	.317
Baerga, Clev	135	557	87	175	.314
Thome, Clev	137	452	92	142	.314

HOME RUNS

Belle, Clev	50
Buhner, Sea	40
F. Thomas, Chi	40
McGwire, Oak	39
Palmeiro, Balt	39
Vaughn, Bos	39
Gaetti, KC	35
Salmon, Cal	34

DOUBLES

Belle, Clev	52
E. Martinez, Sea	52
Puckett, Minn	39
Valentin, Bos	37
T. Martinez, Sea	35

TRIPLES

Lofton, Clev	13
Johnson, Chi	12
Anderson, Balt	10
B. Williams, NY	9
Knoblauch, Minn	8

RUNS

Belle, Clev	121
E. Martinez, Sea	121
Edmonds, Cal	120
Phillips, Cal	119

RUNS BATTED IN

Belle, Clev	126
Vaughn, Bos	126
Buhner, Sea	121
E. Martinez, Sea	113
T. Martinez, Sea	111
F. Thomas, Chi	111
Edmonds, Cal	107
Ramirez, Clev	107
Salmon, Cal	105

HITS

Johnson, Chi	186
E. Martinez, Sea	182
Knoblauch, Min	179
Salmon, Cal	177
Baerga, Clev	175
Nixon, Tex	174
Belle, Clev	173
B. Williams, NY	173

STOLEN BASES

Lofton, Clev	54
Goodwin, KC	50
Nixon, Tex	50
Knoblauch, Min	46
Coleman, Sea	42
Johnson, Chi	40

TOTAL BASES

Belle, Clev	377
Palmeiro, Balt	323
E. Martinez, Sea	321
Salmon, Cal	319
Vaughn, Bos	316
Edmonds, Cal	299

WALKS

F. Thomas, Chi	136
E. Martinez, Sea	116
Phillips, Cal	113
Tettleton, Tex	107
Thome, Clev	97
Salmon, Cal	91

SLUGGING PCT.*

Belle, Clev	.690
E. Martinez, Sea	.628
F. Thomas, Chi	.606
Salmon, Cal	.594
Palmeiro, Balt	.583
Vaughn, Bos	.575

ON-BASE PCT.*

E. Martinez, Sea	.479
F. Thomas, Chi	.454
Thome, Clev	.438
Salmon, Cal	.429
Davis, Cal	.429
Knoblauch, Min	.424

Pitching

VICTORIES

Mussina, Balt	19-9
Johnson, Sea	18-2
Cone, Tor -NY	18-8
Rogers, Tex	17-7
Hershiser, Clev	16-6
Nagy, Clev	16-6
Wakefield, Bos	16-8

ERA

Johnson, Sea	2.48
Wakefield, Bos	2.95
Martinez, Clev	3.08
Mussina, Balt	3.29
Rogers, Tex	3.38

SAVES

Mesa, Clev	46
Smith, Cal	37
Aguilera, Bos	32
Hernandez, Chi	32
Montgomery, KC	31

COMPLETE GAMES

McDowell, NY	8
Erickson, Balt	7
Mussina, Balt	7
Cone, Tor -NY	6

STRIKEOUTS

Johnson, Sea	294
Stottlemyre, Oak	205
Finley, Cal	195
Cone, Tor -NY	191
Appier, KC	185

INNINGS

Cone, Tor -NY	229.1
Mussina, Balt	221.2
McDowell, NY	217.2
Johnson, Sea	214.1
Gubicza, KC	213.1
Stotlmyre, Oak	209.2

GAMES

Orosco, Balt	65
McDowell, Tex	64
Ayala, Sea	63
Belinda, Bos	63
Wickman, NY	63

SHUTOUTS

Mussina, Balt	4
Johnson, Sea	3
Cone, Tor -NY	2
Erickson, Balt	2
Fernandez, Chi	2

*Based on 3.1 plate appearances for each game a player's team has played.

National League Leaders: 1995 statistics

Batting

BATTING AVERAGE*

BATTING AVERAGE*	G	AB	R	H	Avg
Gwynn, SD	135	535	82	197	.368
Piazza, LA	112	434	82	150	.346
Bichette, Col	139	579	102	197	.340
Bell, Hou	112	452	63	151	.334
Grace, Chi	143	552	97	180	.326
Larkin, Cin	131	496	98	158	.319
Castilla, Col	139	527	82	163	.309
Segui, NY-Mtl	130	456	68	141	.309
Jefferies, Phil	114	480	69	147	.306
R. Sanders, Cin	133	484	91	148	.306

HOME RUNS

Bichette, Col	40
Sosa, Chi	36
Walker, Col	36
Bonds, SF	33
Castilla, Col	32
Karros, LA	32
Piazza, LA	32

DOUBLES

Grace, Chi	51
Bichette, Col	38
McRae, Chi	38
R. Sanders, Cin	36
Cordero, Mtl	35
Lankford, StL	35

TRIPLES

Butler, NY-LA	9
Young, Col	9
Finley, SD	8
Gonzalez, Hou -Chi	8
Sanders, Cin -SF	8

RUNS

Biggio, Hou	123
Bonds, SF	109
Finley, SD	104
Bichette, Col	102
Larkin, Cin	98
Grace, Chi	97

RUNS BATTED IN

Bichette, Col	128
Sosa, Chi	119
Galarraga, Col	106
Conine, Fla	105
Karros, LA	105
Bonds, SF	104
Walker, Col	101
R. Sanders, Cin	99
Caminiti, SD	94

HITS

Bichette, Col	197
Gwynn, SD	197
Grace, Chi	180
Biggio, Hou	167
Finley, SD	167
McRae, Chi	167
Karros, LA	164
Castilla, Col	163

STOLEN BASES

Veras, Fla	56
Larkin, Cin	51
DeShields, LA	39
Finley, SD	36
R. Sanders, Cin	36
Young, Col	35
Sosa, Chi	34

TOTAL BASES

Bichette, Col	359
Walker, Col	300
Castilla, Col	297
Karros, LA	295
Bonds, SF	292
Grace, Chi	285

WALKS

Bonds, SF	120
Weiss, Col	98
Biggio, Hou	80
Veras, Fla	80
Bagwell, Hou	79
Gant, Cin	74

SLUGGING PCT.*

Bichette, Col	.620
Walker, Col	.607
Piazza, LA	.606
R. Sanders, Cin	.579
Bonds, SF	.577
Castilla, Col	.564

ON-BASE PCT.*

Bonds, SF	.431
Biggio, Hou	.406
Gwynn, SD	.404
Weiss, Col	.403
Piazza, LA	.400
Bagwell, Hou	.399

Pitching

VICTORIES

Maddux, Atl	19-2
Schourek, Cin	18-7
Martinez, LA	17-7
Glavine, Atl	16-7
Navarro, Chi	14-6
Rapp, Fla	14-7
Martinez, Mtl	14-10

ERA

Maddux, Atl	1.63
Nomo, LA	2.54
Ashby, SD	2.94
Valdes, LA	3.05

SAVES

Myers, Chi	38
Henke, StL	36
Beck, SF	33
Slocumb, Phil	32
Worrell, LA	32
Hoffman, SD	31

COMPLETE GAMES

Maddux, Atl	10
Leiter, SF	7
Valdes, LA	6
Neagle, Pitt	5

STRIKEOUTS

Nomo, LA	236
Smoltz, Atl	193
Maddux, Atl	181
Reynolds, Hou	175
Martinez, Mtl	174
Fassero, Mtl	164
Schourek, Cin	160

INNINGS

Maddux, Atl	209.2
Neagle, Pitt	209.2
Martinez, LA	206.1
Hamilton, SD	204.1
Navarro, Chi	200.1
Glavine, Atl	198.2
Valdes, LA	197.2

GAMES

Leskanic, Col	76
Veres, Hou	72
Reed, Col	71
Perez, Fla	69
Holmes, Col	68
Jones, Hou	68
Perez, Chi	68

SHUTOUTS

Maddux, Atl	3
Nomo, LA	3

30

1996 BASEBALL WEEKLY ALMANAC

*Based on 3.1 plate appearances for each game a player's team has played.

Postseason

▸ **AL and NL Division playoffs**

▸ **NLCS and ALCS game** descriptions and composite box scores

▸ **World Series game-by-game wrapups and box scores**

▸ *and more . . .*

USA SNAPSHOTS®

A look at statistics that shape the sports world

Baseball in the air

Ages of adults who say they listen to big-league baseball on radio:

| 11% | 22% | 27% | 16% | 11% | 12% |
| 18-24 | 25-34 | 35-44 | 45-54 | 55-64 | 65+ |

Source: The Interep Radio Store

By Scott Boeck and Nick Galifianakis, USA TODAY

SEATTLE 3, NEW YORK 2

SERIES BATTING / SEATTLE

	G	AB	R	H	2B	3B	HR	RBI	SO	BB	AVG
EMartinez dh	5	21	6	12	3	0	2	10	2	6	.571
Buhner rf	5	24	2	11	1	0	1	3	4	2	.458
TMartinez 1b	5	22	4	9	1	0	1	5	4	3	.409
Griffey cf	5	23	9	9	0	0	5	7	3	2	.391
ADiaz ph-lf	2	3	0	1	0	0	0	0	1	1	.333
Cora 2b	5	19	7	6	1	0	1	1	1	3	.316
Sojo ss	5	20	0	5	0	0	0	3	3	0	.250
Colman lf	5	23	6	5	0	1	1	1	4	2	.217
Blowers 3b	5	18	0	3	0	0	0	1	7	3	.167
DWilson c	5	17	0	2	0	0	0	1	6	2	.118
Strnge ph-3b	2	4	0	0	0	0	0	1	1	1	.000
Widger c	2	3	0	0	0	0	0	0	3	0	.000
Fermin 2b	3	1	0	0	0	0	0	0	1	0	.000
Rdrgz pr-ss	1	1	1	0	0	0	0	0	0	0	.000
Newson ph	1	1	0	0	0	0	0	0	1	0	.000
Totals	5	200	35	63	6	1	11	33	41	25	.315

SERIES PITCHING / SEATTLE

	G	CG	IP	H	R	BB	SO	HB	WP	W	L	S	ER	ERA
Charlton	4	0	7.1	4	2	3	9	1	1	1	0	1	2	2.45
Johnson	2	0	10	5	3	6	16	0	0	2	0	0	3	2.70
JNelson	3	0	5.2	7	2	3	7	1	0	0	1	0	2	3.18
Benes	2	0	11.2	10	7	9	8	0	0	0	0	0	7	5.40
Risley	4	0	3	2	2	0	1	1	0	0	0	1	2	6.00
Belcher	2	0	4.1	4	3	5	0	1	0	0	1	0	3	6.23
BWells	1	0	1	2	1	1	0	0	0	0	0	0	1	9.00
Bosio	2	0	7.2	10	9	4	2	0	0	0	0	0	9	10.57
Ayala	2	0	.2	6	4	1	0	0	0	0	0	0	4	54.00
Totals	5	0	51.1	50	33	32	43	4	1	3	2	2	33	5.79

SERIES BATTING / NEW YORK

	G	AB	R	H	2B	3B	HR	RBI	SO	BB	AVG
BWilliams cf	5	21	8	9	2	0	2	5	3	7	.429
Mattingly 1b	5	24	3	10	4	0	1	6	5	1	.417
O'Neill rf	5	18	5	6	0	0	3	6	5	5	.333
Stanley c	5	16	2	5	0	0	1	3	1	2	.313
Boggs 3b	4	19	4	5	2	0	1	3	5	3	.263
Fernandez ss	5	21	0	5	2	0	0	0	2	2	.238
RDavis 3b	2	5	0	1	0	0	0	0	2	0	.200
Velarde 2b-3b-lf	5	17	3	3	0	0	0	1	4	6	.176
Sierra dh	5	23	2	4	2	0	2	5	7	2	.174
Leyritz c	2	7	1	1	0	0	1	2	1	0	.143
James lf	4	12	0	1	0	0	0	0	1	1	.083
GWilms pr-lf-rf	5	5	1	0	0	0	0	0	3	2	.000
Kelly pr-2b	4	3	3	0	0	0	0	1	3	1	.000
Strawberry ph	2	2	0	0	0	0	0	0	1	0	.000
Posada pr	1	0	1	0	0	0	0	0	0	0	—
Totals	5	193	33	50	12	0	11	32	43	32	.259

SERIES PITCHING / NEW YORK

	G	CG	IP	H	R	BB	SO	HB	WP	W	L	S	ER	ERA
Rivera	3	0	5.1	3	0	1	8	0	0	1	0	0	0	0.00
Wckmn	3	0	3	5	0	0	3	0	0	0	0	0	0	0.00
Cone	2	0	15.2	15	8	9	14	0	2	1	0	0	8	4.60
Pettitte	1	0	7	9	4	3	0	0	0	0	0	0	4	5.14
Htchck	2	0	1.2	2	2	2	1	0	0	0	0	0	1	5.40
Kmniecki	1	0	5	9	5	4	4	0	0	0	0	0	4	7.20
McDwell	3	0	7	8	7	4	6	1	1	0	2	0	7	9.00
Wttland	3	0	4.1	8	7	2	5	1	0	0	1	0	7	14.55
Howe	2	0	1	4	2	0	0	0	0	0	0	0	2	18.00
Totals	5	0	50	63	35	25	41	2	3	2	3	0	33	5.94

Mo Vaughn's big bat was silenced by the Indians' pitching, and Boston paid the price—Cleveland went on to the ALCS.

By Russell Beeker, Baseball Weekly

AL Division Playoffs: Seattle refused to lose, Cleveland kept right on winning

The Yankees had quieted the Seattle fans, amazing considering that they numbered 57,180 in the Kingdome. New York was up 5-0 in Game Four and needed only this one win to bury the Mariners. Up came Edgar Martinez.

Martinez is overshadowed nationally by superstar Ken Griffey Jr. and by the "Big Unit," Randy Johnson. The 32-year-old designated hitter is quiet and unassuming. He's also the AL batting champion who hit .356 with 29 home runs and 113 RBI. The Yankees know all about him.

"The best way to pitch him is to try to keep him in the ballpark and hope that he hits a line drive right at somebody," said Yankees manager Buck Showalter.

Right-hander Scott Kamieniecki didn't do that. Martinez hit a three-run home run in the third, and Seattle—and the crowd—was back in the game.

"The fans really get your adrenaline going so fast—they play a big part in our team," Martinez said.

With the score tied 6-6 in the eighth, Yankees closer John Wetteland was in the game. Vince Coleman walked, Joey Cora reached base on an infield single, and Ken Griffey Jr. was hit in the left foot with a pitch.

Up came Martinez. The count went to 2-2. Then Wetteland tried to blow a fastball past him. It landed beyond the 405-foot center-field fence, prompting an 11-8 Mariners win and a final Game Five.

Pandemonium in the crowd.

Playing their first postseason game in 41 years, the Indians beat the Boston Red Sox 5-4 in Game One on a home run with two outs in the 13th inning. Who in the Murder Inc. lineup slugged it? Try Light-hitter Inc. Tony Pena.

"We broke out our secret weapon," Cleveland manager Mike Hargrove said. "You look at Tony Pena, and you don't think home run. But Tony's a clutch player. He's been a clutch player all his life."

Pena, who spent four years with the Red Sox (1990–93) drove a 3-0 pitch from Zane Smith just over the bleacher railing in left field.

The Indians slammed a major-league-high 207 home runs during the season. Pena had five.

He didn't get in until after the Indians pinch-ran for starting catcher Sandy Alomar in the 11th inning.

"With a 3-0 count, I thought he'd be thinking I would take a pitch," the 38-year-old Pena said. "He threw a fastball, and I hit it hard."

The win was Cleveland's 28th victory on its last at-bat.

This is how the Indians won 100 games in the regular season.

Fifteen innings of high drama, long balls and fan rowdiness ended when Jim Leyritz belted an opposite-field, two-run homer over Yankee Stadium's right-field fence in Game Two.

At home plate, teammates mobbed Leyritz, who had his only hit after catching every inning of the five-hour, 12-minute marathon that ended at 1:19 a.m. Thursday with the score 7-5.

Leyritz slammed a 3-1 pitch off right-hander Tim Belcher, Seattle's fifth pitcher, with one out and Pat Kelly on first base after a walk.

"He got the slider up, and I hit it out," Leyritz said. "Besides being exhausted, I'm really elated."

During the wild celebration, rain-soaked fans from the sellout crowd of 57,126 sang along with Frank Sinatra's rendition of "New York, New York." Belcher had some fireworks after the game, slamming his glove into a wall in the tunnel leading from the dugout and angrily slapping a television camera out of a cameraman's hands.

In addition to the home run, he allowed a two-out, RBI double to Ruben Sierra that tied it in the 12th.

A few minutes later, Belcher appeared calm as he answered questions.

"I gave up the homer to Leyritz because I didn't throw strikes, got behind 3-0, had to come in with the ball and he hit it," he said. "But the key was earlier when I got Paul O'Neill on a popup, and then all I have to do is give a split-finger down to Sierra, and it's over a lot earlier."

Box score: AL division playoffs

CLEVELAND 3, BOSTON 0

SERIES BATTING / BOSTON

	G	AB	R	H	2B	3B	HR	RBI	SO	BB	AVG
Alicea 2b	3	10	1	6	1	0	1	1	2	2	.600
Mcfarlane c	3	9	0	3	0	0	0	1	3	0	.333
McGee rf-ph	2	4	0	1	0	0	0	1	2	0	.333
Naehring 3b	3	13	2	4	0	0	1	1	1	0	.308
JnValentin ss	3	12	1	3	1	0	1	2	1	3	.250
Jefferson dh	1	4	1	1	0	0	0	0	1	0	.250
Greenwell lf	3	15	0	3	0	0	0	0	1	0	.200
Canseco dh	3	13	0	0	0	0	0	0	2	2	.000
Hosey rf	3	12	1	0	0	0	0	0	3	2	.000
Haselman c	1	2	0	0	0	0	0	0	0	0	.000
Stairs ph	1	1	0	0	0	0	0	0	1	0	.000
Tinsley cf	1	5	0	0	0	0	0	0	2	1	.000
MVaughn 1b	3	14	0	0	0	0	0	0	7	1	.000
Totals	3	114	6	21	2	0	3	6	26	11	.184

SERIES PITCHING / BOSTON

	G	CG	IP	H	R	BB	SO	HB	WP	W	L	S	ER	ERA
Belinda	1	0	.1	0	0	0	0	0	0	0	0	0	0	0.00
MMaddux	2	0	3	2	0	1	1	1	0	0	0	0	0	0.00
Hudson	1	0	1	2	0	1	0	0	1	0	0	0	0	0.00
Stanton	1	0	2.1	1	0	0	4	0	0	0	0	0	0	0.00
Clemens	1	0	7	5	3	1	5	0	0	0	0	0	3	3.86
Hanson	1	0	8	4	4	4	5	1	0	0	1	0	4	4.50
ZSmith	1	0	1.1	1	1	0	0	0	0	0	1	0	1	6.75
Wakefield	1	0	5.1	5	7	5	4	1	0	0	1	0	7	11.81
Cormier	2	0	.2	2	1	1	2	1	0	0	0	0	1	13.49
Aguilera	1	0	.2	3	1	0	1	0	0	0	0	0	1	13.50
Totals	3	0	29.2	25	17	13	22	4	1	0	3	0	17	5.16

SERIES BATTING / INDIANS

	G	AB	R	H	2B	3B	HR	RBI	SO	BB	AVG
Kirby pr-rf	2	1	0	1	0	0	0	0	0	0	1.000
Pena c	2	2	1	1	0	0	1	1	0	0	.500
Murray dh	3	13	3	5	0	1	1	3	1	2	.385
Sorrento 1b	3	10	2	3	0	0	0	1	3	2	.300
Baerga 2b	3	14	2	4	1	0	0	1	1	0	.286
Belle lf	3	11	3	3	1	0	1	3	3	4	.273
SAlomar c	3	11	1	2	1	0	0	1	1	0	.182
Vizquel ss	3	12	2	2	1	0	0	4	2	2	.167
Lofton cf	3	13	1	2	0	0	0	0	3	1	.154
Thome 3b	3	13	1	2	0	0	1	3	6	1	.154
HPerry 1b	1	1	0	0	0	0	0	0	0	0	.000
MRamirez rf	3	12	1	0	0	0	0	0	2	1	.000
Espinoza 3b	1	1	0	0	0	0	0	0	0	0	.000
Totals	3	114	17	25	4	1	4	17	22	13	.219

SERIES PITCHING / CLEVELAND

	G	CG	IP	H	R	BB	SO	HB	WP	W	L	S	ER	ERA
Assnmchr	3	0	1.2	0	0	0	3	0	0	0	0	0	0	0.00
Hershiser	1	0	7.1	3	0	2	7	0	1	1	0	0	0	0.00
KHill	1	0	1.1	1	0	0	2	0	0	1	0	0	0	0.00
Mesa	2	0	2	0	0	2	0	0	0	0	0	1	0	0.00
Plunk	1	0	1.1	1	0	1	1	0	0	0	0	0	0	0.00
Nagy	1	0	7	4	1	5	6	0	0	1	0	0	1	0.78
DeMrtnz	1	0	6	5	2	0	2	0	0	0	0	0	2	3.00
Poole	1	0	1.2	2	1	1	2	0	0	0	0	0	1	5.40
Tavarez	3	0	2.2	5	2	0	3	0	0	0	0	0	2	6.75
Totals	3	0	31	21	6	11	26	0	1	3	0	1	6	1.74

CINCINNATI 3, LOS ANGELES 0

SERIES BATTING / CINCINNATI

	G	AB	R	H	2B	3B	HR	RBI	SO	BB	AVG
MJackson p	3	1	0	1	1	0	0	3	0	0	1.000
Duncan ph-2b	2	3	1	2	0	0	0	1	0	0	.667
Morris 1b	3	10	5	5	1	0	0	2	1	3	.500
MLewis ph-3b	2	2	2	1	0	0	1	5	0	1	.500
Larkin ss	3	13	2	5	0	0	0	1	2	1	.385
Santiago c	3	9	2	3	0	0	1	3	3	2	.333
DWells p	1	3	0	1	0	0	0	0	1	0	.333
Boone 2b	3	10	4	3	1	0	1	1	3	1	.300
Branson 3b	3	7	0	2	1	0	0	2	0	2	.286
Gant lf	3	13	3	3	0	0	1	2	3	0	.231
RSanders rf	3	13	3	2	1	0	1	2	9	2	.154
Howard cf	3	10	0	1	1	0	0	0	2	0	.100
DLewis ph-cf	3	3	0	0	0	0	0	0	1	0	.000
Walton ph-cf-lf	3	3	0	0	0	0	0	0	1	1	.000
Schourek p	1	2	0	0	0	0	0	0	1	0	.000
Smiley p	1	2	0	0	0	0	0	0	1	0	.000
Totals	3	104	22	29	6	0	5	22	28	13	.279

SERIES PITCHING / CINCINNATI

	G	CG	IP	H	R	BB	SO	HB	WP	W	L	S	ER	ERA
DWells	1	0	6.1	6	1	1	8	1	0	1	0	0	0	0.00
MJackson	3	0	3.2	4	0	0	1	0	0	0	0	0	0	0.00
Burba	1	0	1	2	0	1	0	0	0	1	0	0	0	0.00
Schourek	1	0	7	5	2	3	5	0	0	1	0	0	2	2.57
Smiley	1	0	6	9	2	0	1	0	0	0	0	0	2	3.00
JBrantley	3	0	3	5	2	0	2	0	0	0	0	1	2	6.00
Totals	3	0	27	31	7	5	17	1	0	3	0	1	6	2.00

SERIES BATTING / LOS ANGELES

	G	AB	R	H	2B	3B	HR	RBI	SO	BB	AVG
Hansen ph	3	3	0	2	0	0	0	0	0	0	.667
Fonville ss	3	12	1	6	0	0	0	0	1	0	.500
Karros 1b	3	12	3	6	1	0	2	4	0	1	.500
RKelly lf	3	11	0	4	0	0	0	0	1	0	.364
Butler cf	3	15	1	4	0	0	0	1	3	0	.267
DeShields 2b	3	12	1	3	0	0	0	0	3	1	.250
Piazza c	3	14	1	3	1	0	1	1	2	0	.214
Mondesi rf	3	9	0	2	0	0	0	1	2	0	.222
Wallach 3b	3	12	0	1	0	0	0	0	3	1	.083
Valdes p	1	3	0	0	0	0	0	0	0	0	.000
Hollndswrth rf	2	2	0	0	0	0	0	0	0	0	.000
Webster ph	2	2	0	0	0	0	0	0	0	0	.000
Nomo p	1	2	0	0	0	0	0	0	2	0	.000
RMartinez p	1	1	0	0	0	0	0	0	0	0	.000
CGwynn p	1	1	0	0	0	0	0	0	1	0	.000
Nomo p	1	2	0	0	0	0	0	0	2	0	.000
Totals	3	111	7	31	2	0	3	7	17	5	.279

SERIES PITCHING / LOS ANGELES

	G	CG	IP	H	R	BB	SO	HB	WP	W	L	S	ER	ERA
Valdes	1	0	7	3	2	1	6	0	0	0	0	0	0	0.00
Astacio	3	0	3.1	1	0	0	5	0	0	0	0	0	0	0.00
Osuna	3	0	3.1	3	1	1	3	0	0	0	1	0	1	2.70
Guthrie	3	0	1.1	2	1	1	1	0	0	0	0	0	1	6.75
Nomo	1	0	5	7	5	2	6	0	1	0	1	0	5	9.00
RMartinez	1	0	4.1	10	7	2	3	0	0	0	1	0	7	14.54
JCmmngs	2	0	1.1	3	3	2	3	0	0	0	0	0	3	20.25
Tapani	2	0	.1	0	3	4	1	0	0	0	0	0	3	81.00
Totals	3	0	26	29	22	13	28	0	1	0	3	0	20	6.92

By H.Darr Beiser, USA TODAY

Steve Avery's ineffective performance in the divisional playoffs (⅔ inning, 1 run, 13.50 ERA) didn't stop the Braves from winning.

NL Division Playoffs: Cincy swept the series, but Atlanta had to work for it

Fred McGriff had been virtually silent all series. The Braves first baseman entered Game Four of the Division Series against the Colorado Rockies with just three hits—all singles—in 13 at-bats.

It had been a particularly frustrating series for a player who led Atlanta in home runs (27) this season, breaking a seven-year streak of hitting 30 or more.

Then came the third inning of Game Four. With the Braves trailing 4-2, McGriff homered to left off Rockies starter Bret Saberhagen, scoring Chipper Jones and tying the score 4-4. McGriff added a solo shot in the fifth and a two-run single in the sixth, finishing the series 6-for-18 (.333) with six RBI.

McGriff thus joined Chipper Jones in Game One and Marquis Grissom in Game Two, and become one of three Braves players who had two-home-run games in one postseason series, the first time it had happened since the 1932 New York Yankees.

Afterward, with champagne flying in the Braves clubhouse, McGriff shrugged off his late-series flurry. "It was just a matter of making some adjustments," he said. "Sooner or later, you're going to get your hits."

In the clubhouse, Benito Santiago showed off his bat—a Cooper C271 model, caramel-colored and glistening—that served notice in inning one of Game One that the Dodgers were doomed. "I saved it for the playoffs," Santiago said of his prized bat. "I used it for just a couple of [regular-season] games and I hit the ball so well with it. It's superstitious."

Santiago took Ramon Martinez deep with a two-run home run, which highlighted a four-run Reds outburst. The Reds went on to win 7-2.

"The four-run first kind of helped," said Reds starter Pete Schourek. "Obviously, it's huge to get this first one."

In Game Three, Mark Lewis slammed the door.

In the sixth, after Hal Morris and Benito Santiago singled, Dodgers skipper Tommy Lasorda pulled starter Hideo Nomo, who had thrown 92 pitches. In came Kevin Tapani, who promptly walked Bret Boone to load the bases.

With left-handed Jeff Branson due up, the Dodgers replaced Tapani with lefty Mark Guthrie.

Reds manager Davey Johnson responded by sending up the right-handed Mark Lewis.

Lewis worked the count to 2-and-2 before lifting a high ball toward left field. He stopped at first base to watch his shot travel, then thrust both arms skyward once the ball vanished.

Presto, the first pinch-hit grand slam in major league postseason history, turning a relatively close game into a 10-1 rout and leading to a Reds sweep.

The ball seemed like a routine out to Chipper Jones. In other parks, perhaps it would have been. But by the time the Atlanta Braves rookie rounded first base in the ninth inning of Game One, he remembered that he was in Coors Field, the park that turns fly balls into round-trippers.

As Colorado Rockies center fielder Mike Kingery futilely scaled the wall in right center field, Jones knew he had his second home run of the game. He thrust his fists into the air and flew around the bases. It was, he said later, "like I was running two feet off the ground."

It was Jones's second home run of the game.

The home run put Atlanta ahead 5-4. Three Mark Wohlers outs later, the Braves had an unlikely win in a game in which the Rockies had led 3-1 after five innings and gotten the better of Braves ace Greg Maddux.

ATLANTA 3, COLORADO 1

SERIES BATTING / ATLANTA

	G	AB	R	H	2B	3B	HR	RBI	SO	BB	AVG
DwSmith ph	4	3	0	2	1	0	0	1	0	0	.667
Mordecai ph	2	3	1	2	1	0	0	2	0	0	.667
Grissom cf	4	21	5	11	2	0	3	4	3	0	.524
Klesko lf	4	15	5	7	1	0	0	1	3	0	.467
JLopez c	3	9	0	4	0	0	0	3	3	0	.444
CpJones 3b	4	18	4	7	2	0	2	4	2	2	.389
McGriff 1b	4	18	4	6	0	0	2	6	3	2	.333
Glavine p	1	3	0	1	0	0	0	0	1	0	.333
Polonia ph	3	3	0	1	0	0	0	2	1	0	.333
Justice rf	4	13	2	3	0	0	0	0	2	5	.231
Lemke 2b	4	19	3	4	1	0	0	1	3	1	.211
Devreaux ph-lf	4	5	1	1	0	0	0	0	0	0	.200
O'Brien c	2	5	0	1	0	0	0	0	1	1	.200
GMaddux p	2	6	1	1	0	0	0	0	1	0	.167
Blauser ss	3	6	0	0	0	0	0	0	3	1	.000
Belliard ss	4	5	1	0	0	0	0	0	1	0	.000
Smoltz p	1	2	0	0	0	0	0	0	0	0	.000
Totals	4	154	27	51	8	0	7	24	27	12	.331

SERIES PITCHING / ATLANTA

	G	CG	IP	H	R	BB	SO	HB	W	P	W	L	S	ER	ERA
Clontz	1	0	1.1	0	0	2	0	0	0	0	0	0	0	0	0.00
APena	3	0	3	3	0	1	2	1	0	2	0	0	0	0	0.00
Borbon	1	0	1	1	0	0	3	0	0	0	0	0	0	0	0.00
Mercker	1	0	.1	0	0	0	0	0	0	0	0	0	0	0	0.00
Glavine	1	0	7	5	3	1	3	0	0	0	0	0	0	2	2.57
GMaddux	2	0	14	19	7	2	7	1	0	1	0	0	7		4.50
Wohlers	3	0	2.2	6	2	2	4	0	0	0	1	2	2	6	6.75
McMichael	3	0	1.1	1	1	2	1	0	0	0	0	0	1		6.75
Smoltz	1	0	5.2	5	5	1	6	1	0	0	0	5			7.94
Avery	1	0	.2	1	1	0	1	0	0	0	0	0	1		13.50
Totals	4	0	37	41	19	9	29	3	1	3	1	2	18		4.38

SERIES BATTING / COLORADO

	G	AB	R	H	2B	3B	HR	RBI	SO	BB	AVG
Bichette lf	4	17	6	10	3	0	1	3	3	1	.588
Castilla 3b	4	15	3	7	1	0	3	6	1	0	.467
EYoung 2b	4	16	3	7	1	0	1	2	2	2	.438
Burks cf	2	6	1	2	1	0	0	2	1	0	.333
Galarraga 1b	4	18	1	5	1	0	2	6	0	0	.278
Bates ph-3b	4	4	0	1	0	0	0	0	0	0	.250
LWalker rf	4	14	3	3	0	0	1	3	4	3	.214
Kingery cf	4	10	1	2	0	0	0	1	0	0	.200
Weiss ss	4	12	1	2	0	0	0	0	2	3	.167
Girardi c	4	16	0	2	0	0	0	0	2	0	.125
VanderWal ph	4	4	0	0	0	0	0	0	2	0	.000
Swift p	1	3	0	0	0	0	0	0	2	0	.000
Painter p-ph	2	2	0	0	0	0	0	0	1	0	.000
Ritz p	2	2	0	0	0	0	0	0	0	0	.000
Hubbard pr-ph	3	2	0	0	0	0	0	0	0	0	.000
Owens c	1	1	0	0	0	0	0	0	1	0	.000
Saberhagen p	1	1	0	0	0	0	0	0	1	0	.000
Totals	4	143	19	41	7	0	6	18	29	9	.287

SERIES PITCHING / COLORADO

	G	CG	IP	H	R	BB	SO	HB	W	P	W	L	S	ER	ERA
SReed	3	0	2.2	2	0	1	3	0	0	0	0	0	0	0	0.00
Holmes	3	0	1.2	6	2	0	2	0	0	1	0	0	0	0	0.00
MThsn	1	0	1	0	0	0	0	0	0	0	0	1	0	0	0.00
Reynoso	1	0	1	2	0	0	0	0	0	0	0	1	0	0	0.00
BRuffin	4	0	3.1	3	1	2	2	0	0	0	0	0	1	1	2.70
Painter	1	0	5	5	3	2	4	0	0	0	0	0	3		5.40
Swift	1	0	6	7	4	2	3	0	0	0	0	0	4		6.00
Leskanic	3	0	3	3	2	0	4	0	0	0	1	2	6		6.00
Ritz	2	0	7	12	7	3	5	0	0	0	0	0	6	7	7.71
Sbhgen	1	0	4	7	6	1	3	0	0	0	1	0	5		11.25
MMunoz	4	0	1.1	4	2	1	1	1	0	0	1	0	2		13.50
Totals	4	0	36	51	27	12	27	1	0	1	3	1	23		5.75

POSTSEASON

Game Five of the National League Championship Series couldn't have been more appropriate. It took Atlanta's Mark Wohlers just three pitches to blow away Reggie Sanders, ending The Hunt for Reds October in four games and bringing a merciful conclusion to Sanders's nightmarish postseason.

After an MVP-quality regular season, he hit just .125 (2 for 16) against Atlanta and set a record for an NLCS of five or fewer games with 10 strikeouts. The previous mark was seven. Including the Division Series, Sanders was 4 for 29 with 19 strikeouts. He hit into a double play to end Game One with the tying run on third base. He struck out with the potential winning run on third in the eighth inning of Game Two. He struck out with the bases loaded in Game Three, when the momentum was ripe for the picking.

Yet Sanders faced the music after each game with the same diplomacy. Hiding in the trainer's room is not part of his repertoire.

"What I do on and off the field is nobody else's problem. It's my problem," he explained midway through the series. "I don't have to show my frustrations to you just because of what has happened to myself."

Sanders wasn't alone in his agony. Slugger Ron Gant, who could have taken revenge upon the team that released him after his leg injury, was 3 for 16 with just one RBI against the Braves. First baseman Hal Morris was 2 for 12 and was robbed by at least three spectacular plays. Catcher Benito Santiago was 3 for 13. Infielder Jeff Branson was 1 for 9.

Barry Larkin (.389) was the only Reds regular to hit within 52

(Continued on next page)

Cleveland's Kenny Lofton was just one of many players who added thrills to the playoffs and reminded fans of why they love baseball.

By Robert Hanashiro, USA TODAY

Playoffs jogged our memories, Seattle stole our hearts

It all came back to us. We started to remember exactly what it is that makes the postseason so special. The playoffs were missing for only one year, but it seemed like they had been gone much longer than that.

We had forgotten the excitement of postseason extra-inning epics until Game Five of the Seattle-New York series, when the crowd was whipped into a frenzy as Randy Johnson made a relief appearance. We had forgotten the anxiety of the tense, nervous moments when a home team takes its final at-bat, on the verge of elimination, needing a pair of runs to survive.

Thank goodness for the "Refuse to Lose" Mariners.

No one pictured Seattle as the team to wake us up, but they grabbed us by the shoulders and gave us a good shake. They reminded us what an exciting playoff run can do—for a city and for a sport. Baseball took its share of bashing in 1995, and rightly so. But ever since Seattle and California met in a one-game playoff for the AL West title, baseball has been very, very good to us.

There were record postseason games on consecutive nights, extra-inning thrillers between Cleveland-Boston and Seattle-New York. Then there was the ninth-inning magic from Atlanta, scoring in its final at-bat in each victory against Colorado. The Braves employed fantastic finishes in the NLCS as well, bagging a pair of extra-inning wins. More drama: The rise and fall of Cincinnati—they swept Los Angeles but got swept by Atlanta.

But it was Seattle that captured our imaginations. America still loves the underdog. The Kingdome, previously baseball's mausoleum, was transformed into the game's most energetic facility since the Metrodome during Minnesota's heyday. Players and coaches alike commented on the noise, fireworks, music, and chants that filled the gray, ugly building. With startling swiftness, the dome changed from dark and lonely to bright and bustling. After 19 seasons, the baseball bug finally bit Seattle. And the Mariners—fighting to stay in town and gain a new stadium—responded by biting right back, chewing up the Angels and then the Yankees in a total of four must-win games at the Kingdome.

It's difficult to put the Division Series against the Yankees in proper historical perspective. After all, exactly how significant is a playoff series if the league or world championship isn't at stake? But based solely on excitement, drama, tension and entertainment, many observers believe it ranks among the best postseason matchups. Fortune smiled on baseball for a change, clearing the stage for Game Five, perhaps the game that will be credited with starting baseball's road to recovery. It was the first 1995 playoff game broadcast to the entire country, and it was an exhilarating reminder of the national pastime's glory days. We saw 57,000 fans—screaming, shouting and waving homemade signs—imploring their team in a loser-goes-home battle. We saw pitchers on short rest, giving their all and damning possible consequences to their arms and careers. We saw several ties and lead changes, down to the 11th inning, when the visitors scored once and the home team twice, ending the game on a bang-bang play at the plate that set off pandemonium.

As manager Lou Piniella said, "If you didn't enjoy that, you don't enjoy baseball."

He was right. Many of us fans had allowed ourselves to forget how much we love baseball. We stayed away and tuned out. We began to confuse baseball with owners meetings and players strikes, with lockouts and replacements. But that has never been what the game is about. The game is about gaining a lead and trying to shut down the opposition, hitting homers and mounting comebacks, taking away base hits with breathless glovework—with championships on the line.

Thanks to the thrilling 1995 postseason, it's all coming back to us now. We're beginning to remember what we started to forget.

—by Paul White

points of his season average.

As a team: The Reds hit .209 in the series. After scoring 747 runs—second in the league—this season, they scored just five in the NLCS. That shattered the previous record for a four-game series (10 runs by Pittsburgh in 1974).

"We didn't have this much trouble scoring runs during our 1-8 start," Larkin said, "but we weren't facing the Atlanta pitching staff, either."

The Reds were just 3 for 29 with runners in scoring position. They hit into eight double plays, five in the first game.

They became the fourth team in NLCS history to go without a home run in the NLCS. Oddly, they did not go four consecutive games in the regular season without a home run. They hit 161 homers during the season, then added five more in the Division Series against the Dodgers.

They stole just four bases—none in the last two games—after leading the majors with 190 during the season.

It was just the third time the Reds were swept in a postseason series. In 1979, they lost three consecutive in a best-of-five NLCS against Pittsburgh. In 1939, they were swept by the New York Yankees in the World Series.

Larkin is one of just four Reds still around from the 1990 World Series sweep of Oakland.

"Now I'm on the other side of a sweep," he said. "But that's the game of baseball."

ALCS: Bats drew raves, arms won games

Postgame talk after Games Four and Five centered around a familiar topic: the potent Cleveland attack. Albert Belle and Sandy Alomar sat out Game Four with injuries. Eddie Murray moved into Belle's cleanup spot and belted a three-run homer in the first inning, providing the only runs necessary for Ken Hill and the bullpen in a six-hit shutout. Jim Thome threw another log on the fire, just in case, with a two-run dinger in the third. Those same two were at it again in Game Five. Murray (3 for 3) singled home a run for a 1-0 lead in the first. And Thome's blast put Cleveland up 3-2—the final score and the series advantage that the Indians carried to Seattle.

The Indians' offense was the talk of baseball all year, but they didn't really break out until the 7-zip blanking in Game Four. They won Games Two and Five with modest run production. Orel Hershiser won both contests, receiving spectacular defense in Game Two and overcoming horrendous defense in Game Five.

What people seemed to forget was that Cleveland had led the league in pitching as well as hitting. After winning the AL Central by 30 games, clinching the title with three weeks remaining in the season, there was speculation that Cleveland might wilt at the first sign of adversity in the postseason. Cleveland's season had the nature of a leisurely Sunday drive, while Seattle's was more like a demolition derby held on an obstacle course.

First-base coach Dave Nelson said that Seattle adopted the slogan, "Refuse to

(Continued on next page)

NLCS composite box score: Atlanta 4, Cincinnati 0

ATLANTA BRAVES BATTING

Player	G	AB	R	H	2B	3B	HR	RBI	BB	SO	AVG
Polonia pr-lf	3	2	0	1	0	0	0	1	0	0	.500
Avery p	2	2	0	1	0	0	0	0	0	0	.500
Jones 3b	4	16	3	7	0	0	1	3	3	1	.438
McGriff 1b	4	16	5	7	4	0	0	0	3	0	.438
O'Brien c	2	5	1	2	0	0	1	3	0	1	.400
Lopez c	3	14	2	5	1	0	1	3	0	1	.357
Smoltz p	1	3	0	1	0	0	0	0	0	1	.333
Devereaux rf	4	13	2	4	1	0	1	5	1	2	.308
Belliard ss	4	11	1	3	0	0	0	0	0	3	.273
Justice rf	3	11	1	3	0	0	0	1	2	1	.273
Grissom cf	4	19	2	5	0	1	0	0	1	4	.263
Lemke 2b	4	18	2	3	0	0	0	1	1	0	.167
Klesko lf	4	7	0	0	0	0	0	0	3	4	.000
Blauser ss	1	4	0	0	0	0	0	0	1	2	.000
Maddux p	1	3	0	0	0	0	0	0	0	1	.000
Mordecai ph-ss	2	2	0	0	0	0	0	0	0	1	.000
Smith ph	2	2	0	0	0	0	0	0	0	0	.000
Glavine p	1	1	0	0	0	0	0	0	1	0	.000
Totals	4	149	19	42	6	1	4	17	16	22	.282

ATLANTA BRAVES PITCHING

Player	G	CG	IP	H	R	BB	SO	HB	WP	W	L	S	ER	ERA
Avery	2	0	6	2	0	4	6	0	0	1	0	0	0	0.00
APena	3	0	3	2	0	1	4	0	0	0	0	0	0	0.00
McMichael	3	0	2.2	0	0	1	2	0	0	1	0	1	0	0.00
Clontz	1	0	.1	1	0	0	0	0	0	0	0	0	0	0.00
Maddux	1	0	8	7	1	2	4	1	1	1	0	0	1	1.12
Glavine	1	0	7	7	1	2	5	1	0	0	0	0	1	1.29
Wohlers	4	0	5	2	1	0	8	0	0	1	0	0	1	1.80
Smoltz	1	0	7	7	2	2	2	0	0	0	0	0	2	2.57
Totals	4	0	39	28	5	12	31	2	1	4	0	1	5	1.15

CINCINNATI REDS BATTING

Player	G	AB	R	H	2B	3B	HR	RBI	BB	SO	AVG
Harris ph	3	2	0	2	0	0	0	1	0	0	1.000
Taubensee c	2	2	0	1	0	0	0	0	0	0	.500
Wells p	1	2	0	1	0	0	0	0	0	0	.500
Larkin ss	4	18	1	7	2	1	0	0	1	1	.389
Howard ph	4	8	0	2	1	0	0	1	2	0	.250
MLewis 3b	2	4	0	1	0	0	0	0	1	1	.250
Santiago c	4	13	0	3	0	0	0	0	2	3	.231
Boone 2b	4	14	1	3	0	0	0	0	1	2	.214
Gant lf	4	16	1	3	0	0	0	1	0	3	.188
Morris 1b	4	12	0	2	1	0	0	1	1	1	.167
Sanders rf	4	16	0	2	0	0	0	0	2	10	.125
Branson ph-3b	4	9	2	1	1	0	0	0	0	2	.111
Walton cf-lf	2	7	0	0	0	0	0	0	0	2	.000
Schourek p	2	5	0	0	0	0	0	0	0	4	.000
Duncan ph	3	3	0	0	0	0	0	0	1	1	.000
Anthony ph	2	1	0	0	0	0	0	0	1	1	.000
DLewis cf	2	1	0	0	0	0	0	0	0	0	.000
Smiley p	1	1	0	0	0	0	0	0	0	0	.000
Totals	4	134	5	28	5	1	0	4	12	31	.209

CINCINNATI REDS BATTING

Player	G	CG	IP	H	R	BB	SO	HB	WP	W	L	S	ER	ERA
Brantley	2	0	2.2	0	0	2	1	0	0	0	0	0	0	0.00
Burba	2	0	3.2	3	0	4	0	0	1	0	0	0	0	0.00
Carrasco	1	0	1.1	1	0	0	3	0	0	0	0	0	0	0.00
Schourek	2	0	14.1	14	2	3	13	0	1	0	1	0	2	1.26
Smiley	1	0	5	5	2	0	1	0	0	0	0	0	2	3.60
Wells	1	0	6	8	3	2	3	0	0	0	1	0	3	4.50
Jackson	3	0	2.1	5	6	4	1	0	0	0	1	0	6	23.14
XHernandez	1	0	.2	3	2	0	0	0	0	0	0	0	2	27.00
Portugal	1	0	1	3	4	1	0	0	1	0	1	0	4	36.00
Totals	4	0	37	42	19	16	22	0	3	0	4	0	19	4.62

ALCS composite box score: Cleveland 4, Seattle 2

CLEVELAND INDIANS BATTING

Player	G	AB	R	H	2B	3B	HR	RBI	BB	SO	AVG
Lofton cf	6	24	4	11	0	2	0	3	4	6	.458
Baerga 2b	6	25	3	10	0	0	1	4	2	3	.400
Pena c	4	6	1	2	1	0	0	0	1	0	.333
MRamirez rf	6	21	2	6	0	0	2	2	2	5	.286
Alomar c	5	15	0	4	1	1	0	1	1	1	.267
Thome 3b	5	15	2	4	0	0	2	5	2	3	.267
Murray dh	6	24	2	6	1	0	1	3	2	3	.250
Belle lf	5	18	1	4	1	0	1	1	3	5	.222
Kirby rf-lf	5	5	2	1	0	0	0	0	0	0	.200
Sorrento 1b	4	13	2	2	1	0	0	0	2	3	.154
Espinoza 3b	4	8	1	1	0	0	0	0	0	3	.125
Vizquel ss	6	23	2	2	1	0	0	2	5	2	.087
Perry 1b	3	8	0	0	0	0	0	0	1	3	.000
Amaro pr	3	1	1	0	0	0	0	0	0	0	.000
Totals	**6**	**206**	**23**	**53**	**6**	**3**	**7**	**21**	**25**	**37**	**.257**

CLEVELAND INDIANS BATTING

Player	G	CG	IP	H	R	BB	SO	HB	WP	W	L	S	ER	ERA
Hill	1	0	7	5	0	3	6	0	0	1	0	0	0	0.00
Assenmacher	3	0	1.1	0	0	1	2	0	0	0	0	0	0	0.00
Poole	1	0	1	0	0	0	2	0	0	0	0	0	0	0.00
Ogea	1	0	.2	1	0	0	2	0	1	0	0	0	0	0.00
Embree	1	0	.1	0	0	0	1	0	0	0	0	0	0	0.00
Nagy	1	0	8	5	2	0	6	1	0	0	0	0	1	1.12
Hershiser	2	0	14	9	3	3	15	1	1	2	0	0	2	1.29
DMartinez	2	0	13.1	10	3	3	7	1	0	1	1	0	3	2.03
Mesa	4	0	4	3	1	1	1	0	0	0	0	1	1	2.25
Tavarez	4	0	3.1	3	1	1	2	0	0	0	1	0	1	2.70
Plunk	3	0	2	1	2	3	2	0	0	0	0	0	2	9.00
Totals	**6**	**0**	**55**	**37**	**12**	**15**	**46**	**3**	**2**	**4**	**2**	**1**	**10**	**1.64**

SEATTLE MARINERS BATTING

Player	G	AB	R	H	2B	3B	HR	RBI	BB	SO	AVG
ADiaz ph-lf	4	7	0	3	1	0	0	0	1	1	.429
Griffey Jr cf	6	21	7	7	2	0	1	2	4	4	.333
Buhner rf	6	23	5	7	2	0	3	5	2	8	.304
Sojo ss	6	20	2	5	2	0	0	1	0	2	.250
Cora 2b	6	23	2	4	1	0	0	0	1	0	.174
Blowers 3b	6	18	1	4	0	0	1	2	0	4	.222
TMartinez 1b	6	22	0	3	0	0	0	0	3	7	.136
Coleman lf	6	20	0	2	0	0	0	0	2	6	.100
EMartinez dh	6	23	0	2	0	0	0	0	2	5	.087
DWilson c	6	16	0	0	0	0	0	0	0	4	.000
Strange ph-3b	4	4	0	0	0	0	0	0	0	2	.000
Amaral ph	2	2	0	0	0	0	0	0	0	1	.000
Rodriguez ph	1	1	0	0	0	0	0	0	0	1	.000
Widger c	3	1	0	0	0	0	0	0	0	1	.000
Fermin 2b-ss	1	0	0	0	0	0	0	0	0	0	—
Totals	**6**	**201**	**12**	**37**	**8**	**0**	**5**	**10**	**15**	**46**	**.184**

SEATTLE MARINERS PITCHING

Player	G	CG	IP	H	R	BB	SO	HB	WP	W	L	S	ER	ERA
Charlton	3	0	6	1	0	1	5	1	1	1	0	1	0	0.00
Nelson	3	0	3	3	0	5	3	0	0	0	0	0	0	0.00
Risley	3	0	2.2	2	0	1	2	0	0	0	0	0	0	0.00
Johnson	2	0	15.1	12	6	2	13	0	0	1	0	0	4	2.35
Ayala	2	0	3.2	3	1	3	3	0	0	0	0	1	1	2.45
Wolcott	1	0	7	8	2	5	2	0	1	0	0	0	2	2.57
Wells	1	0	3	2	1	2	2	0	0	0	0	0	1	3.00
Bosio	1	0	5.1	7	3	2	3	0	0	0	1	0	2	3.38
Belcher	1	0	5.2	9	4	2	1	0	0	0	1	0	4	6.35
Benes	1	0	2.1	6	6	2	3	0	0	1	0	0	6	23.14
Totals	**6**	**0**	**54**	**53**	**23**	**25**	**37**	**1**	**1**	**2**	**4**	**1**	**20**	**3.33**

Lose," but Cleveland lived it all season long with a major-league-leading 27 wins in the last at-bat.

"We've faced adversity in this organization," Nelson said. "From the boating accident a couple of years ago, to the pressure where fans expect us to win and anything less is failure."

The nation was enamored of the Indians' big bats all season, but in the LCS, the pitchers got their due. They had just as big a role in Cleveland's 3-2 series lead as anyone else, shutting down a red-hot Mariners club. They kept games close until the offense did its thing; then the top-notch bullpen and Jose Mesa took over. After that, it was on to the clubhouse for another victorious postgame celebration.

Tribal leaders

39

Batting average

Team	BA
1. Cleveland Indians	.291
2. Chicago White Sox	.280
3. Boston Red Sox	.280

Home runs

Team	HR
1. Cleveland Indians	207
2. California Angels	186
3. Boston Red Sox	182

Earned-run average

Team	ERA
1. Cleveland Indians	3.83
2. Baltimore Orioles	4.31
3. Boston Red Sox	4.39

Manager Mike Hargrove (Indians) shook hands with manager Bobby Cox (Braves) before the Series—afterward it was all second-guesswork.

1995 World Series

▶**Game One:** Oct. 21
Atlanta 3, Cleveland 2

▶**Game Two:** Oct. 22
Atlanta 4, Cleveland 3

▶**Game Three:** Oct. 24
Cleveland 7, Atlanta 6, (11 inn.)

▶**Game Four:** Oct. 25
Atlanta 5, Cleveland 2

▶**Game Five:** Oct. 26
Cleveland 5, Atlanta 4

▶**Game Six:** Oct. 28
Atlanta 1, Cleveland 0

Atlanta wins series 4-2

World Series 1995: One man's victory, another's scrutiny

"So, did you even think about walking Lopez?"

"Why did you stay with Nagy so long?"

"When is the last time Poole batted?"

"Is there any particular reason we haven't seen Ogea?"

"Do you think Albert is pressing?"

Mike Hargrove was warned.

Managers with World Series experience told the Cleveland Indians skipper to anticipate intense scrutiny of every move in his first postseason.

"It's more than I thought," Hargrove admitted, calmly fielding another string of questions as smoothly as Omar Vizquel turns base hits into double plays.

Atlanta's Bobby Cox could have filled him in.

Good moves? Bad moves? They're good if they work, bad if they don't.

In a six-game Series, with five games decided by one run, 31 pitching changes (too many? not quite enough?), double switches, lefty-righty matchups, action in the bullpen...and don't forget daily pre- and postgame trips to the media interview room, win or lose...the losing manager inevitably gets second-guessed more.

Did Bobby Cox, veteran of every postseason since

1991, outmanage Hargrove? The results might suggest that. Is Cox any different from the guy who lost a World Series when a starting pitcher failed in a relief role, who lost a World Series when his bullpen buckled, who lost a 3-games-to-1 lead in a League Championship Series?

No, but the talent at his disposal was different. There was more of it in the right roles, allowing Cox to remove Tom Glavine from a one-hitter and expect Mark Wohlers to finish the job, to signal for a squeeze and know Rafael Belliard would get the bunt down.

If ever there was a year that Cox should have felt and, more important, reacted to the unseen heat of October, surely this was it.

There were the great expectations, certainly, but Cox displayed a serenity that indicated that he had come to grips with that portion of the job.

"I'm very proud of my career," he said when still a victory short of the championship, as he had been in 1991. "I tell our players that they should walk around like winners because that's what they are. It hasn't taken its toll on me."

Perhaps the biggest toll came from the highly publicized domestic dispute between Cox and his wife earlier in the season.

It left him facing second-guessing of another level, an obviously uncomfortable exposure far beyond the daily baseball banter he's accustomed to.

"A lot of people say he's under pressure," rookie third baseman Chipper Jones says. "But he doesn't show it in the dugout, in the clubhouse."

This was Atlanta's win-or-else year. World Series title or bust. Team on a mission. "The fans don't get mad at you the first year," Cox said, comparing his situation to that of Hargrove and the Indians' love affair with the Cleveland fans who had waited 41 years for a World Series game, 47 years to win just one of those games. "They give you a big parade. The next year they boo you."

Cox had never imagined that he would spend 20 seasons running somebody's ballclub when Yankees general manager Lee McPhail asked him to take over the Fort Lauderdale team in '71.

"I guess he saw in me what we see in a lot of organization guys," Cox says. "Guys that keep plugging, keep trying."

Hargrove, still eight years in arrears of Cox after celebrating his 46th birthday with a Game Five victory on Oct. 26, was plugging along quite nicely, thank you, in his first try at a postseason since he took Kinston to the Carolina League finals in 1987, his first year as a manager.

He took the stepped-up scrutiny in stride, as evidenced by one exchange with reporters:

ATLANTA 3, CLEVELAND 2

Cleveland 1 0 0   0 0 0   0 0 1

Atlanta   0 1 0   0 0 0   2 0 x

BATTING

Cleveland	ab	r	h	bi	bb	so	lo	avg
Lofton cf	4	2	1	0	0	0	1	.250
Vizquel ss	4	0	0	0	0	1	1	.000
Baerga 2b	4	0	0	1	0	1	0	.000
Belle lf	3	0	0	0	0	0	0	.000
Murray 1b	3	0	0	0	0	0	0	.000
Tavarez p	0	0	0	0	0	0	0	.000
Embree p	0	0	0	0	0	0	0	.000
Thome 3b	3	0	1	0	0	0	0	.333
Ramirez rf	3	0	0	0	0	2	1	.000
Alomar c	3	0	0	0	0	0	1	.000
Hershiser p	2	0	0	0	0	0	0	.000
Assnmchr p	0	0	0	0	0	0	0	.000
Sorrento 1b	1	0	0	0	0	0	0	.000
Totals	30	2	2	1	0	4	4	

BATTING

Atlanta	ab	r	h	bi	bb	so	lo	avg
Grissom cf	4	0	1	0	0	1	0	.250
Lemke 2b	3	0	1	0	1	1	0	.333
Jones 3b	4	0	0	0	0	2	3	.000
McGriff 1b	3	2	1	1	1	1	1	.333
Justice rf	1	1	0	0	2	0	0	.000
Klesko lf	2	0	0	0	0	2	1	.000
a-Dvrx ph-lf	0	0	0	0	1	0	0	.000
O'Brien c	2	0	0	0	0	1	1	.000
b-Plnia ph	1	0	0	1	0	0	3	.000
Lopez c	0	0	0	0	0	0	0	.000
Belliard ss	2	0	0	1	0	0	1	.000
Maddux p	3	0	0	0	0	1	1	.000
Totals	25	3	3	3	5	9	11	

a-walked for Klesko in the 7th; b-hit into fielder's choice for O'Brien in the 7th.

PITCHING

Cleveland	ip	h	r	er	bb	so	hr	era
Hrshiser (L, 0-1)	6	3	3	3	3	7	1	4.50
Assenmacher	0	0	0	0	1	0	0	0.00
Tavarez	1.1	0	0	0	1	0	0	0.00
Embree	.2	0	0	0	0	2	0	0.00

PITCHING

Atlanta	ip	h	r	er	bb	so	hr	era
Mddux (W, 1-0)	9	2	2	0	0	4	0	0.00

41

World Series: Game Two

ATLANTA 4, CLEVELAND 3

Cleveland 020 000 100

Atlanta   002 002 00x

BATTING

Cleveland	ab	r	h	bi	bb	so	lo	avg
Lofton cf	5	1	1	0	0	0	1	.222
Vizquel ss	4	0	1	0	1	0	1	.125
Baerga 2b	4	0	0	0	1	0	3	.000
Belle lf	3	1	1	0	1	1	2	.167
Murray 1b	3	1	1	2	1	0	1	.167
Ramirez rf	4	0	2	0	0	1	1	.286
Thome 3b	3	0	0	0	1	1	3	.167
TPena c	3	0	0	0	0	0	0	.000
b-Srnto ph	1	0	0	0	0	0	1	.000
Alomar c	0	0	0	0	0	0	0	.000
Martinez p	2	0	0	0	0	0	0	.000
Embree p	0	0	0	0	0	0	0	.000
a-Kirby ph	1	0	0	0	0	1	0	.000
Poole p	0	0	0	0	0	0	0	.000
Tavarez p	0	0	0	0	0	0	0	.000
c-Amro ph	1	0	0	0	0	1	0	.000
Totals	34	3	6	2	5	5	13	

a-struck out for Embree in the 7th; b-flied to center for Pena in the 8th; c-struck out for Tavarez in the 9th.

BATTING

Atlanta	ab	r	h	bi	bb	so	lo	avg
Grissom cf	3	1	1	0	0	0	1	.286
Lemke 2b	3	1	1	0	1	0	2	.333
Jones 3b	3	0	2	1	0	0	1	.286
McGriff 1b	4	0	0	0	0	0	3	.143
Justice rf	3	1	2	1	1	0	0	.500
Wohlers p	0	0	0	0	0	0	0	.000
Klesko lf	3	0	0	0	0	1	4	.000
Devereaux lf-rf	1	0	0	0	0	0	0	.000
Lopez c	3	1	1	2	0	0	0	.333
Belliard ss	4	0	0	0	0	1	1	.000
Glavine p	1	0	0	0	1	1	0	.000
a-Smith ph	1	0	1	0	0	0	0	1.000
McMichael p	0	0	0	0	0	0	0	.000
APena p	0	0	0	0	0	0	0	.000
Polonia lf	0	0	0	0	0	0	0	.000
Totals	29	4	8	4	3	3	12	

a-singled for Glavine in the 6th.

PITCHING

Cleveland	ip	h	r	er	bb	so	hr	era
Mrtnz (L, 0-1)	5.2	8	4	4	3	3	1	6.35
Embree	.1	0	0	0	0	0	0	0.00
Poole	1	0	0	0	0	0	0	0.00
Tavarez	1	0	0	0	0	0	0	0.00

PITCHING

Atlanta	ip	h	r	er	bb	so	hr	era
Glvine (W, 1-0)	6	3	2	2	3	3	1	3.00
McMchl (H, 1)	.2	1	1	0	1	1	0	0.00
APena (H, 1)	1	1	0	0	1	0	0	0.00
Wohlrs (S, 1)	1.1	1	0	0	0	1	0	0.00

By Robert Deutsch, USA TODAY

Braves catcher Javy Lopez leaps into pitcher Mark Wohlers' arms to celebrate the long-awaited World Series victory in Atlanta.

Q: How much do you read the papers to find out how you should have managed?

Hargrove: I read the papers every day. I don't know that I read it to find out how I should have managed.

Q: Have you ever read an article that really did enlighten you in a baseball sense?

Hargrove, nodding affirmative as the question unfolded, shot back: "No." The reporters laughed. He added, "I certainly couldn't do your job either."

Or, when asked what the Indians could do to hit better against Atlanta's pitchers: "I think it's real difficult when we try to hit with both eyes closed."

But this isn't a Casey Stengel talking circles around questions or a John McKay deflecting issues with a series of one-liners. Hargrove continued from the joke to the point he intended to make.

"I've watched and read and listened in the ALCS that Seattle's lineup didn't hit because of our pitching and now in the World Series our lineup isn't hitting because we're in a slump. I think you do a disservice to Atlanta pitching. It's a combination of us being impatient and them getting us to swing at pitches they want us to swing at."

That good pitching often took the managers out of the game for long stretches.

"You look up and it's the seventh inning," Cox says. "You haven't used a player. You think you have to do something."

He and Hargrove got their opportunities nightly, usually in the late innings when the squeaky-tight games tilted on the managers' moves and on how their players performed after the moves.

Game Two swung on Javy Lopez's swing, a sixth-inning two-run homer off Dennis Martinez after Hargrove elected not to put him on vacant first base with one out and to pitch to Belliard, who never did get a hit in the series.

Game Three almost got away from the Indians when starting pitcher Charles Nagy began the eighth by allowing the two hits that launched a three-run rally.

Nagy had thrown but 81 pitches and had handled the two hitters, Marquis Grissom and Luis Polonia, making Hargrove believe he could get past them before using his standard move of using a left-handed reliever against the lefty-laden middle of the Braves lineup.

Logical. But another of Hargrove's standard moves all season set off the second-guessing. It came partly because Nagy and the bullpen faltered and mostly because everyone was accustomed to seeing Julian Tavarez pitch eighth innings before Jose Mesa's mail-it-in ninths.

There was little talk about Mesa entering a Game Three ninth-inning tie rather than with a lead. After all, the Indians had to win that game, and eventually they did.

But had Mark Lemke, the first batter Mesa faced, gotten his line drive to the right field wall a few inches higher and thus over the wall, would putting the closer in an unaccustomed situation suddenly have been transformed into a managerial miscue?

And as for Cox, who lifted Tom Glavine, despite his having a one-hitter, for a two-out, nobody-on pinch-hitter. There he goes, being too loyal to his closer, the mumbling went. Hadn't he learned in '92?

What about it, Bobby?

"Tommy came and told us he was tired."

Oh.

But as long as there's a World Series, don't expect anyone to tire of second-guessing the manager.

World Series: Game Three

CLEVELAND 7, ATLANTA 6

Atlanta	100	001	130	00	
Cleveland	202	000	110	01	

BATTING

Atlanta	ab	r	h	bi	bb	so	lo	avg
Grissom cf	6	1	2	0	0	2	2	.308
Polonia lf	4	1	1	1	1	1	0	.200
Jones 3b	3	2	1	0	2	0	2	.300
McGriff 1b	5	1	3	2	0	1	1	.333
Justice rf	5	0	0	1	0	0	3	.222
Klesko dh	3	1	2	1	0	0	0	.250
b-Dvreux ph-dh	2	0	1	1	0	1	1	.333
Lopez c	5	0	0	0	0	0	4	.125
Lemke 2b	5	0	2	0	0	0	0	.364
Belliard ss	2	0	0	0	0	1	0	.000
a-Smith ph	1	0	0	0	0	0	0	.500
Mordecai ss	1	0	0	0	0	1	1	.000
Totals	**42**	**6**	**12**	**6**	**3**	**7**	**14**	

a-grounded to first for Belliard in the 7th; b-singled for Klesko in the 8th.

BATTING

Cleveland	ab	r	h	bi	bb	so	lo	avg
Lofton cf	3	3	3	0	3	0	0	.417
Vizquel ss	6	2	2	1	0	1	5	.214
Baerga 2b	6	0	3	3	0	0	3	.214
Espinoza pr	0	1	0	0	0	0	0	.000
Belle lf	4	0	1	1	2	0	0	.200
Murray dh	6	0	1	1	0	3	0	.167
Thome 3b	4	0	0	0	1	1	0	.100
Ramirez rf	2	1	0	0	3	0	2	.222
Sorrento 1b	4	0	1	0	0	3	1	.167
Kirby pr	0	0	0	0	0	0	0	.000
Perry 1b	1	0	0	0	0	1	1	.000
Alomar c	5	0	1	1	0	1	1	.125
Totals	**41**	**7**	**12**	**7**	**9**	**10**	**18**	

PITCHING

Atlanta	ip	h	r	er	bb	so	hr	era
Smoltz	2.1	6	4	4	2	4	0	15.43
Clontz	2.1	1	0	0	0	1	0	0.00
Mercker	2	1	1	1	2	2	0	4.50
McMichael	.2	1	1	1	1	1	0	6.75
Whlrs (BS, 1)	2.2	1	0	0	3	2	0	0.00
APena (L, 0-1)	0	2	1	1	1	0	0	9.00

PITCHING

Cleveland	ip	h	r	er	bb	so	hr	era
Nagy	7	8	5	5	1	4	2	6.43
Amchr (BS, 1)	.1	0	1	1	1	0	0	27.00
Tavarez	.2	1	0	0	0	0	0	0.00
Mesa (W, 1-0)	3	3	0	0	1	3	0	0.00

Braves refused to give in

ATLANTA 5, CLEVELAND 2

Atlanta	000	001	301
Cleveland	000	001	001

BATTING

Atlanta	ab	r	h	bi	bb	so	lo	avg
Grissm cf	4	1	3	0	1	0	0	.412
Polonia lf	4	1	2	1	0	0	1	.333
Dvreaux lf	0	0	0	0	1	0	0	.333
Jones 3b	4	1	0	0	1	0	3	.214
McGriff 1b	3	1	1	0	2	1	3	.333
Justice rf	5	0	1	2	0	0	5	.214
Klesko dh	3	1	1	1	1	1	1	.273
a-Mrdchai ph	1	0	0	0	0	0	1	.000
Lopez c	5	0	2	1	0	1	1	.231
Lemke 2b	5	0	1	0	0	0	2	.313
Belliard ss	3	0	0	0	0	1	2	.000
Totals	**37**	**5**	**11**	**5**	**6**	**4**	**19**	

a-flied to left for Klesko in the 9th.

BATTING

Cleveland	ab	r	h	bi	bb	so	lo	avg
Lofton cf	5	0	0	0	0	1	2	.294
Vizquel ss	3	0	0	0	1	0	1	.176
Baerga 2b	4	0	1	0	0	0	1	.222
Belle lf	3	1	1	1	1	1	0	.231
Murray dh	2	0	0	0	2	0	2	.143
Ramirez rf	3	1	1	1	0	0	1	.250
Perry 1b	3	0	0	0	0	1	3	.000
b-Sorrento ph	1	0	1	0	0	0	0	.286
Espinoza 3b	2	0	1	0	0	0	1	.500
a-Thome ph-3b	2	0	1	0	0	1	1	.167
Alomar c	4	0	0	0	0	1	2	.083
Totals	**32**	**2**	**6**	**2**	**5**	**5**	**14**	

a-doubled for Espinoza in the 7th; b-doubled for Perry in the 9th.

PITCHING

Atlanta	ip	h	r	er	bb	so	hr	era
Avery (W, 1-0)	6	3	1	1	5	3	1	1.50
McMichl (H, 2)	2	1	0	0	0	0	0	2.70
Wohlers	0	2	1	1	0	0	1	2.25
Borbon (S, 1)	1	0	0	0	0	2	0	0.00

PITCHING

Cleveland	ip	h	r	er	bb	so	hr	era
Hill (L, 0-1)	6.1	6	3	3	4	1	1	4.26
Assenmacher	.2	1	1	0	1	2	0	9.00
Tavarez	.2	2	0	0	1	1	0	0.00
Embree	1.1	2	1	1	0	0	0	3.86

After 17 postseason losses in three seasons, 13 of them by one run, would the Braves ever win a World Series? When monkeys fly, it seemed. Then the Braves exorcised their demons.

"The monkey was camped outside my house all day long," said Braves outfielder David Justice, who freed the Atlanta Nine with his Game Six home run, the only tally of the deciding game. "Now, he's going to Cleveland."

Actually, David had invited the monkey over the morning before Game Six with a newspaper interview questioning the support of Atlanta fans. "If we don't win, they'll probably burn our houses down," he said.

"My stomach hurt so bad before the game, I didn't eat," he said. "I thought 50,000 people were going to boo me in the World Series." No way. Not when he trotted to right field in the seventh inning after THE home run. Was that his cap he tipped or an olive branch?

Fence cleared and fences mended, his Louisville Slugger on its way to the Hall of Fame, Justice regains spokesman status for the Atlanta Nine, not the generic nine but the group that's lived the entire saga. From the worst-to-first-but-not-quite-best season of '91 to Carlos Baerga's final fly ball in '95, nine players have persevered with manager Bobby Cox and the same coaching staff. It was fitting the group included Justice; Mark Wohlers, who blossomed into the closer who pitched the final inning; and Tom Glavine, whose dominant one-hitter for the first eight innings clinched the Series MVP award, plus John Smoltz, Jeff Blauser, Rafael Belliard, Steve Avery, Kent Mercker and Mark Lemke. But why did they win this time?

"This is a better team," Justice responds, as if there could be no doubt. "Think about it."

But the Braves were next to last in the league in hitting (.250), with Justice himself at a career-low .253. No team had won a World Series with so low an average since the 1988 Dodgers (.248), and that team had Orel. So dominant was Hershiser that he was MVP of the playoffs and the Series.

The batting stats don't reveal, however, that these Braves were second in drawing walks and came to the Fall Classic having won 29 games in their last at-bat, nine games when they trailed after eight innings, 13 more when tied after eight. They had a 33-17 record in one-run games. And they ended Hershiser's 7-0 career postseason run in this year's Game One, scoring the decisive two runs in the seventh inning without a base hit.

Get it? Clutch.

Justice is a prime example. When he came to the plate to hit the homer that won the Series, he was in a 1-for-15 funk. His one hit had been a two-run single in the seventh inning of Game Four that gave Atlanta a 4-1 lead in the 5-2 victory. Then there's the pitching.

"Glavine used to be No. 1," Justice explains. Now, he's No. 1 with an asterisk since we added Mad Dog [Maddux]." Maddux was a two-hit magician in Game One, but the Indians lived up to their boasts of being able to adjust once they had seen a pitcher and prolonged the Series with a 5-4 win in Game Five. Glavine out-gutted Dennis Martinez in Game Two when neither had his best stuff. In Game Six, the Indians didn't get a hit until, or after, Tony Pena's flare to left leading off the sixth. That's the longest a World Series starter had carried a no-hitter since 1985. But this is the third season for the dream rotation of Maddux, Glavine, Smoltz and Avery. There must be more to it.

Before Justice's game-winner, four of Atlanta's six home runs had been hit by the two men up immediately after his No. 5 batting spot. Sixth-hitter Ryan Klesko hit one in each of the three games in Cleveland, and No. 7 Javy Lopez ripped the Game Two winner.

The Braves had additional punch in the bullpen, too.

"Wohlers stepped forward to be a dominant closer," says Justice. Which sets off an effective chain reaction. Cox never had the luxury of a deep, dependable relief corps, each with a defined role, a bullpen that outpitched the opposition. That's not easy against the Jose Mesa-led group given significant credit for Cleveland's 100 victories. Each bullpen allowed five runs in 15-plus innings during the series, but look deeper. Until Poole whiffed McGriff in Game Six with two men on, Alan Embree was the only Indians reliever to enter a game with base runners and escape the inning without any scoring. The only Brave to fail in those situations was Wohlers, who was the victim of Sandy Alomar's inside-out double to force extra innings in Game Three.

But wait, there's more.

"We have a deeper bench," Justice says. "It used to be pretty much just Lonnie Smith." That's where Mike Devereaux, the NLCS MVP, and Luis Polonia come in. That outfield depth even allowed the Braves to make the cost-cutting move of not pursuing free-agent-to-be Fred McGriff and moving Ryan Klesko to first base, despite fans' post-Series chants of "Sign McGriff."

"Experience and preparation are the difference," Avery says. "We were able to set our rotation, get people healthy. Other years, we got in [the playoffs] at the last minute.... Winning the one-run games, a lot can be said for experience. It's not hard to keep your concentration level up in the World Series."

CLEVELAND 5, ATLANTA 4

Atlanta	000	110	002
Cleveland	200	002	01x

BATTING

Atlanta	ab	r	h	bi	bb	so	lo	avg
Grissom cf	4	0	1	1	0	0	1	.381
Polonia lf	4	1	1	1	0	1	2	.308
C.Jones 3b	4	0	1	0	0	1	0	.222
McGriff 1b	4	1	1	0	0	2	1	.316
Justice rf	4	0	0	0	0	1	0	.167
Klesko dh	4	2	2	2	0	0	0	.333
Lemke 2b	4	0	0	0	0	1	1	.250
O'Brien c	1	0	0	0	0	0	0	.000
b-Lopez ph-c	1	0	0	0	0	0	0	.214
Belliard ss	1	0	0	0	0	1	0	.000
a-Smith ph	0	0	0	0	1	0	0	.500
Mordecai ss	1	0	1	0	0	0	0	.333
Totals	32	4	7	4	1	7	5	

a-intentionally walked for Belliard in the 5th; b-grounded to catcher for O'Brien in the 7th.

BATTING

Cleveland	ab	r	h	bi	bb	so	lo	avg
Lofton cf	4	0	0	0	0	0	2	.238
Vizquel ss	3	1	1	0	1	1	1	.200
Baerga 2b	4	1	1	0	0	0	2	.227
Belle lf	3	2	1	2	1	2	0	.250
E.Murray dh	3	0	0	0	1	0	1	.118
Thome 3b	4	1	2	2	0	0	0	.250
M.Ramirez rf	3	0	1	1	0	1	0	.267
1b	1	0	0	0	0	0	0	.000
Sorrento 1b	3	0	0	0	0	1	2	.200
rf	0	0	0	0	0	0	0	.000
S.Alomar c	3	0	2	0	0	0	0	.200
Totals	31	5	8	5	3	5	8	

PITCHING

Atlanta	ip	h	r	er	bb	so	hr	era
Mddx (L, 1-1)	7	7	4	4	3	4	1	2.25
Clontz	1	1	1	1	0	1	1	2.70

PITCHING

Cleveland	ip	h	r	er	bb	so	hr	era
Hrshsr (W, 1-1)	8	5	2	1	1	6	1	2.57
Mesa (S, 1)	1	2	2	2	0	1	1	4.50

1995 World Series: Between the lines

ATLANTA 1, CLEVELAND 0

Atlanta   0 0 0   0 0 0   0 0 0

Cleveland 0 0 0   0 0 1   0 0 x

BATTING

Cleveland	ab	r	h	bi	bb	so	lo	avg
Lofton cf	4	0	0	0	0	0	1	.200
Vizquel ss	3	0	0	0	0	2	1	.174
a-Sorrento ph	1	0	0	0	0	0	0	.182
Baerga 2b	4	0	0	0	0	0	0	.192
Belle lf	1	0	0	0	2	1	0	.235
Murray 1b	2	0	0	0	1	1	1	.105
Ramirez rf	3	0	0	0	0	1	2	.222
Embree p	0	0	0	0	0	0	0	.000
Tavarez p	0	0	0	0	0	0	0	.000
Assenmacher p	0	0	0	0	0	0	0	.000
Thome 3b	3	0	0	0	0	2	1	.211
TPena c	3	0	1	0	0	0	0	.167
Martinez p	1	0	0	0	0	1	0	.000
Poole p	1	0	0	0	0	0	1	.000
Hill p	0	0	0	0	0	0	0	.000
Amaro rf	1	0	0	0	0	0	0	.000
Totals	**27**	**0**	**1**	**0**	**3**	**8**	**7**	

a-flied to center for Vizquel in the 9th.

BATTING

Atlanta	ab	r	h	bi	bb	so	lo	avg
Grissom cf	4	0	1	0	0	0	0	.360
Lemke 2b	2	0	1	0	1	0	0	.273
Jones 3b	3	0	2	0	1	0	0	.286
McGriff 1b	4	0	0	0	0	2	5	.261
Justice rf	2	1	2	1	2	0	0	.250
Klesko lf	1	0	0	0	2	0	0	.313
Devereaux lf	1	0	0	0	0	0	3	.250
Lopez c	3	0	0	0	1	0	2	.176
Belliard ss	4	0	0	0	0	0	4	.000
Glavine p	3	0	0	0	0	1	1	.000
a-Polonia ph	1	0	0	0	0	1	0	.286
Wohlers p	0	0	0	0	0	0	0	.000
Totals	**28**	**1**	**6**	**1**	**7**	**4**	**15**	

a-struck out for Glavine in the 8th.

PITCHING

Cleveland	ip	h	r	er	bb	so	hr	era
Martinez	4.2	4	0	0	5	2	0	3.48
Poole (L, 0-1)	1.1	1	1	1	1	0	1	3.86
Hill	0	1	0	0	0	0	0	4.26
Embree	1	0	0	0	2	0	0	2.70
Tavarez	.2	0	0	0	0	0	0	0.00
Assenmacher	.1	0	0	0	0	1	0	6.75

PITCHING

Atlanta	ip	h	r	er	bb	so	hr	era
Glvine (W, 2-0)	8	1	0	0	3	8	0	1.29
Wohlers (S, 2)	1	0	0	0	0	0	0	1.80

▶**A cliche comes true:** "Great pitching beats great hitting," as the No. 1 staff in baseball held the No. 1 lineup to 19 runs in six games—12 of them came in Game No. 3 and Game No. 5—and a .179 average.

▶**Series-turning start:** Braves manager Bobby Cox gave lefty Steve Avery the ball for Game 4. Almost everyone clamored for Greg Maddux, but Cox wisely remembered Avery's great Game 4 start (six shutout innings) against Cincinnati in the NLCS. Avery was at least as sharp this time: six innings, one run (a homer).

▶**Redemption theory:** Braves CF Marquis Grissom did not hit or steal to his standards during the season. He redeemed it all with a record 25 postseason hits, including a 9-for-25 (.360) Series.

▶**AWOL:** From Cleveland—1B-DH Eddie Murray (.105), 2B Carlos Baerga (.192) and RF Manny Ramirez (.222). They did have 9 RBI, but these guys combined for 67 homers and 279 RBI this season. More was expected.

▶**Disappearing act:** In Games 1-3, Cleveland CF Kenny Lofton was 5-for-12, walked three times, reached twice on errors and scored six times. In Games 4-6, he was 0-for-13 and did not score.

▶**Timely outburst:** David Justice ripped Braves fans as front-runners, and quiet ones at that. He won back their love by knocking his first postseason extra-base hits in Game 6, including the winning HR.

▶**Ill-timed outburst:** Belle directed expletives at TV's Hannah Storm and later apologized. P.S.: He curses print reporters often, but it did not become an issue until a TV figure was the subject.

▶**A new Wiz:** Forget the Gold Glove; give Cleveland SS Omar Vizquel a Platinum Glove. He was the leather king of the Series.

▶**Cranky clubhouse:** With angry Albert Belle, silent Eddie Murray and a few other surly characters, the Indians' clubhouse ranked near the top on the media's World Series unpleasant scale.

▶**Boom-boom Belliard:** The Braves SS was 0-for-16. He was not in the lineup for his bat, but if Jeff Blauser had been healthy, he would not have been in at all.

▶**We'll be back:** Braves because of 3B Chipper Jones and LF Ryan Klesko; Indians because of RF Manny Ramirez and Lofton.

For the record

▸ All-time single-season, league and club records

▸ Career records

▸ Top fielding marks

▸ Active player and individual records

▸ All no-hitters

▸ Perfect game box scores

Record qualifications

All-time records
1000 games played minimum for BA and other hitting categories.
1500 innings pitched minimum for ERA.
100 wins minimum for winning percentage.

Active-player records
One-half above all-time minimum requirements.

Club records
Same as active player records.

Season records
3.1 plate appearances per game for BA.
1 inning pitched per game for ERA.
15 victories for winning percentage.

Active player records

Players listed through 1995 season.

Hitters

Games played: Most, career active players

2973	Dave Winfield, 1973-1995
2819	Eddie Murray, 1977-1995
2585	Andre Dawson, 1976-1995
2491	Ozzie Smith, 1978-1995
2390	Lou Whitaker, 1977-1995
2261	Paul Molitor, 1978-1995
2227	Alan Trammell, 1977-1995
2218	Cal Ripken, 1981-1995
2192	Rickey Henderson, 1979-1995
2183	Harold Baines, 1980-1995

At-bats: Most, career, active players

11,003	Dave Winfield, 1973-1995
10,603	Eddie Murray, 1977-1995
9869	Andre Dawson, 1976-1995
9169	Ozzie Smith, 1978-1995
9135	Paul Molitor, 1978-1995
8577	Cal Ripken, 1981-1995
8570	Lou Whitaker, 1977-1995
8095	Alan Trammell, 1977-1995
8063	Rickey Henderson, 1979-1995
7871	Harold Baines, 1980-1995

Runs: Most, career, active players

1719	Rickey Henderson, 1979-1995
1669	Dave Winfield, 1973-1995
1545	Paul Molitor, 1978-1995
1545	Eddie Murray, 1977-1995
1386	Lou Whitaker, 1977-1995
1374	Tim Raines, 1979-1995
1367	Andre Dawson, 1976-1995
1287	Wade Boggs, 1982-1995
1285	Brett Butler, 1981-1995
1272	Cal Ripken, 1981-1995

Hits: Most, career, active players

3110	Dave Winfield, 1973-1995
3071	Eddie Murray, 1977-1995
2789	Paul Molitor, 1978-1995
2758	Andre Dawson, 1976-1995
2541	Wade Boggs, 1982-1995
2401	Tony Gwynn, 1982-1995
2396	Ozzie Smith, 1978-1995
2371	Cal Ripken, 1981-1995
2369	Lou Whitaker, 1977-1995
2338	Rickey Henderson, 1979-1995

Total bases: Most, career, active players

5221	Dave Winfield, 1973-1995
5108	Eddie Murray, 1977-1995

4763	Andre Dawson, 1976-1995
4119	Paul Molitor, 1978-1995
3883	Cal Ripken, 1981-1995
3657	Harold Baines, 1980-1995
3651	Lou Whitaker, 1977-1995
3552	Rickey Henderson, 1979-1995
3453	Kirby Puckett, 1984-1995
3445	Wade Boggs, 1982-1995

2B: Most, career, active players

540	Dave Winfield, 1973-1995
532	Eddie Murray, 1977-1995
503	Paul Molitor, 1978-1995
501	Andre Dawson, 1976-1995
489	Wade Boggs, 1982-1995
447	Cal Ripken, 1981-1995
442	Don Mattingly, 1982-1995
422	Tim Wallach, 1980-1995
420	Lou Whitaker, 1977-1995
414	Kirby Puckett, 1984-1995

3B: Most, career, active players

127	Brett Butler, 1981-1995
109	Tim Raines, 1979-1995
98	Andre Dawson, 1976-1995
97	Paul Molitor, 1978-1995
95	Juan Samuel, 1983-1995
91	Andy Van Slyke, 1983-1995
89	Tony Fernandez, 1983-1995
88	Vince Coleman, 1985-1995
88	Dave Winfield, 1973-1995
87	Willie McGee, 1982-1995

HR: Most, career, active players

479	Eddie Murray, 1977-1995
465	Dave Winfield, 1973-1995
436	Andre Dawson, 1976-1995
327	Joe Carter, 1983-1995
327	Cal Ripken, 1981-1995
324	Lance Parrish, 1977-1995
301	Harold Baines, 1980-1995
300	Jose Canseco, 1985-1995
297	Darryl Strawberry, 1983-1995
292	Barry Bonds, 1986-1995
292	Gary Gaetti, 1981-1995

RBI: Most, career, active players

1833	Dave Winfield, 1973-1995
1820	Eddie Murray, 1977-1995
1577	Andre Dawson, 1976-1995
1267	Cal Ripken, 1981-1995
1261	Harold Baines, 1980-1995
1173	Joe Carter, 1983-1995
1100	Chili Davis, 1981-1995
1099	Don Mattingly, 1982-1995
1085	Kirby Puckett, 1984-1995
1084	Lou Whitaker, 1977-1995

SB: Most, career, active players

1149	Rickey Henderson, 1979-1995
777	Tim Raines, 1979-1995
740	Vince Coleman, 1985-1995
573	Ozzie Smith, 1978-1995
535	Brett Butler, 1981-1995

466	Paul Molitor, 1978-1995
444	Otis Nixon, 1983-1995
369	Juan Samuel, 1983-1995
340	Barry Bonds, 1986-1995
325	Willie McGee, 1982-1995

BB: Most, career, active players

1550	Rickey Henderson, 1979-1995
1257	Eddie Murray, 1977-1995
1216	Dave Winfield, 1973-1995
1213	Wade Boggs, 1982-1995
1197	Lou Whitaker, 1977-1995
1134	Tim Raines, 1979-1995
1078	Brett Butler, 1981-1995
1047	Ozzie Smith, 1978-1995
974	Tony Phillips, 1982-1995
948	Paul Molitor, 1978-1995

HBP: Most, career, active players

110	Andre Dawson, 1976-1995
79	Mike Macfarlane, 1987-1995
78	Andres Galarraga, 1985-1995
75	Tim Wallach, 1980-1995
74	Joe Carter, 1983-1995
70	Gary Gaetti, 1981-1995
68	Juan Samuel, 1983-1995
63	Rickey Henderson, 1979-1995
63	Dave Valle, 1984-1995
61	Kirk Gibson, 1979-1995
61	Robby Thompson, 1986-1995

GIDP: Most, career, active players

319	Dave Winfield, 1973-1995
286	Eddie Murray, 1977-1995
255	Cal Ripken, 1981-1995
225	Harold Baines, 1980-1995
223	Tony Pena, 1980-1995
216	Andre Dawson, 1976-1995
197	Lance Parrish, 1977-1995
196	Wade Boggs, 1982-1995
196	Tony Gwynn, 1982-1995
191	Don Mattingly, 1982-1995

BA: Highest, career, active players

.336	Tony Gwynn, 1982-1995
.334	Wade Boggs, 1982-1995
.323	Frank Thomas, 1990-1995
.318	Kirby Puckett, 1984-1995
.313	Edgar Martinez, 1987-1995
.312	Kenny Lofton, 1991-1995
.308	Hal Morris, 1988-1995
.307	Don Mattingly, 1982-1995
.306	Jeff Bagwell, 1991-1995
.306	Mark Grace, 1988-1995

Slug avg: Highest, career, active players

.593	Frank Thomas, 1990-1995
.571	Albert Belle, 1989-1995
.541	Barry Bonds, 1986-1995
.536	Ken Griffey, 1989-1995
.535	Fred McGriff, 1986-1995

.533 Juan Gonzalez, 1989-1995
.523 Mark McGwire, 1986-1995
.515 Jose Canseco, 1985-1995
.515 Jeff Bagwell, 1991-1995
.510 Mo Vaughn, 1991-1995

Extra-base hits: Most, career, active players

1093 Dave Winfield, 1973-1995
1045 Eddie Murray, 1977-1995
1035 Andre Dawson, 1976-1995
816 Cal Ripken, 1981-1995
811 Paul Molitor, 1978-1995
736 Harold Baines, 1980-1995
729 Lou Whitaker, 1977-1995
713 Joe Carter, 1983-1995
705 Tim Wallach, 1980-1995
687 Rickey Henderson, 1979-1995

Pitchers

Games: Most, career, active players

943 Lee Smith, 1980-1995
901 Dennis Eckersley, 1975-1995
819 Jesse Orosco, 1979-1995
734 Rick Honeycutt, 1977-1995
732 Steve Bedrosian, 1981-1995
718 Dave Righetti, 1979-1995
703 Greg Harris, 1981-1995
682 Roger McDowell, 1985-1995
661 John Franco, 1984-1995
642 Tom Henke, 1982-1995

Complete games: Most, career, active players

120 Dennis Martinez, 1976-1995
112 Fernando Valenzuela, 1980-1995
100 Dennis Eckersley, 1975-1995
94 Roger Clemens, 1984-1995
79 Mark Langston, 1984-1995
79 Mike Moore, 1982-1995
76 Bret Saberhagen, 1984-1995
74 Frank Viola, 1982-1995
70 Greg Maddux, 1986-1995
66 Orel Hershiser, 1983-1995

Shutouts: Most, career, active players

36 Roger Clemens, 1984-1995
31 Fernando Valenzuela, 1980-1995
28 Dennis Martinez, 1976-1995
25 Orel Hershiser, 1983-1995
21 David Cone, 1986-1995
21 Doug Drabek, 1986-1995
20 Dennis Eckersley, 1975-1995
20 Greg Maddux, 1986-1995
18 Mark Langston, 1984-1995
18 Ramon Martinez, 1988-1995

Wins: Most, career, active players

231 Dennis Martinez, 1976-1995
192 Dennis Eckersley, 1975-1995
182 Roger Clemens, 1984-1995

175 Frank Viola, 1982-1995
168 Dave Stewart, 1978-1995
166 Mark Langston, 1984-1995
163 Scott Sanderson, 1978-1995
161 Mike Moore, 1982-1995
158 Fernando Valenzuela, 1980-1995
152 Jimmy Key, 1984-1995

Losses: Most, career, active players

176 Dennis Martinez, 1976-1995
176 Mike Moore, 1982-1995
159 Dennis Eckersley, 1975-1995
150 Danny Darwin, 1978-1995
149 Kevin Gross, 1983-1995
147 Frank Viola, 1982-1995
144 Mike Morgan, 1978-1995
142 Rick Honeycutt, 1977-1995
141 Mark Langston, 1984-1995
141 Scott Sanderson, 1978-1995

HR allowed: Most, career, active players

344 Dennis Martinez, 1976-1995
324 Dennis Eckersley, 1975-1995
292 Scott Sanderson, 1978-1995
291 Mike Moore, 1982-1995
288 Frank Viola, 1982-1995
265 Mark Langston, 1984-1995
264 Dave Stewart, 1978-1995
256 Danny Darwin, 1978-1995
239 Ron Darling, 1983-1995
236 Tom Browning, 1984-1995

BB: Most career, active players

1156 Mike Moore, 1982-1995
1145 Mark Langston, 1984-1995
1080 Dennis Martinez, 1976-1995
1038 Fernando Valenzuela, 1980-1995
1034 Dave Stewart, 1978-1995
1025 Bobby Witt, 1986-1995
916 Kevin Gross, 1983-1995
906 Ron Darling, 1983-1995
843 Frank Viola, 1982-1995
841 Jose DeLeon, 1983-1995

K: Most, career, active players

2333 Roger Clemens, 1984-1995
2285 Dennis Eckersley, 1975-1995
2252 Mark Langston, 1984-1995
2022 Dennis Martinez, 1976-1995
1918 Fernando Valenzuela, 1980-1995
1826 Frank Viola, 1982-1995
1741 David Cone, 1986-1995
1741 Dave Stewart, 1978-1995
1673 Danny Darwin, 1978-1995
1667 Mike Moore, 1982-1995

Wild pitches: Most, career, active players

135 Mike Moore, 1982-1995
119 Dave Stewart, 1978-1995
108 Fernando Valenzuela, 1980-1995

102 Mark Gubicza, 1984-1995
101 Bobby Witt, 1986-1995
98 David Cone, 1986-1995
97 Ron Darling, 1983-1995
94 John Smoltz, 1988-1995
87 Mike Morgan, 1978-1995
86 Tom Candiotti, 1983-1995

Win pct: Highest, career, active players

.703 Mike Mussina, 1991-1995
.650 Roger Clemens, 1984-1995
.623 David Cone, 1986-1995
.620 Mike Henneman, 1987-1995
.620 Jimmy Key, 1984-1995
.617 Greg Maddux, 1986-1995
.609 Juan Guzman, 1991-1995
.609 Jack McDowell, 1987-1995
.607 Randy Johnson, 1988-1995
.602 Tom Glavine, 1987-1995

ERA: Lowest, career, active players

2.62 John Franco, 1984-1995
2.67 Tom Henke, 1982-1995
2.88 Greg Maddux, 1986-1995
2.95 Lee Smith, 1980-1995
2.96 Jesse Orosco, 1979-1995
3.00 Roger Clemens, 1984-1995
3.06 Orel Hershiser, 1983-1995
3.10 Alejandro Pena, 1981-1995
3.16 Jose Rijo, 1984-1995
3.17 David Cone, 1986-1995

Innings: Most, career, active players

3747.7 Dennis Martinez, 1976-1995
3133.0 Dennis Eckersley, 1975-1995
2831.7 Mike Moore, 1982-1995
2806.0 Frank Viola, 1982-1995
2669.3 Fernando Valenzuela, 1980-1995
2648.7 Mark Langston, 1984-1995
2629.7 Dave Stewart, 1978-1995
2546.0 Danny Darwin, 1978-1995
2543.7 Scott Sanderson, 1978-1995
2533.3 Roger Clemens, 1984-1995

American League single-season records

Hitters

ACTIVE PLAYERS IN CAPS

At-bats: Most, season, AL

705 Willie Wilson, KC-1980
692 Bobby Richardson, NY-1962
691 KIRBY PUCKETT, Min-1985
689 Sandy Alomar Sr., Cal-1971
687 TONY FERNANDEZ, Tor-1986
686 Horace Clarke, NY-1970

680	KIRBY PUCKETT, Min-1986
679	Harvey Kuenn, Det-1953
679	Bobby Richardson, NY-1964
677	DON MATTINGLY, NY-1986
677	Jim Rice, Bos-1978

Runs: Most, season, AL

177	Babe Ruth, NY-1921
167	Lou Gehrig, NY-1936
163	Lou Gehrig, NY-1931
163	Babe Ruth, NY-1928
158	Babe Ruth, NY-1920
158	Babe Ruth, NY-1927
152	Al Simmons, Phi-1930
151	Joe DiMaggio, NY-1937
151	Jimmie Foxx, Phi-1932
151	Babe Ruth, NY-1923

Hits: Most, season, AL

257	George Sisler, StL-1920
253	Al Simmons, Phi-1925
248	Ty Cobb, Det-1911
246	George Sisler, StL-1922
241	Heinie Manush, StL-1928
240	WADE BOGGS, Bos-1985
239	Rod Carew, Min-1977
238	DON MATTINGLY, NY-1986
237	Harry Heilmann, Det-1921
236	Jack Tobin, StL-1921

Total bases: Most, season, AL

457	Babe Ruth, NY-1921
447	Lou Gehrig, NY-1927
438	Jimmie Foxx, Phi-1932
419	Lou Gehrig, NY-1930
418	Joe DiMaggio, NY-1937
417	Babe Ruth, NY-1927
410	Lou Gehrig, NY-1931
409	Lou Gehrig, NY-1934
406	Jim Rice, Bos-1978
405	Hal Trosky, Cle-1936

2B: Most, season, AL

67	Earl Webb, Bos-1931
64	George Burns, Cle-1926
63	Hank Greenberg, Det-1934
60	Charlie Gehringer, Det-1936
59	Tris Speaker, Cle-1923
56	George Kell, Det-1950
55	Gee Walker, Det-1936
54	Hal McRae, KC-1977
54	JOHN OLERUD, Tor-1993
53	DON MATTINGLY, NY-1986
53	Al Simmons, Phi-1926
53	Tris Speaker, Bos-1912

3B: Most, season, AL

26	Sam Crawford, Det-1914
26	Joe Jackson, Cle-1912
25	Sam Crawford, Det-1903
24	Ty Cobb, Det-1911
24	Ty Cobb, Det-1917
23	Ty Cobb, Det-1912
23	Earle Combs, NY-1927
23	Sam Crawford, Det-1913
23	Dale Mitchell, Cle-1949

22	Bill Bradley, Cle-1903
22	Earle Combs, NY-1930
22	Birdie Cree, NY-1911
22	Elmer Flick, Cle-1906
22	Tris Speaker, Bos-1913
22	Snuffy Stirnweiss, NY-1945

HR: Most, season, AL

61	Roger Maris, NY-1961
60	Babe Ruth, NY-1927
59	Babe Ruth, NY-1921
58	Jimmie Foxx, Phi-1932
58	Hank Greenberg, Det-1938
54	Mickey Mantle, NY-1961
54	Babe Ruth, NY-1920
54	Babe Ruth, NY-1928
52	Mickey Mantle, NY-1956
51	CECIL FIELDER, Det-1990

RBI: Most, season, AL

184	Lou Gehrig, NY-1931
183	Hank Greenberg, Det-1937
175	Jimmie Foxx, Bos-1938
175	Lou Gehrig, NY-1927
174	Lou Gehrig, NY-1930
171	Babe Ruth, NY-1921
170	Hank Greenberg, Det-1935
169	Jimmie Foxx, Phi-1932
167	Joe DiMaggio, NY-1937
165	Lou Gehrig, NY-1934
165	Al Simmons, Phi-1930

SB: Most, season, AL

130	RICKEY HENDERSON, Oak-1982
108	RICKEY HENDERSON, Oak-1983
100	RICKEY HENDERSON, Oak-1980
96	Ty Cobb, Det-1915
93	RICKEY HENDERSON, NY-1988
88	Clyde Milan, Was-1912
87	RICKEY HENDERSON, NY-1986
83	Ty Cobb, Det-1911
83	Willie Wilson, KC-1979
81	Eddie Collins, Phi-1910

BB: Most, season, AL

170	Babe Ruth, NY-1923
162	Ted Williams, Bos-1947
162	Ted Williams, Bos-1949
156	Ted Williams, Bos-1946
151	Eddie Yost, Was-1956
149	Eddie Joost, Phi-1949
148	Babe Ruth, NY-1920
146	Mickey Mantle, NY-1957
145	Harmon Killebrew, Min-1969
145	Ted Williams, Bos-1941
145	Ted Williams, Bos-1942

K: Most, season, AL

186	Rob Deer, Mil-1987
185	Pete Incaviglia, Tex-1986
182	CECIL FIELDER, Det-1990

179	Rob Deer, Mil-1986
175	JOSE CANSECO, Oak-1986
175	Rob Deer, Det-1991
175	Dave Nicholson, Chi-1963
175	Gorman Thomas, Mil-1979
172	Bo Jackson, KC-1989
172	Jim Presley, Sea-1986

GIDP: Most, season, AL

36	Jim Rice, Bos-1984
35	Jim Rice, Bos-1985
32	Jackie Jensen, Bos-1954
32	CAL RIPKEN, Bal-1985
31	Tony Armas, Bos-1983
31	Bobby Doerr, Bos-1949
31	Jim Rice, Bos-1983
30	Billy Hitchcock, Phi-1950
30	DAVE WINFIELD, NY-1983
30	Carl Yastrzemski, Bos-1964

BA: Highest, season, AL

.426	Nap Lajoie, Phi-1901.
420	Ty Cobb, Det-1911
420	George Sisler, StL-1922
.409	Ty Cobb, Det-1912
.408	Joe Jackson, Cle-1911
.407	George Sisler, StL-1920
.406	Ted Williams, Bos-1941
.403	Harry Heilmann, Det-1923
.401	Ty Cobb, Det-1922
.398	Harry Heilmann, Det-1927

Slug avg: Highest, season, AL

.847	Babe Ruth, NY-1920
.846	Babe Ruth, NY-1921
.772	Babe Ruth, NY-1927
.765	Lou Gehrig, NY-1927
.764	Babe Ruth, NY-1923
.749	Jimmie Foxx, Phi-1932
.739	Babe Ruth, NY-1924
.737	Babe Ruth, NY-1926
.735	Ted Williams, Bos-1941
.732	Babe Ruth, NY-1930

Extra-base hits: Most, season, AL

119	Babe Ruth, NY-1921
117	Lou Gehrig, NY-1927
103	ALBERT BELLE, Cle-1995
103	Hank Greenberg, Det-1937
100	Jimmie Foxx, Phi-1932
100	Lou Gehrig, NY-1930
99	Hank Greenberg, Det-1940
99	Babe Ruth, NY-1920
99	Babe Ruth, NY-1923
98	Hank Greenberg, Det-1935

Pitchers

Games: Most, season, AL

90	Mike Marshall, Min-1979
89	Mark Eichhorn, Tor-1987
88	Wilbur Wood, Chi-1968
85	MITCH WILLIAMS, Tex-1987
84	Dan Quisenberry, KC-1985
83	Ken Sanders, Mil-1971
82	Eddie Fisher, Chi-1965

81	KENNY ROGERS, Tex-1992
81	DUANE WARD, Tor-1991
81	John Wyatt, KC-1964

Complete games: Most, season, AL

48	Jack Chesbro, NY-1904
42	George Mullin, Det-1904
42	Ed Walsh, Chi-1908
41	Cy Young, Bos-1902
40	Cy Young, Bos-1904
39	Bill Dinneen, Bos-1902
39	Joe McGinnity, Bal-1901
39	Rube Waddell, Phi-1904
38	Walter Johnson, Was-1910
38	Jack Powell, NY-1904
38	Cy Young, Bos-1901

Saves: Most, season, AL

57	Bobby Thigpen, Chi-1990
51	DENNIS ECKERSLEY, Oak-1992
48	DENNIS ECKERSLEY, Oak-1990
46	BRYAN HARVEY, Cal-1991
46	JOSE MESA, Cle-1995
46	DAVE RIGHETTI, NY-1986
45	DENNIS ECKERSLEY, Oak-1988
45	JEFF MONTGOMERY, KC-1993
45	Dan Quisenberry, KC-1983
45	DUANE WARD, Tor-1993

Shutouts: Most, season, AL

13	Jack Coombs, Phi-1910
11	Dean Chance, LA-1964
11	Walter Johnson, Was-1913
11	Ed Walsh, Chi-1908
10	Bob Feller, Cle-1946
10	Bob Lemon, Cle-1948
10	Jim Palmer, Bal-1975
10	Ed Walsh, Chi-1906
10	Joe Wood, Bos-1912
10	Cy Young, Bos-1904

Wins: Most, season, AL

41	Jack Chesbro, NY-1904
40	Ed Walsh, Chi-1908
36	Walter Johnson, Was-1913
34	Joe Wood, Bos-1912
33	Walter Johnson, Was-1912
33	Cy Young, Bos-1901
32	Cy Young, Bos-1902
31	Jim Bagby, Cle-1920
31	Jack Coombs, Phi-1910
31	Lefty Grove, Phi-1931
31	Denny McLain, Det-1968

Losses: Most, season, AL

26	Pete Dowling, Mil-Cle-1901
26	Bob Groom, Was-1909
26	Happy Townsend, Was-1904
25	Patsy Flaherty, Chi-1903
25	Fred Glade, StL-1905
25	Walter Johnson, Was-1909
25	Scott Perry, Phi-1920

25	Red Ruffing, Bos-1928
24	Joe Bush, Phi-1916
24	Pat Caraway, Chi-1931
24	Sam Gray, StL-1931
24	Tom Hughes, NY-Was-1904

HR allowed: Most, season, AL

50	Bert Blyleven, Min-1986
46	Bert Blyleven, Min-1987
43	Pedro Ramos, Was-1957
42	Denny McLain, Det-1966
40	Fergie Jenkins, Tex-1979
40	Jack Morris, Det-1986
40	Orlando Pena, KC-1964
40	Ralph Terry, NY-1962
39	Catfish Hunter, Oak-1973
39	Jack Morris, Det-1987
39	Jim Perry, Min-1971
39	Pedro Ramos, Min-1961

BB: Most, season, AL

208	Bob Feller, Cle-1938
204	Nolan Ryan, Cal-1977
202	Nolan Ryan, Cal-1974
194	Bob Feller, Cle-1941
192	Bobo Newsom, StL-1938
183	Nolan Ryan, Cal-1976
181	Bob Turley, Bal-1954
179	Tommy Byrne, NY-1949
177	Bob Turley, NY-1955
171	Bump Hadley, Chi-StL-1932

K: Most, season, AL

383	Nolan Ryan, Cal-1973
367	Nolan Ryan, Cal-1974
349	Rube Waddell, Phi-1904
348	Bob Feller, Cle-1946
341	Nolan Ryan, Cal-1977
329	Nolan Ryan, Cal-1972
327	Nolan Ryan, Cal-1976
325	Sam McDowell, Cle-1965
313	Walter Johnson, Was-1910
308	RANDY JOHNSON, Sea-1993
308	Mickey Lolich, Det-1971

Win pct: Highest, season, AL

.938	Johnny Allen, Cle-1937
.900	RANDY JOHNSON, Sea-1995
.893	Ron Guidry, NY-1978
.886	Lefty Grove, Phi-1931
.882	Bob Stanley, Bos-1978
.872	Joe Wood, Bos-1912
.862	Bill Donovan, Det-1907
.862	Whitey Ford, NY-1961
.857	ROGER CLEMENS, Bos-1986
.850	Chief Bender, Phi-1914

ERA: Lowest, season, AL

0.96	Dutch Leonard, Bos-1914
1.14	Walter Johnson, Was-1913
1.16	Addie Joss, Cle-1908
1.26	Cy Young, Bos-1908
1.27	Walter Johnson, Was-1918
1.27	Ed Walsh, Chi-1910

1.30	Jack Coombs, Phi-1910
1.36	Walter Johnson, Was-1910
1.39	Walter Johnson, Was-1912
1.39	Harry Krause, Phi-1909

Innings: Most, season, AL

464.0	Ed Walsh, Chi-1908
454.2	Jack Chesbro, NY-1904
422.1	Ed Walsh, Chi-1907
393.0	Ed Walsh, Chi-1912
390.1	Jack Powell, NY-1904
384.2	Cy Young, Bos-1902
383.0	Rube Waddell, Phi-1904
382.1	George Mullin, Det-1904
382.0	Joe McGinnity, Bal-1901
380.0	Cy Young, Bos-1904

American League club records

BA: Highest, season, AL

.316	Detroit, 1921
.313	St. Louis, 1922
.309	New York, 1930
.308	Cleveland, 1921
.308	St. Louis, 1920

BA: Lowest, season, AL

.211	Chicago, 1910
.214	New York, 1968
.217	Texas, 1972
.218	St. Louis, 1910
.221	Chicago, 1909

Slug avg: Highest, season, AL

.489	New York, 1927
.488	New York, 1930
.484	Cleveland, 1994
.483	New York, 1936
.470	Cleveland, 1995

Runs: Most, season, AL

1067	New York, 1931
1065	New York, 1936
1062	New York, 1930
1027	Boston, 1950
1002	New York, 1932

Homers: Most, season, AL

240	New York, 1961
225	Detroit, 1987
225	Minnesota, 1963
221	Minnesota, 1964
216	Milwaukee, 1982

Stolen bases: Most, season, AL

341	Oakland, 1976
288	New York, 1910
287	Washington, 1913
280	Chicago, 1901
280	Detroit, 1909

GIDP: Most, season, AL

174	Boston, 1990
171	Boston, 1982
171	Boston, 1983
170	Philadelphia, 1950
169	Boston, 1949
169	Boston, 1951
169	Boston, 1989

Fielding average: Highest, season, AL

.986	Baltimore, 1995
.986	New York, 1995
.986	Baltimore, 1994
.986	Toronto, 1990
.986	Baltimore, 1989

Errors: Most, season, AL

410	Detroit, 1901
401	Baltimore, 1901
393	Milwaukee, 1901
385	St. Louis, 1910
382	New York, 1912

Errors: Fewest, season, AL

84	Minnesota, 1988
86	Toronto, 1990
87	Baltimore, 1989
87	Oakland, 1990
89	Milwaukee, 1992

Double plays: Most, season, AL

217	Philadelphia, 1949
214	New York, 1956
208	Philadelphia, 1950
207	Boston, 1949
206	Boston, 1980
206	Toronto, 1980

ERA: Lowest, season, AL

1.78	Philadelphia, 1910
1.93	Philadelphia, 1909
1.99	Chicago, 1905
2.02	Cleveland, 1908
2.03	Chicago, 1910

Shutouts: Most, season, AL

32	Chicago, 1906
28	Los Angeles, 1964
27	Cleveland, 1906
27	Philadelphia, 1907
27	Philadelphia, 1909

Homers allowed: Most, season, AL

226	Baltimore, 1987
220	Kansas City, 1964
219	Cleveland, 1987
212	California, 1987
210	Minnesota, 1987
210	Minnesota, 1995

Homers allowed: Fewest, season, AL

6	Boston, 1913
7	St. Louis, 1908
8	Chicago, 1909

8	Cleveland, 1907
8	Detroit, 1907
8	Philadelphia, 1910

Walks allowed: Most, season, AL

827	Philadelphia, 1915
812	New York, 1949
801	St. Louis, 1951
779	Washington, 1949
770	Cleveland, 1971

National League single-season records

Hitters

ACTIVE PLAYERS IN CAPS

At-bats: Most, season, NL

701	JUAN SAMUEL, Phi-1984
699	Dave Cash, Phi-1975
698	Matty Alou, Pit-1969
696	Woody Jensen, Pit-1936
695	Omar Moreno, Pit-1979
695	Maury Wills, LA-1962
689	Lou Brock, StL-1967
687	Dave Cash, Phi-1974
681	Jo-Jo Moore, NY-1935
681	Lloyd Waner, Pit-1931

Runs: Most, season, NL

192	Billy Hamilton, Phi-1894
166	Billy Hamilton, Phi-1895
165	Willie Keeler, Bal-1894
165	Joe Kelley, Bal-1894
162	Willie Keeler, Bal-1895
160	Jesse Burkett, Cle-1896
160	Hugh Duffy, Bos-1894
159	Hughie Jennings, Bal-1895
158	Chuck Klein, Phi-1930
158	Bobby Lowe, Bos-1894

Hits: Most, season, NL

254	Lefty O'Doul, Phi-1929
254	Bill Terry, NY-1930
250	Rogers Hornsby, StL-1922
250	Chuck Klein, Phi-1930
241	Babe Herman, Bro-1930
240	Jesse Burkett, Cle-1896
239	Willie Keeler, Bal-1897
238	Ed Delahanty, Phi-1899
237	Hugh Duffy, Bos-1894
237	Joe Medwick, StL-1937
237	Paul Waner, Pit-1927

Total bases: Most, season, NL

450	Rogers Hornsby, StL-1922
445	Chuck Klein, Phi-1930
429	Stan Musial, StL-1948
423	Hack Wilson, Chi-1930
420	Chuck Klein, Phi-1932
416	Babe Herman, Bro-1930

409	Rogers Hornsby, Chi-1929
406	Joe Medwick, StL-1937
405	Chuck Klein, Phi-1929
400	Hank Aaron, Mil-1959

2B: Most, season, NL

64	Joe Medwick, StL-1936
62	Paul Waner, Pit-1932
59	Chuck Klein, Phi-1930
57	Billy Herman, Chi-1935
57	Billy Herman, Chi-1936
56	Joe Medwick, StL-1937
55	Ed Delahanty, Phi-1899
53	Stan Musial, StL-1953
53	Paul Waner, Pit-1936
52	Johnny Frederick, Bro-1929
52	Enos Slaughter, StL-1939

3B: Most, season, NL

36	Chief Wilson, Pit-1912
31	Heinie Reitz, Bal-1894
29	Perry Werden, StL-1893
28	Harry Davis, Pit-1897
27	George Davis, NY-1893
27	Sam Thompson, Phi-1894
27	Jimmy Williams, Pit-1899
26	Kiki Cuyler, Pit-1925
26	John Reilly, Cin-1890
26	George Treadway, Bro-1894

HR: Most, season, NL

56	Hack Wilson, Chi-1930
54	Ralph Kiner, Pit-1949
52	George Foster, Cin-1977
52	Willie Mays, SF-1965
51	Ralph Kiner, Pit-1947
51	Willie Mays, NY-1955
51	Johnny Mize, NY-1947
49	ANDRE DAWSON, Chi-1987
49	Ted Kluszewski, Cin-1954
49	Willie Mays, SF-1962

RBI: Most, season, NL

190	Hack Wilson, Chi-1930
170	Chuck Klein, Phi-1930
166	Sam Thompson, Det-1887
165	Sam Thompson, Phi-1895
159	Hack Wilson, Chi-1929
154	Joe Medwick, StL-1937
153	Tommy Davis, LA-1962
152	Rogers Hornsby, StL-1922
151	Mel Ott, NY-1929
149	George Foster, Cin-1977
149	Rogers Hornsby, Chi-1929

SB: Most, season, NL

118	Lou Brock, StL-1974
111	Billy Hamilton, Phi-1891
111	John Ward, NY-1887
110	VINCE COLEMAN, StL-1985
109	VINCE COLEMAN, StL-1987
107	VINCE COLEMAN, StL-1986
104	Maury Wills, LA-1962
102	Jim Fogarty, Phi-1887
102	Billy Hamilton, Phi-1890
99	Jim Fogarty, Phi-1889

BB: Most, season, NL

148	Eddie Stanky, Bro-1945
148	Jim Wynn, Hou-1969
147	Jimmy Sheckard, Chi-1911
144	Eddie Stanky, NY-1950
137	Ralph Kiner, Pit-1951
137	Willie McCovey, SF-1970
137	Eddie Stanky, Bro-1946
136	Jack Clark, StL-1987
136	Jack Crooks, StL-1892
132	Jack Clark, SD-1989
132	Joe Morgan, Cin-1975

K: Most, season, NL

189	Bobby Bonds, SF-1970
187	Bobby Bonds, SF-1969
180	Mike Schmidt, Phi-1975
169	ANDRES GALARRAGA, Mon-1990
168	JUAN SAMUEL, Phi-1984
163	Donn Clendenon, Pit-1968
162	JUAN SAMUEL, Phi-1987
161	Dick Allen, Phi-1968
158	ANDRES GALARRAGA, Mon-1989
156	Tommie Agee, NY-1970
156	Dave Kingman, NY-1982

GIDP: Most, season, NL

30	Ernie Lombardi, Cin-1938
29	Ted Simmons, StL-1973
28	Sid Gordon, Bos-1951
27	John Bateman, Mon-1971
27	Carl Furillo, Bro-1956
27	Ron Santo, Chi-1973
27	Ken Singleton, Mon-1973
26	Sid Gordon, NY-1943
26	Cleon Jones, NY-1970
26	Billy Jurges, NY-1939
26	Ernie Lombardi, Cin-1933
26	Willie Montanez, Phi-SF-1975
26	Willie Montanez, SF-Atl-1976
26	Dave Parker, Cin-1985
26	Joe Torre, Mil-1964

BA: Highest, season, NL

.440	Hugh Duffy, Bos-1894
.424	Willie Keeler, Bal-1897
.424	Rogers Hornsby, StL-1924
.410	Jesse Burkett, Cle-1896
.410	Ed Delahanty, Phi-1899
.409	Jesse Burkett, Cle-1895
.407	Ed Delahanty, Phi-1894
.404	Ed Delahanty, Phi-1895
.404	Billy Hamilton, Phi-1894
.403	Rogers Hornsby, StL-1925

Slug avg: Highest, season, NL

.756	Rogers Hornsby, StL-1925
.750	JEFF BAGWELL, Hou-1994
.723	Hack Wilson, Chi-1930
.722	Rogers Hornsby, StL-1922
.702	Stan Musial, StL-1948
.696	Rogers Hornsby, StL-1924
.694	Hugh Duffy, Bos-1894
.687	Chuck Klein, Phi-1930

.681	Kevin Mitchell, Cin-1994
.679	Rogers Hornsby, Chi-1929

Extra-base hits: Most, season, NL

107	Chuck Klein, Phi-1930
103	Chuck Klein, Phi-1932
103	Stan Musial, StL-1948
102	Rogers Hornsby, StL-1922
97	Joe Medwick, StL-1937
97	Hack Wilson, Chi-1930
95	Joe Medwick, StL-1936
94	Babe Herman, Bro-1930
94	Rogers Hornsby, Chi-1929
94	Chuck Klein, Phi-1929

Pitchers

Games: Most, season, NL

106	Mike Marshall, LA-1974
94	Kent Tekulve, Pit-1979
92	Mike Marshall, Mon-1973
91	Kent Tekulve, Pit-1978
90	Wayne Granger, Cin-1969
90	Kent Tekulve, Phi-1987
87	ROB MURPHY, Cin-1987
85	Kent Tekulve, Pit-1982
85	Frank Williams, Cin-1987
84	Ted Abernathy, Chi-1965
84	Enrique Romo, Pit-1979

Complete games: Most, season, NL

75	Will White, Cin-1879
73	Charley Radbourn, Pro-1884
72	Pud Galvin, Buf-1883
72	Jim McCormick, Cle-1880
71	Pud Galvin, Buf-1884
68	John Clarkson, Chi-1885
68	John Clarkson, Bos-1889
67	Bill Hutchison, Chi-1892
66	Jim Devlin, Lou-1876
66	Charley Radbourn, Pro-1883

Saves: Most, season, NL

53	RANDY MYERS, Chi-1993
48	ROD BECK, SF-1993
47	LEE SMITH, StL-1991
45	BRYAN HARVEY, Fla-1993
45	Bruce Sutter, StL-1984
44	Mark Davis, SD-1989
43	LEE SMITH, StL-1992
43	LEE SMITH, StL-1993
43	JOHN WETTELAND, Mon-1993
43	MITCH WILLIAMS, Phi-1993

Shutouts: Most, season, NL

16	Pete Alexander, Phi-1916
16	George Bradley, StL-1876
13	Bob Gibson, StL-1968
12	Pete Alexander, Phi-1915
12	Pud Galvin, Buf-1884
11	Tommy Bond, Bos-1879
11	Sandy Koufax, LA-1963
11	Christy Mathewson, NY-1908
11	Charley Radbourn, Pro-1884
10	John Clarkson, Chi-1885

10	Mort Cooper, StL-1942
10	Carl Hubbell, NY-1933
10	Juan Marichal, SF-1965
10	John Tudor, StL-1985

Wins: Most, season, NL

59	Charley Radbourn, Pro-1884
53	John Clarkson, Chi-1885
49	John Clarkson, Bos-1889
48	Charlie Buffinton, Bos-1884
48	Charley Radbourn, Pro-1883
47	Al Spalding, Chi-1876
47	John Ward, Pro-1879
46	Pud Galvin, Buf-1883
46	Pud Galvin, Buf-1884
45	George Bradley, StL-1876
45	Jim McCormick, Cle-1880

Losses: Most, season, NL

48	John Coleman, Phi-1883
42	Will White, Cin-1880
40	George Bradley, Tro-1879
40	Jim McCormick, Cle-1879
37	George Cobb, Bal-1892
36	Bill Hutchison, Chi-1892
36	Stump Wiedman, KC-1886
35	Jim Devlin, Lou-1876
35	Red Donahue, StL-1897
35	Pud Galvin, Buf-1880

HR allowed: Most, season, NL

46	Robin Roberts, Phi-1956
41	Phil Niekro, Atl-1979
41	Robin Roberts, Phi-1955
40	Phil Niekro, Atl-1970
40	Robin Roberts, Phi-1957
39	Murry Dickson, StL-1948
38	Lew Burdette, Mil-1959
38	Warren Hacker, Chi-1955
38	Don Sutton, LA-1970
36	TOM BROWNING, Cin-1988
36	Larry Jansen, NY-1949
36	Art Mahaffey, Phi-1962
36	Ed Whitson, SD-1987

BB: Most, season, NL

289	Amos Rusie, NY-1890
267	Amos Rusie, NY-1892
262	Amos Rusie, NY-1891
227	Mark Baldwin, Pit-1891
218	Amos Rusie, NY-1893
213	Cy Seymour, NY-1898
203	John Clarkson, Bos-1889
200	Amos Rusie, NY-1894
199	Bill Hutchison, Chi-1890
194	Mark Baldwin, Pit-1892

K: Most, season, NL

441	Charley Radbourn, Pro-1884
417	Charlie Buffinton, Bos-1884
382	Sandy Koufax, LA-1965
369	Pud Galvin, Buf-1884
345	Mickey Welch, NY-1884
345	Jim Whitney, Bos-1883
341	Amos Rusie, NY-1890
337	Amos Rusie, NY-1891

| 335 | Tim Keefe, NY-1888 |
| 323 | Lady Baldwin, Det-1886 |

Win pct: Highest, season, NL

.947	Roy Face, Pit-1959
.941	Rick Sutcliffe, Chi-1984
.905	GREG MADDUX, Atl-1995
.889	Freddie Fitzsimmons, Bro-1940
.880	Preacher Roe, Bro-1951
.875	Fred Goldsmith, Chi-1880
.870	DAVID CONE, NY-1988
.864	OREL HERSHISER, LA-1985
.857	DWIGHT GOODEN, NY-1985
.842	Ron Perranoski, LA-1963
.842	Emil Yde, Pit-1924
.842	Tom Hughes, Bos-1916

ERA: Lowest, season, NL

1.04	Mordecai Brown, Chi-1906
1.12	Bob Gibson, StL-1968
1.14	Christy Mathewson, NY-1909
1.15	Jack Pfiester, Chi-1907
1.17	Carl Lundgren, Chi-1907
1.22	Pete Alexander, Phi-1915
1.23	George Bradley, StL-1876
1.28	Christy Mathewson, NY-1905
1.31	Mordecai Brown, Chi-1909
1.33	Jack Taylor, Chi-1902

Innings: Most, season, NL

680.0	Will White, Cin-1879
678.2	Charley Radbourn, Pro-1884
657.2	Jim McCormick, Cle-1880
656.1	Jim Galvin, Buf-1883
636.1	Jim Galvin, Buf-1884
632.1	Charley Radbourn, Pro-1883
627.0	Bill Hutchison, Chi-1892
623.0	John Clarkson, Chi-1885
622.0	Jim Devlin, Lou-1876
620.0	John Clarkson, Bos-1889

National League club records

BA: Highest, season, NL

.349	Philadelphia, 1894
.343	Baltimore, 1894
.337	Chicago, 1876
.331	Boston, 1894
.330	Philadelphia, 1895

BA: Lowest, season, NL

.208	Detroit, 1884
.208	Washington, 1888
.210	Washington, 1886
.213	Brooklyn, 1908
.219	New York, 1963

Slug avg: Highest, season, NL

| .484 | Boston, 1894 |

.483	Baltimore, 1894
.481	Chicago, 1930
.476	Philadelphia, 1894
.474	Brooklyn, 1953

Runs: Most, season, NL

1220	Boston, 1894
1171	Baltimore, 1894
1143	Philadelphia, 1894
1068	Philadelphia, 1895
1041	Chicago, 1894

Homers: Most, season, NL

221	Cincinnati, 1956
221	New York, 1947
209	Chicago, 1987
208	Brooklyn, 1953
207	Atlanta, 1966

Stolen bases: Most, season, NL

441	Baltimore, 1896
415	New York, 1887
409	Brooklyn, 1892
401	Baltimore, 1897
382	Chicago, 1887

GIDP: Most, season, NL

166	St. Louis, 1958
157	Chicago, 1938
154	Atlanta, 1985
153	New York, 1939
151	Brooklyn, 1952

Fielding average: Highest, season, NL

.986	Cincinnati, 1995
.985	St. Louis, 1992
.985	San Francisco, 1994
.984	Cincinnati, 1977
.984	Pittsburgh, 1992

Errors: Most, season, NL

639	Philadelphia, 1883
607	Pittsburgh, 1890
595	Chicago, 1884
584	Baltimore, 1892
565	New York, 1892

Errors: Fewest, season, NL

94	St. Louis, 1992
95	Cincinnati, 1977
96	Cincinnati, 1992
100	Cincinnati, 1958
101	Pittsburgh, 1992
101	San Francisco, 1993

Double plays: Most, season, NL

215	Pittsburgh, 1966
198	Los Angeles, 1958
197	Atlanta, 1985
195	Pittsburgh, 1963
195	Pittsburgh, 1970

ERA: Lowest, season, NL

1.22	St. Louis, 1876
1.61	Providence, 1884
1.64	Providence, 1880
1.67	Hartford, 1876
1.69	Louisville, 1876

Shutouts: Most, season, NL

32	Chicago, 1907
32	Chicago, 1909
30	Chicago, 1906
30	St. Louis, 1968
29	Chicago, 1908

Homers allowed: Most, season, NL

192	New York, 1962
185	St. Louis, 1955
185	Atlanta, 1970
184	Chicago, 1966
181	Colorado, 1993

Homers allowed: Fewest, season, NL

5	Cincinnati, 1909
6	Chicago, 1909
8	Philadelphia, 1908
11	Chicago, 1907
12	Chicago, 1906
12	Pittsburgh, 1909
12	Pittsburgh, 1907
12	Pittsburgh, 1905

Walks allowed: Most, season, NL

716	Montreal, 1970
715	San Diego, 1974
702	Montreal, 1969
701	Atlanta, 1977
701	St. Louis, 1911

Career records

Hitters

ACTIVE PLAYERS IN CAPS

Games played: Most, career, all-time

3562	Pete Rose, 1963-1986
3308	Carl Yastrzemski, 1961-1983
3298	Hank Aaron, 1954-1976
3035	Ty Cobb, 1905-1928
3026	Stan Musial, 1941-1963
2992	Willie Mays, 1951-1973
2973	DAVE WINFIELD, 1973-1995
2951	Rusty Staub, 1963-1985
2896	Brooks Robinson, 1955-1977
2856	Robin Yount, 1974-1993
2834	Al Kaline, 1953-1974
2826	Eddie Collins, 1906-1930
2820	Reggie Jackson, 1967-1987
2819	EDDIE MURRAY, 1977-1995
2808	Frank Robinson, 1956-1976
2792	Honus Wagner, 1897-1917
2789	Tris Speaker, 1907-1928
2777	Tony Perez, 1964-1986
2730	Mel Ott, 1926-1947
2707	George Brett, 1973-1993

At-bats: Most, career, all-time

14,053	Pete Rose, 1963-1986
12,364	Hank Aaron, 1954-1976
11,988	Carl Yastrzemski, 1961-1983
11,434	Ty Cobb, 1905-1928

11,008 Robin Yount, 1974-1993
11,003 DAVE WINFIELD, 1973-1995
10,972 Stan Musial, 1941-1963
10,881 Willie Mays, 1951-1973
10,654 Brooks Robinson, 1955-1977
10,603 EDDIE MURRAY, 1977-1995
10,430 Honus Wagner, 1897-1917
10,349 George Brett, 1973-1993
10,332 Lou Brock, 1961-1979
10,274 Cap Anson, 1871-1897
10,230 Luis Aparicio, 1956-1973
10,195 Tris Speaker, 1907-1928
10,116 Al Kaline, 1953-1974
10,078 Rabbit Maranville, 1912-1935,
10,006 Frank Robinson, 1956-1976
9949 Eddie Collins, 1906-1930

Runs: Most, career, all-time

2246 Ty Cobb, 1905-1928
2174 Hank Aaron, 1954-1976
2174 Babe Ruth, 1914-1935
2165 Pete Rose, 1963-1986
2062 Willie Mays, 1951-1973
1996 Cap Anson, 1871-1897
1949 Stan Musial, 1941-1963
1888 Lou Gehrig, 1923-1939
1882 Tris Speaker, 1907-1928
1859 Mel Ott, 1926-1947
1829 Frank Robinson, 1956-1976
1821 Eddie Collins, 1906-1930
1816 Carl Yastrzemski, 1961-1983
1798 Ted Williams, 1939-1960
1774 Charlie Gehringer, 1924-1942
1751 Jimmie Foxx, 1925-1945
1736 Honus Wagner, 1897-1917
1732 Jim O'Rourke, 1872-1904
1720 Jesse Burkett, 1890-1905
1719 RICKEY HENDERSON,
        1979-1995
1719 Willie Keeler, 1892-1910

Hits: Most, career, all-time

4256 Pete Rose, 1963-1986
4189 Ty Cobb, 1905-1928
3771 Hank Aaron, 1954-1976
3630 Stan Musial, 1941-1963
3514 Tris Speaker, 1907-1928
3419 Carl Yastrzemski, 1961-1983
3415 Cap Anson, 1871-1897
3415 Honus Wagner, 1897-1917
3312 Eddie Collins, 1906-1930
3283 Willie Mays, 1951-1973
3242 Nap Lajoie, 1896-1916
3154 George Brett, 1973-1993
3152 Paul Waner, 1926-1945
3142 Robin Yount, 1974-1993
3110 DAVE WINFIELD, 1973-1995
3053 Rod Carew, 1967-1985
3023 Lou Brock, 1961-1979
3007 Al Kaline, 1953-1974
3000 Roberto Clemente,
        1955-1972
3071 EDDIE MURRAY, 1977-1995

Total bases: Most, career, all-time

6856 Hank Aaron, 1954-1976
6134 Stan Musial, 1941-1963
6066 Willie Mays, 1951-1973
5854 Ty Cobb, 1905-1928
5793 Babe Ruth, 1914-1935
5752 Pete Rose, 1963-1986
5539 Carl Yastrzemski, 1961-1983
5373 Frank Robinson, 1956-1976
5221 DAVE WINFIELD, 1973-1995
5108 EDDIE MURRAY, 1977-1995
5101 Tris Speaker, 1907-1928
5060 Lou Gehrig, 1923-1939
5044 George Brett, 1973-1993
5041 Mel Ott, 1926-1947
4956 Jimmie Foxx, 1925-1945
4884 Ted Williams, 1939-1960
4862 Honus Wagner, 1897-1917
4852 Al Kaline, 1953-1974
4834 Reggie Jackson, 1967-1987
4763 ANDRE DAWSON, 1976-1995

2B: Most, career, all-time

792 Tris Speaker, 1907-1928
746 Pete Rose, 1963-1986
725 Stan Musial, 1941-1963
724 Ty Cobb, 1905-1928
665 George Brett, 1973-1993
657 Nap Lajoie, 1896-1916
646 Carl Yastrzemski, 1961-1983
640 Honus Wagner, 1897-1917
624 Hank Aaron, 1954-1976
605 Paul Waner, 1926-1945
583 Robin Yount, 1974-1993
582 Cap Anson, 1871-1897
574 Charlie Gehringer, 1924-1942
542 Harry Heilmann, 1914-1932
541 Rogers Hornsby, 1915-1937
540 DAVE WINFIELD, 1973-1995
540 Joe Medwick, 1932-1948
539 Al Simmons, 1924-1944
534 Lou Gehrig, 1923-1939
532 EDDIE MURRAY, 1977-1995

3B: Most, career, all-time

309 Sam Crawford, 1899-1917
295 Ty Cobb, 1905-1928
252 Honus Wagner, 1897-1917
243 Jake Beckley, 1888-1907
233 Roger Connor, 1880-1897
222 Tris Speaker, 1907-1928
220 Fred Clarke, 1894-1915
205 Dan Brouthers, 1879-1904
194 Joe Kelley, 1891-1908
191 Paul Waner, 1926-1945
188 Bid McPhee, 1882-1899
186 Eddie Collins, 1906-1930
185 Ed Delahanty, 1888-1903
184 Sam Rice, 1915-1934
182 Jesse Burkett, 1890-1905
182 Edd Roush, 1913-1931
181 Ed Konetchy, 1907-1921
178 Buck Ewing, 1880-1897
177 Rabbit Maranville, 1912-1935
177 Stan Musial, 1941-1963

HR: Most, career, all-time

755 Hank Aaron, 1954-1976
714 Babe Ruth, 1914-1935
660 Willie Mays, 1951-1973
586 Frank Robinson, 1956-1976
573 Harmon Killebrew, 1954-1975
563 Reggie Jackson, 1967-1987
548 Mike Schmidt, 1972-1989
536 Mickey Mantle, 1951-1968
534 Jimmie Foxx, 1925-1945
521 Willie McCovey, 1959-1980
521 Ted Williams, 1939-1960
512 Ernie Banks, 1953-1971
512 Eddie Mathews, 1952-1968
511 Mel Ott, 1926-1947
493 Lou Gehrig, 1923-1939
479 EDDIE MURRAY, 1977-1995
475 Stan Musial, 1941-1963
475 Willie Stargell, 1962-1982
465 DAVE WINFIELD, 1973-1995
452 Carl Yastrzemski, 1961-1983

RBI: Most, career, all-time

2297 Hank Aaron, 1954-1976
2213 Babe Ruth, 1914-1935
1995 Lou Gehrig, 1923-1939
1981 Cap Anson, 1871-1897
1951 Stan Musial, 1941-1963
1937 Ty Cobb, 1905-1928
1922 Jimmie Foxx, 1925-1945
1903 Willie Mays, 1951-1973
1860 Mel Ott, 1926-1947
1844 Carl Yastrzemski, 1961-1983
1839 Ted Williams, 1939-1960
1833 DAVE WINFIELD, 1973-1995
1827 Al Simmons, 1924-1944
1820 EDDIE MURRAY, 1977-1995
1812 Frank Robinson, 1956-1976
1732 Honus Wagner, 1897-1917
1702 Reggie Jackson, 1967-1987
1652 Tony Perez, 1964-1986
1636 Ernie Banks, 1953-1971
1609 Goose Goslin, 1921-1938

SB: Most, career, all-time

1149 RICKEY HENDERSON,
        1979-1995
938 Lou Brock, 1961-1979
912 Billy Hamilton, 1888-1901
892 Ty Cobb, 1905-1928
777 TIM RAINES, 1979-1995
744 Eddie Collins, 1906-1930
740 VINCE COLEMAN,
        1985-1995
739 Arlie Latham, 1880-1909
738 Max Carey, 1910-1929
722 Honus Wagner, 1897-1917
689 Joe Morgan, 1963-1984
668 Willie Wilson, 1976-1994
657 Tom Brown, 1882-1898
649 Bert Campaneris, 1964-1983
616 George Davis, 1890-1909
594 Dummy Hoy, 1888-1902
586 Maury Wills, 1959-1972
583 George Vanhaltren,
        1887-1903
574 Hugh Duffy, 1888-1906
573 OZZIE SMITH, 1978-1995

BB: Most, career, all-time

2056	Babe Ruth, 1914-1935
2019	Ted Williams, 1939-1960
1865	Joe Morgan, 1963-1984
1845	Carl Yastrzemski, 1961-1983
1733	Mickey Mantle, 1951-1968
1708	Mel Ott, 1926-1947
1614	Eddie Yost, 1944-1962
1605	Darrell Evans, 1969-1989
1599	Stan Musial, 1941-1963
1566	Pete Rose, 1963-1986
1559	Harmon Killebrew, 1954-1975
1550	RICKEY HENDERSON, 1979-1995
1508	Lou Gehrig, 1923-1939
1507	Mike Schmidt, 1972-1989
1499	Eddie Collins, 1906-1930
1464	Willie Mays, 1951-1973
1452	Jimmie Foxx, 1925-1945
1444	Eddie Mathews, 1952-1968
1420	Frank Robinson, 1956-1976
1402	Hank Aaron, 1954-1976

HBP: Most, career, all-time

287	Hughie Jennings, 1891-1918
272	Tommy Tucker, 1887-1899
267	Don Baylor, 1970-1988
243	Ron Hunt, 1963-1974
230	Dan McGann, 1896-1908
198	Frank Robinson, 1956-1976
192	Minnie Minoso, 1949-1980
183	Jake Beckley, 1888-1907
173	Curt Welch, 1884-1893
165	Kid Elberfeld, 1898-1914
153	Fred Clarke, 1894-1915
151	Chet Lemon, 1975-1990
143	Carlton Fisk, 1969-1993
142	Nellie Fox, 1947-1965
141	Art Fletcher, 1909-1922
140	Bill Dahlen, 1891-1911
137	Frank Chance, 1898-1914
134	Nap Lajoie, 1896-1916
134	John McGraw, 1891-1906
134	Dummy Hoy, 1888-1902

K: Most, career, all-time

2597	Reggie Jackson, 1967-1987
1936	Willie Stargell, 1962-1982
1883	Mike Schmidt, 1972-1989
1867	Tony Perez, 1964-1986
1816	Dave Kingman, 1971-1986
1757	Bobby Bonds, 1968-1981
1748	Dale Murphy, 1976-1993
1730	Lou Brock, 1961-1979
1710	Mickey Mantle, 1951-1968
1699	Harmon Killebrew, 1954-1975
1697	Dwight Evans, 1972-1991
1686	DAVE WINFIELD, 1973-1995
1570	Lee May, 1965-1982
1556	Dick Allen, 1963-1977
1550	Willie McCovey, 1959-1980
1537	Dave Parker, 1973-1991
1532	Frank Robinson, 1956-1976
1527	Lance Parrish, 1977-1995
1526	Willie Mays, 1951-1973

1513	Rick Monday, 1966-1984

GIDP: Most, career, all-time

328	Hank Aaron, 1954-1976
323	Carl Yastrzemski, 1961-1983
319	DAVE WINFIELD, 1973-1995
315	Jim Rice, 1974-1989
297	Brooks Robinson, 1955-1977
297	Rusty Staub, 1963-1985
287	Ted Simmons, 1968-1988
286	EDDIE MURRAY, 1977-1995
284	Joe Torre, 1960-1977
277	George Scott, 1966-1979
275	Roberto Clemente, 1955-1972
271	Al Kaline, 1953-1974
270	Frank Robinson, 1956-1976
268	Tony Perez, 1964-1986
266	Dave Concepcion, 1970-1988
261	Ernie Lombardi, 1931-1947
256	Ron Santo, 1960-1974
255	Buddy Bell, 1972-1989
255	CAL RIPKEN, JR., 1981-1995
254	Al Oliver, 1968-1985

BA: Highest, career, all-time

.366	Ty Cobb, 1905-1928
.359	Rogers Hornsby, 1915-1937
.356	Joe Jackson, 1908-1920
.346	Ed Delahanty, 1888-1903
.345	Tris Speaker, 1907-1928
.344	Ted Williams, 1939-1960
.344	Billy Hamilton, 1888-1901
.342	Dan Brouthers, 1879-1904
.342	Babe Ruth, 1914-1935
.342	Harry Heilmann, 1914-1932
.342	Pete Browning, 1882-1894
.341	Willie Keeler, 1892-1910
.341	Bill Terry, 1923-1936
.340	George Sisler, 1915-1930
.340	Lou Gehrig, 1923-1939
.338	Jesse Burkett, 1890-1905
.338	Nap Lajoie, 1896-1916
.336	TONY GWYNN, 1982-1995
.336	Riggs Stephenson, 1921-1934
.334	WADE BOGGS, 1982-1995

Slug avg: Highest, career, all-time

.690	Babe Ruth, 1914-1935
.634	Ted Williams, 1939-1960
.632	Lou Gehrig, 1923-1939
.609	Jimmie Foxx, 1925-1945
.605	Hank Greenberg, 1930-1947
.579	Joe DiMaggio, 1936-1951
.577	Rogers Hornsby, 1915-1937
.562	Johnny Mize, 1936-1953
.559	Stan Musial, 1941-1963
.558	Willie Mays, 1951-1973
.557	Mickey Mantle, 1951-1968
.554	Hank Aaron, 1954-1976
.548	Ralph Kiner, 1946-1955
.545	Hack Wilson, 1923-1934
.543	Chuck Klein, 1928-1944
.541	BARRY BONDS, 1986-1995

.540	Duke Snider, 1947-1964
.537	Frank Robinson, 1956-1976
.535	FRED McGRIFF, 1986-1995
.535	Al Simmons, 1924-1944

Extra-base hits: Most, career, all-time

1477	Hank Aaron, 1954-1976
1377	Stan Musial, 1941-1963
1356	Babe Ruth, 1914-1935
1323	Willie Mays, 1951-1973
1190	Lou Gehrig, 1923-1939
1186	Frank Robinson, 1956-1976
1157	Carl Yastrzemski, 1961-1983
1136	Ty Cobb, 1905-1928
1131	Tris Speaker, 1907-1928
1119	George Brett, 1973-1993
1117	Jimmie Foxx, 1925-1945
1117	Ted Williams, 1939-1960
1093	DAVE WINFIELD, 1973-1995
1075	Reggie Jackson, 1967-1987
1071	Mel Ott, 1926-1947
1045	EDDIE MURRAY, 1977-1995
1041	Pete Rose, 1963-1986
1035	ANDRE DAWSON, 1976-1995
1015	Mike Schmidt, 1972-1989
1011	Rogers Hornsby, 1915-1937
1009	Ernie Banks, 1953-1971

Pitchers

Games: Most, career, all-time

1070	Hoyt Wilhelm, 1952-1972
1050	Kent Tekulve, 1974-1989
1002	Rich Gossage, 1972-1994
987	Lindy McDaniel, 1955-1975
944	Rollie Fingers, 1968-1985
943	LEE SMITH, 1980-1995
931	Gene Garber, 1969-1988
906	Cy Young, 1890-1911
901	DENNIS ECKERSLEY, 1975-1995
899	Sparky Lyle, 1967-1982
898	Jim Kaat, 1959-1983
880	Jeff Reardon, 1979-1994
874	Don McMahon, 1957-1974
864	Phil Niekro, 1964-1987
858	Charlie Hough, 1970-1994
848	Roy Face, 1953-1969
824	Tug McGraw, 1965-1984
819	JESSE OROSCO, 1979-1995
807	Nolan Ryan, 1966-1993
802	Walter Johnson, 1907-1927

Complete games: Most, career, all-time

749	Cy Young, 1890-1911
646	Pud Galvin, 1875-1892
554	Tim Keefe, 1880-1893
531	Walter Johnson, 1907-1927
531	Kid Nichols, 1890-1906
525	Bobby Mathews, 1871-1887
525	Mickey Welch, 1880-1892
489	Charley Radbourn, 1880-1891

485	John Clarkson, 1882-1894
468	Tony Mullane, 1881-1894
466	Jim McCormick, 1878-1887
448	Gus Weyhing, 1887-1901
437	Pete Alexander, 1911-1930
434	Christy Mathewson, 1900-1916
422	Jack Powell, 1897-1912
410	Eddie Plank, 1901-1917
394	Will White, 1877-1886
392	Amos Rusie, 1889-1901
388	Vic Willis, 1898-1910
386	Tommy Bond, 1874-1884

Saves: Most, career, all-time

471	LEE SMITH, 1980-1995
367	Jeff Reardon, 1979-1994
341	Rollie Fingers, 1968-1985
323	DENNIS ECKERSLEY, 1975-1995
311	TOM HENKE, 1982-1995
310	Rich Gossage, 1972-1994
300	Bruce Sutter, 1976-1988
295	JOHN FRANCO, 1984-1995
252	DAVE RIGHETTI, 1979-1995
244	Dan Quisenberry, 1979-1990
243	RANDY MYERS, 1985-1995
239	DOUG JONES, 1982-1995
238	Sparky Lyle, 1967-1982
227	Hoyt Wilhelm, 1952-1972
218	Gene Garber, 1969-1988
218	JEFF MONTGOMERY, 1987-1995
216	Dave Smith, 1980-1992
211	RICK AGUILERA, 1985-1995
201	Bobby Thigpen, 1986-1994
193	Roy Face, 1953-1969
192	MITCH WILLIAMS, 1986-1995
188	Mike Marshall, 1967-1981
184	STEVE BEDROSIAN, 1981-1995
184	Kent Tekulve, 1974-1989
183	JEFF RUSSELL, 1983-1995
180	Tug McGraw, 1965-1984
179	Ron Perranoski, 1961-1973
177	BRYAN HARVEY, 1987-1995
177	TODD WORRELL, 1983-1995
172	Lindy McDaniel, 1955-1975

Shutouts: Most, career, all-time

110	Walter Johnson, 1907-1927
90	Pete Alexander, 1911-1930
79	Christy Mathewson, 1900-1916
76	Cy Young, 1890-1911
69	Eddie Plank, 1901-1917
63	Warren Spahn, 1942-1965
61	Nolan Ryan, 1966-1993
61	Tom Seaver, 1967-1986
60	Bert Blyleven, 1970-1992
58	Don Sutton, 1966-1988
58	Pud Galvin, 1875-1892
57	Ed Walsh, 1904-1917
56	Bob Gibson, 1959-1975
55	Mordecai Brown, 1903-1916
55	Steve Carlton, 1965-1988
53	Jim Palmer, 1965-1984
53	Gaylord Perry, 1962-1983
52	Juan Marichal, 1960-1975
50	Rube Waddell, 1897-1910
50	Vic Willis, 1898-1910

Wins: Most, career, all-time

511	Cy Young, 1890-1911
417	Walter Johnson, 1907-1927
373	Pete Alexander, 1911-1930
373	Christy Mathewson, 1900-1916
364	Pud Galvin, 1875-1892
363	Warren Spahn, 1942-1965
361	Kid Nichols, 1890-1906
342	Tim Keefe, 1880-1893
329	Steve Carlton, 1965-1988
328	John Clarkson, 1882-1894
326	Eddie Plank, 1901-1917
324	Nolan Ryan, 1966-1993
324	Don Sutton, 1966-1988
318	Phil Niekro, 1964-1987
314	Gaylord Perry, 1962-1983
311	Tom Seaver, 1967-1986
309	Charley Radbourn, 1880-1891
307	Mickey Welch, 1880-1892
300	Lefty Grove, 1925-1941
300	Early Wynn, 1939-1963

Losses: Most, career, all-time

316	Cy Young, 1890-1911
310	Pud Galvin, 1875-1892
292	Nolan Ryan, 1966-1993
279	Walter Johnson, 1907-1927
274	Phil Niekro, 1964-1987
265	Gaylord Perry, 1962-1983
256	Don Sutton, 1966-1988
254	Jack Powell, 1897-1912
251	Eppa Rixey, 1912-1933
250	Bert Blyleven, 1970-1992
248	Bobby Mathews, 1871-1887
245	Robin Roberts, 1948-1966
245	Warren Spahn, 1942-1965
244	Steve Carlton, 1965-1988
244	Early Wynn, 1939-1963
237	Jim Kaat, 1959-1983
236	Frank Tanana, 1973-1993
232	Gus Weyhing, 1887-1901
231	Tommy John, 1963-1989
230	Bob Friend, 1951-1966
230	Ted Lyons, 1923-1946

HR allowed: Most, career, all-time

505	Robin Roberts, 1948-1966
484	Fergie Jenkins, 1965-1983
482	Phil Niekro, 1964-1987
472	Don Sutton, 1966-1988
448	Frank Tanana, 1973-1993
434	Warren Spahn, 1942-1965
430	Bert Blyleven, 1970-1992
414	Steve Carlton, 1965-1988
399	Gaylord Perry, 1962-1983
395	Jim Kaat, 1959-1983
389	Jack Morris, 1977-1994
383	Charlie Hough, 1970-1994
380	Tom Seaver, 1967-1986
374	Catfish Hunter, 1965-1979
372	Jim Bunning, 1955-1971
347	Mickey Lolich, 1963-1979
346	Luis Tiant, 1964-1982
344	DENNIS MARTINEZ, 1976-1995
338	Early Wynn, 1939-1963
324	Doyle Alexander, 1971-1989
324	DENNIS ECKERSLEY, 1975-1995

BB: Most, career, all-time

2795	Nolan Ryan, 1966-1993
1833	Steve Carlton, 1965-1988
1809	Phil Niekro, 1964-1987
1775	Early Wynn, 1939-1963
1764	Bob Feller, 1936-1956
1732	Bobo Newsom, 1929-1953
1704	Amos Rusie, 1889-1901
1665	Charlie Hough, 1970-1994
1566	Gus Weyhing, 1887-1901
1541	Red Ruffing, 1924-1947
1442	Bump Hadley, 1926-1941
1434	Warren Spahn, 1942-1965
1431	Earl Whitehill, 1923-1939
1408	Tony Mullane, 1881-1894
1396	Sam Jones, 1914-1935
1390	Tom Seaver, 1967-1986
1390	Jack Morris, 1977-1994
1379	Gaylord Perry, 1962-1983
1371	Mike Torrez, 1967-1984
1363	Walter Johnson, 1907-1927

K: Most, career, all-time

5714	Nolan Ryan, 1966-1993
4136	Steve Carlton, 1965-1988
3701	Bert Blyleven, 1970-1992
3640	Tom Seaver, 1967-1986
3574	Don Sutton, 1966-1988
3534	Gaylord Perry, 1962-1983
3509	Walter Johnson, 1907-1927
3342	Phil Niekro, 1964-1987
3192	Fergie Jenkins, 1965-1983
3117	Bob Gibson, 1959-1975
2855	Jim Bunning, 1955-1971
2832	Mickey Lolich, 1963-1979
2803	Cy Young, 1890-1911
2773	Frank Tanana, 1973-1993
2583	Warren Spahn, 1942-1965
2581	Bob Feller, 1936-1956
2556	Jerry Koosman, 1967-1985
2543	Tim Keefe, 1880-1893
2502	Christy Mathewson, 1900-1916
2486	Don Drysdale, 1956-1969

Wild pitches: Most, career, all-time

343	Tony Mullane, 1881-1894
277	Nolan Ryan, 1966-1993
274	Mickey Welch, 1880-1892
240	Tim Keefe, 1880-1893
240	Gus Weyhing, 1887-1901

226	Phil Niekro, 1964-1987
221	Mark Baldwin, 1887-1893
221	Will White, 1877-1886
220	Pud Galvin, 1875-1892
214	Charley Radbourn, 1880-1891
214	Jim Whitney, 1881-1890
206	Adonis Terry, 1884-1897
206	Jack Morris, 1977-1993
203	Matt Kilroy, 1886-1898
187	Tommy John, 1963-1989
185	Bobby Mathews, 1871-1887
183	Steve Carlton, 1965-1988
182	John Clarkson, 1882-1894
179	Toad Ramsey, 1885-1890
179	Charlie Hough, 1970-1994

Win pct: Highest, career, all-time

.796	Al Spalding, 1871-1878
.717	Spud Chandler, 1937-1947
.690	Dave Foutz, 1884-1896
.690	Whitey Ford, 1950-1967
.688	Bob Caruthers, 1884-1893
.686	Don Gullett, 1970-1978
.680	Lefty Grove, 1925-1941
.671	Joe Wood, 1908-1922
.667	Vic Raschi, 1946-1955
.665	Larry Corcoran, 1880-1887
.665	Christy Mathewson, 1900-1916
.660	Sam Leever, 1898-1910
.657	Sal Maglie, 1945-1958
.656	Dick McBride, 1871-1876
.655	Sandy Koufax, 1955-1966
.654	Johnny Allen, 1932-1944
.651	Ron Guidry, 1975-1988
.650	ROGER CLEMENS, 1984-1995
.650	Lefty Gomez, 1930-1943
.649	DWIGHT GOODEN, 1984-1994

ERA: Lowest, career, all-time

1.82	Ed Walsh, 1904-1917
1.89	Addie Joss, 1902-1910
2.06	Mordecai Brown, 1903-1916
2.10	John Ward, 1878-1894
2.13	Christy Mathewson, 1900-1916
2.14	Al Spalding, 1871-1878
2.16	Rube Waddell, 1897-1910
2.17	Walter Johnson, 1907-1927
2.23	Orval Overall, 1905-1913
2.28	Will White, 1877-1886
2.28	Ed Reulbach, 1905-1917
2.30	Jim Scott, 1909-1917
2.31	Tommy Bond, 1874-1884
2.35	Eddie Plank, 1901-1917
2.35	Larry Corcoran, 1880-1887
2.38	George McQuillan, 1907-1918
2.38	Eddie Cicotte, 1905-1920
2.38	Ed Killian, 1903-1910
2.39	Doc White, 1901-1913
2.42	George Bradley, 1875-1888

Innings: Most, career, all-time

7356.2	Cy Young, 1890-1911
6003.1	Pud Galvin, 1875-1892
5914.2	Walter Johnson, 1907-1927
5404.1	Phil Niekro, 1964-1987
5386.0	Nolan Ryan, 1966-1993
5350.1	Gaylord Perry, 1962-1983
5282.1	Don Sutton, 1966-1988
5243.2	Warren Spahn, 1942-1965
5217.1	Steve Carlton, 1965-1988
5190.0	Pete Alexander, 1911-1930
5056.1	Kid Nichols, 1890-1906
5047.1	Tim Keefe, 1880-1893
4970.0	Bert Blyleven, 1970-1992
4956.1	Bobby Mathews, 1871-1887
4802.0	Mickey Welch, 1880-1892
4782.2	Tom Seaver, 1967-1986
4780.2	Christy Mathewson, 1900-1916
4710.1	Tommy John, 1963-1989
4688.2	Robin Roberts, 1948-1966
4564.0	Early Wynn, 1939-1963

General club records

Highest percentage for league champion

.832	St. Louis, UA-1884
.798	Chicago, NL-1880
.788	Chicago, NL-1876
.777	Chicago, NL-1885
.763	Chicago, NL-1906

Lowest percentage for league champion

.509	New York, NL-1973
.525	Minnesota, AL-1987
.551	New York, AL-1981
.556	Oakland, AL-1974
.556	Philadelphia, NL-1983

Most wins

116	Chicago, NL-1906
111	Cleveland, AL-1954
110	Pittsburgh, NL-1909
110	New York, AL-1927
109	New York, AL-1961
109	Baltimore, AL-1969

Fewest wins

36	Philadelphia, AL-1916
38	Washington, AL-1904
38	Boston, NL-1935
40	New York, NL-1962
42	Washington, AL-1909
42	Philadelphia, NL-1942
42	Pittsburgh, NL-1952

Most league championships

33	New York, AL
21	Brooklyn-Los Angeles, NL
19	New York-San Francisco, NL
16	Chicago, NL
15	St. Louis, NL
15	Philadelphia-Oakland, AL

Individual fielding records

Gold Gloves: Most, pitcher

16	Jim Kaat
9	Bob Gibson
8	Bobby Shantz
7	MARK LANGSTON
6	GREG MADDUX
5	Ron Guidry
5	Phil Niekro
4	Jim Palmer
3	Harvey Haddix
2	Andy Messersmith
2	Mike Norris
2	Rick Reuschel

Gold Gloves: Most, catcher

10	Johnny Bench
7	Bob Boone
6	Jim Sundberg
5	Bill Freehan
4	Del Crandall
4	TONY PENA
4	IVAN RODRIGUEZ
3	Earl Battey
3	Gary Carter
3	Sherm Lollar
3	Thurman Munson
3	TOM PAGNOZZI
3	LANCE PARRISH
3	BENITO SANTIAGO

Gold Gloves: Most, first base

11	Keith Hernandez
9	DON MATTINGLY
8	George Scott
7	Vic Power
7	Bill White
6	Wes Parker
4	Steve Garvey
3	Gil Hodges
3	MARK GRACE
3	EDDIE MURRAY
3	Joe Pepitone

Gold Gloves: Most, second base

9	Ryne Sandberg
8	Bill Mazeroski
8	Frank White
5	Bobby Richardson
5	Joe Morgan
4	ROBERTO ALOMAR
4	Bobby Grich
3	Nellie Fox
3	Bobby Knoop
3	Davey Johnson
3	Manny Trillo
3	LOU WHITAKER
3	Harold Reynolds

Gold Gloves: Most, third base

16	Brooks Robinson
10	Mike Schmidt
6	Buddy Bell
5	Ken Boyer
5	Doug Rader
5	Ron Santo
4	GARY GAETTI
3	Frank Malzone
3	TERRY PENDLETON
3	ROBIN VENTURA
3	TIM WALLACH
3	MATT WILLIAMS

Gold Gloves: Most, shortstop

13	OZZIE SMITH
9	Luis Aparicio
8	Mark Belanger
5	Dave Concepcion
4	TONY FERNANDEZ
4	ALAN TRAMMELL
3	Roy McMillan
3	OMAR VIZQUEL
2	Gene Alley
2	Larry Bowa
2	Don Kessinger
2	BARRY LARKIN
2	CAL RIPKEN JR.
2	Zoilo Versalles
2	Maury Wills

Gold Gloves: Most, outfield

12	Roberto Clemente
12	Willie Mays
10	Al Kaline
8	Paul Blair
8	ANDRE DAWSON
8	Dwight Evans
8	Garry Maddox
7	Curt Flood
7	DEVON WHITE
7	DAVE WINFIELD
7	Carl Yastrzemski

Fielding average, pitcher (92 chances accepted)

1.000	Kid Nichols, Bos/N-1896
1.000	Frank Owen, Chi/A-1904
1.000	Mordecai Brown, Chi/N-1908
1.000	Pete Alexander, Phi/N-1913
1.000	Walter Johnson, Was/A-1913
1.000	Eppa Rixey, Phi/N-1917
1.000	Walter Johnson, Was/A-1917
1.000	Hal Schumacher, NY/N-1935
1.000	Larry Jackson, Chi/N-1964
1.000	Randy Jones, SD/N-1976
1.000	GREG MADDUX, Chi/N-1990

Fielding average, catcher

1.000	Spud Davis, Phi/N-1939
1.000	Buddy Rosar, Phi/A-1946
1.000	Lou Berberet, Was/A-1957
1.000	Pete Daley, Bos/A-1957
1.000	Yogi Berra, NY/A-1958
1.000	Rick Cerone, Bos/A-1988
.999	TOM PAGNOZZI, StL/N-1992

.999	Joe Azcue, Cle/A-1967
.999	Wes Westrum, NY/N-1950
.998	TERRY STEINBACH, Oak/A-1994

Fielding average, first base

1.000	Steve Garvey, SD/N-1984
.999	Stuffy McInnis, Bos/A-1921
.999	Frank McCormick, Phi/N-1946
.999	Steve Garvey, LA/N-1981
.999	Jim Spencer, Cal-Tex/A-1973
.999	Wes Parker, LA/N-1968
.999	EDDIE MURRAY, Bal/A-1981
.999	HAL MORRIS, Cin/N-1992
.998	Jim Spencer, Chi/A-1976
.998	Jim Spencer, NY-Oak/A-1981

Fielding average, second base

.997	Bobby Grich, Cal/A-1985
.996	JOSE OQUENDO, StL/N-1990
.995	Ryne Sandberg, Chi/N-1991
.995	JODY REED, Mil/A-1994
.995	Rob Wilfong, Min/A-1980
.995	Bobby Grich, Bal/A-1973
.994	Frank White, KC/A-1988
.994	MARK LEMKE, Atl/N-1994
.994	JOSE OQUENDO, StL/N-1989
.994	BRET BOONE, Cin/N-1995

Fielding average, shortstop

.996	CAL RIPKEN JR., Bal/A-1990
.992	TONY FERNANDEZ, Tor/A-1989
.991	Larry Bowa, Phi/N-1979
.990	Ed Brinkman, Det/A-1972
.990	CAL RIPKEN JR., Bal/A-1989
.989	SPIKE OWEN, Mon/N-1990
.989	OMAR VIZQUEL, Sea/A-1992
.989	TONY FERNANDEZ, Tor/A-1990
.989	CAL RIPKEN JR., Bal/A-1995
.988	DICK SCHOFIELD, NY/N-1992

Fielding average, third base

.991	TONY FERNANDEZ, Cin/N-1994
.991	STEVE BUECHELE, Tex/A-1991 (counting Pit/N in 1991, Buechele's average was .983)
.989	Don Money, Mil/A-1974
.988	Hank Majeski, Phi/A-1947
.987	Aurelio Rodriguez, Det/A-1978
.984	Willie Kamm, Cle/A-1933
.983	George Kell, Phi-Det/A-1946
.983	Heinie Groh, NY/N-1924
.983	Carney Lansford, Cal/A-1979
.982	GARY GAETTI, KC/A-1994

Fielding average, outfield

1.000	Danny Litwhiler, Phi/N-1942
1.000	Willard Marshall, Bos/N-1951
1.000	Tony Gonzalez, Phi/N-1962

1.000	Don Demeter, Phi/N-1963
1.000	Rocky Colavito, Cle/A-1965
1.000	Curt Flood, StL/N-1966
1.000	Johnny Callison, Phi/N-1968
1.000	Mickey Stanley, Det/A-1968
1.000	Ken Harrelson, Bos/A-1968
1.000	Ken Berry, Chi/A-1969
1.000	Mickey Stanley, Det/A-1970
1.000	Roy White, NY/A-1971
1.000	Al Kaline, Det/A-1971
1.000	Ken Berry, Cal/A-1972
1.000	Carl Yastrzemski, Bos/A-1977
1.000	Terry Puhl, Hou/N-1979
1.000	Gary Roenicke, Bal/A-1980
1.000	Ken Landreaux, LA/N-1981
1.000	Terry Puhl, Hou/N-1981
1.000	Ken Singleton, Bal/A-1981
1.000	Brian Downing, Cal/A-1982
1.000	John Lowenstein, Bal/A-1982
1.000	Brian Downing, Cal/A-1984
1.000	BRETT BUTLER, LA/N-1991
1.000	DARRYL HAMILTON, Mil/A-1992
1.000	BRETT BUTLER, LA/N-1993
1.000	DARREN LEWIS, SF/N-1993
1.000	TIM RAINES, Chi/A-1993
1.000	MILT THOMPSON, Phi-Hou/N-1994
1.000	LANCE JOHNSON, Chi/A-1994
1.000	JIM EISENREICH, Phi/N-1995

Fielding average, pitcher, active players (60 chances accepted)

1.000	Greg Maddux, Chi/N-1990
1.000	Tom Glavine, Atl/N-1991
1.000	Jimmy Key, Tor/A-1986
1.000	Jose Rijo, Cin/N-1993
1.000	Bob Tewksbury, StL/N-1993
1.000	Mark Gubicza, KC/A-1995
1.000	Greg Maddux, Atl/N-1995

Fielding average, catcher, active players

.999	Tom Pagnozzi, StL/N-1992
.998	Terry Steinbach, Oak/A-1994
.998	Mike LaValliere, Pit/N-1991
.998	Chris Hoiles, Bal/A-1991
.998	Damon Berryhill, Atl/N-1992
.998	Tom Pagnozzi, StL/N-1994
.998	Kirt Manwaring, SF/N-1993
.998	Wally Joyner, KC/A-1995
.998	Rico Brogna, NY/N-1995

Fielding average, first base, active players

.999	Eddie Murray, Bal/A-1981
.999	Hal Morris, Cin/N-1992
.998	Don Mattingly, NY/A-1994
.998	Dave Magadan, NY/N-1990
.998	Don Mattingly, NY/A-1993
.998	Mark Grace, Chi/N-1992
.998	Kevin Young, Pit/N-1993

Fielding average, second base, active players

.996	Jose Oquendo, StL/N-1990
.995	Jody Reed, Mil/A-1994
.994	Mark Lemke, Atl/N-1994
.994	Jose Oquendo, StL/N-1989
.994	Chuck Knoblauch, Min/A-1994
.994	Jose Lind, KC/A-1993
.994	Lou Whitaker, Det/A-1991
.994	Bret Boone, Cin/N-1995
.994	Jody Reed, SD/N-1995
.994	Roberto Alomar, Tor/A-1995

Fielding average, shortstop, active players

.996	Cal Ripken JR, Bal/A-1990
.992	Tony Fernandez, Tor/A-1989
.990	Cal Ripken JR, Bal/A-1989
.989	Spike Owen, Mon/N-1990
.989	Omar Vizquel, Sea/A-1992
.989	Tony Fernandez, Tor/A-1990
.989	Cal Ripken, Jr., Bal/A-1995

Fielding average, third base, active players

.991	Tony Fernandez, Cin/N-1994
.991	Steve Buechele, Tex/A-1991 (counting Pit/N in 1991, Buechele's average was .983)
.982	Gary Gaetti, KC/A-1994
.981	Wade Boggs, NY/A-1995
.977	Gary Gaetti, Min/A-1988

Fielding average, outfield, active players

1.000	Brett Butler, LA/N-1991
1.000	Darryl Hamilton, Mil/A-1992
1.000	Brett Butler, LA/N-1993
1.000	Darren Lewis, SF/N-1993
1.000	Tim Raines, Chi/A-1993
1.000	Milt Thompson, Phi-Hou/N-1994
1.000	Lance Johnson, Chi/A-1994
1.000	Jim Eisenreich, Phi/N-1995
1.000	Stan Javier, Oak/A-1995

Assists, pitcher

227	Ed Walsh, Chi/A-1907
223	Will White, Cin/A-1882
190	Ed Walsh, Chi/A-1908
178	Harry Howell, StL/A-1905
177	Tony Mullane, Lou/A-1882
174	John Clarkson, Chi/N-1885
172	John Clarkson, Bos/N-1889
166	Jack Chesbro, NY/A-1904
163	George Mullin, Det/A-1904
160	Ed Walsh, Chi/A-1911

Assists, catcher

238	Bill Rariden, New/F-1915
215	Bill Rariden, Ind/F-1914
214	Pat Moran, Bos/N-1903
212	Oscar Stanage, Det/A-1911
212	Art Wilson, Chi/F-1914
210	Gabby Street, Was/A-1909

204	Frank Snyder, StL/N-1915
203	George Gibson, Pit/N-1910
202	Bill Bergen, Bro/N-1909
202	Claude Berry, Pit/F-1914

Assists, first base

184	Bill Buckner, Bos/A-1985
180	MARK GRACE, Chi/N-1990
167	MARK GRACE, Chi/N-1991
166	Sid Bream, Pit/N-1986
161	Bill Buckner, Chi/N-1983
159	Bill Buckner, Chi/N-1982
157	Bill Buckner, Bos/A-1986
155	Mickey Vernon, Cle/A-1949
152	Fred Tenney, Bos/N-1905
152	EDDIE MURRAY, Bal/A-1985

Assists, second base

641	Frankie Frisch, StL/N-1927
588	Hughie Critz, Cin/N-1926
582	Rogers Hornsby, NY/N-1927
572	Ski Melillo, StL/A-1930
571	Ryne Sandberg, Chi/N-1983
568	Rabbit Maranville, Pit/N-1924
562	Frank Parkinson, Phi/N-1922
559	Tony Cuccinello, Bos/N-1936
557	Johnny Hodapp, Cle/A-1930
555	Lou Bierbauer, Pit/N-1892

Assists, shortstop

621	OZZIE SMITH, SD/N-1980
601	Glenn Wright, Pit/N-1924
598	Dave Bancroft, Phi-NY/N-1920
597	Tommy Thevenow, StL/N-1926
595	Ivan DeJesus, Chi/N-1977
583	CAL RIPKEN JR., Bal/A-1984
581	Whitey Wietelmann, Bos/N-1943
579	Dave Bancroft, NY/N-1922
574	Rabbit Maranville, Bos/N-1914
573	Don Kessinger, Chi/N-1968

Assists, third base

412	Graig Nettles, Cle/A-1971
410	Graig Nettles, NY/A-1973
410	Brooks Robinson, Bal/A-1974
405	Harlond Clift, StL/A-1937
405	Brooks Robinson, Bal/A-1967
404	Mike Schmidt, Phi/N-1974
399	Doug DeCinces, Cal/A-1982
396	Clete Boyer, NY/A-1962
396	Mike Schmidt, Phi/N-1977
396	Buddy Bell, Tex/A-1982

Assists, outfield

50	Orator Shaffer, Chi/N-1879
48	Hugh Nicol, StL/A-1884
45	Hardy Richardson, Buf/N-1881
44	Tommy McCarthy, StL/A-1888
44	Chuck Klein, Phi/N-1930
43	Charlie Duffee, StL/A-1889
43	Jimmy Bannon, Bos/N-1894
42	Jim Fogarty, Phi/N-1889
41	Orator Shaffer, Buf/N-1883
41	Jim Lillie, Buf/N-1884

Assists, pitcher, active players

64	Fernando Valenzuela, LA/N-1982
64	Greg Maddux, Chi/N-1992
60	Orel Hershiser, LA/N-1988
59	Dennis Martinez, Bal/A-1979
59	Greg Maddux, Atl/N-1993

Assists, catcher, active players

100	Tony Pena, Pit/N-1985
100	Benito Santiago, SD/N-1991
99	Tony Pena, Pit/N-1986
99	Mike Piazza, LA/N-1993
95	Tony Pena, Pit/N-1984

Assists, first base, active players

180	Mark Grace, Chi/N-1990
167	Mark Grace, Chi/N-1991
152	Eddie Murray, Bal/A-1985
147	Eric Karros, LA/N-1993
146	Rafael Palmeiro, Tex/A-1993

Assists, second base, active players

500	Jose Oquendo, StL/N-1989
475	Carlos Baerga, Cle/A-1992
473	Jose Lind, Pit/N-1988
472	Roberto Alomar, SD/N-1989
472	Jody Reed, Bos/A-1992

Assists, shortstop, active players

621	Ozzie Smith, SD/N-1980
583	Cal Ripken Jr., Bal/A-1984
570	Ozzie Guillen, Chi/A-1988
555	Ozzie Smith, SD/N-1979
549	Ozzie Smith, StL/N-1985

Assists, third base, active players

392	Terry Pendleton, StL/N-1989
383	Tim Wallach, Mon/N-1985
372	Robin Ventura, Chi/A-1992
371	Terry Pendleton, StL/N-1986
369	Terry Pendleton, StL/N-1987

Assists, outfield, active players

22	Joe Orsulak, Bal/A-1991
21	Tim Raines, Mon/N-1983
20	Dave Winfield, SD/N-1980
19	Brett Butler, Cle/A-1985
19	Kirby Puckett, Min/A-1985
19	Tony Gwynn, SD/N-1986
19	Bernard Gilkey, StL/N-1993
19	Wayne Kirby, Cle/A-1993

Individual records

Hitters

ACTIVE PLAYERS IN CAPS

Most consecutive games played, lifetime

2153	CAL RIPKEN JR., 1982-1995
2130	Lou Gehrig, 1925-1939

1307	Everett Scott, 1916-1925	25	Brian Harper, Min/AL-1990	6	Dave Clark, 1986-1995
1207	Steve Garvey, 1975-1983	25	Lance Johnson, Chi/AL-1992	6	Chris Gwynn,1987-1995
1117	Billy Williams, 1963-1970	24	Rafael Palmiero, Bal/A-1994	6	Rex Hudler, 1984-1995
1103	Joe Sewell, 1922-1930			6	Kevin Roberson, 1993-1995
895	Stan Musial, 1951-1957			6	John Vander Wal, 1991-1995
829	Eddie Yost, 1949-1955				

Most pinch-hits, lifetime

822	Gus Suhr, 1931-1937
798	Nellie Fox, 1955-1960

150	Manny Mota, 1962-1982
145	Smoky Burgess, 1949-1967
143	Greg Gross, 1973-1989

Most consecutive games played, lifetime, active players

2153	Cal Ripken, 1982-1995
259	Frank Thomas, 1993-1995

123	Jose Morales, 1973-1984
116	Jerry Lynch, 1954-1966
114	Red Lucas, 1923-1938
113	Steve Braun, 1971-1985
108	Terry Crowley, 1969-1983
108	Denny Walling, 1975-1992
107	Gates Brown, 1963-1975
103	Mike Lum, 1967-1981
102	Jim Dwyer, 1973-1990
100	Rusty Staub, 1963-1985

Most consecutive games batted safely, season

56	Joe DiMaggio, NY/AL-1941
44	Willie Keeler, Bal/NL-1897
44	Pete Rose, Cin/NL-1978
42	Bill Dahlen, Chi/NL-1894
41	George Sisler, StL/AL-1922
40	Ty Cobb, Det/AL-1911
39	PAUL MOLITOR, Mil/AL-1987
37	Tommy Holmes, Bos/NL-1945
36	Billy Hamilton, Phi/NL-1894
35	Fred Clarke, Lou/NL-1895
35	Ty Cobb, Det/AL-1917
34	George Sisler, StL/AL-1925
34	George McQuinn, StL/AL-1938
34	Dom DiMaggio, Bos/AL-1949
34	BENITO SANTIAGO, SD/NL-1987
33	Hal Chase, NY/AL-1907
33	George Davis, NY/NL-1893
33	Rogers Hornsby, StL/NL-1922
33	Heinie Manush, Was/AL-1933
31	Ed Delahanty, Phi/NL-1899
31	Nap Lajoie, Cle/AL-1906
31	Sam Rice, Was/AL-1924
31	Willie Davis, LA/NL-1969
31	Rico Carty, Atl/NL-1970
31	Ken Landreaux, Min/AL-1980
30	Elmer Smith, Cin/NL-1898
30	Tris Speaker, Bos/AL-1912
30	Bing Miller, Phi/NL-1929
30	Goose Goslin, Det/AL-1934
30	Stan Musial, StL/NL-1950
30	Ron LeFlore, Det/AL-1976
30	George Brett, KC/AL-1980
30	JEROME WALTON, Chi/NL-1989

Most pinch-hits, lifetime, active players

95	Gerald Perry, 1983-1995
80	Kevin Bass, 1982-1995
79	Milt Thompson, 1984-1995
78	Gary Varsho, 1988-1995
71	Dwight Smith, 1989-1995
63	Mitch Webster, 1983-1995
61	Mike Aldrete, 1986-1995
60	Chris Gwynn, 1987-1995
56	John Cangelosi, 1985-1995
56	John Vander Wal, 1991-1995

Most pinch-hit home runs, lifetime

20	Cliff Johnson, 1972-1986
18	Jerry Lynch, 1954-1966
16	Gates Brown, 1963-1975
16	Smoky Burgess, 1949-1967
16	Willie McCovey, 1959-1980
14	George Crowe, 1952-1961
12	Joe Adcock, 1950-1966
12	Bob Cerv, 1951-1962
12	Jose Morales, 1973-1984
12	Graig Nettles, 1967-1988
11	Jeff Burroughs, 1970-1985
11	Jay Johnstone, 1966-1985
11	Fred Whitfield, 1962-1970
11	Cy Williams, 1912-1930
11	CANDY MALDONADO, 1981-1995
10	Jim Dwyer, 1973-1990
10	Mike Lum, 1967-1981
10	Ken McMullen, 1962-1977
10	Don Mincher, 1960-1972
10	Wally Post, 1949-1964
10	Champ Summers, 1974-1984
10	Jerry Turner, 1974-1983
10	Gus Zernial, 1949-1959

Most consecutive games batted safely, season, active players

39	Paul Molitor, Mil/AL-1987
34	Benito Santiago, SD/NL-1987
30	George Brett, KC/AL-1980
30	Jerome Walton, Chi/NL-1989
28	Wade Boggs, Bos/AL-1985
26	John Olerud, Tor/AL-1993
25	Tony Gwynn, SD/NL-1983
25	Steve Sax, LA/NL-1986
25	Wade Boggs, Bos/AL-1987

Most pinch-hit home runs, lifetime, active players

11	Candy Maldonado, 1981-1994
9	Mark Carreon, 1987-1994
9	Howard Johnson, 1982-1995
7	Gerald Perry, 1983-1995
7	Chris James, 1986-1995
7	Mike Aldrete, 1986-1995

Pitchers

Most consecutive scoreless innings, season

59	OREL HERSHISER, LA/NL - Aug. 30 to Sept. 28, 1988 (end of season)
58	Don Drysdale, LA/NL - May 14 to June 8, 1968
55.2	Walter Johnson, Was/AL - April 10 to May 14, 1913
53	Jack Coombs, Phi/AL - Sept. 5 to 25, 1910
47	Bob Gibson, StL/NL - June 2 to 26, 1968
45.1	Carl Hubbell, NY/NL - July 13 to Aug. 1, 1933 (allowed a run charged to starter in a relief appearance on July 19, after 12 scoreless innings, had a 33-inning string afterwards)
45	Cy Young, Bos/AL - April 25 to May 17, 1904
45	Doc White, Chi/AL - Sept. 12 to 30, 1904
45	Sal Maglie, NY/NL - Aug. 16 to Sept. 13, 1950
44	Ed Reulbach, Chi/NL - Sept. 17 to Oct. 3, 1908 (end of season) (added 6 more innings on April 17, 1909, for a total of 50 over 2 years)
43.2	Rube Waddell, Phi/AL - Aug. 22 to Sept. 5, 1905
42	Rube Foster, Bos/AL - May 1 to 26, 1914
41	Jack Chesbro, Pit/NL - June 26 to July 16, 1902
41	Grover Cleveland Alexander, Phi/NL - Sept. 7 to 24, 1911
41	Art Nehf, Bos/NL - Sept. 13 to Oct. 4, 1917
41	Luis Tiant, Cle/AL - April 28 to May 17, 1968
41	GREGG OLSON, Bal/AL had a streak of 41 scoreless innings over two seasons from Aug. 4, 1989 to May 4, 1990, 26 in 1989 and 15 in 1990)
40	Walter Johnson, Was/AL - May 7 to 26, 1918
40	Gaylord Perry, SF/NL - Aug. 28 to Sept. 10, 1967
40	Luis Tiant, Bos/AL - Aug. 19 to Sept. 8, 1972
39.2	Mordecai Brown, Chi/NL - June 8 to July 8, 1908
39.2	Billy Pierce, Chi/AL - Aug. 3 to 19, 1953

39 Ed Walsh, Chi/AL - Aug. 10 to 22, 1906

39 Christy Mathewson, NY/NL - May 3 to 21, 1901

39 Don Newcombe, Bro/NL - July 25 to Aug. 11, 1956

39 Ray Culp, Bos/AL - Sept. 7 to 25, 1968

39 Gaylord Perry, SF/NL - Sept. 1 to 23, 1970

38.1 Bill Lee, Chi/NL - Sept. 5 to 26, 1938

38 Pud Galvin, Buf/NL - Aug. 2 to 8, 1884

38 John Clarkson, Chi/NL - May 18 to 27, 1885

38 Jim Bagby, Cle/AL - June 30 to July 16, 1917

38 Ray Herbert, Chi/AL - May 1 to 14, 1963

37 George Bradley, StL/NL - July 8 to 18, 1876

37 Cy Young, Bos/AL - June 13 to July 1, 1903

37 Walter Johnson, Was/AL - June 27 to July 13, 1913

37 Ed Walsh, Chi/AL - July 31 to Aug. 14, 1910

37 Joel Horlen, Chi/AL - May 11 to 29, 1968

37 Mike Torrez, Oak/AL - Aug. 29 to Sept. 15, 1976

Most strikeouts, game

21 Tom Cheney, Was/AL - Sept. 12, 1962 (16 innings)

20 ROGER CLEMENS, Bos/AL - April 29, 1986

19 Charlie Sweeney, Pro/NL - June 7, 1884

19 Hugh (One Arm) Daily, Chi/UA - July 7, 1884

19 Luis Tiant, Cle/AL - July 3, 1968 (10 innings)

19 Steve Carlton, StL/NL- Sept. 15, 1969

19 Tom Seaver, NY/NL - April 22, 1970

19 Nolan Ryan, Cal/AL - June 14, 1974 (12 innings)

19 Nolan Ryan, Cal/AL - Aug. 12, 1974

19 Nolan Ryan, Cal/AL - Aug. 20, 1974 (11 innings)

19 Nolan Ryan, Cal/AL - June 8, 1977 (10 innings)

19 DAVID CONE, NY/NL - Oct. 6, 1991

18 Jim Whitney, Bos/NL - June 14, 1884 (15 innings)

18 Dupee Shaw, Bos/UA - July 19, 1884

18 Henry Porter, Mil/UA - Oct. 3, 1884

18 Jack Coombs, Phi/AL - Sept. 1, 1906 (24 innings)

18 Bob Feller, Cle/AL - Oct. 2, 1938 (1st game)

18 Warren Spahn, Bos/NL - June 14, 1952 (15 innings)

18 Sandy Koufax, LA/NL - Aug. 31, 1959

18 Sandy Koufax, LA/NL - April 24, 1962

18 Jim Maloney, Cin/NL - June 14, 1965 (11 innings)

18 Chris Short, Phi/NL - Oct. 2, 1965 (15 innings in an 18-inning game)

18 Don Wilson, Hou/NL - July 14, 1968

18 Nolan Ryan, Cal/AL - Sept. 10, 1976

18 Ron Guidry, NY/AL - June 17, 1978

18 Bill Gullickson, Mon/NL - Sept. 10, 1980

18 RAMON MARTINEZ, LA/NL - June 4, 1990

18 RANDY JOHNSON, Sea/AL - Sept. 27, 1992

Most bases on balls, game

16 Bill George, NY/NL - May 30, 1887 (1st game)

16 George Van Haltren, Chi/NL - June 27, 1887

16 Henry Gruber, Cle/PL - April 19, 1890

16 Bruno Haas, Phi/AL - June 23, 1915

16 Tommy Byrne, NY/AL - Aug. 22, 1951 (13 innings)

15 Carroll Brown, Phi/AL - July 12, 1913

14 Ed Crane, Was/NL - Sept. 1, 1886

14 Charlie Hickman, Bos/NL - Aug. 16, 1899 (2nd game)

14 Henry Mathewson, NY/NL - Oct. 5, 1906

14 Skipper Friday, Was/AL - June 17, 1923

No-hit games, nine or more innings (number to left is career total if greater than 1)

Joe Borden, Phi vs Chi NA, 4-0; July 28, 1875.

George Bradley, StL vs Har NL, 2-0; July 15, 1876.Lee Richmond, Wor vs Cle NL, 1-0; June 12, 1880 (perfect game).

Monte Ward, Pro vs Buf NL, 5-0; June 17, 1880 (perfect game).

Larry Corcoran, Chi vs Bos NL, 6-0; Aug. 19, 1880.

Pud Galvin, Buf at Wor NL, 1-0; Aug. 20, 1880.

Tony Mullane, Lou at Cin AA, 2-0; Sept. 11, 1882.

Guy Hecker, Lou at Pit AA, 3-1; Sept. 19, 1882.

2 Larry Corcoran, Chi vs Wor NL, 5-0; Sept. 20, 1882.

Charley Radbourn, Pro at Cle NL, 8-0; July 25, 1883.

Hugh (One Arm) Daily, Cle at Phi NL; 1-0; Sept. 13, 1883.

Al Atkisson, Phi vs Pit AA, 10-1; May 24, 1884.

Ed Morris, Col at Pit AA, 5-0; May 29, 1884.

Frank Mountain, Col at Was AA, 12-0; June 5, 1884.

3 Larry Corcoran, Chi vs Pro NL, 6-0; June 27, 1884.

2 Pud Galvin, Buf at Det NL, 18-0; Aug. 4, 1884.

Dick Burns, Cin at KC UA, 3-1; Aug. 26, 1884.

Ed Cushman, Mil vs Was UA, 5-0; Sept. 28, 1884.

Sam Kimber, Bro vs Tol AA, 0-0; Oct. 4, 1884 (10 innings, called because of darkness).

John Clarkson, Chi at Pro NL, 4-0; July 27, 1885.

Charlie Ferguson, Phi vs Pro NL, 1-0; Aug. 29, 1885.

2 Al Atkisson, Phi vs NY AA, 3-2; May 1, 1886.

Adonis Terry, Bro vs StL AA, 1-0; July 24, 1886.

Matt Kilroy, Bal at Pit AA, 6-0; Oct. 6, 1886.

2 Adonis Terry, Bro vs Lou AA, 4-0; May 27, 1888.

Henry Porter, KC at Bal AA, 4-0; June 6, 1888.

Ed Seward, Phi vs Cin AA, 12-2; July 26, 1888.

Gus Weyhing, Phi vs KC AA, 4-0; July 31, 1888.

Silver King, Chi vs Bro PL, 0-1; June 21, 1890, (8 innings, lost the game; bottom of 9th not played).

Cannonball Titcomb, Roch vs Syr AA, 7-0; Sept. 15, 1890.

Tom Lovett, Bro vs NY NL, 4-0; June 22, 1891.

Amos Rusie, NY vs Bro NL, 6-0; July 31, 1891.

Ted Breitenstein, StL vs Lou AA, 8-0; Oct. 4, 1891 (1st game, first start in the major leagues).

Jack Stivetts, Bos vs Bro NL, 11-0; Aug. 6, 1892.

Ben Sanders, Lou vs Bal NL, 6-2; Aug. 22, 1892.

Bumpus Jones, Cin vs Pit NL, 7-1; Oct. 15, 1892 (first game in the major leagues).

Bill Hawke, Bal vs Was NL, 5-0; Aug. 16, 1893.

Cy Young, Cle vs Cin NL, 6-0;
 Sept. 18, 1897 (1st game).
2 Ted Breitenstein, Cin vs Pit NL,
 11-0; April 22, 1898.
Jim Hughes, Bal vs Bos NL, 8-0;
 April 22, 1898.
Red Donahue, Phi vs Bos NL, 5-0;
 July 8, 1898.
Walter Thornton, Chi vs Bro NL, 2-0;
 Aug. 21, 1898 (2nd game).
Deacon Phillippe, Lou vs NY NL, 7-0;
 May 25, 1899.
Noodles Hahn, Cin vs Phi NL, 4-0;
 July 12, 1900.
Earl Moore, Cle vs Chi AL, 2-4;
 May 9, 1901 (lost on two hits in
 the 10th).
Christy Mathewson, NY at StL NL,
 5-0; July 15, 1901.
Nixey Callahan, Chi vs Det AL, 3-0;
 Sept. 20, 1902 (1st game).
Chick Fraser, Phi at Chi NL; 10-0;
 Sept. 18, 1903 (2nd game).
2 Cy Young, Bos vs Phi AL, 3-0;
 May 5, 1904 (perfect game).
Bob Wicker, Chi at NY NL, 1-0;
 June 11, 1904 (won in 12 innings
 after allowing 1 hit in the 10th).
Jesse Tannehill, Bos at Chi AL, 6-0;
 Aug. 17, 1904.
2 Christy Mathewson, NY at Chi NL,
 1-0; June 13, 1905.
Weldon Henley, Phi at StL AL, 6-0;
 July 22, 1905 (1st game).
Frank Smith, Chi at Det AL, 15-0;
 Sept. 6, 1905 (2nd game).
Bill Dinneen, Bos vs Chi AL, 2-0;
 Sept. 27, 1905 (1st game).
Johnny Lush, Phi at Bro NL, 6-0;
 May 1, 1906.
Mal Eason, Bro at StL NL, 2-0;
 July 20, 1906.
Harry McIntyre, Bro vs Pit NL, 0-1;
 Aug. 1, 1906 (lost on 4 hits in 13
 innings after allowing the first hit
 in the 11th).
Frank (Jeff) Pfeffer, Bos vs Cin NL,
 6-0; May 8, 1907.
Nick Maddox, Pit vs Bro NL, 2-1;
 Sept. 20, 1907.
3 Cy Young, Bos at NY AL, 8-0;
 June 30, 1908.
Hooks Wiltse, NY vs Phi NL, 1-0;
 July 4, 1908 (1st game, 10 innings).
Nap Rucker, Bro vs Bos NL, 6-0;
 Sept. 5, 1908 (2nd game).
Dusty Rhoades, Cle vs Bos AL, 2-1;
 Sept. 18, 1908.
2 Frank Smith, Chi vs Phi AL, 1-0;
 Sept. 20, 1908.
Addie Joss, Cle vs Chi AL, 1-0;
 Oct. 2, 1908 (perfect game).
Red Ames, NY vs Bro NL. 0-3;
 April 15, 1909 (lost on 7 hits in 13
 innings after allowing the first hit
 in the 10th).

2 Addie Joss, Cle vs Chi AL, 1-0;
 April 20, 1910.
Chief Bender, Phi vs Cle AL, 4-0;
 May 12, 1910.
Tom L. Hughes, NY vs Cle AL, 0-5;
 Aug. 30, 1910 (2nd game) (lost on
 7 hits in 11 innings after allowing
 the first hit in the 10th).
Joe Wood, Bos vs StL AL, 5-0;
 July 29, 1911 (1st game).
Ed Walsh, Chi vs Bos AL, 5-0;
 Aug. 27, 1911.
George Mullin, Det vs StL AL, 7-0;
 July 4, 1912 (2nd game).
Earl Hamilton, StL at Det AL, 5-1;
 Aug. 30, 1912.
Jeff Tesreau, NY at Phi NL, 3-0; Sept. 6,
 1912 (1st game).
Jim Scott, Chi at Was AL, 0-1; May 14,
 1914 (lost on 2 hits in the 10th).
Joe Benz, Chi vs Cle AL, 6-1;
 May 31, 1914.
George Davis, Bos vs Phi NL, 7-0;
 Sept. 9, 1914 (2nd game).
Ed Lafitte, Bro vs KC FL, 6-2;
 Sept. 19, 1914.
Rube Marquard, NY vs Bro NL, 2-0;
 April 15, 1915.
Frank Allen, Pit vs StL FL, 2-0;
 April 24, 1915.
Claude Hendrix, Chi vs Pit FL, 10-0;
 May 15, 1915.
Alex Main, KC vs Buf FL, 5-0;
 Aug. 16, 1915.
Jimmy Lavender, Chi at NY NL, 2-0;
 Aug. 31, 1915 (1st game).
Dave Davenport, StL vs Chi FL, 3-0;
 Sept. 7, 1915.
2 Tom L. Hughes, Bos vs Pit NL, 2-0;
 June 16, 1916.
Rube Foster, Bos vs NY AL, 2-0; June
 21, 1916.
Joe Bush, Phi vs Cle AL, 5-0;
 Aug. 26, 1916.
Dutch Leonard, Bos vs StL AL, 4-0;
 Aug. 30, 1916.
Eddie Cicotte, Chi at StL AL, 11-0;
 April 14, 1917.
George Mogridge, NY at Bos AL, 2-1;
 April 24, 1917.
Fred Toney, Cin at Chi NL, 1-0;
 May 2, 1917 (10 innings).
Hippo Vaughn, Chi vs Cin NL, 0-1;
 May 2, 1917 (lost on 2 hits in the
 10t; Toney pitched a no-hitter in
 this game).
Ernie Koob, StL vs Chi AL, 1-0;
 May 5, 1917.
Bob Groom, StL vs Chi AL, 3-0;
 May 6, 1917 (2nd game).
Ernie Shore, Bos vs Was AL, 4-0; June
 23, 1917 (1st game, perfect game)
 (Shore relieved Babe Ruth in the
 first inning after Ruth had been
 thrown out of the game
 for protesting a walk to the first

batter. The runner was caught
 stealing, and Shore retired the
 remaining 26 batters in order).
2 Dutch Leonard, Bos at Det AL, 5-0;
 June 3, 1918.
Hod Eller, Cin vs StL NL, 6-0;
 May 11, 1919.
Ray Caldwell, Cle at NY AL, 3-0;
 Sept. 10, 1919 (1st game).
Walter Johnson, Was at Bos AL, 1-0;
 July 1, 1920.
Charlie Robertson, Chi at Det AL, 2-0;
 April 30, 1922 (perfect game).
Jesse Barnes, NY vs Phi NL, 6-0;
 May 7, 1922.
Sam Jones, NY at Phi AL, 2-0;
 Sept. 4, 1923.
Howard Ehmke, Bos at Phi AL, 4-0;
 Sept. 7, 1923.
Jesse Haines, StL vs Bos NL, 5-0;
 July 17, 1924.
Dazzy Vance, Bro vs Phi NL, 10-1;
 Sept. 13, 1925 (1st game).
Ted Lyons, Chi at Bos AL, 6-0;
 Aug. 21, 1926.
Carl Hubbell, NY vs Pit NL, 11-0;
 May 8, 1929.
Wes Ferrell, Cle vs StL AL, 9-0;
 April 29, 1931.
Bobby Burke, Was vs Bos AL, 5-0;
 Aug. 8, 1931.
Bobo Newsom, StL vs Bos AL, 1-2;
 Sept. 18, 1934 (lost on 1 hit in the
 10th).
Paul Dean, StL at Bro NL, 3-0;
 Sept. 21, 1934 (2nd game).
Vern Kennedy, Chi vs Cle AL, 5-0;
 Aug. 31, 1935.
Bill Dietrich, Chi vs StL AL, 8-0;
 June 1, 1937.
Johnny Vander Meer, Cin vs Bos NL,
 3-0; June 11, 1938.
2 Johnny Vander Meer, Cin at Bro
 NL, 6-0; June 15, 1938 (next start
 after June 11).
Monte Pearson, NY vs Cle AL, 13-0;
 Aug. 27, 1938 (2nd game).
Bob Feller, Cle at Chi AL, 1-0;
 April 16, 1940 (opening day).
Tex Carleton, Bro at Cin NL, 3-0;
 April 30, 1940.
Lon Warneke, StL at Cin NL, 2-0;
 Aug. 30, 1941.
Jim Tobin, Bos vs Bro NL, 2-0;
 April 27, 1944.
Clyde Shoun, Cin vs Bos NL, 1-0;
 May 15, 1944.
Dick Fowler, Phi vs StL AL, 1-0;
 Sept. 9, 1945 (2nd game).
Ed Head, Bro vs Bos NL, 5-0;
 April 23, 1946.
2 Bob Feller, Cle at NY AL, 1-0;
 April 30, 1946.
Ewell Blackwell, Cin vs Bos NL, 6-0;
 June 18, 1947.

Don Black, Cle vs Phi AL, 3-0;
July 10, 1947 (1st game).
Bill McCahan, Phi vs Was AL, 3-0;
Sept. 3, 1947.
Bob Lemon, Cle at Det AL, 2-0;
June 30, 1948.
Rex Barney, Bro at NY NL, 2-0;
Sept. 9, 1948.
Vern Bickford, Bos vs Bro NL, 7-0;
Aug. 11, 1950.
Cliff Chambers, Pit at Bos NL, 3-0;
May 6, 1951 (2nd game).
3 Bob Feller, Cle vs Det AL, 2-1;
July 1, 1951 (1st game).
Allie Reynolds, NY at Cle AL, 1-0;
July 12, 1951.
2 Allie Reynolds, NY vs Bos AL, 8-0;
Sept. 28, 1951 (1st game).
Virgil Trucks, Det vs Was AL, 1-0;
May 15, 1952.
Carl Erskine, Bro vs Chi NL, 5-0;
June 19, 1952.
2 Virgil Trucks, Det at NY AL, 1-0;
Aug. 25, 1952.
Bobo Holloman, StL vs Phi AL, 6-0;
May 6, 1953 (first start in the
major leagues).
Jim Wilson, Mil vs Phi NL, 2-0;
June 12, 1954.
Sam Jones, Chi vs Pit NL, 4-0;
May 12, 1955.
2 Carl Erskine, Bro vs NY NL, 3-0;
May 12, 1956.
Johnny Klippstein (7 innings),
Hershell Freeman (1 inning) and
Joe Black (3 innings), Cin at Mil
NL, 1-2; May 26, 1956 (lost on 3
hits in 11 innings after allowing
the first hit in the 10th).
Mel Parnell, Bos vs Chi AL, 4-0;
July 14, 1956.
Sal Maglie, Bro vs Phi NL, 5-0;
Sept. 25, 1956.
Don Larsen, NY AL vs Bro NL, 2-0;
Oct. 8, 1956 (World Series, per-
fect game).
Bob Keegan, Chi vs Was AL, 6-0;
Aug. 20, 1957 (2nd game).
Jim Bunning, Det at Bos AL, 3-0;
July 20, 1958 (1st game).
Hoyt Wilhelm, Bal vs NY AL, 1-0;
Sept. 20, 1958.
Harvey Haddix, Pit at Mil NL, 0-1;
May 26, 1959 (lost on 1 hit in 13
innings after pitching 12 perfect
innings).
Don Cardwell, Chi vs StL NL, 4-0;
May 15, 1960 (2nd game).
Lew Burdette, Mil vs Phi NL, 1-0;
Aug. 18, 1960.
Warren Spahn, Mil vs Phi NL, 4-0;
Sept. 16, 1960.
2 Warren Spahn, Mil vs SF NL, 1-0;
April 28, 1961.
Bo Belinsky, LA vs Bal AL, 2-0;
May 5, 1962.

Earl Wilson, Bos vs LA AL, 2-0;
June 26, 1962.
Sandy Koufax, LA vs NY NL, 5-0;
June 30, 1962.
Bill Monbouquette, Bos at Chi AL,
1-0; Aug. 1, 1962.
Jack Kralick, Min vs KC AL, 1-0
Aug. 26, 1962.
2 Sandy Koufax, LA vs SF NL, 8-0;
May 11, 1963.
Don Nottebart, Hou vs Phi NL, 4-1;
May 17, 1963.
Juan Marichal, SF vs Hou NL, 1-0;
June 15, 1963.
Ken T. Johnson, Hou vs Cin NL, 0-1;
April 23, 1964 (lost the game).
3 Sandy Koufax, LA at Phi NL, 3-0;
June 4, 1964.
2 Jim Bunning, Phi at NY NL, 6-0;
June 21, 1964 (1st game, perfect
game).
Jim Maloney, Cin vs NY NL, 0-1;
June 14, 1965 (lost on 2 hits in 11
innings after pitching 10 hitless
innings).
2 Jim Maloney, Cin at Chi NL, 1-0;
Aug. 19, 1965 (1st game, 10
innings).
4 Sandy Koufax, LA vs Chi NL, 1-0;
Sept. 9, 1965 (perfect game).
Dave Morehead, Bos vs Cle AL, 2-0;
Sept. 16, 1965.
Sonny Siebert, Cle vs Was AL, 2-0;
June 10, 1966.
Steve D. Barber (8⅔ innings) and Stu
Miller (⅓ inning) Bal vs Det AL,
1-2; April 30, 1967 (1st game, lost
the game).
Don Wilson, Hou vs Atl NL, 2-0;
June 18, 1967.
Dean Chance, Min at Cle AL, 2-1;
Aug. 25, 1967 (2nd game).
Joe Horlen, Chi vs Det AL, 6-0;
Sept. 10, 1967 (1st game).
Tom Phoebus, Bal vs Bos AL, 6-0;
April 27, 1968.
Catfish Hunter, Oak vs Min AL, 4-0;
May 8, 1968 (perfect game).
George Culver, Cin at Phi NL, 6-1;
July 29, 1968 (2nd game).
Gaylord Perry, SF vs StL NL, 1-0;
Sept. 17, 1968.
Ray Washburn, StL at SF NL, 2-0;
Sept. 18, 1968.
Bill Stoneman, Mon at Phi NL, 7-0;
April 17, 1969.
3 Jim Maloney, Cin vs Hou NL, 10-0;
April 30, 1969.
2 Don Wilson, Hou at Cin NL, 4-0;
May 1, 1969.
Jim Palmer, Bal vs Oak AL, 8-0;
Aug. 13, 1969.
Ken Holtzman, Chi vs Atl NL, 3-0;
Aug. 19, 1969.
Bob Moose, Pit at NY NL, 4-0;
Sept. 20, 1969.

Dock Ellis, Pit at SD NL, 2-0; June 12,
1970 (1st game).
Clyde Wright, Cal vs Oak AL, 4-0;
July 3, 1970.
Bill Singer, LA vs Phi NL, 5-0; July 20,
1970.
Vida Blue, Oak vs Min AL, 6-0;
Sept. 21, 1970.
2 Ken Holtzman, Chi at Cin NL, 1-0;
June 3, 1971.
Rick Wise, Phi at Cin NL, 4-0;
June 23, 1971.
Bob Gibson, StL at Pit NL, 11-0;
Aug. 14, 1971.
Burt Hooton, Chi vs Phi NL, 4-0;
April 16, 1972.
Milt Pappas, Chi vs SD NL, 8-0;
Sept. 2, 1972.
2 Bill Stoneman, Mon vs NY NL, 7-0;
Oct. 2, 1972 (1st game).
Steve Busby, KC at Det AL, 3-0;
April 16, 1973.
Nolan Ryan, Cal at KC AL, 3-0;
May 15, 1973.
2 Nolan Ryan, Cal at Det AL, 6-0;
July 15, 1973.
Jim Bibby, Tex at Oak AL, 6-0;
July 20, 1973.
Phil Niekro, Atl vs SD NL, 9-0;
Aug. 5, 1973.
2 Steve Busby, KC at Mil AL, 2-0;
June 19, 1974.
Dick Bosman, Cle vs Oak AL, 4-0;
July 19, 1974.
3 Nolan Ryan, Cal vs Min AL, 4-0;
Sept. 28, 1974.
4 Nolan Ryan, Cal vs Bal AL, 1-0;
June 1, 1975.
Ed Halicki, SF vs NY NL, 6-0;
Aug. 24, 1975 (2nd game).
Vida Blue (5 innings), Glenn Abbott
(1 inning), Paul Lindblad
(1 inning) and Rollie Fingers
(2 innings), Oak vs Cal AL,
5-0; Sept. 28, 1975.
Larry Dierker, Hou vs Mon NL, 6-0;
July 9, 1976.
Blue Moon Odom (5 innings) and
Francisco Barrios (4 innings), Chi
at Oak AL, 2-1; July 28, 1976.
John Candelaria, Pit vs LA NL,
2-0; Aug. 9, 1976.
John Montefusco, SF at Atl NL, 9-0;
Sept. 29, 1976.
Jim Colborn, KC vs Tex AL, 6-0;
May 14, 1977.
DENNIS ECKERSLEY, Cle vs Cal AL,
1-0; May 30, 1977.
Bert Blyleven, Tex at Cal AL, 6-0;
Sept. 22, 1977.
Bob Forsch, StL vs Phi NL, 5-0;
April 16, 1978.
Tom Seaver, Cin vs StL NL, 4-0;
June 16, 1978.
Ken Forsch, Hou vs Atl NL, 6-0;
April 7, 1979.

Jerry Reuss, LA at SF NL, 8-0; June 27, 1980.

Charlie Lea, Mon vs SF NL, 4-0; May 10, 1981 (2nd game).

Len Barker, Cle vs Tor AL, 3-0; May 15, 1981 (perfect game).

5 Nolan Ryan, Hou vs LA NL, 5-0; Sept. 26, 1981.

DAVE RIGHETTI, NY vs Bos AL, 4-0; July 4, 1983.

2 Bob Forsch, StL vs Mon NL, 3-0; Sept. 26, 1983.

Mike Warren, Oak vs Chi AL, 3-0; Sept. 29, 1983.

Jack Morris, Det at Chi AL, 4-0; April 7, 1984.

Mike Witt, Cal at Tex AL, 1-0; Sept. 30, 1984 (perfect game).

Joe Cowley, Chi at Cal AL, 7-1; Sept. 19, 1986.

Mike Scott, Hou vs SF NL, 2-0; Sept. 25, 1986.

Juan Nieves, Mil at Bal AL, 7-0; April 15, 1987.

TOM BROWNING, Cin vs LA NL, 1-0; Sept. 16, 1988 (perfect game).

MARK LANGSTON (7 innings) and Mike Witt (2 innings), Cal vs Sea AL, 1-0; April 11, 1990.

RANDY JOHNSON, Sea vs Det AL, 2-0; June 2, 1990.

6 Nolan Ryan, Tex at Oak AL, 5-0; June 11, 1990.

DAVE STEWART, Oak at Tor AL, 5-0; June 29, 1990.

FERNANDO VALENZUELA, LA vs StL NL, 6-0; June 29, 1990.

Andy Hawkins, NY at Chi AL, 0-4; July 1, 1990 (8 innings, lost the game; bottom of 9th not played).

TERRY MULHOLLAND, Phi vs SF NL, 6-0; Aug. 15, 1990.

Dave Stieb, Tor at Det AL, 3-0; Sept. 2, 1990.

7 Nolan Ryan, Tex vs Tor AL, 3-0; May 1, 1991.

TOMMY GREENE, Phi at Mon NL, 2-0; May 23, 1991.

Bob Milacki (6 innings), Mike Flanagan (1 inning), Mark Williamson, (1 inning) and GREGG OLSON (1 inning), Bal at Oak AL, 2-0; July 13, 1991.

MARK GARDNER, Mon at LA NL, 0-1; July 26, 1991 (9 innings, lost on 2 hits in 10th, relieved by JEFF FASSERO, who allowed 1 more hit).

DENNIS MARTINEZ, Mon at LA NL, 2-0; July 28, 1991 (perfect game).

WILSON ALVAREZ, Chi at Bal AL, 7-0; Aug. 11, 1991.

BRET SABERHAGEN, KC vs Chi AL, 7-0; Aug. 26, 1991.

KENT MERCKER (6 innings), MARK WOHLERS (2 innings) and

ALEJANDRO PENA (1 inning), Atl at SD NL, 1-0; Sept. 11, 1991.

Matt Young, Bos at Cle AL, 1-2; April 12, 1992 (1st game) (8 innings, lost the game, bottom of 9th not played).

KEVIN GROSS, LA vs SF NL, 2-0; Aug. 17, 1992.

CHRIS BOSIO, Sea vs Bos AL, 7-0; April 22, 1993.

JIM ABBOTT, NY vs Cle AL, 4-0; Sept. 4, 1993.

DARRYL KILE, Hou vs NY NL, 7-1; Sept. 8, 1993.

KENT MERCKER, Atl at LA NL, 6-0; April 8, 1994.

SCOTT ERICKSON, Min vs. Mil AL, 6-0; April 27, 1994.

KENNY ROGERS, Tex vs Cal AL, 4-0; July 28, 1994 (perfect game).

RAMON MARTINEZ, LA vs Fla NL, 7-0; July 14, 1995.

No-hit games, less than 9 innings

Larry McKeon, 6 innings, rain, Ind at Cin AA, 0-0; May 6, 1884.

Charlie Gagus, 8 innings, darkness, Was vs Wil UA, 12-1; Aug. 21, 1884.

Charlie Getzien, 6 innings, rain, Det vs Phi NL, 1-0; Oct. 1, 1884.

Charlie Sweeney (2 innings) and Henry Boyle (3 innings), 5 innings, rain, StL vs StP UA, 0-1; Oct. 5,1884.

Dupee Shaw, 5 innings, agreement, Pro at Buf NL, 4-0; Oct. 7, 1885 (1st game).

George Van Haltren, 6 innings, rain, Chi vs Pit NL, 1-0, June 21,1888.

Ed Crane, 7 innings, darkness, NY vs Was NL, 3-0; Sept. 27, 1888.

Matt Kilroy, 7 innings, darkness, Bal vs StL AA, 0-0; July 29, 1889 (2nd game).

George Nicol, 7 innings, darkness, StL vs Phi AA, 21-2; Sept. 23, 1890.

Hank Gastright, 8 innings, darkness, Col vs Tol AA, 6-0; Oct. 12, 1890.

Jack Stivetts, 5 innings, called so Boston could catch train to Cleveland for Temple Cub playoffs, Bos at Was NL, 6-0; Oct. 15, 1892 (2nd game).

Elton Chamberlain, 7 innings, darkness, Cin vs Bos NL, 6-0; Sept. 23, 1893 (2nd game).

Ed Stein, 6 innings, rain, Bro vs Chi NL, 6-0; June 2, 1894.

Red Ames, 5 innings, darkness, NY at StL NL, 5-0; Sept. 14, 1903 (2nd game, his first game in the major leagues).

Rube Waddell, 5 innings, rain, Phi vs StL AL, 2-0; Aug. 15, 1905.

Jake Weimer, 7 innings,

agreement, Cin vs Bro NL, 1-0; Aug. 24, 1906 (2nd game).

Jimmy Dygert (3 innings) and Rube Waddell (2 innings), 5 innings, rain, Phi vs Chi AL, 4-3; Aug. 29, 1906. (Waddell allowed 1 hit and 2 runs in 6th, but rain caused game to revert to 5 innings).

Stoney McGlynn, 7 innings, agreement, StL at Bro NL, 1-1; Sept. 24, 1906 (2nd game).

Lefty Leifield, 6 innings, darkness, Pit at Phi NL, 8-0; Sept. 26, 1906 (2nd game).

Ed Walsh, 5 innings, rain, Chi vs NY AL, 8-1; May 26, 1907.

Ed Karger, 7 perfect innings, agreement, StL vs Bos NL, 4-0; Aug. 11, 1907 (2nd game).

Howie Camnitz, 5 innings, agreement, Pit at NY NL, 1-0; Aug. 23, 1907 (2nd game).

Rube Vickers, 5 perfect innings, darkness, Phi at Was AL, 4-0; Oct. 5, 1907 (2nd game).

Johnny Lush, 6 innings, rain, StL at Bro NL, 2-0; Aug. 6, 1908.

King Cole, 7 innings, called so Chicago could catch train, Chi at StL NL, 4-0; July 31, 1910 (2nd game).

Jay Cashion, 6 innings, called so Cleveland could catch train, Was vs Cle AL, 2-0; Aug. 20, 1912 (2nd game).

Walter Johnson, 7 innings, rain, Was vs StL AL, 2-0; Aug. 25, 1924.

Fred Frankhouse, 7⅔ innings, rain, Bro vs Cin NL, 5-0; Aug. 27, 1937.

John Whitehead, 6 innings, rain, StL vs Det AL, 4-0; Aug. 5, 1940 (2nd game).

Jim Tobin, 5 innings, darkness, Bos vs Phi NL, 7-0; June 22, 1944 (2nd game).

Mike McCormick, 5 innings, rain, SF at Phi NL, 3-0; June 12, 1959. (allowed hit in 6th, but rain caused game to revert to 5 innings).

Sam Jones, 7 innings, rain, SF at StL NL, 4-0; Sept. 26, 1959.

Dean Chance, 5 perfect innings, rain, Min vs Bos AL, 2-0; Aug. 6, 1967.

David Palmer, 5 perfect innings, rain, Mon at StL NL, 4-0; April 21, 1984 (2nd game).

Pascual Perez, 5 innings, rain, Mon at Phi NL, 1-0; Sept. 24, 1988

MELIDO PEREZ, 6 innings, rain, Chi at NY AL, 8-0; July 12, 1990.

Lee Richmond, Wor vs Cle NL, 1-0; June 12, 1880

CLEVELAND	ab	r	h	po	a	e
Dunlap, 2b	3	0	0	4	2	2
Hankinson, 3b	3	0	0	0	0	0
Kennedy, c	3	0	0	9	1	0
Phillips, 1b	3	0	0	7	0	0
Shaffer, rf	3	0	0	2	0	0
McCormick, p	3	0	0	0	10	0
Gilligan, cf	3	0	0	1	0	0
Glasscock, ss	3	0	0	0	2	0
Hanlon, lf	3	0	0	1	0	0
Team	27	0	0	24	15	2

WORCESTER	ab	r	h	po	a	e
Wood, lf	4	0	0	0	0	0
Richmond, p	3	0	1	0	6	0
Knight, rf	3	0	0	1	1	0
Irwin, ss	3	0	2	2	3	0
Bennett, c	2	0	0	8	0	0
Whitney, 3b	3	0	0	1	2	0
Sullivan, 1b	3	0	0	14	0	0
Corey, cf	3	0	0	1	0	0
Creamer, 2b	3	0	0	0	4	0
Team	27	1	3	27	16	0

Cleveland   000 000 000–0
Worcester   000 010 00x–1

Runs batted in - none
Double play - Glasscock, Dunlap and Phillips

	ip	h	r	er	bb	so
McCormick (L)	8	3	1	0	1	7
Richmond (W)	9	0	0	0	0	5

Time - 1:27
Umpire - Bradley
Attendance - 700

John Montgomery Ward, Pro vs Buf NL, 5-0; June 17, 1880 (A.M.)

PROVIDENCE	ab	r	h	po	a	e
Hines, cf	5	0	2	2	0	0
Start, 1b	5	1	1	14	0	0
Dorgan, rf	5	0	2	0	0	0
Gross, c	5	0	0	5	1	0
Farrell, 2b	4	3	3	0	2	0
Ward, p	4	0	1	2	6	0
Peters, ss	4	0	1	0	6	0
York, lf	4	0	2	3	0	0
Bradley, 3b	4	1	1	1	4	0
Team	40	5	13	27	19	0

BUFFALO	ab	r	h	po	a	e
Crowley, rf-c	3	0	0	4	0	2
Richardson, 3b	3	0	0	0	1	0
Rowe, c-rf	3	0	0	3	1	0
Walker, lf	3	0	0	3	0	1
Hornung, 2b	3	0	0	2	3	0
Mack, ss	3	0	0	3	3	1
Esterbrook, 1b	3	0	0	10	0	0
Poorman, cf	3	0	0	2	0	1
Galvin, p	3	0	0	0	5	0
Team	27	0	0	27	13	5

Providence   010 100 111–5
Buffalo   000 000 000–0

Double - Farrell
Triples - Start, York, Bradley

Runs batted in - Ward, Hines, Dorgan
Passed ball - Crowley

	ip	h	r	er	bb	so
Ward (W)	9	0	0	0	0	6
Galvin (L)	9	13	5	3	0	2

Wild pitches - Galvin 2
Time - 1:40
Umpire - Daniels
Attendance - 2,000

Cy Young, Bos vs Phi AL, 3-0; May 5, 1904

PHILADELPHIA	ab	r	h	po	a	e
Hartsel, lf	1	0	0	0	0	0
Hoffman, lf	2	0	0	2	1	0
Pickering, cf	3	0	0	1	0	0
Davis, 1b	3	0	0	5	0	1
L. Cross, 3b	3	0	0	4	1	0
Seybold, rf	3	0	0	2	0	0
Murphy, 2b	3	0	0	1	2	0
M. Cross, ss	3	0	0	2	3	0
Schreck, c	3	0	0	7	0	0
Waddell, p	3	0	0	0	1	0
Team	27	0	0	24	8	1

BOSTON	ab	r	h	po	a	e
Dougherty, lf	4	0	1	1	0	0
Collins, 3b	4	0	2	2	0	0
Stahl, cf	4	1	1	3	0	0
Freeman, rf	4	0	1	2	0	0
Parent, ss	4	0	2	1	4	0
LaChance, 1b	3	0	1	9	0	0
Ferris, 2b	3	1	1	0	3	0
Criger, c	3	1	1	9	0	0
Young, p	3	0	0	0	2	0
Team	32	3	10	27	9	0

Philadelphia   000 000 000–0
Boston   000 001 20x–3

Doubles - Collins, Criger
Triples - Stahl, Freeman, Ferris
Runs batted in - Freeman, Criger
Sacrifice - LaChance
Double plays - Hoffman and Schreck; L.Cross and Davis

	ip	h	r	er	bb	so
Waddell (L)	8	10	3	2	0	6
Young (W)	9	0	0	0	0	8

Time - 1:30
Umpire - Dwyer
Attendance - 10,267

Addie Joss, Cle vs Chi AL, 1-0; October 2, 1908

CHICAGO	ab	r	h	po	a	e
Hahn, rf	3	0	0	1	0	0
Jones, cf	3	0	0	0	0	0
Isbell, 1b	3	0	0	6	1	1
Dougherty, lf	3	0	0	0	0	0
Davis, 2b	3	0	0	1	0	0
Parent, ss	3	0	0	0	3	0
Schreck, c	2	0	0	13	1	0
Shaw, c	0	0	0	2	0	0
White, ph	1	0	0	0	0	0
Tannehill, 3b	2	0	0	0	0	0
Donohue, ph	1	0	0	0	0	0
Walsh, p	2	0	0	1	3	0
Anderson, ph	1	0	0	0	0	0
Team	27	0	0	24	8	1

CLEVELAND

CLEVELAND	ab	r	h	po	a	e
Good, rf	4	0	0	1	0	0
Bradley, 3b	4	0	0	0	1	0
Hinchman, lf	3	0	0	3	0	0
Lajoie, 2b	3	0	1	2	8	0
Stovall, 1b	3	0	0	16	0	0
Clarke, c	3	0	0	4	1	0
Birmingham, cf	4	1	2	0	0	0
Perring, ss	2	0	1	1	1	0
Joss, p	3	0	0	0	5	0
Team	29	1	4	27	16	0

Chicago   000 000 000–0
Cleveland   001 000 00x–1
Runs batted in - none
Stolen bases - Birmingham 2

	ip	h	r	er	bb	so
Walsh (L)	8	4	1	0	1	15
Joss (W)	9	0	0	0	0	3

Wild pitch - Walsh
Time - 1:40
Umpires - Connolly and O'Loughlin
Attendance - 10,598

Ernie Shore, Bos vs Was AL, 4-0; June 23, 1917 (1st game)

WASHINGTON	ab	r	h	po	a	e
Morgan, 2b	2	0	0	4	2	0
Foster, 3b	3	0	0	1	3	2
Leonard, 3b	0	0	0	0	1	0
Milan, cf	3	0	0	1	0	0
Rice, r	3	0	0	3	0	1
Gharrity, 1b	0	0	0	0	0	0
Judge, 1b	3	0	0	11	1	0
Jamieson, lf	3	0	0	0	0	0
Shanks, ss	3	0	0	1	2	0
Henry, c	3	0	0	1	0	0
Ayers, p	2	0	0	2	8	0
Menosky, ph	1	0	0	0	0	0
Team	26	0	0	24	17	3

BOSTON	ab	r	h	po	a	e
Hooper, rf	4	0	1	0	0	0
Barry, 2b	4	0	0	2	1	0
Hoblitzel, 1b	4	0	0	12	2	0
Gardner, 3b	4	1	1	2	1	0
Lewis, lf	4	0	3	2	0	0
Walker, cf	3	1	1	4	0	0
Scott, ss	3	0	0	1	5	0
Thomas, c	0	0	0	0	0	0
Agnew, c	3	1	3	2	1	0
Ruth, p	0	0	0	0	0	0
Shore, p	2	1	0	2	6	0
Team	31	4	9	27	16	0

Washington   000 000 000–0
Boston   010 000 30x–4
Doubles - Walker, Agnew
Runs batted in - Agnew 2, Hooper 2
Sacrifices - Walker, Shore, Scott
Caught stealing - Morgan
Double plays - Ayers, Foster and Judge; Ayers and Judge

	ip	h	r	er	bb	so
Ayers (L)	8	9	4	2	0	0
#Ruth	0	0	0	0	1	0
Shore (W)	9	0	0	0	0	2

- Ruth faced one batter in 1st inning
Time - 1:40
Umpires - Owens, McCormick and Dinneen
Attendance - 16,158

Charlie Robertson, Chi at Det AL, 2-0; April 30, 1922

CHICAGO	ab	r	h	po	a	e
Mulligan, ss	4	0	1	0	0	0
McClellan, 3b	3	0	1	1	3	0
Collins, 2b	3	0	1	4	3	0
Hooper, rf	3	1	0	3	0	0
Mostil, lf	4	1	1	3	0	0
Strunk, cf	3	0	0	0	0	0
Sheely, 1b	4	0	2	9	0	0
Schalk, c	4	0	1	7	1	0
Robertson, p	4	0	0	0	1	0
Team	32	2	7	27	8	0

DETROIT	ab	r	h	po	a	e
Blue, 1b	3	0	0	11	3	1
Cutshaw, 2b	3	0	0	2	3	0
Cobb, cf	3	0	0	1	0	0
Veach, lf	3	0	0	2	0	0
Heilmann, rf	3	0	0	1	0	0
Jones, 3b	3	0	0	1	5	0
Rigney, ss	2	0	0	2	1	0
Clark, ph	1	0	0	0	0	0
Manion, c	3	0	0	7	1	0
Pillette, p	2	0	0	0	3	0
Bassler, ph	1	0	0	0	0	0
Team	27	0	0	27	16	1

Chicago   020 000 000–2
Detroit   000 000 000–0
Doubles - Mulligan, Sheely
Runs batted in - Sheely 2
Sacrifices - McClellan, Collins, Strunk

	ip	h	r	er	bb	so
Robertson (W)	9	0	0	0	0	6
Pillette (L)	9	7	2	2	2	5

Time - 1:55
Umpires - Nallin and Evans
Attendance - 25,000

Don Larsen, NY AL vs Bro NL, 2-0; October 8, 1956 (World Series)

BROOKLYN	ab	r	h	po	a	e
Gilliam, 2b	3	0	0	2	0	0
Reese, ss	3	0	0	4	2	0
Snider, cf	3	0	0	1	0	0
Robinson, 2b	3	0	0	2	4	0
Hodges, 1b	3	0	0	5	1	0
Amoros, lf	3	0	0	3	0	0
Furillo, rf	3	0	0	0	0	0
Campanella, c	3	0	0	7	2	0
Maglie, p	2	0	0	0	1	0
Mitchell, ph	1	0	0	0	0	0
Team	27	0	0	24	10	0

NEW YORK	ab	r	h	po	a	e
Bauer, rf	4	0	1	4	0	0
Collins, 1b	4	0	1	7	0	0
Mantle, cf	3	1	1	4	0	0
Berra, c	3	0	0	7	0	0
Slaughter, lf	2	0	0	1	0	0
Martin, 2b	3	0	1	3	4	0
McDougald, ss	2	0	0	0	2	0
Carey, 3b	3	1	1	1	1	0
Larsen, p	2	0	0	0	1	0
Team	26	2	5	27	8	0

Brooklyn   000 000 000–0
New York   000 101 00x–2
Home run - Mantle
Runs batted in - Mantle, Bauer

Sacrifice - Larsen
Double plays - Reese and Hodges; Hodges, Campanella, Robinson, Campanella and Robinson

	ip	h	r	er	bb	so
Maglie (L)	8	5	2	2	2	5
Larsen (W)	9	0	0	0	0	7

Time - 2:06
Umpires - Pinelli, Soar, Boggess, Napp, Gorman, Runge
Attendance - 64,519

Harvey Haddix, Pit at Mil NL, 0-1;
May 26, 1959 (12 perfect innings, lost on one hit in the 13th inning)

PITTSBURGH	ab	r	h	po	a	e
Schofield, ss	6	0	3	2	4	0
Virdon, cf	6	0	1	8	0	0
Burgess, c	5	0	0	8	0	0
Nelson, lb	5	0	2	14	0	0
Skinner, lf	5	0	1	4	0	0
Mazeroski, 2b	5	0	1	1	1	0
Hoak, 3b	5	0	2	0	6	1
Mejias, rf	3	0	1	1	0	0
Stuart, ph	1	0	0	0	0	0
Christopher, rf	1	0	0	0	0	0
Haddix, p	5	0	1	0	2	0
Team	47	0	12	38	13	1

MILWAUKEE	ab	r	h	po	a	e
O'Brien, 2b	3	0	0	2	5	0
Rice, ph	1	0	0	0	0	0
Mantilla, 2b	1	1	0	1	2	0
Mathews, 3b	4	0	0	2	3	0
Aaron, rf	4	0	0	1	0	0
Adcock, lb	5	0	1	17	3	0
Covington, lf	4	0	0	4	0	0
Crandall, c	4	0	0	3	5	0
Pafko, cf	4	0	0	6	0	0
Logan, ss	4	0	0	3	5	0
Burdette, p	4	0	0	1	3	0
Team	38	1	1	39	22	0

Pittsburgh   000 000 000 000 0–0
Milwaukee   000 000 000 000 1–1
Double - Adcock
Run batted in - Adcock
Sacrifice - Mathews
Double plays - Adcock, Logan and Adcock; Mathews, O'Brien and Adcock; Adcock and Logan

	ip	h	r	er	bb	so
Haddix (L)	12⅔	1	1	0	1	8
Burdette (W)	13	12	0	0	0	2

Time - 2:54
Umpires - Smith, Dascoli, Secory and Dixon
Attendance - 19,194

Jim Bunning, Phi at NY NL, 6-0;
June 21, 1964

PHILADELPHIA	ab	r	h	po	a	e
Briggs, cf	4	1	0	2	0	0
Herrnstein, lb	4	0	0	7	0	0
Callison, rf	4	1	2	1	0	0
Allen, 3b	3	0	1	0	2	0
Covington, lf	2	0	0	1	0	0
Wine, pr-ss	1	1	0	2	1	0
T. Taylor, 2b	3	2	1	0	3	0
Rojas, ss-lf	3	0	1	3	0	0
Triandos, c	4	1	2	11	1	0
Bunning, p	4	0	1	0	0	0
Team	32	6	8	27	7	0

NEW YORK	ab	r	h	po	a	e
Hickman, cf	3	0	0	2	0	0
Hunt, 2b	3	0	0	3	2	0
Kranepool, lb	3	0	0	8	1	0
Christopher, rf	3	0	0	4	0	0
Gonder, c	3	0	0	6	2	0
R. Taylor, lf	3	0	0	1	0	0
C. Smith, ss	3	0	0	2	1	0
Samuel, 3b	2	0	0	0	1	0
Altman, ph	1	0	0	0	0	0
Stallard, p	1	0	0	0	2	0
Wakefield, p	0	0	0	0	0	0
Kanehl, ph	1	0	0	0	0	0
Sturdivant, p	0	0	0	1	0	0
Stephenson, ph	1	0	0	0	0	0
Team	27	0	0	27	9	0

Philadelphia   110 004 000–6
New York   000 000 000–0
Doubles - Triandos, Bunning
Home run - Callison
Runs batted in - Callison, Allen, Triandos 2, Bunning 2
Sacrifices - Hernstein, Rojas

	ip	h	r	er	bb	so
Bunning (W)	9	0	0	0	0	10
Stallard (L)	5⅔	7	6	6	4	3
Wakefield	⅓	0	0	0	0	0
Sturdivant	3	1	0	0	0	3

Wild pitch - Stallard
Time - 2:19
Umpires - Sudol, Pryor, Secory and Burkhart
Attendance - 32,026

Sandy Koufax, LA vs Chi NL, 1-0;
September 9, 1965

CHICAGO	ab	r	h	po	a	e
Young, cf	3	0	0	5	0	0
Beckert, 2b	3	0	0	1	1	0
Williams, rf	3	0	0	0	0	0
Santo, 3b	3	0	0	1	2	0
Banks, lb	3	0	0	13	0	0
Browne, lf	3	0	0	1	0	0
Krug, c	3	0	0	3	0	1
Kessinger, ss	2	0	0	0	2	0
Amalfitano, ph	1	0	0	0	0	0
Hendley, p	2	0	0	0	5	0
Kuenn, ph	1	0	0	0	0	0
Team	27	0	0	24	10	1

LOS ANGELES	ab	r	h	po	a	e
Wills, ss	3	0	0	0	2	0
Gilliam, 3b	3	0	0	0	1	0
W. Davis, cf	3	0	0	2	0	0
Johnson, lf	2	1	1	2	0	0
Fairly, rf	2	0	0	3	0	0
Lefebvre, 2b	3	0	0	1	0	0
Tracewski, 2b	0	0	0	0	0	0
Parker, lb	3	0	0	4	0	0
Torborg, c	3	0	0	15	0	0
Koufax, p	2	0	0	0	0	0
Team	24	1	1	27	3	0

Chicago   000 000 000–0
Los Angeles   000 010 00x–1
Double - Johnson
Runs batted in - none
Sacrifice - Fairly
Stolen base - Johnson

	ip	h	r	er	bb	so
Hendley (L)	8	1	1	0	1	3
Koufax (W)	9	0	0	0	0	14

Time - 1:43

Umpires - Vargo, Pelekoudas, Jackowski and Pryor

Attendance - 29,139

Jim "Catfish" Hunter, Oak vs Min AL, 4-0; May 8, 1968

MINNESOTA	ab	r	h	po	a	e
Tovar, 3b	3	0	0	1	2	0
Carew, 2b	3	0	0	4	1	0
Killebrew, 1b	3	0	0	5	0	0
Oliva, rf	3	0	0	3	0	0
Uhlaender, cf	3	0	0	2	0	0
Allison, lf	3	0	0	0	0	0
Hernandez, ss	2	0	0	2	4	0
Roseboro, ph	1	0	0	0	0	0
Look, c	3	0	0	7	2	0
Boswell, p	2	0	0	0	1	1
Perranoski, p	0	0	0	0	0	0
Reese, ph	1	0	0	0	0	0
Team	27	0	0	24	10	1

OAKLAND	ab	r	h	po	a	e
Campaneris, ss	4	0	2	1	3	0
Jackson, rf	4	0	0	3	0	0
Bando, 3b	3	0	1	0	2	0
Webster, 1b	4	1	2	7	0	0
Donaldson, 2b	3	0	0	1	2	0
Pagliaroni, c	3	1	0	11	0	0
Monday, cf	3	2	2	2	0	0
Rudi, lf	3	0	0	2	0	0
Robinson, ph	0	0	0	0	0	0
Cater, ph	0	0	0	0	0	0
Hershberger, lf	0	0	0	0	0	0
Hunter, p	4	0	3	0	0	0
Team	31	4	10	27	7	0

Minnesota   000 000 000–0
Oakland   000 000 13x–4

Doubles - Hunter, Monday

Runs batted in - Hunter 3, Cater

Stolen base - Campaneris

Double plays - Boswell, Hernandez and Killebrew; Hernandez, Carew and Killebrew

	ip	h	r	er	bb	so
Boswell (L)	7⅔	9	4	4	4	6
Perranoski	⅓	1	0	0	1	0
Hunter (W)	9	0	0	0	0	11

Hit by pitch - by Boswell (Donaldson)

Wild pitches - Boswell 2

Time - 2:28

Umpires - Napp, Salerno, Haller and Neudecker

Attendance - 6,298

Len Barker, Cle vs Tor AL, 3-0; May 15, 1981

TORONTO	ab	r	h	po	a	e
Griffin, ss	3	0	0	1	1	1
Moseby, rf	3	0	0	4	0	0
Bell, lf	3	0	0	2	0	0
Mayberry, 1b	3	0	0	4	1	1
Upshaw, dh	3	0	0	0	0	0
Garcia, 2b	3	0	0	3	2	1
Bosetti, cf	3	0	0	3	0	0
Ainge, 3b	2	0	0	1	0	0
Woods, ph	1	0	0	0	0	0
B. Martinez, c	2	0	0	5	1	0
Whitt, ph	1	0	0	0	0	0

	ab	r	h	po	a	e
Leal, p	0	0	0	1	1	0
Team	27	0	0	24	6	3

CLEVELAND	ab	r	h	po	a	e
Manning, cf	4	1	1	4	0	0
Orta, rf	4	1	3	0	0	0
Hargrove, 1b	4	1	1	9	0	0
Thornton, dh	3	0	0	0	0	0
Hassey, c	4	0	1	11	0	0
Harrah, 3b	4	0	1	2	0	0
Charbonneau, lf	3	0	0	1	0	0
Kuiper, 2b	3	0	0	0	4	0
Veryzer, ss	3	0	0	0	3	0
Barker, p	0	0	0	0	0	0
Team	32	3	7	27	7	0

Toronto   000 000 000–0
Cleveland   200 000 01x–3

Home run - Orta

Runs batted in - Thornton, Hassey, Orta

Sacrifice - Thornton

	ip	h	r	er	bb	so
Leal (L)	8	7	3	1	0	5
Barker (W)	9	0	0	0	0	11

Time - 2:09

Umpires - Garcia, Kosc, Denkinger and McKean

Attendance - 7,290

Mike Witt, Cal at Tex AL, 1-0; September 30, 1984

(last game of the season)

CALIFORNIA	ab	r	h	po	a	e
Wilfong, 2b	4	0	0	0	8	0
Sconiers, 1b	3	0	0	10	1	0
Grich, 1b	0	0	0	2	0	0
Lynn, cf-rf	4	0	2	1	0	0
DeCinces, 3b	4	1	2	0	1	0
Downing, lf	4	0	0	1	0	0
Thomas, lf	0	0	0	0	0	0
Re. Jackson, dh	4	0	0	0	0	0
M. Brown, rf	3	0	3	2	0	0
Pettis, cf	0	0	0	0	0	0
Boone, c	3	0	0	10	0	0
Schofield, ss	2	0	0	0	3	0
Witt, p	0	0	0	1	0	0
Team	31	1	7	27	13	0

TEXAS	ab	r	h	po	a	e
Rivers, dh	3	0	0	0	0	0
Tolleson, 2b	3	0	0	4	5	0
Ward, lf	3	0	0	0	0	0
Parrish, 3b	3	0	0	0	3	0
O'Brien, 1b	3	0	0	13	0	0
G. Wright, cf	3	0	0	3	0	0
Dunbar, rf	3	0	0	1	0	0
Scott, c	2	0	0	4	3	0
B. Jones, ph	1	0	0	0	0	0
Wilkerson, ss	2	0	0	2	4	0
Foley, ph	1	0	0	0	0	0
Hough, p	0	0	0	0	2	0
Team	27	0	0	27	17	0

California   000 000 100–1
Texas   000 000 000–0

Double - Brown

Triple - Brown

Run batted in - Jackson

Double plays - Parrish, Tolleson and O'Brien; Tolleson, Wilkerson and O'Brien

Passed ball - Scott

	ip	h	r	er	bb	so
Witt (W)	9	0	0	0	0	10
Hough (L)	9	7	1	0	3	3

Wild pitch - Hough
Time - 1:49
Umpires - Kosc, Hendry, Coble and Evans
Attendance - 8,375

Tom Browning, Cin vs LA NL, 1-0; September 16, 1988

LOS ANGELES	ab	r	h	po	a	e
Griffin, ss	3	0	0	0	4	0
Hatcher, 1b	3	0	0	10	0	0
Gibson, lf	3	0	0	1	0	0
Gonzalez, lf	0	0	0	0	0	0
Marshall, rf	3	0	0	2	0	0
Shelby, cf	3	0	0	2	0	0
Hamilton, 3b	3	0	0	0	1	1
Dempsey, c	3	0	0	7	0	0
Sax, 2b	3	0	0	2	2	0
Belcher, p	2	0	0	0	2	0
Woodson, ph	1	0	0	0	0	0
Team	27	0	0	24	9	0

CINCINNATI	ab	r	h	po	a	e
Larkin, ss	3	1	1	0	4	0
Sabo, 3b	3	0	1	0	3	0
Daniels, lf	3	0	0	3	0	0
Davis, cf	2	0	0	1	0	0
O'Neill, rf	3	0	0	4	0	0
Esasky, 1b	3	0	0	10	1	0
Reed, c	3	0	0	7	0	0
Oester, 2b	3	0	1	1	1	0
Browning, p	3	0	0	1	0	0
Team	26	1	3	27	9	0

Los Angeles   000 000 000–0
Cincinnati   000 001 00x–1
Double - Larkin
Run batted in - none

	ip	h	r	er	bb	so
Belcher (L)	8	3	1	0	1	7
Browning (W)	9	0	0	0	0	7

Time - 1:51
Umpires - Quick, Hirschbeck, Kibler and Gregg
Attendance - 16,591

Dennis Martinez, Mon at LA NL, 2-0; July 28, 1991

MONTREAL	ab	r	h	po	a	e
DeShields, 2b	3	0	1	0	9	0
Grissom, cf	4	0	0	2	0	0
Da. Martinez, rf	4	1	0	0	0	0
Calderon, lf	3	0	0	2	0	0
Wallach, 3b	4	0	0	1	1	0
Walker, 1b	4	1	1	17	0	0
Hassey, c	3	0	1	5	0	0
Owen, ss	3	0	0	0	2	0
De. Martinez, p	3	0	1	0	2	0
Team	31	2	4	27	14	0

LOS ANGELES	ab	r	h	po	a	e
Butler, cf	3	0	0	1	0	0
Samuel, 2b	3	0	0	1	3	0
Murray, 1b	3	0	0	8	2	0
Strawberry, rf	3	0	0	4	0	0
Daniels, lf	3	0	0	3	0	0
Harris, 3b	3	0	0	0	0	0
Scioscia, c	3	0	0	5	1	0
Griffin, ss	2	0	0	4	4	2
Javier, ph	1	0	0	0	0	0

Morgan, p	2	0	0	1	2	0
Gwynn, ph	1	0	0	0	0	0
Team	27	0	0	26	12	2

Montreal   000 000 200–2
Los Angeles   000 000 000–0
Triple - Walker
Run batted in - Walker
Caught stealing - Hassey

	ip	h	r	er	bb	so
De. Martinez (W)	9	0	0	0	0	5
Morgan (L)	9	4	2	0	1	5

Wild pitch - Morgan
Time - 2:14
Umpires - Poncino, Froemming, DeMuth and Bonin
Attendance - 45,560

Kenny Rogers, Tex vs Cal AL, 4-0; July 28, 1994

CALIFORNIA	ab	r	h	po	a	e
Curtis, cf	3	0	0	3	0	0
Owen, 3b	3	0	0	0	4	0
Edmonds, lf	3	0	0	2	0	0
Davis, dh	3	0	0	0	0	0
Jackson, rf	3	0	0	2	0	0
Snow, 1b	3	0	0	8	1	0
Hudler, 2b	3	0	0	3	0	0
Turner, c	3	0	0	4	1	0
DiSarcina, ss	3	0	0	1	2	0
Lorraine, p	0	0	0	1	0	0
Springer, p	0	0	0	0	0	0
Team	27	0	0	24	8	0

TEXAS	ab	r	h	po	a	e
Davis, rf	4	0	0	0	0	0
Rodriguez, c	3	1	1	8	0	0
Canseco, dh	4	2	2	0	0	0
Clark, 1b	3	1	0	8	0	0
Gonzalez, lf	4	0	2	4	0	0
Palmer, 3b	4	0	1	1	3	0
Greer, cf	3	0	0	5	0	0
Lee, 2b	3	0	0	0	1	0
Beltre, ss	2	0	0	1	2	0
Rogers, p	0	0	0	0	1	0
Team	30	4	6	27	7	0

California   000 000 000–0
Texas   202 000 00x–4
Home runs - Canseco 2, Rodriguez
Runs batted in - Canseco 2, Rodriguez, Palmer

	ip	h	r	er	bb	so
Lorraine (L)	6⅔	4	4	4	2	4
Springer	1⅓	0	0	0	1	1
Rogers (W)	9	0	0	0	0	8

Wild pitch - Springer
Time - 2:08
Umpires - Bean, Denkinger, Shulock, and Tschida
Attendance - 46,581

*M*ajor

league

report

Boston Red Sox

By Neil Seiler, USA TODAY

Knuckleballer Tim Wakefield's comeback (16-8, 2.95 ERA) helped the Red Sox win the AL East.

1995 Red Sox: No one thought they'd win

Manager Kevin Kennedy stood in front of the dugout late in spring training and talked about the many folks who predicted his team would finish fourth, or worse, in the American League East.

"They can all pick us fourth—we'll be lying in the woods," Kennedy said that sunny Florida day. Was Kennedy just trying to encourage the troops, or did he know something? Maybe a bit of both, because the Sox got off to a quick start and never looked back, easily winning the division before dropping three in a row to the Indians in the divisional playoffs.

In any other town, Sox fever would have been a way of life. But the strike and a history of close calls left the fans subdued. When it was over, most people just shrugged.

But it was a season that shouldn't be ignored. Led by burly first baseman Mo Vaughn, the Sox moved into first place May 13 and never moved out. They were threatened by the Yankees, but blew it open with a 20-2 run before the stretch even started. It was a remarkable feat for what seemed to be a ragtag team. Erik Hanson and Zane Smith, hostages at the free agent refugee camp in Homestead, Fla., at the start of spring training, combined for 23 wins. Tim Wakefield, who lost more games than any minor league pitcher in 1994, came off the scrap heap and jumped to a 14-1 start. Players like Troy O'Leary, claimed off waivers from Milwaukee, were coming out of the woodwork.

Many faces weren't around long. Most were around long enough to do something positive. Even Wes Chamberlain won a game with a home run. Backup catcher Bill Haselman won another with a broken-bat homer.

It never stopped—center fielder Dwayne Hosey, a 28-year-old minor leaguer claimed from Kansas City, excited Boston fans the last month of the season. His coach turned into a pumpkin in the playoffs and he's probably played his last game in a Sox uniform, but he put an exclamation point on the general manager's great year.

There were flops—like Mark Whiten and Dave Hollins—but the successes far outweighed the failures. General manager Dan Duquette kept picking people out of oblivion as other GMs marveled at how much he knew about the people he was getting. The man does his homework, and the studying paid off. The Sox won when they were just striving for respectability.

John Valentin became a 20-20 man and was even a 100-100 man when it came to RBI and runs scored. Tim Naehring shook off his well-earned injury label to hit .307. Jose Canseco, battered through the first half of the season, was an MVP performer in the second half. Mike Greenwell did his usual damage in the .300 neighborhood. Roger Clemens recovered from injury in the second half. Rick Aguilera blew only one save after coming over from the Twins—until the playoffs, when he served up a homer to Albert Belle that cost the Sox Game 1.

1996 Red Sox: Preview

Most fans know that the Sox could use a Craig Biggio type at second base and that a couple of outfielders, a left-handed starter and a catcher wouldn't hurt. But what general manager Dan Duquette has known all along is that the Red Sox farm system is on its way back. The plan he started will continue to be followed. His success in 1995 won't change the rebuilding process, except to prove what he can really do when he has some money at his disposal.

1995 Red Sox: Week-by-week notes

These notes were excerpted from the following issues of Baseball Weekly.

▶**May 3:** The Red Sox got off to a 3-0 start—Aaron Sele, Rheal Cormier and Erik Hanson compiled a 1.20 ERA—despite shuffling the starting rotation. Roger Clemens was disabled with a shoulder injury, and Zane Smith had a rib-cage problem. Tim VanEgmond, slated to start the fourth game, was disabled with a groin pull, which put rookie Frankie Rodriguez into the starting rotation. The Sox signed knuckleballer Tim Wakefield, who was working with Colorado Silver Bullets manager Phil Niekro before heading to Class AAA.

▶**May 10:** Lee Tinsley and Tim Naehring were on 10-game hitting streaks. Tinsley was batting .439 with four steals and 10 RBI.

▶**May 17:** Red Sox pitching continued to excel—sparked by the surprise contribution of rookie Vaughn Eshelman. He threw 18⅔ consecutive scoreless innings to start his big-league career and was working on a no-hitter when he gave up his first run. Zane Smith tossed six shutout innings in his Red Sox (and AL) debut. Meanwhile, Mo Vaughn led the majors in homers (eight).

▶**May 31:** Knuckleballer Tim Wakefield won his AL debut.

▶**June 7:** The Red Sox got Roger Clemens back on June 2, and Aaron Sele took Clemens's place on the DL, joining Vaughn Eshelman, Jose Canseco, Mark Whiten and Lee Tinsley. Despite all the injuries, the Sox had an eight-game lead in the AL East through June 4.

▶**June 14:** Tim Wakefield continued to write his great comeback story, almost pitching a no-hitter on June 9 for his fourth win in his first 14 days with the Red Sox.

▶**June 21:** Originally not due back until after the All-Star break, Canseco was to rejoin the Red Sox lineup in Cleveland on June 20. Also expected back was Troy O'Leary.

▶**July 5:** The Red Sox lead stood at five games, but there were a couple of question marks on their pitching staff. With Aaron Sele's return from shoulder trouble on hold and Vaughn Eshelman's getting hammered (12.56 ERA in five starts) since his return from the disabled list, the Red Sox were looking for a fifth starter for Eshelman's next turn. Reliever Mike Maddux was a possibility, as was Class AA righty Jeff Suppan, just 20 but impressive in the minor leagues. With the bullpen continuing to struggle, the Sox were talking to the Twins about closer Rick Aguilera, but the price was said to be too high. Meanwhile, Ken Ryan continued to look for answers to his problems, and even Stan Belinda, who had been sailing along, had hit a snag. One guy who was rounding into form was Jose Canseco, whose four-hit game raised his batting average to .267. The previous night, Canseco had words with the Tiger battery of Mike Gardiner and Ron Tingley after a pitch was thrown under his helmet. On the next pitch, Canseco received another life when an apparent third strike was called a ball. The slugger lined a homer on the next pitch.

▶**July 13:** The Red Sox finally got their closer on July 6, dealing Frankie Rodriguez and a player to be named later to the Twins for Rick Aguilera, during a series with the Twins. Aguilera didn't take long to join the Sox bandwagon, saving the game at the Metrodome the next night. Outfielder Lee Tinsley surrendered his No. 38 to Aguilera, switching to his high school number, 26. Aguilera and lefty Brian Bark became the 43rd and 44th players for the Sox in 1995—22 of them pitchers. The club record for most players is 48, set in 1948 and matched in 1951.

▶**July 26:** After an 0-for-5 night at Fenway with three strikeouts, Mo

Vaughn blasted the park's lack of a hitting background, a problem that is acute during day games with pitches coming out of white shirts. "Blow it up, blow the damned place up," Vaughn said.

▶**Aug. 16:** The Red Sox's lead in the AL East approached double figures, and Tim Wakefield looked like the Comeback Player of the Year. Dick Williams, who managed the Sox to their Impossible Dream season of 1967, was in Boston scouting for the Yankees and noted that the 1995 Sox team is "possessed" the way the '67 club was.

▶**Aug. 23:** With the acquisitions of reliever Eric Gunderson and outfielder Chris James, the Sox's roster for the season grew to 49, an all-time club record. Gunderson responded to landing on a first-place team by picking up wins on consecutive days, his second and third outings with the club.

▶**Aug. 30:** Tim Wakefield, a strong candidate for both MVP and Cy Young honors, was suffering through his first pitching slump of the year, going 0-1 in two starts that saw him allow 12 runs in 10 innings. Over his last 10⅓ innings dating back to a third start, Wakefield had yielded 13 hits and 13 runs as his ERA jumped to 2.30.

▶**Sept. 13:** Tim Wakefield, who carried the Red Sox through much of the season, continued to struggle. He gave up just two hits in six innings in a game at Yankee Stadium Sept. 8, but both were homers. He walked seven. After issuing just 32 walks in his first 16 starts, Wakefield yielded 29 in his last six, covering 38⅓ innings. He also won just once in those six starts, falling to 15-4 as his ERA jumped to 2.63. He allowed nine homers in that span, raising his team-leading total to 20.

▶**Sept. 20:** Manager Kevin Kennedy said that as early as spring training, he feared the September road trip to New York, Baltimore and Cleveland. His fears were realized as the Sox finished at 3-7 on the 10-game trip, beating Cleveland on Sept. 17 in the finale. The Sox started the trip by being outscored 26-8 and losing all three in New York, breathing serious life into the rival Yankees' wild-card chances. They then lost two of three in Baltimore and were down 2-1 in Cleveland after Roger Clemens was beaten on Sept. 16. The bit of good news for the starters was Tim Wakefield, putting an end to a personal six-game struggle by combining with Aguilera on a two-hit shutout in Baltimore. But Clemens had two tough starts on the trip, with home plate umpires giving him a rough time in both.

▶**Sept. 27:** With their first AL East title since 1990—and fourth in the past 10 years—in the bank, Boston turned to the task of lining up its pitching rotation and setting the postseason roster. Roger Clemens would open the playoffs. Tim Wakefield and Erik Hanson would be the other starters for the short series.

▶**Oct. 4:** Roger Clemens finished the regular season with seven wins in his last eight decisions and wound up 10-5.

Team directory

▶**Owners:** JRY Corporation and John Harrington
▶**General manager:** Dan Duquette
▶**Ballpark:**
Fenway Park
4 Yawkey Way, Boston, Mass.
617-267-9440
Capacity 33,871
Public transportation available
Family, wheelchair, and vision-impaired sections, ramps, sound amplification and TDD ticket information for hearing-impaired
▶**Team publications:**
Media guide, official scorebook, yearbook
617-267-9440
▶**TV, radio broadcast stations:**
WEEI 850 AM, UPN Channel 38, New England Sports Network Cable TV
▶**Spring training:**
City of Palms Park
Fort Myers, Fla.
Capacity 6,850
813-334-4700

BOSTON RED SOX 1995 final stats

BATTERS	BA	SLG	OB	G	AB	R	H	TB	2B	3B	HR	RBI	BB	SO	SB	CS	E
Hatteberg	.500	.500	.500	2	2	1	1	1	0	0	0	0	0	0	0	0	0
Hosey	.338	.618	.408	24	68	20	23	42	8	1	3	7	8	16	6	0	0
C. Rodriguez	.333	.400	.394	13	30	5	10	12	2	0	0	5	2	2	0	0	1
O'Leary	.308	.491	.355	112	399	60	123	196	31	6	10	49	29	64	5	3	5
Naehring	.307	.448	.415	126	433	61	133	194	27	2	10	57	77	66	0	2	16
Canseco	.306	.556	.378	102	396	64	121	220	25	1	24	81	42	93	4	0	0
Vaughn	.300	.575	.388	140	550	98	165	316	28	3	39	126	68	150	11	4	11
Valentin	.298	.533	.399	135	520	108	155	277	37	2	27	102	81	67	20	5	18
Greenwell	.297	.459	.349	120	481	67	143	221	25	4	15	76	38	35	9	5	6
Jefferson	.289	.479	.333	46	121	21	35	58	8	0	5	26	9	24	0	0	0
McGee	.285	.400	.311	67	200	32	57	80	11	3	2	15	9	41	5	2	3
Tinsley	.284	.402	.359	100	341	61	97	137	17	1	7	41	39	74	18	8	5
Alicea	.270	.375	.367	132	419	64	113	157	20	3	6	44	63	61	13	10	16
James	.268	.390	.326	42	82	8	22	32	4	0	2	8	7	14	1	0	0
Stairs	.261	.398	.298	39	88	8	23	35	7	1	1	17	4	14	0	1	2
Donnels	.253	.385	.317	40	91	13	23	35	2	2	2	11	9	18	0	0	4
Haselman	.243	.395	.322	64	152	22	37	60	6	1	5	23	17	30	0	2	3
Shumpert	.234	.298	.294	21	47	6	11	14	3	0	0	3	4	13	3	1	2
Macfarlane	.225	.404	.319	115	364	45	82	147	18	1	15	51	38	78	2	1	5
Mahay	.200	.450	.273	5	20	3	4	9	2	0	1	3	1	6	0	0	0
Whiten	.185	.241	.239	32	108	13	20	26	3	0	0	10	8	23	1	0	0
Rowland	.172	.207	.172	14	29	1	5	6	1	0	0	1	0	11	0	0	1
Bell	.154	.346	.207	17	26	7	4	9	2	0	1	2	2	10	0	0	3
Hollins	.154	.154	.353	5	13	2	2	2	0	0	0	1	4	7	0	0	0
Chamberlain	.119	.214	.178	19	42	4	5	9	1	0	1	1	3	11	1	0	1
Rhodes	.080	.120	.179	10	25	2	2	3	1	0	0	1	3	4	0	0	1

PITCHERS	W-L	ERA	G	GS	CG	GF	Sho	SV	IP	H	R	ER	HR	BB	SO
Bark	0-0	0.00	3	0	0	2	0	0	2.1	2	0	0	0	1	0
Aguilera	3-3	2.60	52	0	0	51	0	32	55.1	46	16	16	6	13	52
Wakefield	16-8	2.95	27	27	6	0	1	0	195.1	163	76	64	22	68	119
Stanton	1-0	3.00	22	0	0	12	0	0	21.0	17	9	7	3	8	10
Sele	3-1	3.06	6	6	0	0	0	0	32.1	32	14	11	3	14	21
Belinda	8-1	3.10	63	0	0	30	0	10	69.2	51	25	24	5	28	57
Maddux	4-1	3.61	36	4	0	6	0	1	89.2	86	40	36	5	15	65
Cormier	7-5	4.07	48	12	0	3	0	0	115.0	131	60	52	12	31	69
Hudson	0-1	4.11	39	0	0	11	0	1	46.0	53	21	21	2	23	29
Clemens	10-5	4.18	23	23	0	0	0	0	140.0	141	70	65	15	60	132
Hanson	15-5	4.24	29	29	1	0	1	0	186.2	187	94	88	17	59	139
Eshelman	6-3	4.85	23	14	0	4	0	0	81.2	86	47	44	3	36	41
Ryan	0-4	4.96	28	0	0	20	0	7	32.2	34	20	18	4	24	34
Gunderson	2-1	5.11	19	0	0	1	0	0	12.1	13	7	7	0	9	9
Smith	8-8	5.61	24	21	0	0	0	0	110.2	144	78	69	7	23	47
Suppan	1-2	5.96	8	3	0	1	0	0	22.2	29	15	15	4	5	19
Lilliquist	2-1	6.26	28	0	0	6	0	0	23.0	27	17	16	7	9	9
Pierce	0-3	6.60	12	0	0	2	0	0	15.0	16	12	11	0	14	12
Pena	1-1	7.40	17	0	0	5	0	0	24.1	33	23	20	5	12	25
VanEgmond	0-1	9.45	4	1	0	1	0	0	6.2	9	7	7	2	6	5
Johnston	0-1	11.25	4	0	0	0	0	0	4.0	2	5	5	1	3	4
Looney	0-1	17.36	3	1	0	0	0	0	4.2	12	9	9	1	4	2
Murray	0-1	18.90	2	1	0	0	0	0	3.1	11	10	7	1	3	1
Shepherd	0-0	36.00	2	0	0	0	0	0	1.0	4	4	4	0	2	0

1996 preliminary roster

PITCHERS (20)
Brian Bark
Stan Belinda
Rich Betti
Roger Clemens
Rheal Cormier
Joe Crawford
Vaughn Eshelman
Eric Gunderson
Butch Henry
Joe Hudson
Matt Murray
Rafael Orellano
Brad Pennington
Ken Ryan
Aaron Sele
Mike Stanton
Jeff Suppan
JJ Thobe
Tim Van Egmond
Tim Wakefield

CATCHERS (2)
Bill Haselman
Scott Hatteberg

INFIELDERS (9)
Luis Alicea
Dave Hollins
Reggie Jefferson
Ryan McGuire
Tim Naehring
Carlos Rodriguez
Jim Tatum
John Valentin
Mo Vaughn

OUTFIELDERS (9)
Jose Canseco
Brent Cookson
Mike Greenwell
Dwayne Hosey
Jose Malave
Glenn Murray
Trot Nixon
Troy O'Leary
Lee Tinsley

Games played by position

PLAYER	G	C	1B	2B	3B	SS	OF	DH
Alicea	132	0	0	132	0	0	0	0
Bell	17	0	0	5	1	6	0	0
Canseco	102	0	0	0	0	0	1	101
Chamberlain	19	0	0	0	0	0	12	5
Donnels	40	0	8	3	27	0	0	0
Greenwell	120	0	0	0	0	0	118	2
Haselman	64	48	1	0	1	0	0	11
Hatteberg	2	2	0	0	0	0	0	0
Hollins	5	0	0	0	0	0	2	3
Hosey	24	0	0	0	0	0	21	1
James	42	0	0	0	0	0	13	20
Jefferson	46	0	7	0	0	0	2	32
Macfarlane	115	111	0	0	0	0	0	3
Mahay	5	0	0	0	0	0	5	0
McGee	67	0	0	0	0	0	64	0
Naehring	126	0	0	0	124	0	0	1
O'Leary	112	0	0	0	0	0	105	3
Rhodes	10	0	0	0	0	0	9	0
C. Rodriguez	13	0	0	7	1	6	0	0
Rowland	14	11	0	0	0	0	0	3
Shumpert	21	0	0	8	5	3	0	1
Stairs	39	0	0	0	0	0	23	2
Tinsley	100	0	0	0	0	0	97	0
Valentin	135	0	0	0	0	135	0	0
Vaughn	140	0	138	0	0	0	0	2
Whiten	32	0	0	0	0	0	31	1

Minor Leagues

Tops in the organization

Batter	Club	Avg.	G	AB	R	H	HR	RBI
Ryan McGuire	Tre	.333	109	414	59	138	7	59
Chris Allison	Mch	.315	87	298	46	94	0	22
Walt McKeel	Sar	.305	92	282	37	86	10	46
Chris Stasio	Mch	.305	87	315	44	96	7	47
Nathan Tebbs	Sar	.291	118	440	58	128	2	52

Home Runs			Wins		
P. Chop Pough	Paw	26	Ethan Merrill	Sar	11
Glenn Murray	Paw	25	Shawn Senior	Paw	11
Jose Malave	Paw	23	Rafael Orellano	Tre	11
Eric Wedge	Paw	20	Brent Hansen	Paw	11
Ben Shelton	Tre	17	Brett Cederblad	Tre	10

RBI			Saves		
P. Chop Pough	Paw	92	Shayne Bennett	Tre	27
David Gibralter	Mch	82	Scott Jones	Mch	13
Eric Wedge	Paw	68	Mike Blais	Tre	10
Bill Selby	Tre	68	Several tied		8
Glenn Murray	Paw	66			

Stolen Bases			Strikeouts		
Donnie Sadler	Mch	41	Rafael Orellano	Tre	160
Chris Allison	Mch	36	Carl Pavano	Mch	138
N. Garciaparra	Tre	35	Jeff Suppan	Paw	120
Marc Lewis	Uti	34	Brett Cederblad	Tre	107
Michael Coleman	Mch	29	Brian Rose	Mch	105

Pitcher	Club	W-L	ERA	IP	H	BB	SO
Rafael Orellano	Tre	11-7	2.99	187	146	72	160
J. Fernandez	Tre	8-6	3.17	105	94	37	63
Kurt Bogott	Tre	6-6	3.18	96	99	45	66
Brian Barkley	Sar	8-10	3.25	147	147	37	70
Jeff Suppan	Paw	8-5	3.30	145	136	35	120

Sick call: 1995 DL Report

Player	Days on the DL
Stan Belinda	11
Jose Canseco	36
Roger Clemens	38
Vaughn Eshelman	52**
Mike Greenwell	21
Dave Hollins	54
Chris James	15
Reggie Jefferson	71
Aaron Sele	131
Keith Shepherd	35
Zane Smith	38*
Lee Tinsley	36*
Tim Vanegmond	15
Mark Whiten	18

Indicates two separate terms on Disabled List.
** Indicates three separate terms on DL.

1995 Amateur draft picks

Players are listed with position and college or high school. Most players were assigned to rookie or Class A leagues. List provided by Major League Baseball.

Lakevie Austin, rf, Emmanuel College; Andrew Beinbrink, ss, Scripps Ranch HS, San Diego; Timothy Boeth, ss, Leon HS, Tallahassee, Fla.; Clifford Brand, rhp, Central Gwinnett HS, Lawrenceville, Ga.; Kristopher Brown, rhp, Kalamazoo (Mich.) Central HS; Matthew Burch, rhp, Thomas A. Edison HS, Horseheads, N.Y.; Patrick Burrell, 3b, Bellarmine College Prep, Boulder Creek, Calif.; Kevan Cannon, lhp, Ohio State; Luis Cardona, c, Manuel Mendez Liciaga HS, San Sebastian, P.R.; Juan Chaidez, c, Dade Christian, Hialeah, Fla.; James Chamblee, ss, Odessa College; Paxton Crawford, rhp, Carlsbad (N.M.) HS; Angel Diaz, c, Hillsborough JC; James Farrell, rhp, Kent; Dwight Ferguson, lf, Dade Christian, Carol City, Fla.; Nicholas Gruber, c, Haddon Township HS, Westmont, N.J.; Kaleb Harp, c, Dekalb (Texas) HS; Corey Jenkins, lf, Dreher HS, Columbia, S.C.; Rontrez Johnson, cf, Marshall (Texas) HS; Matthew Jones, rhp, Miami (Ohio); Matthew Kinney, rhp, Bangor (Maine) HS; Derrick Lewis, rhp, Central Alabama CC; Cole Liniak, ss, San Dieguito HS, Encinitas, Calif.; Steven Lomasney, c, Peabody (Mass.) HS; Chuck Lopez, cf, Gahr HS, Cerritos, Calif.; Brian Messer, rhp, Northwest HS, Shawnee, Kan.; Cordele Mincey, rhp, Dodge County HS, Milan, Ga.; Andrew Noffke, rhp, Ohio State; Jose Olmeda, ss, Dr. Veve Calzada HS, Fajardo, P.R.; Juan Pena, rhp, Miami Dade CC; Peter Prodanov, 3b-of, Oklahoma State; Robert Rauch, rhp, Lamar; Robert Rodgers, rhp, Wake Forest; Moises Rojas, cf-rf, Brito Miami Private School, Hialeah, Fla.; Felipe Roman, lf, Metropolitana Universidad, Rio Piedras, P.R.; Curtis Romboli, lhp, Boston College; Jeffrey Sauve, rhp, Clemson; Michael Spinelli, lhp, Revere (Mass.) HS; Benjamin Stallings, rhp, Apollo HS, Owensboro, Ky.; Christopher Toomey, cf-rhp, Dana (Calif.) Hills HS; Mark Varriano, c, North Dakota; Barton Vaughn, rhp, Mount Dora Bible HS, Orlando, Fla.; Jason Wilson, rhp, South Broward HS, Hollywood, Fla.; Bryan Wright, ss, Escambia HS, Pensacola, Fla.; Jay Yennaco, rhp, Pinkerton Academy, Windham, N.H.; Andrew Yount, rhp, Kingwood (Texas) HS.

Boston (1901-1995)

Runs: Most, career, all-time

1816	Carl Yastrzemski, 1961-1983
1798	Ted Williams, 1939-1960
1435	Dwight Evans, 1972-1990
1249	Jim Rice, 1974-1989
1094	Bobby Doerr, 1937-1951

Hits: Most, career, all-time

3419	Carl Yastrzemski, 1961-1983
2654	Ted Williams, 1939-1960
2452	Jim Rice, 1974-1989
2373	Dwight Evans, 1972-1990
2098	WADE BOGGS, 1982-1992

2B: Most, career, all-time

646	Carl Yastrzemski, 1961-1983
525	Ted Williams, 1939-1960
474	Dwight Evans, 1972-1990
422	WADE BOGGS, 1982-1992
381	Bobby Doerr, 1937-1951

3B: Most, career, all-time

130	Harry Hooper, 1909-1920
106	Tris Speaker, 1907-1915
90	Buck Freeman, 1901-1907
89	Bobby Doerr, 1937-1951
87	Larry Gardner, 1908-1917

HR: Most, career, all-time

521	Ted Williams, 1939-1960
452	Carl Yastrzemski, 1961-1983
382	Jim Rice, 1974-1989
379	Dwight Evans, 1972-1990
223	Bobby Doerr, 1937-1951

RBI: Most, career, all-time

1844	Carl Yastrzemski, 1961-1983
1839	Ted Williams, 1939-1960
1451	Jim Rice, 1974-1989
1346	Dwight Evans, 1972-1990
1247	Bobby Doerr, 1937-1951

SB: Most, career, all-time

300	Harry Hooper, 1909-1920
267	Tris Speaker, 1907-1915
168	Carl Yastrzemski, 1961-1983
141	Heinie Wagner, 1906-1918
134	Larry Gardner, 1908-1917

BB: Most, career, all-time

2019	Ted Williams, 1939-1960
1845	Carl Yastrzemski, 1961-1983
1337	Dwight Evans, 1972-1990
1004	WADE BOGGS, 1982-1992
826	Harry Hooper, 1909-1920

BA: Highest, career, all-time

.344	Ted Williams, 1939-1960
.338	WADE BOGGS, 1982-1992
.337	Tris Speaker, 1907-1915
.320	Pete Runnels, 1958-1962
.320	Jimmie Foxx, 1936-1942

Slug avg: Highest, career, all-time

.634	Ted Williams, 1939-1960
.605	Jimmie Foxx, 1936-1942
.520	Fred Lynn, 1974-1980
.510	MO VAUGHN, 1991-1995
.502	Jim Rice, 1974-1989

Games started: Most, career, all-time

348	ROGER CLEMENS, 1984-1995
297	Cy Young, 1901-1908
238	Luis Tiant, 1971-1978
232	Mel Parnell, 1947-1956
228	Bill Monbouquette, 1958-1965

Saves: Most, career, all-time

132	Bob Stanley, 1977-1989
104	Dick Radatz, 1962-1966
91	Ellis Kinder, 1948-1955
88	Jeff Reardon, 1990-1992
69	Sparky Lyle, 1967-1971

Shutouts: Most, career, all-time

38	Cy Young, 1901-1908
36	ROGER CLEMENS, 1984-1995
28	Joe Wood, 1908-1915
26	Luis Tiant, 1971-1978
25	Dutch Leonard, 1913-1918

Wins: Most, career, all-time

192	Cy Young, 1901-1908
182	ROGER CLEMENS, 1984-1995
123	Mel Parnell, 1947-1956
122	Luis Tiant, 1971-1978
116	Joe Wood, 1908-1915

K: Most, career, all-time

2333	ROGER CLEMENS, 1984-1995
1341	Cy Young, 1901-1908
1075	Luis Tiant, 1971-1978
1043	Bruce Hurst, 1980-1988
986	Joe Wood, 1908-1915

Win pct: Highest, career, all-time

.695	Roger Moret, 1970-1975
.684	Dave Ferriss, 1945-1950
.674	Joe Wood, 1908-1915
.659	Babe Ruth, 1914-1919
.650	ROGER CLEMENS, 1984-1995

ERA: Lowest, career, all-time

1.99	Joe Wood, 1908-1915
2.00	Cy Young, 1901-1908
2.12	Ernie Shore, 1914-1917
2.13	Dutch Leonard, 1913-1918
2.19	Babe Ruth, 1914-1919

Runs: Most, season

150	Ted Williams, 1949
142	Ted Williams, 1946
141	Ted Williams, 1942
139	Jimmie Foxx, 1938
136	Tris Speaker, 1912

Hits: Most, season

240	WADE BOGGS, 1985
222	Tris Speaker, 1912
214	WADE BOGGS, 1988
213	Jim Rice, 1978
210	WADE BOGGS, 1983

2B: Most, season

67	Earl Webb, 1931
53	Tris Speaker, 1912
51	WADE BOGGS, 1989
51	Joe Cronin, 1938
47	WADE BOGGS, 1986
47	George Burns, 1923
47	Fred Lynn, 1975

3B: Most, season

22	Tris Speaker, 1913
20	Buck Freeman, 1903
19	Buck Freeman, 1902
19	Buck Freeman, 1904
19	Larry Gardner, 1914
19	Chick Stahl, 1904

HR: Most, season

50	Jimmie Foxx, 1938
46	Jim Rice, 1978
44	Carl Yastrzemski, 1967
43	Tony Armas, 1984
43	Ted Williams, 1949

RBI: Most, season

175	Jimmie Foxx, 1938
159	Vern Stephens, 1949
159	Ted Williams, 1949
145	Ted Williams, 1939
144	Walt Dropo, 1950
144	Vern Stephens, 1950

BOSTN RED SOX / AL EAST

1996 BASEBALL WEEKLY ALMANAC

SB: Most, season

54	Tommy Harper, 1973
52	Tris Speaker, 1912
46	Tris Speaker, 1913
42	Tris Speaker, 1914
42	OTIS NIXON, 1994

BB: Most, season

162	Ted Williams, 1947
162	Ted Williams, 1949
156	Ted Williams, 1946
145	Ted Williams, 1941
145	Ted Williams, 1942

BA: Highest, season

.406	Ted Williams, 1941
.388	Ted Williams, 1957
.383	Tris Speaker, 1912
.369	Ted Williams, 1948
.368	WADE BOGGS, 1985

Slug avg: Highest, season

.735	Ted Williams, 1941
.731	Ted Williams, 1957
.704	Jimmie Foxx, 1938
.694	Jimmie Foxx, 1939
.667	Ted Williams, 1946

Games started: Most, season

43	Cy Young, 1902
42	Bill Dinneen, 1902
41	Babe Ruth, 1916
41	Cy Young, 1901
41	Cy Young, 1904

Saves: Most, season

40	Jeff Reardon, 1991
33	JEFF RUSSELL, 1993
33	Bob Stanley, 1983
31	Bill Campbell, 1977
29	Dick Radatz, 1964
29	LEE SMITH, 1988

Shutouts: Most, season

10	Joe Wood, 1912
10	Cy Young, 1904
9	Babe Ruth, 1916
8	ROGER CLEMENS, 1988
8	Carl Mays, 1918

Wins: Most, season

34	Joe Wood, 1912
33	Cy Young, 1901
32	Cy Young, 1902
28	Cy Young, 1903
26	Cy Young, 1904

K: Most, season

291	ROGER CLEMENS, 1988
258	Joe Wood, 1912
256	ROGER CLEMENS, 1987
246	Jim Lonborg, 1967
241	ROGER CLEMENS, 1991

Win pct: Highest, season

.882	Bob Stanley, 1978
.872	Joe Wood, 1912
.857	ROGER CLEMENS, 1986
.806	Dave Ferriss, 1946
.793	Ellis Kinder, 1949

ERA: Lowest, season

0.96	Dutch Leonard, 1914
1.26	Cy Young, 1908
1.49	Joe Wood, 1915
1.62	Ray Collins, 1910
1.62	Cy Young, 1901

Most pinch-hit homers, season

5	Joe Cronin, 1943
4	Del Wilber, 1953

Most pinch-hit homers, career

7	Ted Williams, 1939-1960

Most consecutive games batting safely

34	Dom DiMaggio, 1949
30	Tris Speaker, 1912

Most consecutive scoreless innings

45	Cy Young, 1904
42	Rube Foster, 1914
40	Luis Tiant, 1972
39	Ray Culp, 1968
37	Cy Young, 1903

No-hit games

Cy Young, Bos vs Phi AL, 3-0; May 5, 1904 (perfect game).

Jesse Tannehill, Bos at Chi AL, 6-0; August 17, 1904.

Bill Dinneen, Bos vs Chi AL, 2-0; September 27, 1905 (1st game).

Cy Young, Bos at NY AL, 8-0; June 30, 1908.

Joe Wood, Bos vs StL AL, 5-0; July 29, 1911 (1st game).

Rube Foster, Bos vs NY AL, 2-0; June 21, 1916.

Hubert (Dutch) Leonard, Bos vs StL AL, 4-0; August 30, 1916.

Ernie Shore, Bos vs Was AL, 4-0; June 23, 1917 (1st game, perfect game) (Shore relieved Babe Ruth in the first inning after Ruth had been thrown out of the game for protesting a walk to the first batter. The runner was caught stealing, and Shore retired the remaining 26 batters in order).

Hubert (Dutch) Leonard, Bos at Det AL, 5-0; June 3, 1918.

Howard Ehmke, Bos at Phi AL, 4-0; September 7, 1923.

Mel Parnell, Bos vs Chi AL, 4-0; July 14, 1956.

Earl Wilson, Bos vs LA AL, 2-0; June 26, 1962.

Bill Monbouquette, Bos at Chi AL, 1-0; August 1, 1962.

Dave Morehead, Bos vs Cle AL, 2-0; September 16, 1965.

Matt Young, Bos at Cle AL, 1-2; April 12, 1992 (1st game) (8 innings, lost the game, bottom of 9th not played).

ACTIVE PLAYERS in caps.

Players' years of service are listed by the first and last years with this team and are not necessarily consecutive; all statistics record performances for this team only.

New York Yankees

Paul O'Neill (.300, 22 homers, 96 RBI) helped the Yankees win a wild-card berth in the AL playoffs.

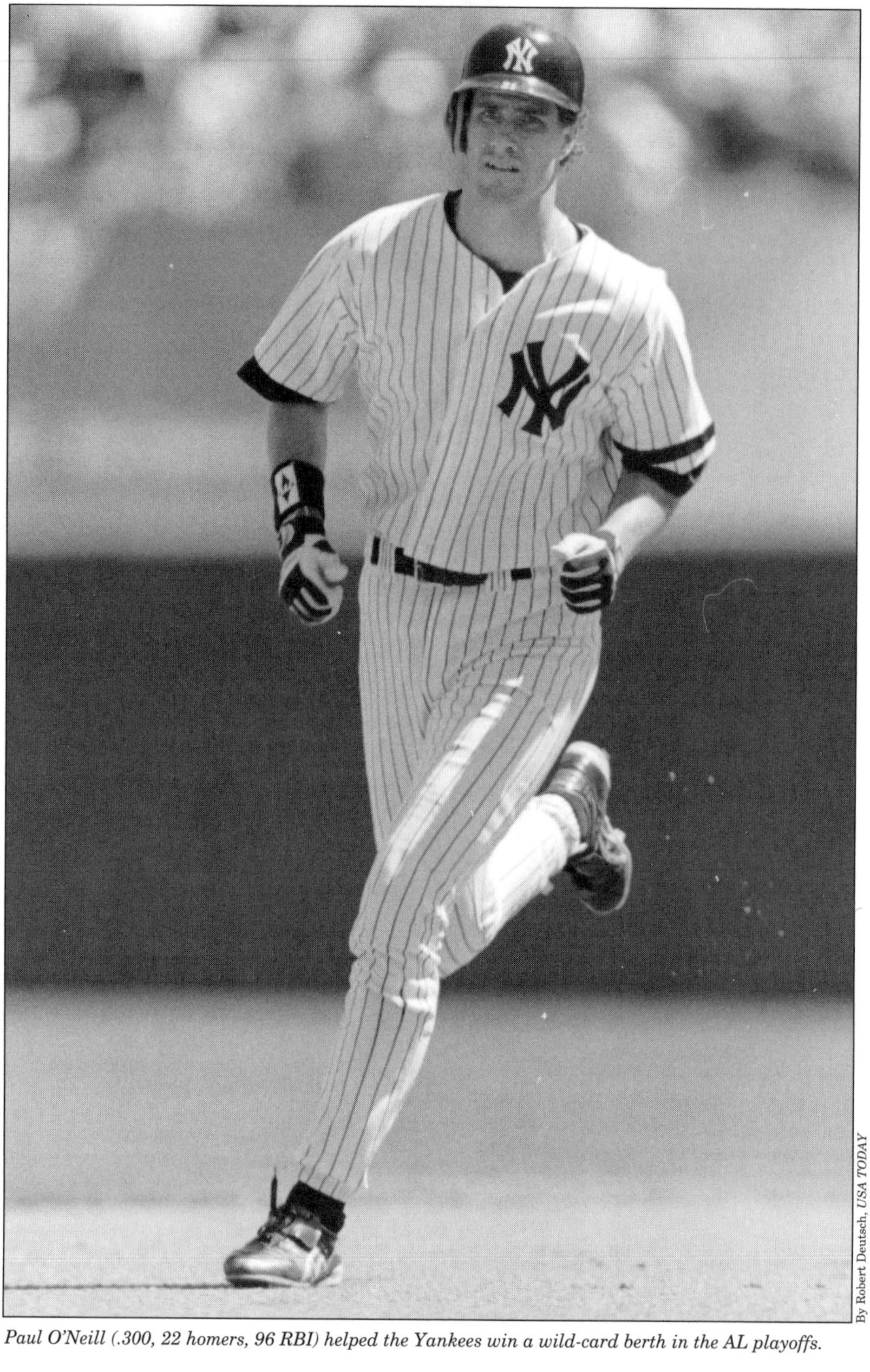

By Robert Deutsch, USA TODAY

1995 Yankees: Mattingly reached October

The Yankees started out full of determination after finishing 1994 with an AL-best record of 70-43 and nothing to show for it. They had added former Cy Young winner Jack McDowell, closer John Wetteland and shortstop Tony Fernandez. But manager Buck Showalter bemoaned the shortened spring training. He said his veteran team would have needed every bit of a normal spring training had it been available. It wasn't.

His words proved prophetic. McDowell didn't really come around until September. Jimmy Key, Scott Kamieniecki, Melido Perez—60% of the starting rotation—missed large chunks of the season with injuries. Key, who made just five starts in 1995 after winning 17 games in 1994, underwent reconstructive left shoulder surgery in early July and might not ever pitch again. Don Mattingly was hampered for nearly six weeks by a mysterious eye infection.

The nagging injuries took their toll. New York was in fourth place (eight games out) at the All-Star break. By the end of August, they trailed the Red Sox by 15 games. Then, inexplicably, the Yankees caught fire. They were led primarily by the bats of Bernie Williams (.256 before the break, .350 after) and Wade Boggs (.295 and .335) and by some key RBI by Ruben Sierra, Paul O'Neill, and Mike Stanley. Although they finished well behind Boston in the AL East, they captured the wild card by winning 11 of their final 12 games.

It wasn't all offense that got them to the playoffs for the first time since 1981, though. The starting pitching, an Achilles' elbow most of the season, found its rhythm in September. McDowell finished with victories in his last four decisions before a back injury caused him to miss his final two regular-season starts. Cone went 9-2 after being acquired from Toronto in late

July, and rookie Andy Pettitte, given an opportunity when Key was lost for the season, went 6-1 beginning on Aug. 30. And, while the rest of the bullpen continued to be erratic, Wetteland overcame a shaky midseason to record saves in his last seven opportunities.

Williams made a case for team MVP with his strong showing. The 27-year-old center fielder finished with career highs in batting (.307), homers (18) and RBI (82). Boggs, even at age 37, hit .324 and played the final two weeks of the season and the playoffs with a badly pulled hamstring.

The defending AL batting champ, O'Neill, dropped from .359 in 1994 to an even .300. But he had a career-high 96 RBI to become the first Yankee since Mattingly in 1985-86 to lead the team in homers and RBI in consecutive seasons.

Stanley batted below .300 (.268) for the first time in three seasons but added 18 homers and 83 RBI. Mattingly, who advanced to the postseason for the first time in his career, had a 10-game hitting streak to finish at .288.

1996 Yankees: Preview

With the notable exceptions of 23-year-old Andy Pettitte and 27-year-old Bernie Williams, the Yankees are an aging team. While 21-year-old Derek Jeter is expected to get a long look at shortstop during spring training, the nucleus of the club—Paul O'Neill, Mike Stanley, Jimmy Key, Ruben Sierra, Darryl Strawberry and newcomer Dwight Gooden—is over 30. Despite all the big names, this is not a deep team, and the Yankees cannot afford another rash of injuries.

1995 Yankees: Week-by-week notes

These notes were excerpted from the following issues of Baseball Weekly.

▸**May 24:** Jimmy Key was placed on the 15-day disabled list and sounded unusually pessimistic. In his two most recent starts, he allowed 19 hits and 11 earned runs over 11⅓ innings.

▸**May 31:** George Steinbrenner laid low, preferring to let his employees react initially to an agent's claim that the Yankees were interested in signing free-agent outfielder Darryl Strawberry, then serving a 60-day suspension for violating baseball's anti drug policy after having been released by the Giants for violating his aftercare program. He had also been suspended the year before as a Dodger for violating the league's drug policy.

▸**June 7:** Showalter was severely criticized by the Angels' Tony Phillips after the Yankees manager had umpires confiscate his bat at the start of the game June 4. The bat was X-rayed and pronounced clean and legal. "It's insulting," Phillips said. "I spent 12 years busting my butt to become the hitter I am, and they accuse me of cheating. I lost a lot of respect for Buck Showalter. If that's all he has to worry about, it's no wonder they're getting their butts kicked."

▸**July 13:** Don Mattingly didn't exactly welcome Dave Pavlas from Class AAA with open arms. Pavlas was the ninth replacement player called up this season. He sat by himself in the Yankee bullpen the night after his call-up while the other relievers sat bunched together. And he sat alone in the dugout after pitching a scoreless seventh inning. "I have my thoughts on it, but I don't think it would do any good to make them public," Mattingly said. "He came here as a scab, to tell you the truth. But he's a scab on our team. He's out there with us on the field, but after that...." Pavlas, who was given a locker away from the rest of the players in the vast

visitors' clubhouse, said he understood Mattingly's feelings but hoped the other players would understand his. Pavlas last pitched in the majors in 1992 with the Cubs and since played in Taiwan, Italy and Mexico. "If people knew where I'd spent the last three years playing ball, I think they'd understand," he said.

▸**July 26:** Jack McDowell barely had time to put his finger back in his pocket (after making an obscene gesture at fans who booed him when he was removed from a subpar outing) when yet another controversy began swirling around the frenetic Yankees. Steve Howe, livid over the public airing of old clubhouse rumors that he had provided amphetamines to teammates, had been suspended seven times for cocaine and alcohol offenses and figured the accusations were absurd in view: "I'm a guy who's tested every day for everything....Why would I even think about it?" Meanwhile, not-yet-Yankee (and famed good sport) Darryl Strawberry hit a snag in his contract negotiations when he refused to set aside a substantial amount of salary for charitable work.

▸**Aug. 2:** While David Cone and Ruben Sierra joined the Yankees, the team still braced for the anticipated arrival of Darryl Strawberry. Strawberry's agent demanded his client be promoted the minute final contract details were worked out, and the Yankees called the demand "bush league" and "counterproductive. Steinbrenner insisted that Strawberry would not join the Yankees until his "baseball people say he's ready." In his first 17 games for Columbus, Strawberry was batting .309 with six homers and 25 RBI, but the Yankees said he still wasn't ready because he has not played enough games in the outfield.

▸**Aug. 16:** David Cone (13-6) was everything the Yankees had hoped for since they got him from Toronto—he won four consecutive games and kept New York's wild-card, if not AL East title, hopes alive. His ERA as a Yankee was 2.25.

▶**Aug. 23:** Ironically, the Yankees, with the highest payroll in the majors, at $55 million, found themselves battling with some of baseball's bargain-basement teams—Kansas City, Milwaukee and Seattle—for the-wild card spot in the AL playoffs.

▶**Aug. 30:** Few Yankees road trips were more damaging than the latest journey to Anaheim, Oakland and Seattle. After dropping two of three games to the Red Sox to fall 10 games off the pace, they took the first of a three-game series with the Angels before losing eight consecutive games (through Aug. 26). It marked the first time the Yankees had lost 10 games on the same road trip since 1967. By Aug. 28, they trailed Boston by 15½ games and were 4½ games behind Texas in the wild-card race.

▶**Sept. 6:** Don Mattingly thought he was answering a simple question honestly. Sure, he'd consider playing in Japan next season if there was no deal to be struck in the major leagues. But even the 13-year veteran of dealing with the New York press was surprised by the mass hysteria that followed. A day later, Mattingly was in full retreat, saying he was "semi-embarrassed" by the furor his comments had caused. The 34-year-old first baseman, in the final year of his contract, said he didn't want to be a distraction as his team bids for a wild-card playoff berth, but he believed all season that owner George Steinbrenner was behind a plot to force him from the Bronx—a charge the owner denied. Mattingly, who was said to have a hankering to play with the St. Louis Cardinals, sounded more and more like he was convinced his days in a Yankees uniform were just about over. "There is a day you prepare for the thought you might have to [wear another uniform]," he said.

▶**Sept. 6:** Mattingly scored the 1,000th run of his major league career. He became the 227th player in history to score that many and the ninth Yankee.

▶**Sept. 27:** If you want a reason for the resurgence—the Yankees had won 21 of their last 28 through Sept. 24—look no

further than the top of the lineup. Since being placed No. 1 and No. 2 after Luis Polonia was designated for assignment on Aug. 4, leadoff batter Wade Boggs hit .359 (60-for-167) with 34 runs scored, while Bernie Williams batted .370 (61-for-165) with 33 runs scored.

▶**Oct. 4:** When the Yankees needed a victory or a California loss on the season's final day to reach the playoffs for the first time since 1981, manager Buck Showalter decided to hold David Cone back a day and start Sterling Hitchcock. Without a playoff, Showalter was able to start Cone on Tuesday for the first game of the playoffs at Yankee Stadium. Following Cone would be rookie Andy Pettitte; the ailing Jack McDowell would start Game Three.

Team directory

▶**Owner:** George Steinbrenner
▶**General manager:** Bob Watson
▶**Ballpark:**
Yankee Stadium
East 161st Street and River Avenue, Bronx, N.Y.
718-293-4300
Capacity 57,545
Parking (independently owned); $5
Public transportation available
Family and wheelchair sections, ramps, Senior Citizen Discount ($2 tickets day of game), group discounts, monument park behind right center field with plaques honoring famous Yankees
▶**Team publications:**
Yankees Magazine, media guide, scorecard, yearbook
718-293-4300
▶**TV, radio broadcast stations:**
WABC 770 AM, WPIX Channel 11, MSG Network
▶**Spring training:**
To open for spring 1996
3802 Martin Luther King Blvd.
Tampa, Fla.
Capacity 8,340
813-879-2244
Capacity: 10,000

NEW YORK YANKEES 1995 final stats

BATTERS	BA	SLG	OB	G	AB	R	H	TB	2B	3B	HR	RBI	BB	SO	SB	CS	E
Boggs	.324	.422	.412	126	460	76	149	194	22	4	5	63	74	50	1	1	5
B. Williams	.307	.487	.392	144	563	93	173	274	29	9	18	82	75	98	8	6	8
O'Neill	.300	.526	.387	127	460	82	138	242	30	4	22	96	71	76	1	2	3
Mattingly	.288	.413	.341	128	458	59	132	189	32	2	7	49	40	35	0	2	7
James	.287	.354	.346	85	209	22	60	74	6	1	2	26	20	16	4	1	1
Velarde	.278	.392	.375	111	367	60	102	144	19	1	7	46	55	64	5	1	10
Strawberry	.276	.448	.364	32	87	15	24	39	4	1	3	13	10	22	0	0	2
Davis	.276	.429	.349	40	98	14	27	42	5	2	2	12	10	26	0	0	2
Leyritz	.269	.394	.374	77	264	37	71	104	12	0	7	37	37	73	1	1	3
Stanley	.268	.481	.360	118	399	63	107	192	29	1	18	83	57	106	1	1	5
Sierra	.263	.449	.323	126	479	73	126	215	32	0	19	86	46	76	5	4	5
Polonia	.261	.349	.326	67	238	37	62	83	9	3	2	15	25	29	10	4	0
Jeter	.250	.375	.294	15	48	5	12	18	4	1	0	7	3	11	0	0	2
G. Williams	.247	.467	.327	100	182	33	45	85	18	2	6	28	22	34	4	2	1
Fernandez	.245	.346	.322	108	384	57	94	133	20	2	5	45	42	40	6	6	10
Kelly	.237	.333	.307	89	270	32	64	90	12	1	4	29	23	65	8	3	7
Eenhoorn	.143	.214	.200	5	14	1	2	3	1	0	0	2	1	3	0	0	1
Elster	.118	.176	.167	10	17	1	2	3	1	0	0	0	1	5	0	0	0
Silvestri	.095	.238	.259	17	21	4	2	5	0	0	1	4	4	9	0	0	0
R. Rivera	.000	.000	.000	5	1	0	0	0	0	0	0	0	0	1	0	0	0
Posada	—	—	—	1	0	0	0	0	0	0	0	0	0	0	0	0	0

PITCHERS	W-L	ERA	G	GS	CG	GF	Sho	SV	IP	H	R	ER	HR	BB	SO
Manzanillo	0-0	2.08	11	0	0	4	0	0	17.1	19	4	4	1	9	11
Patterson	0-0	2.70	3	0	0	3	0	0	3.1	3	1	1	1	3	3
Wetteland	1-5	2.93	60	0	0	56	0	31	61.1	40	22	20	6	14	66
Honeycutt	5-1	2.96	52	0	0	6	0	2	45.2	39	16	15	6	10	21
Pavlas	0-0	3.18	4	0	0	1	0	0	5.2	8	2	2	0	0	3
Cone	18-8	3.57	30	30	6	0	2	0	229.1	195	95	91	24	88	191
McDowell	15-10	3.93	30	30	4	0	2	0	217.2	211	106	95	25	78	157
Kamieniecki	7-6	4.01	17	16	1	1	0	0	89.2	83	43	40	8	49	43
Wickman	2-4	4.05	63	1	0	14	0	1	80.0	77	38	36	6	33	51
Pettitte	12-9	4.17	31	26	3	1	0	0	175.0	183	86	81	15	63	114
Hitchcock	11-10	4.70	27	27	4	0	1	0	168.1	155	91	88	22	68	121
MacDonald	1-1	4.86	33	0	0	5	0	0	46.1	50	25	25	7	22	41
Howe	6-3	4.96	56	0	0	20	0	2	49.0	66	29	27	7	17	28
M. Rivera	5-3	5.51	19	10	0	2	0	0	67.0	71	43	41	11	30	51
Perez	5-5	5.58	13	12	1	1	0	0	69.1	70	46	43	10	31	44
Key	1-2	5.64	5	5	0	0	0	0	30.1	40	20	19	3	6	14
Ausanio	2-0	5.73	28	0	0	10	0	1	37.2	42	24	24	9	23	36
Bankhead	1-1	6.00	20	1	0	8	0	0	39.0	44	26	26	9	16	20
Eiland	1-1	6.30	4	1	0	1	0	0	10.0	16	10	7	1	3	6
Boehringer	0-3	13.75	7	3	0	0	0	0	17.2	24	27	27	5	22	10

1996 preliminary roster

PITCHERS (18)
Brian Boehringer
Andy Croghan
Chris Cumberland
Dwight Gooden
Mark Hutton
Scott Kamieniecki
Jimmy Key
Jim Mecir
Ramiro Mendoza
Jeff Nelson
Kirt Ojala
Melido Perez
Andy Pettitte
Mariano Rivera
Brien Taylor
Kent Wallace
John Wetteland
Bob Wickman

CATCHERS (5)
Mike Figga
Joe Girardi
Jim Leyritz
Jorge Posada
Marc Ronan

INFIELDERS (9)
Wade Boggs
Mariano Duncan
Robert Eenhoorn
Tony Fernandez
Andy Fox
Derek Jeter
Pat Kelly
Tino Martinez
Tate Seefried

OUTFIELDERS (6)
Matt Luke
Paul O'Neill
Ruben Rivera
Ruben Sierra
Bernie Williams
Gerald Williams

Games played by position

PLAYER	G	C	1B	2B	3B	SS	OF	DH
Boggs	126	0	9	0	117	0	0	0
Davis	40	0	2	0	34	0	0	4
Eenhoorn	5	0	0	3	0	2	0	0
Elster	10	0	0	1	0	10	0	0
Fernandez	108	0	0	4	0	103	0	0
James	85	0	6	0	0	0	29	27
Jeter	15	0	0	0	0	15	0	0
Kelly	89	0	0	87	0	0	0	1
Leyritz	77	46	18	0	0	0	0	15
Mattingly	128	0	125	0	0	0	0	1
O'Neill	127	0	0	0	0	0	121	4
Polonia	67	0	0	0	0	0	64	1
Posada	1	1	0	0	0	0	0	0
R. Rivera	5	0	0	0	0	0	4	0
Sierra	126	0	0	0	0	0	72	53
Silvestri	17	0	4	7	0	1	0	4
Stanley	118	107	0	0	0	0	0	10
Strawberry	32	0	0	0	0	0	11	15
Velarde	111	0	0	62	19	28	20	0
B. Williams	144	0	0	0	0	0	144	0
G. Williams	100	0	0	0	0	0	92	2

Sick call: 1995 DL Report

Player	Days on the DL
Tony Fernandez	18
Scott Kamieniecki	70
Pat Kelly	41
Jimmy Key	138
Josias Manzanillo	88
Paul O'Neill	16
Melido Perez	69
Dave Silvestri	17

1995 Amateur draft picks

Players are listed with position and college or high school. Most players were assigned to rookie or Class A leagues. List provided by Major League Baseball.

Patrick Antrim, ss, Saddleback CC; Brian Aylor, cf, Oklahoma State; Jason Becker, 2b, Bremen HS, Midlothian, Ill.; Casey Blake, 3b, Wichita State; Eric Boardman, rhp, Cerritos College; Scott Brand, rhp, McLennan CC; Richard Brown, cf, Nova HS, Plantation, Fla.; Barry Brown, cf, Grossmont College; Travis Brummitt, rhp, Cleveland State CC; Brian Buchanan, lhp, Oviedo (Fla.) HS; Dorian Cameron, ss, Northern HS, Durham, N.C.; Jude Campbell, cf, Chabot; Orlando Carey, of, Motlow State CC; Justin Carpenter, rhp, Prague (Okla.) HS; Benjamin Chestnut, of, Sacramento CC; Chad Clements, ss, Centreville HS, Fairfax, Va.; Darryl Craig, lhp-1b, Douglas College; Christopher Crawford, rhp, Wheeler HS, Marietta, Ga.; Richard Cremer, lhp, W. Frankfort (Ill.) HS; Daunte Culpepper, rf, Vanguard HS, Ocala, Fla.; Mark Davis, rhp, Rice; Isnardo Decastro, 1b-of, Florida Bible Christian, Sunrise, Fla.; Lesley Dennis, ss, Portland; Douglas Dixon, rhp, Northside HS, Belhaven, N.C.; William Duncan, c, Burlington Edison HS, Burlington, Wash.; Darrell Einertson, rhp, Iowa Wesleyan; Jason Ellison, rhp, Navarro College; Scott Emmons, c, Cal.-Riverside; Peter Fisher, rhp, Stoneham (Mass.) HS; Phillip Haigler, rhp, Vanderbilt; Michael Hamm, c, Shoals CC; Scott Hardesty, rhp, Illinois; Lance Hawkins, cf, Lake Charles–Boston HS, Lake Charles, La.; Brandon Hemmings, cf, Columbus (Ga.) HS; Brian Hervey, rhp, Tallahassee CC; Joshua Hochgesang, ss, Sunny Hills HS, Fullerton, Calif.; Jared Hoerman, rhp, Plainview HS, Armore, Okla.; Joseph Horgan, lhp, Cordova (Calif.) HS; Jason Imrisek, c, Evansville; Brandon James, cf, Sacramento CC; Jeremiah Johnson, rhp, Homer (Minn.) HS; Michael Judd, rhp, Grossmont College; Danny Kanell, rhp, Florida State; Scott Kingston, 1b, Columbus (Ga.) HS; Nathan Koepke, rf-cf, Long Beach CC; Jerry Lail, rhp, Wingate College; Mike Lowell, 2b-c, Florida International; Cody McCormick, c, California; Donzell McDonald, of-cf, Yavapai College; Ryan Mills, lhp, Horizon HS, Scottsdale, Ariz.; Shea Morenz, rf, Texas; Benjamin Phillips, rhp, Howard College; Denis Pujals, rhp, Miami; Stephen Randolph, lhp, Texas; Jason Ryan, lhp, Indian River CC; Jeffrey Saffer, of, Pima CC; Michael Schnautz, lhp, San Jacinto College North; Charles Shipp, cf, Chicago Vocational HS; William Snellings, lhp, Seminole (Fla.) HS; Michael Spence, rhp, Lake City CC; Timothy Spindler, rhp-ss, Orange County CC; Bobby St. Pierre, rhp, Richmond; Jay Tessmer, rhp, Miami; Daniel Thomas, rhp, Poway (Calif.) HS; Charles Thomas, rf, Harlan (Ky.) Sr. HS; Lateef Vaughn, ss, Southwestern College; Cesar Verdin, lhp, Crawford HS, San Diego; Daniel Washburn, rhp, Nova HS, Pembroke Pines, Fla.; Christopher Wilcox, rf, Western Michigan; Bradford Williams, lhp, Sabino HS, Tucson, Ariz.; Jason Wright, rhp, Martinsville (Ind.) HS; Jake Zajc, rhp, Bradley-Bourbonnais HS, Bourbonnais, Ill.

Minor Leagues

Tops in the organization

Batter	Club	Avg.	G	AB	R	H	HR	RBI
Derek Jeter	Col	.317	123	486	96	154	2	45
Daniel Donato	Tam	.316	111	395	56	125	8	70
Don Sparks	Col	.312	137	545	67	170	7	90
Shane Spencer	Tam	.300	134	500	87	150	16	88
Brian Turner	Nrw	.296	86	311	39	92	4	43

Home Runs			Wins		
Ruben Rivera	Col	24	Matthew Drews	Tam	15
Nick Delvecchio	Nrw	19	Brett Schlomann	Tam	12
Tyrone Horne	Nrw	16	David Meyer	Gbo	11
Shane Spencer	Tam	16	Kent Wallace	Col	11
Several tied		14	Marty Janzen	Nrw	11

RBI			Saves		
Don Sparks	Col	90	Chris Corn	Tam	24
Shane Spencer	Tam	88	Dan Rios	Tam	24
Ruben Rivera	Col	74	Jay Tessmer	One	20
Nick Delvecchio	Nrw	74	Mike DeJean	Nrw	20
Daniel Donato	Tam	70	Dave Pavlas	Col	18

Stolen Bases			Strikeouts		
Rod Smith	One	41	Ray Ricken	Nrw	178
Kraig Hawkins	Tam	35	Brett Schlomann	Tam	145
R.D. Long	Tam	30	Matthew Drews	Tam	140
Andy Fox	Col	30	Rafael Medina	Tam	133
Robert Hinds	Nrw	27	Marty Janzen	Nrw	120

Pitcher	Club	W-L	ERA	IP	H	BB	SO
Matthew Drews	Tam	15-7	2.27	182	142	58	140
Ray Ricken	Nrw	10-8	2.33	193	133	67	178
S. Shoemaker	Tam	4-5	2.76	98	71	65	94
B. Boehringer	Col	8-6	2.77	104	101	31	58
Marty Janzen	Nrw	11-5	2.96	134	119	37	120

New York (1903-1995)

86

Runs: Most, career, all-time

1959	Babe Ruth,	1920-1934
1888	Lou Gehrig,	1923-1939
1677	Mickey Mantle,	1951-1968
1390	Joe DiMaggio,	1936-1951
1186	Earle Combs,	1924-1935

Hits: Most, career, all-time

2721	Lou Gehrig,	1923-1939
2518	Babe Ruth,	1920-1934
2415	Mickey Mantle,	1951-1968
2214	Joe DiMaggio,	1936-1951
2153	DON MATTINGLY,	1982-1994

2B: Most, career, all-time

534	Lou Gehrig,	1923-1939
442	DON MATTINGLY,	1982-1995
424	Babe Ruth,	1920-1934
389	Joe DiMaggio,	1936-1951
344	Mickey Mantle,	1951-1968

3B: Most, career, all-time

163	Lou Gehrig,	1923-1939
154	Earle Combs,	1924-1935
131	Joe DiMaggio,	1936-1951
121	Wally Pipp,	1915-1925
115	Tony Lazzeri,	1926-1937

HR: Most, career, all-time

659	Babe Ruth,	1920-1934
536	Mickey Mantle,	1951-1968
493	Lou Gehrig,	1923-1939
361	Joe DiMaggio,	1936-1951
358	Yogi Berra,	1946-1963

RBI: Most, career, all-time

1995	Lou Gehrig,	1923-1939
1971	Babe Ruth,	1920-1934
1537	Joe DiMaggio,	1936-1951
1509	Mickey Mantle,	1951-1968
1430	Yogi Berra,	1946-1963

SB: Most, career, all-time

326	RICKEY HENDERSON,	1985-1989
251	Willie Randolph,	1976-1988
248	Hal Chase,	1905-1913
233	Roy White,	1965-1979
184	Ben Chapman,	1930-1936
184	Wid Conroy,	1903-1908

BB: Most, career, all-time

1847	Babe Ruth,	1920-1934
1733	Mickey Mantle,	1951-1968
1508	Lou Gehrig,	1923-1939
1005	Willie Randolph,	1976-1988
934	Roy White,	1965-1979

BA: Highest, career, all-time

.349	Babe Ruth,	1920-1934
.340	Lou Gehrig,	1923-1939
.325	Earle Combs,	1924-1935
.325	Joe DiMaggio,	1936-1951
.313	Bill Dickey,	1928-1946

Slug avg: Highest, career, all-time

.711	Babe Ruth,	1920-1934
.632	Lou Gehrig,	1923-1939
.579	Joe DiMaggio,	1936-1951
.557	Mickey Mantle,	1951-1968
.526	Reggie Jackson,	1977-1981

Games started: Most, career, all-time

438	Whitey Ford,	1950-1967
391	Red Ruffing,	1930-1946
356	Mel Stottlemyre,	1964-1974
323	Ron Guidry,	1975-1988
319	Lefty Gomez,	1930-1942

Saves: Most, career, all-time

224	DAVE RIGHETTI,	1979-1990
151	Rich Gossage,	1978-1989
141	Sparky Lyle,	1972-1978
104	Johnny Murphy,	1932-1946
78	Steve Farr,	1991-1993

Shutouts: Most, career, all-time

45	Whitey Ford,	1950-1967
40	Red Ruffing,	1930-1946
40	Mel Stottlemyre,	1964-1974
28	Lefty Gomez,	1930-1942
27	Allie Reynolds,	1947-1954

Wins: Most, career, all-time

236	Whitey Ford,	1950-1967
231	Red Ruffing,	1930-1946
189	Lefty Gomez,	1930-1942
170	Ron Guidry,	1975-1988
168	Bob Shawkey,	1915-1927

K: Most, career, all-time

1956	Whitey Ford,	1950-1967
1778	Ron Guidry,	1975-1988
1526	Red Ruffing,	1930-1946
1468	Lefty Gomez,	1930-1942
1257	Mel Stottlemyre,	1964-1974

Win pct: Highest, career, all-time

.725	Johnny Allen,	1932-1935
.717	Spud Chandler,	1937-1947
.706	Vic Raschi,	1946-1953
.700	Monte Pearson,	1936-1940
.690	Whitey Ford,	1950-1967

ERA: Lowest, career, all-time

2.54	Russ Ford,	1909-1913
2.58	Jack Chesbro,	1903-1909
2.72	Al Orth,	1904-1909
2.73	Tiny Bonham,	1940-1946
2.73	George Mogridge,	1915-1920

Runs: Most, season

177	Babe Ruth,	1921
167	Lou Gehrig,	1936
163	Lou Gehrig,	1931
163	Babe Ruth,	1928
158	Babe Ruth,	1920
158	Babe Ruth,	1927

Hits: Most, season

238	DON MATTINGLY,	1986
231	Earle Combs,	1927
220	Lou Gehrig,	1930
218	Lou Gehrig,	1927
215	Joe DiMaggio,	1937

2B: Most, season

53	DON MATTINGLY,	1986
52	Lou Gehrig,	1927
48	DON MATTINGLY,	1985
47	Lou Gehrig,	1926
47	Lou Gehrig,	1928
47	Bob Meusel,	1927

3B: Most, season

23	Earle Combs,	1927
22	Earle Combs,	1930
22	Birdie Cree,	1911
22	Snuffy Stirnweiss,	1945
21	Earle Combs,	1928

HR: Most, season

61	Roger Maris,	1961
60	Babe Ruth,	1927
59	Babe Ruth,	1921
54	Mickey Mantle,	1961
54	Babe Ruth,	1920
54	Babe Ruth,	1928

RBI: Most, season

184	Lou Gehrig,	1931
175	Lou Gehrig,	1927
174	Lou Gehrig,	1930
171	Babe Ruth,	1921
167	Joe DiMaggio,	1937

SB: Most, season

93	RICKEY HENDERSON,	1988
87	RICKEY HENDERSON,	1986
80	RICKEY HENDERSON,	1985
74	Fritz Maisel,	1914
61	Ben Chapman,	1931

BB: Most, season

170	Babe Ruth, 1923
148	Babe Ruth, 1920
146	Mickey Mantle, 1957
144	Babe Ruth, 1921
144	Babe Ruth, 1926

BA: Highest, season

.393	Babe Ruth, 1923
.381	Joe DiMaggio, 1939
.379	Lou Gehrig, 1930
.378	Babe Ruth, 1924
.378	Babe Ruth, 1921

Slug avg: Highest, season

.847	Babe Ruth, 1920
.846	Babe Ruth, 1921
.772	Babe Ruth, 1927
.765	Lou Gehrig, 1927
.764	Babe Ruth, 1923

Games started: Most, season

51	Jack Chesbro, 1904
45	Jack Powell, 1904
42	Jack Chesbro, 1906
39	Pat Dobson, 1974
39	Whitey Ford, 1961
39	Catfish Hunter, 1975
39	Al Orth, 1906
39	Mel Stottlemyre, 1969
39	Ralph Terry, 1962

Saves: Most, season

46	DAVE RIGHETTI, 1986
36	DAVE RIGHETTI, 1990
35	Sparky Lyle, 1972
33	Rich Gossage, 1980
31	DAVE RIGHETTI, 1984
31	DAVE RIGHETTI, 1987
31	JOHN WETTELAND, 1995

Shutouts: Most, season

9	Ron Guidry, 1978
8	Whitey Ford, 1964
8	Russ Ford, 1910
7	Whitey Ford, 1958
7	Catfish Hunter, 1975
7	Allie Reynolds, 1951
7	Mel Stottlemyre, 1971
7	Mel Stottlemyre, 1972

Wins: Most, season

41	Jack Chesbro, 1904
27	Carl Mays, 1921
27	Al Orth, 1906
26	Joe Bush, 1922
26	Russ Ford, 1910
26	Lefty Gomez, 1934
26	Carl Mays, 1920

K: Most, season

248	Ron Guidry, 1978
239	Jack Chesbro, 1904
218	MELIDO PEREZ, 1992
217	Al Downing, 1964
210	Bob Turley, 1955

Win pct: Highest, season

.893	Ron Guidry, 1978
.862	Whitey Ford, 1961
.842	Ralph Terry, 1961
.839	Lefty Gomez, 1934
.833	Spud Chandler, 1943

ERA: Lowest, season

1.64	Spud Chandler, 1943
1.65	Russ Ford, 1910
1.74	Ron Guidry, 1978
1.82	Jack Chesbro, 1904
1.83	Hippo Vaughn, 1910

Most pinch-hit homers season

4	Johnny Blanchard, 1961

Most pinch-hit homers, career

9	Yogi Berra, 1946-1963

Most consecutive games batting safely

56	Joe DiMaggio, 1941
33	Hal Chase, 1907

Most consecutive scoreless innings

33	Jack Aker, 1969

No-hit games

Tom L. Hughes, NY vs Cle AL, 0-5; August 30, 1910 (2nd game) (lost on 7 hits in 11 innings after allowing the first hit in the 10th).

George Mogridge, NY at Bos AL, 2-1; April 24, 1917.

Sam Jones, NY at Phi AL, 2-0; September 4, 1923.

Monte Pearson, NY vs Cle AL, 13-0; August 27, 1938 (2nd game).

Allie Reynolds, NY at Cle AL, 1-0; July 12, 1951.

Allie Reynolds, NY vs Bos AL, 8-0; September 28, 1951 (1st game).

Don Larsen, NY AL vs Bro NL, 2-0; October 8, 1956 (World Series, perfect game).

DAVE RIGHETTI, NY vs Bos AL, 4-0; July 4, 1983.

JIM ABBOTT, NY vs Cle AL, 4-0; September 4, 1993.

Andy Hawkins, NY at Chi AL, 0-4; July 1, 1990 (8 innings, lost the game; bottom of 9th not played).

ACTIVE PLAYERS in caps.

Players' years of service are listed by the first and last years with this team and are not necessarily consecutive; all statistics record performances for this team only.

Baltimore Orioles

By Russell Beeker, *Baseball Weekly*

Rafael Palmiero led the Oriole offense at .310 with 39 homers and 104 RBI.

1995 Orioles: The big disappointment

Picked by some to win the American League East or at least to give the Yankees a serious run for their money, the O's slipped to a 71-73 record—and that was only after winning 11 of their last 13 games, including five consecutive shutouts to end the season.

The third-place finish—15 games behind—cost first-year manager Phil Regan and veteran general manager Roland Hemond their jobs. Regan was fired with one year left on his contract, while Hemond resigned under pressure.

Despite the lack of success, the Orioles did provide baseball with its brightest shining moment Sept. 5-6, when shortstop Cal Ripken tied, then broke Lou Gehrig's "unbreakable" record of 2,130 consecutive games. In the middle of the fifth inning, when the game became official, Ripken was given a 22-minute standing ovation and responded with eight curtain calls from the dugout and a victory lap around the field at Camden Yards. Myriad celebrities, from Hank Aaron to Joe DiMaggio, joined Ripken on the field for postgame festivities. And just to put an exclamation point on the entire affair, Ripken hit a home run in both games.

Giddy moments such as that were few and far between, though. Despite a payroll of $42 million, the Orioles spent just three days above .500. A 10-16 start put them behind the eight ball for the first month of the season.

At one point, the Orioles had $12 million worth of pitchers on the disabled list simultaneously. Ben McDonald won just three games, while Kevin Brown (10-9, 3.60) went two months without a victory in midseason.

Injury-plagued outfielder Jeffrey Hammonds, third baseman Leo Gomez and catcher Chris Hoiles also missed significant time.

"I don't feel too bad personally about the job we've done here," Regan said. "We played as well as we could play with all the injuries."

To be sure, there was some individual brilliance. First baseman Rafael Palmeiro hit .310 with a career-high 39 home runs and 104 RBI. Mike Mussina (19-9, 3.29 ERA) led the league in victories and shutouts (four). Ripken (.262-17-88) finished the year with 2,153 consecutive games and played the final 70 games in the national spotlight without making an error. The game's goodwill ambassador also signed about five zillion consecutive autographs. Bobby Bonilla hit .333 in 61 games after the Orioles acquired him from the Mets on July 29. Harold Baines quietly hit .299 with 24 home runs.

And, despite the shortened season, the O's drew 3,098,475 in 72 home dates (average 43,034) to lead the AL. Their average crowd was 17,759 more than the rest of the league (25,275).

1996 Orioles: Preview

The Orioles will get a fresh start with new manager Davey Johnson, formerly a Gold Glove second baseman with the O's and a successful manager with the Mets and Reds (.576 winning percentage, highest among active managers).

"We're going to win next year," he promised when he was hired Oct. 30. "And we're going to win a world championship while I'm here. This ball club coming out of spring training should be the odds-on favorite to win our division."

This season, the Orioles will have Bonilla and pitcher Scott Erickson (13-10, 4.81) for the full season. And Hoiles has to bounce back from an off-year. If Mussina throws a complete-game shutout on Opening Day against the Royals, the Orioles will tie their league record of 54 consecutive scoreless innings.

1995 Orioles: Week-by-week notes

These notes were excerpted from the following issues of Baseball Weekly.

▶**May 3:** The Orioles' bullpen allowed 36 baserunners in 13⅓ innings, allowed 10 of 19 inherited runners to score and posted a 12.15 ERA.

▶**May 10:** Rookie Armando Benitez allowed just four hits in 7⅔ innings during his first seven games.

▶**May 24:** Arthur Rhodes and Sid Fernandez were struggling—Rhodes lasted only three innings and Fernandez 2⅓ in back-to-back starts at Yankee Stadium. After a rocky start, the bullpen went 2-2 in a 14-game stretch May 4-20, with a 1.84 ERA, and converted four of five saves.

▶**May 31:** The Orioles recorded two dubious feats in two days, matching a club record by allowing 14 walks in Oakland on May 25 and setting a club mark by striking out 17 times in Seattle May 26.

▶**June 7:** The Orioles put together their longest winning streak of the season after pitcher Mike Mussina questioned the heart of the team and Rafael Palmeiro bought T-shirts that said, "It's not how good you are. It's how bad you want it."

▶**June 14:** Jeff Manto, the Orioles' third baseman, became only the 24th player in major league history to hit home runs in four consecutive at-bats. He had only four career homers before the season started.

▶**June 21:** Just when it appeared they were ready to make a run at first place, the Orioles lost a season-high seven consecutive games, including three in Cleveland in which they were outscored 20-5. "This definitely stinks, to say the least," third baseman Jeff Manto said. "If we were losing once in a while, that would be fine. But you've got to watch it before it becomes a habit." Mike Mussina and Ben McDonald had combined to win only seven of their first 21 starts, and Kevin Brown lost three in a row after opening the season 5-2.

▶**June 28:** Another week, another set of faces. Catcher Greg Zaun replaced the released Matt Nokes; reliever Gene Harris replaced the demoted Alan Mills; relievers Jimmy Myers and Armando Benitez replaced Brown and McDonald. Nokes left with harsh words, saying, "I'm out on parole," complaining that he didn't know his role and accusing the front office of lacking a plan. Manager Phil Regan said Nokes didn't work hard enough on his hitting.

▶**July 5:** Center fielder Curtis Goodwin was emerging as a Rookie of the Year candidate, even though he didn't join the club until June 2. The lefty had two or more hits in 16 of his first 30 games and also stole 11 bases. He reached 40 hits faster than any rookie in Orioles history and hit his first homer—an opposite-field shot off left-hander Al Leiter—on July 1. On the opposite end of the scale, veteran left-hander Sid Fernandez said he was considering retirement after yielding three homers in 3⅔ innings in a 5-0 loss to Toronto on July 29. "Maybe it's over. Maybe it's done and time to get out of the way," said Fernandez, who had not won since July 1994 and stood at 0-4 with a 7.67 ERA for 1995.

▶**July 13:** The Orioles entered the All-Star break on a 14-7 run and planned to activate pitchers Kevin Brown and Ben McDonald, as well as third baseman Jeff Manto, from the disabled list when the season resumed. The club went 11-5 without Brown and McDonald, two of its top starters, to move within six games of first-place Boston for the first time since May 28. They gained ground with three rookie starters—John DeSilva, Rick Krivda and Scott Klingenbeck, who has since has been traded to Minnesota.

▶**Aug. 16:** The trip to New York and Boston was make-or-break, but after going 1-6, the Orioles' postseason chances were in serious jeopardy. They trailed the Red Sox by 14 games in the AL East and dropped to sixth place in the wild-card race, 4½ games behind Texas. Bobby Bonilla drove in nine runs in his first 14 games with the club but also was forced to play three positions—right field, left field and third base.

▶**Aug. 23:** Newcomer Bobby Bonilla called a players-only meeting to discuss pitches thrown at Rafael Palmeiro during the ninth inning of the Orioles' 8-4 victory against Oakland on Aug. 18. The game included four hit batsmen, two on each club. Afterward, the Orioles blamed Oakland manager Tony La Russa for the alleged brushbacks. "It was obvious," said Palmeiro, "which is fine. If that's the way La Russa is going to play, he's going to get somebody on his team killed."

▶**Aug. 30:** In a span of two days, the Orioles released a former replacement player after promoting him to the majors, then lost their Class AAA shortstop because he, too, was a former replacement player. Owner Peter Angelos, who refused to use replacement players in spring training, said, "The signing and promotion of a replacement player would be inconsistent with our stated policy."

▶**Sept. 6:** Cal Ripken grew emotional about the fifth-inning ovations he got at Camden Yards as he began his final countdown to Lou Gehrig's consecutive-games record. "They make you feel really good," Ripken said of the nightly ovations. "They almost make you want to cry sometimes when you start to think about it." The Orioles posted the numbers of how many games his streak had reached on the warehouse, then changed them when each game became official. Ripken appeared to get emotional for the first time on Aug. 31, when Oakland manager Tony La Russa stood in the dugout clapping.

▶**Sept. 27:** The day after he broke Lou Gehrig's consecutive-game record, Cal Ripken went into a dreadful slump, going 3-for-44 over the next two weeks.

▶**Oct. 4:** Mike Mussina hurled his final shutout on the last day of the season. He also began the team's shutout streak by blanking the Blue Jays on Sept. 26. Capping a wonderful season for the 26-year-old hurler, the Oct. 1 two-hitter gave Mussina the lead league in victories (19) and shutouts (four).

In his final 21 starts, the Orioles ace went 14-4 with a 2.45 ERA. He finished fourth in the AL with a 3.29 ERA and was second in innings pitched (221⅔).

Team directory

▶**Owner:** Peter Angelos
▶**General manager:** Pat Gillick
▶**Ballpark:**
Oriole Park at Camden Yards
Baltimore, Md.
410-685-9800
Capacity 48,262
Pay parking for over 5,000 cars
Public transportation available
Disability seating, ramps, elevators, sound-amplification devices for the hearing impaired, special menu selection board for the speaking-impaired
▶**Team publications:**
Orioles Magazine, media guide, yearbook
410-685-9800
▶**TV, radio broadcast stations:**
WBAL 1090 AM, Home Team
 Sports Cable, WJZ Channel 13
▶**Camps and/or clinics:**
Fantasy Camp (ages 30+), February, 410-799-0005
Cal Ripken Sr. Baseball School
(ages 8-18), Mount St. Mary's, Emmitsburg, Md., late June
and early July, 301-791-3512
Elrod Hendricks Camp, McDonough School, McDonough, Md., July, 410-685-9800
Summer clinics, the Orioles region, during the season, 410-685-9800
▶**Spring training:**
Al Lang Stadium
St. Petersburg, Fla.
Capacity 6,500
813-893-7490

BALTIMORE ORIOLES 1995 final stats

BATTERS	BA	SLG	OB	G	AB	R	H	TB	2B	3B	HR	RBI	BB	SO	SB	CS	E
Bonilla	.333	.544	.392	61	237	47	79	129	12	4	10	46	23	31	0	2	5
Palmeiro	.310	.583	.380	143	554	89	172	323	30	2	39	104	62	65	3	1	4
Baines	.299	.540	.403	127	385	60	115	208	19	1	24	63	70	45	0	2	0
Obando	.263	.289	.293	16	38	0	10	11	1	0	0	3	2	12	1	0	1
Goodwin	.263	.332	.301	87	289	40	76	96	11	3	1	24	15	53	22	4	2
Ripken	.262	.422	.324	144	550	71	144	232	33	2	17	88	52	59	0	1	7
Anderson	.262	.444	.371	143	554	108	145	246	33	10	16	64	87	111	26	7	3
Zaun	.260	.394	.358	40	104	18	27	41	5	0	3	14	16	14	1	1	3
Manto	.256	.492	.325	89	254	31	65	125	9	0	17	38	24	69	0	3	6
Hoiles	.250	.460	.373	114	352	53	88	162	15	1	19	58	67	80	1	0	3
Huson	.248	.317	.315	66	161	24	40	51	4	2	1	19	15	20	5	4	1
Bass	.244	.336	.303	111	295	32	72	99	12	0	5	32	24	47	8	8	2
Hammonds	.242	.371	.279	57	178	18	43	66	9	1	4	23	9	30	4	2	1
Barberie	.241	.325	.351	90	237	32	57	77	14	0	2	25	36	50	3	3	7
Gomez	.236	.370	.336	53	127	16	30	47	5	0	4	12	18	23	0	1	2
Alexander	.236	.318	.299	94	242	35	57	77	9	1	3	23	20	30	11	4	10
Smith	.231	.365	.314	37	104	11	24	38	5	0	3	15	12	22	3	0	0
Van Slyke	.159	.317	.221	17	63	6	10	20	1	0	3	8	5	15	0	0	1
J. Brown	.148	.185	.324	18	27	2	4	5	1	0	0	1	7	9	1	1	0
Nokes	.122	.265	.185	26	49	4	6	13	1	0	2	6	4	11	0	0	1
Buford	.063	.063	.205	24	32	6	2	2	0	0	0	2	6	7	3	1	0
Devarez	.000	.000	.000	6	4	0	0	0	0	0	0	0	0	0	0	0	0

PITCHERS	W-L	ERA	G	GS	CG	GF	Sho	SV	IP	H	R	ER	HR	BB	SO
Borowski	0-0	1.23	6	0	0	3	0	0	7.1	5	1	1	0	4	3
Haynes	2-1	2.25	4	3	0	0	0	0	24.0	11	6	6	2	12	22
Dedrick	0-0	2.35	6	0	0	1	0	0	7.2	8	2	2	1	6	3
Orosco	2-4	3.26	65	0	0	23	0	3	49.2	28	19	18	4	27	58
Mussina	19-9	3.29	32	32	7	0	4	0	221.2	187	86	81	24	50	158
Clark	2-5	3.46	38	0	0	12	0	1	39.0	40	15	15	3	15	18
K. Brown	10-9	3.60	26	26	3	0	1	0	172.1	155	73	69	10	48	117
McDonald	3-6	4.16	14	13	1	1	0	0	80.0	67	40	37	10	38	62
Oquist	2-1	4.17	27	0	0	2	0	0	54.0	51	27	25	6	41	27
Harris	0-0	4.50	3	0	0	0	0	0	4.0	4	2	2	0	1	4
Krivda	2-7	4.54	13	13	1	0	0	0	75.1	76	40	38	9	25	53
Erickson	13-10	4.81	32	31	7	1	2	0	196.1	213	108	105	18	67	106
Lee	2-0	4.86	39	0	0	7	0	1	33.1	31	18	18	5	18	27
Jones	0-4	5.01	52	0	0	47	0	22	46.2	55	30	26	6	16	42
Hartley	1-0	5.14	8	0	0	2	0	0	14.0	13	8	8	1	3	6
Moyer	8-6	5.21	27	18	0	3	0	0	115.2	117	70	67	18	30	65
Benitez	1-5	5.66	44	0	0	18	0	2	47.2	37	33	30	8	37	56
Rhodes	2-5	6.21	19	9	0	3	0	0	75.1	68	53	52	13	48	77
DeSilva	1-0	7.27	2	2	0	0	0	0	8.2	8	7	7	3	7	1
Fernandez	0-4	7.39	8	7	0	1	0	0	28.0	36	26	23	9	17	31
Mills	3-0	7.43	21	0	0	1	0	0	23.0	30	20	19	4	18	16
Pennington	0-1	8.10	8	0	0	2	0	0	6.2	3	7	6	1	11	10

1996 preliminary roster

PITCHERS (19)
Armando Benitez
Joe Borowski
Terry Clark
Scott Erickson
Mike Hartley
Jimmy Haynes
Rick Krivda
Aaron Lane
Mark Lee
Calvin Maduro
Ben McDonald
Alan Mills

Oscar Munoz
Mike Mussina
Jesse Orosco
Billy Percibal
Arthur Rhodes
Brian Sackinsky
Garrett Stephenson

CATCHERS (4)
Cesar Devarez
Chris Hoiles
B.J. Wazsgis
Gregg Zaun

INFIELDERS (11)
Manny Alexander
Bret Barberie
Juan Bautista
Bobby Bonilla
Leo Gomez
Jeff Huson
Jeff Manto
Scott McClain
Rafael Palmeiro
Cal Ripken
Brad Tyler

OUTFIELDERS (6)
Brady Anderson
Kimera Bartee
Curtis Goodwin
Jeffrey Hammonds
Sherman Obando
Mark Smith

Games played by position

PLAYER	G	C	1B	2B	3B	SS	OF	DH
Alexander	94	0	0	81	2	7	0	1
Anderson	143	0	0	0	0	0	142	0
Baines	127	0	0	0	0	0	0	122
Barberie	90	0	0	74	3	0	0	5
Bass	111	0	0	0	0	0	77	19
Bonilla	61	0	0	0	24	0	39	0
J. Brown	18	0	0	0	0	0	17	0
Buford	24	0	0	0	0	0	24	0
Devarez	6	6	0	0	0	0	0	0
Gomez	53	0	3	0	44	0	0	5
Goodwin	87	0	0	0	0	0	84	3
Hammonds	57	0	0	0	0	0	46	5
Hoiles	114	107	0	0	0	0	0	6
Huson	66	0	0	21	33	1	0	3
Manto	89	0	4	0	69	0	0	13
Nokes	26	16	0	0	0	0	0	2
Obando	16	0	0	0	0	0	7	7
Palmeiro	143	0	142	0	0	0	0	0
Ripken	144	0	0	0	0	144	0	0
Smith	37	0	0	0	0	0	32	3
Van Slyke	17	0	0	0	0	0	17	0
Zaun	40	39	0	0	0	0	0	1

Sick call: 1995 DL Report

Player	Days on the DL
Jarvis Brown	24
Mark Eichhorn	160
Sid Fernandez	23
Leo Gomez	63
Curtis Goodwin	15
Jeffrey Hammonds	47
Gene Harris	99
Chris Hoiles	15
Jeff Manto	17
Ben McDonald	80*
Arthur Rhodes	38
Andy VanSlyke	31

Indicates two separate terms on Disabled List.

1995 Amateur draft picks

Players are listed with position and college or high school. Most players were assigned to rookie or Class A leagues. List provided by Major League Baseball.

Matthew Achilles, rhp, Black Hawk JC; Lawrence Adams, 1b, Creekside HS, Fairburn, Ga.; Carlos Akins, cf, Western Kentucky; Jason Albert, 2b, Central Connecticut State; William Alley, c, Palm Beach (Fla.) Lakes HS; John Bale, lhp, Southern Mississippi; Christopher Bray, rhp, Mount Olive; Christopher Bryant, ss, North Carolina Wesleyan; Carlos Casillas, 1b, St. Monica HS, Los Angeles; Corey Coil, rhp, Francis Scott Key HS, Taneytown, Md.; Michael Cosgrove, rhp, Cypress College; Greg Dean, rhp, Oklahoma State; David Dellucci, cf, Mississippi; Darrell Dent, cf, Montclair Prep HS, Panorama City, Calif.; Gaylon Dixon, lhp, Seminole JC; Scott Eibey, lhp, Northern Iowa; Louis Fisher, rhp, Fremont HS, Oakland, Calif.; Jason Glover, cf, Georgia State; Jerry Hairston, 2b, Naperville (Ill.) North HS; Luke Hudson, rhp, Fountain Valley (Calif.) HS; Johnny Isom, of, Texas Wesleyan; Craig Jones, rhp, La Quinta HS, Westminster, Calif.; Daniel Keller, rhp, Fountain Valley (Calif.) HS; Brion King, lf, Oviedo (Fla.) HS; Jason LeCronier, of, McNeese State; Andrew Marquardt, of, Columbia Basin CC; Kevin Miller, 3b, Ballard HS, Seattle; Darin Moore, rhp, Lodi HS, Acampo, Calif.; Robert Morseman, lhp, Salem Teikyo; William Morstad, 3b, Windsor Academy, Macon, Ga.; Timothy Olszewski, rhp, Triton; Robert O'Toole, c, Providence; Christopher Paxton, c, Palmdale (Calif.) HS; Calvin Pickering, lf-1b, King HS, Terrace, Fla.; Daniel Reed, lhp, Stanford; Thomas Russin, 1b, Eckerd; John Santos, rhp, Corcoran HS, Tulare, Calif.; Cory Scott, rhp, Currituck County HS, Knotts Island, N.C.; Joaquin Serra, ss, no school, Beverly Hills, Calif.; Alvie Shepherd, rhp, Nebraska; Kenneth Sims, rhp, New Mexico JC; Zach Sorensen, ss, Highland HS, Salt Lake City; Joel Stephens, of, Notre Dame HS, Tioga, Pa; Avery Taylor, ss, Long Beach (Miss.) HS; Joshua Taylor, ss, Shawnee (Okla.) HS; Douglas Thompson, rhp, Mississippi Gulf Coast JC; Robert Williams, c, Edgewater HS, Winter Park, Fla.; Wess Winn, ss, Texas; Robert Wooden, rhp, North County HS, Baltimore.

Minor Leagues

Tops in the organization

Batter	Club	Avg.	G	AB	R	H	HR	RBI
Sherman Obando	Roc	.296	85	324	42	96	9	53
T.R. Lewis	Roc	.295	108	387	69	114	9	63
Kevin Curtis	Hds	.293	112	399	70	117	21	70
Ed Fully	Hds	.289	90	304	47	88	9	43
Jim Wawruck	Roc	.288	95	361	50	104	7	53

Home Runs			Wins		
Danny Clyburn	Hds	23	Rocky Coppinger	Roc	16
Scott McClain	Bow	21	Jimmy Haynes	Roc	12
Kevin Curtis	Hds	21	Jimmy Williams	Roc	12
Tommy Davis	Bow	18	Kevin McGehee	Roc	11
Several tied		17	John DeSilva	Roc	11

RBI			Saves		
Billy Owens	Bow	92	Chris Lemp	Bow	23
Scott McClain	Bow	83	Joe Borowski	Roc	13
Danny Clyburn	Hds	82	F. Hernandez	Fre	12
Kim Batiste	Bow	74	Jim Newlin	Bow	11
Kevin Curtis	Hds	70	Several tied		8

Stolen Bases			Strikeouts		
Miguel Mejia	Blu	52	Rocky Coppinger	Roc	172
Rolando Avila	Bow	36	C. Maduro	Bow	146
Trovin Valdez	Fre	34	Rachaad Stewart	Fre	140
Denio Gabriel	Blu	31	Jimmy Haynes	Roc	140
Several tied		23	G. Stephenson	Bow	139

Pitcher	Club	W-L	ERA	IP	H	BB	SO
R. Coppinger	Roc	16-3	1.97	187	127	84	172
Jim Dedrick	Roc	8-2	2.46	106	104	39	79
Billy Percibal	Bow	8-6	2.92	142	130	62	112
Joe Rhodes	Fre	6-4	3.03	107	107	38	78
Brad Crills	Fre	6-7	3.03	98	97	25	58

Baltimore (1954-1995), includes St. Louis (1902-1953)

Runs: Most, career, all-time

1272	CAL RIPKEN JR., 1981-1995	
1232	Brooks Robinson, 1955-1977	
1091	George Sisler, 1915-1927	
1048	EDDIE MURRAY, 1977-1988	
1013	Harlond Clift, 1934-1943	

Hits: Most, career, all-time

2848	Brooks Robinson, 1955-1977
2371	CAL RIPKEN JR., 1981-1995
2295	George Sisler, 1915-1927
2021	EDDIE MURRAY, 1977-1988
1574	Boog Powell, 1961-1974

2B: Most, career, all-time

482	Brooks Robinson, 1955-1977
447	CAL RIPKEN JR., 1981-1995
351	EDDIE MURRAY, 1977-1988
343	George Sisler, 1915-1927
294	Harlond Clift, 1934-1943

3B: Most, career, all-time

145	George Sisler, 1915-1927
88	Baby Doll Jacobson, 1915-1926
72	Del Pratt, 1912-1917
72	Jack Tobin, 1916-1925
70	Ken Williams, 1918-1927
68	Brooks Robinson, 1955-1977 (6)

HR: Most, career, all-time

333	EDDIE MURRAY, 1977-1988
327	CAL RIPKEN JR., 1981-1995
303	Boog Powell, 1961-1974
268	Brooks Robinson, 1955-1977
185	Ken Williams, 1918-1927

RBI: Most, career, all-time

1357	Brooks Robinson, 1955-1977
1267	CAL RIPKEN JR., 1981-1995
1190	EDDIE MURRAY, 1977-1988
1063	Boog Powell, 1961-1974
959	George Sisler, 1915-1927

SB: Most, career, all-time

351	George Sisler, 1915-1927
252	Al Bumbry, 1972-1984
247	Burt Shotton, 1909-1917
192	Jimmy Austin, 1911-1929
183	BRADY ANDERSON, 1988-1995

BB: Most, career, all-time

986	Harlond Clift, 1934-1943
901	CAL RIPKEN JR., 1981-1995
889	Boog Powell, 1961-1974
886	Ken Singleton, 1975-1984
860	Brooks Robinson, 1955-1977

BA: Highest, career, all-time

.344	George Sisler, 1915-1927
.326	Ken Williams, 1918-1927
.318	Jack Tobin, 1916-1925
.317	Baby Doll Jacobson, 1915-1926
.309	Bob Dillinger, 1946-1949
.301	Bob Boyd, 1956-1960 (8)

Slug avg: Highest, career, all-time

.558	Ken Williams, 1918-1927
.543	Frank Robinson, 1966-1971
.512	Jim Gentile, 1960-1963
.500	EDDIE MURRAY, 1977-1988
.486	Bob Nieman, 1951-1959

Games started: Most, career, all-time

521	Jim Palmer, 1965-1984
384	Dave McNally, 1962-1974
328	Mike Flanagan, 1975-1992
309	Scott McGregor, 1976-1988
283	Mike Cuellar, 1969-1976

Saves: Most, career, all-time

160	GREGG OLSON, 1988-1993
105	Tippy Martinez, 1976-1986
100	Stu Miller, 1963-1967
74	Eddie Watt, 1966-1973
58	Dick Hall, 1961-1971

Shutouts: Most, career, all-time

53	Jim Palmer, 1965-1984
33	Dave McNally, 1962-1974
30	Mike Cuellar, 1969-1976
27	Jack Powell, 1902-1912
26	Milt Pappas, 1957-1965

Wins: Most, career, all-time

268	Jim Palmer, 1965-1984
181	Dave McNally, 1962-1974
143	Mike Cuellar, 1969-1976
141	Mike Flanagan, 1975-1992
138	Scott McGregor, 1976-1988

K: Most, career, all-time

2212	Jim Palmer, 1965-1984
1476	Dave McNally, 1962-1974
1297	Mike Flanagan, 1975-1992
1011	Mike Cuellar, 1969-1976
944	Milt Pappas, 1957-1965

Win pct: Highest, career, all-time

.703	MIKE MUSSINA, 1991-1995
.638	Jim Palmer, 1965-1984
.620	Wally Bunker, 1963-1968
.619	Dick Hall, 1961-1971
.619	Mike Cuellar, 1969-1976

ERA: Lowest, career, all-time

2.06	Harry Howell, 1904-1910
2.52	Fred Glade, 1904-1907
2.62	Barney Pelty, 1903-1912
2.63	Jack Powell, 1902-1912
2.67	Carl Weilman, 1912-1920
2.86	Jim Palmer, 1965-1984 (6)

Runs: Most, season

145	Harlond Clift, 1936
137	George Sisler, 1920
134	George Sisler, 1922
132	Jack Tobin, 1921
128	Ken Williams, 1922
122	Frank Robinson, 1966 (7)

Hits: Most, season

257	George Sisler, 1920
246	George Sisler, 1922
241	Heinie Manush, 1928
236	Jack Tobin, 1921
224	George Sisler, 1925
211	CAL RIPKEN JR., 1983 (10)

2B: Most, season

51	Beau Bell, 1937
49	George Sisler, 1920
47	Heinie Manush, 1928
47	CAL RIPKEN JR., 1983
47	Joe Vosmik, 1937

3B: Most, season

20	Heinie Manush, 1928
20	George Stone, 1906
18	George Sisler, 1920
18	George Sisler, 1921
18	George Sisler, 1922
18	Jack Tobin, 1921
12	Paul Blair, 1967 (24)

HR: Most, season

49	Frank Robinson, 1966
46	Jim Gentile, 1961
39	RAFAEL PALMEIRO, 1995
39	Boog Powell, 1964
39	Ken Williams, 1922

RBI: Most, season

155	Ken Williams, 1922
141	Jim Gentile, 1961
134	Moose Solters, 1936
124	EDDIE MURRAY, 1985
123	Beau Bell, 1936

SB: Most, season

57	Luis Aparicio, 1964
53	BRADY ANDERSON, 1992
51	George Sisler, 1922
46	Armando Marsans, 1916
45	George Sisler, 1918

BB: Most, season

126	Lu Blue, 1929
121	Roy Cullenbine, 1941
118	Harlond Clift, 1938
118	Burt Shotton, 1915
118	Ken Singleton, 1975

BA: Highest, season

.420	George Sisler, 1922
.407	George Sisler, 1920
.378	Heinie Manush, 1928
.371	George Sisler, 1921
.358	George Stone, 1906
.328	Ken Singleton, 1977 (*)

Slug avg: Highest, season

.646	Jim Gentile, 1961
.637	Frank Robinson, 1966
.632	George Sisler, 1920
.627	Ken Williams, 1922
.623	Ken Williams, 1923

Games started: Most, season

40	Mike Cuellar, 1970
40	Mike Flanagan, 1978
40	Dave McNally, 1969
40	Dave McNally, 1970
40	Bobo Newsom, 1938
40	Jim Palmer, 1976

Saves: Most, season

37	GREGG OLSON, 1990
36	GREGG OLSON, 1992
34	Don Aase, 1986
31	GREGG OLSON, 1991
29	LEE SMITH, 1994

Shutouts: Most, season

10	Jim Palmer, 1975
8	Steve Barber, 1961
7	Milt Pappas, 1964
6	Fred Glade, 1904
6	Harry Howell, 1906
6	Dave McNally, 1972
6	Jim Palmer, 1969
6	Jim Palmer, 1973
6	Jim Palmer, 1976
6	Jim Palmer, 1978

Wins: Most, season

27	Urban Shocker, 1921
25	Steve Stone, 1980
24	Mike Cuellar, 1970
24	Dave McNally, 1970
24	Urban Shocker, 1922

K: Most, season

232	Rube Waddell, 1908
226	Bobo Newsom, 1938
202	Dave McNally, 1968
199	Jim Palmer, 1970
198	Harry Howell, 1905

Win pct: Highest, season

.808	Alvin Crowder, 1928
.808	Dave McNally, 1971
.800	Jim Palmer, 1969
.792	Wally Bunker, 1964
.783	MIKE MUSSINA, 1992

ERA: Lowest, season

1.59	Barney Pelty, 1906
1.77	Jack Powell, 1906
1.89	Harry Howell, 1908
1.89	Rube Waddell, 1908
1.93	Harry Howell, 1907
1.95	Dave McNally, 1968 (7)

Most pinch-hit homers, season

3	Whitey Herzog, 1962
3	Sam Bowens, 1967
3	Pat Kelly, 1979
3	Jim Dwyer, 1986
3	SAM HORN, 1991

Most pinch-hit homers, career

9	Jim Dwyer, 1980-1988

Most consecutive games batting safely

41	George Sisler, 1922
34	George Sisler, 1925
34	George McQuinn, 1938
24	RAFAEL PALMEIRO, 1994
22	EDDIE MURRAY, 1982
22	Doug DeCinces, 1978-1979

Most consecutive scoreless innings

41	GREGG OLSON, 1989-1990
36	Hal Brown, 1961

No-hit games

Earl Hamilton, StL at Det AL, 5-1; August 30, 1912.

Ernie Koob, StL vs Chi AL, 1-0; May 5, 1917.

Bob Groom, StL vs Chi AL, 3-0; May 6, 1917 (2nd game).

Bobo Newsom, StL vs Bos AL, 1-2; September 18, 1934 (lost on 1 hit in the 10th).

Bobo Holloman, StL vs Phi AL, 6-0; May 6, 1953 (first start in the major leagues).

Hoyt Wilhelm, Bal vs NY AL, 1-0; September 20, 1958.

Steve D. Barber (8⅔ innings) and Stu Miller (⅓ inning) Bal vs Det AL, 1-2; April 30, 1967 (1st game, lost the game).

Tom Phoebus, Bal vs Bos AL, 6-0; April 27, 1968.

Jim Palmer, Bal vs Oak AL, 8-0; August 13, 1969.

Bob Milacki (6 innings), Mike Flanagan (1 inning), Mark WIlliamson, (1 inning) and GREGG OLSON (1 inning), Bal at Oak AL, 2-0; July 13, 1991.

John Whitehead, 6 innings, rain, StL vs Det AL, 4-0; August 5, 1940 (2nd game).

ACTIVE PLAYERS in caps.

Leader from the franchise's current location is included. If not in the top five, leader's rank is listed in parenthesis; asterisk (*) indicates player is not in top 25.

Players' years of service are listed by the first and last years with this team and are not necessarily consecutive; all statistics record performances for this team only.

Detroit Tigers

By Russell Beeker, *Baseball Weekly*

Third baseman Travis Fryman led the Tigers with his bat (.275) and his glove (337 assists).

1995 Tigers: Another second-half slide

By the numbers, it looked like another awful season with another disastrous second half. The Tigers, four games over .500 and three games out of first place at the All-Star break, lost 36 of their next 46 games. They finished 24 games under .500, and they were held out of last place only by the even worse Blue Jays.

They had the worst ERA in club history. They were outscored by nearly 200 runs. They were last in the league in hitting, next to last in pitching, and near the bottom in fielding. They didn't even come close to leading the league in home runs, unless you're talking home runs allowed. Opponents hit nearly .300 against them, and they couldn't even hit .250 themselves.

It was bad.

But there were some successes, considering that they knew they couldn't win and were just trying to progress. They rang out the old—trading Tony Phillips, David Wells, and Mike Henneman and watching Kirk Gibson retire—and rang in the new. By the end of the year, 25-year-old Sean Bergman was the old man and only non-rookie in the starting rotation.

A day after the season ended, Sparky Anderson announced he was leaving the team he had managed for the last 17 years. Tiger fans cheered Anderson at the final home game and saluted Alan Trammell and Lou Whitaker, who finished a record 19th (and final) season together as teammates. Even Tiger Stadium itself seemed to be on the way out, after an agreement with the state and city governments about financing for a new ballpark. By the time the new stadium opens—Opening Day 1998 is the target—the Tigers hope to be on their way toward contending for another championship.

Fifteen of the 45 players who appeared in a Tigers uniform in 1995 were making their major league debuts. Four others still qualified as rookies, and several more just missed. Not all will be back. Among those who showed promise were Bergman (the only pitcher to shut out Boston), Jose Lima (2.25 ERA, .157 opposition batting average in his last five starts), Clint Sodowsky (won two of his first three starts and left with a lead in the other one), C.J. Nitkowski (six scoreless innings one night and five another).

Not all the youngsters proved to be ready. Rudy Pemberton debuted on Opening Day as the left fielder and No. 3 hitter. By the end of May, he was back at Class AAA Toledo for good. Bobby Higginson led the league with 13 outfield assists, but his batting average slipped to .224 by the end of the year, and his 14th and final home run came with more than a month to go in the season. Despite the encouraging finish, Lima had a 6.11 ERA. Despite the one outstanding start, Bergman won only seven times in 28 starts. Despite the couple of good outings, Nitkowski allowed opponents to hit .335 against him.

1996: Tigers: Preview

The rebuilding process will continue, even if occasionally a young player comes in over his head. The team won't change completely, because Cecil Fielder is still signed for big money for another two years. Travis Fryman, who'll be 27 by Opening Day, and Chad Curtis, 28, are also signed. Most of the pitchers who got chances in '95 will get more. High hopes are attached to Justin Thompson, Mike Drumright and others coming up.

Eventually, the rebuilding will pay off and the expectations the Tigers raise with a good first half won't be false ones.

These notes were excerpted from the following issues of Baseball Weekly.

▶**May 3:** The 1995 Tigers started out even worse than the 1994 team that led the majors with 897 strikeouts in 115 games. Through three games in '95, Tiger hitters reached double digits in strikeouts three times in a row. The '94 Tigers fanned in double figures 32 times, but never in three consecutive games.

▶**May 10:** Pitchers were supposed to be the front line of the Tigers' youth movement, but through the first nine games, under-30 pitchers were 0-5 with a 9.00 ERA while the over-30 staff combined to go 3-1, with a 5.25 ERA. Manager Sparky Anderson said he planned to keep pitching the kids. "If you don't find out about the kids, what good are you doing?" Anderson asked. "If you think you can beat Baltimore, Toronto or New York, you ought to be in a sanitarium."

▶**May 17:** Lou Whitaker said he would retire at the end of the season: "I don't have to think twice—I could play; I'm choosing not to play."

▶**May 31:** After surviving for almost two weeks with a nine-man staff, the Tigers called up 24-year-old right-hander Brian Maxcy on May 26 to be their 10th pitcher. He got his first win in his major league debut—Kirk Gibson won it with a two-run pinch homer in the ninth inning.

▶**June 7:** A four-home-run week propelled Cecil Fielder into a tie for the major-league lead.

▶**June 14:** The Tigers won the final three games of their longest trip of the year to finish with a 5-8 record. But they did it in strange fashion. They played the three games in Minnesota without Lou Whitaker and Kirk Gibson, who were hurt, and without Alan Trammell, who was held out by manager Sparky Anderson because of the Metrodome's artificial turf. The Tigers even won one game in which they allowed the Twins 20 baserunners. "Oh, my God, it's almost like losing," said manager Sparky Anderson, who with the win moved within eight of passing Bucky Harris for third-place all-time. "If it takes eight more of these, they can have it. I don't want it."

▶**June 21:** When Felipe Lira made his first major-league start, manager Sparky Anderson said it was "written in stone" that he would never start again. Four starts later, Lira was in the Tiger rotation. In each of his first four starts, he pitched at least five innings and gave up three runs or fewer. He won two starts and left the other two trailing 1-0 and tied 3-3. Meanwhile, Anderson passed former Washington Senators skipper Bucky Harris as the third-winningest manager of all time, with 2,158 victories.

▶**June 28:** The Tigers had been winning, but hardly anyone noticed. On a Saturday night in late June, a crowd of 12,062 was embarrassingly small. "We're making a big deal of it, but we've never had crowds," said Cecil Fielder, a Tiger since 1990. He was right. In 1994, the average attendance was the worst in the American League.

▶**July 5:** The Tigers went to a four-man rotation, at least for the week before the All-Star break and maybe beyond. Felipe Lira would make at least two starts on three days' rest, and David Wells, Mike Moore and Brian Bohanon would make at least one start apiece. After the All-Star Game, manager Sparky Anderson said Sean Bergman would either make it a five-man rotation or replace Bohanon. "Lefty Phillips used to say to me, 'If you use five, which one's the worst?' " Anderson said, referring to his baseball mentor. "He'd say, 'Then why use him?' I believe you should be able to go every four days. If you can't pitch 260 innings a year, what use are you?" Anderson had talked before about trying a four-man rotation—he routinely does it at the start of a season—but this was the first time he had attempted it during the middle of the year.

▶**July 13:** Several players gave Sparky Anderson some credit for the better-than-expected first half. "I think this is the best managing he's done since I've been here," said Travis Fryman, who came to Detroit in 1990. "The way he's handled young players, stayed with guys, he's the best manager in baseball."

▶**July 19:** In spring training, Sparky Anderson refused to manage replacement players. Now he had to decide whether to deal with replacement writers. In the midst of a newspaper strike, *The Detroit News* sent a non-union worker to cover a Tiger game. "He introduced himself, but he never asked me a question," said Anderson, who admitted he was uncomfortable at having a strike-breaker covering his team. Several Tiger players said they wouldn't talk to the replacement writer.

▶**July 26:** Kirk Gibson became the third Tiger veteran to say he'll retire at the end of the season. Mike Henneman said it the day he arrived for spring training. Lou Whitaker followed in May. Another veteran, Alan Trammell, said he wouldn't make a decision on his future until the end of the year.

▶**Aug. 2:** The Tigers lost 13 of 16 games after the All-Star break.

▶**Aug. 30:** Alan Trammell will finish his career as a Tiger—and he won't have any regrets. Cleveland was interested in Trammell as a free agent and might have traded for him in July or August if he had been interested. He could have been on a first-place team, maybe headed for another trip to the World Series. "It's not going to happen," Trammell said. "I don't want to look at my baseball card and see another team at the end. It's not me. I'm a Tiger."

▶**Sept. 6:** As they reached the end of arguably their worst month in 20 years, the Tigers also reached a pair of milestones—Alan Trammell and Lou Whitaker played their 1,914th game together on Aug. 30 in Chicago. They tied the AL record, set by Kansas City's George Brett and Frank White. The major league record is 2,015, set by Billy Williams and Ron Santo of the Cubs. "We'll take it in stride," said Whitaker. "I don't sit back much and think about it." Sparky Anderson didn't think much about managing his 4,000th game, since it was a 14-4 loss to the Indians, but he became the fourth manager in history to manage that many, joining Connie Mack, John McGraw and Bucky Harris.

▶**Sept. 20:** Cecil Fielder hit the 250th home run of his career on Sept. 15.

▶**Oct. 4:** Sparky Anderson ended his Tigers career, but he said he'd like to keep managing next season. "I love being in the dugout," he said. "I truly love it."

Team directory

▶**Owner:** Michael Ilitch
▶**General manager:** Randy Smith
▶**Ballpark:**
Tiger Stadium
2121 Trumbull Ave., Detroit, Mich.
313-962-4000
Capacity 52,416
Pay parking lot (independently owned)
Public transportation available
Wheelchair section, ramps, Group
Sales department
▶**Team publications:**
Scorebook/program
▶**TV, radio broadcast stations:**
WJR 760 AM, WKBO Channel 50,
PASS Cable
▶**Camps and/or clinics:**
Tigers' Fantasy Camp
▶**Spring Training:**
Marchant Stadium
Lakeland, Fla.
Capacity 7,027
813-499-8229

DETROIT TIGERS 1995 final stats

BATTERS	BA	SLG	OB	G	AB	R	H	TB	2B	3B	HR	RBI	BB	SO	SB	CS	E
Penn	.333	.333	.400	3	9	0	3	3	0	0	0	0	1	2	0	0	3
Pemberton	.300	.467	.344	12	30	3	9	14	3	1	0	3	1	5	0	0	0
Whitaker	.293	.518	.372	84	249	36	73	129	14	0	14	44	31	41	4	0	4
Fryman	.275	.409	.347	144	567	79	156	232	21	5	15	81	63	100	4	2	14
Trammell	.269	.350	.345	74	223	28	60	78	12	0	2	23	27	19	3	1	5
Curtis	.268	.435	.349	144	586	96	157	255	29	3	21	67	70	93	27	15	3
Steverson	.262	.405	.340	30	42	11	11	17	0	0	2	6	6	10	2	0	0
Gibson	.260	.449	.358	70	227	37	59	102	12	2	9	35	33	61	9	2	0
Stubbs	.250	.397	.358	62	116	13	29	46	11	0	2	19	19	27	0	1	5
Flaherty	.243	.404	.284	112	354	39	86	143	22	1	11	40	18	47	0	0	11
Fielder	.243	.472	.346	136	494	70	120	233	18	1	31	82	75	116	0	1	5
Clark	.238	.396	.294	27	101	10	24	40	5	1	3	11	8	30	0	0	4
Fletcher	.231	.313	.312	67	182	19	42	57	10	1	1	17	19	27	1	0	0
Tingley	.226	.403	.307	54	124	14	28	50	8	1	4	18	15	38	0	1	2
Higginson	.224	.393	.329	131	410	61	92	161	17	5	14	43	62	107	6	4	4
Gomez	.223	.355	.292	123	431	49	96	153	20	2	11	50	41	96	4	1	15
Nevin	.219	.333	.318	29	96	9	21	32	3	1	2	12	11	27	0	0	2
Cuyler	.205	.307	.271	41	88	15	18	27	1	4	0	5	8	16	2	1	4
Bautista	.203	.314	.237	89	271	28	55	85	9	0	7	27	12	68	4	1	2
White	.188	.229	.188	39	48	3	9	11	2	0	0	2	0	7	1	0	2
Rodriguez	.179	.205	.289	18	39	5	7	8	1	0	0	0	6	10	2	2	2
Hall	.133	.133	.235	7	15	2	2	2	0	0	0	0	2	3	0	0	0
PITCHERS	W-L	ERA	G	GS	CG	GF	Sho	SV	IP	H	R	ER	HR	BB	SO		
Gohr	1-0	0.87	10	0	0	1	0	0	10.1	9	1	1	0	3	12		
Henneman	0-1	1.53	29	0	0	26	0	18	29.1	24	5	5	0	9	24		
Wells	10-3	3.04	18	18	3	0	0	0	130.1	120	54	44	17	37	83		
Christopher	4-0	3.82	36	0	0	11	0	1	61.1	71	28	26	8	14	34		
Lira	9-13	4.31	37	22	0	7	0	1	146.1	151	74	70	17	56	89		
Sodowsky	2-2	5.01	6	6	0	0	0	0	23.1	24	15	13	4	18	14		
Doherty	5-9	5.10	48	2	0	18	0	6	113.0	130	66	64	10	37	46		
Bergman	7-10	5.12	28	28	1	0	1	0	135.1	169	95	77	19	67	86		
Bohanon	1-1	5.54	52	10	0	7	0	1	105.2	121	68	65	10	41	63		
Lima	3-9	6.11	15	15	0	0	0	0	73.2	85	52	50	10	18	37		
Henry	1-0	6.23	10	0	0	6	0	5	8.2	11	6	6	0	10	9		
Boever	5-7	6.39	60	0	0	27	0	3	98.2	128	74	70	17	44	71		
Maxcy	4-5	6.88	41	0	0	14	0	0	52.1	61	48	40	6	31	20		
Nitkowski	1-4	7.09	11	11	0	0	0	0	39.1	53	32	31	7	20	13		
Groom	1-3	7.52	23	4	0	6	0	1	40.2	55	35	34	6	26	23		
Moore	5-15	7.53	25	25	1	0	0	0	132.2	179	118	111	24	68	64		
Blomdahl	0-0	7.77	14	0	0	5	0	1	24.1	36	21	21	5	13	15		
Myers	1-0	9.95	11	0	0	3	0	0	6.1	10	7	7	1	4	4		
Ahearne	0-2	11.70	4	3	0	0	0	0	10.0	20	13	13	2	5	4		
Gardiner	0-0	14.59	9	0	0	1	0	0	12.1	27	20	20	5	2	7		
Whiteside	0-0	14.73	2	0	0	0	0	0	3.2	7	6	6	1	4	2		

1996 preliminary roster

PITCHERS (21)
Sean Bergman
Ben Blomdahl
Joe Boever
Mike Christopher
John Doherty
Greg Gohr
Rick Greene
Greg Keagle
Jose Lima
Felipe Lira
Brian Maxcy
Jeff McCurry
Trever Miller
Brian Moehler
Mike Myers
C.J. Nitkowski
Jon Ratliff
Henry Santos
Cam Smith
Clint Sodowsky
Justin Thompson

CATCHERS (1)
John Flaherty

INFIELDERS (10)
Tony Clark
Cecil Fielder
Travis Fryman
Chris Gomez
Mark Lewis
Phil Nevin
Shannon Penn
Steve Rodriguez
Tom Schmidt
Alan Trammell

OUTFIELDERS (6)
Danny Bautista
Chad Curtis
Micah Franklin
Phil Hiatt
Bob Higginson
Phil Plantier
Todd Steverson

Games played by position

PLAYER	G	C	1B	2B	3B	SS	OF	DH
Bautista	89	0	0	0	0	0	86	1
Clark	27	0	27	0	0	0	0	0
Curtis	144	0	0	0	0	0	144	0
Cuyler	41	0	0	0	0	0	36	2
Fielder	136	0	77	0	0	0	0	58
Flaherty	112	112	0	0	0	0	0	0
Fletcher	67	0	1	63	0	3	0	1
Fryman	144	0	0	0	144	0	0	0
Gibson	70	0	0	0	0	0	1	63
Gomez	123	0	0	31	0	97	0	2
Hall	7	0	0	0	0	0	5	2
Higginson	131	0	0	0	0	0	123	2
Nevin	29	0	0	0	0	0	27	2
Pemberton	12	0	0	0	0	0	8	3
Penn	3	0	0	3	0	0	0	0
Rodriguez	18	0	0	13	0	5	0	1
Steverson	30	0	0	0	0	0	27	1
Stubbs	62	0	20	0	0	0	20	3
Tingley	54	53	1	0	0	0	0	0
Trammell	74	0	0	0	0	60	0	6
Whitaker	84	0	0	63	0	0	0	8
White	39	0	16	0	0	0	9	11

Sick call: 1995 DL Report

Player	Days on the DL
Sean Bergman	21
Scott Fletcher	21
Mike Gardiner	105*
Greg Gohr	129
Todd Steverson	77
Franklin Stubbs	26
Alan Trammell	11
Lou Whitaker	17
Kevin Wickander	21

Indicates two separate terms on Disabled List.

Minor Leagues

Tops in the organization

Batter	Club	Avg.	G	AB	R	H	HR	RBI
Joe Hall	Tol	.320	91	319	52	102	11	47
David Roberts	Lak	.303	92	357	67	108	3	30
Chris Facione	Lak	.293	110	400	44	117	5	56
Sean Freeman	Lak	.290	119	414	42	120	6	65
Mike Darr	Fay	.289	112	395	58	114	5	66

Home Runs			Wins		
Ivan Cruz	Jax	31	Cam Smith	Fay	13
Gary Cooper	Jax	18	Mickey Weston	Tol	11
Bubba Trammell	Lak	16	Jason Jordan	Fay	11
J. Encarnacion	Fay	16	Clint Sodowsky	Tol	10
Several tied		14	Several tied		9

RBI			Saves		
Daryle Ward	Fay	106	Brandon Reed	Fay	41
Ivan Cruz	Jax	96	John Kelly	Jax	29
Bubba Trammell	Lak	72	Eddy Gaillard	Lak	25
J. Encarnacion	Fay	72	Mike Christopher	Tol	21
Several tied		66	Brent Stentz	Lak	16

Stolen Bases			Strikeouts		
Richard Almanzar	Fay	50	Cam Smith	Fay	166
Glen Barker	Jax	39	Greg Whiteman	Fay	156
Jamie Borel	Fay	38	Scott Gardner	Fay	126
David Roberts	Lak	30	Justin Thompson	Jax	118
Carlos Delacruz	Lak	28	Jason Jordan	Fay	111

Pitcher	Club	W-L	ERA	IP	H	BB	SO
Scott Gardner	Fay	6-3	2.15	100	72	31	126
Randy Marshall	Tol	7-3	2.30	109	99	29	67
Clint Sodowsky	Tol	10-6	2.65	184	149	80	109
Trever Miller	Jax	8-2	2.72	122	122	34	77
Jason Jordan	Fay	11-7	2.74	158	160	50	111

1995 Amateur draft picks

Players are listed with position and college or high school. Most players were assigned to rookie or Class A leagues. List provided by Major League Baseball.

Lukas Bonner, rhp, Divine Child HS, Inkster, Mich.; David Borkowski, rhp, Sterling Heights (Mich.) HS; Clayton Bruner, rhp, Weatherford (Okla.) HS; Clint Bryant, 3b, Texas Tech; Manuel Caballero, c, Grand Canyon; Christopher Clark, cf, Arkansas; Chad Cook, rhp, Fallbrook (Calif.) HS; Charles Crowder, lhp, Crestwood HS, Mantua, Ohio; Brian Cummins, lhp, Northwestern; Joshua Davis, rhp, Pensacola (Fla.) Catholic HS; Michael Davis, ss, Chicago Vocational HS; Michael Drumright, rhp, Wichita State; Peter Durkovic, lhp, Fordham; Douglas Engleka, ss, Ohio U.; Robert Fick, c, Cal State Northridge; Pedro Flores, lhp, Sierra Vista HS, Baldwin Park, Calif.; John Foran, rhp, Central Florida; Brian Fuller, c, Northwestern; Jeremy Giambi, of, Cal State Fullerton; Richard Gray, cf, Embry-Riddle Aeronautical, Orland, Maine; Steven Hartsburg, ss, Schaumburg (Ill.) HS; Jason Haynie, lhp, South Carolina; Mark Hendrickson, lhp, Washington State; Bryan Houston, cf, Escambia HS, Pensacola, Fla.; Darrell Hussman, rhp, Quartz Hill HS, Lancaster, Calif.; Kevin Jordan, ss, Robert E. Lee, Midland, Texas; Brian Justine, lhp, William T. Dwyer HS, Palm Beach Lakes, Fla.; Gabriel Kapler, 3b, Moorpark; Derek Kopacz, 3b, Triton; John Kremer, rhp, Chatard HS, Indianapolis; Jason Lawrie, rhp, Independence HS, San Jose, Calif.; Charles Lehr, rhp-c, West Covina (Calif.) HS; Jeremiah Lignitz, c, Davison (Mich.) HS; Errick Lowe, rf, Lake Worth (Fla.) HS; Christopher Manser, rhp-rf, Hillsborough HS, Lutz, Fla.; Ronald Marietta, lhp, Bishop Ford Central, Brooklyn, N.Y.; Joseph McFarlane, rhp, Anacortes (Wash.) HS; Michael Miller, 3b, Hofstra; Lawyer Milloy, of, Washington; Clausel Milord, cf, New York Tech; Derek Mitchell, ss, Triton; Mark Mulder, 1b, Thornwood HS, Holland, Ill.; Jose Nunez, 2b, Northeast Texas CC; Rosario Ortiz, rhp, Arizona Western; William Powell, rhp, Georgia; David Reinfelder, lhp, Michigan State; Ronald Rojas, 2b, Northwestern; Philip Rosengren, rhp, Rye (N.Y.) Day School; Gregory Ryan, lhp, Divine Child HS, Garden City, Mich.; Thomas Shipman, cf, River Ridge HS, Port Richey, Fla.; Gregory Sprehn, rhp, Bangor (Wis.) HS; Matthew Thornton, lhp, Centerville HS, Sturgis, Mich.; Eric Valent, cf-rf, Canyon HS, Anaheim, Calif.; Winkle Van Judd, lhp, Spartanburg Methodist; Jay Waggoner, 1b-of, Auburn; Maurice Watkins, rhp, Prosser HS, Chicago; Scott Weaver, lf, Michigan; J.D. Webb, c, Texas; Michael Whiteman, lhp, Potomac State JC.

Detroit (1901-1995)

Runs: Most, career, all-time

2088 Ty Cobb, 1905-1926
1774 Charlie Gehringer, 1924-1942
1622 Al Kaline, 1953-1974
1386 LOU WHITAKER, 1977-1995
1242 Donie Bush, 1908-1921

Hits: Most, career, all-time

3900 Ty Cobb, 1905-1926
3007 Al Kaline, 1953-1974
2839 Charlie Gehringer, 1924-1942
2499 Harry Heilmann, 1914-1929
2466 Sam Crawford, 1903-1917

2B: Most, career, all-time

665 Ty Cobb, 1905-1926
574 Charlie Gehringer, 1924-1942
498 Al Kaline, 1953-1974
497 Harry Heilmann, 1914-1929
420 LOU WHITAKER, 1977-1995

3B: Most, career, all-time

284 Ty Cobb, 1905-1926
249 Sam Crawford, 1903-1917
146 Charlie Gehringer, 1924-1942
145 Harry Heilmann, 1914-1929
136 Bobby Veach, 1912-1923

HR: Most, career, all-time

399 Al Kaline, 1953-1974
373 Norm Cash, 1960-1974
306 Hank Greenberg, 1930-1946
262 Willie Horton, 1963-1977
244 LOU WHITAKER, 1977-1995

RBI: Most, career, all-time

1804 Ty Cobb, 1905-1926
1583 Al Kaline, 1953-1974
1442 Harry Heilmann, 1914-1929
1427 Charlie Gehringer, 1924-1942
1264 Sam Crawford, 1903-1917

SB: Most, career, all-time

865 Ty Cobb, 1905-1926
400 Donie Bush, 1908-1921
317 Sam Crawford, 1903-1917
294 Ron LeFlore, 1974-1979
230 ALAN TRAMMELL, 1977-1995

BB: Most, career, all-time

1277 Al Kaline, 1953-1974
1197 LOU WHITAKER, 1977-1995
1186 Charlie Gehringer, 1924-1942
1148 Ty Cobb, 1905-1926
1125 Donie Bush, 1908-1921

BA: Highest, career, all-time

.368 Ty Cobb, 1905-1926
.342 Harry Heilmann, 1914-1929
.337 Bob Fothergill, 1922-1930
.325 George Kell, 1946-1952
.321 Heinie Manush, 1923-1927

Slug avg: Highest, career, all-time

.616 Hank Greenberg, 1930-1946
.518 Harry Heilmann, 1914-1929
.516 Ty Cobb, 1905-1926
.503 Rudy York, 1934-1945
.501 Rocky Colavito, 1960-1963

Games started: Most, career, all-time

459 Mickey Lolich, 1963-1975
408 Jack Morris, 1977-1990
395 George Mullin, 1902-1913
388 Hooks Dauss, 1912-1926
373 Hal Newhouser, 1939-1953

Saves: Most, career, all-time

154 MIKE HENNEMAN, 1987-1995
125 John Hiller, 1965-1980
120 Willie Hernandez, 1984-1989
85 Aurelio Lopez, 1979-1985
55 Terry Fox, 1961-1966

Shutouts: Most, career, all-time

39 Mickey Lolich, 1963-1975
34 George Mullin, 1902-1913
33 Tommy Bridges, 1930-1946
33 Hal Newhouser, 1939-1953
29 Bill Donovan, 1903-1918

Wins: Most, career, all-time

222 Hooks Dauss, 1912-1926
209 George Mullin, 1902-1913
207 Mickey Lolich, 1963-1975
200 Hal Newhouser, 1939-1953
198 Jack Morris, 1977-1990

K: Most, career, all-time

2679 Mickey Lolich, 1963-1975
1980 Jack Morris, 1977-1990
1770 Hal Newhouser, 1939-1953
1674 Tommy Bridges, 1930-1946
1406 Jim Bunning, 1955-1963

Win pct: Highest, career, all-time

.654 Denny McLain, 1963-1970
.639 Aurelio Lopez, 1979-1985
.626 MIKE HENNEMAN, 1987-1995
.629 Schoolboy Rowe, 1933-1942
.616 Harry Coveleski, 1914-1918

ERA: Lowest, career, all-time

2.34 Harry Coveleski, 1914-1918
2.38 Ed Killian, 1904-1910
2.42 Ed Summers, 1908-1912
2.49 Bill Donovan, 1903-1918
2.61 Ed Siever, 1901-1908

Runs: Most, season

147 Ty Cobb, 1911
144 Ty Cobb, 1915
144 Charlie Gehringer, 1930
144 Charlie Gehringer, 1936
144 Hank Greenberg, 1938

Hits: Most, season

248 Ty Cobb, 1911
237 Harry Heilmann, 1921
227 Charlie Gehringer, 1936
226 Ty Cobb, 1912
225 Ty Cobb, 1917
225 Harry Heilmann, 1925

2B: Most, season

63 Hank Greenberg, 1934
60 Charlie Gehringer, 1936
56 George Kell, 1950
55 Gee Walker, 1936
50 Charlie Gehringer, 1934
50 Hank Greenberg, 1940
50 Harry Heilmann, 1927

3B: Most, season

26 Sam Crawford, 1914
25 Sam Crawford, 1903
24 Ty Cobb, 1911
24 Ty Cobb, 1917
23 Ty Cobb, 1912
23 Sam Crawford, 1913

HR: Most, season

58 Hank Greenberg, 1938
51 CECIL FIELDER, 1990
45 Rocky Colavito, 1961
44 CECIL FIELDER, 1991
44 Hank Greenberg, 1946

RBI: Most, season

183 Hank Greenberg, 1937
170 Hank Greenberg, 1935
150 Hank Greenberg, 1940
146 Hank Greenberg, 1938
140 Rocky Colavito, 1961

SB: Most, season

96	Ty Cobb, 1915
83	Ty Cobb, 1911
78	Ron LeFlore, 1979
76	Ty Cobb, 1909
68	Ty Cobb, 1916
68	Ron LeFlore, 1978

BB: Most, season

137	Roy Cullenbine, 1947
135	Eddie Yost, 1959
132	TONY PHILLIPS, 1993
125	Eddie Yost, 1960
124	Norm Cash, 1961

BA: Highest, season

.420	Ty Cobb, 1911
.409	Ty Cobb, 1912
.403	Harry Heilmann, 1923
.401	Ty Cobb, 1922
.398	Harry Heilmann, 1927

Slug avg: Highest, season

.683	Hank Greenberg, 1938
.670	Hank Greenberg, 1940
.668	Hank Greenberg, 1937
.662	Norm Cash, 1961
.632	Harry Heilmann, 1923

Games started: Most, season

45	Mickey Lolich, 1971
44	George Mullin, 1904
42	Mickey Lolich, 1973
42	George Mullin, 1907
41	Joe Coleman, 1974
41	Mickey Lolich, 1972
41	Mickey Lolich, 1974
41	Denny McLain, 1968
41	Denny McLain, 1969
41	George Mullin, 1905

Saves: Most, season

38	John Hiller, 1973
32	Willie Hernandez, 1984
31	Willie Hernandez, 1985
27	Tom Timmermann, 1970
24	MIKE HENNEMAN, 1992
24	MIKE HENNEMAN, 1993
24	Willie Hernandez, 1986

Shutouts: Most, season

9	Denny McLain, 1969
8	Ed Killian, 1905
8	Hal Newhouser, 1945
7	Billy Hoeft, 1955
7	George Mullin, 1904
7	Dizzy Trout, 1944

Wins: Most, season

31	Denny McLain, 1968
29	George Mullin, 1909
29	Hal Newhouser, 1944
27	Dizzy Trout, 1944
26	Hal Newhouser, 1946

K: Most, season

308	Mickey Lolich, 1971
280	Denny McLain, 1968
275	Hal Newhouser, 1946
271	Mickey Lolich, 1969
250	Mickey Lolich, 1972

Win pct: Highest, season

.862	Bill Donovan, 1907
.842	Schoolboy Rowe, 1940
.838	Denny McLain, 1968
.808	Bobo Newsom, 1940
.784	George Mullin, 1909

ERA: Lowest, season

1.64	Ed Summers, 1908
1.71	Ed Killian, 1909
1.78	Ed Killian, 1907
1.81	Hal Newhouser, 1945
1.91	Ed Siever, 1902

Most pinch-hit homers, season

3	Gus Zernial, 1958
3	Norm Cash, 1960
3	Vic Wertz, 1962
3	Gates Brown, 1968
3	Ben Oglivie, 1976
3	John Grubb, 1984
3	Larry Herndon, 1986

Most pinch-hit homers, career

16	Gates Brown, 1963-1975

Most consecutive games batting safely

40	Ty Cobb, 1911
35	Ty Cobb, 1917
30	Goose Goslin, 1934
30	Ron LeFlore, 1976

Most consecutive scoreless innings

33	Harry Coveleski, 1914

No-hit games

George Mullin, Det vs StL AL, 7-0; July 4, 1912 (2nd game).

Virgil Trucks, Det vs Was AL, 1-0; May 15, 1952.

Virgil Trucks, Det at NY AL, 1-0; August 25, 1952.

Jim Bunning, Det at Bos AL, 3-0; July 20, 1958 (1st game).

Jack Morris, Det at Chi AL, 4-0; April 7, 1984.

ACTIVE PLAYERS in caps.

Players' years of service are listed by the first and last years with this team and are not necessarily consecutive; all statistics record performances for this team only.

Toronto Blue Jays

By Neil Seiler, USA TODAY

Seemingly ageless Joe Carter once again stood out, leading the Jays with 25 homers and 76 RBI.

1995 Blue Jays: Tied for worst in the AL

Some teams, like the Red Sox or the Cubs, start the season with a monkey on their back—decades between World Series appearances will do that to a team. But the Toronto Blue Jays began 1995 with a giant asterisk around their neck—they were the defending World Series champs in spite of the fact that they had a losing record in the strike-shortened '94 season. By mid-May, it was apparent that the asterisk was moot.

The youth movement—except for strong-throwing catcher Sandy Martinez and right fielder Shawn Green—wasn't too successful. Green set a rookie record for extra-base hits and equaled the club mark for a consecutive-game hitting streak. Only Fred McGriff and Jesse Barfield homered more in their inaugural Blue Jays seasons.

Shortstop Alex Gonzalez shared playing time with Domingo Cedeno and Perez. Center fielder Shannon Stewart—elevated after Devon White broke a bone in his foot with five weeks to play—saw little action. Randy Knorr couldn't hold the catching job after Carlos Delgado was demoted because his shoulder prevented him from catching.

Pitchers Darren Hall, Tim Crabtree and Giovanni Carrara didn't deliver, but Paul Menhart, Jeff Ware and Ken Robinson were better than scouts or teammates expected.

"We had a lot of young players come into a bad environment," said White after he was injured for the remainder of the season. "In spring training we expected Pat Hentgen to win 15 games, Joe Carter to drive in 100 runs, Juan Guzman to win 15, Robbie Alomar would hit .300, and I was supposed to steal 30 bases. The only thing that happened was that Robbie hit .300. Instead of coming into a winning environment like Pat Hentgen came into, these young guys came up and had to produce."

Carter failed to crack his customary 100-RBI barrier, finishing with 25 homers and 76 RBI. Olerud raised his average to .291 but managed only eight homers—just one at SkyDome—and 54 RBI.

Third baseman Ed Sprague played every day, and although his average slipped in the second half, he hit .244 with 18 homers and 74 RBIs.

Reliever Tony Castillo was asked to be the closer when optimistic early reports on reliever Duane Ward turned out to be inaccurate. Castillo had 13 saves but blew nine chances.

1996 Blue Jays: Preview

The biggest problem the Jays face with their team up for sale and a smaller budget is whether to spend their money on re-signing Alomar, perhaps the best player in franchise history, or to spend their money on much-needed starting pitching. Even with Alomar on board, they finished last, tied for the worst record in the league, with a paltry 56 wins.

The Jays start their 1996 season with only four players signed: Hentgen, Castillo, Carter and Olerud. On the horizon are plenty of holes in the rotation. Juan Guzman earned $2.8 million, and the Jays will have to decide whether to tender him a contract after a second-straight sub-par season. Barring trades they can count on returning everyday players in Martinez, Olerud, Gonzalez and Sprague in the infield, Carter and Green in the outfield, and Carlos Delgado as the DH, unless Paul Molitor is re-signed.

1995 Blue Jays: Week-by-week notes

These notes were excerpted from the following issues of Baseball Weekly.

▶**May 3:** The Blue Jays' bullpen had allowed one run in 10 innings before Woody Williams was tagged for a pair of runs on April 30. Unfortunately, the bullpen woes continued a couple of nights later in California as right-hander Paul Menhart allowed two runs on one hit in two-thirds of an inning. "I have no excuses," Menhart said. "I just couldn't throw strikes." Manager Cito Gaston moved Roberto Alomar down to sixth in the batting order and put rookie shortstop Alex Gonzalez in the No. 2 slot between Devon White and Paul Molitor. Under those circumstances, Alomar could lose 60 plate appearances on the season.

▶**May 10:** Roberto Alomar wasn't bothered hitting in the No. 6 hole, where he was moved to protect John Olerud. In fact, he was hitting .341 and was able to bunt and steal as well as deliver the big hit.

▶**May 17:** Despite batting eighth in the lineup, third baseman Ed Sprague led the team and was third in the AL with 17 RBI. Roberto Alomar and Sprague shared the club lead with five home runs apiece, second in the AL.

▶**June 7:** Roberto Alomar's streak of 80 errorless games survived June 4 after Cleveland scorekeeper Hank Kozloski changed a call in the ninth inning. Alomar was charged with an error, but Kozloski changed his decision after the game and gave Albert Belle a hit. The league record for consecutive errorless games by a second baseman is 89 by Baltimore's Jerry Adair in 1964-65.

▶**June 21:** Roberto Alomar figured was sure to find his way into the record book sooner or later—the only unknown was whether it would be his bat or glove that got him there. He and his glove set an American League mark for second basemen on June 17 when he played his 90th consecutive game without an error.

▶**June 28:** Two acoustical panels (2½ feet by 8 feet) fell from the facing of SkyDome's 500 seating level to the 200 level below, hitting seven people. The panels floated down on unsuspecting fans like leaves. Two people were treated for injuries, including one woman who was taken to a hospital with a laceration and later released.

▶**July 5:** The Blue Jays ended an eight-game losing streak in Boston and then won three of their next five, including two of a four-game series with Baltimore. Was this sudden burst too little, too late? Gord Ash had talked to every GM about whom he had available with the July 31 trade deadline approaching. A number of clubs expressed interest in right-hander David Cone, whose contract was up at the end of the season and who would be eligible for free agency. With problems in their rotation, the Yankees wanted Cone—as did a number of contenders who think they're one pitcher away. Cone is the best starter on the market. The Jays acquired Cone in 1992 from the Mets for Jeff Kent and Ryan Thompson. Now the shoe is on the other foot. "I spoke to Gord when we got back from Boston," said Cone. "He told me the trade would likely come sooner than later." In the news, a distraught female fan seeking a relationship with Roberto Alomar was arrested at the SkyDome hotel Sunday after threatening to kill him. Tricia Miller, 31, a factory worker from Port Hope, Ontario, was found with a gun and arrested at the hotel, which overlooks the field, while Alomar was playing. He was removed in the ninth inning. "I left the game because someone was threatening me, she said she had a pistol and she was going to kill me," Alomar said. "They took me out for my own safety."

▶**July 13:** Only Minnesota and Florida had fewer wins than the Jays' 27 going into the break. So much for the chance of a historic "three-peat," however tainted by last season's sub-.500 record and the cancellation of the World Series. Gord Ash was at the All-Star Game talking with other executives, trying to better his club for next season. One club made an offer of two young players for right-hander David Cone but wanted the Jays to pick up part of his remaining contract. "All we're asking for is the same as what we gave up when we acquired David Cone three years ago or Rickey Henderson two years ago," Ash said. The Jays sent Jeff Kent and Ryan Thompson to the Mets for Cone; they sent former No. 1 pick Steve Karsay and outfield prospect Jose Herrera to the A's for Henderson. They didn't ask either club to pick up any of Cone's or Henderson's contracts.

▸**July 26:** Toronto pitching had allowed teams to bat around in an inning 20 times.

▸**Aug. 2:** The Jays received a package of strong-armed pitchers in the David Cone trade. Right-handers Marty Janzen, 22; Mike Gordon, 22; and Jason Jarvis, 21, were a combined 57-49 in the minors for the Yankees. All three throw more than 90 miles an hour.

▸**Aug. 30:** Paul Molitor wielded a torrid bat against Chicago on Aug. 26 and 27, going 4-for-4 on both days. The eight consecutive hits by Molitor tied a Blue Jays record, set by Rance Mulliniks in 1984. He also reached base nine consecutive times, one short of Mulliniks's team mark, and provided the game-winning hit in each game. "It's been a fun couple of days," said Molitor.

▸**Last-day recap:** *Heroes*—In a year in which the Blue Jays finished last for the first time since 1982 and had a sub-.400 winning percentage for the first time since 1979, Heroes were relatively hard to come by. Still, one can't overlook the continued superlative play of Roberto Alomar. The All-Star second baseman hit .300—two points above his career average—belted 13 homers (the second-highest total of his career) and drove in 66 runs while batting second in the lineup. He stole 30 bases and fielded his position in his typically outstanding manner.

Rookie outfielder Shawn Green came into his own this year. Batting .288 with 15 homers and 54 RBI, Green had more home runs as a Jays rookie than any other player except Fred McGriff and Jesse Barfield. He broke the franchise record for rookies with 50 extra-base hits and tied the club's longest hitting streak for rookies (14). While Jays pitching faltered, Al Leiter performed well. The six-year veteran set personal records for most wins (11) and innings pitched (183) while posting a 3.64 ERA in 28 starts.

Unsung Hero—Alex Gonzalez knocked in 42 runs and hit 10 home runs as a shortstop. Perhaps more impressively, he never complained or sulked when he was benched, once for eight consecutive games.

Team directory

▸**Owner:** Labatt's Breweries and the Canadian Imperial Bank of Commerce
▸**General manager:** Gord Ash
▸**Ballpark:**
SkyDome
Toronto, Ontario
416-341-1000
Capacity 51,000
Public transportation available
Family and wheelchair sections, no-alcohol sections, ramps, Playland
▸**Team publications:**
Scorebook Magazine (Buzz Communications), 416-961-3319
▸**TV, radio broadcast stations:**
TSN and Baton Broadcasting,
FAN 590, CBCTV
▸**Spring training:**
Dunedin Stadium at Grant Field
311 Douglas Ave.
Dunedin, Fla.
Capacity 6,218
813-733-9302

TORONTO BLUE JAYS 1995 final stats

BATTERS	BA	SLG	OB	G	AB	R	H	TB	2B	3B	HR	RBI	BB	SO	SB	CS	E
Alomar	.300	.449	.354	130	517	71	155	232	24	7	13	66	47	45	30	3	4
Olerud	.291	.404	.398	135	492	72	143	199	32	0	8	54	84	54	0	0	4
Green	.288	.509	.326	121	379	52	109	193	31	4	15	54	20	68	1	2	6
White	.283	.431	.334	101	427	61	121	184	23	5	10	53	29	97	11	2	3
Molitor	.270	.423	.350	130	525	63	142	222	31	2	15	60	61	57	12	0	0
Carter	.253	.428	.300	139	558	70	141	239	23	0	25	76	37	87	12	1	7
T. Perez	.245	.327	.292	41	98	12	24	32	3	1	1	8	7	18	0	1	5
Sprague	.244	.407	.333	144	521	77	127	212	27	2	18	74	58	96	0	0	17
Gonzalez	.243	.398	.322	111	367	51	89	146	19	4	10	42	44	114	4	4	19
Martinez	.241	.335	.270	62	191	12	46	64	12	0	2	25	7	45	0	0	5
Cedeno	.236	.360	.289	51	161	18	38	58	6	1	4	14	10	35	0	1	3
Huff	.232	.333	.337	61	138	14	32	46	9	1	1	9	22	21	1	1	2
Knorr	.212	.341	.273	45	132	18	28	45	8	0	3	16	11	28	0	0	8
Stewart	.211	.211	.318	12	38	2	8	8	0	0	0	1	5	5	2	0	1
Parrish	.202	.320	.265	70	178	15	36	57	9	0	4	22	15	52	0	0	0
Battle	.200	.200	.368	9	15	3	3	3	0	0	0	0	4	8	1	0	0
R. Perez	.188	.292	.188	17	48	2	9	14	2	0	1	3	0	5	0	0	0
Delgado	.165	.297	.212	37	91	7	15	27	3	0	3	11	6	26	0	0	0

PITCHERS	W-L	ERA	G	GS	CG	GF	Sho	SV	IP	H	R	ER	HR	BB	SO
Timlin	4-3	2.14	31	0	0	19	0	5	42.0	38	13	10	1	17	36
Crabtree	0-2	3.09	31	0	0	19	0	0	32.0	30	16	11	1	13	21
Castillo	1-5	3.22	55	0	0	31	0	13	72.2	64	27	26	7	24	38
Leiter	11-11	3.64	28	28	2	0	1	0	183.0	162	80	74	15	108	153
Williams	1-2	3.69	23	3	0	10	0	0	53.2	44	23	22	6	28	41
Robinson	1-2	3.69	21	0	0	9	0	0	39.0	25	21	16	7	22	31
Hall	0-2	4.41	17	0	0	11	0	3	16.1	21	9	8	2	9	11
Menhart	1-4	4.92	21	9	1	6	0	0	78.2	72	49	43	9	47	50
Hentgen	10-14	5.11	30	30	2	0	0	0	200.2	236	129	114	24	90	135
Hurtado	5-2	5.45	14	10	1	0	0	0	77.2	81	50	47	11	40	33
Ware	2-1	5.47	5	5	0	0	0	0	26.1	28	18	16	2	21	18
Rogers	2-4	5.70	19	0	0	9	0	0	23.2	21	15	15	4	18	13
Guzman	4-14	6.32	24	24	3	0	0	0	135.1	151	101	95	13	73	94
Jordan	1-0	6.60	15	0	0	3	0	1	15.0	18	11	11	3	13	10
Carrara	2-4	7.21	12	7	1	2	0	0	48.2	64	46	39	10	25	27
Cox	1-3	7.40	24	0	0	7	0	0	45.0	57	40	37	4	33	38
Cornett	0-0	9.00	5	0	0	2	0	0	5.0	9	6	5	1	3	4
Ward	0-1	27.00	4	0	0	0	0	0	2.2	11	10	8	0	5	3

108

1996 preliminary roster

PITCHERS (19)
Giovanni Carrara
Tony Castillo
Tim Crabtree
Mike Gordon
Juan Guzman
Pat Hentgen
Edwin Hurtado
Marty Jantzen
Paul Menhart
Carey Paige
Paul Quantrill
Ken Robinson
Jimmy Rogers
Mark Sievert
Jose Silva
Paul Spoljaric

Mike Timlin
Jeff Ware
Woody Williams

CATCHERS (3)
Randy Knorr
Sandy Martinez
Julio Mosquera

INFIELDERS (10)
D.J. Boston
Tilson Brito
Domingo Cedeno
Felipe Crespo
Carlos Delgado
Tom Evans
Alex Gonzalez

John Olerud
Tomas Perez
Ed Sprague

OUTFIELDERS (7)
Joe Carter
Shawn Green
Otis Nixon
Robert Perez
Angel Ramirez
Lonell Roberts
Shannon Stewart

Games played by position

PLAYER	G	C	1B	2B	3B	SS	OF	DH
Alomar	130	0	0	128	0	0	0	0
Battle	9	0	0	0	6	0	0	1
Carter	139	0	7	0	0	0	128	5
Cedeno	51	0	0	20	1	30	0	0
Delgado	37	0	4	0	0	0	17	7
Gonzalez	111	0	0	0	9	97	0	3
Green	121	0	0	0	0	0	109	0
Huff	61	0	0	0	0	0	55	0
Knorr	45	45	0	0	0	0	0	0
Martinez	62	61	0	0	0	0	0	0
Molitor	130	0	0	0	0	0	0	129
Olerud	135	0	133	0	0	0	0	0
Parrish	70	67	0	0	0	0	0	1
R. Perez	17	0	0	0	0	0	15	0
T. Perez	41	0	0	7	1	31	0	0
Sprague	144	0	7	0	139	0	0	2
Stewart	12	0	0	0	0	0	12	0
White	101	0	0	0	0	0	99	0

Minor Leagues

Tops in the organization

Batter	Club Avg.	G	AB	R	H	HR	RBI
Robert Perez	Syr .343	122	502	70	172	9	66
John Curl	Mh .319	69	270	47	86	7	63
Carlos Delgado	Syr .318	91	333	59	106	22	74
Michael Peeples	Mht.312	72	285	55	89	3	50
Chris Hayes	Stc .306	70	271	39	83	2	36

Home Runs			Wins		
Carlos Delgado	Syr	22	Mark Sievert	Hag	12
John Ramos	Syr	20	Jason Jarvis	Hag	12
Jeff Ladd	Knx	19	Michael Romano	Dun	11
Ryan Jones	Dun	18	Keilan Smith	Dun	11
Several tied		17	Scott Pace	Knx	10

RBI			Saves		
Ryan Jones	Dun	78	Brian Smith	Hag	21
John Ramos	Syr	75	Tim Adkins	Dun	17
Jeff Patzke	Dun	75	Kendall Rhine	Hag	13
Carlos Delgado	Syr	74	John Mitchell	Mht	11
D.J. Boston	Knx	71	Several tied		10

Stolen Bases			Strikeouts		
Lonell Roberts	Knx	57	Mark Sievert	Hag	140
Shannon Stewart	Knx	42	Mike Gordon	Dun	132
Omar Sanchez	Stc	32	Scott Pace	Knx	128
Michael Peeples	Mht	27	Jason Jarvis	Hag	124
Anthony Sanders	Hag	26	Jeremy Lee	Hag	118

Pitcher	Club W-L	ERA	IP	H	BB	SO
Brian Smith	Hag 9-1	0.87	104	77	16	101
Mark Sievert	Hag 12-6	2.91	161	126	46	140
Doug Meiners	Hag 8-4	2.99	117	121	14	73
Jason Jarvis	Hag 12-10	3.19	161	152	51	124
Scott Pace	Knx 10-10	3.32	160	149	60	128

Sick call: 1995 DL Report

Player	Days on the DL
Brad Cornett	30
Danny Cox	39
Juan Guzman	39*
Darren Hall	85*
Mike Huff	34*
Randy Knorr	41
Mike Timlin	57
Duane Ward	122*
Woody Williams	77

Indicates two separate terms on Disabled List.

1995 Amateur draft picks

Players are listed with position and college or high school. Most players were assigned to rookie or Class A leagues. List provided by Major League Baseball.

Kyle Adams, lhp, Creighton Prep, Papillion, Neb.; Randy Albaral, cf, Jesuit HS, River Ridge, La.; Jesse Bechard, ss, Washington HS, Brantford, Ont.; Brian Bejarano, 3b, Central Arizona; William Brabec, rhp, Illinois State; Ryan Bundy, c, Lake Stevens HS, Everett, Wash.; Kyle Burchart, rhp, Bixby HS, Tulsa; Johnny Byrd, rhp, University Christian HS, Jacksonville, Fla.; Ryan Cisar, ss, Magnolia HS, Martinsville, W.Va.; Albert Colon, rf, Apopka (Fla.) HS; Robert Corraro, rhp, Xavier HS, Madison, Conn.; John Curl, 1b, Texas A&M; Mark Curtis, lhp, Bellerose HS, St. Albert, Ont.; Frank Dent, rhp, San Juan HS, Citrus Heights, Calif.; John Douglas, ss, Catholic U.; Brandon Duckworth, rhp, College of Southern Idaho; Scott Fitterer, rhp, Louisiana State; Brian Fitts, rhp, Gallatin (Tenn.) HS; Blaine Fortin, c-rhp, Lundar School, Manitoba; Douglas Franklin, 2b, Pensacola JC; Ryan Freel, 2b-ss, Tallahassee CC; Stanley Gay, lhp, Covington (Tenn.) HS; Tyrone Gracia, 3b, Dennis Yarmouth Reg HS, Dennis, Mass.; Travis Grant, rhp, Skyline HS, Salt Lake City; Claude Greene, 1b, O Dea HS, Renton, Wash.; Harry Halladay, rhp, Arvada West HS, Golden, Colo.; Sidney Harden, rhp, Middle Georgia JC; Chris Hayes, 3b, Jacksonville; Jonathan Herring, lhp, Alabama Christian Academy, Montgomery, Ala.; Derek Hines, cf, Arvada West HS, Arvada, Colo.; Antonio Jackson, cf, A.H. Parker HS, Birmingham, Ala.; Justin Johnson, lf, Diamond Bar (Calif.) HS; John Kehoe, 2b, Cumberland; Brian Leach, rhp, Osceola HS, Seminole, Fla.; Allen Levrault, rhp, Westport (Mass.) HS; Theodore Lilly, lhp, Fresno CC; Jeffrey Maloney, ss, Ridge (N.J.) HS; David Marciniak, ss, Woodbridge (N.J.) HS; Eduardo Marquez, cf, Mater Dei HS, Orange, Calif.; Andrew McCormick, cf, Grand Canyon; Robert Medina, c, Eloisa Pascual HS, Moderno Caguas, P.R.; Logan Miller, c, Texas Tech; John Mitchell, rhp, Cal State Sacramento; Todd Moser, lhp, Manatee JC; Thomas Peck, of, Rollins; Joseph Pierson, ss, Huntington (W.Va.) HS; Jason Pomar, rhp, Vero Beach (Fla.) HS; Jeremi Rudolph, cf, Apopka (Fla.) HS; Jeremy Satterfield, rhp, College of Southern Idaho; Patrick Schultz, lf, CC of Rhode Island; Jaron Seabury, rhp, Bellevue CC; Paxton Stewart, 1b, Florida International; Andrew Tarpley, rhp, California; Thomas Taylor, ss, Tate HS, Gonzales, Fla.; Jay Veniard, lhp, Central Florida; James Whitehead, 1b-c, Meridian CC; Michael Whitlock, 1b, San Lorenzo HS, Oakland, Calif.; Brian Williams, c, Southwest Texas State; Craig Wilson, c, Marina HS, Huntington Beach, Calif.

Toronto (1977-1995)

Runs: Most, career, all-time

768	Lloyd Moseby, 1980-1989
641	George Bell, 1981-1990
555	TONY FERNANDEZ, 1983-1993
538	Willie Upshaw, 1978-1987
530	Jesse Barfield, 1981-1989

Hits: Most, career, all-time

1319	Lloyd Moseby, 1980-1989
1294	George Bell, 1981-1990
1250	TONY FERNANDEZ, 1983-1993
1028	Damaso Garcia, 1980-1986
982	Willie Upshaw, 1978-1987

2B: Most, career, all-time

242	Lloyd Moseby, 1980-1989
237	George Bell, 1981-1990
210	TONY FERNANDEZ, 1983-1993
204	Rance Mulliniks, 1982-1992
188	JOHN OLERUD, 1989-1995

3B: Most, career, all-time

70	TONY FERNANDEZ, 1983-1993
60	Lloyd Moseby, 1980-1989
50	Alfredo Griffin, 1979-1993
42	Willie Upshaw, 1978-1987
36	ROBERTO ALOMAR, 1991-1995

HR: Most, career, all-time

202	George Bell, 1981-1990
179	Jesse Barfield, 1981-1989
152	JOE CARTER, 1991-1995
149	Lloyd Moseby, 1980-1989
131	Ernie Whitt, 1977-1989

RBI: Most, career, all-time

740	George Bell, 1981-1990
651	Lloyd Moseby, 1980-1989
527	Jesse Barfield, 1981-1989
527	JOE CARTER, 1991-1995
518	Ernie Whitt, 1977-1989

SB: Most, career, all-time

255	Lloyd Moseby, 1980-1989
204	ROBERTO ALOMAR, 1991-1995
194	Damaso Garcia, 1980-1986
153	TONY FERNANDEZ, 1983-1993
126	DEVON WHITE, 1991-1995

BB: Most, career, all-time

547	Lloyd Moseby, 1980-1989
454	JOHN OLERUD, 1989-1995
416	Rance Mulliniks, 1982-1992
403	Ernie Whitt, 1977-1989
390	Willie Upshaw, 1978-1987

BA: Highest, career, all-time

.307	ROBERTO ALOMAR, 1991-1995
.296	JOHN OLERUD, 1989-1995
.290	TONY FERNANDEZ, 1983-1993
.288	Damaso Garcia, 1980-1986
.286	George Bell, 1981-1990

Slug avg: Highest, career, all-time

.530	FRED McGRIFF, 1986-1990
.488	JOE CARTER, 1991-1995
.486	George Bell, 1981-1990
.483	Jesse Barfield, 1981-1989
.471	JOHN OLERUD, 1989-1995

Games started: Most, career, all-time

405	Dave Stieb, 1979-1992
345	Jim Clancy, 1977-1988
250	JIMMY KEY, 1984-1992
175	TODD STOTTLEMYRE, 1988-1994
151	Luis Leal, 1980-1985

Saves: Most, career, all-time

217	TOM HENKE, 1985-1992
121	DUANE WARD, 1986-1993
31	Joey McLaughlin, 1980-1984
30	Roy Lee Jackson, 1981-1984
20	DARREN HALL, 1994-1995

Shutouts: Most, career, all-time

30	Dave Stieb, 1979-1992
11	Jim Clancy, 1977-1988
10	JIMMY KEY, 1984-1992
4	Jesse Jefferson, 1977-1980
4	TODD STOTTLEMYRE, 1988-1994

Wins: Most, career, all-time

174	Dave Stieb, 1979-1992
128	Jim Clancy, 1977-1988
116	JIMMY KEY, 1984-1992
69	TODD STOTTLEMYRE, 1988-1994
56	JUAN GUZMAN, 1991-1995

K: Most, career, all-time

1631	Dave Stieb, 1979-1992
1237	Jim Clancy, 1977-1988
944	JIMMY KEY, 1984-1992
700	JUAN GUZMAN, 1991-1995
671	DUANE WARD, 1986-1995

Win pct: Highest, career, all-time

.639	Doyle Alexander, 1983-1986
.609	JUAN GUZMAN, 1991-1995
.589	JIMMY KEY, 1984-1992
.587	PAT HENTGEN, 1991-1995
.569	Dave Stieb, 1979-1992

ERA: Lowest, career, all-time

3.39	Dave Stieb, 1979-1992
3.42	JIMMY KEY, 1984-1992
3.56	Doyle Alexander, 1983-1986
3.87	John Cerutti, 1985-1990
4.10	Jim Clancy, 1977-1988

Runs: Most, season

121	PAUL MOLITOR, 1993
116	DEVON WHITE, 1993
111	George Bell, 1987
110	DEVON WHITE, 1991
109	ROBERTO ALOMAR, 1993
109	JOHN OLERUD, 1993

Hits: Most, season

213	TONY FERNANDEZ, 1986
211	PAUL MOLITOR, 1993
200	JOHN OLERUD, 1993
198	George Bell, 1986
192	ROBERTO ALOMAR, 1993

2B: Most, season

54	JOHN OLERUD, 1993
42	JOE CARTER, 1991
42	DEVON WHITE, 1993
41	ROBERTO ALOMAR, 1991
41	George Bell, 1989
41	TONY FERNANDEZ, 1988

3B: Most, season

17	TONY FERNANDEZ, 1990
15	Dave Collins, 1984
15	Alfredo Griffin, 1980
15	Lloyd Moseby, 1984
11	ROBERTO ALOMAR, 1991

HR: Most, season

47	George Bell, 1987
40	Jesse Barfield, 1986
36	FRED McGRIFF, 1989
35	FRED McGRIFF, 1990
34	JOE CARTER, 1992
34	FRED McGRIFF, 1988

RBI: Most, season

134	George Bell, 1987
121	JOE CARTER, 1993
119	JOE CARTER, 1992
118	Kelly Gruber, 1990
111	PAUL MOLITOR, 1993

SB: Most, season

60	Dave Collins, 1984
55	ROBERTO ALOMAR, 1993
54	Damaso Garcia, 1982
53	ROBERTO ALOMAR, 1991
49	ROBERTO ALOMAR, 1992

BB: Most, season

119	FRED McGRIFF, 1989
114	JOHN OLERUD, 1993
94	FRED McGRIFF, 1990
87	ROBERTO ALOMAR, 1992
84	JOHN OLERUD, 1995

BA: Highest, season

.363	JOHN OLERUD, 1993
.341	PAUL MOLITOR, 1994
.332	PAUL MOLITOR, 1993
.326	ROBERTO ALOMAR, 1993
.322	TONY FERNANDEZ, 1987

Slug avg: Highest, season

.605	George Bell, 1987
.599	JOHN OLERUD, 1993
.559	Jesse Barfield, 1986
.552	FRED McGRIFF, 1988
.536	Jesse Barfield, 1985

Games started: Most, season

40	Jim Clancy, 1982
38	Luis Leal, 1982
38	Dave Stieb, 1982
37	Jim Clancy, 1987
36	Doyle Alexander, 1985
36	Jim Clancy, 1984
36	JIMMY KEY, 1987
36	Dave Stieb, 1983
36	Dave Stieb, 1985

Saves: Most, season

45	DUANE WARD, 1993
34	TOM HENKE, 1987
34	TOM HENKE, 1992
32	TOM HENKE, 1990
22	TOM HENKE, 1991

Shutouts: Most, season

5	Dave Stieb, 1982
4	Dave Stieb, 1980
4	Dave Stieb, 1983
4	Dave Stieb, 1988
3	Jim Clancy, 1982
3	Jim Clancy, 1986
3	PAT HENTGEN, 1994
3	Dave Lemanczyk, 1979

Wins: Most, season

21	Jack Morris, 1992
19	PAT HENTGEN, 1993
18	Dave Stieb, 1990
17	Doyle Alexander, 1984
17	Doyle Alexander, 1985
17	JIMMY KEY, 1987
17	Dave Stieb, 1982
17	Dave Stieb, 1983
17	Dave Stieb, 1989

K: Most, season

198	Dave Stieb, 1984
194	JUAN GUZMAN, 1993
187	Dave Stieb, 1983
180	Jim Clancy, 1987
167	Dave Stieb, 1985

Win pct: Highest, season

.778	Jack Morris, 1992
.762	JUAN GUZMAN, 1992
.750	Dave Stieb, 1990
.739	Doyle Alexander, 1984
.680	JIMMY KEY, 1987
.680	Dave Stieb, 1989

ERA: Lowest, season

2.48	Dave Stieb, 1985
2.64	JUAN GUZMAN, 1992
2.76	JIMMY KEY, 1987
2.83	Dave Stieb, 1984
2.93	Dave Stieb, 1990

Most pinch-hit homers, season

2	Al Woods, 1977
2	Otto Velez, 1979
2	Rico Carty, 1979
2	Ernie Whitt, 1982
2	Jeff Burroughs, 1985

Most pinch-hit homers, career

4	Ernie Whitt, 1977-1989
4	Jesse Barfield, 1981-1989

Most consecutive games batting safely

26	JOHN OLERUD, 1993
22	George Bell, 1989
21	Damaso Garcia, 1983
21	Lloyd Moseby, 1983

Most consecutive scoreless innings

31	Dave Stieb, 1988

No-hit game

Dave Stieb, Tor at Det AL, 3-0;
September 2, 1990.

ACTIVE PLAYERS in caps.

Players' years of service are listed by the first and last years with this team and are not necessarily consecutive; all statistics record performances for this team only.

111

Cleveland Indians

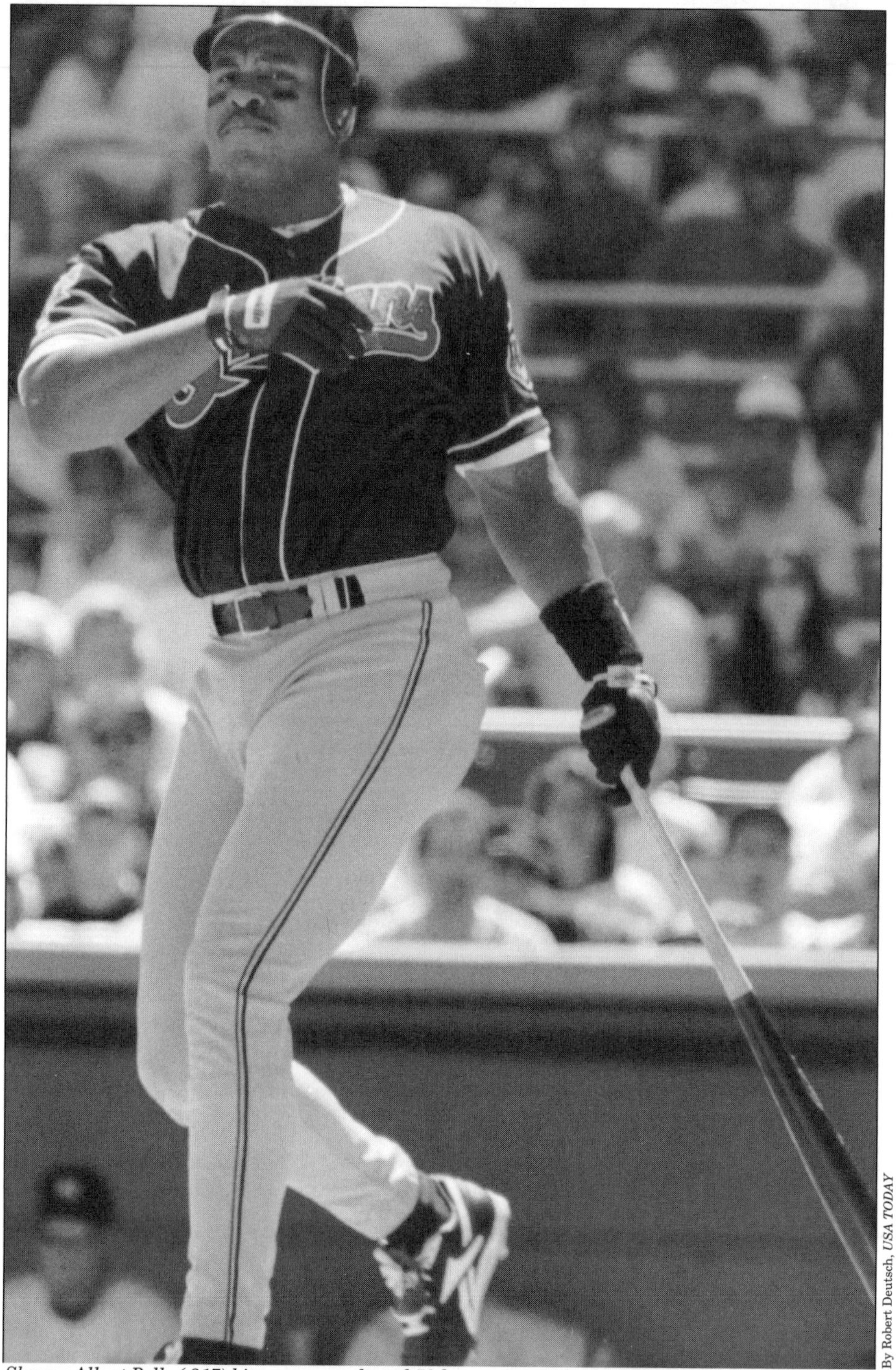

By Robert Deutsch, USA TODAY

Slugger Albert Belle (.317) hit an unprecedented 50 home runs with 126 RBI in just 142 games.

1995 Indians: The best in baseball

The Indians, built with match-sticks and airplane glue for almost 40 years, finally fielded a team to challenge the long season in 1995. They led the American League with a .291 team batting average and a 3.83 earned run average on the way to winning 100 games for just the second time in franchise history. And best of all, for the first time in 41 years, they reached the postseason, winning the AL Central Division by 30 games—the largest margin ever.

The Tribe was so dominant that they moved into first place on May 11 and stayed there until the end of the season. They won games in their last at-bat 27 times, 17 of them coming in Jacobs Field. Eleven times they ended games with home runs. Their power at the plate was dazzling, epecially at home, where they were 54-18.

The Indians went 13-0 in extra innings because of that kind of late-inning power. Albert Belle led all of baseball with 50 homers—36 of them came after the All-Star break, including 17 in September. He became the first player in history to hit 50 or more homers and doubles in one season.

The Indians' lineup had a little bit of everything. Lead-off hitter Kenny Lofton won his fourth straight AL stolen base title in spite of leg and rib-cage problems. Omar Vizquel proved to be a valuable No. 2 hitter, finishing fifth in the league in sacrifice bunts and stealing 29 bases. Then came the heart of the order—Carlos Baerga, Belle, and Eddie Murray. Baerga, who walked 35 times compared with 10 times in 1994, hit over .300 for the fourth straight season, adding 15 homers and 90 RBI. Murray became the 20th man in history to reach 3,000 hits and drove in 82 runs in spite of missing a month with two broken ribs. Murray has had at least 75 RBI in each of his 19 big-league seasons. There was no break in the Indians' lineup. The bottom of the order featured Jim Thome (.314, 25 HR, 73 RBI), Manny Ramirez (.308, 31 HR, 107 RBI), Paul Sorrento (.235, 25 HR, 79 RBI) and Sandy Alomar Jr. (.300, 10 HR, 35 RBI).

Then there was the pitching. The biggest story was Jose Mesa, who became the closer because the Indians didn't have anyone else and ended up with 46 saves, setting a major league record by converting 38 straight save opportunities. Mesa was the last line of defense on a staff that produced 10 complete games, 10 shutouts and 50 saves. Their 3.83 ERA was the only one in the league below 4.00. The rotation featured 16-game winners Orel Hershiser and Charles Nagy. Dennis Martinez, battling knee, shoulder and elbow problems, squeezed 12 wins out of his 40-year-old right arm, while rookie Julian Tavarez led all AL relievers with 10 victories. The strength of the staff was the bullpen, which led the league with a 3.05 ERA and 32 wins.

1996 Indians: Preview

This could be the last year that the current team will terrorize the league. Belle will be in his option year, as will Vizquel and Sorrento. Murray, Assenmacher, Ken Hill, Tony Pena, Dave Winfield and Alvaro Espinoza were free agents at the end of last year. GM John Hart said he thinks he can keep the club together through 1996. After that, there will be some difficult choices to make.

"But we're going to stay competitive," said Hart. "We want a team that can compete for a pennant every year."

These notes were excerpted from the following issues of Baseball Weekly.

▸**May 3:** Another season, another stretch on the disabled list for Sandy Alomar Jr. For the second time in five months, the catcher underwent surgery on April 25 on his left knee, to be sidelined for two months. David Bell became the third generation of his family to reach the big leagues with his Indians debut on April 27. His father, Buddy, played for 18 years in the majors, for and his grandfather, Gus, played for 15 years.

▸**May 17:** Eddie Murray hit his 463rd homer on May 14, tying him with teammate Dave Winfield for the lead among active major leaguers.

▸**June 14:** Not only were the Indians leading the AL in hitting and pitching, they were doing it with style. In a 9-1 home stand, they won five games in their last at-bat—twice with homers. Tribe relievers were 5-0 with five saves. In 19 appearances, they pitched 27⅔ innings and allowed just two earned runs for a 0.65 ERA. The starters were 4-1 with a 3.55 ERA (25 ER, 63⅓ IP). Dennis Martinez and Orel Hershiser threw shutouts.

▸**June 21:** Jose Mesa, for years a struggling starter with a high-voltage arm, had taken the job of closer as if he were born to it. Through the first 46 games, Mesa went 17 for 17 in save situations, and the club had won all 20 games in which he appeared. In his 17 saves, he faced the minimum number of batters 10 times. In nine of those games, he retired the side in order. In the other save, he relieved with one out in the ninth inning and retired the next two batters.

▸**June 28:** Orel Hershiser was placed on the disabled list, and Dennis Martinez was pitching with torn cartilage in his left knee.

▸**July 5:** Life imitates Hollywood— when the real-life Indians took batting practice in Jacobs Field, a troll-like creature watched from a post on the dugout. His face appeared to be made of clay, and long strands of green grass grew out of the holes on the top of his head. His name, like the voodoo doll in the movie *Major League*, was Joeboo (or Jobu, depending on your dictionary). "Joeboo likes to watch BP," said Tom Foster, one of the clubhouse assistants. "The sun is good for him. It makes his hair grow. During the games, we put him by the exercise pool in the clubhouse. He needs the moisture." It's believed a fan mailed Joeboo to the Indians at the start of the year. "Joeboo was out in the dugout when we were playing Detroit," said Foster. "Cecil Fielder saw him and was going to take his bat to him. He thought we were putting a hex on the Tigers."

▸**July 13:** Catcher Sandy Alomar Jr. wasted little time swinging the bat since coming off the disabled list on June 29. In seven games after being activated, he hit .500. He also threw out four of the nine base stealers attempting to run against him. Other news: Two days after reaching 3,000 hits, Eddie Murray landed on the disabled list for just the second time in 19 seasons when Twins catcher Matt Walbeck kneed him in the side in a collision at the plate.

▸**July 19:** Orel Hershiser, his trademark sinker working impeccably, won for the first time in more than a month. In his previous four starts—a stretch interrupted by a stint on the disabled list for a sprained back—Hershiser was 0-3 with a 6.55 ERA. Meanwhile, Cleveland's three rookie pitchers—Chad Ogea, Alan Embree and Julian Tavarez—were a combined 11-1 with a 1.69 ERA. Murray a-go-go: When Eddie Murray reached 3,000 hits on June 30, he wore four jerseys during the game. One will go to the Hall of Fame, one to the Indians' museum, one will be auctioned off for charity, and one (the one he actually wore when he got hit No. 3,000) will stay with Murray.

▸**Aug. 23:** The Indians had ended six games with game-winning homers—the sixth came on Aug. 19 when Eddie Murray started the bottom of the ninth with a homer into the right-field seats to give the club a 4-3 victory against Milwaukee in Jacobs Field. "I'm sure the fans enjoy these late-inning heroics a lot more than we do," said Murray. "We'd like to win these kind of games a little earlier."

▸**Aug. 30:** Albert Belle became the first Indian in history to hit 30 or more homers in four consecutive seasons when he homered twice on Aug. 25, to celebrate his 29th birthday. "It's a nice thing to do," said Belle. "But it should be five years in a row."

▸**Sept. 6:** These were good times for Albert Belle. On Aug. 30, he homered in the 14th inning to beat Toronto 4-3. On Aug. 31, he homered in the 10th inning to beat the Blue Jays 6-4. On Sept. 1, he hit a grand slam in a 14-4 blowout against Detroit. "When Albert gets hot, he can do just about anything," said Carlos Baerga. Belle was named the AL Player of the Month for August after hitting .381 (45-for-118) with 14 homers and 30 RBI. The Indians had won 24 games in their last at-bat and hit nine game-ending homers—including three by Belle.

▸**Sept. 13:** In the clinching party in the Tribe's locker room on Sept. 8, the Indians went through 10 cases of champagne, 14 cases of beer, two gallons of milk, a half-gallon of orange juice and a half-gallon of mouthwash. The alcohol was poured over players' heads and over anyone else who was nearby—but milk, mouthwash and orange juice? "Tony Pena poured a gallon of milk over Wayne Kirby, so Wayne poured a gallon of milk over Pena," said clubhouse manager Stan Hunter. "I don't know who got hit with the orange juice and mouthwash."

▸**Oct. 4:** Would baseball writers name Albert Belle the AL MVP? "It's going to be tough," said Belle. "I'm not consid-

ered a media darling." But Belle's numbers were awesome. On Sept. 30, he became just the 12th man in history to hit 50 homers in a season. He is the only man in history to hit 50 homers and 50 doubles in a season. In August and September he hit 31 homers to set a major league record. His 17 homers in September tied Babe Ruth's record. Belle finished at .317 with 52 doubles, 50 homers and 126 RBI. His 103 extra-base hits were the most in the league. The Indians won their 100th game on Oct. 1 against Kansas City—just the second time in team history the Tribe had won 100.

Team directory

▸**Owner:** Richard E. Jacobs
▸**General manager:** John Hart
▸**Ballpark:**
Jacobs Field
2401 Ontario St., Cleveland, Ohio
216-420-4200
Capacity 42,865
Downtown parking available; public transportation; handicapped seating; extremely accessible with escalators, elevators and ramps; all 38 bathrooms have diaper-changing areas; two unisex bathrooms for physically challenged and kids.
▸**Team publications:**
Game Face Magazine, Tribe Talk
216-420-4200
▸**TV, radio broadcast stations:**
WKNR 1220 AM, WUAB Channel 43, SportsChannel Ohio
▸**Camps and/or clinics:**
Cleveland Indians Baseball Heaven (fantasy camp), January, 800-75-TRIBE
▸**Spring training:**
Chain O'Lakes Park
Winter Haven, Fla.
Capacity 4,520
813-291-5803

CLEVELAND INDIANS 1995 final stats

BATTERS	BA	SLG	OB	G	AB	R	H	TB	2B	3B	HR	RBI	BB	SO	SB	CS	E
Burnitz	.571	.714	.571	9	7	4	4	5	1	0	0	0	0	0	0	0	0
Giles	.556	.889	.556	6	9	6	5	8	0	0	1	3	0	1	0	0	0
Ripken	.412	.765	.412	8	17	4	7	13	0	0	2	3	0	3	0	0	0
Levis	.333	.444	.333	12	18	1	6	8	2	0	0	3	1	0	0	0	0
Murray	.323	.516	.375	113	436	68	141	225	21	0	21	82	39	65	5	1	3
Belle	.317	.690	.401	143	546	121	173	377	52	1	50	126	73	80	5	2	6
Perry	.315	.463	.376	52	162	23	51	75	13	1	3	23	13	28	1	3	0
Baerga	.314	.452	.355	135	557	87	175	252	28	2	15	90	35	31	11	2	19
Thome	.314	.558	.438	137	452	92	142	252	29	3	25	73	97	113	4	3	16
Lofton	.310	.453	.362	118	481	93	149	218	22	13	7	53	40	49	54	15	6
Ramirez	.308	.558	.402	137	484	85	149	270	26	1	31	107	75	112	6	6	5
Alomar	.300	.478	.332	66	203	32	61	97	6	0	10	35	7	26	3	1	2
Vizquel	.266	.351	.333	136	542	87	144	190	28	0	6	56	59	59	29	11	9
Pena	.262	.376	.302	91	263	25	69	99	15	0	5	28	14	44	1	0	7
Espinoza	.252	.322	.264	66	143	15	36	46	4	0	2	17	2	16	0	2	5
Sorrento	.235	.511	.336	104	323	50	76	165	14	0	25	79	51	71	1	1	7
Kirby	.207	.298	.260	101	188	29	39	56	10	2	1	14	13	32	10	3	1
Amaro	.200	.300	.273	28	60	5	12	18	3	0	1	7	4	6	1	3	0
Winfield	.191	.287	.285	46	115	11	22	33	5	0	2	4	14	26	1	0	0
Bell	.000	.000	.000	2	2	0	0	0	0	0	0	0	0	0	0	0	0
Tucker	.000	.000	.231	17	20	2	0	0	0	0	0	0	0	5	4	0	1

PITCHERS	W-L	ERA	G	GS	CG	GF	Sho	SV	IP	H	R	ER	HR	BB	SO
Mesa	3-0	1.13	62	0	0	57	0	46	64.0	49	9	8	3	17	58
Tavarez	10-2	2.44	57	0	0	15	0	0	85.0	76	36	23	7	21	68
Plunk	6-2	2.67	56	0	0	22	0	2	64.0	64	19	19	5	27	71
Assenmacher	6-2	2.82	47	0	0	12	0	0	38.1	32	13	12	3	12	40
Ogea	8-3	3.05	20	14	1	3	0	0	106.1	95	38	36	11	29	57
Martinez	12-5	3.08	28	28	3	0	2	0	187.0	174	71	64	17	46	99
Lopez	0-0	3.13	6	2	0	0	0	0	23.0	17	8	8	4	7	22
Poole	3-3	3.75	42	0	0	9	0	0	50.1	40	22	21	7	17	41
Farrell	0-0	3.86	1	0	0	0	0	0	4.2	7	4	2	0	0	4
Hershiser	16-6	3.87	26	26	1	0	1	0	167.1	151	76	72	21	51	111
Hill	4-1	3.98	12	11	1	0	0	0	74.2	77	36	33	5	32	48
Shuey	0-2	4.26	7	0	0	3	0	0	6.1	5	4	3	0	5	5
Nagy	16-6	4.55	29	29	2	0	1	0	178.0	194	95	90	20	61	139
Embree	3-2	5.11	23	0	0	8	0	1	24.2	23	16	14	2	16	23
Clark	9-7	5.27	22	21	2	0	0	0	124.2	143	77	73	13	42	68
Roa	0-1	6.00	1	1	0	0	0	0	6.0	9	4	4	1	2	0
Grimsley	0-0	6.09	15	2	0	2	0	1	34.0	37	24	23	4	32	25
Black	4-2	6.85	11	10	0	0	0	0	47.1	63	42	36	8	16	34

1996 preliminary roster

PITCHERS (21)
Paul Assenmacher
Mark Clark
Maximo DeLa Rosa
Alan Embree
Pep Harris
Orel Hershiser
Daron Kirkreit
Steve Kline
Jim Lewis
Albie Lopez
Dennis Martinez
Jose Mesa
Charles Nagy
Chad Ogea
Eric Plunk

Jim Poole
Joe Roa
Jeff Sexton
Paul Shuey
Julian Tavarez
Casey Whitten

CATCHERS (4)
Sandy Alomar
Einar Diaz
Jesse Levis
Tony Pena

INFIELDERS (9)
Carlos Baerga
Julio Franco

Damian Jackson
Eddie Murray
Herbert Perry
Paul Sorrento
Jim Thome
Omar Vizquel
Enrique Wilson

OUTFIELDERS (6)
Albert Belle
Jeromy Burnitz
Brian Giles
Wayne Kirby
Kenny Lofton
Manny Ramirez

Games played by position

PLAYER	G	C	1B	2B	3B	SS	OF	DH
Alomar	66	61	0	0	0	0	0	0
Amaro	28	0	0	0	0	0	22	3
Baerga	135	0	0	134	0	0	0	1
Bell	2	0	0	0	2	0	0	0
Belle	143	0	0	0	0	0	142	1
Burnitz	9	0	0	0	0	0	6	2
Espinoza	66	0	2	22	22	19	0	3
Giles	6	0	0	0	0	0	3	1
Kirby	101	0	0	0	0	0	68	7
Levis	12	12	0	0	0	0	0	0
Lofton	118	0	0	0	0	0	114	2
Murray	113	0	18	0	0	0	0	95
Pena	91	91	0	0	0	0	0	0
Perry	52	0	45	0	1	0	0	6
Ramirez	137	0	0	0	0	0	131	5
Ripken	8	0	0	7	1	0	0	0
Sorrento	104	0	91	0	0	0	0	11
Thome	137	0	0	0	134	0	0	1
Tucker	17	17	0	0	0	0	0	0
Vizquel	136	0	0	0	0	136	0	0
Winfield	46	0	0	0	0	0	0	39

Minor Leagues

Tops in the organization

Batter	Club	Avg.	G	AB	R	H	HR	RBI
Tim Jorgensen	Wtn	.325	73	295	44	96	8	52
Rod McCall	Can	.318	122	440	77	140	29	88
Eric White	Clm	.317	112	369	49	117	6	46
Brian Giles	Buf	.310	123	413	67	128	15	67
Richie Sexson	Kin	.306	131	494	80	151	22	85

Home Runs			Wins		
Rod McCall	Can	29	Joe Roa	Buf	17
James Betzsold	Kin	25	Bartolo Colon	Kin	13
Bruce Aven	Kin	23	Eric Bell	Buf	13
Richie Sexson	Kin	22	Several tied		11
Several tied		19			

RBI			Saves		
Rod McCall	Can	88	Daniel Graves	Buf	31
Jeromy Burnitz	Buf	85	Wilmer Montoya	Clm	31
Richie Sexson	Kin	85	Scott Winchester	Wtn	11
Marc Marini	Buf	71	Paul Shuey	Buf	11
James Betzsold	Kin	71	Several tied		10

Stolen Bases			Strikeouts		
Ricky Gutierrez	Kin	43	Bartolo Colon	Kin	152
Damian Jackson	Can	40	Roland Delamaza	Kin	127
Milt Anderson	Kin	38	Teddy Warrecker	Clm	125
Chip Glass	Clm	37	Jaret Wright	Clm	113
Patricio Claudio	Kin	32	Jeff Sexton	Kin	112

Pitcher	Club	W-L	ERA	IP	H	BB	SO
Bartolo Colon	Kin	13-3	1.96	129	91	39	152
Jeff Sexton	Kin	11-3	2.33	139	118	23	112
Pep Harris	Can	8-4	2.41	116	110	38	58
Chris Granata	Clm	11-5	2.47	113	94	53	93
R. Delamaza	Kin	8-1	2.80	148	134	46	127

Sick call: 1995 DL Report

Player	Days on the DL
Sandy Alomar Jr.	65
Ruben Amaro	34
Orel Hershiser	15
Kenny Lofton	15
Eddie Murray	29
Paul Shuey	18
Dave Winfield	56*

Indicates two separate terms on Disabled List.

1995 Amateur draft picks

Players are listed with position and college or high school. Most players were assigned to rookie or Class A leagues. List provided by Major League Baseball.

Jason Adge, rhp, Miami; Brian Anderson, rhp, East Tennessee State; Dannon Atkins, rhp, Wake Forest; Ryan Bailey, rhp, Rancho Bernardo HS, San Diego; Jason Bennett, rhp, Shippensburg; Michael Bishop, 3b, Willis (Texas) HS; Thomas Blythe, c, N. Little Rock (Ark.) HS; Jamie Brown, rhp, W. Lauderdale HS, Meridian, Miss.; Mark Budzinski, of, Richmond; Sean Casey, 1b, Richmond; Frank Chapman, rhp, San Jacinto College; Nathan Coats, c, San Francisco City College; Rex Crosnoe, c, Southwest Missouri State; Michael Custer, rhp, Linn Benton CC; Marc Deschenes, ss, Massachusetts; Brandon Driggers, rhp, Whitehouse (Texas) HS; Kevin Eberwein, of, Green Valley HS, Las Vegas; Jon Edwards, rhp, Whitman College; Michael Edwards, ss, Mechanicsburg (Pa.) HS; Luis Estrella, rhp, Rancho Santiago JC; Tony Fleetwood, lhp, Oklahoma State; Alberto Garza, rhp, Wapato (Wash.) HS; Michael Glavine, 1b, Northeastern; Richard Gonzalez, c, Miami; Bryan Hardy, 1b, Arlington (Texas) Martin HS; Scott Harrison, rhp, John Swett HS, Pinole, Calif.; Terry Harvey, rhp, North Carolina State; Keith Horn, rhp, Arkansas State; Kirk Irvine, rhp, Rancho Santiago JC; Tim Jorgensen, 3b, Wisconsin-Oshkosh; Randy Keisler, lhp, Navarro JC; Damien Kolb, of, Capital HS, Olympia, Wash.; Peter Lopez, rhp, Manchester (N.H.) Central HS; Darren Loudermilk, rhp, Oklahoma City; Dennis Martinez Jr., rhp, St. Thomas Univ.; Sammie Mathis, rhp, Southern Arkansas; Brett Merrick, lhp, Washington; Jacob Messner, of, Rio Americano HS, Sacto, Calif.; David Miller, 1b, Clemson; Jason Minici, of, Long Beach State; Scott Morgan, of, Gonzaga; Michael Ploharz, rhp, Clovis (Calif.) HS; Jason Rakers, rhp, New Mexico State; Cody Ransom, 2b, South Mountain CC; Corey Richardson, ss-of, Daingerfield HS, Lone Star, Texas; Gary Rodriguez, of, Seminole JC; Frankie Sanders, rhp, Pasco Hernando CC; Scott Schultz, rhp, Louisiana State; Michael Spiegal, lhp, Sacramento City College; Jerry Taylor, of, Texas; Chad Thornhill, inf-of, Cal State Northridge; Kenneth Wagner, rhp, Florida Atlantic; Chad Whitaker, of, St. Thomas Aquinas HS, Fort Lauderdale, Fla.; Jewell Williams, of, Las Vegas HS; Scott Winchester, rhp, Clemson.

Cleveland (1901-1995)

118

Runs: Most, career, all-time

1154	Earl Averill,	1929-1939
1079	Tris Speaker,	1916-1926
942	Charlie Jamieson,	1919-1932
865	Nap Lajoie,	1902-1914
857	Joe Sewell,	1920-1930

Hits: Most, career, all-time

2046	Nap Lajoie,	1902-1914
1965	Tris Speaker,	1916-1926
1903	Earl Averill,	1929-1939
1800	Joe Sewell,	1920-1930
1753	Charlie Jamieson,	1919-1932

2B: Most, career, all-time

486	Tris Speaker,	1916-1926
424	Nap Lajoie,	1902-1914
377	Earl Averill,	1929-1939
375	Joe Sewell,	1920-1930
367	Lou Boudreau,	1938-1950

3B: Most, career, all-time

121	Earl Averill,	1929-1939
108	Tris Speaker,	1916-1926
106	Elmer Flick,	1902-1910
89	Joe Jackson,	1910-1915
83	Jeff Heath,	1936-1945

HR: Most, career, all-time

226	Earl Averill,	1929-1939
216	Hal Trosky,	1933-1941
215	Larry Doby,	1947-1958
214	Andy Thornton,	1977-1987
194	ALBERT BELLE,	1989-1995

RBI: Most, career, all-time

1084	Earl Averill,	1929-1939
919	Nap Lajoie,	1902-1914
911	Hal Trosky,	1933-1941
884	Tris Speaker,	1916-1926
869	Joe Sewell,	1920-1930

SB: Most, career, all-time

254	Terry Turner,	1904-1918
250	KENNY LOFTON,	1992-1995
240	Nap Lajoie,	1902-1914
233	Ray Chapman,	1912-1920
207	Elmer Flick,	1902-1910

BB: Most, career, all-time

857	Tris Speaker,	1916-1926
766	Lou Boudreau,	1938-1950
725	Earl Averill,	1929-1939
712	Jack Graney,	1908-1922
703	Larry Doby,	1947-1958

BA: Highest, career, all-time

.375	Joe Jackson,	1910-1915
.354	Tris Speaker,	1916-1926
.339	Nap Lajoie,	1902-1914
.327	George Burns,	1920-1928
.323	Ed Morgan,	1928-1933

Slug avg: Highest, career, all-time

.571	ALBERT BELLE,	1989-1995
.551	Hal Trosky,	1933-1941
.542	Joe Jackson,	1910-1915
.542	Earl Averill,	1929-1939
.520	Tris Speaker,	1916-1926

Games started: Most, career, all-time

484	Bob Feller,	1936-1956
433	Mel Harder,	1928-1947
350	Bob Lemon,	1941-1958
320	Willis Hudlin,	1926-1940
305	Stan Coveleski,	1916-1924

Saves: Most, career, all-time

128	DOUG JONES,	1986-1991
53	Ray Narleski,	1954-1958
48	JOSE MESA,	1992-1995
48	Steve Olin,	1989-1992
46	Jim Kern,	1974-1986
46	Sid Monge,	1977-1981

Shutouts: Most, career, all-time

45	Addie Joss,	1902-1910
44	Bob Feller,	1936-1956
31	Stan Coveleski,	1916-1924
31	Bob Lemon,	1941-1958
27	Mike Garcia,	1948-1959

Wins: Most, career, all-time

266	Bob Feller,	1936-1956
223	Mel Harder,	1928-1947
207	Bob Lemon,	1941-1958
172	Stan Coveleski,	1916-1924
164	Early Wynn,	1949-1963

K: Most, career, all-time

2581	Bob Feller,	1936-1956
2159	Sam McDowell,	1961-1971
1277	Bob Lemon,	1941-1958
1277	Early Wynn,	1949-1963
1161	Mel Harder,	1928-1947

Win pct: Highest, career, all-time

.667	Vean Gregg,	1911-1914
.663	Johnny Allen,	1936-1940
.630	Cal McLish,	1956-1959
.623	Addie Joss,	1902-1910
.622	Wes Ferrell,	1927-1933

ERA: Lowest, career, all-time

1.89	Addie Joss,	1902-1910
2.31	Vean Gregg,	1911-1914
2.39	Bob Rhoads,	1903-1909
2.45	Bill Bernhard,	1902-1907
2.50	Otto Hess,	1902-1908

Runs: Most, season

140	Earl Averill,	1931
137	Tris Speaker,	1920
136	Earl Averill,	1936
133	Tris Speaker,	1923
130	Charlie Jamieson,	1923

Hits: Most, season

233	Joe Jackson,	1911
232	Earl Averill,	1936
227	Nap Lajoie,	1910
226	Joe Jackson,	1912
225	Johnny Hodapp,	1930

2B: Most, season

64	George Burns,	1926
59	Tris Speaker,	1923
52	ALBERT BELLE,	1995
52	Tris Speaker,	1921
52	Tris Speaker,	1926

3B: Most, season

26	Joe Jackson,	1912
23	Dale Mitchell,	1949
22	Bill Bradley,	1903
22	Elmer Flick,	1906
20	Jeff Heath,	1941
20	Joe Vosmik,	1935

HR: Most, season

50	ALBERT BELLE,	1995
43	Al Rosen,	1953
42	Rocky Colavito,	1959
42	Hal Trosky,	1936
41	Rocky Colavito,	1958

RBI: Most, season

162	Hal Trosky,	1936
145	Al Rosen,	1953
143	Earl Averill,	1931
142	Hal Trosky,	1934
136	Ed Morgan,	1930

SB: Most, season

70	KENNY LOFTON,	1993
66	KENNY LOFTON,	1992
61	Miguel Dilone,	1980
60	KENNY LOFTON,	1994
54	KENNY LOFTON,	1995

BB: Most, season

111	Mike Hargrove	1980
109	Andy Thornton	1982
106	Les Fleming	1942
105	Jack Graney	1919
102	Jack Graney	1916

BA: Highest, season

.408	Joe Jackson	1911
.395	Joe Jackson	1912
.389	Tris Speaker	1925
.388	Tris Speaker	1920
.386	Tris Speaker	1916

Slug avg: Highest, season

.714	ALBERT BELLE	1994
.690	ALBERT BELLE	1995
.644	Hal Trosky	1936
.627	Earl Averill	1936
.620	Rocky Colavito	1958

Games started: Most, season

44	George Uhle	1923
42	Bob Feller	1946
41	Gaylord Perry	1973
40	Stan Coveleski	1921
40	Bob Feller	1941
40	Gaylord Perry	1972
40	Dick Tidrow	1973
40	George Uhle	1922

Saves: Most, season

46	JOSE MESA	1995
43	DOUG JONES	1990
37	DOUG JONES	1988
32	DOUG JONES	1989
29	Steve Olin	1992

Shutouts: Most, season

10	Bob Feller	1946
10	Bob Lemon	1948
9	Stan Coveleski	1917
9	Addie Joss	1906
9	Addie Joss	1908
9	Luis Tiant	1968

Wins: Most, season

31	Jim Bagby	1920
27	Bob Feller	1940
27	Addie Joss	1907
27	George Uhle	1926
26	Bob Feller	1946
26	George Uhle	1923

K: Most, season

348	Bob Feller	1946
325	Sam McDowell	1965
304	Sam McDowell	1970
283	Sam McDowell	1968
279	Sam McDowell	1969

Win pct: Highest, season

.938	Johnny Allen	1937
.773	Bill Bernhard	1902
.767	Vean Gregg	1911
.767	Bob Lemon	1954
.741	Gene Bearden	1948

ERA: Lowest, season

1.16	Addie Joss	1908
1.59	Addie Joss	1904
1.60	Luis Tiant	1968
1.71	Addie Joss	1909
1.72	Addie Joss	1906

Most pinch-hit homers, season

3	Gene Green	1962
3	Fred Whitfield	1965
3	Ted Uhlaender	1970
3	Ron Kittle	1987

Most pinch-hit homers, career

8	Fred Whitfield	1963-1967

Most consecutive games batting safely

31	Nap Lajoie	1906
29	Bill Bradley	1902

Most consecutive scoreless innings

41	Luis Tiant	1968
38	Jim Bagby	1917

No-hit games

Earl Moore, Cle vs Chi AL, 2-4;
May 9, 1901 (lost on 2 hits in
the 10th).

Dusty Rhoades, Cle vs Bos AL, 2-1;
September 18, 1908.

Addie Joss, Cle vs Chi AL, 1-0;
October 2, 1908 (perfect
game).

Addie Joss, Cle vs Chi AL, 1-0;
April 20, 1910.

Ray Caldwell, Cle at NY AL, 3-0;
September 10, 1919 (1st
game).

Wes Ferrell, Cle vs StL AL, 9-0;
April 29, 1931.

Bob Feller, Cle at Chi AL, 1-0;
April 16, 1940 (opening day).

Bob Feller, Cle at NY AL, 1-0;
April 30, 1946.

Don Black, Cle vs Phi AL, 3-0;
July 10, 1947 (1st game).

Bob Lemon, Cle at Det AL, 2-0;
June 30, 1948.

Bob Feller, Cle vs Det AL, 2-1;
July 1, 1951 (1st game).

Sonny Siebert, Cle vs Was AL, 2-0;
June 10, 1966.

Dick Bosman, Cle vs Oak AL, 4-0;
July 19, 1974.

DENNIS ECKERSLEY, Cle vs Cal
AL, 1-0; May 30, 1977.

Len Barker, Cle vs Tor AL, 3-0;
May 15, 1981 (perfect game).

ACTIVE PLAYERS in caps.

*Players' years of service are listed by
the first and last years with this team
and are not necessarily consecutive;
all statistics record performances for
this team only.*

CLEVELAND INDIANS / AL CENTRAL

Kansas City Royals

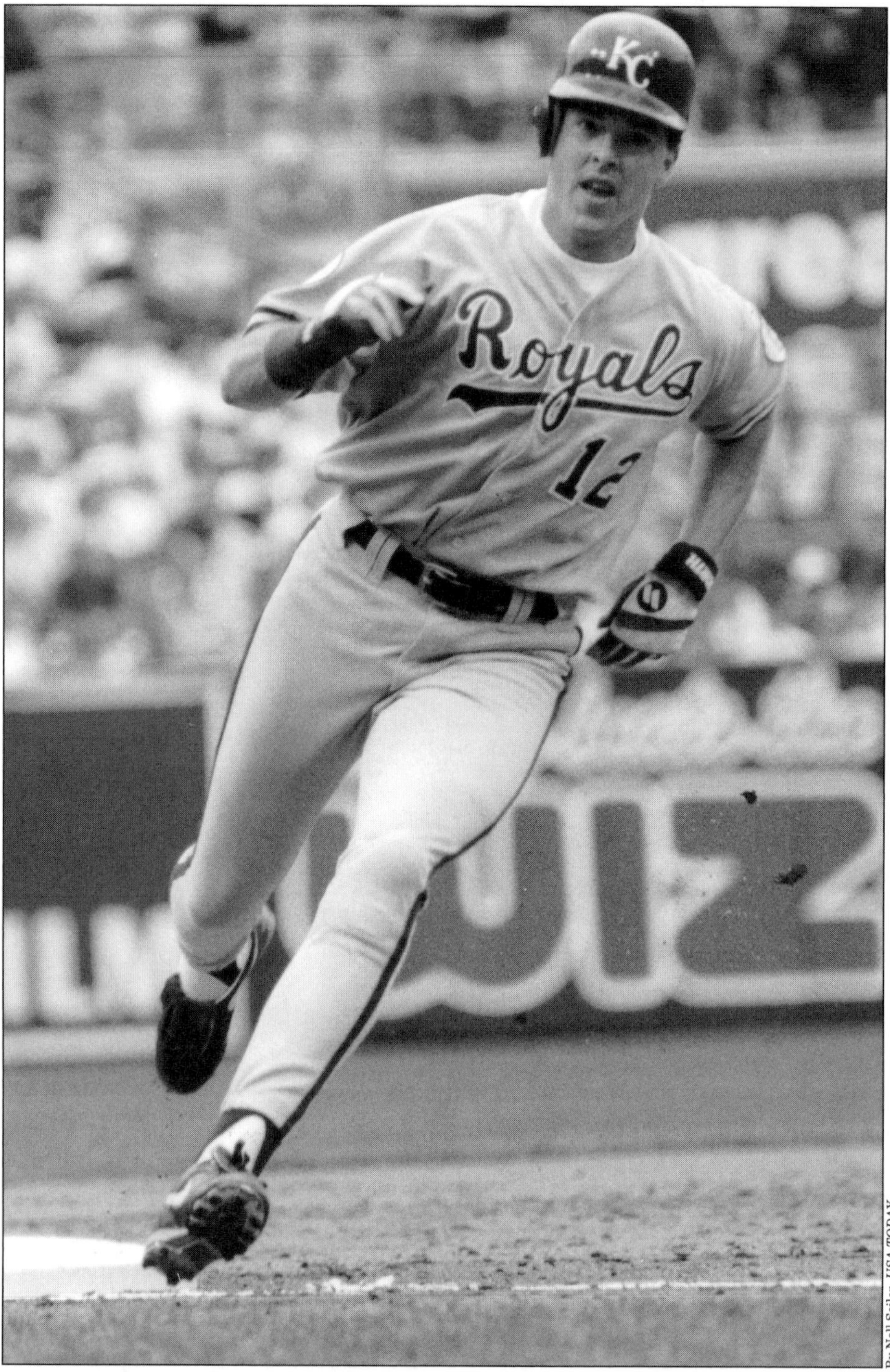

By Nell Seiler, USA TODAY

First baseman Wally Joyner led the Royals in batting (.310) and was second in RBI (82).

1995 Royals: A distant second

The Royals needed field glasses to spot the Indians, 30 games ahead of them. Still, they nearly made the playoffs as the wild card—they were not eliminated until the final week of the season, after they ran totally out of gas. They lost 11 of their last 13 games, including four straight to the last-place Twins.

Gary Gaetti belted a career-high 35 home runs and drove in 96 runs. But he slumped in late September after Wally Joyner, who hit .310 with 12 home runs and 83 RBI, went out with an ankle injury. Bob Hamelin was the club's biggest disappointment. After winning 1994 AL Rookie of the Year honors with 24 HR, 65 RBI and a .282 average, Hamelin slumped to .168, 7 HR and 25 RBI. Twice he was demoted to AAA Omaha.

Three pleasant surprises were Keith Lockhart, Tom Goodwin and Jon Nunnally. Lockhart, a 30-year-old rookie, was called up in early June after second baseman Chico Lind went AWOL. Lockhart responded by hitting .321 with a .478 slugging percentage. Goodwin inherited center field after Brian McRae was traded to the Cubs in spring training. No one knew if the career .232 hitter, would hit enough, but he finished at .288 and tied for second in the AL with 50 stolen bases. Defensively, he was superb. Nunnally, who was a Rule V draft pick from the Indians, had never played above Class A. He homered in his first at-bat and was second on the club with 14 home runs. Unfortunately, he did not hit a home run after Aug. 6, and his average dropped from .275 to .244 in the final weeks of the season.

Catcher Brent Mayne had an up-and-down season, hitting .306 on May 28, but by the end of August his average sagged to .211. However, he hit .400 the final month to finish at .251. After not having an extra-base hit and driving in only two runs in August, Mayne had eight doubles and eight RBI in his final 20 games. The Royals went 53-42 in

games he started as pitchers lauded his game-calling abilities.

While Kevin Appier led the pitching staff with 15 victories, he won only four times after June 23. After starting the season 11-2 with a 2.04 ERA, Appier was placed on the disabled list on July 26 with tendinitis of his rotator cuff but returned to make 11 more starts. He was 4-8 in his final 17 starts. Mark Gubicza led the team in innings (213⅓), shutouts (two) and ERA (3.75), even though he had a losing record (12-14)—the club scored two or fewer runs in 10 of his losses. Chris Haney was 3-1 with a 2.09 ERA on June 18 and could have had more victories, leaving with leads only to have the bullpen lose. He did not pitch after July 12, however, and had back surgery on Aug. 3.

The Royals got a glimpse of the future when they promoted Johnny Damon, Michael Tucker and Joe Vitiello. Damon hit .282 with three home runs and 23 RBI in 47 games and could move Goodwin from center to left. Damon led the pros with 198 hits—145 at AA Wichita and 53 for the Royals. Tucker hit .260 in 62 games with four HR and 17 RBI, while Vitiello hit seven HR in only 130 at-bats.

1996 Royals: Preview

"Our goal is to catch the Indians," Royals manager Bob Boone said, but both he and the front office know it will not be achieved overnight—or within a year, for that matter. They are hoping the experience that Damon, Tucker, Nunnally and Vitiello gained will send their numbers upward in 1996, enough to make a good run at the wild card. The Royals need to add right-handed hitting to their lefty lineup, which went 14-27 against left-handed pitching in 1995.

1995 Royals: Week-by-week notes

These notes were excerpted from the following issues of Baseball Weekly.

▶**May 3:** If not for the strike and the short spring, Kevin Appier might have tossed a no-hitter in the Royals' 5-1 Opening Day victory against Baltimore. He was relieved after 6⅔ hitless innings when his pitch count reached 98, more than enough after only 11⅓ innings in spring training. In his second start—on three days' rest—Appier limited the Yankees to three hits and one earned run over six innings to pick up his second victory. On April 29 outfielder Jon Nunnally became the 70th major leaguer—and the first Royal—to homer in his first at-bat.

▶**May 10:** Kevin Appier, 3-0 with a 0.46 ERA in his first three starts, allowed just eight hits and one earned run and struck out 27 in 19⅔ consecutive innings. Vince Coleman joined the club on May 7.

▶**May 17:** Veteran left-hander Tom Browning was called up from Class AAA on May 14 and immediately inserted into the rotation. To make room for him, the Royals released outfielder Felix Jose, who hit .303 in 1994. Meanwhile, Kevin Appier owned four of the Royals' first seven victories and recorded the club's first complete game May 13. He led the majors with 41 strikeouts in his 4-1 start.

▶**May 31:** Gary Gaetti hit two home runs and drove in four runs on May 26 at Milwaukee to reach 1,000 career RBI. "I kept the ball (from the 1,000th RBI)," Gaetti said. "At least I stayed around long enough to do that."

▶**June 7:** Second baseman Jose Lind might have decided to quit baseball because of personal problems, GM Herk Robinson said. He missed a series with Milwaukee, June 2-4, and was placed on the disqualified list, which cost him $18,056 in salary for each missed game. He had returned to Puerto Rico to be with his family. Robinson said Lind would have to be evaluated "both physically and emotionally" before a decision could be made on whether he would return to the Royals.

▶**June 14:** Bob Hamelin was sent down to Class AAA. Kevin Appier became the first eight-game winner in the majors when he tossed a complete-game four-hitter on June 10 to beat Toronto 8-2. He retired the last 13 batters he faced, not allowing the ball out of the infield. He lowered his ERA to 2.13, third in the AL.

▶**June 21:** Pitcher Chris Haney was moving into an elite group of left-handers in the AL, although he didn't have the victories to show for it. "He should be about 5-1, but we've coughed up two for him," manager Bob Boone said. Haney's ERA was 2.09, which ranks third in the league, but his record still stands at 3-1.

▶**June 28:** Prized rookie pitcher Jim Pittsley learned that he could face Tommy John surgery and was sent home to rest his arm for a month.

▶**July 5:** Bob Hamelin took the circuitous route back to Kansas City when he was called up on June 28. He was in five cities in 24 hours in reporting to Kansas City. He started in Nashville, was re-routed because of bad weather to Indianapolis, where he sat on the ground for five hours, then Chicago, Omaha and finally Kansas City. A .175 batting average, two homers and 10 RBI in 30 games to start 1995 had prompted the Royals to demote Hamelin on June 11 to Omaha. "I wasn't saying I was expecting it, but it was hard not to expect it when you're hitting .175," Hamelin said. "You can't be really surprised when you're hitting that." In a dozen games for Omaha, Hamelin hit .378 with six doubles, four homers and 11 RBI. On July 1, his second game back, Hamelin had an RBI double in a loss against the White Sox.

July 13: Left-hander Dave Fleming, a 17-game winner as a rookie with the Seattle Mariners in 1992, was obtained by the Royals for pitcher Bob Milacki, who was 8-3 with a 3.33 ERA in 15 starts for Class AAA Omaha. Fleming, who joined the Royals July 8, was 1-5 with a 7.50 ERA with the Mariners in 1995 and had walked 34. Meanwhile, Kevin Appier, after starting the season 11-2, lost his final three decisions before the All-Star Game.

July 26: Jason Jacome was obtained in a four-player trade with the New York Mets. Jacome opened the season with the Mets but was sent back to AAA May 22 with an 0-4 record and 10.29 ERA in five starts. The Royals were 30-21 on June 23 but fell below .500 as July was coming to a close.

Aug. 2: Did All-Star Kevin Appier break down because of the reliance on a four-man rotation instead of five? Placed on the 15-day DL with tendinitis in his right shoulder, Appier had five losses in six starts after beginning the season 11-2. He had been leading the majors in innings pitched (133⅓) and starts (20). Bob Boone said the four-man rotation wasn't the primary factor for the injury: "Anytime you pitch a lot, you're going to feel it. There are very few pitchers walking around who haven't experienced tendinitis."

Aug. 16: The Royals made a mind-boggling 11 roster moves, including designating Vince Coleman for assignment—they had 10 days to move him or release him. "Vince didn't fit into our plans for 1996," general manager Herk Robinson said.

Aug. 23: Wally Joyner had 64 RBI, seven more than in 1994. Joyner and Gary Gaetti combined for 34% of the club's RBI. "I'd hate to think where we'd be if Wally wasn't doing what he was doing," Bob Boone said.

Aug. 30: The Kevin Appier of May and June is what the Kansas City Royals needed to make an earnest run for the wild-card playoff spot—not the Kevin Appier who showed up in his past two starts, when he allowed 13 runs on 14 hits and six walks, inflating his ERA

to 4.04. Meanwhile, Aug. 25 was a rare day for Mark Gubicza. The Royals scored nine runs for him as he beat Texas. Gubicza, who had been supported by an average of 3.6 runs in his previous 25 starts, picked up his first home victory against the Rangers since May 31, 1986. "Most of these guys were in the first grade the last time I beat them here," Gubicza said.

Sept. 6: On Aug. 23, the Royals were four games below .500 and 5½ games out in the wild-card race, but a six-game winning streak, which ended Sept. 2 in Texas, pushed the Royals into the lead in the wild-card standings. Through Sept. 3, the Royals trailed Seattle by one game. The last time the Royals were in the playoffs was 1985, when they topped the Cardinals in the World Series. Between 1976 and 1985 they reached the playoffs seven times.

Oct. 4: In the Royals' final home game of the year, Mark Gubicza restricted Chicago to four singles for his 15th career shutout.

Team directory

▶**Owner:** Community Foundation, board of directors; David Glass, chairman of the board; Michael Herman, president
▶**General manager:** Herk Robinson
▶**Ballpark:**
Ewing Kauffman Stadium
1 Royal Way, Kansas City, Mo.
816-921-2200
Capacity 40,625
Pay parking lot; $5
Public transportation available
Wheelchair section and ramps, handicapped accessible
▶**Team publications:**
Yearbook, scorecard, media guide
▶**TV, radio broadcast stations:**
WDAF 610 AM, KSMO Channel 62
▶**Spring Training:**
Baseball City Stadium
Baseball City, Fla.
Capacity 7,000 (1,000 on grass)
813-424-7211

KANSAS CITY ROYALS 1995 final stats

BATTERS	BA	SLG	OB	G	AB	R	H	TB	2B	3B	HR	RBI	BB	SO	SB	CS	E
Miller	.333	.533	.412	9	15	2	5	8	0	0	1	3	2	4	0	0	0
Lockhart	.321	.478	.355	94	274	41	88	131	19	3	6	33	14	21	8	1	8
Joyner	.310	.447	.394	131	465	69	144	208	28	0	12	83	69	65	3	2	3
Goodwin	.288	.358	.346	133	480	72	138	172	16	3	4	28	38	72	50	18	3
Damon	.282	.324	.324	47	188	32	53	83	11	5	3	23	12	22	7	0	1
Grotewold	.278	.389	.422	15	36	4	10	14	1	0	1	6	9	7	0	0	1
Samuel	.263	.498	.360	91	205	31	54	102	10	1	12	39	29	49	6	4	9
Gaetti	.261	.518	.329	137	514	76	134	266	27	0	35	96	47	91	3	3	16
Tucker	.260	.384	.332	62	177	23	46	68	10	0	4	17	18	51	2	3	1
Gagne	.256	.374	.316	120	430	58	110	161	25	4	6	49	38	60	3	5	18
Mercedes	.256	.302	.370	23	43	7	11	13	2	0	0	9	8	13	0	0	1
Vitiello	.254	.446	.317	53	130	13	33	58	4	0	7	21	8	25	0	0	1
Mayne	.251	.326	.313	110	307	23	77	100	18	1	1	27	25	41	0	1	3
Sweeney	.250	.250	.250	4	4	1	1	1	0	0	0	0	0	0	0	0	0
Nunnally	.244	.472	.357	119	303	51	74	143	15	6	14	42	51	86	6	4	6
Howard	.243	.325	.310	95	255	23	62	83	13	4	0	19	24	41	6	1	6
Caceres	.239	.350	.291	55	117	13	28	41	6	2	1	17	8	15	2	2	1
Borders	.231	.385	.267	52	143	14	33	55	8	1	4	13	7	22	0	0	0
Norman	.225	.275	.326	24	40	6	9	11	0	1	0	4	6	6	0	1	1
Hiatt	.204	.363	.262	52	113	11	23	41	6	0	4	12	9	37	1	0	3
Randa	.171	.243	.237	34	70	6	12	17	2	0	1	5	6	17	0	1	3
Stynes	.171	.200	.256	22	35	7	6	7	1	0	0	2	4	3	0	0	1
Hamelin	.168	.313	.278	72	208	20	35	65	7	1	7	25	26	56	0	1	0
Cookson	.143	.171	.189	22	35	2	5	6	1	0	0	5	2	7	1	0	0
Jose	.133	.167	.188	9	30	2	4	5	1	0	0	1	2	9	0	0	0
McGinnis	.000	.000	.167	3	5	1	0	0	0	0	0	0	0	1	1	0	0	0
Mota	.000	.000	.000	2	2	0	0	0	0	0	0	0	0	0	0	0	0

PITCHERS	W-L	ERA	G	GS	CG	GF	Sho	SV	IP	H	R	ER	HR	BB	SO
Montgomery	2-3	3.43	54	0	0	46	0	31	65.2	60	27	25	7	25	49
Haney	3-4	3.65	16	13	1	0	0	0	81.1	78	35	33	7	33	31
Gubicza	12-14	3.75	33	33	3	0	2	0	213.1	222	97	89	21	62	81
Appier	15-10	3.89	31	31	4	0	1	0	201.1	163	90	87	14	80	185
Olson	3-3	4.09	23	0	0	12	0	3	33.0	28	15	15	4	19	21
Magnante	1-1	4.23	28	0	0	7	0	0	44.2	45	23	21	6	16	28
Pichardo	8-4	4.36	44	0	0	16	0	1	64.0	66	34	31	4	30	43
Gordon	12-12	4.43	31	31	2	0	0	0	189.0	204	110	93	12	89	119
Meacham	4-3	4.98	49	0	0	26	0	2	59.2	72	36	33	6	19	30
Anderson	1-0	5.33	6	4	0	0	0	0	25.1	29	15	15	3	8	6
Jacome	4-6	5.36	15	14	1	0	0	0	84.0	101	52	50	15	21	39
Brewer	2-4	5.56	48	0	0	13	0	0	45.1	54	28	28	9	20	31
Bunch	1-3	5.63	13	5	0	3	0	0	40.0	42	25	25	11	14	19
Fleming	1-6	5.96	25	12	1	3	0	0	80.0	84	61	53	19	53	40
Torres	1-2	6.09	24	2	0	7	0	0	44.1	56	30	30	6	17	28
Converse	1-3	6.56	15	1	0	4	0	1	23.1	28	17	17	2	16	14
Linton	0-1	7.25	7	2	0	0	0	0	22.1	22	21	18	4	10	13
Huisman	0-0	7.45	7	0	0	2	0	0	9.2	14	8	8	2	1	12
Browning	0-2	8.10	2	2	0	0	0	0	10.0	13	9	9	2	5	3
Rasmussen	0-1	9.00	5	1	0	1	0	0	10.0	13	10	10	3	8	6
Pittsley	0-0	13.50	1	1	0	0	0	0	3.1	7	5	5	3	1	0

1996 preliminary roster

PITCHERS (19)
Kevin Appier
Brian Bevil
Mike Bovee
Billy Brewer
Mel Bunch
Jim Converse
Bart Evans
Dave Fleming
Jeff Granger
Mark Gubicza
Chris Haney
Rick Huisman
Jason Jacome
Mike Magnante
Rusty Meacham
Hipolito Pichardo
Jim Pittsley
Kris Ralston
Dilson Torres

CATCHERS (4)
Sal Pasano
Brent Mayne
Henry Mercedes
Mike Sweeney

INFIELDERS (9)
Bob Hamelin
David Howard
Wally Joyner
Keith Lockhart
Mendy Lopez
Sergio Nunez
Joe Randa
Chris Stynes
Joe Vitiello

OUTFIELDERS (7)
Darren Burton
Johnny Damon
Tom Goodwin
Rod Myers
Les Norman
Jon Nunnally
Michael Tucker

Games played by position

PLAYER	G	C	1B	2B	3B	SS	OF	DH
Borders	52	45	0	0	0	0	0	3
Caceres	55	0	6	36	3	8	0	3
Cookson	22	0	0	0	0	0	12	2
Damon	47	0	0	0	0	0	47	0
Gaetti	137	0	11	0	123	0	0	6
Gagne	120	0	0	0	0	118	0	2
Goodwin	133	0	0	0	0	0	130	2
Grotewold	15	0	1	0	0	0	0	11
Hamelin	72	0	8	0	0	0	0	56
Hiatt	52	0	0	0	0	0	47	2
Howard	95	0	1	41	0	33	30	1
Jose	9	0	0	0	0	0	7	0
Joyner	131	0	126	0	0	0	0	2
Lockhart	94	0	0	61	17	0	0	14
Mayne	110	103	0	0	0	0	0	0
McGinnis	3	0	1	0	1	0	1	0
Mercedes	23	22	0	0	0	0	0	0
Miller	9	0	0	0	0	0	4	4
Mota	2	0	0	2	0	0	0	0
Norman	24	0	0	0	0	0	17	5
Nunnally	119	0	0	0	0	0	107	4
Randa	34	0	0	9	22	0	0	2
Samuel	91	0	38	6	0	0	14	23
Stynes	22	0	0	17	0	0	0	2
Sweeney	4	4	0	0	0	0	0	0
Tucker	62	0	0	0	0	0	36	22
Vitiello	53	0	8	0	0	0	0	38

Sick call: 1995 DL Report

Player	Days on the DL
Kevin Appier	17
Tom Browning	135
Edgar Caceres	15
Greg Gagne	21
Tom Gordon	16
Chris Haney	81
Phil Hiatt	15
David Howard	21
Chris James	66
Jose Mota	94
Hipolito Pichardo	17
Jim Pittsley	46

1995 Amateur draft picks

Players are listed with position and college or high school. Most players were assigned to rookie or Class A leagues. List provided by Major League Baseball.

Alonzo Aguilar, rhp, East Los Angeles JC; Jonathan Albrecht, lhp, Kansas St.; Jeremy Albritton, c, Parklane Academy, Chitto, Miss.; Greg Arnold, lhp, Smithtown HS, Nesconset, N.Y.; Lance Awbrey, c, Sinagua HS, Flagstaff, Ariz.; Taylor Bales, c, Lee College; Carlos Beltran, cf, Fernando Callejo, Manati, P.R.; Douglas Blosser, 1b, Sarasota (Fla.) HS; Adam Bolthouse, lhp, Spring Lake (Mich.) HS; Jaime Bonilla, lhp, Zayas Santana HS, Villaalba, P.R.; Brandon Buckley, c, San Ramon HS, Danville, Calif.; Rudy Bulgar, of, New Bedford (Mass.) HS; Alan Bundy, rhp, E.O. Smith HS, Mansfield, Conn.; Michael Cabales, rhp, East Islip (N.Y.) HS; Ralph Cadima, cf, Mount San Antonio; Melvin Dasher, cf, Palatka (Fla.) HS; Michael Degruy, rhp, Harrison Central HS, Gulfport, Miss.; Stephen Donaghey, rhp, Woburn (Mass.) HS; Emiliano Escandon, ss, Pomona-Pitzer; Adam Finnieston, cf, Miami; Hallmark James, c, Rice; Ham Scott, c, Palestine (Ill.) HS; William Hodge, lhp, Jacksonville St.; Francis Key, rhp, Pensacola JC; Scott Kortmeyer, lf, Grand Canyon; Juan Lebron, rf, Carmen B. Huyke, Arroyo, P.R.; Merrell Ligons, 2b, Palisades HS, Culver City, Calif.; Jesus Liz, lhp, Miami Dade CC North; Andy Lynch, lhp, Bridgton Academy HS, Mattapoisett, Mass.; Jeffrey Martin, rhp, Bishop Gorman HS, Las Vegas; Denton McDaniel, lhp, Lake Travis HS, West Austin, Texas; Todd Meady, rhp, Milford Academy, Middlebury, Conn.; Steve Medrano, ss, Bishop Amat HS, La Puente, Calif.; Mark Melito, ss, Wake Forest; Mario Miranda, of, Cal State Fullerton; David Moore, rhp, Northeast HS, Fort Lauderdale, Fla.; Steven Mullis, lhp, Brevard College; Randel Paulin, c, Pacific; Monoleto Penny, rhp, Newberry (S.C.) HS; Paul Phillips, c, West Lauderdale HS, Bailey, Miss.; Jamison Powers, rhp, Sullivan East HS, Bluff City, Tenn.; Stephen Prihoda, lhp, Sam Houston St.; Mark Quinn, of, Rice; Victor Radcliff, ss, North Augusta HS, Beech Island, S.C.; Adam Reikowski, rhp, Providence HS, Charlotte, N.C.; Michael Robbins, lhp, Stanford; Michael Rodriguez, ss, Chaffey HS, Ontario, Calif.; Matthew Saier, rhp, Georgia Tech; James Sanders, rhp, Lee College; John Sanders, rhp, Nebraska; James Scarborough, cf, Lawrence Elkins HS, Sugarland, Texas; Brett Schafer, of, UCLA; Glen School, lf, Brookdale CC; Chad Schroeder, rhp, Northwestern; Robert Shabansky, lhp, Bishop Gorman HS, Las Vegas; Bobby Shannon, lhp, Shippensburg (Pa.) Area HS; Brian Starcich, rhp, Blinn College; Paul Stryhas, 3b, Sarasota (Fla.) HS; Seth Tate, ss, Wenatchee (Wash.) HS; Courtney Thornton, rhp, Tallassee (Ala.) HS; Jason Vancuren, rhp, Monte Vista HS, San Ramon, Calif.; James Vida, 1b, Florida Southern College; Jeffrey Wallace, lhp, Minerva HS, Paris, Ohio; Stephen Watson, rhp, Galveston College; Brian Wiese, rhp, Central HS, Greenwell Springs, La.; Jeremy Williamson, lhp, Southern Mississippi; Cliff Wilson, 3b, Byrnes HS, Lyman, S.C.; Dustin Wilson, rhp, Columbia Basin CC; Brian Winders, rhp, Louisiana State; Tommy Worthy, ss, Etowah HS, Attalla, Ala.

Minor Leagues

Tops in the organization

Batter	Club	Avg.	G	AB	R	H	HR	RBI
Johnny Damon	Wch	.343	111	423	83	145	16	54
Lino Diaz	Wch	.328	113	399	60	131	8	66
James Vida	Spo	.323	74	291	38	94	4	39
Mike Sweeney	Wil	.310	99	332	61	103	18	53
Rod Myers	Wch	.307	131	499	71	153	7	62

Home Runs			Wins		
Sal Fasano	Wch	22	Glendon Rusch	Wil	14
Mandy Romero	Wch	21	Eric Anderson	Wil	12
Mike Sweeney	Wil	18	Tim Byrdak	Wil	11
Jeff Grotewold	Oma	17	Jose Rosado	Wil	10
Johnny Damon	Wch	16	Ken Ray	Wch	10

RBI			Saves		
Mandy Romero	Wch	82	Jaime Bluma	Oma	26
Sean McNally	Spr	79	Mike MacDonald	Spr	12
Sal Fasano	Wch	73	Jose DeJesus	Oma	10
Rudolfo Mendez	Spr	72	Don Strange	Wch	9
Lino Diaz	Wch	66	John Dickens	Wil	9

Stolen Bases			Strikeouts		
Jeremy Carr	Bak	52	Glendon Rusch	Wil	147
Felix Martinez	Wch	44	Tim Byrdak	Wil	127
Jed Hansen	Spr	44	Lance Carter	Spr	118
Luke Oglesby	Wil	43	Jose Rosado	Wil	117
Rudolfo Mendez	Spr	40	Ken Ray	Wch	116

Pitcher	Club	W-L	ERA	IP	H	BB	SO
Glendon Rusch	Wil	14-6	1.74	166	110	34	147
Tim Byrdak	Wil	11-5	2.16	166	118	45	127
Robert Toth	Oma	9-6	2.62	151	148	35	108
Jose Rosado	Wil	10-7	3.13	138	128	30	117
Eric Anderson	Wil	12-6	3.30	120	117	38	71

Runs: Most, career, all-time

1583	George Brett, 1973-1993	
1074	Amos Otis, 1970-1983	
1060	Willie Wilson, 1976-1990	
912	Frank White, 1973-1990	
873	Hal McRae, 1973-1987	

Hits: Most, career, all-time

3154	George Brett, 1973-1993
2006	Frank White, 1973-1990
1977	Amos Otis, 1970-1983
1968	Willie Wilson, 1976-1990
1924	Hal McRae, 1973-1987

2B: Most, career, all-time

665	George Brett, 1973-1993
449	Hal McRae, 1973-1987
407	Frank White, 1973-1990
365	Amos Otis, 1970-1983
241	Willie Wilson, 1976-1990

3B: Most, career, all-time

137	George Brett, 1973-1993
133	Willie Wilson, 1976-1990
65	Amos Otis, 1970-1983
63	Hal McRae, 1973-1987
58	Frank White, 1973-1990

HR: Most, career, all-time

317	George Brett, 1973-1993
193	Amos Otis, 1970-1983
169	Hal McRae, 1973-1987
160	Frank White, 1973-1990
143	John Mayberry, 1972-1977

RBI: Most, career, all-time

1595	George Brett, 1973-1993
1012	Hal McRae, 1973-1987
992	Amos Otis, 1970-1983
886	Frank White, 1973-1990
552	John Mayberry, 1972-1977

SB: Most, career, all-time

612	Willie Wilson, 1976-1990
340	Amos Otis, 1970-1983
336	Freddie Patek, 1971-1979
201	George Brett, 1973-1993
178	Frank White, 1973-1990

BB: Most, career, all-time

1096	George Brett, 1973-1993
739	Amos Otis, 1970-1983
616	Hal McRae, 1973-1987
561	John Mayberry, 1972-1977
413	Freddie Patek, 1971-1979

BA: Highest, career, all-time

.305	George Brett, 1973-1993
.294	KEVIN SEITZER, 1986-1991
.293	Hal McRae, 1973-1987
.290	DANNY TARTABULL, 1987-1991
.293	WALLY JOYNER, 1992-1995

Slug avg: Highest, career, all-time

.518	DANNY TARTABULL, 1987-1991
.487	George Brett, 1973-1993
.480	Bo Jackson, 1986-1990
.469	Willie Aikens, 1980-1983
.459	Steve Balboni, 1984-1988

Games started: Most, career, all-time

392	Paul Splittorff, 1970-1984
308	MARK GUBICZA, 1984-1995
302	Dennis Leonard, 1974-1986
226	BRET SABERHAGEN, 1984-1991
219	Larry Gura, 1976-1985

Saves: Most, career, all-time

238	Dan Quisenberry, 1979-1988
218	JEFF MONTGOMERY, 1988-1995
58	Doug Bird, 1973-1978
49	STEVE FARR, 1985-1990
40	Ted Abernathy, 1970-1972

Shutouts: Most, career, all-time

23	Dennis Leonard, 1974-1986
17	Paul Splittorff, 1970-1984
15	MARK GUBICZA, 1984-1995
14	Larry Gura, 1976-1985
14	BRET SABERHAGEN, 1984-1991

Wins: Most, career, all-time

166	Paul Splittorff, 1970-1984
144	Dennis Leonard, 1974-1986
128	MARK GUBICZA, 1984-1995
111	Larry Gura, 1976-1985
110	BRET SABERHAGEN, 1984-1991

K: Most, career, all-time

1323	Dennis Leonard, 1974-1986
1311	MARK GUBICZA, 1984-1995
1093	BRET SABERHAGEN, 1984-1991
1057	Paul Splittorff, 1970-1984
999	TOM GORDON, 1988-1995

Win pct: Highest, career, all-time

.600	KEVIN APPIER, 1989-1995
.593	Al Fitzmorris, 1969-1976
.587	Larry Gura, 1976-1985
.585	BRET SABERHAGEN, 1984-1991
.576	Doug Bird, 1973-1978

ERA: Lowest, career, all-time

2.55	Dan Quisenberry, 1979-1988
3.21	BRET SABERHAGEN, 1984-1991
3.22	KEVIN APPIER, 1989-1995
3.46	Al Fitzmorris, 1969-1976
3.48	Marty Pattin, 1974-1980

Runs: Most, season

133	Willie Wilson, 1980
119	George Brett, 1979
113	Willie Wilson, 1979
108	George Brett, 1985
105	George Brett, 1977
105	KEVIN SEITZER, 1987

Hits: Most, season

230	Willie Wilson, 1980
215	George Brett, 1976
212	George Brett, 1979
207	KEVIN SEITZER, 1987
195	George Brett, 1975

2B: Most, season

54	Hal McRae, 1977
46	Hal McRae, 1982
45	George Brett, 1978
45	George Brett, 1990
45	Frank White, 1982

3B: Most, season

21	Willie Wilson, 1985
20	George Brett, 1979
15	Willie Wilson, 1980
15	Willie Wilson, 1982
15	Willie Wilson, 1987

HR: Most, season

36	Steve Balboni, 1985
35	GARY GAETTI, 1995
34	John Mayberry, 1975
34	DANNY TARTABULL, 1987
32	Bo Jackson, 1989

RBI: Most, season

133	Hal McRae, 1982
118	George Brett, 1980
112	George Brett, 1985
112	Al Cowens, 1977
112	Darrell Porter, 1979

SB: Most, season

83	Willie Wilson, 1979
79	Willie Wilson, 1980
59	Willie Wilson, 1983
59	Willie Wilson, 1987
53	Freddie Patek, 1977

BB: Most, season

122	John Mayberry, 1973
121	Darrell Porter, 1979
119	John Mayberry, 1975
103	George Brett, 1985
103	Paul Schaal, 1971

BA: Highest, season

.390	George Brett, 1980
.335	George Brett, 1985
.333	George Brett, 1976
.332	Hal McRae, 1976
.332	Willie Wilson, 1982

Slug avg: Highest, season

.664	George Brett, 1980
.599	BOB HAMELIN, 1994
.593	DANNY TARTABULL, 1991
.585	George Brett, 1985
.563	George Brett, 1979
.563	George Brett, 1983

Games started: Most, season

40	Dennis Leonard, 1978
38	Steve Busby, 1974
38	Dennis Leonard, 1980
38	Paul Splittorff, 1973
38	Paul Splittorff, 1978

Saves: Most, season

45	JEFF MONTGOMERY, 1993
45	Dan Quisenberry, 1983
44	Dan Quisenberry, 1984
39	JEFF MONTGOMERY, 1992
37	Dan Quisenberry, 1985

Shutouts: Most, season

6	Roger Nelson, 1972
5	Dennis Leonard, 1977
5	Dennis Leonard, 1979
4	Bill Butler, 1969
4	Dick Drago, 1971
4	Al Fitzmorris, 1974
4	MARK GUBICZA, 1988
4	Larry Gura, 1980
4	Dennis Leonard, 1978
4	BRET SABERHAGEN, 1987
4	BRET SABERHAGEN, 1989

Wins: Most, season

23	BRET SABERHAGEN, 1989
22	Steve Busby, 1974
21	Dennis Leonard, 1978
20	MARK GUBICZA, 1988
20	Dennis Leonard, 1977
20	Dennis Leonard, 1980
20	BRET SABERHAGEN, 1985
20	Paul Splittorff, 1973

K: Most, season

244	Dennis Leonard, 1977
206	Bob Johnson, 1970
198	Steve Busby, 1974
193	BRET SABERHAGEN, 1989
191	DAVID CONE, 1993

Win pct: Highest, season

.800	Larry Gura, 1978
.793	BRET SABERHAGEN, 1989
.769	BRET SABERHAGEN, 1985
.762	DAVID CONE, 1994
.727	Paul Splittorff, 1977

ERA: Lowest, season

2.08	Roger Nelson, 1972
2.16	BRET SABERHAGEN, 1989
2.46	KEVIN APPIER, 1992
2.56	KEVIN APPIER, 1993
2.69	Charlie Leibrandt, 1985

Most pinch-hit homers, season

2	Hal McRae, 1986
2	Carmelo Martinez, 1991

Most pinch-hit homers, career

2	Chuck Harrison, 1969-1971
2	Bob Oliver, 1969-1972
2	Amos Otis, 1970-1983
2	Hal McRae, 1973-1987
2	Steve Balboni, 1984-1988
2	JIM EISENREICH, 1987-1991
2	Carmelo Martinez, 1991

Most consecutive games batting safely

30	George Brett, 1980
22	BRIAN McRAE, 1991

Most consecutive scoreless innings

31	BRET SABERHAGEN, 1989

No-hit games

Steve Busby, KC at Det AL, 3-0; April 16, 1973.
Steve Busby, KC at Mil AL, 2-0; June 19, 1974.
Jim Colborn, KC vs Tex AL, 6-0; May 14, 1977.
BRET SABERHAGEN, KC vs Chi AL, 7-0; August 26, 1991.

ACTIVE PLAYERS in caps.

Players' years of service are listed by the first and last years with this team and are not necessarily consecutive; all statistics record performances for this team only.

Chicago White Sox

By AnneRyan, *USA TODAY*

Once again, "The Big Hurt" Frank Thomas dominated the team at .308 with 40 homers and 111 RBI.

1995 White Sox: Revolving-door disaster

To say 1995 was a disaster for the White Sox is like saying the strike hurt players and owners. The Sox season was lost in the spring when manager Gene Lamont tried to run things like he always had. By the time the real season started, the Sox still weren't ready. They made 22 errors in less than two weeks and their staff ERA was near double figures when Lamont was fired June 2, and replaced on an interim basis by third base coach Terry Bevington.

By the All-Star break, general manager Ron Schueler had watched two DH's, Chris Sabo and John Kruk, come and go, and he began to unload veterans in exchange for young players.

By the time the season ended, the Sox had used 15 players making their major league debuts, including nine pitchers, with six of them winning their first games. Almost every minor league prospect from Class AA up had seen some duty with the big club.

The revolving door did not stop with players. There were three pitching coaches and two bullpen coaches employed. This was a team that had finished one game ahead of Cleveland when the strike stopped the 1994 season and returned a veteran team with baseball's fifth-highest payroll. But the pitching staff, which had led the league in ERA the year before, fell to near the bottom, and the defense was the worst in the league.

There were few bright spots, except for another record-breaking year for Frank Thomas, who became the first player ever to have five straight seasons with a batting average over .300 and at least 20 homers, 100 RBI, 100 runs, and 100 walks. The rest of the offense also chipped in, giving the Sox the second-highest batting average in the league, but it wasn't enough to redeem the horrible pitching and defense.

Alex Fernandez, Wilson Alvarez and Jason Bere finished 28-34 combined. To his credit, Fernandez turned around at the end, going undefeated in his last 10 starts. The other two spots in the rotation were passed around like it was a tryout camp, from 37-year-old Dave Righetti to 22-year-old Luis Andujar. Kids also got a chance in the bullpen, but the closer's role stayed with Roberto Hernandez, who saved his last 10 chances, even though he had blown 10 of his first 32 tries.

Andujar was one of the bright spots from the youth movement. So were Ray Durham, who played every day at second base; Lyle Mouton, who earned an everyday spot in the outfield; and Chris Snopek, who proved he could play either third base or shortstop.

As the season ended, there was some order to what had been season-long chaos. Lance Johnson handled the pressures of batting leadoff for the first time in the big leagues while playing flawless center field, Robin Ventura continued to quietly put up big numbers, and Thomas, for the first time in his career, agreed to batting cleanup and being the DH on a part-time basis.

1996 White Sox: Preview

General manager Ron Schueler does not expect major changes, although he would like to add veteran help at several spots. The emphasis will be on youth, as the Sox try to rebound from their lost season. A third of the 25-man roster could be taken up by first- and second-year players, including some in the starting lineup and rotation, such as outfielder Lyle Mouton, infielder Ray Durham and pitcher Luis Andujar. Schueler believes that the Sox will be able to contend in 1996 because of the nucleus of Frank Thomas, Robin Ventura, Alex Fernandez and Wilson Alvarez.

1995 White Sox: Week-by-week notes

These notes were excerpted from the following issues of Baseball Weekly.

▸**May 3:** Pitching was supposed to be the strength of the '95 White Sox, but it was the weakest of many weak links the first week. Alex Fernandez, Jim Abbott, Jason Bere and Wilson Alvarez all lost their first starts, allowing a combined 16 walks in 13⅔ innings. The Sox were outscored 39-11 and committed 13 errors—a very bad start for a team that was a preseason favorite. Ozzie Guillen played only two games before flying home to Venezuela following the murder of his best friend, Gus Polidor.

▸**May 10:** Wilson Alvarez became the first Sox starter to post a victory (vs. Kansas City, game nine). White Sox pitchers allowed at least eight runs in each of the first seven games (five in the next two), while fielders made 24 errors (22 unearned runs).

▸**May 17:** Alex Fernandez started out 1-2 in his first four games. There was concern after he allowed 29 hits and 11 walks in his first 18⅔ innings. Meanwhile, Tim Raines tied the American League record for consecutive stolen bases with his 32nd. He shares the mark with Willie Wilson and Julio Cruz.

▸**May 31:** Frank Thomas was on pace to break Babe Ruth's record for walks in one season (170). The White Sox hoped that would stop with the arrival of new cleanup hitter John Kruk, who took the place of Chris Sabo. "I don't want to put everything on [Thomas's] shoulders," general manager Ron Schueler said. "He shouldn't have to carry the club. But it's time to win."

▸**June 7:** Gene Lamont was fired, and Terry Bevington took over as manager with the White Sox already 11 games behind the Indians. The question had already become whether the Sox were good enough to be a wild-card playoff team. Frank Thomas said, "To lose the players we lost and come back to where we were, that's not going to happen. We've still got some obvious holes, and they haven't been filled. This team is not as good as last year's."

▸**June 21:** With the White Sox reaching a new low almost every day, interim manager Terry Bevington was finding himself the subject of rumors, the most popular involving the return of Oakland manager Tony La Russa. La Russa said he wouldn't touch the situation "with a 10-foot pole."

▸**June 28:** Ron Schueler had predicted that the Sox were "going to break out against someone," but no one knew it would be the Cleveland Indians, who were outscored 23-10 as the White Sox swept the three-game series at Comiskey Park. Strangely, the mood change came right after the team finished a 1-7 road trip and split four games with Seattle at home.

▸**July 5:** White Sox hitters and pitchers awoke at the same time during a stretch of nine victories in 11 games that included seven consecutive victories over three different teams. It didn't move the Sox much closer to Cleveland in the Central Division, but it did raise their hopes for a wild-card playoff berth. They raised their average to .280, second in the league behind the Indians, and their starting pitchers put up a 10-game 7-2 record with a 3.69 ERA—quite an improvement over 9-22 record (5.44 ERA) in the first 48 games. "There is enough time," said Frank Thomas, "and guys are getting their confidence back."

▸**July 13:** Even after winning nine of 11 games, the White Sox were in danger of falling out of wild-card contention as they fell behind the Brewers into fourth place. Meanwhile, Frank Thomas had 15 intentional walks, a pace to draw 33 on the season, which would tie him for the American League mark with Ted Williams and John Olerud. The major league record, since 1955, is 45, set by Willie McCovey in 1969.

July 19: Tired of watching walks by his pitchers, Terry Bevington issued a new rule because he "had seen enough." He allowed starting pitchers no more than two walks leading to runs. Any more and the pitcher would be removed, even in the first inning. It began after Sox pitchers allowed nine of 14 walks to score in two losses to the Brewers. "I've been more than patient with the guys," Bevington said. "It's not a move made out of frustration, panic or bad mood. It's something I've done before and found drastic improvement."

Aug. 2: The trade of Jim Abbott, who led the White Sox in victories, ERA and innings pitched, met with almost unanimous disapproval from players who believed they were still alive in the wild-card race. "I'm definitely upset about it," said third baseman Robin Ventura, who had become good friends with Abbott. "I think it was bad timing for the team," Frank Thomas said. General manager Ron Schueler admitted Abbott's trade "creates a big hole. If I wasn't overwhelmed [by the deal], I wouldn't have done it."

Aug. 16: Frank Thomas became only the second player in history with more than 100 walks in each of his first five full seasons. The other was Roy Thomas, who did it with the Phillies in 1899-1904.

Aug. 23: Frank Thomas, who bought a Ping-Pong table for the White Sox clubhouse three years ago, replaced it with picnic tables and furniture. "We need a new attitude, a new decor," he said.

Aug. 30: Jason Bere, who led the league in walks most of the season, showed signs of getting his game turned around as he won his first game in more than a month (including a stint on the DL).

Sept. 6: Lance Johnson had been one of the pleasant surprises in an otherwise dull season. He raised his average to better than .300—.364 in July and .317 in August—and stole 35 bases while being caught only four times. Still, the Sox were officially eliminated from the NL Central race before Labor Day and were in danger of finishing more than 30 games out of first place, something that has happened only once since 1968.

Sept. 27: Frank Thomas—who appeared to be on the verge of becoming the first major leaguer in history with five consecutive seasons with at least a .300 average, 100 runs scored, 100 RBI, 100 walks and 20 home runs—all but conceded he would not win his third consecutive MVP award. His concession speech came after Cleveland's Albert Belle hit five homers in two nights at Comiskey Park. "He's had an awesome season," Thomas said. "Right now, he's put himself in his own class. He's going to run away with the MVP award this year."

Team directory

Owner: Jerry Reinsdorf (chairman), Eddie Einhorn (vice-chairman) and a board of directors
General manager: Ron Schueler
Ballpark:
Comiskey Park
333 W. 35th St., Chicago, Ill.
312-924-1000
Capacity 44,321
Parking for 7,000 vehicles; $8
Public transportation available
Kids Corner (with photo booth and uniforms for imitation baseball cards), elevators and seating for the handicapped, escalators, ramps, cash station, Hall of Fame
Team publications:
Program, yearbook, media guide, calendar, team photos and player photos, 312-451-5300
TV, radio broadcast stations:
WMVP 1000 AM, WGN TV-9, Sports Channel Chicago
Camps and/or clinics:
Chicago White Sox Training Centers
708-752-9225
Spring training:
Ed Smith Stadium
Sarasota, Fla.
Capacity 7,500
813-953-3388

CHICAGO WHITE SOX 1995 final stats

BATTERS	BA	SLG	OB	G	AB	R	H	TB	2B	3B	HR	RBI	BB	SO	SB	CS	E
Snopek	.324	.426	.403	22	68	12	22	29	4	0	1	7	9	12	1	0	2
F. Thomas	.308	.606	.454	145	493	102	152	299	27	0	40	111	136	74	3	2	7
Kruk	.308	.390	.399	45	159	13	49	62	7	0	2	23	26	33	0	1	1
Martinez	.307	.436	.371	119	303	49	93	132	16	4	5	37	32	41	8	2	3
Johnson	.306	.425	.341	142	607	98	186	258	18	12	10	57	32	31	40	6	3
Devereaux	.306	.465	.352	92	333	48	102	155	21	1	10	55	25	51	6	6	3
Mouton	.302	.475	.373	58	179	23	54	85	16	0	5	27	19	46	1	0	1
Ventura	.295	.498	.384	135	492	79	145	245	22	0	26	93	75	98	4	3	19
Raines	.285	.422	.374	133	502	81	143	212	25	4	12	67	70	52	13	2	4
Martin	.269	.400	.281	72	160	17	43	64	7	4	2	17	3	25	5	0	7
Lyons	.266	.531	.304	27	64	8	17	34	2	0	5	16	4	14	0	0	2
Grebeck	.260	.357	.360	53	154	19	40	55	12	0	1	18	21	23	0	0	7
Durham	.257	.384	.309	125	471	68	121	181	27	6	7	51	31	83	18	5	15
Sabo	.254	.366	.295	20	71	10	18	26	5	0	1	8	3	12	2	0	1
Guillen	.248	.318	.270	122	415	50	103	132	20	3	1	41	13	25	6	7	12
LaValliere	.245	.337	.303	46	98	7	24	33	6	0	1	19	9	15	0	0	1
Karkovice	.217	.387	.306	113	323	44	70	125	14	1	13	51	39	84	2	3	6
Brady	.190	.238	.261	12	21	4	4	5	1	0	0	3	2	4	0	1	0
Cameron	.184	.316	.244	28	38	4	7	12	2	0	1	2	3	15	0	0	0
Tremie	.167	.167	.200	10	24	0	4	4	0	0	0	0	1	2	0	0	1

PITCHERS	W-L	ERA	G	GS	CG	GF	Sho	SV	IP	H	R	ER	HR	BB	SO
Martinez	0-0	0.00	1	0	0	1	0	0	1.0	0	0	0	0	0	2	0
L. Thomas	0-0	1.32	17	0	0	5	0	0	13.2	8	2	2	1	6	12
Karchner	4-2	1.69	31	0	0	10	0	0	32.0	33	8	6	2	12	24
Simas	1-1	2.57	14	0	0	4	0	0	14.0	15	5	4	1	10	16
Andujar	2-1	3.26	5	5	0	0	0	0	30.1	26	12	11	4	14	9
Lorraine	0-0	3.38	5	0	0	2	0	0	8.0	3	3	3	0	2	5
Fernandez	12-8	3.80	30	30	5	0	2	0	203.2	200	98	86	19	65	159
Hernandez	3-7	3.92	60	0	0	57	0	32	59.2	63	30	26	9	28	84
Sirotka	1-2	4.19	6	6	0	0	0	0	34.1	39	16	16	2	17	19
Righetti	3-2	4.20	10	9	0	1	0	0	49.1	65	24	23	6	18	29
Alvarez	8-11	4.32	29	29	3	0	0	0	175.0	171	96	84	21	93	118
McCaskill	6-4	4.89	55	1	0	17	0	2	81.0	97	50	44	10	33	50
Keyser	5-6	4.97	23	10	0	0	0	0	92.1	114	53	51	10	27	48
DeLeon	5-3	5.19	38	0	0	4	0	0	67.2	60	41	39	10	28	53
Radinsky	2-1	5.45	46	0	0	10	0	1	38.0	46	23	23	7	17	14
Fortugno	1-3	5.59	37	0	0	11	0	0	38.2	30	24	24	7	19	24
Shaw	0-0	6.52	9	0	0	1	0	0	9.2	12	7	7	2	1	6
Marquez	0-1	6.75	7	0	0	2	0	0	6.2	9	5	5	3	2	8
Bere	8-15	7.19	27	27	1	0	0	0	137.2	151	120	110	21	106	110
Ruffcorn	0-0	7.88	4	0	0	0	0	0	8.0	10	7	7	0	13	5
Bolton	0-2	8.18	8	3	0	2	0	0	22.0	33	23	20	4	14	10
Bertotti	1-1	12.56	4	4	0	0	0	0	14.1	23	20	20	6	11	15
Hammaker	0-0	12.79	13	0	0	2	0	0	6.1	11	9	9	2	8	3
Baldwin	0-1	12.89	6	4	0	0	0	0	14.2	32	22	21	6	9	10

1996 preliminary roster

PITCHERS (22)
Wilson Alvarez
Luis Andujar
James Baldwin
Jason Bere
Mike Bertotti
Rodney Bolton
Jeff Darwin
Robert Ellis
Alex Fernandez
Roberto Hernandez
Matt Karchner
Brian Keyser
Andrew Lorraine
Kirk McCaskill
Scott Radinsky
Scott Ruffcorn
Steve Schrenk
Jeff Shaw
Bill Simas
Mike Sirotka
Larry Thomas
Brian Woods

CATCHERS (3)
Ron Karkovice
Julio Vinas
Scott Vollmer

INFIELDERS (10)
Doug Brady
Ray Durham
Craig Grebeck
Ozzie Guillen
Paco Martin
Greg Norton
Olmedo Saenz
Chris Snopek
Frank Thomas
Robin Ventura

OUTFIELDERS (5)
Mike Cameron
Jimmy Hurst
Dave Martinez
Lyle Mouton
Tim Raines

Games played by position

PLAYER	G	C	1B	2B	3B	SS	OF	DH
Brady	12	0	0	6	0	0	0	3
Cameron	28	0	0	0	0	0	28	0
Devereaux	92	0	0	0	0	0	90	0
Durham	125	0	0	122	0	0	0	0
Grebeck	53	0	0	8	18	31	0	0
Guillen	122	0	0	0	0	120	0	1
Johnson	142	0	0	0	0	0	140	1
Karkovice	113	113	0	0	0	0	0	0
Kruk	45	0	1	0	0	0	0	42
LaValliere	46	46	0	0	0	0	0	0
Lyons	27	16	4	0	0	0	0	6
Martin	72	0	0	17	9	7	12	10
Martinez	119	0	47	0	0	0	59	5
Mouton	58	0	0	0	0	0	53	2
Raines	133	0	0	0	0	0	107	22
Sabo	20	0	1	0	1	0	0	15
Snopek	22	0	0	0	17	6	0	0
F. Thomas	145	0	90	0	0	0	0	54
Tremie	10	9	0	0	0	0	0	1
Ventura	135	0	18	0	121	0	0	1

Minor Leagues

Tops in the organization

Batter	Club	Avg.	G	AB	R	H	HR	RBI
Kevin Coughlin	Bir	.372	106	349	56	130	3	49
Jeff Abbott	Bir	.336	125	461	66	155	7	55
Chris Snopek	Nvl	.323	113	393	56	127	12	55
F. Ramsey	Nvl	.310	98	406	61	126	5	45
Olmedo Saenz	Nvl	.304	111	415	60	126	13	74

Home Runs			Wins		
Juan Thomas	Prw	26	Tom Fordham	Bir	15
Nilson Robledo	Sbn	20	Luis Andujar	Bir	14
Mike Robertson	Nvl	19	Rodney Bolton	Nvl	14
Melvin Rosario	Sbn	15	Charles Smith	Sbn	10
Several tied		14	Several tied		9

RBI			Saves		
Nilson Robledo	Sbn	108	Archie Vazquez	Prw	20
Jeff Abbott	Bir	75	Chris Woodfin	Bir	20
Carlos Lee	Brs	75	Dane Johnson	Nvl	15
Olmedo Saenz	Nvl	74	Jamie Surratt	Sbn	14
Harold Williams	Prw	72	Nelson Cruz	Prw	10

Stolen Bases			Strikeouts		
Essex Burton	Bir	60	Russell Herbert	Sbn	163
Andres Levias	But	40	Jack Ford	Hck	157
Sandy McKinnon	Prw	35	Luis Andujar	Bir	146
Chernan Albert	Brs	34	Charles Smith	Sbn	145
Brandon Moore	Sbn	34	Tom Fordham	Bir	139

Pitcher	Club	W-L	ERA	IP	H	BB	SO
Charles Smith	Sbn	10-10	2.69	167	128	61	145
Tom Fordham	Bir	15-3	2.70	167	145	63	139
Luis Andujar	Bir	14-8	2.85	167	147	44	146
Rodney Bolton	Nvl	14-3	2.88	131	125	23	76
Russell Herbert	Sbn	5-12	2.95	168	129	73	163

Sick call: 1995 DL Report

Player	Days on the DL
Jason Bere	15
John Kruk	16
Mike LaValliere	34*
Scott Radinsky	29

Indicates two separate terms on Disabled List.

1995 Amateur draft picks

Players are listed with position and college or high school. Most players were assigned to rookie or Class A leagues. List provided by Major League Baseball.

Franklin Anderson, c, Southern Union State JC; Christopher Beck, cf, El Dorado HS, Placentia, Calif.; Kevin Beirne, rhp, Texas A&M; Michael Biasucci, 2b, South Broward HS, Hollywood, Fla.; Brian Bowness, 1b-3b, Villanova; Tighe Brown, rhp, St. Xavier HS, Louisville, Ky.; Thomas Buckman, rhp, Edison CC; Brian Bullock, rhp, Itawamba JC; Keeron Clarke, of-2b, South Plantation HS, Plantation, Fla.; Kristopher Conrad, rhp, Killian HS, Miami; Pedro Demorejon, rhp, Miami; Erik Desrosiers, rhp, Grand Canyon; Brian Downs, c, Riverside CC; Joshua Fauske, c, Central Washington; Jason Fennell, rf, Baldwin HS, Pittsburgh; Joel Garber, lhp, Nevada; Aaron Gentry, ss, Labette CC; Nestor Gonzales, c, Rio Grande HS, Albuquerque; Jason Gray, rhp, Coconut Creek HS, N. Fort Lauderdale, Fla.; Claudius Halley, rhp, South Alabama; David Harden, lhp, Allen County CC; Derek Hasselhoff, rhp, Towson State; Darren Hayes, lf, Wingate; Darontaye Hollins, cf, Sierra College; David Hostetter, cf, Fannett Metal HS, Fort Loudan, Pa.; Matthew Howe, ss, Mayde Creek HS, Houston.; John Hunt, lhp, Ohio U.; Jeffrey Johnson, ss, Mississippi; Charles Klee, ss, Cardinal Gibbons HS, Lighthouse Point, Fla.; Timothy Kraus, rhp, Notre Dame; Kelly Kruse, rhp, Southwest Missouri State; Jason Lakman, rhp, Woodinville (Wash.) Sr. HS; Eric Leblanc, rhp, St. Rose; Jeffrey Liefer, rf-lf, Long Beach State; Manuel Lutz, 3b, Southwestern JC; Joseph Putz, rhp, Trenton (Mich.) HS; Aaron Randle, 2b-ss, Northeast HS, Fort Lauderdale, Fla.; Justin Rayment, lhp, San Diego St.; Nathan Robertson, lhp, Maize HS, Wichita, Kan.; Peter Rodriguez of, Broward JC; Jason Secoda, rhp, Cal State; Barry Shelton, 3b, West Virginia St.; Brian Simmons, cf, Michigan; Stephen Sparks, rhp, Faulkner St JC; Eric Stanton, 1b, Newberry HS, Silverstreet S.C.; Wade Sterling, c, Allen County CC; Strasser John, ss, Mesa CC; Andrew Tellez, of, Fullerton College; Brian Thrash of, Rising Sun HS, Elkton, Md.; Ryan Topham, rf, Notre Dame; Adam Virchis, rhp, San Diego State; Michael Vota, rhp, Towson State; Christopher Weekly, ss, Highland HS, Gilbert, Ariz.; Brent Wilhelm, 3b, Kansas.

Runs: Most, career, all-time

1319	Luke Appling,	1930-1950
1187	Nellie Fox,	1950-1963
1065	Eddie Collins,	1915-1926
893	Minnie Minoso,	1951-1980
791	Luis Aparicio,	1956-1970

Hits: Most, career, all-time

2749	Luke Appling,	1930-1950
2470	Nellie Fox,	1950-1963
2007	Eddie Collins,	1915-1926
1576	Luis Aparicio,	1956-1970
1523	Minnie Minoso,	1951-1980

2B: Most, career, all-time

440	Luke Appling,	1930-1950
335	Nellie Fox,	1950-1963
267	HAROLD BAINES,	1980-1989
266	Eddie Collins,	1915-1926
260	Minnie Minoso,	1951-1980

3B: Most, career, all-time

104	Shano Collins,	1910-1920
104	Nellie Fox,	1950-1963
102	Luke Appling,	1930-1950
102	Eddie Collins,	1915-1926
82	Johnny Mostil,	1918-1929

HR: Most, career, all-time

214	Carlton Fisk,	1981-1993
186	HAROLD BAINES,	1980-1989
182	FRANK THOMAS,	1990-1995
154	Bill Melton,	1968-1975
140	Ron Kittle,	1982-1991

RBI: Most, career, all-time

1116	Luke Appling,	1930-1950
819	HAROLD BAINES,	1980-1989
808	Minnie Minoso,	1951-1980
804	Eddie Collins,	1915-1926
762	Carlton Fisk,	1981-1993

SB: Most, career, all-time

368	Eddie Collins,	1915-1926
318	Luis Aparicio,	1956-1970
250	Frank Isbell,	1901-1909
206	Fielder Jones,	1901-1908
226	LANCE JOHNSON,	1988-1995

BB: Most, career, all-time

1302	Luke Appling,	1930-1950
965	Eddie Collins,	1915-1926
661	FRANK THOMAS,	1990-1995
658	Nellie Fox,	1950-1963
658	Minnie Minoso,	1951-1980

BA: Highest, career, all-time

.340	Joe Jackson,	1915-1920
.331	Eddie Collins,	1915-1926
.323	FRANK THOMAS,	1990-1995
.317	Zeke Bonura,	1934-1937
.315	Bibb Falk,	1920-1928

Slug avg: Highest, career, all-time

.593	FRANK THOMAS,	1990-1995
.518	Zeke Bonura,	1934-1937
.499	Joe Jackson,	1915-1920
.470	Ron Kittle,	1982-1991
.468	Minnie Minoso,	1951-1980

Games started: Most, career, all-time

484	Ted Lyons,	1923-1946
483	Red Faber,	1914-1933
390	Billy Pierce,	1949-1961
312	Ed Walsh,	1904-1916
301	Doc White,	1903-1913

Saves: Most, career, all-time

201	Bobby Thigpen,	1986-1993
98	Hoyt Wilhelm,	1963-1968
96	ROBERTO HERNANDEZ,	1991-1995
75	Terry Forster,	1971-1976
57	Wilbur Wood,	1967-1978

Shutouts: Most, career, all-time

57	Ed Walsh,	1904-1916
42	Doc White,	1903-1913
35	Billy Pierce,	1949-1961
29	Red Faber,	1914-1933
28	Eddie Cicotte,	1912-1920

Wins: Most, career, all-time

260	Ted Lyons,	1923-1946
254	Red Faber,	1914-1933
195	Ed Walsh,	1904-1916
186	Billy Pierce,	1949-1961
163	Wilbur Wood,	1967-1978

K: Most, career, all-time

1796	Billy Pierce,	1949-1961
1732	Ed Walsh,	1904-1916
1471	Red Faber,	1914-1933
1332	Wilbur Wood,	1967-1978
1098	Gary Peters,	1959-1969

Win pct: Highest, career, all-time

.648	Lefty Williams,	1916-1920
.644	Virgil Trucks,	1953-1955
.616	Jim Kaat,	1973-1975
.615	Juan Pizarro,	1961-1966
.611	JACK McDOWELL,	1987-1994

ERA: Lowest, career, all-time

1.81	Ed Walsh,	1904-1916
2.18	Frank Smith,	1904-1910
2.25	Eddie Cicotte,	1912-1920
2.30	Jim Scott,	1909-1917
2.30	Doc White,	1903-1913

Runs: Most, season

135	Johnny Mostil,	1925
120	Zeke Bonura,	1936
120	Fielder Jones,	1901
120	Johnny Mostil,	1926
120	Rip Radcliff,	1936

Hits: Most, season

224	Eddie Collins,	1920
218	Joe Jackson,	1920
208	Buck Weaver,	1920
207	Rip Radcliff,	1936
204	Luke Appling,	1936

2B: Most, season

46	FRANK THOMAS,	1992
45	Floyd Robinson,	1962
44	Ivan Calderon,	1990
44	Chet Lemon,	1979
43	Bibb Falk,	1926
43	Earl Sheely,	1925

3B: Most, season

21	Joe Jackson,	1916
20	Joe Jackson,	1920
18	Jack Fournier,	1915
18	Harry Lord,	1911
18	Minnie Minoso,	1954
18	Carl Reynolds,	1930

HR: Most, season

41	FRANK THOMAS,	1993
40	FRANK THOMAS,	1995
38	FRANK THOMAS,	1994
37	Dick Allen,	1972
37	Carlton Fisk,	1985
35	Ron Kittle,	1983

RBI: Most, season

138	Zeke Bonura,	1936
128	Luke Appling,	1936
128	FRANK THOMAS,	1993
121	Joe Jackson,	1920
119	Al Simmons,	1933

SB: Most, season

77	Rudy Law,	1983
56	Luis Aparicio,	1959
56	Wally Moses,	1943
53	Luis Aparicio,	1961
53	Eddie Collins,	1917

BB: Most, season

138	FRANK THOMAS, 1991
136	FRANK THOMAS, 1995
127	Lu Blue, 1931
122	Luke Appling, 1935
122	FRANK THOMAS, 1992

BA: Highest, season

.388	Luke Appling, 1936
.382	Joe Jackson, 1920
.372	Eddie Collins, 1920
.360	Eddie Collins, 1923
.359	Carl Reynolds, 1930

Slug avg: Highest, season

.729	FRANK THOMAS, 1994
.607	FRANK THOMAS, 1993
.607	FRANK THOMAS, 1995
.603	Dick Allen, 1972
.589	Joe Jackson, 1920

Games started: Most, season

49	Ed Walsh, 1908
49	Wilbur Wood, 1972
48	Wilbur Wood, 1973
46	Ed Walsh, 1907
43	Wilbur Wood, 1975

Saves: Most, season

57	Bobby Thigpen, 1990
38	ROBERTO HERNANDEZ, 1993
34	Bobby Thigpen, 1988
34	Bobby Thigpen, 1989
32	ROBERTO HERNANDEZ, 1995
32	Bob James, 1985

Shutouts: Most, season

11	Ed Walsh, 1908
10	Ed Walsh, 1906
8	Reb Russell, 1913
8	Ed Walsh, 1909
8	Wilbur Wood, 1972

Wins: Most, season

40	Ed Walsh, 1908
29	Eddie Cicotte, 1919
28	Eddie Cicotte, 1917
27	Ed Walsh, 1911
27	Ed Walsh, 1912
27	Doc White, 1907

K: Most, season

269	Ed Walsh, 1908
258	Ed Walsh, 1910
255	Ed Walsh, 1911
254	Ed Walsh, 1912
215	Gary Peters, 1967

Win pct: Highest, season

.842	Sandy Consuegra, 1954
.806	Eddie Cicotte, 1919
.774	Clark Griffith, 1901
.759	Richard Dotson, 1983
.750	Reb Russell, 1917
.750	Bob Shaw, 1959
.750	Monty Stratton, 1937
.750	Doc White, 1906

ERA: Lowest, season

1.27	Ed Walsh, 1910
1.41	Ed Walsh, 1909
1.42	Ed Walsh, 1908
1.52	Doc White, 1906
1.53	Eddie Cicotte, 1917

Most pinch-hit homers, season

3	Ron Northey, 1956
3	John Romano, 1959
3	Oscar Gamble, 1977

Most pinch-hit homers, career

7	Jerry Hairston, 1973-1989

Most consecutive games batting safely

27	Luke Appling, 1936
26	Guy Curtwright, 1943
25	LANCE JOHNSON, 1992

Most consecutive scoreless innings

45	Doc White, 1904
39	Billy Pierce, 1953
39	Ed Walsh, 1906
38	Ray Herbert, 1963
37	Ed Walsh, 1910
37	Joel Horlen, 1968

No-hit games

Nixey Callahan, Chi vs Det AL, 3-0; September 20, 1902 (1st game).

Frank Smith, Chi at Det AL, 15-0; September 6, 1905 (2nd game).

Frank Smith, Chi vs Phi AL, 1-0; September 20, 1908.

Ed Walsh, Chi vs Bos AL, 5-0; August 27, 1911.

Jim Scott, Chi at Was AL, 0-1; May 14, 1914 (lost on 2 hits in the 10th).

Joe Benz, Chi vs Cle AL, 6-1; May 31, 1914.

Eddie Cicotte, Chi at StL AL, 11-0; April 14, 1917.

Charlie Robertson, Chi at Det AL, 2-0; April 30, 1922 (perfect game).

Ted Lyons, Chi at Bos AL, 6-0; August 21, 1926.

Vern Kennedy, Chi vs Cle AL, 5-0; August 31, 1935.

Bill Dietrich, Chi vs StL AL, 8-0; June 1, 1937.

Bob Keegan, Chi vs Was AL, 6-0; August 20, 1957 (2nd game).

Joe Horlen, Chi vs Det AL, 6-0; September 10, 1967 (1st game).

Blue Moon Odom (5 innings) and Francisco Barrios (4 innings), Chi at Oak AL, 2-1; July 28, 1976.

Joe Cowley, Chi at Cal AL, 7-1; September 19, 1986.

WILSON ALVAREZ, Chi at Bal AL, 7-0; August 11, 1991.

Ed Walsh, 5 innings, rain, Chi vs NY AL, 8-1; May 26, 1907.

MELIDO PEREZ, 6 innings, rain, Chi at NY AL, 8-0; July 12, 1990.

ACTIVE PLAYERS in caps.

Players' years of service are listed by the first and last years with this team and are not necessarily consecutive; all statistics record performances for this team only.

135

Milwaukee Brewers

By Anne Ryan, USA TODAY

First baseman / outfielder B.J. Surhoff led the sagging Brewers in batting (.320) and RBI (46).

1995 Brewers: Lost the season, won a park

A few years from now, 1995 might be remembered as the year the Brewers were saved—not from a dismal record (65-79), but from losing their home in Milwaukee. After bitter debate, the State Assembly and Senate narrowly passed a stadium financing plan that paved the way for a new $250 million, retractable-roof stadium to open in 1999.

Sal Bando, vice president of baseball operations, and manager Phil Garner now face the task of building the Brewers to the point where they are a competitive, entertaining team when they play in their expensive new home. It won't be easy, but there were some signs in 1995 of a nucleus for the future. They were in the wild-card hunt until the last month, when they went 7-25.

"The collapse the last month made it difficult to assess things," Garner said. "We were in the race, and then just couldn't get it done. That made us take a second look at what direction to go. There were some good signs though."

First baseman John Jaha finally arrived, with a .313 average, a team-high 20 home runs and 65 RBI despite two stints on the disabled list. Dave Nilsson recovered from Ross River fever, a rare disease from an Australian mosquito, and ended up at .278 with 12 homers and 53 RBI in 263 at-bats. B.J. Surhoff played everywhere and hit .320. Infielder Jeff Cirillo saw plenty of action and finished at .277. Infielder Jose Valentin and catcher Mike Matheny also showed signs they could be regulars in the majors. Together these players form the nucleus of position players.

Injuries opened the gates for rookie pitchers—at one time there were four in the staring rotation. Knuckleballer Steve Sparks (9-11, 4.63), Scott Karl (6-7, 4.14) and Brian Givens (5-7, 4.95) should be back next season. Jamie McAndrew, who had a couple of good starts before injuring his arm, also could get a shot.

After an All-Star season in 1994, Ricky Bones (10-12, 4.63) was a major disappointment. The Brewers hope he can bounce back in 1996.

Angel Miranda and Bob Scanlan, veterans who had injury problems during the season, also could be a big help if they bounce back.

Mike Fetters established himself as the closer in the bullpen with 22 saves but had some arm problems at times during the season.

1996 Brewers: Preview

Bando and Garner are talking about being committed to youth. That could mean that two first-round draft picks get a shot at the parent club before the end of the '96 season. Third baseman Antone Williamson and outfielder Geoff Jenkins could make the jump from Class AA. Garner said Williamson has to improve defensively if he is to live up to his potential. Jenkins showed power but lacks the speed to play center, where the biggest hole in the Brewers' outfield could be. Pitcher Jeff D'Amico also could get a look before the end of the '96 season.

Two veterans likely to be back in '96 because their high salaries make them almost unmoveable are outfielder Greg Vaughn and infielder Pat Listach. Together, they make up almost half of the Brewers' payroll in '96, with Vaughn making more than $5 million and Listach making $2 million.

As a survival technique until the new stadium is ready, the Brewers will probably have to go with youth. The model for rebuilding is Cleveland; the hope is that the youngsters will blossom by 1999. With increased revenue from a new stadium, some veterans can then be added to make the Brewers contenders.

1995 Brewers: Week-by-week notes

These notes were excerpted from the following issues of Baseball Weekly.

▶ **May 3:** The Brewers had two grand slams in their first three games: John Jaha's on April 26 and Joe Oliver's on April 28. Defensively, though, Jaha had a couple of miscues at first base, in part because of a quadriceps problem that slowed his movement. Catcher Oliver had three passed balls in the first four games.

▶ **May 17:** Bill Wegman was moved to the bullpen after a disastrous start in which he threw only 12 pitches and gave up four runs. With a 9.23 ERA as a starter, Wegman said retirement wouldn't be out of the question if he couldn't find his lost velocity—he was hitting the upper 70s on the radar gun. The Brewers went to a four-man rotation of Ricky Bones, Cal Eldred, Angel Miranda and Bob Scanlan.

▶ **June 14:** Manager Phil Garner continued to have to juggle his starting rotation because of ineffectiveness and injuries. Cal Eldred was headed for more tests on his ailing right elbow. Ricky Bones had his scheduled start on June 12 delayed one day because a line drive hit him in the knee.

▶ **June 21:** Cal Eldred decided to have surgery on his ailing elbow rather than rest it and try to pitch, which meant he was out for the year. Knuckleballer Steve Sparks pitched the Brewers' first complete game since June 27, 1994, when he went the distance in a 9-1 win against the Red Sox on June 17 at Fenway Park. Sparks faced hard-throwing Roger Clemens in a contest that pitted two distinctly different pitching styles.

▶ **June 28:** Steve Sparks continued to help fill the gap in the starting rotation created by elbow injuries to right-hander Cal Eldred and Bob Scanlan. Sparks began throwing the knuckler after suffering a career-threatening shoulder injury in 1993 spring training—he had

tried to rip a Phoenix-area phone book in two after watching a motivational speaker do it.

▶ **July 5:** Phil Garner said he was flattered to be named a coach for the AL All-Star team. "I played in three of them and enjoyed the experience," he said. "They've made it even more of a show, and even better for the participants. I'm looking forward to it." Garner was just as happy about the selection of his son, Eric, to be bullpen catcher for the AL team. Eric played at Texas Christian this past season.

▶ **July 13:** The Brewers play the White Sox in five consecutive games immediately after the All-Star break. The last time they played (June 29), there was a bench-clearing brawl after Rob Dibble knocked down Pat Listach with a pitch. Several Brewers said the hard feelings weren't over, and they applauded when Dibble was handed a suspension.

▶ **July 26:** The main event on July 22 was a wrestling match between White Sox manager Terry Bevington and Brewers skipper Phil Garner. The bad blood boiled up in the seventh inning after Jeff Cirillo and Ozzie Guillen got tangled up at third base. Garner and a few Brewers players came out of the dugout and went to third base, as did Bevington; then both benches cleared. Garner had a cut on his right cheek after the game but claimed he cut himself shaving.

▶ **Aug. 2:** Rob Dibble was sent to New Orleans to work on mechanics. He would have to serve his suspension for the Brewers–White Sox feud that he started if called up from the minors. "That's ironic. It's also typical of my life," said Dibble, who has been dogged by controversy much of his career.

▶ **Aug. 16:** Rob Dibble could turn out to be a fan favorite. When he made his debut on Aug. 9, fans chanted, "Dibble, Dibble." On his second pitch, he unloaded a fastball and fell from the mound.

Fans cheered again.

▶ **Aug. 30:** The Brewers admitted they were doing some scoreboard watching and reading the newspapers as they hung in the AL wild-card race. "We don't even look at our division anymore," outfielder Darryl Hamilton said. Phil Garner, who originally opposed the wild card, also said the race is adding incentive.

▶ **Sept. 6:** The Brewers hoped their dwindling wild-card chances could be rejuvenated with a three-game series versus the Rangers on Sept. 8-10, at home. It would be their last chance to play any of the Western or Central teams contending for the wild-card slot

▶ **Last-day recap: *Heroes*—**Despite the Brewers' collapse the last month, several players had seasons that qualify them as Heroes. Utility player B.J. Surhoff, who signed a minor-league contract to stay with the Brewers in the spring, hit well over .300 all season and hung in the batting race until the last few weeks. He ended at a .320 clip. He also played a handful of positions. Infielder Kevin Seitzer hit .311 and made the All-Star team. First baseman John Jaha hit .313 and had 19 homers despite a couple of stints on the DL.

Unsung Heroes—Dave Nilsson could qualify as an Unsung Hero. He started the season on the DL because of a rare disease, Ross River fever, returning to play solid baseball. Nilsson hit .275 and provided some power with 11 homers and 50 RBI in 80 games. He played in the outfield, where he had virtually no experience. And, throughout, he didn't whine. Catchers Joe Oliver and Mike Matheny also qualify as Unsung Heroes. Oliver came back from an abbreviated season to hit .270, even after suffering a broken left wrist. Matheny provided backup despite little experience.

Disappointments—The two major Disappointments were outfielder Greg Vaughn and pitcher Ricky Bones. Vaughn hit a meager .224 and provided little power. He caught heat because his $4 million salary was almost a third of the Brewers' total payroll. Bones, expected to be the ace of the staff, was

10-12, with a 4.63 ERA. His struggles, coupled with a season-ending elbow injury to Cal Eldred, had to qualify as the major Disappointments in the pitching area.

Infielder Pat Listach, who hit .219, also was a Disappointment, although after injury-riddled seasons in '93 and '94, expectations for him were limited.

Team directory

▶ **Owner:** Allan H. (Bud) Selig
▶ **General manager:** Sal Bando
▶ **Ballpark:**
Milwaukee County Stadium
201 South 46th St., Milwaukee, Wis.
414-933-4114
Capacity 53,192
Pay parking lot; $5 or $7 (11,000 spaces)
Public transportation available
Family and wheelchair sections, ramps, Designated Driver Program including free taxi transportation for single ticket holders participating in the DDP
▶ **Team publications:**
Media guide, *Lead Off*
▶ **TV, radio broadcast stations:**
WTMJ 620 AM, WVTV-TV 18
▶ **Camps and/or clinics:**
Gatorade Youth Camp, during the season, 414-933-4114
Fantasy Camp, winter, 414-933-4114, 800-336-CAMP
▶ **Spring training:**
Compadre Stadium
Chandler, Ariz.
Capacity 5,000 (10,000 including lawn)
602-895-1200

MILWAUKEE BREWERS 1995 final stats

BATTERS	BA	SLG	OB	G	AB	R	H	TB	2B	3B	HR	RBI	BB	SO	SB	CS	E
Surhoff	.320	.492	.378	117	415	72	133	204	26	3	13	73	37	43	7	3	5
Jaha	.313	.579	.389	88	316	59	99	183	20	2	20	65	36	66	2	1	2
Seitzer	.311	.421	.395	132	492	56	153	207	33	3	5	69	64	57	2	0	10
Nilsson	.278	.468	.337	81	263	41	73	123	12	1	12	53	24	41	2	0	2
Cirillo	.277	.442	.371	125	328	57	91	145	19	4	9	39	47	42	7	2	15
Oliver	.273	.439	.332	97	337	43	92	148	20	0	12	51	27	66	2	4	8
Hamilton	.271	.389	.350	112	398	54	108	155	20	6	5	44	47	35	11	1	3
Ward	.264	.395	.338	44	129	19	34	51	3	1	4	16	14	21	6	1	1
Loretta	.260	.380	.327	19	50	13	13	19	3	0	1	3	4	7	1	1	1
Vina	.257	.361	.327	113	288	46	74	104	7	7	3	29	22	28	6	3	8
Mieske	.251	.442	.323	117	267	42	67	118	13	1	12	48	27	45	2	4	4
Hulse	.251	.345	.285	119	339	46	85	117	11	6	3	47	18	60	15	3	3
Unroe	.250	.250	.250	2	4	0	1	1	0	0	0	0	0	0	0	0	0
May	.248	.319	.286	32	113	15	28	36	3	1	1	9	5	18	0	1	2
Matheny	.247	.313	.306	80	166	13	41	52	9	1	0	21	12	28	2	1	4
Vaughn	.224	.408	.317	108	392	67	88	160	19	1	17	59	55	89	10	4	0
Valentin	.219	.402	.293	112	338	62	74	136	23	3	11	49	37	83	16	8	15
Listach	.219	.254	.276	101	334	35	73	85	8	2	0	25	25	61	13	3	6
Singleton	.065	.065	.094	13	31	0	2	2	0	0	0	0	1	10	1	0	0

PITCHERS	W-L	ERA	G	GS	CG	GF	Sho	SV	IP	H	R	ER	HR	BB	SO
Thomas	0-0	0.00	1	0	0	0	0	0	1.1	2	0	0	0	1	0
Wickander	0-0	1.93	29	0	0	9	0	1	23.1	19	6	5	1	12	11
Reyes	1-1	2.43	27	0	0	13	0	1	33.1	19	9	9	3	18	29
Fetters	0-3	3.38	40	0	0	34	0	22	34.2	40	16	13	3	20	33
Eldred	1-1	3.42	4	4	0	0	0	0	23.2	24	10	9	4	10	18
Kiefer	4-1	3.44	24	0	0	7	0	0	49.2	37	20	19	6	27	41
Bronkey	0-0	3.65	8	0	0	4	0	0	12.1	15	6	5	0	6	5
Karl	6-7	4.14	25	18	1	3	0	0	124.0	141	65	57	10	50	59
Lloyd	0-5	4.50	33	0	0	14	0	4	32.0	28	16	16	4	8	13
Bones	10-12	4.63	32	31	3	0	0	0	200.1	218	108	103	26	83	77
Sparks	9-11	4.63	33	27	3	2	0	0	202.0	210	111	104	17	86	96
McAndrew	2-3	4.71	10	4	0	2	0	0	36.1	37	21	19	2	12	19
Givens	5-7	4.95	19	19	0	0	0	0	107.1	116	71	59	11	54	73
Miranda	4-5	5.23	30	10	0	5	0	1	74.0	83	47	43	8	49	45
Wegman	5-7	5.35	37	4	0	17	0	2	70.2	89	45	42	14	21	50
Rightnowar	2-1	5.40	34	0	0	13	0	1	36.2	35	23	22	3	18	22
Slusarski	1-1	5.40	12	0	0	6	0	0	15.0	21	11	9	3	6	6
Roberson	6-4	5.76	26	13	0	8	0	0	84.1	102	55	54	16	37	40
Ignasiak	4-1	5.90	25	0	0	2	0	0	39.2	51	27	26	5	23	26
Scanlan	4-7	6.59	17	14	0	1	0	0	83.1	101	66	61	9	44	29
Dibble	1-2	7.18	31	0	0	8	0	1	26.1	16	21	21	2	46	26
Mercedes	0-1	9.82	5	0	0	0	0	0	7.1	12	9	8	1	8	6

1996 preliminary roster

PITCHERS (17)
Ricky Bones
Marshall Boze
Byron Browne
Cal Eldred
Mike Fetters
Brian Givens
Scott Karl
Mark Kiefer
Graeme Lloyd
Jamie McAndrew
Angel Miranda
Tyrone Narcisse
Alberto Reyes
Sid Roberson
Bob Scanlan
Steve Sparks

Kevin Wickander

CATCHERS (3)
Bobby Hughes
Mike Matheny
Dave Nilsson

INFIELDERS (10)
Jeff Cirillo
John Jaha
Pat Listach
Mark Loretta
Gabby Martinez
Kevin Setzer
Tim Unroe
Jose Valentin
Fernando Vina

Wes Weger

OUTFIELDERS (10)
Brian Banks
Chuck Carr
Todd Dunn
Kenny Felder
David Hulse
Matt Mieske
Danny Perez
Duane Singleton
Greg Vaughn
Turner Ward

Games played by position

PLAYER	G	C	1B	2B	3B	SS	OF	DH
Cirillo	125	0	3	25	108	2	0	0
Hamilton	112	0	0	0	0	0	109	2
Hulse	119	0	0	0	0	0	115	0
Jaha	88	0	81	0	0	0	0	6
Listach	101	0	0	59	2	36	11	0
Loretta	19	0	0	4	0	13	0	1
Matheny	80	80	0	0	0	0	0	0
May	32	0	0	0	0	0	32	0
Mieske	117	0	0	0	0	0	108	2
Nilsson	81	2	7	0	0	0	58	14
Oliver	97	91	2	0	0	0	0	6
Seitzer	132	0	36	0	88	0	0	14
Singleton	13	0	0	0	0	0	11	0
Surhoff	117	18	55	0	0	0	60	3
Unroe	2	0	2	0	0	0	0	0
Valentin	112	0	0	0	1	104	0	4
Vaughn	108	0	0	0	0	0	0	104
Vina	113	0	0	99	2	6	0	0
Ward	44	0	0	0	0	0	40	1

Sick call: 1995 DL Report

Player	Days on the DL
Jeff Bronkey	115*
Cal Eldred	140
Mike Fetters	15
Mike Ignasiak	35
John Jaha	49*
Graeme Lloyd	47
Jamie McAndrew	30
Jose Mercedes	141
Angel Miranda	32
Dave Nilsson	60
Joe Oliver	32
Al Reyes	75
Bob Scanlan	70
Mike Thomas	17
Turner Ward	15
Turner Ward	87*

Indicates two separate terms on Disabled List.

Minor Leagues

Tops in the organization

Batter	Club Avg.	G	AB	R	H	HR	RBI
Mike Kinkade	Hel .353	69	266	76	94	4	39
Jonas Hamlin	Stk .332	99	388	65	129	16	69
Derek Hacopian	Blt .324	123	442	75	143	23	92
Bo Dodson	No .322	125	426	75	137	16	77
Roberto Lopez	Elp .312	114	417	80	130	1	44

Home Runs			Wins		
Derek Hacopian	Blt	23	Brian Tollberg	Blt	13
Dave Staton	No	19	Jeff D'Amico	Blt	13
Bo Dodson	No	16	Joe Ganote	No	12
Jonas Hamlin	Stk	16	Jeff Kramer	Stk	12
Todd Landry	Elp	16	Several tied		11

RBI			Saves		
Derek Hacopian	Blt	92	Doug Webb	Elp	30
A. Williamson	Elp	90	Chris Burt	Blt	27
Mark Loretta	No	79	Sean Maloney	Elp	15
Todd Landry	Elp	79	Tony Pavlovich	Hel	14
Brian Banks	Elp	78	Joe Slusarski	No	11

Stolen Bases			Strikeouts		
Greg Martinez	Stk	55	Joshua Bishop	Brw	134
Mike Dumas	Blt	32	Frankie Rodriguez	Elp	129
Duane Singleton	No	31	Kelly Wunsch	Stk	128
Darrell Nicholas	Stk	30	Kevin Kloek	Elp	121
Several tied		26	Jeff D'Amico	Blt	119

Pitcher	Club W-L	ERA	IP	H	BB	SO
Joshua Bishop	Brw 8-2	2.16	96	64	29	134
Jeff D'Amico	Blt 13-3	2.39	132	102	31	95
Joe Ganote	No 12-5	2.73	132	128	37	95
Cory Lidle	Elp 5-4	3.36	110	126	36	78
Brian Tollberg	Blt 13-4	3.41	132	119	27	110

1995 Amateur draft picks

Players are listed with position and college or high school. Most players were assigned to rookie or Class A leagues. List provided by Major League Baseball.

Jeffrey Alfano, c, Mount Whitney HS, Visalia, Calif.; Alex Andreopoulos, c, Seton Hall; Ryan Arevalos, ss, Texas; Eric Armour, rf, Palm Beach CC; Kenny Avera, rhp, Pace (Fla.) HS; Travis Bailey, ss, Wellington Community HS, West Palm Beach, Fla.; Carlos Barbosa, c, Dinuba (Calif.) HS; Darren Berninger, rhp, Nicholls State; Joshua Bishop, rhp, Missouri; Jared Camp, rhp, Indian River CC; Richard Cercy, rhp, Seabreeze HS, Ormond Beach, Fla.; Robert Cornett, c, North Hall HS, Gainesville, Ga.; Mark Cridland, rf, Galveston College; Alain Cruz, c, Miami Dade CC North; Zane Curry, c, Ball HS, Galveston, Texas; Jason Dawsey, lhp, Clemson; David Elliott, cf, Western Michigan; Edward French, of, Seabreeze HS, Ormond Beach, Fla.; Sergio Guerrero, 2b, Laredo JC; Jonathan Guzman, lhp, Pedro Albizu Campos HS, Levittown, P.R.; Brian Hommel, lhp, Louisville; Charlie Hunter, rhp, Notre Dame HS, Ooltewah, Tenn.; Geoff Jenkins, rf, Southern California; Richard Jennings, ss, Overland HS, Aurora, Colo.; Ledowick Johnson, cf, North Carolina State; Beau Johnson, 1b-of, Mendocino CC; Lance Jordan, rhp, Whittier Christian HS, Hacienda Heights, Calif.; Michael Kinkade, 1b, Washington State; Scott Kirby, 3b, Lake Gibson HS, Lakeland, Fla.; Toby Kominek, 3b, Central Michigan; James Landingham, rf, South Miami (Fla.) HS; Austin Lawes, cf, North Miami (Fla.) HS; Steven Lawson, rhp, Damien HS, La Verne, Calif.; Michael Leach, rhp, Palm Beach CC; James Leary, rhp, South Grand Prairie (Texas) HS; Eric Leiser, cf-rf, Antioch (Calif.) Sr. HS, Dirk Lewallen, 1b, Victor Valley JC; Mickey Lopez, 2b, Florida State; Kevin McDougal, of, Arvada (Colo.) West HS, Eric McMaster, 2b, Arvada (Colo.) West HS; Shawn Miller, rhp, Northeastern Illinois; Donald Moore, cf, Dallastown HS, York, Pa.; Blair Murphy, rhp, De Anza JC; Gerald Parent, cf, Merrimack College; Michael Pasqualicchio, lhp, Lamar; Brad Pautz, rhp, Reedsville (Wis.) HS; Ara Petrosian, rhp, Cypress College; Phillips George, ss, Demopolis (Ala.) HS; Jesse Richardson, lhp, Northern Illinois; Ryan Ritter, 2b, Georgia Tech; Michael Roche, 2b, Brevard JC; Anthony Rodriguez, rhp, Cooper City HS, Pembroke Pines, Fla.; Migues Rodriguez, ss, Sonora HS, Brea, Calif.; Johnathan Rose, lhp, Brevard JC; Jason Ross, rf, Hawaii; Gregory Schaub, rhp-cf, Solanco HS, Oxford Pa.; Samuel Singleton, ss, Dupont HS, Rand, W.Va.; Travis Smith, rhp, Texas Tech; Richard Smith, 1b, Central Michigan; Derek Torres, rhp, Miami Dade CC North; Byron Tribe, rhp, Galveston College; Paul Turco, ss, Sarasota (Fla.) HS; Douglas Wakefield, lhp, Victor Valley CC; Christopher Walther, cf, Vivian Gaither HS, Tampa; Walter Ward, of, Northern HS, Chesapeake Beach, Md.; Monty Ward, rhp, Monterey HS, Lubbock, Texas; Robert Wells, rhp, Lawrence E. Elkins HS, Missouri City, Texas; Stanford Woods, cf, William R. Boone HS, Orlando, Fla.

Milwaukee (1970-1995), incl. Seattle (1969)

Runs: Most, career, all-time

1632	Robin Yount,	1974-1993
1275	PAUL MOLITOR,	1978-1992
821	Cecil Cooper,	1977-1987
726	Jim Gantner,	1976-1992
596	Don Money,	1973-1983

Hits: Most, career, all-time

3142	Robin Yount,	1974-1993
2281	PAUL MOLITOR,	1978-1992
1815	Cecil Cooper,	1977-1987
1696	Jim Gantner,	1976-1992
1168	Don Money,	1973-1983

2B: Most, career, all-time

583	Robin Yount,	1974-1993
405	PAUL MOLITOR,	1978-1992
345	Cecil Cooper,	1977-1987
262	Jim Gantner,	1976-1992
215	Don Money,	1973-1983

3B: Most, career, all-time

126	Robin Yount,	1974-1993
86	PAUL MOLITOR,	1978-1992
42	Charlie Moore,	1973-1986
38	Jim Gantner,	1976-1992
33	Cecil Cooper,	1977-1987

HR: Most, career, all-time

251	Robin Yount,	1974-1993
208	Gorman Thomas,	1973-1986
201	Cecil Cooper,	1977-1987
176	Ben Oglivie,	1978-1986
160	PAUL MOLITOR,	1978-1992

RBI: Most, career, all-time

1406	Robin Yount,	1974-1993
944	Cecil Cooper,	1977-1987
790	PAUL MOLITOR,	1978-1992
685	Ben Oglivie,	1978-1986
605	Gorman Thomas,	1973-1986

SB: Most, career, all-time

412	PAUL MOLITOR,	1978-1992
271	Robin Yount,	1974-1993
137	Jim Gantner,	1976-1992
136	Tommy Harper,	1969-1971
109	DARRYL HAMILTON,	1988-1995

BB: Most, career, all-time

966	Robin Yount,	1974-1993
755	PAUL MOLITOR,	1978-1992
501	Gorman Thomas,	1973-1986
440	Don Money,	1973-1983
432	Ben Oglivie,	1978-1986

BA: Highest, career, all-time

.303	PAUL MOLITOR,	1978-1992
.302	Cecil Cooper,	1977-1987
.290	DARRYL HAMILTON,	1988-1995
.285	Robin Yount,	1974-1993
.283	George Scott,	1972-1976

Slug avg: Highest, career, all-time

.470	Cecil Cooper,	1977-1987
.461	Gorman Thomas,	1973-1986
.461	Ben Oglivie,	1978-1986
.456	George Scott,	1972-1976
.452	Sixto Lezcano,	1974-1980

Games started: Most, career, all-time

268	Jim Slaton,	1971-1983
231	Moose Haas,	1976-1985
217	Mike Caldwell,	1977-1984
216	BILL WEGMAN,	1985-1995
205	Teddy Higuera,	1985-1994

Saves: Most, career, all-time

133	DAN PLESAC,	1986-1992
97	Rollie Fingers,	1981-1985
61	DOUG HENRY,	1991-1994
61	Ken Sanders,	1970-1972
44	Bill Castro,	1974-1980

Shutouts: Most, career, all-time

19	Jim Slaton,	1971-1983
18	Mike Caldwell,	1977-1984
12	Teddy Higuera,	1985-1994
10	Bill Travers,	1974-1980
8	CHRIS BOSIO,	1986-1992
8	Moose Haas,	1976-1985

Wins: Most, career, all-time

117	Jim Slaton,	1971-1983
102	Mike Caldwell,	1977-1984
94	Teddy Higuera,	1985-1994
91	Moose Haas,	1976-1985
81	BILL WEGMAN,	1985-1995

K: Most, career, all-time

1081	Teddy Higuera,	1985-1994
929	Jim Slaton,	1971-1983
800	Moose Haas,	1976-1985
749	CHRIS BOSIO,	1986-1992
696	BILL WEGMAN,	1985-1995

Win pct: Highest, career, all-time

.606	Pete Vuckovich,	1981-1986
.595	Teddy Higuera,	1985-1994
.577	CAL ELDRED,	1991-1995
.560	Mike Caldwell,	1977-1984
.535	Moose Haas,	1976-1985

ERA: Lowest, career, all-time

3.46	Teddy Higuera,	1985-1994
3.65	Jim Colborn,	1972-1976
3.72	Lary Sorensen,	1977-1980
3.74	Mike Caldwell,	1977-1984
3.76	CHRIS BOSIO,	1986-1992

Runs: Most, season

136	PAUL MOLITOR,	1982
133	PAUL MOLITOR,	1991
129	Robin Yount,	1982
121	Robin Yount,	1980
115	PAUL MOLITOR,	1988

Hits: Most, season

219	Cecil Cooper,	1980
216	PAUL MOLITOR,	1991
210	Robin Yount,	1982
205	Cecil Cooper,	1982
203	Cecil Cooper,	1983

2B: Most, season

49	Robin Yount,	1980
46	Robin Yount,	1982
44	Cecil Cooper,	1979
42	Robin Yount,	1983
41	PAUL MOLITOR,	1987

3B: Most, season

16	PAUL MOLITOR,	1979
13	PAUL MOLITOR,	1991
12	Robin Yount,	1982
11	Robin Yount,	1988
10	Robin Yount,	1980
10	Robin Yount,	1983

HR: Most, season

45	Gorman Thomas,	1979
41	Ben Oglivie,	1980
39	Gorman Thomas,	1982
38	Gorman Thomas,	1980
36	George Scott,	1975

RBI: Most, season

126	Cecil Cooper,	1983
123	Gorman Thomas,	1979
122	Cecil Cooper,	1980
121	Cecil Cooper,	1982
118	Ben Oglivie,	1980

SB: Most, season

73	Tommy Harper,	1969
54	PAT LISTACH,	1992
45	PAUL MOLITOR,	1987
41	DARRYL HAMILTON,	1992
41	PAUL MOLITOR,	1982
41	PAUL MOLITOR,	1983
41	PAUL MOLITOR,	1988

BB: Most, season

98	Gorman Thomas, 1979
95	Tommy Harper, 1969
89	Darrell Porter, 1975
89	GREG VAUGHN, 1993
87	Johnny Briggs, 1973

BA: Highest, season

.353	PAUL MOLITOR, 1987
.352	Cecil Cooper, 1980
.331	Robin Yount, 1982
.327	Willie Randolph, 1991
.325	PAUL MOLITOR, 1991

Slug avg: Highest, season

.578	Robin Yount, 1982
.573	Sixto Lezcano, 1979
.566	PAUL MOLITOR, 1987
.563	Ben Oglivie, 1980
.539	Cecil Cooper, 1980
.539	Gorman Thomas, 1979

Games started: Most, season

38	Jim Slaton, 1973
38	Jim Slaton, 1976
36	Jim Colborn, 1973
36	CAL ELDRED, 1993
36	Marty Pattin, 1971
36	Lary Sorensen, 1978

Saves: Most, season

33	DAN PLESAC, 1989
31	Ken Sanders, 1971
30	DAN PLESAC, 1988
29	Rollie Fingers, 1982
29	DOUG HENRY, 1992

Shutouts: Most, season

6	Mike Caldwell, 1978
5	Marty Pattin, 1971
4	Mike Caldwell, 1979
4	Jim Colborn, 1973
4	Teddy Higuera, 1986
4	Bill Parsons, 1971
4	Jim Slaton, 1971

Wins: Most, season

22	Mike Caldwell, 1978
20	Jim Colborn, 1973
20	Teddy Higuera, 1986
18	Teddy Higuera, 1987
18	Lary Sorensen, 1978
18	Pete Vuckovich, 1982

K: Most, season

240	Teddy Higuera, 1987
207	Teddy Higuera, 1986
192	Teddy Higuera, 1988
180	CAL ELDRED, 1993
173	CHRIS BOSIO, 1989

Win pct: Highest, season

.750	Pete Vuckovich, 1982
.727	Mike Caldwell, 1979
.727	CHRIS BOSIO, 1992
.710	Mike Caldwell, 1978
.682	BILL WEGMAN, 1991

ERA: Lowest, season

2.36	Mike Caldwell, 1978
2.45	Teddy Higuera, 1988
2.79	Teddy Higuera, 1986
2.81	Bill Travers, 1976
2.83	Jim Lonborg, 1972

Most pinch-hit homers, season

2	Max Alvis, 1970
2	Bobby Darwin, 1975
2	Bob Hansen, 1974
2	Andy Kosco, 1971
2	Ken McMullen, 1977
2	MATT MIESKE, 1995

Most pinch-hit homers, career

2	Max Alvis, 1970
2	Bobby Darwin, 1975-1976
2	Bob Hansen, 1974-1976
2	Mike Hegan,1969-1977
2	Andy Kosco, 1971
2	Ken McMullen, 1977
2	MATT MIESKE, 1995

Most consecutive games batting safely

39	PAUL MOLITOR, 1987
24	Dave May, 1973

Most consecutive scoreless innings

32	TEDDY HIGUERA, 1987

No-hit game

Juan Nieves, Mil at Bal AL, 7-0; April 15, 1987.

ACTIVE PLAYERS in caps.

Players' years of service are listed by the first and last years with this team and are not necessarily consecutive; all statistics record performances for this team only.

Minnesota Twins

Chuck Knoblauch is the Twins' double threat—he led in batting (.333) and stolen bases (46).

By Russell Beeker, *Baseball Weekly*

1995 Twins: It couldn't get much worse

The Twins were the worst of teams in the worst of times. They finished tied with the Toronto Blue Jays for lowest winning percentage in a shortened season, traded away four veteran pitchers, and set a franchise record for rookies and players used.

The rotation had four right-handed, 22-year-old rookies—Brad Radke, Frank Rodriguez, Jose Parra and LaTroy Hawkins. The fifth starter was Rich Robertson, who was claimed off waivers from Pittsburgh in the off-season.

The Twins traded closer Rick Aguilera to Boston on July 6, starter Scott Erickson, a key to their 1991 World Series championship, to Baltimore on July 7, and starter Kevin Tapani and reliever Mark Guthrie to the Dodgers on July 31. They played a bit better as a team after that but wound up with the worst ERA in the majors for the second consecutive year.

Veterans Kirby Puckett and Chuck Knoblauch, at first angry about the trades, said later they were encouraged by the development of the young pitchers. Radke had a super season for someone who had never pitched above Class AA, leading the team in victories—and, unfortunately, leading the majors in home runs allowed. Rodriguez had the best arm on the staff. Parra needs to get stronger and develop a sharper breaking pitch. Hawkins failed his first time up, then showed marked improvement at Class AAA and in a September call-up.

At the plate, right fielder Kirby Puckett overcame a slow start and second baseman Chuck Knoblauch set a career high for homers. Left fielder Marty Cordova was the first 20-20 rookie since 1987, with 24 home runs and 20 stolen bases—the third Twin ever to do so. Center fielder Rich Becker, given every opportunity to win the everyday job after Alex Cole broke his leg in May, struggled.

Shortstop Pat Meares stabilized a position that had been in flux since Greg Gagne left in free agency after 1992. Jeff Reboulet was an above-average utility player, and Chip Hale continued to be one of the better pinch-hitters. Designated hitter Pedro Munoz remained a liability in the field, but he had a career high in homers and provided much of what little power this team had.

The corners weren't up to par. First baseman Scott Stahoviak fielded well but didn't hit for power. Scott Leius was horrid at third base and was waived after the season.

The Twins hit only 15 homers from the left side of the plate in 1995, an embarrassing number in a ballpark that favors lefties.

"It was a tough year," general manager Terry Ryan says. "I suspect I'm going to gain from it. But I sure as hell don't want to go through another one like it."

1996 Twins: Preview

The few moves general manager Terry Ryan plans to make will be aimed at 1997, when the Twins hope they can contend for a wild-card playoff spot.

He'll try to sign a left-handed-hitting cleanup hitter to protect Kirby Puckett in the lineup and generate lefty power in the Metrodome. Pedro Munoz is better suited to hitting sixth or seventh in the order, Ryan says.

Also on the list are a free agent pitcher to provide leadership to a green pitching staff and an upgrade in the catching. Ryan hopes other problems will be resolved as the youngsters mature. Two big concerns are first base and center field, where prospects Scott Stahoviak and Rich Becker failed to secure jobs. Third base was another problem area. Todd Walker, the first-round pick in '94, will win the job if his fielding improved in the Arizona Fall League.

1995 Twins: Week-by-week notes

These notes were excerpted from the following issues of Baseball Weekly.

▶ **May 3:** The Twins announced before their home opener that they would retire Kent Hrbek's No. 14 jersey. (Hrbek retired after the 1994 strike.) His number will join Tony Oliva's No. 6, Rod Carew's No. 29 and Harmon Killebrew's No. 3 on the outfield wall.

▶ **May 10:** Brad Radke won his first major league start by beating the Indians 5-2 at Jacobs Field. He pitched 5⅔ innings, allowing six hits and two runs and walking none.

▶ **May 17:** Through 16 games, the Twins displayed the worst starting pitching in baseball.

Also, with Kent Hrbek gone, the Twins had already used six different first basemen and five different cleanup hitters.

▶ **May 24:** Marty Cordova had his string of consecutive games with a home run stopped at five, three short of the major-league record. Still, his streak tied the major league rookie record shared by Rudy York, George Alusik and Ron Kittle and also matched the team mark set by Harmon Killebrew in 1970. Seattle pitcher Randy Johnson stopped the streak on May 21.

▶ **May 31:** Kirby Puckett was off to his slowest start ever, hitting .241 after 29 games. Only three times in his career had he been below .290 this far into a season.

▶ **June 14:** The Twins had been outscored by exactly two runs per game this season—not in losses, but in all games. They were 12-31, baseball's worst, and couldn't even compete with teams considered equally inept, such as the Brewers and the Tigers, who were a combined 9-3 against them this season.

▶ **June 21:** Pitcher Pat Mahomes was back—from shoulder stiffness and his banishment. Mahomes begged his way back into the rotation, then was late to the park on June 11, causing manager Tom Kelly to remove him from the rotation. But with Eddie Guardado having convinced Kelly that he's not a major-league starter, Mahomes was the only alternative.

▶ **June 28:** The Twins became the last major-league team to win a series this season when they took a two of three from the A's. To achieve that milestone, they required a 10-inning, 8-5 victory and a ninth-inning rally, with rookie center fielder Rich Becker driving home the winning run with a single. Becker had struck out in his previous two at-bats. "I don't know why I left him in there," manager Tom Kelly said. "He wasn't swinging worth [expletive]. And I still send him up there to hit. I don't know why, but he hit a bullet." The Twins won 3-2. It was their first victory in which they scored three runs or fewer, after 22 such losses.

▶ **July 13:** The Twins consummated two expected trades within less than 24 hours July 6-7, sending closer Rick Aguilera to the Red Sox and starter Scott Erickson to the Orioles. They received top pitching prospect Frankie Rodriguez and a player to be named later from the Red Sox and young starter Scott Klingenbeck and a player to be named from the Orioles. Twins veterans were livid after the Aguilera deal and worried after the Erickson deal. "I think this is a bunch of...," star outfielder Kirby Puckett said. "He's our all-time saves leader. This doesn't make sense. To me it seems the organization doesn't want to win. I think that's the message they're sending. Who's going to want to come here and play? You trade your best players, and what free agent at the end of the year is going to want to come here? It's not a good message. I think it's garbage. We've got nobody to take his place. I'm not saying Frankie Rodriguez can't pitch, but we have a lot of holes as it is, and now it's worse." Pitcher Kevin Tapani seemed close to tears. "It's bad—I don't understand it," he said. "I don't see how you get better by subtracting an All-Star who's a strong presence in your clubhouse. This is hard to take."

July 19: Puckett said he was through ripping the Twins for trading Aguilera and Erickson and made a point of praising rookie pitcher Frankie Rodriguez, acquired in the Aguilera deal: "Frankie Rodriguez is going to be an All-Star pitcher one day, and you can quote me on that."

July 26: After dealing away their star closer and a workhorse starter, the Twins were playing their best baseball of the season. They were 10-9 in July after having losing records in each of the season's three months while building baseball's worst record. "We've got nothing to lose," Puckett said. "We might as well play with reckless abandon."

Aug. 16: The second-largest crowd of the season, 35,796, watched the retirement of Kent Hrbek's No. 14 jersey on Aug. 13. Some athletes get Rolexes when they're honored—Hrbek got a cow. Bullpen coach and longtime lockermate Rick Stelmaszek gave him a pig. Why? "Stelly always called me a pig," Hrbek said. "Now he gave me one. But I don't know why they got me a cow. They didn't know what to get me." The franchise's foremost practitioner of barnyard humor watched as two of the three other Twins whose numbers have been retired—Tony Oliva and Rod Carew—peeled off part of the outfield wall to reveal Hrbek's surname and his old No. 14. "It's beyond dreams," Hrbek said.

Aug. 23: Twins rookie pitcher Brad Radke was the unquestioned ace of the Twins staff at just 9-11—more than 20% of the Twins' victories.

Aug. 30: Kirby Puckett and Chuck Knoblauch were two of the harshest critics of the Twins' willingness to trade their veteran pitchers. But after watching Frankie Rodriguez and Jose Parra put a couple of good starts together, they have decided there is reason for optimism. "Rebuilding is a funny word," Knoblauch said. "You see some of these young guys pitch, and you think a few of them are going to be great pitchers. If

guys like Frankie and Jose Parra and Brad Radke can finish this season strong, who knows what will happen next year?"

Oct. 4: Twins rookie left fielder Marty Cordova stole his 20th base on Sept. 30, making him the third Twin ever, and the first rookie since 1987, to compile 20 homers and 20 steals in a season.

Last-day recap: *Heroes*—Despite an unusually sluggish start, Kirby Puckett had another great year, batting .314 with 23 home runs and 99 RBI. Chuck Knoblauch hit .333 while reaching career highs in home runs with 11 and RBI with 63. With 46 stolen bases and a slick glove complementing his hitting prowess, Knoblauch is vying with Roberto Alomar and Carlos Baerga to become the best second baseman in the AL. Brad Radke was the ace of the Twins' staff. Though his 11-14 record and 5.32 ERA were not particularly noteworthy, he was the top starter on the team.

Team directory

Owner: Carl R. Pohlad
General manager: Terry Ryan
Ballpark:
Hubert H. Humphrey Metrodome
501 Chicago Ave. S.,
Minneapolis, Minn.
612-375-1366
Capacity 56,144
Public transportation available
Family and wheelchair sections, elevators
Team publications:
Twins Magazine
612-375-7458
TV, radio broadcast stations:
WCCO 830 AM, WCCO-TV Channel 4, Midwest Sports Channel
Camps and/or clinics:
Twins Clinics, weekends throughout the summer, 612-375-7498
Spring training:
Lee County Sports Complex
Fort Myers, Fla.
Capacity 7,500
813-768-4200

MINNESOTA TWINS 1995 final stats

BATTERS	BA	SLG	OB	G	AB	R	H	TB	2B	3B	HR	RBI	BB	SO	SB	CS	E
Cole	.342	.468	.409	28	79	10	27	37	3	2	1	14	8	15	1	3	3
Clark	.339	.550	.354	36	109	17	37	60	8	3	3	15	2	11	3	0	0
Knoblauch	.333	.487	.424	136	538	107	179	262	34	8	11	63	78	95	46	18	10
Lawton	.317	.467	.414	21	60	11	19	28	4	1	1	12	7	11	1	1	1
Puckett	.314	.515	.379	137	538	83	169	277	39	0	23	99	56	89	3	2	4
P. Munoz	.301	.489	.338	104	376	45	113	184	17	0	18	58	19	86	0	3	5
Reboulet	.292	.398	.373	87	216	39	63	86	11	0	4	23	27	34	1	2	4
Merullo	.282	.379	.335	76	195	19	55	74	14	1	1	27	14	27	0	1	3
Cordova	.277	.486	.352	137	512	81	142	249	27	4	24	84	52	111	20	7	5
Meares	.269	.431	.311	116	390	57	105	168	19	4	12	49	15	68	10	4	18
Stahoviak	.266	.373	.341	94	263	28	70	98	19	0	3	23	30	61	5	1	5
Hale	.262	.373	.333	69	103	10	27	37	4	0	2	18	11	20	0	0	0
Coomer	.257	.455	.324	37	101	15	26	46	3	1	5	19	9	11	0	1	2
Walbeck	.257	.316	.302	115	393	40	101	124	18	1	1	44	25	71	3	1	6
Leius	.247	.349	.335	117	372	51	92	130	16	5	4	45	49	54	2	1	14
Masteller	.237	.343	.303	71	198	21	47	68	12	0	3	21	18	19	1	2	2
Becker	.237	.296	.303	106	392	45	93	116	15	1	2	33	34	95	8	9	4
McCarty	.218	.309	.279	25	55	10	12	17	3	1	0	4	4	18	0	1	1
Raabe	.214	.214	.267	6	14	4	3	3	0	0	0	0	1	1	0	0	0
Brito	.200	.800	.333	5	5	1	1	4	0	0	1	1	0	3	0	0	0
Hocking	.200	.360	.259	9	25	4	5	9	0	2	0	3	2	2	1	0	1
Maas	.193	.316	.281	22	57	5	11	18	4	0	1	5	7	11	0	0	3
Ingram	.125	.125	.300	4	8	0	1	1	0	0	0	1	2	1	0	0	0
Dunn	.000	.000	.143	5	6	0	0	0	0	0	0	0	1	3	0	0	0

PITCHERS	W-L	ERA	G	GS	CG	GF	Sho	SV	IP	H	R	ER	HR	BB	SO
Robertson	2-0	3.83	25	4	1	8	0	0	51.2	48	28	22	4	31	38
Guthrie	5-3	4.46	36	0	0	7	0	0	42.1	47	22	21	5	16	48
Campbell	0-0	4.66	6	0	0	1	0	0	9.2	8	5	5	0	5	5
Tapani	6-11	4.92	20	20	3	0	1	0	133.2	155	79	73	21	34	88
Stevens	5-4	5.07	56	0	0	34	0	10	65.2	74	40	37	14	32	47
Guardado	4-9	5.12	51	5	0	10	0	2	91.1	99	54	52	13	45	71
Sanford	0-0	5.30	11	0	0	6	0	0	18.2	16	11	11	7	16	17
Radke	11-14	5.32	29	28	2	0	1	0	181.0	195	112	107	32	47	75
Watkins	0-0	5.40	27	0	0	7	0	0	21.2	22	14	13	2	11	11
O. Munoz	2-1	5.60	10	3	0	4	0	0	35.1	40	28	22	6	17	25
Trombley	4-8	5.62	20	18	0	0	0	0	97.2	107	68	61	18	42	68
Rodriguez	5-8	6.13	25	18	0	1	0	0	105.2	114	83	72	11	57	59
Mahomes	4-10	6.37	47	7	0	16	0	3	94.2	100	74	67	22	47	67
Schullstrom	0-0	6.89	37	0	0	16	0	0	47.0	66	36	36	8	22	21
Horsman	0-0	7.00	6	0	0	3	0	0	9.0	12	8	7	2	4	4
Klingenbeck	2-4	7.12	24	9	0	4	0	0	79.2	101	65	63	22	42	42
Parra	1-5	7.59	12	12	0	0	0	0	61.2	83	59	52	11	22	29
Hawkins	2-3	8.67	6	6	1	0	0	0	27.0	39	29	26	3	12	9
Harris	0-5	8.82	7	6	0	0	0	0	32.2	50	35	32	5	16	21
Willis	0-0	94.50	3	0	0	0	0	0	0.2	5	7	7	5	0	0

1996 preliminary roster

PITCHERS (21)
Rick Aguilera
Marc Barcello
Gus Gandarillas
Eddie Guardado
Greg Hansell
Latroy Hawkins
Joe Jacobsen
Scott Klingenbeck
Pat Mahomes
Mike Misuraca
Dan Naulty
Jose Parra
Brad Radke
Todd Ritchie
Brett Roberts
Rich Robertson
Frankie Rodriguez
Dan Serafini
Dave Stevens
Hector Trinidad
Scott Watkins

CATCHERS (3)
Mike Durant
Greg Myers
Matt Walbeck

INFIELDERS (9)
Ron Coomer
Denny Hocking
Chuck Knoblauch
Pat Meares
Paul Molitor
Jamie Ogden
Jeff Reboulet
Chad Roper
Scott Stahoviak

OUTFIELDERS (7)
Rich Becker
Marty Cordova
J.J. Johnson
Chris Latham
Matt Lawton
Pedro Munoz
Kirby Puckett

Games played by position

PLAYER	G	C	1B	2B	3B	SS	OF	DH
Becker	106	0	0	0	0	0	105	0
Brito	5	0	0	0	0	0	0	3
Clark	36	0	11	0	0	0	23	3
Cole	28	0	0	0	0	0	23	4
Coomer	37	0	22	0	13	0	1	4
Cordova	137	0	0	0	0	0	137	0
Dunn	5	0	3	0	0	0	0	0
Hale	69	0	3	7	5	0	0	27
Hocking	9	0	0	0	0	6	0	0
Ingram	4	0	0	0	0	0	0	3
Knoblauch	136	0	0	136	0	2	0	0
Lawton	21	0	0	0	0	0	19	1
Leius	117	0	0	0	112	7	0	3
Maas	22	0	8	0	0	0	0	12
Masteller	71	0	48	0	0	0	22	8
McCarty	25	0	18	0	0	0	5	0
Meares	116	0	0	0	0	114	3	0
Merullo	76	46	2	0	0	0	0	13
P. Munoz	104	0	3	0	0	0	25	77
Puckett	137	0	0	1	1	1	109	28
Raabe	6	0	0	4	2	0	0	0
Reboulet	87	1	17	15	22	39	0	0
Stahoviak	94	0	69	0	22	0	0	1
Walbeck	115	113	0	0	0	0	0	0

Minor Leagues

Tops in the organization

Batter	Club	Avg.	G	AB	R	H	HR	RBI
Riccardo Ingram	Slk	.348	122	477	80	166	12	85
A.J. Pierzynski	Elz	.325	78	289	39	94	9	59
Mitch Simons	Slk	.325	130	480	87	156	3	46
Jose Valentin	Ftw	.324	112	383	59	124	19	65
Steve Dunn	Slk	.316	109	402	57	127	12	83

Home Runs			Wins		
Todd Walker	Nbr	21	Tom Mott	Ftw	13
Bubba Smith	Nbr	19	Shane Bowers	Ftm	13
Jose Valentin	Ftw	19	Troy Carrasco	Ftm	12
Tom Quinlan	Slk	17	Dan Serafini	Slk	12
Corey Koskie	Ftw	16	Several tied		11

RBI			Saves		
Tom Quinlan	Slk	88	Scott Watkins	Slk	20
Todd Walker	Nbr	85	Paul Morse	Ftm	15
Riccardo Ingram	Slk	85	Darren Fidge	Ftw	13
Steve Dunn	Slk	83	Fred Rath	Elz	12
Corey Koskie	Ftw	78	Sean Gavaghan	Slk	10

Stolen Bases			Strikeouts		
Carlos Garcia	Elz	38	Travis Miller	Nbr	151
Mitch Simons	Slk	32	Aaron Fultz	Ftm	139
Armann Brown	Ftw	27	Brett Roberts	Nbr	135
Onofre Astacio	Twi	26	Dan Serafini	Slk	127
Matt Lawton	Nbr	26	Darren Fidge	Ftw	106

Pitcher	Club	W-L	ERA	IP	H	BB	SO
Keith Linebarger	Ftm	7-4	2.10	103	74	35	73
Shane Bowers	Ftm	13-5	2.16	146	119	32	103
Mike Nartker	Ftw	5-5	3.10	96	87	20	79
Troy Carrasco	Ftm	12-4	3.13	138	131	63	96
Brett Roberts	Nbr	11-9	3.41	174	162	50	135

Sick call: 1995 DL Report

Player	Days on the DL
Jerald Clark	106*
Alex Cole	111
Kevin Maas	16

Indicates two separate terms on Disabled List.

1995 Amateur draft picks

Players are listed with position and college or high school. Most players were assigned to rookie or Class A leagues. List provided by Major League Baseball.

Todd Bartels, rhp, Stanford; Jason Bell, rhp, Oklahoma State; Craig Black, 2b, Palm Beach Lakes (Fla.) HS; John Blank, lhp, William Carey; Brian Bodwell, rhp, Ocosta HS, Westport, Wash.; Harold Boggs, rhp, West Virginia State; Paul Boykin, of, Columbine HS, W. Littleton, Colo.; Michael Brunet, rhp, Land O'Lakes (Fla.) HS; John Chapman, lhp, St. Josephs College; Nelson Correa, 1b, Florida Air Academy, Melbourne, Fla.; Andres Cruz, c, Stella Marquez HS, Salinas, P.R.; Edmond Daniels, rhp, Polk CC; John Danner, rhp, South Florida; Scott Dobson, rhp, West Potomac HS, Alexandria, Va.; Gary Forster, rhp, Montesano (Wash.) HS; Joseph Fraser, 2b, Cal State Fullerton; Jeffrey Garff, rhp, Dixie College; Shane Gunderson, 1b-c, Minnesota; Jeffrey Harris, rhp, San Francisco; Lewis Harrison, 1b, Palo Alto (Calif.) HS; A.J. Hinch, c, Stanford; Joshua Holliday, c, Stillwater (Okla.) HS; James Hood, ss, Germantown (Tenn.) HS; Carlisle Johnson, ss-cf, T. Dewitt Taylor HS, Pierson, Fla.; Travis Johnson, lf-rf, North Dakota; Ivory Jones, rf-cf, San Francisco State; Kyle Kane, cf-rf, The Linfield School, Temecula, Calif.; Alan Mahaffey, lhp, Arkansas; Bryan Malko, rhp, Piscataway (N.J.) HS; Charles Marshall, rhp, Enterprise HS, Ariton, Ala.; Joseph McHenry, rf-lf, Oakland HS, Murfreesboro, Tenn.; Jason McKenzie, rhp, Mississippi; Javier Mejia, rhp, Southern California; Douglas Mientkiewicz, 1b, Florida State; Brian Mitchell, 3b, Iowa City (Iowa) HS; Michael Moriarty, ss, Seton Hall; Kevin Nelson, 1b, Bryant HS, Alexander, Ark.; Brad Niedermaier, rhp, Northwestern; Matthew Noe, lhp, Riverside CC; David Orndorff, c, Shippensburg (Pa.) Area HS; Edgar Oropeza, rhp, CC of San Francisco; Timothy Peters, lhp, Baylor; Robert Ramsay, lhp, Washington State; Mark Redman, lhp, Oklahoma; Sean Reilly, lhp, Aldershot HS, Burlington, Ont.; Freddy Reyes, 1b-3b, Jefferson HS, Levittown, P.R.; William Rushing, lhp, Georgia Southern; Jeffrey Smith, c, Stetson; James Splittorff, rhp, Kansas; William Tanksley, rhp, Mississippi State; Leonardo Torres, lhp, Cibola HS, Somerton, Ariz.; Jamie Vallis, lhp, Charles P. Allen HS, Bedford, Nova Scotia.; Matthew Vanderbush, lhp, William Paterson; Toby Wilmot, lhp, Oklahoma.

Minnesota (1961-1995), includes Washington (1901-1960)

Runs: Most, career, all-time

1466	Sam Rice, 1915-1933
1258	Harmon Killebrew, 1954-1974
1154	Joe Judge, 1915-1932
1071	KIRBY PUCKETT, 1984-1995
1037	Buddy Myer, 1925-1941

Hits: Most, career, all-time

2889	Sam Rice, 1915-1933
2304	KIRBY PUCKETT, 1984-1995
2291	Joe Judge, 1915-1932
2100	Clyde Milan, 1907-1922
2085	Rod Carew, 1967-1978

2B: Most, career, all-time

479	Sam Rice, 1915-1933
421	Joe Judge, 1915-1932
414	KIRBY PUCKETT, 1984-1995
391	Mickey Vernon, 1939-1955
329	Tony Oliva, 1962-1976

3B: Most, career, all-time

183	Sam Rice, 1915-1933
157	Joe Judge, 1915-1932
125	Goose Goslin, 1921-1938
113	Buddy Myer, 1925-1941
108	Mickey Vernon, 1939-1955
90	Rod Carew, 1967-1978 (8)

HR: Most, career, all-time

559	Harmon Killebrew, 1954-1974
293	Kent Hrbek, 1981-1994
256	Bob Allison, 1958-1970
220	Tony Oliva, 1962-1976
207	KIRBY PUCKETT, 1984-1995

RBI: Most, career, all-time

1540	Harmon Killebrew, 1954-1974
1086	Kent Hrbek, 1981-1994
1085	KIRBY PUCKETT, 1984-1995
1045	Sam Rice, 1915-1933
1026	Mickey Vernon, 1939-1955

SB: Most, career, all-time

495	Clyde Milan, 1907-1922
346	Sam Rice, 1915-1933
321	George Case, 1937-1947
271	Rod Carew, 1967-1978
210	Joe Judge, 1915-1932

BB: Most, career, all-time

1505	Harmon Killebrew, 1954-1974
1274	Eddie Yost, 1944-1958
943	Joe Judge, 1915-1932
864	Buddy Myer, 1925-1941
838	Kent Hrbek, 1981-1994

BA: Highest, career, all-time

.334	Rod Carew, 1967-1978
.328	Heinie Manush, 1930-1935
.323	Sam Rice, 1915-1933
.323	Goose Goslin, 1921-1938
.318	KIRBY PUCKETT, 1984-1995

Slug avg: Highest, career, all-time

.514	Harmon Killebrew, 1954-1974
.502	Goose Goslin, 1921-1938
.500	Roy Sievers, 1954-1959
.481	Jimmie Hall, 1963-1966
.481	Kent Hrbek, 1981-1994

Games started: Most, career, all-time

666	Walter Johnson, 1907-1927
433	Jim Kaat, 1959-1973
345	Bert Blyleven, 1970-1988
331	Camilo Pascual, 1954-1966
259	FRANK VIOLA, 1982-1989

Saves: Most, career, all-time

184	RICK AGUILERA, 1989-1995
108	Ron Davis, 1982-1986
104	Jeff Reardon, 1987-1989
96	Firpo Marberry, 1923-1936
88	Al Worthington, 1964-1969

Shutouts: Most, career, all-time

110	Walter Johnson, 1907-1927
31	Camilo Pascual, 1954-1966
29	Bert Blyleven, 1970-1988
23	Jim Kaat, 1959-1973
23	Dutch Leonard, 1938-1946

Wins: Most, career, all-time

417	Walter Johnson, 1907-1927
190	Jim Kaat, 1959-1973
149	Bert Blyleven, 1970-1988
145	Camilo Pascual, 1954-1966
128	Jim Perry, 1963-1972

K: Most, career, all-time

3509	Walter Johnson, 1907-1927
2035	Bert Blyleven, 1970-1988
1885	Camilo Pascual, 1954-1966
1851	Jim Kaat, 1959-1973
1214	FRANK VIOLA, 1982-1989

Win pct: Highest, career, all-time

.622	Firpo Marberry, 1923-1936
.602	Sam Jones, 1928-1931
.599	Walter Johnson, 1907-1927
.598	Earl Whitehill, 1933-1936
.588	Mudcat Grant, 1964-1967

ERA: Lowest, career, all-time

2.17	Walter Johnson, 1907-1927
2.64	Doc Ayers, 1913-1919
2.75	Harry Harper, 1913-1919
2.76	Charlie Smith, 1906-1909
2.83	Bert Gallia, 1912-1917
3.15	Jim Perry, 1963-1972 (10)

Runs: Most, season

128	Rod Carew, 1977
127	Joe Cronin, 1930
126	Zoilo Versalles, 1965
122	Buddy Lewis, 1938
121	Heinie Manush, 1932
121	Sam Rice, 1930

Hits: Most, season

239	Rod Carew, 1977
234	KIRBY PUCKETT, 1988
227	Sam Rice, 1925
223	KIRBY PUCKETT, 1986
221	Heinie Manush, 1933

2B: Most, season

51	Mickey Vernon, 1946
50	Stan Spence, 1946
45	Joe Cronin, 1933
45	KIRBY PUCKETT, 1989
45	Zoilo Versalles, 1965
45	CHUCK KNOBLACH, 1994

3B: Most, season

20	Goose Goslin, 1925
19	Joe Cassidy, 1904
19	Cecil Travis, 1941
18	Joe Cronin, 1932
18	Goose Goslin, 1923
18	Sam Rice, 1923
18	Howie Shanks, 1921
18	John Stone, 1935
16	Rod Carew, 1977 (11)

HR: Most, season

49	Harmon Killebrew, 1964
49	Harmon Killebrew, 1969
48	Harmon Killebrew, 1962
46	Harmon Killebrew, 1961
45	Harmon Killebrew, 1963

RBI: Most, season

140	Harmon Killebrew, 1969
129	Goose Goslin, 1924
126	Joe Cronin, 1930
126	Joe Cronin, 1931
126	Harmon Killebrew, 1962

SB: Most, season

88	Clyde Milan, 1912
75	Clyde Milan, 1913
63	Sam Rice, 1920
62	Danny Moeller, 1913
61	George Case, 1943
49	Rod Carew, 1976 (8)

BB: Most, season

151	Eddie Yost, 1956
145	Harmon Killebrew, 1969
141	Eddie Yost, 1950
131	Harmon Killebrew, 1967
131	Eddie Yost, 1954

BA: Highest, season

.388	Rod Carew, 1977
.379	Goose Goslin, 1928
.376	Ed Delahanty, 1902
.364	Rod Carew, 1974
.359	Rod Carew, 1975

Slug avg: Highest, season

.614	Goose Goslin, 1928
.606	Harmon Killebrew, 1961
.590	Ed Delahanty, 1902
.584	Harmon Killebrew, 1969
.579	Roy Sievers, 1957

Games started: Most, season

42	Walter Johnson, 1910
42	Jim Kaat, 1965
41	Jim Kaat, 1966
40	Bert Blyleven, 1973
40	Bob Groom, 1912
40	Walter Johnson, 1914
40	Jim Perry, 1970

Saves: Most, season

42	RICK AGUILERA, 1991
42	Jeff Reardon, 1988
41	RICK AGUILERA, 1992
34	RICK AGUILERA, 1993
34	Ron Perranoski, 1970

Shutouts: Most, season

11	Walter Johnson, 1913
9	Bert Blyleven, 1973
9	Walter Johnson, 1914
9	Bob Porterfield, 1953
8	Walter Johnson, 1910
8	Walter Johnson, 1917
8	Walter Johnson, 1918
8	Camilo Pascual, 1961

Wins: Most, season

36	Walter Johnson, 1913
33	Walter Johnson, 1912
28	Walter Johnson, 1914
27	Walter Johnson, 1915
26	Alvin Crowder, 1932
25	Jim Kaat, 1966 (6)

K: Most, season

313	Walter Johnson, 1910
303	Walter Johnson, 1912
258	Bert Blyleven, 1973
249	Bert Blyleven, 1974
243	Walter Johnson, 1913

Win pct: Highest, season

.837	Walter Johnson, 1913
.800	Stan Coveleski, 1925
.800	Firpo Marberry, 1931
.774	FRANK VIOLA, 1988
.773	Bill Campbell, 1976

ERA: Lowest, season

1.14	Walter Johnson, 1913
1.27	Walter Johnson, 1918
1.36	Walter Johnson, 1910
1.39	Walter Johnson, 1912
1.49	Walter Johnson, 1919
2.49	Dave Goltz, 1978 (*)

Most pinch-hit homers, season

4	Don Mincher, 1964

Most pinch-hit homers, career

8	Bob Allison, 1961-1970 (none with Was, 1958-1960)

Most consecutive games batting safely

33	Heine Manush, 1933
31	Sam Rice, 1924
31	Ken Landreaux, 1980

Most consecutive scoreless innings

55	Walter Johnson, 1913
40	Walter Johnson, 1918
37	Walter Johnson, 1913

No-hit games

Walter Johnson, Was at Bos AL, 1-0; July 1, 1920.

Bobby Burke, Was vs Bos AL, 5-0; August 8, 1931.

Jack Kralick, Min vs KC AL, 1-0; August 26, 1962.

Dean Chance, Min at Cle AL, 2-1; August 25, 1967 (2nd game).

SCOTT ERICKSON, Min vs Mil AL, 6-0; April 27, 1994.

Jay Cashion, 6 innings, called so Cleveland could catch train, Was vs Cle AL, 2-0; August 20, 1912 (2nd game).

Walter Johnson, 7 innings, rain, Was vs StL AL, 2-0; August 25, 1924.

Dean Chance, 5 perfect innings, rain, Min vs Bos AL, 2-0; August 6, 1967.

ACTIVE PLAYERS in caps.

Leader from the franchise's current location is included. If not in the top five, leader's rank is listed in parenthesis; asterisk (*) indicates player is not in top 25.

Players' years of service are listed by the first and last years with this team and are not necessarily consecutive; all statistics record performances for this team only.

Seattle Mariners

By Neil Seiler, USA TODAY

Cy Young winner Randy Johnson was one victory short of a triple crown (18-2, 294 SO, 2.48 ERA).

1995 Mariners: They "refused to lose"

It's not often that a team can claim it has both the batting champion and a Cy Young winner. But that was far from the biggest story in Seattle. The Mariners won the AL West in a one-game playoff against the California Angels and went to the playoffs for the first time in their history.

The team knew they weren't expected to win, especially with the half-season absence of their main man, Ken Griffey Jr. But there was plenty of help.

Edgar Martinez hit .356 and never went more than two games or eight at-bats without a hit. Johnson finished 18-2 (the Mariners won 27 of his 30 starts), won his fourth straight strikeout crown (294), and had the league's best ERA (2.48) and the lowest opponents' batting average (.201). He set a major league single-season record for strikeouts per nine innings—12.35.

Jay Buhner, Tino Martinez and Mike Blowers also had career years. Buhner (40 HR, 121 RBI) and Tino (31, 111) joined Edgar in the 100-RBI club. Griffey returned to the lineup on Aug. 15 and managed 17 home runs and 42 RBI playing with a steel plate and seven screws still in his wrist. The acquisition of Vince Coleman gave the club a solid leadoff hitter and speed—he stole 16 bases in 21 attempts. Luis Sojo played solid shortstop, Joey Cora hit .297, and catcher Dan Wilson had career numbers for average (.278), HR (nine) and RBI (51) and was superior in handling the staff and calling games.

Tim Belcher (10-12) and Andy Benes (7-2) were acquired in trades, and Norm Charlton was claimed on waivers to replace struggling Bobby Ayala as the closer—he had 12 saves and two wins in his final 15 outings.

"We weren't supposed to win," Charlton said. "We were supposed to be home watching" the LCS against Cleveland. Instead, they were front and center in the national spotlight. They brought baseball fever to Seattle and stole America's heart with their "Refuse to Lose" attitude. The loyal, raucous home crowds put the Kingdome on opponents' lists of most-dreaded places to play. So when no one left after Cleveland won Game 6, 4-0, ending Cinderella's night at the ball, the Mariners were touched. And they took advantage of the opportunity to express some gratitude of their own.

"They showed that win or lose, they're behind us 100%," Griffey said. "It was great, and it was something we've never had before. I have to take my hat off to them. They made a difference in this town and in this ballpark."

1996 Mariners: Preview

The Mariners may spend more money but have less talent. They have a large investment tied up in a handful of long-term contracts—Ken Griffey Jr., Jay Buhner, Chris Bosio and Randy Johnson eat up about $21 million of the $34 million payroll. The club also has a $3 million-plus option on Edgar Martinez, which it exercised; will keep closer Norm Charlton and infielder Joey Cora; and will arbitrate higher pay levels with first baseman Tino Martinez and relievers Bobby Ayala and Jeff Nelson.

The leaves plenty of decisions on players acquired during the stretch drive or replacements for them. Players' salaries are still being drained by pitcher Greg Hibbard, who has missed a season and a half with shoulder surgery—he's signed through 1996. It's time for Alex Rodriguez to plant his roots at shortstop. Bob Wolcott, who gave the club some critical help as the fifth starter in September (3-2, 4.42 ERA), will have a spot in the rotation come spring. Tim Davis, who had shoulder surgery but should be fully recovered, is likely to move out of the rotation competition and back to the bullpen.

1995 Mariners: Week-by-week notes

These notes were excerpted from the following issues of Baseball Weekly.

▶**May 3:** The Mariners started out 3-0 for 1995. Starters Dave Fleming, Randy Johnson and Chris Bosio all won their first starts against Detroit, for a combined 1.13 ERA. Ken Griffey Jr. hit two home runs in his first three games.

▶**May 10:** Relief pitching was the major reason the Mariners shot out to their fastest start ever—winning 14 of their first 15 games. Closer Bobby Ayala, Bill Risley and Jeff Nelson combined to allow just one run in 16⅔ innings.

▶**May 17:** In his last two starts, Dave Fleming had worked 9⅔ innings, allowing 11 runs and 13 hits while, walking seven—his ERA ballooned to 7.36.

▶**May 24:** Fleming—at 1-3 with a 7.71 ERA—was relegated to the bullpen. In his first relief appearance he allowed a three-run homer to the second batter he faced.

▶**May 31:** Mike Blowers tied a club record with eight RBI and set a record for most extra-base hits in one game, with two doubles, a triple and a home run.

▶**June 7:** Randy Johnson angered the Yankees when he hit catcher Jim Leyritz—the ball glanced off Leyritz's wrist and into his face, and both benches emptied. Leyritz suggested he might stalk Johnson off the field for revenge, but Johnson made light of the threats, suggesting that he and Leyritz could duel "like the 1600s, with swords or pistols at 10 paces. I can see it now," he said, " 'High Noon at Times Square.' "

▶**June 14:** Dave Fleming returned to the rotation only to bomb again. The rumor was that he'd be optioned back to the minor leagues or released. A possible replacement candidate was 21-year-old Bob Wolcott.

▶**June 21:** Injuries were finally catching up to the Mariners. The absence of Griffey with a broken list and Jay

Buhner with a tender hamstring put a heavier burden on the remaining roster. One player who was definitely doing his part was Edgar Martinez, vying for the AL batting lead, who tied a club record with at least one RBI in eight consecutive games (15 total).

▶**June 28:** Lou Piniella figured out a way to use Randy Johnson as often as possible—a four-man rotation that corresponded with the start of a 10-game homestand against their three AL West rivals. Johnson's season strikeout ratio was 12.99 per nine innings, on pace to easily surpass the single season mark of 11.48 set by Nolan Ryan in 1987.

▶**July 5:** The team ERA had gone from 4.46 to 5.38, and walks issued were up 12%. The four-man rotation consisted of Randy Johnson, Chris Bosio, Tim Belcher and Salomon Torres, but Piniella wanted to go back to a five-man rotation for the final two series before the All-Star break. Erstwhile starters Dave Fleming and Bob Wells seemed fixed in the bullpen, so the club wanted a trade.

▶**Aug. 16:** Seattle was making the most of its first-ever chance at postseason play. They put together a season-high six-game win streak to move among the front-runners in the wild-card race, encouraged by the healthy return of Randy Johnson and the pending return of Ken Griffey Jr. The Mariners were 18-3 in Johnson's 21 starts—he won 14 of his past 16 decisions. Norm Charlton picked up two consecutive saves in the first week of August, his first in two years.

▶**Aug. 23:** The Mariners had never had a leadoff hitter with the legs and experience that Vince Coleman brought them, so they hoped he could bring them something else they'd never had—a postseason berth. Coleman cost the Mariners only about $55,000, but he could prove to be invaluable. Meanwhile, Bob Wolcott made his big-league debut with a 9-3 victory over Boston.

Aug. 30: The team earned what was the most pivotal victory of the season Aug. 24 against New York. It started a four-game win streak, the first-ever four-game sweep of the Yankees, and moved the club within two games of the wild-card spot. Randy Johnson had 229 strikeouts for 1995 (best in baseball), a 13-2 record (second in the AL), and a 2.68 ERA (second in the AL). The Mariners were 21-3 in games he started. Mike Blowers, who hit three grand slams in August, was 7 for 13 with three home runs, a triple, three doubles and 26 RBI with the bases loaded. Edgar Martinez, the AL hitting leader with a peak .370 average on Aug. 27, had a .504 on-base percentage.

Sept. 6: The Mariners went through the most important road trip in their 19-year history without Randy Johnson. He came up with shoulder stiffness before his start on Aug. 31 and was held out. Meanwhile, the Mariners decided to use Norm Charlton as their closer until Bobby Ayala improved. Charlton had three saves and an 0.99 ERA in August.

Sept. 13: Randy Johnson missed 13 days—two starts—but when he returned on Sept. 8, he helped beat Kansas City 4-1. The victory moved the Mariners into a tie with the Royals for first place in the wild-card race. He lowered his ERA to 2.63, matching Boston's Tim Wakefield for the league low. He was also leading in strikeouts with 237. The Mariners were 22-3 in his 25 starts. Through Sept. 9, the Mariners had the AL's top three RBI producers—Edgar Martinez and Jay Buhner led with one every 4.1 at-bats. Mike Blowers was third at 4.3.

Sept. 20: "There's no reason we can't win the West," Mike Blowers said. "For me, the Angels have let us back in." Wolcott wasn't on the Mariners' post-season roster and was slated to go home on Oct. 1, no matter what.

Sept. 27: Seattle's lineup was putting together a season that could be compared favorably with some of the most powerful teams this century. Even though the season was shortened by 18 games, the Mariners had three players with 100 RBI and a fourth on the verge.

There have been 14 clubs in major league history to have at least four 100-RBI guys, but only two since 1940. "I don't remember any team like this," Piniella said. "But these kids are hitting the ball and hitting for damage."

Oct. 4: Jay Buhner, who set a club record with 13 home runs in September to help drive his team into playoff contention, had his best season—by far. He had 40 home runs (previous high was 27) and set a club record with 121 RBI in 120 games—on 122 hits, the best RBI-to-hits ratio (.992) in baseball history among players with a minimum of 100 hits. Randy Johnson finished atop the league in ERA (2.54), strikeouts, (282), opponents' batting average, (.202), shutouts (three, tied with Mike Mussina) and winning percentage (17-2, .895). The Mariners were 26-3 in his 29 starts. Edgar Martinez won his second batting title with a .356 average. He is only the fifth AL right-hander to win two.

Team directory

Owner: Baseball Club of Seattle
General manager: Woody Woodward
Ballpark:
The Kingdome
201 South King St., Seattle, Wash.
206-296-3663
Capacity 59,158
Public transportation available
Parking for 3,500 cars,
30,000 within a mile;
Family and wheelchair sections,
birthday package, anniversary
package
Team publications:
Mariners Magazine, Mariners Newsletter, scorecard, media guide
206-296-3663
TV, radio broadcast stations:
KIRO 710 AM, KSTW Channel 11,
Prime Sports Northwest Cable
Spring training:
Peoria Sports Complex
Peoria, Ariz.
Capacity 10,000 (3,000 on grass)
602-412-9000

SEATTLE MARINERS 1995 final stats

BATTERS	BA	SLG	OB	G	AB	R	H	TB	2B	3B	HR	RBI	BB	SO	SB	CS	E
E. Martinez	.356	.628	.479	145	511	121	182	321	52	0	29	113	116	87	4	3	2
Thurman	.320	.400	.333	13	25	3	8	10	2	0	0	3	1	3	5	2	0
Cora	.297	.372	.359	120	427	64	127	159	19	2	3	39	37	31	18	7	23
T. Martinez	.293	.551	.369	141	519	92	152	286	35	3	31	111	62	91	0	0	8
Sojo	.289	.416	.335	102	339	50	98	141	18	2	7	39	23	19	4	2	9
Coleman	.288	.398	.343	115	455	66	131	181	23	6	5	29	37	80	42	16	4
Amaral	.282	.382	.342	90	238	45	67	91	14	2	2	19	21	33	21	2	1
Wilson	.278	.416	.336	119	399	40	111	166	22	3	9	51	33	63	2	1	5
Strange	.271	.394	.323	74	155	19	42	61	9	2	2	21	10	25	0	3	5
Buhner	.262	.566	.343	126	470	86	123	266	23	0	40	121	60	120	0	1	2
Newson	.261	.395	.411	84	157	34	41	62	2	2	5	15	39	45	2	1	2
Griffey	.258	.481	.379	72	260	52	67	125	7	0	17	42	52	53	4	2	2
Blowers	.257	.474	.335	134	439	59	113	208	24	1	23	96	53	128	2	1	16
Diaz	.248	.333	.286	103	270	44	67	90	14	0	3	27	13	27	18	8	2
Pirkl	.235	.235	.278	10	17	2	4	4	0	0	0	0	1	7	0	0	0
Bragg	.234	.345	.331	52	145	20	34	50	5	1	3	12	18	37	9	0	1
Rodriguez	.232	.408	.264	48	142	15	33	58	6	2	5	19	6	42	4	2	8
Kreuter	.227	.333	.293	26	75	12	17	25	5	0	1	8	5	22	0	0	4
Widger	.200	.267	.245	23	45	2	9	12	0	0	1	2	3	11	0	0	0
Fermin	.195	.225	.232	73	200	21	39	45	6	0	0	15	6	6	2	0	6
Newfield	.188	.329	.225	24	85	7	16	28	3	0	3	14	3	16	0	0	0
Pozo	.000	.000	.000	1	1	0	0	0	0	0	0	0	0	0	0	0	0

PITCHERS	W-L	ERA	G	GS	CG	GF	Sho	SV	IP	H	R	ER	HR	BB	SO
Mecir	0-0	0.00	2	0	0	1	0	0	4.2	5	1	0	0	2	3
Charlton	2-1	1.51	30	0	0	22	0	14	47.2	23	12	8	2	16	58
Nelson	7-3	2.17	62	0	0	24	0	2	78.2	58	21	19	4	27	96
Johnson	18-2	2.48	30	30	6	0	3	0	214.1	159	65	59	12	65	294
Risley	2-1	3.13	45	0	0	5	0	1	60.1	55	21	21	7	18	65
Wolcott	3-2	4.42	7	6	0	0	0	0	36.2	43	18	18	6	14	19
Ayala	6-5	4.44	63	0	0	50	0	19	71.0	73	42	35	9	30	77
Belcher	10-12	4.52	28	28	1	0	0	0	179.1	188	101	90	19	88	96
Frey	0-3	4.76	13	0	0	3	0	0	11.1	16	7	6	0	6	7
Bosio	10-8	4.92	31	31	0	0	0	0	170.0	211	98	93	18	69	85
Carmona	2-4	5.66	15	3	0	6	0	1	47.2	55	31	30	9	34	28
Wells	4-3	5.75	30	4	0	3	0	0	76.2	88	51	49	11	39	38
Krueger	2-1	5.85	6	5	0	1	0	0	20.0	37	17	13	4	4	10
Benes	7-2	5.86	12	12	0	0	0	0	63.0	72	42	41	8	33	45
Torres	3-8	6.00	16	13	1	2	0	0	72.0	87	53	48	12	42	45
Davison	0-0	6.23	3	0	0	3	0	0	4.1	7	3	3	1	1	3
Davis	2-1	6.38	5	5	0	0	0	0	24.0	30	21	17	2	18	19
Guetterman	0-0	6.88	23	0	0	3	0	1	17.0	21	13	13	1	11	11
Villone	0-2	7.91	19	0	0	7	0	0	19.1	20	19	17	6	23	26
Cummings	0-0	11.81	4	0	0	0	0	0	5.1	8	8	7	0	7	4
King	0-0	12.27	2	0	0	0	0	0	3.2	7	5	5	0	1	3
Harikkala	0-0	16.20	1	0	0	1	0	0	3.1	7	6	6	1	1	1

1996 preliminary roster

PITCHERS (17)
Bobby Ayala
Chris Bosio
Rafael Carmona
Norm Charlton
Dean Crow
Tim Davis
Scott Davison
Tim Harikkala
Greg Hibbard
Sterling Hitchcock
Randy Johnson
Derek Lowe
Bill Risley
Mac Suzuki
Salomon Torres
Sal Urso
Bob Wolcott

CATCHERS (3)
Raul Ibanez
Chris Widger
Dan Wilson

INFIELDERS (15)
Rich Amaral
Miguel Cairo
Joey Cora
Russ Davis
Felix Fermin
Giomar Guevara
Edgar Martinez
Willis Otanez
Greg Pirkl
Arquimedez Pozo
Desi Relaford
Alex Rodriguez
Andy Sheets
Luis Sojo
Doug Strange

OUTFIELDERS (4)
Darren Bragg
Jay Buhner
Alex Diaz
Ken Griffey Jr.

Games played by position

PLAYER	G	C	1B	2B	3B	SS	OF	DH
Amaral	90	0	0	0	0	0	73	1
Blowers	134	0	7	0	126	0	5	0
Bragg	52	0	0	0	0	0	47	2
Buhner	126	0	0	0	0	0	120	4
Coleman	115	0	0	0	0	0	107	4
Cora	120	0	0	112	0	1	0	1
Diaz	103	0	0	0	0	0	88	0
Fermin	73	0	0	29	0	46	0	0
Griffey	72	0	0	0	0	0	70	2
Kreuter	26	23	0	0	0	0	0	0
T. Martinez	141	0	139	0	0	0	0	1
E. Martinez	145	0	3	0	4	0	0	138
Newfield	24	0	0	0	0	0	24	0
Newson	84	0	0	0	0	0	47	7
Pirkl	10	0	6	0	0	0	0	1
Pozo	1	0	0	1	0	0	0	0
Rodriguez	48	0	0	0	0	46	0	1
Sojo	102	0	0	19	0	80	6	0
Strange	74	0	0	5	41	0	4	1
Thurman	13	0	0	0	0	0	9	0
Widger	23	19	0	0	0	0	3	1
Wilson	119	119	0	0	0	0	0	0

Minor Leagues

Tops in the organization

Batter	Club	Avg.	G	AB	R	H	HR	RBI
Raul Ibanez	Riv	.332	95	361	59	120	20	108
Mike Barger	Riv	.317	82	344	77	109	2	41
Greg Litton	Tac	.309	117	388	58	120	9	56
Rick Ladjevich	Riv	.309	122	470	74	145	7	71
Gary Thurman	Tac	.300	93	363	65	109	5	46

Home Runs			Wins		
Raul Ibanez	Riv	20	Trey Moore	Riv	14
James Bonnici	Pcy	20	Bob Wolcott	Tac	13
Roberto Ramirez	Pcy	17	O. Fernandez	Pcy	12
Eddy Diaz	Pcy	16	Chris Beck	Wsc	12
Several tied		15	Several tied		11

RBI			Saves		
Raul Ibanez	Riv	108	Dean Crow	Riv	22
Randy Jorgensen	Riv	97	John Thompson	Tac	19
James Bonnici	Pcy	91	Ron Villone	Tac	13
Roberto Ramirez	Pcy	82	Jeff Darwin	Tac	12
Rick Ladjevich	Riv	71	Trey Witte	Pcy	11

Stolen Bases			Strikeouts		
Kyle Towner	Wsc	34	Marino Santana	Riv	167
Mike Barger	Riv	33	O. Fernandez	Pcy	160
Desi Relaford	Tac	31	Craig Clayton	Riv	156
M. Sturdivant	Riv	31	Matt Wagner	Tac	144
Chad Sheffer	Evr	28	Ken Cloude	Wsc	140

Pitcher	Club	W-L	ERA	IP	H	BB	SO
Trey Moore	Riv	14-6	3.09	148	122	58	134
Bob Wolcott	Tac	13-6	3.10	165	154	29	96
Ryan Smith	Riv	10-7	3.11	142	142	50	108
Derek Bieniasz	Wsc	11-10	3.13	175	145	54	99
Marino Santana	Riv	11-8	3.24	145	101	50	167

Sick call: 1995 DL Report

Player	Days on the DL
Jay Buhner	16
Tim Davis	25
Felix Fermin	21
Steve Frey	20
Ken Griffey Jr.	80
Greg Hibbard	161
Chad Kreuter	17
Greg Pirkl	71
Bill Risley	15
Luis Sojo	16

1995 Amateur draft picks

Players are listed with position and college or high school. Most players were assigned to rookie or Class A leagues. List provided by Major League Baseball.

Michael Anderson, of, Jones County HS, Gray, Ga.; Jason Balcom, of, Mount Desales HS, Macon, Ga.; Seth Brizek, ss, Clemson; Nathan Burnett, rhp, Rutherford HS, Panama City, Fla.; Timothy Burton, rhp, St. Thomas Aquinas HS, Coral Springs, Fla.; Isaac Burton, rhp, Arizona State; Michael Campbell, rf, Coronado HS, Mesa, Ariz.; Brian Cawaring, cf, Alhambra HS, Martinez, Calif.; Charles Christianson, rhp, Chaffey College; Robert Collett, rhp-1b, Loyola Marymount; Leron Cook, rf, Fresno City College; Jose Cruz Jr., cf-lf, Rice; Joe Devisser, ss, Mattawan HS, Schoolcraft, Mich.; Greg Donahue, c, Rockland CC; Gerald Eady, of, Seminole CC; Harvey Farmer, of, Duke; Harold Frazier, rhp, Oral Roberts; Brian Fuentes, lhp, Merced; Joel Greene, lhp, Linn Benton CC; Brian Grubbs, lhp, Cooper HS, Abilene, Texas; Kevin Gryboski, rhp, Wilkes; Yusef Hamilton, cf, St. Martin Deporres Sr. HS, Detroit; Sean Hamilton, rhp, Dunedin (Fla.) HS; Jeffrey Hammond, of, Flomaton (Ala.) HS; Sean Hansen, 1b, Norco (Calif.) HS; Shaylar Hatch, rhp, Gilbert (Ariz.) HS; Timothy Henley, of, Eastside HS, Gainesville, Fla.; Jacob Hermann, lhp, Eagle Point (Ore.) HS; Joseph Hunt, of, Sante Fe CC; Joseph Johnson, ss, St. Pauls (N.C.) High; Justin Kaye, rhp, Bishop Gorman HS, Las Vegas; Sean Kelley, rhp, Miramar HS, Miami; Gary Kinnie, rhp, Chippewa Valley HS, Clinton Township, Mich.; Travis Knight, 2b, Kent (Wash.) Meridian HS; Harold Koehler, rhp, Chemeketa CC; Steven Kokinda, 3b, Palm Beach JC; Daniel Kurtz, rhp, Le Moyne; Keith Law, ss, East Paulding HS, Hiram, Ga.; Brett Laxton, rhp, Louisiana State; Eric Lloyd, rhp, Charlton County HS, Folkston, Ga.; Jason Marr, rhp, Cerritos College; Scott Maynard, c, Dana Hills HS, Laguna Niguel, Calif.; Brandon McNab, 1b, Boerne HS, Fair Oaks Ranch, Texas; Shane Monahan, cf-rf, Clemson; Robert Morrison, rhp, Wellington Community HS, Loxahatchee, Fla.; Eric Mouten, of, Grant HS, Portland, Ore.; Aaron Myette, rhp, Johnston Heights Secondary, Surrey, B.C.; Brian Nelson, c, Edison CC; Todd Niemeier, lhp, Southern Indiana; Brandon Nogowski, lhp, Hood River (Ore.) Valley HS; Todd Ozias, rhp, Miami Dade CC; Jeremy Palki, rhp, Clackamas CC; Wynter Phoenix, cf, Cal State Santa Barbara; Juan Pierre, cf, Alexandria (La.) HS; James Pietraszko, c, Forest Heights HS, Kitchener, Ont.; Travis Ray, rhp, Cairo (Ga.) HS; Anthony Rice, 3b, CC of San Francisco; Rafael Rivera, rhp, Miami Dade CC; Shane Roland, rf, Cook County HS, Adel, Ga.; Roy Roundy, c, Coronado HS, Scottsdale, Ariz.; Gregory Scheer, lhp, Jacksonville; Lawrence Severence, c, Bryan HS, Archbold, Ohio; Joseph Seymour, c, Southside HS, Elmira, N.Y.; Chadwick Sheffer, ss-2b, Central Florida; Brian Shultz, lf, Blinn JC; Wendell Simmons, rhp, Southwest HS, Macon, Ga.; Brian Smith, cf, Granite Hills HS, El Cajon, Calif.; Chad Soden, lhp, Arkansas State; Richard Sundstrom, rhp, John F. Kennedy HS, La Palma, Calif.; Zachary Tharp, 1b, Boone HS, Orlando, Fla.; Karl Thompson, c, Santa Clara; Ernest Tolbert, of, Abraham Lincoln Prep, San Diego; Ramon Vazquez, ss, Indian Hills CC; Adam Walker, lhp, Yavapai JC; Damon Warren, rhp, Lower Columbia CC; Martin Weymouth, rhp, Brother Rice HS, Romeo, Mich.; Gregory Wooten, rhp, Portland State.

Seattle (1977-1995)

Runs: Most, career, all-time

570	KEN GRIFFEY JR., 1989-1995
563	Alvin Davis, 1984-1991
543	Harold Reynolds, 1983-1992
483	EDGAR MARTINEZ, 1987-1995
455	JAY BUHNER, 1988-1995

Hits: Most, career, all-time

1163	Alvin Davis, 1984-1991
1063	Harold Reynolds, 1983-1992
1039	KEN GRIFFEY JR., 1989-1995
868	EDGAR MARTINEZ, 1987-1995
751	JAY BUHNER, 1988-1995

2B: Most, career, all-time

212	Alvin Davis, 1984-1991
204	EDGAR MARTINEZ, 1987-1995
201	KEN GRIFFEY JR., 1989-1995
200	Harold Reynolds, 1983-1992
147	Jim Presley, 1984-1989

3B: Most, career, all-time

48	Harold Reynolds, 1983-1992
26	Phil Bradley, 1983-1987
23	SPIKE OWEN, 1983-1986
20	Ruppert Jones, 1977-1979
19	KEN GRIFFEY JR., 1989-1995
19	Dan Meyer, 1977-1981

HR: Most, career, all-time

189	KEN GRIFFEY JR., 1989-1995
166	JAY BUHNER, 1988-1995
160	Alvin Davis, 1984-1991
115	Jim Presley, 1984-1989
105	Ken Phelps, 1983-1988

RBI: Most, career, all-time

667	Alvin Davis, 1984-1991
585	KEN GRIFFEY JR., 1989-1995
534	JAY BUHNER, 1988-1995
418	Jim Presley, 1984-1989
381	EDGAR MARTINEZ, 1987-1995

SB: Most, career, all-time

290	Julio Cruz, 1977-1983
228	Harold Reynolds, 1983-1992
107	Phil Bradley, 1983-1987
102	Henry Cotto, 1988-1993
92	KEN GRIFFEY JR., 1989-1995

BB: Most, career, all-time

672	Alvin Davis, 1984-1991
432	EDGAR MARTINEZ, 1987-1995
423	KEN GRIFFEY JR., 1989-1995
411	JAY BUHNER, 1988-1995
391	Harold Reynolds, 1983-1992

BA: Highest, career, all-time

.313	EDGAR MARTINEZ, 1987-1995
.302	KEN GRIFFEY JR., 1989-1995
.301	Phil Bradley, 1983-1987
.290	Bruce Bochte, 1978-1982
.281	Alvin Davis, 1984-1991

Slug avg: Highest, career, all-time

.536	KEN GRIFFEY JR., 1989-1995
.521	Ken Phelps, 1983-1988
.492	JAY BUHNER, 1988-1995
.491	EDGAR MARTINEZ, 1987-1995
.466	TINO MARTINEZ, 1990-1995

Games started: Most, career, all-time

217	MIKE MOORE, 1982-1988
206	RANDY JOHNSON, 1989-1995
173	MARK LANGSTON, 1984-1989
147	Jim Beattie, 1980-1986
146	Glenn Abbott, 1977-1983

Saves: Most, career, all-time

98	Mike Schooler, 1988-1992
52	Bill Caudill, 1982-1983
37	BOBBY AYALA, 1994-95
36	Shane Rawley, 1978-1981
35	Edwin Nunez, 1982-1988

Shutouts: Most, career, all-time

15	RANDY JOHNSON, 1989-1995
9	MARK LANGSTON, 1984-1989
9	MIKE MOORE, 1982-1988
7	Floyd Bannister, 1979-1982
6	Jim Beattie, 1980-1986

Wins: Most, career, all-time

96	RANDY JOHNSON, 1989-1995
74	MARK LANGSTON, 1984-1989
66	MIKE MOORE, 1982-1988
56	ERIK HANSON, 1988-1993
45	Matt Young, 1983-1990

K: Most, career, all-time

1573	RANDY JOHNSON, 1989-1995
1078	MARK LANGSTON, 1984-1989
937	MIKE MOORE, 1982-1988
740	ERIK HANSON, 1988-1993
597	Matt Young, 1983-1990

Win pct: Highest, career, all-time

.615	RANDY JOHNSON, 1989-1995
.525	MARK LANGSTON, 1984-1989
.509	ERIK HANSON, 1988-1993
.444	Floyd Bannister, 1979-1982
.415	Glenn Abbott, 1977-1983

ERA: Lowest, career, all-time

3.47	RANDY JOHNSON, 1989-1995
3.69	ERIK HANSON, 1988-1993
3.75	Floyd Bannister, 1979-1982
4.01	MARK LANGSTON, 1984-1989
4.04	BILL SWIFT, 1985-1991

Runs: Most, season

121	EDGAR MARTINEZ, 1995
113	KEN GRIFFEY JR., 1993
109	Ruppert Jones, 1979
101	Phil Bradley, 1987
100	Phil Bradley, 1985
100	EDGAR MARTINEZ, 1992
100	Harold Reynolds, 1990

Hits: Most, season

192	Phil Bradley, 1985
184	HAROLD REYNOLDS, 1989
182	EDGAR MARTINEZ, 1995
181	EDGAR MARTINEZ, 1992
180	KEN GRIFFEY JR., 1993
180	Willie Horton, 1979
180	Jack Perconte, 1984

2B: Most, season

52	EDGAR MARTINEZ, 1995
46	EDGAR MARTINEZ, 1992
42	KEN GRIFFEY JR., 1991
39	Al Cowens, 1982
39	KEN GRIFFEY JR., 1992

3B: Most, season

11	Harold Reynolds, 1988
10	Phil Bradley, 1987
9	Ruppert Jones, 1979
9	Harold Reynolds, 1989
8	Phil Bradley, 1985
8	Al Cowens, 1982
8	Ruppert Jones, 1977
8	SPIKE OWEN, 1984
8	Harold Reynolds, 1987

HR: Most, season

45	KEN GRIFFEY JR., 1993
40	JAY BUHNER, 1995
40	KEN GRIFFEY JR., 1994
32	Gorman Thomas, 1985
31	TINO MARTINEZ, 1995

RBI: Most, season

121	JAY BUHNER, 1995
116	Alvin Davis, 1984
113	EDGAR MARTINEZ, 1995
111	TINO MARTINEZ, 1995
109	KEN GRIFFEY JR., 1993

SB: Most, season

60	Harold Reynolds, 1987
59	Julio Cruz, 1978
49	Julio Cruz, 1979
46	Julio Cruz, 1982
45	Julio Cruz, 1980

BB: Most, season

116	EDGAR MARTINEZ, 1995
101	Alvin Davis, 1989
100	JAY BUHNER, 1993
97	Alvin Davis, 1984
96	KEN GRIFFEY JR., 1993

BA: Highest, season

.356	EDGAR MARTINEZ, 1995
.343	EDGAR MARTINEZ, 1992
.327	KEN GRIFFEY JR., 1991
.326	Tom Paciorek, 1981
.323	KEN GRIFFEY JR., 1994

Slug avg: Highest, season

.674	KEN GRIFFEY JR., 1994
.628	EDGAR MARTINEZ, 1995
.617	KEN GRIFFEY JR., 1993
.566	JAY BUHNER, 1995
.551	TINO MARTINEZ, 1995

Games started: Most, season

37	MIKE MOORE, 1986
36	MARK LANGSTON, 1986
35	Floyd Bannister, 1982
35	MARK LANGSTON, 1987
35	MARK LANGSTON, 1988
35	Matt Young, 1985

Saves: Most, season

33	Mike Schooler, 1989
30	Mike Schooler, 1990
26	Bill Caudill, 1982
26	Bill Caudill, 1983
19	BOBBY AYALA, 1995

Shutouts: Most, season

4	DAVE FLEMING, 1992
4	RANDY JOHNSON, 1994
3	Floyd Bannister, 1982
3	Brian Holman, 1991
3	RANDY JOHNSON, 1993
3	RANDY JOHNSON, 1995
3	MARK LANGSTON, 1987
3	MARK LANGSTON, 1988
3	MIKE MOORE, 1988

Wins: Most, season

19	RANDY JOHNSON, 1993
19	MARK LANGSTON, 1987
18	ERIK HANSON, 1990
18	RANDY JOHNSON, 1995
17	DAVE FLEMING, 1992
17	MARK LANGSTON, 1984
17	MIKE MOORE, 1985

K: Most, season

308	RANDY JOHNSON, 1993
294	RANDY JOHNSON, 1995
262	MARK LANGSTON, 1987
245	MARK LANGSTON, 1986
241	RANDY JOHNSON, 1992

Win pct: Highest, season

.900	RANDY JOHNSON, 1995
.704	RANDY JOHNSON, 1993
.667	ERIK HANSON, 1990
.630	DAVE FLEMING, 1992
.630	MARK LANGSTON, 1984
.630	MIKE MOORE, 1985

ERA: Lowest, season

2.48	RANDY JOHNSON, 1995
3.19	RANDY JOHNSON, 1994
3.24	ERIK HANSON, 1990
3.24	RANDY JOHNSON, 1993
3.27	Matt Young, 1983

Most pinch-hit homers, season

2	Leon Roberts, 1978
2	Gary Gray, 1981
2	Ken Phelps, 1986
2	Greg Briley, 1992

Most pinch-hit homers, career

4	Ken Phelps, 1983-1988

Most consecutive games batting safely

21	Dan Meyer, 1979
21	Richie Zisk, 1982

Most consecutive scoreless innings

34	MARK LANGSTON, 1988

No-hit games

RANDY JOHNSON, Sea vs Det AL, 2-0; June 2, 1990.
CHRIS BOSIO, Sea vs Bos AL, 7-0; April 22, 1993.

ACTIVE PLAYERS in caps.

Players' years of service are listed by the first and last years with this team and are not necessarily consecutive; all statistics record performances for this team only.

California Angels

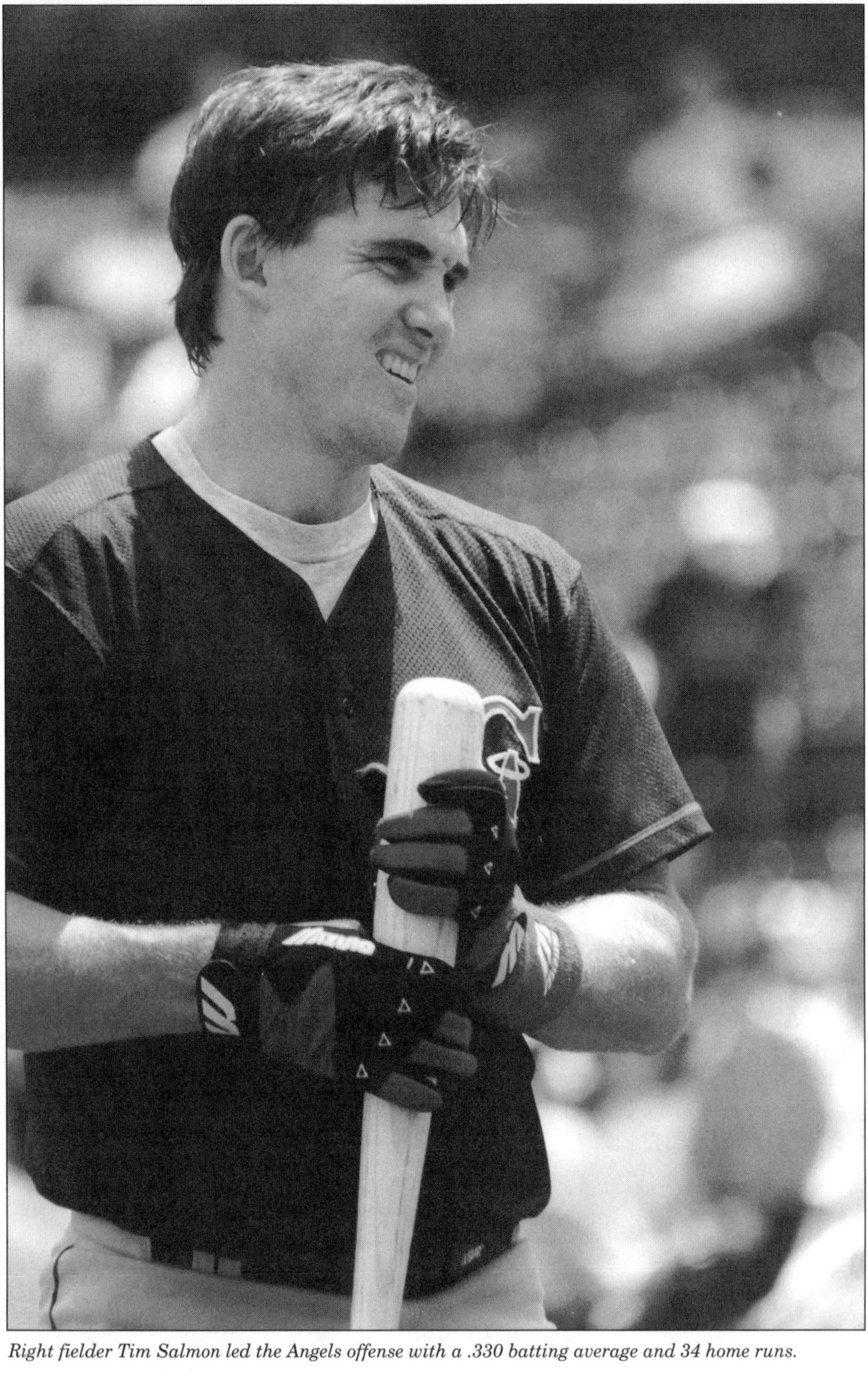

By Nell Seiler, USA TODAY

Right fielder Tim Salmon led the Angels offense with a .330 batting average and 34 home runs.

1995 Angels: Close enough to taste it

The Angels never wanted it to end in a skid—and they prefer to avoid the word "choke" altogether—but general manager Bill Bavasi believes the anger inherent in the Great Collapse of 1995 might best be channeled into winning in '96.

Sure, the Angels lost nine games in a row twice within a month, and 27 of 35 overall. Sure, they coughed up a 13-game lead over the Seattle Mariners. But they never lost more than three in a row until Aug. 9.

"We were a tough, tough club," Bavasi says. "We got the lead because another team collapsed.... We chose later to collapse."

Manager Marcel Lachemann heaped the blame for the Angels' collapse on his own shoulders at every opportunity, even for factors over which he had no control, like Mark Langston's and Chuck Finley's getting bombed. Although the players appreciated such comments at first, they privately said those remarks rang hollow after a while. He even said he should be fired if the club didn't win, the strongest of his many self-blaming remarks. Bavasi finally told him to clam up. After all, Bavasi endured severe criticism when he fired Buck Rodgers and hired the inexperienced Lachemann. The Angels finished 1995 painfully, but Bavasi tips his cap to Lachemann anyway.

"By and large, we were picked last," Bavasi said. "He did a great job of planning and turned it around. He did a good enough job where we expect things of ourselves now."

Plenty of other Angels did a good enough job as well. Start with the outfield of Garrett Anderson, Jim Edmonds and Tim Salmon. That's a Rookie of the Year candidate in left field, an All-Star in center field, and a Triple Crown contender in right field.

The slump seemed to start with an injury to shortstop Gary DiSarcina on Aug. 3. He had established himself as the key to the infield defense, and he combined with third baseman Tony Phillips and first baseman J.T. Snow to provide far more offense than anticipated.

The addition of Jim Abbott, partially in anticipation of a possible postseason matchup with Cleveland, gave the Angels powerful left-handed starting pitching, including Finley and Langston. That allowed Lachemann to get plenty of games to fireballing closer-in-waiting Troy Percival in the eighth inning and all-time save leader Lee Smith in the ninth.

1996 Angels: Preview

Strong starting pitching is Bavasi's focus. Troy Percival is ready to become a closer, but Bavasi isn't interested.

"Our plan is for Troy to close out the eighth inning and Lee the ninth," he said.

The lineup has few openings, though second and third base could be up for grabs. Damion Easley didn't distinguish himself at second, and Eduardo Perez could get another look at third.

Catcher remains in flux, though the position could be determined by how soon powerful Todd Greene is ready to handle the defensive portion of the major league job, after two seasons of being converted from the outfield. His bat is a big plus—as *Baseball Weekly*'s minor league player of the year, Greene hit 40 home runs between Vancouver and Class AA Midland.

1995 Angels: Week-by-week notes

These notes were excerpted from the following issues of Baseball Weekly.

▶**May 3:** As soon as the Toronto crowd could make out the 99 on the back of his uniform, they stood and saluted the Angels' new pitcher with a warm round of applause. Now pitching for the Angels, and pitching in Toronto for the first time since Joe Carter homered off him to win the World Series two years ago: No. 99, Mitch Williams. Williams had predicted it all: "There'll be a standing ovation, I imagine. They sure as hell have nothing to boo me about."

▶**May 10:** Pitcher Shawn Boskie chipped two teeth and suffered a slightly sprained neck in a brawl against Oakland. What upset him the most, he said, was that he failed to knock over his target, A's pitcher Jim Corsi. "That was pretty brutal," Boskie said. "I need to work on my tackling technique."

▶**May 24:** The Angels tried jazzing up their uniforms, but Chuck Finley wasn't quite sure what to make of the new Saturday uniform tops, a dark-on-dark mess of red letters and numbers on navy blue shirts: "I thought they were robes at first, the kind you wear when you get your hair done so you don't mess up your good shirt."

▶**May 31:** Left-hander Mitch Williams was trying the patience of the Angels and their fans, who tossed hundreds of giveaway seat cushions onto the field May 27 after he gave up a home run to Boston's Mo Vaughn that gave the Red Sox a 10-1 lead. Williams had given up three runs on back-to-back nights, as his ERA shot from 3.00 to 9.82. "So far, I haven't done nothing," Williams said. "I'm just filling up a uniform."

▶**June 7:** Lee Smith recorded his 14th save on June 3, one more than former closer Joe Grahe had in all of 1994. Smith's ERA hadn't budged from 0.00. Chuck Finley made 269 pitches over consecutive starts, but manager Marcel

Lachemann trusts him to speak up in case of trouble. "If I was hurt, I'd tell him," Finley said. "But I'd probably lie to him as long as I could. I'm all right until they knock me out."

▶**June 14:** Mitch Williams all but dared the Angels to release him, rejecting their suggestion that he spend some time in the minor leagues in an attempt to rediscover the strike zone. In six of his past 12 appearances, Williams had failed to retire a batter. In 11 of those appearances, however, he had either walked or hit a batter. "Of course, they're getting impatient," Williams said. "They'd be fools not to be....This team was in first place, and I've done nothing but hold them back."

▶**June 28:** With DH Chili Davis on the disabled list (strained hamstring), the Angels lost the AL's second-leading hitter as well as the club leader in hits, runs scored and RBI. Catcher Greg Myers was activated to fill the roster spot, and Lachemann said he would rotate players, including Myers, in the DH spot.

▶**July 5:** While catcher Greg Myers was on the disabled list, Jorge Fabregas started all but one game and wowed the Angels by throwing out runners aplenty and hitting in nine consecutive games, the longest such streak by an Angels catcher since Lance Parrish hit in nine in a row in 1990. And, with DH Chili Davis on the DL, the Angels used Myers as a DH and kept Fabregas behind the plate. "He's done a fabulous job," general manager Bill Bavasi said. "He's done well enough to stay in the big leagues, I'll tell you that." Meanwhile, center fielder Jim Edmonds ended a 23-game hitting streak on June 30, tied for the longest in the majors this season. In other news, Mitch Williams retired. It had been tough enough to accept a setup role, but an assignment to the minors was too much. Lee Smith, baseball's all-time save leader, said he'd never have gone even as far as Williams did to stay in the game. "If I have to be a setup man, I'm losing valuable time with my young'uns," Smith said. "I'm looking good financially. I ain't no extravagant dresser, and a Chevrolet truck can't cost that much."

▸**July 19:** The Angels led the majors in runs scored at the All-Star break, with a wonderfully diversified attack. Tony Phillips and Jim Edmonds, the first two hitters in the lineup, had combined for 27 homers. Tim Salmon and Chili Davis, the third and fourth hitters, had combined for 24. The fifth hitter, J.T. Snow, had 51 RBI, the same as Albert Belle and Cecil Fielder. The ninth hitter, shortstop Gary DiSarcina, took a .324 average into the All-Star Game and had driven in 33 runs, two fewer than starting shortstop Cal Ripken.

▸**Aug. 2:** Chili Davis, preparing to bat in the third inning of the July 30 game in Milwaukee, walked off the on-deck circle and struck a fan in the face. Davis was being taunted as he stood in the on-deck circle. Witnesses said Davis walked over to the first row of box seats on the third-base side and struck a 26-year-old man with an open hand under his chin, then grabbed his cheek. The fan who was struck was not heckling Davis, witnesses said. The actual hecklers were nearby. Davis was booed when he went to the plate and tipped his helmet to the taunting crowd. He singled, and when the inning was over, he motioned for fans to bring on more boos. Davis was charged with disorderly conduct but was not taken into police custody. He was given a citation that carries a $287 fine.

▸**Aug. 23:** Jim Edmonds scored his 100th run of the season, the first Angel to do so since 1987.

▸**Sept. 6:** In the worst of ways, Tony Phillips was proving just how valuable he is to the Angels. The club's leadoff hitter and offensive catalyst, Phillips had not reached base in the first inning in any game during a losing streak that hit nine games on Sept. 3. The Angels hadn't had a lead in 69 innings. In July, when the Angels scored more runs in a month than any major league club had

in four decades, Phillips hit .352 and scored 37 runs. In August, Phillips hit .188, scored 21 runs and struck out 41 times in 101 at-bats. With three hits in 31 at-bats, Phillips' average had fallen to .270, its lowest point since June 13.

▸**Sept. 27:** The Angels blew an 11-game lead, and the folks at home loved it—if you believe Marcel Lachemann's view of his team's fickle fan base. "There's an awful lot of people gloating right now that couldn't wait for this to happen," Lachemann said. "People all around Southern California are saying, 'We knew it, we knew it.' The only support these guys have is themselves."

▸**Oct. 4:** In his first appearance in 13 days and longest appearance in seven weeks, Mike Harkey rescued the Angels with 6⅔ shutout innings to beat Oakland on Sept. 30. If the Angels hadn't won, the final day of the season wouldn't have mattered.

Team directory

▸**Owner:** Gene Autry
▸**General manager:** Bill Bavasi
▸**Ballpark:**
Anaheim Stadium
2000 Gene Autry Way, Anaheim, Calif., 714-937-6700
Capacity 64,593
Parking for 15,000 vehicles; $6
Public transportation available
Family and wheelchair sections, elevators, ramps, picnic section
▸**Team publications:**
Halo Magazine, media guide, yearbook
714-937-6700, ext. 7281
▸**TV, radio broadcast stations:**
KMPC 710 AM, KTLA Channel 5, Prime Sports
▸**Camps and/or clinics:**
Angels Clinic, on Saturdays during the season, 714-937-7282
▸**Spring training:**
Tempe Diablo Stadium
Tempe, Ariz.
Capacity 7,285 (9,785 including lawn)
602-438-4300

CALIFORNIA ANGELS 1995 final stats

BATTERS	BA	SLG	OB	G	AB	R	H	TB	2B	3B	HR	RBI	BB	SO	SB	CS	E
Palmeiro	.350	.350	.381	15	20	3	7	7	0	0	0	1	1	1	0	0	0
Gonzales	.333	.556	.333	30	18	1	6	10	1	0	1	3	0	4	0	0	0
Salmon	.330	.594	.429	143	537	111	177	319	34	3	34	105	91	111	5	5	4
G. Anderson	.321	.505	.352	106	374	50	120	189	19	1	16	69	19	65	6	2	5
Davis	.318	.514	.429	119	424	81	135	218	23	0	20	86	89	79	3	3	0
DiSarcina	.307	.459	.344	99	362	61	111	166	28	6	5	41	20	25	7	4	6
Edmonds	.290	.536	.352	141	558	120	162	299	30	4	33	107	51	130	1	4	1
Snow	.289	.465	.353	143	544	80	157	253	22	1	24	102	52	91	2	1	4
Aldrete	.268	.403	.349	78	149	19	40	60	8	0	4	24	19	31	0	0	3
Hudler	.265	.417	.310	84	223	30	59	93	16	0	6	27	10	48	12	0	4
Phillips	.261	.459	.394	139	525	119	137	241	21	1	27	61	113	135	13	10	20
Myers	.260	.418	.304	85	273	35	71	114	12	2	9	38	17	49	0	1	4
Schofield	.250	.250	.375	12	20	1	5	5	0	0	0	2	4	2	0	0	0
Fabregas	.247	.304	.298	73	227	24	56	69	10	0	1	22	17	28	0	2	6
Correia	.238	.381	.238	14	21	3	5	8	1	1	0	3	0	5	0	0	5
Lind	.236	.271	.267	44	140	9	33	38	5	0	0	7	6	12	0	1	1
Owen	.229	.312	.288	82	218	17	50	68	9	3	1	28	18	22	3	2	6
Easley	.216	.300	.288	114	357	35	77	107	14	2	4	35	32	47	5	2	10
Gallagher	.188	.250	.278	11	16	1	3	4	1	0	0	0	2	1	0	0	0
Martinez	.180	.246	.265	26	61	7	11	15	1	0	1	9	6	7	0	0	1
Allanson	.171	.317	.244	35	82	5	14	26	3	0	3	10	7	12	0	1	1
Perez	.169	.296	.302	29	71	9	12	21	4	1	1	7	12	9	0	2	7
Dalesandro	.100	.200	.100	11	10	1	1	2	1	0	0	0	0	2	0	0	0
Turner	.100	.100	.100	5	10	0	1	1	0	0	0	0	1	0	0	0	0
Flora	.000	.000	.000	2	1	1	0	0	0	0	0	0	0	1	0	0	0

PITCHERS	W-L	ERA	G	GS	CG	GF	Sho	SV	IP	H	R	ER	HR	BB	SO
Bennett	0-0	0.00	1	0	0	1	0	0	0.1	0	0	0	0	0	0
Percival	3-2	1.95	62	0	0	16	0	3	74.0	37	19	16	6	26	94
Monteleone	1-0	2.00	9	0	0	2	0	0	9.0	8	2	2	1	3	5
Patterson	5-2	3.04	62	0	0	20	0	0	53.1	48	18	18	6	13	41
Smith	0-5	3.47	52	0	0	51	0	37	49.1	42	19	19	3	25	43
Abbott	11-8	3.70	30	30	4	0	1	0	197.0	209	93	81	14	64	86
James	3-0	3.88	46	0	0	11	0	1	55.2	49	27	24	6	26	36
Sanderson	1-3	4.12	7	7	0	0	0	0	39.1	48	23	18	6	4	23
Habyan	1-2	4.13	28	0	0	7	0	0	32.2	36	16	15	2	12	25
Finley	15-12	4.21	32	32	2	0	1	0	203.0	192	106	95	20	93	195
Edenfield	0-0	4.26	7	0	0	3	0	0	12.2	15	7	6	1	5	6
Langston	15-7	4.63	31	31	2	0	1	0	200.1	212	109	103	21	64	142
Butcher	6-1	4.73	40	0	0	13	0	0	51.1	49	28	27	7	31	29
Holzemer	0-1	5.40	12	0	0	5	0	0	8.1	11	6	5	1	7	5
Harkey	8-9	5.44	26	20	1	1	0	0	127.1	155	78	77	24	47	56
Boskie	7-7	5.64	20	20	1	0	0	0	111.2	127	73	70	16	25	51
B. Anderson	6-8	5.87	18	17	1	0	0	0	99.2	110	66	65	24	30	45
Bielecki	4-6	5.97	22	11	0	2	0	0	75.1	80	56	50	15	31	45
Springer	1-2	6.10	19	6	0	3	0	1	51.2	60	37	35	11	25	38
Williams	1-2	6.75	20	0	0	3	0	0	10.2	13	10	8	1	21	9

1996 preliminary roster

PITCHERS (18)
Brian Anderson
Shawn Boskie
Ken Edenfield
Geoff Edsell
Ryan Hancock
Mike Harkey
David Holdridge
Mark Holzemer
Mike James
Pete Janicki
Mark Langston
Phil Leftwich
Rich Monteleone
Troy Percival
Jeff Schmidt
Lee Smith
Ben VanRyn
Shad Williams

CATCHERS (3)
Jorge Fabregas
Todd Greene
Chris Turner

INFIELDERS (10)
George Arias
Rod Correia
Gary DiSarcina
Damion Easley
Tim Harkrider
Rex Hudler
Orlando Palmeiro
Eduardo Perez
J.T. Snow
Randy Velarde

OUTFIELDERS (5)
Garret Anderson
Chili Davis
Jim Edmonds
Marquis Riley
Tim Salmon

Games played by position

PLAYER	G	C	1B	2B	3B	SS	OF	DH
Aldrete	78	0	36	0	0	0	18	2
Allanson	35	35	0	0	0	0	0	0
G. Anderson	106	0	0	0	0	0	100	1
Correia	14	0	0	3	2	7	0	1
Dalesandro	11	8	0	0	0	0	1	1
Davis	119	0	0	0	0	0	0	119
DiSarcina	99	0	0	0	0	98	0	0
Easley	114	0	0	88	0	25	0	0
Edmonds	141	0	0	0	0	0	139	0
Fabregas	73	73	0	0	0	0	0	0
Flora	2	0	0	0	0	0	0	1
Gallagher	11	0	0	0	0	0	6	1
Gonzales	30	0	0	6	18	1	0	1
Hudler	84	0	2	52	0	0	22	3
Lind	44	0	0	44	0	0	0	0
Martinez	26	0	4	0	16	0	0	2
Myers	85	61	0	0	0	0	0	16
Owen	82	0	0	16	29	25	0	0
Palmeiro	15	0	0	0	0	0	7	1
Perez	29	0	0	0	23	0	0	1
Phillips	139	0	0	0	88	0	48	2
Salmon	143	0	0	0	0	0	142	1
Schofield	12	0	0	0	0	12	0	0
Snow	143	0	143	0	0	0	0	0
Turner	5	4	0	0	0	0	0	1

Sick call: 1995 DL Report

Player	Days on the DL
Andy Allanson	21
Brian Anderson	45
Mike Bielecki	78
Shawn Boskie	89
Chili Davis	28
Gary DiSarcina	44
Dave Gallagher	20
Mike James	21
Phil Leftwich	124
Greg Myers	34**
Spike Owen	26
Scott Sanderson	124

* Indicates three separate terms on Disabled List.*

1995 Amateur draft picks

Players are listed with position and college or high school. Most players were assigned to rookie or Class A leagues. List provided by Major League Baseball.

Javier Baretti, c, Elisa Pascual HS, Caguas, P.R.; Esteban Barrios, of, Miami Dade CC; Justin Baughman, ss, Lewis-Clark State; Randy Betten, 2b, Arizona State; Ty Bilderback, lf-rf, Arkansas; David Bittler, lhp, Florida CC; Douglas Blackman, c, Warren Easton HS, New Orleans; Jeremy Blevins, rhp, Sullivan East HS, Bristol, Tenn.; Sterling Bullock, 3b, Carson HS, Compton, Calif.; Kurt Bultmann, ss-2b, Seminole (Fla.) HS; Daniel Buxbaum, 1b-3b, Miami; Robert Bystrowski, 3b-cf, Jesuit HS, Fair Oaks, Calif.; Michael Clarke, rhp, St. Petersburg JC; Brian Cooper, rhp, Southern California; Jed Dalton, 3b-of, Nebraska; Thomas Darrell, rhp, Garrett CC; Joshua Deakman, 3b-rhp, Arizona State; Antonio Diaz, ss, Gulf Coast CC; Darin Erstad, lf, Nebraska; David Farfan, rhp, Fresno State; Michael Gauger, lhp, Wakulla HS, St. Marks, Fla.; Bryan Graves, c, Southern A&M; Moses Herrera, rhp, Colton (Calif.) HS; Daren Hooper, cf, Aragon HS, Woodside, Calif.; Douglas Hurst, rhp, Fresno CC; Douglas Hurst, rhp, Okaloosa Walton CC; Mario Iglesias, rhp, Stanford; Stanisles James, of, James A. Shanks HS, Quincy, Fla.; Khalif Jefferson, ss, Serra HS, Compton, Calif.; Jacob Jensen, ss-2b, Washington Union HS, Fresno, Calif.; Gregory Jones, c, Seminole (Fla.) HS; Ryan Kane, 3b, Presbyterian College; Joel Katte, 3b, Sheboygan (Wis.) North HS; Matthew Koziara, rhp, Franklin (Pa.) HS; Alexis Llanos, 2b, Lola Rodriguez De Tio HS, Carolina, P.R.; Steven Maris, ss-2b, Oak Hall HS, Gainesville, Fla.; Eddie Marquez, 2b-ss, Pasco Hernando CC; John McAninch, c, Lewis-Clark State; Brandon McGuire, ss, Coahoma HS, Big Spring, Texas; Steven Mikesell, c, Glendale College; Gregory Millichap, cf, Serra HS, Woodside, Calif.; John Opina, ss, La Sierra, Riverside, Calif.; James O'Quinn, lhp, Florida CC; Christopher Pine, rhp, Tualatin HS, Tigard, Ore.; Robert Prather, lhp, Lassiter HS, Atlanta; Robb Quinlan, ss, Hill-Murray HS, Maplewood, Minn.; John Romero, rhp, Mission JC; Derek Ryder, c, Penn St.; Brian Scutero, rhp, Central Florida; Fernando Sordo, rhp, Spanish River HS, Boca Raton, Fla.; Jason Stockstill, lhp, Katella HS, Villa Park, Calif.; Donnell Tate, ss-c, Oakland (Calif.) HS; Evert Thoen, ss, Indian River CC; Jason Townsell, rhp, Marianna (Fla.) HS; Gar Vallone, ss, UCLA; Jonathan VanderGriend, of, Washington; Derrick Vargas, lhp, Newark (Calif.) Memorial HS; Kyle Wagner, c, Wake Forest; Jarrod Washburn, lhp, Wisconsin-Oshkosh; Widd Workman, rhp-of, Brigham Young.

Minor Leagues

Tops in the organization

Batter	Club	Avg.	G	AB	R	H	HR	RBI
Greg Shockey	Lke	.327	114	441	85	144	20	88
Tom Redington	Lke	.320	85	303	55	97	6	57
Jovino Carvajal	Van	.317	120	511	83	162	3	33
Joe Urso	Lke	.317	77	281	54	89	3	38
Orlando Munoz	Mdl	.307	91	319	39	98	1	44

Home Runs			Wins		
Todd Greene	Van	40	Matt Beaumont	Lke	16
George Arias	Mdl	30	Keith Morrison	Van	14
Tony Moeder	Cr	21	Jason Dickson	Cr	14
Greg Shockey	Lke	20	Nicholas Skuse	Cr	13
Leon Glenn	Mdl	17	Several tied		12

RBI			Saves		
George Arias	Mdl	104	Carlos Castillo	Lke	32
Todd Greene	Van	92	Michael Freehill	Cr	28
Greg Shockey	Lke	88	Mike Schooler	Mdl	20
John Donati	Cr	75	Brian Scutero	Boi	12
Tony Moeder	Cr	73	Julian Heredia	Van	10

Stolen Bases			Strikeouts		
Jovino Carvajal	Van	49	Geoff Edsell	Mdl	153
Juan Henderson	Cr	47	Matt Beaumont	Lke	149
Paul Failla	Cr	30	Travis Thurmond	Boi	148
Marquis Riley	Van	29	Pete Janicki	Van	140
Derek Vaughn	Lke	23	Jason Dickson	Cr	134

Pitcher	Club	W-L	ERA	IP	H	BB	SO
Jason Dickson	Cr	14-6	2.86	173	151	45	134
Matt Beaumont	Lke	16-9	3.29	175	162	57	149
Shad Williams	Van	9-7	3.37	150	142	48	114
Jon DeClue	Lke	11-6	3.52	143	145	32	112
Korey Keling	Mdl	8-7	3.54	140	131	58	117

California (1965-1995), includes Los Angeles (1961-1964)

Runs: Most, career, all-time

889	Brian Downing, 1978-1990
691	Jim Fregosi, 1961-1971
601	Bobby Grich, 1977-1986
481	Don Baylor, 1977-1982
474	Rod Carew, 1979-1985

Hits: Most, career, all-time

1588	Brian Downing, 1978-1990
1408	Jim Fregosi, 1961-1971
1103	Bobby Grich, 1977-1986
968	Rod Carew, 1979-1985
925	WALLY JOYNER, 1986-1991

2B: Most, career, all-time

282	Brian Downing, 1978-1990
219	Jim Fregosi, 1961-1971
183	Bobby Grich, 1977-1986
170	WALLY JOYNER, 1986-1991
149	Doug DeCinces, 1982-1987

3B: Most, career, all-time

70	Jim Fregosi, 1961-1971
32	Mickey Rivers, 1970-1975
27	LUIS POLONIA, 1990-1993
27	DICK SCHOFIELD, 1983-1992
25	Bobby Knoop, 1964-1969

HR: Most, career, all-time

222	Brian Downing, 1978-1990
154	Bobby Grich, 1977-1986
141	Don Baylor, 1977-1982
130	Doug DeCinces, 1982-1987
128	CHILI DAVIS, 1988-1995

RBI: Most, career, all-time

846	Brian Downing, 1978-1990
557	Bobby Grich, 1977-1986
546	Jim Fregosi, 1961-1971
523	Don Baylor, 1977-1982
523	CHILI DAVIS, 1988-1995

SB: Most, career, all-time

186	Gary Pettis, 1982-1987
174	LUIS POLONIA, 1990-1993
139	Sandy Alomar, 1969-1974
126	Mickey Rivers, 1970-1975
123	DEVON WHITE, 1985-1990

BB: Most, career, all-time

866	Brian Downing, 1978-1990
630	Bobby Grich, 1977-1986
558	Jim Fregosi, 1961-1971
407	CHILI DAVIS, 1988-1995
405	Rod Carew, 1979-1985

BA: Highest, career, all-time

.314	Rod Carew, 1979-1985
.294	LUIS POLONIA, 1990-1993
.293	Juan Beniquez, 1981-1985
.288	WALLY JOYNER, 1986-1991
.276	CHILI DAVIS, 1988-1995

Slug avg: Highest, career, all-time

.463	Doug DeCinces, 1982-1987
.458	CHILI DAVIS, 1988-1995
.455	WALLY JOYNER, 1986-1991
.448	Don Baylor, 1977-1982
.441	Brian Downing, 1978-1990

Games started: Most, career, all-time

288	Nolan Ryan, 1972-1979
272	Mike Witt, 1981-1990
252	CHUCK FINLEY, 1986-1995
218	Frank Tanana, 1973-1980
189	KIRK McCASKILL, 1985-1991
189	Clyde Wright, 1966-1973

Saves: Most, career, all-time

126	BRYAN HARVEY, 1987-1992
65	Dave LaRoche, 1970-1980
61	Donnie Moore, 1985-1988
58	Bob Lee, 1964-1966
45	JOE GRAHE, 1990-1994

Shutouts: Most, career, all-time

40	Nolan Ryan, 1972-1979
24	Frank Tanana, 1973-1980
21	Dean Chance, 1961-1966
14	George Brunet, 1964-1969
13	Geoff Zahn, 1981-1985

Wins: Most, career, all-time

138	Nolan Ryan, 1972-1979
114	CHUCK FINLEY, 1986-1995
109	Mike Witt, 1981-1990
102	Frank Tanana, 1973-1980
87	Clyde Wright, 1966-1973

K: Most, career, all-time

2416	Nolan Ryan, 1972-1979
1369	CHUCK FINLEY, 1986-1995
1283	Mike Witt, 1981-1990
1233	Frank Tanana, 1973-1980
999	MARK LANGSTON, 1990-1995

Win pct: Highest, career, all-time

.567	Frank Tanana, 1973-1980
.557	Andy Messersmith, 1968-1972
.553	Geoff Zahn, 1981-1985
.552	MARK LANGSTON, 1990-1995
.538	CHUCK FINLEY, 1986-1995

ERA: Lowest, career, all-time

2.78	Andy Messersmith, 1968-1972
2.83	Dean Chance, 1961-1966
3.07	Nolan Ryan, 1972-1979
3.08	Frank Tanana, 1973-1980
3.13	George Brunet, 1964-1969

Runs: Most, season

120	Don Baylor, 1979
120	JIM EDMONDS, 1995
119	TONY PHILLIPS, 1995
115	Albie Pearson, 1962
114	Carney Lansford, 1979

Hits: Most, season

202	Alex Johnson, 1970
188	Carney Lansford, 1979
186	Don Baylor, 1979
186	Billy Moran, 1962
184	Johnny Ray, 1988

2B: Most, season

42	Doug DeCinces, 1982
42	Johnny Ray, 1988
38	Fred Lynn, 1982
37	Brian Downing, 1982
35	TIM SALMON, 1993

3B: Most, season

13	Jim Fregosi, 1968
13	Mickey Rivers, 1975
13	DEVON WHITE, 1989
12	Jim Fregosi, 1963
11	Bobby Knoop, 1966
11	Mickey Rivers, 1974

HR: Most, season

39	Reggie Jackson, 1982
37	Bobby Bonds, 1977
37	Leon Wagner, 1962
36	Don Baylor, 1979
34	Don Baylor, 1978
34	WALLY JOYNER, 1987
34	TIM SALMON, 1995

RBI: Most, season

139	Don Baylor, 1979	
117	WALLY JOYNER, 1987	
115	Bobby Bonds, 1977	
112	CHILI DAVIS, 1993	
107	JIM EDMONDS, 1995	
107	Leon Wagner, 1962	

SB: Most, season

70	Mickey Rivers, 1975
56	Gary Pettis, 1985
55	LUIS POLONIA, 1993
51	LUIS POLONIA, 1992
50	Gary Pettis, 1986

BB: Most, season

113	TONY PHILLIPS, 1995
106	Brian Downing, 1987
96	Albie Pearson, 1961
95	Albie Pearson, 1962
93	Jim Fregosi, 1969

BA: Highest, season

.339	Rod Carew, 1983
.331	Rod Carew, 1980
.330	TIM SALMON, 1995
.329	Alex Johnson, 1970
.326	Brian Downing, 1979

Slug avg: Highest, season

.594	TIM SALMON, 1995
.561	CHILI DAVIS, 1994
.548	Doug DeCinces, 1982
.543	Bobby Grich, 1981
.537	Bobby Grich, 1979

Games started: Most, season

41	Nolan Ryan, 1974
40	Bill Singer, 1973
39	Nolan Ryan, 1972
39	Nolan Ryan, 1973
39	Nolan Ryan, 1976
39	Clyde Wright, 1970

Saves: Most, season

46	BRYAN HARVEY, 1991
37	LEE SMITH, 1995
31	Donnie Moore, 1985
27	Minnie Rojas, 1967
25	BRYAN HARVEY, 1989
25	BRYAN HARVEY, 1990
25	Dave LaRoche, 1978

Shutouts: Most, season

11	Dean Chance, 1964
9	Nolan Ryan, 1972
7	Nolan Ryan, 1976
7	Frank Tanana, 1977
6	Jim McGlothlin, 1967

Wins: Most, season

22	Nolan Ryan, 1974
22	Clyde Wright, 1970
21	Nolan Ryan, 1973
20	Dean Chance, 1964
20	Andy Messersmith, 1971
20	Bill Singer, 1973

K: Most, season

383	Nolan Ryan, 1973
367	Nolan Ryan, 1974
341	Nolan Ryan, 1977
329	Nolan Ryan, 1972
327	Nolan Ryan, 1976

Win pct: Highest, season

.773	Bert Blyleven, 1989
.704	MARK LANGSTON, 1991
.692	Geoff Zahn, 1982
.690	Dean Chance, 1964
.682	MARK LANGSTON, 1995

ERA: Lowest, season

1.65	Dean Chance, 1964
2.28	Nolan Ryan, 1972
2.40	CHUCK FINLEY, 1990
2.43	Frank Tanana, 1976
2.52	Andy Messersmith, 1969

Most pinch-hit homers, season

3	Joe Adcock, 1966
3	George Hendrick, 1987

Most pinch-hit homers, career

4	Ruppert Jones, 1985-1987
4	George Hendrick, 1985-1988

Most consecutive games batting safely

25	Rod Carew, 1982
23	JIM EDMONDS, 1995

Most consecutive scoreless innings

36	Jim McGlothlin, 1967

No-hit games

Bo Belinsky, LA vs Bal AL, 2-0; May 5, 1962.

Clyde Wright, Cal vs Oak AL, 4-0; July 3, 1970.

Nolan Ryan, Cal at KC AL, 3-0; May 15, 1973.

Nolan Ryan, Cal at Det AL, 6-0; July 15, 1973.

Nolan Ryan, Cal vs Min AL, 4-0; September 28, 1974.

Nolan Ryan, Cal vs Bal AL, 1-0; June 1, 1975.

Mike Witt, Cal at Tex AL, 1-0; September 30, 1984 (perfect game).

MARK LANGSTON (7 innings) and Mike Witt (2 innings), Cal vs Sea AL, 1-0; April 11, 1990.

ACTIVE PLAYERS in caps.

Leader from the franchise's current location is included. If not in the top five, leader's rank is listed in parenthesis; asterisk (*) indicates player is not in top 25.

Players' years of service are listed by the first and last years with this team and are not necessarily consecutive; all statistics record performances for this team only.

Texas Rangers

Will Clark was the RBI-meister in Texas with 92—and a .302 batting average for good measure.

By Russell Beeker, *Baseball Weekly*

1995 Rangers: Always a bridesmaid . . .

A season that began with promise ended like every other one in the franchise's 24 years in Arlington: without a postseason appearance. The Rangers teased their fans with hope that 1995 might finally be the year they made the playoffs. They were tied for the division lead at the All-Star break and led the wild-card standings into September. But like so many teams before them, they faded.

Midway through spring training, new general manager Doug Melvin and first-year manager Johnny Oates appeared to have assembled a team that could challenge for the American League West title. The batting order featured speed at the top in center fielder Otis Nixon and second baseman Mark McLemore, a career .300 hitter in the three hole in Will Clark, power in the middle from Juan Gonzalez, Mickey Tettleton and Dean Palmer, and good hitters lower down in Ivan Rodriguez and Rusty Greer. The pitching rotation seemed to be solid with Kenny Rogers, Bob Tewksbury, Kevin Gross and Roger Pavlik holding down the first four spots.

Gonzalez missed the first 33 games of the season and later was plagued by continuing injuries that kept him out of the lineup. He played just 88 games—83 at DH—but still hit 27 homers with 82 RBI. Palmer got off to an All-Star start but injured his arm June 3 and was out until the final week. Clark suffered a hairline fracture in his elbow early in the season and ended up with just 16 homers. The pitching staff was also plagued. Darren Oliver tore his rotator cuff and was out for the season by June 27. Closer Jeff Russell went on the DL twice with back injuries. And Gross, the team's big free-agent signing in the off-season, began the year 1-6.

Nevertheless, the Rangers won games. Nixon, McLemore, Tettleton, Rodriguez and Greer carried the offense. Rogers and Tewksbury carried the pitching staff. The team was 39-30 at the All-Star break, tied for first. They won three of four in Boston after the break, and hopes for that first-ever playoff appearance were high.

Then they went into a free fall, lost 10 straight and lost sight of first place. They hit .235 in July, lowest in the AL. Melvin didn't give up, though. He traded for starting pitcher Bobby Witt to help down the stretch, and the team was leading the wild-card standings in late August.

Then they hit another skid—losing 10 of 12—and were out of the race. A three-game sweep by Seattle in the middle of September was the final nail in the coffin.

Highlights: Rodriguez (.303) made the All-Star team for the fourth consecutive year and led major league catchers by throwing out 48% of runners attempting to steal. Leadoff hitter Nixon played good defense, hit .295 and stole 50 bases. And Rogers made the All-Star team and finished 17-7, a team record for victories by a lefty.

1996 Rangers: Preview

The core of the Rangers' potent offense returns—Gonzalez, Clark and McLemore—were signed; the club held an option on Nixon; Palmer and Rodriguez were arbitration-eligible; and Greer and Gil were players with less than three years and thus under control. Roger Pavlik, Gross and Oliver were the only starting pitchers definitely set to return when the season ended. Oliver is expected to be at full strength before spring training and ready to resume a spot in the rotation. Minor leaguers Rick Helling and Julio Santana could challenge for jobs. Setup reliever Matt Whiteside will be back in the bullpen, and could be joined by right-handers Jose Alberro and Mark Brandenburg, along with lefty Terry Burrows, who got some experience in the majors in '95.

These notes were excerpted from the following issues of Baseball Weekly.

▶**May 3:** Early returns indicated that the Rangers invested $1.5 million wisely in Bob Tewksbury. The 34-year-old right-hander held the Indians, a great hitting team, to one run in six innings of his first start. Kenny Rogers, the Opening Day starter, says no one can be called the ace until the end of the year: "The last two years I've pitched as well as anybody on the staff, but I've still got to pitch well this year. The one who wins the most games and pitches the best is the staff ace."

▶**May 10:** Rookie shortstop Benji Gil hit home runs in three consecutive games, raised his average to .310 and was playing stellar defense.

▶**May 17:** Any thoughts the Rangers had of a closer-by-committee arrangement died when Darren Oliver had problems in the first few games and Jeff Russell converted four of his first five save opportunities. Oliver struggled with control (eight walks in his first 8⅓ innings) and velocity, while Russell had a 1.35 ERA in his first six appearances. So Oliver joined Matt Whiteside as the setup men, and Russell became the closer.

▶**May 24:** Darren Oliver was moved into the rotation. In his first major league start. he allowed one run on three hits before running out of gas after 58 pitches—3⅓ innings.

▶**May 31:** Kenny Rogers was within 12 innings of the AL record for consecutive shutout innings for a left-hander after extending his streak to 33. He had won five consecutive games and had lowered his ERA to 1.42, the best in the majors.

▶**June 7:** The Rangers suffered a serious blow when third baseman Dean Palmer sustained a season-ending injury. He led the Rangers in home runs (nine), RBI (24), runs (30), slugging percentage (.623) and on-base percentage (.450). He was second in batting average

at .333. Meanwhile, Kenny Rogers ran his scoreless-innings streak to 39 before giving up a run in the seventh inning on June 1. He broke the club record of 36 set by Charlie Hough.

▶**June 14:** Juan Gonzalez's continuing back problems forced Johnny Oates to go with a new-look lineup—Gonzalez moved to DH, Mickey Tettleton moved to right field, and Rusty Greer moved to left. Gonzalez missed the first 33 games of the season because of a herniated disc, then returned to start five, including four in left and one at DH. But he had to leave the fifth game after two innings because of a stiff back and missed the next two contests. He returned at DH in the next two games.

▶**June 21:** Kevin Gross continued to struggle. He fell to 1-6 with a 9.89 ERA and was worst among major league starters in runs (52) and earned runs (48).

▶**July 5:** The Rangers' experiment with Darren Oliver as a starter appeared to have backfired. He went on the DL a day after pulling himself out of a start after one inning. He went 3-2 with a 2.91 ERA in his first six starts but said he felt something pulling in his shoulder on June 20. "I asked the doctor, and he said this thing could have happened pitching out of the bullpen," general manager Doug Melvin said. "I still think he's going to be a fine starting pitcher in the majors. I think he's got a bright future as a starter." Meanwhile, Juan Gonzalez was beginning to reclaim his place as one of the top sluggers in the game, hitting eight homers in June, a pace that would mean more than 40 over the course of a full season.

▶**July 19:** Kevin Gross—the worst pitcher in the majors with an 8.83 ERA in mid-June—allowed just one run on five hits in 7⅔ innings to beat Boston, his second victory in his last three starts. "Personally, it's just nice to throw good a couple of times in a row," he said.

July 26: The Rangers were tied for first at the All-Star break and won three out of four in Boston to open the second half but then lost a season-worst six consecutive games to fall a season-high five games behind the Angels. The collapse involved both pitching, which allowed seven runs per game, and hitting, as the offense averaged 3.2 runs in the skid.

Aug. 2: The beleaguered pitching staff took another hit when Bob Tewksbury was diagnosed with a stress fracture on the left side of his rib cage, possibly jeopardizing the rest of his season. Tewksbury was 7-4 with a 3.98 ERA in 108⅔ innings. He was second on the club in innings pitched and victories and second among starters in ERA.

Aug. 16: Bobby Witt made a triumphant return to Texas on Aug. 12 by holding the Blue Jays scoreless through the first six innings and notching a 6-3 victory. It was the first appearance for Witt in a Rangers uniform in three years

Aug. 23: Will Clark and Juan Gonzalez were back in the lineup. They each homered in the same game and combined for five RBI in a 9-6 victory against the White Sox on Aug. 19. Kevin Gross was 3-0 with a 1.78 ERA in his last three starts.

Aug. 30: The rotation, a weakness for much of the season, finally seemed to be at strength: Bobby Witt was 2-1 with a 1.99 ERA in his first three starts after being acquired from the Marlins; Bob Tewksbury returned from the DL to win his first start; Roger Pavlik allowed just one run in four of his last six starts to improve to 8-4; Kevin Gross was 6-6 in his last 14 starts; and Kenny Rogers was an All-Star. Ironically, the weak link was Rogers, with a 5.33 ERA in his last 14 starts. But the Rangers were 8-6 in those outings and had won five times in Rogers' last six starts.

Sept. 6: The Rangers had a chance to get back into the race in the West as the Angels were slumping but were unable to make a move. Instead, they lost ground in the wild-card race by dropping six of seven on a road trip to Kansas City and Minnesota. They were

swept by the Twins, the team with the worst record in the majors. The Rangers hit just .160 in the three-game series and scored five runs in 28 innings. Combined with a loss to open their subsequent homestand, the Rangers went 3-for-31 with runners in scoring position in a four-game stretch.

Sept. 13: The Rangers went 4-12 in a 16-game period ending on Sept. 9 to go from a 3½-game lead in the wild-card race to fourth place, two games out. The main culprit was the offense, which batted .214 in the last 13 games of that stretch.

Team directory

Owner: J. Thomas Schieffer and Edward W. Rose, managing general partners

General manager: Doug Melvin

Ballpark:
The Ballpark in Arlington
1000 Ballpark Way, Arlington, Texas
817-273-5222
Capacity 49,178
Parking for 12,500 cars; $5
No public transportation
Approximately 480 wheelchair seats with additional handicapped seating; restrooms with diaper-changing areas; ramps, escalators and elevators to serve all areas

Team publications:
On Deck Newsletter, yearbook, *Program Magazine*
817-273-5222

TV, radio broadcast stations:
KRLD-AM 1080, KXEB 910 AM (Spanish), KTVT-TV 11, Prime Sports Entertainment

Camps and/or clinics:
Texas Ranger Coaches Clinic, June, 817-273-5222

Spring training:
Charlotte County Stadium
Port Charlotte, Fla.
Capacity 6,026
813-625-9500

TEXAS RANGERS 1995 final stats

BATTERS	BA	SLG	OB	G	AB	R	H	TB	2B	3B	HR	RBI	BB	SO	SB	CS	E
Palmer	.336	.613	.448	36	119	30	40	73	6	0	9	24	21	21	1	1	5
Marzano	.333	.333	.333	2	6	1	2	2	0	0	0	0	0	0	0	0	0
Rodriguez	.303	.449	.327	130	492	56	149	221	32	2	12	67	16	48	0	2	8
Clark	.302	.480	.389	123	454	85	137	218	27	3	16	92	68	50	0	1	7
Gonzalez	.295	.594	.324	90	352	57	104	209	20	2	27	82	17	66	0	0	0
Nixon	.295	.338	.357	139	589	87	174	199	21	2	0	45	58	85	50	21	4
Frye	.278	.377	.335	90	313	38	87	118	15	2	4	29	24	45	3	3	11
Greer	.271	.424	.355	131	417	58	113	177	21	2	13	61	55	66	3	1	6
Maldonado	.263	.489	.370	74	190	28	50	93	16	0	9	30	32	50	1	2	1
McLemore	.261	.358	.346	129	467	73	122	167	20	5	5	41	59	71	21	11	4
Hare	.250	.292	.357	18	24	2	6	7	1	0	0	2	4	6	0	0	0
Valle	.240	.280	.305	36	75	7	18	21	3	0	0	5	6	18	1	0	1
Tettleton	.238	.510	.396	134	429	76	102	219	19	1	32	78	107	110	0	0	3
Pagliarulo	.232	.349	.277	86	241	27	56	84	16	0	4	27	15	49	0	0	7
Ortiz	.231	.343	.270	41	108	10	25	37	5	2	1	18	6	18	0	1	8
Worthington	.221	.368	.293	26	68	4	15	25	4	0	2	6	7	8	0	0	1
Gil	.219	.347	.266	130	415	36	91	144	20	3	9	46	26	147	2	4	17
Beltre	.217	.304	.250	54	92	7	20	28	8	0	0	7	4	15	0	0	5
Frazier	.212	.232	.278	49	99	19	21	23	2	0	0	8	7	20	9	1	2
Voigt	.175	.317	.284	36	63	9	11	20	3	0	2	8	10	14	0	0	1
Buechele	.125	.125	.250	9	24	0	3	3	0	0	0	0	4	3	0	0	0
Horn	.111	.111	.200	11	9	0	1	1	0	0	0	0	1	6	0	0	0
Hatcher	.083	.167	.154	6	12	2	1	2	1	0	0	0	1	1	0	0	0
Fox	.000	.000	.167	10	15	2	0	0	0	0	0	0	3	4	0	0	0

PITCHERS	W-L	ERA	G	GS	CG	GF	Sho	SV	IP	H	R	ER	HR	BB	SO
Howard	0-0	0.00	4	0	0	1	0	0	4.0	3	0	0	0	1	2
Vosberg	5-5	3.00	44	0	0	20	0	4	36.0	32	15	12	3	16	36
Russell	1-0	3.03	37	0	0	32	0	20	32.2	36	12	11	3	9	21
Rogers	17-7	3.38	31	31	3	0	1	0	208.0	192	87	78	26	76	140
Heredia	0-1	3.75	6	0	0	0	0	0	12.0	9	5	5	2	15	6
McDowell	7-4	4.02	64	0	0	26	0	4	85.0	86	39	38	5	34	49
Whiteside	5-4	4.08	40	0	0	18	0	3	53.0	48	24	24	5	19	46
Oliver	4-2	4.22	17	7	0	2	0	0	49.0	47	25	23	3	32	39
Pavlik	10-10	4.37	31	31	2	0	1	0	191.2	174	96	93	19	90	149
Cook	0-2	4.53	46	1	0	10	0	2	57.2	63	32	29	9	26	53
Witt	3-4	4.55	10	10	1	0	0	0	61.1	81	35	31	4	21	46
Tewksbury	8-7	4.58	21	21	4	0	1	0	129.2	169	75	66	8	20	53
Gross	9-15	5.54	31	30	4	0	0	0	183.2	200	124	113	27	89	106
Brandenburg	0-1	5.93	11	0	0	5	0	0	27.1	36	18	18	5	7	21
Burrows	2-2	6.45	28	3	0	6	0	1	44.2	60	37	32	11	19	22
Helling	0-2	6.57	3	3	0	0	0	0	12.1	17	11	9	2	8	5
Nichting	0-0	7.03	13	0	0	3	0	0	24.1	36	19	19	1	13	6
Alberro	0-0	7.40	12	0	0	7	0	0	20.2	26	18	17	2	12	10
Darwin	3-10	7.45	20	15	1	0	0	0	99.0	131	87	82	25	31	58
Fajardo	0-0	7.80	5	0	0	1	0	0	15.0	19	13	13	2	5	9
Taylor	1-2	9.39	3	3	0	0	0	0	15.1	25	16	16	6	5	10
Dettmer	0-0	27.00	1	0	0	0	0	0	0.1	2	1	1	0	0	0

1996 preliminary roster

PITCHERS (19)
Jose Alberro
Mark Brandenburg
Dennis Cook
Chris Curtis
Jeff Davis
Kevin Gross
Rick Helling
Chris Howard
Kerry Lacy
Mark Mimbs
Chris Nichting
Darren Oliver
Danny Patterson
Roger Pavlik
Tim Rumer
Julio Santana
Dan Smith
Ed Vosberg
Matt Whiteside

CATCHERS (2)
Ivan Rodriguez
Dave Valle

INFIELDERS (8)
Esteban Beltre
Will Clark
Jeff Frye
Benji Gil
Mark McLemore
Luis Ortiz
Dean Palmer
Craig Worthington

OUTFIELDERS (6)
Rikkert Faneyte
Lou Frazier
Juan Gonzalez
Rusty Greer
Terrell Lowery
Warren Newson

Games played by position

PLAYER	G	C	1B	2B	3B	SS	OF	DH
Beltre	54	0	0	15	1	36	0	0
Buechele	9	0	0	0	9	0	0	0
Clark	123	0	122	0	0	0	0	1
Fox	10	0	0	0	0	0	8	1
Frazier	49	0	0	0	0	0	47	2
Frye	90	0	0	83	0	0	0	0
Gil	130	0	0	0	0	130	0	0
Gonzalez	90	0	0	0	0	0	5	83
Greer	131	0	3	0	0	0	125	0
Hare	18	0	1	0	0	0	9	3
Hatcher	6	0	0	0	0	0	5	1
Horn	11	0	0	0	0	0	0	1
Maldonado	74	0	0	0	0	0	69	1
Marzano	2	2	0	0	0	0	0	0
McLemore	129	0	0	66	0	0	73	2
Nixon	139	0	0	0	0	0	138	0
Ortiz	41	0	0	0	35	0	0	3
Pagliarulo	86	0	11	0	68	0	0	0
Palmer	36	0	0	0	36	0	0	0
Rodriguez	130	127	0	0	0	0	0	1
Tettleton	134	3	9	0	0	0	63	58
Valle	36	29	7	0	0	0	0	0
Voigt	36	0	6	0	0	0	25	3
Worthington	26	0	0	0	26	0	0	0

Minor Leagues

Tops in the organization

Batter	Club	Avg.	G	AB	R	H	HR	RBI
C. Brumbaugh	Hdv	.358	74	282	44	101	2	45
John Marzano	Okc	.309	120	427	55	132	9	56
Johnny Monell	Tul	.306	121	434	55	133	12	64
Fernando Tatis	CSc	.303	131	499	74	151	15	84
Hanley Frias	Tul	.294	126	480	67	141	0	41

Home Runs

Mike Smith	Tul	16
Fernando Tatis	CSc	15
Frank Charles	Tul	13
Several tied		12

Wins

Jeff Davis	Chl	13
Michael Venafro	Hdv	9
Joseph Keusch	Tul	9
Gardner O'Flynn	CSc	9
David Manning	Chl	9

RBI

Fernando Tatis	CSc	84
Andrew Vessel	Chl	78
Frank Charles	Tul	72
Several tied		64

Saves

Brian Martineau	Hdv	18
Bucky Buckles	Chl	16
Rodney Cook	CSc	11
Kerry Lacy	Okc	10
Several tied		8

Stolen Bases

Dom Gatti	CSc	39
Ryan Rutz	CSc	36
Juan Nunez	Rng	26
Several tied		22

Strikeouts

Nelson Perpetuo	CSc	132
Jim Brower	Chl	110
Gardner O'Flynn	CSc	110
Jeff Davis	Chl	109
Julio Santana	Tul	104

Pitcher	Club	W-L	ERA	IP	H	BB	SO
Scott Mudd	Hdv	7-1	2.24	101	91	18	62
Rodney Cook	CSc	3-8	2.53	96	83	39	88
Jeff Davis	Chl	13-7	2.77	172	161	38	109
G. O'Flynn	CSc	9-10	2.96	167	156	61	110
Rob Wishnevski	Okc	6-3	3.47	109	101	53	78

Sick call: 1995 DL Report

Player	Days on the DL
Steve Dreyer	61
Jeff Frye	30*
Juan Gonzalez	57*
Darren Oliver	97
Mike Pagliarulo	16
Dean Palmer	110
Jeff Russell	31*
Dan Smith	160
Bob Tewksbury	34
Matt Whiteside	16

* Indicates two separate terms on Disabled List.

1995 Amateur draft picks

Players are listed with position and college or high school. Most players were assigned to rookie or Class A leagues. List provided by Major League Baseball.

Charles Bauer, rhp, St. Rose; Russell Bratton, rhp, Central HS, Columbia, Tenn.; David Brazeal, c, Mustang (Okla.) HS; Christopher Briones, c, Nevada; Clifford Brumbaugh, 3b, Delaware; Braxford Bryant, lhp, Sulphur (La.) HS; Danny Carrasco, rhp, Hayward (Calif.) HS; Jorge Carrion, rhp-ss, DeWitt Clinton HS, Bronx, N.Y.; Timothy Codd, rhp, Edinboro; Ryan Dempster, rhp, Elphinstone Secondary, Gibsons, Ont.; Mark Draeger, rhp, Slippery Rock; Mandell Echols, of, William Carey; Emar Fleming, rhp, Allegany CC; Shawn Gallagher, 1b, New Hanover HS, Wilmington, N.C.; Joseph Garibaldi, lhp, Terra Nova HS, Pacifica, Calif.; Ryan Glynn, rhp-of, VMI; Joseph Goodwin, c, George Mason; Ryan Gorecki, 2b, Seton Hall; Ryan Haley, rhp, no school, Loxahachee, Fla.; Jonathan Johnson, rhp, Florida State; Gary Johnson, of, East Los Angeles JC; Bobby Kahlon, rhp, California; Brandon Knight, rhp, Ventura; Daniel Kolb, rhp, no school, Sterling, Ill.; Amury Leon, ss, Tucson (Ariz.) HS.; Bryan Link, lhp, Winthrop; Brian Llibre, c, West Covina (Calif.) HS; Phillip Lowery, lhp, Casa Grande HS, Petaluma, Calif.; Brian Martineau, rhp, Rancho Santiago College; John McAulay, c, William Carey College; Michael McHugh, lhp, Penn State; Julio Mercado, of, Brook Pointe HS, Stafford, Va.; Craig Monroe, ss-rf, Texas HS, Texarkana, Texas; Robert Moore, rhp, Hawaii; Leslie Mudd, rhp, Indiana; William Reed, ss, Auburn; Juan Rivera, c, Dr. Jose M. Lazaro HS, Rio Grande, P.R.; Damian Rose, cf, William Overfelt HS, San Jose, Calif.; Brent Sagedal, rhp, Carthage College; Ted Silva, rhp, Cal State Fullerton; Thomas Smith, rhp, Petaluma (Calif.) HS; Kelly Stratton, of, Utah; Bobby Styles, rhp, East Henderson HS, Hendersonville, N.C.; Manuel Torres, rhp, St. Joseph's, Bridgeport, N.Y.; Michael Venafro, lhp, James Madison; Nathan Vopata, 3b-2b, Lewis-Clark State; Joseph Williams, 3b, Chaffey HS, Ontario, Calif.

Texas (1972-1995), includes Washington (1961-1971)

Runs: Most, career, all-time

631	Toby Harrah, 1969-1986	
571	RUBEN SIERRA, 1986-1992	
544	Frank Howard, 1965-1972	
482	Jim Sundberg, 1974-1989	
471	Buddy Bell, 1979-1989	
471	RAFAEL PALMEIRO, 1989-1993	

Hits: Most, career, all-time

1180	Jim Sundberg, 1974-1989
1174	Toby Harrah, 1969-1986
1141	Frank Howard, 1965-1972
1132	RUBEN SIERRA, 1986-1992
1060	Buddy Bell, 1979-1989

2B: Most, career, all-time

226	RUBEN SIERRA, 1986-1992
200	Jim Sundberg, 1974-1989
197	Buddy Bell, 1979-1989
187	Toby Harrah, 1969-1986
174	RAFAEL PALMEIRO, 1989-1993

3B: Most, career, all-time

43	RUBEN SIERRA, 1986-1992
30	Chuck Hinton, 1961-1964
27	Ed Brinkman, 1961-1975
27	Jim Sundberg, 1974-1989
24	Ed Stroud, 1967-1970

HR: Most, career, all-time

246	Frank Howard, 1965-1972
167	JUAN GONZALEZ, 1989-1995
153	RUBEN SIERRA, 1986-1992
149	Larry Parrish, 1982-1988
124	Toby Harrah, 1969-1986
124	Pete Incaviglia, 1986-1990

RBI: Most, career, all-time

701	Frank Howard, 1965-1972
656	RUBEN SIERRA, 1986-1992
568	Toby Harrah, 1969-1986
522	Larry Parrish, 1982-1988
515	JUAN GONZALES, 1989-1995

SB: Most, career, all-time

161	Bump Wills, 1977-1981
153	Toby Harrah, 1969-1986
144	Dave Nelson, 1970-1975
129	Oddibe McDowell, 1985-1994
98	Julio Franco, 1989-1993

BB: Most, career, all-time

708	Toby Harrah, 1969-1986
575	Frank Howard, 1965-1972
544	Jim Sundberg, 1974-1989
435	Mike Hargrove, 1974-1978
404	Pete O'Brien, 1982-1988

BA: Highest, career, all-time

.319	Al Oliver, 1978-1981
.307	Julio Franco, 1989-1993
.303	Mickey Rivers, 1979-1984
.296	RAFAEL PALMEIRO, 1989-1993
.293	Mike Hargrove, 1974-1978

Slug avg: Highest, career, all-time

.533	JUAN GONZALEZ, 1989-1995
.503	Frank Howard, 1965-1972
.474	RAFAEL PALMEIRO, 1989-1993
.471	RUBEN SIERRA, 1986-1992
.466	Al Oliver, 1978-1981

Games started: Most, career, all-time

313	Charlie Hough, 1980-1990
192	BOBBY WITT, 1986-1995
190	Fergie Jenkins, 1974-1981
186	KEVIN BROWN, 1986-1994
155	Dick Bosman, 1966-1973

Saves: Most, career, all-time

131	JEFF RUSSELL, 1985-1995
83	Ron Kline, 1963-1966
64	Darold Knowles, 1967-1977
58	TOM HENKE, 1982-1994
37	Jim Kern, 1979-1981

Shutouts: Most, career, all-time

17	Fergie Jenkins, 1974-1981
12	Gaylord Perry, 1975-1980
11	Charlie Hough, 1980-1990
9	Dick Bosman, 1966-1973
8	Jim Bibby, 1973-1984

Wins: Most, career, all-time

139	Charlie Hough, 1980-1990
93	Fergie Jenkins, 1974-1981
78	KEVIN BROWN, 1986-1994
71	BOBBY WITT, 1986-1995
70	KENNY ROGERS, 1989-1995

K: Most, career, all-time

1452	Charlie Hough, 1980-1990
1097	BOBBY WITT, 1986-1995
939	Nolan Ryan, 1989-1993
895	Fergie Jenkins, 1974-1981
742	KEVIN BROWN, 1986-1994

Win pct: Highest, career, all-time

.567	Nolan Ryan, 1989-1993
.564	Fergie Jenkins, 1974-1981
.549	KEVIN BROWN, 1986-1994
.578	KENNY ROGERS, 1989-1995
.538	Doc Medich, 1978-1982

ERA: Lowest, career, all-time

3.26	Gaylord Perry, 1975-1980
3.35	Dick Bosman, 1966-1973
3.41	Jon Matlack, 1978-1983
3.43	Nolan Ryan, 1989-1993
3.51	Joe Coleman, 1965-1970

Runs: Most, season

124	RAFAEL PALMEIRO, 1993
115	RAFAEL PALMEIRO, 1991
111	Frank Howard, 1969
110	RUBEN SIERRA, 1991
108	Julio Franco, 1991

Hits: Most, season

210	Mickey Rivers, 1980
209	Al Oliver, 1980
203	RAFAEL PALMEIRO, 1991
203	RUBEN SIERRA, 1991
201	Julio Franco, 1991

2B: Most, season

49	RAFAEL PALMEIRO, 1991
44	RUBEN SIERRA, 1991
43	Al Oliver, 1980
42	Buddy Bell, 1979
42	Larry Parrish, 1984

3B: Most, season

14	RUBEN SIERRA, 1989
12	Chuck Hinton, 1963
10	DAVID HULSE, 1993
10	RUBEN SIERRA, 1986
10	Ed Stroud, 1968

HR: Most, season

48	Frank Howard, 1969
46	JUAN GONZALEZ, 1993
44	Frank Howard, 1968
44	Frank Howard, 1970
43	JUAN GONZALEZ, 1992

RBI: Most, season

126	Frank Howard, 1970	
119	RUBEN SIERRA, 1989	
118	Jeff Burroughs, 1974	
118	JUAN GONZALEZ, 1993	
117	Al Oliver, 1980	

SB: Most, season

52	Bump Wills, 1978
51	Dave Nelson, 1972
50	OTIS NIXON, 1995
45	Cecil Espy, 1989
44	Bill Sample, 1983

BB: Most, season

132	Frank Howard, 1970
113	Toby Harrah, 1985
109	Toby Harrah, 1977
107	Mike Hargrove, 1978
107	MICKEY TETTLETON, 1995

BA: Highest, season

.341	JULIO FRANCO, 1991
.333	Mickey Rivers, 1980
.329	WILL CLARK, 1994
.329	Buddy Bell, 1980
.324	Al Oliver, 1978

Slug avg: Highest, season

.632	JUAN GONZALEZ, 1993
.574	Frank Howard, 1969
.554	RAFAEL PALMEIRO, 1993
.552	JOSE CANSECO, 1994
.552	Frank Howard, 1968

Games started: Most, season

41	Jim Bibby, 1974
41	Fergie Jenkins, 1974
40	Charlie Hough, 1987
37	Fergie Jenkins, 1975
37	Fergie Jenkins, 1979

Saves: Most, season

40	TOM HENKE, 1993
38	JEFF RUSSELL, 1989
30	JEFF RUSSELL, 1991
29	Jim Kern, 1979
29	Ron Kline, 1965

Shutouts: Most, season

6	Bert Blyleven, 1976
6	Fergie Jenkins, 1974
5	Jim Bibby, 1974
5	Bert Blyleven, 1977
4	Tom Cheney, 1963
4	Joe Coleman, 1969
4	Fergie Jenkins, 1975
4	Fergie Jenkins, 1978
4	Doc Medich, 1981
4	Camilo Pascual, 1968
4	Gaylord Perry, 1975
4	Gaylord Perry, 1977

Wins: Most, season

25	Fergie Jenkins, 1974
21	KEVIN BROWN, 1992
19	Jim Bibby, 1974
18	Charlie Hough, 1987
18	Fergie Jenkins, 1978

K: Most, season

301	Nolan Ryan, 1989
232	Nolan Ryan, 1990
225	Fergie Jenkins, 1974
223	Charlie Hough, 1987
221	BOBBY WITT, 1990

Win pct: Highest, season

.708	KENNY ROGERS, 1995
.692	Fergie Jenkins, 1978
.676	Fergie Jenkins, 1974
.656	KEVIN BROWN, 1992
.630	CHARLIE HOUGH, 1986
.630	BOBBY WITT, 1990

ERA: Lowest, season

2.19	Dick Bosman, 1969
2.27	Jon Matlack, 1978
2.40	Dick Donovan, 1961
2.42	RICK HONEYCUTT, 1983
2.60	Pete Richert, 1965

Most pinch-hit homers, season

3	Don Lock, 1966
3	Brant Alyea, 1969
3	Rick Reichardt, 1970
3	Tom McCraw, 1971
3	Darrell Porter, 1987

Most pinch-hit homers, career

6	Brant Alyea, 1965-1969
6	Geno Petralli, 1985-1993

Most consecutive games batting safely

24	Mickey Rivers, 1980
22	Jim Sundberg, 1978

Most consecutive scoreless innings

36	Charlie Hough, 1983

No-hit games

Jim Bibby, Tex at Oak AL, 6-0; July 20, 1973.

Bert Blyleven, Tex at Cal AL, 6-0; September 22, 1977.

Nolan Ryan, Tex at Oak AL, 5-0; June 11, 1990.

Nolan Ryan, Tex vs Tor AL, 3-0; May 1, 1991.

KENNY ROGERS, Tex vs Cal AL, 4-0; July 28, 1994 (perfect game).

ACTIVE PLAYERS in caps.

Leader in the franchise's current location is included. If not in the top five, leader's rank is listed in paren- thesis; asterisk (*) indicates player is not in top 25.

Players' years of service are listed by the first and last years with this team and are not necessarily consecutive; all statistics record performances for this team only.

Oakland Athletics

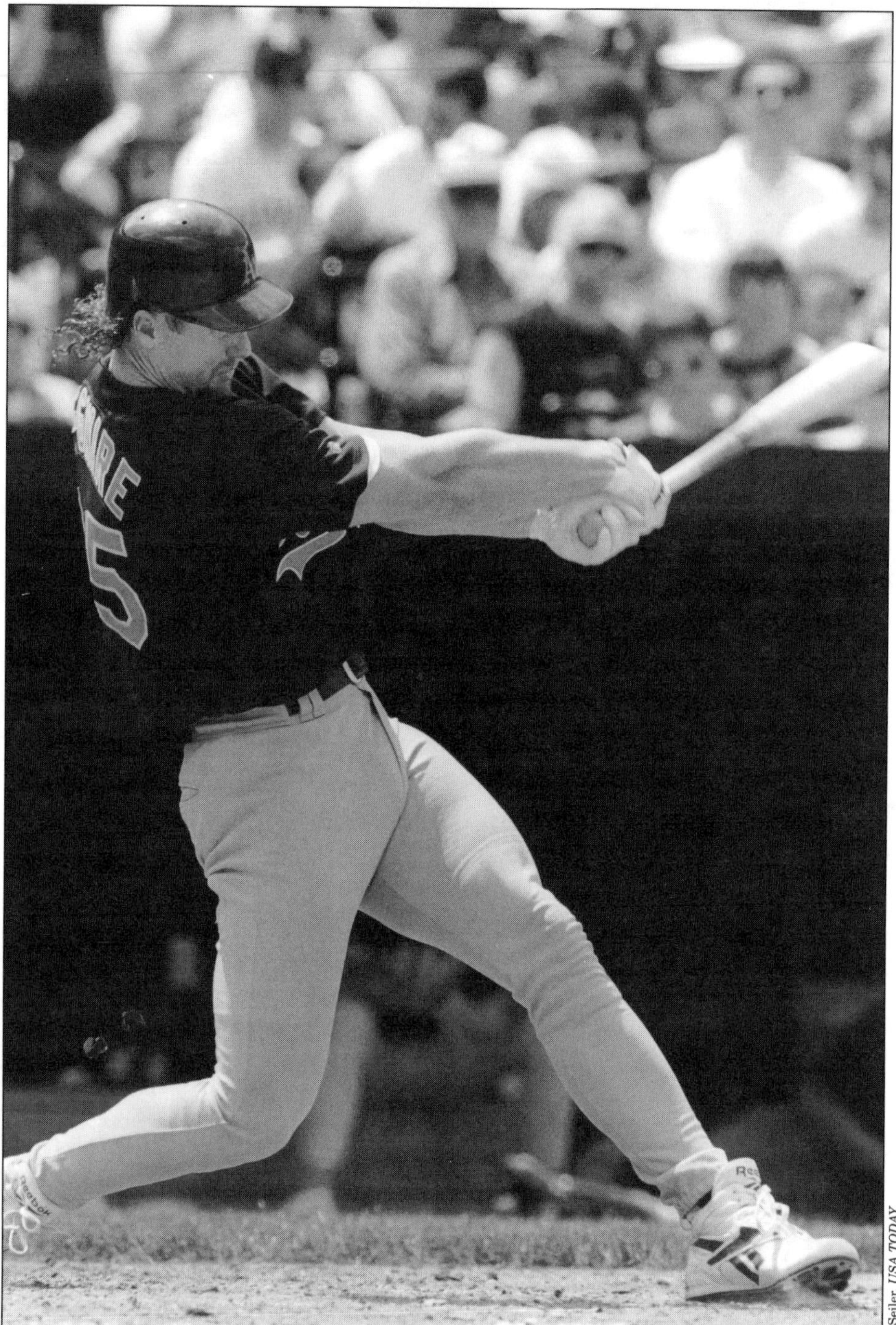

By Neil Seiler, USA TODAY

Despite injuries, Mark McGwire thrilled A's fans with 39 homers and 90 RBI in just 91 games.

1995 Athletics: McGwire was the key

The 1995 season in Oakland can best be defined by one pitch: On July 8 in Oakland, David Cone, then pitching for Toronto, hit A's first baseman Mark McGwire in the head. McGwire missed the next seven games, plus the All-Star game, and the A's season was never the same. McGwire was injured twice more with foot and back problems and didn't start more than three games in succession at first base until the first week of September.

And as McGwire went, so went the A's. A few days before the incident, Oakland was six games over .500 and 2½ games out of first place. By the time the explosive McGwire (he had one homer every 8.13 at-bats and was on a pace to break Babe Ruth's home run percentage record) was fully functional, the A's were four under .500 and nine games out. Last place was a lock.

The season started with considerable promise—starting pitchers Dave Stewart and Todd Stottlemyre, together with 1994 ERA champ Steve Ontiveros, seemed to have the makings of a good starting rotation. But Stewart retired, Ron Darling was released, and Ontiveros eventually succumbed to the injuries that have plagued his entire career. Only Stottlemyre persevered, winning 14 games. Dennis Eckersley blew eight saves during the second half of the season; left fielder Rickey Henderson hit a club-best .300, but manager Tony La Russa was constantly on his case for not playing through pain; and right fielder Ruben Sierra was on such bad terms with LaRussa that in June La Russa called him the "village idiot," and he was soon traded to New York for Danny Tartabull, who went on the disabled list after 11 at-bats.

Still, the A's had some highly encouraging performances in 1995. Mike Bordick's defensive wizardry at shortstop put him near the top of his profession. Geronimo Berroa reached new career highs in home runs and RBI after taking over in right field for Sierra. Rookie third baseman Jason Giambi showed signs of the skills that got him on the 1992 Olympic team.

All that—and being in one of the worst divisions in baseball—led to a late-September winning streak that pushed the A's within one game of .500 and five of first place. Less than two hours after the final win of the streak, unfortunately, Walter Haas, the beloved owner of the club for the last 15 seasons, died, and it was a somber group that headed into their last road trip needing to win seven of nine to have a chance at honoring Haas with another trip to the postseason. Oakland lost all nine games, then lost again when La Russa escaped to St. Louis.

1996 Athletics: Preview

The A's field one of the youngest teams in their history with new manager Art Howe, known for his patience and leadership in developing young players.

The starting rotation could consist of Todd Van Poppel, Doug Johns, Ariel Prieto, John Wasdin and Steve Wojciechowski. All of them except Van Poppel were rookies in 1995; Wasdin and Wojciechowski will be rookies in 1996, too.

The A's will need rookie contributions on offense as well, mostly from switch-hitting catcher George Williams and strong-armed outfielder Jose Herrera.

But Oakland won't be entirely without name value. Mark McGwire is slated to return, along with catcher Terry Steinbach and outfielders Danny Tartabull and Geronimo Berroa. Mike Bordick and Brent Gates are set up the middle, and Jason Giambi seems to have taken over third base from Scott Brosius. Brosius could wind up starting in center.

1995 Athletics: Week-by-week notes

These notes were excerpted from the following issues of Baseball Weekly.

May 10: Ruben Sierra was struggling, hitting .205 and leaving men on base all over the place. Both manager Tony La Russa and general manager Sandy Alderson talked with him. Finding separation from his family was too much, catcher Brian Harper announced his retirement after an 18-year career.

May 17: Todd Van Poppel had given the A's four strong performances in relief, allowing a two-run homer but otherwise dominating. Then there was Ron Darling, who hadn't made it through five innings in any of his first four starts.

May 31: Catcher Terry Steinbach had a huge week. First he homered off A's killer Mike Mussina of Baltimore, a two-run shot that erased a 3-1 deficit; then he hit an eighth-inning grand slam off Armando Benitez to rally the A's from a 6-5 deficit to a 9-6 win; to top it off, he hit a two-run seventh-inning homer off the Yankees' Sterling Hitchcock to lift Oakland from a 3-2 deficit to a 4-3 win. "When I was pitching against the A's," starter Todd Stottlemyre said, "Terry was the one guy I didn't want to face with men in scoring position."

June 7: Rick Honeycutt said if he had to consider retiring, so be it. He had a 9.54 ERA, and opposing hitters had averaged .500 (12-for-24) against him: "I've got to get myself on track or I've got a decision to make."

June 14: Relief pitcher Jim Corsi had given up just one run in 17 games (21⅔ innings)—and that came when he had a six-run lead. He had inherited 10 baserunners and let none score. He didn't allow a run in his first 15 games, the best in the AL.

June 21: Pitcher Steve Karsay was slated for Tommy John surgery and would be lost to the A's for the rest of 1995 and probably all of 1996 as well.

July 5: The Ariel Prieto era was scheduled to begin. Prieto, the Cuban emigrant who spent his first week in the majors in the bullpen, would make his first against Toronto on July 8. Tony La Russa said he told Prieto not to think in terms of pressure: "I told him, 'Remember when you pitched for Cuba, and Fidel Castro said to win or you'd disappear off the face of the earth?' That's pressure. This is not the same."

July 13: Mark McGwire didn't know when he'd be playing again after he was beaned by Toronto's David Cone on July 8. He suggested that when he came back, he wouldn't be so hesitant to go to the mound. He had already been hit eight times in 1995 and had not charged the mound on a pitcher. "I'm a pretty easy-going guy, but I'm fed up," he said.

July 19: Ariel Prieto lost his first two starts but won respect in the A's clubhouse. "He hasn't won," reliever Dennis Eckersley said. "But the quality is there, and that is all that matters." Prieto lost a 1-0 game to hot-hitting Cleveland but completely stifled the Indians' hitters. Two infield hits and a balk gave the Tribe their run. "You can't pitch the Cleveland lineup any better than Ariel did," A's hitting coach Jimmy Lefebvre said. And Terry Steinbach just kept getting better—he had thrown out 23 of 61 (37.7%) runners attempting to steal against him through July 15, the best record in the league.

July 26: Mark McGwire and Steve Ontiveros were both placed on the DL. McGwire was the club leader in homers (24) and RBI (59). Ontiveros was tied with Todd Stottlemyre for the club lead in wins (eight). Owner Walter Haas, confined to a wheelchair because of an ongoing battle with cancer, paid a rare visit to the clubhouse on July 22, just 24 hours after the club's sale to Bay Area developers Steve Schott and Ken Hofmann was made official. Starting pitcher Dave Stewart had chosen that day to tell his teammates about his retirement, and the appearance by Haas was special because it was the 79-year-old owner's first venture outside his San Francisco home in three weeks.

▶**Aug. 2:** For Rickey Henderson, who lost two of his best friends in a week—Dave Stewart to retirement and Ruben Sierra to trade—July was looking even bleaker as the A's 8-20 tumble made even a wild-card berth remote. "We've got a chance," he said guardedly. "But you've got to have something to win with. Right now, we've got nothing to win with. Everybody is either hurt or gone."

▶**Aug. 23:** The A's continued to see their links with past glory dismantled when they released starting pitcher Ron Darling. Dave Stewart, who had retired just a month before and had moved to the front office, said, "You won't find a better guy in the game. He was the perfect teammate, as far as I was concerned."

▶**Aug. 30:** At the end of July, the A's were batting .252, worst in the AL and close to the worst in the majors. But since then, they hit .311 and improved their team average to .265.

▶**Sept. 6:** Rickey Henderson and Tony La Russa apparently patched things together after their falling out over rumors that Henderson was being considered for trade to Cleveland. Henderson had said: "You can bet that if I think they don't want me, I'll be sitting Thursday." On Thursday La Russa said Henderson was "mentally unavailable." The manager said he got the word from baseball's all-time stolen-base leader after Wednesday's game that, in Henderson's words, "my head was not on straight." Those were not words designed to make La Russa smile. "I believe he's got special talent," La Russa said. "He's done some great things with stolen bases and as a leadoff hitter, but he's not a great player. To be a great player in a team game, you've got to be interested in the team as much as you are in yourself. That piece is missing with Rickey." Later La Russa admitted he had misunderstood Henderson's remark. "I believe a lot of what was bothering him had to do with wanting to be part of our club and being part of our final rush," La Russa said.

▶**Sept. 20:** Mark McGwire is in the record books, all by himself. A five-homer week gave him 271 for his Oakland career and moved him past Reggie Jackson (268) as Oakland's all-time long-ball leader. And that was after losing six weeks to injury in 1995 and missing 202 of 276 games to injury in 1993 and 1994. Even in 1992, when he hit 42 homers, he missed three weeks. "I'd like to play for one year without any injuries," McGwire said. "I don't think I've gotten into my prime yet.

▶**Sept. 27:** The A's wore patches on the right sleeves of their game in memory of owner Walter A. Haas Jr., who had died a week earlier.

Team directory

▶**Owner:** Steve Schott and Ken Hofman
▶**General manager:** Sandy Alderson
▶**Ballpark:**
Oakland Coliseum
Nimitz Freeway & Hegenberger Road, Oakland, Calif.
510-568-5600
Capacity 46,942
Public transportation available
Wheelchair sections and ramps, picnic areas
▶**Team publications:**
A's Magazine, media guide
510-638-4900, ext. 223 or 233
▶**TV, radio broadcast stations:**
KFRC 610 AM, KRON Channel 4, SportsChannel
▶**Spring training:**
Phoenix Municipal Stadium
Phoenix, Ariz.
Capacity 8,500
602-392-0074

OAKLAND ATHLETICS 1995 final stats

BATTERS	BA	SLG	OB	G	AB	R	H	TB	2B	3B	HR	RBI	BB	SO	SB	CS	E
Henderson	.300	.447	.407	112	407	67	122	182	31	1	9	54	72	66	32	10	2
Williams	.291	.494	.383	29	79	13	23	39	5	1	3	14	11	21	0	0	3
Berroa	.278	.451	.351	141	546	87	152	246	22	3	22	88	63	98	7	4	4
Steinbach	.278	.458	.322	114	406	43	113	186	26	1	15	65	25	74	1	3	6
Javier	.278	.387	.353	130	442	81	123	171	20	2	8	56	49	63	36	5	0
McGwire	.274	.685	.441	104	317	75	87	217	13	0	39	90	88	77	1	1	12
Bordick	.264	.350	.325	126	428	46	113	150	13	0	8	44	35	48	11	3	10
Brosius	.263	.454	.342	123	388	69	102	176	19	2	17	46	41	67	4	2	15
Giambi	.256	.398	.364	54	176	27	45	70	7	0	6	25	28	31	2	1	4
Gates	.254	.344	.308	136	524	60	133	180	24	4	5	56	46	84	3	3	12
Herrera	.243	.314	.299	33	70	9	17	22	1	2	0	2	6	11	1	3	2
Tartabull	.236	.379	.335	83	280	34	66	106	16	0	8	35	43	82	0	2	0
Gallego	.233	.233	.292	43	120	11	28	28	0	0	0	8	9	24	0	1	5
Paquette	.226	.417	.256	105	283	42	64	118	13	1	13	49	12	88	5	2	8
Cruz	.217	.217	.286	8	23	0	5	5	0	0	0	5	3	5	1	1	1
Tomberlin	.212	.353	.256	46	85	15	18	30	0	0	4	10	5	22	4	1	1
Young	.200	.380	.310	26	50	9	10	19	3	0	2	5	8	12	0	0	2
Helfand	.163	.209	.265	38	86	9	14	18	2	1	0	7	11	25	0	0	1
Harper	.000	.000	.000	2	7	0	0	0	0	0	0	0	0	1	0	0	0
PITCHERS	W-L	ERA	G	GS	CG	GF	Sho	SV	IP	H	R	ER	HR	BB	SO		
Corsi	2-4	2.20	38	0	0	7	0	2	45.0	31	14	11	2	26	26		
Mohler	1-1	3.04	28	0	0	6	0	1	23.2	16	8	8	0	18	15		
Wengert	1-1	3.34	19	0	0	10	0	0	29.2	30	14	11	3	12	16		
Leiper	1-1	3.57	24	0	0	3	0	0	22.2	23	10	9	3	13	10		
Ontiveros	9-6	4.37	22	22	2	0	1	0	129.2	144	75	63	12	38	77		
Stottlemyre	14-7	4.55	31	31	2	0	0	0	209.2	228	117	106	26	80	205		
Johns	5-3	4.61	11	9	1	1	1	0	54.2	44	32	28	5	26	25		
Wasdin	1-1	4.67	5	2	0	3	0	0	17.1	14	9	9	4	3	6		
Eckersley	4-6	4.83	52	0	0	48	0	29	50.1	53	29	27	5	11	40		
Van Poppel	4-8	4.88	36	14	1	10	0	0	138.1	125	77	75	16	56	122		
Prieto	2-6	4.97	14	9	1	1	0	0	58.0	57	35	32	4	32	37		
Reyes	4-6	5.09	40	1	0	19	0	0	69.0	71	43	39	10	28	48		
Wojciechowski	2-3	5.18	14	7	0	3	0	0	48.2	51	28	28	7	28	13		
Acre	1-2	5.71	43	0	0	10	0	0	52.0	52	35	33	7	28	47		
Darling	4-7	6.23	21	21	1	0	0	0	104.0	124	79	72	16	46	69		
Stewart	3-7	6.89	16	16	0	0	0	0	81.0	101	65	62	11	39	58		
Eddy	0-0	7.36	6	0	0	0	0	0	3.2	7	3	3	0	2	2		
Briscoe	0-1	8.35	16	0	0	7	0	0	18.1	25	17	17	4	21	19		
Baker	0-0	9.82	1	0	0	0	0	0	3.2	5	4	4	0	5	3		
Fermin	0-0	13.50	1	0	0	1	0	0	1.1	4	2	2	0	1	0		
Phoenix	0-0	32.40	1	0	0	0	0	0	1.2	3	6	6	1	3	3		

1996 preliminary roster

PITCHERS (17)
Mark Acre
Willie Adams
Jim Corsi
Dennis Eckersley
Ramon Fermin
Stacy Hollins
Doug Johns
Steve Karsay
Mike Mohler
Ariel Prieto
Carlos Reyes
Todd Stottlemyre
Todd Van Poppel
John Wasdin
Don Wengert

Todd Williams
Steve Wojociechowski

CATCHERS (2)
Terry Steinbach
George Williams

INFIELDERS (11)
Tony Batista
Mike Bordick
Scott Brosius
Steve Cox
Fausto Cruz
Brent Gates
Jason Giambi
Jason McDonald

Mark McGwire
Craig Paquette
Scott Spiezio

OUTFIELDERS (6)
Geronimo Berroa
Jose Herrera
Brian Lesher
Scott Lydy
Danny Tartabull
Ernie Young

Games played by position

PLAYER	G	C	1B	2B	3B	SS	OF	DH
Berroa	141	0	0	0	0	0	71	72
Bordick	126	0	0	0	0	126	0	1
Brosius	123	0	18	3	60	3	49	2
Cruz	8	0	0	0	0	8	0	0
Gallego	43	0	0	18	12	14	0	0
Gates	136	0	1	132	0	0	0	3
Giambi	54	0	26	0	30	0	0	2
Harper	2	2	0	0	0	0	0	0
Helfand	38	36	0	0	0	0	0	0
Henderson	112	0	0	0	0	0	90	19
Herrera	33	0	0	0	0	0	25	5
Javier	130	0	0	0	1	0	124	0
McGwire	104	0	91	0	0	0	0	10
Paquette	105	0	3	0	75	8	20	0
Steinbach	114	111	2	0	0	0	0	0
Tartabull	83	0	0	0	0	0	19	61
Tomberlin	46	0	0	0	0	0	42	2
Williams	29	13	0	0	0	0	0	10
Young	26	0	0	0	0	0	24	0

Sick call: 1995 DL Report

Player	Days on the DL
Mark Acre	22
Mike Bordick	19
John Briscoe	91
Jim Corsi	47
Mike Gallego	84
Steve Karsay	160
Mark McGwire	36*
Steve Ontiveros	39
Ariel Prieto	15
Ruben Sierra	15
Terry Steinbach	16
Danny Tartabull	29
Billy Taylor	160
Don Wengert	19

Indicates two separate terms on Disabled List.

Minor Leagues

Tops in the organization

Batter	Club	Avg.	G	AB	R	H	HR	RBI
Demond Smith	Wmi	.338	87	349	70	118	9	44
George Williams	Edm	.310	81	290	53	90	13	55
Damon Mashore	Edm	.300	117	337	50	101	1	37
Paul Faries	Edm	.300	117	424	67	127	0	45
Steve Cox	Mod	.298	132	483	95	144	30	110

Home Runs			Wins		
Jason White	Mod	30	Bobby Chouinard	Hvl	14
Steve Cox	Mod	30	John Wasdin	Edm	12
Gary Hust	Mod	27	Brad Rigby	Mod	11
Brian Lesher	Hvl	19	Derek Manning	Mod	11
Several tied		16	Juan Perez	Wmi	11

RBI			Saves		
Steve Cox	Mo	110	Mike Maurer	Mod	24
Jason White	Mod	98	Jason Rajotte	Wmi	13
Gary Hust	Mod	87	Scott Rose	Hvl	13
Scott Spiezio	Hvl	86	Robert Kazmirski	Ath	10
Ben Grieve	Mod	76	Todd Revenig	Edm	10

Stolen Bases			Strikeouts	
Jason McDonald	Mod	70	Brad Rigby	Mod 145
Jose Castro	Wmi	51	Derek Manning	Mod 124
Fred Soriano	Wmi	40	Juan Perez	Wmi
Demond Smith	Wmi	40		117
Several tied		35	Willie Adams	Edm 112

Pitcher	Club	W-L	ERA	IP	H	BB	SO
Derek Manning	Mod	11-3	2.85	139	138	32	124
Gary Haught	Hvl	10-6	2.95	110	99	32	101
Bill King	Wmi	9-7	3.34	148	152	41	95
Doug Johns	Edm	9-5	3.41	132	148	43	70
B. Chouinard	Hvl	14-8	3.62	167	155	50	106

1995 Amateur draft picks

Players are listed with position and college or high school. Most players were assigned to rookie or Class A leagues. List provided by Major League Baseball.

William Abbott, rhp, Arkansas; Daniel Ardoin, c, McNeese State; William Batchelder, rhp, New Hampshire; Mark Bellhorn, ss, Auburn; Thomas Bennett, rhp, Ohlone College; Stephen Bess, rhp, Montgomery Bell Academy, Nashville; William Brown, cf, Saint Thomas Aquinas HS, Plantation, Fla.; Brian Callahan, rhp, The Citadel; Victor Chambers, 2b-CC of San Francisco; Ryan Christenson, cf, Pepperdine; Rodney Clifton, cf, Elgin (Ill.) HS; Steven Connelly, rhp, Oklahoma; Terrance Costello, lhp, Montclair State; Jeffrey DaVanon, cf-2b, San Diego State; Matthew Dornfeld, cf, Arizona Western; Byron Embry, rhp, Madison Central HS, Richmond, Ky.; Duane Filchner, cf, Radford; Jon French, rhp, Arkansas State; Ryan Gill, rhp, Woodlawn School, Baton Rouge; Kevin Gunther, rhp, Fresno State; Gregory Halvorson, c, Canyon Del Oro HS, Tucson, Ariz.; Robert Harris, ss, Texas A&M; Victor Hernandez, of, Maria T. Pimeiro HS, Ciales, P.R.; Jason Hill, c, Monte Vista HS, Alamo, Calif.; Willard Hilton, rhp, Eastern Illinois; Jace Johnson, of, Scottsdale CC; Timothy Jones, of, Buena Park (Calif.) HS; Ryan Kjos, rhp, Texas; Michael Klostermeyer, 1b, Louisiana State; Thomas Knickerbocker, of, Kirkwood CC; William Knight, rf, Massachusetts; Kevin Mlodik, rhp, Wisconsin-Oshkosh; Christopher Morrison, rhp, Auburn; Chris Nelson, rhp, Oklahoma State; David Newhan, of, Pepperdine; Wayne Nix, rhp, Monroe HS, North Hills, Calif.; Robert Norman, rhp, Columbia Academy, Mount Pleasant, Tenn.; Jamey Price, rhp, Mississippi; Ariel Prieto, rhp, no school, Beverly Hills, Calif.; Troy Rauer, of, Arizona State; Scott Rivette, rhp, Long Beach State; David Shepard, rhp, Mansfield; David Slemmer, ss-2b, Southwest Missouri State; Brandon Welch, of, Texas Tech.

Oakland (1968-1995), incl. Philadelphia (1901-1952) and Kansas City (1953-1967)

Runs: Most, career, all-time

1169	RICKEY HENDERSON, 1979-1995
997	Bob Johnson, 1933-1942
983	Bert Campaneris, 1964-1976
975	Jimmie Foxx, 1925-1935
969	Al Simmons, 1924-1944

Hits: Most, career, all-time

1882	Bert Campaneris, 1964-1976
1827	Al Simmons, 1924-1944
1705	Jimmy Dykes, 1918-1932
1640	RICKEY HENDERSON, 1979-1995
1617	Bob Johnson, 1933-1942

2B: Most, career, all-time

365	Jimmy Dykes, 1918-1932
348	Al Simmons, 1924-1944
319	Harry Davis, 1901-1917
307	Bob Johnson, 1933-1942
292	Bing Miller, 1922-1934
273	RICKEY HENDERSON (8), 1979-1995

3B: Most, career, all-time

102	Danny Murphy, 1902-1913
98	Al Simmons, 1924-1944
88	Frank Baker, 1908-1914
84	Eddie Collins, 1906-1930
82	Harry Davis, 1901-1917
70	Bert Campaneris, 1964-1976 (12)

HR: Most, career, all-time

302	Jimmie Foxx, 1925-1935
269	Reggie Jackson, 1967-1987
252	Bob Johnson, 1933-1942
277	MARK McGWIRE, 1986-1995
231	JOSE CANSECO, 1985-1992

RBI: Most, career, all-time

1178	Al Simmons, 1924-1944
1075	Jimmie Foxx, 1925-1935
1040	Bob Johnson, 1933-1942
796	Sal Bando, 1966-1976
776	Reggie Jackson, 1967-1987

SB: Most, career, all-time

801	RICKEY HENDERSON, 1979-1995
566	Bert Campaneris, 1964-1976
376	Eddie Collins, 1906-1930
232	Billy North, 1973-1978
223	Harry Davis, 1901-1917

BB: Most, career, all-time

1109	RICKEY HENDERSON, 1979-1995
1043	Max Bishop, 1924-1933
853	Bob Johnson, 1933-1942
820	Elmer Valo, 1940-1956
792	Sal Bando, 1966-1976

BA: Highest, career, all-time

.356	Al Simmons, 1924-1944
.339	Jimmie Foxx, 1925-1935
.336	Eddie Collins, 1906-1930
.321	Mickey Cochrane, 1925-1933
.321	Frank Baker, 1908-1914
.293	RICKEY HENDERSON, 1979-1995 (17)

Slug avg: Highest, career, all-time

.640	Jimmie Foxx, 1925-1935
.584	Al Simmons, 1924-1944
.523	MARK McGWIRE, 1986-1995
.520	Bob Johnson, 1933-1942
.512	JOSE CANSECO, 1985-1992

Games started: Most, career, all-time

458	Eddie Plank, 1901-1914
340	Catfish Hunter, 1965-1974
288	Chief Bender, 1903-1914
267	Lefty Grove, 1925-1933
267	Rube Walberg, 1923-1933

Saves: Most, career, all-time

320	DENNIS ECKERSLEY, 1987-1995
136	Rollie Fingers, 1968-1976
73	John Wyatt, 1961-1969
61	JAY HOWELL, 1985-1987
58	Jack Aker, 1964-1968

Shutouts: Most, career, all-time

59	Eddie Plank, 1901-1914
37	Rube Waddell, 1902-1907
36	Chief Bender, 1903-1914
31	Catfish Hunter, 1965-1974
28	Vida Blue, 1969-1977
28	Jack Coombs, 1906-1914

Wins: Most, career, all-time

284	Eddie Plank, 1901-1914
195	Lefty Grove, 1925-1933
193	Chief Bender, 1903-1914
171	Eddie Rommel, 1920-1932
161	Catfish Hunter, 1965-1974

K: Most, career, all-time

1985	Eddie Plank, 1901-1914
1576	Rube Waddell, 1902-1907
1536	Chief Bender, 1903-1914
1523	Lefty Grove, 1925-1933
1520	Catfish Hunter, 1965-1974

Win pct: Highest, career, all-time

.712	Lefty Grove, 1925-1933
.654	Chief Bender, 1903-1914
.637	Eddie Plank, 1901-1914
.632	Jack Coombs, 1906-1914
.628	George Earnshaw, 1928-1933
.615	Bob Welch, 1988-1994 (6)

ERA: Lowest, career, all-time

1.97	Rube Waddell, 1902-1907
2.15	Cy Morgan, 1909-1912
2.32	Chief Bender, 1903-1914
2.39	Eddie Plank, 1901-1914
2.60	Jack Coombs, 1906-1914
2.91	Rollie Fingers, 1968-1976 (8)

Runs: Most, season

152	Al Simmons, 1930
151	Jimmie Foxx, 1932
145	Nap Lajoie, 1901
144	Al Simmons, 1932
137	Eddie Collins, 1912
123	Reggie Jackson, 1969 (10)

Hits: Most, season

253	Al Simmons, 1925
232	Nap Lajoie, 1901
216	Al Simmons, 1932
214	Doc Cramer, 1935
213	Jimmie Foxx, 1932
187	JOSE CANSECO, 1988 (*)

2B: Most, season

53	Al Simmons, 1926
48	Nap Lajoie, 1901
48	Wally Moses, 1937
47	Harry Davis, 1905
47	Eric McNair, 1932
39	Reggie Jackson, 1975 (22)

3B: Most, season

21	Frank Baker, 1912	
19	Frank Baker, 1909	
18	Danny Murphy, 1910	
17	Danny Murphy, 1904	
16	Bing Miller, 1929	
16	Al Simmons, 1930	
16	Amos Strunk, 1915	
12	Bert Campaneris, 1965 (*)	
12	Phil Garner, 1976 (*)	

HR: Most, season

58	Jimmie Foxx, 1932
49	MARK McGWIRE, 1987
48	Jimmie Foxx, 1933
47	Reggie Jackson, 1969
44	JOSE CANSECO, 1991
44	Jimmie Foxx, 1934

RBI: Most, season

169	Jimmie Foxx, 1932
165	Al Simmons, 1930
163	Jimmie Foxx, 1933
157	Al Simmons, 1929
156	Jimmie Foxx, 1930
124	JOSE CANSECO, 1988 (13)

SB: Most, season

130	RICKEY HENDERSON, 1982
108	RICKEY HENDERSON, 1983
100	RICKEY HENDERSON, 1980
81	Eddie Collins, 1910
75	Billy North, 1976

BB: Most, season

149	Eddie Joost, 1949
136	Ferris Fain, 1949
133	Ferris Fain, 1950
128	Max Bishop, 1929
128	Max Bishop, 1930
118	Sal Bando, 1970 (10)

BA: Highest, season

.426	Nap Lajoie, 1901
.390	Al Simmons, 1931
.387	Al Simmons, 1925
.381	Al Simmons, 1930
.365	Eddie Collins, 1911
.325	RICKEY HENDERSON, 1990 (*)

Slug avg: Highest, season

.749	Jimmie Foxx, 1932
.708	Al Simmons, 1930
.703	Jimmie Foxx, 1933
.653	Jimmie Foxx, 1934
.643	Nap Lajoie, 1901
.618	MARK McGWIRE, 1987 (11)

Games started: Most, season

46	Rube Waddell, 1904
43	Eddie Plank, 1904
41	Catfish Hunter, 1974
41	Eddie Plank, 1905
40	Vida Blue, 1974
40	George Caster, 1938
40	Jack Coombs, 1911
40	Chuck Dobson, 1970
40	Ken Holtzman, 1973
40	Catfish Hunter, 1970
40	Eddie Plank, 1903
40	Eddie Plank, 1907

Saves: Most, season

51	DENNIS ECKERSLEY, 1992
48	DENNIS ECKERSLEY, 1990
45	DENNIS ECKERSLEY, 1988
43	DENNIS ECKERSLEY, 1991
36	Bill Caudill, 1984
36	DENNIS ECKERSLEY, 1993

Shutouts: Most, season

13	Jack Coombs, 1910
8	Vida Blue, 1971
8	Joe Bush, 1916
8	Eddie Plank, 1907
8	Rube Waddell, 1904
8	Rube Waddell, 1906

Wins: Most, season

31	Jack Coombs, 1910
31	Lefty Grove, 1931
28	Jack Coombs, 1911
28	Lefty Grove, 1930
27	Eddie Rommel, 1922
27	Rube Waddell, 1905
27	Bob Welch, 1990

K: Most, season

349	Rube Waddell, 1904
302	Rube Waddell, 1903
301	Vida Blue, 1971
287	Rube Waddell, 1905
232	Rube Waddell, 1907

Win pct: Highest, season

.886	Lefty Grove, 1931
.850	Chief Bender, 1914
.849	Lefty Grove, 1930
.821	Chief Bender, 1910
.818	Bob Welch, 1990

ERA: Lowest, season

1.30	Jack Coombs, 1910
1.39	Harry Krause, 1909
1.48	Rube Waddell, 1905
1.55	Cy Morgan, 1910
1.58	Chief Bender, 1910
1.82	Vida Blue, 1971 (10)

Most pinch-hit homers, season

4	Jeff Burroughs, 1982

Most pinch-hit homers, career

5	Jeff Burroughs, 1982-1984
5	MIKE ALDRETE, 1993-1995

Most consecutive games batting safely

30	Bing Miller, 1929
29	Billy Lamar, 1925
24	Carney Lansford, 1984

Most consecutive scoreless innings

53	Jack Coombs, 1910
43	Rube Waddell, 1905
37	Mike Torrez, 1976

No-hit games

Weldon Henley, Phi at StL AL, 6-0; July 22, 1905 (1st game).

Chief Bender, Phi vs Cle AL, 4-0; May 12, 1910.

Joe Bush, Phi vs Cle AL, 5-0; August 26, 1916.

Dick Fowler, Phi vs StL AL, 1-0; September 9, 1945 (2nd game).

Bill McCahan, Phi vs Was AL, 3-0; September 3, 1947.

Catfish Hunter, Oak vs Min AL, 4-0; May 8, 1968 (perfect game).

Vida Blue, Oak vs Min AL, 6-0; September 21, 1970.

Vida Blue (5 innings), Glenn Abbott (1 inning), Paul Lindblad (1 inning) and Rollie Fingers (2 innings), Oak vs Cal AL, 5-0; September 28, 1975.

Mike Warren, Oak vs Chi AL, 3-0; September 29, 1983.

DAVE STEWART, Oak at Tor AL, 5-0; June 29, 1990.

Rube Waddell, 5 innings, rain, Phi vs StL AL, 2-0; August 15, 1905.

Jimmy Dygert (3 innings) and Rube Waddell (2 innings), five innings, rain, Phi vs Chi AL, 4-3; August 29, 1906. (Waddell allowed hit and two runs in 6th, but rain caused game to revert to 5 innings).

Rube Vickers, five perfect innings, darkness, Phi at Was AL, 4-0; October 5, 1907 (2nd game).

ACTIVE PLAYERS in caps.

Leader from the franchise's current location is included. If not in the top five, leader's rank is listed in parenthesis; asterisk (*) indicates player is not in top 25.

Players' years of service are listed by the first and last years with this team and are not necessarily consecutive; all statistics record performances for this team only.

Atlanta Braves

184

By Russell Beeker, Baseball Weekly

Cy Young winner Greg Maddux went 19-2 with a 1.63 ERA and 181 strikeouts in 192.2 innings.

1995 Braves: They finally caught the rings

On the night the Braves defeated the Cleveland Indians and earned their World Series rings, nine players—plus manager Bobby Cox and his coaching staff—could say they had lived the whole saga of Atlanta's unfulfilled dream, beginning with the miracle season of 1991 that ended with a seven-game World Series loss. The players were David Justice, Mark Wohlers, Tom Glavine, John Smoltz, Jeff Blauser, Rafael Belliard, Steve Avery, Kent Mercker and Mark Lemke.

They won the series at last, but they didn't do it with big bats. During the regular season, in fact, they were next to last in the league in hitting (.250). One of the keys to their success despite such flat performance at the plate was their ability to come through in the clutch. They won 29 games in their last at-bat, nine games when they trailed after eight innings, 13 more when tied after eight. They had a 33-17 record in one-run games.

Combine that with the starting pitching of Glavine (16-7), Smoltz (12-7) and Greg Maddux (19-2), and the NL East race was a relative cakewalk. Maddux, with his 1.63 ERA, became the first pitcher since Walter Johnson in 1918-19 to achieve an ERA under 1.80 in consecutive seasons. He walked only 23 batters all season and went 51 walkless innings at one stretch.

The bullpen was the strongest it had been in the '90s. When Wohlers stepped forward to become a dominant closer, the rest of the relief roles fell comfortably to Greg McMichael, Brad Clontz, Pedro Borbon, and Alejandro Pena. Pena was one of GM John Schuerholz's late-season acquisitions that may have finally put the Braves over the top. Adding Mike Devereaux and Luis Polonia gave Atlanta a deeper bench and more flexibility.

But the regular lineup was deeper, too. Chipper Jones took over at third base and became the league's top everyday rookie. Javy Lopez continued to blossom behind the plate, and left fielder Ryan Klesko graduated from platoon to nearly regular status. Jones, after missing a season due to injury, hit .265 with 23 home runs. He helped set up Justice (24 home runs) and Fred McGriff (27 HR), especially with shortstop and usual No. 2 hitter Jeff Blauser struggling all year to a .211 finish.

Cox took an "if it ain't broke, don't fix it" attitude to Blauser's problems for much of the season but finally moved second baseman Mark Lemke to the No. 2 spot, especially when injuries further curtailed the shortstop's availability.

Little else went wrong for Atlanta, especially after Philadelphia slipped from its early-season success. A 20-7 July ended any semblance of a race.

But that was only the prelude to what really counted for the team and the city, and what they finally got—the World Series championship.

1996 Braves: Preview

"We'll have enough youth on this club to carry it for...years," says Bobby Cox, and that's more bad news for the National League. The Braves will remain as intact as owner Ted Turner and GM John Schuerholz want them to be. The money that brought in key stars such as Fred McGriff and Marquis Grissom is still there, but so is the productive farm system that allowed the Braves to permit McGriff to be a free agent, knowing that Ryan Klesko could return to his more comfortable first base position and left field could be filled with little problem.

"We got a sense this year, with the changing economics of the game, that we won't all be here forever," says pitcher John Smoltz.

1995 Braves: Week-by-week notes

186

These notes were excerpted from the following issues of Baseball Weekly.

▶**May 3:** In three appearances, reliever Mark Wohlers faced 13 batters—he walked six, two intentionally, hit another, threw a wild pitch and gave up a home run. He said the problem was mechanical—he couldn't control his fastball.

▶**May 10:** The Braves lost Ryan Klesko for three weeks to a thumb injury and filled his role in left field with third baseman Chipper Jones. Meanwhile, the Braves completed their $20 million rotation by signing Steve Avery to a one-year, $4 million deal.

▶**May 17:** General manager John Schuerholz wasn't worried about the Braves' 8-9 start: "It doesn't bother me at all. Statistics don't lie. If you look at the records of the players we have, I think they bode very well for a successful and exciting season."

▶**May 24:** David Justice revealed a hoop ring in his left nipple. He refused to have the nipple ring photographed, though he admitted he is into body adornments—his left ear is pierced twice, he has a black panther tattoo on his right ankle and a tattoo on his left shoulder. His wife, actress Halle Berry, has a tattoo on her backside.

▶**June 7:** Already struggling at the plate as a team, the Braves received a major blow when David Justice found out he had torn ligaments in his right shoulder. He was placed on the 15-day disabled list and slated for possible postseason surgery.

▶**June 14:** Steve Avery had just four wins in his last 24 starts, and his ERA had ballooned to 4.56. Said Avery, "It's either time to say, 'Let's go, let's kick it in,' or 'Let's quit.' I'm too young to quit."

▶**June 21:** Steve Avery won for the first time in nearly a month, and David Justice returned to the lineup.

▶**June 28:** Mike Stanton, with a 5.40 ERA, was basically dropped into a mop-up role. "If you go back through my career, there has always been a span of time where I haven't pitched well," said Stanton. "But I have always snapped out of it."

▶**July 5:** Greg Maddux, 8-1, had won 11 consecutive road starts, six consecutive games overall and pushed his streak of walkless innings to 41, which covered 156 hitters. Meanwhile he lowered his ERA to 1.78.

▶**July 13:** The Braves brought in an old sidewinder to work with their new one. Former Kansas City closer Dan Quisenberry was in Atlanta tutoring Braves right-hander Brad Clontz. The idea to bring in Quisenberry was that of Braves general manager John Schuerholz. The two worked together in Kansas City. Schuerholz said he saw Quisenberry at the 10th reunion of the 1985 Royals World Championship team. "Dan told me that the best advice he ever got was when he was young and the Royals brought in Kent Tekulve to talk to him," Schuerholz said. The Braves didn't pay Quisenberry, but they did pick up his travel expenses.

▶**Aug. 16:** With his ERA a team-high 6.11 and his arm having grown tired after almost 13 major league seasons, reliever Steve Bedrosian retired on Aug. 11, with a career 184 saves, 76-79 record and 3.38 ERA in 732 games. His teammates honored him that night by wearing their stockings pulled up high, a fashion Bedrosian loved.

▶**Aug. 30:** The Braves filled the hole in the right-handed pinch-hitting slot by acquiring Mike Devereaux from the White Sox. Devereaux was hitting .306 with 10 home runs and 55 RBI with Chicago and would be used primarily as a pinch hitter and late-inning defensive replacement for Ryan Klesko in left field. Braves pinch-hitters were batting just .214 (28-for-131).

▶**Sept. 6:** As if the Braves didn't already have an imposing pitching staff, they added rookie Jason Schmidt, who held the Cubs scoreless over eight innings in his first big league start.

▶**Sept. 20:** Greg Maddux just kept on piling up wins and records. The three-time Cy Young Award winner—a favorite to win a fourth consecutive—pitched seven shutout innings on Sept. 16 for a 6-1 win against the Cincinnati Reds. It was a record-setting 17th consecutive road win. Maddux, 17-2 in a shortened season, had gone 17-0 in 19 road starts since July 2, 1994, allowing just 17 earned runs (1.03 ERA).

▶**Oct. 4:** There comes a time when words don't do justice to a story. Such is the case with Maddux. The best way to describe what the Braves right-hander did over these last five months is by the numbers. Winning the 150th game of his career seven months before his 30th birthday, Maddux notched his 19th win of the season. He threw six shutout innings as the Braves blew past the Phillies 6-0 on Sept. 27. Maddux finished the regular season with just two losses; an incredible .905 winning percentage, a major league record for pitchers with 20 or more decisions; a 1.63 ERA; and a string of 21 scoreless innings. Maddux became the first pitcher since Walter Johnson in 1918-19 to have an ERA of less than 1.80 in two consecutive years.

▶**Last-day recap:** *Heroes*—In a season in which they had the division wrapped up by early August, the Braves had a lot of Heroes, but several Disappointments. The Heroes begin with Greg Maddux. What else can be said about the right-hander? He led the league with 10 complete games. He also went 51 consecutive innings without walking anyone. Chipper Jones, in any other year, would have won the rookie honors in a landslide. Jones finished with 23 home runs and 86 RBI and saved the club several times with his glove at third base. He started 140 games and helped out in left field when needed. Mark Wohlers turned into a closer, and his fastball was clocked at 100 mph on many nights. He finished with 25 saves, including 21 in a row. He struck out 90 in just 64⅔ innings and compiled a 2.09 ERA.

Unsung Heroes—Rafael Belliard filled in on several occasions for Blauser at short and Mark Lemke at second (because of injuries). The club did not miss a beat with him. Ryan Klesko, though overshadowed by Jones, hit .310 with 23 homers in just 329 at-bats. Javy Lopez led the team in hitting at .315, though his defense was spotty at times.

Disappointments—Until his final three outings of the season, Steve Avery was one of the league's most unproductive starters. He finished the season at 7-13, with an ERA of 4.67, and that figure had been much higher before September. Jeff Blauser also had a tough year. After reporting late to spring training because of a contract squabble, Blauser ended up having the worst season of his career, hitting .211 with 12 homers and 31 RBI.

Team directory

▶**Owner:** Ted Turner
▶**General manager:** John Schuerholz
▶**Ballpark:**
Atlanta–Fulton County Stadium
521 Capitol Ave., SW, Atlanta, Ga.
404-522-7630
Capacity 52,710
Parking for 3,500 cars; $5
Public transportation available by bus
Family and wheelchair sections,
no-alcohol section
▶**Team publications:**
Fan Magazine, Chop Talk
404-522-7630
▶**TV, radio broadcast stations:**
WSB 750 AM, WTBS Channel 17,
Sport South
▶**Camps and/or clinics:**
Braves Fantasy Camp (ages 30+),
February, 800-8-BRAVES
▶**Spring training:**
Municipal Stadium
West Palm Beach, Fla.
Capacity 7,200
407-683-6100

ATLANTA BRAVES 1995 final stats

BATTERS	BA	SLG	OB	G	AB	R	H	TB	2B	3B	HR	RBI	BB	SO	SB	CS	E
Lopez	.315	.498	.344	100	333	37	105	166	11	4	14	51	14	57	0	1	8
Klesko	.310	.608	.396	107	329	48	102	200	25	2	23	70	47	72	5	4	8
Perez	.308	.615	.308	7	13	1	4	8	1	0	1	4	0	2	0	0	0
McGriff	.280	.489	.361	144	528	85	148	258	27	1	27	93	65	99	3	6	5
Mordecai	.280	.480	.353	69	75	10	21	36	6	0	3	11	9	16	0	0	0
Jones	.265	.450	.353	140	524	87	139	236	22	3	23	86	73	99	8	4	25
Polonia	.264	.396	.304	28	53	6	14	21	7	0	0	2	3	9	3	0	0
Grissom	.258	.376	.317	139	551	80	142	207	23	3	12	42	47	61	29	9	2
Devereaux	.255	.364	.281	29	55	7	14	20	3	0	1	8	2	11	2	0	0
Lemke	.253	.356	.325	116	399	42	101	142	16	5	5	38	44	40	2	2	5
Justice	.253	.479	.365	120	411	73	104	197	17	2	24	78	73	68	4	2	4
Smith	.252	.412	.327	103	131	16	33	54	8	2	3	21	13	35	0	3	2
O'Brien	.227	.399	.343	67	198	18	45	79	7	0	9	23	29	40	0	1	4
Belliard	.222	.244	.255	75	180	12	40	44	2	1	0	7	6	28	2	2	1
Blauser	.211	.341	.319	115	431	60	91	147	16	2	12	31	57	107	8	5	15
Kelly	.190	.314	.258	97	137	26	26	43	6	1	3	17	11	49	7	3	4
Kowitz	.167	.208	.259	10	24	3	4	5	1	0	0	3	2	5	0	1	0
Sharperson	.143	.286	.143	7	7	1	1	2	1	0	0	0	2	0	2	0	0
Giovanola	.071	.071	.235	13	14	2	1	1	0	0	0	0	3	5	0	0	0

PITCHERS	W-L	ERA	G	GS	CG	GF	Sho	SV	IP	H	R	ER	HR	BB	SO
Maddux	19-2	1.63	28	28	10	0	3	0	209.2	147	39	38	8	23	181
Wohlers	7-3	2.09	65	0	0	49	0	25	64.2	51	16	15	2	24	90
Pena	2-0	2.61	27	0	0	6	0	0	31	22	9	9	3	7	39
McMichael	7-2	2.79	67	0	0	16	0	2	80.2	64	27	25	8	32	74
Glavine	16-7	3.08	29	29	3	0	1	0	198.2	182	76	68	9	66	127
Borbon	2-2	3.09	41	0	0	19	0	2	32	29	12	11	2	17	33
Smoltz	12-7	3.18	29	29	2	0	1	0	192.2	166	76	68	15	72	193
Clontz	8-1	3.65	59	0	0	14	0	4	69	71	29	28	5	22	55
Mercker	7-8	4.15	29	26	0	1	0	0	143	140	73	66	16	61	102
Wade	0-1	4.50	3	0	0	0	0	0	4	3	2	2	1	4	3
Avery	7-13	4.67	29	29	3	0	1	0	173.1	165	92	90	22	52	141
Clark	0-0	4.91	3	0	0	1	0	0	3.2	3	2	2	0	5	2
Nichols	0-0	5.40	5	0	0	0	0	0	6.2	14	11	4	3	5	3
Stanton	1-1	5.59	26	0	0	10	0	1	19.1	31	14	12	3	6	13
Schmidt	2-2	5.76	9	2	0	1	0	0	25	27	17	16	2	18	19
Woodall	1-1	6.10	9	0	0	3	0	0	10.1	13	10	7	1	8	5
Bedrosian	1-2	6.11	29	0	0	7	0	0	28	40	21	19	6	12	22
Murray	0-2	6.75	4	1	0	1	0	0	10.2	10	8	8	3	5	3
Thobe	0-0	10.80	3	0	0	1	0	0	3.1	7	4	4	0	0	2
May	0-0	11.25	2	0	0	1	0	0	4	10	5	5	0	0	1

1996 preliminary roster

PITCHERS (17)
Steve Avery
Pedro Borbon
Chris Brock
Brad Clontz
Lee Daniels
Tom Glavine
Greg Maddux
Darrell May
Greg McMichael
Kent Mercker
Mike Potts
Jason Schmidt
John Smoltz
Tom Thobe
Terrell Wade
Mark Wohlers
Brad Woodall

CATCHERS (4)
Joe Ayrault
Tyler Houston
Javy Lopez
Eddie Perez

INFIELDERS (8)
Rafael Belliard
Jeff Blauser
Ed Giovanola
Tony Graffanino
Chipper Jones
Mark Lemke

Fred McGriff
Mike Mordecai

OUTFIELDERS (4)
Marquis Grissom
David Justice
Mike Kelly
Ryan Klesko

Games played by position

PLAYER	G	C	1B	2B	3B	SS	OF
Belliard	75	0	0	32	0	40	0
Blauser	115	0	0	0	0	115	0
Devereaux	29	0	0	0	0	0	27
Giovanola	13	0	0	7	3	1	0
Grissom	139	0	0	0	0	0	136
Jones	140	0	0	0	123	0	20
Justice	120	0	0	0	0	0	120
Kelly	97	0	0	0	0	0	83
Klesko	107	0	4	0	0	0	102
Kowitz	10	0	0	0	0	0	8
Lemke	116	0	0	115	0	0	0
Lopez	100	93	0	0	0	0	0
McGriff	144	0	144	0	0	0	0
Mordecai	69	0	9	21	6	6	1
O'Brien	67	64	0	0	0	0	0
Perez	7	5	1	0	0	0	0
Polonia	28	0	0	0	0	0	15
Sharperson	7	0	0	0	1	0	0
Smith	103	0	0	0	0	0	25

Minor Leagues

Tops in the organization

Batter	Club	Avg.	G	AB	R	H	HR	RBI
Aldo Pecorilli	Rmd	.344	119	392	67	135	13	59
Kevin Grijak	Rmd	.324	127	383	49	124	14	67
Ed Giovanola	Rmd	.321	99	321	45	103	4	36
M Sharperson	Rmd	.319	87	298	42	95	3	47
Pedro Swann	Grv	.313	117	377	59	118	11	67

Home Runs			Wins		
Ron Wright	Mac	32	Derrin Ebert	Mac	14
Andruw Jones	Mac	25	Matt Murray	Rmd	14
Gus Kennedy	Mac	24	Ryan Jacobs	Dur	11
Juan Williams	Rmd	19	Tom Harrison	Rmd	11
Miguel Correa	Dur	19	Several tied		10

RBI			Saves		
Ron Wright	Mac	104	Matt Byrd	Dur	27
Andruw Jones	Mac	100	Carl Schutz	Grv	26
Wes Helms	Mac	85	Rod Nichols	Rmd	25
Randall Simon	Dur	79	Ken Raines	Mac	14
Damon Hollins	Grv	77	Adam Butler	Eug	8

Stolen Bases			Strikeouts		
Andruw Jones	Mac	56	Damian Moss	Mac	177
George Lombard	Eug	51	John Rocker	Eug	135
Scott Pagano	Dur	41	C. Seelbach	Rmd	130
Mike Eaglin	Mac	41	Micah Bowie	Dur	127
W. Monds	Dur	30	Several tied		124

Pitcher	Club	W-L	ERA	IP	H	BB	SO
Tom Thobe	Rmd	7-0	1.84	88	65	26	57
Jason Schmidt	Rmd	8-6	2.25	116	97	48	95
Matt Murray	Rmd	14-3	2.54	152	128	42	103
Anthony Briggs	Mac	8-5	2.99	147	145	56	114
Chris Seelbach	Rmd	10-6	3.30	134	102	69	130

Sick call: 1995 DL Report

Player	Days on the DL
Dave Justice	15
Ryan Klesko	15
Mark Lemke	23

1995 Amateur draft picks

Players are listed with position and college or high school. Most players were assigned to rookie or Class A leagues. List provided by Major League Baseball.

Waylon Anglen, 2b, Arkansas State; Joseph Bauldree, rhp, Wake Forest (N.C.) Rolesville HS; Robert Bell, rhp, Marlboro (N.Y.) Central HS; Nathan Bennett, lhp, Coastal Christian HS, Arroyo Grande, Calif.; Darren Blakely, cf, Pensacola (Fla.) HS; Antone Brooks, lhp, Norfolk State; Andrew Cochrane, lhp, Pacific Lutheran; Ariel Colon, 1b, Jose M. Lazaro HS, Carolina, P.R.; Craig Cozart, rhp, Central Florida; Casey Crawford, 1b-of, Dennis J. O'Connell HS, Falls Church, Va.; Charlie Cruz, lhp, Florida State; Charlie Curry, ss-2b, Centennial HS, Portland, Ore.; Keith Dougherty, 3b, Columbus College; Watson Ellison, lf, Dixie College; Robert Fishel, lhp, Pflugerville (Texas) HS; Benjamin Fowler, rhp, Pace Academy, Alpharetta, Ga.; Mike Goldstein, of, Cherry Creek HS, Englewood, Colo.; Steve Hacker, 1b, Southwest Missouri State; Jason Hart, ss, Fair Grove (Mo.) HS; Zachery Hines, ss, DeKalb College; Randy Hodges, of, Florida State; Craig House, rhp, Christian Brothers HS, Memphis, Chad Hutchinson, rhp, Torrey Pines HS, San Diego; Brian Jolliffe, lhp, Maine; Yan Lagrandeur, rhp, CEGEP Montmorency, Granby, Que.; Kevin Loewe, lhp, Maryland; Michael Mahoney, c, Creighton; Lester Mayhew, rhp, Ferrum (Cal.); Jamal McAdory, 1b, Jackson State; Kevin McGlinchy, rhp, Malden (Mass.) HS; Jeremy McMullen, lhp, Portland State; Matt McWilliams, rhp, North Carolina; Chad Mead, lhp, Woodward (Okla.) HS; Matthew Middleton, ss, Graham HS, Conover, Ohio; David Noyce, lhp, Marietta (Ga.) HS; James Osting, lhp, Trinity HS, Louisville; Oscar Otero, 3b, Benjamin Harrison HS, Cayey, P.R.; Craig Owens, rf, Chowan College; Thomas Reynolds, rhp, Berry; Jacob Ruotsinoja, cf, Seminole (Fla.) HS; Brian Rust, 3b, Lewis-Clark State; Luther Salinas, rhp-1b, Laverne Lutheran HS, Whittier, Calif.; Troy Satterfield, lhp, Jonesboro (Ga.) HS; James Scharrer, lf, Cathedral Prep, Erie, Pa.; Curt Schnur, rhp, Delaware; Ryan Schurman, rhp, Tualatin (Ore.) HS; Jason Shiell, rhp, Windsor-Forest, Savannah, Ga.; Jason Shy, c, Butte College; Phillip Smith, lf, Phillipsburg (N.J.) HS; Matthew Taylor, ss, California St.; Donnie Thomas, lhp, Andrew College; Gerald Vecchioni, ss, Patapsco School, Baltimore; Corey Walker, of, Westmar; Eric White, rhp, Enrico Fermi HS, Enfield, Conn.; James Wise, lhp, Abraham Baldwin CC; Benjamin Wyatt, lhp, J.A. Fair HS, Little Rock.

Atlanta (1966-1995), incl. Boston (1876-1952) and Milwaukee (1953-1965)

Runs: Most, career, all-time

2107 Hank Aaron, 1954-1974
1452 Eddie Mathews, 1952-1966
1291 Herman Long, 1890-1902
1134 Fred Tenney, 1894-1911
1103 Dale Murphy, 1976-1990

Hits: Most, career, all-time

3600 Hank Aaron, 1954-1974
2201 Eddie Mathews, 1952-1966
1994 Fred Tenney, 1894-1911
1901 Dale Murphy, 1976-1990
1900 Herman Long, 1890-1902

2B: Most, career, all-time

600 Hank Aaron, 1954-1974
338 Eddie Mathews, 1952-1966
306 Dale Murphy, 1976-1990
295 Herman Long, 1890-1902
291 Tommy Holmes, 1942-1951

3B: Most, career, all-time

103 Rabbit Maranville, 1912-1935
96   Hank Aaron, 1954-1974
91   Herman Long, 1890-1902
80   John Morrill, 1876-1888
79   Bill Bruton, 1953-1960

HR: Most, career, all-time

733 Hank Aaron, 1954-1974
493 Eddie Mathews, 1952-1966
371 Dale Murphy, 1976-1990
239 Joe Adcock, 1953-1962
215 Bob Horner, 1978-1986

RBI: Most, career, all-time

2202 Hank Aaron, 1954-1974
1388 Eddie Mathews, 1952-1966
1143 Dale Murphy, 1976-1990
964   Herman Long, 1890-1902
927   Hugh Duffy, 1892-1900

SB: Most, career, all-time

431 Herman Long, 1890-1902
331 Hugh Duffy, 1892-1900
274 Billy Hamilton, 1896-1901
260 Bobby Lowe, 1890-1901
260 Fred Tenney, 1894-1911
240 Hank Aaron, 1954-1974 (6)

BB: Most, career, all-time

1376 Eddie Mathews, 1952-1966
1297 Hank Aaron, 1954-1974
912   Dale Murphy, 1976-1990
750   Fred Tenney, 1894-1911
598   Billy Nash, 1885-1895

BA: Highest, career, all-time

.338 Billy Hamilton, 1896-1901
.332 Hugh Duffy, 1892-1900
.327 Chick Stahl, 1897-1900
.317 Rico Carty, 1963-1972
.317 Ralph Garr, 1968-1975

Slug avg: Highest, career, all-time

.567 Hank Aaron, 1954-1974
.533 Wally Berger, 1930-1937
.517 Eddie Mathews, 1952-1966
.511 Joe Adcock, 1953-1962
.508 Bob Horner, 1978-1986

Games started: Most, career, all-time

635 Warren Spahn, 1942-1964
595 Phil Niekro, 1964-1987
501 Kid Nichols, 1890-1901
330 Lew Burdette, 1951-1963
302 Vic Willis, 1898-1905

Saves: Most, career, all-time

141 Gene Garber, 1978-1987
78   Cecil Upshaw, 1966-1973
57   Rick Camp, 1976-1985
55   MIKE STANTON, 1989-1995
50   Don McMahon, 1957-1962

Shutouts: Most, career, all-time

63 Warren Spahn, 1942-1964
44 Kid Nichols, 1890-1901
43 Phil Niekro, 1964-1987
30 Lew Burdette, 1951-1963
29 Tommy Bond, 1877-1881

Wins: Most, career, all-time

356 Warren Spahn, 1942-1964
329 Kid Nichols, 1890-1901
268 Phil Niekro, 1964-1987
179 Lew Burdette, 1951-1963
151 Vic Willis, 1898-1905

K: Most, career, all-time

2912 Phil Niekro, 1964-1987
2493 Warren Spahn, 1942-1964
1667 Kid Nichols, 1890-1901
1252 JOHN SMOLTZ, 1988-1995
1161 Vic Willis, 1898-1905

Win pct: Highest, career, all-time

.753 GREG MADDUX, 1993-1995
.679 Fred Klobedanz, 1896-1902
.655 Harry Staley, 1891-1894
.645 John Clarkson, 1888-1892
.643 Kid Nichols, 1890-1901

ERA: Lowest, career, all-time

2.21 Tommy Bond, 1877-1881
2.49 Jim Whitney, 1881-1885
2.52 Art Nehf, 1915-1919
2.62 Dick Rudolph, 1913-1927
2.74 Pat Ragan, 1915-1919
3.20 Phil Niekro, 1964-1987 (16)

Runs: Most, season

160 Hugh Duffy, 1894
158 Bobby Lowe, 1894
152 Billy Hamilton, 1896
152 Billy Hamilton, 1897
149 Herman Long, 1893
131 Dale Murphy, 1983 (9)

Hits: Most, season

237 Hugh Duffy, 1894
224 Tommy Holmes, 1945
223 Hank Aaron, 1959
219 Ralph Garr, 1971
218 Felipe Alou, 1966

2B: Most, season

51 Hugh Duffy, 1894
47 Tommy Holmes, 1945
46 Hank Aaron, 1959
44 Wally Berger, 1931
44 Lee Maye, 1964
39 TERRY PENDLETON, 1992 (12)

3B: Most, season

20 Dick Johnston, 1887
20 Harry Stovey, 1891
19 Chick Stahl, 1899
18 Dick Johnston, 1888
18 Ray Powell, 1921
17 Ralph Garr, 1974 (6)

HR: Most, season

47	Hank Aaron, 1971
47	Eddie Mathews, 1953
46	Eddie Mathews, 1959
45	Hank Aaron, 1962
44	Hank Aaron, 1957
44	Hank Aaron, 1963
44	Hank Aaron, 1966
44	Hank Aaron, 1969
44	Dale Murphy, 1987

RBI: Most, season

145	Hugh Duffy, 1894
135	Eddie Mathews, 1953
132	Hank Aaron, 1957
132	Jimmy Collins, 1897
130	Hank Aaron, 1963
130	Wally Berger, 1935
127	Hank Aaron, 1966 (9)

SB: Most, season

84	King Kelly, 1887
83	Billy Hamilton, 1896
72	OTIS NIXON, 1991
68	King Kelly, 1889
66	Billy Hamilton, 1897

BB: Most, season

131	Bob Elliott, 1948
127	Jim Wynn, 1976
126	Darrell Evans, 1974
124	Darrell Evans, 1973
124	Eddie Mathews, 1963

BA: Highest, season

.440	Hugh Duffy, 1894
.387	Rogers Hornsby, 1928
.373	Dan Brouthers, 1889
.369	Billy Hamilton, 1898
.366	Rico Carty, 1970

Slug avg: Highest, season

.694	Hugh Duffy, 1894
.669	Hank Aaron, 1971
.636	Hank Aaron, 1959
.632	Rogers Hornsby, 1928
.627	Eddie Mathews, 1953

Games started: Most, season

72	John Clarkson, 1889
67	Charlie Buffinton, 1884
64	Tommy Bond, 1879
63	Jim Whitney, 1881
59	Tommy Bond, 1878
44	Phil Niekro, 1979 (22)

Saves: Most, season

30	Gene Garber, 1982
27	MIKE STANTON, 1993
27	Cecil Upshaw, 1969
25	Gene Garber, 1979
25	MARK WOHLERS, 1995

Shutouts: Most, season

11	Tommy Bond, 1879
9	Tommy Bond, 1878
8	Charlie Buffinton, 1884
8	John Clarkson, 1889
7	Kid Nichols, 1890
7	Togie Pittinger, 1902
7	Warren Spahn, 1947
7	Warren Spahn, 1951
7	Warren Spahn, 1963
7	Irv Young, 1905
6	Phil Niekro, 1974 (11)

Wins: Most, season

49	John Clarkson, 1889
48	Charlie Buffinton, 1884
43	Tommy Bond, 1879
40	Tommy Bond, 1877
40	Tommy Bond, 1878
23	Phil Niekro, 1969 (*)

K: Most, season

417	Charlie Buffinton, 1884
345	Jim Whitney, 1883
284	John Clarkson, 1889
270	Jim Whitney, 1884
262	Phil Niekro, 1977

Win pct: Highest, season

.905	GREG MADDUX, 1995
.842	Tom Hughes, 1916
.810	Phil Niekro, 1982
.788	Fred Klobedanz, 1897
.788	Bill James, 1914

ERA: Lowest, season

1.56	GREG MADDUX, 1994
1.63	GREG MADDUX, 1995
1.87	Phil Niekro, 1967
1.90	Bill James, 1914
1.96	Tommy Bond, 1879

Most pinch-hit homers, season

5	Butch Nieman, 1945
4	TOMMY GREGG, 1990

Most pinch-hit homers, career

7	Joe Adcock, 1953-1962
6	TOMMY GREGG, 1988-1992

Most consecutive games batting safely

37	Tommy Holmes, 1945
31	Rico Carty, 1970

Most consecutive scoreless innings

41	Art Nehf, 1917
29	Phil Niekro, 1974

No-hit games

Jack Stivetts, Bos vs Bro NL, 11-0; August 6, 1892.

Frank (Jeff) Pfeffer, Bos vs Cin NL, 6-0; May 8, 1907.

George Davis, Bos vs Phi NL, 7-0; September 9, 1914 (2nd game).

Tom L. Hughes, Bos vs Pit NL, 2-0; June 16, 1916.

Jim Tobin, Bos vs Bro NL, 2-0; April 27, 1944.

Vern Bickford, Bos vs Bro NL, 7-0; August 11, 1950.

Jim Wilson, Mil vs Phi NL, 2-0; June 12, 1954.

Lew Burdette, Mil vs Phi NL, 1-0; August 18, 1960.

Warren Spahn, Mil vs Phi NL, 4-0; September 16, 1960.

Warren Spahn, Mil vs SF NL, 1-0; April 28, 1961.

Phil Niekro, Atl vs SD NL, 9-0; August 5, 1973.

KENT MERCKER (6 innings), MARK WOHLERS (2 innings) and ALEJANDRO PENA (1 inning), Atl at SD NL, 1-0; September 11, 1991.

KENT MERCKER, Atl at LA NL, 6-0; April 8, 1994.

Jack Stivetts, 5 innings, called so Boston could catch train to Cleveland for Temple Cub playoffs, Bos at Was NL, 6-0; October 15, 1892 (2nd game).

Jim Tobin, 5 innings, darkness, Bos vs Phi NL, 7-0; June 22, 1944 (2nd game).

ACTIVE PLAYERS in caps.

Leader from franchise's current location is included. If not in the top five, leader's rank is listed in parenthesis; asterisk (*) indicates player is not in top 25.

Players' years of service are listed by the first and last years with this team and are not necessarily consecutive; all statistics record performances for this team only.

New York Mets

By Anne Ryan, *USA TODAY*

Catcher Todd Hundley boosted the Mets offense with 15 homers and 51 RBI in 89 games.

1995 Mets: Young talent brought new vitality

The 1995 season was a snapshot of two different seasons—before and after—for the New York Mets. In the first picture, there were several veteran players on the team, including Bret Saberhagen, Bobby Bonilla and Brett Butler. In the second picture, the only veteran remaining was closer John Franco, surrounded by a bunch of fresh-faced, no-name—but very promising—youngsters.

When they arrived, the Mets thrived. One statistic tells the story: The Mets were 22 games under .500 after losing their first five games in August. They went 34-18 after they sent Saberhagen to Colorado, dealt Bonilla to Baltimore and returned Butler to Los Angeles, thus becoming baseball's youngest team. The enthusiasm revived the team and energized the clubhouse. Bill Pulsipher and his 20-something cohorts bounced around in baggy jeans and backwards caps—a far cry from gray-haired Butler and his tailored suits.

Jason Isringhausen, a 44th-round draft pick in 1991, dazzled with a 9-2 record and 2.81 ERA. He won 20 games all told in Binghamton, Norfolk and New York. Pulsipher made 17 starts and pitched into the seventh inning in 16 of them. The two young pitchers formed the heart of the rotation, along with fellow rookie Reid Cornelius and Bobby Jones. Another rookie, Dave Mlicki, showed a lot of promise while going 4-1 in his last nine starts.

New York's position players also took steady steps in their career tracks. First baseman Rico Brogna proved to be one of the best defenders at his position, while batting .289 with 22 home runs and 76 RBI. Rookie third baseman Edgardo Alfonzo was hampered by a herniated disc but played good defense and hit .278. The Bonilla trade brought prized prospect Alex Ochoa, who could team with Carl Everett and Ryan Thompson in the outfield of the future. Everett has a gun in the outfield and wound up with 54 RBI in 79 games. Thompson has the greatest natural talent on the team, but his poor work habits and stubbornness kept him from reaching his potential.

With the infusion of youth, the Mets went 44-31 after the All-Star break, the NL's second-best mark in the second half. And things never seemed better than the last two home stands. The Mets won their final 11 games at Shea and swept a pair of three-game series from playoff teams Cincinnati and Atlanta.

"It shows that we have enough talent to play with the best," said manager Dallas Green, who was rewarded with a one-year contract extension.

1996 Mets: Preview

Judging from the record of the final two months of last season (34-18), a return to the top seems imminent for the Mets. They go into the 1996 season with a probable starting rotation of Pulsipher, Isring-hausen, Mlicki, Jones and Paul Wilson. The infield could include Rey Ordonez at shortstop, Butch Huskey at third base, Brogna at first and Alfonzo at second.

There are at least six legitimate outfield candidates, including Ochoa, Everett and Jay Payton.

"I don't want the fans to push these kids and think they're going to win a World Series title next year," Green said. "We still have to realize we're going to have the youngest team in the league here, and any additions we make will be young guys, not veterans, so we're going to need growing time."

1995 Mets: Week-by-week notes

These notes were excerpted from the following issues of Baseball Weekly.

▶**May 3:** The Mets came out hitting, scoring 31 runs on 48 hits in four games. But key lapses by the bullpen meant they won only two games and nearly blew a third. Over those four games, the bullpen made 19 appearances and gave up five leads. Exception: Blas Minor. He pitched twice, allowing no runs in four innings, and picked up a win.

▶**May 10:** Todd Hundley had 11 RBI in the club's first 10 games—eight of them came on grand slams in just over a week. Leadoff man Brett Butler hit .353 through the 10 games.

▶**June 14:** A sub-.500 trip to the West Coast increased the likelihood of a long and lonely summer at Shea Stadium. After visits to Los Angeles and San Francisco, the Mets entered a three-game series in San Diego with a chance to break even on the 10-game sojourn. But they promptly lost the first two to the Padres, despite leading 2-0 in both. With their 6-3 defeat on June 11, the Mets fell to 16-27. Going into a three-game series against Florida, they faced the possibility of falling into last place. Attendance was already down, and the team had to be wondering what it could offer fans the rest of the way.

▶**June 21:** They came to praise Bill Pulsipher and wound up burying Brett Butler, who didn't exactly help the pitcher's debut by missing a catchable fly ball in a five-run first inning, misplaying another ball into a triple in the third, and getting thrown out on the basepaths to abort a rally in the eighth. By then he had inherited the boos normally reserved for Bobby Bonilla as the fans reacted to a team that appeared to be racing toward prime position for the next year's amateur draft.

▶**June 28:** With a 9-3 victory against Atlanta on June 23, the Mets not only snapped a four-game losing streak but opened a road trip with a sign of life. Still, they stood 20-34 at that point, just one game ahead of their 103-loss pace in the disastrous 1993 campaign. The spiral left manager Dallas Green virtually without answers, as he twice refused to grant post-game interviews during the recent homestand. Then again, what could he say? The Mets left town after allowing 19 hits to Philadelphia in an 8-2 loss. In a four-game sweep by the Phillies, the Mets were outscored 28-9.

▶**July 5:** More than two months into the season, the Mets finally assembled their first three-game winning streak. In what they hoped was a preview of more to come, rookie Bill Pulsipher started with a strong performance against Florida. Then came two games in which the offense overcame three-run deficits. The streak ended July 1 when the Reds hammered Pete Harnisch, but even a modest string of victories stood out when the team was 15 games under .500.

▶**July 13:** Dallas Green, who had been remarkably quiet considering the poor quality of his team's play, finally lost his temper after an 8-4 defeat against the Chicago Cubs on July 6. He ripped into his players after the game, and even though he declined to share exactly what he said, you could make some educated guesses. The Mets made four errors, resulting in six unearned runs. You name the mistake, and the Mets made it: a ball lost in the sun, a misplayed pickoff throw, a wide throw to first after a third strike, a throw not backed up. "I'm embarrassed all the time," Green said. "Nobody likes to watch that happen." On top of everything else, Pete Harnisch left after six innings with soreness in his shoulder—but if the shoulder didn't force him to miss work, his pitching might have. He was 1-7 with a 4.23 ERA. Meanwhile, the Mets called up Jason Isringhausen from Class AAA. Isringhausen, considered one of the Mets' best right-handed prospects since Tom Seaver, was 9-0 with a 1.29 ERA.

▶**July 19:** Bret Saberhagen, bothered by various ailments in his four-year stint with the Mets, was hurt again. The injury might have created a reprieve for Dave Mlicki, who had been headed for the bullpen in advance of rookie Jason Isringhausen's arrival. Mlicki had delivered a series of respectable outings, and his four wins ranked him third on the staff. Meanwhile, lack of speed and defense continued to plague the Mets. Not only did they rank last in the league in steals, but Brett Butler, with 14, owned nearly half of their 29. And through the All-Star break, no NL team had allowed more unearned runs.

▶**July 26:** The Mets came charging out of the All-Star break with a 7-3 record, mostly on the road. They assembled their first four-game winning streak of the season and took four of six from Colorado. Bill Pulsipher and Jason Isringhausen energized the pitching staff, the bullpen cleaned up its act, Brett Butler came within one hit of tying the major-league record of 16 hits over a four-game span as he had a 15-for-20 tear that included three four-hit games in a row. But the biggest laurels belonged to Bonilla, who raised his average to .330, hit his 16th homer, and notched his 51st RBI.

▶**Aug. 2:** Bobby Bonilla was traded to Baltimore.

▶**Aug. 16:** The Mets won 16 of their first 30 games after the All-Star break, a marked improvement over their first-half performance.

▶**Aug. 30:** Suddenly, the Mets could hardly lose. On Aug. 18-20, they took three in a row from the Dodgers. A week later, they entered their Aug. 27 game against San Diego with a chance to complete a four-game sweep. In between, the Mets lost two of three to the Giants but in one of them an umpire's call took away what appeared to have been a game-tying home run by Chris Jones. They were so hot that they even gave up a ninth-inning grand slam on Aug. 26—

and still won the game. At one point, they had won nine of 11 and 15 of 20. With such spoiler potential, the Mets began their longest trip of the year, a 13-game excursion taking them to the West Coast and then to Montreal—a team they could suddenly dream of catching for third place.

Team directory

▶**Owners:** Fred Wilpon (president and CEO) and Nelson Doubleday (chairman of the board)

▶**President of baseball operations:** Joseph McIlvaine

▶**Ballpark:**
William A. Shea Municipal Stadium
126th Street and Roosevelt Avenue
Flushing, N.Y.
718-507-METS
Capacity 55,777
Parking for 6,000 cars; $5
Public transportation available
Family and wheelchair sections, ramps, elevators

▶**Team publications:**
Inside Pitch, yearbook, scorecard, press guide
919-688-0218

▶**TV, radio broadcast stations:**
WFAN 660 AM, WWOR Channel 9, SportsChannel

▶**Camps and/or clinics:**
Baseball Heaven, 800-898-METS

▶**Spring training:**
Thomas J. White Stadium
Port St. Lucie, Fla.
Capacity 7,347
407-871-2100

NEW YORK METS 1995 final stats

BATTERS	BA	SLG	OB	G	AB	R	H	TB	2B	3B	HR	RBI	BB	SO	SB	CS	E
Fordyce	.500	1.000	.667	4	2	1	1	2	1	0	0	0	1	0	0	0	0
Bonilla	.325	.599	.385	80	317	49	103	190	25	4	18	53	31	48	0	3	14
Ochoa	.297	.324	.333	11	37	7	11	12	1	0	0	0	2	10	1	0	0
Bogar	.290	.359	.329	78	145	17	42	52	7	0	1	21	9	25	1	0	6
Brogna	.289	.485	.342	134	495	72	143	240	27	2	22	76	39	111	0	0	3
Vizcaino	.287	.365	.332	135	509	66	146	186	21	5	3	56	35	76	8	3	10
Orsulak	.283	.372	.323	108	290	41	82	108	19	2	1	37	19	35	1	3	4
C. Jones	.280	.467	.327	79	182	33	51	85	6	2	8	31	13	45	2	1	2
Hundley	.280	.484	.382	90	275	39	77	133	11	0	15	51	42	64	1	0	7
Alfonzo	.278	.382	.301	101	335	26	93	128	13	5	4	41	12	37	1	1	7
Kent	.278	.464	.327	125	472	65	131	219	22	3	20	65	29	89	3	3	10
Everett	.260	.436	.352	79	289	48	75	126	13	1	12	54	39	67	2	5	3
Thompson	.251	.378	.306	75	267	39	67	101	13	0	7	31	19	77	3	1	3
Ledesma	.242	.242	.359	21	33	4	8	8	0	0	0	3	6	7	0	0	2
Buford	.235	.360	.346	44	136	24	32	49	5	0	4	12	19	28	7	7	2
Stinnett	.219	.332	.338	77	196	23	43	65	8	1	4	18	29	65	2	0	7
Spiers	.208	.264	.314	63	72	5	15	19	2	1	0	11	12	15	0	1	7
Huskey	.189	.300	.267	28	90	8	17	27	1	0	3	11	10	16	1	0	6
Otero	.137	.176	.185	35	51	5	7	9	2	0	0	1	3	10	2	1	0
Barry	.133	.200	.188	15	15	2	2	3	1	0	0	0	1	8	0	0	0
Castillo	.103	.103	.212	13	29	2	3	3	0	0	0	0	3	9	1	0	2

PITCHERS	W-L	ERA	G	GS	CG	GF	Sho	SV	IP	H	R	ER	HR	BB	SO
Person	1-0	0.75	3	1	0	0	0	0	12	5	1	1	1	2	10
Florence	3-0	1.50	14	0	0	3	0	0	12	17	3	2	0	6	5
Birkbeck	0-1	1.63	4	4	0	0	0	0	27.2	22	5	5	2	2	14
Byrd	2-0	2.05	17	0	0	6	0	0	22	18	6	5	1	7	26
Franco	5-3	2.44	48	0	0	41	0	29	51.2	48	17	14	4	17	41
Isringhausen	9-2	2.81	14	14	1	0	0	0	93	88	29	29	6	31	55
Henry	3-6	2.96	51	0	0	20	0	4	67	48	23	22	7	25	62
Minor	4-2	3.66	35	0	0	10	0	1	46.2	44	21	19	6	13	43
Harnisch	2-8	3.68	18	18	0	0	0	0	110	111	55	45	13	24	82
Gunderson	1-1	3.70	30	0	0	7	0	0	24.1	25	10	10	2	8	19
DiPoto	4-6	3.78	58	0	0	26	0	2	78.2	77	41	33	2	29	49
Pulsipher	5-7	3.98	17	17	2	0	0	0	126.2	122	58	56	11	45	81
B. Jones	10-10	4.19	30	30	3	0	1	0	195.2	209	107	91	20	53	127
Mlicki	9-7	4.26	29	25	0	1	0	0	160.2	160	82	76	23	54	123
Walker	1-0	4.58	13	0	0	10	0	0	17.2	24	9	9	3	5	5
Cornelius	3-7	5.54	18	10	0	1	0	0	66.2	75	44	41	11	30	39
Telgheder	1-2	5.61	7	4	0	2	0	0	25.2	34	18	16	4	7	16
Lomon	0-1	6.75	6	0	0	1	0	0	9.1	17	8	7	0	5	6
Manzanillo	1-2	7.88	12	0	0	4	0	0	16	18	15	14	3	6	14
Jacome	0-4	10.29	5	5	0	0	0	0	21	33	24	24	3	15	11

1996 preliminary roster

PITCHERS (21)
Juan Acevedo
Paul Byrd
John Carter
Reid Cornelius
Jerry DiPoto
Brian Edmondson
John Franco
Pete Harnisch
Doug Henry
Jason Isringhausen
Bobby Jones
Eric Ludwick
Blas Minor
Dave Mlicki
Chris Nabholz
Robert Person

Bill Pulsipher
Hector Ramirez
Bryan Rodgers
Pete Walker
Derek Wallace

CATCHERS (4)
Alberto Castillo
Charlie Green
Todd Hundley
Kelly Stinnett

INFIELDERS (7)
Edgardo Alfonzo
Tim Bogar
Rico Brogna
Butch Huskey

Jeff Kent
Aaron Ledesma
Jose Vizcaino

OUTFIELDERS (5)
Damon Buford
Carl Everett
Chris Jones
Alex Ochoa
Ryan Thompson

Games played by position

PLAYER	G	C	1B	2B	3B	SS	OF
Alfonzo	101	0	0	29	58	6	0
Barry	15	0	0	0	0	0	2
Bogar	78	0	10	7	25	27	1
Bonilla	80	0	10	0	46	0	31
Brogna	134	0	131	0	0	0	0
Buford	44	0	0	0	0	0	39
Castillo	13	12	0	0	0	0	0
Everett	79	0	0	0	0	0	77
Fordyce	4	0	0	0	0	0	0
Hundley	90	89	0	0	0	0	0
Huskey	28	0	0	0	27	0	1
C. Jones	79	0	5	0	0	0	52
Kent	125	0	0	122	0	0	0
Ledesma	21	0	2	0	10	2	0
Ochoa	11	0	0	0	0	0	10
Orsulak	108	0	1	0	0	0	86
Otero	35	0	0	0	0	0	23
Spiers	63	0	0	6	11	0	0
Stinnett	77	67	0	0	0	0	0
Thompson	75	0	0	0	0	0	74
Vizcaino	135	0	0	1	0	134	0

Minor Leagues

Tops in the organization

Batter	Club	Avg.	G	AB	R	H	HR	RBI
Omar Garcia	Bng	.318	120	449	59	143	3	65
Fletcher Bates	Bng	.317	77	284	53	90	6	37
Jay Payton	Nor	.307	135	553	92	170	18	84
Tom Arvelo	Ptf	.295	75	295	45	87	0	17
Bob Daly	Bng	.290	77	307	44	89	3	60

Home Runs			Wins		
Butch Huskey	Nor	28	Eric Ludwick	Nor	13
Preston Wilson	Clb	20	Paul Wilson	Nor	11
Jay Payton	Nor	18	Sean Johnston	Clb	11
Derek Lee	Nor	18	Mark Guerra	Bng	11
Bryon Gainey	Clb	14	J. Isringhausen	Nor	11

RBI			Saves		
Butch Huskey	Nor	87	Mike Welch	Bng	15
Jay Payton	Nor	84	Joseph Lisio	Ptf	12
Chris Saunders	Bng	73	Steve Pack	Clb	12
Brian Daubach	Nor	72	Brent Knackert	Bng	11
Randy Warner	Slu	70	Bryan Rogers	Nor	10

Stolen Bases			Strikeouts		
Julio Zorrilla	Clb	42	Paul Wilson	Nor	194
Yudith Ozario	Clb	40	Jesus Sanchez	Clb	177
Sandy Pichardo	Slu	29	Eric Ludwick	Nor	140
Carlos Mendoza	Kpt	28	Erik Hiljus	Bng	138
Jay Payton	Nor	27	Toby Larson	Slu	135

Pitcher	Club	W-L	ERA	IP	H	BB	SO
J. Isringhausen	Nor	11-2	1.97	128	90	36	134
Dave Telgheder	Nor	5-4	2.24	92	77	8	75
Paul Wilson	Nor	11-6	2.41	187	148	44	194
Toby Larson	Slu	9-10	2.55	173	165	49	135
Andy Trumpour	Ptf	7-6	2.57	105	95	32	75

Sick call: 1995 DL Report

Player	Days on the DL
Edgardo Alfonzo	20
Pete Harnisch	61
Todd Hundley	71
Jeff Kent	15
Blas Minor	31
Kevin Northrup	160
Bill Spiers	41*
Ryan Thompson	66*

Indicates two separate terms on Disabled List.

1995 Amateur draft picks

Players are listed with position and college or high school. Most players were assigned to rookie or Class A leagues. List provided by Major League Baseball.

Christopher Adolph, of, Clovis West HS, Fresno, Calif.; Jacob Bailey, rhp, Hutchinson CC; Preston Ballew, lhp, Carlsbad (N.M.) HS; Brandon Black, rf, Pensacola JC; Michael Blang, rhp, Southern Illinois; Kevin Bowers, c, Pineview HS, St. George, Utah; Corey Brittan, rhp, Hutchinson CC; Allan Burnett, rhp, Central Arkansas Christian, Little Rock, Ark.; Jerrell Carver, 1b, Northeastern HS, Elizabeth City, N.C.; Luis Castillo, c, American HS, Miami Lakes, Fla.; Chadwick Cooper, rhp, Potomac State JC; Brandon Copeland, of, Washburn Rural HS, Topeka, Kan.; Quinn Cravens, of, Valley Center (Kan.) HS; Todd Cutchins, lhp, Tallahassee CC; Derek Daugherty, of, Kingfisher (Okla.) HS; Christopher Dewitt, rhp, St. Andrews Presbyterian, Ozark, Mo.; Darren Dyt, of, Porterville JC; Mark Enloe, lhp, Tarkington HS, Cleveland, Texas; Corey Erickson, ss, Lanphier HS, Springfield, Ill.; Hector Esparza, 3b, San Jose CC; Matthew Ferullo, rhp, Michigan; Nelson Figueroa, rhp, Brandeis; Sean Gill, of, Wright State; Lindsay Gulin, lhp, Issaquah (Wash.) HS; Jacob Handy, rhp, Arvin HS, Bakersfield, Calif.; Shawn Hannah, rhp, Clovis (Calif.) HS; Brett Herbison, rhp, Central HS, Elgin, Ill.; Benjaman Hickman, rhp, Bryant (Ark.) HS; Jeffrey Howatt, rhp, UCLA; Ryan Jaroncyk, ss, Orange Glen HS, Valley Center, Calif.; Anthony Johnson, cf-c, Oakland HS, Clinton Johnston, 1b, John Carroll HS, Vero Beach, Fla.; Donald Loland, rhp, Ascension Catholic HS, Donaldsonville, La.; Richard Martinez, c, St. Mary's, Texas; John Mattson, rhp, South Kitsap HS, Port Orchard, Wash.; Eric McQueen, c, North Cobb HS, Alworth, Ga.; Tydus Meadows, cf, Evans HS, Evans, Ga.; Ryan Minor, 3b-rhp, Oklahoma; Damon Minor, 1b, Oklahoma; Stephen Minus, rhp-c, Judson HS, San Antonio; Tylor More, of, East HS, Cheyenne, Wyo.; Tony Moreno, c, Riverside HS, El Paso, Texas; Ryan Morrison, of, Onondaga CC; Daniel Murray, rhp, San Diego State; Philip Olson, rhp, Florida State; Jeffrey Parsons, ss, Arkansas; Casey Patterson, rhp, Fresno CC; Cory Patton, of, Olney Central College; Robert Piercy, c, Crest HS, Shelby, N.C.; Mark Pileski, ss, Massachusetts; Scott Proctor, rhp, Martin County HS, Jensen Beach, Fla.; Joseph Pyrtle, rhp, North Carolina; Christopher Reinike, rhp, Long Beach (Miss.) HS; Grant Roberts, rhp, Grossmont HS, El Cajon, Calif.; Jaime Rodgers, rhp, Friendship Christian HS, Mount Juliet, Tenn.; Aaron Rowand, ss, Glendora (Calif.) HS; Lee Stephens, 1b, Florida HS, Tallahassee, Fla.; Timothy Tessmar, lhp, Eastern Michigan; Erick Torres, rhp, Segundo Ruiz Belvi HS, Mayaguez P.R.; Clifton Wren, c, Petal (Miss.) HS; Paul Yoder, of, Alvernia; Randel Young, of, Wichita State; Andrew Zwirchitz, rhp-ss, Okaloosa Walton CC.

New York (1962-1995)

Runs: Most, career, all-time

662	DARRYL STRAWBERRY, 1983-1990	
627	HOWARD JOHNSON, 1985-1993	
592	Mookie Wilson, 1980-1989	
563	Cleon Jones, 1963-1975	
536	Ed Kranepool, 1962-1979	

Hits: Most, career, all-time

1418	Ed Kranepool, 1962-1979
1188	Cleon Jones, 1963-1975
1112	Mookie Wilson, 1980-1989
1029	Bud Harrelson, 1965-1977
1025	DARRYL STRAWBERRY, 1983-1990

2B: Most, career, all-time

225	Ed Kranepool, 1962-1979
214	HOWARD JOHNSON, 1985-1993
187	DARRYL STRAWBERRY, 1983-1990
182	Cleon Jones, 1963-1975
170	Mookie Wilson, 1980-1989

3B: Most, career, all-time

62	Mookie Wilson, 1980-1989
45	Bud Harrelson, 1965-1977
33	Cleon Jones, 1963-1975
31	Steve Henderson, 1977-1980
30	DARRYL STRAWBERRY, 1983-1990

HR: Most, career, all-time

252	DARRYL STRAWBERRY, 1983-1990
192	HOWARD JOHNSON, 1985-1993
154	Dave Kingman, 1975-1983
122	Kevin McReynolds, 1987-1994
118	Ed Kranepool, 1962-1979

RBI: Most, career, all-time

733	DARRYL STRAWBERRY, 1983-1990
629	HOWARD JOHNSON, 1985-1993
614	Ed Kranepool, 1962-1979
521	Cleon Jones, 1963-1975
468	Keith Hernandez, 1983-1989

SB: Most, career, all-time

281	Mookie Wilson, 1980-1989
202	HOWARD JOHNSON, 1985-1993
191	DARRYL STRAWBERRY, 1983-1990
152	Lee Mazzilli, 1976-1989
116	LENNY DYKSTRA, 1985-1989

BB: Most, career, all-time

580	DARRYL STRAWBERRY, 1983-1990
573	Bud Harrelson, 1965-1977
556	HOWARD JOHNSON, 1985-1993
482	Wayne Garrett, 1969-1976
471	Keith Hernandez, 1983-1989

BA: Highest, career, all-time

.297	Keith Hernandez, 1983-1989
.292	DAVE MAGADAN, 1986-1992
.283	Wally Backman, 1980-1988
.281	Cleon Jones, 1963-1975
.278	LENNY DYKSTRA, 1985-1989

Slug avg: Highest, career, all-time

.520	DARRYL STRAWBERRY, 1983-1990
.460	Kevin McReynolds, 1987-1994
.459	HOWARD JOHNSON, 1985-1993
.453	Dave Kingman, 1975-1983
.429	Keith Hernandez, 1983-1989

Games started: Most, career, all-time

395	Tom Seaver, 1967-1983
346	Jerry Koosman, 1967-1978
303	DWIGHT GOODEN, 1984-1994
250	SID FERNANDEZ, 1984-1993
241	RON DARLING, 1983-1991

Saves: Most, career, all-time

147	JOHN FRANCO, 1990-1995
107	JESSE OROSCO, 1979-1987
86	Tug McGraw, 1965-1974
84	ROGER McDOWELL, 1985-1989
69	Neil Allen, 1979-1983

Shutouts: Most, career, all-time

44	Tom Seaver, 1967-1983
26	Jerry Koosman, 1967-1978
26	Jon Matlack, 1971-1977
23	DWIGHT GOODEN, 1984-1994
15	DAVID CONE, 1987-1992

Wins: Most, career, all-time

198	Tom Seaver, 1967-1983
157	DWIGHT GOODEN, 1984-1994
140	Jerry Koosman, 1967-1978
99	RON DARLING, 1983-1991
98	SID FERNANDEZ, 1984-1993

K: Most, career, all-time

2541	Tom Seaver, 1967-1983
1875	DWIGHT GOODEN, 1984-1994
1799	Jerry Koosman, 1967-1978
1449	SID FERNANDEZ, 1984-1993
1159	DAVID CONE, 1987-1992

Win pct: Highest, career, all-time

.649	DWIGHT GOODEN, 1984-1994
.625	DAVID CONE, 1987-1992
.615	Tom Seaver, 1967-1983
.586	RON DARLING, 1983-1991
.560	Bob Ojeda, 1986-1990

ERA: Lowest, career, all-time

2.57	Tom Seaver, 1967-1983
3.03	Jon Matlack, 1971-1977
3.08	DAVID CONE, 1987-1992
3.09	Jerry Koosman, 1967-1978
3.10	DWIGHT GOODEN, 1984-1994

Runs: Most, season

108	HOWARD JOHNSON, 1991
108	DARRYL STRAWBERRY, 1987
107	Tommie Agee, 1970
104	HOWARD JOHNSON, 1989
101	DARRYL STRAWBERRY, 1988

Hits: Most, season

191	Felix Millan, 1975
185	Felix Millan, 1973
183	Keith Hernandez, 1985
182	Tommie Agee, 1970
181	Lee Mazzilli, 1979

2B: Most, season

41	HOWARD JOHNSON, 1989
40	GREGG JEFFERIES, 1990
37	LENNY DYKSTRA, 1987
37	HOWARD JOHNSON, 1990
37	Felix Millan, 1975
37	EDDIE MURRAY, 1992
37	Joel Youngblood, 1979

3B: Most, season

10	Mookie Wilson, 1984
9	Steve Henderson, 1978
9	Charlie Neal, 1962
9	Frank Taveras, 1979
9	Mookie Wilson, 1982

HR: Most, season

39	DARRYL STRAWBERRY, 1987
39	DARRYL STRAWBERRY, 1988
38	HOWARD JOHNSON, 1991
37	Dave Kingman, 1976
37	Dave Kingman, 1982
37	DARRYL STRAWBERRY, 1990

RBI: Most, season

117	HOWARD JOHNSON, 1991
108	DARRYL STRAWBERRY, 1990
105	Gary Carter, 1986
105	Rusty Staub, 1975
104	DARRYL STRAWBERRY, 1987

SB: Most, season

58	Mookie Wilson, 1982
54	Mookie Wilson, 1983
46	Mookie Wilson, 1984
42	Frank Taveras, 1979
41	HOWARD JOHNSON, 1989
41	Lee Mazzilli, 1980

BB: Most, season

97	Keith Hernandez, 1984
97	DARRYL STRAWBERRY, 1987
95	Bud Harrelson, 1970
94	Keith Hernandez, 1986
93	Lee Mazzilli, 1979

BA: Highest, season

.340	Cleon Jones, 1969
.328	DAVE MAGADAN, 1990
.319	Cleon Jones, 1971
.311	Keith Hernandez, 1984
.310	Keith Hernandez, 1986

Slug avg: Highest, season

.583	DARRYL STRAWBERRY, 1987
.559	HOWARD JOHNSON, 1989
.545	DARRYL STRAWBERRY, 1988
.535	HOWARD JOHNSON, 1991
.522	BOBBY BONILLA, 1993

Games started: Most, season

36	Jack Fisher, 1965
36	Tom Seaver, 1970
36	Tom Seaver, 1973
36	Tom Seaver, 1975
35	RON DARLING, 1985
35	Gary Gentry, 1969
35	DWIGHT GOODEN, 1985
35	Jerry Koosman, 1973
35	Jerry Koosman, 1974
35	Jon Matlack, 1976
35	Tom Seaver, 1968
35	Tom Seaver, 1969
35	Tom Seaver, 1971
35	Tom Seaver, 1972
35	Craig Swan, 1979
35	FRANK VIOLA, 1990
35	FRANK VIOLA, 1991

Saves: Most, season

33	JOHN FRANCO, 1990
31	JESSE OROSCO, 1984
30	JOHN FRANCO, 1991
30	JOHN FRANCO, 1994
29	JOHN FRANCO, 1995

Shutouts: Most, season

8	DWIGHT GOODEN, 1985
7	Jerry Koosman, 1968
7	Jon Matlack, 1974
6	Jerry Koosman, 1969
6	Jon Matlack, 1976

Wins: Most, season

25	Tom Seaver, 1969
24	DWIGHT GOODEN, 1985
22	Tom Seaver, 1975
21	Jerry Koosman, 1976
21	Tom Seaver, 1972

K: Most, season

289	Tom Seaver, 1971
283	Tom Seaver, 1970
276	DWIGHT GOODEN, 1984
268	DWIGHT GOODEN, 1985
251	Tom Seaver, 1973

Win pct: Highest, season

.870	DAVID CONE, 1988
.857	DWIGHT GOODEN, 1985
.783	Bob Ojeda, 1986
.781	Tom Seaver, 1969
.739	DWIGHT GOODEN, 1986

ERA: Lowest, season

1.53	DWIGHT GOODEN, 1985
1.76	Tom Seaver, 1971
2.08	Tom Seaver, 1973
2.08	Jerry Koosman, 1968
2.20	Tom Seaver, 1968

Most pinch-hit homers, season

4	Danny Heep, 1983
4	MARK CARREON, 1989

Most pinch-hit homers, career

8	MARK CARREON, 1987-1991

Most consecutive games batting safely

24	Hubie Brooks, 1984
23	Cleon Jones, 1970
23	Mike Vail, 1975

Most consecutive scoreless innings

31	Jerry Koosman, 1973

No-hit games

None

ACTIVE PLAYERS in caps.

Players' years of service are listed by the first and last years with this team and are not necessarily consecutive; all statistics record performances for this team only.

199

Philadelphia Phillies

By Eileen Blass, *USA TODAY*

Closer Heathcliff Slocumb maintained a 2.89 ERA while notching 32 saves for the Phillies.

1995 Phillies: A Jekyll-and-Hyde season

When the 1995 season finally ended for the Phillies, Jim Fregosi leaned back in his chair and sighed: "I guess the best way to sum up this year is to say that I started out managing a replacement team. And I ended up managing a replacement team."

In between, though, Fregosi and the Phillies experienced a Jekyll-and-Hyde season. On June 25, they were 37-18 and led second-place Atlanta by five games. One month later, after losing 20 of 26 games, they trailed the Braves by 8½.

By then, the epidemic of injuries that began in spring training had caught up with the team. They slipped out of wild-card contention. They didn't even achieve their final goal, to finish alone in second in the division. They lost five of their last six to end up 69-75, tied with the Mets for the runner-up spot. In the process, they used 50 different players, including 26 pitchers. Tommy Greene and Bobby Munoz, expected to be in the rotation, opened the season on the disabled list. David West had shoulder surgery after just eight starts. Curt Schilling, the staff ace, made 17 starts before his season was ended by shoulder surgery.

For the first two months, though, it didn't seem to matter. Rookie Tyler Green got off to an 8-4 start and made the All-Star team. Michael Mimbs, who had never pitched above Class AA, won six of his first seven decisions. Paul Quantrill was 7-2 late in June. It all seemed too good to be true. And it was. Green didn't win a game after June 30. Mimbs and Quantrill both faded and were moved at least temporarily to the bullpen.

The hitting was an unexpected problem. After signing free agent Gregg Jefferies to a four-year, $20 million contract, general manager Lee Thomas was convinced he had a club that would score tons of runs. But the lineup never jelled. Dave Hollins got off to a slow start, was benched and then traded on July 24 to the Red Sox. Lenny Dykstra had a sore back and then a bad knee that required season-ending surgery with two months left. Jefferies, bothered by numerous injuries and the pressure of trying to live up to the expectations generated by his big contract, got off to a slow start. Darren Daulton was batting only .249 when he injured his right knee on Aug. 25.

It wasn't just injuries that doomed the Phillies, though. The front office made some moves that raised eyebrows in the clubhouse—trading Hollins, releasing reliever Norm Charlton, letting Mariano Duncan go on a waiver trade and trading Dave Gallagher. Duncan and Gallagher were traded for minor leaguers and unproven players.

Despite all that, the Phillies took advantage of an Astros skid and actually led the wild-card standings as late as Aug. 27. After that, they headed for California, lost six of nine and dropped out of contention for good.

1996 Phillies: Preview

Late last season, Fregosi admitted he couldn't be absolutely certain about the identity of a single starting pitcher for 1996. Giles admitted that 1996 could be a "difficult" year. The best prospects are at least a year away from being ready to help at the big-league level. And the Phillies are backed into a financial corner. Dykstra, Daulton and Jefferies are guaranteed a total of $16.2 million, well over half the total payroll. And that's not counting Sid Fernandez or Mickey Morandini. The bullpen seems to be the main strength, and on that the Phillies may have to rely.

1995 Phillies: Week-by-week notes

These notes were excerpted from the following issues of Baseball Weekly.

▶**May 3:** Club president Bill Giles was thrilled with an announced crowd of 47,088 for the home opener on April 28. A day earlier Giles admitted he was worried about how quickly fans would forgive baseball for the strike. Instead, the game attracted the largest crowd for a night home opener since 1981.

▶**May 17:** In less than a week, the Phillies beat three pitchers who have won the past five National League Cy Young Awards: Greg Maddux, Tom Glavine and Doug Drabek.

▶**June 7:** The Phils lost to the Giants on June 2 and 3, marking the first time in 1995 the Phillies lost back-to-back games. It had taken 35 games for that to happen, an NL record that surpassed the 1907 Chicago Cubs, who didn't lose consecutive games until 34 games into the schedule. Dropping two to the Giants also marked the first time in 1995 the Phillies lost a series.

▶**June 14:** In the four years preceding 1995, when Lenny Dykstra was in the lineup, the Phillies were 212-180. That's a respectable .540 winning percentage. When he was out with an assortment of injuries, they were 85-123. That's .409. So when manager Jim Fregosi let it be known that Dykstra's sore lower back would land him on the disabled list, it was bad news indeed. So far in 1995, the Phillies were 4-4 when Dykstra wasn't available and 21-10 when he had played.

▶**June 21:** The Phillies announced June 18 they had acquired veteran outfielder Andy Van Slyke from the Baltimore Orioles for reliever Gene Harris. Van Slyke batted .159 in 17 games with the Orioles and had been on the disabled list twice.

▶**June 28:** The Phillies had traded for Andy Van Slyke because Lenny Dykstra and Gregg Jefferies were on the disabled list, while outfielders Dave Gallagher and Tony Longmire were playing with nagging injuries. But on June 20, in just his second game for the Phillies, Van Slyke joined the wounded when he bruised his chest sliding head-first into second. "I wanted to fit in," he said. "But this isn't what I had in mind."

▶**July 5:** On June 29, catcher Darren Daulton was ejected in the first inning by home plate umpire Ed Rapuano for questioning a balk call, even though Daulton never turned his head. Catchers usually are allowed to protest a call as long as they keep facing the pitcher. On July 1, Daulton was tossed in the fourth inning by home plate umpire Charlie Reliford after mildly disputing a called third strike. "I think an umpire's job is to control the game and keep order," Daulton said, "...and [not to] let his calls decide who wins and who loses. The best way to know an umpire has done a good job is, when the game is over, you don't even know he was there. But, in some cases, you're asking guys who want to be Prime Time not to be noticed." What can be done? "It can be as simple as keeping your ego in check," he said. "We all make mistakes. As long as you realize you've made a mistake, that's going to help."

▶**July 13:** Manager Jim Fregosi said he'll never make a prediction again. "I said in spring training that this was a team that was going to score a ton of runs," the Phillies manager said, shaking his head. Even as the Phillies got off to a 37-18 start to build a five-game lead over the Atlanta Braves, the offense wasn't clicking. And then came the skid. They lost 10 out of 12 to fall three games behind Atlanta. During that streak, the Phils hit .202 as a team. When the Phillies fell apart, it was a team effort. Lenny Dykstra, Gregg Jefferies, Dave Hollins and Darren Daulton were hitting well below what might have been expected. For some reason, though, Hollins seemed to become the lightning rod for local fan discontent. The talk radio shows, particularly, seemed to focus on Hollins as the root of all the team's offensive problems. It was variously suggested that he should be traded, dropped from the cleanup spot, or forced to stop switch-hitting and bat exclusively right-handed. Said Hollins: "If I'm [the whipping boy], there's not much I can do. I didn't appoint myself." Meanwhile, the Phillies released reliever Norm Charlton. "This is a business," he said. "It's a business for them and it's a business for me. I'll just wait for a call from somebody else and go from there."

▶**July 19:** The Phillies beat the Cardinals at Busch Stadium on June 25 and flew home with a five-game lead in the NL East. From that point through July 16, though, they lost 14 of 17 and fell six behind the Braves. During the streak they scored more than four runs just twice.

▶**Aug. 30:** The Phillies had pulled to within a half-game of the lead in the wild-card race when Darren Daulton hurt his knee rounding second on Aug. 25. Daulton is the Phillies' acknowledged team leader, both on and off the field. "Believe it our not, we will continue to show up," Jim Fregosi said. "Whoever is available to play will play, and we'll do the best that we can."

▶**Sept. 6:** The Phillies continued to be mystified by the abrupt turn rookie Tyler Green's fortunes were taking. After he beat the Braves at the end of June, he was named to the All-Star team, but by Sept. 2, he had gone 11 starts in a row without a win. In those gams he was 0-4 with an 8.58 ERA, giving up 73 hits and 25 walks in 50⅓ innings. The Phillies lost five of the seven games in which he did not get a decision. "He just hasn't pitched very well," said Jim Fregosi. No kidding. Another rookie righty, Mike Grace, joined the Phillies' youthfest to pitch against the Padres on Sept. 1. He was the 12th starting pitcher the club had used in 1995. He was knocked out after 4⅓ innings but made a good impression

on Fregosi: "I liked the way he went after the hitters."

▶**Sept. 13:** One day after the National League announced that Sid Fernandez had been named Pitcher of the Month for August, the Phillies discovered their prime lefty had a sore shoulder and wouldn't be able to make his next start. Then, true to the Phils' 1995 run of luck, it turned out Fernandez would need an MRI exam and might be through for the season. To make matters worse for the ailing staff—which set a club record by having used 25 different pitchers through Sept. 8—Tyler Green was axed from the rotation after Fregosi determined that Green couldn't "get back what he had earlier [in the season]."

▶**Oct. 4:** Despite the shortened season, the Phillies drew more than 2 million in home attendance for the 13th time in the 25-year history of Veterans Stadium.

Team directory

▶**Owner:** Bill Giles
▶**General manager:** Lee Thomas
▶**Ballpark:**
Veterans Stadium
Broad Street & Pattison Avenue,
Philadelphia, Pa.
215-463-1000
Capacity 62,530
Parking for 10,000 cars; $5
Public transportation available
Wheelchair section and ramps, TDD ticket information for hearing impaired (215-463-2998)
▶**Team publications:**
Media guide, yearbook, scorebook
▶**TV, radio broadcast stations:**
WPHL Channel 17, WGMP 1210 AM
SportsChannel, Prism Cable
▶**Spring training:**
Jack Russell Memorial Stadium
Clearwater, Fla.
Capacity 7,195
813-441-8638

PHILADELPHIA PHILLIES 1995 final stats

BATTERS	BA	SLG	OB	G	AB	R	H	TB	2B	3B	HR	RBI	BB	SO	SB	CS	E
Longmire	.356	.510	.419	59	104	21	37	53	7	0	3	19	11	19	1	1	0
Gallagher	.318	.414	.379	62	157	12	50	65	12	0	1	12	16	20	0	0	0
Eisenreich	.316	.464	.375	129	377	46	119	175	22	2	10	55	38	44	10	0	0
Jefferies	.306	.448	.349	114	480	69	147	215	31	2	11	56	35	26	9	5	3
Marsh	.294	.422	.316	43	109	13	32	46	3	1	3	15	4	25	0	1	3
Morandini	.283	.417	.350	127	494	65	140	206	34	7	6	49	42	80	9	6	7
Hayes	.276	.406	.340	141	529	58	146	215	30	3	11	85	50	88	5	1	14
Whiten	.269	.481	.365	60	212	38	57	102	10	1	11	37	31	63	7	0	4
Webster	.267	.407	.337	49	150	18	40	61	9	0	4	14	16	27	0	0	3
Dykstra	.264	.354	.353	62	254	37	67	90	15	1	2	18	33	28	10	5	2
Lieberthal	.255	.298	.327	16	47	1	12	14	2	0	0	4	5	5	0	0	1
Varsho	.252	.282	.310	72	103	7	26	29	1	1	0	11	7	17	2	0	2
Daulton	.249	.401	.359	98	342	44	85	137	19	3	9	55	55	52	3	0	4
Van Slyke	.243	.350	.333	63	214	26	52	75	10	2	3	16	28	41	7	0	2
Schall	.231	.262	.306	24	65	2	15	17	2	0	0	5	6	16	0	0	2
Hollins	.229	.410	.393	65	205	46	47	84	12	2	7	25	53	38	1	1	7
Stocker	.218	.274	.304	125	412	42	90	113	14	3	1	32	43	75	6	1	17
Flora	.213	.333	.253	24	75	12	16	25	3	0	2	7	4	22	1	0	0
Elster	.208	.377	.302	26	53	10	11	20	4	1	1	9	7	14	0	0	1
Jordan	.185	.315	.228	24	54	6	10	17	1	0	2	6	2	9	0	0	1
Ready	.138	.138	.219	23	29	3	4	4	0	0	0	0	3	6	0	1	1
Bennett	.000	.000	.000	1	1	0	0	0	0	0	0	0	0	1	0	0	0
Sefcik	.000	.000	.000	5	4	1	0	0	0	0	0	0	0	2	0	0	0

PITCHERS	W-L	ERA	G	GS	CG	GF	Sho	SV	IP	H	R	ER	HR	BB	SO
Ricci	1-0	1.80	7	0	0	3	0	0	10	9	2	2	0	3	9
Frey	0-1	2.12	18	0	0	4	0	1	17	10	7	4	2	4	7
Bottalico	5-3	2.46	62	0	0	20	0	1	87.2	50	25	24	7	42	87
Slocumb	5-6	2.89	61	0	0	54	0	32	65.1	64	26	21	2	35	63
Grace	1-1	3.18	2	2	0	0	0	0	11.1	10	4	4	0	4	7
Williams	3-3	3.29	33	8	0	7	0	0	87.2	78	37	32	10	29	57
Fernandez	6-1	3.34	11	11	0	0	0	0	64.2	48	25	24	11	21	79
Schilling	7-5	3.57	17	17	1	0	0	0	116	96	52	46	12	26	114
R. Springer	0-0	3.71	14	0	0	3	0	0	26.2	22	11	11	5	10	32
Borland	1-3	3.77	50	0	0	18	0	6	74	81	37	31	3	37	59
West	3-2	3.79	8	8	0	0	0	0	38	34	17	16	5	19	25
Abbott	2-0	3.81	18	0	0	3	0	0	28.1	28	12	12	3	16	21
Juden	2-4	4.02	13	10	1	0	0	0	62.2	53	31	28	6	31	47
Mimbs	9-7	4.15	35	19	2	6	1	1	136.2	127	70	63	10	75	93
Harris	2-2	4.26	21	0	0	5	0	0	19	19	9	9	2	8	9
Karp	0-0	4.50	1	0	0	0	0	0	2	1	1	1	0	3	2
Quantrill	11-12	4.67	33	29	0	1	0	0	179.1	212	102	93	20	44	103
D. Springer	0-3	4.84	4	4	0	0	0	0	22.1	21	15	12	3	9	15
Green	8-9	5.31	26	25	4	0	2	0	140.2	157	86	83	15	66	85
Fletcher	1-0	5.40	10	0	0	1	0	0	13.1	15	8	8	2	9	10
Munoz	0-2	5.74	3	3	0	0	0	0	15.2	15	13	10	2	9	6
Carter	0-0	6.14	4	0	0	1	0	0	7.1	4	5	5	3	2	6
Olivares	1-4	6.91	16	6	0	4	0	0	41.2	55	34	32	5	23	22
Charlton	2-5	7.36	25	0	0	5	0	0	22	23	19	18	2	15	12
Greene	0-5	8.29	11	6	0	3	0	0	33.2	45	32	31	6	20	24
Deshaies	0-1	20.25	2	2	0	0	0	0	5.1	15	12	12	3	1	6

1996 preliminary roster

PITCHERS (22)
Willie Banks
Ron Blazier
Toby Borland
Ricky Bottalico
Carlos Crawford
Sid Fernandez
Wayne Gomes
Mike Grace
Tyler Green
Tommy Greene
Ricardo Jordan
Ryan Karp
Mike Mimbs
Larry Mitchell
Bobby Munoz
Curt Schilling
Heathcliff Slocumb
Dennis Springer
Russ Springer
B.J. Wallace
David West
Mike Williams

CATCHERS (3)
Darren Daulton
Mike Lieberthal
Lenny Webster

INFIELDERS (9)
Howard Battle
Mike Benjamin
David Doster
Gregg Jefferies
Kevin Jordan
Mickey Morandini
Gene Schall
Kevin Sefcik
Kevin Stocker

OUTFIELDERS (6)
Lenny Dykstra
Jim Eisenreich
Rick Holifield
Tony Longmire
Tom Marsh
Mark Whiten

Games played by position

PLAYER	G	C	1B	2B	3B	SS	OF
Bennett	1	0	0	0	0	0	0
Daulton	98	95	0	0	0	0	0
Dykstra	62	0	0	0	0	0	61
Eisenreich	129	0	0	0	0	0	111
Elster	26	0	4	0	2	19	0
Flora	24	0	0	0	0	0	20
Gallagher	62	0	0	0	0	0	55
Hayes	141	0	0	0	141	0	0
Hollins	65	0	61	0	0	0	0
Jefferies	114	0	59	0	0	0	55
Jordan	24	0	0	9	1	0	0
Lieberthal	16	14	0	0	0	0	0
Longmire	59	0	0	0	0	0	23
Marsh	43	0	0	0	0	0	29
Morandini	127	0	0	122	0	0	0
Ready	23	0	3	1	0	0	0
Schall	24	0	14	0	0	0	4
Sefcik	5	0	0	0	2	0	0
Stocker	125	0	0	0	0	125	0
Van Slyke	63	0	0	0	0	0	56
Varsho	72	0	0	0	0	0	25
Webster	49	43	0	0	0	0	0
Whiten	60	0	0	0	0	0	55

Minor Leagues

Tops in the organization

Batter	Club	Avg.	G	AB	R	H	HR	RBI
Wendell Magee	Rea	.338	135	524	84	177	9	67
Gene Schall	Swb	.313	92	320	52	100	12	63
Kevin Jordan	Swb	.310	106	410	61	127	5	60
Robert Butler	Swb	.300	92	327	46	98	3	35
Adam Millan	Pdt	.297	117	414	72	123	11	71

Home Runs			Wins		
Fred McNair	Rea	23	Rich Hunter	Rea	19
Dan Held	Rea	22	Mike Grace	Swb	15
David Doster	Rea	21	Ryan Nye	Clw	12
Rob Grable	Rea	19	Several tied		11
Bobby Estalella	Rea	17			

RBI			Saves		
Dan Held	Rea	85	Brian Stumpf	Pdt	28
David Doster	Rea	79	Chuck Ricci	Swb	25
Rob Grable	Rea	78	Bronson Heflin	Rea	21
Adam Millan	Pdt	71	Blake Doolan	Rea	16
Fred McNair	Rea	70	Brian Ford	Bat	10

Stolen Bases			Strikeouts		
Scott Shores	Clw	30	Matt Beech	Rea	155
Rick Holifield	Rea	26	Len Manning	Pdt	154
Larry Huff	Pdt	26	Rich Hunter	Rea	143
Jose Flores	Pdt	23	Larry Wimberly	Pdt	139
Several tied		22	Mike Grace	Swb	131

Pitcher	Club	W-L	ERA	IP	H	BB	SO
Len Manning	Pdt	10-10	2.64	160	130	58	154
Larry Wimberly	Pdt	10-3	2.67	135	99	44	139
Rich Hunter	Rea	19-2	2.73	184	155	32	143
Carlton Loewer	Rea	11-6	2.95	165	166	67	118
Bo Hamilton	Bat	8-2	3.01	105	97	30	72

Sick call: 1995 DL Report

Player	Days on the DL
Kyle Abbott	70
Toby Borland	24
Darren Daulton	37
Lenny Dykstra	86*
Tommy Greene	112**
Dave Hollins	15
Gregg Jefferies	15
Tony Longmire	56
Tom Marsh	47
Bobby Munoz	148*
Curt Schilling	75
Andy VanSlyke	26
Gary Varsho	23
David West	120*

Indicates two separate terms on Disabled List.
**Indicates three separate terms on DL.*

1995 Amateur draft picks

Players are listed with position and college or high school. Most players were assigned to rookie or Class A leagues. List provided by Major League Baseball.

Marlon Anderson, 2b, South Alabama; Martin Barnett, rhp, South Alabama; Christopher Bauer, rhp-ss, Wichita State; Jason Bell, of, Atwater (Calif.) HS; Casey Brookens, rhp, James Madison; Matthew Buckles, c, Palatka (Fla.) HS; Steven Carver, 1b-ss, Stanford; David Coggin, rhp, Upland (Calif.) HS; Jonathon Cornelius, of, California St.; Charles Cox, c, Texas-Pan American; Todd Crane, of, Georgia; Walter Dawkins, of, Southern California; Brian Dunne, lhp, Kansas Newman; Zachary Elliott, 2b-ss, California; Brian Ford, lhp, Methodist College; Robert Gaiko, rhp, Oklahoma State; Joshua Glenn, rhp, Riley HS, South Bend, Ind.; Michael Heidemann, 1b, Yavapai College; Kevin Hooker, 2b-rhp, Oregon State; Jared Janke, 1b, California; Kyle Kawabata, rhp, Washington State; Justin Kennedy, of, Bastrop (La.) HS; Jason Kershner, lhp, Saguaro HS, Scottsdale, Ariz.; Matthew Kimm, ss, Creighton; Randy Knoll, rhp, Corona (Calif.) Senior HS; Kory Kosek, rhp, Mankato (Minn.) State; Jeffrey Leaman, 3b, Indiana State; Benito Lemos, c, Royal HS, Simi Valley, Calif.; Ryan Lentz, 3b, Woodinville (Wash.) Sr HS; Clyde Livingston, c, Newberry; Rafael Lopez, c, Westminster Christian, Miami; Charles Marino, of, John F. Kennedy HS, La Palma, Calif.; Caleb Martinez, 1b-lhp, Florida Bible Christian, Hialeah, Fla.; Jaime Mendes, rhp, New Mexico State; Brian Mensink, rhp, Minnesota; Marques Meshack, rhp, Lincoln Prep HS, San Diego; Brian Miller, rhp, Marian College, of, Fond Du Lac, Wisc.; Courtney Moore, of, Shoals CC; William Noone, rhp, Wilkes; Richard O'Connor, ss, Valparaiso; Kirk Pierce, c, Long Beach State; Melvin Pizarro, lhp, Luz A. Calderon HS, Carolina, P.R.; Mark Raynor, ss, Barton College; David Robinson, of, Rio Grande; Jose Sandoval, ss, Polytechnic HS, Sun Valley, Calif.; Anthony Shumaker, lhp, Cardinal Stritch College; Christopher Snusz, c, Mercyhurst; Reginald Taylor, cf-rhp, Newberry (S.C.) HS; Scott Tebbetts, rhp, Cal. State Riverside; Jason Wallace, cf, Callaway HS, Jackson, Miss.; Timothy Walton, rhp, Oklahoma; Errick Williams, cf, Patrick Henry HS, San Diego; Bryan Williamson, rhp, Kamiakin HS, Kennewick, Wash.; Gary Yeager, rhp, Elizabethtown.

Philadelphia (1883-1995)

206

Runs: Most, career, all-time

1506	Mike Schmidt, 1972-1989
1367	Ed Delahanty, 1888-1901
1114	Richie Ashburn, 1948-1959
963	Chuck Klein, 1928-1944
924	Sam Thompson, 1889-1898

Hits: Most, career, all-time

2234	Mike Schmidt, 1972-1989
2217	Richie Ashburn, 1948-1959
2213	Ed Delahanty, 1888-1901
1812	Del Ennis, 1946-1956
1798	Larry Bowa, 1970-1981

2B: Most, career, all-time

442	Ed Delahanty, 1888-1901
408	Mike Schmidt, 1972-1989
337	Sherry Magee, 1904-1914
336	Chuck Klein, 1928-1944
310	Del Ennis, 1946-1956

3B: Most, career, all-time

157	Ed Delahanty, 1888-1901
127	Sherry Magee, 1904-1914
106	Sam Thompson, 1889-1898
97	Richie Ashburn, 1948-1959
84	Johnny Callison, 1960-1969

HR: Most, career, all-time

548	Mike Schmidt, 1972-1989
259	Del Ennis, 1946-1956
243	Chuck Klein, 1928-1944
223	Greg Luzinski, 1970-1980
217	Cy Williams, 1918-1930

RBI: Most, career, all-time

1595	Mike Schmidt, 1972-1989
1286	Ed Delahanty, 1888-1901
1124	Del Ennis, 1946-1956
983	Chuck Klein, 1928-1944
957	Sam Thompson, 1889-1898

SB: Most, career, all-time

508	Billy Hamilton, 1890-1895
411	Ed Delahanty, 1888-1901
387	Sherry Magee, 1904-1914
289	Jim Fogarty, 1884-1889
288	Larry Bowa, 1970-1981

BB: Most, career, all-time

1507	Mike Schmidt, 1972-1989
946	Richie Ashburn, 1948-1959
946	Roy Thomas, 1899-1911
693	Willie Jones, 1947-1959
643	Ed Delahanty, 1888-1901

BA: Highest, career, all-time

.361	Billy Hamilton, 1890-1895
.348	Ed Delahanty, 1888-1901
.338	Elmer Flick, 1898-1901
.333	Sam Thompson, 1889-1898
.326	Chuck Klein, 1928-1944

Slug avg: Highest, career, all-time

.553	Chuck Klein, 1928-1944
.530	Dick Allen, 1963-1976
.527	Mike Schmidt, 1972-1989
.510	Dolph Camilli, 1934-1937
.508	Ed Delahanty, 1888-1901

Games started: Most, career, all-time

499	Steve Carlton, 1972-1986
472	Robin Roberts, 1948-1961
301	Chris Short, 1959-1972
280	Pete Alexander, 1911-1930
262	Curt Simmons, 1947-1960

Saves: Most, career, all-time

103	STEVE BEDROSIAN, 1986-1989
102	MITCH WILLIAMS, 1991-1993
94	Tug McGraw, 1975-1984
90	Ron Reed, 1976-1983
65	Turk Farrell, 1956-1969

Shutouts: Most, career, all-time

61	Pete Alexander, 1911-1930
39	Steve Carlton, 1972-1986
35	Robin Roberts, 1948-1961
24	Chris Short, 1959-1972
23	Jim Bunning, 1964-1971

Wins: Most, career, all-time

241	Steve Carlton, 1972-1986
234	Robin Roberts, 1948-1961
190	Pete Alexander, 1911-1930
132	Chris Short, 1959-1972
115	Curt Simmons, 1947-1960

K: Most, career, all-time

3031	Steve Carlton, 1972-1986
1871	Robin Roberts, 1948-1961
1585	Chris Short, 1959-1972
1409	Pete Alexander, 1911-1930
1197	Jim Bunning, 1964-1971

Win pct: Highest, career, all-time

.676	Pete Alexander, 1911-1930
.642	Tom Seaton, 1912-1913
.607	Charlie Ferguson, 1884-1887
.606	Charlie Buffinton, 1887-1889
.603	Red Donahue, 1898-1901

ERA: Lowest, career, all-time

1.79	George McQuillan, 1907-1916
2.18	Pete Alexander, 1911-1930
2.48	Tully Sparks, 1897-1910
2.61	Frank Corridon, 1904-1909
2.63	Earl Moore, 1908-1913

Runs: Most, season

192	Billy Hamilton, 1894
166	Billy Hamilton, 1895
158	Chuck Klein, 1930
152	Chuck Klein, 1932
152	Lefty O'Doul, 1929

Hits: Most, season

254	Lefty O'Doul, 1929
250	Chuck Klein, 1930
238	Ed Delahanty, 1899
226	Chuck Klein, 1932
223	Chuck Klein, 1933

2B: Most, season

59	Chuck Klein, 1930
55	Ed Delahanty, 1899
50	Chuck Klein, 1932
49	Ed Delahanty, 1895
48	Dick Bartell, 1932

3B: Most, season

27	Sam Thompson, 1894
23	Nap Lajoie, 1897
21	Ed Delahanty, 1892
21	Sam Thompson, 1895
19	JUAN SAMUEL, 1984
19	George Wood, 1887

HR: Most, season

48	Mike Schmidt, 1980
45	Mike Schmidt, 1979
43	Chuck Klein, 1929
41	Cy Williams, 1923
40	Dick Allen, 1966
40	Chuck Klein, 1930
40	Mike Schmidt, 1983

RBI: Most, season

170	Chuck Klein, 1930
165	Sam Thompson, 1895
146	Ed Delahanty, 1893
145	Chuck Klein, 1929
143	Don Hurst, 1932

SB: Most, season

111	Billy Hamilton, 1891
102	Jim Fogarty, 1887
102	Billy Hamilton, 1890
99	Jim Fogarty, 1889
98	Billy Hamilton, 1894
72	JUAN SAMUEL, 1984 (7)

BB: Most, season

129	LENNY DYKSTRA, 1993
128	Mike Schmidt, 1983
126	Billy Hamilton, 1894
125	Richie Ashburn, 1954
121	Von Hayes, 1987

BA: Highest, season

.410	Ed Delahanty, 1899
.407	Ed Delahanty, 1894
.404	Billy Hamilton, 1894
.404	Ed Delahanty, 1895
.398	Lefty O'Doul, 1929

Slug avg: Highest, season

.687	Chuck Klein, 1930
.657	Chuck Klein, 1929
.654	Sam Thompson, 1895
.646	Chuck Klein, 1932
.644	Mike Schmidt, 1981

Games started: Most, season

61	John Coleman, 1883
55	Kid Gleason, 1890
50	Ed Daily, 1885
49	Gus Weyhing, 1892
47	Charlie Ferguson, 1884
45	Pete Alexander, 1916 (8)

Saves: Most, season

43	MITCH WILLIAMS, 1993
40	STEVE BEDROSIAN, 1987
32	HEATHCLIFF SLOCUMB, 1995
30	MITCH WILLIAMS, 1991
29	STEVE BEDROSIAN, 1986
29	Al Holland, 1984
29	MITCH WILLIAMS, 1992

Shutouts: Most, season

16	Pete Alexander, 1916
12	Pete Alexander, 1915
9	Pete Alexander, 1913
8	Pete Alexander, 1917
8	Steve Carlton, 1972
8	Ben Sanders, 1888

Wins: Most, season

38	Kid Gleason, 1890
33	Pete Alexander, 1916
32	Gus Weyhing, 1892
31	Pete Alexander, 1915
30	Pete Alexander, 1917
30	Charlie Ferguson, 1886

K: Most, season

310	Steve Carlton, 1972
286	Steve Carlton, 1980
286	Steve Carlton, 1982
275	Steve Carlton, 1983
268	Jim Bunning, 1965

Win pct: Highest, season

.800	TOMMY GREENE, 1993
.800	Robin Roberts, 1952
.769	Charlie Ferguson, 1886
.765	Steve Carlton, 1981
.760	Larry Christenson, 1977
.760	John Denny, 1983

ERA: Lowest, season

1.22	Pete Alexander, 1915
1.53	George McQuillan, 1908
1.55	Pete Alexander, 1916
1.83	Lew Richie, 1908
1.83	Pete Alexander, 1917

Most pinch-hit homers, season

5	Gene Freese, 1959
4	Rip Repulski, 1958
4	Del Unser, 1979

Most pinch-hit homers, career

9	Cy Williams, 1918-1930

Most consecutive games batting safely

36	Billy Hamilton, 1894
31	Ed Delahanty, 1899
26	Chuck Klein, 1930 (2 streaks)

Most consecutive scoreless innings

41	Grover Cleveland Alexander, 1911

No-hit games

Joe Borden, Phi vs Chi NA, 4-0; July 28, 1875.

Charlie Ferguson, Phi vs Pro NL, 1-0; August 29, 1885.

Red Donahue, Phi vs Bos NL, 5-0; July 8, 1898.

Chick Fraser, Phi at Chi NL, 10-0; September 18, 1903 (2nd game).

Johnny Lush, Phi at Bro NL, 6-0; May 1, 1906.

Jim Bunning, Phi at NY NL, 6-0; June 21, 1964 (1st game, perfect game).

Rick Wise, Phi at Cin NL, 4-0; June 23, 1971.

TERRY MULHOLLAND, Phi vs SF NL, 6-0; August 15, 1990.

TOMMY GREENE, Phi at Mon NL, 2-0; May 23, 1991.

Florida Marlins

By Robert Deutsch, USA TODAY

All-Star MVP Jeff Conine led the Marlins in average (.302), homers (25) and RBI (105).

1995 Marlins: Getting better all the time

It's tough to see how a team that finished 22½ games out of first place could come away feeling encouraged by its performance, but the Florida Marlins had plenty of reasons to smile after a season that saw them rebound from the worst start in the majors (9-26) to a 67-77 finish and put the third-year franchise in position for playoff contention soon.

The club has stuck to its plans for long-range success, grooming younger players and refusing to trade any of its top prospects. In 1995, that philosophy began to pay dividends. First and foremost, rookie catcher Charles Johnson led the National League by throwing out base-stealers at a 41% clip. Johnson, 24, who skipped Class AAA ball, was widely hailed as the top defensive catcher in the NL in 1995. And after batting below .150 through late June, he came around to hit .337 the rest of the season.

Several questions were also answered by the youthful infield. First baseman Greg Colbrunn showed what he can do if healthy for an entire season, batting .277 with 23 home runs and 89 RBI. Rookie second baseman Quilvio Veras led the league in stolen bases with 56 and had a .387 on-base percentage, fourth highest among NL leadoff men. And shortstop Kurt Abbott, despite 110 strikeouts and a sluggish second half, showed improved defense and exceptional power for his position, with 17 home runs and 60 RBI.

Anchoring the infield was third baseman Terry Pendleton, who came to Florida as a free agent and hit .290 with 78 RBI while providing the leadership the Marlins had sorely lacked during their first two season.

Left fielder Jeff Conine signed a long-term contract and had a career-best season, batting .302 with 25 home runs and 105 RBI and providing the Marlins with a moment to remember—a game-winning home run that made him the MVP of the All-Star Game.

Despite missing most of the season with a torn thumb ligament, right fielder Gary Sheffield posted a .324 average with 16 homers, 46 RBI and 19 stolen bases in 63 games. Projected over 162 games, that comes to 41 homers, 118 RBI and 48 steals—which is why Gary Sheffield, 27, is considered a franchise cornerstone.

The starting rotation may still need a little help, but steady John Burkett was 14-14 with a 4.30 ERA in his first season away from the San Francisco Giants, Pat Rapp (14-7, 3.44) went 11-2 after the All-Star break, and lefty Chris Hammond (9-6, 3.80) was dominant before the break, even though he had a third consecutive second-half slide.

1996 Marlins: Preview

The Marlins say they can contend in 1996. They went into the 1995 off-season hoping to fill their two main weaknesses by adding a standout center fielder and one or two starting pitchers. Florida players and management believe that those moves, plus a healthy Gary Sheffield, would make the club a force to be reckoned with in 1996. General manager Dave Dombrowski doesn't claim they'll beat the Braves, but a wild-card spot is in his sights.

If closer Bryan Harvey, who underwent Tommy John surgery, is re-signed, he'll likely serve as a setup man for hard-throwing Robb Nen. With or without Harvey, the bullpen should be solid with Terry Mathews, Randy Veres and youngsters such as Jay Powell, Matt Mantei, Kurt Miller and Aaron Small.

For the first time, the Marlins can also turn to their minor league system for depth, especially in the middle infield. Shortstop Edgar Renteria and second baseman Ralph Milliard will be in Charlotte and could fill in if needed.

1995 Marlins: Week-by-week notes

These notes were excerpted from the following issues of Baseball Weekly.

▶**May 3:** Bryan Harvey hurt his elbow again on April 28, 10 pitches into his 1995 regular-season debut, and was out for the year, slated for Tommy John surgery.

▶**May 10:** Quilvio Veras became the third Marlin to hit a grand slam for his first major league home run. Jeff Conine and Chuck Carr did it in 1993.

▶**May 17:** The Marlins couldn't win a game in a bet, but Gary Sheffield was leading the league in stolen bases (10), averaging better than a walk a game (18 in 17 games) and leading the team in on-base percentage (.506). He had a 14-game hitting streak and had been on base 41 times in 17 games.

▶**May 24:** Off to the worst start in their brief history, the Marlins showed the strain during a week in which Terry Pendleton was suspended for four games, Andre Dawson accused an umpire of showing him no respect, Gary Sheffield flung his helmet in disgust and manager Rene Lachemann didn't move fast enough to satisfy a crew chief.

▶**June 7:** Andre Dawson, 40, said the difficulties he has had adjusting to part-time status have him considering retirement. "You start to feel like, quite possibly, it's time," Dawson said. "I'm not at all pleased with my performance. You can go as far as saying it's embarrassing, from my standpoint. Because I know what's out on the field, and it's not me. And it has nothing to do with age." Dawson was hitting .150 in 40 at-bats.

▶**June 14:** Gary Sheffield suffered a season-ending injury on June 10. Center fielder Jesus Tavarez pulled his left hamstring about 15 minutes after Sheffield's injury. He, too, was placed on the DL, though he isn't expected to miss the year. The events of the night cast a pall over the clubhouse, which 24 hours earlier had been celebrating a fourth consecutive win and a return to competitiveness. Sheffield was hitting .315 when injured, with a team-high six home runs and 19 RBI.

▶**June 21:** One of the people cheering after Andre Dawson's 400th National League homer on June 16 was Rene Lachemann. "The kinds of numbers he's put up, those get you to upstate New York," Lachemann said. "I don't think I even had 400 major league at-bats." Just seven more long balls would tie Dawson with Duke Snider at 407 for 10th place in NL history.

▶**June 28:** Asked to explain the Florida Marlins' two-year struggle against left-handed pitching, Jeff Conine was stumped. "Maybe there's some astrological thing," he ventured. "We're a predominantly right-handed hitting team. We should be able to hit them. It's something that defies baseball logic." Thus far in 1995, the Marlins were 3-13 against lefties.

▶**July 5:** The Marlins set a club record for home runs in a month with 31 in June, a feat made more notable by the loss of Gary Sheffield on June 10. Jeff Conine led the way with nine, one short of Sheffield's club record of 10 for a single month, set in April 1994. In Conine's final 14 games in June, he had a slugging percentage of .870. He finished the month by going 4-for-5 with two home runs and 4 RBI against the Expos. June was the Marlins' third non-losing month in history. Terry Pendleton raised his average 79 points, from .214 to .293.

▶**July 19:** Jeff Conine became the Most Valuable Player of the 66th All-Star Game. His eighth-inning homer in his first All-Star at-bat gave the NL a 3-2 win. Meanwhile 47-year-old retired knuckleballer Charlie Hough, visiting the Marlins' clubhouse with his son Aaron, was respectfully asked to leave so the team could conduct a private pregame meeting. "I've been kicked out of better places than this," cracked Hough.

Aug. 16: The red-hot Marlins won 13 of 15. They got strong starting pitching. They got the bounces, including Kurt Abbott's second inside-the-park home run in four days. And they got a big contribution from a player who hasn't made much of one all year, Bob Natal, who hit a homer and a two-run double. "When you are hot, all kinds of things fall into place," said manager Rene Lachemann, whose team was nine games back of Houston in the NL wild-card race. "There is no explanation for it."

Aug. 23: The youthful Marlins broke a 10-game losing streak with the help of Andre Dawson and Alejandro Pena, whose combined age is close to 80. Dawson, 41, hit two homers, including a first-inning grand slam, to supply the offense. And Pena, 36, came in to throttle the Braves when they were beginning to close the gap in the late innings. The grand slam was the seventh in Dawson's career.

Aug. 30: Blistered and beaten, the Marlins came home to Joe Robbie Stadium on Aug. 25 and began winning again. Three quick wins against the Astros gave the Marlins 13 consecutive victories at home and helped soothe the wounds of a road trip to Atlanta, Pittsburgh and Chicago in which Florida went 2-9. The Marlins hadn't lost at Joe Robbie since July 26.

Oct. 4: John Burkett cautioned people not to label any pitcher as the ace of the Florida staff until the season closed. But with three games left, he finally gave in after watching Pat Rapp throw seven more scoreless innings on Sept. 27 in a 9-3 win against the Expos. "Go ahead," said Burkett, who signed a two-year, $6.9 million contract to be the Marlins' ace this spring. "Pat Rapp deserves it." Rapp ended the season 14-7. He allowed just eight hits in his last 23⅔ innings. His 14th win tied him with Burkett for the most wins in a season by a Marlins pitcher. His ninth consecutive win also is a new team record, eclipsing the mark set by Chris Hammond in 1993. In addition, his 24⅔ consecutive scoreless innings is a team record, passing the mark set by Hammond last year. It was also the best

streak in the NL in 1995. Only Greg Maddux of Atlanta had as many wins as Rapp (11) in the second half of the season.

Last-day recap: *Heroes*—The Marlins found a legitimate No. 1 starter this year in 28-year-old right-hander Pat Rapp. He compiled a 3.44 ERA while going 14-7. Jeff Conine had another superlative season. He hit .302 with 25 home runs and 105 RBI. The home run and RBI totals were career highs. And the only thing standing between Gary Sheffield and another monster season was his old bugaboo—injuries. He was back on Sept. 1 from a torn ligament in his right thumb. In only 59 games, he hit 16 home runs and knocked in 46 runs, while batting .324.

***Unsung Hero*—**First baseman Greg Colbrunn quietly put together a banner season that hinted that the 26-year-old former Expo might be on the brink of stardom. Colbrunn hit 23 homers and had 89 RBI—both second on the club to Conine—while hitting a solid .277.

Team directory

Owner: Wayne Huizenga
General manager:
David Dombrowski
Ballpark:
Joe Robbie Stadium
2267 N.W. 199th St., Miami, Fla.
305-626-7400
Capacity 46,238
Parking 14,970 cars ; $5
Public transportation available
Wheelchair section, family section, alcohol-free section, ramps and elevators
TV, radio broadcast stations:
WQAM 560 AM (English), WCMQ 1210 AM (Spanish), WBFS Channel 33, Sunshine Network
Spring Training:
Space Coast Stadium
Melbourne, Fla.
Capacity 7,200
407-633-9200

FLORIDA MARLINS 1995 final stats

BATTERS	BA	SLG	OB	G	AB	R	H	TB	2B	3B	HR	RBI	BB	SO	SB	CS	E
Sheffield	.324	.587	.467	63	213	46	69	125	8	0	16	46	55	45	19	4	7
Conine	.302	.520	.379	133	483	72	146	251	26	2	25	105	66	94	2	0	6
Pendleton	.290	.439	.339	133	513	70	149	225	32	1	14	78	38	84	1	2	18
Tavarez	.289	.374	.346	63	190	31	55	71	6	2	2	13	16	27	7	5	0
Morman	.278	.458	.316	34	72	9	20	33	2	1	3	7	3	12	0	0	1
Colbrunn	.277	.453	.311	138	528	70	146	239	22	1	23	89	22	69	11	3	5
Arias	.269	.370	.337	94	216	22	58	80	9	2	3	26	22	20	1	0	9
Veras	.261	.373	.384	124	440	86	115	164	20	7	5	32	80	68	56	21	9
Dawson	.257	.434	.305	79	226	30	58	98	10	3	8	37	9	45	0	0	8
Browne	.255	.293	.346	77	184	21	47	54	4	0	1	17	25	20	1	1	3
Abbott	.255	.452	.318	120	420	60	107	190	18	7	17	60	36	110	4	3	19
Johnson	.251	.410	.351	97	315	40	79	129	15	1	11	39	46	71	0	2	6
Gregg	.237	.385	.313	72	156	20	37	60	5	0	6	20	16	33	3	1	1
Natal	.233	.465	.244	16	43	2	10	20	2	1	2	6	1	9	0	0	1
Diaz	.230	.299	.239	49	87	5	20	26	3	0	1	6	1	12	0	0	2
Carr	.227	.312	.330	105	308	54	70	96	20	0	2	20	46	49	25	11	3
Decker	.226	.323	.318	51	133	12	30	43	2	1	3	13	19	22	1	0	5
Zosky	.200	.200	.200	6	5	0	1	1	0	0	0	0	0	0	0	0	1
Whitmore	.190	.276	.250	27	58	6	11	16	2	0	1	2	5	15	0	0	1

PITCHERS	W-L	ERA	G	GS	CG	GF	Sho	SV	IP	H	R	ER	HR	BB	SO
Myers	0-0	0.00	2	0	0	2	0	0	2	1	0	0	0	3	0
Powell	0-0	1.08	9	0	0	1	0	0	8.1	7	2	1	0	6	4
Small	1-0	1.42	7	0	0	1	0	0	6.1	7	2	1	1	6	5
Nen	0-7	3.29	62	0	0	54	0	23	65.2	62	26	24	6	23	68
Mathews	4-4	3.38	57	0	0	14	0	3	82.2	70	32	31	9	27	72
Rapp	14-7	3.44	28	28	3	0	2	0	167.1	158	72	64	10	76	102
Lewis	0-1	3.75	21	1	0	6	0	0	36	30	15	15	9	15	32
Bowen	2-0	3.78	4	3	0	0	0	0	16.2	23	11	7	3	12	15
Hammond	9-6	3.80	25	24	3	0	2	0	161	157	73	68	17	47	126
Johnstone	0-0	3.86	4	0	0	0	0	0	4.2	7	2	2	1	2	3
Veres	4-4	3.88	47	0	0	15	0	1	48.2	46	25	21	6	22	31
Witt	2-7	3.90	19	19	1	0	0	0	110.2	104	52	48	8	47	95
Burkett	14-14	4.30	30	30	4	0	0	0	188.1	208	95	90	22	57	126
Garces	0-2	4.44	18	0	0	7	0	0	24.1	25	15	12	1	11	22
Gardner	5-5	4.49	39	11	1	7	1	1	102.1	109	60	51	14	43	87
Mantei	0-1	4.73	12	0	0	3	0	0	13.1	12	8	7	1	13	15
Perez	2-6	5.21	69	0	0	11	0	1	46.2	35	29	27	6	28	47
Banks	2-6	5.66	25	15	0	2	0	0	90.2	106	71	57	14	58	62
Weathers	4-5	5.98	28	15	0	0	0	0	90.1	104	68	60	8	52	60
Scheid	0-0	6.10	6	0	0	1	0	0	10.1	14	7	7	1	7	10
Groom	1-2	7.20	14	0	0	5	0	0	15	26	12	12	2	6	12
Murphy	1-2	10.95	14	0	0	1	0	0	12.1	14	16	15	3	8	7
Dunbar	0-1	11.57	8	0	0	1	0	0	7	12	9	9	0	11	5
Hernandez	0-0	11.57	7	0	0	3	0	0	7	12	9	9	2	3	5
Valdes	0-0	14.14	3	3	0	0	0	0	7	17	13	11	1	9	2
Harvey	0-0	∞	1	0	0	0	0	0	0	2	3	3	1	1	0

1996 preliminary roster

PITCHERS (26)
Joel Adamson
Antonio Alfonseca
Miguel Batista
Ryan Bowen
John Burkett
Victor Darensbourg
Chris Hammond
Wilson Heredia
Bill Hurst
John Johnstone
Jarod Juelsgaard
Andy Larkin
Matt Mantei

Terry Mathews
Kurt Miller
Robb Nen
Yorkis Perez
Jay Powell
Pat Rapp
Chris Seelbach
Aaron Small
Marc Valdes
Randy Veres
Bryan Ward
David Weathers
Matt Whisenant

CATCHERS (2)
Charles Johnson
Bob Natal

INFIELDERS (6)
Kurt Abbott
Alex Arias
Greg Colbrunn
Terry Pendleton
Edgar Renteria
Quilvio Veras

OUTFIELDERS (6)
Jeff Conine

Billy McMillon
Joe Orsulak
Gary Sheffield
Jesus Tavarez
Devon White

Games played by position

PLAYER	G	C	1B	2B	3B	SS	OF
Abbott	120	0	0	0	0	115	0
Arias	94	0	0	6	21	36	0
Browne	77	0	0	27	7	0	29
Carr	105	0	0	0	0	0	103
Colbrunn	138	0	134	0	0	0	0
Conine	133	0	14	0	0	0	118
Dawson	79	0	0	0	0	0	59
Decker	51	46	2	0	0	0	0
Diaz	49	0	0	9	3	5	0
Gregg	72	0	2	0	0	0	38
Johnson	97	97	0	0	0	0	0
Morman	34	0	3	0	0	0	18
Natal	16	13	0	0	0	0	0
Pendleton	133	0	0	0	129	0	0
Sheffield	63	0	0	0	0	0	61
Tavarez	63	0	0	0	0	0	61
Veras	124	0	0	122	0	0	2
Whitmore	27	0	0	0	0	0	16
Zosky	6	0	0	1	0	4	0

Minor Leagues

Tops in the organization

Batter	Club	Avg.	G	AB	R	H	HR	RBI
Luis Castillo	Knc	.326	89	340	71	111	0	23
Billy McMillon	Prt	.313	141	518	92	162	14	93
Rob Katzaroff	Prt	.304	116	441	87	134	10	49
David Berg	Bre	.298	114	382	71	114	3	39
John Roskos	Knc	.297	114	418	74	124	12	88

Home Runs			Wins		
Todd Dunwoody	Knc	14	Bryan Ward	Bre	12
Billy McMillon	Prt	14	Clemente Nunez	Bre	12
Kevin Millar	Bre	13	Michael Parisi	Knc	11
John Roskos	Knc	12	Greg Press	Knc	10
Chris Sheff	Prt	12	Matt Whisenant	Prt	10

RBI			Saves		
Billy McMillon	Prt	93	Jay Powell	Prt	24
Chris Sheff	Prt	91	Todd Bussa	Knc	14
Todd Dunwoody	Knc	89	William Hurst	Bre	12
Tim Clark	Prt	88	Aaron Small	Chr	10
John Roskos	Knc	88	Nigel Alejo	Knc	7

Stolen Bases			Strikeouts		
Amaury Garcia	Elm	46	Bryan Ward	Bre	136
Luis Castillo	Knc	41	Reynol Mendoza	Prt	120
Todd Dunwoody	Knc	39	Michael Parisi	Knc	113
Edgar Renteria	Prt	30	Matt Whisenant	Prt	107
Several tied		23	Walter Miranda	Knc	106

Pitcher	Club	W-L	ERA	IP	H	BB	SO
C. Nunez	Bre	12-6	2.48	123	99	22	79
Jamie Ybarra	Knc	5-5	3.00	96	62	40	104
Michael Parisi	Knc	11-8	3.29	164	152	42	113
Joel Adamson	Chr	8-4	3.29	115	113	20	80
R. Mendoza	Prt	9-10	3.43	168	163	69	120

Sick call: 1995 DL Report

Player	Days on the DL
Kurt Abbott	11
Ryan Bowen	131
Jerry Browne	43*
Chuck Carr	27
Vic Darensbourg	17
Andre Dawson	29
Tommy Gregg	21
Chris Hammond	34*
Bryan Harvey	156
Jeremy Hernandez	114*
Charles Johnson	23
John Johnstone	147
Matt Mantei	84*
Terry Mathews	15
Russ Morman	21
Gary Sheffield	82
Jesus Tavarez	16
Randy Veres	15
David Weathers	17
Darrell Whitmore	120

1995 Amateur draft picks

Players are listed with position and college or high school. Most players were assigned to rookie or Class A leagues. List provided by Major League Baseball.

Joel Atwater, cf, Southern Alamance HS, Graham, N.C.; Swan Austin, rhp, no school, Douglasville, Ga.; Wayne Bair, lhp, Calvert Hall College HS, Manchester, Md.; Darin Baker, cf, Fallon (Nev.) HS; Dion Battee, of, St. Bernard HS, Los Angeles; Howard Bell, rhp, Westchester HS, Los Angeles; Jason Berry, rhp, Mountain View HS, W. Orem, Utah; Clarence Blank, lhp, Galveston College; Stephen Blevins, 1b, Spotsylvania (Va.) HS; William Boughey, rhp, Berkmar HS, Lawrenceville, Ga.; Todd Bramble, ss, Sprague HS, Salem, Ore.; Travis Burgus, lhp, Univ. of San Diego; Brian Bush, cf, Howland HS, Warren, Ohio; Aaron Cames, rhp, Sacramento CC; Shannon Carter, rhp, Gate City HS, Weber City, Va.; Jeffrey Cermak, of, Mesa CC; Richard Circuit, ss, La Jolla (Calif.) HS; Letarvius Copeland, cf, Miami (Fla) Jackson HS; Brian Dallimore, 2b-3b, Stanford; James Detwiler, lhp, Valley Forge Military Academy, Pottsville, Pa.; Kenneth Duebelbeis, lhp, De Anza College; Michael Duvall, lhp, Potomac State; Anthony Enard, rhp, Fresno State; Mathew Erwin, c, Nevada; Scott Esker, 3b, College of the Redwoods; Kevin Fitzmaurice, rhp, Silver Creek HS, San Jose, Calif.; William Fleck, rhp, Mercer County CC; Quincy Foster, rf, Spartanburg Methodist; Joseph Funaro, 2b, Eastern Connecticut St.; Ricky Garcia, rhp, Oklahoma City U.; Jason Garrett, 1b, Texas-Arlington; Gabriel Gonzalez, lhp, Long Beach State; Steven Goodell, ss, Arizona State; Jay Gospodarek, rhp, Pima JC; Kevin Green, cf, Mohawk Valley CC; Raymond Green, c, Sonoma St.; Mark Greenlee, lhp, Triton; Robert Hammock, c, South Cobb HS, Marietta, Ga.; Brian Haught, ss, Jesuit HS, Tampa, Fla.; Robert Hernandez, c, Oklahoma State; Timothy Hicks, rf, Gordon College; Rhett Ingerick, rhp, Davidson College; Hansel Izquierdo, rhp, Southwest Miami (Fla.) HS; James Jones, cf-1b, Rancho Bernardo HS, Poway, Calif.; Carl Jones, cf, Andress HS, El Paso, Texas; Eric Kalie, ss, Martin County HS, Stuart, Fla.; Dustin Keppen, rhp, Central Gwinnett HS, Lawrenceville, Ga.; Gary Knotts, rhp, Brewer HS, Decatur, Ala.; Michael Laine, rhp, Connally HS, Waco, Texas; Andrew Lecrone, 3b, Downers Grove (Ill.) North HS; Kerthatis Lovely, cf, Glades Central HS, South Bay, Fla.; Druen Mahony, ss, Hillcrest HS, Fountain Inn, S.C.; Michael Marriott, rhp, Spring (Texas) HS; Timothy McClaskey, rhp, Muscatine CC; Scott McKee, c, Riverdale Baptist School, Bowie, Md.; David Miller, rhp, North Carolina-Charlotte; Alexander Morris, rhp, Westlake HS, Austin, Texas; Dwaine Neal, cf, Miami (Fla.) Norland HS; James Nederostek, lhp, St Mary's HS, Lodi, Calif.; George Oleksik, rhp, Middle Tennessee State; Robert Pailthorpe, rhp, Santa Clara; Matthew Pidgeon, ss, Eureka (Calif.) HS; Rene Rascon, rf, Sonoma State; William Reed, lf, Westchester HS, Inglewood, Calif.; Jerrod Riggan, rhp, San Diego State; Rafael Riguiero, rhp, John W North HS, Riverside, Calif.; Ryan Roberts, ss, Brigham Young; Jorge Rodriguez, ss, Adolfo Gram Rivera, Penuelas P.R.; Euclides Rodriguez, rhp, no school, Beverly Hills, Calif.; Nathan Rolison, 1b-lf, Petal (Miss.) HS; Michael Rose, rhp, Southwood HS, Shreveport, La.; Derek Rowen, lf, Mesa CC; Joel Sajiun, of, Miami Springs HS, Hialeah, Fla.; Gary Santoro, rhp, Flagler College; John Schmitz, cf, College of San Mateo; Brett Schreyer, rhp, Paul VI HS, Waterford, N.J.; Jason Shanahan, 3b, Cal State Northridge; Shannon Stephens, rhp, Cal Poly-SLO; Ryan Tack, rhp, Durango HS, Las Vegas; Michael Tejera, lhp, Southwest Miami (Fla.) HS; David Themeau, rhp, Navarro College; Kevin Tolan, rhp, Citrus College; William Tull, rhp, Gloucester County College; Mark Watson, lhp, Clemson; Jonathan Widerski, rhp, Holy Angels HS, Winn, lf, Santa Clara.

213

Florida (1993-1995)

Runs: Most, career, all-time

207	JEFF CONINE, 1993-1995
190	CHUCK CARR, 1993-1995
140	GARY SHEFFIELD, 1993-1995
101	KURT ABBOTT, 1994-1995
87	GREG COLBRUNN, 1994-1995

Hits: Most, career, all-time

464	JEFF CONINE, 1993-1995
331	CHUCK CARR, 1993-1995
227	GARY SHEFFIELD, 1993-1995
216	BRET BARBERIE, 1993-1994
200	BENITO SANTIAGO, 1993-1994

2B: Most, career, all-time

77	JEFF CONINE, 1993-1995
58	CHUCK CARR, 1993-1995
36	BRET BARBERIE, 1993-1994
35	KURT ABBOTT, 1994-1995
33	BENITO SANTIAGO, 1993-1994

3B: Most, career, all-time

11	JEFF CONINE, 1993-1995
10	KURT ABBOTT, 1994-1995
8	BENITO SANTIAGO, 1993-1994
7	QUILVIO VERAS, 1995-1995
4	BRET BARBERIE, 1993-1994
4	JERRY BROWNE, 1994-1995
4	CHUCK CARR, 1993-1995
4	GARY SHEFFIELD, 1993-1995

HR: Most, career, all-time

55	JEFF CONINE, 1993-1995
53	GARY SHEFFIELD, 1993-1995
29	GREG COLBRUNN, 1994-1995
26	KURT ABBOTT, 1994-1995
25	Orestes Destrade, 1993-1994

RBI: Most, career, all-time

266	JEFF CONINE, 1993-1995
161	GARY SHEFFIELD, 1993-1995
120	GREG COLBRUNN, 1994-1995
102	Orestes Destrade, 1993-1994
93	KURT ABBOTT, 1994-1995

SB: Most, career, all-time

115	CHUCK CARR, 1993-1995
56	QUILVIO VERAS, 1995
43	GARY SHEFFIELD, 1993-1995
12	GREG COLBRUNN, 1994-1995
11	BENITO SANTIAGO, 1993-1994

BB: Most, career, all-time

158	JEFF CONINE, 1993-1995
135	GARY SHEFFIELD, 1993-1995
117	CHUCK CARR, 1993-1995
83	DAVE MAGADAN, 1993-1994
80	QUILVIO VERAS, 1995

BA: Highest, career, all-time

.303	JEFF CONINE, 1993-1995
.294	GARY SHEFFIELD, 1993-1995
.289	BRET BARBERIE, 1993-1994
.283	GREG COLBRUNN, 1994-1995
.281	JERRY BROWNE, 1994-1995

Slug avg: Highest, career, all-time

.553	GARY SHEFFIELD, 1993-1995
.476	JEFF CONINE, 1993-1995
.460	GREG COLBRUNN, 1994-1995
.426	KURT ABBOTT, 1994-1995
.398	BENITO SANTIAGO, 1993-1994

Games started: Most, career, all-time

69	CHRIS HAMMOND, 1993-1995
67	PAT RAPP, 1993-1995
55	Charlie Hough, 1993-1994
45	DAVE WEATHERS, 1993-1995
38	RYAN BOWEN, 1993-1995

Saves: Most, career, all-time

51	BRYAN HARVEY, 1993-1995
38	ROBB NEN, 1993-1995
9	JEREMY HERNANDEZ, 1994-1995
3	TERRY MATHEWS, 1994-1995
2	TREVOR HOFFMAN, 1993

Shutouts: Most, career, all-time

3	CHRIS HAMMOND, 1993-1995
3	PAT RAPP, 1993-1995
1	RYAN BOWEN, 1993-1995
1	MARK GARDNER, 1994-1995
1	Charlie Hough, 1993-1994

Wins: Most, career, all-time

25	PAT RAPP, 1993-1995
24	CHRIS HAMMOND, 1993-1994
14	JOHN BURKETT, 1995
14	Charlie Hough, 1993-1994
14	DAVE WEATHERS, 1993-1995

K: Most, career, all-time

274	CHRIS HAMMOND, 1993-1995
234	PAT RAPP, 1993-1995
191	Charlie Hough, 1993-1994
166	DAVE WEATHERS, 1993-1995
155	ROBB NEN, 1993-1995

Win pct: Highest, career, all-time

.522	CHRIS HAMMOND, 1993-1995
.543	PAT RAPP, 1993-1995
.500	JOHN BURKETT, 1995
.412	DAVE WEATHERS, 1993-1995
.393	RYAN BOWEN, 1993-1995

ERA: Lowest, career, all-time

3.51	LUIS AQUINO, 1993-1994
3.72	PAT RAPP, 1993-1995
3.96	ROBB NEN, 1993-1995
4.06	CHRIS HAMMOND, 1993-1994
4.14	RICHIE LEWIS, 1993-1995

Runs: Most, season

86	QUILVIO VERAS, 1995
75	CHUCK CARR, 1993
75	JEFF CONINE, 1993
72	JEFF CONINE, 1995
70	GREG COLBRUNN, 1995
70	TERRY PENDLETON, 1995

Hits: Most, season

174	JEFF CONINE, 1993	
149	TERRY PENDLETON, 1995	
147	CHUCK CARR, 1993	
146	GREG COLBRUNN, 1995	
146	JEFF CONINE, 1995	

2B: Most, season

32	TERRY PENDLETON, 1995
27	JEFF CONINE, 1994
26	JEFF CONINE, 1995
24	JEFF CONINE, 1993
22	GREG COLBRUNN, 1995

3B: Most, season

7	KURT ABBOTT, 1995
7	QUILVIO VERAS, 1995
6	JEFF CONINE, 1994
6	BENITO SANTIAGO, 1993
4	JERRY BROWNE, 1994

HR: Most, season

27	GARY SHEFFIELD, 1994
25	JEFF CONINE, 1995
23	GREG COLBRUNN, 1995
20	Orestes Destrade, 1993
18	JEFF CONINE, 1994

RBI: Most, season

105	JEFF CONINE, 1995
89	GREG COLBRUNN, 1995
87	Orestes Destrade, 1993
82	JEFF CONINE, 1994
79	JEFF CONINE, 1993

SB: Most, season

58	CHUCK CARR, 1993
56	QUILVIO VERAS, 1995
32	CHUCK CARR, 1994
25	CHUCK CARR, 1995
19	GARY SHEFFIELD, 1995

BB: Most, season

80	QUILVIO VERAS, 1995
79	WALT WEISS, 1993
66	JEFF CONINE, 1995
58	Orestes Destrade, 1993
52	JERRY BROWNE, 1994
52	JEFF CONINE, 1993

BA: Highest, season

.319	JEFF CONINE, 1994
.302	JEFF CONINE, 1995
.301	BRET BARBERIE, 1994
.295	JERRY BROWNE, 1994
.292	JEFF CONINE, 1993

Slug avg: Highest, season

.584	GARY SHEFFIELD, 1994
.526	JEFF CONINE, 1994
.520	JEFF CONINE, 1995
.453	GREG COLBRUNN, 1995
.452	KURT ABBOTT, 1995

Games started: Most, season

34	Charlie Hough, 1993
33	Jack Armstrong 1993
32	CHRIS HAMMOND, 1993
30	JOHN BURKETT, 1995
28	PAT RAPP, 1995

Saves: Most, season

45	BRYAN HARVEY, 1993
23	ROBB NEN, 1995
15	ROBB NEN, 1994
9	JEREMY HERNANDEZ, 1994
3	TERRY MATHEWS, 1995

Shutouts: Most, season

2	CHRIS HAMMOND, 1995
2	PAT RAPP, 1995
1	RYAN BOWEN, 1993
1	MARK GARDNER, 1995
1	CHRIS HAMMOND, 1994
1	Charlie Hough, 1994
1	PAT RAPP, 1994

Wins: Most, season

14	JOHN BURKETT, 1995
14	PAT RAPP, 1995
11	CHRIS HAMMOND, 1993
9	Jack Armstrong, 1993
9	CHRIS HAMMOND, 1995
9	Charlie Hough, 1993

K: Most, season

126	JOHN BURKETT, 1995
126	CHRIS HAMMOND, 1995
126	Charlie Hough, 1993
118	JACK ARMSTRONG, 1993
108	CHRIS HAMMOND, 1993

Win pct: Highest, season

.667	PAT RAPP, 1995
.500	JOHN BURKETT, 1995

ERA: Lowest, season

3.44	PAT RAPP, 1995
3.80	CHRIS HAMMOND, 1995
3.85	PAT RAPP, 1994
4.27	Charlie Hough, 1993
4.30	JOHN BURKETT, 1995

Most pinch-hit homers, season

1	GARY SHEFFIELD, 1994

Most pinch-hit homers, career

1	GARY SHEFFIELD, 1993-1994

Most consecutive games batting safely

17	GREG COLBRUNN, 1995
15	BRET BARBERIE, 1993
15	CHUCK CARR, 1993

Most consecutive scoreless innings

26⅓	LUIS AQUINO, 1994
24	CHRIS HAMMOND, 1994

No-hit games

None

Players' years of service are listed by the first and last years with this team and are not necessarily consecutive; all statistics record performances for this team only.

FLORIDA MARLINS / NL EAST

Montreal Expos

By Eileen Blass, *USA TODAY*

First baseman David Segui led the Expos in batting (.309) and RBI (68).

1995 Expos: The owners threw it all away

The Expos went from the best team in baseball to a last-place team that counted pitchers Greg Harris and Dave Leiper as among the best performers. What happened? Ken Hill—gone. John Wetteland—gone. Marquis Grissom—adieu. Larry Walker—bon voyage. Making matters worse were injuries to Cliff Floyd (shattered left wrist), left-hander Butch Henry (Tommy John elbow surgery) and outfielder Moises Alou (torn left and right shoulders.)

By the time the season ended—with a 66-78 record and a 31-41 home mark that was their worst since 1976—Kevin Malone decided that unemployment was a better option than staying on as vice president and general manager of a club with such a miserly payroll.

The remaining players hardly had banner years. Wil Cordero, counted on to pick up some of the slack with the departure of Grissom and Walker, went 109 plate appearances between RBI at one point. A throwing funk put the All-Star shortstop in left field, which basically sums up all you need to know about the season.

Jeff Fassero finished 13-14 with a 4.33 ERA. Pitching coach Joe Kerrigan suggested Fassero see a sports psychologist to improve his body language. Outfielder Moises Alou's season was cut short by shoulder surgery. He wasn't the offensive force the team expected him to be, anyway. Without the protection afforded by Walker and Grissom, he was easy to pitch around. Closer Mel Rojas saved 30 games but blew nine others. Tim Scott, counted on to replace Rojas as a setup man, was inconsistent and was often forced to leave in the eighth inning.

But there were some good performances. A 7-2 road trip (including a three-game sweep of the Astros in Houston) from Aug. 8-16 gave the team a glimmer of hope for a wild-card bid after having been out of contention at the All-Star break. Center fielder Rondell White became a polished defensive player and put up eye-opening numbers (.295, 13 HR, 57 RBI, 25 steals) as well as hitting for the cycle on June 11. Switch-hitting David Segui came over from the New York Mets in a trade for minor leaguer Reid Cornelius and briefly climbed into the NL batting race before settling down at .309. His defense was Gold Glove caliber. And Pedro Martinez continued to mature as a starter, going 14-10 (3.51) while flirting with a perfect game on June 3, losing it in the 10th inning. Sean Berry and Mike Lansing had career years.

Harris (who became the first pitcher in modern baseball to throw ambidextrously in a game) and Leiper bailed out their bullpen comrades on a number of occasions, and rookie Carlos Perez (10-8, 3.69) represented the team in the All-Star Game.

1996 Expos: Preview

As long as manager Felipe Alou is pulling the strings, the Expos will most likely be competitive. But amid rumors of yet another fire sale, it is clear that new GM Jim Beattie has a major task in front of him. A decision must be made whether Cordero will stay in the crowded outfield or play at shortstop instead of defensive whiz Mark Grudzielanek. Sean Berry must be given a full-time job or be part of a good trade. At least one more starting pitcher must be added, and the bullpen needs someone who can save a few games and fill setup duty.

The farm system is stripped, with little to offer above Class A. Shane Andrews might take over at third if Berry goes, and Alou has already said that Tim Laker deserves to be the everyday catcher. With a healthy Floyd and Moises Alou and a more consistent Tony Tarasco back to join budding superstar White, there is some hope.

1995 Expos: Week-by-week notes

These notes were excerpted from the following issues of Baseball Weekly.

▶**May 3:** Prospect Rondell White and newly acquired Tony Tarasco got off to a strong start. White homered in his first at-bat, and Tarasco was hitting .333 in three starts with outstanding defense as well.

▶**May 10:** Carlos Perez, younger brother of Melido and Pascual, was moved to the starting rotation when the Expos sent Kirk Rueter and Curt Schmidt down to Class AAA. Rueter started his career 10-0.

▶**May 24:** Cliff Floyd was lost due to a fracture dislocation of the left wrist. He underwent a two-hour operation the following day and faced two additional operations in July. Doctors said the injury could be career-threatening.

▶**June 7:** "I know I'm still young, but I've been around long enough now that I think I've shown people what I can do," said 23-year-old Pedro Martinez after his bid for a perfect game was undone by a Bip Roberts double in the 10th inning. He settled instead for a one-hitter and his fourth win of the year.

▶**June 14:** Moises Alou found out he would need arthroscopic surgery on his shoulder but didn't know whether it would be done during the season or afterward.

▶**June 21:** Rondell White hit for the cycle on June 11 against the Giants. White went 6-for-7 and showed once again why the Expos felt justified in trading Roberto Kelly to the Dodgers. In the same game, catcher Darrin Fletcher set a career high by collecting four hits in the same game, including a three-run homer.

▶**June 28:** The Expos were livid about the treatment pitcher Pedro Martinez was getting from opposing players and umpires, with manager Felipe Alou going so far as suggesting discrimination was behind it. Martinez was given a warning in a game against the Astros after hitting the third batter in the first inning, Jeff Bagwell. This came after Martinez was given a warning earlier this year by umpire Bruce Froemming after his third pitch of a game against the Giants. Alou called a meeting with VP and GM Kevin Malone and team president Claude Brochu to discuss the matter. "We're going to do whatever it takes to back Pedro in this," Malone said. "It seems to me that he's being singled out for some reason, and we want to know what it is. It doesn't seem fair to us." Martinez, for his part, agreed with Alou's claim that at least part of the reason was because "I'm a young black kid from the Dominican Republic." The Expos were particularly incensed at comments by Reds veteran broadcaster Marty Brennaman, who said Martinez and left-hander Carlos Perez (who hit Reds pitcher Kevin Jarvis with a pitch while he was squaring to bunt with two runners on base) tried to hit people. Malone barged into Brennaman's booth between innings to complain about the statement and the two became embroiled in a war of words in the media.

▶**July 5:** Felipe Alou had been worried about how the loss of Larry Walker and Marquis Grissom would affect the pitches his son saw. "What I don't want to see happen with Moises is the same thing that happened with Andy Van Slyke when the Pirates lost Bobby Bonilla and Barry Bonds," the manager said. "All of sudden it was Van Slyke who became the object of everyone's strategy. Everything was geared so that Andy Van Slyke wouldn't be the guy who beat you. In Moises' case you have to be particularly concerned because he's not a very patient hitter." The younger Alou said, "We still have a pretty good team here." But, he added, the club's first losing month in 15 months (a 10-16 record in June) showed "we just don't have the horses around like we used to. Now it's like if I get myself out, a lot of people lose faith. We need some guys to step forward.... It just can't be me carrying the team."

▶**July 19:** The day after his brother Ramon pitched a no-hitter, Pedro Martinez—who has twice in the past two years flirted with a perfect game—knew the question was going to come. "There's a chance, still," the Expos right-hander said when asked about the intriguing prospect of brothers pitching no-hitters in the same year. "Every time you go out, there's a chance for it. Remember that." He watched his brother's gem at the home of teammate Henry Rodriguez. "They showed the last three outs live on TV, and I was more nervous watching that than when I was out there in my own game," said Martinez. "I was calling each pitch."

▶**Aug. 30:** In a major step to gear up for the final sprint to the wild-card spot, the Expos shifted All-Star shortstop Wil Cordero to left field and called up Mark Grudzielanek from Class AAA. The move was made to shore up the defense on the left side of the infield as well as prepare for the likelihood that Moises Alou's season was over. "This is a big move," said Felipe Alou. "I don't believe it's the end of Wil Cordero at shortstop, because I'll do some things. And I won't hesitate to bring him in. I don't know how long I'll manage here or how long Wil will be here, but if he addresses his throwing problem, I'll return him to shortstop." General manager Kevin Malone made it sound a lot more permanent. "He's a productive offensive player," Malone said of Cordero. "But his arm isn't of major-league caliber."

▶**Sept. 13:** It wasn't quite the Night Flight to Terror, but the charter flight from San Francisco to Montreal in the wee hours of Sept. 7 will go down as one of the most notorious events in club history. It started with reports that 18 seats were damaged on the Air Canada charter and that some carpeting had to be replaced, leading one wire service to call it a "beer-soaked party flight." Air Canada said the plane could not be used for a 9 a.m. Montreal-Toronto business flight (it arrived in Montreal at 8:30) and that the 18 seats were out of commission for the rest of the day. Expos management said the responsible players would pick up the tab. But what made the flight even more notorious was a statement by second baseman Mike Lansing. He criticized flight attendants for speaking over the P.A. system in French (in addition to English), a comment that turned into yet one more flashpoint in Quebec's long-running language dispute. Lansing, who three days later would surpass the club record for RBI by a second baseman (breaking Delino De-Shields' club mark of 56 set in 1992), made a public apology. The damaged seats were caused by players removing pins to push the seats forward to be used as card tables, something that's common practice on team charters.

Team directory

▶**Owner:** Montreal Baseball Club Inc., Claude R. Brochu (president and general partner)

▶**General manager:** Jim Beattie

▶**Ballpark:**
Olympic Stadium
4549 Avenue Pierre-de-Coubertin, Montreal, Quebec
514-253-3434
Capacity 46,500
Parking for 4,000 cars; $8
Public transportation available
Wheelchair sections, ramps, extensive food concessions, outfield bleachers

▶**Team publications:**
Media Guide, *Expos Magazine*
P.O. Box 500, Station M, Montreal, Que., Canada H1V 3P2

▶**TV, radio broadcast stations:**
CIQC 600 AM, C-TV, TSN (English); CKAC 730 AM, FSRC-TV, RDS (French)

▶**Spring training:**
Municipal Stadium
West Palm Beach, Fla.
Capacity 7,500
407-684-6801

219

MONTREAL EXPOS 1995 final stats

BATTERS	BA	SLG	OB	G	AB	R	H	TB	2B	3B	HR	RBI	BB	SO	SB	CS	E
Benitez	.385	.641	.400	14	39	8	15	25	2	1	2	7	1	7	0	2	1
Berry	.318	.529	.367	103	314	38	100	166	22	1	14	55	25	53	3	8	12
Segui	.309	.461	.367	130	456	68	141	210	25	4	12	68	40	47	2	7	3
Siddall	.300	.300	.500	7	10	4	3	3	0	0	0	1	3	3	0	0	2
Santangelo	.296	.398	.384	35	98	11	29	39	5	1	1	9	12	9	1	1	1
R. White	.295	.464	.356	130	474	87	140	220	33	4	13	57	41	87	25	5	4
Cordero	.286	.420	.341	131	514	64	147	216	35	2	10	49	36	88	9	5	22
Fletcher	.286	.446	.351	110	350	42	100	156	21	1	11	45	32	23	0	1	4
Alou	.273	.459	.342	93	344	48	94	158	22	0	14	58	29	56	4	3	3
Silvestri	.264	.431	.341	39	72	12	19	31	6	0	2	7	9	27	2	0	1
Spehr	.257	.486	.366	41	35	4	9	17	5	0	1	3	6	7	0	0	1
Lansing	.255	.392	.299	127	467	47	119	183	30	2	10	62	28	65	27	4	6
Tarasco	.249	.404	.329	126	438	64	109	177	18	4	14	40	51	78	24	3	5
Grudzielanek	.245	.316	.300	78	269	27	66	85	12	2	1	20	14	47	8	3	10
Rodriguez	.239	.326	.293	45	138	13	33	45	4	1	2	15	11	28	0	1	1
Laker	.234	.369	.306	64	141	17	33	52	8	1	3	20	14	38	0	1	7
Andrews	.214	.377	.271	84	220	27	47	83	10	1	8	31	17	68	1	1	7
Treadway	.209	.269	.264	58	67	6	14	18	2	1	0	13	5	4	0	1	0
Foley	.208	.292	.269	11	24	2	5	7	2	0	0	2	2	4	1	0	0
Frazier	.190	.222	.297	35	63	6	12	14	2	0	0	3	8	12	4	0	1
Pride	.175	.190	.235	48	63	10	11	12	1	0	0	2	5	16	3	2	2
Floyd	.130	.188	.221	29	69	6	9	13	1	0	1	8	7	22	3	0	3

PITCHERS	W-L	ERA	G	GS	CG	GF	Sho	SV	IP	H	R	ER	HR	BB	SO
Harris	2-3	2.61	45	0	0	12	0	0	48.1	45	18	14	6	16	47
Henry	7-9	2.84	21	21	1	0	1	0	126.2	133	47	40	11	28	60
Leiper	0-2	2.86	26	0	0	7	0	2	22	16	8	7	2	6	12
Rueter	5-3	3.23	9	9	1	0	1	0	47.1	38	17	17	3	9	28
Martinez	14-10	3.51	30	30	2	0	2	0	194.2	158	79	76	21	66	174
Perez	10-8	3.69	28	23	2	2	1	0	141.1	142	61	58	18	28	106
Scott	2-0	3.98	62	0	0	15	0	2	63.1	52	30	28	6	23	57
Rojas	1-4	4.12	59	0	0	48	0	30	67.2	69	32	31	2	29	61
Heredia	5-6	4.31	40	18	0	5	0	1	119	137	60	57	7	21	74
Fassero	13-14	4.33	30	30	1	0	0	0	189	207	102	91	15	74	164
Shaw	1-6	4.62	50	0	0	17	0	3	62.1	58	35	32	4	26	45
Eversgerd	0-0	5.14	25	0	0	5	0	0	21	22	13	12	2	9	8
Fraser	2-1	5.61	22	0	0	6	0	2	25.2	25	17	16	6	9	12
Urbina	2-2	6.17	7	4	0	0	0	0	23.1	26	17	16	6	14	15
Alvarez	1-5	6.75	8	8	0	0	0	0	37.1	46	30	28	2	14	17
Schmidt	0-0	6.97	11	0	0	0	0	0	10.1	15	8	8	1	9	7
G. White	1-2	7.01	19	1	0	8	0	0	25.2	26	21	20	7	9	25
DeLeon	0-1	7.56	7	0	0	1	0	0	8.1	7	7	7	2	7	12
Thobe	0-0	9.00	4	0	0	2	0	0	4	6	4	4	0	3	0

1996 preliminary roster

PITCHERS (22)
Tavo Alvarez
Derek Aucoin
Bryan Eversgerd
Steve Faltersek
Jeff Fassero
Scott Gentile
Rodney Henderson
Gil Heredia
Dave Leiper
Pedro Martinez
Alex Pacheo
Jose Panaigua
Carlos Perez
Mel Rojas
Kirk Rueter
Tim Scott
Everett Stull
Ugueth Urbina
Neil Weber
Gabe White
Trey Witte
Esteban Yan

CATCHERS (3)
Darrin Fletcher
Tim Laker
Tim Spehr

INFIELDERS (10)
Israel Alcantara
Shane Andrews
Sean Berry
Wil Cordero
Cliff Floyd
Mark Grudzielanek
Mike Lansing
Henry Rodriguez
David Segui
Dave Silvestri

OUTFIELDERS (5)
Moises Alou
Yamil Benitez
Darond Stovall
Tony Tarasco
Rondell White

Games played by position

PLAYER	G	C	1B	2B	3B	SS	OF
Alou	93	0	0	0	0	0	92
Andrews	84	0	29	0	51	0	0
Benitez	14	0	0	0	0	0	14
Berry	103	0	3	0	83	0	0
Cordero	131	0	0	0	0	105	26
Fletcher	110	98	0	0	0	0	0
Floyd	29	0	18	0	0	0	4
Foley	11	0	4	3	0	0	0
Frazier	35	0	0	1	0	0	25
Grudzielanek	78	0	0	13	31	34	0
Laker	64	61	0	0	0	0	0
Lansing	127	0	0	127	0	2	0
Pride	48	0	0	0	0	0	24
Rodriguez	45	0	11	0	0	0	28
Santangelo	35	0	0	5	0	0	25
Segui	130	0	104	0	0	0	20
Siddall	7	7	0	0	0	0	0
Silvestri	39	0	4	3	8	9	3
Spehr	41	38	0	0	0	0	0
Tarasco	126	0	0	0	0	0	116
Treadway	58	0	0	12	3	0	0
R. White	130	0	0	0	0	0	119

Minor Leagues

Tops in the organization

Batter	Club	Avg.	G	AB	R	H	HR	RBI
V. Guerrero	Aby	.333	110	421	77	140	16	63
Edward Bady	Vmt	.329	72	295	51	97	2	25
Brad Fullmer	Aby	.323	123	468	69	151	8	67
Jon Saffer	HRb	.303	112	400	69	121	4	39
Frank Jacobs	HRb	.302	120	394	67	119	14	70

Home Runs			Wins		
Julian Yan	Ott	22	Chris Weidert	Vmt	12
Tony Barron	Ott	20	Steve Falteisek	Ott	11
Yamil Benitez	Ott	18	Tommy Phelps	Aby	10
Vladimir Guerrero	Aby	16	Alex Pacheco	Ott	10
Frank Jacobs	HRb	14	Several tied		9

RBI			Saves		
Julian Yan	Ott	78	Jake Benz	WPb	22
Frank Jacobs	HRb	70	Robert Marquez	Vmt	21
Yamil Benitez	Ott	69	Jason Woodring	Aby	16
Brad Fullmer	Aby	67	Curt Schmidt	Ott	15
F. Seguignol	Aby	66	Scott Gentile	HRb	11

Stolen Bases			Strikeouts		
Hiram Bocabica	Aby	47	Everett Stull	HRb	132
Jim Buccheri	Ott	43	Steve Falteisek	Ott	130
Edward Bady	Vmt	34	Tommy Phelps	Aby	124
Jason Camilli	Vmt	30	David Moraga	Aby	119
Chris Martin	Ott	30	Neil Weber	HRb	119

Pitcher	Club	W-L	ERA	IP	H	BB	SO
Chris Weidert	Vmt	12-3	2.38	106	83	26	69
Steve Falteisek	Ott	11-6	2.73	191	169	69	130
David Moraga	Aby	9-9	2.80	164	156	56	119
Kirk Rueter	Ott	9-7	3.06	121	120	25	67
Esteban Yan	WPb	6-8	3.07	138	139	33	89

Sick call: 1995 DL Report

Player	Days on the DL
Moises Alou	38*
Cliff Floyd	118
Tom Foley	18
Rod Henderson	160
Butch Henry	47
Mike Lansing	15
Henry Rodriguez	122
Tim Spehr	63
Jeff Treadway	18
B.J. Wallace	160

Indicates two separate terms on Disabled List.

1995 Amateur draft picks

Players are listed with position and college or high school. Most players were assigned to rookie or Class A leagues. List provided by Major League Baseball.

Jeffrey Austin, rhp, Kingwood (Texas) HS; Michael Barrett, ss, Pace Academy, Alpharetta, Ga.; Stanley Baston, lf-3b, North Florida Christian HS, Tallahassee, Fla.; Michael Bell, lhp, Florida State; Darrell Blakeney, cf, Elon College; Thomas Brady, c, Serra HS, San Mateo, Calif.; Jeremiah Colson, rf, St. Paul's (N.C.) High; Jesse Crespo, c, Camuy (P.R.) HS; Ronney Daniels, lhp, Lake Wales (Fla.) HS; Torrance Davis, lf-cf, Liberty Eylau HS, Texarkana, Texas; Matthew Dehner, 3b, El Dorado HS, Las Vegas; Wes Denning, cf, Minnesota; Philip Derryman, rhp, Moorpark JC; Timothy Dixon, rhp, Cal State Fullerton; Robert Everett, rhp, Lake City CC; Peter Fortune, lhp, Rockland CC; Brandon Gadke, of, Orange (Ohio) HS; Jaime Garcia, c, New Mexico; Noah Hall, cf, Aptos (Calif.) HS; David Herr, rhp, Villanova; Adam Huxhold, lhp, Lindbergh HS, Maple Valley, Wash.; Kennouth James, lf, Sebring (Fla.) HS; Joseph Kerrigan, ss, Radnor HS, Rosemont Pa.; James Lacey, rhp, Coconut Creek HS, North Lauderdale, Fla.; Pierre LaForest, ss-3b, Polyvalente Edouard Montp., Gatineau, Que.; Robert Marquez, rhp, McNeese State; Cleburne Martin, rhp, Arcadia HS, Phoenix; Henry Mateo, 2b, Escuela Central, Santurce PR; Toby McDermott, lhp, Tacoma CC; Scott Mitchell, rhp, Pacific; D.C. Olsen, 1b, Cal State Fullerton; Shawn Peterson, c-cf, Orem (Utah) High; Scott Porter, rhp, Middleburg (Fla.) HS; Daniel Prata, lhp, Kells Academy, Repentigny, Que.; Bienvenido Sanchez, rhp, no school, Arecibo P.R.; Brian Schneider, c, Northhampton HS, Cherryville, Pa.; James Shearin, cf, Wake Forest (N.C.) Rolesville HS; J.D. Smart, rhp, Texas; Jacob Steinkemper, c, Arizona State; Jimmy Turman, rhp, Shelton St. CC.; Aaron Underwood, rhp, Lehigh HS, Lehigh Acres, Fla.; Bruno Vaillancourt, lhp, Cegep Montmorency, Le Gardeur, Que.; Ryan Van Oeveren, ss, Michigan; Michael Wolger, lhp, California; Shane Wright, rhp, Hayden HS, Topeka, Kan.; Mitch Wylie, rhp, North Scott HS, Princeton, Iowa.

Montreal (1969-1995)

222

Runs: Most, career, all-time

934	TIM RAINES, 1979-1990	
828	ANDRE DAWSON, 1976-1986	
737	TIM WALLACH, 1980-1992	
707	Gary Carter, 1974-1992	
446	Warren Cromartie, 1974-1983	

Hits: Most, career, all-time

1694	TIM WALLACH, 1980-1992	
1598	TIM RAINES, 1979-1990	
1575	ANDRE DAWSON, 1976-1986	
1427	Gary Carter, 1974-1992	
1063	Warren Cromartie, 1974-1983	

2B: Most, career, all-time

360	TIM WALLACH, 1980-1992	
295	ANDRE DAWSON, 1976-1986	
274	Gary Carter, 1974-1992	
273	TIM RAINES, 1979-1990	
222	Warren Cromartie, 1974-1983	

3B: Most, career, all-time

81	TIM RAINES, 1979-1990	
67	ANDRE DAWSON, 1976-1986	
31	TIM WALLACH, 1980-1992	
30	Warren Cromartie, 1974-1983	
25	DELINO DeSHIELDS, 1990-1993	
25	MITCH WEBSTER, 1985-1988	

HR: Most, career, all-time

225	ANDRE DAWSON, 1976-1986	
220	Gary Carter, 1974-1992	
204	TIM WALLACH, 1980-1992	
118	Bob Bailey, 1969-1975	
106	ANDRES GALARRAGA, 1985-1991	

RBI: Most, career, all-time

905	TIM WALLACH, 1980-1992	
838	ANDRE DAWSON, 1976-1986	
823	Gary Carter, 1974-1992	
552	TIM RAINES, 1979-1990	
466	Bob Bailey, 1969-1975	

SB: Most, career, all-time

634	TIM RAINES, 1979-1990	
266	MARQUIS GRISSOM, 1989-1994	
253	ANDRE DAWSON, 1976-1986	
187	DELINO DeSHIELDS, 1990-1993	
139	Rodney Scott, 1976-1982	

BB: Most, career, all-time

775	TIM RAINES, 1979-1990	
582	Gary Carter, 1974-1992	
514	TIM WALLACH, 1980-1992	
502	Bob Bailey, 1969-1975	
370	Ron Fairly, 1969-1974	

BA: Highest, career, all-time

.301	TIM RAINES, 1979-1990	
.294	Rusty Staub, 1969-1979	
.288	Ellis Valentine, 1975-1981	
.282	LARRY WALKER, 1989-1994	
.280	Warren Cromartie, 1974-1983	

Slug avg: Highest, career, all-time

.497	Rusty Staub, 1969-1979	
.483	LARRY WALKER, 1989-1994	
.476	ANDRE DAWSON, 1976-1986	
.476	Ellis Valentine, 1975-1981	
.454	Gary Carter, 1974-1992	

Games started: Most, career, all-time

393	Steve Rogers, 1973-1985	
233	DENNIS MARTINEZ, 1986-1993	
193	Bryn Smith, 1981-1989	
192	Steve Renko, 1969-1976	
170	Bill Gullickson, 1979-1985	

Saves: Most, career, all-time

152	Jeff Reardon, 1981-1986	
105	JOHN WETTELAND, 1992-1994	
101	Tim Burke, 1985-1991	
75	Mike Marshall, 1970-1973	
73	MEL ROJAS, 1990-1995	

Shutouts: Most, career, all-time

37	Steve Rogers, 1973-1985	
15	Bill Stoneman, 1969-1973	
13	DENNIS MARTINEZ, 1986-1993	
8	Woodie Fryman, 1975-1983	
8	Charlie Lea, 1980-1987	
8	SCOTT SANDERSON, 1978-1983	
8	Bryn Smith, 1981-1989	

Wins: Most, career, all-time

158	Steve Rogers, 1973-1985	
100	DENNIS MARTINEZ, 1986-1993	
81	Bryn Smith, 1981-1989	
72	Bill Gullickson, 1979-1985	
68	Steve Renko, 1969-1976	

K: Most, career, all-time

1621	Steve Rogers, 1973-1985	
973	DENNIS MARTINEZ, 1986-1993	
838	Bryn Smith, 1981-1989	
831	Bill Stoneman, 1969-1973	
810	Steve Renko, 1969-1976	

Win pct: Highest, career, all-time

.661	KEN HILL, 1992-1994	
.623	Tim Burke, 1985-1991	
.581	DENNIS MARTINEZ, 1986-1993	
.573	Charlie Lea, 1980-1987	
.556	Mike Torrez, 1971-1974	

ERA: Lowest, career, all-time

3.06	DENNIS MARTINEZ, 1986-1993	
3.17	Steve Rogers, 1973-1985	
3.28	Bryn Smith, 1981-1989	
3.32	Charlie Lea, 1980-1987	
3.33	SCOTT SANDERSON, 1978-1983	

Runs: Most, season

133	TIM RAINES, 1983	
123	TIM RAINES, 1987	
115	TIM RAINES, 1985	
107	ANDRE DAWSON, 1982	
106	TIM RAINES, 1984	

Hits: Most, season

204	Al Oliver, 1982	
194	TIM RAINES, 1986	
192	TIM RAINES, 1984	
189	ANDRE DAWSON, 1983	
188	Dave Cash, 1977	
188	MARQUIS GRISSOM, 1993	

2B: Most, season

46	Warren Cromartie, 1979	
44	LARRY WALKER, 1994	
43	Al Oliver, 1982	
42	Dave Cash, 1977	
42	ANDRES GALARRAGA, 1988	
42	TIM WALLACH, 1987	
42	TIM WALLACH, 1989	

3B: Most, season

13	TIM RAINES, 1985	
13	Rodney Scott, 1980	
13	MITCH WEBSTER, 1986	
12	ANDRE DAWSON, 1979	
11	Ron LeFlore, 1980	

HR: Most, season

32	ANDRE DAWSON, 1983
31	Gary Carter, 1977
30	Larry Parrish, 1979
30	Rusty Staub, 1970
29	Gary Carter, 1980
29	Gary Carter, 1982
29	ANDRES GALARRAGA, 1988
29	Rusty Staub, 1969

RBI: Most, season

123	TIM WALLACH, 1987
113	ANDRE DAWSON, 1983
109	Al Oliver, 1982
106	Gary Carter, 1984
103	Ken Singleton, 1973

SB: Most, season

97	Ron LeFlore, 1980
90	TIM RAINES, 1983
78	MARQUIS GRISSOM, 1992
78	TIM RAINES, 1982
76	MARQUIS GRISSOM, 1991

BB: Most, season

123	Ken Singleton, 1973
112	Rusty Staub, 1970
110	Rusty Staub, 1969
100	Bob Bailey, 1974
97	Bob Bailey, 1971
97	TIM RAINES, 1983

BA: Highest, season

.339	MOISES ALOU, 1994
.334	TIM RAINES, 1986
.331	Al Oliver, 1982
.330	TIM RAINES, 1987
.322	LARRY WALKER, 1994

Slug avg: Highest, season

.592	MOISES ALOU, 1994
.587	LARRY WALKER, 1994
.553	ANDRE DAWSON, 1981
.551	Larry Parrish, 1979
.540	ANDRES GALARRAGA, 1988

Games started: Most, season

40	Steve Rogers, 1977
39	Bill Stoneman, 1971
38	Steve Rogers, 1974
37	Carl Morton, 1970
37	Steve Renko, 1971
37	Steve Rogers, 1979
37	Steve Rogers, 1980

Saves: Most, season

43	JOHN WETTELAND, 1993
41	JEFF REARDON, 1985
37	JOHN WETTELAND, 1992
35	JEFF REARDON, 1986
31	Mike Marshall, 1973

Shutouts: Most, season

5	DENNIS MARTINEZ, 1991
5	Steve Rogers, 1979
5	Steve Rogers, 1983
5	Bill Stoneman, 1969
4	MARK LANGSTON, 1989
4	Charlie Lea, 1983
4	Carl Morton, 1970
4	Steve Rogers, 1976
4	Steve Rogers, 1977
4	Steve Rogers, 1980
4	Steve Rogers, 1982
4	Bill Stoneman, 1972

Wins: Most, season

20	Ross Grimsley, 1978
19	Steve Rogers, 1982
18	Carl Morton, 1970
18	Bryn Smith, 1985
17	Bill Gullickson, 1983
17	Steve Rogers, 1977
17	Steve Rogers, 1983
17	Bill Stoneman, 1971

K: Most, season

251	Bill Stoneman, 1971
206	Steve Rogers, 1977
202	Floyd Youmans, 1986
185	Bill Stoneman, 1969
179	Steve Rogers, 1982

Win pct: Highest, season

.783	Bryn Smith, 1985
.762	KEN HILL, 1994
.704	Steve Rogers, 1982
.696	DENNIS MARTINEZ, 1989
.652	Mike Torrez, 1974
.652	Dale Murray, 1975

ERA: Lowest, season

2.39	DENNIS MARTINEZ, 1991
2.39	MARK LANGSTON, 1989
2.40	Steve Rogers, 1982
2.44	Pascual Perez, 1988
2.47	DENNIS MARTINEZ, 1992

Most pinch-hit homers, season

4	Hal Breeden, 1973

Most pinch-hit homers, career

5	Jose Morales. 1973-1977

Most consecutive games batting safely

21	DELINO DeSHIELDS, 1993
19	Warren Cromartie, 1979
19	ANDRE DAWSON, 1980

Most consecutive scoreless innings

32	Woodie Fryman, 1975

No-hit games

Bill Stoneman, Mon at Phi NL, 7-0; April 17, 1969.

Bill Stoneman, Mon vs NY NL, 7-0; October 2, 1972 (1st game).

Charlie Lea, Mon vs SF NL, 4-0; May 10, 1981 (2nd game).

MARK GARDNER, Mon at LA NL, 0-1; July 26, 1991 (9 innings, lost on 2 hits in 10th, relieved by JEFF FASSERO, who allowed 1 more hit).

DENNIS MARTINEZ, Mon at LA NL, 2-0; July 28, 1991 (perfect game).

David Palmer, 5 perfect innings, rain, Mon at StL NL, 4-0; April 21, 1984 (2nd game).

Pascual Perez, 5 innings, rain, Mon at Phi NL, 1-0; September 24, 1988.

ACTIVE PLAYERS in caps.

Players' years of service are listed by the first and last years with this team and are not necessarily consecutive; all statistics record performances for this team only.

Cincinnati Reds

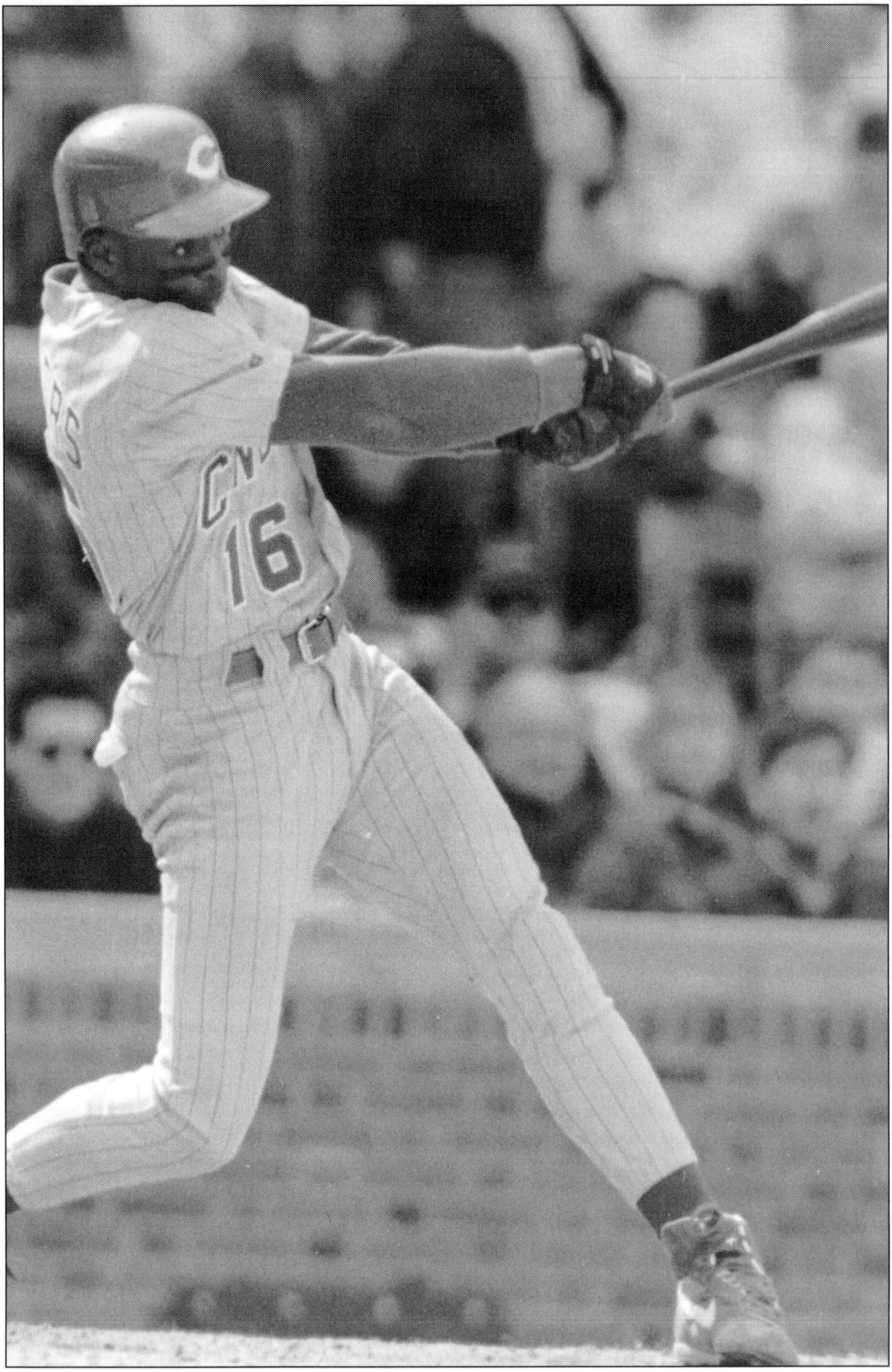

Slugger Reggie Sanders hit .306 with 28 homers and led the Reds with 99 RBI.

1995 Reds: Bad start, great middle, sad end

The finish mirrored the start of the season—and it was a reflection the Reds wish they'd never seen. When they lost four in a row to the Atlanta Braves in the National League Championship Series, it was as if they had traveled back in time to their six consecutive losses (eight of their first nine) of the season.

In between, there was much to remember, including a three-game sweep of the Los Angeles Dodgers in the division series.

A bad omen surfaced early when pitcher Jose Rijo, after a sensational spring, developed elbow pain. After a pair of stints on the disabled list and 14 starts, he underwent Tommy John surgery in August. Fortunately, Pete Schourek, a reclamation project off the waiver wire, pitched well enough to win the Cy Young—if Greg Maddux hadn't been around. Schourek was the ace with an 18-7 record; he went 13-1 with an 1.86 ERA in Riverfront Stadium, and the Reds won 20 of his 29 starts. Veteran John Smiley was 11-1 through Aug. 4 but won only one of his final nine starts after a groin injury.

To shore up the pitching, general manager Jim Bowden made two gigantic deals. First, he sent outfielder Deion Sanders, who was crippled with an ankle injury, John Roper and Scott Service to the Giants for pitchers Mark Portugal and Dave Burba and outfielder Darren Lewis on July 21. The surprise out of the deal was Burba, a reliever-turned-starter who won four in a row and went 7-1. Portugal, the main piece of the trade, went 5-5. On July 31, just hours before the trading deadline, Bowden acquired left-hander David Wells from the Tigers for pitcher C.J. Nitkowski and a player to be named. Wells won four of his first five starts and finished 6-4 down the stretch.

The bullpen was a major problem. Only closer Jeff Brantley, with 28 saves, was an exception. Mike Jackson started slowly because of elbow problems, while Xavier Hernandez, Hector Carrasco and Chuck McElroy (the only lefty in the bullpen) never got on track.

Shortstop Barry Larkin did what he always does—led off and on the field. He and Bret Boone combined to provide spectacular defense up the middle—Larkin was second among shortstops with a .960 fielding average, and Boone led second basemen at .994 with only four errors, none before the All-Star break.

Reggie Sanders put together a career year, hitting .306 with 28 homers, 99 RBI and 36 stolen bases. Ron Gant came off Atlanta's scrap heap—and paid back the Reds for taking a chance on him—with 29 homers and 88 RBI.

Third basemen Jeff Branson and Mark Lewis combined for 15 homers and 75 RBI. Catcher Benito Santiago, plucked from Camp Homestead, the free-agent tryout camp, recovered from elbow surgery to hit .286 with 11 homers.

1996 Reds: Preview

With 11 players signed for $29.6 million, general manager Jim Bowden has little room to maneuver. Due to his elbow surgery, Jose Rijo isn't expected to pitch competitively until midseason, if at all. Reggie Sanders, a young, budding player, put together a career year only to fall flat in the playoffs.

It's time for young pitchers Kevin Jarvis and Tim Pugh to join veterans John Smiley and David Wells, along with fast-developing Pete Schourek. Jeff Brantley is back to anchor the bullpen as stopper, but the middle relief remains a question.

Not much is ready in the minor league system. Willie Greene has failed twice at third base. Shortstop Pokey Reese is ready but homeless with Barry Larkin around for another year. First baseman Tim Belk could make it.

1995 Reds: Week-by-week notes

These notes were excerpted from the following issues of Baseball Weekly.

▶**May 3:** The Reds, picked by nearly everybody to stroll to the NL Central title, lost their first four games. Starting pitchers gave up 19 runs in 19 innings. Relief pitchers gave up 12 runs in 16 innings. Leadoff hitter Deion Sanders was 3-for-20, first baseman Hal Morris was 1-for-18, and third baseman Willie Greene was 1 for 11.

▶**May 10:** General manager Jim Bowden sent a message little more than a week into the season—produce or pack. Third baseman Willie Greene and middle reliever Johnny Ruffin were optioned to Class AAA after the Reds' 1-8 start. Bowden also issued a warning to members of his 28-man roster, indicating there could be surprises when teams cut down to 25 on May 15.

▶**May 31:** The Reds major turnaround was all in the pitching. They started off 1-8—the starters were 0-4 with a 6.86 ERA, and the bullpen was 1-4 with a 4.81 ERA and a blown save—then they won 16 of 19, the starters were 9-3 with a 3.32 ERA, and the bullpen was 7-0 with seven saves in seven opportunities.

▶**June 7:** In one day, the Reds placed $7.2 million worth of talent on the DL and held their breath on $3.3 million more. Pitcher Jose Rijo (elbow tendinitis) and outfielder Deion Sanders (sprained left ankle) were disabled on June 3. First baseman Hal Morris, bothered by a strained left hamstring, was battling to stay off the list.

▶**June 14:** Ron Gant went down. Barry Larkin went down. Deion Sanders, Hal Morris, Benito Santiago and Jose Rijo already were down. But the Reds kept right on winning. After their 1-8 start, the Reds won 27 of their next 33 and became The Road Warriors. Their 16-6 record away from home was baseball's best.

▶**June 21:** Three consecutive losses had left the Reds in need of a hair-raising experience. They got one, courtesy of Marge Schott and her inexhaustible supply of dog fur, before their 5-4 victory June 17 against the Expos. As she did on May 6, when Cincinnati began its resurgence from a 1-8 start, Schott rubbed hair from Schottzie, her late St. Bernard, on team members—and the Reds won, scoring three runs in the third inning, with two outs and nobody on base, although just one of their three hits made it out of the infield—and breaking a 4-4 tie in the eighth with Jeff Branson's broken-bat single.

▶**June 28:** What had been a strength evaporated into a mess when the starting staff couldn't get beyond the fourth inning—in a span of 10 games, starters didn't make it out of the fourth inning seven times. Over those 10 starts, Tim Pugh, Pete Schourek, John Smiley, Jose Rijo, Kevin Jarvis, C.J. Nitkowski and John Roper combined to pitch only 47 innings, giving up 45 earned runs (8.62 ERA) and 10 home runs. And that included one game during which Smiley pitched seven shutout innings.

▶**July 5:** Davey Johnson firmly believed the Reds could make it into the post-season with their existing pitching staff, despite trade rumors involving David Cone. "You have young guys who need to stand up and other guys who are capable of turning some things around," he said. "If you look at where this staff and the ball club are, if Jose [Rijo] starts doing the things he's capable of, to go with [C.J.] Nitkowski, [John] Smiley and [Pete] Schourek, that elevates our pitching." Cincinnati might have been able to tempt the Blue Jays with its excess of talented young pitchers, but Johnson said, "You don't want to sacrifice tomorrow or the future for today."

▶**July 13:** Dazzled by the success of Hideo Nomo, GM Jim Bowden was exploring ways to make a trade with the

Japanese leagues and said the commissioner's office had given him the go-ahead. "We're told there are at least four pitchers in Japan better than Nomo," he said.

▶**July 19:** Second baseman Bret Boone made his first error of the season. He and shortstop Barry Larkin had made just four errors all season—Boone led NL second basemen with a .997 fielding average and Larkin led NL shortstops at .989 (three errors).

▶**July 26:** Deion Sanders went from the disabled list to being part of an eight-player trade with the Giants to restock Cincinnati's pitching staff. The Reds obtained starting pitcher Mark Portugal; reliever Dave Burba, who'll also be an emergency starter; and center fielder Darren Lewis. Going to the Giants with Sanders were pitcher John Roper, minor league first baseman David McCarty, minor league pitcher Scott Service and minor league pitcher Ricky Pickett.

▶**Aug. 2:** It took four starts, but John Smiley finally reached the 100-victory plateau and raised his season record to 10-1.

▶**Aug. 23:** Dave Burba pitched a complete-game, two-hit 8-0 win—his first major league shutout and complete game. He was a relief pitcher for the Giants but was pressed into a starting role for the Reds. In four starts he was 3-0 with a 1.04 ERA (26 innings, three runs) and 4-0 overall for the Reds. And he was on a string of 15 consecutive scoreless innings. "As I've been saying, I know I can pitch," Burba said.

▶**Aug. 30:** Frank Viola's return to a major league pitching mound on Aug. 26 after a 15-month absence wasn't a film clip they'll send to Cooperstown. But considering from whence he came, Viola accepts it. Gladly. After undergoing Tommy John surgery to reconstruct a ligament in his elbow in May 1994, Viola made his Reds' debut in Pittsburgh. He left with a 5-3 lead after 4⅔ innings. For four innings, he was passable—two runs on solo home runs and five hits—before the 35-year-old petrol tank slipped to empty, and he needed

help in the fifth. "I felt like a little kid," he said. "I had the adrenaline flow, the rush was there, but it was gone real quick."

▶**Sept. 13:** Even with a shortened season, Reggie Sanders was on pace to become only the second Red to join the 30-30-100 club—30 homers, 30 stolen bases and 100 RBI. With 20 games left, Sanders already had 31 stolen bases, 27 home runs and 93 RBI. Only six NL players have done it—the last was Barry Bonds for the 1990 Pirates.

▶**Oct. 4:** It was a wobbly finish for the Reds, who staggered into the playoffs against the Dodgers with a 12-17 record in September, their only losing month other than an 0-5 April. Shortstop Barry Larkin stole his 50th base (in 55 tries, .909), a career high. In his career, Larkin had stolen 238 bases and been caught only 30 times, an .888 success ratio.

Team directory

▶**Owner:** Marge Schott and a limited partnership
▶**General manager:** James G. Bowden
▶**Ballpark:**
Riverfront Stadium
Pete Rose Way, Cincinnati, Ohio
513-421-4510
Capacity 52,952
Parking for 5,022 cars; $3.50-$5
Wheelchair locations, ramps
▶**Team publications:**
Media guide, yearbook/program, *Reds Report*, 513-421-4510
▶**TV, radio broadcast stations:**
WLW 700 AM, WLWT Channel 5, SportsChannel-Cincinnati
▶**Spring training:**
Plant City Stadium
Plant City, Fla.
Capacity 6,700
813-752-1878

CINCINNATI REDS 1995 final stats

BATTERS	BA	SLG	OB	G	AB	R	H	TB	2B	3B	HR	RBI	BB	SO	SB	CS	E
Owens	1.000	1.000	1.000	2	2	0	2	2	0	0	0	1	0	0	0	0	0
M. Lewis	.339	.480	.407	81	171	25	58	82	13	1	3	30	21	33	0	3	4
Gibralter	.333	.333	.333	4	3	0	1	1	0	0	0	0	0	0	0	0	0
Larkin	.319	.492	.394	131	496	98	158	244	29	6	15	66	61	49	51	5	11
R. Sanders	.306	.579	.397	133	484	91	148	280	36	6	28	99	69	122	36	12	5
Howard	.302	.402	.350	113	281	42	85	113	15	2	3	26	20	37	17	8	2
Walton	.290	.525	.368	102	162	32	47	85	12	1	8	22	17	25	10	7	2
Duncan	.287	.423	.297	81	265	36	76	112	14	2	6	36	5	62	1	3	11
Santiago	.286	.485	.351	81	266	40	76	129	20	0	11	44	24	48	2	2	2
Taubensee	.284	.491	.354	80	218	32	62	107	14	2	9	44	22	52	2	2	6
Morris	.279	.451	.333	101	359	53	100	162	25	2	11	51	29	58	1	1	5
Worthington	.278	.500	.350	10	18	1	5	9	1	0	1	2	2	1	0	0	0
Gant	.276	.554	.386	119	410	79	113	227	19	4	29	88	74	108	23	8	3
Anthony	.269	.425	.327	47	134	19	36	57	6	0	5	23	13	30	2	1	4
Boone	.267	.429	.326	138	513	63	137	220	34	2	15	68	41	84	5	1	4
Branson	.260	.435	.345	122	331	43	86	144	18	2	12	45	44	69	2	1	9
D. Lewis	.250	.297	.311	132	472	66	118	140	13	3	1	24	34	57	32	18	2
Hunter	.215	.329	.312	40	79	9	17	26	6	0	1	9	11	21	2	1	3
Harris	.208	.310	.259	101	197	32	41	61	8	3	2	16	14	20	10	1	4
Berryhill	.183	.293	.260	34	82	6	15	24	3	0	2	11	10	19	0	0	2
Greene	.105	.105	.227	8	19	1	2	2	0	0	0	0	3	7	0	0	0
Wilson	.000	.000	.000	5	7	0	0	0	0	0	0	0	0	4	0	0	0

PITCHERS	W-L	ERA	G	GS	CG	GF	Sho	SV	IP	H	R	ER	HR	BB	SO
Ruffin	0-0	1.35	10	0	0	6	0	0	13.1	4	3	2	0	11	11
Jackson	6-1	2.39	40	0	0	10	0	2	49	38	13	13	5	19	41
Brantley	3-2	2.82	56	0	0	49	0	28	70.1	53	22	22	11	20	62
Schourek	18-7	3.22	29	29	2	0	0	0	190.1	158	72	68	17	45	160
Smiley	12-5	3.46	28	27	1	0	0	0	176.2	173	72	68	11	39	124
Wells	6-5	3.59	11	11	3	0	0	0	72.2	74	34	29	6	16	50
Pugh	6-5	3.84	28	12	0	4	0	0	98.1	100	46	42	13	32	38
Burba	10-4	3.97	52	9	1	7	1	0	106.2	90	50	47	9	51	96
Portugal	11-10	4.01	31	31	1	0	0	0	181.2	185	91	81	17	56	96
Carrasco	2-7	4.12	64	0	0	28	0	5	87.1	86	45	40	1	46	64
Rijo	5-4	4.17	14	14	0	0	0	0	69	76	33	32	6	22	62
Hernandez	7-2	4.60	59	0	0	19	0	3	90	95	47	46	8	31	84
Sullivan	0-0	4.91	3	0	0	1	0	0	3.2	4	2	2	0	2	2
Pennington	0-0	5.59	6	0	0	2	0	0	9.2	9	8	6	0	11	7
Jarvis	3-4	5.70	19	11	1	2	1	0	79	91	56	50	13	32	33
Reed	0-0	5.82	4	3	0	1	0	0	17	18	12	11	5	3	10
McElroy	3-4	6.02	44	0	0	11	0	0	40.1	46	29	27	5	15	27
Nitkowski	1-3	6.12	9	7	0	0	0	0	32.1	41	25	22	4	15	18
Viola	0-1	6.28	3	3	0	0	0	0	14.1	20	11	10	3	3	4
Smith	1-2	6.66	11	2	0	3	0	0	24.1	30	19	18	8	7	14
Remlinger	0-1	6.75	7	0	0	4	0	0	6.2	9	6	5	1	5	7
Courtright	0-0	9.00	1	0	0	0	0	0	1	2	1	1	0	0	0
Grott	0-0	21.60	2	0	0	0	0	0	1.2	6	4	4	1	0	2

1996 preliminary roster

PITCHERS (18)
Jeff Brantley
Dave Burba
Hector Carrasco
Chad Fox
Xavier Hernandez
Kevin Jarvis
Chuck McElroy
Marcus Moore
Mark Portugal
Tim Pugh
Jose Rijo
John Roper
Johnny Ruffin
Roger Salkeld
Pete Schourek
John Smiley
Scott Sullivan
David Wells

CATCHERS (2)
Damon Berryhill
Eddie Taubensee

INFIELDERS (10)
Tim Belk
Bret Boone
Jeff Branson
Willie Greene
Lenny Harris
Brian Hunter
Barry Larkin
Hal Morris
Eric Owens
Pokey Reese

OUTFIELDERS (10)
Eric Anthony
Steve Gibralter
Thomas Howard
Andre King
Cleveland Ladell
Chad Mottola
Reggie Sanders
Jerome Walton
Pat Watkins
Nigel Wilson

Games played by position

PLAYER	G	C	1B	2B	3B	SS	OF
Anthony	47	0	17	0	0	0	24
Berryhill	34	29	1	0	0	0	0
Boone	138	0	0	0	0	0	0
Branson	122	0	1	6	98	32	0
Duncan	81	0	18	31	1	20	3
Gant	119	0	0	0	0	0	117
Gibralter	4	0	0	0	0	0	2
Greene	8	0	0	0	7	0	0
Harris	101	0	23	1	24	0	8
Howard	113	0	0	0	0	0	82
Hunter	40	0	23	0	0	0	4
Larkin	131	0	0	0	0	130	0
D. Lewis	132	0	0	0	0	0	130
M. Lewis	81	0	0	2	72	2	0
Morris	101	0	99	0	0	0	0
Owens	2	0	0	0	2	0	0
R. Sanders	133	0	0	0	0	0	130
Santiago	81	75	8	0	0	0	0
Taubensee	80	65	3	0	0	0	0
Walton	102	0	3	0	0	0	89
Wilson	5	0	0	0	0	0	2
Worthington	10	0	4	0	2	0	0

Sick call: 1995 DL Report

Player	Days on the DL
Eric Anthony	88**
Damon Berryhill	39
Steve Gibralter	1
Brian Hunter	53*
Mike Jackson	41
Chuck McElroy	16
Hal Morris	25
Eric Owens	1
Jose Rijo	90*
John Roper	42
Johnny Ruffin	31
Reggie Sanders	45
Benito Santiago	57
John Smiley	15
Frank Viola	10

Indicates two separate terms on Disabled List.
**Indicates three separate terms on DL.*

1995 Amateur draft picks

Players are listed with position and college or high school. Most players were assigned to rookie or Class A leagues. List provided by Major League Baseball.

Justin Atchley, lhp, Texas A&M; Benjamin Bailey, rhp, Glen Oaks CC; Andrew Burress, c, Telfair County HS, McRae, Ga.; Stephen Claybrook, cf, Texas A&M; Antonia Cloud, rhp, Spartanburg Methodist; Mark Corey, rhp, Edinboro; Dwayne Cushman, rhp, Valdosta State; Michael Daniel, rhp, John C. Calhoun CC; Johnny Davis, lhp, Lake Gibson HS, Polk City, Fla.; James Davis, c, Western Kentucky; Todd Fehrenbach, c, Citrus HS, Inverness, Fla.; Zachary Frachiseur, rhp, Rockdale County HS, Conyers, Ga.; Steven Goodhart, 2b, Ohio Wesleyan; Herbert Goodman of, North Greenville JC; David Guthrie, ss, North Carolina State; Jason Hubbard, lhp, Angelina JC; Jason Johnson of, Montclair (Calif.) HS; Jeffery Juarez, cf, New Braunfels (Texas) HS; Raymond King, lhp, Lambuth University; Michael Larue, c, Dallas Baptist; Richard Lawrence, rhp, Central Florida; Brian Loyd, c, Cal State Fullerton; Robert Mackoviak, ss-2b, South Suburban College; Scott Macrae, rhp, Valdosta State; James Maddox, rhp, Florida CC; William Mapp, rf, Lamar; Justin Marine, rhp, Moorpark College; Lamont Mason, 2b-ss, Lubbock Christian; Andre Montgomery, ss, Pleasure Ridge Park HS, Louisville, Ky.; Joseph Montgomery, rhp, Jacksonville State; Christopher Murphy, lhp, Cincinnati; Jason Parsons, 1b, Dallas Baptist; Anthony Patellis, 3b, Kent; Schleuss Del, lhp, Alabama; Thomas Scott cf, Linfield College; James Sparks, rhp, St. Mary's; Larfeyette Stanley, rhp, Jordan HS, Columbus, Ga.; Brett Tomko, rhp, Florida Southern; Andrew Tracy, 1b, Bowling Green; Chad Truby, 3b, Yavapai College; Bobby Walters, cf, Sallisaw (Okla.) HS; Brian Willman, rhp, North Carolina; Scott Wright, rhp, Missouri Southern State.

Minor Leagues

Tops in the organization

Batter	Club	Avg.	G	AB	R	H	HR	RBI
Brandon Wilson	Cng	.316	106	405	67	128	10	60
Dan Rohrmeier	Cng	.315	128	460	82	145	17	79
Eric Owens	Ind	.314	108	427	86	134	12	63
Nigel Wilson	Ind	.313	82	304	53	95	17	51
Brian Koelling	Cng	.296	107	432	71	128	3	45

Home Runs			Wins		
Mike Meggers	W-S	20	Cedric Allen	Cwv	13
Jamie Dismuke	Cng	20	Roger Salkeld	Ind	12
Ray Brown	Cwv	19	Tommy Kramer	Cng	12
Willie Greene	Ind	19	Several tied		11
Several tied		18			

RBI			Saves		
Dan Rohrmeier	Cng	79	Rusty Kilgo	Cng	29
Ruben Santana	Cng	79	Scott McKenzie	W-S	20
Ray Brown	Cwv	77	Emiliano Giron	Cwv	20
Chad Mottola	Ind	76	Scott Service	Ind	18
Marlon Allen	Cwv	76	Rich Sauveur	Ind	15

Stolen Bases			Strikeouts		
Terry Wright	Cwv	46	Tommy Kramer	Cng	126
Johnny Carvajal	Cwv	44	Curt Lyons	W-S	122
Nick Morrow	Cwv	41	Clint Koppe	Cwv	119
Eric Owens	Ind	33	Cedric Allen	Cwv	108
Brian Koelling	Cng	30	Jason Robbins	W-S	106

Pitcher	Club	W-L	ERA	IP	H	BB	SO
John Burgos	Cng	3-5	2.78	100	95	19	82
Cedric Allen	Cwv	13-7	2.85	170	143	46	108
Curt Lyons	W-S	9-9	2.98	160	139	67	122
Jason Robbins	W-S	9-6	3.06	141	113	42	106
Chris Reed	W-S	10-7	3.32	149	116	68	104

Cincinnati (1890-1995)

Runs: Most, career, all-time

1741	Pete Rose, 1963-1986
1091	Johnny Bench, 1967-1983
1043	Frank Robinson, 1956-1965
993	Dave Concepcion, 1970-1988
978	Vada Pinson, 1958-1968

Hits: Most, career, all-time

3358	Pete Rose, 1963-1986
2326	Dave Concepcion, 1970-1988
2048	Johnny Bench, 1967-1983
1934	Tony Perez, 1964-1986
1881	Vada Pinson, 1958-1968

2B: Most, career, all-time

601	Pete Rose, 1963-1986
389	Dave Concepcion, 1970-1988
381	Johnny Bench, 1967-1983
342	Vada Pinson, 1958-1968
339	Tony Perez, 1964-1986

3B: Most, career, all-time

152	Edd Roush, 1916-1931
115	Pete Rose, 1963-1986
112	Bid McPhee, 1890-1899
96	Vada Pinson, 1958-1968
94	Curt Walker, 1924-1930

HR: Most, career, all-time

389	Johnny Bench, 1967-1983
324	Frank Robinson, 1956-1965
287	Tony Perez, 1964-1986
251	Ted Kluszewski, 1947-1957
244	George Foster, 1971-1981

RBI: Most, career, all-time

1376	Johnny Bench, 1967-1983
1192	Tony Perez, 1964-1986
1036	Pete Rose, 1963-1986
1009	Frank Robinson, 1956-1965
950	Dave Concepcion, 1970-1988

SB: Most, career, all-time

406	Joe Morgan, 1972-1979
337	Arlie Latham, 1890-1895
321	Dave Concepcion, 1970-1988
320	Bob Bescher, 1908-1913
316	Bid McPhee, 1890-1899

BB: Most, career, all-time

1210	Pete Rose, 1963-1986
891	Johnny Bench, 1967-1983
881	Joe Morgan, 1972-1979
736	Dave Concepcion, 1970-1988
698	Frank Robinson, 1956-1965

BA: Highest, career, all-time

.332	Cy Seymour, 1902-1906
.331	Edd Roush, 1916-1931
.325	Jake Beckley, 1897-1903
.314	Bubbles Hargrave, 1921-1928
.311	Rube Bressler, 1917-1927

Slug avg: Highest, career, all-time

.554	Frank Robinson, 1956-1965
.514	George Foster, 1971-1981
.512	Ted Kluszewski, 1947-1957
.509	Eric Davis, 1984-1991
.498	Wally Post, 1949-1963

Games started: Most, career, all-time

356	Eppa Rixey, 1921-1933
322	Paul Derringer, 1933-1942
319	Dolf Luque, 1918-1929
298	TOM BROWNING, 1984-1994
296	Bucky Walters, 1938-1948

Saves: Most, career, all-time

148	JOHN FRANCO, 1984-1989
119	Clay Carroll, 1968-1975
88	ROB DIBBLE, 1988-1993
88	Tom Hume, 1977-1987
76	Pedro Borbon, 1970-1979

Shutouts: Most, career, all-time

32	Bucky Walters, 1938-1948
30	Jim Maloney, 1960-1970
29	Johnny Vander Meer, 1937-1949
25	Ken Raffensberger, 1947-1954
24	Paul Derringer, 1933-1942
24	Noodles Hahn, 1899-1905
24	Dolf Luque, 1918-1929

Wins: Most, career, all-time

179	Eppa Rixey, 1921-1933
161	Paul Derringer, 1933-1942
160	Bucky Walters, 1938-1948
154	Dolf Luque, 1918-1929
134	Jim Maloney, 1960-1970

K: Most, career, all-time

1592	Jim Maloney, 1960-1970
1449	Mario Soto, 1977-1988
1289	Joe Nuxhall, 1944-1966
1251	Johnny Vander Meer, 1937-1949
1201	JOSE RIJO, 1988-1995

Win pct: Highest, career, all-time

.674	Don Gullett, 1970-1976
.653	Pedro Borbon, 1970-1979
.623	Jim Maloney, 1960-1970
.623	Clay Carroll, 1968-1975
.621	Gary Nolan, 1967-1977

ERA: Lowest, career, all-time

2.18	Fred Toney, 1915-1918
2.37	Bob Ewing, 1902-1909
2.52	Noodles Hahn, 1899-1905
2.62	Hod Eller, 1917-1921
2.65	Pete Schneider, 1914-18

Runs: Most, season

134	Frank Robinson, 1962
131	Vada Pinson, 1959
130	Pete Rose, 1976
129	Arlie Latham, 1894
126	Tommy Harper, 1965

Hits: Most, season

230	Pete Rose, 1973
219	Cy Seymour, 1905
218	Pete Rose, 1969
215	Pete Rose, 1976
210	Pete Rose, 1968
210	Pete Rose, 1975

2B: Most, season

51	Frank Robinson, 1962
51	Pete Rose, 1978
47	Vada Pinson, 1959
47	Pete Rose, 1975
45	George Kelly, 1929
45	Pete Rose, 1974

3B: Most, season

26	John Reilly, 1890
22	Sam Crawford, 1902
22	Jake Daubert, 1922
22	Bid McPhee, 1890
22	Mike Mitchell, 1911

HR: Most, season

52	George Foster, 1977
49	Ted Kluszewski, 1954
47	Ted Kluszewski, 1955
45	Johnny Bench, 1970
40	Johnny Bench, 1972
40	George Foster, 1978
40	Ted Kluszewski, 1953
40	Tony Perez, 1970
40	Wally Post, 1955

RBI: Most, season

149	George Foster, 1977	
148	Johnny Bench, 1970	
141	Ted Kluszewski, 1954	
136	Frank Robinson, 1962	
130	Deron Johnson, 1965	

SB: Most, season

87	Arlie Latham, 1891
81	Bob Bescher, 1911
80	Eric Davis, 1986
79	Dave Collins, 1980
76	Dusty Miller, 1896

BB: Most, season

132	Joe Morgan, 1975
120	Joe Morgan, 1974
117	Joe Morgan, 1977
115	Joe Morgan, 1972
114	Joe Morgan, 1976

BA: Highest, season

.377	Cy Seymour, 1905
.372	Bug Holliday, 1894
.351	Edd Roush, 1923
.351	Mike Donlin, 1903
.348	Edd Roush, 1924
.348	Pete Rose, 1969

Slug avg: Highest, season

.642	Ted Kluszewski, 1954
.631	George Foster, 1977
.624	Frank Robinson, 1962
.611	Frank Robinson, 1961
.595	Frank Robinson, 1960

Games started: Most, season

49	Elton Chamberlain, 1892
47	Tony Mullane, 1891
45	Billy Rhines, 1890
43	Billy Rhines, 1891
42	Noodles Hahn, 1901
42	Pete Schneider, 1917
42	Fred Toney, 1917

Saves: Most, season

39	JOHN FRANCO, 1988
37	Clay Carroll, 1972
35	Wayne Granger, 1970
32	JOHN FRANCO, 1987
32	JOHN FRANCO, 1989

Shutouts: Most, season

7	Jack Billingham, 1973
7	Hod Eller, 1919
7	Fred Toney, 1917
6	Ewell Blackwell, 1947
6	Noodles Hahn, 1902
6	Jack Harper, 1904
6	DANNY JACKSON, 1988
6	Dolf Luque, 1923
6	Jim Maloney, 1963
6	Ken Raffensberger, 1952
6	Billy Rhines, 1890
6	Fred Toney, 1915
6	Johnny Vander Meer, 1941
6	Bucky Walters, 1944
6	Jake Weimer, 1906

Wins: Most, season

28	Billy Rhines, 1890
27	Pink Hawley, 1898
27	Dolf Luque, 1923
27	Bucky Walters, 1939
25	Paul Derringer, 1939
25	Eppa Rixey, 1922

K: Most, season

274	Mario Soto, 1982
265	Jim Maloney, 1963
244	Jim Maloney, 1965
242	Mario Soto, 1983
239	Noodles Hahn, 1901

Win pct: Highest, season

.826	Elmer Riddle, 1941
.821	Bob Purkey, 1962
.789	Don Gullett, 1975
.783	TOM BROWNING, 1988
.781	Paul Derringer, 1939

ERA: Lowest, season

1.58	Fred Toney, 1915
1.73	Bob Ewing, 1907
1.77	Noodles Hahn, 1902
1.82	Dutch Ruether, 1919
1.86	Andy Coakley, 1908

Most pinch-hit homers, season

5	Jerry Lynch, 1961
4	Bob Thurman, 1957

Most pinch-hit homers, career

13	Jerry Lynch, 1957-1963

Most consecutive games batting safely

44	Pete Rose, 1978
30	Elmer Smith, 1898

Most consecutive scoreless innings

32	Jim Maloney, 1968-1969
27	Tom Seaver, 1977

No-hit games

Bumpus Jones, Cin vs Pit NL, 7-1; October 15, 1892 (first game in the major leagues).

Ted Breitenstein, Cin vs Pit NL, 11-0; April 22, 1898.

Noodles Hahn, Cin vs Phi NL, 4-0; July 12, 1900.

Fred Toney, Cin at Chi NL, 1-0; May 2, 1917 (10 innings).

Hod Eller, Cin vs StL NL, 6-0; May 11, 1919.

Johnny Vander Meer, Cin vs Bos NL, 3-0; June 11, 1938.

Johnny Vander Meer, Cin at Bro NL, 6-0; June 15, 1938 (next start after June 11).

Clyde Shoun, Cin vs Bos NL, 1-0; May 15, 1944.

Ewell Blackwell, Cin vs Bos NL, 6-0; June 18, 1947.

Johnny Klippstein (7 innings), Hershell Freeman (1 inning) and Joe Black (3 innings), Cin at Mil NL, 1-2; May 26, 1956 (lost on 3 hits in 11 innings after allowing the first hit in the 10th).

Jim Maloney, Cin vs NY NL, 0-1; June 14, 1965 (lost on 2 hits in 11 innings after pitching 10 hitless innings).

Jim Maloney, Cin at Chi NL, 1-0; August 19, 1965 (1st game, 10 innings).

George Culver, Cin at Phi NL, 6-1; July 29, 1968 (2nd game).

Jim Maloney, Cin vs Hou NL, 10-0; April 30, 1969.

Tom Seaver, Cin vs StL NL, 4-0; June 16, 1978.

TOM BROWNING, Cin vs LA NL, 1-0; September 16, 1988 (perfect game).

Elton Chamberlain, 7 innings, darkness, Cin vs Bos NL, 6-0; September 23, 1893 (2nd game).

Jake Weimer, 7 innings, agreement, Cin vs Bro NL, 1-0; August 24, 1906 (2nd game).

ACTIVE PLAYERS in caps.

Players' years of service are listed by the first and last years with this team and are not necessarily consecutive; all statistics record performances for this team only.

Houston Astros

By Anne Ryan, USA TODAY

Right fielder Derek Bell led the Astros in batting at .334, stole 27 bases, and was second in RBI with 86.

1995 Astros: Injuries killed wild-card hopes

The Astros went to the final day with a chance to earn the first wild-card berth but finished one game behind Colorado. The fact they were that close was surprising, given all the injuries they were forced to overcome. First baseman Jeff Bagwell, right fielder Derek Bell, catcher Rick Wilkins and reliever John Hudek all missed significant time due to injuries. The Astros were forced to use role players like Dave Magadan, John Cangelosi and Derrick May more than anticipated but got better than expected production from each of them. In addition, they made several trades that changed the chemistry in the clubhouse and the lineup. Popular veterans Luis Gonzalez and Scott Servais were sent to the Cubs in late June for Wilkins. Unfortunately, Wilkins was diagnosed with a neck disk problem after two games and had major surgery in July.

The key injury came July 30 when Bagwell was hit by a pitch and suffered a broken bone in his left hand for the third straight season. While he sat out the month of August, the Astros lost a club-record 11 consecutive games. They fell out of the race in the NL Central and lost what appeared to be a commanding lead for the wild-card spot. Bagwell finished at .290 with 21 homers and a team-best 87 RBIs, but this was subpar for him.

Shaky starting pitching and a poor home record kept the Astros under .500 the first six weeks of the season, but Bagwell and the rest of the offense started to perk up when rookie center fielder Brian Hunter was called up from the minors in mid-June. With Hunter, Craig Biggio, Bagwell and Derek Bell at the top of the lineup, the Astros scored 181 runs in July, the most by an NL team in any month since June 1977. The Astros set a franchise record with a 19-10 record that month, and both Bagwell and Bell set a club mark with 31 RBI. Bagwell, Bell and Biggio combined for a .325 average, 17 homers, 80 RBI and 80 runs.

Then came Bagwell's injury and the down days of August. The starting pitching slumped badly, as well. Doug Drabek and Greg Swindell, expected to provide veteran leadership down the stretch, combined for one win in August. Younger pitchers Shane Reynolds and Mike Hampton seemed to tire as the season wore on. At the end of the year, no Astros starter had more than 10 wins.

The bullpen held things together for most of the season, despite losing Hudek in June. Todd Jones moved into the closer's spot, but he faltered and veteran Mike Henneman was acquired from Detroit in August. The Astros had 32 saves, third fewest in the league.

When the team regrouped to get back into the wild-card race in September, they had to do it without Bell, their top hitter (.334), who was hit by a pitch in August and never returned. Rookie shortstop Orlando Miller suffered a knee injury that month that knocked him out for the rest of the year, too.

The constant through all the injuries and trades was Biggio, who led the majors with 123 runs and hit .302 with 22 homers, 77 RBI and 33 stolen bases.

1996 Astros: Preview

The Astros have more than $15 million committed to Drabek, Swindell and Bagwell for '96, and there are signs that the team wants to hold down costs. Look for a younger, less expensive team. Many players that fit that description already have major league experience—Hunter, Miller, Reynolds, Hampton, Jones, Dave Veres, Tony Eusebio and James Mouton. Also look for pitchers Donne Wall and Billy Wagner, second baseman Dave Hajek and outfielder Bobby Abreu. Wall was named player of the year in the Pacific Coast League after leading in wins, strikeouts and ERA. It might not be enough to get the Astros a playoff berth, but they should be a contender again.

1995 Astros: Week-by-week notes

These notes were excerpted from the following issues of Baseball Weekly.

▶**May 3:** After a 10-run season-opener win at San Diego, the Astros lost their steam, scoring a total of four runs over the next four games, all losses. Jeff Bagwell struck out three times in a game, something that happened just once in 1994. Through four games, the Astros struck out 35 times and left 39 runners stranded.

▶**May 10:** Through 10 games, Jeff Bagwell was hitting .121, but he was second in the league with 13 walks—teams were pitching around him. Meanwhile, cleanup hitter Derek Bell had eight RBI through May 7, six with two men out.

▶**May 24:** The big three in the Astros' bullpen—closer John Hudek and setup men Todd Jones and Dave Veres—were virtually perfect through the first three weeks of the season. With 11 consecutive shutout innings through May 20, the Astros' bullpen ERA dropped to 2.97, second in the league behind Chicago's. Relievers were 6-0, the only bullpen in the league not to have lost a game yet. In addition, the bullpen was 4-for-4 in save situations. The key pitchers were Veres, who had not allowed a run in 15 ⅔ innings; Jones, who allowed just two in 18⅔; and Hudek, who had not been scored on in 7⅔. They combined for a 3-0 record, four saves and a 0.43 ERA.

▶**May 31:** Through May 27, Derek Bell was hitting .355 with one home run, 17 RBI and eight stolen bases. In addition, he was doing little things like sliding hard into second to break up double plays and running out routine infield ground balls. "All he does is play hard," said pitcher Doug Drabek. "He runs out every ground ball and every fly ball, and he dives all over the place in the outfield. He just runs all over the place."

▶**June 7:** Considering that the starting rotation had an 8-15 record through June 3, the Astros were fortunate their bullpen had been nearly perfect—9-1 with seven saves in seven chances. Closers John Hudek (2-0, six saves) and Todd Jones (3-0, one save) attracted most of the attention, but middle reliever Dave Veres was just as important. He was 1-1 with a 0.76 ERA and had allowed only two runs in 23⅔ innings.

▶**June 14:** As the Astros continued to struggle at home, manager Terry Collins let his players know he was not happy. "I'm baffled by this," said Collins. "I just want us to go out and get the job done. I don't want to hear about how we're snakebit or how the other guys make good plays. The other guys are supposed to make good plays—this is the major leagues."

▶**June 21:** Third baseman Phil Nevin, who went 2-for-21 in his first week after coming up from the minors, suffered a mild concussion June 17 during a freak accident in the first inning of a game at New York. He was hit by a foul ball that went off the end of his bat, rolled backward and struck him in the right temple. Nevin was wobbly as he walked off the field to the Astros' clubhouse, but he was coherent within a few minutes.

▶**June 28:** When the Astros concluded a 7-2 swing to Philadelphia, New York and Montreal on June 21, it was their third winning trip in 1995. Already, that was more winning trips than 12 previous Houston teams since the club began play in 1962. The record for winning trips in a season is six, accomplished three times.

▶**July 5:** After scoring 77 runs in their first 25 home games, the Astros scored 61 runs in winning five of six games. The key was rookie center fielder Brian Hunter, who scored 21 runs in his first 18 games after being called up. The Astros were 13-5 since his arrival. He was hitting .374.

▶**July 26:** The Astros were 44-34, 2½ games ahead of Philadelphia in the wild-card race. They had the third-best record in the league but trailed the Reds by 6½ games in the Central Division.

▶**Aug. 2:** The Astros were in position to break several franchise records. Through July 29, they had scored a league-high 478 runs in 85 games, a pace that would give them 810 runs for the season. The team record was 744 in 1970, in 162 games. Led by Derek Bell's .339 and 75 RBI, the Astros had a team average of .276 and 438 RBI. The club record for average was .267, set in 1993. The team was on a pace to drive in 753 runs, which would break the previous record of 694, set in 1970.

▶**Aug. 16:** In the middle of one of their worst stretches of the season, the Astros suddenly had to deal with their first replacement player being called up to the majors. Veteran pitcher Craig McMurtry was recalled from Class AAA during a six-game losing streak. "We've been struggling as it is, so we don't need this kind of distraction," said relief pitcher Dave Veres. "If we hadn't come back, he would still be here with our job. He wouldn't think twice about us. It's going to be hard to ignore him." McMurtry played in the majors with Atlanta and Texas for parts of seven seasons. "I definitely don't approve of what was done," said relief pitcher Todd Jones, the Astros' player representative, "especially for a guy that has six years of major league service. He bit the hand that feeds him."

▶**Aug. 23:** It didn't take a math genius to figure out why the Astros faded from the NL Central race—through Aug. 20, they were 0-10 against first-place Cincinnati. They trailed the Reds by those 10 games.

▶**Aug. 30:** The Astros' worst fears about a lineup without first baseman Jeff Bagwell came true when they suffered through a 10-game losing streak and dropped out of the lead for the NL wild-card spot. After scoring 6.2 runs per game in July, the Astros averaged 3.3 in August (through Aug. 26). Their record without Bagwell was 7-10, and they had lost 17 out of 20 Aug. 5-27. The 10-game losing streak tied a club record and was their longest since 1974.

▶**Sept. 6:** After hitting rock bottom while losing a franchise-record 11 consecutive games, the Astros showed signs of coming to life as the final month of the season began. Though the return of Jeff Bagwell on Sept. 1 perked up the Astros' offense, things had already started to get better. The Astros scored 15 runs in taking two out of three at Atlanta Aug. 29-31, including an 11-9 win that snapped the long losing streak. "We're lucky," said Bagwell. "We lost a lot of games the last three weeks, but we're still in good shape."

▶**Oct. 4:** Although the Astros lost three consecutive extra-inning games the final week—killing their playoff chances—Terry Collins was upbeat about the effort he got from his team. "Workers, grinders, that's us," said Collins. "We've got our two stars in [Craig] Biggio and [Jeff] Bagwell ... the rest of the group is just a bunch of guys doing their jobs."

Team directory

▶**Owner:** Drayton McLane Jr.
▶**General manager:** Gerry Hunsicker
▶**Ballpark:**
Houston Astrodome
8400 Kirby Dr., Houston, Texas
713-799-9500
Capacity 54,313
Parking for 26,000 cars; $4
Public transportation by bus
Wheelchair section and ramps
▶**Team publications:**
Astros Magazine, Astros Media Guide
713-799-9600
▶**TV, radio broadcast stations:**
KPRC 950 AM, UPN Channel 20, Prime Sports Entertainment Cable
▶**Camps and/or clinics:**
Astros Youth Clinics, during the season, 713-799-9877
▶**Spring training:**
Osceola County Stadium
Kissimmee, Fla.
Capacity 5,130
407-933-5400

HOUSTON ASTROS 1995 final stats

BATTERS	BA	SLG	OB	G	AB	R	H	TB	2B	3B	HR	RBI	BB	SO	SB	CS	E
Bell	.334	.442	.385	112	452	63	151	200	21	2	8	86	33	71	27	9	8
Cangelosi	.318	.393	.457	90	201	46	64	79	5	2	2	18	48	42	21	5	5
Magadan	.313	.399	.428	127	348	44	109	139	24	0	2	51	71	56	2	1	18
Hunter	.302	.396	.346	78	321	52	97	127	14	5	2	28	21	52	24	7	9
Biggio	.302	.483	.406	141	553	123	167	267	30	2	22	77	80	85	33	8	10
May	.301	.500	.358	78	206	29	62	103	15	1	8	41	19	24	5	0	2
Donnels	.300	.300	.364	19	30	4	9	9	0	0	0	2	3	6	0	0	2
Eusebio	.299	.410	.354	113	368	46	110	151	21	1	6	58	31	59	0	2	5
Bagwell	.290	.496	.399	114	448	88	130	222	29	0	21	87	79	102	12	5	7
Tucker	.286	.714	.286	5	7	1	2	5	0	0	1	1	0	0	0	0	0
Gutierrez	.276	.314	.321	52	156	22	43	49	6	0	0	12	10	33	5	0	8
Shipley	.263	.345	.291	92	232	23	61	80	8	1	3	24	8	28	6	1	3
Miller	.262	.377	.319	92	324	36	85	122	20	1	5	36	22	71	3	4	15
Mouton	.262	.376	.326	104	298	42	78	112	18	2	4	27	25	59	25	8	0
Simms	.256	.512	.341	50	121	14	31	62	4	0	9	24	13	28	1	2	1
Thompson	.220	.333	.297	92	132	14	29	44	9	0	2	19	14	37	4	2	1
Wilkins	.203	.322	.351	65	202	30	41	65	3	0	7	19	46	61	0	0	4
Goff	.154	.346	.267	12	26	2	4	9	2	0	1	3	4	13	0	0	0
Nevin	.117	.133	.221	18	60	4	7	8	1	0	0	1	7	13	1	0	3
Stankiewicz	.115	.135	.281	43	52	6	6	7	1	0	0	7	12	19	4	2	1
Borders	.114	.114	.162	11	35	1	4	4	0	0	0	0	2	7	0	0	1
Brumley	.056	.222	.056	18	18	1	1	4	0	0	1	2	0	6	1	0	1
Hajek	.000	.000	.333	5	2	0	0	0	0	0	0	0	1	1	1	1	0

PITCHERS	W-L	ERA	G	GS	CG	GF	Sho	SV	IP	H	R	ER	HR	BB	SO
Cangelosi	0-0	0.00	1	0	0	1	0	0	1	0	0	0	0	1	0
Wagner	0-0	0.00	1	0	0	0	0	0	0.1	0	0	0	0	0	0
Veres	5-1	2.26	72	0	0	15	0	1	103.1	89	29	26	5	30	94
Henneman	0-1	3.00	21	0	0	18	0	8	21	21	7	7	1	4	19
Jones	6-5	3.07	68	0	0	40	0	15	99.2	89	38	34	8	52	96
Hartgraves	2-0	3.22	40	0	0	11	0	0	36.1	30	14	13	2	16	24
Tabaka	1-0	3.23	34	0	0	6	0	0	30.2	27	11	11	2	17	25
Hampton	9-8	3.35	24	24	0	0	0	0	150.2	141	73	56	13	49	115
Reynolds	10-11	3.47	30	30	3	0	2	0	189.1	196	87	73	15	37	175
Brocail	6-4	4.19	36	7	0	12	0	1	77.1	87	40	36	10	22	39
Swindell	10-9	4.47	33	26	1	3	1	0	153	180	86	76	21	39	96
Drabek	10-9	4.77	31	31	2	0	1	0	185	205	104	98	18	54	143
Dougherty	8-4	4.92	56	0	0	11	0	0	67.2	76	37	37	7	25	49
Kile	4-12	4.96	25	21	0	1	0	0	127	114	81	70	5	73	113
Hudek	2-2	5.40	19	0	0	16	0	7	20	19	12	12	3	5	29
Wall	3-1	5.55	6	5	0	0	0	0	24.1	33	19	15	5	5	16
Martinez	0-0	7.40	25	0	0	3	0	0	20.2	29	18	17	3	16	17
McMurtry	0-1	7.84	11	0	0	3	0	0	10.1	15	11	9	0	9	4

1996 preliminary roster

PITCHERS (23)
Doug Brocail
Ryan Creek
Jim Dougherty
Doug Drabek
Kevin Gallaher
Mike Grzanich
Mike Hampton
Dean Hartgraves
Oscar Henriquez
Chris Holt
John Hudek
Todd Jones
Darryl Kile
Rich Loiselle
Doug Mlicki
Alvin Morman
Shane Reynolds
Mark Small
Greg Swindell
Jeff Tabaka
David Veres
Billy Wagner
Donne Wall

CATCHERS (2)
Tony Eusebio
Rick Wilkins

INFIELDERS (6)
Jeff Bagwell
Ricky Gutierrez
Dave Hajek
Ray Holbert
Orlando Miller
Craig Shipley

OUTFIELDERS (7)
Bob Abreu
Derek Bell
Richard Hidalgo
Brian Hunter
Derrick May
James Mouton
Mike Simms

Games played by position

PLAYER	G	C	1B	2B	3B	SS	OF
Bagwell	114	0	114	0	0	0	0
Bell	112	0	0	0	0	0	110
Biggio	141	0	0	141	0	0	0
Borders	11	11	0	0	0	0	0
Brumley	18	0	1	0	1	3	3
Cangelosi	90	0	0	0	0	0	59
Donnels	19	0	0	1	9	0	0
Eusebio	113	103	0	0	0	0	0
Goff	12	11	0	0	0	0	0
Gutierrez	52	0	0	0	2	44	0
Hajek	5	0	0	0	0	0	0
Hunter	78	0	0	0	0	0	74
Magadan	127	0	11	0	100	0	0
May	78	0	1	0	0	0	55
Miller	92	0	0	0	0	89	0
Mouton	104	0	0	0	0	0	94
Nevin	18	0	0	0	16	0	0
Shipley	92	0	1	4	65	11	0
Simms	50	0	25	0	0	0	12
Stankiewicz	43	0	0	6	3	14	0
Thompson	92	0	0	0	0	0	34
Tucker	5	3	0	0	0	0	0
Wilkins	65	62	2	0	0	0	0

Sick call: 1995 DL Report

Player	Days on the DL
Jeff Bagwell	32
Chris Donnels	17
Mike Hampton	29
John Hudek	101
Brian Lee Hunter	18
Orlando Miller	15
James Mouton	18
Phil Plantier	51
Andy Stankiewicz	28
Rick Wilkins	65

1995 Amateur draft picks

Players are listed with position and college or high school. Most players were assigned to rookie or Class A leagues. List provided by Major League Baseball.

Jason Adams, ss, Wichita State; James Alarcon, rhp, Jupiter (Fla.) Community HS; Chad Alexander, cf, Texas A&M; Brock Ashby, cf, Saint Francis Xavier HS, Edmonton; Adam Bell, c, Helena (Mont.) HS; Brian Berryman, rhp, Redford (Mich.) Union HS; Ryan Block, rhp, Walla Walla (Wash.) HS; Frank Bludau, rhp, Halletsville (Texas) HS; Andy Bovender, 3b, North Carolina-Charlotte; Caleb Brown, lhp, Howard College; Brett Brown, lhp, Delaware Tech; Darren Brown, rhp, Brophy Jesuit Prep School, Scottsdale, Ariz.; Mark Burnett, ss, Bryant HS, Benton, Ark.; Charles Carter, 1b, McLennan CC; Christopher Castleberry, c, Americus (Ga.) HS; Mark Chambers, Navarro College; Ryan Channel, lhp, Satellite Beach (Fla.) HS; Scott Chapman, c, Alexander HS, Albany, Ohio; Wayne Chinapen, rhp-of, York Mills (Ont.) Institute; Ryan Coe, c, Kennesaw State; Eric Cole, 3b, Antelope Valley JC; Javier Contreras, rhp, La Providencia HS, Rio Piedras P.R.; Michael Corominas, lhp, Arizona State; James Crossley, 3b, Chabot College; Jeremy Deshazer, cf, Lake Washington Senior HS, Kirkland, Wash.; Stephen Dye, rhp, Middle Georgia JC; Bill Eaton, ss-rhp, Indian River CC; Eric Eckenstahler, lhp, Antioch HS, Lindenhurst, Ill.; Roger Foltynowicz, 3b, Lakeside HS, Evans, Ga.; Brian Fritz, 1b, Santa Ynez HS, Solvang, Calif.; Peter Fukuhara, cf, Canada College; Gabriel Garcia, c-rhp, James Logan HS, Union City, Calif.; Marty Godwin, lf, Osceola Senior HS, Kissimmee, Fla.; Timothy Hamulack, of-lhp, Edgewood (Md.) HS; Christopher Hargett, 1b, Jeffersonville (Ind.) HS; Walter Harrington, rhp, Palomar College; Corey Hart, 2b, Connors State; James Hawkins, rhp, Santa Margarita HS, Niguel, Calif.; Christopher Hill, rhp, Long Beach CC; David Huggins, rhp, Galveston College; Eric Ireland, rhp, Robert A. Millikan HS, Long Beach, Calif.; Brian Issett, of, Kimball HS, Royal Oak, Mich.; Shawn Jacob, c, Brandon (Miss.) HS; Ric Johnson, cf, Indiana State; Brian Jordan, rhp, Gordon College; Bryan King, rhp, Brawley Union HS, Brawley, Calif.; Corbett Leonard, c, Spring Grove (Pa.) HS; Joshua Maloney, rhp, Butte (Mont.) Central HS; Jason McCarter, rhp, Monterey Peninsula College; Tony McKnight, rhp, Arkansas HS, Texarkana, Ark.; Aaron McNeal, 1b, Castro Valley (Calif.) HS; Marlon Mejia, ss, Westchester CC; Jorge Mesa, c, Braddock HS, Miami; Christopher Meyer, rhp, Dakota Collegiate HS, Winnipeg; Michael Meyers, rhp, Annandale HS, Tillsonburg, Can.; Aaron Miles, 2b, Antioch (Calif.) Sr HS; Brian Moon, c, Newton County HS, South Mansfield, Ga.; Troy Norrell, c, Brazoswood HS, Jackson, Texas; Christopher Oldham, c, Sullivan (Mo.) HS; Joshua Pascarella, rhp, Rancho Bernardo (Calif.) HS; Scott Pasonage, rhp, Fullerton College; George Pickard, 1b, The Hill School, Austin, Texas; Robert Porter, lhp, McComb (Miss.) HS; Luis Ramos, rhp, Providencia HS, Rio Piedras P.R.; Blake Ricken, lhp, Fresno CC; Juan Rivera, ss, Palm Beach JC; Jerome Robertson, lhp, Exeter (Calif.) Union HS; Michael Rose, c, Jesuit HS, Elk Grove, Calif.; Scott Sandusky, c, Seward County CC; Stephen Schwartz, rhp, Aurora U.; Christopher Sheldon, of, Glendale (Calif.) HS; Brian Sikorski, rhp, Western Michigan; Eric Smith, rhp, Butler County CC; Gregg Smyth, lhp, Rollins; Shawn Sonnier, rhp, Chipola JC; Eric Stachler, rhp, Bowling Green; Troy Stoppa, lhp, Havre (Mont.) HS; Adrian Taylor, ss, Oakland (Calif.) Tech HS; Mark Tomse, lhp, Aurora (Ill.) Central Catholic HS; Nelson Ubaldo, of, Massachusetts; Aaron Vincent, rhp, Porterville College; Jason Von Haefen, rhp, Blinn College; Derek Wallace, cf, Neville HS, Monroe, La.; Jason Welch, rf, Edison CC; Barry Wesson, cf, Brandon HS, Glenn Allan, Miss.; Charles Wheeler, lhp, Connors State.

Minor Leagues

Tops in the organization

Batter	Club	Avg.	G	AB	R	H	HR	RBI
D. Mitchell	Qc	.329	111	383	72	126	4	42
Dave Hajek	Tcn	.327	131	502	99	164	4	78
Ken Ramos	Tcn	.315	112	327	57	103	3	47
Noel Rodriguez	Qc	.311	109	386	48	120	8	71
Bryant Nelson	Qc	.309	111	421	48	130	3	54

Home Runs			Wins		
Ray Montgomery	Tcn	21	Donne Wall	Tcn	17
Tony Mitchell	Jck	19	Tony Mounce	Qc	16
Chris Hatcher	Tcn	15	Scott Elarton	Qc	13
Alejandro Freire	Qc	15	Tim Kester	Qc	12
Richard Hidalgo	Jck	14	Several tied		9

RBI			Saves		
Ray Montgomery	Tcn	92	Manuel Barrios	Qc	23
Dave Hajek	Tcn	78	Mark Small	Tcn	19
Bob Abreu	Tcn	75	Dave Evans	Tcn	18
Noel Rodriguez	Qc	71	Rich Humphrey	Jck	14
Mike Simms	Tcn	66	Brian Sikorski	Qc	12

Stolen Bases			Strikeouts		
C. Hernandez	Qc	58	Billy Wagner	Tcn	157
Chris Truby	Qc	27	Tony Mounce	Qc	143
Melvin Mora	Tcn	23	Ryan Creek	Jck	120
Johnny Perez	Kis	23	Donne Wall	Tcn	119
Roy Marsh	Kis	22	Scott Elarton	Qc	112

Pitcher	Club	W-L	ERA	IP	H	BB	SO
Tony Mounce	Qc	16-8	2.43	159	118	57	143
Billy Wagner	Tcn	7-5	2.89	146	119	68	157
Tim Kester	Qc	12-5	2.97	161	158	20	111
Donnie Dault	Kis	4-7	3.08	108	95	36	95
Dennis Shrum	Kis	7-6	3.24	92	96	28	69

Houston (1962-1995)

Runs: Most, career, all-time

890	Cesar Cedeno, 1970-1981
871	Jose Cruz, 1975-1987
829	Jim Wynn, 1963-1973
676	Terry Puhl, 1977-1990
640	Bob Watson, 1966-1979

Hits: Most, career, all-time

1937	Jose Cruz, 1975-1987
1659	Cesar Cedeno, 1970-1981
1448	Bob Watson, 1966-1979
1357	Terry Puhl, 1977-1990
1291	Jim Wynn, 1963-1973

2B: Most, career, all-time

343	Cesar Cedeno, 1970-1981
335	Jose Cruz, 1975-1987
241	Bob Watson, 1966-1979
228	Jim Wynn, 1963-1973
226	Terry Puhl, 1977-1990

3B: Most, career, all-time

80	Jose Cruz, 1975-1987
63	Joe Morgan, 1963-1980
62	Roger Metzger, 1971-1978
56	Terry Puhl, 1977-1990
55	Cesar Cedeno, 1970-1981
55	Craig Reynolds, 1979-1989

HR: Most, career, all-time

223	Jim Wynn, 1963-1973
166	Glenn Davis, 1984-1990
163	Cesar Cedeno, 1970-1981
139	Bob Watson, 1966-1979
138	Jose Cruz, 1975-1987

RBI: Most, career, all-time

942	Jose Cruz, 1975-1987
782	Bob Watson, 1966-1979
778	Cesar Cedeno, 1970-1981
719	Jim Wynn, 1963-1973
600	Doug Rader, 1967-1975

SB: Most, career, all-time

487	Cesar Cedeno, 1970-1981
288	Jose Cruz, 1975-1987
219	Joe Morgan, 1963-1980
217	Terry Puhl, 1977-1990
196	CRAIG BIGGIO, 1988-1995

BB: Most, career, all-time

847	Jim Wynn, 1963-1973
730	Jose Cruz, 1975-1987
678	Joe Morgan, 1963-1980
585	Bill Doran, 1982-1990
534	Cesar Cedeno, 1970-1981

BA: Highest, career, all-time

.306	JEFF BAGWELL, 1991-1995
.297	Bob Watson, 1966-1979
.292	Jose Cruz, 1975-1987
.289	Cesar Cedeno, 1970-1981
.285	CRAIG BIGGIO, 1988-1995

Slug avg: Highest, career, all-time

.515	JEFF BAGWELL, 1991-1995
.483	Glenn Davis, 1984-1990
.454	Cesar Cedeno, 1970-1981
.445	Jim Wynn, 1963-1973
.444	Bob Watson, 1966-1979

Games started: Most, career, all-time

320	Larry Dierker, 1964-1976
301	Joe Niekro, 1975-1985
282	Nolan Ryan, 1980-1988
267	Bob Knepper, 1981-1989
259	Mike Scott, 1983-1991

Saves: Most, career, all-time

199	Dave Smith, 1980-1990
76	Fred Gladding, 1968-1973
72	Joe Sambito, 1976-1984
62	DOUG JONES, 1992-1993
50	Ken Forsch, 1970-1980

Shutouts: Most, career, all-time

25	Larry Dierker, 1964-1976
21	Joe Niekro, 1975-1985
21	Mike Scott, 1983-1991
20	Don Wilson, 1966-1974
19	J.R. Richard, 1971-1980

Wins: Most, career, all-time

144	Joe Niekro, 1975-1985
137	Larry Dierker, 1964-1976
110	Mike Scott, 1983-1991
107	J.R. Richard, 1971-1980
106	Nolan Ryan, 1980-1988

K: Most, career, all-time

1866	Nolan Ryan, 1980-1988
1493	J.R. Richard, 1971-1980
1487	Larry Dierker, 1964-1976
1318	Mike Scott, 1983-1991
1283	Don Wilson, 1966-1974

Win pct: Highest, career, all-time

.634	MARK PORTUGAL, 1989-1993
.609	Jim Ray, 1965-1973
.601	J.R. Richard, 1971-1980
.577	PETE HARNISCH, 1991-1994
.576	Mike Scott, 1983-1991

ERA: Lowest, career, all-time

2.53	Dave Smith, 1980-1990
3.13	Nolan Ryan, 1980-1988
3.15	Don Wilson, 1966-1974
3.15	J.R. Richard, 1971-1980
3.18	Ken Forsch, 1970-1980

Runs: Most, season

123	CRAIG BIGGIO, 1995
117	Jim Wynn, 1972
113	Jim Wynn, 1969
104	JEFF BAGWELL, 1994
103	Cesar Cedeno, 1972

Hits: Most, season

195	Enos Cabell, 1978
189	Jose Cruz, 1983
187	Jose Cruz, 1984
185	Jose Cruz, 1980
185	Greg Gross, 1974

2B: Most, season

44	Rusty Staub, 1967
44	CRAIG BIGGIO, 1994
41	CRAIG BIGGIO, 1993
40	Cesar Cedeno, 1971
39	Cesar Cedeno, 1972

3B: Most, season

14	Roger Metzger, 1973
13	Jose Cruz, 1984
13	STEVE FINLEY, 1992
13	STEVE FINLEY, 1993
12	Joe Morgan, 1965
12	Craig Reynolds, 1981

HR: Most, season

39	JEFF BAGWELL, 1994
37	Jim Wynn, 1967
34	Glenn Davis, 1989
33	Jim Wynn, 1969
31	Glenn Davis, 1986

RBI: Most, season

116	JEFF BAGWELL, 1994
110	Bob Watson, 1977
107	Jim Wynn, 1967
105	Lee May, 1973
102	Cesar Cedeno, 1974
102	Bob Watson, 1976

SB: Most, season

65	Gerald Young, 1988
64	Eric Yelding, 1990
61	Cesar Cedeno, 1977
58	Cesar Cedeno, 1976
57	Cesar Cedeno, 1974

238

BB: Most, season

148 Jim Wynn, 1969
110 Joe Morgan, 1969
106 Jim Wynn, 1970
103 Jim Wynn, 1972
102 Joe Morgan, 1970

BA: Highest, season

.368 JEFF BAGWELL, 1994
.334 DEREK BELL, 1995
.333 Rusty Staub, 1967
.324 Bob Watson, 1975
.320 Cesar Cedeno, 1972

Slug avg: Highest, season

.750 JEFF BAGWELL, 1994
.537 Cesar Cedeno, 1972
.537 Cesar Cedeno, 1973
.516 JEFF BAGWELL, 1993
.507 Jim Wynn, 1969

Games started: Most, season

40 Jerry Reuss, 1973
39 J.R. Richard, 1976
38 Bob Knepper, 1986
38 Joe Niekro, 1979
38 Joe Niekro, 1983
38 Joe Niekro, 1984
38 J.R. Richard, 1979

Saves: Most, season

36 DOUG JONES, 1992
33 Dave Smith, 1986
29 Fred Gladding, 1969
27 Dave Smith, 1985
27 Dave Smith, 1988

Shutouts: Most, season

6 Dave Roberts, 1973
5 Larry Dierker, 1972
5 Bob Knepper, 1981
5 Bob Knepper, 1986
5 Joe Niekro, 1979
5 Joe Niekro, 1982
5 Mike Scott, 1986
5 Mike Scott, 1988

Wins: Most, season

21 Joe Niekro, 1979
20 Larry Dierker, 1969
20 Joe Niekro, 1980
20 J.R. Richard, 1976
20 Mike Scott, 1989

K: Most, season

313 J.R. Richard, 1979
306 Mike Scott, 1986
303 J.R. Richard, 1978
270 Nolan Ryan, 1987
245 Nolan Ryan, 1982

Win pct: Highest, season

.818 MARK PORTUGAL, 1993
.692 Mike Scott, 1985
.667 Mike Scott, 1989
.656 Joe Niekro, 1979
.652 DARRYL KILE, 1993
.652 Larry Dierker, 1972

ERA: Lowest, season

1.69 Nolan Ryan, 1981
2.18 Bob Knepper, 1981
2.21 DANNY DARWIN, 1990
2.22 Mike Cuellar, 1966
2.22 Mike Scott, 1986

Most pinch-hit homers, season

5 Cliff Johnson, 1974

Most pinch-hit homers, career

8 Cliff Johnson, 1972-1977

Most consecutive games batting safely

23 Art Howe, 1981
22 Cesar Cedeno, 1977

Most consecutive scoreless innings

31 J.R. Richard, 1980

No-hit games

Don Nottebart, Hou vs Phi NL, 4-1;
　　May 17, 1963.
Ken T. Johnson, Hou vs Cin NL, 0-1;
　　April 23, 1964 (lost the game).
Don Wilson, Hou vs Atl NL, 2-0;
　　June 18, 1967.
Don Wilson, Hou at Cin NL, 4-0;
　　May 1, 1969.
Larry Dierker, Hou vs Mon NL, 6-0;
　　July 9, 1976.
Ken Forsch, Hou vs Atl NL, 6-0;
　　April 7, 1979.
Nolan Ryan, Hou vs LA NL, 5-0;
　　September 26, 1981.
Mike Scott, Hou vs SF NL, 2-0;
　　September 25, 1986.
DARRYL KILE, Hou vs NY NL, 7-1;
　　September 8, 1993.

ACTIVE PLAYERS in caps.

Players' years of service are listed by the first and last years with this team and are not necessarily consecutive; all statistics record performances for this team only.

239

Chicago Cubs

By Eileen Blass, USA TODAY

Sammy Sosa was tops on the Cubs in home runs (36), RBI (119) and stolen bases (34).

1995 Cubs: Most improved, more to come

The Cubs threw off the distractions of three years of front-office meddling to improve by 8½ games in the standings and stay in the wild-card hunt until the final weekend. The rebirth started with the hiring of Andy MacPhail, the team's first president in four years and two-time American League Executive of the Year with the Twins. It continued with the hiring of general manager Ed Lynch to replace Larry Himes, manager Jim Riggleman for Tom Trebelhorn, and farm director Jim Hendry for Al Goldis, who remained as scouting director.

Lynch moved quickly after the strike. He traded two marginal minor league prospects for Kansas City center fielder Brian McRae and signed overlooked free agent Jaime Navarro after being assured by Navarro's agent that the right-hander was in good shape and eager to come back from two bad seasons in Milwaukee. The effects were immediate: The Cubs were in first place from May 13 to June 7. When they struggled the rest of June, Lynch traded veteran starter Mike Morgan to the Cardinals for third baseman Todd Zeile and sent catcher Rick Wilkins to the Astros for outfielder Luis Gonzalez and catcher Scott Servais.

Again, the effects were immediate. The Cubs went on an 8-1 spree before the All-Star Game to make a run at eventual division champion Cincinnati. But coming out of the All-Star break they went 1-11 and spent the rest of the season trying to get over .500, finally succeeding at the end (73-71).

Navarro headed the pitching staff with 14 wins and a 3.28 ERA. Randy Myers led the league in saves for the second time in three seasons with 38. Sammy Sosa had his second consecutive 30-30 season (home runs and stolen bases) with 36 and 34, respectively, as well as a career-high 119 RBI. Mark Grace hit .326 with career highs in runs (97), homers (16) and doubles (51). McRae solved a longtime center-field problem

with only three errors while batting .288 in the unfamiliar leadoff spot, scoring 92 runs and stealing 27 bases. Shawon Dunston batted a career-best .296.

The only disappointment was a continued inability to win at home, where Wrigley Field is supposed to be the "friendly confines." The Cubs were better on the road for the third consecutive year.

Still, eight Cubs were in double figures in home runs, and that doesn't count Mark Parent, who hit 15 of his 18 homers with the Pirates, or the combined 10 of part-timers Ozzie Timmons and Scott Bullett. Without a true leadoff hitter, Riggleman had to use McRae. It worked, but when Rey Sanchez in the No. 2 spot failed to move runners along, Riggleman was forced to bat players out of their slots.

The pitching staff led the league in ERA early in the season under new coach and Hall of Famer Fergie Jenkins before settling for fifth with 4.06. Four starters had double-digit victories: Navarro (14-6), Jim Bullinger (12-8), Kevin Foster (12-11) and Frank Castillo (11-10), who came within an out of a no-hitter late in September.

1996 Cubs: Preview

The reformation should continue, thanks in part to instruction in the farm system that helped its minor league teams improve from a combined .446 winning percentage in 1994 to .546 in 1995. Expected to help are outfielder Brooks Kieschnick, who hit .295 at Class AAA Iowa with 23 home runs; reliever Terry Adams, who had a 1.43 ERA at Class AA Orlando; and catcher Mike Hubbard. Free agents and trades helped in 1995, but it will be a few more years before the Cubs are contenders. Some middle relievers and another starting pitcher capable of 200 innings would help.

1995 Cubs: Week-by-week notes

These notes were excerpted from the following issues of Baseball Weekly.

▶**May 3:** Key players were excited, but cautious about the 4-0 start, best since the ill-fated 1969 team blew a 9½-game lead in August. First baseman Mark Grace praised new manager Jim Riggleman, general manager Ed Lynch and president Andy MacPhail: "We've already had more fun in 2½ weeks under these new guys than all of last year."

▶**May 10:** Jaime Navarro was off to a 2-0 start in his prediction of 20. Steve Trachsel was off to a slow start, no thanks to giving up four home runs in two starts. "The trick is not to put anyone on base in the first place," said pitching coach Ferguson Jenkins, who one year gave up 41 homers.

▶**May 31:** The Cubs' remarkable success of starting pitching carried through May, with Kevin Foster the only one over 3.00 in earned run average. Unfortunately, league ERA leader Jim Bullinger, at 1.95, went on the disabled list with elbow inflammation.

▶**June 7:** Shawon Dunston, off to his best season in 10 years with a .348 average and 26 RBI, said he wanted to play five more years to break Don Kessinger's club record for shortstop games of 1,618. Also ahead are Joe Tinker (1,500) and Ernie Banks (1,125).

▶**June 14:** Riggleman was trying Shawon Dunston in the fifth spot behind Mark Grace. Dunston liked No. 5 for its RBI opportunities. "I don't mind facing right-handers," he said. "It's nice to bat behind Grace."

▶**June 21:** The acquisition of Cardinals third baseman Todd Zeile for veteran pitcher Mike Morgan was another "we mean business" signal from the new management team. "Things haven't been this upbeat in a long time," first baseman Mark Grace said. "All these [acquisitions] show a strong commitment to winning."

▶**June 28:** Frank Castillo didn't inherit the role of ace on the Cubs' pitching staff. He earned it with six victories and an ERA among the league's 10 best all season. "Coming out of winter ball, I thought this would be a make-or-break year for me," he said. "I've been trying to stay aggressive, and it's paying off." Meanwhile, the Cubs weren't too concerned about the slump by Sammy Sosa that caused his average to fall to the .280s from the .340s. He still took over the league RBI lead with five in one game at Houston. "I guess 40-plus RBI indicates you can't argue with the way he swings," manager Jim Riggleman said.

▶**July 5:** The Cubs scored more points with their players and fans by gaining an experienced left fielder in Luis Gonzalez and a replacement catcher in Scott Servais for Rick Wilkins, who went to the Astros with a .191 average. "I hate to lose a friend, but this shows the club has made another commitment," Mark Grace said. "They got us Brian McRae, Jaime Navarro, Todd Zeile and now these two guys. They're not giving up, and neither are we." Gonzalez was attractive for his .391 Wrigley Field average and his .350 lifetime mark against the Cubs. The Cubs were 9-20 in June, compared with 16-10 in May and 4-1 in April.

▶**July 13:** In a six-game span just before the All-Star break, the rotation of Jim Bullinger, Jaime Navarro, Frank Castillo, Kevin Foster and Steve Trachsel went 5-0 with a 1.98 ERA. Veteran third baseman Steve Buechele was not bitter after his release just before the All-Star break. Buechele, who was hitting .189, had been replaced by Todd Zeile. "I think they needed another bat, and it just so happened he was a third baseman," he said. "I think that was a good move. For every move, someone is affected, and I happened to be that guy."

▶**July 19:** The Cubs spun out of control—and possibly contention—with four consecutive losses after the All-Star break, leaving even a wild-card spot an uphill fight. Through July 16, the Cubs were three games behind the wild-card Astros. "The wild card is interesting, but you have to focus on the whole thing, and the whole thing to us is to resume winning," manager Jim Riggleman said.

▶**Aug. 2:** Shawon Dunston, at .340-plus, had a chance to unseat league batting champion Tony Gwynn. "No, no. That's an insult to Tony Gwynn," the shortstop said. "Tony's the best. I'm not even the best hitter on our team. I'm not a .300 hitter, either. We've got one of those on this team, Mark Grace. It'd be nice to hit .300, but getting into the playoffs is my only goal."

▶**Aug. 16:** Randy Myers joined Lee Smith and Bruce Sutter as the only Cubs with 100 saves. Smith needed 305 appearances to reach his 100th and Sutter required 224. Myers did it in his 148th.

▶**Last-day recap:** *Heroes*—The surprising Cubs, who improved 8½ games from a year ago, had superior seasons from Sammy Sosa (36 home runs, 34 steals) and Mark Grace (.326 and career-high 16 homers and 51 doubles). But the manager, coaches and players felt Brian McRae was their most valuable player for stellar center-field defense, leadoff hitting (.288 with 27 stolen bases) and leadership. McRae, new GM Ed Lynch's first major acquisition, took himself out of games only when he couldn't stand the pain of thigh and hamstring problems and hand tendinitis. "I've had players in 10 years of managing who didn't like to play when they were hurt or when they faced certain pitching, but I have not seen that with Brian," manager Jim Riggleman said. McRae lost 11 points off his average during the last three weeks because of the hand injury. It was aggravated each time McRae swung and missed, but one of his last hits was a home run to beat the Pirates in 10 innings. Still, McRae not only finished in five Top 10 league offensive categories—runs (92), hits (167), doubles (38), triples (seven) and multihit games (51)—he also led NL outfielders in chances (346), while committing only three errors.

Unsung Hero—Jaime Navarro led a trio of overachieving starting pitchers—with Jim Bullinger and Frank Castillo—by compiling a 14-6 record with a 3.28 ERA.

Disappointments—The club might have won the wild-card spot if Steve Trachsel had come close to his 1993 rookie season of 9-7 with a 3.21 ERA. Instead, he was 7-13 with a 5.15 ERA. Of equal concern is Trachsel's two-year Wrigley Field record of 2-16. Riggleman pitched Trachsel and Kevin Foster, another struggling second-year man, to the end of the season. Foster justified Riggleman's faith with 13 strikeouts in his last start to keep the playoff hopes flickering. Another disappointment was the 34-38 Wrigley Field record, for the third consecutive sub-.500 year at home.

Team directory

▶**Owner:** Tribune Company
▶**General manager:** Ed Lynch
▶**Ballpark:**
Wrigley Field
Clark and Addison Streets,
Chicago, Ill.
312-404-2827
Capacity 38,765
Parking for 900; $10 (private lots available)
Public transportation available
Family and wheelchair sections, ramps
▶**Team publications:**
Yearbook, *Vineline, Scorecard Magazine, Cubs Quarterly*
312-404-2827
▶**TV, radio broadcast stations:**
WGN 720 AM, WGN Channel 9
▶**Spring Training:**
HoHoKam Park
Mesa, Ariz.
Capacity 8,963
602-644-2149

CHICAGO CUBS 1995 final stats

BATTERS	BA	SLG	OB	G	AB	R	H	TB	2B	3B	HR	RBI	BB	SO	SB	CS	E
Haney	.411	.603	.463	25	73	11	30	44	8	0	2	6	7	11	0	0	2
Grace	.326	.516	.395	143	552	97	180	285	51	3	16	92	65	46	6	2	7
Dunston	.296	.472	.317	127	477	58	141	225	30	6	14	69	10	75	10	5	17
Franco	.294	.353	.294	16	17	3	5	6	1	0	0	1	0	4	0	0	0
McRae	.288	.440	.348	137	580	92	167	255	38	7	12	48	47	92	27	8	3
Sanchez	.278	.360	.301	114	428	57	119	154	22	2	3	27	14	48	6	4	7
Gonzalez	.276	.454	.357	133	471	69	130	214	29	8	13	69	57	63	6	8	6
Bullett	.273	.460	.331	104	150	19	41	69	5	7	3	22	12	30	8	3	2
Sosa	.268	.500	.340	144	564	89	151	282	17	3	36	119	58	134	34	7	13
Servais	.265	.496	.348	80	264	38	70	131	22	0	13	47	32	52	2	2	12
Timmons	.263	.474	.314	77	171	30	45	81	10	1	8	28	13	32	3	0	2
Zeile	.246	.397	.305	113	426	50	105	169	22	0	14	52	34	76	1	0	19
Kmak	.245	.358	.328	19	53	7	13	19	3	0	1	6	6	12	0	0	0
Hernandez	.245	.482	.281	93	245	37	60	118	11	4	13	40	13	69	1	0	9
Parent	.234	.479	.302	81	265	30	62	127	11	0	18	38	26	69	0	0	4
Johnson	.195	.355	.330	87	169	26	33	60	4	1	7	22	34	46	1	1	7
Buechele	.189	.236	.265	32	106	10	20	25	2	0	1	9	11	19	0	0	5
Roberson	.184	.526	.311	32	38	5	7	20	1	0	4	6	6	14	0	1	0
Hubbard	.174	.174	.240	15	23	2	4	4	0	0	0	1	2	2	0	0	1
Pratt	.133	.167	.209	25	60	3	8	10	2	0	0	4	6	21	0	0	3
Rhodes	.125	.125	.118	13	16	2	2	2	0	0	0	2	0	4	0	0	1

PITCHERS	W-L	ERA	G	GS	CG	GF	Sho	SV	IP	H	R	ER	HR	BB	SO
Swartzbaugh	0-0	0.00	7	0	0	0	0	0	7.1	5	2	0	0	3	5
Casian	1-0	1.93	42	0	0	5	0	0	23.1	23	6	5	1	15	11
Castillo	11-10	3.21	29	29	2	0	2	0	188	179	75	67	22	52	135
Walker	1-3	3.22	42	0	0	12	0	1	44.2	45	22	16	2	24	20
Navarro	14-6	3.28	29	29	1	0	1	0	200.1	194	79	73	19	56	128
Perez	2-6	3.66	68	0	0	18	0	2	71.1	72	30	29	8	27	49
Young	3-4	3.70	32	1	0	8	0	2	41.1	47	20	17	5	14	15
Myers	1-2	3.88	57	0	0	47	0	38	55.2	49	25	24	7	28	59
Bullinger	12-8	4.14	24	24	1	0	1	0	150	152	80	69	14	65	93
Foster	12-11	4.51	30	28	0	1	0	0	167.2	149	90	84	32	65	146
Wendell	3-1	4.92	43	0	0	17	0	0	60.1	71	35	33	11	24	50
Trachsel	7-13	5.15	30	29	2	0	0	0	160.2	174	104	92	25	76	117
Nabholz	0-1	5.40	34	0	0	0	0	0	23.1	22	15	14	4	14	21
Rivera	0-0	5.40	7	0	0	2	0	0	5	8	3	3	1	2	2
Edens	1-0	6.00	5	0	0	1	0	0	3	6	3	2	0	3	2
Adams	1-1	6.50	18	0	0	7	0	1	18	22	15	13	0	10	15
Sturtze	0-0	9.00	2	0	0	0	0	0	2	2	2	2	1	1	0

1996 preliminary roster

PITCHERS (18)
Terry Adams
Jim Bullinger
Larry Casian
Frank Castillo
Kevin Foster
Jose Guzman
Scott Moten
Rod Myers
Jaime Navarro
Mike Perez
Roberto Rivera
Tanyon Sturtze
David Swartzbaugh
Amaury Telamaco
Steve Trachsel
Wade Walker
Turk Wendell
Anthony Young

CATCHERS (2)
Mike Hubbard
Scott Servais

INFIELDERS (10)
Brant Brown
Matt Franco
Todd Haney
Jose Hernandez
Jason Maxwell
Bobby Morris
Kevin Orie

Rey Sanchez
Ryne Sandberg
Todd Zeile

OUTFIELDERS (10)
Scott Bullett
Doug Glanville
Luis Gonzalez
Vee Hightower
Robin Jennings
Brooks Kieschnick
Brian McRae
Sammy Sosa
Ozzie Timmons
Pedro Valdes

Games played by position

PLAYER	G	C	1B	2B	3B	SS	OF
Buechele	32	0	0	0	32	0	0
Bullett	104	0	0	0	0	0	64
Dunston	127	0	0	0	0	125	0
Franco	16	0	1	3	1	0	0
Gonzalez	133	0	0	0	0	0	131
Grace	143	0	143	0	0	0	0
Haney	25	0	0	17	4	0	0
Hernandez	93	0	0	29	20	43	0
Hubbard	15	9	0	0	0	0	0
Johnson	87	0	3	8	34	1	13
Kmak	19	18	0	0	1	0	0
McRae	137	0	0	0	0	0	137
Parent	81	77	0	0	0	0	0
Pratt	25	25	0	0	0	0	0
Rhodes	13	0	0	0	0	0	11
Roberson	32	0	0	0	0	0	11
Sanchez	114	0	0	111	0	4	0
Servais	80	80	0	0	0	0	0
Sosa	144	0	0	0	0	0	143
Timmons	77	0	0	0	0	0	55
Zeile	113	0	35	0	75	0	2

Minor Leagues

Tops in the organization

Batter	Club	Avg.	G	AB	R	H	HR	RBI
Mike Carter	Iwa	.325	107	421	57	137	8	40
Scott Samuels	Day	.325	117	409	95	133	3	46
Todd Haney	Iwa	.313	90	326	38	102	4	30
Bobby Morris	Day	.308	95	344	44	106	2	55
Pedro Valdes	Orl	.300	114	426	57	128	7	68

Home Runs / Wins

B. Kieschnick	Iwa	23	Alfredo Garcia	Rkf	14
Robin Jennings	Orl	17	Dax Winslett	Day	12
Bryn Kosco	Iwa	15	Jason Ryan	Day	11
Pat Cline	Rkf	13	Several tied		10
Doug Kimbler	Rkf	12			

RBI / Saves

Robin Jennings	Orl	79	Jason Hart	Orl	27
Pat Cline	Rkf	77	Terry Adams	Iwa	24
Gabe Duross	Day	74	Steve Rain	Rkf	23
B. Kieschnick	Iwa	73	Rob Taylor	Iwa	18
Pedro Valdes	Orl	68	Justin Speier	WPt	12

Stolen Bases / Strikeouts

Steve Walker	Rkf	40	A. Telemaco	Orl	151
Scott Samuels	Day	40	Paul Abbott	Iwa	127
Elinton Jasco	WPt	31	Mike Anderson	Iwa	123
Dee Dowler	Day	27	Matt Connolly	Orl	120
Ken Coleman	Orl	25	Alfredo Garcia	Rkf	120

Pitcher	Club	W-L	ERA	IP	H	BB	SO
Dennis Bair	Rkf	6-5	1.55	93	74	8	71
Matt Connolly	Orl	10-5	2.27	95	71	20	120
Mike Campbell	Iwa	9-3	2.45	103	93	29	88
Wade Walker	Day	8-6	2.53	135	113	36	117
Dax Winslett	Day	12-6	2.78	152	148	39	111

Sick call: 1995 DL Report

Player	Days on the DL
Steve Buechele	24
Jim Bullinger	32
Larry Casian	48
Jose Guzman	160
Joe Kmak	35
Mike Morgan	30
Chris Nabholz	35
Rey Sanchez	16
Scott Servais	24
Turk Wendell	32
Anthony Young	77*

Indicates two separate terms on Disabled List.

1995 Amateur draft picks

Players are listed with position and college or high school. Most players were assigned to rookie or Class A leagues. List provided by Major League Baseball.

Anthony Aaron, 3b, Middle Georgia JC; Dennis Bair, rhp, Northeast Louisiana; Steven Bechard, rhp, Oneida (N.Y.) HS; Kevin Bentley, cf, Southern Mississippi; Christopher Booker, rhp, Monroe County HS, Monroeville, Ala.; Casey Burns, rhp, Hopewell Valley Central HS Trenton, N.J.; Brian Conley ss-2b, Volunteer State CC; Gerald Connell cf-rf, Colonia HS, Avenel, N.J.; Brett Cornwell, rhp, Hobbs (NM) HS.; Timothy Currens, of, Volunteer State CC; Anthony Ellison, of, North Carolina State; Jeffrey Everett, ss, Harrison HS, Kennesaw, Ga.; Ryan Fuller, rhp, Monroe CC; Donald Gordon, c, Bridgewater College; Brian Greene, rhp, Indiana; Christopher Grubbs, c, West Orange HS, Ocoee, Fla.; Brandon Hammack, rhp, Texas; Matthew Hammons, rhp, Mission Bay HS, San Diego; Lance Haver, c, Molalla (Ore.) HS; Chris Humpert, cf, Arcadia (Calif.) HS; Terry Joseph, cf, Northwestern (La.) State; David Kelly, rhp, Leon HS Tallahassee, Fla.; Robert Kern, cf-rf, Central HS, Cape Girardeau, Mo.; Donald Kinnie, cf, Ronald Licciardi, lhp, Jack Koch, rhp, Miami Dade CC North; Connecticut-Avery Point; Thomas Maleski, 3b-c, Houston; Andrew Mallory, rhp, Dixie Hollins HS, St. Petersburg, Fla.; Barret Markey, rhp, St. Petersburg JC; Jason Martino, rhp, Vorhees HS, Pittstown, N.J.; Arturo Mata, ss-2b, New Mexico JC; Ashanti McDonald, ss-of, Olivet Nazarene; John McNeese, lhp, Mississippi; Brian McNichol, lhp, James Madison; Chris Mollor, 1b, Alabama; Daniel Mooney, c, Monsignor Donovan HS, Forked River, N.J.; Timothy Mosley, rhp, Arkansas; Steven Norris, c, Alabama; John Ogden, c, Palm Beach JC; Michael Perez, 2b, Texas; Dave Phillips, 2b, Gloucester CC; Richard Pressley, 1b, Dr. Phillips HS, Orlando, Fla.; James Putko, 1b, Akron; Robert Ricketts, rhp, Polk CC; Ryan Seidel, cf, Southern California College; Michael Smosna, rhp, Burroughs HS, Ridgecrest, Calif.; Dorian Speed, lf, Florida International; Justin Speier, c-rhp, Nicholls State; Seth Spiker, c, Blinn College; Bobby Sprauge Queen, of, Peace HS, North Arlington, N.J.; Kristofer Stading, lhp, Trevor Browne HS, Phoenix; Scott Stephens, lhp, Manatee JC; Gregery Strickland, lf, Volunteer State CC; Mark Taylor, lhp, Rice; Scott Vieira, c, Tennessee; Ismael Villegas, rhp, Margarita Janer HS, Caguas P.R.; Brandon Ward, rhp, Cerro Coso JC; Kristopher Williams, rhp, Westfield (N.J.) HS; Kerry Wood, rhp, Grand Prairie (Texas) HS; Jeffrey Yoder, rhp, Pottsville (Pa.) Area HS; Jerry Zaffis, rhp, Eustis HS, Mount Dora, Fla.

Chicago (1876-1995)

Runs: Most, career, all-time

1719	Cap Anson, 1876-1897
1409	Jimmy Ryan, 1885-1900
1306	Billy Williams, 1959-1974
1305	Ernie Banks, 1953-1971
1239	Stan Hack, 1932-1947

Hits: Most, career, all-time

2995	Cap Anson, 1876-1897
2583	Ernie Banks, 1953-1971
2510	Billy Williams, 1959-1974
2193	Stan Hack, 1932-1947
2171	Ron Santo, 1960-1973

2B: Most, career, all-time

528	Cap Anson, 1876-1897
407	Ernie Banks, 1953-1971
402	Billy Williams, 1959-1974
391	Gabby Hartnett, 1922-1940
363	Stan Hack, 1932-1947

3B: Most, career, all-time

142	Jimmy Ryan, 1885-1900
124	Cap Anson, 1876-1897
117	Frank Schulte, 1904-1916
106	Bill Dahlen, 1891-1898
99	Phil Cavarretta, 1934-1953

HR: Most, career, all-time

512	Ernie Banks, 1953-1971
392	Billy Williams, 1959-1974
337	Ron Santo, 1960-1973
245	RYNE SANDBERG, 1982-1994
231	Gabby Hartnett, 1922-1940

RBI: Most, career, all-time

1879	Cap Anson, 1876-1897
1636	Ernie Banks, 1953-1971
1353	Billy Williams, 1959-1974
1290	Ron Santo, 1960-1973
1153	Gabby Hartnett, 1922-1940

SB: Most, career, all-time

400	Frank Chance, 1898-1912
399	Bill Lange, 1893-1899
369	Jimmy Ryan, 1885-1900
325	RYNE SANDBERG, 1982-1994
304	Joe Tinker, 1902-1916

BB: Most, career, all-time

1092	Stan Hack, 1932-1947
1071	Ron Santo, 1960-1973
952	Cap Anson, 1876-1897
911	Billy Williams, 1959-1974
794	Phil Cavarretta, 1934-1953

BA: Highest, career, all-time

.336	Riggs Stephenson, 1926-1934
.330	Bill Lange, 1893-1899
.329	Cap Anson, 1876-1897
.325	Kiki Cuyler, 1928-1935
.323	Bill Everitt, 1895-1900

Slug avg: Highest, career, all-time

.590	Hack Wilson, 1926-1931
.512	Hank Sauer, 1949-1955
.507	ANDRE DAWSON, 1987-1992
.503	Billy Williams, 1959-1974
.500	Ernie Banks, 1953-1971

Games started: Most, career, all-time

347	Fergie Jenkins, 1966-1983
343	Rick Reuschel, 1972-1984
340	Bill Hutchison, 1889-1895
339	Charlie Root, 1926-1941
296	Bill Lee, 1934-1947

Saves: Most, career, all-time

180	LEE SMITH, 1980-1987
133	Bruce Sutter, 1976-1980
112	RANDY MYERS, 1993-1995
63	Don Elston, 1953-1964
60	Phil Regan, 1968-1972

Shutouts: Most, career, all-time

48	Mordecai Brown, 1904-1916
35	Hippo Vaughn, 1913-1921
31	Ed Reulbach, 1905-1913
29	Fergie Jenkins, 1966-1983
28	Orval Overall, 1906-1913

Wins: Most, career, all-time

201	Charlie Root, 1926-1941
188	Mordecai Brown, 1904-1916
182	Bill Hutchison, 1889-1895
175	Larry Corcoran, 1880-1885
167	Fergie Jenkins, 1966-1983

K: Most, career, all-time

2038	Fergie Jenkins, 1966-1983
1432	Charlie Root, 1926-1941
1367	Rick Reuschel, 1972-1984
1226	Bill Hutchison, 1889-1895
1138	Hippo Vaughn, 1913-1921

Win pct: Highest, career, all-time

.800	Al Spalding, 1876-1878
.773	Jim McCormick, 1885-1886
.706	John Clarkson, 1884-1887
.686	Mordecai Brown, 1904-1916
.677	Ed Reulbach, 1905-1913

ERA: Lowest, career, all-time

1.80	Mordecai Brown, 1904-1916
1.85	Jack Pfiester, 1906-1911
1.91	Orval Overall, 1906-1913
2.14	Jake Weimer, 1903-1905
2.24	Ed Reulbach, 1905-1913

Runs: Most, season

156	Rogers Hornsby, 1929
155	Kiki Cuyler, 1930
155	King Kelly, 1886
152	Woody English, 1930
150	George Gore, 1886

Hits: Most, season

229	Rogers Hornsby, 1929
228	Kiki Cuyler, 1930
227	Billy Herman, 1935
214	Woody English, 1930
212	Frank Demaree, 1936

2B: Most, season

57	Billy Herman, 1935
57	Billy Herman, 1936
50	Kiki Cuyler, 1930
51	MARK GRACE, 1995
49	Riggs Stephenson, 1932
49	Ned Williamson, 1893

3B: Most, season

21	Vic Saier, 1913
21	Frank Schulte, 1911
19	Bill Dahlen, 1892
19	Bill Dahlen, 1896
19	RYNE SANDBERG, 1984

HR: Most, season

56	Hack Wilson, 1930
49	ANDRE DAWSON, 1987
48	Dave Kingman, 1979
47	Ernie Banks, 1958
45	Ernie Banks, 1959

RBI: Most, season

190	Hack Wilson, 1930
159	Hack Wilson, 1929
149	Rogers Hornsby, 1929
147	Cap Anson, 1886
143	Ernie Banks, 1959

SB: Most, season

84	Bill Lange, 1896
76	Walt Wilmot, 1890
74	Walt Wilmot, 1894
73	Bill Lange, 1897
67	Frank Chance, 1903
67	Bill Lange, 1895

BB: Most, season

147	Jimmy Sheckard, 1911
122	Jimmy Sheckard, 1912
116	Richie Ashburn, 1960
113	Cap Anson, 1890
108	Johnny Evers, 1910

BA: Highest, season

.389	Bill Lange, 1895
.388	King Kelly, 1886
.380	Rogers Hornsby, 1929
.372	Heinie Zimmerman, 1912
.371	Cap Anson, 1886

Slug avg: Highest, season

.723	Hack Wilson, 1930
.679	Rogers Hornsby, 1929
.630	Gabby Hartnett, 1930
.618	Hack Wilson, 1929
.614	Ernie Banks, 1958

Games started: Most, season

71	Bill Hutchison, 1892
70	John Clarkson, 1885
66	Bill Hutchison, 1890
60	Larry Corcoran, 1880
60	Al Spalding, 1876
42	Fergie Jenkins, 1969 (18)

Saves: Most, season

53	RANDY MYERS, 1993
38	RANDY MYERS, 1995
37	Bruce Sutter, 1979
36	LEE SMITH, 1987
36	MITCH WILLIAMS, 1989

Shutouts: Most, season

10	John Clarkson, 1885
9	Pete Alexander, 1919
9	Mordecai Brown, 1906
9	Mordecai Brown, 1908
9	Bill Lee, 1938
9	Orval Overall, 1909

Wins: Most, season

53	John Clarkson, 1885
47	Al Spalding, 1876
44	Bill Hutchison, 1891
43	Larry Corcoran, 1880
42	Bill Hutchison, 1890
29	Mordecai Brown, 1908 (14)

K: Most, season

316	Bill Hutchison, 1892
313	John Clarkson, 1886
308	John Clarkson, 1885
289	Bill Hutchison, 1890
274	Fergie Jenkins, 1970

Win pct: Highest, season

.941	RICK SUTCLIFFE, 1984
.875	Fred Goldsmith, 1880
.833	King Cole, 1910
.833	Jim McCormick, 1885
.826	Ed Reulbach, 1906

ERA: Lowest, season

1.04	Mordecai Brown, 1906
1.15	Jack Pfiester, 1907
1.17	Carl Lundgren, 1907
1.31	Mordecai Brown, 1909
1.33	Jack Taylor, 1902

Most pinch-hit homers, season

3	Willie Smith, 1969
3	Thad Bosley, 1985
3	KEVIN ROBERSON, 1994

Most pinch-hit homers, career

6	Thad Bosley, 1983-1986

Most consecutive games batting safely

42	Bill Dahlen, 1894
30	JEROME WALTON, 1989

Most consecutive scoreless innings

50	Ed Reulbach, 1908-1909
39	Mordecai Brown, 1908
38	Bill Lee, 1938
38	John Clarkson, 1885

No-hit games

Larry Corcoran, Chi vs Bos NL, 6-0; August 19, 1880.

Larry Corcoran, Chi vs Wor NL, 5-0; September 20, 1882.

Larry Corcoran, Chi vs Pro NL, 6-0; June 27, 1884.

John Clarkson, Chi at Pro NL, 4-0; July 27, 1885.

Walter Thornton, Chi vs Bro NL, 2-0; August 21, 1898 (2nd game).

Bob Wicker, Chi at NY NL, 1-0; June 11, 1904 (won in 12 innings after allowing 1 hit in the 10th).

Jimmy Lavender, Chi at NY NL, 2-0; August 31, 1915 (1st game).

Hippo Vaughn, Chi vs Cin NL, 0-1; May 2, 1917 (lost on 2 hits in the 10th; Fred Toney pitched a no-hitter in this game).

Sam Jones, Chi vs Pit NL, 4-0; May 12, 1955.

Don Cardwell, Chi vs StL NL, 4-0; May 15, 1960 (2nd game).

Ken Holtzman, Chi vs Atl NL, 3-0; August 19, 1969.

Ken Holtzman, Chi at Cin NL, 1-0; June 3, 1971.

Burt Hooton, Chi vs Phi NL, 4-0; April 16, 1972.

Milt Pappas, Chi vs SD NL, 8-0; September 2, 1972.

George Van Haltren, 6 innings, rain, Chi vs Pit NL, 1-0, June 21,1888.

King Cole, 7 innings, called so Chicago could catch train, Chi at StL NL, 4-0; July 31, 1910 (2nd game).

ACTIVE PLAYERS in caps.

Leaders since 1900 are included. If not in the top five, leader's rank is listed in parenthesis.

Players' years of service are listed by the first and last years with this team and are not necessarily consecutive; all statistics record performances for this team only.

St. Louis Cardinals

Ray Lankford led the Cardinals with 25 homers, 82 RBI and 24 stolen bases (tied with Brian Jordan).

By Anne Ryan, USA TODAY

1995 Cardinals: It was a forgettable year

The Cardinals' first three-game sweep was not until Aug. 25-27—a good gauge of how the season went for the Redbirds, whose 23-48 road record was their worst since 1919.

The biggest news came on June 16 when they traded cleanup hitter Todd Zeile to the Chicago Cubs and fired manager Joe Torre to deflect attention from the trade. Torre was 20-27. New manager Mike Jorgensen, who used a plethora of lineups, finished 42-54.

The most valuable player was reliever Tom Henke, who was thought to be on the decline. He saved 36 games in 38 opportunities and captured his first Rolaids Relief Pitcher of the Year honors. Center fielder Ray Lankford had his best power season with 25 home runs among 62 extra-base hits. Brian Jordan hit 22 homers, drove in 81 runs and made just one error in the outfield. The most pleasant surprise was outfielder–first baseman John Mabry, who started out as a replacement for Zeile and eventually won the job for good. His .307 average was highest on the club.

Veteran left-handed reliever Tony Fossas was another surprise. Fossas had an ERA of 1.47 (0.44 at Busch Stadium), and opposing batsmen hit just .214 against him.

There were a few disappointments. Left-hander Danny Jackson had a harder time than he expected recovering from thyroid cancer surgery. He finished 2-12 with a 5.90 ERA. Former All-Star Scott Cooper hit .230 with just three homers. Ozzie Smith missed three months after shoulder surgery and hit just .199. Tom Pagnozzi, who hit .215, hurt his left knee for the third consecutive year and missed two months. Geronimo Pena was invisible at second base, batting just 101 times and spending three tours on the disabled list. Ken Hill, who was only 6-7 with a 5.06 ERA before being traded to Cleveland, was not the leader the Cardinals needed.

St. Louis finished last in the league in batting average, runs, slugging percentage and on-base percentage. Their run total of 563 was 58 runs behind the 13th-ranked Expos. The offense was blanked an astounding 19 times. One particularly galling stretch was a West Coast trip in August—they went 1-8, with the only victory coming by forfeit when Dodger fans pelted the field with autographed baseballs.

The pitching staff finished sixth in ERA, but only because the bullpen was tops in the National League. Relievers contributed 26 of the 62 wins in addition to 38 saves.

1996 Cardinals: Preview

Tony La Russa brings a wealth of championship experience to the Cardinals, but he needs better players to manage. General manager Walt Jocketty says the Cardinals need a "bopper," but they also need a leadoff man. Their 79 stolen bases in 1995 were 11th in the league. Brian Jordan, Ray Lank-ford and Bernard Gilkey make up a great outfield. But problems are acute at second base, third base and catcher. Look for at least 30% of the 25-man roster to be overturned, though the pitching staff might not be disturbed that much. Pitching is one area Jocketty says doesn't need much help, even though reliever Rich DeLucia's mere eight victories led the team. The GM is counting on Jackson and has been encouraged by the development of Allen Watson and the return of Donovan Osborne, who won his last four decisions after going two years without a victory.

Busch Stadium, once among the hardest parks in which to hit a home run, will become friendlier in left center with the distance to the fence shrinking to possibly 365 feet in the new configuration that features bullpens beyond the outfield.

249

1995 Cardinals: Week-by-week notes

These notes were excerpted from the following issues of Baseball Weekly.

▶**May 3:** In a week marked by injuries and inconsistent play, manager Joe Torre seemed most concerned about a healthy starting pitcher, Allen Watson, who failed to hang on to a big lead, losing much of a five-run cushion against New York in a game that turned into a 10-8 loss. Watson admitted he had been "too cute" in trying to protect the lead. "It didn't look cute to me," Torre snapped.

▶**May 17:** After three ineffective starts, Allen Watson was banished to the bullpen, with the possibility of going to the minors. He was hitting .667 (4-for-6) and his slugging percentage was 1.000 (six bases in six at-bats)—but his ERA was even higher, at 10.75. "Maybe I'll become a hitter," he said.

▶**May 24:** Closer Tom Henke had eight saves with a 0.90 ERA.

▶**May 31:** After losing seven games in nine, the Cardinals' clubhouse was very quiet, a fact that worried Todd Zeile. "Losing is a bad trend," he said. "Accepting losing is a worse trend. It's dead. There's no spark in here."

▶**June 7:** Ozzie Smith said he would not play another position, such as second base, to save his arm. "There's no reason for me to do it," said Smith. "When all is said and done, I'll be noted as a shortstop. And a shortstop alone." Smith had played more games defensively at only one position than any player in NL history—2,435.

▶**June 14:** The Cardinals made 39 errors in their first 43 games, and coach Bob Gibson, back in the game after 11 years, said, "This organization has always been known for its defense. Right now, I don't see it."

▶**June 21:** The Cardinals became probably the first team in baseball history to trade their cleanup hitter and fire their manager on the same day. Todd Zeile

went to the Cubs June 16 for oft-injured right-hander Mike Morgan and two prospects. Joe Torre, with a 351-354 record, was canned after six seasons in favor of Mike Jorgensen, a former minor league manager who had been the club's director of player development.

▶**June 28:** In the Cardinals' ongoing remodeling process, they acquired a 35-year-old pitcher (Mike Morgan) and a 33-year-old infielder (Chris Sabo) and disposed of a 29-year-old first baseman (Todd Zeile)—making the National League's oldest team even older, at 31.6 years, counting disabled players 40-year-old Ozzie Smith and 33-year-old Danny Jackson. They had let go their Nos. 3-4-5 hitters and their top starting pitcher from 1994—Gregg Jefferies, Zeile, Mark Whiten, and Bob Tewksbury. Seth Levinson, agent for Zeile, said club president Mark Lamping "has done some nice things with the stadium and all the amenities. It's all shine but no substance. They create this wonderful picture—we're going to win for the fans—but you've lost your 3-4-5 hitters and you've lost your ace. How does this rebuild the organization?"

▶**July 5:** In three games at the Astrodome, the Cardinals were pounded 26-2, with one of those runs scoring on a balk. They had been over .500 for just one day—the first day of this season— since July 4, 1994. Catcher Tom Pagnozzi said, "I'm embarrassed every time I take the field right now." Outfielder Brian Jordan said, simply, "It's sickening."

▶**July 13:** Danny Jackson, having broken his losing streak at nine games (10 over two seasons) with a shutout against Florida, said a great weight had been lifted. "I've got King Kong off my back," said Jackson. "I wanted to show the team I was a much better pitcher and, more important, I wanted to show the fans. The fans have been great. People would stop you on the street and say, 'Keep your head up. You'll turn it around.' That really made me feel good. It would have been totally different in Chicago."

July 19: Ken Hill asked the club to trade him and the Cardinals were trying to accommodate him. He had been shut out four times in his six losses, and said he would prefer to go to Cincinnati, Colorado or Cleveland—all teams with potent offenses.

July 26: The Cardinals continued to fade into the sunset and, after losing three of four games in Pittsburgh, center fielder Ray Lankford had had enough. "We've got to change some things," he said. "Right now, some Little League team would beat us."

Aug. 16: The Cardinals won just one of their first six games on a West Coast trip—umpire Jim Quick called a forfeit in Dodger Stadium after fans threw baseballs onto the field for a third time. Reliever Tom Henke, who gained his 299th save by pitching to just one batter before the game was called, said, "You've ruined a good game by stupidity. I'm glad that wasn't my 300th."

Aug. 23: Tom Henke's 300th career save came the old-fashioned way—he earned it. Henke had to retire three Atlanta Braves hitters with the tying run at third and nobody out. "I was as nervous as I've been in a long, long time," said Henke. "I've had my so-called easy [saves]. I'm just glad this one is over."

Aug. 30: Danny Jackson's season, not exactly one to write home about, came to a premature end due to stretched tendons and ligaments in his right ankle. "This just ends a year of frustration," said Jackson, who had been battling the aftereffects of off-season thyroid cancer surgery.

Sept. 13: Ray Lankford went on one his tears in early September, pounding five homers, driving in 10 runs and batting .515 over a nine-game span. "I just want to have a good September, try to finish up strong as far as the team is concerned," Lankford said. "It will make a better winter if we finish by winning."

Oct. 4: The Cardinals finished with the worst road record in baseball and their worst in 76 years when they finished 23-48 away from Busch Stadium.

Team directory

Owner: August A. Busch III
General manager: Walt Jocketty
Ballpark:
Busch Stadium
250 Stadium Plaza, St. Louis, Mo.
314-421-3060
Capacity 57,078 (includes 1,500 standing)
Parking for over 7,000 cars; $5
Public transportation available
Wheelchair section, ramps
Team publications:
Yearbook, media guide, *The Cardinals Magazine*
314-982-7336
TV, radio broadcast stations:
KMOX 1120 AM, KPLR Channel 11, Prime Sports
Spring training:
Al Lang Stadium
St. Petersburg, Fla.
Capacity 7,227
813-893-7490

ST. LOUIS CARDINALS 1995 final stats

BATTERS	BA	SLG	OB	G	AB	R	H	TB	2B	3B	HR	RBI	BB	SO	SB	CS	E
Lee	1.000	1.000	1.000	1	1	1	1	1	0	0	0	0	0	0	0	0	1
Mabry	.307	.405	.347	129	388	35	119	157	21	1	5	41	24	45	0	3	4
Gilkey	.298	.490	.358	121	480	73	143	235	33	4	17	69	42	70	12	6	3
Jordan	.296	.488	.339	131	490	83	145	239	20	4	22	81	22	79	24	9	1
Lankford	.277	.513	.360	132	483	81	134	248	35	2	25	82	63	110	24	8	3
Sweeney	.273	.377	.348	37	77	5	21	29	2	0	2	13	10	15	1	1	2
Battle	.271	.314	.358	61	118	13	32	37	5	0	0	2	15	26	3	3	1
Pena	.267	.376	.367	32	101	20	27	38	6	1	1	8	16	30	3	2	3
Bell	.250	.368	.278	39	144	13	36	53	7	2	2	19	4	25	1	2	7
Sheaffer	.231	.361	.306	76	208	24	48	75	10	1	5	30	23	38	0	0	3
Cooper	.230	.313	.321	118	374	29	86	117	18	2	3	40	49	85	0	3	18
Bradshaw	.227	.295	.261	19	44	6	10	13	1	1	0	2	2	10	1	2	1
Cromer	.226	.325	.261	105	345	36	78	112	19	0	5	18	14	66	0	0	17
Coles	.225	.341	.316	63	138	13	31	47	7	0	3	16	16	20	0	0	3
Pagnozzi	.215	.315	.254	62	219	17	47	69	14	1	2	15	11	31	0	1	2
Oquendo	.209	.300	.316	88	220	31	46	66	8	3	2	17	35	21	1	1	6
Caraballo	.202	.323	.269	34	99	10	20	32	4	1	2	3	6	33	3	2	6
Smith	.199	.244	.282	44	156	16	31	38	5	1	0	11	17	12	4	3	7
Hulett	.182	.182	.182	4	11	0	2	2	0	0	0	0	0	3	0	0	2
Perry	.165	.215	.224	65	79	4	13	17	4	0	0	5	6	12	0	0	0
Sabo	.154	.231	.214	5	13	0	2	3	1	0	0	3	1	2	1	0	1
Hemond	.144	.229	.233	57	118	11	17	27	1	0	3	9	12	31	0	0	3
Oliva	.142	.284	.202	70	183	15	26	52	5	0	7	20	12	46	0	0	7
Giannelli	.091	.091	.286	9	11	0	1	1	0	0	0	0	3	4	0	0	0

PITCHERS	W-L	ERA	G	GS	CG	GF	Sho	SV	IP	H	R	ER	HR	BB	SO
Creek	0-0	0.00	6	0	0	1	0	0	6.2	2	0	0	0	3	10
Rodriguez	0-0	0.00	1	0	0	0	0	0	1.2	0	0	0	0	0	0
Fossas	3-0	1.47	58	0	0	20	0	0	36.2	28	6	6	1	10	40
Mathews	1-1	1.52	23	0	0	12	0	2	29.2	21	7	5	1	11	28
Henke	1-1	1.82	52	0	0	47	0	36	54.1	42	11	11	2	18	48
Habyan	3-2	2.88	31	0	0	9	0	0	40.2	32	18	13	0	15	35
DeLucia	8-7	3.39	56	1	0	8	0	0	82.1	63	38	31	9	36	76
Morgan	7-7	3.56	21	21	1	0	0	0	131.1	133	56	52	12	34	61
Parrett	4-7	3.64	59	0	0	17	0	0	76.2	71	33	31	8	28	71
Urbani	3-5	3.70	24	13	0	2	0	0	82.2	99	40	34	11	21	52
Osborne	4-6	3.81	19	19	0	0	0	0	113.1	112	58	48	17	34	82
Arocha	3-5	3.99	41	0	0	13	0	0	49.2	55	24	22	6	18	25
Petkovsek	6-6	4.00	26	21	1	1	1	0	137.1	136	71	61	11	35	71
Frascatore	1-1	4.41	14	4	0	3	0	0	32.2	39	19	16	3	16	21
Watson	7-9	4.96	21	19	0	1	0	0	114.1	126	68	63	17	41	49
Hill	6-7	5.06	18	18	0	0	0	0	110.1	125	71	62	16	45	50
Barber	2-1	5.22	9	4	0	2	0	0	29.1	31	17	17	4	16	27
Palacios	2-3	5.80	20	5	0	3	0	0	40.1	48	29	26	7	19	34
Jackson	2-12	5.90	19	19	2	0	1	0	100.2	120	82	66	10	48	52
Bailey	0-0	7.36	3	0	0	0	0	0	3.2	2	3	3	0	2	5
Benes	1-2	8.44	3	3	0	0	0	0	16	24	15	15	2	4	20

1996 preliminary roster

PITCHERS (18)
Manuel Aybar
Cory Bailey
Brian Barber
Alan Benes
Mike Busby
Doug Creek
Rich DeLucia
Tony Fossas
John Frascatore
Danny Jackson
T.J. Mathews
Steve Montgomery

Donovan Osborne
Jeff Parrett
Mark Petkovsek
Tom Urbani
Allen Watson
Jay Witasick

CATCHERS (4)
Scott Hemond
Elieser Marrero
Tom Pagnozzi
Danny Sheaffer

INFIELDERS (11)
David Bell
Scott Cooper
Tripp Cromer
Mike Gulan
Aaron Holbert
Keith Johns
Jose Oliva
Geronimo Pena
Ozzie Smith
Mark Sweeney
Dmitri Young

OUTFIELDERS (7)
Allen Battle
Terry Bradshaw
Bernard Gilkey
Brian Jordan
Ray Lankford
John Mabry
Miguel Mejia

Games played by position

PLAYER	G	C	1B	2B	3B	SS	OF
Battle	61	0	0	0	0	0	32
Bell	39	0	0	37	3	0	0
Bradshaw	19	0	0	0	0	0	10
Caraballo	34	0	0	24	0	0	0
Coles	63	0	18	0	22	0	1
Cooper	118	0	0	0	110	0	0
Cromer	105	0	0	11	0	95	0
Giannelli	9	0	2	0	0	0	2
Gilkey	121	0	0	0	0	0	118
Hemond	57	38	0	6	0	0	0
Hulett	4	0	0	2	0	1	0
Jordan	131	0	0	0	0	0	126
Lankford	132	0	0	0	0	0	129
Lee	1	0	0	1	0	0	0
Mabry	129	0	73	0	0	0	39
Oliva	70	0	3	0	43	0	0
Oquendo	88	0	0	62	2	24	1
Pagnozzi	62	61	0	0	0	0	0
Pena	32	0	0	25	0	0	0
Perry	65	0	11	0	0	0	0
Sabo	5	0	2	0	1	0	0
Sheaffer	76	67	3	0	1	0	0
Smith	44	0	0	0	0	41	0
Sweeney	37	0	19	0	0	0	1

Minor Leagues

Tops in the organization

Batter	Club	Avg.	G	AB	R	H	HR	RBI
Jeff Berblinger	Ark	.319	87	332	66	106	5	29
Ray Giannelli	Lou	.295	119	390	56	115	16	70
Chris Fick	Stp	.293	113	348	56	102	13	52
Dmitri Young	Lou	.291	99	374	57	109	10	62
Brian Rupp	Ark	.286	113	402	40	115	0	29

Home Runs			Wins		
Anthony Lewis	Ark	24	Brian Reed	Peo	11
Tracy Woodson	Lou	18	Scott Simmons	Ark	11
Mike Gulan	Lou	17	Blake Stein	Peo	10
Ray Giannelli	Lou	16	Kris Detmers	Stp	10
Dan Cholowsky	Lou	14	Several tied		9

RBI			Saves		
Anthony Lewis	Ark	85	S. Montgomery	Ark	36
Tracy Woodson	Lou	76	Travis Welch	Peo	31
Mike Gulan	Lou	75	Jeff Matulevich	Stp	30
Ray Giannelli	Lou	70	Frank Garcia	Stp	25
Dave Madsen	Stp	64	Cory Bailey	Lou	25

Stolen Bases			Strikeouts		
Anton French	Peo	57	Kris Detmers	Stp	150
Bert Green	Sav	26	Manuel Aybar	Stp	142
Osmel Garcia	Stp	24	Jay Witasick	Ark	135
Steve Grandizio	Peo	21	Blake Stein	Peo	133
Several tied		20	Mike Busby	Lou	121

Pitcher	Club	W-L	ERA	IP	H	BB	SO
Cory Corrigan	Peo	4-7	2.32	113	90	23	84
Bret Wagner	Ark	6-6	2.42	130	111	46	90
Curtis King	Stp	7-8	2.58	136	117	49	65
Brady Raggio	Stp	5-3	2.81	96	85	15	69
Carl Dale	Peo	9-9	2.94	144	124	62	104

Sick call: 1995 DL Report

Player	Days on the DL
Rene Arocha	63
Bernard Gilkey	19
Tim Hulett	13
Danny Jackson	69*
Manuel Lee	158
Mike Morgan	20
Donovan Osborne	60
Tom Pagnozzi	39
Vincente Palacios	102
Geronimo Pena	101**
Rich Rodriguez	158
Chris Sabo	77
Ozzie Smith	92
Tom Urbani	22
Allen Watson	31
Todd Zeile	14

Indicates two separate terms on Disabled List.
**Indicates three separate terms on DL.*

1995 Amateur draft picks

Players are listed with position and college or high school. Most players were assigned to rookie or Class A leagues. List provided by Major League Baseball.

Rodney Barfield, rhp, DeKalb College; Adam Benes, rhp, Evansville; Darrell Betts, ss, Ball State; James Birr, ss, North Florida; Gavin Brown, of, California; Dean Brueggemann, lhp, Bellville JC; George Burgos, of, American Senior HS, Miami; Kenneth Cameron, rf, Washington State; Ruben Cardona, 2b, Belhaven; Anthony Clark, lhp, Mississippi St.; Robert Cooke, rhp, Mount Olive; Bryce Darnell, c, Missouri Southern State; William Deck, cf-1b, Potomac Senior HS, Dumfries, Va.; Michael Delano, lhp, North Hollywood (Calif.) HS; Nicholas Deluca, ss, Bellevue College; Louis Deman, c, Long Island; Mathew Dewitt, rhp-3b, Valley HS, Las Vegas; Robert Donnelly, rhp, Fresno State; Anthony Falciglia, c, Fairleigh Dickinson; Cheron Farley, 2b, Lincolnton (N.C.) HS; Brandon Folkers, 1b, Pasco JC; Joseph Freitas, rf, Fresno State; Ryan Gladwin, of, Martin County HS, Stuart, Fla.; Michael Glendenning, 3b-of, Pierce JC; Michael Gray, rhp, North Florida JC; Christopher Haas, 3b, St Mary HS, Paducah, Ky.; Andrew Hall, 2b, Cal Poly-SLO; Michael Hogan, rf, Middle Georgia College; Miguel Insunza, ss, Lewis-Clark State; Wade Jackson, 2b, Nevada; Brian Jorgensen, 3b, Missouri; Nicklous Kast, lhp, Oral Roberts; Michael Kimbrell, lhp, Southeastern Louisiana; Matthew King, rhp, Galveston College; Jason Lariviere, of-2b, Southern Maine; Jason Lee, of, Burlington (Iowa) HS; Christopher Mazur, lhp, East Bladen HS, Elizabethtown, N.C.; Travis McClendon, c, Nevada-Las Vegas; Ryan McHugh, rf, Florida Southern; Cody McKay, 3b-ss, Arizona State; William McNally, cf-ss, Auburn; Kevin Miedreich, rhp, St. Thomas Aquinas; Craig Moore, 3b, Bergail HS, Freemont, Neb.; Matthew Morris, rhp, Seton Hall; Bret Mueller, rf, Cal Poly-SLO; Juan Munoz, cf, Florida International; Ryan Pene, lhp, Grand County HS, Moab, Utah; Clifford Politte, rhp, Jefferson College; William Reames, rhp, Citadel; Chris Richard, of-1b, Oklahoma State; Nick Roberts, rhp, South Sevibic HS, West Annabella, Utah; Kerry Robinson, of, Southeast Missouri State; Jorge Roque, rhp, Interamericana De Culpe, Santurce P.R.; Jeffrey Ryan, ss, Grand Prairie (Texas) HS; Rusty Sarnes, lhp, Lincoln Land CC; Andrew Schofield, rf, Illinois State; Scott Spaulding, rhp, Eastern Connecticut State; Ernest Spivey, 2b, Cowley County CC; Michael Swenson, lhp, South Florida; Thomas Truselo, rhp, Delcastle Technical, New Castle, Del.; Jose Villafana, rhp, Mission JC; Nolan Vincent, 3b-of, Hollister (Mo.) HS; Matthew Wagner, rhp, Lewis-Clark State; Jon Ward, rhp, Cal State Fullerton; Kyle West, ss, Pineview HS, Santa Clara, Utah; Jason Woolf, ss, American Senior HS, Miami.

St. Louis (1892-1995)

Runs: Most, career, all-time

1949	Stan Musial, 1941-1963
1427	Lou Brock, 1964-1979
1089	Rogers Hornsby, 1915-1933
1071	Enos Slaughter, 1938-1953
1025	Red Schoendienst, 1945-1963

Hits: Most, career, all-time

3630	Stan Musial, 1941-1963
2713	Lou Brock, 1964-1979
2110	Rogers Hornsby, 1915-1933
2064	Enos Slaughter, 1938-1953
1980	Red Schoendienst, 1945-1963

2B: Most, career, all-time

725	Stan Musial, 1941-1963
434	Lou Brock, 1964-1979
377	Joe Medwick, 1932-1948
367	Rogers Hornsby, 1915-1933
366	Enos Slaughter, 1938-1953

3B: Most, career, all-time

177	Stan Musial, 1941-1963
143	Rogers Hornsby, 1915-1933
135	Enos Slaughter, 1938-1953
121	Lou Brock, 1964-1979
119	Jim Bottomley, 1922-1932

HR: Most, career, all-time

475	Stan Musial, 1941-1963
255	Ken Boyer, 1955-1965
193	Rogers Hornsby, 1915-1933
181	Jim Bottomley, 1922-1932
172	Ted Simmons, 1968-1980

RBI: Most, career, all-time

1951	Stan Musial, 1941-1963
1148	Enos Slaughter, 1938-1953
1105	Jim Bottomley, 1922-1932
1072	Rogers Hornsby, 1915-1933
1001	Ken Boyer, 1955-1965

SB: Most, career, all-time

888	Lou Brock, 1964-1979
549	VINCE COLEMAN, 1985-1990
426	OZZIE SMITH, 1982-1995
274	WILLIE McGEE, 1982-1990
203	Jack Smith, 1915-1926

BB: Most, career, all-time

1599	Stan Musial, 1941-1963
851	OZZIE SMITH, 1982-1995
838	Enos Slaughter, 1938-1953
681	Lou Brock, 1964-1979
660	Rogers Hornsby, 1915-1933

BA: Highest, career, all-time

.359	Rogers Hornsby, 1915-1933
.336	Johnny Mize, 1936-1941
.335	Joe Medwick, 1932-1948
.331	Stan Musial, 1941-1963
.326	Chick Hafey, 1924-1931

Slug avg: Highest, career, all-time

.600	Johnny Mize, 1936-1941
.568	Rogers Hornsby, 1915-1933
.568	Chick Hafey, 1924-1931
.559	Stan Musial, 1941-1963
.545	Joe Medwick, 1932-1948

Games started: Most, career, all-time

482	Bob Gibson, 1959-1975
401	Bob Forsch, 1974-1988
388	Jesse Haines, 1920-1937
319	Bill Doak, 1913-1929
243	Bill Sherdel, 1918-1932

Saves: Most, career, all-time

160	LEE SMITH, 1990-1993
129	TODD WORRELL, 1985-1992
127	Bruce Sutter, 1981-1984
64	Lindy McDaniel, 1955-1962
60	Al Brazle, 1943-1954
60	Joe Hoerner, 1966-1969

Shutouts: Most, career, all-time

56	Bob Gibson, 1959-1975
30	Bill Doak, 1913-1929
28	Mort Cooper, 1938-1945
25	Harry Brecheen, 1940-1952
24	Jesse Haines, 1920-1937

Wins: Most, career, all-time

251	Bob Gibson, 1959-1975
210	Jesse Haines, 1920-1937
163	Bob Forsch, 1974-1988
153	Bill Sherdel, 1918-1932
144	Bill Doak, 1913-1929

K: Most, career, all-time

3117	Bob Gibson, 1959-1975
1095	Dizzy Dean, 1930-1937
1079	Bob Forsch, 1974-1988
979	Jesse Haines, 1920-1937
951	Steve Carlton, 1965-1971

Win pct: Highest, career, all-time

.718	Ted Wilks, 1944-1951
.705	John Tudor, 1985-1990
.677	Mort Cooper, 1938-1945
.667	Al Hrabosky, 1970-1977
.641	Dizzy Dean, 1930-1937

ERA: Lowest, career, all-time

2.52	John Tudor, 1985-1990
2.67	Slim Sallee, 1908-1916
2.67	Jack Taylor, 1904-1906
2.74	Johnny Lush, 1907-1910
2.74	Red Ames, 1915-1919

Runs: Most, season

142	Jesse Burkett, 1901
141	Rogers Hornsby, 1922
135	Stan Musial, 1948
133	Rogers Hornsby, 1925
132	Joe Medwick, 1935

Hits: Most, season

250	Rogers Hornsby, 1922
237	Joe Medwick, 1937
235	Rogers Hornsby, 1921
230	Stan Musial, 1948
230	Joe Torre, 1971

2B: Most, season

64	Joe Medwick, 1936
56	Joe Medwick, 1937
53	Stan Musial, 1953
52	Enos Slaughter, 1939
51	Stan Musial, 1944

3B: Most, season

29	Perry Werden, 1893
25	Roger Connor, 1894
25	Tom Long, 1915
20	Jim Bottomley, 1928
20	Duff Cooley, 1895
20	Rogers Hornsby, 1920
20	Stan Musial, 1943
20	Stan Musial, 1946

HR: Most, season

43	Johnny Mize, 1940
42	Rogers Hornsby, 1922
39	Rogers Hornsby, 1925
39	Stan Musial, 1948
36	Stan Musial, 1949

RBI: Most, season

154	Joe Medwick, 1937
152	Rogers Hornsby, 1922
143	Rogers Hornsby, 1925
138	Joe Medwick, 1936
137	Jim Bottomley, 1929
137	Johnny Mize, 1940
137	Joe Torre, 1971

SB: Most, season

118	Lou Brock, 1974
110	VINCE COLEMAN, 1985
109	VINCE COLEMAN, 1987
107	VINCE COLEMAN, 1986
81	VINCE COLEMAN, 1988

BB: Most, season

136	Jack Clark, 1987
136	Jack Crooks, 1892
121	Jack Crooks, 1893
116	Miller Huggins, 1910
107	Stan Musial, 1949

BA: Highest, season

.424	Rogers Hornsby, 1924
.403	Rogers Hornsby, 1925
.401	Rogers Hornsby, 1922
.397	Rogers Hornsby, 1921
.396	Jesse Burkett, 1899

Slug avg: Highest, season

.756	Rogers Hornsby, 1925
.722	Rogers Hornsby, 1922
.702	Stan Musial, 1948
.696	Rogers Hornsby, 1924
.652	Chick Hafey, 1930

Games started: Most, season

50	Ted Breitenstein, 1894
50	Ted Breitenstein, 1895
47	Jack Taylor, 1898
45	Kid Gleason, 1892
45	Kid Gleason, 1893
41	Bob Harmon, 1911 (11)

Saves: Most, season

47	LEE SMITH, 1991
45	Bruce Sutter, 1984
43	LEE SMITH, 1992
43	LEE SMITH, 1993
36	TOM HENKE, 1995
36	Bruce Sutter, 1982
36	TODD WORRELL, 1986

Shutouts: Most, season

13	Bob Gibson, 1968
10	Mort Cooper, 1942
10	John Tudor, 1985
7	Harry Brecheen, 1948
7	Mort Cooper, 1944
7	Dizzy Dean, 1934
7	Bill Doak, 1914

Wins: Most, season

30	Dizzy Dean, 1934
28	Dizzy Dean, 1935
27	Ted Breitenstein, 1894
26	Cy Young, 1899
24	Dizzy Dean, 1936
24	Jesse Haines, 1927

K: Most, season

274	Bob Gibson, 1970
270	Bob Gibson, 1965
269	Bob Gibson, 1969
268	Bob Gibson, 1968
245	Bob Gibson, 1964

Win pct: Highest, season

.811	Dizzy Dean, 1934
.810	Ted Wilks, 1944
.789	Harry Brecheen, 1945
.778	Johnny Beazley, 1942
.767	Bob Gibson, 1970

ERA: Lowest, season

1.12	Bob Gibson, 1968
1.72	Bill Doak, 1914
1.78	Mort Cooper, 1942
1.90	Max Lanier, 1943
1.93	John Tudor, 1985

Most pinch-hit homers, season

4	George Crowe, 1959
4	George Crowe, 1960
4	Carl Sawatski, 1961

Most pinch-hit homers, career

8	George Crowe, 1959-1961

Most consecutive games batting safely

33	Rogers Hornsby, 1922
30	Stan Musial, 1950

Most consecutive scoreless innings

47	Bob Gibson, 1968
37	George Bradley, 1876

No-hit games

George Bradley, StL vs Har NL, 2-0; July 15, 1876.

Jesse Haines, StL vs Bos NL, 5-0; July 17, 1924.

Paul Dean, StL at Bro NL, 3-0; September 21, 1934 (2nd game).

Lon Warneke, StL at Cin NL, 2-0; August 30, 1941.

Ray Washburn, StL at SF NL, 2-0; September 18, 1968.

Bob Gibson, StL at Pit NL, 11-0; August 14, 1971.

Bob Forsch, StL vs Phi NL, 5-0; April 16, 1978.

Bob Forsch, StL vs Mon NL, 3-0; September 26, 1983.

Stoney McGlynn, 7 innings, agreement, StL at Bro NL, 1-1; September 24, 1906 (2nd game).

Ed Karger, 7 perfect innings, agreement, StL vs Bos NL, 4-0; August 11, 1907 (2nd game).

Johnny Lush, 6 innings, rain, StL at Bro NL, 2-0; August 6, 1908.

ACTIVE PLAYERS in caps.

Leaders since 1900 are included. If not in the top five, the leader's rank is listed in parenthesis.

Players' years of service are listed by the first and last years with this team and are not necessarily consecutive; all statistics record performances for this team only.

Pittsburgh Pirates

By Anne Ryan, USA TODAY

Jeff King was one of a few bright spots on the Bucs offense, leading the team with 18 homers and 87 RBI.

1995 Pirates: Earned the top draft pick

It took a lot of bad playing and poor pitching, but the Pirates did get something positive out of the 1995 season—the No. 1 pick in the June draft. They paid dearly for it, though. Their "losing percentage" of .597 (58-86) was their worst since 1986.

On the positive side, left-hander Denny Neagle emerged as a bona fide major league starter. He finished 13-8 with a 3.43 earned run average. Rookie left-hander Jason Christiansen showed he can be a weapon in the bullpen, his 4.15 ERA notwithstanding. Right-hander Dan Miceli had 21 saves in his first full season as the closer. Right-handers John Ericks and Steve Parris, both coming back from arm surgeries, opened some eyes as starting prospects. Even Paul Wagner, who finished 5-16, earned some points with some good starts down the stretch. That includes his near no-hitter against Colorado on Aug. 29, when Andres Galarraga singled with two outs in the ninth.

And, believe it or not, there was a point in the season when the Pirates had a right to think about a wild-card spot. On July 22, they were 35-40, a half-game behind the third-place Chicago Cubs, and winners of nine of 12 games.

But in short order, they lost pitcher Jim Gott, catcher Don Slaught, second baseman Carlos Garcia and outfielder Dave Clark to injuries, and the season went into the tank. They lost 46 of their last 69 games.

Another reason for the Pirates' record was the slow starts by outfielder Al Martin and shortstop Jay Bell, both of whom were heavily involved in union meetings during the off-season. Martin's batting average cowered at .215 as late as July 2. Bell's mark was .216 as late as July 7.

The Pirates also had to contend with abysmal outfield defense much of the season. A firmer outfield defense would have taken a little off the pitching staff's 4.70 earned-run average. Another disappointment? The attendance was slightly more than 900,000—the first time since 1985 that the Pirates failed to draw one million at home. Only 11,190 showed up for the last home game on Sept. 20, with the team's fate undecided and the money-losing franchise's relocation apparently imminent. But after the game, fans staged an impromptu 20-minute demonstration, chanting "Don't go, Bucs" and "Keep our Bucs."

1996 Pirates: Preview

The Pirates lack an impact player in the middle of their lineup, a player who excels offensively and defensively. There was some reason to hope that hole could be filled during the off-season via free agency.

"If you're going to win championships, you have to be able to spend money at the major-league level," general manager Cam Bonifay said.

With the Pirates' impending sale, manager Jim Leyland saw reason for optimism.

"I feel confident our pockets will be deeper," he said. "We won't be able to spend wildly and do silly things, but I think we can make some adjustments and understand what it takes to be competitive."

Bonifay and Leyland entered the off-season armed with great job security. In mid-October, the Pirates announced that Leyland's contract had been extended through 2000 and that Bonifay's contract had been extended through 1998.

"People shouldn't expect an overnight miracle," Leyland said. "But I just refuse to give up. I'm in it to the end. And I think we can get it done within five years."

1995 Pirates: Week-by-week notes

These notes were excerpted from the following issues of Baseball Weekly.

▶**May 24:** In a clear-cut message that they intended to ride out the season with young players, the Pirates released catcher Mackey Sasser and right-hander Mike Maddux and sent left-hander Ravelo Manzanillo to their Calgary farm team—leaving nine rookies on the 25-man roster.

▶**June 21:** Jim Leyland didn't start Jay Bell on June 15 for the second time in four games. "I'm getting him out of there," Leyland said. "He's fighting himself. He's really treading water right now. I'm going to get him away from it for a day or two." Bell hadn't had an extra-base hit since May 25—with just four all season. With more than a quarter of the season gone, he had just nine RBI and had struck out 42 times in 43 games.

▶**July 19:** Denny Neagle became the first 10-game winner in the National League with a 9-2 complete-game victory against the St. Louis Cardinals. The Pirates—the lowest-scoring team in the league—had scored 97 runs in Neagle's 17 starts, an average of 5.71 per game, but for the rest of the rotation, they averaged 3.81.

▶**July 26:** Jason Christiansen's ERA had been under 2.00 most of the season—and left-handed batters were 4-for-42 (.095) against him.

▶**Aug. 16:** You'd have to be a really huge Pirate fan to remember Jake Stenzel, but Jeff King brought the old outfielder to the forefront in the Bucs' 9-5 win against San Francisco on Aug. 8. King hit two home runs in a nine-run second inning to become only the second Pirate to accomplish the feat, after Stenzel, who did it 101 years ago on June 6, 1894. Think any of the Pirates knew who Jake Stenzel was? "I think there are a few people in our dugout who never heard of Babe Ruth," manager Jim Leyland joked.

▶**Aug. 23:** Jim Leyland's briefcase contained a piece of paper on which every Pirate wished his name were written in the column on the left side. The headings on the paper read "Yes," "Maybe," and "No," from left to right. It's Leyland's list of how he feels about keeping players for next season. So while division races were going on elsewhere, the Pirates were involved in a roster race. "They have to show us whether they want to be members of this organization or move on," Leyland said.

▶**Aug. 30:** Dave Clark celebrated the one-month anniversary of his crash with teammate Jacob Brumfield in the outfield by playing catch for the first time. Clark, recovering from a broken collarbone, caught throws from trainer Kent Biggerstaff and passed the ultimate test by being able to reach above his head for a ball. "He's right on schedule," Biggerstaff said. "He's the kind of go-getter who wants to play so bad that you have to be careful not to let him rush himself. But it's definitely never a problem getting him to do what he has to do." On the day of the injury, Clark was hitting .314 with four homers and 24 RBI. He was an astonishing 9-for-20 with five RBI as a pinch-hitter.

▶**Sept. 13:** The slumping Pirates lost their fifth in a row on Sept. 10 and were a season-low 22 games under .500. "Same story. When you're not hitting, you've got to pitch, and we pitched bad," manager Jim Leyland said after the fourth loss. "We didn't pitch, we just threw. Paul Wagner threw some right in the wheelhouse, and they hit them out of the ballpark," Leyland said. "They add up quick, those two-run homers."

▶**Oct. 4:** The Pirates finished No. 1—in next June's draft. With a 2-0 loss in Houston on Sept. 26, they assured themselves of finishing with the worst record in the NL, which gets the top pick in 1996.

▶**Last-day recap:** *Heroes*—There

weren't many Heroes for the 1995 Pirates—unless you count Dave Clark, who caught the ball for the final out of a miserable season.

However, Denny Neagle stood out. The left-hander, who was 9-10 with a 5.12 ERA in 1994, blossomed into a quality major league starter in '95. He was 13-8 with a 3.43 ERA and was named to the All-Star team. He also worked 209⅔ innings in 31 starts, making him the most consistent of the Pirates' starters.

"Denny has it pretty well figured out now," manager Jim Leyland said. "He has a feel for pitching."

Neagle's change-up was his best pitch. In his first three years with the Pirates, he pitched a lot in relief and wasn't able to use his change-up much.

"But now I can use it," he said. "It makes my fastball better."

Jeff King and Orlando Merced also had solid seasons.

King hit .265 with a career-high 18 home runs and 87 RBI despite missing two weeks with a wrist injury. Merced batted .300 for the second time in three years, hit a career-high 15 home runs and drove in a career-high 83 runs.

"He's learned how to drive in runs," Leyland said. "It takes time for a player to learn that. He was our best hitter—period."

Unsung Hero—Infielder Nelson Liriano, acquired to give second baseman Carlos Garcia a backup, had to rank as the Pirates' Unsung Hero. He appeared in 107 games and batted .286 with five home runs and 38 RBI in only 259 at-bats. He also hit over .300 with runners in scoring position.

Disappointments—Right-hander Paul Wagner ranked as a Disappointment, finishing 5-16 with a 4.80 ERA. But he pitched better in the final month, trying to add a palm ball as an off-speed pitch to complement his outstanding hard stuff.

"I think he's learned something," catcher Don Slaught said. "Every year I kind of expect him to just blossom. Things didn't work out this year, although he showed signs that he could do things to help himself."

What hurt the Pirates, too, was their outfield defense. It wasn't the errors as much as the balls that weren't caught or cut off.

Another disappointment?

The attendance was just over 900,000, marking the first year since 1985 the Pirates failed to draw a million at home.

Team directory

▸**Owner:** Pittsburgh Baseball Associates
▸**General manager:** Cam Bonifay
▸**Ballpark:**
Three Rivers Stadium
600 Stadium Circle, Pittsburgh, Pa.
412-323-5000
Capacity 47,972
Pay parking lot; $4
Public transportation available
Family and wheelchair sections, ramps, guest relations
▸**Team publications:**
Yearbook, scorecard,
Info Guide
▸**TV, radio broadcast stations:**
KDKA 1020 AM, WPXI Channel 11,
TCI Cable, KLB Sports Network
▸**Camps and/or clinics:**
Youth Camps, 412-323-5098
Fantasy Camp for Adults, 412-323-5025
▸**Spring Training:**
McKechnie Field
Bradenton, Fla.
Capacity 6,562
813-743-3031

PITTSBURGH PIRATES 1995 final stats

BATTERS	BA	SLG	OB	G	AB	R	H	TB	2B	3B	HR	RBI	BB	SO	SB	CS	E
Wehner	.308	.364	.361	52	107	13	33	39	0	3	0	5	10	17	3	1	0
Slaught	.304	.357	.361	35	112	13	34	40	6	0	0	13	9	8	0	0	1
Merced	.300	.468	.365	132	487	75	146	228	29	4	15	83	52	74	7	2	6
C. Garcia	.294	.420	.340	104	367	41	108	154	24	2	6	50	25	55	8	4	15
Liriano	.286	.398	.347	107	259	29	74	103	12	1	5	38	24	34	2	2	5
Martin	.282	.442	.351	124	439	70	124	194	25	3	13	41	44	92	20	11	5
Clark	.281	.372	.359	77	196	30	55	73	6	0	4	24	24	38	3	3	4
Brumfield	.271	.368	.339	116	402	64	109	148	23	2	4	26	37	71	22	12	8
King	.265	.456	.342	122	445	61	118	203	27	2	18	87	55	63	7	4	17
Bell	.262	.404	.336	138	530	79	139	214	28	4	13	55	55	110	2	5	14
Aude	.248	.376	.287	42	109	10	27	41	8	0	2	19	6	20	1	2	1
Pegues	.246	.398	.263	82	171	17	42	68	8	0	6	16	4	36	1	2	4
Cummings	.243	.342	.303	59	152	13	37	52	7	1	2	15	13	30	1	0	1
Young	.232	.381	.268	56	181	13	42	69	9	0	6	22	8	53	1	3	12
Encarnacion	.226	.333	.285	58	159	18	36	53	7	2	2	10	13	28	1	1	7
Johnson	.208	.421	.326	79	221	32	46	93	6	1	13	28	37	66	5	2	8
Sasser	.154	.192	.154	14	26	1	4	5	1	0	0	0	0	0	0	0	0
F. Garcia	.140	.193	.246	42	57	5	8	11	1	1	0	1	8	17	0	1	1

PITCHERS	W-L	ERA	G	GS	CG	GF	Sho	SV	IP	H	R	ER	HR	BB	SO
Hancock	0-0	1.93	11	0	0	3	0	0	14	10	3	3	0	2	6
Morel	0-1	2.84	5	0	0	0	0	0	6.1	6	2	2	0	2	3
Neagle	13-8	3.43	31	31	5	0	1	0	209.2	221	91	80	20	45	150
Plesac	4-4	3.58	58	0	0	16	0	3	60.1	53	26	24	3	27	57
Christiansen	1-3	4.15	63	0	0	13	0	0	56.1	49	28	26	5	34	53
Dyer	4-5	4.34	55	0	0	15	0	0	74.2	81	40	36	9	30	53
Ericks	3-9	4.58	19	18	1	0	0	0	106	108	59	54	7	50	80
Miceli	4-4	4.66	58	0	0	51	0	21	58	61	30	30	7	28	56
White	2-3	4.75	15	9	0	2	0	0	55	66	33	29	3	18	29
Wagner	5-16	4.80	33	25	3	1	1	1	165	174	96	88	18	72	120
Manzanillo	0-0	4.91	5	0	0	0	0	0	3.2	3	3	2	0	2	1
McCurry	1-4	5.02	55	0	0	10	0	1	61	82	38	34	9	30	27
Wilson	0-1	5.02	10	0	0	1	0	0	14.1	13	8	8	2	5	8
Loaiza	8-9	5.16	32	31	1	0	0	0	172.2	205	115	99	21	55	85
Parris	6-6	5.38	15	15	1	0	1	0	82	89	49	49	12	33	61
Gott	2-4	6.03	25	0	0	12	0	3	31.1	38	26	21	2	12	19
Lieber	4-7	6.32	21	12	0	3	0	0	72.2	103	56	51	7	14	45
Powell	0-2	6.98	27	3	0	6	0	0	29.2	36	26	23	6	21	20
Maddux	1-0	9.00	8	0	0	1	0	0	9	14	9	9	0	3	4
Hope	0-0	30.86	3	0	0	0	0	0	2.1	8	8	8	0	4	2
Konuszewski	0-0	54.00	1	0	0	0	0	0	0.1	3	2	2	0	1	0

1996 preliminary roster

PITCHERS (18)
Jason Christiansen
Mariano Delossantos
Mike Dyer
John Ericks
Lee Hancock
Jon Lieber
Esteban Loaiza
Dan Miceli
Ramon Morel
Denny Neagle
Steve Parris
Chris Peters
Marc Piscioatta
Dan Plesac
Kevin Rogers

Matt Ruebel
Matt Ryan
Paul Wagner

CATCHERS (2)
Angelo Encarnacion
Jason Kendall

INFIELDERS (10)
Rich Aude
Jay Bell
Carlos Garcia
Freddy Garcia
Mark Johnson
Jeff King
Nelson Liriano

John Wehner
Tony Womack
Kevin Young

OUTFIELDERS (9)
Jermaine Allensworth
Trey Beamon
Jacob Brumfield
Dave Clark
Patricio Claudio
Midre Cummings
Al Martin
Orlando Merced
Charles Peterson

Games played by position

PLAYER	G	C	1B	2B	3B	SS	OF
Aude	42	0	32	0	0	0	0
Bell	138	0	0	0	3	136	0
Brumfield	116	0	0	0	0	0	104
Clark	77	0	0	0	0	0	61
Cummings	59	0	0	0	0	0	41
Encarnacion	58	55	0	0	0	0	0
C. Garcia	104	0	0	92	0	15	0
F. Garcia	42	0	0	0	8	0	10
Johnson	79	0	70	0	0	0	0
King	122	0	35	8	84	2	0
Liriano	107	0	0	67	5	1	0
Martin	124	0	0	0	0	0	121
Merced	132	0	35	0	0	0	107
Pegues	82	0	0	0	0	0	53
Sasser	14	11	0	0	0	0	0
Slaught	35	33	0	0	0	0	0
Wehner	52	1	0	0	19	1	23
Young	56	0	6	0	48	0	0

Sick call: 1995 DL Report

Player	Days on the DL
Jacob Brumfield	15
Dave Clark	47
Steve Cooke	160
Carlos Garcia	17
Jim Gott	91**
Jeff King	15
Don Slaught	89*
Paul Wagner	18
Rick White	22
Kevin Young	15

Indicates two separate terms on Disabled List.
**Indicates three separate terms on DL.*

Minor Leagues

Tops in the organization

Batter	Club	Avg.	G	AB	R	H	HR	RBI
Keith Osik	CGy	.336	90	301	40	101	10	59
Trey Beamon	CGy	.334	118	452	74	151	5	62
Daryl Ratliff	CGy	.332	111	349	51	116	1	42
Jason Kendall	Car	.326	117	429	87	140	8	71
F. Matos	CGy	.323	100	341	36	110	3	40

Home Runs			Wins		
Micah Franklin	CGy	21	Elmer Dessens	Car	15
George Canale	Car	21	Chris Peters	Car	13
Reed Secrist	Lyn	19	Matt Ruebel	Car	13
Jose Guillen	Aug	14	Kane Davis	Aug	12
Rob Leary	Car	14	Brian Shouse	Car	11

RBI			Saves		
George Canale	Car	102	Matt Ryan	Car	27
Reed Secrist	Lyn	75	Rafael Chaves	Aug	24
Rob Leary	Car	73	Joe Maskivish	Aug	20
Jason Kendall	Car	71	Randy St. Claire	CGy	19
Micah Franklin	CGy	71	Tim Collie	Eri	11

Stolen Bases			Strikeouts		
Derek Swafford	Aug	52	Chris Peters	Car	139
Adrian Brown	Lyn	36	Matt Ruebel	Car	136
Jeff Conger	Car	34	Jeff Kelly	Aug	114
Tony Womack	Car	34	Brett Backlund	CGy	109
Charles Peterson	Car	33	Jimmy Anderson	Lyn	107

Pitcher	Club	W-L	ERA	IP	H	BB	SO
Chris Peters	Car	13-5	2.33	159	135	37	139
Aaron France	Aug	6-6	2.47	95	80	26	77
Elmer Dessens	Car	15-8	2.49	152	170	21	68
J. Anderson	Lyn	5-7	2.58	129	107	52	107
Kevin Pickford	Aug	7-6	2.71	113	116	16	74

1995 Amateur draft picks

Players are listed with position and college or high school. Most players were assigned to rookie or Class A leagues. List provided by Major League Baseball.

Bronson Arroyo, rhp, Hernando HS, Brooksville, Fla.; Scott Beach, rhp, Pittsburg State; Aljereau Benjamin, cf, Charles H Milby HS, Houston; Cory Bigler, rhp, Wisconsin; Ronald Brooks, rhp, Leon HS, Tallahassee, Fla.; Derek Bullock, rhp, Briar Cliff; John Canetto, 3b, Coastal Carolina; Michael Carney, lhp, Merritt Island (Fla.) HS; Timothy Collie, rhp, North Carolina-Charlotte; Orenthal Cook, rhp, Liberty HS, Bethlehem, Pa.; Daniel Delgado, ss, Miami (Fla.) Killian HS; Dawan Elliott, lf-cf, Long Branch (N.J.) HS; Jason Farrow, rhp, Houston; Steven Flanigan, c, California, Pa.; Travis Gaerte, rhp, Fremont HS, Lake Fremont, Ind.; Ryan Gillispie, rhp, Rancho Bernardo HS, San Diego; Christopher Heck, lhp, Northeast Catholic HS, Philadelphia; Chad Hermansen, ss, Green Valley HS, Henderson, Nev.; Alexander Hernandez, of, Juan Rios Serpa HS, Levitown P.R.; George Hlodan, rhp, Elizabeth (Pa) Forward HS; Matthew Hoffman, rhp, Claremore (Okla.) HS; Brock Hundt, 3b, John A. Logan College; Brandon Larson, ss, Blinn College; Joshua Loggins, c, Harrison HS, West Lafayette, Ind.; Garrett Long, rf, Bellaire HS, Houston; Freddie May, cf, John F Kennedy HS, Seattle; Neal McDade, rhp, Florida CC; Chris Miller, rhp-3b, Winter Haven (Fla.) HS; Christopher Miyake, ss, Cal State San Diego; Brian O'Connor, lhp, Reading HS, Cincinnati; Elton Pollock, of, Presbyterian College; Ian Rauls, cf, Ewing HS, Trenton, N.J.; Ronald Ricks, rhp, Tallahassee CC; Jason Saenz, lhp, Mater Dei HS, Santa Ana, Calif.; Brian Settle, rhp, Woodrow Wilson HS, Portsmouth, Va.; Jason Shelley, ss, Plainfield (Ill.) HS; Travis Siegel, of, Choctaw HS, Midwest City, Okla.; Maika Symmonds, lhp, Old Dominion; Robert Thomas, lhp, Texas A&M; Brad Weber, cf, De Kalb HS, Auburn, Ind.; Jacob Whitfield, lhp, Tallahassee CC.; Jason Wright, rhp, Palomar College; Joseph Wroble, lhp, South Suburban College; Arthur Young, cf, New Rochelle (N.Y.) HS.

Pittsburgh (1887-1995)

Runs: Most, career, all-time

1521	Honus Wagner, 1900-1917
1493	Paul Waner, 1926-1940
1416	Roberto Clemente, 1955-1972
1414	Max Carey, 1910-1926
1195	Willie Stargell, 1962-1982

Hits: Most, career, all-time

3000	Roberto Clemente, 1955-1972
2967	Honus Wagner, 1900-1917
2868	Paul Waner, 1926-1940
2416	Max Carey, 1910-1926
2416	Pie Traynor, 1920-1937

2B: Most, career, all-time

558	Paul Waner, 1926-1940
551	Honus Wagner, 1900-1917
440	Roberto Clemente, 1955-1972
423	Willie Stargell, 1962-1982
375	Max Carey, 1910-1926

3B: Most, career, all-time

232	Honus Wagner, 1900-1917
187	Paul Waner, 1926-1940
166	Roberto Clemente, 1955-1972
164	Pie Traynor, 1920-1937
156	Fred Clarke, 1900-1915

262

HR: Most, career, all-time

475	Willie Stargell, 1962-1982
301	Ralph Kiner, 1946-1953
240	Roberto Clemente, 1955-1972
176	BARRY BONDS, 1986-1992
166	Dave Parker, 1973-1983

RBI: Most, career, all-time

1540	Willie Stargell, 1962-1982
1475	Honus Wagner, 1900-1917
1305	Roberto Clemente, 1955-1972
1273	Pie Traynor, 1920-1937
1177	Paul Waner, 1926-1940

SB: Most, career, all-time

688	Max Carey, 1910-1926
639	Honus Wagner, 1900-1917
412	Omar Moreno, 1975-1982
312	Patsy Donovan, 1892-1899
271	Tommy Leach, 1900-1918

BB: Most, career, all-time

937	Willie Stargell, 1962-1982
918	Max Carey, 1910-1926
909	Paul Waner, 1926-1940
877	Honus Wagner, 1900-1917
795	Ralph Kiner, 1946-1953

BA: Highest, career, all-time

.340	Paul Waner, 1926-1940
.336	Kiki Cuyler, 1921-1927
.328	Honus Wagner, 1900-1917
.327	Matty Alou, 1966-1970
.324	Arky Vaughan, 1932-1941
.324	Elmer Smith, 1892-1901

Slug avg: Highest, career, all-time

.567	Ralph Kiner, 1946-1953
.529	Willie Stargell, 1962-1982
.513	Kiki Cuyler, 1921-1927
.512	Dick Stuart, 1958-1962
.503	BARRY BONDS, 1986-1992

Games started: Most, career, all-time

477	Bob Friend, 1951-1965
371	Wilbur Cooper, 1912-1924
364	Vern Law, 1950-1967
354	Babe Adams, 1907-1926
299	Sam Leever, 1898-1910

Saves: Most, career, all-time

188	Roy Face, 1953-1968
158	Kent Tekulve, 1974-1985
133	Dave Giusti, 1970-1976
61	STAN BELINDA, 1989-1993
59	Al McBean, 1961-1970

Shutouts: Most, career, all-time

44	Babe Adams, 1907-1926
39	Sam Leever, 1898-1910
35	Bob Friend, 1951-1965
33	Wilbur Cooper, 1912-1924
29	Lefty Leifield, 1905-1912

Wins: Most, career, all-time

202	Wilbur Cooper, 1912-1924
194	Babe Adams, 1907-1926
194	Sam Leever, 1898-1910
191	Bob Friend, 1951-1965
168	Deacon Phillippe, 1900-1911

K: Most, career, all-time

1682	Bob Friend, 1951-1965
1652	Bob Veale, 1962-1972
1191	Wilbur Cooper, 1912-1924
1159	John Candelaria, 1975-1993
1092	Vern Law, 1950-1967

Win pct: Highest, career, all-time

.683	Nick Maddox, 1907-1910
.667	Jesse Tannehill, 1897-1902
.660	Sam Leever, 1898-1910
.659	Vic Willis, 1906-1909
.656	Emil Yde, 1924-1927

ERA: Lowest, career, all-time

2.08	Vic Willis, 1906-1909
2.38	Lefty Leifield, 1905-1912
2.47	Sam Leever, 1898-1910
2.50	Deacon Phillippe, 1900-1911
2.60	Bob Harmon, 1914-1918

Runs: Most, season

148	Jake Stenzel, 1894
145	Patsy Donovan, 1894
144	Kiki Cuyler, 1925
142	Paul Waner, 1928
140	Max Carey, 1922

Hits: Most, season

237	Paul Waner, 1927
234	Lloyd Waner, 1929
231	Matty Alou, 1969
223	Lloyd Waner, 1927
223	Paul Waner, 1928

2B: Most, season

62	Paul Waner, 1932
53	Paul Waner, 1936
50	Paul Waner, 1928
47	Adam Comorosky, 1930
45	Dave Parker, 1979
45	ANDY VAN SLYKE, 1992
45	Honus Wagner, 1900

3B: Most, season

36	Chief Wilson, 1912
28	Harry Davis, 1897
27	Jimmy Williams, 1899
26	Kiki Cuyler, 1925
23	Adam Comorosky, 1930
23	Elmer Smith, 1893

HR: Most, season

54	Ralph Kiner, 1949
51	Ralph Kiner, 1947
48	Willie Stargell, 1971
47	Ralph Kiner, 1950
44	Willie Stargell, 1973

RBI: Most, season

131	Paul Waner, 1927
127	Ralph Kiner, 1947
127	Ralph Kiner, 1949
126	Honus Wagner, 1901
125	Willie Stargell, 1971

SB: Most, season

96	Omar Moreno, 1980
77	Omar Moreno, 1979
71	Omar Moreno, 1978
71	Billy Sunday, 1888
70	Frank Taveras, 1977

BB: Most, season

137	Ralph Kiner, 1951
127	BARRY BONDS, 1992
122	Ralph Kiner, 1950
119	Elbie Fletcher, 1940
118	Elbie Fletcher, 1941
118	Arky Vaughan, 1936

BA: Highest, season

.385	Arky Vaughan, 1935
.381	Honus Wagner, 1900
.380	Paul Waner, 1927
.374	Jake Stenzel, 1895
.373	Paul Waner, 1936

Slug avg: Highest, season

.658	Ralph Kiner, 1949
.646	Willie Stargell, 1973
.639	Ralph Kiner, 1947
.628	Willie Stargell, 1971
.627	Ralph Kiner, 1951

Games started: Most, season

55	Ed Morris, 1888
53	Mark Baldwin, 1892
50	Mark Baldwin, 1891
50	Pud Galvin, 1888
50	Pink Hawley, 1895
50	Frank Killen, 1896
42	Bob Friend, 1956 (12)

Saves: Most, season

34	JIM GOTT, 1988
31	Kent Tekulve, 1978
31	Kent Tekulve, 1979
30	Dave Giusti, 1971
28	Roy Face, 1962

Shutouts: Most, season

8	Babe Adams, 1920
8	Jack Chesbro, 1902
8	Lefty Leifield, 1906
8	Al Mamaux, 1915
7	Steve Blass, 1968
7	Wilbur Cooper, 1917
7	Sam Leever, 1903
7	Bob Veale, 1965
7	Vic Willis, 1908

Wins: Most, season

36	Frank Killen, 1893
31	Pink Hawley, 1895
30	Frank Killen, 1896
29	Ed Morris, 1888
28	Jack Chesbro, 1902
28	Pud Galvin, 1887

K: Most, season

276	Bob Veale, 1965
250	Bob Veale, 1964
229	Bob Veale, 1966
213	Bob Veale, 1969
199	Larry McWilliams, 1983

Win pct: Highest, season

.947	Roy Face, 1959
.842	Emil Yde, 1924
.824	Jack Chesbro, 1902
.806	Howie Camnitz, 1909
.800	John Candelaria, 1977
.800	Ed Doheny, 1902
.800	Sam Leever, 1905

ERA: Lowest, season

1.56	Howie Camnitz, 1908
1.62	Howie Camnitz, 1909
1.66	Sam Leever, 1907
1.73	Vic Willis, 1906
1.87	Lefty Leifield, 1906

Most pinch-hit homers, season

3	Ham Hyatt, 1913
3	Al Rubeling, 1944
3	Bob Skinner, 1956
3	Dick Stuart, 1959
3	Gene Freese, 1964
3	Jose Pagan, 1969
3	Willie Stargell, 1982

Most pinch-hit homers, career

7	Willie Stargell 1962-1982

Most consecutive games batting safely

27	Jimmy Williams, 1899
26	Danny O'Connell, 1953

Most consecutive scoreless innings

41	Jack Chesbro, 1902
36	Ed Morris, 1888

No-hit games

Nick Maddox, Pit vs Bro NL, 2-1; September 20, 1907.

Cliff Chambers, Pit at Bos NL, 3-0; May 6, 1951 (2nd game).

Harvey Haddix, Pit at Mil NL, 0-1; May 26, 1959 (lost on 1 hit in 13 innings after pitching 12 perfect innings).

Bob Moose, Pit at NY NL, 4-0; September 20, 1969.

Dock Ellis, Pit at SD NL, 2-0; June 12, 1970 (1st game).

John Candelaria, Pit vs LA NL, 2-0; August 9, 1976.

Lefty Leifield, 6 innings, darkness, Pit at Phi NL, 8-0; September 26, 1906 (2nd game).

Howie Camnitz, 5 innings, agreement, Pit at NY NL, 1-0; August 23, 1907 (2nd game).

ACTIVE PLAYERS in caps.

Leaders since 1900 are included. If not in the top five, leader's rank is listed in parenthesis.

Players' years of service are listed by the first and last years with this team and are not necessarily consecutive; all statistics record performances for this team only.

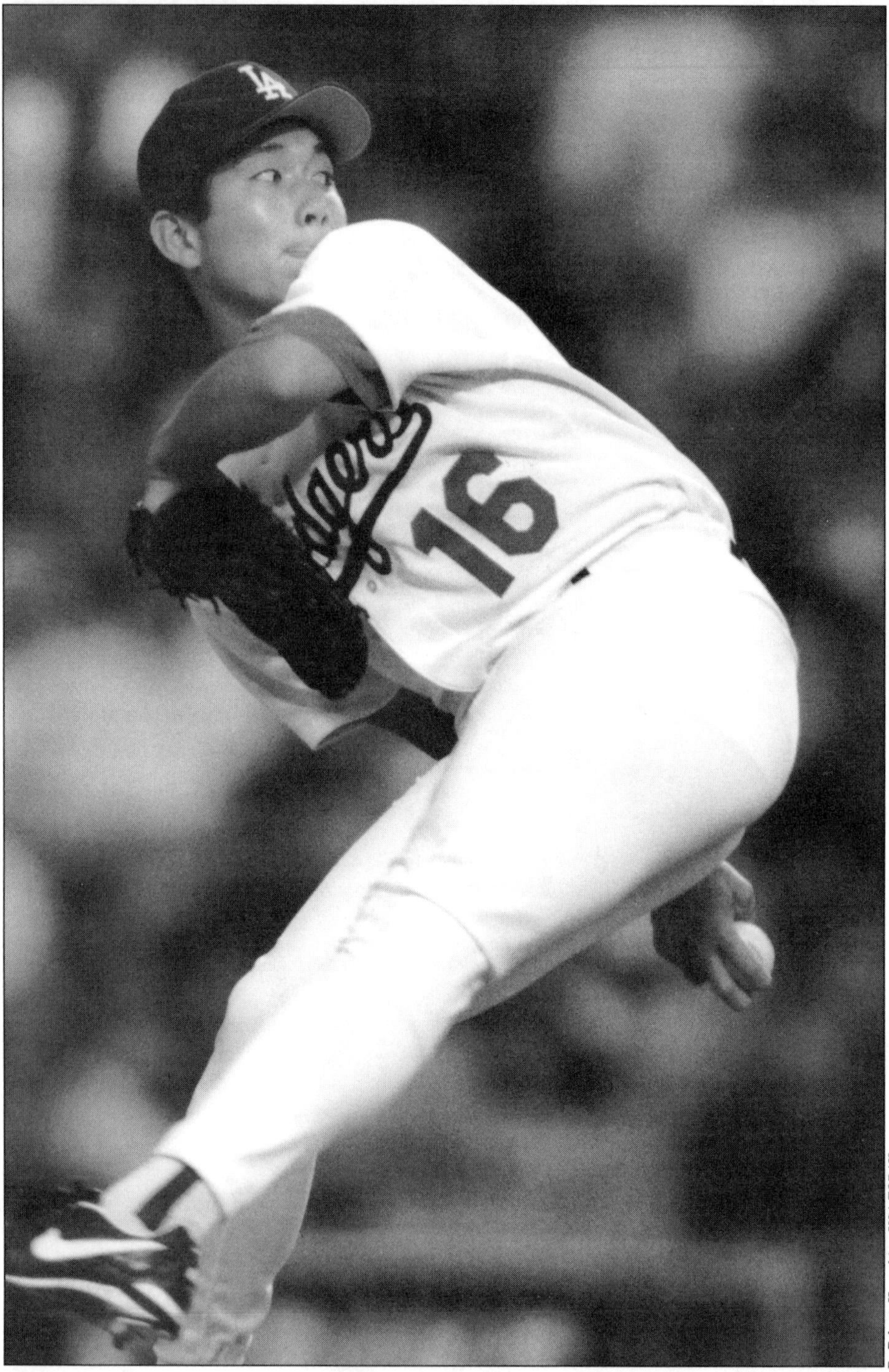

By Robert Hanashiro, *USA TODAY*

Hideo Nomo (13-6), who led the team in ERA (2.52) and strikeouts (236), was the team's biggest draw.

1995 Dodgers: Could they have done better?

The Dodgers won the National League West for the first since 1988, but when they were eliminated in three consecutive games by the Cincinnati Reds in the division series, it resurrected those haunting accusations about their being underachievers.

It was a year that brought Dodger fans Hideo Nomo. It had them screaming once again at Jose Offerman. It resurrected the career of Todd Worrell. It may have ended the career of Tim Wallach. It left fans feeling exasperated, excited, but, in the end, utterly confused. The Dodgers were labeled underachievers not only by the public but also by many of their peers in the National League, wondering why in the world they couldn't run away from the pack in the National League West. How can you have five All-Stars, two MVP candidates, acquire Brett Butler, Roberto Kelly and Kevin Tapani, and still almost not reach the playoffs?

Executive vice president Fred Claire let Orel Hershiser, Kevin Gross and Brett Butler walk away, but he discovered that his organization is rich in young talent. Nomo (13-6), the first Japanese major league pitcher in 30 years, was given a $2 million signing bonus and became the talk of baseball. Ismael Valdes (13-11) emerged as one of the finest young starters in all of baseball. Antonio Osuna proved by the end of the season that he will be a bona fide closer within a year. And Chad Fonville proved that the San Francisco Giants made a serious blunder leaving him in Class A for all those years.

While the debate most of the year focused on whether the team MVP should be Mike Piazza (.346, 32 homers, 93 RBIs) or first baseman Eric Karros (.298, 32 homers, 105 RBI), second baseman Delino DeShields cast his vote for shortstop/second baseman/left fielder Fonville. Fonville, a Rule V selection, became an everyday player in June and by the end of the season proved to be the team's spark plug (.276, 41 runs and 20 stolen bases in just 308 at-bats).

"When Chad started to play," DeShields said, "that energy level went up for all us. He's a big ball of energy. He's always in high gear, so we have to get up to bring ourselves to his level. The excitement is genuine, too. He's not diving, jumping around just trying to get a reaction from the crowd. That's just him."

1996 Dodgers: Preview

The Dodgers' outfield should be set with All-Star Raul Mondesi (.285, 26 homers, 88 RBI), Brett Butler (.300), and Todd Hollandsworth, but that could change depending on the progress of young outfielders. Billy Ashley will likely get one more chance to be the everyday left fielder, which could move Hollandsworth to center and Butler to the bench. Rookie Roger Cedeno will be given a chance to be the starting center fielder, although there are doubts about whether he will be ready.

The entire left side of the infield departed after the season. Offerman had been benched all of September, and Wallach, plagued by injuries all season, needs knee surgery and six months of rehabilitation. The Dodgers' dilemma during the winter was where to play Fonville. They may use his many talents to use him as a super utility man, making sure he's in the lineup every day, just as Detroit used to do with Tony Phillips.

The Dodgers are counting on a starting rotation of Ramon Martinez (17-7), Valdes, Nomo and rookie Chan Ho Park next season, leaving one opening. They'll definitely try to bring back closer Todd Worrell.

These notes were excerpted from the following issues of Baseball Weekly.

▶**May 3:** Catcher Mike Piazza suffered a strained right hamstring on April 26, and although he missed the entire opening series against the Braves, he avoided the disabled list. Manager Tom Lasorda's reaction the moment he saw Piazza clutch at his leg was, "If somebody was robbing your Rolls-Royce, wouldn't you come out of your house fast?"

▶**May 10:** In his first two major league starts, Japanese-born Hideo Nomo saw the best and worst of times. On May 2, fans in Candlestick Park unfurled the Japanese flag. Many had tears streaming down their faces as the Dodgers pitcher emerged from the dugout and slowly walked to the mound. Nomo, the first Japanese-born player to pitch in the major leagues in 30 years, was brilliant in his major league debut, pitching five shutout innings, yielding one hit and striking out seven. In his next start, though, he was tagged for seven runs and nine hits, including three homers, in 4⅔ innings. Asked if he had underestimated the power of major leaguers, Nomo said, "No, those were just missed pitches."

▶**May 24:** Ramon Martinez let the Dodgers and the rest of the baseball world know that he was back, entering the week with a 4-2 record and 3.32 ERA. "This is the best I've ever seen him," said teammate Tom Candiotti. "He's unbelievable right now. He just dominates hitters. What can you say—with Orel [Hershiser] and Kevin [Gross] gone, he's our ace."

▶**May 31:** Henry Rodriguez and Jeff Treadway were traded to the Expos for Roberto Kelly and rookie reliever Joey Eischen. Three days later, they found themselves playing against their former teammates and picking up the belongings they left behind. "I just never imagined something like this could happen

to me," Rodriguez said. "I thought I'd be with the Dodgers for the rest of my life. I cried. I was so sad. I still am sad."

▶**June 7:** When Mike Piazza returned June 4, the Dodgers were able to put their starting lineup on the field for the first time since the season started. "I don't think we can just say, 'OK, now the division's ours,'" pitcher Tom Candiotti said, "but I think the rest of the division has got to be worried." The Dodgers went 8-14 in Piazza's absence.

▶**June 14:** No matter what he does or how good he pitches, Tom Candiotti couldn't seem to win a game. "You want to just stand there and scream," Candiotti said, "but what good will it do except hurt your throat? This stuff can drive you crazy." He had a 1.30 ERA, but his record was 2-5.

▶**June 21:** The novelty factor surrounding Nomo had faded somewhat and he was beginning to be recognized as one of the finest pitchers in the league. After Nomo (3-0, 2.84) set a franchise rookie record with 16 strikeouts in eight innings in a victory over Pittsburgh, Pirates shortstop Jay Bell was asked if Nomo reminded him of anybody. "Yeah," Bell answered. "Cy Young."

▶**June 28:** Nomo hoped that his allure would eventually pass as the season went on, but his pitching continued to keep him in the spotlight, especially after he pitched a two-hit complete-game shutout against the Giants. The crowd cheered wildly for each of his 13 strikeouts and gave him a standing ovation after the seventh and eighth innings. Nomo wasn't just winning, he was dominating—over his last five starts, his ERA was 1.09 with 46 strikeouts in only 41⅓ innings.

▶**July 5:** Nomo led the Dodgers into first place in the NL West with a 3-0 victory against the Colorado Rockies, striking out 13 batters for his second consecutive shutout. The crowd, infamous for their early exits, refused to leave. Fans stood during the entire ninth inning and screamed to the heavens the moment Nomo struck out Walt Weiss, ending the game. It was Nomo's 50th strikeout victim in his last four games, setting a Dodger franchise record and eclipsing Sandy Koufax's mark of 49 set in 1965.

In shutting down the most powerful hitting team in the league, Nomo won his league-high sixth consecutive victory. His ERA: 0.89 during that span. Nomomania was in full force. "I never thought I'd see anything like Fernandomania again in my life," said Dodgers broadcaster Jaime Jarrin, Fernando Valenzuela's interpreter. "But it's coming. Believe me, it is coming."

▶**July 13:** The Dodgers limped into the All-Star break with nine losses in 12 games. They had been shut out a National League–leading nine times. One of the tough losses was a 4-1 decision in Atlanta when Chipper Jones's three-run home run against reliever Rudy Seanez broke up what had been a masterful pitching duel between Hideo Nomo and John Smoltz. Nomo went seven innings, allowing two hits and one run, striking out 10. "The guy [Nomo] was phenomenal," Jones said. "He's worth all of the hype and press that he's getting. I know that a lot of people are touting me as Rookie of the Year, but after what he [Nomo] has done the past month, even I'd consider him Rookie of the Year."

▶**July 26:** The Dodgers entered the week trailing the third-year Colorado Rockies by five games and have never overcome a greater second-half deficit to earn a playoff berth. Second baseman Delino DeShields, benched for four games, said he believes he no longer has a future in the organization past this season and would retire at the season's conclusion if his lower left leg pains continue.

▶**Aug. 23:** Brett Butler was a Dodger again. Saying they never wanted to break up in the first place, the Dodgers resumed their love affair Aug. 18 by re-acquiring Butler from the Mets. "We

should win this now, no?" said Dodgers right fielder Raul Mondesi.

▶**Sept. 6:** For the first time since Aug. 11 the Dodgers had fallen out of first place, and the entire division entered the week separated by just five games. "That's the worst thing of all," Dodgers catcher Mike Piazza said. "We let the Giants back in the race. That hurts."

▶**Sept. 13:** Tom Lasorda, realizing his team was in a must-win situation, benched All-Star shortstop Jose Offerman until further notice. An angry Offerman said he'd probably request a trade at the season's conclusion.

▶**Oct. 4:** All of the ridicule and criticism were buried on Sept. 30 under the mass of Dodger humanity that piled onto the field celebrating the 1995 NL West Division title. The Dodgers clinched their eighth division title with a 7-2 victory against the Padres, earning their first playoff berth since winning the 1988 World Series.

Team directory

▶**Owner:** Peter O'Malley
▶**General manager:** Fred Claire
▶**Ballpark:**
Dodger Stadium
1000 Elysian Park Ave.,
Los Angeles, Calif.
213-224-1400
Capacity 56,000
Parking for 16,000 cars; $4
Wheelchair section and ramps
▶**Team publications:**
Dodger Magazine, media guide
▶**TV, radio broadcast stations:**
KABC 790 AM, KWKW 1330 AM
(Spanish), KTLA Channel 5
▶**Camps and/or clinics:**
Twenty clinics per year, 213-224-1435
▶**Spring training:**
Holman Stadium
Dodgertown
Vero Beach, Fla.
Capacity 7,000
407-569-4900

LOS ANGELES DODGERS 1995 final stats

BATTERS	BA	SLG	OB	G	AB	R	H	TB	2B	3B	HR	RBI	BB	SO	SB	CS	E
Piazza	.346	.606	.400	112	434	82	150	263	17	0	32	93	39	80	1	0	9
Butler	.300	.376	.377	129	513	78	154	193	18	9	1	38	67	51	32	8	2
Karros	.298	.535	.369	143	551	83	164	295	29	3	32	105	61	115	4	4	7
Hansen	.287	.359	.384	100	181	19	52	65	10	0	1	14	28	28	0	0	7
Offerman	.287	.375	.389	119	429	69	123	161	14	6	4	33	69	67	2	7	35
Mondesi	.285	.496	.328	139	536	91	153	266	23	6	26	88	33	96	27	4	6
Fonville	.278	.303	.328	102	320	43	89	97	6	1	0	16	23	42	20	7	11
Kelly	.278	.373	.312	136	504	58	140	188	23	2	7	57	22	79	19	10	6
Parker	.276	.276	.323	27	29	3	8	8	0	0	0	4	2	4	1	1	0
Wallach	.266	.428	.326	97	327	24	87	140	22	2	9	38	27	69	0	0	5
Deshields	.256	.369	.353	127	425	66	109	157	18	3	8	37	63	83	39	14	11
Castro	.250	.250	.400	11	4	0	1	1	0	0	0	0	1	1	0	0	0
Cedeno	.238	.286	.283	40	42	4	10	12	2	0	0	3	3	10	1	0	1
Ashley	.237	.372	.320	81	215	17	51	80	5	0	8	27	25	88	0	0	3
Busch	.235	.765	.235	13	17	3	4	13	0	0	3	6	0	7	0	0	1
Hollandsworth	.233	.398	.304	41	103	16	24	41	2	0	5	13	10	29	2	1	4
Gwynn	.214	.333	.272	67	84	8	18	28	3	2	1	10	6	23	0	0	0
Garcia	.200	.200	.200	13	20	1	4	4	0	0	0	0	0	4	0	0	0
Ingram	.200	.236	.313	44	55	5	11	13	2	0	0	3	9	8	3	0	8
Prince	.200	.375	.273	18	40	3	8	15	2	1	1	4	4	10	0	0	1
Webster	.179	.286	.246	54	56	6	10	16	1	1	1	3	4	14	0	0	0
Hernandez	.149	.223	.216	45	94	3	14	21	1	0	2	8	7	25	0	0	4
Schofield	.100	.100	.182	9	10	0	1	1	0	0	0	0	1	3	0	0	0
R. Williams	.091	.091	.231	15	11	2	1	1	0	0	0	0	1	2	3	0	0
Munoz	.000	.000	.000	2	1	0	0	0	0	0	0	0	0	0	0	0	0
Pye	.000	.000	.000	7	8	0	0	0	0	0	0	0	0	4	0	0	0

PITCHERS	W-L	ERA	G	GS	CG	GF	Sho	SV	IP	H	R	ER	HR	BB	SO
Worrell	4-1	2.02	59	0	0	53	0	32	62.1	50	15	14	4	19	61
F. Rodriguez	1-1	2.53	11	0	0	5	0	0	10.2	11	3	3	2	5	5
Nomo	13-6	2.54	28	28	4	0	3	0	191.1	124	63	54	14	78	236
Cummings	3-1	3.00	35	0	0	11	0	0	39	38	16	13	3	10	21
Valdes	13-11	3.05	33	27	6	1	2	1	197.2	168	76	67	17	51	150
Eischen	0-0	3.10	17	0	0	8	0	0	20.1	19	9	7	1	11	15
Candiotti	7-14	3.50	30	30	1	0	1	0	190.1	187	93	74	18	58	141
Guthrie	0-2	3.66	24	0	0	7	0	0	19.2	19	11	8	1	9	19
Martinez	17-7	3.66	30	30	4	0	2	0	206.1	176	95	84	19	81	138
Astacio	7-8	4.24	48	11	1	7	1	0	104	103	53	49	12	29	80
Parra	0-0	4.35	8	0	0	0	0	0	10.1	10	8	5	2	6	7
Osuna	2-4	4.43	39	0	0	8	0	0	44.2	39	22	22	5	20	46
Bruske	0-0	4.50	9	0	0	3	0	1	10	12	7	5	0	4	5
Park	0-0	4.50	2	1	0	0	0	0	4	2	2	2	1	2	7
Tapani	4-2	5.05	13	11	0	0	0	0	57	72	37	32	8	14	43
T. Williams	2-2	5.12	16	0	0	5	0	0	19.1	19	11	11	3	7	8
Seanez	1-3	6.75	37	0	0	12	0	3	34.2	39	27	26	5	18	29
Daal	4-0	7.20	28	0	0	6	0	0	20	29	16	16	1	15	11
Hansell	0-1	7.45	20	0	0	7	0	0	19.1	29	17	16	5	6	13

1996 preliminary roster

PITCHERS (20)
Pedro Astacio
Ramser Correa
John Cummings
Darren Dreifort
Roberto Duran
Joey Eischen
Rick Gorecki
Mark Guthrie
Darren Hall
Jesus Martinez
Ramon Martinez
Hideo Nomo
Antonio Osuna
Chan Ho Park
Felix Rodriguez
Kevin Tapani
Ismael Valdes
Brandon Watts
Eric Weaver
Todd Worrell

CATCHERS (3)
Carlos Hernandez
Ken Huckaday
Mike Piazza

INFIELDERS (11)
Mike Blowers
Mike Busch
Juan Castro
Delino DeShields
Chad Fonville
Greg Gagne
Wilton Guerrero
Dave Hansen
Garey Ingram
Eric Karros
Jose Offerman

OUTFIELDERS (6)
Billy Ashley
Brett Butler
Roger Cedeno
Karim Garcia
Todd Hollandsworth
Raul Mondesi

Games played by position

PLAYER	G	C	1B	2B	3B	SS	OF
Ashley	81	0	0	0	0	0	69
Busch	13	0	2	0	10	0	0
Butler	129	0	0	0	0	0	128
Castro	11	0	0	0	7	4	0
Cedeno	40	0	0	0	0	0	36
DeShields	127	0	0	113	0	0	0
Fonville	102	0	0	38	0	38	11
Garcia	13	0	0	0	0	0	5
Gwynn	67	0	2	0	0	0	17
Hansen	100	0	0	0	58	0	0
Hernandez	45	41	0	0	0	0	0
Hollandsworth	41	0	0	0	0	0	37
Ingram	44	0	0	7	12	0	4
Karros	143	0	143	0	0	0	0
Kelly	136	0	0	0	0	0	134
Mondesi	139	0	0	0	0	0	138
Munoz	2	2	0	0	0	0	0
Offerman	119	0	0	0	0	115	0
Parker	27	0	0	0	2	2	21
Piazza	112	112	0	0	0	0	0
Prince	18	17	0	0	0	0	0
Pye	7	0	0	0	2	0	0
Schofield	9	0	0	0	1	3	0
Wallach	97	0	1	0	96	0	0
Webster	54	0	0	0	0	0	25
R. Williams	15	0	0	0	0	0	14

Minor Leagues

Tops in the organization

Batter	Club	Avg.	G	AB	R	H	HR	RBI
Adam Riggs	Sbr	.362	134	542	111	196	24	106
Wilton Guerrero	Abq	.346	109	431	63	149	0	28
Brad Dandridge	Sbr	.323	85	334	57	108	11	62
Ron Coomer	Abq	.322	85	323	54	104	16	76
Karim Garcia	Abq	.319	124	474	88	151	20	90

Home Runs

Adam Riggs	Sbr	24		
Oreste Marrero	Abq	23		
Karim Garcia	Abq	20		
Paul Konerko	Sbr	19		
Mike Busch	Abq	18		

Wins

Gary Rath	Abq	16
William Brunson	San	14
Kevin Pincavitch	Sbr	12
Dave Pyc	Abq	12
Several tied		11

RBI

Adam Riggs	Sbr	106
Oreste Marrero	Abq	92
Karim Garcia	Abq	90
Chris Latham	Abq	79
Paul Konerko	Sbr	77

Saves

Joe Jacobsen	Sbr	34
Rich Linares	Bak	20
Ramser Correa	Abq	17
Julio Colon	Sbr	12
Several tied		11

Stolen Bases

Mike Metcalfe	Vb	61
Chris Latham	Abq	54
V. Spearman	Sbr	45
Kevin Gibbs	Sbr	40
Several tied		33

Strikeouts

Mike Iglesias	Sbr	120
Roberto Duran	Vb	114
William Brunson	San	114
Kevin Pincavitch	Sbr	113
Eric Weaver	San	105

Pitcher	Club	W-L	ERA	IP	H	BB	SO
K. Pincavitch	Sbr	12-7	1.74	135	91	54	113
Tom Price	Sbr	10-5	2.20	152	145	14	82
Rafael Montalvo	Abq	3-5	2.65	98	105	34	65
Mark Mimbs	Abq	6-5	2.97	106	105	22	96
Gary Rath	Abq	16-8	3.35	156	142	68	104

Sick call: 1995 DL Report

Player	Days on the DL
Darren Dreifort	160
Rick Gorecki	160
Chris Gwynn	21
Todd Hollandsworth	30*
Antonio Osuna	28
Mike Piazza	24
Tom Prince	36
Rudy Seanez	19
Tim Wallach	40*
Mitch Webster	21

* Indicates two separate terms on Disabled List.

1995 Amateur draft picks

Players are listed with position and college or high school. Most players were assigned to rookie or Class A leagues. List provided by Major League Baseball.

Cesar Acosta, lf, Yuma (Ariz.) HS; Joel Ainsworth, lhp, Sarnia Collegiate Inst., Sarnia, Ont.; Craig Allen, rhp, Notre Dame; Neal Atchison, rhp, Central Huron, Clinton, Can.; Paul Auton, c, Harry Ainlay HS, Edmonton, Alta.; Darrin Babineaux, rhp, Southwestern Louisiana.; Larry Bethea, 1b, Red Springs (N.C.) HS; Trevor Bishop, rhp, Assiniboia (Sask.) Composite HS; Brad Block, rhp, Lake Michigan College; Michael Bourbakis, rhp, F.D. Roosevelt HS, Brooklyn, N.Y.; Brandon Bowe, rhp, Delta CC; Brad Brewer, ss, Sacramento City College; Eric Brown, 3b, East St. John Laplace, La.; Ryan Cail, rhp, Kwantlen College; Michael Carpentier, ss, Cal State Sacramento; Cesar Castenada, 3b, Lincoln HS, Los Angeles; Peter Cervantes, rhp, East Los Angeles JC; Norman Chambers, rhp, John A. Logan College; Gregory Clark, c, Paradise Valley HS, Phoenix; Gregory Conley, c, Sequim (Wash.) HS; Vance Cozier, rhp, Pickering HS, Ajax, Ont.; Bobby Cripps, c, Max Cameron Secondary, Powell River, Can.; Trent Cueves, ss, El Dorado HS, Placentia, Calif.; Xavier Curley, 3b, Marshall County HS, Lewisburg, Tenn.; John Davis, rhp, Bethune-Cookman College; Brian Dawson, rhp, San Bernardino Valley, Highland, Calif.; Jeffrey Deno, lhp, Franklin HS, Los Angeles; Andrew Dougherty, c, Glassboro (N.J.) HS; Stephen Dupont, rhp, Nicholls State; Harold Featherstone, rhp, Hendersonville (N.C.) HS; Pedro Feliciano, lhp, Jose S. Alegria HC, Puerto Dorado, P.R.; Eric Flores, ss, Rio Mesa HS, Camarillo, Calif.; Kevin Gibbs, cf-rf, Old Dominion; Judd Granzow, of-1b, Faith Baptist HS, Granada Hills, Calif.; Steve Green, rhp, Polyvalente Edouard Montpelier, Longueuil, Que., Can.; Lazaro Gutierrez, lhp, Brito Miami Private School, Hialeah, Fla.; Timothy Hackman, rhp, Vernon Secondary, Vernon, Can.; Maurice Hightower, lhp, Arlington (Texas) HS; Kevin Hodge, ss, Bryan (Texas) HS; Brett Illig, 3b, Phoenixville (Pa.) HS; Tony James, 2b, Chaffey College; Christian Keating, rhp, Brother Rice HS, Country Club Hills, Ill.; Jeffrey Keppen, rhp, Georgia Southern; Charles Koone, cf, Spartanburg Methodist JC; Onan Masaoka, lhp, Waiakea HS, Hilo, Hawaii.; Dennis Mauch, c, Cosumnes River College; Terrence McClain, ss, Cumberland; Mitchell McNeely, lhp, Centenary; Travis Meyer, c, East Carolina; Spencer Micunek, rhp, Henry Ford CC; Kendrick Miller, ss, Providence Catholic HS, Joliet, Ill.; Ken Morimoto, cf, Hawaii; Ryan Moskau, 1b-lhp, Sabino HS, Tucson, Ariz.; Antonio Mota, cf-lf, Miami Springs Sr HS, Miami; James O'Shaughnessy, rhp, Northeastern; Brian Oliver, ss, Antioch (Calif.) Sr HS; Scott Oliver, rhp, Richland NE HS, Columbia, S.C.; Andrew Owen, of, California; Mark Paschal, rf, Fontana HS, Bloomington, Calif.; Gwynne Pearsall, lhp, South Carolina; Mathew Randel, rhp, Ridgefield (Wash.) HS; Jose Rijo-Berger, cf, Walla Walla CC; William Riley, rf, Trinity Christian Academy, Irving, Texas; Rabell Rivera, ss, Rafael Cordero HS, Las Lomas PR; Jeffrey Rodriguez, c, Coral Gables HS, Miami; Chad Roney, c, Jacksonville; David Ross, c, Florida HS, Tallahassee, Fla.; Justin Rumfield, ss-3b, McLennan CC; Vincent Sanchez, rhp, Chaffey College; David Schmidt, c, Oregon State; Jason Smith, ss, Demopolis HS, Coatopa, Ala.; Seferino Soto, rhp, Palomar College; Cary Stover, rhp, American River College; Todd Sutton, cf, Angola HS, Pleasant Lake, Ind.; Michael Tablit, rhp, Yuba CC; Craig Taczy, lhp, Shepard HS, Crestwood, Ill.; Joseph Thomas, rhp, West Covina HS, La Puente, Calif.; Jonathan Tucker, 1b, Chatsworth HS, Northridge, Calif.; Mark Vallecorsa, lhp, Damien HS, San Dimas, Calif.; Christopher Vollaro, rhp, Alvin CC; Brian Wagner, c, Sacramento CC; A.J. Walkanoff, c, Creighton; Peyton Warren, rhp, West Florence (S.C.) HS; Stephan Wilkerson, lhp, Apollo HS, Owensboro, Ky.; David Yocum, lhp, Florida State.

269

Los Angeles (1958-1995), includes Brooklyn (1890-1957)

Runs: Most, career, all-time

1338	Pee Wee Reese, 1940-1958
1255	Zack Wheat, 1909-1926
1199	Duke Snider, 1947-1962
1163	Jim Gilliam, 1953-1966
1088	Gil Hodges, 1943-1961

Hits: Most, career, all-time

2804	Zack Wheat, 1909-1926
2170	Pee Wee Reese, 1940-1958
2091	Willie Davis, 1960-1973
1995	Duke Snider, 1947-1962
1968	Steve Garvey, 1969-1982

2B: Most, career, all-time

464	Zack Wheat, 1909-1926
343	Duke Snider, 1947-1962
333	Steve Garvey, 1969-1982
330	Pee Wee Reese, 1940-1958
324	Carl Furillo, 1946-1960

3B: Most, career, all-time

171	Zack Wheat, 1909-1926
110	Willie Davis, 1960-1973
97	Hy Myers, 1909-1922
87	Jake Daubert, 1910-1918
82	John Hummel, 1905-1915
82	Duke Snider, 1947-1962

270

HR: Most, career, all-time

389	Duke Snider, 1947-1962
361	Gil Hodges, 1943-1961
242	Roy Campanella, 1948-1957
228	Ron Cey, 1971-1982
211	Steve Garvey, 1969-1982

RBI: Most, career, all-time

1271	Duke Snider, 1947-1962
1254	Gil Hodges, 1943-1961
1210	Zack Wheat, 1909-1926
1058	Carl Furillo, 1946-1960
992	Steve Garvey, 1969-1982

SB: Most, career, all-time

490	Maury Wills, 1959-1972
418	Davey Lopes, 1972-1981
335	Willie Davis, 1960-1973
298	Tom Daly, 1890-1901
290	Steve Sax, 1981-1988

BB: Most, career, all-time

1210	Pee Wee Reese, 1940-1958
1036	Jim Gilliam, 1953-1966
925	Gil Hodges, 1943-1961
893	Duke Snider, 1947-1962
765	Ron Cey, 1971-1982

BA: Highest, career, all-time

.352	Willie Keeler, 1893-1902
.339	Babe Herman, 1926-1945
.337	Jack Fournier, 1923-1926
.317	Zack Wheat, 1909-1926
.315	Babe Phelps, 1935-1941
.315	Manny Mota, 1969-1982 (6)

Slug avg: Highest, career, all-time

.557	Babe Herman, 1926-1945
.553	Duke Snider, 1947-1962
.552	Jack Fournier, 1923-1926
.528	Reggie Smith, 1976-1981
.512	Pedro Guerrero, 1978-1988

Games started: Most, career, all-time

533	Don Sutton, 1966-1988
465	Don Drysdale, 1956-1969
335	Claude Osteen, 1965-1973
332	Brickyard Kennedy, 1892-1901
326	Dazzy Vance, 1922-1935

Saves: Most, career, all-time

125	Jim Brewer, 1964-1975
101	Ron Perranoski, 1961-1972
85	Jay Howell, 1988-1992
83	Clem Labine, 1950-1960
64	Tom Niedenfuer, 1981-1987

Shutouts: Most, career, all-time

52	Don Sutton, 1966-1988
49	Don Drysdale, 1956-1969
40	Sandy Koufax, 1955-1966
38	Nap Rucker, 1907-1916
34	Claude Osteen, 1965-1973

Wins: Most, career, all-time

233	Don Sutton, 1966-1988
209	Don Drysdale, 1956-1969
190	Dazzy Vance, 1922-1935
177	Brickyard Kennedy, 1892-1901
165	Sandy Koufax, 1955-1966

K: Most, career, all-time

2696	Don Sutton, 1966-1988
2486	Don Drysdale, 1956-1969
2396	Sandy Koufax, 1955-1966
1918	Dazzy Vance, 1922-1935
1759	FERNANDO VALENZUELA, 1980-1990

Win pct: Highest, career, all-time

.715	Preacher Roe, 1948-1954
.674	Tommy John, 1972-1978
.674	Jim Hughes, 1899-1902
.658	Billy Loes, 1950-1956
.655	Sandy Koufax, 1955-1966

ERA: Lowest, career, all-time

2.31	Jeff Pfeffer, 1913-1921
2.42	Nap Rucker, 1907-1916
2.56	Ron Perranoski, 1961-1972
2.58	Rube Marquard, 1915-1920
2.62	Jim Brewer, 1964-1975

Runs: Most, season

148	Hub Collins, 1890
143	Babe Herman, 1930
140	Mike Griffin, 1895
140	Willie Keeler, 1899
136	Mike Griffin, 1897
130	Maury Wills, 1962 (10)

Hits: Most, season

241	Babe Herman, 1930
230	Tommy Davis, 1962
221	Zack Wheat, 1925
219	Lefty O'Doul, 1932
217	Babe Herman, 1929

2B: Most, season

52	Johnny Frederick, 1929
48	Babe Herman, 1930
47	Wes Parker, 1970
44	Johnny Frederick, 1930
43	Augie Galan, 1944
43	Babe Herman, 1931
43	Steve Sax, 1986

3B: Most, season

26	George Treadway, 1894
22	Hy Myers, 1920
20	Dan Brouthers, 1892
20	Tommy Corcoran, 1894
19	Jimmy Sheckard, 1901
16	Willie Davis, 1970 (12)

HR: Most, season

43	Duke Snider, 1956
42	Gil Hodges, 1954
42	Duke Snider, 1953
42	Duke Snider, 1955
41	Roy Campanella, 1953
35	MIKE PIAZZA, 1993 (9)

RBI: Most, season

153	Tommy Davis,	1962
142	Roy Campanella,	1953
136	Duke Snider,	1955
130	Jack Fournier,	1925
130	Babe Herman,	1930
130	Gil Hodges,	1954
130	Duke Snider,	1954

SB: Most, season

104	Maury Wills,	1962
94	Maury Wills,	1965
88	John Ward,	1892
85	Hub Collins,	1890
77	Davey Lopes,	1975

BB: Most, season

148	Eddie Stanky,	1945
137	Eddie Stanky,	1946
119	Dolph Camilli,	1938
116	Pee Wee Reese,	1949
114	Augie Galan,	1945
110	Jim Wynn, 1975 (6)	

BA: Highest, season

.393	Babe Herman,	1930
.381	Babe Herman,	1929
.379	Willie Keeler,	1899
.375	Zack Wheat,	1924
.368	Lefty O'Doul,	1932
.346	Tommy Davis, 1962 (16)	

Slug avg: Highest, season

.678	Babe Herman,	1930
.647	Duke Snider,	1954
.628	Duke Snider,	1955
.627	Duke Snider,	1953
.612	Babe Herman,	1929
.606	MIKE PIAZZA, 1995 (7)	

Games started: Most, season

44	George Haddock,	1892
44	Brickyard Kennedy,	1893
44	Adonis Terry,	1890
43	Tom Lovett,	1891
42	Don Drysdale,	1963
42	Don Drysdale,	1965
42	Ed Stein,	1892

Saves: Most, season

28	Jay Howell,	1989
25	JIM GOTT,	1993
24	Jim Brewer,	1970
24	Jim Hughes,	1954
32	TODD WORRELL,	1995

Shutouts: Most, season

11	Sandy Koufax,	1963
9	Don Sutton,	1972
8	TIM BELCHER,	1989
8	Don Drysdale,	1968
8	OREL HERSHISER,	1988
8	Sandy Koufax,	1965
8	FERNANDO VALENZUELA, 1981	

Wins: Most, season

30	Tom Lovett,	1890
29	George Haddock,	1892
28	Jim Hughes,	1899
28	Joe McGinnity,	1900
28	Dazzy Vance,	1924
27	Sandy Koufax, 1966 (6)	

K: Most, season

382	Sandy Koufax,	1965
317	Sandy Koufax,	1966
306	Sandy Koufax,	1963
269	Sandy Koufax,	1961
262	Dazzy Vance,	1924

Win pct: Highest, season

.889	Freddie Fitzsimmons,	1940
.880	Preacher Roe,	1951
.864	OREL HERSHISER,	1985
.842	Ron Perranoski,	1963
.833	Sandy Koufax,	1963

ERA: Lowest, season

1.58	Rube Marquard,	1916
1.68	Ned Garvin,	1904
1.73	Sandy Koufax,	1966
1.74	Sandy Koufax,	1964
1.87	Kaiser Wilhelm,	1908

Most pinch-hit homers, season

6	Johnny Frederick,	1932
5	Lee Lacy,	1978

Most pinch-hit homers, career

8	Johnny Frederick,	1929-1934
8	Lee Lacy,	1972-1978

Most consecutive games batting safely

31	Willie Davis,	1969
29	Zach Wheat, Bro-1916	

Most consecutive scoreless innings

59	OREL HERSHISER,	1988
58	Don Drysdale,	1968
39	Don Newcombe,	1956

No-hit games

Tom Lovett, Bro vs NY NL, 4-0; June 22, 1891.

Mal Eason, Bro at StL NL, 2-0; July 20, 1906.

Harry McIntyre, Bro vs Pit NL, 0-1; August 1, 1906 (lost on 4 hits in 13 innings after allowing the first hit in the 11th).

Nap Rucker, Bro vs Bos NL, 6-0; September 5, 1908 (2nd game).

Dazzy Vance, Bro vs Phi NL, 10-1; September 13, 1925 (1st game).

Tex Carleton, Bro at Cin NL, 3-0; April 30, 1940.

Ed Head, Bro vs Bos NL, 5-0; April 23, 1946.

Rex Barney, Bro at NY NL, 2-0; September 9, 1948.

Carl Erskine, Bro vs Chi NL, 5-0; June 19, 1952.

Carl Erskine, Bro vs NY NL, 3-0; May 12, 1956.

Sal Maglie, Bro vs Phi NL, 5-0; September 25, 1956.

Sandy Koufax, LA vs NY NL, 5-0; June 30, 1962.

Sandy Koufax, LA vs SF NL, 8-0; May 11, 1963.

Sandy Koufax, LA at Phi NL, 3-0; June 4, 1964.

Sandy Koufax, LA vs Chi NL, 1-0; September 9, 1965 (perfect game).

Bill Singer, LA vs Phi NL, 5-0; July 20, 1970.

Jerry Reuss, LA at SF NL, 8-0; June 27, 1980.

FERNANDO VALENZUELA, LA vs StL NL, 6-0; June 29, 1990.

KEVIN GROSS, LA vs SF NL, 2-0; August 17, 1992.

RAMON MARTINEZ, LA vs Fla NL, 7-0; July 14, 1995.

Ed Stein, 6 innings, rain, Bro vs Chi NL, 6-0; June 2, 1894.

Fred Frankhouse, 7⅔ innings, rain, Bro vs Cin NL, 5-0; August 27, 1937.

ACTIVE PLAYERS in caps.

Leader from franchise's current location is included. If not in the top five, leader's rank is listed in parenthesis; asterisk (*) indicates player is not in top 25.

Players' years of service are listed by the first and last years with this team and are not necessarily consecutive; all statistics record performances for this team only.

Colorado Rockies

By Anne Ryan, USA TODAY

Dante Bichette was one of the league's top hitters at .340, with 40 homers and 128 RBI in 120 games.

1995 Rockies: The best expansion team yet

The Colorado Rockies made history by qualifying for postseason play in their third year of existence. The closest any previous expansion team has come was eight years (New York Mets and Kansas City Royals). When they clinched a wild-card berth Oct. 1, Don Baylor and his players thanked the Coors Field crowd with a postgame victory lap.

Opening Day was equally memorable. Dante Bichette christened Coors Field with a towering homer and an 11-9, 14-inning victory against the Mets—the temperature in Denver was barely 30 degrees.

While major-league baseball attendance declined about 18 percent from 1994, the Rockies bucked the trend. They finished the season with 55 sell-outs—51 in succession—and led the NL in attendance for the third consecutive season.

The Rockies never lost more than five games in a row all season. Baylor knew he could count on his team to score runs—especially at home. When Andres Galarraga homered against Willie Blair Sept. 19 in San Diego, he joined Bichette, Larry Walker and Vinny Castilla in the 30-homer club. They became the first four teammates to hit 30 homers since Steve Garvey, Reggie Smith, Ron Cey and Dusty Baker did it for the 1977 Los Angeles Dodgers. Cozy Coors Field obviously helped. Bichette, Walker, Castilla and Galarraga—the Blake Street Bombers—combined to hit 96 of their 137 home runs at home.

The Rockies went 77-67 and qualified as the National League's wild-card entry despite a league-worst 4.97 ERA. Kevin Ritz, the team's leading winner, went 11-11. Marvin Freeman finished 3-7 and spent much of the season on the disabled list. Bill Swift and Bret Saberhagen each pitched with shoulder pain in September and October. Rookies Bryan Rekar and Roger Bailey came up from the minors to provide a major lift down the stretch. And in the absence of an overpowering starter, the Colorado bullpen worked overtime. Leskanic, Steve Reed and Darren Holmes ranked in the top six in the league in appearances. Along with Mike Munoz, they were part of the exclusive 60-60-60-60 appearance club.

The Colorado bullpen finally ran out of gas against Atlanta in the divisional playoffs. The Braves beat the Rockies twice in their final at-bats at Coors Field. Eric Young and Castilla homered to give Colorado a 7-5 victory in Game 3 at Atlanta–Fulton County Stadium. But Greg Maddux beat Saberhagen 10-4 in the series finale to send the Rockies home for the winter.

1996 Rockies: Preview

The Rockies are an organization on the rise. They've proven they can light up a scoreboard. Whether they can make an even greater impression in October depends in large part on improved pitching.

They've made a commitment to developing young pitchers. But Swift, Saberhagen and Freeman—veterans with a history of injuries—will give a major boost if they can stay healthy in 1996.

Can Castilla match his production of 1995, when he hit 32 homers and made the All-Star team? Can Galarraga remain productive at age 35? And can Ellis Burks stay healthy in the final year of a three-year contract? The answers to these and other questions will help determine how the Rockies fare in 1996.

1995 Rockies: Week-by-week notes

These notes were excerpted from the following issues of Baseball Weekly.

▶**May 3:** Manager Don Baylor used his bullpen liberally through the first four games, and they responded by assisting in a 4-0 start. The Rockies went 3-0 in one-run games.

▶**May 10:** Marvin Freeman, who signed a two-year, $4 million deal with the Rockies over the winter, was 0-0 with a 20.77 ERA in his first two appearances. He walked eight batters in his first 4⅓ innings, and opponents were hitting .524 against him.

▶**May 17:** Starting pitching gave Baylor cause for concern. No Colorado pitcher lasted seven innings in the club's first 16 games. Bill Swift compiled a 6.95 ERA in his first four starts, and Marvin Freeman had a 16.20 ERA after three. But the bats were healthy—Larry Walker homered in four consecutive games to set a club record.

▶**May 24:** In their first 11 home games at Coors Field, the Rockies scored 98 runs and batted .336 (142-for-423) as a team. In their first 12 road games, they scored 43 runs and hit .231 (90-for-390).

▶**May 31:** Andres Galarraga was hitting .239 and had struck out 38 times in 29 games—a pace to strike out 189 times in a 144-game season. "In most slumps, the No. 1 problem is not swinging at strikes," Baylor said. "He [Galarraga] is swinging at pitches that Superman would have a hard time hitting."

▶**June 7:** Darren Holmes was back in the spotlight as closer. He reassumed his old role when the Rockies placed Bruce Ruffin on the disabled list. In his first three games as a closer, he picked up saves against St. Louis and Pittsburgh and raised his record to 4-0 in a 7-4 victory against the Pirates. Meanwhile, Larry Walker broke an 0-for-24 slump with a homer and a double and joked that he hadn't reached base for so long, he wasn't sure whether to turn left or right when he touched first.

▶**June 14:** With three members of their projected starting rotation and their closer on the DL, the Rockies won eight of nine games and moved into first place in the NL West. During a six-game homestand, the Rockies managed to lower their team ERA to 5.38 from 5.67. That's tough to do at Coors Field, where double-figure scores are a regular occurrence. "The fans might not have enjoyed this as much," said Rockies manager Don Baylor. "But I did."

▶**June 21:** Through 47 games, third baseman Vinny Castilla was tied with teammate Dante Bichette for the National League lead with 112 total bases. He also ranked among the league leaders in batting average (.341), home runs (12), RBI (36), hits (59) and doubles (13). And the front-line pitchers were starting to get healthy—Bill Swift and Bruce Ruffin came off the disabled list.

▶**June 28:** On June 25 in San Diego, Andres Galarraga almost had a chance to do what no major leaguer had ever done—hit a homer in four consecutive innings. He homered in the sixth, seventh and eighth innings but lost his chance in the ninth when Dante Bichette and Larry Walker struck out with the bases loaded. Galarraga was on deck when the third out was made. "Believe me, I wanted to hit so bad," said Galarraga, who had a career-high seven RBI. He reached base safely all five times he came to bat and was the fourth major leaguer to homer in three consecutive innings. The last to do it was Larry Parrish of Montreal on July 30, 1978.

▶**July 5:** The Rockies ranked first in the league in hitting, and last in team ERA. But starters were improving—Bill Swift, Armando Reynoso, Marvin Freeman, Kevin Ritz and Joe Grahe compiled a 1.93 ERA on the first eight games of a 10-game trip to San Diego, San Francisco and Los Angeles. Dante

Bichette, whose average peaked at .367 after a 23-game hitting streak, fell to .339. And Vinny Castilla, an All-Star reserve at third base, dropped from .349 to .314.

▶**July 13:** First the Rockies released second baseman Harold Reynolds the day before the season opener then they optioned second baseman Roberto Mejia to Class AAA in late June, and just when it appeared Jason Bates had won the everyday job, he hurt his left wrist and went into a slump—so now the Rockies' new second baseman is their old second baseman, Eric Young. Young, who held down the position in 1993 before moving to the outfield, seemed to have been rejuvenated in a return to the infield. He hit safely in Colorado's first eight games in July (16-for-37, .432) and scored at least one run in each of those games. He also assumed the club lead with his 10th stolen base. "I'm like a kid who has some candy and can still go out and play baseball, too," he said. "I enjoy playing second base. Now I can go home and look in the mirror and say I gave it my best."

▶**July 19:** How much does playing in Denver mean to Bichette? Through July 16, he was hitting .377 (57-for-151) with 13 homers and 36 RBI in Denver and .293 (41-for-140) with no homers and 15 RBI on the road.

▶**Aug. 2:** After starting out with 17 consecutive homers at Coors Field, Bichette hit three on the road. He and teammates Larry Walker, Vinny Castilla and Andres Galarraga have 20 apiece. Only two other clubs have even two players with 20 homers—Cleveland, with Manny Ramirez and Jim Thome, and California, with Jim Edmonds and Tim Salmon.

▶**Aug. 23:** Bret Saberhagen lasted only one-third of an inning in the Rockies' 26-7 loss to Chicago on Aug. 18. It was the shortest outing of his major league career. The club said a doctor examined Saberhagen after the game and found nothing medically wrong.

▶**Aug. 30:** Through Aug. 27, the Rockies had dropped six of 10 to the Cubs, Pirates and Cardinals at Coors Field. "Everybody's talking about home field advantage," Baylor said. "But we haven't dominated at all. We've been dominated."

▶**Sept. 13:** Bill Swift, making his first appearance since July 26, threw five innings of one-run ball in a 6-2 win against Cincinnati. A productive Swift and Bret Saberhagen could make the Rockies formidable for September and the post-season.

▶**Last-day recap:** *Heroes*—The Rockies and Indians were the only major league teams to finish with 200 home runs. Colorado reached 200 on the final day of the regular season, when Andres Galarraga took San Francisco reliever Scott Service deep. Dante Bichette, Larry Walker, Galarraga and Vinny Castilla—the Blake Street Bombers—combined for 137 homers, or 68.5% of the Rockies' total. The Rockies were only the second team to have four 30-homer men in a season.

Team directory

▶**Owner:** Jerry McMorris (Colorado Baseball Partnership)
▶**General manager:** Bob Gebhard
▶**Ballpark:**
Coors Field
2001 Blake St., Denver, Colo.
303-762-5437
Capacity 50,200
Parking for 4,600 cars, 200 handicapped, 18,000 within a 15 min. walk
Public transportation available
Wheelchair section, family sections in all price ranges
▶**Team publications:**
High & Inside (for season ticket holders only), media guide, game program, yearbook
▶**TV, radio broadcast stations:**
KOA 850 AM, KWGN Channel 2
▶**Spring training:**
Hi Corbett Field
Tucson, Ariz.
Capacity 8,000
602-327-9467

COLORADO ROCKIES 1995 final stats

BATTERS	BA	SLG	OB	G	AB	R	H	TB	2B	3B	HR	RBI	BB	SO	SB	CS	E
Pulliam	.400	1.200	.400	5	5	1	2	6	1	0	1	3	0	2	0	0	0
Vander Wal	.347	.594	.432	105	101	15	35	60	8	1	5	21	16	23	1	1	2
Bichette	.340	.620	.364	139	579	102	197	359	38	2	40	128	22	96	13	9	3
Young	.317	.473	.404	120	366	68	116	173	21	9	6	36	49	29	35	12	11
Hubbard	.310	.534	.394	24	58	13	18	31	4	0	3	9	8	6	2	1	0
Castilla	.309	.564	.347	139	527	82	163	297	34	2	32	90	30	87	2	8	15
Walker	.306	.607	.381	131	494	96	151	300	31	5	36	101	49	72	16	3	3
Galarraga	.280	.511	.329	143	554	89	155	283	29	3	31	106	32	146	12	2	13
Kingery	.269	.411	.351	119	350	66	94	144	18	4	8	37	45	40	13	5	5
Bates	.267	.419	.355	116	322	42	86	135	17	4	8	46	42	70	3	6	5
Burks	.266	.496	.359	103	278	41	74	138	10	6	14	49	39	72	7	3	5
Girardi	.262	.359	.308	125	462	63	121	166	17	2	8	55	29	76	3	3	10
Weiss	.260	.321	.403	137	427	65	111	137	17	3	1	25	98	57	15	3	16
Owens	.244	.556	.286	18	45	7	11	25	2	0	4	12	2	15	0	0	1
Tatum	.235	.324	.257	34	34	4	8	11	1	1	0	4	1	7	0	0	1
Brito	.216	.275	.259	18	51	5	11	14	3	0	0	7	2	17	1	0	1
Nokes	.182	.273	.250	10	11	1	2	3	1	0	0	0	1	4	0	0	1
Mejia	.154	.231	.167	23	52	5	8	12	1	0	1	4	0	17	0	1	2
Castellano	.000	.000	.286	4	5	0	0	0	0	0	0	0	2	3	0	0	0
Counsell	.000	.000	.500	3	1	0	0	0	0	0	0	0	1	0	0	0	0
McCracken	.000	.000	.000	3	1	0	0	0	0	0	0	0	0	1	0	0	0

PITCHERS	W-L	ERA	G	GS	CG	GF	Sho	SV	IP	H	R	ER	HR	BB	SO
Ruffin	0-1	2.12	37	0	0	19	0	11	34	26	8	8	1	19	23
Reed	5-2	2.14	71	0	0	15	0	3	84	61	24	20	8	21	79
Holmes	6-1	3.24	68	0	0	33	0	14	66.2	59	26	24	3	28	61
Leskanic	6-3	3.40	76	0	0	27	0	10	98	83	38	37	7	33	107
Saberhagen	7-6	4.18	25	25	3	0	0	0	153	165	78	71	21	33	100
Ritz	11-11	4.21	31	28	0	3	0	2	173.1	171	91	81	16	65	120
Painter	3-0	4.37	33	1	0	7	0	1	45.1	55	23	22	9	10	36
Swift	9-3	4.94	19	19	0	0	0	0	105.2	122	62	58	12	43	68
Rekar	4-6	4.98	15	14	1	0	0	0	85	95	51	47	11	24	60
Bailey	7-6	4.98	39	6	0	9	0	0	81.1	88	49	45	9	39	33
Grahe	4-3	5.08	17	9	0	0	0	0	56.2	69	42	32	6	27	27
Reynoso	7-7	5.32	20	18	0	0	0	0	93	116	61	55	12	36	40
Freeman	3-7	5.89	22	18	0	0	0	0	94.2	122	64	62	15	41	61
Acevedo	4-6	6.44	17	11	0	0	0	0	65.2	82	53	47	15	20	40
Thompson	2-3	6.53	21	5	0	3	0	0	51	73	42	37	7	22	30
Sager	0-0	7.36	10	0	0	2	0	0	14.2	19	16	12	1	7	10
Munoz	2-4	7.42	64	0	0	19	0	2	43.2	54	38	36	9	27	37
Hickerson	3-3	8.57	56	0	0	13	0	1	48.1	69	52	46	8	28	40
Nied	0-0	20.77	2	0	0	0	0	0	4.1	11	10	10	2	3	3

1996 preliminary roster

PITCHERS (22)
Garvin Alston
Ivan Arteaga
Roger Bailey
John Burke
Mike Farmer
Marvin Freeman
Darren Holmes
Bobby Jones
Curtis Leskanic
Mike Munoz
David Nied
Lance Painter
Steve Reed
Bryan Rekar
Armando Reynoso
Kevin Ritz
Bruce Ruffin
Bret Saberhagen
Bill Swift
Mark Thompson
John Thomson
Jake Viano

CATCHERS (2)
Jorge Brito
Jayhawk Owens

INFIELDERS (6)
Jason Bates
Vinny Castilla
Craig Counsell
Andres Galarraga
Roberto Mejia
Walt Weiss

OUTFIELDERS (9)
Dante Bichette
Ellis Burks
Trenidad Hubbard
Terry Jones
Quinton McCracken
Harvey Pulliam
John VanderWal
Larry Walker
Eric Young

Games played by position

PLAYER	G	C	1B	2B	3B	SS	OF
Bates	116	0	0	82	15	20	0
Bichette	139	0	0	0	0	0	136
Brito	18	18	0	0	0	0	0
Burks	103	0	0	0	0	0	80
Castellano	4	0	0	0	3	0	0
Castilla	139	0	0	0	137	5	0
Counsell	3	0	0	0	0	3	0
Galarraga	143	0	142	0	0	0	0
Girardi	125	122	0	0	0	0	0
Hubbard	24	0	0	0	0	0	16
Kingery	119	0	5	0	0	0	108
McCracken	3	0	0	0	0	0	1
Mejia	23	0	0	16	0	0	0
Nokes	10	3	0	0	0	0	0
Owens	18	16	0	0	0	0	0
Pulliam	5	0	0	0	0	0	1
Tatum	34	1	0	0	0	0	2
Vander Wal	105	0	10	0	0	0	10
Walker	131	0	0	0	0	0	129
Weiss	137	0	0	0	0	136	0
Young	120	0	0	77	0	0	19

Sick call: 1995 DL Report

Player	Days on the DL
Ellis Burks	10
Marvin Freeman	19
Joe Grahe	45
David Nied	102
Matt Nokes	35
Lance Painter	11
Armando Reynoso	54
Bruce Ruffin	76*
Bill Swift	56*

Indicates two separate terms on Disabled List.

1995 Amateur draft picks

Players are listed with position and college or high school. Most players were assigned to rookie or Class A leagues. List provided by Major League Baseball.

Blake Barthol, c, Eastern Kentucky; Robert Bevel, lhp, Xavier Univ.; Allen Bost, rhp, Catawba; Brian Bowman, c, Garces Memorial HS, Bakersfield, Calif.; Scott Brent, cf, Linden (Calif.) HS; Marc Brzozoski, rf, Shorter College; John Clark, ss, Samuel Clemens HS, Cibolo, Texas; John Clifford, c, Villanova; Derek Corbett, rhp, Highland HS, Highley, Ariz.; Reginald Douglas, rhp, Dorsey HS, Los Angeles; Justin Drizos, 1b, Nevada; Christopher Druckrey, rhp, Kankakee CC; Brett Elam, ss, McNeese State; James Emiliano, rhp, Florida International; David Feuerstein, of, Yale; Foster Gabriel, rhp, Santa Rosa JC; Rodney Friar, c, Temecula Valley HS; John Garrison, rhp, San Joaquin Delta College; Garfield Gordon, cf, Willingboro (N.J.) HS; Harold Groseclose, ss, VMI; Todd Helton, 1b, Tennessee; Jeremy Jones, c, Raymore (Mo.) Peculiar HS; Joshua Kalinowski, lhp, Natrona County HS, Casper, Wyo.; Casey Kelley, 1b, Ellensburg (Wash.) HS; Brian Kirkpatrick, ss, King City (Calif.) HS; Ryan Kohlmeier, rhp, Chase County HS, Cottonwood Falls, Kan.; Daniel Ledesma, ss, Foy H. Moody, Corpus Christi, Texas; David Lee, rhp, Mercyhurst; Brandon Lenox, ss, Red Mountain HS, Mesa, Ariz.; Tal Light, 3b-1b, Oklahoma State; John Lindsey, 1b, Hattiesburg (Miss.) HS; Christopher Macca, rhp, Saint Leo; John Mahlberg, rhp, Douglas HS, Coquille, Ore.; Chandler Martin, rhp-of, Portland; Michael Medina, c, Foy H. Moody, Corpus Christi, Texas; Damione Merriman, rf, Cheraw (S.C.) HS; Andres Mitchell, ss, Motlow State CC; Matthew Montgomery, rhp, Rancho Santiago CC; Jason Moore, rhp, Burnsville (Minn.) HS; Sean Murphy, rhp, North Carolina; Garrett Neubart, cf, Columbia; Rodney Nye, 3b, Cameron (Okla.) HS; Benjamin Petrick, c, Glencoe HS, Hillsboro, Ore.; Jason Pozo, rhp, Ocean CC; Scott Randall, rhp, Santa Barbara City JC; Brad Reitzenstein, rhp, Portland; Chris Rodriguez, c, Modesto JC; Cristy Rosa, rhp, Aurea E. Quiles HS, Guanica PR; Ali Samadani, rhp, Marin CC; Derek Sawyer, ss, Paradise Valley HS, Phoenix; Bradley Schwartzbauer, 3b, White Bear Lake (Minn.) Area HS; James Slaughter, cf, San Joaquin Delta JC; Anthony Taylor, rhp, Pueblo HS, Tucson, Ariz.; Michael Vavrek, lhp, Lewis U.; Carlos Vidal, c, Miami Dade CC; William Whitley, ss, Tennessee; Patrick Williams, rhp, Mount San Jacinto JC; Kent Zweifel, 1b, Henley HS, Klamath Falls, Ore.

Minor Leagues

Tops in the organization

Batter	Club	Avg.	G	AB	R	H	HR	RBI
Quinton McCracken	CSp	.359	116	465	88	167	4	54
Trent Hubbard	CSp	.340	123	480	102	163	12	66
Harvey Pulliam	CSp	.327	115	407	90	133	25	91
Alan Cockrell	CSp	.313	106	355	58	111	12	58
David Kennedy	Nhv	.306	128	484	75	148	22	96

Home Runs			Wins		
Derrick Gibson	Ash	32	Brent Crowther	CSp	15
Harvey Pulliam	CSp	25	Joel Moore	Nhv	14
Jay Gainer	CSp	23	Luther Hackman	Ash	11
David Kennedy	Nhv	22	Scott Fredrickson	CSp	11
Angel Echevarria	Nhv	21	Several tied		10

RBI			Saves		
Derrick Gibson	Ash	115	Luis Colmenares	Ash	21
Angel Echevarria	Nhv	100	Jake Viano	Nhv	19
David Kennedy	Nhv	96	Jim Czajkowski	CSp	17
Harvey Pulliam	CSp	91	Matt Aminoff	Sal	16
Jay Gainer	CSp	86	James Emiliano	Por	11

Stolen Bases			Strikeouts		
Elvis Pena	Por	51	Brent Crowther	CSp	133
Terry Jones	Nhv	51	Bryan Rekar	CSp	119
Q. McCracken	CSp	43	Bobby Jones	Nhv	118
Trent Hubbard	CSp	37	M. Kusiewicz	Ash	110
Derrick Gibson	Ash	31	Luther Hackman	Ash	108

Pitcher	Club	W-L	ERA	IP	H	BB	SO
Bryan Rekar	CSp	10-5	1.89	129	94	29	119
Scott Randall	Por	7-3	1.99	95	76	28	78
M. Kusiewicz	Ash	8-4	2.03	128	99	34	110
Jamey Wright	Nhv	10-9	2.59	174	166	75	95
Brent Crowther	CSp	15-10	2.66	183	160	52	133

Colorado (1993-1995)

Runs: Most, career, all-time

269	DANTE BICHETTE, 1993-1995
237	ANDRES GALARRAGA, 1993-1995
187	ERIC YOUNG, 1993-1995
145	JOE GIRARDI, 1993-1995
135	CHARLIE HAYES, 1993-1994

Hits: Most, career, all-time

511	DANTE BICHETTE, 1993-1995
462	ANDRES GALARRAGA, 1993-1995
310	ERIC YOUNG, 1993-1995
302	JOE GIRARDI, 1993-1994
297	CHARLIE HAYES, 1993-1994

2B: Most, career, all-time

114	DANTE BICHETTE, 1993-1994
85	ANDRES GALARRAGA, 1993-1994
68	CHARLIE HAYES, 1993-1994
54	VINNY CASTILLA, 1993-1995
50	ERIC YOUNG, 1993-1995

3B: Most, career, all-time

18	ERIC YOUNG, 1993-1995
12	MIKE KINGERY, 1994-1995
11	JOE GIRARDI, 1993-1995
10	VINNY CASTILLA, 1993-1995
9	DANTE BICHETTE, 1993-1995
9	ELLIS BURKS, 1994-1995

HR: Most, career, all-time

88	DANTE BICHETTE, 1993-1995
84	ANDRES GALARRAGA, 1993-1995
44	VINNY CASTILLA, 1993-1995
36	LARRY WALKER, 1995
35	CHARLIE HAYES, 1993-1994

RBI: Most, career, all-time

312	DANTE BICHETTE, 1993-1995
289	ANDRES GALARRAGA, 1993-1995
148	CHARLIE HAYES, 1993-1994
138	VINNY CASTILLA, 1993-1995
120	JOE GIRARDI, 1993-1995

SB: Most, career, all-time

95	ERIC YOUNG, 1993-1995
48	DANTE BICHETTE, 1993-1995
30	ALEX COLE, 1993
22	ANDRES GALARRAGA, 1993-1995
27	WALT WEISS, 1994-1995

BB: Most, career, all-time

154	WALT WEISS, 1994-1995
150	ERIC YOUNG, 1993-1994
79	CHARLIE HAYES, 1993-1994
75	ANDRES GALARRAGA, 1993-1995
75	MIKE KINGERY, 1994-1995

BA: Highest, career, all-time

.321	ANDRES GALARRAGA, 1993-1995
.319	DANTE BICHETTE, 1993-1995
.306	MIKE KINGERY, 1994-1995
.298	CHARLIE HAYES, 1993-1994
.294	JOHN VANDER WAL, 1994-1995

Slug avg: Highest, career, all-time

.567	DANTE BICHETTE, 1993-1995
.564	ANDRES GALARRAGA, 1993-1995
.507	JOHN VANDER WAL, 1994-1995
.501	VINNY CASTILLA, 1993-1995
.484	CHARLIE HAYES, 1993-1994

Games started: Most, career, all-time

57	ARMANDO REYNOSO, 1993-1995
43	KEVIN RITZ, 1994-1995
38	DAVID NIED, 1993-1995
36	MARVIN FREEMAN, 1994-1995
32	GREG HARRIS, 1993-1994

Saves: Most, career, all-time

42	DARREN HOLMES, 1993-1995
29	BRUCE RUFFIN, 1993-1995
10	CURT LESKANIC, 1993-1995
9	STEVE REED, 1993-1995
3	WILLIE BLAIR, 1993-1994
3	MIKE MUNOZ, 1993-1995

Shutouts: Most, career, all-time

1	DAVID NIED, 1993-1995

Wins: Most, career, all-time

22	ARMANDO REYNOSO, 1993-1995
17	STEVE REED, 1993-1995
16	KEVIN RITZ, 1994-1995
14	DAVID NIED, 1993-1995
13	MARVIN FREEMAN, 1994-1995

K: Most, career, all-time

214	BRUCE RUFFIN, 1993-1995
182	ARMANDO REYNOSO, 1993-1995
181	STEVE REED, 1993-1995
173	KEVIN RITZ, 1994-1995
154	DARREN HOLMES, 1993-1995
154	CURT LESKANIC, 1993-1995

Win pct: Highest, career, all-time

.654	STEVE REED, 1993-1995
.591	MARVIN FREEMAN, 1994-1995
.500	ARMANDO REYNOSO, 1993-1995
.485	KEVIN RITZ, 1994-1995
.476	BRUCE RUFFIN, 1993-1995

ERA: Lowest, career, all-time

3.49	STEVE REED, 1993-1995
3.65	BRUCE RUFFIN, 1993-1995
4.12	DARREN HOLMES, 1993-1995
4.21	MARVIN FREEMAN, 1994-1995
4.31	CURT LESKANIC, 1993-1995

Runs: Most, season

102	DANTE BICHETTE, 1995
96	LARRY WALKER, 1995
93	DANTE BICHETTE, 1993
89	ANDRES GALARRAGA, 1995
89	CHARLIE HAYES, 1993

Hits: Most, season

197	DANTE BICHETTE, 1995
175	CHARLIE HAYES, 1993
174	ANDRES GALARRAGA, 1993
167	DANTE BICHETTE, 1993
163	VINNY CASTILLA, 1995

2B: Most, season

45	CHARLIE HAYES, 1993
43	DANTE BICHETTE, 1993
38	DANTE BICHETTE, 1995
35	ANDRES GALARRAGA, 1993
34	VINNY CASTILLA, 1995

3B: Most, season

9	ERIC YOUNG, 1995
8	MIKE KINGERY, 1994
8	ERIC YOUNG, 1993
7	VINNY CASTILLA, 1993
6	ELLIS BURKS, 1995
6	JERALD CLARK, 1993

HR: Most, season

40	DANTE BICHETTE, 1995
36	LARRY WALKER, 1995
32	VINNY CASTILLA, 1995
31	ANDRES GALARRAGA, 1994
31	ANDRES GALARRAGA, 1995

RBI: Most, season

128	DANTE BICHETTE, 1995
106	ANDRES GALARRAGA, 1995
101	LARRY WALKER, 1995
98	ANDRES GALARRAGA, 1993
98	CHARLIE HAYES, 1993

SB: Most, season

42	ERIC YOUNG, 1993
35	ERIC YOUNG, 1995
30	ALEX COLE, 1993
21	DANTE BICHETTE, 1994
18	ERIC YOUNG, 1994

BB: Most, season

98	WALT WEISS, 1995
63	ERIC YOUNG, 1993
56	WALT WEISS, 1994
49	LARRY WALKER, 1995
49	ERIC YOUNG, 1995

BA: Highest, season

.370	ANDRES GALARRAGA, 1993
.340	DANTE BICHETTE, 1995
.319	ANDRES GALARRAGA, 1994
.310	DANTE BICHETTE, 1993
.309	VINNY CASTILLA, 1995

Slug avg: Highest, season

.620	DANTE BICHETTE, 1995
.607	LARRY WALKER, 1995
.602	ANDRES GALARRAGA, 1993
.592	ANDRES GALARRAGA, 1994
.564	VINNY CASTILLA, 1995

Games started: Most, season

30	ARMANDO REYNOSO, 1993
28	KEVIN RITZ, 1995
22	DAVID NIED, 1994
19	GREG HARRIS, 1994
19	BILL SWIFT, 1995

Saves: Most, season

25	DARREN HOLMES, 1993
16	BRUCE RUFFIN, 1994
14	DARREN HOLMES, 1995
11	BRUCE RUFFIN, 1995
10	CURT LESKANIC, 1995

Shutouts: Most, season

1	DAVID NIED, 1994

Wins: Most, season

12	ARMANDO REYNOSO, 1993
11	KEVIN RITZ, 1995
10	MARVIN FREEMAN, 1994
9	DAVID NIED, 1994
9	STEVE REED, 1993
9	BILL SWIFT, 1995

K: Most, season

126	BRUCE RUFFIN, 1993
120	KEVIN RITZ, 1995
117	ARMANDO REYNOSO, 1993
107	CURT LESKANIC, 1995
84	WILLIE BLAIR, 1993

Win pct: Highest, season

.833	MARVIN FREEMAN, 1994
.522	ARMANDO REYNOSO, 1993
.500	KEVIN RITZ, 1995

ERA: Lowest, season

4.00	ARMANDO REYNOSO, 1993
4.21	KEVIN RITZ, 1995
4.79	DAVID NIED, 1994
6.65	GREG HARRIS, 1994

Most pinch-hit homers, season

4	HOWARD JOHNSON, 1994
4	JOHN VANDER WAL, 1995

Most pinch-hit homers, career

5	JOHN VANDER WAL, 1994-1995
4	HOWARD JOHNSON, 1994

Most consecutive games batting safely

19	DANTE BICHETTE, 1995
19	ERIC YOUNG, 1995

Most consecutive scoreless innings

16	BRUCE RUFFIN, 1993

No-hit games

None

ACTIVE PLAYERS in caps.

Players' years of service are listed by the first and last years with this team and are not necessarily consecutive; all statistics record performances for this team only.

279

Tony Gwynn won the National League batting title at .368 and drove in 90 runs for the Padres.

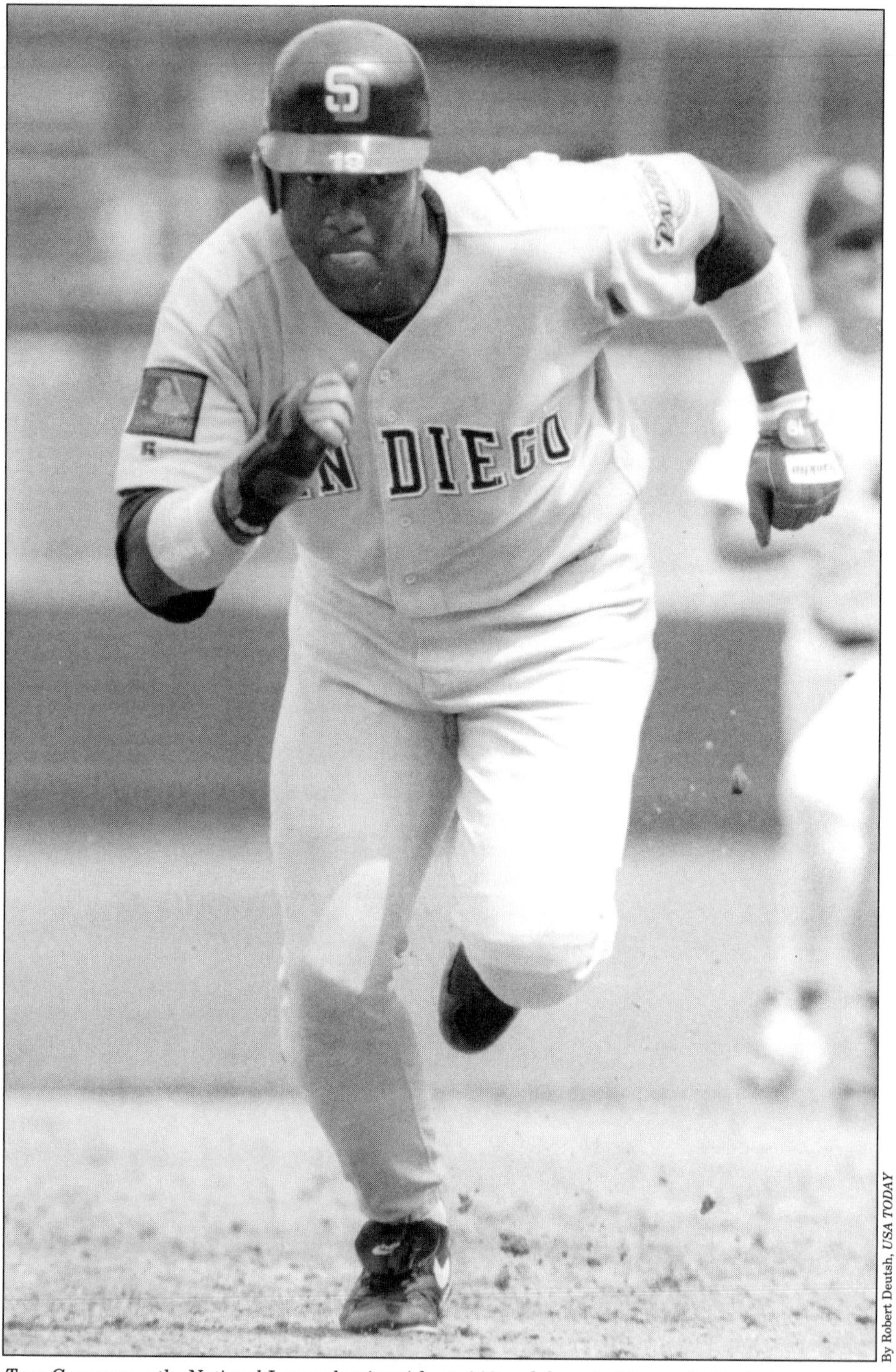

By Robert Deutsh, *USA TODAY*

1995 Padres: They needed more experience

At 70-74, the Padres' 1995 record was a vast improvement over their majors-worst 47-70 mark in '94. But it wasn't enough for Tony Gwynn. Although he claimed his sixth National League batting title with a .368 average, Gwynn knew there was a much more appealing goal to shoot for—the post-season. The Padres didn't make it, though they were in contention well into September.

The final tally for games Gwynn thought the Padres should have won but didn't: 17. The main reason they didn't, according to Gwynn: inexperience. Said Gwynn: "Next year, when we get to those games in the seventh inning and we have the lead, I hope they'll say, 'Hey, remember last year when I made this bad pitch, or I made this bad throw, or I took this bad hack?' ...these are the games where we had the lead and we let it get away from us."

Third baseman Ken Caminiti and center fielder Steve Finley did everything they could to get to the postseason. Caminiti posted career highs in nearly every offensive category, including average (.302), home runs (26) and RBI (94). Finley had career highs in average (.297) and runs scored (104), while brilliantly patrolling center field.

The team didn't lack experienced players; it lacked overall experience—most notably in the bullpen, which included as many as seven rookies down the stretch. The relievers' 4.57 ERA played a large part in a 4.13 team ERA that ranked 20th in the franchise's 27-year history.

Though the Padres traded away long-time ace Andy Benes, both Andy Ashby and Joey Hamilton made huge strides as starters. Ashby had a 12-10 record and a 2.94 ERA—the lowest by a Padres starter since 1990—while Hamilton had an unsightly 6-9 mark but an impressive 3.08 ERA. Closer Trevor Hoffman, meanwhile, became only the fourth Padre to reach the 30-save barrier, finishing with 31.

The team had its share of disappointments in the field. Shortstop Andujar Cedeno struggled mightily, his average plummeting to .210 and his defensive play bogging down in inconsistency. Melvin Nieves, given his first starting assignment at the beginning of the season, had trouble making contact most of the season but let loose with a power surge at the end and finished with 14 homers.

Injury also took its toll. Eddie Williams struggled with hamstring problems all season and never took hold of the starting job at first base. Roberts got off to a blazing start but lost almost two months of the season to a quadriceps injury, returned for a month and then saw his season end when a bone in his right leg was fractured in a freak pregame accident. Right-hander Scott Sanders came up with a sore elbow in midseason and might need surgery that would wipe out 1996 as well.

At the end of the season, Randy Smith parted company with the team with which he'd spent 11 of his first 12 years as a baseball executive. Manager Bruce Bochy, meanwhile, impressed ownership enough that they picked up his option for '96.

1996 Padres: Preview

For the Padres to use 1995 as a springboard to better things, they can't forget what happened a year ago, manager Bruce Bochy said.

Though their core of veterans—led by six-time NL batting champ Tony Gwynn—remains solid, it'll be up to younger players to take the next step in '96. Relievers Bryce Florie, Doug Bochtler and Ron Villone can use some positives from '95 to get better this coming season. Young hitters Melvin Nieves and Marc Newfield will also have the opportunity to grow in stature this year.

1995 Padres: Week-by-week notes

282

These notes were excerpted from the following issues of Baseball Weekly.

▶**May 3:** Leadoff hitter Bip Roberts spent 20 minutes before the season opener handing out complimentary caps to fans, but when the Padres fell behind in their 10-2 loss to Houston, some people got out of hand in Roberts's eyes. "You've got five fights all over the place, you've got guys hanging over the fence [cursing] us, drunk as hell, and they don't realize where they are," Roberts said. "This is a family atmosphere. It's not a porno flick."

▶**May 10:** Staff ace Andy Benes hadn't posted a victory since July 1994, a span of 10 starts and more than 300 days. For 1995 he was 0-2 with a 6.86 ERA.

▶**May 17:** In a game many thought might end his stint with the Padres—and his career—Fernando Valenzuela provided a solid start against his old team, the Dodgers, and survived the roster cuts.

▶**May 24:** Relievers posted seven of the Padres' first 11 victories. Dustin Hermanson (three), Trevor Hoffman (two), Andres Berumen (one) and Fernando Valenzuela (one) all notched victories before starters Andy Benes and Joey Hamilton got their first.

▶**June 7:** When Montreal's Pedro Martinez lost his bid for a perfect game with a 10th-inning single by Bip Roberts on June 3, Jack Murphy Stadium lost what would have been only the second no-hitter pitched there in its 27-year history. The only no-hitter pitched there was back on June 12, 1970, when Pittsburgh's Dock Ellis no-hit the Padres in the first game of a twi-night doubleheader. Ellis later revealed he pitched the game while on LSD.

▶**June 14:** As soon as the ball jumped off Joey Hamilton's bat, the crowd at Jack Murphy Stadium rose to its feet. When the ball hit the ground, Hamilton was applauded as though he had just

sent the Padres to the World Series. It was the first hit of Hamilton's career after an 0-for-57 start that's considered the unofficial major league record for the worst start to a hitting career.

▶**June 21:** Andy Benes finally posted his first victory since July 3, 1994, snapping a string of 10 consecutive losses in 17 starts.

▶**June 28:** Through Joey Hamilton's shutout of the Rockies June 24, the starters posted a 2.22 ERA over their last 25 starts. Over a 33-game span, the overall club ERA shrank to 4.05 from 6.15, elevating the staff to sixth from 13th in the National League. Each of the four right-handed starters—Andy Benes, Andy Ashby, Hamilton and Scott Sanders—delivered shutouts during June, giving the Padres a majors-leading six on the season. Of the Padres' hot starters, Hamilton was the hottest—he allowed only three earned runs in his five June starts for a 0.68 ERA. His four-hit shutout of the Rockies was 1995's fastest game in the majors to date: 1 hour, 55 minutes. The quickest before that was his 1:59 shutout of St. Louis.

▶**July 5:** Ken Caminiti snapped a string of 57 homerless at-bats with a grand slam in L.A. The four RBI on that one swing matched his RBI output for the previous 17 games. The homer felt so good that he went out and hit two more the following night, giving him 11 for the season and tying him with Tony Gwynn for the team RBI lead at 40. "I think I've been trying to do too much, so I went back to the basics—see the ball, hit the ball," Caminiti said.

▶**July 13:** Tony Gwynn found his hitting stroke on the Padres' 14-game road trip before the All-Star break, taking his rightful place atop the National League batting standings, but as the Padres sunk in the NL West standings, Gwynn's frustration mounted. "I think as expectations start to grow with this club, the more you just can't erase games that you should have won," Gwynn said. "We've had too many of those on this road trip." After surrendering late-inning leads in Los Angeles and San Francisco, the Padres gave up leads in the ninth inning in back-to-back games at Houston.

▸**July 19:** The Padres' players were asked their opinion, and they made it perfectly clear—no replacement players in their clubhouse. GM Randy Smith told the club he was considering promoting Ira Smith, a 27-year-old outfielder who played in replacement spring training games and was slated to be on the regular-season replacement roster. The team took a vote and decided that having Smith in the clubhouse was an unwanted distraction. Player representative Andy Benes said Smith and everyone else who played in spring exhibitions knew the ramifications of their actions: "There's going to be bad feelings with everybody, because essentially the guys that played were helping management try to break our union, so they were basically on the other side in the dispute." Meanwhile, on the other side of the fence, veteran Tony Gwynn went to bat for his manager and general manager. Both had only option years left on their contracts for 1996, and the Padres' five-time NL batting champion believed they deserve more. "We've got a manager and a general manager dangling on one-year deals," Gwynn said. "I think both have done a good job.... Give [them] a break. They deserve to be recognized."

▸**Aug. 16:** The Padres made a surge in the NL West, partially due to leadoff hitter Steve Finley. "He needs to get called up to the bigger big leagues pretty soon, because he's just got everything going right now," said Tony Gwynn. Down in the regular big leagues, Finley hit safely in 19 of 22 games, batting at a .430 clip. Through 47 games at the leadoff spot, he hit .390 with 49 runs scored and 22 steals. He also scored his 83rd run, keeping him in second place in the NL behind his former teammate on the Astros, Craig Biggio.

▸**Aug. 23:** Andy Ashby ran his scoreless-innings streak to 18.

▸**Aug. 30:** The Padres tied the NL record for grand slams in one season with nine, but their ninth didn't really do them any good. Melvin Nieves connected on a ninth-inning grand slam Aug. 26 at Shea Stadium, but it wasn't enough for the Padres to erase a seven-run deficit in a 7-6 loss to the Mets. Nieves's slam, his second of the season, tied the NL mark set by the 1929 Cubs. It left the Padres one slam off the major league record, held by the 1938 Tigers and the 1987 Yankees.

▸**Oct. 4:** Tony Gwynn wrapped up his sixth NL batting title. While Gwynn savored the honor, it wasn't his first goal at the start of the season. It wasn't even his second. "I had two goals: I wanted to get to 2,400 hits and I wanted to get through the entire season," Gwynn said. Mission accomplished—on both counts. Gwynn achieved his 2,400th hit on Sept. 30, and on Oct. 1 he played his 135th game of the season. That meant he'd completed an entire season for the first time since 1989.

Team directory

▸**Owner:** San Diego Padres LP
▸**General manager:** Kevin Towers
▸**Ballpark:**
San Diego Jack Murphy Stadium
9449 Friars Rd., San Diego, Calif.
619-283-4494
Capacity 47,750
Parking for 18,751 cars; $4
Public transportation available
Wheelchair sections, ramps, pre-registration for telephone paging, ATM machines
▸**Team publications:**
Padre Spectator (Spectator Sports Publishing)
619-283-4494
▸**TV, radio broadcast stations:**
KFMB 760 AM, XEXX AM (Spanish), KFMB Channel 8, Prime Sports
▸**Spring training:**
Peoria Sports Complex
Peoria, AZ
Capacity 10,000 with grass seating
602-878-4337

SAN DIEGO PADRES 1995 final stats

BATTERS	BA	SLG	OB	G	AB	R	H	TB	2B	3B	HR	RBI	BB	SO	SB	CS	E
Gwynn	.368	.484	.404	135	535	82	197	259	33	1	9	90	35	15	17	5	2
Livingstone	.337	.490	.380	99	196	26	66	96	15	0	5	32	15	22	2	1	3
Newfield	.309	.491	.333	21	55	6	17	27	5	1	1	7	2	8	0	0	0
Roberts	.304	.372	.346	73	296	40	90	110	14	0	2	25	17	36	20	2	4
Caminiti	.302	.513	.380	143	526	74	159	270	33	0	26	94	69	94	12	5	27
Finley	.297	.420	.366	139	562	104	167	236	23	8	10	44	59	62	36	12	7
Ausmus	.293	.412	.353	103	328	44	96	135	16	4	5	34	31	56	16	5	6
Cianfrocco	.263	.449	.333	51	118	22	31	53	7	0	5	31	11	28	0	2	3
E. Williams	.260	.426	.320	97	296	35	77	126	11	1	12	47	23	47	0	0	7
Reed	.256	.328	.348	131	445	58	114	146	18	1	4	40	59	38	6	4	4
Plantier	.255	.407	.339	76	216	33	55	88	6	0	9	34	28	48	1	1	4
Johnson	.251	.338	.287	68	207	20	52	70	9	0	3	29	11	39	0	0	4
Petagine	.234	.371	.367	89	124	15	29	46	8	0	3	17	26	41	0	0	1
Clark	.216	.309	.278	75	97	12	21	30	3	0	2	7	8	18	0	2	0
Cedeno	.210	.308	.271	120	390	42	82	120	16	2	6	31	28	92	5	3	17
Nieves	.205	.419	.276	98	234	32	48	98	6	1	14	38	19	88	2	3	2
Holbert	.178	.315	.277	63	73	11	13	23	2	1	2	5	8	20	4	0	5
McDavid	.176	.176	.263	11	17	2	3	3	0	0	0	0	0	2	6	1	1	0
Bean	.000	.000	.125	4	7	1	0	0	0	0	0	0	1	4	0	0	1
Hyers	.000	.000	.000	6	5	0	0	0	0	0	0	0	0	1	0	0	0

PITCHERS	W-L	ERA	G	GS	CG	GF	Sho	SV	IP	H	R	ER	HR	BB	SO
Elliott	0-0	0.00	1	0	0	1	0	0	2	2	0	0	0	1	3
Ashby	12-10	2.94	31	31	2	0	2	0	192.2	180	79	63	17	62	150
Florie	2-2	3.01	47	0	0	10	0	1	68.2	49	30	23	8	38	68
Hamilton	6-9	3.08	31	30	2	1	2	0	204.1	189	89	70	17	56	123
Bochtler	4-4	3.57	34	0	0	11	0	1	45.1	38	18	18	5	19	45
Hoffman	7-4	3.88	55	0	0	51	0	31	53.1	48	25	23	10	14	52
Benes	4-7	4.17	19	19	1	0	1	0	118.2	121	65	55	10	45	126
Villone	2-1	4.21	19	0	0	8	0	1	25.2	24	12	12	5	11	37
Sanders	5-5	4.30	17	15	0	0	0	0	90	79	46	43	14	31	88
Blair	7-5	4.34	40	12	0	11	0	0	114	112	60	55	11	45	83
Worrell	1-0	4.73	9	0	0	4	0	0	13.1	16	7	7	2	6	13
Valenzuela	8-3	4.98	29	15	0	5	0	0	90.1	101	53	50	16	34	57
Dishman	4-8	5.01	19	16	0	1	0	0	97	104	60	54	11	34	43
Berumen	2-3	5.68	37	0	0	17	0	1	44.1	37	29	28	3	36	42
B. Williams	3-10	6.00	44	6	0	7	0	0	72	79	54	48	3	38	75
Hermanson	3-1	6.82	26	0	0	6	0	0	31.2	35	26	24	8	22	19
Krueger	0-0	7.04	6	0	0	0	0	0	7.2	13	6	6	1	4	6
Mauser	0-1	9.53	5	0	0	1	0	0	5.2	4	6	6	0	9	9
Kroon	0-1	10.80	2	0	0	1	0	0	1.2	1	2	2	0	2	2

1996 preliminary roster

PITCHERS (19)
Andy Ashby
Robbie Beckett
Andres Berumen
Willie Blair
Doug Bochtler
Glenn Dishman
Bryce Florie
Joey Hamilton
Denny Harriger
Dustin Hermanson
Trevor Hoffman
Brad Kaufman
Marc Kroon
Joey Long
Scott Sanders
Fernando Valenzuela
Ron Villone
Brian Williams
Tim Worrell

CATCHERS (4)
Brad Ausmus
Raul Casanova
Brian Johnson
Sean Mulligan

INFIELDERS (11)
Julio Bruno
Homer Bush
Ken Caminiti
Andujar Cedeno
Archi Cianfrocco
Scott Livingstone
Luis Lopez
Roberto Petagine
Bip Roberts
Jorge Velandia
Eddie Williams

OUTFIELDERS (6)
Steve Finley
Tony Gwynn
Earl Johnson
Ray McDavid
Marc Newfield
Melvin Nieves

Games played by position

PLAYER	G	C	1B	2B	3B	SS	OF
Ausmus	103	100	1	0	0	0	0
Bean	4	0	0	0	0	0	4
Caminiti	143	0	0	0	143	0	0
Cedeno	120	0	0	0	1	116	0
Cianfrocco	51	0	30	3	3	15	7
Clark	75	0	2	0	0	0	34
Finley	139	0	0	0	0	0	138
Gwynn	135	0	0	0	0	0	133
Holbert	63	0	0	7	0	30	1
Hyers	6	0	1	0	0	0	0
Johnson	68	55	2	0	0	0	0
Livingstone	99	0	43	4	13	0	0
McDavid	11	0	0	0	0	0	7
Newfield	21	0	0	0	0	0	19
Nieves	98	0	2	0	0	0	79
Petagine	89	0	51	0	0	0	2
Plantier	76	0	0	0	0	0	59
Reed	131	0	0	130	0	5	0
Roberts	73	0	0	25	0	7	50
E. Williams	97	0	81	0	0	0	0

Minor Leagues

Tops in the organization

Batter	Club	Avg.	G	AB	R	H	HR	RBI
Ricardo Gama	Idf	.320	70	266	71	85	8	58
Greg Larocca	Mem	.319	127	473	77	151	8	74
Ira Smith	Lvg	.313	123	447	79	140	8	58
A. Cianfrocco	Lvg	.311	89	322	51	100	10	58
Rico Rossy	Lvg	.301	98	316	44	95	1	45

Home Runs			Wins		
Derrek Lee	Mem	23	Heath Murray	Mem	14
Jason Thompson	Mem	20	Rob Mattson	Mem	12
Rob Deer	Lvg	18	Several tied		11
Larry See	Rc	16			
Several tied		15			

RBI			Saves		
Derrek Lee	Mem	96	Todd Schmitt	Lvg	20
Billy Bean	Lvg	77	Bryan Wolff	Rc	18
Greg Larocca	Mem	74	Chris Logan	Cln	17
Larry See	Rc	70	D. Hermanson	Lvg	11
Sean Watkins	Idf	67	D. Guzman	Idf	11

Stolen Bases			Strikeouts		
Keith Thomas	Mem	43	Shane Dennis	Rc	157
Chris Prieto	Rc	39	Heath Murray	Mem	152
Dario Tena	Cln	35	Greg Keagle	Lvg	142
Earl Johnson	Mem	34	Rob Mattson	Mem	139
Homer Bush	Mem	34	Bubba Dixon	Rc	133

Pitcher	Club	W-L	ERA	IP	H	BB	SO
Glenn Dishman	Lvg	6-3	2.55	106	91	20	64
Brett Walters	Cln	8-7	2.71	146	133	27	122
Heath Murray	Mem	14-8	3.24	170	163	80	152
Bubba Dixon	Rc	10-7	3.24	142	118	46	133
Shane Dennis	Rc	11-11	3.27	165	131	57	157

Sick call: 1995 DL Report

Player	Days on the DL
Andres Berumen	52
Donnie Elliott	146
Ray Holbert	64
Luis Lopez	160
Bip Roberts	54*
Scott Sanders	76*
Tim Worrell	160

Indicates two separate terms on Disabled List.

1995 Amateur draft picks

Players are listed with position and college or high school. Most players were assigned to rookie or Class A leagues. List provided by Major League Baseball.

George Abernathy, lf, Mississippi; William Alexander, rhp, NW Shoals CC; Dustin Allen, rf-1b, Stanford; Gabriel Alvarez, ss, Southern California; Ryan Brown, rhp, Grapevine HS, Colleyville, Texas; Brandon Brown, lhp, Ranger JC; Carmen Bucci, ss, Northwestern; Jesse Cornejo, lhp, Wellington (Kan.) HS; Chuck Crumpton, rhp, Dr. Ralph H. Poteet HS, Mesquite, Texas; Mark Davis, c, Malvern Prep, Aston, Pa.; Anthony Felston, cf, Mississippi Delta JC; Ricardo Gama, 2b-rf, Miami; Robert Gorr, ss, Rancho Buena Vista HS, Vista, Calif.; Allen Goudy, rf, Lake Michigan JC; Andrew Hammerschmidt, lhp, Minnesota; James Henderson, rhp, Miami; Rich Hills, ss, Oklahoma; Steven Hoff, lhp, Mills HS, San Bruno. Calif.; Andrew Hunter, rf, Arlington (Texas) HS; Michael Irvine, rhp, Northern Iowa; Brian Jacobus, of, John R. Rogers HS, Puyallup, Wash.; Kenneth Jones, c, Western Michigan; Davis Kile, rhp, Friday Harbor (Wash.) HS; Donardo Kirkendoll, lhp, Bacone College; Brandon Kolb, rhp, Texas Tech; Brett Kondro, lhp, Fort Saskatchewan (Can.) HS; Rico Lagattuta, lhp, Nevada; Enrique Lazu, rhp, Santa Cruz HS, Alto P.R.; Aaron Looper, rhp, Byng HS, Ada. Okla.; Curt Lowry, of, McNeese State; Anthony Marnell, c, Arizona; Michael Martin, c, Florida State; Damon Minor, of, Green River CC; James Moore, cf, Ranger JC; Damond Nash, rhp, Texarkana JC; Wilbert Nieves, c, Eloisa Pascual HS, Condado, P.R.; Brandon Pernell, of, St. Bernard HS, Torrance, Calif.; Scott Pratt, ss, Tooele (Utah.) HS; Chad Reynolds, rhp, Friendship HS, Lubbock, Texas; John Robertson, rhp, Rockdale (Texas) HS; John Rodriguez, ss, Miller HS, Corpus Christi, Texas; James Sak, rhp, Illinois Benedictine; Justin Sellers, rhp, Evergreen HS, Vancouver, Wash.; Adrian Stewart, 1b, Claremont (Calif.) HS; Jason Totman, 2b, Texas Tech; Ryan Vandeweg, rhp, Western Michigan; Joel Vega, lhp, Academia Milagrosa Arenas, Cidra P.R.; Joseph Victery, cf, Eastern Oklahoma State; Kevin Walker, lhp, Grand Prairie (Texas) HS; Sean Watkins, 1b, Bradley; Clint Weibl, rhp, Odessa College; Mark Wulfert, of, New Mexico.

San Diego (1969-1995)

Runs: Most, career, all-time

1073	TONY GWYNN, 1982-1995
599	DAVE WINFIELD, 1973-1980
484	Gene Richards, 1977-1983
442	Nate Colbert, 1969-1974
430	Garry Templeton, 1982-1991

Hits: Most, career, all-time

2401	TONY GWYNN, 1982-1995
1135	Garry Templeton, 1982-1991
1134	DAVE WINFIELD, 1973-1980
994	Gene Richards, 1977-1983
817	Terry Kennedy, 1981-1986

2B: Most, career, all-time

384	TONY GWYNN, 1982-1995
195	Garry Templeton, 1982-1991
179	DAVE WINFIELD, 1973-1980
158	Terry Kennedy, 1981-1986
130	Nate Colbert, 1969-1974

3B: Most, career, all-time

80	TONY GWYNN, 1982-1995
63	Gene Richards, 1977-1983
39	DAVE WINFIELD, 1973-1980
36	Garry Templeton, 1982-1991
29	Cito Gaston, 1969-1974

HR: Most, career, all-time

163	Nate Colbert, 1969-1974
154	DAVE WINFIELD, 1973-1980
87	TONY GWYNN, 1982-1995
85	BENITO SANTIAGO, 1986-1992
84	FRED McGRIFF, 1991-1993

RBI: Most, career, all-time

804	TONY GWYNN, 1982-1995
626	DAVE WINFIELD, 1973-1980
481	Nate Colbert, 1969-1974
427	Garry Templeton, 1982-1991
424	Terry Kennedy, 1981-1986

SB: Most, career, all-time

285	TONY GWYNN, 1982-1995
242	Gene Richards, 1977-1983
171	Alan Wiggins, 1981-1985
148	BIP ROBERTS, 1986-1995
147	OZZIE SMITH, 1978-1981

BB: Most, career, all-time

625	TONY GWYNN, 1982-1995
463	DAVE WINFIELD, 1973-1980
423	Gene Tenace, 1977-1980
350	Nate Colbert, 1969-1974
338	Gene Richards, 1977-1983

BA: Highest, career, all-time

.336	TONY GWYNN, 1982-1995
.298	BIP ROBERTS, 1986-1995
.291	Gene Richards, 1977-1983
.286	Johnny Grubb, 1972-1976
.284	DAVE WINFIELD, 1973-1980

Slug avg: Highest, career, all-time

.468	Nate Colbert, 1969-1974
.464	DAVE WINFIELD, 1973-1980
.449	TONY GWYNN, 1982-1995
.422	Gene Tenace, 1977-1980
.409	Steve Garvey, 1983-1987

Games started: Most, career, all-time

253	Randy Jones, 1973-1980
230	Eric Show, 1981-1990
208	Ed Whitson, 1983-1991
186	ANDY BENES, 1989-1995
172	Andy Hawkins, 1982-1988

Saves: Most, career, all-time

108	Rollie Fingers, 1977-1980
83	Rich Gossage, 1984-1987
78	Mark Davis, 1987-1994
64	Craig Lefferts, 1984-1992
54	TREVOR HOFFMAN, 1993-1995

Shutouts: Most, career, all-time

18	Randy Jones, 1973-1980
11	Steve Arlin, 1969-1974
11	Eric Show, 1981-1990
10	Bruce Hurst, 1989-1993
8	ANDY BENES, 1989-1995

Wins: Most, career, all-time

100	Eric Show, 1981-1990
92	Randy Jones, 1973-1980
77	Ed Whitson, 1983-1991
69	ANDY BENES, 1989-1995
60	Andy Hawkins, 1982-1988

K: Most, career, all-time

1036	ANDY BENES, 1989-1995
951	Eric Show, 1981-1990
802	Clay Kirby, 1969-1973
767	Ed Whitson, 1983-1991
677	Randy Jones, 1973-1980

Win pct: Highest, career, all-time

.591	Bruce Hurst, 1989-1993
.535	Eric Show, 1981-1990
.517	Ed Whitson, 1983-1991
.515	Dave Dravecky, 1982-1987
.512	GREG HARRIS, 1988-1993

ERA: Lowest, career, all-time

3.12	Dave Dravecky, 1982-1987
3.27	Bruce Hurst, 1989-1993
3.30	Randy Jones, 1973-1980
3.57	ANDY BENES, 1989-1995
3.59	Eric Show, 1981-1990

Runs: Most, season

119	TONY GWYNN, 1987
107	TONY GWYNN, 1986
106	Alan Wiggins, 1984
104	STEVE FINLEY, 1995
104	BIP ROBERTS, 1990
104	DAVE WINFIELD, 1977

Hits: Most, season

218	TONY GWYNN, 1987
213	TONY GWYNN, 1984
211	TONY GWYNN, 1986
203	TONY GWYNN, 1989
197	TONY GWYNN, 1985
197	TONY GWYNN, 1995

2B: Most, season

42	Terry Kennedy, 1982
41	TONY GWYNN, 1993
36	Johnny Grubb, 1975
36	TONY GWYNN, 1987
36	BIP ROBERTS, 1990

3B: Most, season

13	TONY GWYNN, 1987
12	Gene Richards, 1978
12	Gene Richards, 1981
11	Bill Almon, 1977
11	TONY GWYNN, 1991
11	Gene Richards, 1977

HR: Most, season

38	Nate Colbert, 1970
38	Nate Colbert, 1972
35	FRED McGRIFF, 1992
34	PHIL PLANTIER, 1993
34	DAVE WINFIELD, 1979

RBI: Most, season

118	DAVE WINFIELD, 1979
115	JOE CARTER, 1990
111	Nate Colbert, 1972
106	FRED McGRIFF, 1991
104	FRED McGRIFF, 1992

SB: Most, season

70	Alan Wiggins, 1984
66	Alan Wiggins, 1983
61	Gene Richards, 1980
57	OZZIE SMITH, 1980
56	TONY GWYNN, 1987
56	Gene Richards, 1977

BB: Most, season

132	Jack Clark, 1989
125	Gene Tenace, 1977
105	FRED McGRIFF, 1991
105	Gene Tenace, 1979
104	Jack Clark, 1990

BA: Highest, season

.394	TONY GWYNN, 1994
.370	TONY GWYNN, 1987
.368	TONY GWYNN, 1995
.358	TONY GWYNN, 1993
.351	TONY GWYNN, 1984

Slug avg: Highest, season

.580	GARY SHEFFIELD, 1992
.568	TONY GWYNN, 1994
.558	DAVE WINFIELD, 1979
.556	FRED McGRIFF, 1992
.543	Cito Gaston, 1970

Games started: Most, season

40	Randy Jones, 1976
39	Randy Jones, 1979
37	Steve Arlin, 1972
37	Gaylord Perry, 1978
36	Randy Jones, 1975
36	Randy Jones, 1978
36	Clay Kirby, 1971

Saves: Most, season

44	Mark Davis, 1989
38	RANDY MYERS, 1992
37	Rollie Fingers, 1978
35	Rollie Fingers, 1977
31	TREVOR HOFFMAN, 1995

Shutouts: Most, season

6	Randy Jones, 1975
6	Fred Norman, 1972
5	Randy Jones, 1976
4	Steve Arlin, 1971
4	Bruce Hurst, 1990
4	Bruce Hurst, 1992

Wins: Most, season

22	Randy Jones, 1976
21	Gaylord Perry, 1978
20	Randy Jones, 1975
18	Andy Hawkins, 1985
16	LaMarr Hoyt, 1985
16	Tim Lollar, 1982
16	Eric Show, 1988
16	Ed Whitson, 1989

K: Most, season

231	Clay Kirby, 1971
189	ANDY BENES, 1994
185	Pat Dobson, 1970
179	ANDY BENES, 1993
179	Bruce Hurst, 1989

Win pct: Highest, season

.778	Gaylord Perry, 1978
.692	Andy Hawkins, 1985
.667	LaMarr Hoyt, 1985
.652	Bruce Hurst, 1991
.640	Tim Lollar, 1982

ERA: Lowest, season

2.10	Dave Roberts, 1971
2.24	Randy Jones, 1975
2.60	Ed Whitson, 1990
2.66	Ed Whitson, 1989
2.69	BRUCE HURST, 1989

Most pinch-hit homers, season

5	Jerry Turner, 1978
3	ARCHI CIANFROCCO, 1995
3	Luis Salazar, 1989

Most pinch-hit homers, career

9	Jerry Turner, 1974-1983

Most consecutive games batting safely

34	BENITO SANTIAGO, 1987
25	TONY GWYNN, 1983

Most consecutive scoreless innings

30	Randy Jones, 1980

No-hit games

None

ACTIVE PLAYERS in caps.

Players' years of service are listed by the first and last years with this team and are not necessarily consecutive; all statistics record performances for this team only.

Barry Bonds was on-and-off with fans but led the Giants at .294 with 33 homers and 104 RBI.

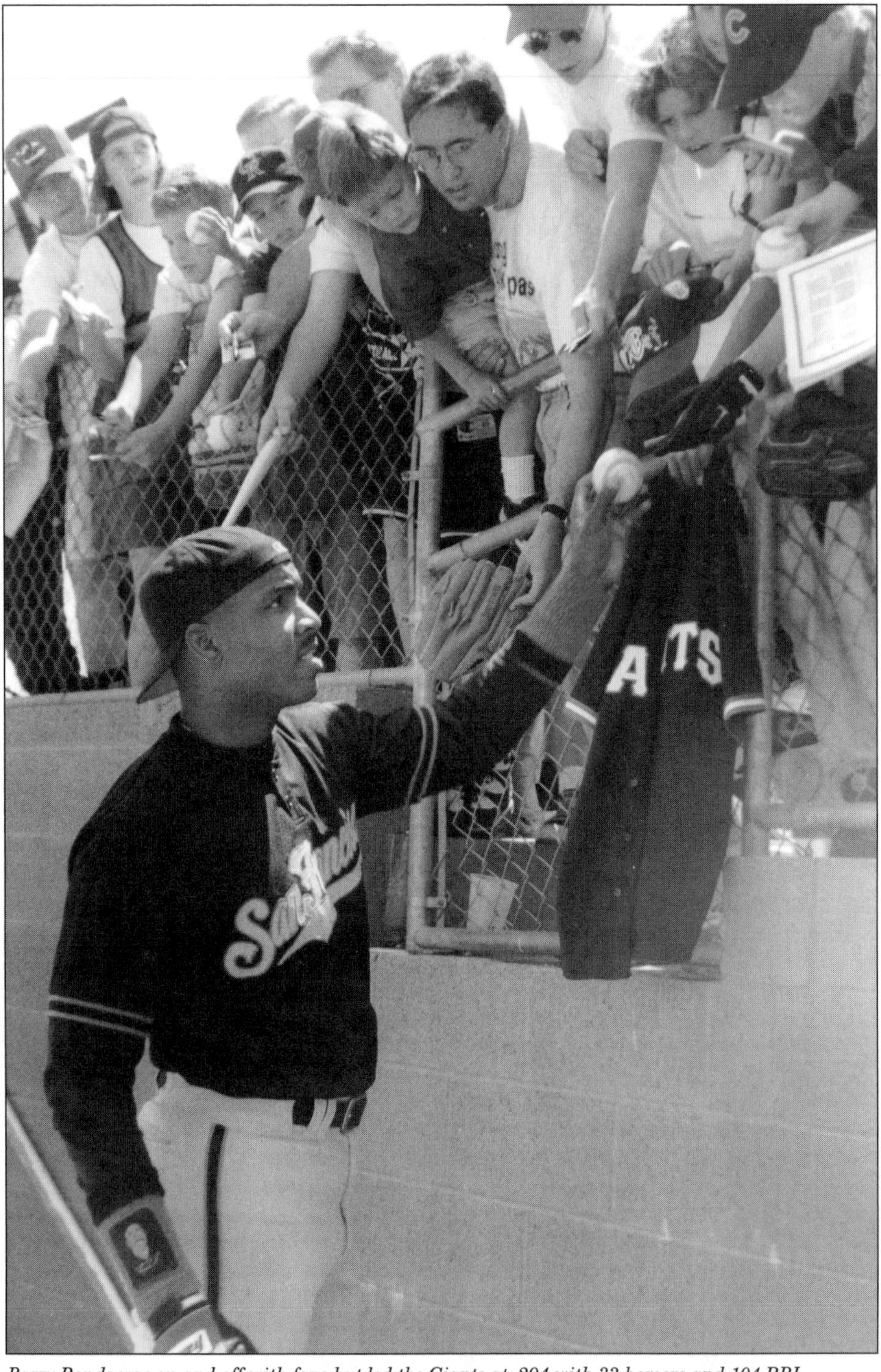

1995 Giants: A team full of holes

It's hard to believe it was just two years ago that the Giants won 103 games and were one of the National League's dominant teams. Since then the Giants have almost completely disintegrated. They still have Matt Williams and Barry Bonds, but surrounding that marvelous nucleus is nothing but holes. The result in 1995 was a 67-77 record and a last-place finish for the first time since 1985. They were among the league's worst in both pitching and hitting—12th in batting (.253) and 13th in ERA (4.86). Even their vaunted defense suffered, as they dropped from first to fifth in the NL with a .981 fielding percentage.

The fielding problems, like many of the team's other woes, can be directly attributed to Williams's fractured foot, injured on June 3, which kept him out for 68 games. When he went down, the Giants were in first place by a half-game, but in his absence, the club went 28-40 to fall to last place, 7½ games out. They made a small run but never recovered from the devastating loss of Williams, who not only was leading the league in all three Triple Crown categories at the time of his injury (.381, 13 HR, 35 RBI) but was providing vital protection for Bonds. Defensively, the loss of Williams's Gold Glove was critical. The team made 60 errors in the 68 games he missed. Williams finished with a career-high .336 average, 23 homers and 65 RBI.

Bonds also put up his usual impressive numbers, batting .294 with 33 homers, 104 RBI, 109 runs, 120 walks, and 31 stolen bases—the third 30-30 season of his career after missing by one steal in each of the past two seasons. But he hit just .203 in August, when the Giants were trying to make a move on the NL West, and became so frustrated in September that he threatened to retire.

The Giants tried to shake things up on July 24, announcing a blockbuster trade: pitchers Mark Portugal and Dave Burba and center fielder Darren Lewis were sent to the Reds for Prime Time himself, Deion

Sanders, along with pitchers John Roper, Scott Service and Ricky Pickett and first baseman Dave McCarty. They no doubt hoped that Sanders would become a Bay Area megastar, but he signed with the Dallas Cowboys. Before bowing out a week early to have ankle surgery, Sanders played well, batting .290.

The long list of disappointments for San Francisco was topped by second baseman Robby Thompson, who for the second straight year was nearly invisible, hitting .223 with eight homers and 23 RBI. Rookie J.R. Phillips failed to hold on to the first base job, hitting just .195 for the season, but his replacement, Mark Carreon, shone in his first opportunity as a regular, batting .301 with 17 homers and 65 RBI. Also shining as a first-time regular was right fielder Glenallen Hill (24 HR, 86 RBI). Closer Rod Beck, previously automatic in the late innings, saved 33 games but led the league with 10 blown opportunities. Just as critical, the team was unable to come up with a consistent setup man to replace Mike Jackson, and Mark Leiter (10-12, 3.82) was the only starting pitcher to last the season in the rotation.

1996 Giants: Preview

The Giants are counting on young arms to turn around their fortunes. Jamie Brewington may come up from Class AA at midseason and Shawn Estes will get a long look, along with Steve Soderstrom, Steve Bourgeois and Edwin Corps. The veteran anchor of the staff will be Leiter. The team is looking to trim the payroll, but they are committed to five players for a total of more than $22 million—Bonds, Williams, Thompson, catcher Kirt Manwaring and Leiter. Crucial to the Giants hopes is a return to form by Thompson, whose $4.65 million salary makes him virtually untradable.

1995 Giants: Week-by-week notes

These notes were excerpted from the following issues of Baseball Weekly.

▶**May 3:** Pitcher Mark Leiter, moved up two days after William VanLandingham was scratched with an injury, blanked the Marlins on two hits—both bunt singles—to win the home opener. The next day, lefty Trevor Wilson, who missed 1994 with shoulder surgery, matched Leiter with six shutout innings.

▶**May 10:** It was only a matter of time, but Barry Bonds rebounded from an 0-for-11 start to bring his average over .300. Glenallen Hill, meanwhile, was a free-agent success story, homering five times in his first 11 games with three stolen bases.

▶**May 24:** After three years of disappointments, the Giants traded Salamon Torres to Seattle for two minor leaguers, pitcher Shawn Estes and infielder Wilson Delgado.

▶**May 31:** Terry Mulholland, whom the Giants expected to be the ace of their staff, was struggling at 2-4 with a 6.69 ERA after seven starts; opponents hit .358 off him.

▶**June 7:** There was no way the Giants could replace injured Matt Williams, but for the time being they went with Steve Scarsone as a fill-in. Scarsone, with a .405 average, had been filling in at first for the benched J.R. Phillips.

▶**June 14:** Barry Bonds failed to go after a ball hit by Mets catcher Kelly Stinnett with the bases loaded, and the ball bounced off the wall. Bonds claimed he didn't see the ball, but to fans it appeared he thought it was a home run and misjudged—and they showered him with boos. "I heard it, but I don't care what they think, man," Bonds said. "They ain't out there. They don't know what's going on. If they can do better, bring your ass out there and do it. If you're better than me, come out here and put my uniform on and do it." The

next day, a contrite Bonds said, "My comment was not toward the fans. The fan support has been great ever since I've been here. If I offended them, I apologize. I wasn't lashing out at them. I was lashing out at the reporter. I just snapped."

▶**June 21:** Mike Benjamin, of all people, turned in one of the greatest hitting stretches in baseball history. The reserve infielder, who once hit .123 in a full season—the fourth-lowest average ever for a non-pitcher with at least 100 at-bats—established a major league record with 14 hits in three games. Benjamin's teammates laid out a path of towels leading to his locker, and they burst into applause. "It shows you anyone with a bat in their hands is dangerous," Dusty Baker said.

▶**June 28:** The Giants considered themselves lucky to have cut themselves free of Darryl Strawberry for only $125,000—the amount they gave the Yankees for Strawberry's 1995 salary after he dropped his grievance against San Francisco. The Giants feared they might get stuck with him for 1995 and were happy to pay what owner/partner Peter Magowan called "a little bit" to avoid that prospect.

▶**July 5:** The Rockies and the Giants have a well-documented history of bad blood, so there was potential for trouble when four players got hit by pitches in a game. But both sides kept their tempers in check, even Andres Galarraga, who had threatened to charge the mound the next time the Giants plunked him. He had his chance when Rod Beck hit him in the back, but he went straight to first. "I like Big Cat [Galarraga], but he issued a warning at Colorado," Baker said. "Evidently, he's not a man of his word." Galarraga said he didn't find the particular pitch offensive. 'It was a slow breaking ball," he said. "It was nothing personal. I had said that [his threat] to protect myself. Maybe if they do it with a fastball, but in that situation, with a breaking ball, it was nothing personal."

▸**July 13:** Barry Bonds was apparently inspired by a column in the San Francisco *Chronicle* suggesting that the Giants trade him. After the article appeared, he won three games in a week with late-inning home runs. He also was named a starter in the All-Star Game as the National League's leading vote-getter. "I want to end my career where my godfather [Willie Mays] and dad [Bobby Bonds] played," he said. "That's my own personal feeling. I want to end my career at home. If that doesn't happen, that doesn't happen. Larry Baer [the Giants executive vice president] came down and said that [trade] is just not going to happen. He said, 'We love what you're doing for the franchise and the team. We make the final decisions. And if we're happy, it doesn't matter what anyone else says.'"

▸**July 19:** For the first time all season, the Giants used the starting rotation which they envisioned at the start of spring training—Terry Mulholland, Mark Portugal, William VanLandingham, Trevor Wilson and Mark Leiter. And they hoped to have Matt Williams back in the lineup by Aug. 1. Without him, they went 13-20 through the All-Star break. Dusty Baker, however, was cautious both about Williams's comeback and the impetus it would provide. "There's no guarantee when Matty comes back, everything will be all right either," Baker said. "You don't know how he's going to come back after a foot injury like that."

▸**July 26:** General manager Bob Quinn conceded the eight-player deal with Cincinnati was financially motivated—Mark Portugal, Darren Lewis, and Dave Burba make an aggregate $6 million in 1995, while Deion Sanders makes $2.25 million with a $1 million bonus if he completes the season. Quinn said the saved money would help him acquire pitching help.

▸**Aug. 2:** Terry Mulholland's career was is hanging by a thread. After losing his ninth consecutive decision to fall to 2-10, he contemplated asking for his release. He said he was incensed by a newspaper column referring to him as "a pile of soot."

▸**Aug. 30:** Terry Mulholland rejoined the rotation after Trevor Wilson went on the disabled list and broke a nine-game losing streak with a four-hitter against the Mets. "Terry battled and battled," Dusty Baker said. "That's the Mulholland we hoped for." Mulholland was actually smiling for a change after retiring 16 consecutive Mets to end the game. "I kind of hit bottom a few weeks ago mentally," he said.

Team directory

▸**Owner:** Peter Magowan (president and managing general partner)
▸**General manager:** Bob Quinn
▸**Ballpark:**
3Com Park
Jamestown Avenue and Harney Way, San Francisco, Calif.
415-468-3700
Capacity 63,000
Parking for 17,000 cars; $4-$5
Public transportation available
Family and wheelchair sections, ramps, battery charger plug-ins for wheelchairs, designated handicapped pick-up and drop-off sights
▸**Team publications:**
Giants Magazine, Giants Info Guide
415-468-3700, ext. 478
▸**TV, radio broadcast stations:**
KNBR 680 AM, KTVU Channel 2, KIQI (Spanish), SportsChannel
▸**Camps and/or clinics:**
Rob Andrews Baseball, June and July, 510-935-3505
▸**Spring training:**
Scottsdale Stadium
Scottsdale, Ariz.
Capacity 7,500 (plus 2,500 on outfield grass)
602-990-7972

SAN FRANCISCO GIANTS 1995 final stats

BATTERS	BA	SLG	OB	G	AB	R	H	TB	2B	3B	HR	RBI	BB	SO	SB	CS	E
Aurilia	.474	.947	.476	9	19	4	9	18	3	0	2	4	1	2	1	0	0
Benard	.382	.529	.400	13	34	5	13	18	2	0	1	4	1	7	1	0	0
Williams	.336	.647	.399	76	283	53	95	183	17	1	23	65	30	58	2	0	10
Carreon	.301	.490	.343	117	396	53	119	194	24	0	17	65	23	37	0	1	7
Bonds	.294	.577	.431	144	506	109	149	292	30	7	33	104	120	83	31	10	6
Lampkin	.276	.342	.360	65	76	8	21	26	2	0	1	9	9	8	2	0	0
Sanders	.268	.399	.327	85	343	48	92	137	11	8	6	28	27	60	24	9	5
Scarsone	.266	.476	.333	80	233	33	62	111	10	3	11	29	18	82	3	2	11
Reed	.265	.283	.376	66	113	12	30	32	2	0	0	9	20	17	0	0	1
Hill	.264	.483	.317	132	497	71	131	240	29	4	24	86	39	98	25	5	10
Manwaring	.251	.332	.314	118	379	21	95	126	15	2	4	36	27	72	1	0	7
McCarty	.250	.300	.318	12	20	1	5	6	1	0	0	2	2	4	1	0	1
Clayton	.244	.342	.298	138	509	56	124	174	29	3	5	58	38	109	24	9	20
Thompson	.223	.339	.317	95	336	51	75	114	15	0	8	23	42	76	1	2	3
Benjamin	.220	.301	.256	68	186	19	41	56	6	0	3	12	8	51	11	1	4
Patterson	.205	.273	.294	95	205	27	42	56	5	3	1	14	14	41	4	2	4
Benzinger	.200	.500	.308	9	10	2	2	5	0	0	1	2	2	3	0	0	0
Faneyte	.198	.267	.289	46	86	7	17	23	4	1	0	4	11	27	1	0	1
Phillips	.195	.351	.256	92	231	27	45	81	9	0	9	28	19	69	1	1	4
Leonard	.190	.381	.346	14	21	4	4	8	1	0	1	4	5	2	0	0	0

PITCHERS	W-L	ERA	G	GS	CG	GF	Sho	SV	IP	H	R	ER	HR	BB	SO
Dewey	1-0	3.13	27	0	0	5	0	0	31.2	30	12	11	2	17	32
Service	3-1	3.19	28	0	0	6	0	0	31	18	11	11	4	20	30
VnLandnghm	6-3	3.67	18	18	1	0	0	0	122.2	124	58	50	14	40	95
Leiter	10-12	3.82	30	29	7	0	1	0	195.2	185	91	83	19	55	129
Wilson	3-4	3.92	17	17	0	0	0	0	82.2	82	42	36	8	38	38
Barton	4-1	4.26	52	0	0	11	0	1	44.1	37	22	21	3	19	22
Beck	5-6	4.45	60	0	0	52	0	33	58.2	60	31	29	7	21	42
Brewington	6-4	4.54	13	13	0	0	0	0	75.1	68	38	38	8	45	45
S. Valdez	4-5	4.75	13	11	1	0	0	0	66.1	78	43	35	12	17	29
Aquino	0-3	5.10	34	0	0	9	0	2	42.1	57	34	24	6	13	26
Gomez	0-0	5.14	18	0	0	3	0	0	14	16	8	8	2	12	15
Greer	0-2	5.25	8	0	0	1	0	0	12	15	12	7	3	5	7
Hook	5-1	5.50	45	0	0	14	0	0	52.1	55	33	32	7	29	40
Mulholland	5-13	5.80	29	24	2	2	0	0	149	190	112	96	25	38	65
C. Valdez	0-1	6.14	11	0	0	3	0	0	14.2	19	10	10	1	8	7
Bautista	3-8	6.44	52	6	0	19	0	0	100.2	120	77	72	24	26	45
Estes	0-3	6.75	3	3	0	0	0	0	17.1	16	14	13	2	5	14
Mintz	1-2	7.45	14	0	0	3	0	0	19.1	26	16	16	4	12	7
Burgos	0-0	8.64	5	0	0	2	0	0	8.1	14	8	8	1	6	12
Rosselli	2-1	8.70	9	5	0	0	0	0	30	39	29	29	5	20	7
Torres	0-1	9.00	4	1	0	2	0	0	8	13	8	8	4	7	2
Roper	0-0	12.38	3	2	0	0	0	0	8	15	12	11	3	6	6

1996 preliminary roster

PITCHERS (17)
Shawn Barton
Jose Bautista
Rod Beck
Steve Bourgeois
Jamie Brewington
Enrique Burgos
Mark Dewey
Shawn Estes
Chris Hook
Jeff Juden
Mark Leiter
Ricky Pickett
Joe Rosselli
Scott Service
Carlos Valdez

Sergio Valdez
William VanLandingham

CATCHERS (3)
Marcus Jensen
Tom Lampkin
Kirt Manwaring

INFIELDERS (11)
Rich Aurilia
Kim Batiste
Jay Canizaro
Royce Clayton
Brett King
David McCarty
Bill Mueller

J.R. Phillips
Steve Scarsone
Robby Thompson
Matt Williams

OUTFIELDERS (9)
Marvin Benard
Barry Bonds
Mark Carreon
Glenallen Hill
Stan Javier
Mark Leonard
Deion Sanders
Chris Singelton
Keith Willliams

Games played by position

PLAYER	G	C	1B	2B	3B	SS	OF
Aurilia	9	0	0	0	0	6	0
Benard	13	0	0	0	0	0	7
Benjamin	68	0	0	8	43	16	0
Benzinger	9	0	5	0	0	0	0
Bonds	144	0	0	0	0	0	143
Carreon	117	0	81	0	0	0	22
Clayton	138	0	0	0	0	136	0
Faneyte	46	0	0	0	0	0	34
Hill	132	0	0	0	0	0	125
Lampkin	65	17	0	0	0	0	6
Leonard	14	0	0	0	0	0	6
Manwaring	118	118	0	0	0	0	0
McCarty	12	0	2	0	0	0	4
Patterson	95	0	0	53	0	0	0
Phillips	92	0	79	0	0	0	1
Reed	66	42	0	0	0	0	0
Sanders	85	0	0	0	0	0	85
Scarsone	80	0	11	13	50	0	0
Thompson	95	0	0	91	0	0	0
Williams	76	0	0	0	74	0	0

Sick call: 1995 DL Report

Player	Days on the DL
Luis Aquino	35
Mark Dewey	89
Pat Gomez	101
Andy Heckman	72
Terry Mulholland	28
Kevin Rogers	160
Joey Rosselli	49
Robby Thompson	15
Bill VanLandingham	15
Matt Williams	76
Trevor Wilson	77*

Indicates two separate terms on Disabled List.

1995 Amateur draft picks

Players are listed with position and college or high school. Most players were assigned to rookie or Class A leagues. List provided by Major League Baseball.

Phillip Bailey, lhp, Central Arkansas; Manuel Bermudez, rhp, Antioch (Calif.) Sr HS; Joseph Blasingim, rhp, Southwest Missouri State; Darin Blood, rhp, Gonzaga; Kirk Bolling, rhp, West Torrance (Calif.) HS; Casey Bookout, 1b, Stroud (Okla.) HS; Jason Brester, lhp, Burlington (Wash.) Edison HS; Billy Coleman, rhp, Davidson (Okla.) HS; Rogelio Colon, rhp, Jose Gautier Benitez HS, Caguas, P.R.; Michael Davis, rhp, Tallahassee CC; Jason Dewey, c, Brandon HS, Valrico, Fla.; Duane Eason, rhp, Brookdale CC; Joseph Fontenot, rhp, Acadiana HS, Scott, La.; Nathan Forbush, c-1b, Central Arizona HS, Naranjito, P.R.; Eduard Guzman, 3b, Interamericana HS, Naranjito, P.R.; Toby Hall, c, American River College; Danny Harmon, rhp, Midland HS, Floral, Ark.; Brandon Hayes, rhp, McLane HS, Fresno, Calif.; Jason Huth, ss, Cherry Creek HS, Englewood, Colo.; Jeffrey Hutzler, rhp, Texas-San Antonio; Kelly Ireland, rf, Mount Hood CC; Jeremy Jackson, cf, Indian Hills CC; Brian Knoll, rhp, Brigham Young; Bradley Lidge, rhp, Cherry Creek HS, Englewood, Colo.; Michael Lincoln, rhp, American River JC; Shawn Lindsey, cf, Franklin HS, Portland, Ore.; Brian Little, 3b, Tulare (Calif) Union HS; Michael Littlefield, rhp, Central Arizona JC; John McMurray, 3b, Monticello (Ark.) Senior HS; Justin Miller, rhp, Torrance (Calif.) HS; Julio Morales, cf, Central Florida; Marc Mosman, rhp, Cal State-Dominguez Hills; Joseph Nathan, ss, Stony Brook; Andrew Norton, c, Gonzaga; Russell Ortiz, rhp, Oklahoma; Mark Peer, rf, St Louis CC; Brian Phelan, c, East Denver HS; Jeffrey Pohl, rhp, Three Rivers CC; Ian Rand, cf, Helix School, La Mesa, Calif.; Lajuan Rice, rf-lf, McNair Senior HS, Atlanta; Matthew Schuldt, c, Howard JC; Kurt Takahashi, rhp, Fresno CC; Bruce Thompson, cf-rf, Miami; Eric Thompson, rhp, Greenon HS, Fairbor, Ohio; Thomas Topaum, c, Centennial HS, Gresham, Ore.; David Townsend, rhp, Delta St.; Benjamin Tucker, rhp, Southern California; Jonathan Watson, 2b, Fairleigh Dickinson; Terry Weaver, ss, Liberty; James Woodrow, rhp, Flagler College.

Minor Leagues

Tops in the organization

Batter	Club	Avg.	G	AB	R	H	HR	RBI
Jesse Ibarra	Sjo	.330	132	446	73	147	34	100
Bill Mueller	Phx	.305	129	502	79	153	3	58
Keith Williams	Phx	.304	99	358	46	109	11	69
Marvin Benard	Phx	.304	111	378	70	115	6	32
Rich Aurilia	Phx	.302	135	484	71	146	9	76

Home Runs			Wins		
Jesse Ibarra	Sjo	34	Keith Foulke	Sjo	13
Brent Cookson	Phx	15	Steve Bourgeois	Phx	13
Andre Keene	Sjo	15	Edwin Corps	Shr	13
Mark Leonard	Phx	14	Bobby Howry	Sjo	12
Several tied		13	Kevin Lake	Bur	10

RBI			Saves		
Jesse Ibarra	Sjo	100	Jeffrey Keith	Bur	23
Mark Leonard	Phx	79	Shawn Purdy	Shr	21
Jacob Cruz	Shr	77	Rich Hyde	Shr	14
Rich Aurilia	Phx	76	Tony Menendez	Phx	13
Armando Rios	Sjo	75	Russell Ortiz	Sjo	12

Stolen Bases			Strikeouts		
Armando Rios	Sjo	51	Keith Foulke	Sjo	168
Dante Powell	Sjo	43	Steve Bourgeois	Phx	114
Chris Singleton	Sjo	33	Shawn Estes	Shr	112
Notorris Bray	But	30	Bobby Howry	Sjo	107
Several tied		28	Bobby Rector	Bur	102

Pitcher	Club	W-L	ERA	IP	H	BB	SO
S. Bourgeois	Phx	13-4	2.95	180	178	66	114
S. Soderstrom	Shr	9-5	3.41	116	106	51	91
Keith Foulke	Sjo	13-6	3.50	177	166	32	168
Bobby Howry	Sjo	12-10	3.54	165	171	54	107
Andy Taulbee	Shr	7-7	3.56	149	157	49	71

San Francisco (1958-1995), includes New York (1883-1957)

Runs: Most, career, all-time

2011	Willie Mays, 1951-1972
1859	Mel Ott, 1926-1947
1313	Mike Tiernan, 1887-1899
1120	Bill Terry, 1923-1936
1113	Willie McCovey, 1959-1980

Hits: Most, career, all-time

3187	Willie Mays, 1951-1972
2876	Mel Ott, 1926-1947
2193	Bill Terry, 1923-1936
1974	Willie McCovey, 1959-1980
1834	Mike Tiernan, 1887-1899

2B: Most, career, all-time

504	Willie Mays, 1951-1972
488	Mel Ott, 1926-1947
373	Bill Terry, 1923-1936
308	Willie McCovey, 1959-1980
291	Travis Jackson, 1922-1936

3B: Most, career, all-time

162	Mike Tiernan, 1887-1899
139	Willie Mays, 1951-1972
131	Roger Connor, 1883-1894
117	Larry Doyle, 1907-1920
112	Bill Terry, 1923-1936

HR: Most, career, all-time

646	Willie Mays, 1951-1972
511	Mel Ott, 1926-1947
469	Willie McCovey, 1959-1980
226	Orlando Cepeda, 1958-1966
225	MATT WILLIAMS, 1987-1995

RBI: Most, career, all-time

1860	Mel Ott, 1926-1947
1859	Willie Mays, 1951-1972
1388	Willie McCovey, 1959-1980
1078	Bill Terry, 1923-1936
929	Travis Jackson, 1922-1936

SB: Most, career, all-time

428	Mike Tiernan, 1887-1899
354	George Davis, 1893-1903
336	Willie Mays, 1951-1972
334	George Burns, 1911-1921
332	John Ward, 1883-1894

BB: Most, career, all-time

1708	Mel Ott, 1926-1947
1394	Willie Mays, 1951-1972
1168	Willie McCovey, 1959-1980
747	Mike Tiernan, 1887-1899
631	George Burns, 1911-1921

BA: Highest, career, all-time

.341	Bill Terry, 1923-1936
.332	George Davis, 1893-1903
.322	Ross Youngs, 1917-1926
.322	Frankie Frisch, 1919-1926
.321	George Van Haltren, 1894-1903
.308	Orlando Cepeda, 1958-1966 (12)

Slug avg: Highest, career, all-time

.564	Willie Mays, 1951-1972
.549	Johnny Mize, 1942-1949
.536	Kevin Mitchell, 1987-1991
.535	Orlando Cepeda, 1958-1966
.533	Mel Ott, 1926-1947

Games started: Most, career, all-time

550	Christy Mathewson, 1900-1916
446	Juan Marichal, 1960-1973
431	Carl Hubbell, 1928-1943
412	Mickey Welch, 1883-1892
403	Amos Rusie, 1890-1898

Saves: Most, career, all-time

127	ROD BECK, 1991-1995
127	Gary Lavelle, 1974-1984
125	Greg Minton, 1975-1987
83	Randy Moffitt, 1972-1981
78	Frank Linzy, 1963-1970

Shutouts: Most, career, all-time

79	Christy Mathewson, 1900-1916
52	Juan Marichal, 1960-1973
36	Carl Hubbell, 1928-1943
29	Amos Rusie, 1890-1898
28	Mickey Welch, 1883-1892

Wins: Most, career, all-time

373	Christy Mathewson, 1900-1916
253	Carl Hubbell, 1928-1943
238	Juan Marichal, 1960-1973
238	Mickey Welch, 1883-1892
233	Amos Rusie, 1890-1898

K: Most, career, all-time

2499	Christy Mathewson, 1900-1916
2281	Juan Marichal, 1960-1973
1819	Amos Rusie, 1890-1898
1677	Carl Hubbell, 1928-1943
1606	Gaylord Perry, 1962-1971

Win pct: Highest, career, all-time

.693	Sal Maglie, 1945-1955
.680	Tim Keefe, 1885-1891
.664	Christy Mathewson, 1900-1916
.656	Jesse Barnes, 1918-1923
.651	Doc Crandall, 1908-1913
.630	Juan Marichal, 1960-1973 (11)

ERA: Lowest, career, all-time

2.12	Christy Mathewson, 1900-1916
2.38	Joe McGinnity, 1902-1908
2.43	Jeff Tesreau, 1912-1918
2.45	Red Ames, 1903-1913
2.48	Hooks Wiltse, 1904-1914
2.82	Gary Lavelle, 1974-1984 (12)

Runs: Most, season

147	Mike Tiernan, 1889
139	Bill Terry, 1930
138	Mel Ott, 1929
137	Johnny Mize, 1947
136	George Van Haltren, 1896
134	Bobby Bonds, 1970 (6)

Hits: Most, season

254	Bill Terry, 1930
231	Freddy Lindstrom, 1928
231	Freddy Lindstrom, 1930
226	Bill Terry, 1929
225	Bill Terry, 1932
208	Willie Mays, 1958 (13)

2B: Most, season

46	Jack Clark, 1978
43	Willie Mays, 1959
43	Bill Terry, 1931
42	George Kelly, 1921
42	Bill Terry, 1932

3B: Most, season

27	George Davis, 1893
25	Larry Doyle, 1911
22	Roger Connor, 1887
21	Mike Tiernan, 1890
21	Mike Tiernan, 1895
21	George Van Haltren, 1896
12	Willie Mays, 1960 (*)

HR: Most, season

52	Willie Mays, 1965
51	Willie Mays, 1955
51	Johnny Mize, 1947
49	Willie Mays, 1962
47	Willie Mays, 1964
47	Kevin Mitchell, 1989

RBI: Most, season

151	Mel Ott, 1929
142	Orlando Cepeda, 1961
141	Willie Mays, 1962
138	Johnny Mize, 1947
136	George Davis, 1897
136	George Kelly, 1924

SB: Most, season

111	John Ward, 1887
65	George Davis, 1897
62	George Burns, 1914
62	John Ward, 1889
61	Josh Devore, 1911
58	Billy North, 1979 (7)

BB: Most, season

144	Eddie Stanky, 1950
137	Willie McCovey, 1970
127	Eddie Stanky, 1951
126	BARRY BONDS, 1993
121	Willie McCovey, 1969

BA: Highest, season

.401	Bill Terry, 1930
.379	Freddy Lindstrom, 1930
.372	Bill Terry, 1929
.371	Roger Connor, 1885
.369	Mike Tiernan, 1896
.347	Willie Mays, 1958 (23)

Slug avg: Highest, season

.677	BARRY BONDS, 1993
.667	Willie Mays, 1954
.659	Willie Mays, 1955
.656	Willie McCovey, 1969
.647	BARRY BONDS, 1994

Games started: Most, season

65	Mickey Welch, 1884
64	Tim Keefe, 1886
63	Amos Rusie, 1890
61	Amos Rusie, 1892
59	Mickey Welch, 1886
41	Gaylord Perry, 1970 (*)

Saves: Most, season

48	ROD BECK, 1993
30	Greg Minton, 1982
24	DAVE RIGHETTI, 1991
33	ROD BECK, 1995
28	ROD BECK, 1994

Shutouts: Most, season

11	Christy Mathewson, 1908
10	Carl Hubbell, 1933
10	Juan Marichal, 1965
9	Joe McGinnity, 1904
8	Tim Keefe, 1888
8	Juan Marichal, 1969
8	Christy Mathewson, 1902
8	Christy Mathewson, 1905
8	Christy Mathewson, 1907
8	Christy Mathewson, 1909
8	Jeff Tesreau, 1914
8	Jeff Tesreau, 1915

Wins: Most, season

44	Mickey Welch, 1885
42	Tim Keefe, 1886
39	Mickey Welch, 1884
37	Christy Mathewson, 1908
36	Amos Rusie, 1894
26	Juan Marichal, 1968 (25)

K: Most, season

345	Mickey Welch, 1884
341	Amos Rusie, 1890
337	Amos Rusie, 1891
335	Tim Keefe, 1888
297	Tim Keefe, 1886
248	Juan Marichal, 1963 (11)

Win pct: Highest, season

.833	Hoyt Wilhelm, 1952
.818	Sal Maglie, 1950
.814	Joe McGinnity, 1904
.813	Carl Hubbell, 1936
.810	Doc Crandall, 1910
.806	Juan Marichal, 1966 (7)

ERA: Lowest, season

1.14	Christy Mathewson, 1909
1.28	Christy Mathewson, 1905
1.43	Christy Mathewson, 1908
1.44	Fred Anderson, 1917
1.57	Tim Keefe, 1885
1.99	Bobby Bolin, 1968 (16)

Most pinch-hit homers, season

4	Ernie Lombardi, 1946
4	Bill Taylor, 1955
4	Mike Ivie, 1978
4	CANDY MALDONADO, 1986
4	ERNIE RILES, 1990

Most pinch-hit homers, career

13	Willie McCovey, 1959-1980

Most consecutive games batting safely

33	George Davis, 1893
26	Jack Clark, 1978

Most consecutive scoreless innings

45	Carl Hubbell, 1933
45	Sal Maglie, 1950
40	Gaylord Perry, 1967
39	Christy Mathewson, 1901
39	Gaylord Perry, 1970

No-hit games

Amos Rusie, NY vs Bro NL, 6-0; July 31, 1891.

Christy Mathewson, NY at StL NL, 5-0; July 15, 1901.

Christy Mathewson, NY at Chi NL, 1-0; June 13, 1905.

Hooks Wiltse, NY vs Phi NL, 1-0; July 4, 1908 (1st game, 10 innings).

Red Ames, NY vs Bro NL. 0-3; April 15, 1909 (lost on 7 hits in 13 innings after allowing the first hit in the 10th).

Jeff Tesreau, NY at Phi NL, 3-0; September 6, 1912 (1st game).

Rube Marquard, NY vs Bro NL, 2-0; April 15, 1915.

Jesse Barnes, NY vs Phi NL, 6-0; May 7, 1922.

Carl Hubbell, NY vs Pit NL, 11-0; May 8, 1929.

Juan Marichal, SF vs Hou NL, 1-0; June 15, 1963.

Gaylord Perry, SF vs StL NL, 1-0; September 17, 1968.

Ed Halicki, SF vs NY NL, 6-0; August 24, 1975 (2nd game).

John Montefusco, SF at Atl NL, 9-0; September 29, 1976.

Ed Crane, 7 innings, darkness, NY vs Was NL, 3-0; September 27, 1888.

Red Ames, 5 innings, darkness, NY at StL NL, 5-0; September 14, 1903 (2nd game, first game in the major leagues).

Mike McCormick, 5 innings, rain, SF at Phi NL, 3-0; June 12, 1959 (allowed hit in 6th, but rain caused game to revert to 5 innings).

Sam Jones, 7 innings, rain, SF at StL NL, 4-0; September 26, 1959.

ACTIVE PLAYERS in caps.

Leader from franchise's current location is included. If not in the top five, leader's rank is listed in parenthesis; asterisk (*) indicates player is not in top 25.

Players' years of service are listed by the first and last years with this team and are not necessarily consecutive; all statistics record performances for this team only.

295

Baseball Weekly's best and worst of '95

Here are the nine most influential people or events of the year as determined by Baseball Weekly's reporters and editors:

Iron Man for all time

Cal Ripken Jr. inspired average workers with a sense of their own nobility as he did his job every day, went about his business, and stayed late to accommodate fans. A Baltimore elementary school devoted streak week to studying his accomplishments. His bat, ankle tapes, and other paraphernalia from the Sept. 6 game, his 2,131st in a row, went to the Hall of Fame.

Wild-card debut

What the strike took away in April the lords added in October, with an extra round of playoffs. The kinks still need to be worked out, but the thrilling five-game series between Mariners and Yankees will get much of the credit for the early success of the divisional round.

Cleveland juggernaut

The Indians were not to be denied playing in the Fall Classic. They won 100 games in a 144-game season, rolled past Boston and Seattle in the playoffs, all the way to their first World Series appearance since 1954.

Lovable underdogs

The Mariners came into their own this year, probably because Ken Griffey Jr. made them. He got hurt. To compensate for his absence, the Mariners produced a Cy Young winner, a Manager of the Year, and a batting champion. They also brewed a new spirit in Seattle and probably saved the franchise.

Labor unrest

Whatever principles triggered the walkout last year were obscured by the time spring training rolled around. People were tired of the mess. The owners' plan to put replacement players on the field further splintered the public. People stayed away in droves and the season ended with still no labor agreement in place.

Mickey Mantle dies

He was one of the game's most conflicted heroes, as he single-mindedly destroyed the body that had once thrilled crowds at Yankee Stadium. He asked for no sympathy as he battled cancer and bared his soul. He died Aug. 13.

Precocious Colorado

The Rockies crawled, then they ran—they skipped the walking stage. No expansion team has made it to the post-season faster. And they did it with a home run-bashing flair that filled Coors Field for virtually every game.

Maddux the Cy-borg

Greg Maddux has flawless mechanics. It's what he does. No matter how much writers gush about the four-time Cy Young winner, the boy-next-door just keeps deflecting the hyperbole.

Nomomania

The Dodgers treat baseball as an international game, scouting for talent throughout the world. This year they delivered their fourth consecutive Rookie of the Year—Hideo Nomo from Japan, who won despite a constant crush of attention from both countries.

League forecasts

▸ **Money still talks**

▸ **East, West and Central Divisions**

▸ **Prophesies**

▸ *and more...*

USA SNAPSHOTS®

A look at statistics that shape the sports world

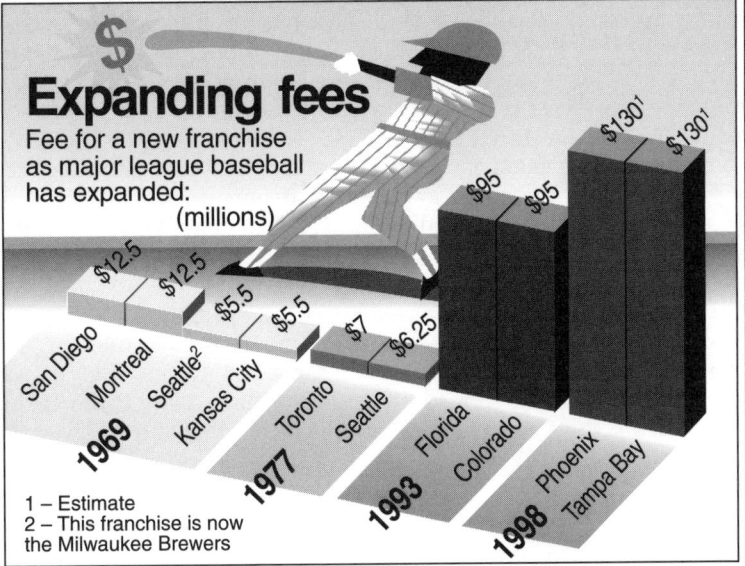

Expanding fees

Fee for a new franchise as major league baseball has expanded:
(millions)

$12.5 — San Diego
$12.5 — Montreal
$5.5 — Seattle[2]
$5.5 — Kansas City
1969

$7 — Toronto
$6.25 — Seattle
1977

$95 — Florida
$95 — Colorado
1993

$130[1] — Phoenix
$130[1] — Tampa Bay
1998

1 – Estimate
2 – This franchise is now the Milwaukee Brewers

Source: Major League Baseball   By John Riley and Sam Ward, USA TODAY

No matter what, money still talks

Last spring a judge set off the wildest signing frenzy baseball has ever seen. More than a hundred free agents scrambling for jobs in a high-stakes game of musical chairs were signed in one three-day period. Many players found themselves in what amounted to a tryout camp at Homestead, Fla., when the Major League Baseball Players Association set up spring training for unsigned players. These weren't utility guys, bench-warmers and long relievers hoping to catch on. This was Benito Santiago, Mariano Duncan, Todd Stottlemyre, Tim Belcher, Dave Magadan, Mickey Tettleton and Andy Van Slyke—begging for a job.

The process wasn't so dramatic this winter, but far more players are likely to have changed teams by the time spring training '96 opens in February. What a lot of those players at Homestead—and scores of others who took huge pay cuts—thought was a one-year aberration is becoming the new way of life.

Team owners have discovered that much of the drag they have been hoping to put on player salaries can be accomplished by the new-style buyer's market—forcing the concept into a new collective bargaining agreement isn't even necessary. If they glut the market with dozens—even hundreds—of mid-level players, the cost of doing business can be reduced. If they build concern among the rank and file that things will never be as good as they used to be, full-scale resentment of the leadership might fester in the union. If they give only the stars megabucks, they can fill in the supporting cast at cut-rate prices.

Within days after the World Series, the Indians decided not to keep 25-homer man Paul Sorrento at his 1995 price. It didn't take much longer for the White Sox to make a similar decision on Lance Johnson, who hit .306 and stole 40 bases. More than 140 players put themselves on this winter's free-agent market, but those kinds of budget decisions by teams pushed the amount of available talent significantly higher.

What that means for fans is less familiarity from year to year, less loyalty from all sides, and more uncertainty in assessing a team's chances.

Yet, even with the new buyer's market, money still talks. Little has changed in terms of which teams have how much to spend. The sizes of the markets haven't changed. The rules haven't changed. In fact, the rules are few. Baseball entered this off-season without the no-movement restrictions of a year ago, but still without anything close to a labor agreement or a method to balance the economic disparities between the richer and poorer clubs.

The Yankees still had money to spend. The Expos still had payroll limits restrictive enough to drive their general manager, Kevin Malone, out of town.

So, while the game could continue to see an annual massive shuffle of names, the balance of power was less likely to tilt quickly. The Braves finally had their World Series rings and as many of their key players back for '96 as they wanted. The Indians had their most potent offensive weapons signed and sealed for the immediate future and merely had to continue their gradual transition from veteran to farm-system-produced pitchers. Up-and-coming teams like the Cinderella Mariners and their AL West stretch-run victims, the Angels, have their core players intact. Other clubs faced with free-agent- and age-induced transition, such as the Yankees and the Red Sox, have the money to make the changes.

Talent-laden farm systems are pushing teams such as the Mets and the Royals back toward prominence. And franchises like Minnesota, Detroit and Pitts-burgh try to reassemble the pieces.

Regardless of the method, virtually every team will have to get reacquainted with its fans come April. But that's still far better than having to get reacquainted with the game itself.

AL 1996: A peek into the crystal ball

Baltimore Orioles

Peter Angelos says he's being treated unfairly when owners approve expansion teams for Washington, D.C., Annapolis, Md., and two Baltimore suburbs.

Boston Red Sox

Dan Duquette signs 83 players to one-year contracts with incentives, says he has plans to use every one during this season.

California Angels

Disney takes over complete control of the team—it turns out the Angels actually won the AL West in 1995 by 17 games.

Chicago White Sox

Dennis Rodman says he wants to play for White Sox: "That Harrelson guy keeps talking on TV about needing players who can tattoo the ball."

Cleveland Indians

Albert Belle gets picked up on a minor traffic violation, and a judge sentences him to 100 hours of interviews with reporters.

Detroit Tigers

Kirk Gibson comes out of retirement in June, says he's looking forward to playing in Detroit's new stadium.

Kansas City Royals

Manager Bob Boone gets Royals to trade for his sons, Bret and Aaron, then convinces ownership to hire Daniel Boone to help fans find their way to the ballpark.

Milwaukee Brewers

Bud Selig finally agrees to become the commissioner. Batman says he'll be glad to be working with such a fine man.

Minnesota Twins

Twins try to boost attendance: Heavy promotion of new Handle-Tie version of right field wall meets with little interest.

New York Yankees

George Steinbrenner mentions a great New Jersey deal to GM Bob Watson. Two days later Watson learns that the home opener is in Hoboken.

Oakland Athletics

Fans are turned away from September home games. Al Davis invokes lease clause that says no outsiders are allowed except on Raiders game days.

Seattle Mariners

Randy Johnson says, "I'm the man, now. It's my turn." All Mariners including Jay Buhner must match Johnson's hair style.

Texas Rangers

Jerry Jones buys the Rangers but is ejected from Opening Day game when he comes down to the on-deck circle in the fourth inning. Rangers players say it's OK, the new shoes are great.

Toronto Blue Jays

Blue Jays make trade for David Cone. No reason, really. It just seemed to be about time to get Cone on the roster.

NL 1996: A peek into the crystal ball

Atlanta Braves

Braves protest lottery to pick two clubs that get to beat Greg Maddux. They wonder who thinks Maddux will lose twice.

Chicago Cubs

Ryne Sandberg no longer feels right in a Cubs uniform: "The people running things seem to know what they're doing."

Cincinnati Reds

June 1: Sparky Anderson tells Ray Knight that Marge Schott said Sparky could be manager that month. Aug. 1: Knight gets nervous, hears scratching at his door.

Colorado Rockies

Rockies trade every pitcher for Albert Belle, Cecil Fielder and Matt Williams, theorizing that visitors will bat in the first inning and never come to the plate again.

Florida Marlins

GM Dave Dombrowski announces a blockbuster deal (the owner gave him free Blockbuster movie rentals for life).

Houston Astros

Drayton McLane defies MLB to move his team. Owners hire Jeff Bagwell to break McLane's wrist so he can't sign the deal.

Los Angeles Dodgers

Tommy Lasorda puts himself on the roster as a rookie, claims, "Hey, somebody here has to be Rookie of the Year."

Montreal Expos

Expos players vote 13-12 against a proposal to secede from the NL and wait for the United League to start up.

New York Mets

So many farm system players make the Opening Day roster, Dallas Green says he'll manage in bib overalls.

Philadelphia Phillies

Lenny Dykstra turns over a new leaf and gives up chewing tobacco. Groundskeepers find mysterious holes in center field turf.

Pittsburgh Pirates

New ownership signs deal for baseball-only stadium. Only seven players from current roster qualify to use it.

St. Louis Cardinals

Tony La Russa's closer takes the field in a horse-drawn beer wagon. It's part of the team's sale agreement.

San Diego Padres

Tony Gwynn wins the batting title. OK, we just wanted to make sure at least one of these predictions comes true.

San Francisco Giants

Barry Bonds completes the cycle: Doesn't run out ball he thinks is a homer; doesn't run after ball he thinks is a homer; forgets to run off field after an inning; refuses to run against wind during home game.

AL East: Don't take your eyes off Boston

The American League East is not the division most likely to produce a World Series winner in 1996, but it certainly is the group most likely to spend whatever it takes in the effort to attain that goal.

Baltimore falls short of expectations? Change managers, shuffle the front office and open the checkbook. No problem.

The Yankees face aging stars who may or may not want to stay and manager who doesn't. Fine. Turn 'em over and turn to the farm system, too.

In Toronto, tying for the worst record in the league hardly seems appropriate. You know this organization can't be accused of sitting on its hands. And there's talent on the farm as well.

The task for the new regime in Detroit is more daunting because the minor league system hasn't been as productive, but the Tigers are shedding their image as an aging, plodding organization.

And don't forget, Boston won this division handily with an awful lot of things going wrong. A full season in the rotation from Roger Clemens and Aaron Sele will take a lot of pressure off Tim Wakefield. Mo Vaughn is among the very best offensive players in the league, John Valentin has quietly emerged as one of the most potent shortstops, and Mike Greenwell seems to finally have gotten beyond injuries and regained All-Star caliber. If Tim Naehring can reproduce his numbers and GM Dan Duquette can continue to create depth on the roster, the onus will be on the big spenders to catch up.

The Yankees probably have the most home-grown talent ready to make major contributions. Left-hander Andy Pettitte is on the verge of stardom, as is Derek Jeter at shortstop. Outfield prospect Ruben Rivera is almost ready. Add third baseman Russ Davis, who has served an effective apprenticeship, and new GM Bob Watson can be selective about how he spends George Steinbrenner's money.

In Baltimore, they just keep growing money. But this might be one team on which changing managers could have a major impact. It's not that Phil Regan did such a bad job last year, but the team lacks spark. That's what Davey Johnson brings to the team he once played for. He didn't take long to say Brady Anderson isn't necessarily the leadoff man, or that Cal Ripken doesn't necessarily play every day. One guy Johnson needs to play more often and more effectively is pitcher Ben McDonald. Mike Mussina is a given as the ace of the staff and as one of the top five pitchers in the league, but McDonald has never attained the consistent brilliance expected of a No. 1 draft pick.

In Toronto, the Blue Jays have eschewed the quick-fix approach in favor of logically retooling their championship teams with what remains of the fertile farm system after talent was skimmed off in previous runs for World Series titles. Outfielder Shawn Green quietly stepped in last season, Carlos Delgado gets another chance to resurrect his power stroke, and Alex Gonzalez needs to step up another notch to be a full-timer in the infield. The setbacks have been on the mound. A series of injuries and disappointments in the minors have accentuated the problem, and that's what still separates Toronto from the other contenders.

Rookie manager Buddy Bell and new GM Randy Smith have a long task ahead of them in Detroit. They begin with most of their key players, but that's not enough without some improvements. Cecil Fielder and Travis Fryman remain the keys to the offense, despite the strikeouts. Bob Higginson got a long, hard baptism in his rookie year and will be asked to step forward. Shortstop Chris Gomez and a host of pitchers also will need to show continued improvement. Jose Lima, Clint Sodowsky and C.J. Nitkowski are the ones most likely to hold down spots in the starting rotation.

AL Central: The only race is the wild card

The Indians are so much better than the rest of the division—which is populated with decent teams, Minnesota excepted—that even a drop-off from their 100 victories in a short season and the likely improvement of the White Sox and Royals still won't create much of a race.

Cleveland general manager John Hart was called a trend-setter when he signed his top young talent to multi-year contracts. That's why Kenny Lofton, Carlos Baerga, Albert Belle, Jim Thome, Manny Ramirez and Sandy Alomar will frighten pitchers almost daily again this year. The fertile farm system now is filling in the pitching staff. Charles Nagy is ready to step up as the staff leader. Chad Ogea and Julian Tavarez have served their apprenticeships. Plus, Jose Mesa has emerged as the league's best closer.

OK, so about that wild-card spot.

The White Sox actually played respectably as the season wore on and adjustments were made after the change to manager Terry Bevington. Now, he has the job full-time and has installed his own coaching staff. Any team with the talent of Robin Ventura and Frank Thomas—and developing youngsters such as second baseman Ray Durham—has the nucleus of a contender. And don't forget, this team's pitching staff was one of the league's best just a year ago.

The exciting team of the division could be Kansas City. The Royals shipped away salaries at the start of 1995 and retooled the lineup with the cream of the farm system in August. A little more pitching depth and manager Bob Boone could have pulled off the surprise of the season. Outfielder Jon Nunnally went from Rule V benchwarmer to Rookie of the Year candidate. Tom Goodwin battled Lofton for the stolen base crown and Johnny Damon was the late-season addition with the biggest impact. His

multidimensional talent is about to burst forth on the league.

While the Royals were using youthful spark to get close, the Milwaukee Brewers were the consummate overachievers. Until the Brewers can get the added boost of a new stadium, GM Sal Bando and manager Phil Garner will continue to scrape together a lineup full of scrappy players in the Garner mold. John Jaha used Dave Nilsson's early-season absence due to illness to finally take hold of the first base job. Nilsson, a converted catcher with sore knees, was to play first but moved to DH and the outfield. He is the top power threat and will be a factor from the beginning. Matt Mieske needs to continue improving as the everyday right fielder. The Brewers will have to continue developing players. Jeff Cirillo has become a significant factor in the infield, and prospect Tim Unroe could move in at third base. The lack of veteran talent could force Milwaukee to push some youngster more quickly than could be prudent.

Yes, there is a fifth team in the division. The Minnesota Twins bottomed out in a tie for the league's worst record with the Toronto Blue Jays. The rebuilding in earnest went into high gear when closer Rick Aguilera was traded to Boston for Frankie Rodriguez, who is looked on as the staff ace of the future. Kirby Puckett, who personifies the franchise, chose to stay at home rather than ask out for one last shot at a ring. But the offense is going to have to be built around outfielder Marty Cordova, the '95 Rookie of the Year. The farm system is not overloaded with prospects at the upper levels, which helped precipitate the trade of Aguilera and starter Kevin Tapani to step up the pace of the overhaul.

AL West: Nobody has it locked up

After the 1995 season, the perception would seem to be: Seattle Mariners, playoff team on the rise with a batting champion and a Cy Young Award winner; California Angels, folded down the stretch, missed the playoffs, a franchise that never quite gets there.

Guess again.

The Mariners and the Angels were separated only by Randy Johnson's brilliance in a one-game playoff, and the Texas Rangers can easily do as much offensively as either of them.

The roar in the Kingdome at the end of 1995 was as deafening as the silence that used to be there. If the fan enthusiasm carries into the new season, a potent new factor has been introduced into this race. Seattle has plenty of other potent factors sure to be there. Johnson, of course, solidified his claim to being the league's most dominant pitcher. Batting champ Edgar Martinez finally received his due as one of baseball's top pure hitters. Ken Griffey will be back full strength, but while he was out, Tino Martinez and Jay Buhner stepped up their roles, and catcher Dan Wilson and second baseman Joey Cora developed into key regulars. Alex Rodriguez will probably make a serious bid for everyday shortstop. Contributions from young players will be necessary on the pitching staff. Bob Wolcott should become a major part of the rotation.

California should retain its unstoppable offense. Tim Salmon, Jim Edmonds, and J.T. Snow headline a group that outscored Cleveland for much of 1995. Shortstop Gary DiSarcina should regain his All-Star status, and Garret Anderson, who nearly grabbed the Rookie of the Year award, makes left field one less question mark. The most likely rookie to have an impact is catcher Todd Greene, *Baseball Weekly*'s Minor League Player of the Year. He's a power hitter who could be the starter if his defense improves at the pace of his offense. Starting pitching has been a strength, but a tenuous one.

The certainty is that Mark Langston will be the No. 1 guy again this year. Also certain is one of the game's best setup-closer situations—Lee Smith is still the man in the ninth inning. The all-time save leader is set up now but will eventually be pushed by hard-throwing closer of the future Troy Percival.

Texas was nearly forgotten by the time the season ended, but the Rangers could be as good as the division's top two clubs if slugger Juan Gonzalez and power-hitting third baseman Dean Palmer are healthy. The Rangers have become a more balanced offensive unit, with Otis Nixon and Mark McLemore providing speed and bat control at the top of the order. First baseman Will Clark and catcher Ivan Rodriguez are among the league's best at their positions, and Texas has improving young players in outfielder Rusty Greer and shortstop Benji Gil. As Greer develops more consistency and Gil cuts down on strikeouts, the offense will get that much better. Pitching has long been the concern in Texas, and that's not likely to change. Kevin Gross was the only starter on a long-term deal when 1995 ended, and he struggled so much at times that he actually considered retiring. Help may finally be arriving via the farm system, but the progress of Darren Oliver was set back by an injury last year and top prospect Jose Alberro might be a bit too green to be a major factor this year.

It's hard to believe, but Oakland has become the team regularly playing catch-up in this division. The departure of manager Tony La Russa and coaches adds to the flux. If healthy, Mark McGwire, Danny Tartabull, Terry Steinbach and Geronimo Berroa can produce runs. But the key to this club is the ongoing supporting cast of guys like Mike Bordick and Scott Brosius. Spotty pitching is a concern. Fading Dennis Eckersley is back in the bullpen, but Todd Van Poppel and Ariel Prieto will have to step forward on the starting staff.

NL East: The Braves still own it

The Atlanta Braves finally have their World Series rings, and they'll remain the standard to strive for in the National League East. No team currently in this division had won the Series since the Mets knocked off Boston in 1986, and the New Yorkers might be the team moving into the best position to challenge the Braves.

While Atlanta was on its way to an easy division championship, the balance of power one rung below was undergoing a noticeable shift. For the first half of the season, the Philadelphia Phillies looked hot, but nothing could hold them together after midseason—not manager Jim Fregosi, not pitching coach Johnny Podres and, most important, not the medical staff. Injuries are the Phillies' biggest concerns for 1996. Center fielder Len Dykstra and catcher Darren Daulton are the guts of the offense and the soul of the clubhouse, but both have become more and more susceptible to time on the sidelines. If they are healthy and first baseman Gregg Jefferies bounces back to the production that made him a key free agent signing a year ago, Philadelphia has the core of a potent offense.

Only a year ago, the Montreal Expos were the best team in the league and seemingly on the way to their first World Series. But after struggling to break even—both in the win-loss column and at the bank—another GM has moved on to greener pastures and the Expos just hope their farm system can continue producing enough to remain competitive. Jim Beattie, who took over the GM job after Kevin Malone resigned, has many young prospects, as well as former super-prospect Cliff Floyd and outfielder Moises Alou (back after injuries). But most of the help must come from within, because the Expos can't afford to go heavily into the free agent market.

The Mets, who made the greatest strides forward in the division during the second half of last season, can afford to go outside but are continuing to make most of their progress from what has resurfaced as one of baseball's strongest farm systems. As in the glory days of the past, the Mets are developing outstanding pitching. Bill Pulsipher and Jason Isringhausen got their first significant looks at the majors in 1995 and showed why they're expected to be staff mainstays for a long time. The next wave of talent is about ready to kick in on the rest of the field, including outfielder Alex Ochoa, shortstop Rey Ordonez and infielder Edgar Alfonzo. It might be asking too much for the Mets to challenge the Braves right away, but their steady progress under Joe McIlvaine and Dallas Green shows that the front office has a plan and is sticking to it.

A step behind the Mets, but more likely to throw money at remaining holes, are the Florida Marlins. Catcher Charles Johnson and second baseman Quilvio Veras, a product of the Mets farm system, became major league regulars last year. More youngsters could begin to make contributions in the bullpen and off the bench. Offense is not a problem, with steady production from Jeff Conine, Gary Sheffield, and Greg Colbrunn. But owner Wayne Huizenga's money probably will have to be directed toward pitching to make this team a serious contender.

All of this leads back to Atlanta, still several steps ahead of the competition and with most of its key parts in place, especially the dominant pitching staff. No team in baseball can match the big four of Greg Maddux, Tom Glavine, John Smoltz and Steve Avery, and the '96 Braves are in an even better position than before thanks to an emerging bullpen with better established roles and a deeper bench. The Braves still own this division. It's unlikely anybody can steal it away from Atlanta unless the Braves find a way to give it away themselves.

NL Central: It's up for grabs

The Cincinnati Reds should be favored to repeat, but the first full-season National League Central winners have nearly as much uncertainty as the teams with a legitimate chance of taking the title away. After getting rid of Davey Johnson, the Reds must regroup under Ray Knight from a disappointing September and October. Last year they won with major contributions from players who hadn't approached such heights before. Now they'll find out if those players can be consistent contributors. Pete Schourek picked up the slack created when ace Jose Rijo was injured and became the No. 2 winner in the league behind Greg Maddux. He will have to lead the staff, along with John Smiley. The third base platoon of Jeff Branson and Mark Lewis filled a major hole when prospect Willie Greene fizzled; they'll have to do it again if Greene doesn't come through. Barry Larkin and Reggie Sanders are still the crux of the offense, but payroll considerations will chip into their supporting cast.

The Houston Astros were the Reds' closest pursuers last year and could have been closer if they had found a way to win a few of the head-to-head meetings—and keep Jeff Bagwell healthy all year. More important was the prospect of entering a season without free agent second baseman Craig Biggio, who was the key to the offense when Bagwell struggled early in the season and when the first baseman was hurt later. The emergence of outfielder Derek Bell reduces some of that sting, but in a season when owner Drayton McLane may put the club up for sale, economic factors become even more crucial. The lower the payroll, the more attractive the property.

The Chicago Cubs stayed in the wildcard race until the final weekend last season. Club president Andy MacPhail made giant strides in instilling confidence that management had a plan that could be successful. Then he found himself and the Tribune Company's money facing a winter in which every key component of his team was unsigned. Most of the free agents were offensive players, but scoring runs won't be the key to the Cubs' '96 success. An overachieving starting staff led by Jaime Navarro, Frank Castillo and Jim Bullinger must repeat its success. And promising youngsters Steve Trachsel and Kevin Foster must develop.

The Cubs will hardly recognize their old archrivals from St. Louis. It's difficult to gauge which will have a bigger impact on the success of the Cardinals, the addition of manager extraordinaire Tony La Russa or the decision by the Busch family to sell the franchise. La Russa can get plenty out of the material he is given, and the Cardinals have been notably frugal during the Busch regime. Given a little more financial leeway, GM Walt Jocketty could accelerate his rebuilding. He's already decided that multitalented outfielder Brian Jordan is the cornerstone and Ray Lankford a close second. The Cardinals also are excited about the emergence of power pitcher Alan Benes, younger brother of Andy.

The only NL Central club without any serious hope of being a contender is Pittsburgh, but the Pirates' recent years of uncertainty appear to be over. With new ownership and manager Jim Leyland's decision to stick around, the franchise could begin moving forward again. The timetable for serious contention would seem to coincide with aspirations for a new baseball-only stadium. Jeff King and Orlando Merced are the best offensive talent, and Denny Neagle has finally emerged as a quality starting pitcher. The farm system has been lean for a while, but catcher Jason Kendall could be ready this year and outfielder Trey Beamon is not far behind as the system regenerates.

The division is up for grabs and probably will be decided not by who spent most but by who spent best.

NL West: Look out for those Rockies

Los Angeles Dodgers were supposed to pull away and win the division in 1995. They won, but they never pulled away, and the Colorado Rockies—continually reminded that they were an expansion team—followed right into the postseason. Now the established Dodgers are making changes to be sure that those Mile High upstarts don't become the power of the NL West.

Unfortunately for the Dodgers, the Rockies already are the power—all they need to do is add the glory. Cozy Coors Field gets much of the credit for the awesome offensive numbers Colorado racks up. But Dante Bichette, Vinny Castilla, Larry Walker and Andres Galarraga aren't exactly hitting pop-ups. This team will continue to score plenty of runs and with Rocky-mania producing plenty of fans, the club will again go after whatever they need to improve the roster. Problem is, it's not easy to persuade a top pitcher to volunteer for Coors Field duty, at any price. Bret Saberhagen, the club's key stretch-drive acquisition, found out just how difficult the Denver adjustment is, though physical woes played a part in his struggles. Kevin Ritz seemed oblivious to, or at least able to cope with, the psychological factors of pitching in the Denver launching pad and now supports Saberhagen as a sure thing in the rotation. Don Baylor was named Manager of the Year for finding ways to win—one of which was manipulating a bullpen that got more than its share of work.

The Dodgers own the Rookie of the Year award, and that should mean a reasonable degree of stability as the roster goes through a transition. Mike Piazza has become the league's best two-way catcher, and first baseman Eric Karros should finally have silenced his critics. Raul Mondesi is a star in right field and gets to stay there because Brett Butler was brought back for another season. That leaves the rest of the best from the farm system to battle for left:

Todd Hollandsworth, Billy Ashley and Roger Cedeno. Reigning Rookie of the Year Hideo Nomo anchors the pitching staff, and look for another youngster, Chan Ho Park, to join the rotation. Also, Rule V surprise Chad Fonville will be a major component of a rebuilt infield.

San Diego and San Francisco are lurking not far behind. The Padres continue to go through front-office turnover, but manager Bruce Bochy has steadily taken the on-field portion of the club through most of the changes. Steve Finley had a career year in center field last season, and with batting champ Tony Gwynn in right and Bip Roberts in left—or maybe another stint at second base—the top of the batting order is stable. If Ken Caminiti can maintain his career-best production of 1995 and regain his third-base defense, he's an All-Star. If San Diego's young pitchers attain the levels predicted for them, this team is a serious contender. Andy Ashby comes off his breakthrough season, and Joey Hamilton continues to grow. Ron Villone, acquired from Seattle in the Andy Benes deal, and Dustin Hermanson should find regular roles.

The prevailing wisdom in San Francisco is that any team with Barry Bonds and Matt Williams in the lineup all season is danger to opponents. Of course, the thought of having Deion Sanders in your lineup all season has inherent dangers for the Giants, too. The underachievers must step up for the Giants to be a threat. Second baseman Robby Thomp-son needs to shake the injuries that have gutted his production, closer Rod Beck must regain his consistency and the starting rotation needs production beyond 1995 surprise Mark Leiter. Jamie Brewington showed some signs of being ready for prime-time duty in the rotation but William Van Landingham and Terry Mulholland will be crucial to the effectiveness of the staff.

*F*inal player statistics

American League

National League

Statistics are provided by the Elias Sports Bureau.

Stats key for pitchers
T–Throws right or left; W–Wins; L–Losses; ERA–Earned run average; G–Games; GS–Games started; CG–Complete games; SHO–Shutouts; GF–Games finished in relief; SV–Saves; IP–Innings pitched; H–Hits; R–Runs; ER–Earned runs; HR–Home runs; BB–Bases on balls; SO–Strikeouts; WP–Wild pitches; BK–Balks; BA–Batting average against; HB–Hit batters; PCT–Winning percentage.

Stats key for pitchers
E–Errors; PO–Put outs; A–Assists; DP–Double plays; PCT–Fielding percentage

Stats key for batters
B–Bats right, left, or both; BA or AVG–Batting average; G–Games; AB–At-bats; R–Runs; H–Hits; TB–Total Bases; 2B–Doubles; 3B–Triples; HR–Home runs; RBI–Runs batted in; SH–Sacrifice hits; SF–Sacrifice flies; BB–Bases on balls; SO–Strikeouts; SB–Stolen bases; CS–Caught stealing; GIDP–Grounded into double play; SLG–Slugging percentage; OBA or OB–On-base average.

Players are listed alphabetically by position, within each league. Each player is listed at the position where he played the most games in 1995; statistics are for all games played in 1995.

American League starting pitchers

Name/Team	T	W	L	ERA	G	GS	CG	SHO	GF	SV	IP	H	R	ER	HR	BB	SO	WP	BK	BA
Abbott, Jim, ChiA-Cal.	L	11	8	3.70	30	30	4	1	0	0	197.0	209	93	81	14	64	86	1	0	.274
Ahearne, Pat, Det.	R	0	2	11.70	4	3	0	0	0	0	10.0	20	13	13	2	5	4	1	0	.400
Alvarez, Wilson, ChiA	L	8	11	4.32	29	29	3	0	0	0	175.0	171	96	84	21	93	118	1	2	.258
Anderson, Brian, Cal.	L	6	8	5.87	18	17	1	0	0	0	99.2	110	66	65	24	30	45	1	3	.282
Anderson, Scott, K.C.	R	1	0	5.33	6	4	0	0	0	0	25.1	29	15	15	3	8	6	0	0	.290
Andujar, Luis, ChiA	R	2	1	3.26	5	5	0	0	0	0	30.1	26	12	11	4	14	9	0	0	.230
Appier, Kevin, K.C.	R	15	10	3.89	31	31	4	1	0	0	201.1	163	90	87	14	80	185	5	0	.221
Baldwin, James, ChiA	R	0	1	12.89	6	4	0	0	0	0	14.2	32	22	21	6	9	10	1	0	.444
Belcher, Tim, Sea.	R	10	12	4.52	28	28	1	0	0	0	179.1	188	101	90	19	88	96	6	0	.269
Benes, Andy, Sea.	R	7	2	5.86	12	12	0	0	0	0	63.0	72	42	41	8	33	45	2	0	.287
Bere, Jason, ChiA	R	8	15	7.19	27	27	1	0	0	0	137.2	151	120	110	21	106	110	8	0	.277
Bergman, Sean, Det.	R	7	10	5.12	28	28	1	1	0	0	135.1	169	95	77	19	67	86	13	0	.307
Bertotti, Mike, ChiA	L	1	1	12.56	4	4	0	0	0	0	14.1	23	20	20	6	11	15	2	1	.365
Black, Bud, Cle.	L	4	2	6.85	11	10	0	0	0	0	47.1	63	42	36	8	16	34	1	1	.317
Bones, Ricky, Mil.	R	10	12	4.63	32	31	3	0	0	0	200.1	218	108	103	26	83	77	5	2	.281
Bosio, Chris, Sea.	R	10	8	4.92	31	31	0	0	0	0	170.0	211	98	93	18	69	85	10	0	.313
Boskie, Shawn, Cal.	R	7	7	5.64	20	20	1	0	0	0	111.2	127	73	70	16	25	51	4	0	.281
Brown, Kevin, Bal.	R	10	9	3.60	26	26	3	1	0	0	172.1	155	73	69	10	48	117	3	0	.241
Browning, Tom, K.C.	L	0	2	8.10	2	2	0	0	0	0	10.0	13	9	9	2	5	3	0	0	.302
Carrara, Giovanni, Tor.	R	2	4	7.21	12	7	1	0	2	0	48.2	64	46	39	10	25	27	1	0	.322
Clark, Mark, Cle.	R	9	7	5.27	22	21	2	0	0	0	124.2	143	77	73	13	42	68	8	0	.288
Clemens, Roger, Bos.	R	10	5	4.18	23	23	0	0	0	0	140.0	141	70	65	15	60	132	9	0	.259
Cone, David, Tor.-NY-A	R	18	8	3.57	30	30	6	2	0	0	229.1	195	95	91	24	88	191	11	1	.228
Darling, Ron, Oak.	R	4	7	6.23	21	21	1	0	0	0	104.0	124	79	72	16	46	69	5	0	.296
Darwin, Danny, Tor.-Tex.	R	3	10	7.45	20	15	1	0	0	0	99.0	131	87	82	25	31	58	2	0	.323
Davis, Tim, Sea.	L	2	1	6.38	5	5	0	0	0	0	24.0	30	21	17	2	18	19	0	0	.306
DeSilva, John, Bal.	R	1	0	7.27	2	2	0	0	0	0	8.2	8	7	7	3	7	1	0	0	.258
Eldred, Cal, Mil.	R	1	1	3.42	4	4	0	0	0	0	23.2	24	10	9	4	10	18	1	1	.261
Erickson, Scott, Min.-Bal.	R	13	10	4.81	32	31	7	2	1	0	196.1	213	108	105	18	67	106	3	2	.281
Eshelman, Vaughn, Bos.	L	6	3	4.85	23	14	0	0	4	0	81.2	86	47	44	3	36	41	4	0	.272
Fernandez, Alex, ChiA	R	12	8	3.80	30	30	5	2	0	0	203.2	200	98	86	19	65	159	3	0	.255
Fernandez, Sid, Bal.	L	0	4	7.39	8	7	0	0	1	0	28.0	36	26	23	9	17	31	0	0	.305
Finley, Chuck, Cal.	L	15	12	4.21	32	32	2	1	0	0	203.0	192	106	95	20	93	195	13	1	.249
Givens, Brian, Mil.	L	5	7	4.95	19	19	0	0	0	0	107.1	116	71	59	11	54	73	3	2	.275
Gordon, Tom, K.C.	R	12	12	4.43	31	31	2	0	0	0	189.0	204	110	93	12	89	119	9	0	.279
Gross, Kevin, Tex.	R	9	15	5.54	31	30	4	0	0	0	183.2	200	124	113	27	89	106	5	0	.279
Gubicza, Mark, K.C.	R	12	14	3.75	33	33	3	2	0	0	213.1	222	97	89	21	62	81	4	1	.272
Guzman, Juan, Tor.	R	4	14	6.32	24	24	3	0	0	0	135.1	151	101	95	13	73	94	8	0	.281
Haney, Chris, K.C.	L	3	4	3.65	16	13	1	0	0	0	81.1	78	35	33	7	33	31	2	0	.262
Hanson, Erik, Bos.	R	15	5	4.24	29	29	1	1	0	0	186.2	187	94	88	17	59	139	5	0	.258
Harkey, Mike, Oak.-Cal.	R	8	9	5.44	26	20	1	0	1	0	127.1	155	78	77	24	47	56	2	0	.302
Harris, Greg W., Min.	R	0	5	8.82	7	6	0	0	0	0	32.2	50	35	32	5	16	21	3	0	.355
Hawkins, LaTroy, Min.	R	2	3	8.67	6	6	1	0	0	0	27.0	39	29	26	3	12	9	1	1	.339
Haynes, Jimmy, Bal.	R	2	1	2.25	4	3	0	0	0	0	24.0	11	6	6	2	12	22	0	0	.136
Helling, Rick, Tex.	R	0	2	6.57	3	3	0	0	0	0	12.1	17	11	9	2	8	5	0	0	.340
Hentgen, Pat, Tor.	R	10	14	5.11	30	30	2	0	0	0	200.2	236	129	114	28	90	135	7	2	.290
Hershiser, Orel, Cle.	R	16	6	3.87	26	26	1	1	0	0	167.1	151	76	72	21	51	111	3	0	.244
Hill, Ken, Cle.	R	4	1	3.98	12	11	1	0	0	0	74.2	77	36	33	5	32	48	3	0	.268
Hitchcock, Sterling, NY-A	L	11	10	4.70	27	27	4	1	0	0	168.1	155	91	88	22	68	121	5	2	.245
Hurtado, Edwin, Tor.	R	5	2	5.45	14	10	1	0	0	0	77.2	81	50	47	11	40	33	11	0	.275
Jacome, Jason, K.C.	L	4	6	5.36	15	14	1	0	0	0	84.0	101	52	50	15	21	39	0	1	.300
Johns, Doug, Oak.	L	5	3	4.61	11	9	1	1	1	0	54.2	44	32	28	5	26	25	5	1	.226
Johnson, Randy, Sea.	L	5	0	3.67	14	8	0	0	2	0	61.1	48	27	25	7	24	85	1	0	.215
Johnson, Randy, Sea.	L	18	2	2.48	30	30	6	3	0	0	214.1	159	65	59	12	65	294	5	2	.201
Kamieniecki, Scott, NY-A	R	7	6	4.01	17	16	1	0	1	0	89.2	83	43	40	8	49	43	4	0	.246
Karl, Scott, Mil.	L	6	7	4.14	25	18	1	0	3	0	124.0	141	65	57	10	50	59	0	0	.288
Key, Jimmy, NY-A	L	1	2	5.64	5	5	0	0	0	0	30.1	40	20	19	3	6	14	1	0	.323
Krivda, Rick, Bal.	L	2	7	4.54	13	13	1	0	0	0	75.1	76	40	38	9	25	53	2	2	.266
Krueger, Bill, Sea.	L	2	1	5.85	6	5	0	0	1	0	20.0	37	13	13	4	4	10	1	0	.407
Langston, Mark, Cal.	L	15	7	4.63	31	31	2	0	0	0	200.1	212	109	103	21	64	142	5	1	.272
Leiter, Al, Tor.	L	11	11	3.64	28	28	2	1	0	0	183.0	162	80	74	15	108	153	14	0	.238
Lima, Jose, Det.	R	3	9	6.11	15	15	0	0	0	0	73.2	85	52	50	10	18	37	5	0	.288
Lira, Felipe, Det.	R	9	13	4.31	37	22	0	0	7	0	146.1	151	74	70	17	56	89	5	1	.271
Martinez, Dennis, Cle.	R	12	5	3.08	28	28	3	2	0	0	187.0	174	71	64	17	46	99	3	0	.247
McDonald, Ben, Bal.	R	3	6	4.16	14	13	1	0	1	0	80.0	67	40	37	10	38	62	4	2	.224
McDowell, Jack, NY-A	R	15	10	3.93	30	30	8	2	0	0	217.2	211	106	95	25	78	157	9	1	.254
Moore, Mike, Det.	R	5	15	7.53	25	25	1	0	0	0	132.2	179	118	111	24	68	64	8	0	.323
Moyer, Jamie, Bal.	L	8	5	5.21	27	18	0	0	3	0	115.2	117	70	67	18	30	65	0	0	.265
Mussina, Mike, Bal.	R	19	9	3.29	32	32	7	4	0	0	221.2	187	86	81	24	50	158	2	0	.226
Nagy, Charles, Cle.	R	16	6	4.55	29	29	2	1	0	0	178.0	194	95	90	20	61	139	2	0	.278
Nitkowski, C.J., Det.	L	1	4	7.09	11	11	0	0	0	0	39.1	53	32	31	7	20	13	1	0	.335

American League starting pitchers

Name/Team	T	W	L	ERA	G	GS	CG	SHO	GF	SV	IP	H	R	ER	HR	BB	SO	WP	BK	BA
Ogea, Chad, Cle.	R	8	3	3.05	20	14	1	0	3	0	106.1	95	38	36	11	29	57	3	1	.234
Ontiveros, Steve, Oak.	R	9	6	4.37	22	22	2	1	0	0	129.2	144	75	63	12	38	77	5	0	.283
Parra, Jose, Min.	R	1	5	7.59	12	12	0	0	0	0	61.2	83	59	52	11	22	29	3	0	.313
Pavlik, Roger, Tex.	R	10	10	4.37	31	31	2	1	0	0	191.2	174	96	93	19	90	149	10	1	.243
Perez, Melido, NY-A	R	5	5	5.58	13	12	1	0	1	0	69.1	70	46	43	10	31	44	4	0	.261
Pettitte, Andy, NY-A	L	12	9	4.17	31	26	3	0	1	0	175.0	183	86	81	15	63	114	8	1	.272
Pittsley, Jim, K.C.	R	0	0	13.50	1	1	0	0	0	0	3.1	7	5	5	3	1	0	0	0	.438
Prieto, Ariel, Oak.	R	2	6	4.97	14	9	1	0	1	0	58.0	57	35	32	4	32	37	4	1	.264
Radke, Brad, Min.	R	11	14	5.32	29	28	2	1	0	0	181.0	195	112	107	32	47	75	4	0	.275
Righetti, Dave, ChiA	L	3	2	4.20	10	9	0	0	1	0	49.1	65	24	23	6	18	29	0	0	.325
Rivera, Mariano, NY-A	R	5	3	5.51	19	10	0	0	2	0	67.0	71	43	41	11	30	51	0	1	.266
Roa, Joe, Cle.	R	0	1	6.00	1	1	0	0	0	0	6.0	9	4	4	1	2	0	0	0	.360
Rodriguez, F., Bos.-Min.	R	5	8	6.13	25	18	0	0	1	0	105.2	114	83	72	11	57	59	9	0	.277
Rogers, Kenny, Tex.	L	17	7	3.38	31	31	3	1	0	0	208.0	192	87	78	26	76	140	8	1	.243
Sanderson, Scott, Cal.	R	1	3	4.12	7	7	0	0	0	0	39.1	48	23	18	6	4	23	0	1	.298
Scanlan, Bob, Mil.	R	4	7	6.59	17	14	0	0	1	0	83.1	101	66	61	9	44	29	3	0	.304
Sele, Aaron, Bos.	R	3	1	3.06	6	6	0	0	0	0	32.1	32	14	11	3	14	21	3	0	.252
Sirotka, Mike, ChiA	L	1	2	4.19	6	6	0	0	0	0	34.1	39	16	16	2	17	19	2	0	.298
Smith, Zane, Bos.	L	8	8	5.61	24	21	0	0	0	0	110.2	144	78	69	7	23	47	0	1	.316
Sodowsky, Clint, Det.	R	2	2	5.01	6	6	0	0	0	0	23.1	24	15	13	4	18	14	1	1	.258
Sparks, Steve, Mil.	R	9	11	4.63	33	27	3	0	2	0	202.0	210	111	104	17	86	96	5	1	.274
Stewart, Dave, Oak.	R	3	7	6.89	16	16	0	0	0	0	81.0	101	65	62	11	39	58	8	1	.305
Stottlemyre, Todd, Oak.	R	14	7	4.55	31	31	2	0	0	0	209.2	228	117	106	26	80	205	11	0	.276
Tapani, Kevin, Min.	R	6	11	4.92	20	20	3	1	0	0	133.2	155	79	73	21	34	88	3	0	.290
Taylor, Scott, Tex.	R	1	2	9.39	3	3	0	0	0	0	15.1	25	16	16	6	5	10	0	0	.379
Tewksbury, Bob, Tex.	R	8	7	4.58	21	21	4	1	0	0	129.2	169	75	66	8	20	53	4	0	.319
Torres, Salomon, Sea.	R	3	8	6.00	16	13	1	0	2	0	72.0	87	53	48	12	42	45	1	2	.291
Trombley, Mike, Min.	R	4	8	5.62	20	18	0	0	0	0	97.2	107	68	61	18	42	68	4	0	.273
Wakefield, Tim, Bos.	R	16	8	2.95	27	27	6	1	0	0	195.1	163	76	64	22	68	119	11	0	.227
Ware, Jeff, Tor.	R	2	1	5.47	5	5	0	0	0	0	26.1	28	18	16	2	21	18	2	0	.277
Wells, David, Det.	L	10	3	3.04	18	18	3	0	0	0	130.1	120	54	44	17	37	83	6	1	.242
Witt, Bobby, Tex.	R	3	4	4.55	10	10	1	0	0	0	61.1	81	35	31	4	21	46	5	0	.324
Wolcott, Bob, Sea.	R	3	2	4.42	7	6	0	0	0	0	36.2	43	18	18	6	14	19	0	0	.297

American League relief pitchers

Name/Team	T	W	L	ERA	G	GS	CG	SHO	GF	SV	IP	H	R	ER	HR	BB	SO	WP	BK	BA
Acre, Mark, Oak.	R	1	2	5.71	43	0	0	0	10	0	52.0	52	35	33	7	28	47	2	1	.256
Aguilera, Rick, Min.-Bos.	R	3	3	2.60	52	0	0	0	51	32	55.1	46	16	16	6	13	52	0	0	.225
Alberro, Jose, Tex.	R	0	0	7.40	12	0	0	0	7	0	20.2	26	18	17	2	12	10	2	0	.299
Assenmacher, Paul, Cle.	L	6	2	2.82	47	0	0	0	12	0	38.1	32	13	12	3	12	40	1	0	.225
Ausanio, Joe, NY-A	R	2	0	5.73	28	0	0	0	10	1	37.2	42	24	24	9	23	36	3	0	.286
Ayala, Bobby, Sea.	R	6	5	4.44	63	0	0	0	50	19	71.0	73	42	35	9	30	77	3	0	.262
Baker, Scott, Oak.	L	0	0	9.82	1	0	0	0	0	0	3.2	5	4	4	0	5	3	0	0	.333
Bankhead, Scott, NY-A	R	1	1	6.00	20	1	0	0	8	0	39.0	44	26	26	9	16	20	1	0	.278
Bark, Brian, Bos.	L	0	0	0.00	3	0	0	0	2	0	2.1	2	0	0	0	1	0	0	0	.286
Belinda, Stan, Bos.	R	8	1	3.10	63	0	0	0	30	10	69.2	51	25	24	5	28	57	2	0	.205
Benitez, Armando, Bal.	R	1	5	5.66	44	0	0	0	18	2	47.2	37	33	30	8	37	56	3	1	.213
Bennett, Erik, Cal.	R	0	0	0.00	1	0	0	0	1	0	0.1	0	0	0	0	0	0	0	0	.000
Bielecki, Mike, Cal.	R	4	6	5.97	22	11	0	0	2	0	75.1	80	56	50	15	31	45	3	0	.273
Blomdahl, Ben, Det.	R	0	0	7.77	14	0	0	0	5	1	24.1	36	21	21	5	13	15	2	0	.356
Boehringer, Brian, NY-A	R	0	3	13.75	7	3	0	0	0	0	17.2	24	27	27	5	22	10	3	0	.320
Boever, Joe, Det.	R	5	7	6.39	60	0	0	0	27	3	98.2	128	74	70	17	44	71	1	1	.319
Bohanon, Brian, Det.	L	1	1	5.54	52	10	0	0	7	1	105.2	121	68	65	10	41	63	3	0	.285
Bolton, Rod, ChiA	R	0	2	8.18	8	3	0	0	2	0	22.0	33	23	20	4	14	10	1	0	.351
Borowski, Joe, Bal.	R	0	0	1.23	6	0	0	0	3	0	7.1	5	1	1	0	4	3	0	0	.192
Brandenburg, Mark, Tex.	R	0	1	5.93	11	0	0	0	5	0	27.1	36	18	18	5	7	21	0	1	.316
Brewer, Billy, K.C.	L	2	4	5.56	48	0	0	0	13	0	45.1	54	28	28	9	20	31	5	1	.290
Briscoe, John, Oak.	R	0	1	8.35	16	0	0	0	7	0	18.1	25	17	17	4	21	19	1	0	.347
Bronkey, Jeff, Mil.	R	0	0	3.65	8	0	0	0	4	0	12.1	15	6	5	0	6	5	1	0	.313
Bunch, Melvin, K.C.	R	1	3	5.63	13	5	0	0	3	0	40.0	42	25	25	11	14	19	6	0	.261
Burrows, Terry, Tex.	L	2	2	6.45	28	3	0	0	6	1	44.2	60	37	32	11	19	22	4	0	.323
Butcher, Mike, Cal.	R	6	1	4.73	40	0	0	0	13	0	51.1	49	28	27	7	31	29	3	0	.257
Campbell, Kevin, Min.	R	0	0	4.66	6	0	0	0	1	0	9.2	8	5	5	0	5	5	1	0	.235
Carmona, Rafael, Sea.	R	2	4	5.66	15	3	0	0	6	1	47.2	55	31	30	9	34	28	3	1	.293
Castillo, Tony J., Tor.	L	1	5	3.22	55	0	0	0	31	13	72.2	64	27	26	7	24	38	0	0	.243
Charlton, Norm, Sea.	L	2	1	1.51	30	0	0	0	22	14	47.2	23	12	8	2	16	58	5	1	.143
Christopher, Mike, Det.	R	4	0	3.82	36	0	0	0	11	1	61.1	71	28	26	8	14	34	5	0	.292
Clark, Terry, Bal.	R	2	5	3.46	38	0	0	0	12	1	39.0	40	15	15	3	15	18	1	0	.276

American League relief pitchers

Name/Team	T	W	L	ERA	G	GS	CG	SHO	GF	SV	IP	H	R	ER	HR	BB	SO	WP	BK	BA
Converse, Jim, Sea.-K.C.	R	1	3	6.56	15	1	0	0	4	1	23.1	28	17	17	2	16	14	2	0	.308
Cook, Dennis, Cle.-Tex.	L	0	2	4.53	46	1	0	0	10	2	57.2	63	32	29	9	26	53	1	0	.289
Cormier, Rheal, Bos.	L	7	5	4.07	48	12	0	0	3	0	115.0	131	60	52	12	31	69	4	0	.294
Cornett, Brad, Tor.	R	0	0	9.00	5	0	0	0	2	0	5.0	9	6	5	1	3	4	1	0	.429
Corsi, Jim, Oak.	R	2	4	2.20	38	0	0	0	7	2	45.0	31	14	11	2	26	26	0	0	.203
Cox, Danny, Tor.	R	1	3	7.40	24	0	0	0	7	0	45.0	57	40	37	4	33	38	7	0	.317
Crabtree, Tim, Tor.	R	0	2	3.09	31	0	0	0	19	0	32.0	30	16	11	1	13	21	2	0	.240
Cummings, John, Sea.	L	0	0	11.81	4	0	0	0	0	0	5.1	8	8	7	0	7	4	4	1	.400
Davison, Scott, Sea.	R	0	0	6.23	3	0	0	0	3	0	4.1	7	3	3	1	1	3	0	0	.350
Dedrick, Jim, Bal.	R	0	0	2.35	6	0	0	0	1	0	7.2	8	2	2	1	6	3	0	0	.308
DeLeon, Jose, ChiA	R	5	3	5.19	38	0	0	0	4	0	67.2	60	41	39	10	28	53	2	1	.238
Dettmer, John, Tex.	R	0	0	27.00	1	0	0	0	0	0	0.1	2	1	1	0	0	0	0	0	.667
Dibble, Rob, ChiA-Mil.	R	1	2	7.18	31	0	0	0	8	1	26.1	16	21	21	2	46	26	8	0	.188
Doherty, John, Det.	R	5	9	5.10	48	2	0	0	18	6	113.0	130	66	64	10	37	46	0	0	.288
Eckersley, Dennis, Oak.	R	4	6	4.83	52	0	0	0	48	29	50.1	53	29	27	5	11	40	0	0	.269
Eddy, Chris, Oak.	L	0	0	7.36	6	0	0	0	0	0	3.2	7	3	3	0	2	2	1	0	.438
Edenfield, Ken, Cal.	R	0	0	4.26	7	0	0	0	3	0	12.2	15	7	6	1	5	6	3	0	.300
Eiland, Dave, NY-A	R	1	1	6.30	4	1	0	0	1	0	10.0	16	10	7	1	3	6	1	0	.348
Embree, Alan, Cle.	L	3	2	5.11	23	0	0	0	8	1	24.2	23	16	14	2	16	23	1	0	.253
Fajardo, Hector, Tex.	R	0	0	7.80	5	0	0	0	1	0	15.0	19	13	13	2	5	9	3	0	.311
Farrell, John E., Cle.	R	0	0	3.86	1	0	0	0	0	0	4.2	7	4	2	0	4	0	0	0	.368
Fermin, Ramon, Oak.	R	0	0	13.50	1	0	0	0	1	0	1.1	4	2	2	0	1	0	1	0	.500
Fetters, Mike, Mil.	R	0	3	3.38	40	0	0	0	34	22	34.2	40	16	13	3	20	33	5	0	.286
Fleming, Dave, Sea.-K.C.	L	1	6	5.96	25	12	1	0	3	0	80.0	84	61	53	19	53	40	5	0	.269
Fortugno, Tim, ChiA	L	1	3	5.59	37	0	0	0	11	0	38.2	30	24	24	7	19	24	5	3	.213
Frey, Steve, Sea.	L	0	3	4.76	13	0	0	0	3	0	11.1	16	7	6	0	6	7	0	0	.356
Gardiner, Mike, Det.	R	0	0	14.59	9	0	0	0	1	0	12.1	27	20	20	5	2	7	1	0	.458
Gohr, Greg, Det.	R	1	0	0.87	10	0	0	0	1	0	10.1	9	1	1	0	3	12	1	0	.243
Grimsley, Jason, Cle.	R	0	0	6.09	15	2	0	0	2	1	34.0	37	24	23	4	32	25	7	0	.289
Groom, Buddy, Det.	L	1	3	7.52	23	4	0	0	6	1	40.2	55	35	34	6	26	23	3	0	.322
Guardado, Eddie, Min.	L	4	9	5.12	51	5	0	0	10	2	91.1	99	54	52	13	45	71	5	1	.280
Guetterman, Lee, Sea.	L	0	0	6.88	23	0	0	0	3	1	17.0	21	13	13	1	11	11	0	0	.300
Gunderson, Eric, Bos.	L	2	1	5.11	19	0	0	0	1	0	12.1	13	7	7	0	9	9	0	0	.295
Guthrie, Mark, Min.	L	5	3	4.46	36	0	0	0	7	0	42.1	47	22	21	5	16	48	3	1	.290
Habyan, John, Cal.	R	1	2	4.13	28	0	0	0	7	0	32.2	36	16	15	2	12	25	2	0	.279
Hall, Darren, Tor.	R	0	2	4.41	17	0	0	0	11	3	16.1	21	9	8	2	9	11	0	0	.309
Hammaker, Atlee, ChiA	L	0	0	12.79	13	0	0	0	2	0	6.1	11	9	9	2	8	3	0	0	.393
Harikkala, Tim, Sea.	R	0	0	16.20	1	0	0	0	1	0	3.1	7	6	6	1	1	1	0	0	.412
Harris, Gene, Bal.	R	0	0	4.50	3	0	0	0	0	0	4.0	4	2	2	0	1	4	2	0	.267
Hartley, Mike, Bos.-Bal.	R	1	0	5.14	8	0	0	0	2	0	14.0	13	8	8	1	3	6	0	0	.265
Henneman, Mike, Det.	R	0	1	1.53	29	0	0	0	26	18	29.1	24	5	5	0	9	24	2	0	.222
Henry, Dwayne, Det.	R	1	0	6.23	10	0	0	0	6	5	8.2	11	6	6	0	10	9	1	0	.306
Heredia, Wilson, Tex.	R	0	1	3.75	6	0	0	0	0	0	12.0	9	5	5	2	15	6	0	0	.225
Hemandez, Roberto, ChiA	R	3	7	3.92	60	0	0	0	57	32	59.2	63	30	26	9	28	84	1	0	.266
Holzemer, Mark, Cal.	L	0	0	5.40	12	0	0	0	5	0	8.1	11	6	5	1	7	5	0	0	.306
Honeycutt, R., Oak.-NY-A	L	5	1	2.96	52	0	0	0	6	2	45.2	39	16	15	6	10	21	0	0	.236
Horsman, Vince, Min.	L	0	0	7.00	6	0	0	0	3	0	9.0	12	8	7	2	4	4	0	0	.333
Howard, Chris, Tex.	L	0	0	0.00	4	0	0	0	1	0	4.0	3	0	0	0	1	2	1	0	.231
Howe, Steve, NY-A	L	6	3	4.96	56	0	0	0	20	2	49.0	66	29	27	7	17	28	1	0	.324
Hudson, Joe, Bos.	R	0	1	4.11	39	0	0	0	11	1	46.0	53	21	21	2	23	29	6	0	.301
Huisman, Rick, K.C.	R	0	0	7.45	7	0	0	0	2	0	9.2	14	8	8	2	1	12	0	0	.333
Ignasiak, Mike, Mil.	R	4	1	5.90	25	0	0	0	2	0	39.2	51	27	26	5	23	26	1	0	.325
James, Mike, Cal.	R	3	0	3.88	46	0	0	0	11	1	55.2	49	27	24	6	26	36	1	0	.238
Johnston, Joel, Bos.	R	0	1	11.25	4	0	0	0	0	0	4.0	2	5	5	1	3	4	0	0	.143
Jones, Doug, Bal.	R	0	4	5.01	52	0	0	0	47	22	46.2	55	30	26	6	16	42	0	0	.286
Jordan, Ricardo, Tor.	L	1	0	6.60	15	0	0	0	3	1	15.0	18	11	11	3	13	10	1	0	.305
Karchner, Matt, ChiA	R	4	2	1.69	31	0	0	0	10	0	32.0	33	8	6	2	12	24	1	0	.275
Keyser, Brian, ChiA	R	5	6	4.97	23	10	0	0	0	0	92.1	114	53	51	10	27	48	1	1	.306
Kiefer, Mark, Mil.	R	4	1	3.44	24	0	0	0	7	0	49.2	37	20	19	6	27	41	4	0	.203
King, Kevin, Sea.	L	0	0	12.27	2	0	0	0	0	0	3.2	7	5	5	0	1	3	1	0	.412
Klingenbeck, S., Bal.-Min.	R	2	4	7.12	24	9	0	0	4	0	79.2	101	65	63	22	42	42	7	0	.314
Lee, Mark O., Bal.	L	2	1	4.86	39	0	0	0	7	1	33.1	31	18	18	5	18	27	0	0	.246
Leiper, Dave, Oak.	L	1	1	3.57	24	0	0	0	3	0	22.2	23	10	9	3	13	10	0	0	.258
Lilliquist, Derek, Bos.	L	2	1	6.26	28	0	0	0	6	0	23.0	27	17	16	7	9	9	1	0	.303
Linton, Doug, K.C.	R	0	0	7.25	7	2	0	0	0	0	22.1	22	21	18	4	10	13	0	0	.256
Lloyd, Graeme, Mil.	L	0	5	4.50	33	0	0	0	14	4	32.0	28	16	16	4	8	13	3	0	.246
Looney, Brian, Bos.	L	0	1	17.36	3	1	0	0	0	0	4.2	12	9	9	1	4	2	0	0	.545
Lopez, Albie, Cle.	R	0	0	3.13	6	2	0	0	0	0	23.0	17	8	8	4	7	22	2	0	.205
Lorraine, Andrew, ChiA	L	0	0	3.38	5	0	0	0	2	0	8.0	3	3	3	0	2	5	0	0	.111
MacDonald, Bob, NY-A	L	1	1	4.86	33	0	0	0	5	0	46.1	50	25	25	7	22	41	1	0	.282

American League relief pitchers

Name/Team	T	W	L	ERA	G	GS	CG	SHO	GF	SV	IP	H	R	ER	HR	BB	SO	WP	BK	BA
Maddux, Mike, Bos.	R	4	1	3.61	36	4	0	0	6	1	89.2	86	40	36	5	15	65	5	0	.247
Magnante, Mike, K.C.	L	1	1	4.23	28	0	0	0	7	0	44.2	45	23	21	6	16	28	2	0	.268
Mahomes, Pat, Min.	R	4	10	6.37	47	7	0	0	16	3	94.2	100	74	67	22	47	67	6	0	.271
Manzanillo, Josias, NY-A	R	0	0	2.08	11	0	0	0	4	0	17.1	19	4	4	1	9	11	1	0	.279
Marquez, Isidro, ChiA	R	0	1	6.75	7	0	0	0	2	0	6.2	9	5	5	3	2	8	0	0	.321
Maxcy, Brian, Det.	R	4	5	6.88	41	0	0	0	14	0	52.1	61	48	40	6	31	20	6	2	.293
McAndrew, Jamie, Mil.	R	2	3	4.71	10	4	0	0	2	0	36.1	37	21	19	2	12	19	0	0	.266
McCaskill, Kirk, ChiA	R	4	4	4.89	55	1	0	0	17	2	81.0	97	50	44	10	33	50	10	0	.302
McDowell, Roger, Tex.	R	7	4	4.02	64	0	0	0	26	4	85.0	86	39	38	5	34	49	1	1	.277
Meacham, Rusty, K.C.	R	4	3	4.98	49	0	0	0	26	2	59.2	72	36	33	6	19	30	0	0	.304
Mecir, Jim, Sea.	R	0	0	0.00	2	0	0	0	1	0	4.2	5	1	0	0	2	3	0	0	.263
Menhart, Paul, Tor.	R	1	4	4.92	21	9	1	0	6	0	78.2	72	49	43	9	47	50	6	0	.248
Mercedes, Jose, Mil.	R	0	1	9.82	5	0	0	0	0	0	7.1	12	9	8	1	8	6	1	0	.375
Mesa, Jose, Cle.	R	3	0	1.13	62	0	0	0	57	46	64.0	49	9	8	3	17	58	5	0	.216
Mills, Alan, Bal.	R	3	0	7.43	21	0	0	0	1	0	23.0	30	20	19	4	18	16	1	0	.309
Miranda, Angel, Mil.	L	4	5	5.23	30	10	0	0	5	1	74.0	83	47	43	8	49	45	5	1	.291
Mohler, Mike, Oak.	L	1	1	3.04	28	0	0	0	6	1	23.2	16	8	8	0	18	15	1	0	.198
Monteleone, Rich, Cal.	R	1	0	2.00	9	0	0	0	2	0	9.0	8	2	2	1	3	5	0	0	.267
Montgomery, Jeff, K.C.	R	2	3	3.43	54	0	0	0	46	31	65.2	60	27	25	7	25	49	1	1	.252
Munoz, Oscar, Min.	R	2	1	5.60	10	3	0	0	4	0	35.1	40	28	22	6	17	25	0	0	.276
Murray, Matt, Bos.	R	0	1	18.90	2	1	0	0	0	0	3.1	11	10	7	1	3	1	0	0	.524
Myers, Mike, Det.	L	1	0	9.95	11	0	0	0	3	0	6.1	10	7	7	1	4	4	0	0	.385
Nelson, Jeff, Sea.	R	7	3	2.17	62	0	0	0	24	2	78.2	58	21	19	4	27	96	1	0	.209
Nichting, Chris, Tex.	R	0	0	7.03	13	0	0	0	3	0	24.1	36	19	19	1	13	6	3	0	.343
Oliver, Darren, Tex.	L	4	2	4.22	17	7	0	0	2	0	49.0	47	25	23	3	32	39	4	0	.257
Olson, Gregg, Cle.-K.C.	R	3	3	4.09	23	0	0	0	12	3	33.0	28	15	15	4	19	21	1	0	.235
Oquist, Mike, Bal.	R	2	1	4.17	27	0	0	0	2	0	54.0	51	27	25	6	41	27	2	0	.246
Orosco, Jesse, Bal.	L	2	4	3.26	65	0	0	0	23	3	49.2	28	19	18	4	27	58	2	1	.169
Patterson, Jeff, NY-A	R	0	0	2.70	3	0	0	0	3	0	3.1	3	1	1	1	3	3	0	0	.231
Patterson, Bob, Cal.	L	5	2	3.04	62	0	0	0	20	0	53.1	48	18	18	6	13	41	0	1	.246
Pavlas, Dave, NY-A	R	0	0	3.18	4	0	0	0	1	0	5.2	8	2	2	0	0	3	0	0	.333
Pena, Alejandro, Bos.	R	1	1	7.40	17	0	0	0	5	0	24.1	33	23	20	5	12	25	0	0	.314
Pennington, Brad, Bal.	L	0	1	8.10	8	0	0	0	2	0	6.2	3	7	6	1	11	10	1	0	.136
Percival, Troy, Cal.	R	3	2	1.95	62	0	0	0	16	3	74.0	37	19	16	6	26	94	2	2	.147
Phoenix, Steve, Oak.	R	0	0	32.40	1	0	0	0	0	0	1.2	3	6	6	1	3	3	0	0	.429
Pichardo, Hipolito, K.C.	R	8	4	4.36	44	0	0	0	16	1	64.0	66	34	31	4	30	43	4	1	.265
Pierce, Jeff, Bos.	R	0	3	6.60	12	0	0	0	2	0	15.0	16	12	11	0	14	12	0	0	.286
Plunk, Eric, Cle.	R	6	2	2.67	56	0	0	0	22	2	64.0	48	19	19	5	27	71	3	0	.211
Poole, Jim Ri., Cle.	L	3	3	3.75	42	0	0	0	9	0	50.1	40	22	21	7	17	41	2	1	.217
Radinsky, Scott, ChiA	L	2	1	5.45	46	0	0	0	10	1	38.0	46	23	23	7	17	14	0	0	.309
Rasmussen, Dennis, K.C.	L	0	1	9.00	5	1	0	0	1	0	10.0	13	10	10	3	8	6	2	0	.302
Reyes, Carlos, Oak.	R	4	6	5.09	40	1	0	0	19	0	69.0	71	43	39	10	28	48	5	0	.264
Reyes, Al, Mil.	R	1	1	2.43	27	0	0	0	13	1	33.1	19	9	9	3	18	29	0	0	.167
Rhodes, Arthur, Bal.	L	2	5	6.21	19	9	0	0	3	0	75.1	68	53	52	13	48	77	3	1	.239
Rightnowar, Ron, Mil.	R	2	1	5.40	34	0	0	0	13	1	36.2	35	23	22	3	18	22	1	0	.271
Risley, Bill, Sea.	R	2	1	3.13	45	0	0	0	5	1	60.1	55	21	21	7	18	65	2	0	.244
Roberson, Sid, Mil.	L	6	4	5.76	26	13	0	0	8	0	84.1	102	55	54	16	37	40	3	0	.307
Robertson, Rich, Min.	L	2	0	3.83	25	4	1	0	8	0	51.2	48	28	22	4	31	38	0	1	.253
Robinson, Ken, Tor.	R	1	2	3.69	21	0	0	0	9	0	39.0	25	21	16	7	22	31	1	0	.179
Rogers, Jimmy, Tor.	R	2	4	5.70	19	0	0	0	9	0	23.2	21	15	15	4	18	13	0	0	.239
Ruffcorn, Scott, ChiA	R	0	0	7.88	4	0	0	0	0	0	8.0	10	7	7	0	13	5	0	0	.333
Russell, Jeff, Tex.	R	1	0	3.03	37	0	0	0	32	20	32.2	36	12	11	3	9	21	1	0	.277
Ryan, Ken, Bos.	R	0	4	4.96	28	0	0	0	20	7	32.2	34	20	18	4	24	34	1	0	.268
Sanford, Mo, Min.	R	0	0	5.30	11	0	0	0	6	0	18.2	16	11	11	7	16	17	1	0	.225
Schullstrom, Erik, Min.	R	0	0	6.89	37	0	0	0	16	0	47.0	66	36	36	8	22	21	5	0	.332
Shaw, Jeff, ChiA	R	0	0	6.52	9	0	0	0	1	0	9.2	12	7	7	2	1	6	0	0	.316
Shepherd, Keith, Bos.	R	0	0	36.00	2	0	0	0	0	0	1.0	4	4	4	0	2	0	0	0	.571
Shuey, Paul, Cle.	R	0	2	4.26	7	0	0	0	3	0	6.1	5	4	3	0	5	5	1	0	.238
Simas, Bill, ChiA	R	1	1	2.57	14	0	0	0	4	0	14.0	15	5	4	1	10	16	1	0	.273
Slusarski, Joe, Mil.	R	1	1	5.40	12	0	0	0	6	0	15.0	21	11	9	3	6	6	0	0	.333
Smith, Lee, Cal.	R	0	5	3.47	52	0	0	0	51	37	49.1	42	19	19	3	25	43	1	0	.237
Springer, Russ, Cal.	R	1	2	6.10	19	6	0	0	3	1	51.2	60	37	35	11	25	38	1	0	.290
Stanton, Mike, Bos.	L	1	0	3.00	22	0	0	0	12	0	21.0	17	9	7	3	8	10	1	0	.224
Stevens, Dave, Min.	R	5	4	5.07	56	0	0	0	34	10	65.2	74	40	37	14	32	47	2	0	.285
Suppan, Jeff, Bos.	R	1	2	5.96	8	3	0	0	1	0	22.2	29	15	15	4	5	19	0	0	.312
Tavarez, Julian, Cle.	R	10	2	2.44	57	0	0	0	15	0	85.0	76	36	23	7	21	68	3	2	.235
Thomas, Larry, ChiA	L	0	0	1.32	17	0	0	0	5	0	13.2	8	2	2	1	6	12	1	0	.167
Thomas, Mike, Mil.	L	0	0	0.00	1	0	0	0	0	0	1.1	2	0	0	0	1	0	0	0	.333
Timlin, Mike, Tor.	R	4	3	2.14	31	0	0	0	19	5	42.0	38	13	10	1	17	36	3	1	.242
Torres, Dilson, K.C.	R	1	2	6.09	24	2	0	0	7	0	44.1	56	30	30	6	17	28	1	0	.311

American League relief pitchers

Name/Team	T	W	L	ERA	G	GS	CG	SHO	GF	SV	IP	H	R	ER	HR	BB	SO	WP	BK	BA
VanEgmond, Tim, Bos.	R	0	1	9.45	4	1	0	0	1	0	6.2	9	7	7	2	6	5	1	0	.310
Van Poppel, Todd, Oak.	R	4	8	4.88	36	14	1	0	10	0	138.1	125	77	75	16	56	122	4	0	.244
Villone, Ron, Sea.	L	0	2	7.91	19	0	0	0	7	0	19.1	20	19	17	6	23	26	1	0	.270
Vosberg, Ed, Tex.	L	5	5	3.00	44	0	0	0	20	4	36.0	32	15	12	3	16	36	3	2	.241
Ward, Duane, Tor.	R	0	1	27.00	4	0	0	0	0	0	2.2	11	10	8	0	5	3	2	0	.579
Wasdin, John, Oak.	R	1	1	4.67	5	2	0	0	3	0	17.1	14	9	9	4	3	6	0	0	.215
Watkins, Scott, Min.	L	0	0	5.40	27	0	0	0	7	0	21.2	22	14	13	2	11	11	0	0	.278
Wegman, Bill, Mil.	R	5	7	5.35	37	4	0	0	17	2	70.2	89	45	42	14	21	50	1	0	.312
Wells, Bob, Sea.	R	4	3	5.75	30	4	0	0	3	0	76.2	88	51	49	11	39	38	1	0	.284
Wengert, Don, Oak.	R	1	1	3.34	19	0	0	0	10	0	29.2	30	14	11	3	12	16	1	0	.263
Wetteland, John, NY-A	R	1	5	2.93	60	0	0	0	56	31	61.1	40	22	20	6	14	66	1	0	.185
Whiteside, Sean, Det.	L	0	0	14.73	2	0	0	0	0	0	3.2	7	6	6	1	4	2	1	0	.438
Whiteside, Matt, Tex.	R	5	4	4.08	40	0	0	0	18	3	53.0	48	24	24	5	19	46	4	0	.242
Wickander, K., Det.-Mil.	L	0	0	1.93	29	0	0	0	9	1	23.1	19	6	5	1	12	11	1	1	.229
Wickman, Bob, NY-A	R	2	4	4.05	63	1	0	0	14	1	80.0	77	38	36	6	33	51	2	0	.253
Williams, Woody, Tor.	R	1	2	3.69	23	3	0	0	10	0	53.2	44	23	22	6	28	41	0	0	.220
Williams, Mitch, Cal.	L	1	2	6.75	20	0	0	0	3	0	10.2	13	10	8	1	21	9	2	1	.317
Willis, Carl, Min.	R	0	0	94.50	3	0	0	0	0	0	0.2	5	7	7	0	5	0	0	0	.833
Wojciechowski, S., Oak.	L	2	3	5.18	14	7	0	0	3	0	48.2	51	28	28	7	28	13	0	0	.273

American League starting pitchers (batting)

Name/Team	B	BA	G	AB	R	H	TB	2B	3B	HR	RBI	SH	SF	BB	SO	SB	CS	GIDP	SLG	OBA
Stottlemyre, Todd, Oak.	L	.000	31	1	0	0	0	0	0	0	0	0	0	0	1	0	0	0	.000	.000
Tewksbury, Bob, Tex.	R	.000	22	1	0	0	0	0	0	0	0	0	0	0	1	0	0	0	.000	.000

American League relief pitchers (batting)

Name/Team	B	BA	G	AB	R	H	TB	2B	3B	HR	RBI	SH	SF	BB	SO	SB	CS	GIDP	SLG	OBA
Pichardo, Hipolito, K.C.	R	.000	44	2	0	0	0	0	0	0	0	0	0	0	0	0	0	0	.000	.000

American League catchers

Name/Team	B	BA	G	AB	R	H	TB	2B	3B	HR	RBI	SH	SF	BB	SO	SB	CS	GIDP	SLG	OBA
Allanson, Andy, Cal.	R	.171	35	82	5	14	26	3	0	3	10	1	0	7	12	0	1	0	.317	.244
Alomar, Sandy Jr., Cle.	R	.300	66	203	32	61	97	6	0	10	35	4	1	7	26	3	1	8	.478	.332
Borders, Pat, K.C.	R	.231	52	143	14	33	55	8	1	4	13	0	0	7	22	0	0	1	.385	.267
Dalesandro, Mark, Cal.	R	.100	11	10	1	1	2	1	0	0	0	0	0	0	2	0	0	0	.200	.100
Devarez, Cesar, Bal.	R	.000	6	4	0	0	0	0	0	0	0	1	0	0	0	0	0	0	.000	.000
Fabregas, Jorge, Cal.	L	.247	73	227	24	56	69	10	0	1	22	3	1	17	28	0	2	9	.304	.298
Flaherty, John, Det.	R	.243	112	354	39	86	143	22	1	11	40	8	2	18	47	0	0	8	.404	.284
Harper, Brian, Oak.	R	.000	2	7	0	0	0	0	0	0	0	0	0	0	1	0	0	0	.000	.000
Haselman, Bill, Bos.	R	.243	64	152	22	37	60	6	1	5	23	0	3	17	30	0	2	4	.395	.322
Hatteberg, Scott, Bos.	L	.500	2	2	1	1	1	0	0	0	0	0	0	0	0	0	0	0	.500	.500
Helfand, Eric, Oak.	L	.163	38	86	9	14	18	2	1	0	7	3	0	11	25	0	0	2	.209	.265
Hoiles, Chris, Bal.	R	.250	114	352	53	88	162	15	1	19	58	0	3	67	80	1	0	11	.460	.373
Karkovice, Ron, ChiA	R	.217	113	323	44	70	125	14	1	13	51	9	6	39	84	2	3	5	.387	.306
Knorr, Randy, Tor.	R	.212	45	132	18	28	45	8	0	3	16	1	0	11	28	0	0	5	.341	.273
Kreuter, Chad, Sea.	B	.227	26	75	12	17	25	5	0	1	8	1	0	5	22	0	0	0	.333	.293
LaValliere, Mike, ChiA	L	.245	46	98	7	24	33	6	0	1	19	0	2	9	15	0	0	3	.337	.303
Levis, Jesse, Cle.	L	.333	12	18	1	6	8	2	0	0	3	1	2	1	0	0	0	1	.444	.333
Leyritz, Jim, NY-A	R	.269	77	264	37	71	104	12	0	7	37	0	1	37	73	1	1	4	.394	.374
Lyons, Barry, ChiA	R	.266	27	64	8	17	34	2	0	5	16	1	1	4	14	0	0	0	.531	.304
Macfarlane, Mike, Bos.	R	.225	115	364	45	82	147	18	1	15	51	0	4	38	78	2	1	9	.404	.319
Martinez, Sandy, Tor.	L	.241	62	191	12	46	64	12	0	2	25	0	1	7	45	0	0	1	.335	.270
Marzano, John, Tex.	R	.333	2	6	1	2	2	0	0	0	0	0	0	0	0	0	0	0	.333	.333
Matheny, Mike, Mil.	R	.247	80	166	13	41	52	9	1	0	21	1	0	12	28	2	1	3	.313	.306
Mayne, Brent, K.C.	L	.251	110	307	23	77	100	18	1	1	27	11	1	25	41	0	1	16	.326	.313
Mercedes, Henry, K.C.	R	.256	23	43	7	11	13	2	0	0	9	1	2	8	13	0	0	0	.302	.370
Merullo, Matt, Min.	L	.282	76	195	19	55	74	14	1	1	27	1	3	14	27	0	1	5	.379	.335
Myers, Greg, Cal.	L	.260	85	273	35	71	114	12	2	9	38	1	2	17	49	0	1	4	.418	.304
Nokes, Matt, Bal.	L	.122	26	49	4	6	13	1	0	2	6	0	1	4	11	0	0	2	.265	.185
Oliver, Joe, Mil.	R	.273	97	337	43	92	148	20	0	12	51	2	0	27	66	2	4	11	.439	.332
Parrish, Lance, Tor.	R	.202	70	178	15	36	57	9	0	4	22	6	2	15	52	0	0	4	.320	.265
Pena, Tony, Cle.	R	.262	91	263	25	69	99	15	0	5	28	1	0	14	44	1	0	9	.376	.302
Rodriguez, Ivan, Tex.	R	.303	130	492	56	149	221	32	2	12	67	0	5	16	48	0	2	11	.449	.327
Rowland, Rich, Bos.	R	.172	14	29	1	5	6	1	0	0	1	0	0	0	11	0	0	0	.207	.172

American League catchers

Name/Team	B	BA	G	AB	R	H	TB	2B	3B	HR	RBI	SH	SF	BB	SO	SB	CS	GIDP	SLG	OBA
Stanley, Mike, NY-A	R	.268	118	399	63	107	192	29	1	18	83	0	9	57	106	1	1	14	.481	.360
Steinbach, Terry, Oak.	R	.278	114	406	43	113	186	26	1	15	65	1	4	25	74	1	3	15	.458	.322
Sweeney, Mike, K.C.	R	.250	4	4	1	1	1	0	0	0	0	0	0	0	0	0	0	0	.250	.250
Tingley, Ron, Det.	R	.226	54	124	14	28	50	8	1	4	18	5	1	15	38	0	1	1	.403	.307
Tremie, Chris, ChiA	R	.167	10	24	0	4	4	0	0	0	0	1	0	1	2	0	0	0	.167	.200
Tucker, Scooter, Cle.	R	.000	17	20	2	0	0	0	0	0	0	1	0	5	4	0	0	0	.000	.231
Turner, Chris, Cal.	R	.100	5	10	0	1	1	0	0	0	1	0	0	0	3	0	0	0	.100	.100
Valle, Dave, Tex.	R	.240	36	75	7	18	21	3	0	0	5	1	0	6	18	1	0	2	.280	.305
Walbeck, Matt, Min.	B	.257	115	393	40	101	124	18	1	1	44	1	2	25	71	3	1	11	.316	.302
Widger, Chris, Sea.	R	.200	23	45	2	9	12	0	0	1	2	0	1	3	11	0	0	0	.267	.245
Williams, George, Oak.	B	.291	29	79	13	23	39	5	1	3	14	0	2	11	21	0	0	1	.494	.383
Wilson, Dan, Sea.	R	.278	119	399	40	111	166	22	3	9	51	5	1	33	63	2	1	12	.416	.336
Zaun, Greg, Bal.	B	.260	40	104	18	27	41	5	0	3	14	2	0	16	14	1	1	2	.394	.358

American League first basemen

Name/Team	B	BA	G	AB	R	H	TB	2B	3B	HR	RBI	SH	SF	BB	SO	SB	CS	GIDP	SLG	OBA
Aldrete, Mike, Oak.-Cal.	L	.268	78	149	19	40	60	8	0	4	24	0	3	19	31	0	0	4	.403	.349
Clark, Tony, Det.	B	.238	27	101	10	24	40	5	1	3	11	0	0	8	30	0	0	2	.396	.294
Clark, Will, Tex.	L	.302	123	454	85	137	218	27	3	16	92	0	11	68	50	0	1	7	.480	.389
Coomer, Ron, Min.	R	.257	37	101	15	26	46	3	1	5	19	0	0	9	11	0	1	9	.455	.324
Dunn, Steve, Min.	L	.000	5	6	0	0	0	0	0	0	0	0	0	1	3	0	0	0	.000	.143
Fielder, Cecil, Det.	R	.243	136	494	70	120	233	18	1	31	82	0	4	75	116	0	1	17	.472	.346
Jaha, John, Mil.	R	.313	88	316	59	99	183	20	2	20	65	0	1	36	66	2	1	8	.579	.389
Joyner, Wally, K.C.	L	.310	131	465	69	144	208	28	0	12	83	5	9	69	65	3	2	10	.447	.394
Martinez, Tino, Sea.	L	.293	141	519	92	152	286	35	3	31	111	2	6	62	91	0	0	10	.551	.369
Martinez, Dave, ChiA	L	.307	119	303	49	93	132	16	4	5	37	9	4	32	41	8	2	6	.436	.371
Masteller, Dan, Min.	L	.237	71	198	21	47	68	12	0	3	21	1	1	18	19	1	2	7	.343	.303
Mattingly, Don, NY-A	L	.288	128	458	59	132	189	32	2	7	49	0	8	40	35	0	2	17	.413	.341
McCarty, David, Min.	R	.218	25	55	10	12	17	3	1	0	4	0	1	4	18	0	1	1	.309	.279
McGinnis, Russ, K.C.	R	.000	3	5	1	0	0	0	0	0	0	0	0	1	1	0	0	0	.000	.167
McGwire, Mark, Oak.	R	.274	104	317	75	87	217	13	0	39	90	0	6	88	77	1	1	9	.685	.441
Olerud, John, Tor.	L	.291	135	492	72	143	199	32	0	8	54	0	1	84	54	0	0	17	.404	.398
Palmeiro, Rafael, Bal.	L	.310	143	554	89	172	323	30	2	39	104	0	5	62	65	3	1	12	.583	.380
Perry, Herbert, Cle.	R	.315	52	162	23	51	75	13	1	3	23	3	2	13	28	1	3	5	.463	.376
Pirkl, Greg, Sea.	R	.235	10	17	2	4	4	0	0	0	0	0	0	1	7	0	0	0	.235	.278
Samuel, Juan, Det.-K.C.	R	.263	91	205	31	54	102	10	1	12	39	1	0	29	49	6	4	3	.498	.360
Snow, J.T., Cal.	B	.289	143	544	80	157	253	22	1	24	102	5	2	52	91	2	1	16	.465	.353
Sorrento, Paul, Cle.	L	.235	104	323	50	76	165	14	0	25	79	0	4	51	71	1	1	10	.511	.336
Stahoviak, Scott, Min.	L	.266	94	263	28	70	98	19	0	3	23	0	2	30	61	5	1	3	.373	.341
Stubbs, Franklin, Det.	L	.250	62	116	13	29	46	11	0	2	19	0	1	19	27	0	1	3	.397	.358
Surhoff, B.J., Mil.	L	.320	117	415	72	133	204	26	3	13	73	2	4	37	43	7	3	7	.492	.378
Thomas, Frank E., ChiA	R	.308	145	493	102	152	299	27	0	40	111	0	12	136	74	3	2	14	.606	.454
Unroe, Tim, Mil.	R	.250	2	4	0	1	1	0	0	0	0	0	0	0	0	0	0	0	.250	.250
Vaughn, Mo, Bos.	L	.300	140	550	98	165	316	28	3	39	126	0	4	68	150	11	4	17	.575	.388
White, Derrick, Det.	R	.188	39	48	3	9	11	2	0	0	2	0	0	0	7	1	0	1	.229	.188

American League second basemen

Name/Team	B	BA	G	AB	R	H	TB	2B	3B	HR	RBI	SH	SF	BB	SO	SB	CS	GIDP	SLG	OBA
Alexander, Manny, Bal.	R	.236	94	242	35	57	77	9	1	3	23	4	0	20	30	11	4	2	.318	.299
Alicea, Luis, Bos.	B	.270	132	419	64	113	157	20	3	6	44	13	9	63	61	13	10	10	.375	.367
Alomar, Roberto, Tor.	B	.300	130	517	71	155	232	24	7	13	66	6	7	47	45	30	3	16	.449	.354
Baerga, Carlos, Cle.	B	.314	135	557	87	175	252	28	2	15	90	0	5	35	31	11	2	15	.452	.355
Barberie, Bret, Bal.	B	.241	90	237	32	57	77	14	0	2	25	6	3	36	50	3	3	6	.325	.351
Brady, Doug, ChiA	B	.190	12	21	4	4	5	1	0	0	3	0	0	2	4	0	1	1	.238	.261
Caceres, Edgar, K.C.	B	.239	55	117	13	28	41	6	2	1	17	3	1	8	15	2	2	3	.350	.291
Cora, Joey, Sea.	B	.297	120	427	64	127	159	19	2	3	39	13	4	37	31	18	7	8	.372	.359
Durham, Ray, ChiA	B	.257	125	471	68	121	181	27	6	7	51	5	4	31	83	18	5	8	.384	.309
Easley, Damion, Cal.	R	.216	114	357	35	77	107	14	2	4	35	4	4	32	47	5	2	11	.300	.288
Eenhoorn, Robert, NY-A	R	.143	5	14	1	2	3	1	0	0	2	0	0	1	3	0	0	1	.214	.200
Espinoza, Alvaro, Cle.	R	.252	66	143	15	36	46	4	0	2	17	2	2	2	16	0	2	3	.322	.264
Fletcher, Scott, Det.	R	.231	67	182	19	42	57	10	1	1	17	4	1	19	27	1	0	2	.313	.312
Frye, Jeff, Tex.	R	.278	90	313	38	87	118	15	2	4	29	8	4	24	45	3	3	7	.377	.335
Gallego, Mike, Oak.	R	.233	43	120	11	28	28	0	0	0	8	2	0	9	24	0	1	3	.233	.292
Gates, Brent, Oak.	B	.254	136	524	60	133	180	24	4	5	56	4	11	46	84	3	3	15	.344	.308
Howard, David, K.C.	B	.243	95	255	23	62	83	13	4	0	19	6	1	24	41	6	1	7	.325	.310
Hudler, Rex, Cal.	R	.265	84	223	30	59	93	16	0	6	27	2	1	10	48	13	0	2	.417	.310

American League second basemen

Name/Team	B	BA	G	AB	R	H	TB	2B	3B	HR	RBI	SH	SF	BB	SO	SB	CS	GIDP	SLG	OBA
Kelly, Pat, NY-A	R	.237	89	270	32	64	90	12	1	4	29	10	2	23	65	8	3	5	.333	.307
Knoblauch, Chuck, Min.	R	.333	136	538	107	179	262	34	8	11	63	0	3	78	95	46	18	15	.487	.424
Lind, Jose, K.C.-Cal.	R	.236	44	140	9	33	38	5	0	0	7	1	0	6	12	0	1	5	.271	.267
Listach, Pat, Mil.	B	.219	101	334	35	73	85	8	2	0	25	7	1	25	61	13	3	6	.254	.276
Lockhart, Keith, K.C.	L	.321	94	274	41	88	131	19	3	6	33	1	7	14	21	8	1	2	.478	.355
Martin, Norberto, ChiA	R	.269	72	160	17	43	64	7	4	2	17	2	3	3	25	5	0	5	.400	.281
Mota, Jose, K.C.	B	.000	2	2	0	0	0	0	0	0	0	0	0	0	0	0	0	0	.000	.000
Penn, Shannon, Det.	B	.333	3	9	0	3	3	0	0	0	0	0	0	1	2	0	0	2	.333	.400
Pozo, Arquimedez, Sea.	R	.000	1	1	0	0	0	0	0	0	0	0	0	0	0	0	0	0	.000	.000
Raabe, Brian, Min.	R	.214	6	14	4	3	3	0	0	0	1	0	0	1	0	0	0	0	.214	.267
Ripken, Billy, Cle.	R	.412	8	17	4	7	13	0	0	2	3	0	0	0	3	0	0	0	.765	.412
Rodriguez, Carlos, Bos.	B	.333	13	30	5	10	12	2	0	0	5	3	0	2	2	0	0	0	.400	.394
Rodriguez, S., Bos.-Det.	R	.179	18	39	5	7	8	1	0	0	0	1	0	6	10	2	2	1	.205	.289
Shumpert, Terry, Bos.	R	.234	21	47	6	11	14	3	0	0	3	0	0	4	13	3	1	0	.298	.294
Silvestri, Dave, NY-A	R	.095	17	21	4	2	5	0	0	1	4	0	1	4	9	0	0	1	.238	.259
Stynes, Chris, K.C.	R	.171	22	35	7	6	7	1	0	0	2	0	0	4	3	0	0	3	.200	.256
Velarde, Randy, NY-A	R	.278	111	367	60	102	144	19	1	7	46	3	3	55	64	5	1	9	.392	.375
Vina, Fernando, Mil.	L	.257	113	288	46	74	104	7	7	3	29	4	2	22	28	6	3	6	.361	.327
Whitaker, Lou, Det.	L	.293	84	249	36	73	129	14	0	14	44	0	3	31	41	4	0	6	.518	.372

American League third basemen

Name/Team	B	BA	G	AB	R	H	TB	2B	3B	HR	RBI	SH	SF	BB	SO	SB	CS	GIDP	SLG	OBA
Battle, Howard, Tor.	R	.200	9	15	3	3	3	0	0	0	0	0	0	4	8	1	0	0	.200	.368
Bell, David, Cle.	R	.000	2	2	0	0	0	0	0	0	0	0	0	0	0	0	0	0	.000	.000
Blowers, Mike, Sea.	R	.257	134	439	59	113	208	24	1	23	96	3	3	53	128	2	1	18	.474	.335
Boggs, Wade, NY-A	L	.324	126	460	76	149	194	22	4	5	63	0	7	74	50	1	1	13	.422	.412
Brosius, Scott, Oak.	R	.262	123	389	69	102	176	19	2	17	46	1	4	41	67	4	2	5	.452	.342
Buechele, Steve, Tex.	R	.125	9	24	0	3	3	0	0	0	0	0	0	4	3	0	0	0	.125	.250
Cirillo, Jeff, Mil.	R	.277	125	328	57	91	145	19	4	9	39	1	4	47	42	7	2	8	.442	.371
Davis, Russ, NY-A	R	.276	40	98	14	27	42	5	2	2	12	0	0	10	26	0	0	0	.429	.349
Donnels, Chris, Bos.	L	.253	40	91	13	23	35	2	2	2	11	0	1	9	18	0	0	1	.385	.317
Fryman, Travis, Det.	R	.275	144	567	79	156	232	21	5	15	81	0	7	63	100	4	2	18	.409	.347
Gaetti, Gary, K.C.	R	.261	137	514	76	134	266	27	0	35	96	3	6	47	91	3	3	7	.518	.329
Giambi, Jason, Oak.	L	.256	54	176	27	45	70	7	0	6	25	1	2	28	31	2	1	4	.398	.364
Gomez, Leo, Bal.	R	.236	53	127	16	30	47	5	0	4	12	0	2	18	23	0	1	0	.370	.336
Gonzales, Rene, Cal.	R	.333	30	18	1	6	10	1	0	1	3	0	0	0	4	0	0	1	.556	.333
Huson, Jeff, Bal.	L	.248	66	161	24	40	51	4	2	1	19	2	1	15	20	5	4	4	.317	.315
Leius, Scott, Min.	R	.247	117	372	51	92	130	16	5	4	45	0	4	49	54	2	1	14	.349	.335
Manto, Jeff, Bal.	R	.256	89	254	31	65	125	9	0	17	38	0	0	24	69	0	3	6	.492	.325
Martinez, Carlos, Cal.	R	.180	26	61	7	11	15	1	0	1	9	0	0	6	7	0	0	2	.246	.265
Naehring, Tim, Bos.	R	.307	126	433	61	133	194	27	2	10	57	4	2	77	66	0	2	16	.448	.415
Ortiz, Luis, Tex.	R	.231	41	108	10	25	37	5	2	1	18	0	1	6	18	0	1	7	.343	.270
Owen, Spike, Cal.	B	.229	82	218	17	50	68	9	3	1	28	1	0	18	22	3	2	7	.312	.288
Pagliarulo, Mike, Tex.	L	.232	86	241	27	56	84	16	0	4	27	2	3	15	49	0	0	10	.349	.277
Palmer, Dean, Tex.	R	.336	36	119	30	40	73	6	0	9	24	0	1	21	21	1	1	2	.613	.448
Paquette, Craig, Oak.	R	.226	105	283	42	64	118	13	1	13	49	3	5	12	88	5	2	5	.417	.256
Perez, Eduardo, Cal.	R	.169	29	71	9	12	21	4	1	1	7	0	1	12	9	0	2	3	.296	.302
Phillips, Tony, Cal.	B	.261	139	525	119	137	241	21	1	27	61	1	1	113	135	13	10	5	.459	.394
Randa, Joe, K.C.	R	.171	34	70	6	12	17	2	0	1	5	0	0	6	17	0	1	2	.243	.237
Seitzer, Kevin, Mil.	R	.311	132	492	56	153	207	33	3	5	69	5	3	64	57	2	0	13	.421	.395
Snopek, Chris, ChiA	R	.324	22	68	12	22	29	4	0	1	7	0	0	9	12	1	0	2	.426	.403
Sprague, Ed Jr., Tor.	R	.244	144	521	77	127	212	27	2	18	74	1	7	58	96	0	0	19	.407	.333
Strange, Doug, Sea.	R	.271	74	155	19	42	61	9	2	2	21	1	0	10	25	0	3	3	.394	.323
Thome, Jim, Cle.	L	.314	137	452	92	142	252	29	3	25	73	0	3	97	113	4	3	8	.558	.438
Ventura, Robin, ChiA	L	.295	135	492	79	145	245	22	0	26	93	1	8	75	98	4	3	8	.498	.384
Worthington, Craig, Tex.	R	.221	26	68	4	15	25	4	0	2	6	2	0	7	8	0	0	6	.368	.293

American League shortstops

Name/Team	B	BA	G	AB	R	H	TB	2B	3B	HR	RBI	SH	SF	BB	SO	SB	CS	GIDP	SLG	OBA
Bell, Juan, Bos.	B	.154	17	26	7	4	9	2	0	1	2	0	1	2	10	0	0	0	.346	.207
Beltre, Esteban, Tex.	R	.217	54	92	7	20	28	8	0	0	7	3	0	4	15	0	0	1	.304	.250
Bordick, Mike, Oak.	R	.264	126	428	46	113	150	13	0	8	44	7	3	35	48	11	3	8	.350	.325
Cedeno, Domingo, Tor.	B	.236	51	161	18	38	58	6	1	4	14	1	0	10	35	0	1	3	.360	.289
Correia, Rod, Cal.	R	.238	14	21	3	5	8	1	1	0	3	1	0	0	5	0	0	1	.381	.238
Cruz, Fausto, Oak.	R	.217	8	23	0	5	5	0	0	0	5	2	2	3	5	1	1	1	.217	.286
DiSarcina, Gary, Cal.	R	.307	99	362	61	111	166	28	6	5	41	7	3	20	25	7	4	10	.459	.344

American League shortstops

Name/Team	B	BA	G	AB	R	H	TB	2B	3B	HR	RBI	SH	SF	BB	SO	SB	CS	GIDP	SLG	OBA
Elster, Kevin, NY-A	R	.118	10	17	1	2	3	1	0	0	0	0	0	1	5	0	0	0	.176	.167
Fermin, Felix, Sea.	R	.195	73	200	21	39	45	6	0	0	15	8	1	6	6	2	0	7	.225	.232
Fernandez, Tony, NY-A	B	.245	108	384	57	94	133	20	2	5	45	3	5	42	40	6	6	14	.346	.322
Gagne, Greg, K.C.	R	.256	120	430	58	110	161	25	4	6	49	7	5	38	60	3	5	11	.374	.316
Gil, Benji, Tex.	R	.219	130	415	36	91	144	20	3	9	46	10	2	26	147	2	4	5	.347	.266
Gomez, Chris, Det.	R	.223	123	431	49	96	153	20	2	11	50	3	4	41	96	4	1	13	.355	.292
Gonzalez, Alex, Tor.	R	.243	111	367	51	89	146	19	4	10	42	9	4	44	114	4	4	7	.398	.322
Grebeck, Craig, ChiA	R	.260	53	154	19	40	55	12	0	1	18	4	0	21	23	0	0	4	.357	.360
Guillen, Ozzie, ChiA	L	.248	122	415	50	103	132	20	3	1	41	4	1	13	25	6	7	11	.318	.270
Hocking, Denny, Min.	B	.200	9	25	4	5	9	0	2	0	3	1	0	2	2	1	0	1	.360	.259
Jeter, Derek, NY-A	R	.250	15	48	5	12	18	4	1	0	7	0	0	3	11	0	0	0	.375	.294
Loretta, Mark, Mil.	R	.260	19	50	13	13	19	3	0	1	3	1	0	4	7	1	1	1	.380	.327
Meares, Pat, Min.	R	.269	116	390	57	105	168	19	4	12	49	4	5	15	68	10	4	17	.431	.311
Perez, Tomas, Tor.	B	.245	41	98	12	24	32	3	1	1	8	0	1	7	18	0	1	6	.327	.292
Reboulet, Jeff, Min.	R	.292	87	216	39	63	86	11	0	4	23	2	0	27	34	1	2	3	.398	.373
Ripken, Cal, Bal.	R	.262	144	550	71	144	232	33	2	17	88	1	8	52	59	0	1	15	.422	.324
Rodriguez, Alex, Sea.	R	.232	48	142	15	33	58	6	2	5	19	1	0	6	42	4	2	0	.408	.264
Schofield, Dick C., Cal.	R	.250	12	20	1	5	5	0	0	0	2	2	0	4	2	0	0	1	.250	.375
Sojo, Luis, Sea.	R	.289	102	339	50	98	141	18	2	7	39	6	1	23	19	4	2	9	.416	.335
Trammell, Alan, Det.	R	.269	74	223	28	60	78	12	0	2	23	3	2	27	19	3	1	8	.350	.345
Valentin, John, Bos.	R	.298	135	520	108	155	277	37	2	27	102	4	6	81	67	20	5	7	.533	.399
Valentin, Jose, Mil.	B	.219	112	338	62	74	136	23	3	11	49	7	4	37	83	16	8	0	.402	.293
Vizquel, Omar, Cle.	B	.266	136	542	87	144	190	28	0	6	56	10	10	59	59	29	11	4	.351	.333

American League outfielders

Name/Team	B	BA	G	AB	R	H	TB	2B	3B	HR	RBI	SH	SF	BB	SO	SB	CS	GIDP	SLG	OBA
Amaral, Rich, Sea.	R	.282	90	238	45	67	91	14	2	2	19	1	0	21	33	21	2	3	.382	.342
Amaro, Ruben Jr., Cle.	B	.200	28	60	5	12	18	3	0	1	7	2	0	4	6	1	3	1	.300	.273
Anderson, Brady, Bal.	L	.262	143	554	108	145	246	33	10	16	64	4	2	87	111	26	7	3	.444	.371
Anderson, Garret, Cal.	L	.321	106	374	50	120	189	19	1	16	69	2	4	19	65	6	2	8	.505	.352
Bass, Kevin, Bal.	B	.244	111	295	32	72	99	12	0	5	32	4	2	24	47	8	8	15	.336	.303
Bautista, Danny, Det.	R	.203	89	271	28	55	85	9	0	7	27	6	0	12	68	4	1	6	.314	.237
Becker, Rich, Min.	L	.237	106	392	45	93	116	15	1	2	33	6	2	34	95	8	9	9	.296	.303
Belle, Albert, Cle.	R	.317	143	546	121	173	377	52	1	50	126	0	4	73	80	5	2	24	.690	.401
Bonilla, Bobby, Bal.	B	.333	61	237	47	79	129	12	4	10	46	0	2	23	31	0	2	11	.544	.392
Bragg, Darren, Sea.	L	.234	52	145	20	34	50	5	1	3	12	1	2	18	37	9	0	2	.345	.331
Brown, Jarvis, Bal.	R	.148	18	27	2	4	5	1	0	0	1	3	0	7	9	1	1	0	.185	.324
Buford, Damon, Bal.	R	.063	24	32	6	2	2	0	0	0	2	3	1	6	7	3	1	0	.063	.205
Buhner, Jay, Sea.	R	.262	126	470	86	123	266	23	0	40	121	2	6	60	120	0	1	15	.566	.343
Burnitz, Jeromy, Cle.	L	.571	9	7	4	4	5	1	0	0	0	0	0	0	0	0	0	0	.714	.571
Cameron, Mike, ChiA	R	.184	28	38	4	7	12	2	0	1	2	3	0	3	15	0	0	0	.316	.244
Carter, Joe, Tor.	R	.253	139	558	70	141	239	23	0	25	76	0	5	37	87	12	1	11	.428	.300
Chamberlain, Wes, Bos.	R	.119	19	42	4	5	9	1	0	1	1	0	0	3	11	1	0	2	.214	.178
Clark, Jerald, Min.	R	.339	36	109	17	37	60	8	3	3	15	0	1	2	11	3	0	5	.550	.354
Cole, Alex, Min.	L	.342	28	79	10	27	37	3	2	1	14	2	0	8	15	1	3	0	.468	.409
Coleman, V., K.C.-Sea.	B	.288	115	455	66	131	181	23	6	5	29	5	1	37	80	42	16	8	.398	.343
Cookson, Brent, K.C.	R	.143	22	35	2	5	6	1	0	0	5	1	0	2	7	1	0	0	.171	.189
Cordova, Marty, Min.	R	.277	137	512	81	142	249	27	4	24	84	0	5	52	111	20	7	10	.486	.352
Curtis, Chad, Det.	R	.268	144	586	96	157	255	29	3	21	67	0	7	70	93	27	15	12	.435	.349
Cuyler, Milt, Det.	B	.205	41	88	15	18	27	1	4	0	5	2	0	8	16	2	1	0	.307	.271
Damon, Johnny, K.C.	L	.282	47	188	32	53	83	11	5	3	23	2	3	12	22	7	0	2	.441	.324
Delgado, Carlos, Tor.	L	.165	37	91	7	15	27	3	0	3	11	0	2	6	26	0	0	1	.297	.212
Devereaux, Mike, ChiA	R	.306	92	333	48	102	155	21	1	10	55	0	3	25	51	6	6	10	.465	.352
Diaz, Alex, Sea.	B	.248	103	270	44	67	90	14	0	3	27	5	2	13	27	18	8	3	.333	.286
Edmonds, Jim, Cal.	L	.290	141	558	120	162	299	30	4	33	107	1	5	51	130	1	4	10	.536	.352
Fox, Eric, Tex.	B	.000	10	15	2	0	0	0	0	0	0	1	0	3	4	0	0	0	.000	.167
Frazier, Lou, Tex.	B	.212	49	99	19	21	23	2	0	0	8	3	0	7	20	9	1	2	.232	.278
Gallagher, Dave, Cal.	R	.188	11	16	1	3	4	1	0	0	0	0	0	2	1	0	0	0	.250	.278
Giles, Brian, Cle.	L	.556	6	9	6	5	8	0	0	1	3	0	0	0	1	0	0	0	.889	.556
Goodwin, Curtis, Bal.	L	.263	87	289	40	76	96	11	3	1	24	7	3	15	53	22	4	5	.332	.301
Goodwin, Tom, K.C.	L	.287	133	480	72	138	172	16	3	4	28	14	0	38	72	50	18	7	.358	.346
Green, Shawn, Tor.	L	.288	121	379	52	109	193	31	4	15	54	0	3	20	68	1	2	4	.509	.326
Greenwell, Mike, Bos.	L	.297	120	481	67	143	221	25	4	15	76	0	4	38	35	9	5	18	.459	.349
Greer, Rusty, Tex.	L	.271	131	417	58	113	177	21	2	13	61	2	3	55	66	3	1	9	.424	.355
Griffey, Ken Jr., Sea.	L	.258	72	260	52	67	125	7	0	17	42	0	2	52	53	4	2	4	.481	.379
Hall, Joe, Det.	R	.133	7	15	2	2	2	0	0	0	0	0	0	2	3	0	0	1	.133	.235
Hamilton, Darryl, Mil.	L	.271	112	398	54	108	155	20	6	5	44	8	3	47	35	11	1	9	.389	.350
Hammonds, Jeffrey, Bal.	R	.242	57	178	18	43	66	9	1	4	23	1	2	9	30	4	2	3	.371	.279

American League outfielders

Name/Team	B	BA	G	AB	R	H	TB	2B	3B	HR	RBI	SH	SF	BB	SO	SB	CS	GIDP	SLG	OBA
Hare, Shawn, Tex.	L	.250	18	24	2	6	7	1	0	0	2	0	0	4	6	0	0	1	.292	.357
Hatcher, Billy, Tex.	R	.083	6	12	2	1	2	1	0	0	0	0	0	1	1	0	0	0	.167	.154
Henderson, Rickey, Oak.	R	.300	112	407	67	122	182	31	1	9	54	1	3	72	66	32	10	8	.447	.407
Herrera, Jose, Oak.	L	.243	33	70	9	17	22	1	2	0	2	0	1	6	11	1	3	1	.314	.299
Hiatt, Phil, K.C.	R	.204	52	113	11	23	41	6	0	4	12	2	0	9	37	1	0	3	.363	.262
Higginson, Bobby, Det.	L	.224	131	410	61	92	161	17	5	14	43	2	7	62	107	6	4	5	.393	.329
Hosey, Dwayne, Bos.	B	.338	24	68	20	23	42	8	1	3	7	1	0	8	16	6	0	0	.618	.408
Huff, Michael, Tor.	R	.232	61	138	14	32	46	9	1	1	9	5	2	22	21	1	1	4	.333	.337
Hulse, David, Mil.	L	.251	119	339	46	85	117	11	6	3	47	2	5	18	60	15	3	3	.345	.285
Javier, Stan, Oak.	B	.278	130	442	81	123	171	20	2	8	56	5	4	49	63	36	5	8	.387	.353
Johnson, Lance, ChiA	L	.306	142	607	98	186	258	18	12	10	57	2	3	32	31	40	6	7	.425	.341
Jose, Felix, K.C.	B	.133	9	30	2	4	5	1	0	0	1	0	0	2	9	0	0	1	.167	.188
Kirby, Wayne, Cle.	L	.207	101	188	29	39	56	10	2	1	14	1	2	13	32	10	3	4	.298	.260
Lawton, Matt, Min.	L	.317	21	60	11	19	28	4	1	1	12	0	0	7	11	1	1	1	.467	.414
Lofton, Kenny, Cle.	L	.310	118	481	93	149	218	22	13	7	53	4	3	40	49	54	15	6	.453	.362
Mahay, Ron, Bos.	L	.200	5	20	3	4	9	2	0	1	3	0	0	1	6	0	0	0	.450	.273
Maldonado, C., Tor.-Tex.	R	.263	74	190	28	50	93	16	0	9	30	0	3	32	50	1	2	6	.489	.370
May, Derrick, Mil.	L	.248	32	113	15	28	36	3	1	1	9	0	0	5	18	0	1	1	.319	.286
McGee, Willie, Bos.	B	.285	67	200	32	57	80	11	3	2	15	5	3	9	41	5	2	5	.400	.311
McLemore, Mark, Tex.	B	.261	129	467	73	122	167	20	5	5	41	10	3	59	71	21	11	10	.358	.346
Mieske, Matt, Mil.	R	.251	117	267	42	67	118	13	1	12	48	0	5	27	45	2	4	8	.442	.323
Miller, Keith A., K.C.	R	.333	9	15	2	5	8	0	0	1	3	0	0	2	4	0	0	1	.533	.412
Mouton, Lyle, ChiA	R	.302	58	179	23	54	85	16	0	5	27	0	1	19	46	1	0	7	.475	.373
Nevin, Phil, Det.	R	.219	29	96	9	21	32	3	1	2	12	0	0	11	27	0	0	3	.333	.318
Newfield, Marc, Sea.	R	.188	24	85	7	16	28	3	0	3	14	0	0	3	16	0	0	2	.329	.225
Newson, W., ChiA-Sea.	L	.261	84	157	34	41	62	2	2	5	15	0	0	39	45	2	1	3	.395	.411
Nilsson, Dave, Mil.	L	.278	81	263	41	73	123	12	1	12	53	0	5	24	41	2	0	9	.468	.337
Nixon, Otis, Tex.	B	.295	139	589	87	174	199	21	2	0	45	6	3	58	85	50	21	6	.338	.357
Norman, Les, K.C.	R	.225	24	40	6	9	11	0	1	0	4	1	0	6	6	0	1	0	.275	.326
Nunnally, Jon, K.C.	L	.244	119	303	51	74	143	15	6	14	42	4	0	51	86	6	4	4	.472	.357
Obando, Sherman, Bal.	R	.263	16	38	0	10	11	1	0	0	3	0	1	2	12	1	0	0	.289	.293
O'Leary, Troy, Bos.	L	.308	112	399	60	123	196	31	6	10	49	3	2	29	64	5	3	8	.491	.355
O'Neill, Paul, NY-A	L	.300	127	460	82	138	242	30	4	22	96	0	11	71	76	1	2	25	.526	.387
Palmeiro, Orlando, Cal.	L	.350	15	20	3	7	7	0	0	0	1	0	0	1	1	0	0	0	.350	.381
Pemberton, Rudy, Det.	R	.300	12	30	3	9	14	3	1	0	3	0	0	1	5	0	0	3	.467	.344
Perez, Robert, Tor.	R	.188	17	48	2	9	14	2	0	1	3	0	0	0	5	0	0	1	.292	.188
Polonia, Luis, NY-A	L	.261	67	238	37	62	83	9	3	2	15	2	4	25	29	10	4	3	.349	.326
Puckett, Kirby, Min.	R	.314	137	538	83	169	277	39	0	23	99	0	5	56	89	3	2	15	.515	.379
Raines, Tim, ChiA	B	.285	133	502	81	143	212	25	4	12	67	3	3	70	52	13	2	8	.422	.374
Ramirez, Manny, Cle.	R	.308	137	484	85	149	270	26	1	31	107	2	5	75	112	6	6	13	.558	.402
Rhodes, Tuffy, Bos.	L	.080	10	25	2	2	3	1	0	0	1	0	0	3	4	0	0	1	.120	.179
Rivera, Ruben, NY-A	R	.000	5	1	0	0	0	0	0	0	0	0	0	0	1	0	0	0	.000	.000
Salmon, Tim, Cal.	R	.330	143	537	111	177	319	34	3	34	105	0	4	91	111	5	5	9	.594	.429
Sierra, R., Oak.-NY-A	B	.263	126	479	73	126	215	32	0	19	86	0	8	46	76	5	4	8	.449	.323
Singleton, Duane, Mil.	L	.065	13	31	0	2	2	0	0	0	0	0	0	1	10	1	0	0	.065	.094
Smith, Mark E., Bal.	R	.231	37	104	11	24	38	5	0	3	15	2	1	12	22	3	0	4	.365	.314
Stairs, Matt, Bos.	L	.261	39	88	8	23	35	7	1	1	17	1	1	4	14	0	1	4	.398	.298
Steverson, Todd, Det.	R	.262	30	42	11	11	17	0	0	2	6	0	2	6	10	2	0	0	.405	.340
Stewart, Shannon, Tor.	R	.211	12	38	2	8	8	0	0	0	1	0	0	5	5	2	0	0	.211	.318
Tettleton, Mickey, Tex.	B	.238	134	429	76	102	219	19	1	32	78	1	3	107	110	0	0	8	.510	.396
Thurman, Gary, Sea.	R	.320	13	25	3	8	10	2	0	0	3	0	1	1	3	5	2	0	.400	.333
Tinsley, Lee, Bos.	B	.284	100	341	61	97	137	17	1	7	41	9	1	39	74	18	8	8	.402	.359
Tomberlin, Andy, Oak.	L	.212	46	85	15	18	30	0	0	4	10	2	0	5	22	4	1	2	.353	.256
Tucker, Michael, K.C.	L	.260	62	177	23	46	68	10	0	4	17	0	0	18	51	2	3	3	.384	.332
Van Slyke, Andy, Bal.	L	.159	17	63	6	10	20	1	0	3	8	0	0	5	15	0	0	1	.317	.221
Voigt, Jack, Bal.-Tex.	R	.175	36	63	9	11	20	3	0	2	8	0	1	10	14	0	0	2	.317	.284
Ward, Turner, Mil.	L	.264	44	129	19	34	51	3	1	4	16	1	1	14	21	6	1	2	.395	.332
White, Devon, Tor.	B	.283	101	427	61	121	184	23	5	10	53	1	3	29	97	11	2	5	.431	.334
Whiten, Mark, Bos.	B	.185	32	108	13	20	26	3	0	1	10	0	1	8	23	1	0	5	.241	.239
Williams, Bernie, NY-A	B	.307	144	563	93	173	274	29	9	18	82	2	3	75	98	8	6	12	.487	.392
Williams, Gerald, NY-A	R	.247	100	182	33	45	85	18	2	6	28	0	3	22	34	4	2	4	.467	.327
Young, Ernie, Oak.	R	.200	26	50	9	10	19	3	0	2	5	0	0	8	12	0	0	1	.380	.310

American League designated hitters

Name/Team	B	BA	G	AB	R	H	TB	2B	3B	HR	RBI	SH	SF	BB	SO	SB	CS	GIDP	SLG	OBA
Baines, Harold, Bal.	L	.299	127	385	60	115	208	19	1	24	63	0	4	70	45	0	2	17	.540	.403
Berroa, Geronimo, Oak.	R	.278	141	546	87	152	246	22	3	22	88	0	6	63	98	7	4	12	.451	.351
Brito, Bernardo, Min.	R	.200	5	5	1	1	4	0	0	1	1	0	0	0	3	0	0	1	.800	.333

American League designated hitters

Name/Team	B	BA	G	AB	R	H	TB	2B	3B	HR	RBI	SH	SF	BB	SO	SB	CS	GIDP	SLG	OBA
Canseco, Jose, Bos.	R	.306	102	396	64	121	220	25	1	24	81	0	5	42	93	4	0	9	.556	.378
Davis, Chili, Cal.	B	.318	119	424	81	135	218	23	0	20	86	0	9	89	79	3	3	12	.514	.429
Flora, Kevin, Cal.	R	.000	2	1	1	0	0	0	0	0	0	0	0	0	1	0	0	0	.000	.000
Gibson, Kirk, Det.	L	.260	70	227	37	59	102	12	2	9	35	0	2	33	61	9	2	6	.449	.358
Gonzalez, Juan, Tex.	R	.295	90	352	57	104	209	20	2	27	82	0	5	17	66	0	0	15	.594	.324
Grotewold, Jeff, K.C.	L	.278	15	36	4	10	14	1	0	1	6	0	0	9	7	0	0	2	.389	.422
Hale, Chip, Min.	L	.262	69	103	10	27	37	4	0	2	18	0	0	11	20	0	0	6	.359	.333
Hamelin, Bob, K.C.	L	.168	72	208	20	35	65	7	1	7	25	0	1	26	56	0	1	6	.313	.278
Hollins, Dave, Bos.	B	.154	5	13	2	2	2	0	0	0	1	0	0	4	7	0	0	0	.154	.353
Horn, Sam, Tex.	L	.111	11	9	0	1	1	0	0	0	0	0	0	1	6	0	0	0	.111	.200
Ingram, Riccardo, Min.	R	.125	4	8	0	1	1	0	0	0	1	0	0	2	1	0	0	1	.125	.300
James, Dion, NY-A	L	.287	85	209	22	60	74	6	1	2	26	0	2	20	16	4	1	5	.354	.346
James, Chris, K.C.-Bos.	R	.268	42	82	8	22	32	4	0	2	8	2	2	7	14	1	0	2	.390	.326
Jefferson, Reggie, Bos.	L	.289	46	121	21	35	58	8	0	5	26	0	2	9	24	0	0	3	.479	.333
Kruk, John, ChiA	L	.308	45	159	13	49	62	7	0	2	23	0	3	26	33	0	1	5	.390	.399
Maas, Kevin, Min.	L	.193	22	57	5	11	18	4	0	1	5	0	0	7	11	0	0	4	.316	.281
Martinez, Edgar, Sea.	R	.356	145	511	121	182	321	52	0	29	113	0	4	116	87	4	3	11	.628	.479
Molitor, Paul, Tor.	R	.270	130	525	63	142	222	31	2	15	60	3	4	61	57	12	0	10	.423	.350
Munoz, Pedro, Min.	R	.301	104	376	45	113	184	17	0	18	58	0	2	19	86	0	3	14	.489	.338
Murray, Eddie, Cle.	B	.323	113	436	68	141	225	21	0	21	82	0	5	39	65	5	1	12	.516	.375
Sabo, Chris, ChiA	R	.254	20	71	10	18	26	5	0	1	8	2	2	3	12	2	0	0	.366	.295
Strawberry, Darryl, NY-A	L	.276	32	87	15	24	39	4	1	3	13	0	0	10	22	0	0	2	.448	.364
Tartabull, D., NY-A-Oak.	R	.236	83	280	34	66	106	16	0	8	35	0	4	43	82	0	2	9	.379	.335
Vaughn, Greg, Mil.	R	.224	108	392	67	88	160	19	1	17	59	0	4	55	89	10	4	10	.408	.317
Vitiello, Joe, K.C.	R	.254	53	130	13	33	58	4	0	7	21	0	0	8	25	0	0	4	.446	.317
Winfield, Dave, Cle.	R	.191	46	115	11	22	33	5	0	2	4	0	0	14	26	1	0	5	.287	.285

American League first baseman (pitching)

Name/Team	T	W	L	ERA	G	GS	CG	SHO	GF	SV	IP	H	R	ER	HR	BB	SO	WP	BK	BA
Martinez, Dave, ChiA	L	0	0	0.00	1	0	0	0	1	0	1.0	0	0	0	0	2	0	0	0	.000

National League starting pitchers

Name/Team	T	W	L	ERA	G	GS	CG	SHO	GF	SV	IP	H	R	ER	HR	BB	SO	WP	BK	BA
Acevedo, Juan, Col.	R	4	6	6.44	17	11	0	0	0	0	65.2	82	53	47	15	20	40	2	1	.317
Alvarez, Tavo, Mon.	R	1	5	6.75	8	8	0	0	0	0	37.1	46	30	28	2	14	17	1	0	.297
Ashby, Andy, S.D.	R	12	10	2.94	31	31	2	2	0	0	192.2	180	79	63	17	62	150	7	0	.253
Avery, Steve, Atl.	L	7	13	4.67	29	29	3	1	0	0	173.1	165	92	90	22	52	141	3	0	.252
Banks, W., ChiN-L.A.-Fla.	R	2	6	5.66	25	15	0	0	2	0	90.2	106	71	57	14	58	62	9	1	.294
Benes, Alan, St.L	R	1	2	8.44	3	3	0	0	0	0	16.0	24	15	15	2	4	20	3	0	.343
Benes, Andy, S.D.	R	4	7	4.17	19	19	1	1	0	0	118.2	121	65	55	10	45	126	3	0	.262
Birkbeck, Mike, NY-N	R	0	1	1.63	4	4	0	0	0	0	27.2	22	5	5	2	2	14	3	1	.220
Bowen, Ryan, Fla.	R	2	0	3.78	4	3	0	0	0	0	16.2	23	11	7	3	12	15	0	0	.329
Brewington, Jamie, S.F.	R	6	4	4.54	13	13	0	0	0	0	75.1	68	38	38	8	45	45	3	0	.245
Bullinger, Jim, ChiN	R	12	8	4.14	24	24	1	1	0	0	150.0	152	80	69	14	65	93	5	1	.265
Burkett, John, Fla.	R	14	14	4.30	30	30	4	0	0	0	188.1	208	95	90	22	57	126	2	1	.282
Candiotti, Tom, L.A.	R	7	14	3.50	30	30	1	1	0	0	190.1	187	93	74	18	58	141	7	0	.255
Castillo, Frank, ChiN	R	11	10	3.21	29	29	2	2	0	0	188.0	179	75	67	22	52	135	3	1	.248
Cornelius, R., Mon.-NY-N	R	3	7	5.54	18	10	0	0	1	0	66.2	75	44	41	11	30	39	2	1	.288
Deshaies, Jim, Phi.	L	0	1	20.25	2	2	0	0	0	0	5.1	15	12	12	3	1	6	0	0	.484
Dishman, Glenn, S.D.	L	4	8	5.01	19	16	0	0	1	0	97.0	104	60	54	11	34	43	3	1	.278
Drabek, Doug, Hou.	R	10	9	4.77	31	31	2	1	0	0	185.0	205	104	98	18	54	143	8	1	.282
Ericks, John, Pit.	R	3	9	4.58	19	18	1	0	0	0	106.0	108	59	54	7	50	80	11	1	.263
Estes, Shawn, S.F.	L	0	3	6.75	3	3	0	0	0	0	17.1	16	14	13	2	5	14	4	0	.229
Fassero, Jeff, Mon.	L	13	14	4.33	30	30	1	0	0	0	189.0	207	102	91	15	74	164	7	1	.283
Fernandez, Sid, Phi.	L	6	1	3.34	11	11	0	0	0	0	64.2	48	25	24	11	21	79	0	1	.200
Foster, Kevin, ChiN	R	12	11	4.51	30	28	0	0	1	0	167.2	149	90	84	32	65	146	2	2	.240
Freeman, Marvin, Col.	R	3	7	5.89	22	18	0	0	0	0	94.2	122	64	62	15	41	61	5	1	.318
Glavine, Tom, Atl.	L	16	7	3.08	29	29	3	1	0	0	198.2	182	76	68	9	66	127	3	0	.246
Grace, Mike, Phi.	R	1	1	3.18	2	2	0	0	0	0	11.1	10	4	4	0	4	7	0	0	.238
Grahe, Joe, Col.	R	4	3	5.08	17	9	0	0	0	0	56.2	69	42	32	6	27	27	3	2	.301
Green, Tyler, Phi.	R	8	9	5.31	26	25	4	2	0	0	140.2	157	86	83	15	66	85	9	2	.290
Greene, Tommy, Phi.	R	0	5	8.29	11	6	0	0	3	0	33.2	45	32	31	6	20	24	3	1	.319
Hamilton, Joey, S.D.	R	6	9	3.08	31	30	2	2	1	0	204.1	189	89	70	17	56	123	2	0	.246
Hammond, Chris, Fla.	L	9	6	3.80	25	24	3	2	0	0	161.0	157	73	68	17	47	126	3	1	.256
Hampton, Mike, Hou.	L	9	8	3.35	24	24	0	0	0	0	150.2	141	73	56	13	49	115	3	1	.247
Harnisch, Pete, NY-N	R	2	8	3.68	18	18	0	0	0	0	110.0	111	55	45	13	24	82	0	1	.261

National League starting pitchers

Name/Team	T	W	L	ERA	G	GS	CG	SHO	GF	SV	IP	H	R	ER	HR	BB	SO	WP	BK	BA
Henry, Butch, Mon.	L	7	9	2.84	21	21	1	1	0	0	126.2	133	47	40	11	28	60	0	1	.275
Hill, Ken, St.L	R	6	7	5.06	18	18	0	0	0	0	110.1	125	71	62	16	45	50	3	0	.286
Isringhausen, J., NY-N	R	9	2	2.81	14	14	1	0	0	0	93.0	88	29	29	6	31	55	4	1	.254
Jackson, Danny, St.L	L	2	12	5.90	19	19	2	1	0	0	100.2	120	82	66	10	48	52	6	0	.303
Jacome, Jason, NY-N	L	0	4	10.29	5	5	0	0	0	0	21.0	33	24	24	3	15	11	1	0	.359
Jarvis, Kevin, Cin.	R	3	4	5.70	19	11	1	1	2	0	79.0	91	56	50	13	32	33	2	0	.292
Jones, Bobby J., NY-N	R	10	10	4.19	30	30	3	1	0	0	195.2	209	107	91	20	53	127	2	1	.274
Juden, Jeff, Phi.	R	2	4	4.02	13	10	1	0	0	0	62.2	53	31	28	6	31	47	4	1	.235
Kile, Darryl, Hou.	R	4	12	4.96	25	21	0	0	1	0	127.0	114	81	70	5	73	113	11	1	.240
Leiter, Mark, S.F.	R	10	12	3.82	30	29	7	1	0	0	195.2	185	91	83	19	55	129	9	3	.254
Lieber, Jon, Pit.	R	4	7	6.32	21	12	0	0	3	0	72.2	103	56	51	7	14	45	3	0	.346
Loaiza, Esteban, Pit.	R	8	9	5.16	32	31	1	0	0	0	172.2	205	115	99	21	55	85	6	1	.300
Maddux, Greg, Atl.	R	19	2	1.63	28	28	10	3	0	0	209.2	147	39	38	8	23	181	1	0	.197
Martinez, Pedro J., Mon.	R	14	10	3.51	30	30	2	2	0	0	194.2	158	79	76	21	66	174	5	2	.227
Martinez, Ramon, L.A.	R	17	7	3.66	30	30	4	2	0	0	206.1	176	95	84	19	81	138	3	0	.231
Mercker, Kent, Atl.	L	7	8	4.15	29	26	0	0	1	0	143.0	140	73	66	16	61	102	6	2	.258
Mimbs, Michael, Phi.	L	9	7	4.15	35	19	2	1	6	1	136.2	127	70	63	10	75	93	9	0	.250
Mlicki, Dave, NY-N	R	9	7	4.26	29	25	0	0	1	0	160.2	160	82	76	23	54	123	5	1	.256
Morgan, Mike, ChiN-St.L	R	7	7	3.56	21	21	1	0	0	0	131.1	133	56	52	12	34	61	6	0	.271
Mulholland, Terry, S.F.	L	5	13	5.80	29	24	2	0	2	0	149.0	190	112	96	25	38	65	4	0	.313
Munoz, Bobby, Phi.	R	0	2	5.74	3	3	0	0	0	0	15.2	15	13	10	2	9	6	0	0	.268
Navarro, Jaime, ChiN	R	14	6	3.28	29	29	1	1	0	0	200.1	194	79	73	19	56	128	1	0	.251
Neagle, Denny, Pit.	L	13	8	3.43	31	31	5	1	0	0	209.2	221	91	80	20	45	150	6	0	.273
Nitkowski, C.J., Cin.	L	1	3	6.12	9	7	0	0	0	0	32.1	41	25	22	4	15	18	1	2	.306
Nomo, Hideo, L.A.	R	16	11	3.19	33	33	3	2	0	0	228.1	180	93	81	23	85	234	9	0	.213
Nomo, Hideo, L.A.	R	13	6	2.54	28	28	4	3	0	0	191.1	124	63	54	14	78	236	19	5	.182
Osborne, Donovan, St.L	L	4	6	3.81	19	19	0	0	0	0	113.1	112	58	48	17	34	82	0	0	.260
Parris, Steve, Pit.	R	6	6	5.38	15	15	1	1	0	0	82.0	89	49	49	12	33	61	4	0	.283
Perez, Carlos, Mon.	L	10	8	3.69	28	23	2	1	2	0	141.1	142	61	58	18	28	106	8	4	.257
Petkovsek, Mark, St.L	R	6	6	4.00	26	21	1	1	1	0	137.1	136	71	61	11	35	71	1	1	.262
Portugal, Mark, S.F.-Cin.	R	11	10	4.01	31	31	1	0	0	0	181.2	185	91	81	17	56	96	7	0	.262
Pulsipher, Bill, NY-N	L	5	7	3.98	17	17	2	0	0	0	126.2	122	58	56	11	45	81	2	1	.255
Quantrill, Paul, Phi.	R	11	12	4.67	33	29	0	0	1	0	179.1	212	102	93	20	44	103	0	3	.295
Rapp, Pat, Fla.	R	14	7	3.44	28	28	3	2	0	0	167.1	158	72	64	10	76	102	7	0	.253
Reed, Rick, Cin.	R	0	0	5.82	4	3	0	0	1	0	17.0	18	12	11	5	3	10	0	0	.273
Rekar, Bryan, Col.	R	4	6	4.98	15	14	1	0	0	0	85.0	95	51	47	11	24	60	3	2	.282
Reynolds, Shane, Hou.	R	10	11	3.47	30	30	3	2	0	0	189.1	196	87	73	15	37	175	7	1	.263
Reynoso, Armando, Col.	R	7	7	5.32	20	18	0	0	0	0	93.0	116	61	55	12	36	40	2	0	.316
Rijo, Jose, Cin.	R	5	4	4.17	14	14	0	0	0	0	69.0	76	33	32	6	22	62	3	0	.285
Ritz, Kevin, Col.	R	11	11	4.21	31	28	0	0	3	2	173.1	171	91	81	16	65	120	6	0	.259
Roper, John, Cin.-S.F.	R	0	0	12.38	3	2	0	0	0	0	8.0	15	12	11	3	6	6	0	1	.417
Rosselli, Joe, S.F.	L	2	1	8.70	9	5	0	0	0	0	30.0	39	29	29	5	20	7	0	1	.342
Rueter, Kirk, Mon.	L	5	3	3.23	9	9	1	1	0	0	47.1	38	17	17	3	9	28	0	0	.224
Saberhagen, B., NY-N-Col.	R	7	6	4.18	25	25	3	0	0	0	153.0	165	78	71	21	33	100	3	0	.273
Sanders, Scott, S.D.	R	5	5	4.30	17	15	1	0	0	0	90.0	79	46	43	14	31	88	6	1	.228
Schilling, Curt, Phi.	R	7	5	3.57	17	17	1	0	0	0	116.0	96	52	46	12	26	114	0	1	.220
Schourek, Pete, Cin.	L	18	7	3.22	29	29	2	0	0	0	190.1	158	72	68	17	45	160	1	2	.228
Smiley, John, Cin.	L	12	5	3.46	28	27	1	0	0	0	176.2	173	72	68	11	39	124	5	1	.263
Smoltz, John, Atl.	R	12	7	3.18	29	29	2	1	0	0	192.2	166	76	68	15	72	193	13	0	.232
Springer, Dennis, Phi.	R	0	3	4.84	4	4	0	0	0	0	22.1	21	15	12	3	9	15	1	0	.256
Swift, Bill C., Col.	R	9	3	4.94	19	19	0	0	0	0	105.2	122	62	58	12	43	68	2	0	.296
Swindell, Greg, Hou.	L	10	9	4.47	33	26	1	1	3	0	153.0	180	86	76	21	39	96	3	0	.297
Tapani, Kevin, L.A.	R	4	2	5.05	13	11	0	0	0	0	57.0	72	37	32	8	14	43	1	0	.306
Telgheder, Dave, NY-N	R	1	2	5.61	7	4	0	0	2	0	25.2	34	18	16	4	7	16	0	1	.318
Trachsel, Steve, ChiN	R	7	13	5.15	30	29	2	0	0	0	160.2	174	104	92	25	76	117	2	1	.277
Urbani, Tom, St.L	L	3	5	3.70	24	13	0	0	2	0	82.2	99	40	34	11	21	52	5	0	.305
Urbina, Ugueth, Mon.	R	2	2	6.17	7	4	0	0	0	0	23.1	26	17	16	6	14	15	2	0	.280
Valdes, Ismael, L.A.	R	13	11	3.05	33	27	6	2	1	1	197.2	168	76	67	17	51	150	1	3	.228
Valdes, Marc, Fla.	R	0	0	14.14	3	3	0	0	0	0	7.0	17	13	11	1	9	2	1	0	.459
Valdez, Sergio, S.F.	R	4	5	4.75	13	11	1	0	0	0	66.1	78	43	35	12	17	29	2	1	.298
Valenzuela, F., S.D.	L	8	3	4.98	29	15	0	0	5	0	90.1	101	53	50	16	34	57	4	0	.289
VanLandingham, W., S.F.	R	6	3	3.67	18	18	1	0	0	0	122.2	124	58	50	14	40	95	5	4	.264
Viola, Frank, Cin.	L	0	1	6.28	3	3	0	0	0	0	14.1	20	11	10	3	4	1	0	0	.333
Wagner, Paul, Pit.	R	5	16	4.80	33	25	3	1	1	1	165.0	174	96	88	18	72	120	8	0	.273
Wall, Donne, Hou.	R	3	1	5.55	6	5	0	0	0	0	24.1	33	19	15	5	5	16	1	0	.320
Watson, Allen, St.L	L	7	9	4.96	21	19	0	0	1	0	114.1	126	68	63	17	41	49	2	2	.285
Weathers, Dave, Fla.	R	4	5	5.98	28	15	0	0	0	0	90.1	104	68	60	8	52	60	3	0	.295
Wells, David, Cin.	L	6	5	3.59	11	11	3	0	0	0	72.2	74	34	29	6	16	50	1	1	.265
West, David, Phi.	L	3	2	3.79	8	8	0	0	0	0	38.0	34	17	16	5	19	25	1	0	.241
White, Rick, Pit.	R	2	3	4.75	15	9	0	0	2	0	55.0	66	33	29	3	18	29	2	0	.299
Wilson, Trevor, S.F.	L	3	4	3.92	17	17	0	0	0	0	82.2	82	42	36	8	38	38	0	1	.269

National League starting pitchers

Name/Team	T	W	L	ERA	G	GS	CG	SHO	GF	SV	IP	H	R	ER	HR	BB	SO	WP	BK	BA
Witt, Bobby, Fla.	R	2	7	3.90	19	19	1	0	0	0	110.2	104	52	48	8	47	95	2	0	.251

National League relief pitchers

Name/Team	T	W	L	ERA	G	GS	CG	SHO	GF	SV	IP	H	R	ER	HR	BB	SO	WP	BK	BA
Abbott, Kyle, Phi.	L	2	0	3.81	18	0	0	0	3	0	28.1	28	12	12	3	16	21	2	1	.267
Adams, Terry, ChiN	R	1	1	6.50	18	0	0	0	7	1	18.0	22	15	13	0	10	15	1	0	.289
Aquino, Luis, Mon.-S.F.	R	0	3	5.10	34	0	0	0	9	2	42.1	57	34	24	6	13	26	3	0	.315
Arocha, Rene, St.L	R	3	5	3.99	41	0	0	0	13	6	49.2	55	24	22	6	18	25	2	0	.297
Astacio, Pedro, L.A.	R	7	8	4.24	48	11	1	1	7	0	104.0	103	53	49	12	29	80	5	0	.261
Bailey, Roger, Col.	R	7	6	4.98	39	6	0	0	9	0	81.1	88	49	45	9	39	33	7	1	.283
Bailey, Cory, St.L	R	0	0	7.36	3	0	0	0	1	0	3.2	2	3	3	0	2	5	1	0	.154
Barber, Brian, St.L	R	2	1	5.22	9	4	0	0	2	0	29.1	31	17	17	4	16	27	3	0	.279
Barton, Shawn, S.F.	L	4	1	4.26	52	0	0	0	11	1	44.1	37	22	21	3	19	22	0	1	.237
Bautista, Jose, S.F.	R	3	8	6.44	52	6	0	0	19	0	100.2	120	77	72	24	26	45	1	2	.295
Beck, Rod, S.F.	R	5	6	4.45	60	0	0	0	52	33	58.2	60	31	29	7	21	42	2	0	.267
Bedrosian, Steve, Atl.	R	1	2	6.11	29	0	0	0	7	0	28.0	40	21	19	6	12	22	0	0	.354
Berumen, Andres, S.D.	R	2	3	5.68	37	0	0	0	17	1	44.1	37	29	28	3	36	42	6	0	.226
Blair, Willie, S.D.	R	7	5	4.34	40	12	0	0	11	0	114.0	112	60	55	11	45	83	4	0	.262
Bochtler, Doug, S.D.	R	4	4	3.57	34	0	0	0	11	1	45.1	38	18	18	5	19	45	1	0	.239
Borbon, Pedro Jr., Atl.	L	2	2	3.09	41	0	0	0	19	2	32.0	29	12	11	2	17	33	0	1	.240
Borland, Toby, Phi.	R	1	3	3.77	50	0	0	0	18	6	74.0	81	37	31	3	37	59	12	0	.277
Bottalico, Ricky, Phi.	R	5	3	2.46	62	0	0	0	20	1	87.2	50	25	24	7	42	87	1	0	.167
Brantley, Jeff, Cin.	R	3	2	2.82	56	0	0	0	49	28	70.1	53	22	22	11	20	62	2	2	.206
Brocail, Doug, Hou.	R	6	4	4.19	36	7	0	0	12	1	77.1	87	40	36	10	22	39	1	1	.280
Bruske, Jim, L.A.	R	0	0	4.50	9	0	0	0	3	1	10.0	12	7	5	0	4	5	1	0	.300
Burba, Dave, S.F.-Cin.	R	10	4	3.97	52	9	1	1	7	0	106.2	90	50	47	9	51	96	5	0	.228
Burgos, Enrique, S.F.	L	0	0	8.64	5	0	0	0	2	0	8.1	14	8	8	1	6	12	2	0	.378
Byrd, Paul, NY-N	R	2	0	2.05	17	0	0	0	6	0	22.0	18	6	5	1	7	26	1	2	.222
Carrasco, Hector, Cin.	R	2	7	4.12	64	0	0	0	28	5	87.1	86	45	40	1	46	64	15	0	.257
Carter, Andy, Phi.	L	0	0	6.14	4	0	0	0	1	0	7.1	4	5	5	3	2	6	0	0	.167
Casian, Larry, ChiN	L	1	0	1.93	42	0	0	0	5	0	23.1	23	6	5	1	15	11	2	0	.258
Charlton, Norm, Phi.	L	2	5	7.36	25	0	0	0	5	0	22.0	23	19	18	2	15	12	1	0	.280
Christiansen, Jason, Pit.	L	1	3	4.15	63	0	0	0	13	0	56.1	49	28	26	5	34	53	4	1	.234
Clark, Terry, Atl.	R	0	0	4.91	3	0	0	0	1	0	3.2	3	2	2	0	5	2	1	0	.231
Clontz, Brad, Atl.	R	8	1	3.65	59	0	0	0	14	4	69.0	71	29	28	5	22	55	0	0	.269
Courtright, John, Cin.	L	0	0	9.00	1	0	0	0	1	0	1.0	2	1	1	0	0	0	0	0	.500
Creek, Doug, St.L	L	0	0	0.00	6	0	0	0	1	0	6.2	2	0	0	0	3	10	0	0	.095
Cummings, John, L.A.	L	3	1	3.00	35	0	0	0	11	0	39.0	38	16	13	3	10	21	1	0	.250
Daal, Omar, L.A.	L	4	0	7.20	28	0	0	0	8	0	20.0	29	16	16	1	15	11	0	1	.354
DeLeon, Jose, Mon.	R	0	1	7.56	7	0	0	0	1	0	8.1	7	7	7	2	7	12	0	0	.233
DeLucia, Rich, St.L	R	8	7	3.39	56	1	0	0	8	0	82.1	63	38	31	9	36	76	5	0	.213
Dewey, Mark, S.F.	R	1	0	3.13	27	0	0	0	5	0	31.2	30	12	11	2	17	32	1	0	.254
DiPoto, Jerry, NY-N	R	4	6	3.78	58	0	0	0	26	2	78.2	77	41	33	2	29	49	3	1	.267
Dougherty, Jim, Hou.	R	8	4	4.92	56	0	0	0	11	0	67.2	76	37	37	7	25	49	1	0	.292
Dunbar, Matt, Fla.	L	0	1	11.57	8	0	0	0	1	0	7.0	12	9	9	0	11	5	1	0	.387
Dyer, Mike, Pit.	R	4	5	4.34	55	0	0	0	15	0	74.2	81	40	36	9	30	53	4	1	.281
Edens, Tom, ChiN	R	1	0	6.00	5	0	0	0	1	0	3.0	6	3	2	0	3	2	0	0	.400
Eischen, Joey, L.A.	L	0	0	3.10	17	0	0	0	8	0	20.1	19	9	7	1	11	15	1	0	.232
Elliott, Donnie, S.D.	R	0	0	0.00	1	0	0	0	1	0	2.0	2	0	0	0	1	3	0	0	.250
Eversgerd, Bryan, Mon.	L	0	0	5.14	25	0	0	0	5	0	21.0	22	13	12	2	9	8	1	0	.268
Fletcher, Paul, Phi.	R	1	0	5.40	10	0	0	0	1	0	13.1	15	8	8	2	9	10	2	0	.288
Florence, Don, NY-N	L	3	0	1.50	14	0	0	0	3	0	12.0	17	3	2	0	6	5	0	0	.340
Florie, Bryce, S.D.	R	2	2	3.01	47	0	0	0	10	1	68.2	49	30	23	8	38	68	7	2	.202
Fossas, Tony, St.L	L	3	0	1.47	58	0	0	0	20	0	36.2	28	6	6	1	10	40	1	0	.214
Franco, John, NY-N	L	5	3	2.44	48	0	0	0	41	29	51.2	48	17	14	4	17	41	0	0	.251
Frascatore, John, St.L	R	1	1	4.41	14	4	0	0	3	0	32.2	39	19	16	3	16	21	0	0	.298
Fraser, Willie, Mon.	R	2	1	5.61	22	0	0	0	6	2	25.2	25	17	16	6	9	12	2	0	.248
Frey, Steve, S.F.-Phi.	L	0	1	2.12	18	0	0	0	4	1	17.0	10	7	4	2	4	7	0	0	.172
Garces, Rich, ChiN-Fla.	R	0	2	4.44	18	0	0	0	7	0	24.1	25	15	12	1	11	22	0	0	.260
Gardner, Mark, Fla.	R	5	5	4.49	39	11	1	1	7	1	102.1	109	60	51	14	43	87	3	1	.272
Gomez, Pat, S.F.	L	0	0	5.14	18	0	0	0	3	0	14.0	16	8	8	2	12	15	0	1	.276
Gott, Jim, Pit.	R	2	4	6.03	25	0	0	0	12	3	31.1	38	26	21	2	12	19	3	0	.288
Greer, Kenny, S.F.	R	0	2	5.25	8	0	0	0	1	0	12.0	15	12	7	3	5	7	0	0	.288
Groom, Buddy, Fla.	L	1	2	7.20	14	0	0	0	5	0	15.0	26	12	12	2	6	12	0	0	.400
Grott, Matt, Cin.	L	0	0	21.60	2	0	0	0	1	0	1.2	6	4	4	1	0	2	0	0	.545
Gunderson, Eric, NY-N	L	1	1	3.70	30	0	0	0	7	0	24.1	25	10	10	2	8	19	1	0	.269
Guthrie, Mark, L.A.	L	0	2	3.66	24	0	0	0	7	0	19.2	19	11	8	1	9	19	2	0	.241
Habyan, John, St.L	R	3	2	2.88	31	0	0	0	9	0	40.2	32	18	13	0	15	35	2	3	.222

National League relief pitchers

Name/Team	T	W	L	ERA	G	GS	CG	SHO	GF	SV	IP	H	R	ER	HR	BB	SO	WP	BK	BA
Hancock, Lee, Pit.	L	0	0	1.93	11	0	0	0	3	0	14.0	10	3	3	0	2	6	2	0	.196
Hansell, Greg, L.A.	R	0	1	7.45	20	0	0	0	7	0	19.1	29	17	16	5	6	13	0	0	.349
Harris, Greg A., Mon.	R	2	3	2.61	45	0	0	0	12	0	48.1	45	18	14	6	16	47	3	0	.245
Harris, Gene, Phi.	R	2	2	4.26	21	0	0	0	5	0	19.0	19	9	9	2	8	9	0	0	.260
Hartgraves, Dean, Hou.	L	2	0	3.22	40	0	0	0	11	0	36.1	30	14	13	2	16	24	1	0	.227
Harvey, Bryan, Fla.	R	0	0	∞	1	0	0	0	0	0	0.0	2	3	3	1	1	0	0	0	1.000
Henke, Tom, St.L	R	1	1	1.82	52	0	0	0	47	36	54.1	42	11	11	2	18	48	1	0	.209
Henneman, Mike, Hou.	R	0	1	3.00	21	0	0	0	18	8	21.0	21	7	7	1	4	19	3	0	.266
Henry, Doug, NY-N	R	3	6	2.96	51	0	0	0	20	4	67.0	48	23	22	7	25	62	6	1	.198
Heredia, Gil, Mon.	R	5	6	4.31	40	18	0	0	5	1	119.0	137	60	57	7	21	74	1	0	.291
Hermanson, Dustin, S.D.	R	3	1	6.82	26	0	0	0	6	0	31.2	35	26	24	8	22	19	3	0	.280
Hernandez, Xavier, Cin.	R	7	2	4.60	59	0	0	0	19	3	90.0	95	47	46	8	31	84	7	0	.273
Hernandez, Jeremy, Fla.	R	0	0	11.57	7	0	0	0	3	0	7.0	12	9	9	2	3	5	0	0	.400
Hickerson, B., ChiN-Col.	L	3	3	8.57	56	0	0	0	13	1	48.1	69	52	46	8	28	40	5	1	.332
Hoffman, Trevor, S.D.	R	7	4	3.88	55	0	0	0	51	31	53.1	48	25	23	10	14	52	1	0	.235
Holmes, Darren, Col.	R	6	1	3.24	68	0	0	0	33	14	66.2	59	26	24	3	28	61	7	1	.237
Hook, Chris, S.F.	R	5	1	5.50	45	0	0	0	14	0	52.1	55	33	32	7	29	40	2	0	.274
Hope, John, Pit.	R	0	0	30.86	3	0	0	0	0	0	2.1	8	8	8	0	4	2	0	0	.615
Hudek, John, Hou.	R	2	2	5.40	19	0	0	0	16	7	20.0	19	12	12	3	5	29	2	0	.247
Jackson, Mike R., Cin.	R	6	1	2.39	40	0	0	0	10	2	49.0	38	13	13	5	19	41	1	1	.213
Johnstone, John, Fla.	R	0	0	3.86	4	0	0	0	0	0	4.2	7	2	2	1	2	3	0	0	.333
Jones, Todd, Hou.	R	6	5	3.07	68	0	0	0	40	15	99.2	89	38	34	8	52	96	5	0	.237
Karp, Ryan, Phi.	L	0	0	4.50	1	0	0	0	0	0	2.0	1	1	1	0	3	2	1	0	.143
Konuszewski, Dennis, Pit.	R	0	0	54.00	1	0	0	0	0	0	0.1	3	2	2	0	1	0	0	0	1.000
Kroon, Marc, S.D.	R	0	1	10.80	2	0	0	0	1	0	1.2	1	2	2	0	2	2	0	0	.200
Krueger, Bill, S.D.	L	0	0	7.04	6	0	0	0	0	0	7.2	13	6	6	1	4	6	2	0	.371
Leiper, Dave, Mon.	L	0	2	2.86	26	0	0	0	7	2	22.0	16	8	7	2	6	12	0	1	.200
Leskanic, Curtis, Col.	R	6	3	3.40	76	0	0	0	27	10	98.0	83	38	37	7	33	107	6	1	.226
Lewis, Richie, Fla.	R	0	1	3.75	21	1	0	0	6	0	36.0	30	15	15	9	15	32	1	2	.224
Lomon, Kevin, NY-N	R	0	1	6.75	6	0	0	0	1	0	9.1	17	8	7	0	5	6	0	0	.405
Maddux, Mike, Pit.	R	1	0	9.00	8	0	0	0	1	0	9.0	14	9	9	0	3	4	1	0	.359
Mantei, Matt, Fla.	R	0	0	4.73	12	0	0	0	3	0	13.1	12	8	7	1	13	15	1	0	.245
Manzanillo, Josias, NY-N	R	1	2	7.88	12	0	0	0	4	0	16.0	18	15	14	3	6	14	5	0	.273
Manzanillo, Ravelo, Pit.	L	0	0	4.91	5	0	0	0	0	0	3.2	3	3	2	0	2	1	0	0	.231
Martinez, Pedro A., Hou.	L	0	0	7.40	25	0	0	0	3	0	20.2	29	18	17	3	16	17	0	1	.330
Mathews, Terry, Fla.	R	4	4	3.38	57	0	0	0	14	3	82.2	70	32	31	9	27	72	3	0	.235
Mathews, T.J., St.L	R	1	1	1.52	23	0	0	0	12	2	29.2	21	7	5	1	11	28	2	0	.200
Mauser, Tim, S.D.	R	0	1	9.53	5	0	0	0	1	0	5.2	4	6	6	0	9	9	0	0	.190
May, Darrell, Atl.	L	0	0	11.25	2	0	0	0	1	0	4.0	10	5	5	0	0	1	0	0	.500
McCurry, Jeff, Pit.	R	1	4	5.02	55	0	0	0	10	1	61.0	82	38	34	9	30	27	2	0	.337
McElroy, Chuck, Cin.	L	3	4	6.02	44	0	0	0	11	0	40.1	46	29	27	5	15	27	1	0	.291
McMichael, Greg, Atl.	R	7	2	2.79	67	0	0	0	16	2	80.2	64	27	25	8	32	74	3	0	.213
McMurtry, Craig, Hou.	R	0	1	7.84	11	0	0	0	3	0	10.1	15	11	9	0	9	4	2	0	.357
Miceli, Dan, Pit.	R	4	4	4.66	58	0	0	0	51	21	58.0	61	30	30	7	28	56	4	0	.270
Minor, Blas, NY-N	R	4	2	3.66	35	0	0	0	10	1	46.2	44	21	19	6	13	43	3	0	.253
Mintz, Steve, S.F.	R	1	2	7.45	14	0	0	0	3	0	19.1	26	16	16	4	12	7	0	0	.329
Morel, Ramon, Pit.	R	0	1	2.84	5	0	0	0	0	0	6.1	6	2	2	0	2	3	0	0	.300
Munoz, Mike, Col.	L	2	4	7.42	64	0	0	0	19	2	43.2	54	38	36	9	27	37	5	0	.307
Murphy, Rob, L.A.-Fla.	L	1	2	10.95	14	0	0	0	1	0	12.1	14	16	15	3	8	7	1	0	.292
Murray, Matt, Atl.	R	0	2	6.75	4	1	0	0	1	0	10.2	10	8	8	3	5	3	0	0	.256
Myers, Mike, Fla.	L	0	0	0.00	2	0	0	0	2	0	2.0	1	0	0	0	3	0	0	0	.167
Myers, Randy, ChiN	L	1	2	3.88	57	0	0	0	47	38	55.2	49	25	24	7	28	59	0	0	.237
Nabholz, Chris, ChiN	L	0	1	5.40	34	0	0	0	4	0	23.1	22	15	14	4	14	21	2	0	.253
Nen, Robb, Fla.	R	0	7	3.29	62	0	0	0	54	23	65.2	62	26	24	6	23	68	2	0	.244
Nichols, Rod, Atl.	R	0	0	5.40	5	0	0	0	0	0	6.2	14	11	4	3	5	3	0	0	.424
Nied, David, Col.	R	0	0	20.77	2	0	0	0	0	0	4.1	11	10	10	2	3	3	0	0	.458
Olivares, Omar, Col.-Phi.	R	1	4	6.91	16	6	0	0	4	0	41.2	55	34	32	5	23	22	4	0	.333
Osuna, Antonio, L.A.	R	2	4	4.43	39	0	0	0	8	0	44.2	39	22	22	5	20	46	1	0	.241
Painter, Lance, Col.	L	3	0	4.37	33	1	0	0	7	1	45.1	55	23	22	9	10	36	4	1	.296
Palacios, Vicente, St.L	R	2	3	5.80	20	5	0	0	3	0	40.1	48	29	26	7	19	34	1	0	.300
Park, Chan Ho, L.A.	R	0	0	4.50	2	0	0	0	0	0	4.0	2	2	2	1	2	7	0	1	.143
Parra, Jose, L.A.	R	0	0	4.35	8	0	0	0	0	0	10.1	10	8	5	2	6	7	0	1	.256
Parrett, Jeff, St.L	R	4	7	3.64	59	0	0	0	17	0	76.2	71	33	31	8	28	71	7	0	.243
Pena, Alejandro, Fla.-Atl.	R	2	0	2.61	27	0	0	0	6	0	31.0	22	9	9	3	7	39	0	0	.193
Pennington, Brad, Cin.	L	0	0	5.59	9	0	0	0	2	0	9.2	9	8	6	0	11	7	3	0	.273
Perez, Mike, ChiN	R	2	6	3.66	68	0	0	0	18	2	71.1	72	30	29	8	27	49	4	0	.268
Perez, Yorkis, Fla.	L	2	6	5.21	69	0	0	0	11	1	46.2	35	29	27	6	28	47	2	0	.203
Person, Robert, NY-N	R	1	0	0.75	3	1	0	0	0	0	12.0	5	1	1	1	2	10	0	0	.119
Plesac, Dan, Pit.	L	4	4	3.58	58	0	0	0	16	3	60.1	53	26	24	3	27	57	1	0	.237
Powell, Jay, Fla.	R	0	0	1.08	9	0	0	0	1	0	8.1	7	2	1	0	6	4	0	0	.241

National League relief pitchers

Name/Team	T	W	L	ERA	G	GS	CG	SHO	GF	SV	IP	H	R	ER	HR	BB	SO	WP	BK	BA
Powell, Ross, Hou.-Pit.	L	0	2	6.98	27	3	0	0	6	0	29.2	36	26	23	6	21	20	4	0	.298
Pugh, Tim, Cin.	R	6	5	3.84	28	12	0	0	4	0	98.1	100	46	42	13	32	38	3	1	.267
Reed, Steve, Col.	R	5	2	2.14	71	0	0	0	15	3	84.0	61	24	20	8	21	79	0	2	.203
Remlinger, M., NY-N-Cin.	L	0	1	6.75	7	0	0	0	4	0	6.2	9	6	5	1	5	7	0	0	.321
Ricci, Chuck, Phi.	R	1	0	1.80	7	0	0	0	3	0	10.0	9	2	2	0	3	9	0	0	.273
Rivera, Roberto, ChiN	L	0	0	5.40	7	0	0	0	2	0	5.0	8	3	3	1	2	2	0	0	.381
Rodriguez, Felix, L.A.	R	1	1	2.53	11	0	0	0	5	0	10.2	11	3	3	2	5	5	0	0	.275
Rodriguez, Rich, St.L	L	0	0	0.00	1	0	0	0	0	0	1.2	0	0	0	0	0	0	0	0	.000
Rojas, Mel, Mon.	R	1	4	4.12	59	0	0	0	48	30	67.2	69	32	31	2	29	61	6	0	.262
Ruffin, Bruce, Col.	L	0	1	2.12	37	0	0	0	19	11	34.0	26	8	8	1	19	23	1	0	.222
Ruffin, Johnny, Cin.	R	0	0	1.35	10	0	0	0	6	0	13.1	4	3	2	0	11	11	3	0	.093
Sager, A.J., Col.	R	0	0	7.36	10	0	0	0	2	0	14.2	19	16	12	1	7	10	0	0	.311
Scheid, Rich, Fla.	L	0	0	6.10	6	0	0	0	1	0	10.1	14	7	7	1	7	10	1	0	.341
Schmidt, Curt, Mon.	R	0	0	6.97	11	0	0	0	0	0	10.1	15	8	8	1	9	7	0	0	.357
Schmidt, Jason, Atl.	R	2	2	5.76	9	2	0	0	1	0	25.0	27	17	16	2	18	19	1	0	.287
Scott, Tim, Mon.	R	2	0	3.98	62	0	0	0	15	2	63.1	52	30	28	6	23	57	4	0	.222
Seanez, Rudy, L.A.	R	1	3	6.75	37	0	0	0	12	3	34.2	39	27	26	5	18	29	0	0	.285
Service, Scott, S.F.	R	3	1	3.19	28	0	0	0	6	0	31.0	18	11	11	4	20	30	3	0	.176
Shaw, Jeff, Mon.	R	1	6	4.62	50	0	0	0	17	3	62.1	58	35	32	4	26	45	0	0	.250
Slocumb, Heathcliff, Phi.	R	5	6	2.89	61	0	0	0	54	32	65.1	64	26	21	2	35	63	3	0	.257
Small, Aaron, Fla.	R	1	0	1.42	7	0	0	0	1	0	6.1	7	2	1	1	6	5	0	0	.269
Smith, Pete J., Cin.	R	1	2	6.66	11	2	0	0	3	0	24.1	30	19	18	8	7	14	1	0	.319
Springer, Russ, Phi.	R	0	0	3.71	14	0	0	0	3	0	26.2	22	11	11	5	10	32	1	0	.227
Stanton, Mike, Atl.	L	1	1	5.59	26	0	0	0	10	1	19.1	31	14	12	3	6	13	1	1	.369
Sturtze, Tanyon, ChiN	R	0	0	9.00	2	0	0	0	0	0	2.0	2	2	2	1	0	1	0	0	.250
Sullivan, Scott, Cin.	R	0	0	4.91	3	0	0	0	1	0	3.2	4	2	2	0	2	2	0	0	.286
Swartzbaugh, Dave, ChiN	R	0	0	0.00	7	0	0	0	2	0	7.1	5	2	0	0	3	5	0	0	.208
Tabaka, Jeff, S.D.-Hou.	L	1	0	3.23	34	0	0	0	6	0	30.2	27	11	11	2	17	25	1	0	.243
Thobe, J.J., Mon.	R	0	0	9.00	4	0	0	0	2	0	4.0	6	4	4	0	3	0	1	0	.333
Thobe, Tom, Atl.	L	0	0	10.80	3	0	0	0	1	0	3.1	7	4	4	0	0	2	0	0	.412
Thompson, Mark, Col.	R	2	3	6.53	21	5	0	0	3	0	51.0	73	42	37	7	22	30	2	0	.349
Torres, Salomon, S.F.	R	0	1	9.00	4	1	0	0	2	0	8.0	13	8	8	4	7	2	0	0	.394
Valdez, Carlos, S.F.	R	0	1	6.14	11	0	0	0	3	0	14.2	19	10	10	1	8	7	1	1	.322
Veres, Dave, Hou.	R	5	1	2.26	72	0	0	0	15	1	103.1	89	29	26	5	30	94	4	0	.241
Veres, Randy, Fla.	R	4	4	3.88	47	0	0	0	15	1	48.2	46	25	21	6	22	31	2	0	.251
Villone, Ron, S.D.	L	2	1	4.21	19	0	0	0	8	1	25.2	24	12	12	5	11	37	2	0	.242
Wade, Terrell, Atl.	L	0	1	4.50	3	0	0	0	0	0	4.0	3	2	2	1	4	3	1	0	.214
Wagner, Billy, Hou.	L	0	0	0.00	1	0	0	0	0	0	0.1	0	0	0	0	0	0	0	0	.000
Walker, Mike C., ChiN	R	1	3	3.22	42	0	0	0	12	1	44.2	45	22	16	2	24	20	3	1	.259
Walker, Pete, NY-N	R	1	0	4.58	13	0	0	0	10	0	17.2	24	9	9	3	5	5	0	0	.329
Wendell, Turk, ChiN	R	3	1	4.92	43	0	0	0	17	0	60.1	71	35	33	11	24	50	1	0	.298
White, Gabe, Mon.	L	1	2	7.01	19	1	0	0	8	0	25.2	26	21	20	7	9	25	0	0	.260
Williams, Brian, S.D.	R	3	10	6.00	44	6	0	0	7	0	72.0	79	54	48	3	38	75	7	1	.279
Williams, Mike, Phi.	R	3	3	3.29	33	8	0	0	7	0	87.2	78	37	32	10	29	57	7	0	.239
Williams, Todd, L.A.	R	2	2	5.12	16	0	0	0	5	0	19.1	19	11	11	3	7	8	0	0	.264
Wilson, Gary, Pit.	R	0	1	5.02	10	0	0	0	1	0	14.1	13	8	8	2	5	8	1	0	.241
Wohlers, Mark, Atl.	R	7	3	2.09	65	0	0	0	49	25	64.2	51	16	15	2	24	90	4	0	.211
Woodall, Brad, Atl.	L	1	1	6.10	9	0	0	0	3	0	10.1	13	10	7	1	8	5	1	0	.310
Worrell, Tim, S.D.	R	1	0	4.73	9	0	0	0	4	0	13.1	16	7	7	2	6	13	1	0	.291
Worrell, Todd, L.A.	R	4	1	2.02	59	0	0	0	53	32	62.1	50	15	14	4	19	61	2	0	.221
Young, Anthony, ChiN	R	3	4	3.70	32	1	0	0	8	2	41.1	47	20	17	5	14	15	6	0	.288

National League catchers

Name/Team	B	BA	G	AB	R	H	TB	2B	3B	HR	RBI	SH	SF	BB	SO	SB	CS	GIDP	SLG	OBA
Ausmus, Brad, S.D.	R	.293	103	328	44	96	135	16	4	5	34	4	4	31	56	16	5	6	.412	.353
Bennett, Gary, Phi.	R	.000	1	1	0	0	0	0	0	0	0	0	0	0	1	0	0	0	.000	.000
Berryhill, Damon, Cin.	B	.183	34	82	6	15	24	3	0	2	11	1	4	10	19	0	0	3	.293	.260
Borders, Pat, Hou.	R	.114	11	35	1	4	4	0	0	0	0	0	0	2	7	0	0	2	.114	.162
Brito, Jorge, Col.	R	.216	18	51	5	11	14	3	0	0	7	1	0	2	17	1	0	1	.275	.259
Castillo, Alberto, NY-N	R	.103	13	29	2	3	3	0	0	0	3	0	0	3	9	1	0	0	.103	.212
Daulton, Darren, Phi.	L	.249	98	342	44	85	137	19	3	9	55	0	2	55	52	3	0	4	.401	.359
Decker, Steve, Fla.	R	.226	51	133	12	30	43	2	1	3	13	0	2	19	22	1	0	1	.323	.318
Encarnacion, Angelo, Pit.	R	.226	58	159	18	36	53	7	2	2	10	3	0	13	28	1	1	3	.333	.285
Eusebio, Tony, Hou.	R	.299	113	368	46	110	151	21	1	6	58	1	5	31	59	0	2	12	.410	.354
Fletcher, Darrin, Mon.	L	.286	110	350	42	100	156	21	1	11	45	1	2	32	23	0	1	15	.446	.351
Fordyce, Brook, NY-N	R	.500	4	2	1	1	2	1	0	0	0	0	0	1	0	0	0	0	1.000	.667
Girardi, Joe, Col.	R	.262	125	462	63	121	166	17	2	8	55	12	1	29	76	3	3	15	.359	.308
Goff, Jerry, Hou.	L	.154	12	26	2	4	9	2	0	1	3	0	0	4	13	0	0	1	.346	.267

National League catchers

Name/Team	B	BA	G	AB	R	H	TB	2B	3B	HR	RBI	SH	SF	BB	SO	SB	CS	GIDP	SLG	OBA
Hemond, Scott, St.L	R	.144	57	118	11	17	27	1	0	3	9	1	1	12	31	0	0	8	.229	.233
Hernandez, Carlos, L.A.	R	.149	45	94	3	14	21	1	0	2	8	1	0	7	25	0	0	5	.223	.216
Hubbard, Mike, ChiN	R	.174	15	23	2	4	4	0	0	0	1	0	0	2	2	0	0	1	.174	.240
Hundley, Todd, NY-N	B	.280	90	275	39	77	133	11	0	15	51	1	3	42	64	1	0	4	.484	.382
Johnson, Brian D., S.D.	R	.251	68	207	20	52	70	9	0	3	29	1	4	11	39	0	0	2	.338	.287
Johnson, Charles, Fla.	R	.251	97	315	40	79	129	15	1	11	39	4	2	46	71	0	2	11	.410	.351
Kmak, Joe, ChiN	R	.245	19	53	7	13	19	3	0	1	6	0	1	6	12	0	0	2	.358	.328
Laker, Tim, Mon.	R	.234	64	141	17	33	52	8	1	3	20	1	1	14	38	0	1	5	.369	.306
Lampkin, Tom, S.F.	L	.276	65	76	8	21	26	2	0	1	9	0	0	9	8	2	0	1	.342	.360
Lieberthal, Mike, Phi.	R	.255	16	47	1	12	14	2	0	0	4	2	0	5	5	0	0	1	.298	.327
Lopez, Javier, Atl.	R	.315	100	333	37	105	166	11	4	14	51	0	3	14	57	0	1	13	.498	.344
Manwaring, Kirt, S.F.	R	.251	118	379	21	95	126	15	2	4	36	4	4	27	72	1	0	8	.332	.314
Munoz, Noe, L.A.	R	.000	2	1	0	0	0	0	0	0	0	0	0	0	0	0	0	0	.000	.000
Natal, Bob, Fla.	R	.233	16	43	2	10	20	2	1	2	6	1	1	1	9	0	0	0	.465	.244
Nokes, Matt, Col.	L	.182	10	11	1	2	3	1	0	0	0	0	0	1	4	0	0	1	.273	.250
O'Brien, Charlie, Atl.	R	.227	67	198	18	45	79	7	0	9	23	0	0	29	40	0	1	8	.399	.343
Owens, Jayhawk, Col.	R	.244	18	45	7	11	25	2	0	4	12	0	1	2	15	0	0	0	.556	.286
Pagnozzi, Tom, St.L	R	.215	62	219	17	47	69	14	1	2	15	0	1	11	31	0	1	9	.315	.254
Parent, Mark, Pit.-ChiN	R	.234	81	265	30	62	127	11	0	18	38	1	0	26	69	0	0	6	.479	.302
Perez, Eddie, Atl.	R	.308	7	13	1	4	8	1	0	1	4	0	0	0	2	0	0	0	.615	.308
Piazza, Mike, L.A.	R	.346	112	434	82	150	263	17	0	32	93	0	1	39	80	1	0	10	.606	.400
Pratt, Todd, ChiN	R	.133	25	60	3	8	10	2	0	0	4	0	1	6	21	0	0	1	.167	.209
Prince, Tom, L.A.	R	.200	18	40	3	8	15	2	1	1	4	0	0	4	10	0	0	0	.375	.273
Reed, Jeff, S.F.	L	.265	66	113	12	30	32	2	0	0	9	1	0	20	17	0	0	3	.283	.376
Santiago, Benito, Cin.	R	.286	81	266	40	76	129	20	0	11	44	0	2	24	48	2	2	7	.485	.351
Sasser, Mackey, Pit.	L	.154	14	26	1	4	5	1	0	0	0	0	0	0	0	0	0	0	.192	.154
Servais, Scott, Hou.-ChiN	R	.265	80	264	38	70	131	22	0	13	47	2	3	32	52	2	2	9	.496	.348
Sheaffer, Danny, St.L	R	.231	76	208	24	48	75	10	1	5	30	0	1	23	38	0	0	8	.361	.306
Siddall, Joe, Mon.	L	.300	7	10	4	3	3	0	0	0	1	0	0	3	3	0	0	0	.300	.500
Slaught, Don, Pit.	R	.304	35	112	13	34	40	6	0	0	13	1	0	9	8	0	0	5	.357	.361
Spehr, Tim, Mon.	R	.257	41	35	4	9	17	5	0	1	3	3	0	6	7	0	0	0	.486	.366
Stinnett, Kelly, NY-N	R	.219	77	196	23	43	65	8	1	4	18	0	0	29	65	2	0	3	.332	.338
Taubensee, Eddie, Cin.	L	.284	80	218	32	62	107	14	2	9	44	1	1	22	52	2	2	2	.491	.354
Tucker, Scooter, Hou.	R	.286	5	7	1	2	5	0	0	1	1	0	0	0	0	0	0	0	.714	.286
Webster, Lenny, Phi.	R	.267	49	150	18	40	61	9	0	4	14	1	0	16	27	0	0	4	.407	.337
Wilkins, Rick, ChiN-Hou.	L	.203	65	202	30	41	65	3	0	7	19	0	2	46	61	0	0	9	.322	.351

National League first basemen

Name/Team	B	BA	G	AB	R	H	TB	2B	3B	HR	RBI	SH	SF	BB	SO	SB	CS	GIDP	SLG	OBA
Aude, Rich, Pit.	R	.248	42	109	10	27	41	8	0	2	19	0	0	6	20	1	2	4	.376	.287
Bagwell, Jeff, Hou.	R	.290	114	448	88	130	222	29	0	21	87	0	6	79	102	12	5	9	.496	.399
Benzinger, Todd, S.F.	B	.200	9	10	2	2	5	0	0	1	2	0	1	2	3	0	0	0	.500	.308
Brogna, Rico, NY-N	L	.289	134	495	72	143	240	27	2	22	76	2	2	39	111	0	0	10	.485	.342
Carreon, Mark, S.F.	R	.301	117	396	53	119	194	24	0	17	65	0	3	23	37	0	1	7	.490	.343
Cianfrocco, Archi, S.D.	R	.263	51	118	22	31	53	7	0	5	31	0	1	11	28	0	2	3	.449	.333
Colbrunn, Greg, Fla.	R	.277	138	528	70	146	239	22	1	23	89	0	4	22	69	11	3	15	.453	.311
Floyd, Cliff, Mon.	L	.130	29	69	6	9	13	1	0	1	8	0	0	7	22	3	0	1	.188	.221
Foley, Tom, Mon.	L	.208	11	24	2	5	7	2	0	0	2	0	0	2	4	1	0	2	.292	.269
Galarraga, Andres, Col.	R	.280	143	554	89	155	283	29	3	31	106	0	5	32	146	12	2	14	.511	.331
Giannelli, Ray, St.L	L	.091	9	11	0	1	1	0	0	0	0	0	0	3	4	0	0	0	.091	.286
Grace, Mark, ChiN	L	.326	143	552	97	180	285	51	3	16	92	1	7	65	46	6	2	10	.516	.395
Hollins, Dave, Phi.	B	.229	65	205	46	47	84	12	2	7	25	0	4	53	38	1	1	4	.410	.393
Hunter, Brian R., Cin.	R	.215	40	79	9	17	26	6	0	1	9	0	2	11	21	2	1	2	.329	.312
Hyers, Tim, S.D.	L	.000	6	5	0	0	0	0	0	0	0	0	0	0	1	0	0	1	.000	.000
Jefferies, Gregg, Phi.	B	.306	114	480	69	147	215	31	2	11	56	0	6	35	26	9	5	15	.448	.349
Johnson, Mark, Pit.	L	.208	79	221	32	46	93	6	1	13	28	0	1	37	66	5	2	2	.421	.326
Karros, Eric, L.A.	R	.298	143	551	83	164	295	29	3	32	105	0	4	61	115	4	4	14	.535	.369
Livingstone, Scott, S.D.	L	.337	99	196	26	66	96	15	0	5	32	0	2	15	22	2	1	3	.490	.380
Mabry, John, St.L	L	.307	129	388	35	119	157	21	1	5	41	0	4	24	45	0	3	6	.405	.347
McGriff, Fred, Atl.	L	.280	144	528	85	148	258	27	1	27	93	0	6	65	99	3	6	19	.489	.361
Morris, Hal, Cin.	L	.279	101	359	53	100	162	25	2	11	51	1	1	29	58	1	1	10	.451	.333
Perry, Gerald, St.L	L	.165	65	79	4	13	17	4	0	0	5	0	0	6	12	0	0	2	.215	.224
Petagine, Roberto, S.D.	L	.234	89	124	15	29	46	8	0	3	17	2	0	26	41	0	0	2	.371	.367
Phillips, J.R., S.F.	L	.195	92	231	27	45	81	9	0	9	28	2	0	19	69	1	1	3	.351	.256
Ready, Randy, Phi.	R	.138	23	29	3	4	4	0	0	0	0	1	0	3	6	0	1	2	.138	.219
Sabo, Chris, St.L	R	.154	5	13	0	2	3	1	0	0	3	0	0	1	2	1	0	1	.231	.214
Schall, Gene, Phi.	R	.231	24	65	2	15	17	2	0	0	5	0	0	6	16	0	0	1	.262	.306
Segui, D., NY-N-Mon.	B	.309	130	456	68	141	210	25	4	12	68	8	3	40	47	2	7	10	.461	.367

National League first basemen

Name/Team	B	BA	G	AB	R	H	TB	2B	3B	HR	RBI	SH	SF	BB	SO	SB	CS	GIDP	SLG	OBA
Simms, Mike, Hou.	R	.256	50	121	14	31	62	4	0	9	24	0	1	13	28	1	2	3	.512	.341
Sweeney, Mark, St.L	L	.273	37	77	5	21	29	2	0	2	13	1	2	10	15	1	1	3	.377	.348
Tatum, Jim, Col.	R	.235	34	34	4	8	11	1	1	0	4	0	0	1	7	0	0	1	.324	.257
Vander Wal, John, Col.	L	.347	105	101	15	35	60	8	1	5	21	0	1	16	23	1	1	2	.594	.432
Williams, Eddie, S.D.	R	.260	97	296	35	77	126	11	1	12	47	0	2	23	47	0	0	21	.426	.320
Worthington, Craig, Cin.	R	.278	10	18	1	5	9	1	0	1	2	0	0	2	1	0	0	0	.500	.350

National League second basemen

Name/Team	B	BA	G	AB	R	H	TB	2B	3B	HR	RBI	SH	SF	BB	SO	SB	CS	GIDP	SLG	OBA
Bates, Jason, Col.	B	.267	116	322	42	86	135	17	4	8	46	2	0	42	70	3	6	4	.419	.355
Bell, David, St.L	R	.250	39	144	13	36	53	7	2	2	19	0	1	4	25	1	2	0	.368	.278
Biggio, Craig, Hou.	R	.302	141	553	123	167	267	30	2	22	77	11	7	80	85	33	8	6	.483	.406
Boone, Bret, Cin.	R	.267	138	513	63	137	220	34	2	15	68	5	5	41	84	5	1	14	.429	.326
Browne, Jerry, Fla.	B	.255	77	184	21	47	54	4	0	1	17	9	1	25	20	1	1	7	.293	.346
Caraballo, Ramon, St.L	B	.202	34	99	10	20	32	4	1	2	3	2	0	6	33	3	2	1	.323	.269
DeShields, Delino, L.A.	L	.256	127	425	66	109	157	18	3	8	37	3	1	63	83	39	14	6	.369	.353
Diaz, Mario, Fla.	R	.230	49	87	5	20	26	3	0	1	6	1	0	1	12	0	0	4	.299	.239
Duncan, M., Phi.-Cin.	R	.287	81	265	36	76	112	14	2	6	36	1	5	5	62	1	3	7	.423	.297
Fonville, Chad, Mon.-L.A.	B	.278	102	320	43	89	97	6	1	0	16	6	0	23	42	20	7	3	.303	.328
Franco, Matt, ChiN	L	.294	16	17	3	5	6	1	0	0	1	0	0	0	4	0	0	0	.353	.294
Garcia, Carlos, Pit.	R	.294	104	367	41	108	154	24	2	6	50	5	3	25	55	8	4	4	.420	.340
Giovanola, Ed, Atl.	L	.071	13	14	2	1	1	0	0	0	0	0	0	3	5	0	0	1	.071	.235
Haney, Todd, ChiN	R	.411	25	73	11	30	44	8	0	2	6	1	0	7	11	0	0	0	.603	.463
Hulett, Tim, St.L	R	.182	4	11	0	2	2	0	0	0	0	0	0	0	3	0	0	0	.182	.182
Jordan, Kevin, Phi.	R	.185	24	54	6	10	17	1	0	2	6	0	0	2	9	0	0	0	.315	.228
Kent, Jeff, NY-N	R	.278	125	472	65	131	219	22	3	20	65	1	4	29	89	3	3	9	.464	.327
Lansing, Mike, Mon.	R	.255	127	467	47	119	183	30	2	10	62	1	3	28	65	27	4	14	.392	.299
Lee, Manuel, St.L	B	1.000	1	1	1	1	1	0	0	0	0	0	0	0	0	0	0	0	1.000	1.000
Lemke, Mark, Atl.	B	.253	116	399	42	101	142	16	5	5	38	7	3	44	40	2	2	17	.356	.325
Liriano, Nelson, Pit.	B	.286	107	259	29	74	103	12	1	5	38	1	3	24	34	2	2	2	.398	.347
Mejia, Roberto, Col.	R	.154	23	52	5	8	12	1	0	1	4	0	1	0	17	0	1	1	.231	.167
Morandini, Mickey, Phi.	L	.283	127	494	65	140	206	34	7	6	49	4	1	42	80	9	6	11	.417	.350
Mordecai, Mike, Atl.	R	.280	69	75	10	21	36	6	0	3	11	2	1	9	16	0	0	0	.480	.353
Oquendo, Jose, St.L	B	.209	88	220	31	46	66	8	3	2	17	4	1	35	21	1	1	1	.300	.316
Patterson, John, S.F.	B	.205	95	205	27	42	56	5	3	1	14	6	0	14	41	4	2	7	.273	.294
Pena, Geronimo, St.L	B	.267	32	101	20	27	38	6	1	1	8	4	2	16	30	3	2	2	.376	.367
Reed, Jody, S.D.	R	.256	131	445	58	114	146	18	1	4	40	3	3	59	38	6	4	9	.328	.348
Sanchez, Rey, ChiN	R	.278	114	428	57	119	154	22	2	3	27	8	2	14	48	6	4	9	.360	.301
Thompson, Robby, S.F.	R	.223	95	336	51	75	114	15	0	8	23	9	0	42	76	1	2	3	.339	.317
Treadway, J., L.A.-Mon.	L	.209	58	67	6	14	18	2	1	0	13	0	0	5	4	0	1	0	.269	.264
Veras, Quilvio, Fla.	B	.261	124	440	86	115	164	20	7	5	32	7	2	80	68	56	21	7	.373	.384
Young, Eric, Col.	R	.317	120	366	68	116	173	21	9	6	36	3	1	49	29	35	12	4	.473	.404

National League third basemen

Name/Team	B	BA	G	AB	R	H	TB	2B	3B	HR	RBI	SH	SF	BB	SO	SB	CS	GIDP	SLG	OBA
Alfonzo, Edgardo, NY-N	R	.278	101	335	26	93	128	13	5	4	41	4	4	12	37	1	1	7	.382	.301
Andrews, Shane, Mon.	R	.214	84	220	27	47	83	10	1	8	31	1	2	17	68	1	1	4	.377	.271
Benjamin, Mike, S.F.	R	.220	68	186	19	41	56	6	0	3	12	7	0	8	51	11	1	3	.301	.256
Berry, Sean, Mon.	R	.318	103	314	38	100	166	22	1	14	55	2	5	25	53	3	8	5	.529	.367
Bonilla, Bobby, NY-N	B	.325	80	317	49	103	190	25	4	18	53	0	2	31	48	0	3	11	.599	.385
Branson, Jeff, Cin.	L	.260	122	331	43	86	144	18	2	12	45	1	6	44	69	2	1	9	.435	.345
Buechele, Steve, ChiN	R	.189	32	106	10	20	25	2	0	1	9	1	0	11	19	0	0	1	.236	.265
Busch, Mike, L.A.	R	.235	13	17	3	4	13	0	0	3	6	0	0	0	7	0	0	0	.765	.235
Caminiti, Ken, S.D.	B	.302	143	526	74	159	270	33	0	26	94	0	6	69	94	12	5	11	.513	.380
Castellano, Pedro, Col.	R	.000	4	5	0	0	0	0	0	0	0	0	0	2	3	0	0	0	.000	.286
Castilla, Vinny, Col.	R	.309	139	527	82	163	297	34	2	32	90	4	6	30	87	2	8	15	.564	.347
Castro, Juan, L.A.	R	.250	11	4	0	1	1	0	0	0	0	0	0	1	1	0	0	0	.250	.400
Coles, Darnell, St.L	R	.225	63	138	13	31	47	7	0	3	16	0	1	16	20	0	0	1	.341	.316
Cooper, Scott, St.L	L	.230	118	374	29	86	117	18	2	3	40	0	4	49	85	0	3	9	.313	.321
Donnels, Chris, Hou.	L	.300	19	30	4	9	9	0	0	0	2	0	0	3	6	0	0	1	.300	.364
Greene, Willie, Cin.	L	.105	8	19	1	2	2	0	0	0	0	0	0	3	7	0	0	1	.105	.227
Hansen, Dave, L.A.	L	.287	100	181	19	52	65	10	0	1	14	0	1	28	28	0	0	4	.359	.384
Harris, Lenny, Cin.	L	.208	101	197	32	41	61	8	3	2	16	3	1	14	20	10	1	6	.310	.259
Hayes, Charlie, Phi.	R	.276	141	529	58	146	215	30	3	11	85	0	6	50	88	5	1	22	.406	.340
Huskey, Butch, NY-N	R	.189	28	90	8	17	27	1	0	3	11	1	1	10	16	1	0	3	.300	.267
Ingram, Garey, L.A.	R	.200	44	55	5	11	13	2	0	0	3	2	0	9	8	3	0	0	.236	.313

National League third basemen

Name/Team	B	BA	G	AB	R	H	TB	2B	3B	HR	RBI	SH	SF	BB	SO	SB	CS	GIDP	SLG	OBA
Johnson, Howard, ChiN	B	.195	87	169	26	33	60	4	1	7	22	0	2	34	46	1	1	2	.355	.330
Jones, Chipper, Atl.	B	.265	140	524	87	139	236	22	3	23	86	1	4	73	99	8	4	10	.450	.353
King, Jeff, Pit.	R	.265	122	445	61	118	203	27	2	18	87	0	8	55	63	7	4	10	.456	.342
Ledesma, Aaron, NY-N	R	.242	21	33	4	8	8	0	0	0	3	0	0	6	7	0	0	2	.242	.359
Lewis, Mark, Cin.	R	.339	81	171	25	58	82	13	1	3	30	0	2	21	33	0	3	1	.480	.407
Magadan, Dave, Hou.	L	.313	127	348	44	109	139	24	0	2	51	1	2	71	56	2	1	9	.399	.428
Nevin, Phil, Hou.	R	.117	18	60	4	7	8	1	0	0	1	1	0	7	13	1	0	2	.133	.221
Oliva, Jose, Atl.-St.L	R	.142	70	183	15	26	52	5	0	7	20	0	1	12	46	0	0	5	.284	.202
Owens, Eric, Cin.	R	1.000	2	2	0	2	2	0	0	0	1	1	0	0	0	0	0	0	1.000	1.000
Pendleton, Terry, Fla.	B	.290	133	513	70	149	225	32	1	14	78	0	4	38	84	1	2	7	.439	.339
Pye, Eddie, L.A.	R	.000	7	8	0	0	0	0	0	0	0	0	0	0	4	0	0	0	.000	.000
Scarsone, Steve, S.F.	R	.266	80	233	33	62	111	10	3	11	29	3	1	18	82	3	2	2	.476	.333
Sefcik, Kevin, Phi.	R	.000	5	4	1	0	0	0	0	0	0	0	0	0	2	0	0	0	.000	.000
Sharperson, Mike, Atl.	R	.143	7	7	1	1	2	1	0	0	2	0	0	0	2	0	0	0	.286	.143
Shipley, Craig, Hou.	R	.263	92	232	23	61	80	8	1	3	24	1	2	8	28	6	1	13	.345	.291
Spiers, Bill, NY-N	L	.208	63	72	5	15	19	2	1	0	11	1	2	12	15	0	1	0	.264	.314
Wallach, Tim, L.A.	R	.266	97	327	24	87	140	22	2	9	38	0	4	27	69	0	0	11	.428	.326
Wehner, John, Pit.	R	.308	52	107	13	33	39	0	3	0	5	4	2	10	17	3	1	2	.364	.361
Williams, Matt, S.F.	R	.336	76	283	53	95	183	17	1	23	65	0	3	30	58	2	0	8	.647	.399
Young, Kevin, Pit.	R	.232	56	181	13	42	69	9	0	6	22	1	3	8	53	1	3	5	.381	.268
Zeile, Todd, St.L-ChiN	R	.246	113	426	50	105	169	22	0	14	52	4	5	34	76	1	0	13	.397	.305

National League shortstops

Name/Team	B	BA	G	AB	R	H	TB	2B	3B	HR	RBI	SH	SF	BB	SO	SB	CS	GIDP	SLG	OBA
Abbott, Kurt, Fla.	R	.255	120	420	60	107	190	18	7	17	60	2	5	36	110	4	3	6	.452	.318
Arias, Alex, Fla.	R	.269	94	216	22	58	80	9	2	3	26	3	3	22	20	1	0	8	.370	.337
Aurilia, Rich, S.F.	R	.474	9	19	4	9	18	3	0	2	4	1	1	1	2	1	0	1	.947	.476
Bell, Jay, Pit.	R	.262	138	530	79	139	214	28	4	13	55	3	1	55	110	2	5	13	.404	.336
Belliard, Rafael, Atl.	R	.222	75	180	12	40	44	2	1	0	7	4	0	6	28	2	2	4	.244	.255
Blauser, Jeff, Atl.	R	.211	115	431	60	91	147	16	2	12	31	2	2	57	107	8	5	6	.341	.319
Bogar, Tim, NY-N	R	.290	78	145	17	42	52	7	0	1	21	2	1	9	25	1	0	2	.359	.329
Brumley, A. Mike, Hou.	B	.056	18	18	1	1	4	0	0	1	2	0	0	6	1	0	0	0	.222	.056
Cedeno, Andujar, S.D.	R	.210	120	390	42	82	120	16	2	6	31	0	1	28	92	5	3	12	.308	.271
Clayton, Royce, S.F.	R	.244	138	509	56	124	174	29	3	5	58	4	3	38	109	24	9	7	.342	.298
Cordero, Wil, Mon.	R	.286	131	514	64	147	216	35	2	10	49	1	4	36	88	9	5	11	.420	.341
Counsell, Craig, Col.	L	.000	3	1	0	0	0	0	0	0	0	0	0	1	0	0	0	0	.000	.500
Cromer, Tripp, St.L	R	.226	105	345	36	78	112	19	0	5	18	1	5	14	66	0	0	14	.325	.261
Dunston, Shawon, ChiN	R	.296	127	477	58	141	225	30	6	14	69	7	3	10	75	10	5	8	.472	.317
Elster, Kevin, Phi.	R	.208	26	53	10	11	20	4	1	1	9	2	2	7	14	0	0	1	.377	.302
Grudzielanek, M., Mon.	R	.245	78	269	27	66	85	12	2	1	20	3	0	14	47	8	3	7	.316	.300
Gutierrez, Ricky, Hou.	R	.276	52	156	22	43	49	6	0	0	12	1	1	10	33	5	0	4	.314	.321
Hernandez, Jose, ChiN	R	.245	93	245	37	60	118	11	4	13	40	8	2	13	69	1	0	8	.482	.281
Holbert, Ray, S.D.	R	.178	63	73	11	13	23	2	1	2	5	3	0	8	20	4	0	3	.315	.277
Larkin, Barry, Cin.	R	.319	131	496	98	158	244	29	6	15	66	3	4	61	49	51	5	6	.492	.394
Miller, Orlando, Hou.	R	.262	92	324	36	85	122	20	1	5	36	4	0	22	71	3	4	7	.377	.319
Offerman, Jose, L.A.	B	.287	119	429	69	123	161	14	6	4	33	10	0	69	67	2	7	5	.375	.389
Schofield, Dick C., L.A.	R	.100	9	10	0	1	1	0	0	0	0	0	0	1	3	0	0	0	.100	.182
Silvestri, Dave, Mon.	R	.264	39	72	12	19	31	6	0	2	7	1	1	9	27	2	0	2	.431	.341
Smith, Ozzie, St.L	B	.199	44	156	16	31	38	5	1	0	11	5	2	17	12	4	3	6	.244	.282
Stankiewicz, Andy, Hou.	R	.115	43	52	6	6	7	1	0	0	7	1	0	12	19	4	2	1	.135	.281
Stocker, Kevin, Phi.	B	.218	125	412	42	90	113	14	3	1	32	10	3	43	75	6	1	7	.274	.304
Vizcaino, Jose, NY-N	B	.287	135	509	66	146	186	21	5	3	56	13	3	35	76	8	3	14	.365	.332
Weiss, Walt, Col.	B	.260	137	427	65	111	137	17	3	1	25	6	1	98	57	15	3	7	.321	.403
Zosky, Eddie, Fla.	R	.200	6	5	0	1	1	0	0	0	0	0	0	0	0	0	0	0	.200	.200

National League outfielders

Name/Team	B	BA	G	AB	R	H	TB	2B	3B	HR	RBI	SH	SF	BB	SO	SB	CS	GIDP	SLG	OBA
Alou, Moises, Mon.	R	.273	93	344	48	94	158	22	0	14	58	0	4	29	56	4	3	9	.459	.342
Anthony, Eric, Cin.	L	.269	47	134	19	36	57	6	0	5	23	0	3	13	30	2	1	1	.425	.327
Ashley, Billy, L.A.	R	.237	81	215	17	51	80	5	0	8	27	0	2	25	88	0	0	8	.372	.320
Barry, Jeff, NY-N	B	.133	15	15	2	2	3	1	0	0	0	0	0	1	8	0	0	0	.200	.188
Battle, Allen, St.L	R	.271	61	118	13	32	37	5	0	0	2	3	0	15	26	3	3	0	.314	.358
Bean, Billy, S.D.	L	.000	4	7	1	0	0	0	0	0	0	0	0	1	4	0	0	0	.000	.125
Bell, Derek, Hou.	R	.334	112	452	63	151	200	21	2	8	86	0	6	33	71	27	9	10	.442	.385
Benard, Marvin, S.F.	L	.382	13	34	5	13	18	2	0	1	4	0	0	1	7	1	0	1	.529	.400
Benitez, Yamil, Mon.	R	.385	14	39	8	15	25	2	1	2	7	0	0	1	7	0	2	1	.641	.400

National League outfielders

Name/Team	B	BA	G	AB	R	H	TB	2B	3B	HR	RBI	SH	SF	BB	SO	SB	CS	GIDP	SLG	OBA
Bichette, Dante, Col.	R	.340	139	579	102	197	359	38	2	40	128	0	7	22	96	13	9	16	.620	.364
Bonds, Barry, S.F.	L	.294	144	506	109	149	292	30	7	33	104	0	4	120	83	31	10	12	.577	.431
Bradshaw, Terry, St.L	L	.227	19	44	6	10	13	1	1	0	2	0	0	2	10	1	2	0	.295	.261
Brumfield, Jacob, Pit.	R	.271	116	402	64	109	148	23	2	4	26	0	1	37	71	22	12	3	.368	.339
Buford, Damon, NY-N	R	.235	44	136	24	32	49	5	0	4	12	0	2	19	28	7	7	3	.360	.346
Bullett, Scott, ChiN	L	.273	104	150	19	41	69	5	7	3	22	1	0	12	30	8	3	4	.460	.331
Burks, Ellis, Col.	R	.266	103	278	41	74	138	10	6	14	49	1	1	39	72	7	3	7	.496	.359
Butler, Brett, NY-N-L.A.	L	.300	129	513	78	154	193	18	9	1	38	10	6	67	51	32	8	5	.376	.377
Cangelosi, John, Hou.	B	.318	90	201	46	64	79	5	2	2	18	2	1	48	42	21	5	3	.393	.457
Carr, Chuck, Fla.	R	.227	105	308	54	70	96	20	0	2	20	7	2	46	49	25	11	2	.312	.330
Cedeno, Roberto, L.A.	B	.238	40	42	4	10	12	2	0	0	3	0	1	3	10	1	0	1	.286	.283
Clark, Dave, Pit.	L	.281	77	196	30	55	73	6	0	4	24	0	2	24	38	3	3	9	.372	.359
Clark, Phil, S.D.	R	.216	75	97	12	21	30	3	0	2	7	0	2	8	18	0	2	3	.309	.278
Conine, Jeff, Fla.	R	.302	133	483	72	146	251	26	2	25	105	0	12	66	94	2	0	13	.520	.379
Cummings, Midre, Pit.	L	.243	59	152	13	37	52	7	1	2	15	0	0	13	30	1	0	1	.342	.303
Dawson, Andre, Fla.	R	.257	79	226	30	58	98	10	3	8	37	0	3	9	45	0	0	7	.434	.305
Devereaux, Mike, Atl.	R	.255	29	55	7	14	20	3	0	1	8	0	0	2	11	2	0	1	.364	.281
Dykstra, Lenny, Phi.	L	.264	62	254	37	67	90	15	1	2	18	0	2	33	28	10	5	1	.354	.353
Eisenreich, Jim, Phi.	L	.316	129	377	46	119	175	22	2	10	55	2	5	38	44	10	0	7	.464	.375
Everett, Carl, NY-N	R	.260	79	289	48	75	126	13	1	12	54	1	0	39	67	2	5	11	.436	.352
Faneyte, Rikkert, S.F.	R	.198	46	86	7	17	23	4	1	0	4	1	0	11	27	1	0	2	.267	.289
Finley, Steve, S.D.	L	.297	139	562	104	167	236	23	8	10	44	4	2	59	62	36	12	8	.420	.366
Flora, Kevin, Phi.	R	.213	24	75	12	16	25	3	0	2	7	2	0	4	22	1	0	0	.333	.253
Frazier, Lou, Mon.	B	.190	35	63	6	12	14	2	0	0	3	0	1	8	12	4	0	1	.222	.297
Gallagher, Dave, Phi.	R	.318	62	157	12	50	65	12	0	1	12	2	1	16	20	0	0	5	.414	.379
Gant, Ron, Cin.	R	.276	119	410	79	113	227	19	4	29	88	1	5	74	108	23	8	11	.554	.386
Garcia, Freddy, Pit.	R	.140	42	57	5	8	11	1	1	0	1	1	0	8	17	0	1	0	.193	.246
Garcia, Karim, L.A.	L	.200	13	20	1	4	4	0	0	0	0	0	0	0	4	0	0	0	.200	.200
Gibralter, Steve, Cin.	R	.333	4	3	0	1	1	0	0	0	0	0	0	0	0	0	0	0	.333	.333
Gilkey, Bernard, St.L	R	.298	121	480	73	143	235	33	4	17	69	1	3	42	70	12	6	17	.490	.358
Gonzalez, Luis, Hou.-ChiN	L	.276	133	471	69	130	214	29	8	13	69	1	6	57	63	6	8	16	.454	.357
Gregg, Tommy, Fla.	L	.237	72	156	20	37	60	5	0	6	20	0	2	16	33	3	1	3	.385	.313
Grissom, Marquis, Atl.	R	.258	139	551	80	142	207	23	3	12	42	1	4	47	61	29	9	8	.376	.317
Gwynn, Tony, S.D.	L	.368	135	535	82	197	259	33	1	9	90	0	6	35	15	17	5	20	.484	.404
Gwynn, Chris, L.A.	L	.214	67	84	8	18	28	3	2	1	10	0	1	6	23	0	0	5	.333	.272
Hajek, Dave, Hou.	R	.000	5	2	0	0	0	0	0	0	0	2	0	1	1	1	0	0	.000	.333
Hill, Glenallen, S.F.	R	.264	132	497	71	131	240	29	4	24	86	0	2	39	98	25	5	11	.483	.317
Hollandsworth, T., L.A.	L	.233	41	103	16	24	41	2	0	5	13	0	1	10	29	2	1	1	.398	.304
Howard, Thomas, Cin.	B	.302	113	281	42	85	113	15	2	3	26	1	1	20	37	17	8	3	.402	.350
Hubbard, Trenidad, Col.	R	.310	24	58	13	18	31	4	0	3	9	1	0	8	6	2	1	2	.534	.394
Hunter, Brian L., Hou.	R	.302	78	321	52	97	127	14	5	2	28	2	3	21	52	24	7	2	.396	.346
Jones, Chris C., NY-N	R	.280	79	182	33	51	85	6	2	8	31	2	3	13	45	2	1	2	.467	.327
Jordan, Brian, St.L	R	.296	131	490	83	145	239	20	4	22	81	0	2	22	79	24	9	5	.488	.339
Justice, David, Atl.	L	.253	120	411	73	104	197	17	2	24	78	0	5	73	68	4	2	5	.479	.365
Kelly, Mike, Atl.	R	.190	97	137	26	26	43	6	1	3	17	2	1	11	49	7	3	2	.314	.258
Kelly, Roberto, Mon.-L.A.	R	.278	136	504	58	140	188	23	2	7	57	0	7	22	79	19	10	14	.373	.312
Kingery, Mike, Col.	L	.269	119	350	66	94	144	18	4	8	37	6	1	45	40	13	5	7	.411	.351
Klesko, Ryan, Atl.	L	.310	107	329	48	102	200	25	2	23	70	0	3	47	72	5	4	8	.608	.396
Kowitz, Brian, Atl.	L	.167	10	24	3	4	5	1	0	0	3	1	0	2	5	0	1	0	.208	.259
Lankford, Ray, St.L	L	.277	132	483	81	134	248	35	2	25	82	0	5	63	110	24	8	10	.513	.360
Leonard, Mark, S.F.	L	.190	14	21	4	4	8	1	0	1	4	0	0	5	2	0	0	0	.381	.346
Lewis, Darren, S.F.-Cin.	R	.250	132	472	66	118	140	13	3	1	24	12	1	34	57	32	18	9	.297	.311
Longmire, Tony, Phi.	L	.356	59	104	21	37	53	7	0	3	19	0	1	11	19	1	1	1	.510	.419
Marsh, Tom, Phi.	R	.294	43	109	13	32	46	3	1	3	15	0	1	4	25	0	1	1	.422	.316
Martin, Al, Pit.	L	.282	124	439	70	124	194	25	3	13	41	1	0	44	92	20	11	5	.442	.351
May, Derrick, Hou.	L	.301	78	206	29	62	103	15	1	8	41	0	3	19	24	5	0	4	.500	.358
McCarty, David, S.F.	R	.250	12	20	1	5	6	1	0	0	2	0	0	2	4	1	0	0	.300	.318
McCracken, Quinton, Col	R	.000	3	0	0	0	0	0	0	0	0	0	0	0	1	0	0	0	.000	.000
McDavid, Ray, S.D.	R	.176	11	17	2	3	3	0	0	0	0	0	0	2	6	1	1	1	.176	.263
McRae, Brian, ChiN	B	.288	137	580	92	167	255	38	7	12	48	3	1	47	92	27	8	12	.440	.348
Merced, Orlando, Pit.	L	.300	132	487	75	146	228	29	4	15	83	0	5	52	74	7	2	9	.468	.365
Mondesi, Raul, L.A.	R	.285	139	536	91	153	266	23	6	26	88	0	7	33	96	27	4	7	.496	.328
Morman, Russ, Fla.	R	.278	34	72	9	20	33	2	1	3	7	0	0	3	12	0	0	5	.458	.316
Mouton, James, Hou.	R	.262	104	298	42	78	112	18	2	4	27	3	1	25	59	25	8	5	.376	.326
Newfield, Marc, S.D.	R	.309	21	55	6	17	27	5	1	1	7	0	0	2	8	0	0	3	.491	.333
Nieves, Melvin, S.D.	B	.205	98	234	32	48	98	6	1	14	38	1	3	19	88	2	3	9	.419	.276
Ochoa, Alex, NY-N	R	.297	11	37	7	11	12	1	0	0	0	0	0	2	10	1	0	1	.324	.333
Orsulak, Joe, NY-N	L	.283	108	290	41	82	108	19	2	1	37	1	6	19	35	1	3	3	.372	.323
Otero, Ricky, NY-N	B	.137	35	51	5	7	9	2	0	0	1	0	0	3	10	2	1	1	.176	.185
Parker, Rick, L.A.	R	.276	27	29	3	8	8	0	0	0	4	2	0	2	4	1	1	1	.276	.323

National League outfielders

Name/Team	B	BA	G	AB	R	H	TB	2B	3B	HR	RBI	SH	SF	BB	SO	SB	CS	GIDP	SLG	OBA
Pegues, Steve, Pit.	R	.246	82	171	17	42	68	8	0	6	16	0	3	4	36	1	2	3	.398	.263
Plantier, Phil, Hou.-S.D.	L	.255	76	216	33	55	88	6	0	9	34	0	3	28	48	1	1	3	.407	.339
Polonia, Luis, Atl.	L	.264	28	53	6	14	21	7	0	0	2	1	0	3	9	3	0	0	.396	.304
Pride, Curtis, Mon.	L	.175	48	63	10	11	12	1	0	0	2	1	0	5	16	3	2	2	.190	.235
Pulliam, Harvey, Col.	R	.400	5	5	1	2	6	1	0	1	3	0	0	0	2	0	0	0	1.200	.400
Rhodes, Tuffy, ChiN	L	.125	13	16	2	2	2	0	0	0	2	0	1	0	4	0	0	1	.125	.118
Roberson, Kevin, ChiN	B	.184	32	38	5	7	20	1	0	4	6	0	0	6	14	0	1	1	.526	.311
Roberts, Bip, S.D.	B	.304	73	296	40	90	110	14	0	2	25	1	0	17	36	20	2	2	.372	.346
Rodriguez, H., L.A.-Mon.	L	.239	45	138	13	33	45	4	1	2	15	0	1	11	28	0	1	5	.326	.293
Sanders, Deion, Cin.-S.F.	L	.268	85	343	48	92	137	11	8	6	28	3	2	27	60	24	9	1	.399	.327
Sanders, Reggie, Cin.	R	.306	133	484	91	148	280	36	6	28	99	0	6	69	122	36	12	9	.579	.397
Santangelo, F. P., Mon.	B	.296	35	98	11	29	39	5	1	1	9	1	0	12	9	1	1	0	.398	.384
Sheffield, Gary, Fla.	R	.324	63	213	46	69	125	8	0	16	46	0	2	55	45	19	4	3	.587	.467
Smith, Dwight, Atl.	L	.252	103	131	16	33	54	8	2	3	21	0	1	13	35	0	3	2	.412	.327
Sosa, Sammy, ChiN	R	.268	144	564	89	151	282	17	3	36	119	0	2	58	134	34	7	8	.500	.344
Tarasco, Tony, Mon.	L	.249	126	438	64	109	177	18	4	14	40	3	1	51	78	24	3	2	.404	.329
Tavarez, Jesus, Fla.	B	.289	63	190	31	55	71	6	2	2	13	3	1	16	27	7	5	1	.374	.346
Thompson, Milt, Hou.	L	.220	92	132	14	29	44	9	0	2	19	2	1	14	37	4	2	3	.333	.297
Thompson, Ryan, NY-N	R	.251	75	267	39	67	101	13	0	7	31	0	4	19	77	3	1	12	.378	.306
Timmons, Ozzie, ChiN	R	.263	77	171	30	45	81	10	1	8	28	0	1	13	32	3	0	8	.474	.314
Van Slyke, Andy, Phi.	L	.243	63	214	26	52	75	10	2	3	16	0	2	28	41	7	0	6	.350	.333
Varsho, Gary, Phi.	L	.252	72	103	7	26	29	1	1	0	11	0	1	7	17	2	0	1	.282	.310
Walker, Larry, Col.	L	.306	131	494	96	151	300	31	5	36	101	0	5	49	72	16	3	13	.607	.381
Walton, Jerome, Cin.	R	.290	102	162	32	47	85	12	1	8	22	3	2	17	25	10	7	0	.525	.368
Webster, Mitch, L.A.	B	.179	54	56	6	10	16	1	1	1	3	2	0	4	14	0	0	1	.286	.246
White, Rondell, Mon.	R	.295	130	474	87	140	220	33	4	13	57	0	4	41	87	25	5	11	.464	.356
Whiten, Mark, Phi.	B	.269	60	212	38	57	102	10	1	11	37	0	0	31	63	7	0	4	.481	.365
Whitmore, Darrell, Fla.	L	.190	27	58	6	11	16	2	0	1	2	1	1	5	15	0	0	1	.276	.250
Williams, Reggie, L.A.	B	.091	15	11	2	1	1	0	0	0	1	0	0	2	3	0	0	0	.091	.231
Wilson, Nigel, Cin.	L	.000	5	7	0	0	0	0	0	0	0	0	0	0	4	0	0	0	.000	.000

National League starting pitchers (batting)

Name/Team	B	BA	G	AB	R	H	TB	2B	3B	HR	RBI	SH	SF	BB	SO	SB	CS	GIDP	SLG	OBA
Acevedo, Juan, Col.	R	.056	17	18	0	1	1	0	0	0	0	0	0	1	6	0	0	2	.056	.105
Alvarez, Tavo, Mon.	R	.000	8	12	1	0	0	0	0	0	0	0	2	0	4	0	0	0	.000	.000
Ashby, Andy, S.D.	R	.163	31	49	2	8	9	1	0	0	3	17	0	1	24	1	0	0	.184	.180
Avery, Steve, Atl.	L	.208	29	53	4	11	20	1	1	2	4	8	1	1	17	0	0	0	.377	.218
Banks, W., ChiN-L.A.-Fla.	R	.269	28	26	2	7	8	1	0	0	1	1	0	1	9	0	0	0	.308	.321
Benes, Alan, St.L	R	.000	3	6	0	0	0	0	0	0	0	0	0	0	3	0	0	0	.000	.000
Benes, Andy, S.D.	R	.150	19	40	2	6	7	1	0	0	3	3	0	1	18	0	0	1	.175	.171
Birkbeck, Mike, NY-N	R	.333	4	6	1	2	2	0	0	0	0	1	0	1	1	0	0	0	.333	.500
Bowen, Ryan, Fla.	R	.333	4	6	1	2	2	0	0	0	0	0	0	0	3	0	0	0	.333	.333
Brewington, Jamie, S.F.	R	.217	14	23	3	5	5	0	0	0	1	4	0	0	7	0	0	0	.217	.217
Bullinger, Jim, ChiN	R	.128	25	47	1	6	9	3	0	0	5	8	2	5	16	0	0	1	.191	.204
Burkett, John, Fla.	R	.106	31	66	3	7	8	1	0	0	3	4	0	2	23	0	0	1	.121	.145
Candiotti, Tom, L.A.	R	.109	30	55	2	6	6	0	0	0	2	5	0	3	16	0	0	1	.109	.155
Castillo, Frank, ChiN	R	.102	29	59	1	6	6	0	0	0	1	7	0	3	25	0	0	0	.102	.145
Cornelius, R., Mon.-NY-N	R	.100	18	20	0	2	2	0	0	0	0	0	0	0	7	0	0	0	.100	.100
Deshaies, Jim, Phi.	L	.000	2	1	0	0	0	0	0	0	0	0	0	0	1	0	0	0	.000	.000
Dishman, Glenn, S.D.	R	.200	19	30	4	6	6	0	0	0	4	2	1	0	13	0	0	0	.200	.219
Drabek, Doug, Hou.	R	.233	33	60	4	14	17	3	0	0	8	8	0	2	17	0	0	0	.283	.258
Ericks, John, Pit.	R	.097	19	31	2	3	4	1	0	0	1	6	0	0	12	0	0	0	.129	.097
Estes, Shawn, S.F.	R	.000	3	5	0	0	0	0	0	0	0	0	0	0	2	0	0	1	.000	.000
Fassero, Jeff, Mon.	L	.070	30	57	6	4	4	0	0	0	1	8	0	5	29	0	0	0	.070	.145
Fernandez, Sid, Phi.	L	.043	11	23	1	1	1	0	0	0	1	1	0	1	15	0	0	0	.043	.083
Foster, Kevin, ChiN	R	.250	33	60	7	15	21	1	1	1	9	5	0	3	16	2	0	0	.350	.286
Freeman, Marvin, Col.	R	.087	22	23	2	2	5	0	0	1	4	6	0	1	16	0	0	0	.217	.125
Glavine, Tom, Atl.	L	.222	29	63	6	14	18	1	0	1	8	8	0	2	15	0	0	0	.286	.258
Grace, Mike, Phi.	R	.000	2	2	0	0	0	0	0	0	0	0	2	0	2	0	0	0	.000	.000
Grahe, Joe, Col.	R	.417	17	12	1	5	6	1	0	0	2	6	0	0	3	0	0	0	.500	.417
Green, Tyler, Phi.	R	.182	27	44	2	8	16	5	0	1	5	8	0	0	16	0	1	0	.364	.182
Greene, Tommy, Phi.	R	.000	11	8	0	0	0	0	0	0	0	1	0	2	3	0	0	0	.000	.200
Hamilton, Joey, S.D.	R	.108	31	65	4	7	9	2	0	0	3	5	1	2	38	0	0	1	.138	.132
Hammond, Chris, Fla.	R	.271	25	48	7	13	18	2	0	1	4	5	0	7	16	0	0	1	.375	.364
Hampton, Mike, Hou.	R	.146	24	48	7	7	7	0	0	0	0	4	0	4	14	0	0	0	.146	.226
Harnisch, Pete, NY-N	R	.091	18	33	0	3	3	0	0	0	0	3	0	0	6	0	0	0	.091	.091
Henry, Butch, Mon.	L	.048	21	42	1	2	2	0	0	0	1	5	0	0	11	0	0	0	.048	.048
Hill, Ken, St.L	R	.194	18	31	1	6	6	0	0	0	3	5	1	2	10	0	0	0	.194	.235

National League starting pitchers (batting)

Name/Team	B	BA	G	AB	R	H	TB	2B	3B	HR	RBI	SH	SF	BB	SO	SB	CS	GIDP	SLG	OBA
Isringhausen, J., NY-N	R	.148	14	27	2	4	5	1	0	0	0	4	0	2	10	0	0	1	.185	.233
Jackson, Danny, St.L	R	.161	19	31	1	5	7	2	0	0	2	4	0	1	16	0	0	0	.226	.188
Jacome, Jason, NY-N	L	.000	5	7	0	0	0	0	0	0	0	1	0	0	6	0	0	0	.000	.000
Jarvis, Kevin, Cin.	L	.143	19	21	2	3	4	1	0	0	0	1	0	0	8	0	0	0	.190	.182
Jones, Bobby J., NY-N	R	.161	30	56	3	9	9	0	0	0	2	18	0	1	25	0	0	0	.161	.175
Juden, Jeff, Phi.	R	.056	13	18	1	1	4	0	0	1	4	3	0	0	12	0	0	0	.222	.056
Kile, Darryl, Hou.	R	.111	25	36	1	4	5	1	0	0	6	5	0	4	20	0	0	1	.139	.200
Leiter, Mark, S.F.	R	.098	30	61	2	6	6	0	0	0	5	9	0	4	33	0	0	2	.098	.154
Lieber, Jon, Pit.	L	.048	21	21	0	1	1	0	0	0	0	0	0	0	14	0	0	1	.048	.048
Loaiza, Esteban, Pit.	R	.192	33	52	4	10	13	1	1	0	2	7	1	1	11	0	0	0	.250	.204
Maddux, Greg, Atl.	R	.153	28	72	8	11	13	2	0	0	6	6	0	3	22	0	0	0	.181	.187
Martinez, Pedro J., Mon.	R	.111	30	63	2	7	7	0	0	0	2	5	2	0	30	0	0	1	.111	.134
Martinez, Ramon, L.A.	L	.172	30	64	2	11	15	4	0	0	4	13	0	1	19	0	0	0	.234	.185
Mercker, Kent, Atl.	L	.104	29	48	1	5	8	3	0	0	5	6	0	0	17	0	0	0	.167	.104
Mimbs, Michael, Phi.	L	.143	35	35	2	5	6	1	0	0	2	8	0	0	12	0	0	0	.171	.143
Mlicki, Dave, NY-N	R	.051	29	39	2	2	2	0	0	0	2	12	0	8	12	0	0	0	.051	.213
Morgan, Mike, ChiN-St.L	R	.053	21	38	2	2	2	0	0	0	0	4	0	3	20	0	0	0	.053	.122
Mulholland, Terry, S.F.	R	.102	30	49	3	5	11	1	1	1	3	3	1	1	22	0	0	1	.224	.118
Munoz, Bobby, Phi.	R	.000	3	5	0	0	0	0	0	0	0	0	0	0	2	0	0	0	.000	.000
Navarro, Jaime, ChiN	R	.185	29	65	0	12	17	5	0	0	7	8	0	1	25	0	0	0	.262	.197
Neagle, Denny, Pit.	L	.122	32	74	5	9	15	3	0	1	8	5	0	4	26	0	0	0	.203	.167
Nitkowski, C.J., Cin.	L	.200	9	10	1	2	2	0	0	0	1	0	0	0	6	0	0	0	.200	.200
Nomo, Hideo, L.A.	R	.091	28	66	2	6	6	0	0	0	4	5	1	0	33	0	0	1	.091	.090
Osborne, Donovan, St.L	L	.161	19	31	1	5	8	3	0	0	4	3	0	3	15	0	0	0	.258	.257
Parris, Steve, Pit.	R	.250	15	28	2	7	9	2	0	0	4	1	0	0	10	0	0	0	.321	.250
Perez, Carlos, Mon.	L	.133	28	45	1	6	12	1	1	1	5	4	0	4	21	0	0	0	.267	.204
Petkovsek, Mark, St.L	R	.081	26	37	4	3	3	0	0	0	2	3	1	5	11	0	0	0	.081	.186
Portugal, Mark, S.F.-Cin.	R	.138	31	58	5	8	13	5	0	0	5	8	0	5	13	0	0	1	.224	.206
Pulsipher, Bill, NY-N	L	.105	17	38	4	4	6	2	0	0	4	4	2	5	19	0	0	0	.158	.200
Quantrill, Paul, Phi.	L	.105	33	57	5	6	6	0	0	0	0	7	0	3	24	0	0	1	.105	.150
Rapp, Pat, Fla.	R	.107	28	56	1	6	7	1	0	0	5	9	0	0	25	0	0	1	.125	.107
Reed, Rick, Cin.	R	.000	4	3	0	0	0	0	0	0	0	0	2	0	0	0	0	0	.000	.000
Rekar, Bryan, Col.	B	.038	15	26	1	1	1	0	0	0	0	4	0	3	15	0	1	2	.038	.138
Reynolds, Shane, Hou.	R	.127	31	63	4	8	9	1	0	0	1	10	0	1	30	0	0	2	.143	.141
Reynoso, Armando, Col.	R	.133	20	30	1	4	4	0	0	0	0	2	0	1	11	0	0	2	.133	.161
Rijo, Jose, Cin.	R	.136	14	22	1	3	4	1	0	0	3	2	0	0	3	0	0	0	.182	.136
Ritz, Kevin, Col.	R	.188	31	48	3	9	10	1	0	0	2	11	0	2	20	1	1	1	.208	.250
Roper, John, Cin.-S.F.	R	.000	3	1	0	0	0	0	0	0	0	1	0	0	0	0	0	0	.000	.000
Rosselli, Joe, S.F.	R	.200	9	10	1	2	2	0	0	0	1	1	0	0	3	0	0	0	.200	.200
Rueter, Kirk, Mon.	L	.000	9	16	0	0	0	0	0	0	1	2	0	0	6	0	0	0	.000	.000
Saberhagen, B., NY-N-Col.	R	.102	25	49	3	5	6	1	0	0	0	5	0	2	12	0	0	0	.122	.137
Sanders, Scott, S.D.	R	.296	17	27	2	8	9	1	0	0	4	3	0	1	3	1	0	0	.333	.321
Schilling, Curt, Phi.	R	.175	17	40	3	7	9	2	0	0	3	5	0	0	15	0	0	1	.225	.175
Schourek, Pete, Cin.	L	.220	29	59	7	13	15	2	0	0	4	12	0	0	12	0	0	1	.254	.220
Smiley, John, Cin.	L	.164	28	55	6	9	16	1	0	2	5	6	1	4	26	0	0	1	.291	.217
Smoltz, John, Atl.	R	.107	29	56	5	6	6	0	0	0	1	6	0	7	25	0	0	0	.107	.206
Springer, Dennis, Phi.	R	.125	4	8	0	1	1	0	0	0	0	0	0	0	3	0	0	0	.125	.125
Swift, Bill C., Col.	R	.194	19	36	5	7	11	1	0	1	4	5	0	2	5	1	0	0	.306	.237
Swindell, Greg, Hou.	R	.240	34	50	4	12	15	3	0	0	5	6	0	3	9	0	0	1	.300	.283
Tapani, Kevin, L.A.	R	.176	13	17	0	3	4	1	0	0	2	3	0	0	7	0	0	0	.235	.176
Telgheder, Dave, NY-N	R	.333	7	6	1	2	2	0	0	0	1	1	0	0	3	0	0	0	.333	.333
Trachsel, Steve, ChiN	R	.265	30	49	3	13	15	2	0	0	4	6	1	2	17	0	0	0	.306	.288
Urbani, Tom, St.L	L	.316	24	19	3	6	10	1	0	1	3	2	0	3	6	0	0	0	.526	.409
Urbina, Ugueth, Mon.	R	.333	7	6	0	2	2	0	0	0	0	0	0	0	4	0	0	0	.333	.333
Valdes, Ismael, L.A.	R	.097	33	62	2	6	6	0	0	0	1	7	0	1	26	1	0	0	.097	.111
Valdes, Marc, Fla.	R	.000	3	2	0	0	0	0	0	0	0	0	0	0	0	0	0	0	.000	.000
Valdez, Sergio, S.F.	R	.095	13	21	1	2	2	0	0	0	1	3	0	0	9	0	0	0	.095	.095
Valenzuela, F., S.D.	L	.250	29	32	3	8	15	1	0	2	8	3	0	0	6	0	0	0	.469	.250
VanLandingham, W., S.F.	R	.152	18	46	1	7	12	2	0	1	3	1	0	0	24	0	0	1	.261	.152
Viola, Frank, Cin.	L	.167	3	6	0	1	2	1	0	0	0	0	0	0	1	0	0	0	.333	.167
Wagner, Paul, Pit.	R	.214	34	42	5	9	10	1	0	0	4	6	0	4	11	0	0	1	.238	.283
Wall, Donne, Hou.	R	.000	6	5	0	0	0	0	0	0	0	0	3	0	2	0	0	0	.000	.000
Watson, Allen, St.L	L	.417	21	36	5	15	19	4	0	0	5	3	0	2	7	0	0	1	.528	.447
Weathers, Dave, Fla.	R	.154	28	26	1	4	4	0	0	0	1	5	0	0	17	0	0	0	.154	.154
Wells, David, Cin.	L	.143	11	28	2	4	4	0	0	0	0	1	0	0	5	0	0	0	.143	.143
West, David, Phi.	L	.125	8	8	1	1	4	0	0	1	3	6	0	1	4	0	0	1	.500	.222
White, Rick, Pit.	R	.067	15	15	1	1	2	1	0	0	1	2	0	0	3	0	0	0	.133	.067
Wilson, Trevor, S.F.	L	.233	19	30	1	7	8	1	0	0	3	3	0	0	8	0	0	0	.267	.233
Witt, Bobby, Fla.	R	.063	21	32	0	2	3	1	0	0	2	4	1	1	10	0	0	0	.094	.088

National League relief pitchers (batting)

Name/Team	B	BA	G	AB	R	H	TB	2B	3B	HR	RBI	SH	SF	BB	SO	SB	CS	GIDP	SLG	OBA
Abbott, Kyle, Phi.	L	.500	18	2	1	1	1	0	0	0	0	0	0	0	1	0	0	0	.500	.500
Aquino, Luis, Mon.-S.F.	R	.250	34	4	0	1	1	0	0	0	0	0	0	1	2	0	0	0	.250	.400
Arocha, Rene, St.L	R	.000	41	1	0	0	0	0	0	0	0	0	0	1	1	0	0	0	.000	.000
Astacio, Pedro, L.A.	R	.125	48	24	0	3	4	1	0	0	0	2	0	1	9	0	0	1	.167	.160
Bailey, Roger, Col.	R	.125	39	16	2	2	2	0	0	0	1	3	0	1	3	0	0	0	.125	.176
Barber, Brian, St.L	R	.125	9	8	0	1	1	0	0	0	0	0	0	1	2	0	0	0	.125	.222
Barton, Shawn, S.F.	R	—	52	0	0	0	0	0	0	0	0	1	0	0	0	0	0	0	—	—
Bautista, Jose, S.F.	R	.000	52	18	0	0	0	0	0	0	0	1	0	1	9	0	0	0	.000	.053
Beck, Rod, S.F.	R	.333	60	3	0	1	1	0	0	0	0	0	0	0	1	0	0	0	.333	.333
Berumen, Andres, S.D.	R	.000	37	1	0	0	0	0	0	0	0	0	0	0	1	0	0	0	.000	.000
Blair, Willie, S.D.	R	.000	40	24	2	0	0	0	0	0	1	4	0	1	17	0	0	0	.000	.040
Bochtler, Doug, S.D.	R	.000	34	2	0	0	0	0	0	0	0	0	0	0	0	0	0	0	.000	.000
Borbon, Pedro Jr., Atl.	R	.000	41	1	0	0	0	0	0	0	0	0	0	0	0	0	0	0	.000	.000
Borland, Toby, Phi.	R	.200	50	5	1	1	1	0	0	0	1	0	1	0	1	0	0	0	.200	.167
Bottalico, Ricky, Phi.	L	.000	62	5	0	0	0	0	0	0	0	1	0	0	4	0	0	0	.000	.000
Brantley, Jeff, Cin.	R	.000	56	3	0	0	0	0	0	0	0	0	0	0	1	0	0	0	.000	.000
Brocail, Doug, Hou.	L	.250	37	16	3	4	6	0	1	0	1	4	0	0	5	0	0	0	.375	.250
Burba, Dave, S.F.-Cin.	R	.067	52	15	2	1	1	0	0	0	0	4	0	3	9	0	0	0	.067	.222
Byrd, Paul, NY-N	R	1.000	17	1	0	1	1	0	0	0	0	0	0	0	0	0	0	0	1.000	1.000
Carrasco, Hector, Cin.	R	.000	64	7	0	0	0	0	0	0	0	0	0	0	4	0	0	0	.000	.000
Carter, Andy, Phi.	L	1.000	4	1	0	1	1	0	0	0	0	0	0	0	0	0	0	0	1.000	1.000
Casian, Larry, ChiN	R	.000	42	2	0	0	0	0	0	0	0	0	0	0	1	0	0	0	.000	.000
Charlton, Norm, Phi.	B	1.000	25	1	0	1	2	1	0	0	1	0	0	0	0	0	0	0	2.000	1.000
Christiansen, Jason, Pit.	R	.000	63	1	0	0	0	0	0	0	0	0	0	0	1	0	0	0	.000	.000
Clontz, Brad, Atl.	R	.000	59	2	0	0	0	0	0	0	0	0	0	0	0	0	0	0	.000	.000
Cummings, John, L.A.	L	.000	35	3	0	0	0	0	0	0	0	0	0	0	1	0	0	0	.000	.000
DeLeon, Jose, Mon.	R	—	7	0	0	0	0	0	0	0	0	1	0	1	0	0	0	0	—	1.000
DeLucia, Rich, St.L	R	.200	56	10	1	2	2	0	0	0	0	1	0	1	3	0	0	1	.200	.273
Dewey, Mark, S.F.	R	.000	27	1	0	0	0	0	0	0	0	0	0	0	1	0	0	0	.000	.000
DiPoto, Jerry, NY-N	R	.000	58	5	0	0	0	0	0	0	0	1	0	0	3	0	0	0	.000	.000
Dougherty, Jim, Hou.	R	.125	56	8	1	1	1	0	0	0	0	1	0	0	2	0	0	0	.125	.125
Dyer, Mike, Pit.	R	.571	55	7	1	4	4	0	0	0	1	1	0	0	2	0	0	0	.571	.571
Eischen, Joey, L.A.	L	.000	17	1	0	0	0	0	0	0	0	0	0	0	1	0	0	0	.000	.000
Eversgerd, Bryan, Mon.	R	.000	25	1	0	0	0	0	0	0	0	0	0	0	0	0	0	0	.000	.000
Florence, Don, NY-N	R	.000	14	1	0	0	0	0	0	0	0	0	0	0	1	0	0	0	.000	.000
Florie, Bryce, S.D.	R	.000	47	2	0	0	0	0	0	0	0	0	0	0	2	0	0	0	.000	.000
Frascatore, John, St.L	R	.000	14	7	0	0	0	0	0	0	0	1	0	1	6	0	0	0	.000	.125
Fraser, Willie, Mon.	R	.000	22	2	0	0	0	0	0	0	0	0	0	0	0	0	0	0	.000	.000
Frey, Steve, S.F.-Phi.	L	.000	18	1	0	0	0	0	0	0	0	0	0	0	1	0	0	0	.000	.000
Garces, Rich, ChiN-Fla.	R	.000	18	1	0	0	0	0	0	0	0	0	0	0	0	0	0	0	.000	.000
Gardner, Mark, Fla.	R	.190	39	21	1	4	4	0	0	0	1	4	0	0	6	0	0	0	.190	.190
Gomez, Pat, S.F.	L	.000	18	1	0	0	0	0	0	0	0	0	0	0	1	0	0	0	.000	.000
Gott, Jim, Pit.	R	.000	25	1	0	0	0	0	0	0	0	0	0	0	1	0	0	0	.000	.000
Greer, Kenny, S.F.	R	.000	8	1	0	0	0	0	0	0	0	0	0	0	0	0	0	0	.000	.000
Gunderson, Eric, NY-N	R	—	30	0	1	0	0	0	0	0	0	0	0	0	0	0	0	0	—	1.000
Guthrie, Mark, L.A.	B	.000	24	1	0	0	0	0	0	0	0	0	0	0	0	0	0	0	.000	.000
Habyan, John, St.L	R	.000	31	2	0	0	0	0	0	0	0	0	0	0	1	0	0	0	.000	.000
Harris, Greg A., Mon.	B	.333	45	3	0	1	2	1	0	0	0	0	0	0	1	0	0	0	.667	.333
Hartgraves, Dean, Hou.	R	.000	40	2	0	0	0	0	0	0	0	1	0	1	1	0	0	0	.000	.000
Henke, Tom, St.L	R	.000	52	1	0	0	0	0	0	0	0	0	0	0	0	0	0	0	.000	.000
Henry, Doug, NY-N	R	1.000	51	1	1	1	1	0	0	0	0	0	0	0	0	0	0	0	1.000	1.000
Heredia, Gil, Mon.	R	.182	40	33	1	6	6	0	0	0	2	5	0	1	3	0	0	0	.182	.206
Hernandez, Xavier, Cin.	L	.000	59	8	0	0	0	0	0	0	0	0	0	0	4	0	0	0	.000	.000
Hernandez, Jeremy, Fla.	R	.000	7	1	0	0	0	0	0	0	0	0	0	0	0	0	0	0	.000	.000
Hickerson, B., ChiN-Col.	L	.667	56	3	1	2	4	0	1	0	3	1	0	1	0	0	0	0	1.333	.750
Hoffman, Trevor, S.D.	R	.500	55	2	1	1	2	1	0	0	2	0	0	0	1	0	0	0	1.000	.500
Holmes, Darren, Col.	R	.000	68	1	0	0	0	0	0	0	0	3	0	0	0	0	0	0	.000	.000
Hook, Chris, S.F.	R	.000	45	3	0	0	0	0	0	0	0	0	0	0	2	0	0	0	.000	.000
Hudek, John, Hou.	B	1.000	19	1	0	1	1	0	0	0	2	0	0	0	0	0	0	0	1.000	1.000
Jackson, Mike R., Cin.	R	.250	40	4	0	1	1	0	0	0	0	0	0	0	0	0	0	0	.250	.250
Jones, Todd, Hou.	L	.200	68	5	1	1	2	1	0	0	0	0	0	0	1	0	0	0	.400	.200
Leiper, Dave, Mon.	L	.000	26	1	0	0	0	0	0	0	0	0	0	0	0	0	0	0	.000	.000
Leskanic, Curtis, Col.	R	.143	76	7	1	1	1	0	0	0	0	2	0	0	1	0	0	1	.143	.143
Lewis, Richie, Fla.	R	.000	21	1	0	0	0	0	0	0	0	0	0	1	1	0	0	0	.000	.500
Lomon, Kevin, NY-N	R	—	6	0	0	0	0	0	0	0	0	1	0	0	0	0	0	0	—	—
Manzanillo, Ravelo, Pit.	L	.000	5	1	0	0	0	0	0	0	0	0	0	0	1	0	0	0	.000	.000
Martinez, Pedro A., Hou.	L	—	25	0	1	0	0	0	0	0	0	0	0	1	0	0	0	0	—	1.000
Mathews, Terry, Fla.	L	.462	57	13	2	6	8	2	0	0	3	0	0	0	4	0	0	1	.615	.462
Mathews, T.J., St.L	R	.000	23	2	0	0	0	0	0	0	0	0	0	0	1	0	0	0	.000	.000
Mauser, Tim, S.D.	R	.000	5	1	0	0	0	0	0	0	0	0	0	0	1	0	0	0	.000	.000

National League relief pitchers (batting)

Name/Team	B	BA	G	AB	R	H	TB	2B	3B	HR	RBI	SH	SF	BB	SO	SB	CS	GIDP	SLG	OBA
McCurry, Jeff, Pit.	R	.000	55	3	0	0	0	0	0	0	0	0	0	0	1	0	0	0	.000	.000
McElroy, Chuck, Cin.	L	.000	44	3	0	0	0	0	0	0	0	0	0	0	0	0	0	0	.000	.000
McMichael, Greg, Atl.	R	.000	67	6	0	0	0	0	0	0	0	0	0	1	4	0	0	0	.000	.143
McMurtry, Craig, Hou.	R	.000	11	1	0	0	0	0	0	0	0	0	0	0	1	0	0	0	.000	.000
Miceli, Dan, Pit.	R	.000	58	1	0	0	0	0	0	0	0	0	0	0	1	0	0	0	.000	.000
Minor, Blas, NY-N	R	.000	35	2	0	0	0	0	0	0	0	0	0	0	0	0	0	0	.000	.000
Mintz, Steve, S.F.	L	.000	14	3	0	0	0	0	0	0	0	0	0	0	3	0	0	0	.000	.000
Munoz, Mike, Col.	L	.500	64	2	1	1	2	1	0	0	1	0	0	2	1	0	0	0	1.000	.750
Murphy, Rob, L.A.-Fla.	L	1.000	14	1	0	1	1	0	0	0	0	0	0	0	0	0	0	0	1.000	1.000
Murray, Matt, Atl.	L	.500	4	2	0	1	1	0	0	0	0	0	0	0	1	0	0	0	.500	.500
Myers, Randy, ChiN	L	—	57	0	0	0	0	0	0	0	1	0	0	1	0	0	0	0	—	1.000
Nabholz, Chris, ChiN	L	.000	34	1	0	0	0	0	0	0	0	0	0	0	0	0	0	0	.000	.000
Olivares, Omar, Col.-Phi.	R	.222	17	9	1	2	6	1	0	1	2	1	0	1	4	0	0	0	.667	.300
Osuna, Antonio, L.A.	R	.000	39	2	0	0	0	0	0	0	0	0	0	0	0	0	0	0	.000	.000
Painter, Lance, Col.	L	.111	33	9	0	1	2	1	0	0	0	1	0	1	4	0	0	0	.222	.200
Palacios, Vicente, St.L	R	.167	20	6	1	1	1	0	0	0	0	1	0	0	4	0	0	0	.167	.167
Park, Chan Ho, L.A.	R	.000	2	1	0	0	0	0	0	0	0	0	0	0	1	0	0	0	.000	.000
Parra, Jose, L.A.	R	—	8	0	0	0	0	0	0	0	0	2	0	0	0	0	0	0	—	—
Parrett, Jeff, St.L	R	.500	59	2	0	1	1	0	0	0	0	0	0	0	1	0	0	0	.500	.500
Pena, Alejandro, Fla.-Atl.	R	.000	27	1	0	0	0	0	0	0	0	0	0	0	1	0	0	0	.000	.000
Pennington, Brad, Cin.	L	.000	6	2	0	0	0	0	0	0	0	0	0	0	1	0	0	0	.000	.000
Perez, Mike, ChiN	R	.000	68	4	1	0	0	0	0	0	0	1	0	2	4	0	0	0	.000	.333
Perez, Yorkis, Fla.	B	.000	69	2	0	0	0	0	0	0	0	0	0	0	1	0	0	0	.000	.000
Person, Robert, NY-N	R	.667	3	3	1	2	2	0	0	0	0	0	0	0	0	0	0	0	.667	.667
Plesac, Dan, Pit.	L	.250	58	4	0	1	1	0	0	0	0	0	0	0	3	0	0	0	.250	.250
Powell, Ross, Hou.-Pit.	L	.000	27	3	0	0	0	0	0	0	0	1	0	0	1	0	0	0	.000	.000
Pugh, Tim, Cin.	R	.143	29	28	2	4	6	2	0	0	1	4	0	1	12	0	0	1	.214	.172
Reed, Steve, Col.	R	.333	71	3	0	1	1	0	0	0	0	0	0	0	1	0	0	0	.333	.333
Remlinger, M., NY-N-Cin.	L	.000	7	1	0	0	0	0	0	0	0	0	0	0	0	0	0	0	.000	.000
Rojas, Mel, Mon.	R	.000	59	6	0	0	0	0	0	0	0	2	0	0	4	0	0	0	.000	.000
Ruffin, Bruce, Col.	B	.000	37	2	0	0	0	0	0	0	0	0	0	0	2	0	0	0	.000	.000
Ruffin, Johnny, Cin.	R	.000	10	2	0	0	0	0	0	0	0	0	0	0	0	0	0	0	.000	.000
Sager, A.J., Col.	R	.000	10	3	0	0	0	0	0	0	0	0	0	0	1	0	0	0	.000	.000
Scheid, Rich, Fla.	L	.000	6	1	0	0	0	0	0	0	0	0	0	0	0	0	0	0	.000	.000
Schmidt, Jason, Atl.	R	.200	9	5	0	1	1	0	0	0	0	1	0	1	2	0	0	0	.200	.333
Scott, Tim, Mon.	R	.250	62	4	0	1	1	0	0	0	0	0	0	0	2	0	0	0	.250	.250
Seanez, Rudy, L.A.	R	.000	37	1	0	0	0	0	0	0	0	0	0	0	1	0	0	0	.000	.000
Service, Scott, S.F.	R	.000	28	1	0	0	0	0	0	0	0	0	0	0	1	0	0	0	.000	.000
Shaw, Jeff, Mon.	R	.000	50	6	2	0	0	0	0	0	0	0	0	2	4	0	0	0	.000	.250
Slocumb, Heathcliff, Phi.	R	.000	61	1	0	0	0	0	0	0	0	0	0	0	0	0	0	0	.000	.000
Smith, Pete J., Cin.	R	.000	11	3	0	0	0	0	0	0	0	0	0	2	2	0	0	0	.000	.400
Springer, Russ, Phi.	R	.000	14	1	0	0	0	0	0	0	0	1	0	0	1	0	0	0	.000	.000
Sullivan, Scott, Cin.	R	.000	3	1	0	0	0	0	0	0	0	0	0	0	1	0	0	0	.000	.000
Tabaka, Jeff, S.D.-Hou.	R	.000	34	1	0	0	0	0	0	0	0	0	0	0	0	0	0	0	.000	.000
Thompson, Mark, Col.	R	.385	21	13	2	5	5	0	0	0	0	1	0	0	7	0	0	0	.385	.385
Torres, Salomon, S.F.	R	.000	4	1	0	0	0	0	0	0	0	0	0	0	0	0	0	0	.000	.000
Valdez, Carlos, S.F.	R	.000	11	1	0	0	0	0	0	0	0	0	0	0	1	0	0	0	.000	.000
Veres, Dave, Hou.	R	.000	72	5	0	0	0	0	0	0	0	1	0	0	4	0	0	0	.000	.000
Veres, Randy, Fla.	R	.000	47	3	0	0	0	0	0	0	0	0	0	0	0	0	0	0	.000	.000
Villone, Ron, S.D.	L	.000	19	1	0	0	0	0	0	0	0	0	0	0	0	0	0	0	.000	.000
Walker, Mike C., ChiN	R	.000	42	3	0	0	0	0	0	0	0	0	0	0	1	0	0	0	.000	.000
Wendell, Turk, ChiN	L	.000	43	7	0	0	0	0	0	0	0	0	0	1	5	0	0	0	.000	.125
White, Gabe, Mon.	L	.000	19	3	0	0	0	0	0	0	0	1	0	0	3	0	0	0	.000	.000
Williams, Brian, S.D.	R	.071	44	14	1	1	2	1	0	0	0	0	0	0	4	0	0	1	.143	.071
Williams, Mike, Phi.	R	.125	33	16	0	2	3	1	0	0	1	7	0	1	5	0	0	0	.188	.176
Williams, Todd, L.A.	R	.500	16	2	0	1	1	0	0	0	0	0	0	0	0	0	0	0	.500	.500
Wilson, Gary, Pit.	R	—	10	0	0	0	0	0	0	0	0	1	0	0	0	0	0	0	—	—
Wohlers, Mark, Atl.	R	.000	65	3	0	0	0	0	0	0	0	0	0	0	3	0	0	0	.000	.000
Woodall, Brad, Atl.	B	1.000	9	1	0	1	1	0	0	0	1	0	0	0	0	0	0	0	1.000	1.000
Worrell, Tim, S.D.	R	.000	9	1	0	0	0	0	0	0	0	0	0	0	0	0	0	0	.000	.000
Worrell, Todd, L.A.	R	.000	59	2	0	0	0	0	0	0	0	0	0	0	2	0	0	0	.000	.000
Young, Anthony, ChiN	R	.667	32	3	2	2	2	0	0	0	0	0	0	0	0	0	0	0	.667	.667

National League outfielders (pitching)

Name/Team	T	W	L	ERA	G	GS	CG	SHO	GF	SV	IP	H	R	ER	HR	BB	SO	WP	BK	BA
Cangelosi, John, Hou.	L	0	0	0.00	1	0	0	0	1	0	1.0	0	0	0	0	1	0	0	0	.000

Major League batting leaders

Extra-base hits

Belle, Cle.	103
E. Martinez, Sea.	81
Bichette, Col.	80
Walker, Col.	72
Palmeiro, Bal.	71
Salmon, Cal.	71
Bonds, S.F.	70
Grace, Chi Cubs	70
R. Sanders, Cin.	70
Vaughn, Bos.	70

Singles

Gwynn, S.D.	154
Nixon, Tex.	151
Johnson, Chi Sox	146
Baerga, Cle.	130
Butler, NYN-L.A.	126
Finley, S.D.	126
Knoblauch, Min.	126
Bell, Hou.	120
Boggs, NY Yanks	118

Lead-assuming RBI

Bonds, S.F.	38
Bichette, Col.	37
F. Thomas, Chi Sox	31
Jones, Atl.	29
Sosa, Chi Cubs	29
Clark, Tex.	28
Grace, Chi Cubs	28
Puckett, Min.	28

Bases on balls

F. Thomas, Chi Sox	136
Bonds, S.F.	120
E. Martinez, Sea.	116
Phillips, Cal.	113
Tettleton, Tex.	107
Weiss, Col.	98
Thome, Cle.	97
Salmon, Cal.	91
Davis, Cal.	89
McGwire, Oak.	88

Intentional walks

F. Thomas, Chi Sox	29
Bonds, S.F.	22
E. Martinez, Sea.	19
Puckett, Min.	18
Vaughn, Bos.	17
T. Martinez, Sea.	15
Branson, Cin.	14
Baines, Bal.	13
Walker, Col.	13

Hit by pitcher

Biggio, Hou.	22
Sprague, Tor.	15
Macfarlane, Bos.	14
Vaughn, Bos.	14
Walker, Col.	14
Galarraga, Col.	13
Blauser, Atl.	12
Patterson, S.F.	12

Strikeouts

Vaughn, Bos.	150
Gil, Tex.	147
Galarraga, Col.	146
Phillips, Cal.	135
Sosa, Chi Cubs	134
Edmonds, Cal.	130
Blowers, Sea.	128
R. Sanders, Cin.	122
Buhner, Sea.	120
Fielder, Det.	116

Caught stealing

Nixon, Tex.	21
Veras, Fla.	21
Goodwin, K.C.	18
Knoblauch, Min.	18
D. Lewis, S.F.-Cin.	18
Coleman, K.C.-Sea.	16
Curtis, Det.	15
Lofton, Cle.	15
DeShields, L.A.	14

Strikeout rate

Gwynn, S.D.	38.5
Johnson, Chi Sox	20.8
Jefferies, Phi.	20.0
Baerga, Cle.	19.4
Cora, Sea.	15.7
Greenwell, Bos.	15.0
Mattingly, NY Yanks	14.5
Grace, Chi Cubs	13.6
Reed, S.D.	13.6
Hamilton, Mil.	13.1

Opp. stolen-base pct.

Rodriguez, Tex.	.519
Johnson, Fla.	.573
Ausmus, S.D.	.581
Parrish, Tor.	.585
Martinez, Tor.	.606
Steinbach, Oak.	.606
Parent, Pit.-Chi Cubs	.607
Fabregas, Cal.	.614
Wilson, Sea.	.629
Pagnozzi, St.L	.632

Games on grass/best

Gwynn, S.D.	.381
Bichette, Col.	.355
Salmon, Cal.	.349
Bell, Hou.	.346
Segui, NY Mets-Mon.	.339
Piazza, L.A.	.338
Gilkey, St.L	.337
Grace, Chi Cubs	.336
Knoblauch, Min.	.335

Games on grass/worst

Grudzielanek, Mon.	.125
Oquendo, St.L	.159
Oliva, Atl.-St.L	.163
Wilkins, Chi Cubs-Hou.	.182
Bautista, Det.	.183
Mouton, Hou.	.189
Griffey, Sea.	.194
Nieves, S.D.	.203
Cromer, St.L	.204
Johnson, Pit.	.207

Games on turf/best

E. Martinez, Sea.	.374
Ripken, Bal.	.373
DiSarcina, Cal.	.373
Nixon, Tex.	.370
Piazza, L.A.	.370
Seitzer, Mil.	.367
Ventura, Chi Sox	.353
Steinbach, Oak.	.352
Thome, Cle.	.352

Games on turf/worst

Kirby, Cle.	.132
Macfarlane, Bos.	.146
Hulse, Mil.	.148
Gomez, Bal.	.152
Blauser, Atl.	.162
Cirillo, Mil.	.163
Carr, Fla.	.171
Karkovice, Chi Sox	.175
Higginson, Det.	.180
Tinsley, Bos.	.182

*M*inor league report

▶ Wacky nicknames and other highlights

▶ 1995 minor league wrapups

▶ Final AAA & AA player stats

▶ Top players and managers

USA SNAPSHOTS®

A look at statistics that shape the nation

Major leagues' troubled past

Length of baseball work stoppages (strikes and lockouts):

	Days
1972	**13** (April 1-13)
1973	**12** (Feb. 14-25)
1976	**17** (March 1-17)
1980	**8** (April 1-8)
1981	**50** (June 12-31)
1985	**2** (Aug. 6-7)
1990	**32** (Feb. 15-March 18)
1994-95	**179** (Aug. 12-present[1])

1 – Includes 52 days of regular season plus postseason

STRIK

Source: USA TODAY research   By John Riley and Elys A. McLean, USA TODAY

1995 wrapup: Goofy nicknames drove licensers batty

The major league baseball strike put the minor leagues in the spotlight on April 6 as the pro season officially got underway at 2:22 p.m. in New Haven, Connecticut. The Ravens opened the season by default, five minutes past Rochester who, like Buffalo and several other cities, was snowed out.

WHAT'S IN A NAME?

The big news before the season began was the trend for minor league teams to adopt new nicknames and logos—from catchy to ridiculous—in an attempt to cash in on the booming souvenir market. The tradition of using the parent club's name was quickly disappearing, replaced by whimsical new logos on everything from boxer shorts to hair scrungies. Finally the licensing bureau cried foul and set up new guidelines for logo and name changes. Before that, however, there were some pretty outrageous monikers floated about. The New Britain, Conn., team, for example, changed its name to the Hardware City Rock Cats. The logo was a cat with sunglasses, an electric guitar, and a gold earring (the earring was 86'd before the season began). The Battle Creek Golden Kazoos—who should have been the Cereal Killers—changed their name to the Battle Cats. In the Midwest League finals, they faced the newly named Beloit Snappers, who were once the Beloit Brewers.

HIGHLIGHTS:

Key individual highlights and achievements in 1995:

▶*Cream of the crop:* California slugging catcher prospect **Todd Greene** was *Baseball Weekly*'s 1995 Minor League Player of the Year, as he became the first minor league player in 10 years to hit 40 homers, splitting his time between Class AA Midland and Class AAA Vancouver.

▶*RBI king also 30-30 man:* Asheville outfielder **Derrick Gibson** led the minors in RBI with 115, adding 32 homers and 31 steals for the Colorado Rockies farm club.

▶*Hit and run:* Macon outfielder **Andruw Jones** became the first minor leaguer since Jose Cardenal in 1961 to hit 20 homers (25), drive in 100 runs (100) and steal 50 bases (56).

▶*More pitching for the Brew Crew:* **Joshua Bishop**, a right-hander taken by the Milwaukee Brewers in the 38th round out of the University of Missouri, may have started at too low a level for a college product, pitching for the Arizona team. But despite that loop's short schedule, he led the Milwaukee farm system in ERA at 2.16 and in strikeouts with 134.

▶*Hitting streaks:* Nashville second baseman **Doug Brady** posted the minors' longest hitting streak of the year—30 games. Behind him were Colorado Springs outfielder **Trenidad Hubbard** (28) and Binghamton outfielder **Jay Payton** (25).

▶*Six-shooters:* Riverside third baseman **Rick Ladjevich** went 6-for-6 on April 15, and **Darryl Monroe** of Fayetteville collected six singles the next night. The feat was achieved just one more time all season—by Carolina's **George Canale** in a 17-inning game against Port City August 12.

▶*Full cycle:* Sept. 1 was a big night for hitting for the cycle—two California League players, Stockton third baseman **Brad Seitzer** and Modesto outfielder **Gary Hust**, each singled, doubled, tripled, and homered that night. Such a double whammy has happened just once in the majors—Sept. 17, 1920. Eight other players hit for the cycle during the season: Rancho Cucamonga's **Derrek Lee**, Elsinore's **Earl Cunningham**, Albany (Ga.)'s **Nate Brown**, Calgary's **Kevin Young**, Gulf Coast Blue Jays'

John Kehoe, Gulf Coast Yankees' Eric Kofler, Orlando's Darren Burton and Louisville's David Bell.

▶**Big bats:** Twenty players had three-homer games, with one—Jesus Ibarra of Burlington—doing it twice in the season. Columbus (Ga.)'s Russell Branyan and Trenton's Greg Blosser homered in five consecutive games; Blosser and Memphis' Tim Killeen each had games in which they hit two homers in one inning. Ty Griffin of Arkansas homered to lead off a game four nights in a row, while Cedar Rapids' Greg Morris had three consecutive two-homer games.

▶**Talk about run production:** Kissimmee infielder Steve Verduzco had a 10-RBI game, tying a Florida State League record. He originally was awarded 12, but a two-run double was changed to an error. Six other players had eight-RBI games: Macon's Andruw Jones; Colorado Springs' Harvey Pulliam; Modesto's Steve Cox; Kinston's Richie Sexson; Helena's Ryan Ritter; and Auburn's Chad Alexander. Several other players had seven-RBI games, most notably Harrisburg's Israel Alcantara, who drove in seven runs in a five-inning game.

▶**Grand larceny:** Miguel Mejia of short-season Bluefield had five steals in a game. Several had four-steal games—Knoxville's Lonell Roberts did it twice.

▶**No-nos:** There were 22 no-hitters thrown—the first and last were among the most noteworthy. On April 8, Brian Woods and Archie Vazquez combined to pitch the first Prince William no-hitter since the team began in 1984. On Sept. 2, the pitcher lost the game. Memphis's Robbie Beckett didn't allow a hit in 6 ⅔ innings, but his team lost, 1-0.

▶**More from the mound:** Joshua Bishop (see above), Paul Wilson of Binghamton and Glendon Rusch of Wilmington each fanned 17 in one game. Wilson got eight in a row. Scott Gardner of Fayetteville struck out five in one inning, as two reached on wild-pitch third strikes. Brent Crowther of Asheville and Salem, and Luis Andujar of Birmingham posted 12-game winning streaks. Matt Golden of Savannah had the longest scoreless-inning streak at 31⅓ innings, while Hagerstown's Brian Smith went 47⅓ innings without allowing an earned run.

TEAM TALK

Bluefield, which had the best winning percentage in the minors, posted a season-best 16-game win streak, while Helena and Colorado Springs each had a 15-game spree. Ogden scored 33 runs in one game, the best output of the year in the minors, while Kane County and Wichita each posted 14-run innings. Great Falls' 32 hits in a single game was tops in that category, while Orlando crushed a season-best seven homers in one slugfest. The longest game of the year—and in California League history—ended May 13, when San Bernardino finally scored to beat San Jose, 1-0, in 21 innings after 5:56 of playing time over two days and three rain delays. The weather wreaked havoc in the Midwest League once again, even without the famous floods of '94—Clinton, already suffering with the worst record in the minors, had its slew of rainouts made up later by 10 consecutive doubleheaders. And in a year marked by many on-field brawls and altercations, perhaps the most ironic occurred in Durham, N.C., when the host Bulls and the visiting Winston-Salem Warthogs racked up a Carolina League record in fines and suspensions in a melee which included a Durham pitcher's kicking a Warthogs reliever unconscious. It was "Stamp Out Domestic Violence Night" at the ball-park.

—by Lisa Winston

Class AAA WRAPUPS

American Association

The Louisville Redbirds beat the Buffalo Bisons to win the American Association title, despite being seeded last. **Mike Carter** of Iowa won the batting crown at .325. Iowa's **Brooks Kieschnick** led the league with 23 homers. **Jeromy Burnitz** of Buffalo had 85 RBI to lead the loop. **Eric Owens** of Indianapolis led the way with 33 steals and was voted MVP. **Rodney Bolton** of Nashville won the ERA title at 2.88. **Joe Roa** of Buffalo was 17-3 to lead the league in wins. **Paul Abbott** of Iowa had a league-high 127 strikeouts as Cubs pitchers notched the top three slots in that category. **Cory Bailey** came over to the Cards from Boston in the off-season and continued St. Louis' minor league dominance in relief, winning the save title for Louisville with 25.

AMERICAN ASSOCIATION (AAA)

	W	L	Pct.	GB
Indianapolis	88	56	.611	—
Buffalo	82	62	.569	6
Omaha	76	68	.528	12
Louisville	74	70	.514	14
Iowa	69	74	.483	18½
Nashville	68	76	.472	20
New Orleans	63	79	.444	24
Oklahoma City	54	89	.378	33½

Semifinals: Louisville 3, Indianapolis 0; Buffalo 3, Omaha 1.
Finals: Louisville 3, Buffalo 2.

\# Switch-hitter
* Left-handed

Final AAA Player Stats

American Association

Buffalo Bisons (Indians) AAA

BATTING	AVG	AB	R	H	2B	3B	HR	RBI	SB
#Amaro, Ruben, OF	.305	213	42	65	15	3	6	22	6
#Bolick, Frank, 3B	.246	65	11	16	6	0	3	10	0
*Burnitz, Jeromy, OF	.284	443	72	126	26	7	19	85	13
#Candaele, C., 2B	.247	364	50	90	10	7	4	38	9
Costo, Tim, 1B	.247	324	41	80	11	2	11	60	2
Flores, Miguel, 2B	.283	113	13	32	8	1	0	12	5
Fordyce, Brook, C	.250	176	18	44	13	0	0	9	1
*Giles, Brian, OF	.310	413	67	128	18	8	15	67	7
*Howitt, Dann, OF	.303	119	19	36	8	3	4	18	0
Humphreys, Mike, OF	.246	126	17	31	4	0	1	5	5
*Levis, Jesse, C	.311	196	26	61	16	0	4	20	0
Lopez, Luis, DH	.262	455	62	119	21	1	17	66	1
#Lovullo, Torey, 2B	.255	474	84	121	20	5	16	61	3
*Marini, Marc, OF	.271	85	12	23	5	0	3	15	0
Martindale, Ryan, C	.161	31	4	5	1	0	0	0	1
Martinez, Carmelo, DH	.278	36	8	10	1	0	2	9	0
Massarelli, John, DH	.000	1	0	0	0	0	0	0	0
McClendon, Lloyd, OF	.278	108	19	30	6	0	5	19	0
Perry, Herb, 1B	.317	180	27	57	14	1	2	17	1
*Riles, Ernest, DH	.278	18	5	5	0	0	1	7	0
Ripken, Billy, SS	.292	448	51	131	34	1	4	56	6
Smith, Ed, OF	.323	31	4	10	0	1	3	9	0
Yelding, Eric, OF	.346	81	13	28	7	0	1	9	3

PITCHING	W	L	ERA	G	SV	IP	H	BB	SO
Austin, Jim	1	1	12.00	2	0	3.0	7	2	1
*Bell, Eric	13	9	3.90	28	0	161.1	177	47	86
Chapin, Darrin	0	1	8.31	6	0	8.2	12	2	4
Clark, Mark	4	0	3.57	5	0	35.1	39	10	17
Crawford, Carlos	0	1	5.64	13	1	30.1	36	12	15
*Embree, Alan	3	4	0.89	30	5	40.2	31	19	56
Farrell, John	11	9	4.54	29	0	184.1	198	61	92
Frohwirth, Todd	0	1	3.34	26	3	32.1	31	12	33
Graves, Daniel	0	0	3.00	3	0	3.0	5	1	2
Grimsley, Jason	5	3	2.91	10	0	68.0	61	19	40
Harris, Pep	2	1	2.48	14	0	32.2	32	15	18
*Klink, Joe	2	1	3.00	45	8	39.0	31	15	32
Lancaster, Les	4	5	4.31	45	0	87.2	90	19	68
Lewis, James	6	4	3.64	18	1	94.0	101	25	50
Lopez, Albie	5	10	4.44	18	0	101.1	101	51	82
*Lynch, David	1	2	4.30	14	0	14.2	16	7	14
Ogea, Chad	0	1	4.58	4	0	17.2	16	8	11
Perschke, Greg	1	1	5.74	3	0	15.2	13	6	11
*Poole, Jim	0	0	27.00	1	0	2.2	7	2	0
Roa, Joe	17	3	3.50	25	0	164.2	168	28	93
Shuey, Paul	1	2	2.63	25	11	27.1	21	7	27
Telford, Anthony	4	1	3.46	16	0	39.0	35	10	24
Turner, Matt	0	1	5.23	13	3	10.1	16	5	10

Indianapolis Indians (Reds) AAA

BATTING	AVG	AB	R	H	2B	3B	HR	RBI	SB
*Anthony, Eric, DH	.292	24	7	7	0	0	4	8	2
#Arias, Amador, 2B	.400	15	2	6	0	0	0	1	1
Belk, Tim, 1B	.301	193	30	58	11	0	4	18	2
#Bess, Johnny, OF	.000	5	0	0	0	0	0	0	0
*Briley, Greg, OF	.233	146	17	34	8	0	3	17	9
Brooks, Jerry, C	.283	325	41	92	19	2	14	52	3
Brown, Chris, 3B	.000	7	0	0	0	0	0	0	0
Denson, Drew, DH	.277	357	59	99	21	0	18	69	1
*Dismuke, Jamie, 1B	.250	36	6	9	1	0	0	2	0
Dorsett, Brian, C	.262	313	40	82	25	1	16	58	1

BATTING	AVG	AB	R	H	2B	3B	HR	RBI	SB
Gibralter, Steve, OF	.316	263	49	83	19	3	18	63	0
Gordon, Keith, OF	.264	265	36	70	14	1	6	38	3
*Greene, Willie, 3B	.243	325	57	79	12	2	19	45	3
Hunter, Brian, OF	.361	36	7	13	5	0	4	11	0
Knapp, Mike, C	.256	39	8	10	2	0	1	6	1
Kremblas, Frank, 3B	.160	75	7	12	2	0	0	3	4
Magdaleno, Ricky, SS	.125	8	1	1	0	0	1	1	0
McCarty, Dave, 1B	.336	140	31	47	10	1	8	32	0
Mitchell, Keith, OF	.244	213	40	52	11	2	11	36	4
*Morris, Hal, 1B	.400	5	2	2	0	0	0	1	0
Mottola, Chad, OF	.259	239	40	62	11	1	8	37	8
Owens, Eric, 2B	.314	427	86	134	24	8	12	63	33
Reese, Pokey, SS	.239	343	51	82	21	1	10	46	8
Rohrmeier, Dan, OF	.176	34	5	6	3	1	0	3	0
Sellers, Rick, C	.263	19	3	5	1	0	3	7	0
#Smith, Greg, 2B	.214	14	1	3	0	0	0	0	0
#Stillwell, Kurt, SS	.264	341	50	90	14	3	7	30	4
Trafton, Todd, Ph	.000	5	0	0	0	0	0	0	0
Wilson, Brandon, SS	.167	12	3	2	0	0	0	0	0
*Wilson, Nigel, OF	.313	304	53	95	27	3	17	51	5
Worthington, Craig, 3B	.318	277	48	88	19	0	9	41	1

PITCHING	W	L	ERA	G	SV	IP	H	BB	SO
*Beatty, Blaine	7	1	3.61	20	0	67.1	80	16	37
Belcher, Tim	0	0	1.80	2	0	10.0	6	1	8
Buckley, Travis	10	9	4.70	23	0	132.0	141	33	85
*Courtright, John	2	1	4.28	13	0	33.2	29	15	13
Davis, Storm	0	0	3.38	4	0	5.1	4	3	4
Donnelly, Brendan	1	1	23.63	3	0	2.2	7	2	1
Drahman, Brian	0	0	0.00	2	0	3.0	3	1	3
Ferry, Mike	1	2	5.19	3	0	17.1	21	3	3
*Grott, Matt	7	3	4.24	25	2	114.2	99	24	74
*Hurst, James	0	0	5.40	3	1	3.1	2	1	1
Jackson, Mike	0	0	0.00	2	0	2.0	0	0	1
Jarvis, Kevin	4	2	4.45	10	0	60.2	62	18	37
Jean, Domingo	1	0	0.00	2	0	2.0	1	0	1
*Kilgo, Rusty	0	0	4.50	2	0	2.0	4	1	1
Mathile, Mike	0	2	2.51	14	0	28.2	22	8	16
Moore, Marcus	1	0	4.97	7	1	12.2	13	14	6
*Nitkowski, C.J.	0	2	5.20	6	0	27.2	28	10	21
*Pennington, Brad	0	0	10.29	11	0	14.0	17	21	11
Pugh, Tim	2	4	4.68	6	0	42.1	42	14	20
Reed, Rick	11	4	3.33	22	0	135.0	127	26	92
*Remlinger, Mike	5	3	4.05	41	0	46.2	40	32	58
Roper, John	2	5	4.97	8	0	41.2	47	16	23
Ruffin, Johnny	3	1	2.90	36	0	49.2	27	37	58
Salkeld, Roger	12	2	4.22	20	0	119.1	96	57	86
*Sauveur, Rich	5	2	2.05	52	15	57.0	43	18	47
Scudder, Scott	1	4	5.17	7	0	38.1	43	9	13
Service, Scott	4	1	2.18	36	18	41.1	33	15	48
Sullivan, Scott	4	3	3.53	44	1	58.2	51	24	54
Vasquez, Marcos	0	0	0.00	2	1	4.0	1	0	1
*Viola, Frank	3	3	4.09	6	0	33.0	33	6	25
Warren, Brian	2	1	1.61	41	2	56.0	56	9	35

Iowa Cubs (Cubs) AAA

BATTING	AVG	AB	R	H	2B	3B	HR	RBI	SB
Benavides, Freddie, SS	.241	315	30	76	14	4	4	26	2
#Bream, Scott, 2B	.159	82	10	13	1	0	2	9	1
Carter, Mike, OF	.325	421	57	137	16	3	8	40	12
#Colon, Cris, 1B	.260	366	35	95	18	1	4	36	1
Cox, Darron, C	.234	94	7	22	6	0	1	14	0
Fanning, Steve, DH	.000	5	0	0	0	0	0	0	0
Fariss, Monty, 1B	.182	33	5	6	0	0	1	2	0
*Franco, Matt, 3B	.281	455	51	128	28	5	6	58	1
*Gardner, Jeff, 2B	.323	235	35	76	11	0	3	24	1
Glanville, Doug, OF	.270	419	48	113	16	2	4	37	13
Gousha, Sean, C	.000	5	0	0	0	0	0	0	0
Haney, Todd, 2B	.313	326	38	102	20	2	4	30	2
Hubbard, Mike, C	.260	254	28	66	6	3	5	23	6
#Jose, Felix, OF	.135	37	2	5	3	0	0	1	0
#Kessinger, Keith, SS	.229	210	21	48	11	0	2	20	1
*Kieschnick, Brooks, OF	.295	505	61	149	30	1	23	73	2
Kmak, Joe, C	.173	98	6	17	3	0	2	7	0

Class AAA WRAPUPS

International League

The Ottawa Lynx became the first Canadian-based team to win an International League championship in nearly 30 years, beating heavily favored Norfolk. Norfolk had cruised to a 86-56 record, starting the season with IL MVP **Butch Huskey** (league-high 28 HRs) and the league's Pitcher of the Year, **Jason Isringhausen**. At the All-Star break they got the players who would receive the same honors in the Eastern League— outfielder **Jay Payton** and pitcher **Paul Wilson**—as reinforcements. Syracuse's **Robert Perez** won the batting title at .343. Veteran **Don Sparks** of Columbus led the league with 90 RBI. Ottawa had the top base-stealer in **Jim Buccheri** (43). Richmond's **Jason Schmidt** won the ERA crown at 2.25. Rochester's **Jimmy Haynes** led in strikeouts (140) and shared the lead in wins with teammate **Jimmy Williams** (12). Richmond's Rod Nichols and Scranton closer **Chuck Ricci** shared the save title with 25.

INTERNATIONAL LEAGUE (AAA)

Eastern Division

	W	L	Pct.	GB
Rochester	73	69	.514	—
Ottawa	72	70	.507	1
Pawtucket	70	71	.496	2½
Scranton/WB	70	72	.493	3
Syracuse	59	82	.418	13½

Western Division

	W	L	Pct.	GB
Norfolk	86	56	.606	—
Richmond	75	66	.532	10½
Columbus	71	68	.511	13½
Toledo	71	71	.500	15
Charlotte	59	81	.421	26

Semifinals: *Ottawa 3, Rochester 2; Norfolk 3, Richmond 2.*
Finals: *Ottawa 3, Norfolk 1.*

Class AAA WRAPUPS

Pacific Coast League

The Colorado Springs Sky Sox won their first championship as a Colorado Rockies farm team, beating the Salt Lake Buzz. The Buzz led the heavy-hitting PCL in batting (.304) thanks to seven regulars hitting .300 or better. The Sox had one of the top outfields in the minors— **Trenidad Hubbard** led the league with 37 steals and 102 runs scored, **Harvey Pulliam** vied for the Triple Crown by leading the loop in homers (25) and RBI (91), and **Quinton McCracken** hit .361 in a half-season. **Riccardo Ingram** won the batting crown (.348) for Salt Lake and led the loop with 43 doubles. **Donne Wall** was MVP, going 17-6 with a 3.30 ERA and 119 strikeouts, the first PCL pitcher to achieve a Triple Crown since 1942. **Scott Watkins** of Salt Lake took the save title (20). **Bob Abreu** of Tucson led the minors in triples with 17.

PACIFIC COAST LEAGUE (AAA)

Northern Division

	W	L	Pct.	GB
Vancouver	81	60	.574	—
Salt Lake	79	65	.549	3½
Edmonton	68	76	.472	14½
Tacoma	68	76	.472	14½
Calgary	58	83	.411	23

Southern Division

	W	L	Pct.	GB
Tucson	87	56	.608	—
Colo. Spgs.	77	66	.538	10
Albuquerque	75	69	.521	12½
Phoenix	62	82	.431	25½
Las Vegas	61	83	.424	26½

Semifinals: *Salt Lake 3, Vancouver 1; Colorado Springs 3, Tucson 1*
Finals: *Colorado Springs 3, Salt Lake 2*

BATTING	AVG	AB	R	H	2B	3B	HR	RBI	SB
*Kosco, Bryn, 1B	.251	363	50	91	24	3	15	52	2
Martinez, Manny, OF	.290	397	63	115	17	8	8	49	11
*O'Halloran, Greg, C	.158	19	1	3	1	0	0	1	0
*Pledger, Kinnis, OF	.083	24	1	2	0	0	0	0	0
Pratt, Todd, C	.328	58	3	19	1	0	0	5	0

PITCHING	W	L	ERA	G	SV	IP	H	BB	SO
Abbott, Paul	7	7	3.67	46	0	115.1	104	64	127
Adams, Terry	0	0	0.00	7	5	6.1	3	2	10
Anderson, Mike	7	9	3.46	27	0	171.2	156	69	123
Campbell, Mike	9	3	2.45	21	0	102.2	93	29	88
*Casian, Larry	0	0	2.13	13	1	12.2	9	2	9
*Dabney, Fred	4	6	5.95	33	0	56.0	68	29	33
Deleon, Luis	0	1	13.50	2	0	2.0	6	0	3
*Dixon, Steve	6	3	2.85	53	0	41.0	34	19	38
Edens, Tom	2	0	3.46	20	1	41.2	36	17	28
Garces, Rich	0	2	2.86	23	7	28.1	25	8	36
Gozzo, Mauro	0	3	4.15	6	0	30.1	37	11	11
Grant, Mark	5	2	3.13	11	0	69.0	58	10	39
Meier, Kevin	1	2	8.44	3	0	10.2	18	3	7
*Morton, Kevin	1	7	4.79	28	0	92.0	97	42	49
*Nabholz, Chris	0	2	6.41	6	0	19.2	27	12	16
Shifflett, Steve	5	1	5.33	26	0	27.0	30	6	10
*Smith, Ottis	1	3	10.45	5	0	20.2	34	13	12
Steenstra, Kennie	9	12	3.89	29	0	171.1	174	48	96
Sturtze, Tanyon	4	7	6.80	23	0	86.0	108	42	48
Swartzbaugh, Dave	3	0	1.53	30	0	47.0	33	18	38
Taylor, Rob	4	2	2.81	54	18	57.2	42	28	48
Walker, Mike	1	1	4.10	16	0	26.1	22	19	13
Young, Anthony	0	1	11.25	3	0	4.0	9	4	6

Louisville Redbirds (Cardinals) AAA

BATTING	AVG	AB	R	H	2B	3B	HR	RBI	SB
#Aversa, Joe, SS	.220	141	23	31	6	0	0	9	7
Battle, Allen, OF	.280	164	28	46	12	1	3	18	7
Bell, David, 2B	.276	76	9	21	3	1	1	9	4
*Bradshaw, Terry, OF	.283	389	65	110	24	8	8	42	20
#Caraballo, Ramon, 2B	.318	245	38	78	10	1	8	25	14
Cholowsky, Dan, OF	.218	238	27	52	9	1	7	25	10
Deak, Brian, C	.228	162	19	37	5	0	6	31	2
#Deak, Darrel, 1B	.241	336	42	81	21	2	7	34	2
DiFelice, Mike, C	.270	63	8	17	4	0	0	3	1
#Diggs, Tony, OF	.250	36	4	9	3	0	0	0	2
*Giannelli, Ray, OF	.295	390	56	115	19	1	16	70	3
Gilkey, Bernard, OF	.333	6	3	2	1	0	0	1	0
Gulan, Mike, 3B	.236	195	21	46	10	4	5	27	2
Hemond, Scott, C	.000	3	1	0	0	0	0	0	0
Holbert, Aaron, SS	.257	401	57	103	16	4	9	40	14
Johns, Keith, 2B	.000	10	0	0	0	0	0	0	0
#Lee, Manuel, SS	.273	22	2	6	0	0	0	0	1
*Mabry, John, OF	.083	12	0	1	0	0	0	0	0
Martinez, Domingo, 1B	.261	222	26	58	15	0	9	31	0
McNeely, Jeff, OF	.236	271	31	64	6	1	0	19	5
Pagnozzi, Tom, C	.500	16	4	8	2	0	1	3	0
#Pena, Geronimo, 2B	.381	21	5	8	1	0	2	6	0
*Prager, Howard, 1B	.255	102	9	26	5	0	6	15	1
*Ronan, Marc, C	.213	225	15	48	8	0	0	8	1
Sabo, Chris, 1B	.393	28	5	11	0	0	1	4	0
*Sweeney, Mark, 1B	.368	76	15	28	8	0	2	22	2
*Thomas, Skeets, OF	.249	273	29	68	15	1	9	34	0
Woodson, Tracy, 3B	.262	431	62	113	35	0	18	76	12
Wrona, Rick, C	.226	31	1	7	1	1	1	2	0
#Young, Dmitri, OF	.286	7	3	2	0	0	0	0	0
Zeile, Todd, 1B	.125	8	0	1	0	0	0	0	0

PITCHING	W	L	ERA	G	SV	IP	H	BB	SO
Bailey, Cory	5	3	4.55	55	25	59.1	51	30	49
Barber, Brian	6	5	4.70	20	0	107.1	105	40	94
Batchelor, Richard	5	4	3.28	50	0	85.0	85	16	61
*Beltran, Rigo	8	9	5.21	24	0	129.2	156	34	92
Benes, Alan	4	2	2.41	11	0	56.0	37	14	54
Buckels, Gary	1	2	5.51	13	5	16.1	18	13	8
Busby, Mike	2	2	3.29	6	0	38.1	28	11	26
*Cadaret, Greg	1	0	3.09	12	0	11.2	14	1	7

PITCHING	W	L	ERA	G	SV	IP	H	BB	SO
Carpenter, Cris	2	5	2.43	49	5	66.2	59	20	41
Cimorelli, Frank	1	1	9.00	6	0	5.0	12	0	3
*Creek, Doug	3	2	3.23	26	0	30.2	20	21	29
Davis, Clint	0	0	12.27	4	0	3.2	6	2	4
Delarosa, Francisco	2	5	4.06	28	0	115.1	104	38	66
Frascatore, John	2	8	3.95	28	5	82.0	89	34	55
*Jackson, Danny	1	0	1.29	1	0	7.0	8	2	2
Martinez, Frankie	2	1	3.61	38	0	52.1	60	21	23
Mathews, T.J.	9	4	2.70	32	1	66.2	60	27	50
Minchey, Nate	8	7	3.73	26	0	147.1	153	42	67
*Osborne, Donovan	0	1	3.86	1	0	7.0	8	0	3
Petkovsek, Mark	4	1	2.32	8	0	54.1	38	8	30
*Prager, Howard	0	0	0.00	2	0	2.0	1	0	1
*Raczka, Mike	5	3	3.86	55	1	49.0	49	20	43
*Simmons, Scott	0	2	8.00	2	0	9.0	11	1	2
*Urbani, Tom	1	1	2.93	2	0	15.1	16	5	11
*Watson, Allen	2	2	2.63	4	0	24.0	20	6	19

Nashville Sounds (White Sox) AAA

BATTING	AVG	AB	R	H	2B	3B	HR	RBI	SB
#Brady, Doug, 2B	.298	450	71	134	15	6	5	27	32
*Cappuccio, C., OF	.273	216	30	59	14	0	5	24	0
Cotto, Henry, DH	.131	61	4	8	1	0	1	4	0
*Coughlin, Kevin, OF	.182	22	0	4	1	0	0	0	0
Cron, Chris, 3B	.217	69	3	15	2	0	2	10	0
Fraraccio, Dan, SS	.250	28	2	7	0	0	0	3	2
*Howard, Tim, 3B	.233	103	8	24	3	1	2	13	4
Lyons, Barry, C	.257	265	37	68	16	1	8	38	0
Machado, Robert, C	.143	49	7	7	3	0	1	5	0
Milstien, Dave, SS	.235	34	1	8	1	0	0	2	0
Mouton, Lyle, OF	.296	267	40	79	17	0	8	41	10
#Noriega, Rey, SS	.164	55	6	9	4	0	1	3	0
Ortiz, Javier, DH	.167	24	3	4	0	0	1	1	0
Ortiz, Junior, C	.186	172	13	32	9	0	1	16	0
Ramsey, Fernando, OF	.310	406	61	126	19	3	5	45	26
*Robertson, Mike, 1B	.248	499	55	124	17	4	19	52	2
Saenz, Olmedo, 3B	.304	415	60	126	26	1	13	74	0
Snopek, Chris, SS	.323	393	56	127	23	4	12	55	2
Tremie, Chris, C	.200	190	13	38	4	0	2	16	0
Valrie, Kerry, OF	.250	544	75	136	30	3	7	55	22
Wolak, Jerry, OF	.229	385	43	88	21	1	14	63	5
Zupcic, Bob, OF	.244	41	9	10	2	0	2	5	1

PITCHING	W	L	ERA	G	SV	IP	H	BB	SO
Baldwin, James	5	9	5.85	18	0	95.1	120	44	89
Bere, Jason	1	0	3.38	1	0	5.1	6	2	7
*Bertotti, Mike	2	3	8.72	7	0	32.0	41	17	35
Bolton, Rodney	14	3	2.88	20	0	131.1	127	23	76
*Bolton, Tom	5	7	4.43	19	0	101.2	106	31	82
Costello, Fred	0	2	5.11	7	0	12.1	17	7	6
Davis, John	1	1	0.00	4	1	3.1	3	3	0
Ellis, Robert	1	1	2.18	4	0	20.2	16	10	9
Gajkowski, Steve	0	1	2.55	15	0	24.2	26	8	12
*Hammaker, Atlee	1	2	1.27	15	1	28.1	27	7	20
Johnson, Dane	4	4	2.41	46	15	56.0	48	28	51
Jones, Calvin	0	0	6.75	5	0	6.2	13	3	5
Karchner, Matt	3	3	1.45	28	9	37.1	39	10	29
Keyser, Brian	2	4	2.36	10	0	72.1	49	9	40
Levine, Alan	0	2	5.14	3	0	14.0	20	7	14
*Lorraine, Andrew	4	1	6.00	7	0	39.0	51	12	26
Marquez, Isidrio	7	4	4.75	46	4	72.0	80	27	57
Mongiello, Mike	3	3	5.14	31	1	91.0	104	37	72
*Novoa, Rafael	0	1	10.80	3	0	10.0	17	9	3
Olsen, Steve	1	7	4.79	14	0	77.0	85	16	45
Pall, Donn	4	3	3.98	44	3	86.0	89	20	79
*Righetti, Dave	4	5	3.23	16	0	83.2	81	20	44
Simas, Bill	1	1	3.86	7	0	11.2	12	3	12
*Sirotka, Mike	1	5	2.83	8	0	54.0	51	13	34
*Vierra, Joey	2	2	4.17	56	4	58.1	47	19	57
*Wilson, Steve	2	2	4.56	20	1	51.1	60	17	26

Class AAA WRAPUPS

Texas League

The Shreveport Captains cruised to the playoffs for a 10th consecutive season and won their first league title since 1991. Wichita's **Johnny Damon** was the league's MVP, hitting .343 and leading the league in on-base average (.434) and slugging (.534). He was edged out in the race for the batting title by San Antonio's **Wilton Guerrero** (.348). Midland's **George Arias** won the home run title with 30, while teammate **Todd Greene** was second with 26 despite being promoted just after the All-Star break. Arias also led the league in RBI with 104. **Felix Martinez** of Wichita led the league with 44 steals. San Antonio's **Gary Rath** won the ERA crown (13-3, 2.77) while Shreveport ace **Steve Bourgeois** (12-3, 2.85) was Pitcher of the Year. Shreveport's **Edwin Corps** shared the league lead in wins (13). Arkansas' **Steve Montgomery** led in saves (36). El Paso's **Frankie Rodriguez'** 129 strikeouts led that department.

TEXAS LEAGUE (AA)
Eastern Division

	W	L	Pct.	GB
Shreveport	88	47	.652	—
Arkansas	70	65	.519	18
Jackson	62	73	.459	26
Tulsa	52	83	.385	36

Western Division

	W	L	Pct.	GB
Wichita	72	64	.529	—
El Paso	68	68	.500	4
Midland	66	70	.485	6
San Antonio	64	72	.471	8

Semifinals: Midland 3, Wichita 2.
Finals: Shreveport 4, Midland 1.

Class AA WRAPUPS

Southern League

The Southern went down to the wire as Carolina outlasted Chattanooga for the championship in five games. **Jason Kendall** of Carolina was league MVP (.326, 71 RBI), while **Luis Andujar** was the Most Outstanding Pitcher (14-8, 2.85 ERA). **Kevin Coughlin** of Birmingham led in batting at .371. **Ivan Cruz** of Jacksonville (31 HR) and **George Canale** of Carolina (102 RBI) had league highs. **Essex Burton** stole 60 bases for Birmingham, edging out Knoxville's **Lonell Roberts** (57) for the league title. Carolina's **Elmer Dessens**, in his first pro season in the U.S., led the league in ERA for Carolina (2.49) and wins (15). **Osvaldo Fernandez**, who came to the U.S. from Cuba on a raft, led the loop with 160 strikeouts for Port City. Jacksonville's **John Kelly** and **Rusty Kilgo** of Chattanooga shared the save lead (29).

SOUTHERN LEAGUE (AA)

Eastern Division

	W	L	Pct.	GB
Carolina	89	55	.618	—
Orlando	76	67	.531	12½
Jacksonville	75	69	.521	14
Port City	62	80	.437	26
Greenville	59	83	.415	29

Western Division

	W	L	Pct.	GB
Chattanooga	83	60	.580	—
Birmingham	80	64	.556	3½
Huntsville	70	74	.486	13½
Memphis	68	74	.479	14½
Knoxville	54	90	.375	29½

Semifinals: *Carolina 3, Orlando 2; Chattanooga 3, Memphis 2.*
Finals: *Carolina 3, Chattanooga 2*

New Orleans Zephyrs (Brewers) AAA

BATTING	AVG	AB	R	H	2B	3B	HR	RBI	SB
Barker, Tim, OF	.258	264	44	68	9	5	1	24	10
*Basse, Mike, OF	.247	381	49	94	14	2	0	35	15
*Dodson, Bo, 1B	.281	203	29	57	5	1	9	34	0
Finn, John, OF	.325	117	20	38	4	1	3	19	9
Gonzalez, Javier, C	.248	113	20	28	11	0	5	15	0
*Harris, Mike, DH	.232	56	3	13	3	0	0	5	1
Jaha, John, DH	.400	10	2	4	1	0	1	3	0
*Koslofski, Kevin, OF	.212	321	41	68	18	4	7	35	4
Lofton, Rodney, 2B	.217	240	30	52	7	0	1	18	9
Lopez, Pedro, C	.000	8	0	0	0	0	0	0	0
Loretta, Mark, SS	.286	479	48	137	22	5	7	79	8
Matheny, Mike, C	.353	17	3	6	2	0	3	4	0
*Nilsson, Dave, DH	.444	9	1	4	0	0	1	4	0
Oliver, Joe, C	.077	13	0	1	1	0	0	0	0
Perez, Danny, DH	.294	34	5	10	1	0	0	0	0
*Singleton, D., OF	.268	355	48	95	10	4	4	29	31
Staton, Dave, 1B	.252	325	42	82	11	1	19	46	0
Stefanski, Mike, C	.246	228	30	56	10	2	2	24	2
Sutko, Glenn, C	.208	101	7	21	8	0	3	14	0
Talanoa, Scott, DH	.143	98	9	14	4	0	1	3	0
Unroe, Tim, 3B	.261	371	43	97	21	2	6	45	4
Wachter, Derek, OF	.257	382	44	98	23	1	8	45	2
#Ward, Turner, OF	.242	33	3	8	1	1	1	3	0
Weger, Wes, 2B	.286	234	28	67	16	0	2	24	0

PITCHING	W	L	ERA	G	SV	IP	H	BB	SO
Archer, Kurt	2	6	3.25	38	2	61.0	57	17	41
Boze, Marshall	3	9	4.27	23	1	111.2	134	45	47
Bronkey, Jeff	0	1	2.25	2	0	8.0	8	1	2
*Combs, Pat	1	1	5.40	12	0	15.0	19	13	10
Dibble, Rob	0	1	0.00	4	0	4.0	1	2	6
Duncan, Chip	1	4	6.29	14	0	34.1	44	18	23
*Farrell, Mike	8	10	4.57	25	0	141.2	173	38	74
Fritz, John	6	3	3.97	41	1	81.2	70	42	56
Ganote, Joe	7	4	3.42	14	0	81.2	88	21	56
*Givens, Brian	7	4	2.55	16	0	77.2	67	33	75
Ignasiak, Mike	1	1	2.50	4	0	18.0	9	8	19
Jones, Stacy	3	2	3.02	34	6	47.2	51	12	39
*Karl, Scott	3	4	3.30	8	0	46.1	47	12	29
Kiefer, Mark	8	2	2.82	12	0	70.1	60	19	52
McAndrew, Jamie	7	5	3.97	17	0	104.1	102	44	62
McClellan, Paul	0	3	6.06	3	0	16.1	19	8	8
Popplewell, Tom	0	2	6.75	10	0	13.1	13	11	16
Rambo, Dan	0	4	5.20	7	0	36.1	39	9	22
Rightnowar, Ron	1	1	2.67	25	10	30.1	37	9	22
*Roberson, Sid	0	2	7.62	4	0	13.0	20	10	8
Scanlan, Bob	0	1	5.40	3	0	11.2	17	3	5
Seminara, Frank	2	3	7.96	11	0	37.1	54	14	19
Shinall, Zak	0	0	7.62	9	0	13.0	15	7	5
Slusarski, Joe	1	1	1.12	33	11	48.1	37	11	30
Swingle, Paul	1	4	4.57	35	0	43.1	42	15	41
*Thomas, Mike	0	1	4.05	35	1	33.1	37	18	28

Oklahoma City 89ers (Rangers) AAA

BATTING	AVG	AB	R	H	2B	3B	HR	RBI	SB
Borrelli, Dean, C	.200	185	17	37	9	1	2	17	0
Brown, Kevin, C	.400	10	1	4	1	0	0	0	0
Brown, Marty, 3B	.168	101	12	17	5	0	3	12	0
Buechele, Steve, 3B	.308	13	1	4	0	0	1	3	0
Byington, John, 3B	.259	390	44	101	15	2	2	29	6
Cameron, Stanton, OF	.167	12	2	2	1	0	0	0	0
Chance, Tony, OF	.214	196	19	42	12	0	2	20	1
Clinton, Jim, 1B	.000	13	0	0	0	0	0	0	0
*Dostal, Bruce, OF	.212	293	35	62	14	6	4	31	11
Figueroa, Bien, SS	.100	20	1	2	0	0	0	2	1
#Fox, Eric, OF	.278	349	52	97	22	5	6	50	5
Goldberg, Lonnie, SS	.233	30	2	7	3	0	1	5	1
*Hare, Shawn, OF	.265	238	27	63	13	3	4	30	3
Harris, Donald, OF	.200	40	4	8	1	1	0	7	0
*Hecht, Steve, 2B	.261	238	26	62	6	3	3	14	9
#Hinzo, Tommy, 2B	.252	254	33	64	10	1	0	20	8

BATTING	AVG	AB	R	H	2B	3B	HR	RBI	SB
*Horn, Sam, DH	.308	156	26	48	9	0	12	42	0
Hulett, Tim, SS	.213	141	14	30	6	1	1	7	0
Kennedy, Darryl, C	.182	11	1	2	0	0	1	3	0
Lindeman, Jim, 1B	.252	294	52	74	16	3	12	36	0
Luce, Roger, C	.000	3	0	0	0	0	0	0	0
Marzano, John, C	.309	427	55	132	41	3	9	56	3
McCoy, Trey, 1B	.310	29	4	9	1	0	0	2	0
Ortiz, Luis, 3B	.306	170	19	52	10	5	2	20	1
#Parra, Franklin, SS	.167	18	0	3	1	0	0	1	1
*Ritchie, Gregg, OF	.179	28	5	5	0	0	1	4	1
Rivera, Luis, SS	.138	58	3	8	4	0	1	3	0
Rolls, David, C	.000	5	0	0	0	0	0	1	0
*Sagmoen, Marc, OF	.223	188	20	42	11	3	3	25	5
Schu, Rick, SS	.271	398	49	108	19	3	12	57	5
Shave, Jon, 2B	.205	83	10	17	1	0	0	5	1
Vargas, Hector, OF	.275	305	38	84	10	2	0	27	6

PITCHING	W	L	ERA	G	SV	IP	H	BB	SO
Alberro, Jose	4	2	3.36	20	0	77.2	73	27	55
*Barfield, John	0	0	0.00	4	1	7.1	4	1	2
Brandenburg, Mark	0	5	2.02	35	2	58.0	52	15	51
Brumley, Duff	1	1	5.40	3	1	5.0	6	2	3
*Burrows, Terry	0	1	10.13	5	0	2.2	5	2	4
Curtis, Chris	3	5	5.00	51	5	77.1	81	39	40
Darwin, Danny	0	0	0.00	1	0	3.0	1	0	4
Dettmer, John	0	0	2.08	5	0	8.2	10	4	10
Geeve, Dave	2	5	5.66	10	0	55.2	72	13	30
Goetz, Barry	4	6	5.72	40	0	89.2	97	49	46
Helling, Rick	4	8	5.33	20	0	109.2	132	41	80
Heredia, Wilson	1	4	6.82	8	0	31.2	40	25	21
Lacy, Kerry	0	0	0.00	1	1	2.1	0	0	1
Nichting, Chris	5	5	2.13	23	0	67.2	58	19	72
Patterson, Danny	1	0	1.65	14	2	27.1	23	9	9
Perez, David	5	12	5.57	20	0	103.1	120	34	74
Santana, Julio	0	2	39.00	2	0	3.0	9	7	6
*Schuermann, Lance	4	7	4.67	33	0	88.2	101	40	44
Taylor, Scott	7	8	3.66	22	0	118.0	122	38	65
Wishnevski, Rob	6	3	3.47	41	3	109.0	101	53	78

Omaha Royals (Royals) AAA

BATTING	AVG	AB	R	H	2B	3B	HR	RBI	SB
*Bruett, J.T., OF	.279	129	20	36	6	1	2	14	6
#Burton, Darren, OF	.000	5	0	0	0	0	0	0	0
#Caceres, Edgar, 3B	.206	107	13	22	3	1	0	12	3
Chamberlain, Wes, OF	.219	64	2	14	3	0	1	6	0
#Coleman, Vince, OF	.395	38	7	15	2	0	1	5	3
Cookson, Brent, OF	.401	137	28	55	13	0	4	20	0
Elster, Kevin, SS	.238	42	5	10	4	0	0	6	0
Garber, Jeff, 3B	.143	14	1	2	0	0	0	0	0
Green, Gary, SS	.169	71	5	12	2	0	0	3	0
*Grotewold, Jeff, 1B	.294	350	70	103	19	0	17	60	0
Halter, Shane, SS	.230	392	42	90	19	3	8	39	2
*Hamelin, Bob, 1B	.294	119	25	35	12	0	10	32	2
Hatcher, Billy, OF	.276	105	14	29	5	1	1	12	4
Hiatt, Phil, OF	.158	76	7	12	5	0	2	8	0
#Hosey, Dwayne, OF	.295	271	59	80	21	4	12	50	15
*Hughes, Keith, OF	.289	342	51	99	22	2	11	46	4
James, Chris, DH	.167	12	3	2	1	0	1	3	0
*Lockhart, Keith, 3B	.378	148	24	56	7	1	5	19	1
*Long, Kevin, OF	.250	64	7	16	3	0	0	0	1
Lyden, Mitch, C	.253	237	26	60	8	1	12	44	0
Mercedes, Henry, C	.215	275	37	59	12	0	11	37	2
Miller, Keith, DH	.250	20	3	5	2	0	0	2	1
#Mota, Jose, SS	.322	87	6	28	4	0	0	10	1
Norman, Les, OF	.284	313	46	89	19	3	9	33	5
Randa, Joe, 3B	.275	233	33	64	10	2	8	33	2
#Reynolds, H., 2B	.202	109	12	22	6	1	1	11	2
Sisco, Steve, 2B	.208	24	4	5	1	0	0	0	0
Stewart, Andy, C	.301	156	24	47	11	0	3	21	0
Strickland, Chad, C	.273	22	3	6	2	0	0	5	0
Stynes, Chris, 2B	.275	306	51	84	12	5	9	42	4
*Tucker, Michael, OF	.305	275	37	84	18	4	4	28	11
Vitiello, Joe, 1B	.279	229	33	64	14	2	12	42	0

Class AA WRAPUPS

Eastern League

In the first game played in pro baseball in 1995, Reading second baseman **David Doster** got the first hit of the season as his team beat New Haven, 3-2. And in the finals, Doster was the star again (6 HR) as his team beat New Haven for its first league title since 1973. Despite being promoted to Class AAA Norfolk at midseason, Binghamton's **Jay Payton** had enough at-bats to win the batting title (.345), while the first pick in the 1994 draft, Binghamton's **Paul Wilson**, was tops in ERA (2.17). **Fred McNair** led the league in homers for Reading (23). New Haven's **Angel Echevarria** (100 RBI) and **Terry Jones** (51 SB) had league highs. Portland's **Billy McMillon** was league MVP. Joel Moore of New Haven led the league with 14 wins. **Rafael Orellano** of Trenton led with 160 strikeouts. **Jay Powell** of Portland was first with 24 saves.

EASTERN LEAGUE (AA)

Northern Division

	W	L	Pct.	GB
Portland	86	56	.606	—
New Haven	79	63	.556	7
Norwich	70	71	.496	15½
Binghamton	67	75	.472	19
Hardware City	65	77	.458	21

Southern Division

	W	L	Pct.	GB
Trenton	73	69	.514	—
Reading	73	69	.514	—
Bowie	68	74	.479	5
Canton-Akron	67	75	.472	6
Harrisburg	61	80	.433	11½

Semifinals: *Reading 3, Trenton 0; New Haven 3, Portland 1.*
Finals: *Reading 3, New Haven 2.*

Class A WRAPUPS

California League

The San Bernardino Spirit, which hit .284, swept the San Jose Giants and their impressive 3.05 ERA in the championship finals. **Adam Riggs** of San Bernardino won the batting title at .362, with 24 homers, 106 RBI and 31 stolen bases. Modesto's **Steve Cox** led in homers (30) and RBI (110); teammate **Jason McDonald** led the minors with 70 steals. **Tom Price** of San Bernardino won the ERA crown at 2.20, (10-5, 14 walks in 152 innings). **Matt Beaumont** of Lake Elsinore was Pitcher of the Year, leading the league with 16 wins. **Masataka Endo** of Visalia led in strikeouts (178). Lake Elsinore's **Carlos Castillo** led the league with 32 saves.

CALIFORNIA LEAGUE (A)

Northern Division

	W	L	Pct.	GB
Modesto	78	62	.557	—
San Jose	77	63	.550	1
Stockton	74	66	.529	4
Bakersfield	58	82	.414	20
Visalia	58	82	.414	20

Southern Division

	W	L	Pct.	GB
S. Bernardino	85	54	.612	—
Lake Elsinore	82	57	.590	3
Riverside	72	67	.518	13
Rcho. Cuca.	68	71	.489	17
High Desert	66	94	.329	39½

Semifinals: San Bernardino 3, Lake Elsinore 0; San Jose 3, Modesto 0.
Finals: San Bernardino 3, San Jose 0.

PITCHING	W	L	ERA	G	SV	IP	H	BB	SO
Anderson, Scott	5	3	4.17	15	0	73.1	63	16	47
Bevil, Brian	1	3	9.41	6	0	22.0	40	14	10
Bluma, Jaime	0	0	3.04	18	4	23.2	21	14	12
*Brewer, Billy	0	0	0.00	6	0	7.0	1	7	5
*Brown, Kevin	0	0	7.62	7	0	13.0	20	12	5
*Browning, Tom	2	1	3.43	5	0	21.0	13	5	5
Bunch, Mel	1	7	4.57	12	0	65.0	63	20	50
Caceres, Edgar	0	0	9.00	1	0	2.0	4	1	1
Converse, Jim	1	0	0.00	4	0	5.0	1	1	9
DeJesus, Jose	3	6	6.13	36	10	61.2	56	52	49
Dorlarque, Aaron	2	2	4.24	24	4	40.1	38	15	24
*Eddy, Chris	1	1	7.27	14	0	17.1	20	12	12
*Fleming, Dave	1	0	3.38	3	0	16.0	17	7	8
Fyhrie, Mike	3	4	4.45	14	0	60.2	71	14	39
Garrelts, Scott	1	2	5.30	9	1	18.2	17	13	15
Harris, Reggie	0	1	18.00	2	0	2.0	5	1	2
Harrison, Brian	4	2	6.13	16	0	54.1	76	10	12
Huisman, Rick	0	0	1.80	5	1	5.0	3	1	13
Kutzler, Jerry	8	5	4.02	37	4	103.0	128	27	45
Linton, Doug	7	7	4.40	18	0	108.1	129	24	85
*Magnante, Mike	5	1	2.84	15	0	57.0	55	13	38
*Mallicoat, Rob	0	1	3.00	3	0	3.0	1	3	1
Melendez, Jose	3	4	4.89	21	0	35.0	44	14	30
Milacki, Bob	8	3	3.33	15	0	105.1	90	31	63
*Munoz, J.J.	2	3	3.38	57	6	56.0	48	19	51
Myers, Rod	4	5	4.10	38	2	48.1	52	19	38
*Perry, Pat	0	0	5.79	5	3	4.2	5	2	4
*Pierce, Ed	0	0	7.36	3	0	3.2	9	1	1
Pittsley, Jim	4	1	3.21	8	0	47.2	38	16	39
*Rasmussen, Dennis	6	3	2.89	10	0	65.1	63	17	51
Strange, Don	0	0	7.47	9	1	15.2	24	6	11
Torres, Dilson	3	1	2.63	5	0	27.1	28	7	12
Toth, Robert	1	2	3.61	8	0	47.1	53	8	31

International League

Charlotte Knights (Marlins) AAA

BATTING	AVG	AB	R	H	2B	3B	HR	RBI	SB
Abbott, Kurt, SS	.278	18	3	5	0	0	1	3	1
*Boston, Daryl, DH	.188	64	7	12	5	0	1	2	0
*Brewer, Rod, 1B	.322	236	31	76	15	1	9	55	0
Capra, Nick, OF	.256	406	60	104	17	1	9	51	22
#Carr, Chuck, OF	.217	23	5	5	0	1	1	2	2
#Carter, Jeff, 2B	.269	428	78	115	20	3	0	22	22
*Carter, Steve, OF	.250	72	9	18	0	3	3	15	0
*Castaldo, Vince, Ph	.200	10	2	2	0	0	0	1	0
#Dascenzo, D., OF	.260	265	51	69	9	0	4	26	14
*Ford, Curt, OF	.305	167	18	51	10	0	3	17	2
*Gregg, Tommy, 1B	.387	124	30	48	10	1	9	32	7
Hernandez, Kiki, C	.240	150	13	36	8	0	7	28	0
Jorgensen, Terry, 3B	.264	356	38	94	14	0	7	52	3
Massarelli, John, OF	.244	254	37	62	7	2	2	8	14
Millette, Joe, 2B	.187	193	22	36	6	0	4	20	1
Morman, Russ, 1B	.314	169	28	53	7	1	6	36	2
Natal, Rob, C	.314	191	23	60	14	0	3	24	0
Pappas, Erik, C	.221	389	48	86	28	3	10	52	10
Rudolph, Mason, C	.250	4	1	1	0	0	0	0	0
Schunk, Jerry, SS	.224	343	36	77	13	0	6	33	8
#Tavarez, Jesus, OF	.300	140	15	42	6	2	1	8	7
Zosky, Eddie, SS	.247	312	27	77	15	2	3	42	2
Zupcic, Bob, OF	.295	254	34	75	12	0	11	47	2

PITCHING	W	L	ERA	G	SV	IP	H	BB	SO
*Adamson, Joel	8	4	3.29	19	0	115.0	113	20	80
Batista, Miguel	6	12	4.80	34	0	116.1	118	60	58
Bowen, Ryan	0	1	9.64	1	0	4.2	5	4	3
Brown, Keith	0	1	2.45	4	0	7.1	6	2	3
Clary, Marty	2	2	4.74	9	0	19.0	26	1	8
*Davis, Mark	0	0	5.00	9	0	9.0	13	1	5
Drahman, Brian	2	1	6.30	21	4	20.0	28	11	17

PITCHING	W	L	ERA	G	SV	IP	H	BB	SO
*Hammond, Chris	0	0	0.00	1	0	4.0	3	2	3
*Hancock, Chris	0	1	13.50	3	0	3.1	6	4	2
Hernandez, Jeremy	0	2	5.58	15	0	30.2	37	15	24
Lemon, Don	0	0	5.40	6	0	11.2	11	3	8
Lewis, Richie	5	2	3.20	17	0	59.0	50	20	45
Long, Steve	5	4	5.96	33	4	74.0	71	46	46
Mantei, Matt	0	1	2.57	6	0	7.0	1	5	10
Mathews, Terry	0	0	4.91	2	0	3.2	5	0	5
Miller, Kurt	8	11	4.62	22	0	126.2	143	55	83
*Murphy, Rob	0	0	0.00	3	2	3.0	2	0	1
*Mutis, Jeff	0	1	3.72	27	2	36.1	31	14	21
Newlin, Jim	0	0	4.26	5	0	6.1	6	1	5
Pena, Alejandro	0	0	0.96	9	5	9.1	2	1	7
Perigny, Don	1	1	5.14	6	0	7.0	8	1	10
Rapp, Pat	0	1	6.00	1	0	6.0	6	1	5
Rojas, Euclides	0	1	3.00	2	0	3.0	2	2	2
*Scheid, Rich	1	4	5.93	19	0	54.2	74	15	37
Shepherd, Keith	1	1	21.21	4	0	4.2	11	3	2
Small, Aaron	2	1	2.88	33	10	40.2	36	10	31
Smith, Pete	2	1	3.86	10	0	49.0	51	17	20
Spencer, Stan	1	4	7.84	9	0	41.1	61	24	19
Spradlin, Jerry	3	3	3.03	41	1	59.1	59	15	38
Valdes, Marc	9	13	4.86	27	0	170.1	189	59	104
Veres, Randy	1	0	2.70	6	1	6.2	3	5	5
Wainhouse, Dave	0	0	9.82	4	0	3.2	6	4	2
Weathers, David	0	1	9.00	1	0	5.0	10	5	0
Zimmerman, Mike	2	2	5.30	31	0	69.2	84	41	30

Columbus Clippers (Yankees) AAA

BATTING	AVG	AB	R	H	2B	3B	HR	RBI	SB
Barnwell, Rich, OF	.231	130	22	30	4	2	1	17	7
#Benzinger, Todd, 1B	.280	50	4	14	3	0	1	4	0
*Carpenter, B., OF	.246	374	57	92	12	3	11	49	13
Davis, Russ, 3B	.250	76	12	19	4	1	2	15	0
*Deberry, Joe, 1B	.292	24	3	7	2	2	0	4	0
Eenhoorn, Robert, 2B	.252	318	36	80	11	3	5	32	2
Epps, Scott, C	.143	7	0	1	0	0	0	0	0
Figga, Mike, C	.280	25	2	7	1	0	1	3	0
#Fleming, Carlton, 2B	.221	86	9	19	6	0	0	5	0
*Fox, Andy, 3B	.348	302	61	105	16	6	9	37	22
#Hill, Lew, OF	.271	144	15	39	5	0	4	20	6
Jeter, Derek, SS	.317	486	96	154	27	9	2	45	20
*Leach, Jalal, OF	.243	272	37	66	12	5	6	31	11
Livesey, Jeff, C	.264	91	8	24	3	0	0	7	0
*Luke, Matt, OF	.299	77	11	23	4	1	3	12	1
*Maas, Kevin, OF	.280	161	28	45	7	2	9	33	0
Masse, Billy, OF	.224	165	19	37	6	2	4	24	3
*McDowell, Oddibe, OF	.217	46	5	10	0	1	1	2	0
Melvin, Bob, C	.288	66	7	19	5	0	1	4	0
Perezchica, Tony, 2B	.257	358	43	92	12	4	7	44	3
#Posada, Jorge, C	.255	368	60	94	32	5	8	51	4
Rivera, Ruben, OF	.270	174	37	47	8	2	15	35	8
*Seefried, Tate, 1B	.164	110	7	18	6	0	1	12	0
Sparks, Don, 1B	.312	545	67	170	26	10	7	90	2
*Strawberry, Darryl, DH	.301	83	20	25	3	1	7	29	1
*Thoutsis, Paul, OF	.215	130	10	28	4	1	0	15	1
Wilson, Tom, C	.258	62	11	16	3	1	0	9	0
PITCHING	W	L	ERA	G	SV	IP	H	BB	SO
Ausanio, Joe	1	0	7.50	11	3	12.0	12	5	20
Boehringer, Brian	8	6	2.77	17	0	104.0	101	31	58
Carper, Mark	8	9	4.82	33	1	106.1	114	55	61
Cook, Andy	2	3	3.36	37	2	56.1	53	19	28
Croghan, Andy	1	1	3.60	20	0	25.0	21	22	22
*Dunbar, Matt	2	3	4.06	36	0	44.1	50	19	33
Eiland, Dave	8	7	3.14	19	0	109.0	109	22	62
Frazier, Ron	1	2	4.50	24	0	54.0	54	23	31
*Hernandez, Willie	2	1	7.67	22	0	27.0	43	12	16
Hutton, Mark	2	6	8.43	11	0	52.1	64	24	23
Kamieniecki, Scott	1	0	0.00	1	0	6.2	2	1	10
*Macdonald, Bob	2	1	2.33	13	0	19.1	22	5	13
Mendoza, Ramiro	1	0	2.57	2	0	14.0	10	2	13
Musset, Jose	0	0	6.23	5	0	4.1	4	2	4
*Ojala, Kirt	8	7	3.95	32	1	145.2	138	54	107

Class A
WRAPUPS

Carolina League

Taking advantage of a bye to the finals and a chance to rest up their fine pitching staff, the Kinston Indians stifled the Wilmington offense, limiting the Blue Rocks to two runs over three games to win the league title in a sweep. **Roland DeLaMaza** took a perfect game into the eighth inning in the 4-0 clincher. Kinston's **Richie Sexson** was playoff and regular season MVP (.306, 23 HR and league-best 85 RBI). Teammate **Bartolo Colon** was the Pitcher of the Year (13-3, 1.96 ERA, league-high 152 strikeouts). Wilmington's **Mike Sweeney** led the league at .310 and a .548 slugging percentage. Teammate **Glendon Rusch** led in wins and ERA (14-6, 1.74). Prince William's **Juan Thomas** led the league with 26 homers. Kinston's **Ricky Gutierrez** led in steals (43). Durham's **Matt Byrd** led with 27 saves.

CAROLINA LEAGUE

Northern Division

	W	L	Pct.	GB
Wilmington	48	21	.696	—
Lynchburg	34	35	.493	14
Frederick	31	38	.449	17
Prince Wm.	27	43	.386	21½

Southern Division

	W	L	Pct.	GB
Kinston	36	32	.529	—
Wnstn.-Slm.	33	34	.493	2½
Salem	34	36	.486	3
Durham	33	37	.471	4

Finals: Kinston 3, Wilmington 0.

Class A WRAPUPS

Florida State League

After posting the best record in Class A, the Daytona Cubs came away with the Florida State League championship—their first trophy since 1981. **Wendell Magee** of Clearwater won the batting title at .353, after winning the starting job only because projected starter **Jeremey Kendall** broke his arm in spring training. His teammate **Dan Held** led the league with 21 homers. Tampa's **Shane Spencer** (.300, 16 HR) led the league with 88 RBI and was MVP. **Mike Metcalfe** of Vero Beach won the stolen base crown (60). **Kevin Pincavitch** of Vero Beach led the league in ERA at 1.66. **Matt Drews** of Tampa had 15 wins to lead the league, while St. Petersburg's **Kris Detmers** was first with 150 strikeouts. Vero Beach's **Joe Jacobsen** notched 32 saves.

FLORIDA STATE LEAGUE (A)

East Division

	W	L	Pct.	GB
Daytona	46	20	.697	—
Vero Beach	35	28	.556	9
Brevard	31	36	.463	15
W. Palm Bch.	29	37	.439	17
St. Lucie	28	38	.424	18
Kissimmee	27	40	.403	19½

West Division

	W	L	Pct.	GB
Fort Myers	41	21	.661	—
Clearwater	41	27	.603	3
St. Petrsbrg.	32	31	.508	9½
Sarasota	31	34	.477	11½
Tampa	31	35	.470	12
Charlotte	30	34	.469	12
Lakeland	28	36	.438	14
Dunedin	28	41	.406	16½

Semifinals: Fort Myers 2, Tampa 1.
Finals: Daytona 3, Fort Myers 2.

PITCHING	W	L	ERA	G	SV	IP	H	BB	SO
Patterson, Jeff	5	3	3.61	33	0	62.1	56	30	36
Pavlas, Dave	3	3	2.61	48	18	58.2	43	20	51
*Pettitte, Andy	0	0	0.00	2	0	11.2	7	0	8
*Quirico, Rafael	0	0	4.70	20	0	23.0	15	14	21
Rivera, Mariano	2	2	2.10	7	0	30.0	25	3	30
*Rumer, Tim	10	8	5.22	28	0	141.1	156	76	110
Segura, Jose	0	2	8.71	11	4	10.1	18	8	8
Smith, Daryl	0	3	4.03	13	0	51.1	54	20	23
Sutherland, John	0	0	9.00	3	0	3.0	5	0	2
Wallace, Kent	4	1	3.02	9	0	50.2	44	11	31

Norfolk Tides (Mets) AAA

BATTING	AVG	AB	R	H	2B	3B	HR	RBI	SB
Abner, Shawn, DH	.258	31	3	8	0	0	0	1	0
#Alicea, Ed, 2B	.245	436	63	107	17	4	3	39	21
Azuaje, Jesus, 2B	.429	14	1	6	1	0	0	0	1
#Barry, Jeff, 1B	.220	41	3	9	2	0	0	6	0
Boka, Ben, C	.143	21	0	3	0	0	0	1	0
Castillo, Alberto, C	.267	217	23	58	13	1	4	31	2
*Daubach, Brian, 1B	.000	7	0	0	0	0	0	0	0
*Davis, Jay, OF	.192	26	1	5	1	1	0	3	0
Diaz, Cesar, C	.182	11	2	2	0	0	0	0	0
#Everett, Carl, OF	.300	260	52	78	16	4	6	35	12
Garcia, Omar, 1B	.309	430	55	133	21	7	3	64	3
#Graham, Greg, 3B	.197	122	14	24	5	0	0	9	1
Greene, Charlie, C	.193	88	6	17	3	0	0	4	0
#Hardtke, Jason, 2B	.286	7	1	2	1	0	0	0	1
Huskey, Butch, 3B	.284	394	66	112	18	1	28	87	8
Jones, Chris, OF	.333	114	20	38	12	1	3	19	5
Ledesma, Aaron, 3B	.299	201	26	60	12	1	0	28	6
*Lee, Derek, OF	.254	351	56	89	17	0	18	60	11
McCoy, Trey, DH	.209	67	6	14	5	0	3	7	0
Morgan, Kevin, 2B	.323	62	10	20	1	0	0	8	1
Ochoa, Alex, OF	.309	123	17	38	6	2	2	15	7
Ordonez, Rey, SS	.214	439	49	94	21	4	2	50	11
Orton, John, C	.288	170	20	49	8	0	3	20	1
#Otero, Ricky, OF	.268	295	37	79	8	6	1	23	16
Payton, Jay, OF	.240	196	33	47	11	4	4	30	11
*Sanders, Tracy, OF	.227	110	21	25	6	0	4	14	3
Saunders, Chris, 3B	.232	56	9	13	3	1	3	7	1
*Spiers, Bill, 2B	.220	41	4	9	2	0	0	4	0
Thompson, Ryan, OF	.340	53	7	18	3	0	2	11	4

PITCHING	W	L	ERA	G	SV	IP	H	BB	SO
Acevedo, Juan	0	0	0.00	2	0	3.0	0	1	2
Birkbeck, Mike	5	3	2.36	9	0	53.1	52	13	39
Byrd, Paul	3	5	2.79	22	6	87.0	71	21	61
Cornelius, Reid	7	0	0.90	10	0	70.1	57	19	43
*Crawford, Joe	1	1	1.93	8	0	18.2	9	4	13
Engle, Tom	0	1	12.00	1	0	3.0	5	3	5
*Florence, Don	0	1	0.96	41	4	47.0	37	17	29
Fuller, Mark	0	0	2.08	4	1	4.1	7	0	2
Isringhausen, Jason	9	1	1.55	12	0	87.0	64	24	75
*Jacome, Jason	2	4	3.92	8	0	43.2	40	13	31
Ludwick, Eric	1	1	5.85	4	0	20.0	22	7	9
McCready, Jim	0	1	2.01	28	0	40.1	41	20	21
*Osuna, Al	3	1	3.00	14	0	42.0	39	12	31
*Paxton, Darrin	0	0	9.00	1	0	2.0	3	2	0
Person, Robert	2	1	4.50	5	0	32.0	30	13	33
*Pulsipher, Bill	6	4	3.14	13	0	91.2	84	33	63
*Roberts, Chris	7	13	5.52	25	0	150.0	197	58	88
Rogers, Bryan	8	3	2.21	56	10	77.1	58	22	50
Stidham, Phil	6	2	3.21	34	1	70.0	56	36	56
Stoddard, Bob	0	1	6.75	3	0	2.2	5	1	1
Telgheder, Dave	5	4	2.24	29	3	92.1	77	8	75
Walker, Pete	5	2	3.91	34	8	48.1	51	16	39
Wilson, Paul	5	3	2.85	10	0	66.1	59	20	67

Ottawa Lynx (Expos) AAA

BATTING	AVG	AB	R	H	2B	3B	HR	RBI	SB
Alvarez, Clemente, C	.231	143	15	33	7	0	4	20	0
Barron, Tony, OF	.245	147	20	36	10	0	10	22	0

BATTING	AVG	AB	R	H	2B	3B	HR	RBI	SB
Benitez, Yamil, OF	.259	474	66	123	24	6	18	69	14
Bournigal, Rafael, SS	.204	54	2	11	4	0	0	6	0
Buccheri, Jim, OF	.268	470	64	126	16	4	0	30	44
Cairo, Sergio, OF	.333	6	1	2	1	0	0	0	0
*Castleberry, Kevin, 2B	.294	428	65	126	18	4	7	56	9
*Delima, Rafael, OF	.259	27	4	7	0	0	0	3	2
#Felix, Junior, OF	.225	160	22	36	7	3	3	24	1
*Foley, Tom, 2B	.306	62	13	19	5	0	0	7	1
#Frazier, Lou, OF	.218	110	11	24	3	0	1	10	10
Grudzielanek, Mark, SS	.298	181	26	54	9	1	1	22	12
*Heffernan, Bert, C	.216	102	13	22	5	0	1	12	1
*Jacobs, Frank, DH	.250	32	9	8	2	2	0	4	0
Martin, Chris, SS	.257	412	55	106	19	1	3	40	30
Martinez, Ray, 3B	.250	108	17	27	6	0	0	9	3
*Pride, Curtis, OF	.279	154	25	43	8	3	4	24	8
*Rodriguez, Henry, DH	.200	15	0	3	1	0	0	2	0
Rundels, Matt, 2B	.250	36	7	9	1	1	0	4	1
#Santangelo, F.P., 3B	.255	267	37	68	15	3	2	25	7
*Siddall, Joe, C	.214	248	26	53	14	2	1	23	3
Tovar, Raul, OF	.304	56	8	17	2	0	0	7	0
*Velasquez, G., 1B	.250	112	11	28	5	0	1	9	1
*Wilstead, Randy, DH	.292	24	6	7	2	1	0	3	0
*Wood, Ted, OF	.267	326	35	87	16	1	8	49	9
Yan, Julian, 1B	.280	372	49	104	22	3	22	79	5

PITCHING	W	L	ERA	G	SV	IP	H	BB	SO
Alvarez, Tavo	2	1	2.49	3	0	21.2	17	5	11
*Baxter, Robert	5	5	3.92	39	0	101.0	125	25	39
*Boucher, Denis	2	3	5.69	14	0	55.1	65	31	22
Diaz, Rafael	0	3	6.56	32	0	48.0	51	25	31
*Eischen, Joey	2	1	1.72	11	0	15.2	9	8	13
*Eversgerd, Bryan	6	2	2.38	38	2	53.0	49	26	45
Fajardo, Hector	0	0	4.11	11	0	15.1	18	6	9
Falteisek, Steve	2	0	1.17	3	0	23.0	17	5	18
Fraser, Willie	7	6	3.19	19	0	107.1	94	18	84
*Garcia, Miguel	0	0	1.35	5	0	6.2	6	3	4
Harris, Greg	3	0	1.06	11	1	17.0	7	3	17
Kerley, Collin	2	0	2.16	5	0	8.1	11	3	3
Layana, Tim	1	1	8.50	26	4	36.0	56	20	27
*Leiper, Dave	0	0	0.00	2	0	3.0	1	1	2
*Magrane, Joe	3	6	4.84	12	0	67.0	69	31	37
Manuel, Barry	5	12	4.59	35	1	127.1	125	50	85
Mitchell, John	0	1	4.32	6	0	8.1	8	3	5
Pacheco, Alex	1	0	6.23	4	0	8.2	8	5	4
*Pena, Jim	0	0	3.68	7	0	7.1	4	8	7
*Rueter, Kirk	9	7	3.06	20	0	120.2	120	25	67
Schmidt, Curt	5	0	2.22	43	15	52.2	40	18	38
Thobe, J.J.	5	8	3.27	55	5	88.0	79	16	36
Torres, Ricky	3	8	5.01	32	0	91.2	90	26	58
Urbina, Ugueth	6	2	3.04	13	0	68.0	46	26	55
*White, Gabe	2	3	3.90	12	0	62.1	58	17	37

Pawtucket Red Sox (Red Sox) AAA

BATTING	AVG	AB	R	H	2B	3B	HR	RBI	SB
*Barbara, Don, 1B	.217	129	19	28	8	0	2	10	2
#Bell, Juan, SS	.263	262	42	69	18	1	6	23	4
*Blosser, Greg, OF	.200	50	5	10	0	0	1	4	0
Brown, Randy, SS	.250	212	27	53	6	1	2	12	5
Canseco, Jose, DH	.167	6	1	1	0	0	0	1	0
Chamberlain, Wes, OF	.350	183	28	64	17	1	12	40	5
Delgado, Alex, C	.252	107	14	27	3	0	5	12	0
*Donnels, Chris, 3B	.400	15	1	6	0	0	1	4	0
*Fulton, Ed, C	.294	17	0	5	2	0	0	2	0
*Greenwell, Mike, DH	.500	4	0	2	2	0	0	0	1
Hardge, Mike, 2B	.253	91	9	23	3	0	1	5	1
*Hatteberg, Scott, C	.271	251	36	68	15	1	7	27	2
*Howard, Tim, OF	.311	90	13	28	5	1	0	11	7
Lennon, Pat, OF	.273	128	20	35	6	2	3	20	6
Levangie, Dana, C	.235	17	1	4	0	0	0	0	0
*Mahay, Ron, OF	.318	44	5	14	4	0	0	3	1
Malave, Jose, OF	.270	318	55	86	12	1	23	57	0
*Malzone, John, 3B	.111	18	0	2	0	0	0	2	0
#McGee, Willie, OF	.476	21	9	10	0	0	0	2	2
Murray, Glenn, OF	.244	336	66	82	15	0	25	66	5

Class A WRAPUPS

Midwest League

The Beloit Snappers swept the Michigan Battle Cats for their first title ever. West Michigan's **Demond Smith** won the batting title (.338). Burlington's **Jesus Ibarra** led the league in homers (34)—second in the minors—and was second in RBI (96) and batting (.330) to win the MVP honors. He posted a minors-best .636 slugging percentage. South Bend's **Nilson Robledo** led in RBI (108). Quad City's **Carlos Hernandez** led with 58 steals. Peoria's **Cory Corrigan** won the ERA crown (2.32); teammate **Travis Welch** had 31 saves. Quad City's **Tony Mounce** led in wins (16). South Bend ace **Charles Smith** struck out a league-best 145.

MIDWEST LEAGUE (A)

Eastern Division

	W	L	Pct.	GB
Fort Wayne	75	65	.536	—
Michigan	75	63	.543	1
W. Michigan	67	69	.493	6
South Bend	66	69	.489	7

Central Division

	W	L	Pct.	GB
Beloit	88	51	.633	—
Rockford	75	65	.536	13½
Kane County	69	69	.500	18½
Wisconsin	63	75	.457	24½

Western Division

	W	L	Pct.	GB
Quad City	76	61	.555	—
Cedar Rapids	76	62	.551	½
Springfield	65	74	.468	12
Peoria	62	72	.463	12½
Burlington	54	81	.400	21
Clinton	51	86	.372	25

Semifinals: Beloit 2, Quad City 1; Michigan 2, West Michigan 1.
Finals: Beloit 3, Michigan 0.

Class A WRAPUPS

South Atlantic League

The Augusta Green Jackets swept Piedmont to win the league title. Asheville's **Derrick Gibson** led the minors in RBI (115) and the league in homers (32), stealing 31 bases and batting .292, but the MVP honors went to 18-year-old **Andruw Jones** of Macon, who led the league with 56 steals, had 25 homers and 100 RBI to become the first minor leaguer in 34 years to hit 20 homers, drive in 100 runs and steal 50 bases. Albany's **Vladimir Guerrero** won the batting title at .333. Michael Kusiewicz of Asheville won the ERA crown at 2.06. **Derrin Ebert** of Macon had a league-high 14 wins. Fayetteville's **Brandon Reed** led the minors in saves with 41.

SOUTH ATLANTIC LEAGUE (A)
Northern Division

	W	L	Pct.	GB
Fayetteville	86	55	.610	—
Piedmont	82	58	.586	3½
Asheville	76	63	.547	9
Chrlston.-W.V.	77	65	.542	9½
Hagerstown	73	68	.518	13
Greensboro	70	70	.500	15½
Hickory	49	89	.355	35½

Southern Division

	W	L	Pct.	GB
Columbus	80	62	.563	—
Augusta	76	62	.551	2
Columbia	72	68	.514	7
Macon	71	70	.504	8½
Albany	62	78	.443	17
Savannah	56	85	.403	13½
Chrlston.-S.C.	50	89	.360	28½

Semifinals: Piedmont 2, Asheville 1; Augusta 2, Columbus 0.
Finals: Augusta 3, Piedmont 0.

BATTING	AVG	AB	R	H	2B	3B	HR	RBI	SB
Pough, PorkChop, 1B	.232	99	12	23	8	1	5	23	0
*Rhodes, Karl, OF	.285	246	40	70	13	3	10	43	8
#Rodriguez, Carlos, SS	.293	133	19	39	7	0	0	13	1
Rodriguez, Steve, 2B	.241	324	39	78	16	3	1	24	12
Rodriguez, Tony, 3B	.268	317	37	85	15	2	0	21	11
Rodriguez, Victor, 3B	.276	116	10	32	5	0	0	8	1
Rowland, Rich, C	.258	124	20	32	7	0	8	24	0
Shumpert, Terry, 3B	.271	133	17	36	7	0	2	11	10
Snyder, Cory, 3B	.227	66	9	15	4	0	3	8	0
*Stairs, Matt, OF	.284	271	40	77	17	0	13	56	3
Wade, Scott, OF	.148	27	2	4	1	0	0	0	0
*Waggoner, Aubrey, OF	.188	48	3	9	1	0	0	8	2
Wedge, Eric, 1B	.234	376	52	88	17	1	20	68	1
#Whiten, Mark, OF	.284	102	19	29	3	1	4	13	4

PITCHING	W	L	ERA	G	SV	IP	H	BB	SO
Bakkum, Scott	1	0	1.71	15	2	26.1	21	7	15
*Bark, Brian	3	1	2.27	30	7	31.2	21	14	21
*Barnes, Brian	7	5	4.23	21	0	106.1	107	30	90
Bennett, Joel	2	4	5.84	20	0	77.0	91	45	50
Cain, Tim	4	0	2.28	14	4	27.2	24	8	19
*Ciccarella, Joe	0	1	3.86	11	0	25.2	22	10	13
Clemens, Roger	0	0	0.00	1	0	5.0	1	3	5
Culberson, Calvain	0	0	6.39	6	0	12.2	18	11	4
Finnvold, Gar	0	0	0.00	1	0	3.2	1	1	3
Gakeler, Dan	0	2	6.10	4	0	20.2	24	9	13
Hansen, Brent	7	5	4.29	14	0	92.1	90	23	50
*Hill, Chris	2	3	6.10	10	0	31.0	31	25	20
Hoeme, Steve	0	2	4.62	15	1	39.0	40	15	21
*Howard, Chris	3	1	3.92	17	0	20.2	25	4	19
Johnston, Joel	1	2	6.75	30	6	41.1	54	19	39
Jones, Calvin	5	2	4.03	33	8	38.0	37	15	36
*Langbehn, Gregg	0	0	0.00	7	0	2.0	0	6	1
Lewis, Scott	0	0	3.86	3	0	4.2	7	0	1
*Looney, Brian	4	7	3.49	18	0	100.2	106	33	78
Pierce, Jeff	4	2	4.14	23	0	41.1	34	16	43
Plummer, Dale	9	9	5.19	34	0	100.2	140	18	47
Rodriguez, Frank	1	1	4.00	13	2	27.0	19	8	18
Ryan, Ken	0	1	6.30	9	0	10.0	12	4	6
Satre, Jason	1	5	6.16	9	0	30.2	38	16	14
Sele, Aaron	0	0	9.00	2	0	5.0	9	2	1
*Senior, Shawn	0	1	6.00	1	0	6.0	9	2	1
*Smith, Zane	0	0	0.00	1	0	7.0	5	0	5
Suppan, Jeff	2	3	5.32	7	0	45.2	50	9	32
Vanegmond, Tim	5	3	3.92	12	0	66.2	66	21	47
Wakefield, Tim	2	1	2.52	4	0	25.0	23	9	14
Wengert, Bill	0	1	5.40	7	0	11.2	17	4	10
Wertz, Bill	4	5	5.80	29	2	63.2	74	31	55
*Wiggs, Johnny	1	0	5.79	14	0	9.1	11	3	6

Richmond Braves (Braves) AAA

BATTING	AVG	AB	R	H	2B	3B	HR	RBI	SB
Cabrera, Francisco, DH	.231	104	7	24	5	0	1	14	0
*Giovanola, Ed, SS	.321	321	45	103	18	2	4	36	8
Graffanino, Tony, 2B	.190	179	20	34	6	0	4	17	2
*Grijak, Kevin, 1B	.298	309	35	92	16	5	12	56	1
*Houston, Tyler, 1B	.255	349	41	89	10	3	12	42	3
Kelly, Mike, OF	.289	45	5	13	1	0	2	8	0
*Kowitz, Brian, OF	.280	353	53	99	14	5	2	34	11
#Martinez, Pablo, SS	.229	48	5	11	0	2	0	4	1
Moore, Bobby, OF	.258	329	45	85	18	2	3	27	9
#Munoz, Jose, 2B	.290	520	65	151	18	5	3	45	7
*O'Connor, Kevin, OF	.222	203	33	45	2	3	4	14	14
#Olmeda, Jose, OF	.253	241	22	61	11	3	1	24	2
Pecorilli, Aldo, 1B	.260	127	16	33	3	0	6	17	0
Perez, Eddie, C	.265	324	31	86	19	0	5	40	1
Reed, Darren, OF	.265	136	11	36	7	0	5	22	0
#Roa, Hector, 3B	.258	120	15	31	5	0	2	7	0
Scott, Gary, 3B	.151	86	7	13	1	0	0	2	0
Sharperson, Mike, 3B	.319	298	42	95	16	1	3	47	7
*Swann, Pedro, OF	.211	38	2	8	1	0	0	3	0
Toth, David, C	.231	13	1	3	0	0	0	1	0
Tucker, Scooter, C	.167	66	5	11	3	1	0	6	0
*Twardoski, Mike, 1B	.138	58	7	8	1	0	0	5	1

BATTING	AVG	AB	R	H	2B	3B	HR	RBI	SB
Villanueva, Hector, Ph	.211	19	1	4	1	0	1	3	0
*Warner, Mike, OF	.206	97	10	20	4	1	2	8	0
*Williams, Juan, OF	.264	129	18	34	5	0	5	11	1

PITCHING	W	L	ERA	G	SV	IP	H	BB	SO
Alvarez, Jose	1	3	3.62	5	0	27.1	26	7	16
Blair, Dirk	1	1	6.48	8	0	8.1	12	4	2
Brock, Chris	2	8	5.40	22	0	60.0	68	27	43
*Brown, Jeff	1	2	3.22	12	1	22.1	23	5	12
Coffman, Kevin	1	0	3.00	2	0	6.0	4	4	7
Harrison, Tom	2	1	3.21	9	1	42.0	34	20	16
King, Richard	1	1	2.57	14	0	14.0	13	6	3
Lomon, Kevin	1	2	3.00	32	1	60.0	62	32	52
*Martin, Tom	0	0	9.00	7	0	9.0	10	10	3
*May, Darrell	4	2	3.71	9	0	51.0	53	16	42
*Minutelli, Gino	0	0	4.41	5	0	16.1	20	3	8
Murray, Matt	10	3	2.78	19	0	123.0	108	34	78
Nichols, Rod	1	2	2.53	41	25	57.0	54	6	57
*Polley, Dale	3	2	1.56	47	7	63.1	51	20	60
*Potts, Mike	5	5	3.79	38	1	73.2	79	37	52
Schmidt, Jason	8	6	2.25	19	0	116.0	97	48	95
Seelbach, Chris	4	6	4.66	14	0	73.1	64	39	65
*Thobe, Tom	7	0	1.84	48	5	88.0	65	26	57
Thomas, Royal	7	7	3.48	39	0	88.0	103	24	39
*Wade, Terrell	10	9	4.56	24	0	142.0	137	63	124
*Woodall, Brad	4	4	5.10	13	0	65.1	70	17	44

Rochester Red Wings (Orioles) AAA

BATTING	AVG	AB	R	H	2B	3B	HR	RBI	SB
Alfonzo, Edgar, SS	.185	54	5	10	3	0	1	6	0
#Bartee, Kimera, OF	.154	52	5	8	2	1	0	3	0
Batiste, Kim, 3B	.281	260	31	73	13	1	3	29	4
Brown, Jarvis, OF	.314	70	12	22	4	2	0	4	1
Buford, Damon, OF	.309	188	40	58	12	3	4	18	17
*Carey, Paul, 1B	.236	284	39	67	13	0	9	50	1
Crowley, Jim, 2B	.173	98	7	17	3	0	1	6	0
#Dejardin, Bobby, 2B	.314	35	6	11	2	0	0	3	1
Devarez, Cesar, C	.250	240	32	60	12	1	1	21	2
*Friedman, Jason, 1B	.377	61	9	23	4	0	4	9	0
*Goodwin, Curtis, OF	.264	140	24	37	3	3	0	7	17
Gresham, Kris, C	.250	64	5	16	2	1	0	4	0
*Huson, Jeff, SS	.251	223	28	56	9	0	3	21	16
Knapp, Mike, C	.183	126	10	23	1	1	1	12	1
Lewis, T.R., DH	.295	78	12	23	7	0	4	19	1
McClain, Scott, 3B	.251	199	32	50	9	1	8	22	0
McGinnis, Russ, DH	.182	55	8	10	2	0	3	11	0
Noboa, Junior, 2B	.100	20	1	2	0	0	0	2	0
Obando, Sherman, DH	.296	324	42	96	26	6	9	53	1
#Owens, Billy, 1B	.143	28	2	4	0	0	0	1	0
#Robertson, Rod, OF	.278	338	54	94	21	2	15	58	8
#Smith, Greg, SS	.229	210	32	48	6	1	4	21	14
Smith, Mark, OF	.277	364	55	101	25	3	12	66	7
*Tyler, Brad, 2B	.258	361	60	93	17	3	17	52	10
*Wawruck, Jim, OF	.302	149	21	45	12	3	1	23	5
Woods, Tyrone, 1B	.261	238	30	62	17	1	8	31	2
#Zaun, Greg, C	.293	140	26	41	13	1	6	18	0

PITCHING	W	L	ERA	G	SV	IP	H	BB	SO
Benitez, Armando	2	2	1.25	17	8	21.2	10	7	37
Borowski, Joe	1	3	4.04	28	6	35.2	32	18	32
Chitren, Steve	0	0	2.45	2	0	3.2	6	3	0
Clark, Terry	1	2	2.70	9	5	10.0	5	2	10
Coppinger, Rocky	3	0	1.04	5	0	34.2	23	17	19
Crowley, Jim	0	0	13.50	1	0	2.0	4	1	3
Dedrick, Jim	4	0	1.77	24	1	45.2	45	14	31
Dettmer, John	4	7	4.68	21	1	82.2	98	16	46
Desilva, John	11	9	4.18	26	0	150.2	156	51	82
Forney, Rick	0	0	3.94	3	0	16.0	19	6	12
Hartley, Mike	0	1	0.82	8	0	11.0	4	2	12
Haynes, Jimmy	12	8	3.29	26	0	167.0	162	49	140
*Hurst, James	1	1	3.79	10	0	19.0	17	4	17
Klingenbeck, Scott	3	1	2.72	8	0	43.0	46	10	29
*Krivda, Rick	6	5	3.19	16	0	101.2	96	32	74
*Lane, Aaron	0	0	6.30	9	0	10.0	11	5	9

Class A WRAPUPS

New York-Penn League

Watertown beat Vermont to win their first-ever New York-Penn League title. Hudson Valley's **Clifford Brumbaugh** won the batting title at .358 and led the league in hits (101) and on-base average (.437). Erie's **Jose Guillen** led the loop with 12 homers. Pittsfield's **Rob Daly** led with 60 RBI and 22 doubles. Elmira's **Amaury Garcia** stole 41 bases. Vermont's **Chris Weidert** led with 11 wins and a 1.79 ERA. Teammate **Robert Marquez** posted 21 saves. Oneonta's **Bob St. Pierre** led the league with 91 strikeouts.

NEW YORK-PENN LEAGUE (SS-A)

McNamara Division

	W	L	Pct.	GB
Vermont	49	27	.645	—
Hudson Vly.	47	27	.635	1
New Jersey	35	41	.461	14
Pittsfield	34	42	.447	15

Pinckney Division

	W	L	Pct.	GB
Watertown	46	27	.630	—
Auburn	40	34	.541	6½
Williamsport	37	39	.487	10½
Oneonta	34	41	.453	13
Utica	33	40	.452	13
Elmira	25	51	.329	22½

Stedler Division

	W	L	Pct.	GB
Batavia	41	34	.547	—
St. Catharines	38	37	.507	3
Erie	34	41	.453	7
Jamestown	32	44	.421	9½

Semifinals: *Watertown 2, Batavia 1; Vermont 2, Hudson Valley 0.*
Finals: *Watertown 2, Vermont 1.*

Class A WRAPUPS

Northwest League

Boise won its third consecutive Northwest League title—and fourth in five years—beating Bellingham in the finals. **Danny Buxbaum** of Boise edged out Spokane's **James Vida** for the batting title by .00033—.32900 to .32867. **Ryan Kane** of Boise led the league with 14 homers and 59 RBI. **Kevin Gibbs** of Yakima had 38 steals to lead the league. Portland's **Scott Randall** won the ERA crown at 1.99. Boise's **Grant Vermillion** led the loop with 12 wins while teammate **Travis Thurmond** led the way with 93 strikeouts. **Russell Ortiz** of Bellingham and Boise's **Brian Scutero** each notched 12 saves.

NORTHWEST LEAGUE (SS-A)

North Division

	W	L	Pct.	GB
Bellingham	43	33	.566	—
Everett	37	39	.487	6
Spokane	36	39	.480	6½
Yakima	27	48	.360	15½

South Division

	W	L	Pct.	GB
Boise	48	27	.640	—
Portland	41	34	.547	7
Eugene	37	39	.487	11½
S. Oregon	33	43	.434	15½

Finals: Boise 2, Bellingham 1.

PITCHING	W	L	ERA	G	SV	IP	H	BB	SO
*Lee, Mark	4	2	1.57	25	3	28.2	18	5	35
Lemp, Chris	0	1	11.25	3	0	4.0	7	3	4
*Magee, Bo	0	0	13.50	2	0	2.0	4	1	1
McDonald, Ben	0	0	2.45	1	0	3.2	1	4	1
McGehee, Kevin	11	9	5.83	27	0	126.2	150	33	84
Mills, Alan	0	1	0.00	1	0	2.2	2	5	2
Myers, Jimmy	0	4	3.06	55	6	64.2	72	29	31
Oquist, Mike	0	0	5.25	7	2	12.0	17	5	11
*Rhodes, Arthur	2	1	2.70	4	0	30.0	27	8	33
Robertson, Rod	0	0	15.43	1	0	2.1	6	0	2
Ryan, Kevin	0	3	9.35	6	0	17.1	27	4	7
Sackinsky, Brian	3	3	4.60	14	0	62.2	70	10	42
Seminara, Frank	1	0	3.28	29	0	35.2	31	14	20
*Shea, John	0	1	2.95	38	4	39.2	38	17	37
Wegmann, Tom	3	2	3.44	9	0	34.0	30	9	23
*Williams, Jimmy	1	2	7.11	5	0	12.2	21	9	12

Scranton/W-B Red Barons (Phillies) AAA

BATTING	AVG	AB	R	H	2B	3B	HR	RBI	SB
Bennett, Gary, C	.150	20	1	3	0	0	0	1	0
#Bieser, Steve, OF	.269	245	37	66	12	6	1	33	14
Brophy, E.J., C	.200	65	7	13	2	0	1	6	0
*Butler, Robert, OF	.300	327	46	98	16	4	3	35	5
Elster, Kevin, SS	.294	17	2	5	3	0	0	2	0
*Geisler, Phil, OF	.186	43	2	8	5	0	1	7	0
Gilbert, Shawn, SS	.263	536	84	141	26	2	2	42	16
Grable, Rob, OF	.229	83	7	19	4	0	3	11	3
Hayden, Dave, 3B	.293	41	6	12	1	0	2	3	0
*Holifield, Rick, OF	.206	223	32	46	6	3	3	24	21
Jordan, Kevin, 2B	.310	410	61	127	29	4	5	60	3
Koelling, Brian, 2B	.264	53	5	14	1	0	0	3	3
Lieberthal, Mike, C	.281	278	44	78	20	2	6	42	1
Manahan, Anthony, 3B	.288	299	36	86	11	1	3	32	6
Marsh, Tom, OF	.307	296	46	91	22	5	10	47	9
McNair, Fred, DH	.240	25	1	6	1	0	0	2	0
Montoyo, Charlie, 3B	.243	288	32	70	13	1	3	34	2
Schall, Gene, OF	.313	320	52	100	25	4	12	63	3
Sefcik, Kevin, 2B	.346	26	5	9	6	1	0	6	0
*Taylor, Sam, OF	.143	7	3	1	0	0	0	1	0
*Tokheim, David, OF	.271	450	64	122	18	8	11	66	6
Vatcher, Jim, OF	.375	24	4	9	1	0	0	2	1
*Zuber, Jon, 1B	.287	418	53	120	19	5	3	50	1

PITCHING	W	L	ERA	G	SV	IP	H	BB	SO
Borland, Toby	0	0	0.00	8	1	11.1	5	6	15
*Carter, Andy	1	2	4.35	14	0	20.2	17	13	18
*Combs, Pat	4	4	5.43	22	0	56.1	71	25	36
*Deshaies, Jim	7	8	3.45	19	0	117.1	105	26	79
*Dubois, Brian	1	5	4.56	49	1	51.1	58	25	48
Fletcher, Paul	4	1	3.10	52	2	61.0	45	28	48
*Frey, Steve	0	0	1.80	4	0	5.0	3	2	3
*Gaddy, Bob	5	7	6.28	17	0	86.0	100	56	42
Grace, Mike	2	0	1.59	2	0	17.0	17	2	13
Greene, Tommy	3	0	2.22	4	0	28.1	18	6	19
Hill, Eric	4	3	4.30	21	2	23.0	24	9	16
*Ilsley, Blaise	8	10	3.88	29	0	185.1	210	34	102
Innis, Jeff	0	2	4.30	15	6	14.2	13	8	14
Juden, Jeff	6	4	4.10	14	0	83.1	73	33	65
*Karp, Ryan	7	1	4.20	13	0	81.1	81	31	73
Melendez, Jose	0	0	6.00	2	0	3.0	6	2	1
Munoz, Bobby	1	0	0.56	2	0	16.0	8	3	10
Olivares, Omar	0	3	4.87	7	0	44.1	49	20	28
Ricci, Chuck	4	3	2.49	68	25	65.0	48	24	66
Springer, Dennis	10	11	4.68	30	0	171.0	163	47	115
Tranberg, Mark	1	4	7.23	11	0	23.2	32	6	15
*West, David	1	0	0.00	1	0	7.0	2	0	6
*Wiegandt, Scott	1	3	2.98	47	2	54.1	55	27	41
Williams, Mike	0	1	4.66	3	0	9.2	8	2	8

Syracuse Chiefs (Blue Jays) AAA

BATTING	AVG	AB	R	H	2B	3B	HR	RBI	SB
Battle, Howard, 3B	.251	443	43	111	17	4	8	48	10
*Bowers, Brent, OF	.252	305	38	77	16	5	5	26	5
Brito, Tilson, SS	.242	327	49	79	16	3	7	32	17
Brooks, Eric, C	.192	120	12	23	3	1	0	5	0
*Butler, Rich, OF	.161	199	20	32	4	2	2	14	2
Canate, Willie, OF	.238	345	48	82	17	2	3	30	8
#Crespo, Felipe, 2B	.294	347	56	102	20	5	13	41	12
*Delgado, Carlos, 1B	.318	333	59	106	23	4	22	74	0
Diaz, Edgar, SS	.302	43	5	13	0	1	0	2	0
Johnson, Matt, SS	.500	6	1	3	2	0	0	0	0
Kelly, Pat, SS	.132	68	6	9	1	0	2	8	0
Knorr, Randy, C	.269	67	6	18	5	1	1	6	0
Lis, Joe, 2B	.262	485	68	127	33	4	17	56	6
Lutz, Brent, C	.163	86	5	14	0	0	1	5	1
Montalvo, Rob, 2B	.038	26	0	1	0	0	0	1	0
Perez, Robert, OF	.343	502	70	172	38	6	9	67	7
Ramos, John, DH	.252	413	59	104	24	1	20	75	2
#Sawkiw, Warren, 3B	.190	42	3	8	1	0	0	0	2
Townley, Jason, C	.261	264	25	69	11	0	8	30	0
*Weinke, Chris, 1B	.226	341	42	77	12	2	10	41	4

PITCHING	W	L	ERA	G	SV	IP	H	BB	SO
*Baptist, Travis	3	4	4.33	15	0	79.0	83	32	52
Brow, Scott	1	5	9.00	11	0	31.0	52	18	14
*Brown, Chad	1	1	3.27	11	0	22.0	21	20	14
Brown, Tim	3	8	6.27	19	0	74.2	95	28	54
Carrara, Giovanni	7	7	3.96	21	0	131.2	116	56	81
Cornett, Brad	0	1	4.91	3	0	11.0	13	4	3
Cox, Danny	0	0	0.00	4	0	7.0	2	5	9
Crabtree, Tim	0	2	5.40	26	5	31.2	38	12	22
*Flener, Huck	6	11	3.94	30	0	134.2	131	41	83
Ganote, Joe	0	2	10.13	3	0	10.2	16	4	3
*Gibson, Paul	0	1	4.81	26	3	24.1	24	6	28
*Gray, Dennis	2	2	4.44	15	0	24.1	27	10	15
Guzman, Juan	0	0	0.00	1	0	5.0	1	3	5
Heble, Kurt	0	0	5.79	4	0	4.2	6	2	5
*Jordan, Ricardo	0	0	6.57	13	0	12.1	15	7	17
Menhart, Paul	2	4	6.31	10	0	51.1	62	25	30
*Montoya, Al	0	0	0.00	7	0	4.1	3	3	2
Robinson, Ken	5	3	3.22	38	2	50.1	37	12	61
Rogers, Jimmy	3	4	3.05	38	1	73.2	65	31	82
*Spoljaric, Paul	2	10	4.93	43	10	87.2	69	54	108
Steed, Rick	4	3	3.72	31	1	55.2	51	23	34
Tilmon, Pat	0	0	1.50	4	0	6.0	8	4	2
Timlin, Mike	1	1	1.04	8	0	17.1	13	4	13
Ward, Duane	1	1	15.00	6	0	6.0	14	2	4
Ware, Jeff	7	4	3.00	16	0	75.0	62	46	76
Weber, Ben	4	5	5.40	25	1	91.2	111	27	38
Whitehurst, Wally	3	1	3.86	6	0	28.0	32	7	21
Williams, Woody	0	0	3.52	5	0	7.2	5	5	13
York, Mike	1	4	7.00	20	0	45.0	55	27	37

Toledo Mud Hens (Tigers) AAA

BATTING	AVG	AB	R	H	2B	3B	HR	RBI	SB
Baez, Kevin, SS	.231	376	30	87	13	2	4	37	1
Bautista, Danny, OF	.241	58	6	14	3	0	0	4	1
*Briley, Greg, OF	.238	84	8	20	4	1	1	7	0
*Brock, Tarrik, OF	.194	31	4	6	1	0	0	0	2
#Clark, Tony, 1B	.242	405	50	98	17	2	14	63	0
*Cruz, Ivan, 1B	.194	36	5	7	2	0	0	3	0
#Cuyler, Milt, OF	.305	203	33	62	10	4	6	28	6
Dellicarri, Joe, 2B	.250	12	4	3	0	0	1	1	1
#Givens, Jim, 2B	.237	219	23	52	5	1	0	14	7
Gonzalez, Pete, C	.211	19	0	4	1	0	0	2	0
Hall, Joe, OF	.320	319	52	102	19	2	11	47	4
*Hecht, Steve, 2B	.236	72	14	17	5	1	0	6	5
*Leiper, Tim, 2B	.212	14	3	3	1	0	0	6	0
*Lukachyk, Rob, OF	.254	346	43	88	24	7	7	26	8
Mashore, Justin, OF	.220	223	32	49	4	3	4	21	12
McGriff, Terry, C	.271	188	14	51	8	0	4	23	0
Mendenhall, Kirk, SS	.200	30	2	6	1	0	1	4	2

Rookie League WRAPUPS

Appalachian League

It was shades of 1969, as the Orioles and Mets squared off for the championship and the Mets were victorious. Kingsport's **Jarrod Patterson** led the league with 57 RBI and extra-base hits with 33. Martinsville's **Zach Elliott** won the batting crown at .358, while Princeton's **Darron Ingram** had 14 homers to lead in that department. Burlington's **Milton Anderson** had 38 steals. **Joel Garber** of Bristol won the ERA crown, going 5-1 with a 1.20; Princeton's **Chris Murphy** wasn't far behind at 7-1, 1.55. Bluefield ace **Chris Fussell** led the league in wins with a 9-1 record and in strikeouts with 98. Johnson City's **Manuel Mendez** continued that club's tradition of ace closers with a league-high 19 saves.

APPALACHIAN LEAGUE (ADV. ROOKIE)

North Division

	W	L	Pct.	GB
Bluefield	49	16	.754	—
Princeton	31	32	.492	17
Martinsville	30	37	.448	20
Burlington	26	38	.406	22½
Danville	27	40	.403	23

South Division

	W	L	Pct.	GB
Kingsport	48	18	.727	—
Elizabethton	33	31	.516	14
Johnson City	35	33	.515	14
Bristol	28	39	.418	20½
Huntington	22	45	.328	26½

Finals: *Kingsport 2, Bluefield 1.*

Rookie League WRAPUPS

Arizona League

Though the league doesn't technically have a post-season, the final three games were played between Oakland and California, with the title on the line. The A's swept the Angels three in a row to earn the championship by two games. Oakland catcher **Ramon Hernandez** won the league's batting title at .371 and tied for the lead in RBI with 37. **Jose Paulino** had nine wins and **Robert Kazmirski** had 10 saves, both tops in the league. The Angels were paced by first baseman **Larry Barnes**, who tied Hernandez for the lead with 37 RBI. **Thomas Darrell** won the ERA crown at 1.71. The Padres had the league's top sluggers—**Peter Paciorek** and **Daryl Rutherford** had five homers apiece. Seattle's **David Arias** (.332) shared the RBI lead and had four homers. Milwaukee's **Rico Harris** led the league in steals with 26 in just 56 games. Teammate **Joshua Bishop** was 8-2 with a 2.16 ERA and struck out 134 in just 96 innings, leading the league by 44 strikeouts.

ARIZONA LEAGUE (ROOKIE)

	W	L	Pct.	GB
Athletics	37	19	.661	—
Angels	35	21	.625	2
Brewers	34	22	.607	3
Padres	24	31	.436	12½
Mariners	24	32	.429	13
Rockies	13	42	.236	23½

No league playoffs.

BATTING	AVG	AB	R	H	2B	3B	HR	RBI	SB
Milne, Darren, OF	.150	20	0	3	1	0	0	4	0
Nevin, Phil, OF	.304	23	3	7	2	0	1	3	0
Pemberton, Rudy, OF	.344	224	31	77	15	3	7	23	8
#Penn, Shannon, 2B	.248	218	41	54	4	1	1	15	15
#Rice, Lance, C	.268	41	2	11	1	0	1	6	0
Springer, Steve, 2B	.265	102	14	27	7	1	2	10	1
Steverson, Todd, OF	.107	28	6	3	0	0	1	1	0
Tackett, Jeff, C	.269	301	32	81	15	0	6	30	2
White, Derrick, OF	.265	309	50	82	15	3	14	49	6
Wilson, Craig, 3B	.263	468	56	123	31	0	9	65	8
#Zinter, Alan, 1B	.222	334	42	74	15	4	13	48	4

PITCHING	W	L	ERA	G	SV	IP	H	BB	SO
Ahearne, Pat	7	9	4.70	25	0	139.2	165	37	54
*Bauer, Matt	2	1	3.46	13	0	13.0	17	4	10
Bergman, Sean	0	1	6.00	1	0	3.0	4	0	4
Blomdahl, Ben	5	4	3.54	41	3	56.0	55	13	39
Bottenfield, Kent	5	11	4.54	27	1	136.2	148	55	68
Buckels, Gary	2	2	2.15	31	0	46.0	37	20	38
Carlyle, Ken	8	8	4.33	32	0	124.2	139	44	63
Christopher, Mike	2	4	2.23	36	21	36.1	38	8	32
Gardiner, Mike	0	1	4.41	11	0	16.1	19	13	10
Gohr, Greg	0	2	2.87	6	0	15.2	16	8	15
*Gonzales, Frank	3	2	3.31	49	0	51.2	43	17	54
*Groom, Buddy	2	3	1.91	6	0	33.0	31	4	24
Henry, Dwayne	1	1	3.35	41	11	48.1	43	24	52
Kiely, John	0	0	1.46	14	0	12.1	13	6	8
Kramer, Tommy	3	1	4.61	6	0	27.1	23	16	15
Lima, Jose	5	3	3.01	11	0	74.2	69	14	40
*Marshall, Randy	7	3	2.30	20	0	109.1	99	29	67
Martel, Ed	0	1	1.59	4	0	5.2	4	5	3
Maxcy, Brian	1	3	5.26	20	2	25.2	32	11	11
*Myers, Mike	0	0	4.32	6	0	8.1	6	3	8
*Santos, Henry	0	1	6.75	1	0	2.2	3	2	4
Sodowsky, Clint	5	1	2.85	9	0	60.0	47	30	32
Tunnell, Lee	0	1	3.14	7	0	14.1	9	2	7
Weston, Mickey	11	7	2.90	28	0	180.0	170	41	69
*Wickander, Kevin	2	1	2.13	16	1	12.2	11	5	8

Pacific Coast League

Albuquerque Dukes (Dodgers) AAA

BATTING	AVG	AB	R	H	2B	3B	HR	RBI	SB
Blanco, Henry, 3B	.227	97	11	22	4	1	2	13	0
Bournigal, Rafael, SS	.129	31	2	4	1	0	0	1	0
Busch, Mike, 3B	.269	443	68	119	32	1	18	62	2
#Candaele, Casey, 2B	.259	27	2	7	0	0	0	2	0
Castro, Juan, SS	.267	341	51	91	18	4	3	43	4
#Cedeno, Roger, OF	.305	367	67	112	19	9	2	44	23
Coomer, Ron, 3B	.322	323	54	104	23	2	16	76	5
*Demetral, Chris, 2B	.278	187	34	52	7	1	3	19	1
*Garcia, Karim, OF	.319	474	88	151	26	10	20	91	2
Guerrero, Wilton, SS	.327	49	10	16	1	1	0	2	2
*Hollandsworth, T., OF	.237	38	9	9	2	0	2	4	1
Huckaby, Ken, C	.324	278	30	90	16	2	1	40	3
Ingram, Garey, 2B	.246	232	28	57	11	4	1	30	10
*Kirkpatrick, Jay, 1B	.250	40	4	10	1	1	1	6	0
#Latham, Chris, OF	.167	18	2	3	0	1	0	3	1
Lott, Billy, OF	.315	146	23	46	7	2	5	26	1
*Marrero, Oreste, OF	.348	23	5	8	2	0	2	6	0
*Martin, Jim, OF	.253	75	8	19	3	1	1	7	3
Maurer, Ron, Ph	.259	185	29	48	14	2	5	25	1
Munoz, Noe, C	.224	58	1	13	1	0	0	3	0
Parker, Rick, OF	.280	175	33	49	7	2	1	14	1
Prince, Tom, C	.318	192	30	61	15	0	7	36	0
Pye, Eddie, 2B	.295	302	49	89	20	1	3	32	11
*Spearman, Vernon, Ph	.172	29	7	5	0	1	0	2	2
*Traxler, Brian, 1B	.283	353	46	100	24	1	11	50	1
Wallach, Tim, 3B	.333	3	1	1	0	0	0	1	0
#Williams, Reggie, OF	.312	234	44	73	15	5	6	29	6

PITCHING	W	L	ERA	G	SV	IP	H	BB	SO
Alicea, Miguel	1	1	4.05	7	3	6.2	6	4	0
*Brosnan, Jason	2	0	4.35	23	2	31.0	30	9	18
Bruske, Jim	7	5	4.11	43	4	114.0	128	41	99
Castro, Nelson	0	0	0.00	2	1	2.1	0	0	2
Correa, Ramser	0	0	0.00	2	0	4.0	5	1	3
*Daal, Omar	2	3	3.88	17	1	53.1	56	26	46
*Edwards, Wayne	1	2	5.06	14	1	16.0	17	17	12
*Eischen, Joey	3	0	0.00	13	2	16.1	8	3	14
Garcia, Jose	1	3	6.32	11	0	15.2	19	7	10
Holman, Shawn	5	6	5.13	49	5	79.0	107	39	60
*Lilliquist, Derek	0	0	2.70	13	5	13.1	18	3	9
*Martinez, Jesus	1	1	4.50	2	0	4.0	4	4	5
McCarthy, Tom	3	3	6.00	13	0	48.0	61	22	28
*Milchin, Mike	8	4	4.32	18	0	83.1	94	30	50
*Mimbs, Mark	6	5	2.97	23	0	106.0	105	22	96
Montalvo, Rafael	3	5	2.65	49	4	98.1	105	34	65
*O'Donoghue, John	5	6	3.82	25	0	92.0	97	25	59
Osuna, Antonio	0	1	4.42	19	11	18.1	15	9	19
Park, Chan Ho	6	7	4.91	23	0	110.0	93	76	101
Parra, Jose	3	2	5.13	12	1	52.2	62	17	33
*Pyc, Dave	0	1	3.86	1	0	7.0	7	2	3
*Rath, Gary	3	5	5.08	8	0	39.0	46	20	23
Rodriguez, Felix	3	2	4.24	14	0	51.0	52	26	46
Treadwell, Jody	7	5	3.96	30	1	125.0	121	32	79
Williams, Todd	4	1	3.38	25	0	45.1	59	15	23

Calgary Cannons (Pirates) AAA

BATTING	AVG	AB	R	H	2B	3B	HR	RBI	SB
Allensworth, J., OF	.316	190	46	60	13	4	3	11	13
Aude, Rich, 1B	.333	195	34	65	14	2	9	42	3
*Beamon, Trey, OF	.334	452	74	151	29	5	5	62	18
Cameron, Stanton, OF	.208	24	8	5	4	0	0	4	0
*Cummings, Midre, OF	.277	159	19	44	9	1	1	16	1
Encarnacion, Angelo, C	.250	80	8	20	3	0	1	6	1
#Franklin, Micah, OF	.293	358	64	105	28	3	21	71	3
Hanel, Marcus, C	.125	8	1	1	0	0	0	0	0
*Horn, Sam, 1B	.333	99	21	33	8	2	8	22	0
Johnson, Erik, 2B	.297	455	64	135	35	6	3	58	5
*Johnson, Mark, 1B	.304	23	7	7	4	0	2	8	1
*Knabenshue, Chris, OF	.000	10	2	0	0	0	0	1	0
Marx, Tim, C	.297	185	27	55	11	1	1	12	2
Matos, Francisco, 2B	.323	341	36	110	11	6	3	40	9
Mercedes, Luis, OF	.262	84	18	22	1	0	1	8	1
Osik, Keith, C	.336	301	40	101	25	1	10	59	2
Polcovich, Kevin, SS	.282	213	31	60	8	1	3	27	5
Ratliff, Daryl, OF	.343	286	41	98	11	1	0	37	6
Richardson, Jeff, 2B	.333	18	4	6	0	0	0	3	0
*Rodriguez, Boi, 1B	.256	39	10	10	2	0	2	10	1
#Simmons, Nelson, OF	.281	299	44	84	17	0	9	58	1
#Sveum, Dale, 3B	.284	408	71	116	34	1	12	70	2
Wehner, John, 3B	.329	158	30	52	12	2	4	24	8
*Womack, Tony, 2B	.280	107	12	30	3	1	0	6	7
Young, Kevin, 3B	.356	163	24	58	23	1	8	34	6

PITCHING	W	L	ERA	G	SV	IP	H	BB	SO
August, Don	0	2	4.50	2	0	8.0	10	4	4
Ayrault, Bob	0	0	4.91	6	0	7.1	7	4	3
Backlund, Brett	2	3	5.22	12	0	50.0	59	9	29
Bennett, Chris	0	0	5.14	4	0	7.0	11	1	7
Corbin, Archie	1	5	8.56	47	1	61.0	76	55	54
Delossantos, Mariano	3	6	6.15	14	0	71.2	85	22	36
Ericks, John	2	1	2.48	5	0	29.0	20	13	25
*Flynt, Bill	1	0	5.40	12	0	21.2	27	12	12
*Gibson, Paul	0	2	3.72	19	1	19.1	21	9	17
*Hancock, Lee	6	10	5.07	34	0	113.2	146	27	49
Hill, Milt	1	3	4.90	24	0	60.2	69	14	31
Hope, John	7	1	2.79	13	0	80.2	76	11	41
Lieber, Jon	1	5	7.01	14	0	77.0	122	19	34
*Manzanillo, Ravelo	0	2	12.75	8	0	12.0	23	10	2
Maysey, Matt	8	7	5.50	44	1	103.0	122	44	71
McCurry, Jeff	0	0	1.80	3	0	5.0	3	2	2
Osik, Keith	0	0	4.50	2	0	2.0	1	1	3
Ralph, Curtis	1	4	8.44	28	1	32.0	43	23	27
Ryan, Matt	0	0	1.93	5	1	4.2	5	1	2

Rookie League WRAPUPS

Pioneer League

Helena won the league championship, sweeping the Medicine Hat Blue Jays in the finals. The league's batting leader, however, came from the independent Ogden club— **Jamie LoPiccolo** hit .388 with 12 homers and 55 RBI. **Sean Watkins** of Idaho Falls wasn't far behind at .372, winning the home run crown with 13. Ogden's **Shane Jones** led the loop with 69 RBI. Two co-op players, **Andres Levias** of Butte and **Tom Hutchison** of Lethbridge, shared the stolen base title (33). Medicine Hat's **Jay Veniard** had a 2.71 ERA to lead the league, while Billings' **Justin Aschley** had 10 wins to lead in that department. Billings' **Adam Bryant** had 11 saves. Lethbridge's **Casey Kirkman** fanned a league-best 91.

PIONEER LEAGUE (ADV. ROOKIE)

North Division

	W	L	Pct.	GB
Billings	49	20	.710	—
Medicine Hat	35	37	.486	15½
Great Falls	31	38	.449	18
Lethbridge	25	47	.347	25½

South Division

	W	L	Pct.	GB
Helena	49	22	.690	—
Idaho Falls	42	29	.592	7
Ogden	32	38	.457	16½
Butte	19	51	.271	29½

Semifinals: *Helena 2, Idaho Falls 1; Medicine Hat 2, Billings 1.*
Finals: *Helena 2, Medicine Hat 0.*

Rookie League WRAPUPS

Gulf Coast League

The Royals swept the Tigers in two games to win the league championship. The Royals' **Gary Coffee** led the league in homers (11) and RBI (45) while hitting .328, and **Jose Cepeda** won the batting crown at .348. Cubs speedster **Elinton Jasco** swiped 29 bases to lead that category. Twins pitcher **Kasey Richardson** won the ERA crown (1.15). White Sox starter **James Nichols** and the Mets' **Octavio Dotel** shared the lead with seven wins apiece. Dotel also led in strikeouts (86). Tigers closer **Brent Stentz** had 16 saves.

GULF COAST LEAGUE (ROOKIE)

Eastern Division

	W	L	Pct.	GB
Marlins	40	16	.714	—
Mets	38	19	.667	2½
Expos	21	35	.375	19
Braves	14	43	.246	26½

Northwest Division

	W	L	Pct.	GB
White Sox	36	22	.621	—
Orioles	34	25	.576	2½
Rangers	24	34	.414	12
Pirates	23	36	.390	13½

Northern Division

	W	L	Pct.	GB
Tigers	33	24	.579	—
Yankees	32	26	.552	1½
Astros	32	26	.552	1½
Blue Jays	19	40	.322	15

Southwest Division

	W	L	Pct.	GB
Royals	37	20	.649	—
Cubs	35	22	.614	2
Red Sox	21	36	.368	16
Twins	20	35	.364	16

Semifinals: *Royals 1, White Sox 0; Tigers 1, Marlins 0.*
Finals: *Royals 2, Tigers 0.*

PITCHING

PITCHING	W	L	ERA	G	SV	IP	H	BB	SO
Rychel, Kevin	0	1	10.38	10	0	8.2	14	6	4
*Shouse, Brian	4	4	6.18	8	0	39.1	62	7	17
St. Claire, Randy	3	5	5.00	54	19	54.0	72	21	43
Sveum, Dale	0	0	0.00	2	0	2.0	1	0	2
*Taylor, Scott	5	8	4.11	27	0	140.0	144	35	83
White, Rick	6	4	4.20	14	0	79.1	97	10	56
Willis, Travis	2	2	7.15	22	0	39.0	57	15	13
Wilson, Gary	1	2	5.51	6	0	16.1	19	9	12
*Winston, Darrin	4	6	4.80	53	2	50.2	59	17	40

Colo. Springs Sky Sox (Rockies) AAA

BATTING	AVG	AB	R	H	2B	3B	HR	RBI	SB
#Bolick, Frank, 3B	.235	68	8	16	3	1	2	7	0
Brito, Jorge, C	.229	96	9	22	4	1	2	15	0
Burks, Ellis, OF	.310	29	9	9	2	1	2	6	0
Case, Mike, 3B	.286	14	2	4	1	0	0	0	1
Castellano, Pete, 3B	.266	334	40	89	23	2	9	47	2
Cockrell, Alan, OF	.313	355	58	111	22	1	12	58	0
Cole, Stu, SS	.274	208	28	57	15	2	2	24	1
*Counsell, Craig, SS	.281	399	60	112	22	6	5	53	10
*Gainer, Jay, 1B	.291	358	57	104	19	1	23	86	2
Garrison, Webster, 2B	.293	460	83	135	32	6	12	77	12
Hubbard, Trent, OF	.340	480	102	163	29	7	12	66	37
*Landrum, Ced, OF	.259	166	31	43	5	2	2	19	12
*Martinez, Chito, OF	.155	110	18	17	8	0	4	6	0
#McCracken, Q., OF	.361	244	55	88	14	6	3	28	17
Mejia, Roberto, 2B	.294	143	18	42	10	2	2	14	0
*Nokes, Matt, C	.216	37	7	8	2	0	4	10	0
Owens, Jayhawk, C	.294	221	47	65	13	5	12	48	2
#Perez, Neifi, SS	.278	36	4	10	4	0	0	2	1
Pulliam, Harvey, OF	.327	407	90	133	30	6	25	91	6
Strittmatter, Mark, C	.294	17	1	5	2	0	0	3	0
Tatum, Jim, 3B	.323	93	17	30	7	0	6	18	0
*VanBurkleo, Ty, 1B	.286	231	43	66	14	2	14	57	2
Walters, Dan, C	.284	155	15	44	9	2	3	23	0

PITCHING	W	L	ERA	G	SV	IP	H	BB	SO
Acevedo, Juan	1	1	6.14	3	0	14.2	18	7	7
Bailey, Roger	0	0	2.70	3	0	16.2	15	8	7
Bullard, Jason	0	0	7.27	4	0	8.2	18	5	5
Burke, John	7	1	4.55	19	1	87.0	79	48	65
Bustillos, Albert	8	4	4.61	34	3	132.2	151	33	77
Conroy, Brian	0	2	6.11	5	0	28.0	36	11	9
Crowther, Brent	0	1	7.50	1	0	6.0	11	2	1
Czajkowski, Jim	3	10	5.06	60	17	83.2	90	52	56
Fredrickson, Scott	11	3	3.45	58	4	75.2	70	47	70
Grahe, Joe	1	1	3.27	2	0	11.0	7	3	4
*Grundt, Ken	0	0	4.76	9	0	5.2	9	4	5
Hawblitzel, Ryan	5	3	4.55	21	0	83.0	88	17	40
Hunter, Jim	2	2	6.96	10	0	32.1	43	17	13
Johnston, Joel	2	2	5.96	18	0	22.2	26	12	14
*Jones, Bobby	1	2	7.30	11	0	40.2	50	33	48
*Kotarski, Mike	2	2	10.80	22	0	30.0	48	20	21
*Logsdon, Kevin	0	0	24.00	2	0	3.0	8	5	2
Nied, David	1	1	4.99	7	0	30.2	31	25	21
Olivares, Omar	0	1	5.40	3	0	11.2	14	2	6
*Painter, Lance	0	3	5.96	11	0	25.2	32	11	12
Peever, Lloyd	3	2	5.36	8	0	42.0	45	16	25
Rekar, Bryan	4	2	1.49	7	0	48.1	29	13	39
Reynoso, Armando	2	1	1.57	5	0	23.0	14	6	17
*Romanoli, Paul	3	1	4.50	31	3	20.0	27	10	23
Sager, A.J.	8	5	3.50	23	0	133.2	153	23	80
Scott, Darryl	4	10	4.70	59	4	95.2	113	41	77
Shifflett, Steve	4	3	6.87	23	0	38.0	61	13	21
Thompson, Mark	5	3	6.10	11	0	62.0	73	25	38

Edmonton Trappers (Athletics) AAA

BATTING	AVG	AB	R	H	2B	3B	HR	RBI	SB
Beard, Garrett, C	.230	61	5	14	2	0	0	10	0
Beauchamp, Kash, OF	.200	5	0	1	0	0	0	1	0
*Bowie, Jim, 1B	.267	531	69	142	26	2	3	70	4
Bryant, Scott, DH	.288	406	58	117	33	3	10	69	1

BATTING	AVG	AB	R	H	2B	3B	HR	RBI	SB
Cruz, Fausto, SS	.281	448	72	126	23	2	11	67	7
Faries, Paul, 2B	.300	424	67	127	15	2	0	46	14
Gallego, Mike, 2B	.278	18	1	5	1	0	0	1	0
*Giambi, Jason, 3B	.342	190	34	65	26	1	3	41	0
*Helfand, Eric, C	.214	56	5	12	4	2	1	12	0
*Jones, Tim, 2B	.500	6	1	3	1	0	0	1	0
Lydy, Scott, OF	.290	400	78	116	29	7	16	65	15
*Maksudian, Mike, C	.265	324	54	86	24	4	3	34	5
#Mashore, Damon, OF	.300	337	50	101	19	5	1	37	17
Molina, Izzy, C	.167	6	0	1	0	0	0	0	0
#Moore, Kerwin, OF	.279	265	53	74	14	4	2	26	10
Northrup, Kevin, OF	.182	44	4	8	2	0	0	1	0
Sheldon, Scott, 3B	.258	128	21	33	7	1	4	12	4
*Tomberlin, Andy, OF	.250	52	9	13	3	0	2	7	0
#Williams, George, C	.310	290	53	90	20	0	13	55	0
Wolfe, Joel, OF	.205	39	4	8	3	0	0	4	0
Wood, Jason, 3B	.235	421	49	99	20	5	2	50	1
Young, Ernie, OF	.277	347	70	96	21	4	15	72	2

PITCHING	W	L	ERA	G	SV	IP	H	BB	SO
Adams, Willie	2	5	4.37	11	0	68.0	73	15	40
*Baker, Scott	4	7	5.28	22	0	107.1	123	46	56
Bankhead, Scott	1	3	7.85	12	1	18.1	28	7	15
Bittiger, Jeff	2	0	5.28	6	0	15.1	17	7	10
*Bowie, Jim	0	0	7.50	7	0	6.0	8	3	4
Brink, Brad	0	1	4.88	9	0	24.0	24	16	15
Briscoe, John	0	0	3.00	3	0	6.0	5	5	3
Brock, Russ	1	8	6.87	18	1	55.0	75	31	44
Bryant, Scott	0	0	0.00	2	0	3.1	3	0	3
Corsi, Jim	0	0	0.00	3	3	3.0	0	1	3
Daspit, Jim	0	1	10.80	2	0	5.0	6	2	5
Haynes, Heath	2	0	6.27	12	0	18.2	21	11	13
Hollins, Stacy	0	7	10.31	7	0	29.2	47	21	25
Hostetler, Tom	0	0	12.60	4	0	5.0	9	8	7
Jimenez, Miguel	0	0	12.27	6	0	7.1	12	10	4
*Johns, Doug	9	5	3.41	23	0	132.0	148	43	70
*Kubinski, Tim	1	2	4.78	6	0	32.0	34	10	12
*Mohler, Mike	2	1	2.60	29	5	45.0	40	20	28
Peek, Tim	0	0	4.57	12	0	21.2	20	7	6
Phoenix, Steve	4	3	4.50	40	5	64.0	66	28	28
Revenig, Todd	4	5	4.31	45	10	54.1	53	15	28
Rose, Scott	0	2	6.30	5	0	10.0	13	7	0
Sanchez, Alex	0	0	5.19	8	0	17.1	18	10	8
*Shaw, Curtis	6	5	4.67	42	2	98.1	91	88	52
Smith, Tim	3	2	6.03	9	0	37.1	44	22	22
Stanhope, Chuck	1	1	4.50	6	0	6.0	8	1	2
*Swan, Russ	3	3	4.34	17	4	18.2	23	11	10
Telford, Anthony	3	2	7.18	8	0	36.1	47	16	17
Wasdin, John	12	8	5.52	29	0	174.1	193	38	111
Wengert, Don	1	1	7.38	16	1	39.0	55	16	20
*Wojciechowski, Steve	6	3	3.69	14	0	78.0	75	21	39

Las Vegas Stars (Padres) AAA

BATTING	AVG	AB	R	H	2B	3B	HR	RBI	SB
*Bean, Billy, OF	.290	445	67	129	34	2	15	77	2
#Bream, Scott, 2B	.241	303	33	73	7	1	0	15	7
Bruno, Julio, 3B	.245	139	13	34	6	1	0	6	1
*Bullock, Eric, Ph	.263	190	32	50	4	1	4	25	6
Cianfrocco, Archi, 1B	.311	322	51	100	20	2	10	58	5
Colbert, Craig, C	.249	241	30	60	8	1	1	24	1
Deer, Rob, OF	.291	223	38	65	18	3	14	45	2
#Hall, Billy, 2B	.225	249	42	56	3	1	1	22	22
Holbert, Ray, 2B	.115	26	3	3	1	0	0	3	1
*Hyers, Tim, 1B	.290	259	46	75	12	1	1	23	0
*McDavid, Ray, OF	.271	166	28	45	8	1	5	27	7
Mulligan, Sean, C	.274	339	34	93	20	1	7	43	0
Newfield, Marc, OF	.343	70	10	24	5	1	3	12	2
*Petagine, Roberto, 1B	.214	56	8	12	2	1	1	5	1
#Roberts, Bip, SS	.333	12	1	4	0	0	0	2	1
Rossy, Rico, SS	.301	316	44	95	11	2	1	45	3
Russo, Paul, 3B	.297	148	17	44	10	0	4	19	0
See, Larry, 1B	.307	114	11	35	8	1	2	20	0
*Smiley, Reuben, OF	.219	96	10	21	4	1	3	17	6
Smith, Ira, OF	.325	209	39	68	19	5	3	22	5

Class AAA Directory

American Association

Buffalo Bisons (Indians)
NorthAmeriCare Park
(capacity 20,900)
Indianapolis Indians (Reds)
Bush Stadium (12,800)
Iowa Cubs (Cubs)
Sec Taylor Stadium
(10,500)
Louisville Redbirds (Cardinals)
Cardinal Stadium (33,500)
Nashville Sounds (White Sox)
Herschel Greer Stadium
(17,000)
New Orleans Zephyrs (Brewers)
Privateer Park (5,116)
Oklahoma City 89ers (Rangers)
All-Sports Stadium
(15,000)
Omaha Royals (Royals)
Rosenblatt Stadium
(19,500)

Switch-hitter
* Left-handed

Class AAA Directory

International League

Charlotte Knights (Marlins)
Knights Castle (10,917)

Columbus Clippers (Yankees)
Harold Cooper Stadium (15,000)

Norfolk Tides (Mets)
Harbor Park (12,000)

Ottawa Lynx (Expos)
Rec Complex (10,000)

Pawtucket Red Sox (Red Sox)
McCoy Stadium (6,010)

Richmond Braves (Braves)
The Diamond (12,500)

Rochester Red Wings (Orioles)
Silver Stadium (12,503)

352

Scranton/Wilkes-Barre Red Barons (Phillies)
Lackawanna County Stadium (10,800)

Syracuse Chiefs (Blue Jays)
MacArthur Stadium (8,316)

Toledo Mud Hens (Tigers)
Ned Skeldon Stadium (10,025)

BATTING	AVG	AB	R	H	2B	3B	HR	RBI	SB
Snyder, Cory, OF	.265	34	4	9	1	0	0	5	0
Springer, Steve, Ph	.218	87	7	19	3	0	1	10	1
Thurston, Jerrey, C	.200	20	2	4	1	0	0	0	0
Vatcher, Jim, OF	.292	356	56	104	31	3	7	43	3
Velandia, Jorge, SS	.262	206	25	54	12	3	0	25	0

PITCHING	W	L	ERA	G	SV	IP	H	BB	SO
Arvesen, Scott	0	0	15.00	2	0	3.0	4	2	0
Berumen, Andres	0	0	5.40	3	0	3.1	4	2	3
Bochtler, Doug	2	3	4.25	18	1	36.0	31	26	32
*Cadaret, Greg	3	5	5.88	28	0	52.0	56	22	52
Cole, Victor	0	2	6.41	4	0	19.2	19	10	12
*Cromwell, Nate	0	2	13.50	9	0	15.1	35	14	11
*Dishman, Glenn	6	3	2.55	14	0	106.0	91	20	64
Elliott, Donnie	1	0	4.50	7	1	8.0	8	4	2
Ettles, Mark	0	0	7.82	10	0	12.2	21	3	10
*Fesh, Sean	2	1	3.32	30	1	38.0	53	16	18
Harriger, Denny	9	9	4.07	29	0	177.0	187	60	97
*Hathaway, Hilly	4	6	6.22	14	0	63.2	76	27	37
Hermanson, Dustin	0	1	3.50	36	11	36.0	35	29	42
Hernandez, Fernando	1	6	7.65	8	0	37.2	43	31	40
Keagle, Greg	7	6	4.28	14	0	75.2	76	42	49
*Long, Joey	1	3	4.60	25	0	31.1	38	16	13
Martinez, Jose	6	10	4.75	27	0	151.2	156	44	64
Mauser, Tim	3	4	4.80	35	0	50.2	63	20	32
McFarlin, Terric	7	6	3.96	58	7	122.2	120	59	85
Merriman, Brett	2	2	8.25	11	0	12.0	14	12	7
Sanders, Scott	0	0	0.00	1	0	3.0	3	1	2
Schmitt, Todd	0	2	7.82	12	2	12.2	16	9	6
*Tabaka, Jeff	0	1	1.99	19	6	22.2	16	14	27
Taylor, Kerry	2	2	4.38	8	0	37.0	44	21	21
Weber, Wes	6	11	4.67	29	0	150.1	170	50	86
Weber, Weston	3	4	4.81	9	0	48.2	59	9	32
Worrell, Tim	0	2	6.00	10	0	24.0	27	17	18

Phoenix Firebirds (Giants) AAA

BATTING	AVG	AB	R	H	2B	3B	HR	RBI	SB
Aurilia, Rich, SS	.279	258	42	72	12	0	5	34	2
Bellinger, Clay, SS	.274	277	34	76	16	1	2	32	3
*Benard, Marvin, OF	.304	378	70	115	14	6	6	32	10
*Brewer, Rod, 1B	.244	45	8	11	4	0	1	8	1
Chimelis, Joel, 1B	.259	398	48	103	32	1	7	66	1
Christopherson, Eric, C	.220	282	21	62	9	1	1	25	1
Cookson, Brent, OF	.300	210	38	63	9	3	15	46	3
#Daugherty, Jack, OF	.152	33	4	5	1	0	0	3	0
Ehmann, Kurt, SS	.269	216	21	58	5	2	0	7	8
Faneyte, Rikkert, OF	.274	135	22	37	8	1	1	17	2
Jones, Dax, OF	.267	404	47	108	21	3	2	45	11
*Leonard, Mark, OF	.296	392	73	116	25	3	14	79	3
McCarty, Dave, 1B	.351	151	31	53	19	2	4	19	1
*Miller, Barry, 1B	.224	156	18	35	8	1	2	21	0
Miller, Roger, C	.212	137	14	29	4	1	1	10	0
Mirabelli, Doug, C	.167	66	3	11	0	1	0	7	1
#Mueller, Bill, 3B	.297	172	23	51	13	6	2	19	0
Murray, Calvin, OF	.180	50	8	9	1	0	4	10	2
*Ortiz, Ray, OF	.242	190	22	46	10	2	4	29	1
Scott, Gary, 3B	.265	219	33	58	16	2	5	26	2
Williams, Keith, OF	.301	83	7	25	4	1	2	14	0
Wimmer, Chris, 2B	.263	449	55	118	23	4	2	44	13

PITCHING	W	L	ERA	G	SV	IP	H	BB	SO
*Barton, Shawn	2	0	1.80	15	0	25.0	20	5	25
Bourgeois, Steve	1	1	3.38	6	0	34.2	38	13	23
Burcham, Tim	1	0	5.06	5	0	10.2	18	2	6
*Burgos, Enrique	2	6	6.14	41	2	58.2	63	40	77
Carlson, Dan	9	5	4.27	23	0	132.2	138	66	93
Clayton, Royal	0	2	5.87	5	0	23.0	35	6	13
*Gamez, Bob	3	5	5.59	36	2	66.0	76	27	41
*Gardella, Mike	0	0	13.50	3	0	4.0	9	1	3
Greer, Ken	5	2	3.98	38	1	63.1	65	19	41
Hook, Chris	0	0	1.50	4	0	6.0	2	3	5
Jones, Stacy	0	1	8.53	4	0	6.1	8	6	4
Knudsen, Kurt	0	1	5.03	11	1	19.2	18	11	20
Menendez, Tony	5	6	3.92	50	13	64.1	67	32	61

Switch-hitter
* Left-handed

PITCHING	W	L	ERA	G	SV	IP	H	BB	SO
Mintz, Steve	5	2	2.39	31	7	49.0	42	21	36
*Mulholland, Terry	0	0	2.25	1	0	4.0	4	1	4
Phillips, Randy	4	13	5.11	25	0	132.0	155	40	66
Piatt, Doug	0	1	5.87	6	0	7.2	7	5	3
Robinson, Scott	5	7	4.66	31	0	123.2	134	37	61
*Rogers, Kevin	0	0	4.15	3	0	4.1	9	2	1
Roper, John	0	1	9.00	1	0	3.0	5	0	2
*Rosselli, Joe	4	3	4.99	13	0	79.1	94	12	34
Trlicek, Rick	5	4	5.29	38	0	63.0	72	21	43
Valdez, Carlos	1	0	2.76	18	2	29.1	29	13	30
Valdez, Sergio	6	7	4.45	18	0	109.1	117	25	64
Vanderweele, Doug	2	4	6.10	11	0	38.1	57	11	20
*Whitaker, Steve	0	5	7.00	16	0	54.0	72	36	30
Whitehurst, Wally	0	1	7.16	4	0	16.1	20	8	7

Salt Lake Buzz (Twins) AAA

BATTING	AVG	AB	R	H	2B	3B	HR	RBI	SB
#Becker, Rich, OF	.309	123	26	38	7	0	6	28	6
Brito, Bernardo, DH	.306	186	31	57	10	1	15	49	1
#Corbin, Ted, 2B	.200	10	0	2	0	0	0	1	0
Delarosa, Juan, OF	.224	49	7	11	2	0	0	5	0
#Duncan, Andres, SS	.278	36	2	10	2	1	0	6	2
*Dunn, Steve, 1B	.316	402	57	127	31	1	12	83	3
Durant, Mike, C	.251	295	40	74	15	3	2	23	11
*Hale, Chip, 3B	.286	49	5	14	4	0	0	2	0
Hazlett, Steve, OF	.300	427	71	128	25	6	4	49	8
#Hocking, Denny, SS	.282	397	51	112	24	2	8	75	12
Horn, Jeff, C	.500	10	0	5	1	0	0	2	0
Ingram, Riccardo, OF	.348	477	80	166	43	2	12	85	4
*Jackson, John, OF	.278	194	39	54	14	3	4	21	8
Lennon, Pat, DH	.400	115	26	46	15	0	6	29	2
*Masteller, Dan, OF	.303	152	25	46	10	7	4	18	4
Miller, Damian, C	.285	295	39	84	23	1	3	41	2
*Pose, Scott, OF	.310	203	41	63	9	1	0	19	13
Quinlan, Tom, 3B	.279	466	78	130	22	6	17	88	6
Raabe, Brian, 2B	.305	440	88	134	32	6	3	60	15
Shelton, Ben, 1B	.242	33	7	8	1	1	1	6	0
Simons, Mitch, 2B	.325	480	87	156	34	4	3	46	32
*Snider, Van, OF	.357	115	25	41	7	0	7	28	1
*Stahoviak, Scott, 3B	.303	33	6	10	1	0	0	5	2

PITCHING	W	L	ERA	G	SV	IP	H	BB	SO
Barcelo, Marc	8	13	7.05	28	0	143.0	214	59	63
*Bryant, Shawn	4	1	4.88	31	0	48.0	62	16	27
*Courtright, John	3	7	6.80	18	0	84.2	108	36	42
Gandarillas, Gus	2	3	6.44	22	2	29.1	34	19	17
Gavaghan, Sean	1	4	5.51	35	5	47.1	53	31	28
Hansell, Greg	3	1	5.01	7	0	32.1	39	4	17
Hawkins, Latroy	9	7	3.55	22	0	144.1	150	40	74
Henry, Jon	1	0	6.75	3	0	12.0	15	2	3
*Horsman, Vince	1	0	10.38	16	0	13.0	23	4	10
*Johnson, Judd	1	1	3.43	17	1	21.0	27	12	11
Misuraca, Mike	9	6	5.34	31	0	143.1	174	36	67
Munoz, Oscar	8	6	4.95	19	0	112.2	121	35	74
Naulty, Dan	2	6	5.18	42	4	90.1	92	47	76
*Pulido, Carlos	8	1	4.67	43	3	71.1	87	20	38
*Robertson, Rich	5	0	2.44	7	0	44.1	31	12	40
Sanford, Mo	0	1	6.35	4	0	5.2	6	4	8
Schullstrom, Erik	2	0	4.66	10	2	9.2	12	4	8
*Serafini, Dan	0	0	6.75	1	1	4.0	4	1	4
Stevens, Matt	0	0	3.52	7	1	7.2	9	2	5
Trombley, Mike	5	3	3.62	12	0	69.2	71	26	59
*Watkins, Scott	4	2	2.80	45	20	54.2	45	13	57
Wissler, Bill	3	3	4.62	37	1	60.1	69	24	26

Tacoma Tigers (Mariners) AAA

BATTING	AVG	AB	R	H	2B	3B	HR	RBI	SB
Barron, Tony, OF	.200	25	4	5	0	0	0	2	0
*Bragg, Darren, OF	.307	212	24	65	13	3	4	31	10
#Diaz, Alex, OF	.250	40	3	10	1	0	0	4	1
Diaz, Eddy, 2B	.333	36	5	12	2	0	0	5	0
Fermin, Felix, SS	.333	3	0	1	0	0	0	0	0

Class AAA Directory

Pacific Coast League

Albuquerque Dukes (Dodgers)
Albuquerque Sports Stadium (10,510)
Calgary Cannons (Pirates)
Foothills Stadium (7,500)
Colorado Springs Sky Sox (Rockies)
Sky Sox Stadium (6,130)
Edmonton Trappers (Athletics)
Telus Field (10,000)
Las Vegas Stars (Padres)
Cashman Field (9,370)
Phoenix Firebirds (Giants)
Scottsdale Stadium (10,000)
Salt Lake Buzz (Twins)
Franklin Quest Field (15,000)
Tacoma Rainiers (Mariners)
Cheney Stadium (8,002)
Tucson Toros (Astros)
Hi Corbett Field (9,500)
Vancouver Canadians (Angels)
Nat Bailey Stadium (6,500)

Switch-hitter
* Left-handed

Class AA Directory

Eastern League

Binghamton Mets (Mets)
Municipal Stadium (6,064)
Bowie Baysox (Orioles)
Prince Georges County Stadium (10,000)
Canton-Akron Indians (Indians)
Thurman Munson Stadium (5,765)
Harrisburg Senators (Expos)
Riverside Stadium (5,600)
New Britain Rock Cats (Twins)
Beehive Field (4,700)
New Haven Ravens (Rockies)
Yale Field (6,200)
Norwich Navigators (Yankees)
Dodd Stadium (6,000)
Portland Sea Dogs (Marlins)
Hadlock Field (6,000)
Reading Phillies (Phillies)
Municipal Stadium (7,500)
Trenton Thunder (Red Sox)
Waterfront Park (6,200)

354

BATTING	AVG	AB	R	H	2B	3B	HR	RBI	SB
*Griffey, Ken, DH	.000	3	0	0	0	0	0	0	0
Hansen, Terrel, 1B	.220	50	5	11	1	0	3	10	0
Howard, Chris, C	.243	268	33	65	14	0	4	31	0
Humphreys, Mike, OF	.200	35	3	7	2	0	0	1	0
#Kreuter, Chad, C	.292	48	6	14	5	0	1	11	0
Litton, Greg, 1B	.309	388	58	120	25	1	9	56	2
*Mack, Quinn, OF	.265	204	30	54	11	0	1	17	9
Maynard, Scott, C	.000	1	0	0	0	0	0	0	0
*Noland, J.D., OF	.275	251	27	69	10	3	5	28	14
#Peguero, Julio, OF	.200	25	2	5	0	1	0	1	0
*Pevey, Marty, C	.105	19	2	2	0	0	0	0	0
Pirkl, Greg, 1B	.293	174	29	51	8	2	15	44	1
Pozo, Arquimedez, 2B	.300	450	57	135	19	6	10	62	3
#Relaford, Desi, 2B	.239	113	20	27	5	1	2	7	6
#Roberson, Kevin, OF	.236	157	17	37	6	1	6	17	1
Rodriguez, Alex, SS	.360	214	37	77	12	3	15	45	2
Saunders, Doug, 3B	.281	135	19	38	5	2	5	24	0
Sealy, Scot, C	.300	10	1	3	0	0	0	0	0
Sheets, Andy, SS	.293	437	57	128	29	9	2	47	8
*Sherman, Darrell, OF	.257	350	59	90	9	3	2	31	19
Sojo, Luis, 2B	.176	17	1	3	0	0	1	1	0
Thurman, Gary, OF	.300	363	65	109	10	12	5	46	22
Turang, Brian, OF	.240	196	22	47	4	1	1	18	7
Wakamatsu, Don, C	.156	32	3	5	1	0	0	6	0
Widger, Chris, C	.276	174	29	48	11	1	9	21	0
#Wilkerson, Curtis, 2B	.222	18	1	4	0	0	0	3	0
*Willard, Jerry, 1B	.268	228	33	61	16	0	9	47	0

PITCHING	W	L	ERA	G	SV	IP	H	BB	SO
Apana, Matt	8	8	4.95	21	0	103.2	121	61	58
Campbell, Kevin	3	2	3.67	31	1	49.0	50	14	34
Carmona, Rafael	4	3	5.06	8	0	48.0	52	19	37
Converse, Jim	4	7	5.99	17	0	73.2	96	36	43
*Cummings, John	0	1	7.71	1	0	2.1	6	3	3
Darwin, Jeff	7	2	2.70	46	12	63.1	51	21	51
*Davis, Tim	0	1	5.40	2	0	13.1	15	4	13
Davison, Scott	1	1	5.32	8	0	22.0	21	4	12
Glinatsis, George	1	2	7.34	8	0	30.2	39	13	13
Graybill, Dave	0	0	6.75	6	0	9.1	12	6	1
*Green, Otis	4	1	5.76	18	0	25.0	26	12	17
*Guetterman, Lee	1	2	2.95	33	4	36.2	33	9	21
Harikkala, Tim	5	12	4.24	25	0	146.1	151	55	73
Holman, Brad	1	0	8.10	5	0	6.2	9	3	1
*King, Kevin	0	0	7.56	16	0	16.2	33	7	10
*Krueger, Bill	5	3	4.26	10	0	50.2	52	9	39
Lewis, Scott	1	1	9.64	3	0	9.1	13	4	11
Mecir, Jim	1	4	3.10	40	8	69.2	63	28	46
Milacki, Bob	6	4	5.27	12	0	71.2	94	23	31
Phillips, Tony	3	2	4.12	47	1	87.1	98	14	44
Salkeld, Roger	1	0	1.80	4	1	15.0	8	7	11
Thompson, John	0	1	0.00	1	0	2.2	3	0	0
Torres, Salomon	1	1	3.21	5	0	28.0	20	13	19
*Villone, Ron	1	0	0.61	22	13	29.2	9	19	43
Wagner, Matt	1	5	6.27	6	0	33.0	43	17	33
Williams, Jeff	0	3	8.22	8	0	23.0	31	12	8
Wolcott, Bob	6	3	4.08	13	0	79.1	94	16	43

Tucson Toros (Astros) AAA

BATTING	AVG	AB	R	H	2B	3B	HR	RBI	SB
*Abreu, Bob, OF	.304	415	72	126	24	17	10	75	16
Ball, Jeff, 3B	.293	362	58	106	25	2	4	56	11
#Brumley, Mike, OF	.261	330	56	86	20	10	4	33	17
#Cangelosi, John, OF	.368	106	18	39	4	1	0	9	11
Chavez, Raul, C	.262	103	14	27	5	0	0	10	0
*Goff, Jerry, C	.222	207	23	46	11	1	6	34	0
Guerrero, Juan, 3B	.294	194	21	57	10	1	2	21	1
Gutierrez, Ricky, SS	.301	236	46	71	12	4	1	26	9
Hajek, Dave, 2B	.327	502	99	164	37	4	4	79	12
Hatcher, Chris, 1B	.286	290	59	83	19	2	14	50	7
Hunter, Brian, OF	.329	155	28	51	5	1	1	16	11
#Kellner, Frank, SS	.180	89	11	16	3	1	0	7	1
Makarewicz, Scott, C	.266	192	21	51	9	0	5	31	1
Montgomery, Ray, OF	.302	291	48	88	19	0	11	68	5
Mora, Melvin, OF	.600	5	3	3	0	1	0	1	1

Switch-hitter
* Left-handed

BATTING	AVG	AB	R	H	2B	3B	HR	RBI	SB
Mouton, James, OF	.455	11	1	5	0	0	1	1	0
Nevin, Phil, 3B	.291	223	31	65	16	0	7	41	2
*Plantier, Phil, OF	.250	24	6	6	2	0	1	4	0
*Ramos, Ken, OF	.315	327	57	103	24	8	3	47	14
#Rohde, Dave, SS	.276	170	27	47	8	2	0	20	2
Simms, Mike, 1B	.295	319	56	94	26	8	13	66	10
Stankiewicz, Andy, SS	.276	87	16	24	4	0	1	15	3
*Wilkins, Rick, C	.333	12	0	4	0	0	0	4	0

PITCHING	W	L	ERA	G	SV	IP	H	BB	SO
Bennett, Erik	3	1	4.76	14	1	22.2	27	14	24
Brocail, Doug	1	0	3.86	3	0	16.1	18	4	16
Castillo, Juan	0	4	10.93	11	0	40.1	66	27	21
Dougherty, Jim	1	0	3.27	8	1	11.0	11	5	12
Evans, Dave	0	0	0.00	2	0	3.0	2	1	4
Gallaher, Kevin	1	1	6.43	3	0	14.0	19	9	11
Gardner, Chris	1	4	8.54	16	0	26.1	43	19	6
*Hartgraves, Dean	3	2	2.11	14	5	21.1	21	5	15
Holt, Chris	5	8	4.10	20	0	118.2	155	32	69
Huisman, Rick	6	1	4.45	42	6	54.2	58	28	47
Jean, Domingo	2	1	6.59	3	0	13.2	15	7	14
Ketchen, Doug	3	6	6.28	19	1	71.2	101	26	30
Kile, Darryl	2	1	8.51	4	0	24.1	29	12	15
Loiselle, Rich	0	0	2.61	2	0	10.1	8	4	4
*Martinez, Pedro	1	1	6.62	20	2	34.0	44	13	21
McMurtry, Craig	6	1	1.29	13	0	69.2	54	19	41
Mlicki, Doug	1	2	5.56	6	0	34.0	44	6	22
*Morman, Alvin	5	1	3.91	45	3	48.1	50	20	36
Patrick, Bronswell	5	1	4.19	43	1	81.2	91	21	62
*Powell, Ross	3	3	3.08	13	1	38.0	37	15	34
Sepeda, Jamie	3	2	4.91	8	0	40.1	52	12	19
Small, Mark	3	3	4.09	51	19	66.0	74	19	51
*Wagner, Billy	5	3	3.18	13	0	76.1	70	32	80
*Waldron, Joe	1	0	4.32	4	0	8.1	6	2	11
Wall, Donne	17	6	3.30	28	0	177.1	190	32	119
Waring, Jim	2	2	8.46	5	0	22.1	30	8	5
Westbrook, Destry	0	0	7.30	5	0	12.1	20	7	8
White, Chris	1	1	8.71	5	0	10.1	16	2	6

Vancouver Canadians (Angels) AAA

BATTING	AVG	AB	R	H	2B	3B	HR	RBI	SB
*Anderson, Garret, OF	.311	61	9	19	7	0	0	12	0
#Carvajal, Jovino, OF	.325	163	25	53	3	3	1	10	10
*Cohick, Emmitt, OF	.333	24	3	8	2	0	0	5	0
Correia, Rod, SS	.303	264	42	80	6	5	1	39	8
Dalesandro, Mark, OF	.333	123	16	41	13	1	1	18	2
*Durham, Leon, DH	.273	55	7	15	1	0	2	10	0
*Fabregas, Jorge, C	.247	73	9	18	3	0	4	10	0
Flora, Kevin, OF	.298	124	22	37	7	0	3	14	7
Forbes, P.J., 2B	.274	369	47	101	22	3	1	52	4
Gonzales, Rene, SS	.273	165	27	45	12	0	4	18	0
Grebeck, Brian, SS	.245	241	41	59	11	2	5	30	4
Greene, Todd, C	.250	168	28	42	3	1	14	35	1
Hosey, Steve, OF	.271	59	10	16	3	0	2	6	2
Jordan, Ricky, DH	.222	63	5	14	2	0	2	6	0
Lind, Jose, 2B	.222	36	2	8	2	0	0	5	1
Martinez, Carlos, 3B	.247	97	17	24	3	0	1	6	1
Molina, Ben, C	.000	2	0	0	0	0	0	0	0
Monzon, Jose, C	.217	23	5	5	1	0	1	5	0
#Munoz, Orlando, 2B	.100	10	0	1	0	0	0	0	0
*Palmeiro, Orlando, OF	.307	398	66	122	21	4	0	47	16
Peguero, Jose, 3B	.254	59	6	15	6	0	0	3	1
Perez, Eduardo, 3B	.325	246	39	80	12	7	6	37	6
*Pritchett, Chris, 1B	.276	434	66	120	27	4	8	53	2
Ramirez, J.D., 2B	.000	4	0	0	0	0	0	0	0
Raven, Luis, 3B	.244	135	18	33	11	1	5	26	3
Riley, Marquis, OF	.262	477	70	125	6	6	0	43	29
Schofield, Dick, SS	.189	53	5	10	4	0	0	9	0
*Sweeney, Mark, OF	.345	226	48	78	14	2	7	59	3
Tejero, Fausto, C	.260	96	10	25	3	0	0	8	2
Turner, Chris, C	.266	282	44	75	20	2	3	48	3
Vaughn, Derek, OF	.667	3	0	2	0	0	0	0	1

Class AA Directory

Southern League

Birmingham Barons (White Sox)
Hoover Met (10,000)
Carolina Mudcats (Pirates)
Five County Stadium (6,000)
Chattanooga Lookouts (Reds)
Engel Stadium (7,500)
Greenville Braves (Braves)
Municipal Stadium (7,027)
Huntsville Stars (Athletics)
Joe W. Davis Stadium (10,200)
Jacksonville Suns (Tigers)
Wolfson Park (8,200)
Knoxville Smokies (Blue Jays)
Bill Meyer Stadium (6,412)
Memphis Chicks (Padres)
Tim McCarver Stadium (10,000)
Orlando Cubs (Cubs)
Tinker Field (6,000)
Port City Roosters (Mariners)
Brooks Field (4,000)

Switch-hitter
* Left-handed

Class AA Directory

Texas League

Arkansas Travelers (Cardinals)
Ray Winder Field (6,083)
El Paso Diablos (Brewers)
Cohen Stadium (10,000)
Jackson Generals (Astros)
Smith-Wills Stadium (5,200)
Midland Angels (Angels)
Christensen Stadium (4,000)
San Antonio Missions (Dodgers)
Missions Stadium (6,500)
Shreveport Captains (Giants)
Fairgrounds Field (6,200)
Tulsa Drillers (Rangers)
Drillers Stadium (10,500)
Wichita Wranglers (Royals)
Lawrence-Dumont Stadium (7,488)

1996 BASEBALL WEEKLY ALMANAC

Switch-hitter
* Left-handed

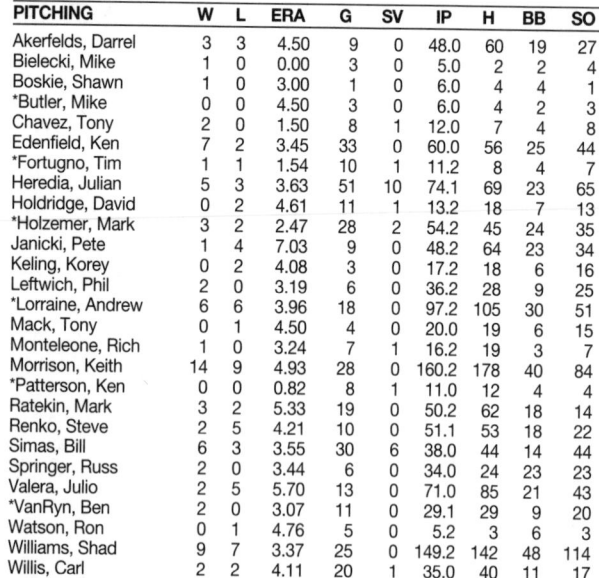

PITCHING	W	L	ERA	G	SV	IP	H	BB	SO
Akerfelds, Darrel	3	3	4.50	9	0	48.0	60	19	27
Bielecki, Mike	1	0	0.00	3	0	5.0	2	2	4
Boskie, Shawn	1	0	3.00	1	0	6.0	4	4	1
*Butler, Mike	0	0	4.50	3	0	6.0	4	2	3
Chavez, Tony	2	0	1.50	8	1	12.0	7	4	8
Edenfield, Ken	7	2	3.45	33	0	60.0	56	25	44
*Fortugno, Tim	1	1	1.54	10	1	11.2	8	4	7
Heredia, Julian	5	3	3.63	51	10	74.1	69	23	65
Holdridge, David	0	2	4.61	11	1	13.2	18	7	13
*Holzemer, Mark	3	2	2.47	28	2	54.2	45	24	35
Janicki, Pete	1	4	7.03	9	0	48.2	64	23	34
Keling, Korey	0	2	4.08	3	0	17.2	18	6	16
Leftwich, Phil	2	0	3.19	6	0	36.2	28	9	25
*Lorraine, Andrew	6	6	3.96	18	0	97.2	105	30	51
Mack, Tony	0	1	4.50	4	0	20.0	19	6	15
Monteleone, Rich	1	0	3.24	7	1	16.2	19	3	7
Morrison, Keith	14	9	4.93	28	0	160.2	178	40	84
*Patterson, Ken	0	0	0.82	8	1	11.0	12	4	4
Ratekin, Mark	3	2	5.33	19	0	50.2	62	18	14
Renko, Steve	2	5	4.21	10	0	51.1	53	18	22
Simas, Bill	6	3	3.55	30	6	38.0	44	14	44
Springer, Russ	2	0	3.44	6	0	34.0	24	23	23
Valera, Julio	2	5	5.70	13	0	71.0	85	21	43
*VanRyn, Ben	2	0	3.07	11	0	29.1	29	9	20
Watson, Ron	0	1	4.76	5	0	5.2	3	6	3
Williams, Shad	9	7	3.37	25	0	149.2	142	48	114
Willis, Carl	2	2	4.11	20	1	35.0	40	11	17

Final AA Player Stats

Eastern League

Binghamton Mets (Mets) AA

BATTING	AVG	AB	R	H	2B	3B	HR	RBI	SB
Agbayani, Benny, OF	.275	295	38	81	11	2	1	26	12
Azuaje, Jesus, 2B	.198	86	10	17	5	0	0	8	1
#Barry, Jeff, OF	.269	290	49	78	17	6	11	53	4
#Bates, Fletcher, OF	.000	8	1	0	0	0	0	0	0
Benbow, Lou, PH	1.000	1	0	1	0	0	0	0	0
*Cradle, Cobi, PH	.000	2	0	0	0	0	0	0	0
Daly, Bob, 1B	.000	4	1	0	0	0	0	0	0
*Daubach, Brian, 1B	.245	469	61	115	25	2	10	72	6
*Davis, Jay, OF	.255	443	64	113	17	6	3	50	11
Diaz, Cesar, C	.170	47	5	8	2	0	0	5	0
#Epperson, Chad, C	.059	17	0	1	0	1	0	0	1
Garcia, Omar, 1B	.526	19	4	10	1	1	0	1	0
Greene, Charlie, C	.237	346	26	82	13	0	2	34	2
#Hardtke, Jason, 2B	.286	455	65	130	42	4	4	52	6
*Keister, Tripp, DH	.219	146	23	32	7	1	1	10	3
Mahalik, John, SS	.225	187	19	42	6	1	5	19	1
Miller, Ryan, SS	.053	19	3	1	0	0	0	0	1
Morgan, Kevin, SS	.277	430	63	119	21	1	4	51	9
Payton, Jay, OF	.345	357	59	123	20	3	14	54	16
*Sanders, Tracy, OF	.281	32	6	9	3	0	2	8	1
Saunders, Chris, 3B	.259	441	58	114	22	5	8	66	3
Smith, Brandon, C	.000	2	0	0	0	0	0	0	0
Smith, John, PH	.083	12	2	1	1	0	0	1	0
Thompson, Ryan, OF	.500	8	2	4	0	0	1	4	0
#Tijerina, Tony, C	.178	118	3	21	5	0	0	9	0
White, Don, OF	.236	314	48	74	17	2	3	20	25
#Wipf, Mark, OF	.091	11	1	1	0	0	0	1	1
Zuniga, David, PR	.000	1	1	0	0	0	0	0	0

PITCHING	W	L	ERA	G	SV	IP	H	BB	SO
*Arffa, Steve	0	0	4.50	1	0	6.0	7	1	1
Bullock, Craig	0	3	6.89	11	0	15.2	20	7	12
Cosman, Jeff	2	4	7.08	10	0	48.1	57	18	23
*Crawford, Joe	7	2	2.23	42	0	60.2	48	17	43

PITCHING	W	L	ERA	G	SV	IP	H	BB	SO
Edmondson, Brian	7	11	4.76	23	0	134.1	150	59	69
Engle, Tom	2	1	5.40	13	0	28.1	28	7	15
*Fiegel, Todd	0	1	15.00	4	0	3.0	4	3	3
Fuller, Mark	4	3	2.95	47	1	79.1	83	22	34
Guerra, Mark	2	1	5.79	6	0	32.2	35	9	24
Hiljus, Erik	2	4	5.86	10	0	55.1	60	32	40
Isringhausen, Jason	2	1	2.85	6	0	41.0	26	12	59
Knackert, Brent	7	7	2.30	48	11	82.1	53	26	69
Ludwick, Eric	12	5	2.95	23	0	143.1	108	68	131
McCready, Jim	1	1	3.23	32	4	39.0	42	14	17
*McDill, Allen	3	5	4.56	12	0	73.0	69	38	44
*Novoa, Rafael	0	1	2.25	4	0	8.0	6	5	6
*Paxton, Darrin	1	1	3.89	21	0	37.0	41	10	20
Person, Robert	5	4	3.11	26	7	66.2	46	25	65
Ramirez, Hector	4	12	4.60	20	0	123.1	127	48	63
Schorr, Brad	0	2	9.18	4	0	16.2	21	20	6
Stidham, Phil	0	0	4.66	7	0	9.2	9	9	7
Tam, Jeff	0	2	4.50	14	3	18.0	20	4	9
Wallace, Derek	0	1	5.28	15	2	15.1	11	9	8
Wilson, Paul	6	3	2.17	16	0	120.1	89	24	127

Bowie Bayson (Orioles) AA

BATTING	AVG	AB	R	H	2B	3B	HR	RBI	SB
Alfonzo, Edgar, 2B	.304	112	14	34	6	0	1	19	1
Arnold, Ken, SS	.000	22	3	0	0	0	0	0	0
Avila, Rolando, OF	.233	43	8	10	2	0	0	4	2
#Bartee, Kimera, OF	.284	218	45	62	9	1	3	19	22
Batiste, Kim, 3B	.358	95	16	34	5	0	4	27	2
Bautista, Juan, SS	.105	38	3	4	2	0	0	0	1
Berrios, Harry, OF	.245	208	32	51	13	0	5	21	12
Brown, Jarvis, OF	.279	219	50	61	12	1	6	23	12
Byrne, Clayton, OF	.218	55	5	12	2	1	1	6	2
Castaldo, Gregg, 2B	.234	265	37	62	12	3	2	26	5
*Castaneda, Hector, C	.154	65	3	10	2	0	0	6	0
Chavez, Eric, 1B	.196	51	5	10	2	0	2	4	0
Crowley, Jim, 3B	.214	98	11	21	5	0	2	13	1
Davis, Tommy, DH	.313	32	5	10	3	0	3	10	0
*Friedman, Jason, 1B	.232	228	22	53	11	0	3	27	1
Fully, Ed, OF	.218	119	15	26	5	0	2	6	2
Gresham, Kris, C	.077	13	1	1	0	0	0	0	1
Hammonds, Jeffrey, OF	.387	31	7	12	3	1	1	11	3
Hodge, Roy, OF	.172	99	11	17	1	1	0	9	2
Howard, Matt, SS	.303	251	42	76	8	2	1	15	22
*Hugo, Sean, OF	.222	117	15	26	3	0	0	10	1
#Lamb, David, SS	.250	4	0	1	0	0	0	1	0
Lewis, T.R., OF	.294	309	57	91	19	1	5	44	12
Manto, Jeff, DH	.250	4	1	1	0	0	0	0	0
McClain, Scott, 3B	.278	259	41	72	14	1	13	61	2
#Mercedes, F., 2B	.150	80	10	12	1	0	0	7	2
Michael, Jeff, SS	.167	12	2	2	0	0	0	0	0
Millares, Jose, DH	.248	411	50	102	30	3	4	50	7
#Owens, Billy, 1B	.269	453	57	122	27	0	17	91	2
Rodriguez, Nerio, C	.000	4	0	0	0	0	0	0	0
*Van Slyke, Andy, OF	.500	6	2	3	0	0	0	2	0
#Virgilio, George, 2B	.234	107	11	25	3	0	1	13	0
Waszgis, B.J., C	.253	438	53	111	22	0	10	50	2
*Wawruck, Jim, OF	.278	212	29	59	7	1	6	30	7

PITCHING	W	L	ERA	G	SV	IP	H	BB	SO
Borowski, Joe	2	2	3.92	16	7	20.2	16	7	32
Chavez, Carlos	0	0	0.00	1	0	2.0	0	1	2
Conner, Scott	5	1	4.17	44	0	82.0	57	74	82
Coppinger, Rocky	6	2	2.69	13	0	83.2	58	43	62
Dedrick, Jim	4	2	2.98	10	0	60.1	59	25	48
Devereux, Charles	0	1	5.21	12	0	19.0	24	17	27
*Faino, Jeff	0	2	2.72	31	0	43.0	34	15	17
*Fernandez, Sid	1	0	0.75	2	0	12.0	4	3	10
Forney, Rick	7	7	5.75	23	0	97.0	110	42	73
Harris, Doug	3	5	4.01	11	0	60.2	66	15	32
*Jarvis, Matt	9	8	5.11	26	0	118.0	154	42	60
Knowles, Greg	5	2	4.14	37	2	74.0	83	26	37
*Lane, Aaron	5	3	4.17	40	2	45.1	45	21	31
Lehman, Toby	1	3	7.94	4	0	17.0	20	11	14
Lemp, Chris	2	4	5.40	18	4	20.0	28	7	14

Class A Directory (full season)

California League

Bakersfield Blaze (co-op)
Sam Lynn Ballpark (3,200)
High Desert Mavericks (Orioles)
Maverick Stadium (3,500)
Lake Elsinore Storm (Angels)
Lake Elsinore Diamond (6,000)
Lancaster Jethawks (Mariners)
Stadium TBA
Modesto A's (Athletics)
Thurman Field (2,500)
Rancho Cucamonga Quakes (Padres)
The Epicenter (4,600)
San Bernardino (Dodgers)
Stadium TBA
San Jose Giants (Giants)
Municipal Stadium (4,500)
Stockton Ports (Brewers)
Billy Hebert Field (3,500)
Visalia Oaks (co-op)
Recreation Park (2,000)

Switch-hitter
* Left-handed

Class A Directory
(full season)

Durham Bulls (Braves)
Athletic Park (6,400)
Frederick Keys (Orioles)
Harry Grove Stadium (5,200)
Kinston Indians (Indians)
Grainger Stadium (4,100)
Lynchburg Hillcats (Pirates)
City Stadium (4,200)
Prince William Cannons (White Sox)
Pfitzner Memorial Stadium (6,000)
Salem Avalanche (Rockies)
Municipal Field (5,000)
Wilmington Blue Rocks (Royals)
Legends Stadium (5,500)
Winston-Salem Warthogs (Reds)
Ernie Shore Field (6,280)

Switch-hitter
* Left-handed

PITCHING	W	L	ERA	G	SV	IP	H	BB	SO
Maduro, Calvin	0	6	5.09	7	0	35.1	39	27	26
*Magee, Bo	1	1	5.40	5	0	8.1	10	6	7
Newlin, Jim	3	5	3.68	40	11	63.2	69	22	51
Nieto, Tony	0	0	15.00	1	0	3.0	6	3	3
Percibal, Billy	1	0	0.00	2	0	14.0	7	7	7
*Pierce, Ed	0	2	6.43	7	1	21.0	32	9	16
Ryan, Kevin	4	3	3.43	39	5	63.0	67	15	31
Shenk, Larry	0	0	6.52	6	0	9.2	6	8	8
Stephenson, Garrett	7	10	3.64	29	0	175.1	154	47	139
Wegmann, Tom	2	3	4.18	14	0	64.2	56	22	49

Canton-Akron Indians (Indians) AA

BATTING	AVG	AB	R	H	2B	3B	HR	RBI	SB
Alomar, Sandy, C	.400	15	3	6	1	0	0	1	0
Biasucci, Joe, DH	.244	135	19	33	8	0	2	16	0
Bryant, Pat, OF	.259	421	60	109	22	3	17	59	16
Cameron, Stanton, OF	.256	82	11	21	8	0	1	12	1
Campbell, Darrin, C	.000	7	1	0	0	0	0	0	0
Castillo, Ben, OF	.224	116	15	26	7	2	2	15	1
*Crosby, Mike, C	.165	224	18	37	5	1	5	20	1
Davenport, Adell, 1B	.276	29	2	8	1	0	0	5	0
Hagy, Gary, SS	.294	17	2	5	2	0	0	3	0
*Harvey, Ray, DH	.259	444	52	115	20	1	3	32	1
Hood, Dennis, OF	.217	23	6	5	1	0	0	2	1
Jackson, Damian, SS	.248	484	67	120	20	2	3	34	40
Lantigua, Eduardo, 3B	.196	46	5	9	2	0	1	4	0
*Marini, Marc, OF	.306	310	41	95	28	1	3	56	3
Martindale, Ryan, C	.375	8	2	3	0	0	0	1	0
Massarelli, John, OF	.281	178	17	50	10	2	2	22	17
*Maxwell, Pat, 3B	.247	267	19	66	7	0	4	25	1
*McCall, Rod, DH	.274	95	16	26	5	0	9	18	1
*McNabb, Buck, OF	.167	48	3	8	0	0	0	1	0
Murphy, Mike, OF	.043	23	3	1	0	0	0	0	0
Neal, Mike, 2B	.267	419	64	112	24	2	5	46	5
Ramirez, Alex, OF	.248	133	15	33	3	4	1	11	3
Ramirez, Omar, DH	.324	34	6	11	0	0	0	3	0
Smith, Ed, 3B	.241	365	41	88	18	2	11	52	0
Soliz, Steve, C	.173	81	9	14	3	0	2	7	0
*Taylor, Jamie, 3B	.000	11	0	0	0	0	0	0	0
*Townsend, Chad, 1B	.262	404	39	106	22	1	9	50	3
Wakamatsu, Don, C	.266	143	16	38	10	0	4	23	0
Yelding, Eric, OF	.351	37	5	13	1	0	0	7	3

PITCHING	W	L	ERA	G	SV	IP	H	BB	SO
Brown, Dickie	8	5	4.67	37	3	98.1	88	67	51
Cabrera, Jose	5	3	3.28	24	0	85.0	83	21	61
Carter, John	1	2	3.95	5	0	27.1	27	13	14
Chapin, Darrin	0	1	4.50	4	0	8.0	12	2	6
Crawford, Carlos	2	2	2.61	8	0	51.2	47	15	36
De La Maza, Roland	2	1	4.10	7	0	37.1	35	18	27
Driskill, Travis	3	4	4.66	33	4	46.1	46	19	39
Fronio, Jason	1	3	7.22	8	0	28.2	32	16	23
Graves, Dan	1	0	0.00	17	10	23.1	10	2	11
Harris, Pep	6	3	2.39	32	10	83.0	78	23	40
Hrusovsky, John	1	7	7.11	35	1	69.2	77	35	59
Kirkreit, Daron	2	9	5.69	14	0	80.2	74	46	67
*Kline, Steve	2	3	2.42	14	0	89.1	86	30	45
Koller, Rod	0	0	7.23	9	1	18.2	26	4	3
*Matthews, Mike	5	8	5.93	15	0	74.1	82	43	37
Perschke, Greg	1	0	3.38	3	0	5.1	4	2	4
Popplewell, Tom	2	0	9.74	15	0	20.1	33	16	14
Steph, Rod	8	10	3.81	32	0	137.0	150	33	82
Taylor, Tommy	1	1	3.72	5	0	9.2	9	6	3
Telford, Anthony	2	0	0.82	2	0	11.0	6	4	4
Trlicek, Rick	5	3	3.05	24	3	38.1	33	16	27
*Whitten, Casey	9	8	3.31	20	0	114.1	100	38	91
*Williams, Greg	0	0	4.23	24	0	27.2	15	21	17

Harrisburg Senators (Expos) AA

BATTING	AVG	AB	R	H	2B	3B	HR	RBI	SB
Alcantara, Israel, 3B	.211	237	25	50	12	2	10	29	1
Allen, Matt, C	.143	14	2	2	0	0	0	1	0

BATTING	AVG	AB	R	H	2B	3B	HR	RBI	SB
Barron, Tony, OF	.291	103	20	30	5	0	10	23	0
Bournigal, Rafael, SS	.221	95	12	21	3	1	0	7	1
Buckley, Troy, C	.291	158	16	46	10	0	2	15	0
Cabrera, Jolbert, SS	.286	35	4	10	2	0	0	1	3
Cairo, Sergio, OF	.000	13	0	0	0	0	0	0	0
*Charbonnet, Mark, OF	.251	407	34	102	14	4	8	57	3
Chick, Bruce, OF	.268	41	4	11	2	1	0	6	0
*Dauphin, Phil, OF	.244	398	53	97	20	2	5	38	17
*Everson, Darin, 1B	.214	14	0	3	1	0	0	1	0
Fitzpatrick, Robert, C	.167	42	3	7	1	0	1	3	0
Grissom, Antonio, OF	.257	237	32	61	10	0	4	23	13
*Hinton, Steve, 1B	.222	18	4	4	0	0	0	0	0
Hymel, Lou, C	.189	302	35	57	10	2	11	36	3
*Jacobs, Frank, 1B	.316	269	44	85	19	0	9	51	1
Kounas, Tony, C	.235	196	15	46	5	0	1	22	1
Lane, Dan, SS	.123	81	5	10	1	0	0	1	0
*Marabella, Tony, 3B	.225	89	10	20	1	0	1	11	0
Martinez, Ray, 2B	.237	152	18	36	6	0	1	13	3
Northrup, Kevin, OF	.309	152	23	47	14	0	1	27	0
Rundels, Matt, 2B	.247	462	72	114	30	4	11	55	19
*Saffer, Jon, OF	.237	76	9	18	4	0	0	4	2
Tovar, Edgar, SS	.202	247	28	50	7	2	3	21	1
#Ventress, Leroy, OF	.220	41	4	9	0	0	0	0	3
#Vidro, Jose, 2B	.260	246	33	64	16	2	4	38	3

PITCHING	W	L	ERA	G	SV	IP	H	BB	SO
Alvarez, Tavo	2	1	2.25	3	0	16.0	17	5	14
Aucoin, Derek	2	4	4.96	29	1	52.2	52	28	48
*Botkin, Alan	0	0	8.31	3	1	4.1	5	2	4
Bullinger, Kirk	5	3	2.42	56	7	67.0	61	25	42
*DeHart, Rick	6	7	4.84	35	0	93.0	94	39	64
Diaz, Ralph	2	2	5.59	11	0	19.1	17	9	16
Falteisek, Steve	9	6	2.95	25	0	168.0	152	64	112
Gentile, Scott	2	2	3.44	37	11	49.2	36	15	48
Henderson, Rod	3	6	4.31	12	0	56.1	51	18	53
Kendrena, Ken	3	2	2.51	30	1	64.2	58	25	46
Kerley, Collin	0	0	0.00	2	0	6.2	5	1	3
Mikkelsen, Linc	1	2	5.37	21	0	53.2	57	24	39
Pacheco, Alex	9	7	4.27	45	4	86.1	76	31	88
Paniagua, Jose	7	12	5.34	25	0	126.1	140	62	89
Pollard, Damon	0	0	8.64	6	0	8.1	11	4	10
Pote, Lou	0	1	5.40	9	0	28.1	32	7	24
*Shaw, Cedric	0	1	4.66	5	0	19.1	25	6	13
Stull, Everett	3	12	5.54	24	0	126.2	114	79	132
Tirado, Aris	1	0	0.77	8	1	11.2	8	5	10
*Weber, Neil	6	11	5.01	28	0	152.2	157	90	119

New Britain Red Sox (Red Sox) AA

BATTING	AVG	AB	R	H	2B	3B	HR	RBI	SB
*Brede, Brent, OF	.274	449	71	123	28	2	3	39	14
Byrd, Anthony, OF	.247	442	54	109	20	8	3	51	21
#Duncan, Andres, SS	.226	230	28	52	5	2	0	10	10
Garrow, David, 3B	.143	14	0	2	0	0	0	1	0
#Gerald, Ed, DH	.111	18	1	2	1	0	0	3	0
Grifol, Pedro, C	.177	226	23	40	9	0	3	21	1
*Hunter, Greg, SS	.077	13	1	1	0	0	0	0	1
*Jackson, John, OF	.298	57	8	17	2	1	3	8	3
*Kontorinis, Andrew, DH	.289	114	12	33	4	0	2	17	1
*Lawton, Matt, OF	.269	412	75	111	19	5	13	54	26
*Legree, Keith, OF	.200	110	10	22	2	0	0	6	3
Lopez, Rene, C	.246	264	22	65	8	0	3	26	0
#Moore, Tim, DH	.241	311	39	75	19	1	9	45	4
#Norman, Kenny, OF	.290	31	4	9	1	0	0	1	0
*Ogden, Jamie, 1B	.284	384	54	109	22	1	13	61	6
Roper, Chad, 3B	.226	443	41	100	22	3	11	61	2
Smith, Bubba, DH	.243	148	20	36	11	0	6	21	0
*Tirpack, Ken, 1B	.250	16	4	4	2	0	2	3	1
Valette, Ramon, SS	.214	346	40	74	11	2	4	32	19
*Walker, Todd, 2B	.290	513	83	149	27	3	21	85	23

PITCHING	W	L	ERA	G	SV	IP	H	BB	SO
*DeJesus, Javier	0	0	1.59	4	0	5.2	8	1	3
*Fultz, Aaron	0	2	6.60	3	0	15.0	11	9	12
Gandarillas, Gus	2	4	6.12	25	7	32.1	38	16	25

Class A Directory
(full season)

Florida State League

Brevard County Manatees (Marlins)
Space Coast Stadium (7,200)

Charlotte Rangers (Rangers)
Charlotte County Stadium (6,026)

Clearwater Phillies (Phillies)
Jack Russell Stadium (7,385)

Daytona Cubs (Cubs)
Jackie Robinson Ballpark (4,900)

Dunedin Blue Jays (Blue Jays)
Grant Field (6,218)

Fort Myers Miracle (Twins)
Lee County Complex (7,500)

Kissimmee Cobras (Astros)
Osceola County Stadium (5,100)

Lakeland Tigers (Tigers)
Joker Marchant Stadium (7,000)

St. Lucie Mets (Mets)
White Stadium (7,400)

St. Petersburg Cardinals (Cardinals)
Al Lang Stadium (7,004)

Sarasota Red Sox (Red Sox)
Ed Smith Stadium (7,500)

Tampa Yankees (Yankees)
Stadium TBA (3,000)

Vero Beach Dodgers (Dodgers)
Holman Stadium (6,500)

West Palm Beach Expos (Expos)
Municipal Stadium (4,400)

Class A Directory

(full season)

Michigan Battle Cats (Red Sox)
Brown Stadium (6,200)
Beloit Snappers (Brewers)
Pohlman Field (3,500)
Burlington Bees (Giants)
Community Field (3,500)
Cedar Rapids Kernels (Angels)
Veterans Memorial Ballpark (6,000)
Clinton Lumber Kings (Padres)
Riverview Stadium (3,400)
Fort Wayne Wizards (Twins)
Memorial Stadium (6,000)
Kane County Cougars (Marlins)
Elfstrom Stadium (4,800)
Lansing Lugnuts (Royals)
Oldsmobile Park (10,000)
Peoria Chiefs (Cardinals)
Pete Vonachen Stadium (6,200)
Quad City River Bandits (Astros)
John O'Donnell Stadium (5,500)
Rockford Cubbies (Cubs)
Marinelli Field (4,300)
South Bend Silver Hawks (White Sox)
Coveleski Stadium (5,000)
West Michigan Whitecaps (Athletics)
Old Kent Park (5,500)
Wisconsin Timber Rattlers (Mariners)
Goodland Field (4,300)

PITCHING	W	L	ERA	G	SV	IP	H	BB	SO
Gavaghan, Sean	2	1	2.20	21	5	28.2	18	10	30
*Konieczki, Dom	0	1	1.95	39	1	32.1	28	19	35
Legault, Kevin	6	1	3.21	47	3	87.0	79	28	52
Maldonado, Jay	0	0	11.81	5	0	5.1	7	3	4
*Mansur, Jeff	0	0	1.42	5	1	6.1	5	2	3
*Miller, Travis	7	9	4.37	28	0	162.2	172	65	151
Moten, Scott	8	5	3.94	40	3	75.1	65	36	43
Norris, Joe	5	6	3.59	46	5	82.2	79	36	81
*Ohme, Kevin	3	4	3.46	35	0	101.1	89	45	52
Ritchie, Todd	4	9	5.73	24	0	113.0	135	54	60
Roberts, Brett	11	9	3.41	28	0	174.0	162	50	135
Saccavino, Craig	1	6	5.66	27	1	41.1	48	32	34
*Serafini, Dan	12	9	3.38	27	0	162.2	155	72	123
Trinidad, Hector	4	11	4.61	23	0	121.0	137	22	92

New Haven Ravens (Rockies) AA

BATTING	AVG	AB	R	H	2B	3B	HR	RBI	SB
Case, Mike, OF	.245	310	55	76	16	2	10	46	6
Dixon, Colin, 3B	.191	47	3	9	2	0	0	7	0
Echevarria, Angel, OF	.300	453	78	136	30	1	21	100	8
#Gonzalez, Mauricio, PH	.268	164	20	44	5	3	0	12	0
Hartung, Andy, 3B	.097	31	4	3	2	0	0	0	1
Higgins, Mike, C	.245	49	4	12	0	0	0	6	0
#Jones, Terry, OF	.269	472	78	127	12	1	1	26	51
Kennedy, David, 1B	.306	484	75	148	22	2	22	96	4
List, Lou, DH	.278	212	26	59	10	4	6	44	2
#McCracken, Q., OF	.357	221	33	79	11	4	1	26	26
Myrow, John, OF	.246	353	52	87	18	1	3	50	16
#Perez, Neifi, SS	.253	427	59	108	28	3	5	43	5
Rogers, Lamarr, 2B	.283	371	68	105	15	0	0	31	21
Scalzitti, Will, C	.187	123	9	23	6	0	1	14	0
Schmidt, Tom, 3B	.217	423	55	92	25	3	6	49	2
Sexton, Chris, SS	.000	3	0	0	0	0	0	0	0
Snyder, Randy, C	.235	17	2	4	1	0	0	2	0
Strittmatter, Mark, C	.243	288	44	70	12	1	7	42	1
*Wells, Forry, OF	.214	14	3	3	0	0	0	1	0
White, Billy, 2B	.232	181	25	42	9	1	3	34	2

PITCHING	W	L	ERA	G	SV	IP	H	BB	SO
Alston, Garvin	4	4	2.84	47	6	66.2	47	26	73
Aminoff, Matt	0	2	1.54	6	0	11.2	9	6	10
Arteaga, Ivan	2	4	5.56	14	0	34.0	36	21	18
Brownson, Mark	0	0	1.50	1	0	6.0	4	1	4
Case, Mike	0	0	0.00	2	0	3.0	0	0	2
*Farmer, Mike	10	5	4.89	40	0	110.1	117	35	77
*Grundt, Ken	2	2	2.13	28	3	38.0	26	10	27
Henderson, Chris	0	0	0.00	3	0	4.0	1	2	2
Holman, Brad	0	0	3.38	7	0	16.0	8	5	9
Hutchins, Jason	0	0	3.86	12	1	14.0	13	14	14
Johnson, Jason	6	3	5.32	19	0	67.2	77	29	37
*Jones, Bobby	5	2	2.58	27	3	73.1	61	36	70
*Kotarski, Mike	2	3	3.24	31	2	50.0	43	36	54
Moore, Joel	14	6	3.20	27	0	157.1	156	67	102
Neier, Chris	10	4	4.16	38	0	123.1	164	47	74
Nied, David	0	0	8.10	1	0	3.1	4	0	0
Rekar, Bryan	6	3	2.13	12	0	80.1	65	16	80
*Ruffin, Bruce	0	0	0.00	2	0	2.0	1	0	2
Salamon, John	1	0	6.10	6	0	10.1	9	16	9
*Schneider, Phil	0	1	7.71	2	0	7.0	8	9	3
Tellers, Dave	2	5	2.87	33	1	69.0	60	14	63
Thomson, John	7	8	4.18	26	0	131.1	132	56	82
Viano, Jake	3	6	3.38	57	19	72.0	51	38	85
Voisard, Mark	2	0	3.23	27	2	30.2	31	14	22
Wright, Jamey	0	1	9.00	1	0	3.0	6	3	0
Zolecki, Mike	3	4	3.25	9	0	55.1	56	20	32

Norwich Navigators (Yankees) AA

BATTING	AVG	AB	R	H	2B	3B	HR	RBI	SB
Burnett, Roger, SS	.222	356	32	79	14	0	3	29	3
Cabreja, Alexis, OF	.091	11	1	1	0	0	0	1	1
*Delvecchio, Nick, 1B	.260	430	66	112	23	4	19	74	2
*Deberry, Joe, DH	.000	4	0	0	0	0	0	0	0

BATTING	AVG	AB	R	H	2B	3B	HR	RBI	SB
Epps, Scott, C	.247	73	6	18	6	0	0	7	0
Figga, Mike, C	.271	399	59	108	22	4	13	61	1
#Fleming, Carlton, 2B	.304	125	15	38	3	1	0	16	5
*Fox, Andy, SS	.206	175	23	36	3	5	5	17	8
#Hawkins, Kraig, OF	.222	45	5	10	0	0	0	3	7
Hinds, Robert, 2B	.252	445	71	112	8	1	1	37	27
*Horne, Tyrone, DH	.283	166	23	47	16	1	2	22	4
Hughes, Troy, OF	.327	55	7	18	2	1	1	8	0
#Long, R.D., SS	.212	33	4	7	3	0	0	5	2
*Luke, Matt, OF	.260	365	48	95	17	5	8	53	5
*Phillips, Steve, OF	.258	31	2	8	1	0	2	7	0
Renteria, Dave, 3B	.105	38	4	4	0	0	0	0	1
*Riggs, Kevin, DH	.330	179	38	59	16	1	4	36	5
Rivera, Ruben, OF	.293	256	49	75	16	8	9	39	16
*Robertson, Jason, OF	.276	456	60	126	29	10	6	54	19
Romano, Scott, 3B	.246	353	43	87	15	1	7	51	7
Salcedo, Edwin, C	.000	2	0	0	0	0	0	0	0
*Seefried, Tate, 1B	.226	274	34	62	18	1	5	33	0
*Turner, Brian, OF	.296	311	39	92	21	3	4	43	3
Wilson, Thomas, C	.143	84	6	12	4	0	0	4	0

PITCHING	W	L	ERA	G	SV	IP	H	BB	SO
Antolick, Jeff	1	1	6.75	2	0	9.1	17	2	5
Buddie, Mike	10	12	4.81	29	1	149.2	155	81	106
Carper, Mark	0	0	10.80	1	0	5.0	9	1	3
*Carter, Tom	3	7	5.57	28	0	97.0	128	47	65
Coleman, Billy	6	4	4.05	46	2	73.1	56	57	64
DeJean, Mike	5	5	2.99	59	20	78.1	58	34	57
*Hines, Rich	3	5	3.63	54	7	62.0	58	34	50
*Hubbard, Mark	4	4	4.21	13	1	72.2	81	25	39
Janzen, Marty	1	2	4.95	3	0	20.0	17	7	16
Kozeniewski, Blaise	1	0	4.91	29	0	55.0	53	27	33
Long, Joe	4	2	4.85	43	2	81.2	103	48	34
Mendoza, Ramiro	5	6	3.21	19	0	89.2	87	33	68
Musselwhite, James	5	9	4.58	24	0	131.2	136	34	96
Musset, Jose	4	1	3.33	34	4	48.2	43	24	42
Pantoja, Johnny	1	2	6.48	11	0	25.0	29	14	19
Perez, Melido	1	0	0.00	2	0	9.0	7	3	9
Ricken, Ray	4	2	2.72	8	0	53.0	44	24	43
Standish, Scott	4	3	5.67	17	0	60.1	73	30	47
Sutherland, John	1	0	2.77	13	2	13.0	12	3	12
*Turner, Brian	0	0	9.00	2	0	2.0	2	2	0
Wallace, Kent	7	6	3.52	18	0	94.2	93	24	72

Portland Sea Dogs (Marlins) AA

BATTING	AVG	AB	R	H	2B	3B	HR	RBI	SB
#Clapinski, Chris, 3B	.236	208	32	49	9	3	4	30	5
*Clark, Tim, 1B	.271	499	62	135	34	2	8	88	0
Johnson, Charles, C	.000	7	0	0	0	0	0	0	0
Katzaroff, Rob, OF	.304	441	87	134	16	4	10	49	18
*Kremers, Jimmy, C	.223	264	32	59	11	5	7	37	1
Lucca, Lou, 3B	.276	388	57	107	28	1	9	64	4
*McMillon, Billy, OF	.313	518	92	162	29	3	14	93	15
Milliard, Ralph, 2B	.267	464	104	124	22	3	11	40	22
Redmond, Mike, C	.255	333	37	85	11	1	3	39	2
Renteria, Edgar, SS	.289	508	70	147	15	7	7	68	30
Rudolph, Mason, PH	.197	76	9	15	4	1	4	16	0
Sheff, Chris, OF	.276	471	85	130	25	7	12	91	23
Torres, Tony, PH	.296	81	15	24	3	2	0	4	9
#Waller, Casey, DH	.222	36	4	8	2	1	0	5	1
*Wilson, Pookie, OF	.273	348	51	95	13	5	3	44	9

PITCHING	W	L	ERA	G	SV	IP	H	BB	SO
Alfonseca, Antonio	9	3	3.64	19	0	96.1	81	42	75
Chergey, Dan	6	7	3.47	55	5	80.1	62	26	75
Cunnane, Will	9	2	3.67	21	0	117.2	120	34	83
Heredia, Wilson	4	0	2.00	4	0	27.0	22	14	19
Juelsgaard, Jarod	3	1	3.89	48	2	71.2	65	44	44
Larkin, Andy	1	2	3.38	9	0	40.0	29	11	23
Leahy, Pat	3	4	4.50	13	0	42.0	32	20	37
Lemon, Don	1	6	3.61	30	1	62.1	60	19	47
Mantei, Matt	1	0	2.38	8	1	11.1	10	5	15
*McGraw, Tom	5	0	1.81	51	2	74.2	69	31	60
Mendoza, Reynol	9	10	3.43	27	0	168.0	163	69	120

South Atlantic League

Asheville Tourists (Rockies)
McCormick Field (4,000)

Augusta Greenjackets (Pirates)
Greenjacket Stadium (4,000)

Capital City Bombers (Mets)
Capital City Stadium (6,100)

Charleston (S.C.) RiverDogs (Rangers)
College Park (4,300)

Charleston (W.Va.) Alley Cats (Reds)
Watt Powell Park (6,000)

Columbus Redstixx (Indians)
Golden Park (5,500)

Delmarva Shorebirds (Expos)
Stadium TBA

Fayetteville Generals (Tigers)
J.P. Riddle Stadium (3,200)

Greensboro Bats (Yankees)
War Memorial Stadium (7,500)

Hagerstown Suns (Blue Jays)
Municipal Stadium (4,500)

Hickory Crawdads (White Sox)
L.P. Frans Stadium (4,500)

Macon Braves (Braves)
Luther Williams Field (3,500)

Piedmont Boll Weevils (Phillies)
Fieldcrest Cannon Stadium (4,600)

Savannah Cardinals (Cardinals)
Grayson Stadium (8,000)

PITCHING (top right table)

PITCHING	W	L	ERA	G	SV	IP	H	BB	SO
Mix, Greg	6	4	4.68	24	0	92.1	98	25	56
Pettit, Doug	3	1	3.69	21	2	31.2	30	6	24
Powell, Jay	5	4	1.87	50	24	53.0	42	15	53
Rojas, Euclides	1	1	7.77	14	1	22.0	27	13	22
Spencer, Stan	1	4	7.38	8	0	39.0	57	19	32
Wainhouse, David	2	1	7.20	17	0	25.0	39	8	16
*Ward, Bryan	7	3	4.50	20	2	72.0	70	31	71
*Whisenant, Matt	10	6	3.50	23	0	128.2	106	65	107

Batting leaders across all leagues

BATTING AVERAGE
(minimum 383 TPA)

Player	Club	Lg.	Avg.
T*Coughlin, K.	Bir	Sou	.372
Riggs, Adam	SBr	Cal	.362
T#McCracken, Q	CSp	PCL	.359
T Lennon, Pat	Slk	PCL	.352
Ingram, R.	Slk	PCL	.348
T Guerrero, W.	Abq	PCL	.346
T Pecorilli, Aldo	Rmd	Int	.344
*Damon, J.	Wch	Tex	.343
Perez, Robert	Syr	Int	.343
T Smith, D.	Wmi	MID	.342
T Cookson, B.	Oma	Ama	.340
Hubbard, Trent	CSp	PCL	.340
T Magee, W.	Rea	East	.338
T Abbott, Jeff	Bir	Sou	.336
*Beamon, Trey	CGy	PCL	.334

HOME RUNS

Player	Club	Lg.	HR
T Greene, Todd	Van	PCL	40
T#Ibarra, Jesse	Sjo	Cal	34
Wright, Ron	Mac	SAL	32
Gibson, Derrick	Ash	SAL	32
T*Cruz, Ivan	Jax	Sou	31
Arias, George	Mdl	Tex	30
*Cox, Steve	Mod	Cal	30
T White, Jason	Mod	Cal	30
T*McCall, Rod	Can	East	29
Huskey, Butch	Nor	Int	28
Hust, Gary	Mod	Cal	27
Thomas, Juan	Prw	Car	26
T Pough, P.	Paw	Int	26
Several tied at			25

RBI

Player	Club	Lg.	RBI
Gibson, Derrick	Ash	SAL	115
*Cox, Steve	Mod	Cal	110
Robledo, Nilson	Sbn	Mid	108
*Ibanez, Raul	Riv	Cal	108
*Ward, Daryle	Fay	SAL	106
Riggs, Adam	Sbr	Cal	106
Arias, George	Mdl	Tex	104
Wright, Ron	Mac	SAL	104
*Canale, G.	Car	Sou	102
Jones, Andruw	Mac	SAL	100
T#Ibarra, Jesse	Sjo	Cal	100
Echevarria, A.	Nhv	East	100
T White, Jason	Mod	Cal	98
*Jorgensen, R.	Riv	Cal	97
Several tied at			96

Switch-hitter
* Left-handed
T Player has been with more than one team; listed with last team.
(Players in major leagues are listed with last minor league club.)

Reading Phillies (Phillies) AA

BATTING	AVG	AB	R	H	2B	3B	HR	RBI	SB
Bennett, Gary, C	.236	271	27	64	11	0	4	40	0
*Bigler, Jeff, 1B	.091	44	4	4	1	0	0	2	0
*Blasingame, Kent, OF	.205	195	38	40	4	2	1	17	9
#Brito, Luis, SS	.333	3	1	1	0	0	0	1	1
Brophy, E.J., C	.500	4	0	2	1	0	0	0	0
Burke, Alan, OF	.200	20	5	4	2	0	1	3	0
Doster, David, 2B	.265	551	84	146	39	3	21	79	11
Eason, Tommy, C	.255	333	43	85	18	3	14	50	2
Estalella, Bobby, C	.235	34	5	8	1	0	2	9	0
Fisher, David, SS	.230	204	18	47	18	1	1	20	4
*Geisler, Phil, OF	.232	272	27	63	10	3	2	35	4
Grable, Rob, OF	.300	353	71	106	24	1	16	67	15
Hayden, Dave, 3B	.234	192	22	45	6	0	3	11	0
Held, Dan, 1B	.500	4	2	2	1	0	1	3	1
*Holifield, Rick, OF	.247	93	18	23	3	1	1	5	5
Magee, Wendell, OF	.294	136	17	40	9	1	3	21	3
McConnell, Chad, OF	.276	319	46	88	12	1	11	52	8
McNair, Fred, 1B	.271	395	64	107	24	1	23	68	3
Millan, Adan, C	.350	20	3	7	3	0	1	7	0
Moler, Jason, 3B	.265	83	17	22	3	0	2	14	2
Mota, Gary, OF	.227	110	13	25	4	2	1	9	0
Rolen, Scott, 3B	.289	76	16	22	3	0	3	15	1
Sefcik, Kevin, SS	.272	508	68	138	18	4	4	46	14
*Solomon, Steve, OF	.228	356	50	81	19	6	3	42	17
Waco, David, DH	.300	10	1	3	0	0	0	1	0

PITCHING	W	L	ERA	G	SV	IP	H	BB	SO
Andersen, Larry	0	0	6.23	5	0	4.1	6	1	7
*Beech, Matt	2	4	2.96	14	0	79.0	67	33	70
Blazier, Ron	4	5	3.29	56	1	106.2	93	31	102
Brown, Dan	1	0	7.71	2	0	2.1	4	0	2
Doolan, Blake	11	5	2.22	60	16	73.0	63	27	50
Fisher, David	0	0	0.00	2	0	2.1	1	0	1
*Foster, Mark	1	1	5.66	25	1	20.2	25	17	15
Gilmore, Joel	2	0	6.25	18	0	36.0	45	18	27
Gomes, Wayne	7	4	3.96	22	0	104.2	89	70	102
Grace, Mike	13	6	3.54	24	0	147.1	137	35	118
Hanselman, Carl	4	3	6.37	24	2	41.0	45	17	35
Hill, Eric	4	3	2.90	38	4	59.0	55	27	52
Holman, Craig	1	1	3.49	32	1	56.2	55	16	40
Hunter, Rich	3	0	2.05	3	0	22.0	14	6	17
*Juhl, Mike	1	8	4.27	49	6	46.1	43	28	39
*Karp, Ryan	1	2	3.06	7	0	47.0	44	15	37
Loewer, Carlton	4	1	2.16	8	0	50.0	42	31	35
Mitchell, Larry	6	11	5.54	25	0	128.1	136	72	107
Munoz, Bobby	0	4	10.80	4	0	15.0	28	3	8
Smith, Eric	0	1	20.25	4	0	4.0	11	4	5
Tranberg, Mark	6	6	3.73	18	0	111.0	110	30	62
Trisler, John	2	4	5.16	30	0	82.0	96	26	50
*West, David	0	0	1.50	1	0	6.0	2	3	8

Trenton Thunder (Tigers) AA

BATTING	AVG	AB	R	H	2B	3B	HR	RBI	SB
*Abad, Andy, OF	.240	287	29	69	14	3	4	32	5
*Blosser, Greg, OF	.246	179	25	44	13	0	11	34	3
Brown, Matt, C	.182	11	1	2	0	0	0	0	0
*Carey, Todd, 3B	.272	228	30	62	11	1	8	36	3
Delgado, Alex, C	.333	72	13	24	1	0	3	14	0
#Fuller, Aaron, OF	.196	204	27	40	7	4	0	10	16
Garciaparra, Nomar, SS	.267	513	77	137	20	8	8	47	35
*Graham, Tim, OF	.160	25	2	4	1	0	0	0	0

BATTING	AVG	AB	R	H	2B	3B	HR	RBI	SB
Hardge, Mike, OF	.244	127	18	31	4	1	0	12	3
Hecker, Doug, 1B	.204	221	20	45	16	0	5	32	2
Johnson, J.J., OF	.500	6	1	3	0	0	0	1	0
#Juday, Rob, 2B	.100	10	0	1	0	0	0	0	0
Lennon, Pat, OF	.398	98	19	39	7	0	1	8	7
Levangie, Dana, C	.178	129	10	23	3	1	0	7	1
*Mahay, Ron, OF	.235	310	37	73	12	3	5	28	5
Martin, Jeff, C	.217	254	25	55	10	1	4	30	3
*McGuire, Ryan, 1B	.333	414	59	138	29	1	7	59	11
McKeel, Walt, C	.238	84	11	20	3	1	2	11	2
Merloni, Lou, 2B	.277	318	42	88	16	1	1	30	7
*Murphy, Pat, OF	.228	114	17	26	4	0	0	11	10
Nava, Lipso, OF	.216	51	7	11	3	0	1	7	1
*Nixon, Trot, OF	.160	94	9	15	3	1	2	8	2
Pough, PorkChop, DH	.278	363	68	101	23	5	21	69	11
*Selby, Bill, 3B	.286	451	64	129	29	2	13	68	4
Shelton, Ben, DH	.186	118	23	22	2	0	4	13	1
#Tinsley, Lee, OF	.389	18	3	7	1	0	0	3	1
Zambrano, Eddie, OF	.147	68	5	10	1	0	1	7	0
Zambrano, Jose, OF	.242	62	7	15	6	0	2	7	2

PITCHING	W	L	ERA	G	SV	IP	H	BB	SO
Amos, Chad	0	0	12.60	6	0	5.0	10	3	1
Bakkum, Scott	6	4	1.34	28	0	47.0	31	9	24
Bennett, Shayne	0	1	5.06	10	3	10.2	16	3	6
Blais, Mike	2	0	2.52	13	0	25.0	19	7	20
*Bogott, Kurt	0	1	2.70	2	0	3.1	3	1	2
Brooks, Wes	5	11	4.12	29	0	161.2	149	43	85
Cain, Tim	4	3	3.73	29	4	50.2	46	17	45
Carter, Glenn	1	1	3.07	14	8	14.2	15	4	10
Caruso, Joe	1	1	11.37	11	0	12.2	21	8	8
Cederblad, Brett	3	2	3.63	8	0	44.2	43	11	36
*Ciccarella, Joe	2	1	2.73	22	0	33.0	31	12	33
*Emerson, Scott	0	0	4.76	4	0	5.2	9	2	5
*Eshelman, Vaughn	0	1	0.00	2	0	7.0	3	0	7
Fernandez, Jared	5	4	3.90	11	0	67.0	64	28	40
Hansen, Brent	4	5	3.26	11	0	77.1	70	17	52
*Hill, Chris	0	0	9.00	7	0	6.0	7	6	10
Hoeme, Steve	2	0	3.33	20	6	24.1	23	8	17
Hudson, Joe	0	1	1.71	22	8	31.2	20	17	24
Ingram, Todd	1	1	5.84	18	0	24.2	27	21	16
Johnson, Dom	1	2	9.42	5	0	14.1	19	12	11
*Langbehn, Gregg	0	1	5.40	14	1	13.1	9	9	11
Malloy, Chuck	0	0	4.76	1	0	5.2	9	1	1
*Orellano, Rafael	11	7	3.09	27	0	186.2	146	72	160
Peterson, Dean	4	8	5.38	20	0	88.2	96	27	47
*Riley, Ed	0	0	2.76	16	1	16.1	14	9	10
Ryan, Ken	0	2	5.82	11	2	17.0	23	5	16
Sele, Aaron	0	1	3.38	2	0	8.0	8	2	9
*Senior, Shawn	11	7	4.52	27	0	151.1	154	68	90
Sullivan, Mike	3	1	1.37	15	2	19.2	17	3	16
Suppan, Jeff	6	2	2.36	15	0	99.0	86	26	88

Southern League

Birmingham Barons (White Sox) AA

BATTING	AVG	AB	R	H	2B	3B	HR	RBI	SB
Abbott, Jeff, OF	.320	197	25	63	11	1	3	28	1
Burton, Essex, 2B	.255	554	95	141	15	2	1	43	60
*Coughlin, Kevin, OF	.385	327	56	126	29	2	3	49	5
*DiSarcina, Glenn, DH	.269	26	4	7	1	0	0	2	0
*Fryman, Troy, 1B	.222	356	48	79	13	3	8	41	9
Hurst, Jimmy, OF	.189	301	47	57	11	0	12	34	12
#Norton, Greg, 3B	.249	469	65	117	23	2	6	60	19
*Pearson, Eddie, 1B	.224	201	20	45	13	0	2	25	1
Poe, Charles, OF	.283	427	75	121	28	2	13	60	19
Vinas, Julio, C	.269	372	47	100	16	2	6	61	3
Vollmer, Scott, C	.236	258	35	61	5	0	6	39	0
Wilson, Craig, SS	.289	471	56	136	19	1	4	46	2

Batting leaders across all leagues

(Cont'd from previous page)

STOLEN BASES

Player	Club	Lg.	SB
#McDonald, J.	Mod	Cal	70
T#Metcalfe, M.	Vb	Fsl	61
T#French, A.	Dur	Car	61
Burton, Essex	Bir	Sou	60
Hernandez, C.	QC	Mid	58
#Roberts, L.	Knx	Sou	57

HITS

Player	Club	Lg.	Hits
Riggs, Adam	Sbr	Cal	196
T Magee, W.	Rea	East	177
Perez, Robert	Syr	Int	172
Sparks, Don	Col	Int	170
T Smith, D.	Wmi	Mid	170
T Payton, Jay	Nor	Int	170
T#McCracken, Q.	Csp	PCL	167

DOUBLES

Player	Club	Lg.	2B
T#Hardtke, J.	Bng	East	43
Ingram, R.	Slk	PCL	43
#Tatis, F.	Csc	SAL	43
Marzano, John	OkC	Ama	41
Jones, Andruw	Mac	SAL	41
#Banks, Brian	Elp	Tex	39
Riggs, Adam	Sbr	Cal	39
Doster, David	Rea	East	39
*Jackson, Ryan	KnC	Mid	39
Perez, Robert	Syr	Int	38
*Fullmer, Brad	Aby	SAL	38
Lane, Ryan	FtW	Mid	37
*Koskie, Corey	FtW	Mid	37
Hajek, Dave	Tcn	PCL	37

TRIPLES

Player	Club	Lg.	3B
*Abreu, Bob	Tcn	PCL	17
DeLaCruz, L	Knx	Sou	12
Thurman, Gary	Tac	PCL	12
Guiliano, Matt	Pdt	SAL	12
T*Samuels, S.	Day	FSL	12
D'Aquila, Tom	Hds	Cal	11
Mendez, R.	Spr	Mid	11
*Glenn, Leon	Mdl	Tex	11
T*Fox, Andy	Col	Int	11

363

Switch-hitter
* Left-handed
T Player has been with more than
one team; listed with last team.
(Players in major leagues are listed
with last minor league club.)

Batting leaders across all leagues

(Cont'd from previous page)

EXTRA BASE HITS

Player	Club	Lg.	EBH
Jones, Andruw	Mac	SAL	71
Riggs, Adam	Sbr	CAL	68
T#Ibarra, Jesse	Sjo	Cal	67
T Greene, Todd	Van	PCL	64
T Pough, P.	Paw	Int	63
Doster, David	Rea	East	63

RUNS

Player	Club	Lg.	Runs
Riggs, Adam	Sbr	Cal	111
#McDonald, J.	Mod	Cal	109
Jones, Andruw	Mac	SAL	104
Milliard, Ralph	Prt	East	104
Sadler, Donnie	Mch	Mid	103
Hubbard, Trent	Csp	PCL	102
T Smith, D.	Wmi	Mid	102

WALKS

Player	Club	Lg.	BB
#McDonald, J.	Mod	Cal	110
T Sexton, Chris	Nhv	East	97
Menechino, F.	Prw	Car	96
*McMillon, Billy	Prt	East	96
Kennedy, Gus	Mac	SAL	95
T#Latham, C.	Abq	PCL	90

364

TOTAL BASES

Player	Club	Lg.	TB
Riggs, Adam	Sbr	Cal	317
T Greene, Todd	Van	PCL	292
T#Ibarra, Jesse	Sjo	Cal	283
Gibson, Derrick	Ash	SAL	280
Jones, Andruw	Mac	SAL	275

STRIKEOUTS

Player	Club	Lg.	SO
Schwab, Chris	Aby	SAL	173
Hust, Gary	Mob	Cal	169
*Gainey, Bryon	Clb	SAL	157
Thomas, Juan	Prw	Car	156
*Dishington, N.	Sav	SAL	154

Switch-hitter
* Left-handed
T Player has been with more than one team; listed with last team.
(Players in major leagues are listed with last minor league club.)

PITCHING	W	L	ERA	G	SV	IP	H	BB	SO
Andujar, Luis	14	8	2.85	27	0	167.1	147	44	146
*Fordham, Tom	6	3	3.38	14	0	82.2	79	28	61
Gajkowski, Steve	4	4	4.18	35	2	51.2	64	16	29
Johnson, Barry	7	4	1.85	47	0	78.0	64	15	53
*Johnston, Sean	5	2	4.21	34	0	98.1	120	36	44
Levine, Alan	4	3	2.34	43	7	73.0	61	25	68
*McCarthy, Greg	3	3	5.04	38	3	44.2	37	29	48
Moore, Tim	7	5	3.68	29	0	120.0	118	40	78
Olsen, Steve	8	3	3.48	14	0	85.1	84	21	56
Ruffcorn, Scott	0	2	5.63	3	0	16.0	17	10	13
Snyder, John	1	0	6.64	5	0	20.1	24	6	13
Woodfin, Chris	3	3	4.50	48	20	64.0	59	24	72

Carolina Mudcats (Pirates) AA

BATTING	AVG	AB	R	H	2B	3B	HR	RBI	SB
Beasley, Tony, 2B	.281	335	59	94	16	4	2	34	20
*Brown, Michael, 1B	.238	223	29	53	13	1	8	33	0
*Canale, George, 1B	.287	487	71	140	30	6	21	102	1
*Conger, Jeff, OF	.289	128	15	37	6	1	1	17	8
Cranford, Jay, 3B	.229	288	30	66	12	1	5	42	3
Edge, Tim, C	.214	126	15	27	5	0	4	19	0
Espinosa, Ramon, OF	.286	489	69	140	28	2	3	48	14
Farrell, Jon, OF	.220	314	34	69	13	0	10	47	3
Kendall, Jason, C	.326	429	87	140	26	1	8	71	10
Krevokuch, Jim, 3B	.282	174	20	49	13	0	1	11	1
*Leary, Rob, 1B	.305	243	38	74	14	3	6	42	3
Munoz, Omer, 2B	.265	234	29	62	10	1	2	25	2
Peterson, Charles, OF	.329	70	13	23	3	1	0	7	2
Rodarte, Raul, 3B	.370	54	8	20	5	1	0	11	2
*Womack, Tony, SS	.256	332	52	85	9	4	1	19	27

PITCHING	W	L	ERA	G	SV	IP	H	BB	SO
*Cooke, Steve	0	0	7.20	1	0	5.0	5	5	4
DeLosSantos, Mariano	1	0	3.62	21	0	27.1	28	14	20
Dessens, Elmer	15	8	2.49	27	0	152.0	170	21	68
Evans, Sean	5	2	5.33	29	0	49.0	47	25	44
Konuszewski, Dennis	7	7	3.65	48	2	61.2	63	26	48
Morel, Ramon	3	3	3.52	10	0	69.0	71	10	34
*Peters, Chris	2	0	1.29	2	0	14.0	9	2	7
Pisciotta, Marc	6	4	4.15	56	9	69.1	60	45	57
Ralph, Curtis	1	1	2.42	18	1	26.0	23	10	17
*Ruebel, Matt	13	5	2.76	27	0	169.1	150	45	136
Ryan, Matt	2	1	1.57	44	26	46.0	33	19	23
Rychel, Kevin	3	2	3.33	40	1	51.1	35	24	60
*Shouse, Brian	7	6	4.47	21	0	114.2	126	19	76
*Tolar, Kevin	1	0	3.65	12	0	12.1	16	7	9
Wilkins, Marc	5	3	3.99	37	0	99.1	91	44	80
Wilson, Gary	0	0	0.00	1	0	4.2	0	3	5

Chattanooga Lookouts (Reds) AA

BATTING	AVG	AB	R	H	2B	3B	HR	RBI	SB
#Arias, Amador, 2B	.222	108	17	24	3	1	0	4	3
*Brown, Adam, C	.266	233	24	62	14	2	5	32	0
*Dismuke, Jamie, 1B	.285	347	56	99	11	0	20	69	0
Hyzdu, Adam, OF	.263	312	55	82	14	1	13	48	3
Kopriva, Dan, 3B	.281	121	14	34	8	0	1	11	1
Kremblas, Frank, 2B	.149	67	8	10	2	0	1	6	1
Ladell, Cleveland, OF	.292	517	76	151	28	7	5	43	28
Rohrmeier, Dan, OF	.326	426	77	139	31	0	17	76	0
Rumfield, Toby, 1B	.264	273	32	72	12	1	8	53	0
Santana, Ruben, 3B	.293	556	89	163	23	10	11	79	2
Sellers, Rick, C	.238	281	40	67	13	3	8	41	2
Watkins, Pat, OF	.291	358	57	104	26	2	12	57	5
Wilson, Brandon, SS	.328	308	56	101	29	1	9	50	12

PITCHING	W	L	ERA	G	SV	IP	H	BB	SO
*Beatty, Blaine	3	2	3.46	8	0	52.0	60	17	34
Brumley, Duff	5	1	1.68	25	1	48.1	31	16	60
Buckley, Travis	1	2	7.53	3	0	14.1	21	5	10
*Burgos, John	3	5	2.78	44	0	100.1	95	19	82
Ferry, Mike	9	5	3.77	24	0	155.0	191	23	74
Fox, Chad	4	5	5.06	20	0	80.0	76	52	56

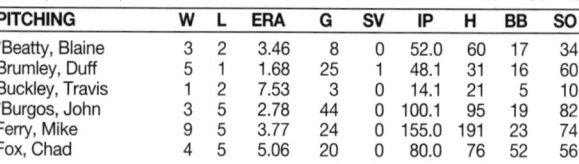

PITCHING	W	L	ERA	G	SV	IP	H	BB	SO
*Kilgo, Rusty	8	2	2.32	54	29	66.0	67	13	61
Kramer, Tommy	12	1	3.33	21	0	127.0	117	28	126
Luebbers, Larry	10	6	4.65	28	0	118.0	112	59	87
Moore, Marcus	6	1	4.98	36	2	43.1	31	34	57
Nix, Jim	3	5	3.20	40	2	84.1	84	30	71
*Tranbarger, Mark	3	1	1.95	48	0	55.1	50	20	46
Vasquez, Marcos	7	6	3.68	26	1	120.0	125	46	80

Greenville Braves (Braves) AA

BATTING	AVG	AB	R	H	2B	3B	HR	RBI	SB
Ayrault, Joe, C	.245	302	27	74	20	0	7	42	2
Dye, Jermaine, OF	.285	403	50	115	26	4	15	71	4
Hollins, Damon, OF	.247	466	64	115	26	2	18	77	6
*Malloy, Marty, 2B	.278	461	73	128	20	3	10	59	11
Nunez, Ramon, 1B	.261	241	34	63	15	2	9	34	1
#Olmeda, Jose, SS	.250	108	16	27	5	1	4	10	1
Ripplemeyer, Brad, C	.182	165	8	30	8	0	2	16	1
Smith, Robert, 3B	.261	444	75	116	27	3	14	58	12
*Sparks, Greg, 1B	.214	145	15	31	6	0	5	21	0
*Swann, Pedro, OF	.324	339	57	110	24	2	11	64	14
*Warner, Mike, OF	.237	173	31	41	12	0	0	7	12
Wollenburg, Doug, 3B	.191	162	22	31	5	0	1	12	4

PITCHING	W	L	ERA	G	SV	IP	H	BB	SO
Arnold, Jamie	1	5	6.35	10	0	56.2	76	25	19
Blair, Dirk	2	2	4.21	40	2	62.0	69	11	38
D'Andrea, Mike	3	6	4.88	40	2	99.2	110	53	61
*Etheridge, Roger	2	10	5.67	32	0	101.2	120	52	47
Hollinger, Adrian	1	4	4.63	7	0	44.2	43	20	28
Hostetler, Mike	10	10	5.26	28	0	162.2	182	46	93
Koller, Jerry	9	12	4.94	25	0	147.2	163	37	84
Paige, Carey	1	4	5.01	7	0	41.1	45	11	26
*Schutz, Carl	3	7	4.94	51	26	58.1	53	36	56
Shafer, Bill	2	2	5.01	42	1	59.1	69	38	44
*Simmons, John	1	5	4.62	48	1	60.1	67	22	54
*Turnier, Aaron	0	1	5.19	8	0	17.1	17	18	16

Huntsville Stars (Athletics) AA

BATTING	AVG	AB	R	H	2B	3B	HR	RBI	SB
Batista, Tony, SS	.255	419	55	107	23	1	16	61	7
Francisco, David, OF	.279	477	75	133	17	1	5	48	30
Gubanich, Creighton, C	.219	274	37	60	7	1	13	43	1
Lesher, Brian, OF	.261	471	78	123	23	2	19	71	7
Molina, Izzy, C	.259	301	38	78	16	1	8	26	3
*Neill, Mike, DH	.299	107	11	32	6	1	2	16	1
Sheldon, Scott, 2B	.217	235	25	51	10	2	4	15	5
Sobolewski, Mark, 2B	.205	307	35	63	14	1	7	34	2
#Spiezio, Scott, 3B	.282	528	78	149	33	8	13	86	10
*Waggoner, Jim, 2B	.200	110	18	22	5	1	0	15	1
*Walker, Dane, DH	.232	370	46	86	13	2	2	35	9
Wolfe, Joel, 1B	.256	399	58	102	15	2	12	41	23

PITCHING	W	L	ERA	G	SV	IP	H	BB	SO
Abbott, Todd	0	0	4.05	4	0	6.2	6	3	4
Banks, Jim	3	2	4.73	44	2	66.2	72	40	52
Bennett, Bob	10	7	4.22	23	0	117.1	119	28	70
Chouinard, Bobby	14	8	3.62	29	0	166.2	155	50	106
Dressendorfer, Kirk	0	1	3.15	9	0	20.0	13	5	18
Fermin, Ramon	6	7	3.86	32	7	100.1	105	45	58
Grigsby, Benji	3	5	4.01	30	3	76.1	66	20	55
Haught, Gary	1	1	4.30	9	0	23.0	23	8	20
Jimenez, Miguel	3	2	3.60	6	0	30.0	25	11	28
Lemke, Steve	4	9	4.38	25	0	125.1	144	29	65
Plaster, Allen	1	0	3.18	43	2	68.0	63	26	47
Rose, Scott	4	6	2.59	38	13	80.0	70	23	35
Shoemaker, Steve	4	4	3.43	43	5	76.0	62	31	63
Waggoner, Jim	0	0	0.00	1	0	2.0	1	0	1
*Zongor, Steve	2	0	7.62	9	0	13.0	13	9	11

(Cont'd from previous page)

SACRIFICE HITS

Player	Club	Lg.	SH
Halter, Shane	Oma	Ama	19
Martinez, R.	Wch	Tex	18
#Soriano, Fred	Wma	Mid	18
Martins, Eric	Mod	Cal	18
*Sbrocco, Jon	Sjo	Cal	17
Jones, Ben	FtM	FSL	16
Rodriguez, V.	KnC	Mid	16
Burton, Essex	Bir	Sou	15
*Sanchez, Yuri	Jax	Sou	15
Soriano, Jose	Wmi	Mid	15
T Medrano, A.	Wil	Car	15

SACRIFICE FLIES

Player	Club	Lg.	SF
Robledo, Nilson	SBn	Mid	16
#Spiezio, Scott	Hvl	Sou	14
Wood, Jason	Edm	PCL	12
T#Barry, Jeff	Bng	East	11
Forbes, P.J.	Van	PCL	10
#Norton, Greg	Bir	Sou	10
#Wilson, E.	Kin	Car	10
*Cox, Steve	MOD	CAL	10
Millar, Kevin	BRE	FSL	10
*Leonard, Mark	PHX	PCL	10

HIT BY PITCH

Player	Club	Lg.	HBP
*Delvecchio, N.	Nrw	East	23
Cooney, Kyle	Vb	FSL	23
Ladjevich, Rick	Riv	CAL	22
Macon, Leland	Chl	FSL	22
T Northeimer, J.	Clw	FSL	22
Millares, Jose	Bow	East	19
T Held, Dan	Rea	East	19
Gibson, Derrick	Ash	SAL	19
Denson, Drew	Ind	Ama	18
T Fasano, Sal	Wch	Tex	17
*Fullmer, Brad	Aby	SAL	17
Hall, Ronnie	Ash	SAL	17
*Dishington, N.	Sav	SAL	17

CAUGHT STEALING

Player	Club	Lg.	CS
T#Metcalfe. Mike	VB	FSL	29
T#Carvajal, J.	Van	PCL	28
Rutz, Ryan	Csc	SAL	26
T Guerrero, W.	Abq	PCL	25
T Almanzar, R.	Fay	SAL	24

Switch-hitter

* Left-handed

T Player has been with more than one team; listed with last team.
(Players in major leagues are listed with last minor league club.)

Batting leaders by position

CATCHER

Player	Club	Lg.	Avg.
*Ibanez, Raul	Riv	Cal	.332
Kendall, Jason	Car	Sou	.326
#Valentin, Jose	FtW	Mid	.324
Sweeney, Mike	Wil	Car	.310
Marzano, John	Oko	Ama	.309

FIRST BASE

Player	Club	Lg.	Avg.
T Pecorilli, Aldo	Rmd	Int	.344
*McGuire, Ryan	Tre	East	.333
Hamlin, Jonas	StK	Cal	.332
T*Grijak, Kevin	Rmd	Int	.324
T*Dodson, Bo	No	Ama	.322

SECOND BASE

Player	Club	Lg.	Avg.
Riggs, Adam	Sbr	Cal	.362
*Mitchell, D.	Qc	Mid	.329
Hajek, Dave	Tcn	PCL	.327
Castillo, Luis	KnC	Mid	.326
Simons, Mitch	SLk	PCL	.325

THIRD BASE

Player	Club	Lg.	Avg.
T Diaz, Lino	Wch	TEX	.328
White, Eric	Clm	SAL	.317
T*Donato, D.	Tam	FSL	.316
*Koskie, Corey	Ftw	Mid	.310
*Williamson, A.	Elp	Tex	.309
Ladjevich, R.	Riv	CA	.309

SHORTSTOP

Player	Club	Lg.	Avg.
T Guerrero, W.	Abq	PCL	.346
Snopek, Chris	Nvl	Ama	.323
*Giovanola, Ed	Rmd	Int	.321
T Larocca, G.	Mem	Sou	.319
Jeter, Derek	Col	Int	.317

OUTFIELD

Player	Club	Lg.	Avg.
T*Coughlin, K.	Bir	Sou	.372
T#McCracken, Q	Csp	PCL	.359
Ingram, R.	SLk	PCL	.348
Damon, J.	Wch	Tex	.343
Perez, Robert	SYR	Int	.343
T Smith, D.	Wmi	Mid	.342

Switch-hitter

* Left-handed

T Player has been with more than one team; listed with last team.

(Players in major leagues are listed with last minor league club.)

Jacksonville Suns (Mariners) AA

BATTING	AVG	AB	R	H	2B	3B	HR	RBI	SB
Barker, Glen, OF	.239	507	74	121	26	4	10	49	39
*Catalanotto, Frank, 2B	.226	491	66	111	19	5	8	48	13
Cooper, Gary, 3B	.276	337	66	93	22	1	18	66	8
*Cruz, Ivan, 1B	.282	397	65	112	17	1	31	93	0
Danapilis, Eric, OF	.258	415	47	107	24	1	10	63	3
Delanuez, Rex, OF	.263	331	47	87	22	1	9	41	10
Fermin, Carlos, SS	.173	127	10	22	4	0	1	9	0
Fernandez, Daniel, C	.165	230	18	38	5	0	4	16	1
Garcia, Luis, SS	.277	47	6	13	0	0	0	5	2
Hansen, Terrel, OF	.223	179	22	40	8	0	9	22	0
*Leiper, Tim, OF	.259	375	60	97	19	1	8	46	3
Mashore, Justin, OF	.243	148	26	36	8	2	4	15	5
*Pevey, Marty, OF	.259	58	2	15	2	0	1	7	0
#Rice, Lance, C	.123	154	8	19	1	1	3	11	0
*Sanchez, Yuri, SS	.213	342	52	73	8	7	6	26	15

PITCHING	W	L	ERA	G	SV	IP	H	BB	SO
*Aldred, Scott	1	0	0.00	2	0	12.0	9	1	11
*Bauer, Matt	1	1	4.12	27	0	43.2	43	22	30
Cedeno, Blas	3	2	3.46	48	0	80.2	71	36	53
Drumright, Mike	0	1	3.69	5	0	31.2	30	15	34
Goldsmith, Gary	4	7	4.61	15	0	82.0	78	31	42
Greene, Rick	6	2	3.49	32	0	38.2	45	15	29
*Guilfoyle, Michael	5	1	2.88	56	3	59.1	55	31	50
Gutierrez, Jim	8	4	2.76	45	4	58.2	60	25	36
Kelly, John	7	7	2.09	66	29	77.1	76	21	47
*Miller, Trever	8	2	2.72	31	0	122.1	122	34	77
Moehler, Brian	8	10	4.82	28	0	162.1	176	52	89
*Thompson, Justin	6	7	3.73	18	0	123.0	110	38	98
*Whiteside, Sean	2	0	3.78	27	0	33.1	34	20	17
Withem, Shannon	5	8	5.75	19	0	108.0	142	24	80

Knoxville Smokies (Blue Jays) AA

BATTING	AVG	AB	R	H	2B	3B	HR	RBI	SB
Adriana, Sharnol, SS	.284	261	33	74	17	1	3	33	12
*Boston, D.J., 1B	.244	479	51	117	27	1	11	71	12
*Butler, Rich, OF	.267	217	27	58	12	3	4	33	11
Coolbaugh, Mike, 3B	.240	500	71	120	32	2	9	56	7
DeLaCruz, Lorenzo, OF	.274	508	63	139	20	12	8	61	11
*Harmes, Kris, C	.228	259	28	59	14	2	4	29	0
Henry, Santiago, 2B	.220	454	47	100	25	4	2	30	16
Johnson, Matt, 2B	.181	144	8	26	4	0	0	11	1
Kelly, Pat, SS	.242	161	22	39	6	1	2	14	1
Ladd, Jeff, C	.292	24	1	7	1	1	0	2	0
Lutz, Brent, C	.132	144	14	19	6	0	2	12	4
#Roberts, Lonell, OF	.236	454	66	107	12	3	1	29	57
#Sawkiw, Warren, DH	.248	121	11	30	4	1	1	11	2
Stewart, Shannon, OF	.287	498	89	143	24	6	5	55	42

PITCHING	W	L	ERA	G	SV	IP	H	BB	SO
Almanzar, Carlos	3	12	3.99	35	2	126.1	144	32	93
Beltran, Alonso	3	6	5.69	28	1	87.0	111	32	54
Brandow, Derek	5	6	4.29	25	1	107.0	95	50	106
Carpenter, Chris	3	7	5.18	12	0	64.1	71	31	53
Freeman, Chris	2	3	5.42	39	8	81.1	78	38	80
*Gray, Dennis	0	3	6.34	24	0	32.2	29	20	22
Heble, Kurt	3	7	6.02	47	6	52.1	52	24	44
Janzen, Marty	5	1	2.63	7	0	48.0	35	14	44
Kotes, Chris	3	9	4.91	36	1	106.1	109	45	74
*Pace, Scott	6	8	4.57	18	0	102.1	117	48	71
Pett, Jose	8	9	4.26	26	0	141.2	132	48	89
Silva, Jose	0	0	9.00	3	0	2.0	3	6	2

Memphis Chicks (Royals) AA

BATTING	AVG	AB	R	H	2B	3B	HR	RBI	SB
Alvarez, Gabe, 2B	.556	9	0	5	1	0	0	4	0
Briggs, Stoney, OF	.247	385	60	95	14	7	8	46	17
Bruno, Julio, 3B	.270	196	16	53	6	3	2	25	3
Bush, Homer, 2B	.280	432	53	121	12	5	5	37	34

366

BATTING	AVG	AB	R	H	2B	3B	HR	RBI	SB
Casanova, Raul, C	.271	306	42	83	18	0	12	44	4
*Cotton, John, OF	.253	407	60	103	19	8	12	47	15
DeLeon, Roberto, SS	.267	236	24	63	10	0	7	34	2
Drinkwater, Sean, 3B	.240	287	29	69	12	1	6	26	3
*Gennaro, Brad, OF	.267	397	46	106	19	1	5	60	11
#Harley, Quentin, 2B	.245	159	21	39	5	3	3	14	7
#Johnson, Earl, OF	.200	10	0	2	0	0	0	0	0
*Killeen, Tim, C	.235	230	27	54	14	0	9	40	2
LaRocca, Greg, SS	.143	7	0	1	0	0	0	0	0
Lee, Derrek, 1B	.111	9	0	1	0	0	0	1	0
*Mack, Quinn, OF	.238	63	6	15	1	0	2	6	2
Schwenke, Matt, C	.242	62	7	15	3	0	0	4	0
#Thomas, Keith, OF	.253	356	66	90	13	4	10	33	43
*Thompson, Jason, 1B	.272	475	62	129	20	1	20	64	7

PITCHING	W	L	ERA	G	SV	IP	H	BB	SO
*Beckett, Robbie	3	4	4.80	36	0	86.1	65	73	98
Clark, Dera	2	2	2.39	23	5	26.1	18	14	29
Cole, Victor	1	0	1.35	8	0	20.0	15	8	17
DeLeon, Roberto	0	0	7.71	2	0	2.1	3	2	3
Freitas, Mike	0	6	3.66	54	2	59.0	55	26	36
*Harrison, Brian	2	1	3.25	38	0	36.0	32	33	29
Hernandez, Fernando	4	6	5.16	12	0	66.1	72	42	74
Kaufman, Brad	11	10	5.76	27	0	148.1	142	90	119
Kroon, Marc	7	5	3.51	22	2	115.1	90	61	123
*Long, Joey	0	2	3.32	25	0	21.2	28	10	18
Mattson, Rob	12	13	4.11	30	0	201.2	199	73	139
*Murray, Heath	5	4	3.38	14	0	77.1	83	42	71
*Plantenberg, Erik	2	0	1.66	20	2	21.2	19	2	16
Thomas, Carlos	1	1	10.13	11	0	13.1	15	14	12
Veras, Dario	7	3	3.81	58	1	82.2	81	27	70

Orlando Cubs (Cubs) AA

BATTING	AVG	AB	R	H	2B	3B	HR	RBI	SB
*Brown, Brant, 1B	.271	446	67	121	27	4	6	53	8
#Burton, Darren, OF	.306	222	40	68	16	2	4	21	7
#Coleman, Ken, 2B	.277	394	82	109	19	3	4	37	25
Erdman, Brad, C	.111	36	4	4	0	0	0	0	0
Gomez, Rudy, 2B	.192	214	18	41	11	1	1	16	0
*Jennings, Robin, OF	.296	490	71	145	27	7	17	79	7
Johnson, Jack, C	.221	68	3	15	0	0	0	4	1
#Kingston, Mark, 3B	.266	199	17	53	13	0	5	24	0
Larregui, Ed, OF	.300	423	55	127	18	1	11	60	3
#Manahan, Austin, OF	.212	260	34	55	12	0	3	19	13
Ortiz, Hector, C	.234	299	13	70	12	0	0	18	0
Petersen, Chris, SS	.212	382	48	81	10	3	4	36	7
*Valdes, Pedro, OF	.300	426	57	128	28	3	7	68	3

PITCHING	W	L	ERA	G	SV	IP	H	BB	SO
Burlingame, Ben	9	2	3.53	37	1	97.0	93	38	73
Connolly, Matt	3	4	4.08	21	2	39.2	34	11	43
*Dabney, Fred	2	1	2.08	13	1	17.1	13	10	9
Harrah, Doug	5	2	1.94	44	5	69.2	58	34	49
Hart, Jason	0	1	2.12	14	3	17.0	14	4	20
Hutcheson, David	8	10	4.01	28	0	168.1	178	45	103
Johnson, Chris	5	4	3.45	46	5	70.1	68	24	49
Petersen, Matt	3	9	5.87	24	0	89.0	107	39	59
Ratliff, Jon	10	5	3.47	26	0	140.0	143	42	94
*Rivera, Roberto	6	2	2.38	49	6	68.0	50	11	34
Telemaco, Amaury	8	8	3.29	22	0	147.2	112	42	151

Port City Roosters (Mariners) AA

BATTING	AVG	AB	R	H	2B	3B	HR	RBI	SB
Adams, Tommy, OF	.220	118	10	26	7	0	3	16	5
Bonnici, James, 1B	.283	508	75	144	36	3	20	91	2
Cardenas, John, C	.226	195	17	44	9	0	0	17	1
#Cora, Manny, 2B	.226	261	17	59	8	3	0	15	1
Diaz, Eddy, SS	.261	421	66	110	22	0	16	47	6
Gipson, Charles, OF	.223	391	36	87	11	2	0	29	10
Griffey, Craig, OF	.177	299	43	53	11	1	0	24	13
#Hickey, Mike, 3B	.262	447	59	117	24	1	6	59	6
*Rackley, Keifer, OF	.256	430	55	110	17	2	6	40	8

Pitching leaders across all leagues

ERA
(MINIMUM 112 LP)

Player	Club	Lg.	ERA
*Rusch, G.	Wil	Car	1.74
T Pincavitch, K.	Sbr	Cal	1.74
T Rekar, Bryan	Csp	PCL	1.89
Colon, Bartolo	Kin	Car	1.96
T Coppinger, R.	Roc	Int	1.97
T Isringhausen, J.	Nor	Int	1.97
T*Kusiewicz, M.	Ash	SAL	2.03
*Byrdak, Tim	Wil	Car	2.16
Bowers, Shane	FtM	FSL	2.16
*Price, Tom	Sbr	Cal	2.20
Schmidt, Jason	Rmd	Int	2.25
Drews, Matthew	Tam	FSL	2.27
Corrigan, Cory	Peo	Mid	2.32
SEVERAL TIED AT 2.33			

WINS

Player	Club	Lg.	Wins
T Hunter, Rich	Rea	East	19
Roa, Joe	Buf	Ama	17
Wall, Donne	Tcn	PCL	17
T Coppinger, R.	Roc	Int	16
*Beaumont, M.	Lke	Cal	16
T Janzen, Marty	Knx	Sou	16
*Mounce, Tony	Qc	Mid	16
T*Rath, Gary	Abq	PCL	16
T*Fordham, T.	Bir	Sou	15
T Kramer, T.	Cng	Sou	15
Drews, Matthew	Tam	FSL	15
T Grace, Mike	Swb	Int	15
T Crowther, B.	Cso	PCL	15
Dessens, Elmer	Car	Sou	15
SEVERAL TIED AT 14			

COMPLETE GAMES

Player	Club	Lg.	CG
Mattson, Rob	Mem	Sou	11
Dickson, Jason	Cr	Mid	9
T Wilson, Paul	Nor	Int	8
Harriger, Denny	Lvg	PCL	7
T Sodowsky, C.	Tol	Int	6
Steenstra, K.	Iwa	Ama	6
T Falteisek, S.	Ott	Int	6
T Cosman, Jeff	Bng	East	6
Endo, Masataka	Vis	Cal	6
T Crowther, B.	Csp	PCL	6
SEVERAL TIED AT 5			

Switch-hitter
* Left-handed
T Player has been with more than one team; listed with last team.
(Players in major leagues are listed with last minor league club.)

367

Pitching leaders across all leagues

(Cont'd from previous page)

SHUTOUTS

Player	Club	Lg.	ShO
T Crowther, B.	Csp	PCL	4
T Coppinger, R.	Roc	Int	3
T Sexton, Jeff	Kin	Car	3
T Sodowsky, C.	Tol	Int	3
Mattson, Rob	Mem	Sou	3
T Isringhausen, J.	Nor	Int	3
T Guerra, Mark	Bng	East	3
T Wilson, Paul	Nor	Int	3
T Tranberg, M.	Swb	Int	3
*Ruebel, Matt	Car	Sou	3
T*Peters, Chris	Car	Sou	3
SEVERAL TIED AT 2			

SAVES

Player	Club	Lg.	Sv
Reed, Brandon	Fay	SAL	41
Montgomery, S.	Ark	Tex	36
T Jacobsen, Joe	Sbr	Cal	34
Castillo, Carlos	Lke	Cal	32
T Montoya, W.	Clm	SAL	31
T Graves, Daniel	Buf	Ama	31
Welch, Travis	Peo	Mid	31
T Webb, Doug	ElP	Tex	30
Matulevich, Jeff	StP	FSL	30
T*Kilgo, Rusty	Cng	Sou	29
Kelly, John	Jax	Sou	29
Freehill, Michael	Cr	Mid	28
Stumpf, Brian	Pdt	SAL	28
SEVERAL TIED AT 27			

GAMES

Player	Club	Lg.	G
Ricci, Chuck	Swb	Int	68
Kelly, John	Jax	Sou	66
Golden, M.	Sav	SAL	64
Reed, Brian	Peo	Mid	63
T Lemp, Chris	Bow	East	62
T Bennett, S.	Tre	East	62
T Trlicek, Rick	Can	East	62
SEVERAL TIED AT 60			

Switch-hitter
* Left-handed
T Player has been with more than one team; listed with last team.
(Players in major leagues are listed with last minor league club.)

BATTING	AVG	AB	R	H	2B	3B	HR	RBI	SB
Ramirez, Roberto, OF	.278	490	67	136	24	6	17	82	11
Saunders, Doug, 3B	.263	114	13	30	9	1	4	16	2
#Varitek, Jason, C	.224	352	42	79	14	2	10	44	0

PITCHING	W	L	ERA	G	SV	IP	H	BB	SO
Adam, Dave	6	10	4.34	31	0	112.0	107	48	85
Apana, Matt	1	3	4.32	6	0	33.1	34	24	28
*Fernandez, Osvaldo	12	7	3.57	27	0	156.1	139	60	160
*Fitzer, Doug	0	0	5.40	4	0	5.0	3	1	4
Franklin, Ryan	6	10	4.32	31	0	146.0	153	43	102
Glinatsis, George	6	7	5.30	18	0	93.1	104	44	68
*King, Kevin	1	2	3.77	20	0	31.0	35	11	19
Lowe, Derek	1	6	6.08	10	0	53.1	70	22	30
Nickell, Jackie	5	8	3.73	27	0	89.1	74	30	81
Russell, Lagrande	4	3	3.24	39	1	72.1	68	43	54
*Tsamis, George	0	0	2.61	7	0	10.1	11	11	3
*Urso, Sal	2	0	2.17	51	1	45.2	41	21	44
Witte, Trey	3	2	1.73	48	11	62.1	48	14	39

Texas League

Arkansas Travelers (Cardinals) AA

BATTING	AVG	AB	R	H	2B	3B	HR	RBI	SB
Anderson, Charlie, 3B	.283	240	31	68	15	2	4	29	1
Berblinger, Jeff, 2B	.319	332	66	106	15	4	5	29	16
*Bethea, Scott, SS	.176	34	6	6	1	0	0	4	1
Cholowsky, Dan, 1B	.311	190	41	59	12	0	7	35	7
Christopher, Chris, OF	.274	62	7	17	1	0	1	3	4
Difelice, Mike, C	.267	176	14	47	10	1	1	24	0
#Diggs, Tony, OF	.268	235	33	63	9	8	2	21	7
*Ellis, Paul, C	.227	229	17	52	6	0	2	25	0
#Griffin, Ty, 2B	.274	263	38	72	16	1	9	44	17
Gulan, Mike, 3B	.314	242	47	76	13	3	12	48	4
Johns, Keith, SS	.280	396	69	111	13	2	2	28	14
*Jones, Keith, PH	.226	84	11	19	2	0	0	4	3
*Lewis, Anthony, OF	.251	407	55	102	21	3	24	85	0
McEwing, Joe, OF	.248	121	16	30	4	0	2	12	3
Norton, Chris, 1B	.240	25	6	6	2	0	0	6	0
Pimentel, Wander, SS	.000	2	0	0	0	0	0	0	0
*Radziewicz, Doug, 1B	.233	116	15	27	5	0	1	13	0
Rupp, Brian, 1B	.325	77	10	25	3	0	0	6	0
Silvia, Brian, C	.241	29	4	7	1	0	0	3	0
Torres, Paul, 1B	.225	231	24	52	11	0	10	33	2
#Velez, Jose, OF	.296	287	37	85	13	1	7	41	5
Warner, Ron, SS	.245	98	9	24	3	0	0	8	0
#Young, Dmitri, OF	.292	367	54	107	18	6	10	62	2

PITCHING	W	L	ERA	G	SV	IP	H	BB	SO
*Alkire, Jeff	0	0	3.00	2	0	3.0	4	0	2
Anderson, Paul	1	0	3.26	38	0	58.0	60	11	31
Arrandale, Matt	3	5	3.28	47	2	68.2	72	22	28
Badorek, Mike	7	5	4.35	18	1	101.1	119	30	50
Busby, Mike	7	6	3.29	20	0	134.0	125	35	95
Carpenter, Brian	2	1	4.96	17	0	52.2	57	21	35
*Corona, John	1	1	7.20	5	0	5.0	7	6	3
*Creek, Doug	4	2	2.88	26	1	34.1	24	16	50
Davis, Ray	7	6	4.50	21	0	110.0	112	30	70
*Long, Tony	4	4	3.74	32	0	55.1	58	14	35
Lowe, Sean	9	8	4.88	24	0	129.0	143	64	77
Martinez, Francisco	1	1	1.29	11	1	21.0	10	7	13
Matranga, Jeff	0	0	0.00	7	0	8.0	1	3	4
*Mesewicz, Mark	0	1	6.75	5	0	9.1	13	1	7
Montgomery, Steve	5	2	3.25	55	36	61.0	52	22	56
*Oehrlein, Dave	4	7	4.87	23	0	77.2	80	28	52
*Osborne, Donovan	0	1	2.45	2	0	11.0	12	2	6
*Simmons, Scott	11	9	3.43	22	0	139.0	145	28	73
*Wagner, Bret	1	2	3.19	6	0	36.2	34	18	31
*Watson, Allen	1	0	0.00	1	0	5.0	4	0	7
Witasick, Jay	2	4	6.88	7	0	34.0	46	16	26

El Paso Diablos (Brewers) AA

BATTING	AVG	AB	R	H	2B	3B	HR	RBI	SB
#Banks, Brian, OF	.308	441	81	136	39	10	12	78	9
*Dodson, Bo, DH	.359	223	46	80	20	4	7	43	1
Dumas, Mike, 2B	.217	23	5	5	0	1	0	4	2
Felder, Ken, OF	.272	367	51	100	24	4	12	55	2
Felix, Lauro, SS	.277	220	51	61	13	1	3	25	6
#Guerrero, Mike, SS	.310	71	14	22	1	0	1	7	0
*Harris, Mike, DH	.333	24	4	8	2	0	1	5	0
Hughes, Bobby, C	.266	173	11	46	12	0	7	27	0
*Jenkins, Geoff, OF	.278	79	12	22	4	2	1	13	3
Kappesser, Bob, C	.191	115	17	22	5	2	1	17	2
Landry, Todd, 1B	.292	511	76	149	33	4	16	79	9
Lopez, Pedro, C	.312	218	32	68	15	2	4	28	0
#Lopez, Roberto, 2B	.312	417	80	130	22	8	1	44	9
Martinez, Gabby, SS	.278	133	13	37	3	2	0	11	5
#Millan, Bernie, PH	.242	33	2	8	1	0	1	3	0
Nevers, Tom, 3B	.254	118	19	30	5	0	1	12	2
Nicholas, Darrell, OF	.205	39	4	8	0	1	0	2	4
*Nilsson, Dave, OF	.467	15	1	7	1	0	1	4	1
Odor, Rouglas, SS	.294	17	2	5	0	0	0	2	0
Perez, Danny, DH	.276	76	16	21	1	1	0	7	1
Richardson, Scott, OF	.254	256	29	65	9	6	1	29	8
Rodriques, Cecil, OF	.266	244	36	65	9	7	2	24	5
Samples, Todd, OF	.000	4	1	0	0	0	0	0	0
Shabazz, Basil, OF	.216	102	19	22	2	3	0	7	8
Stefanski, Mike, 3B	.407	27	5	11	3	0	1	6	1
Sutko, Glenn, C	.277	119	18	33	9	1	4	20	1
Talanoa, Scott, DH	.222	9	0	2	2	0	0	1	0
*Thompson, F., 2B	.192	26	3	5	0	0	0	3	0
Weger, Wes, SS	.256	160	22	41	9	2	0	19	1
*Williamson, Antone, 3B	.309	392	62	121	30	6	7	90	3

PITCHING	W	L	ERA	G	SV	IP	H	BB	SO
Archer, Kurt	0	0	3.00	4	1	6.0	4	1	5
Browne, Byron	10	4	3.43	25	0	126.0	106	78	110
*Caruso, Gene	2	1	6.08	46	2	71.0	87	36	53
Cimorelli, Frank	0	0	4.50	2	0	2.0	1	2	0
Cole, Jim	1	4	8.75	6	0	23.2	42	11	14
Duda, Steve	1	3	4.87	24	1	44.1	58	16	29
Gamez, Francisco	2	1	5.29	27	2	68.0	79	39	32
Ganote, Joe	5	1	1.61	12	1	50.1	40	16	39
*Gerstein, Ron	8	12	4.55	28	1	126.2	155	58	69
Guerrero, Mike	0	0	3.38	2	0	2.2	3	0	0
Jones, Stacy	1	1	2.03	8	3	13.1	12	4	14
Kappesser, Bob	0	0	9.28	8	0	10.2	18	5	2
Kloek, Kevin	7	11	4.93	28	0	157.0	196	48	121
Kosenski, John	3	1	5.72	16	0	28.1	41	17	25
*Langbehn, Gregg	2	1	5.24	16	0	22.1	19	12	20
Lidle, Cory	5	4	3.36	45	2	109.2	126	36	78
Linares, Yfrain	1	1	9.45	8	0	13.1	21	12	9
Maloney, Sean	7	5	4.18	43	15	64.2	69	28	54
*Montoya, Norm	2	5	3.42	51	2	76.1	88	18	43
Popplewell, Tom	0	0	15.00	4	0	3.0	7	6	1
Rodriguez, Frankie	9	8	4.98	28	0	142.2	157	80	129
Wagner, Joe	0	4	9.95	5	0	19.0	32	22	8
Webb, Doug	2	1	4.42	18	8	18.1	11	13	11

Jackson Generals (Astros) AA

BATTING	AVG	AB	R	H	2B	3B	HR	RBI	SB
Bagwell, Jeff, 1B	.167	12	0	2	0	0	0	0	0
*Bridges, Kary, 2B	.301	418	56	126	22	4	3	43	10
#Centeno, Henri, 2B	.256	172	24	44	3	1	2	12	6
Chavez, Raul, C	.287	188	16	54	8	0	4	25	0
*Colon, Dennis, 1B	.225	378	33	85	10	0	5	31	3
*Donnels, Chris, 3B	.167	12	1	2	1	0	0	1	0
*Forkner, Tim, 3B	.269	119	19	32	11	0	3	23	1
Gilmore, Tony, OF	.214	145	10	31	3	0	1	15	0
Groppuso, Mike, 3B	.215	79	5	17	3	1	1	5	2
Hatcher, Chris, OF	.308	39	5	12	1	0	1	3	0
Hidalgo, Richard, OF	.266	489	59	130	28	6	14	59	8
Hunter, Brian, OF	.500	6	1	3	0	0	0	0	0
Johnson, Russ, SS	.248	476	65	118	16	2	9	53	10

(Cont'd from previous page)

INNINGS PITCHED

Player	Club	Lg.	IP
Mattson, Rob	Mem	Sou	201.2
T Ricken, Ray	Nrw	East	193.0
T Guerra, Mark	Bng	East	192.2
T Falteisek, S.	Ott	Int	191.0
T Coppinger, R.	Roc	Int	187.0
*Orellano, R.	Tre	East	186.2
T Wilson, Paul	Nor	Int	186.2
Endo, Masataka	Vis	Cal	186.2
*Ilsley, Blaise	Swb	Int	185.1
Farrell, John	Buf	Ama	184.1
T Hunter, Rich	Rea	East	184.1
T Sodowsky, C.	Tol	Int	183.2
T Crowther, B.	Csp	PCL	183.0
Drews, Matthew	Tam	FSL	182.0
*Ebert, Derrin	Mac	SAL	182.0

STRIKEOUTS

Player	Club	Lg.	SO
T Wilson, Paul	Nor	Int	194
T Ricken, Ray	Nrw	East	178
Endo, Masataka	Vis	Cal	178
*Moss, Damian	Mac	SAL	177
*Sanchez, J.	Clb	SAL	177
T Coppinger, R.	Roc	Int	172
Foulke, Keith	Sjo	Cal	168
T Santana, M.	Riv	Cal	167
Smith, Cam	Fay	SAL	166
T*Whiteman, G.	Fay	SAL	165
T Janzen, Marty	Knx	Sou	164
T Herbert, R.	Sbn	Mid	163
*Orellano, R.	Tre	East	160
*Fernandez, O.	Pcy	Sou	160

SEVERAL TIED AT 157

369

 # Switch-hitter
* Left-handed
T Player has been with more than one team; listed with last team.
(Players in major leagues are listed with last minor league club.)

Player of the Year

Todd Greene, C
California Angels

The Angels' top power prospect, catcher Todd Greene, was *Baseball Weekly*'s 1995 Minor League Player of the Year. He was the first minor leaguer in 10 years to hit 40 homers. Only one other AA or AAA player hit more than 30—Jacksonville's Ivan Cruz, with 31. Greene split his season between AA Midland and AAA Vancouver—between the two stops he hit .300 and drove in 92 runs, all while he was making the transition to catcher. "All those numbers he's put up have been while he's been learning the hardest, most physically demanding position there is," said Ken Forsch, the Angels' director of player development. "To me, that's someone who's got some real drive, ambition and toughness." Greene was drafted as an outfielder in 1993, but the Angels needed a catcher, so he switched positions in '94. "He really struggled at first, but he kept going out there and going out there and taking his bruises," Forsch said. "He's a gamer."

BATTING	AVG	AB	R	H	2B	3B	HR	RBI	SB
#Kellner, Frank, 1B	.316	269	31	85	15	1	0	29	1
Luce, Roger, C	.212	52	4	11	2	1	1	4	0
*McNabb, Buck, OF	.260	50	4	13	1	0	0	3	1
#Mitchell, Tony, OF	.266	331	45	88	17	2	19	61	1
Montgomery, Ray, OF	.299	127	24	38	8	1	10	24	6
Mora, Melvin, OF	.298	467	63	139	32	0	3	45	22
Probst, Alan, C	.236	89	11	21	5	0	1	8	0
Verduzco, Steven, PH	.241	29	4	7	3	0	1	1	0
Wesson, Barry, OF	.667	3	2	2	0	1	0	1	0
#White, Chad, OF	.273	77	11	21	4	0	0	3	2
*White, Jimmy, PH	.000	1	1	0	0	0	0	0	0
*Wilkins, Rick, C	.000	11	0	0	0	0	0	0	0

PITCHING	W	L	ERA	G	SV	IP	H	BB	SO
Allen, Ron	2	0	5.91	4	0	10.2	13	5	3
Castillo, Juan	4	4	4.01	12	0	67.1	68	27	38
Creek, Ryan	9	7	3.63	26	0	143.2	137	64	120
Duey, Kyle	0	2	5.40	7	2	6.2	11	2	4
Evans, Dave	2	9	3.33	49	18	67.2	50	28	54
Gallaher, Kevin	2	2	3.40	6	0	42.1	31	23	28
Grzanich, Mike	5	3	2.74	50	8	65.2	55	38	44
*Hingle, Larry	0	2	11.12	9	0	11.1	11	15	5
Holt, Chris	2	2	1.67	5	0	32.1	27	5	24
Humphrey, Rich	1	1	1.69	9	0	16.0	11	9	9
Kellner, Frank	0	0	4.50	1	0	2.0	3	1	1
Ketchen, Doug	3	3	3.59	15	1	52.2	55	15	45
*Lister, Martin	4	3	4.00	15	0	69.2	80	24	27
*Mercado, Hector	1	4	7.80	8	0	30.0	36	32	20
Mlicki, Doug	8	3	2.79	16	0	96.2	73	33	72
Narcisse, Tyrone	5	14	3.24	27	0	163.2	140	60	93
Sepeda, Jaime	0	1	9.00	1	0	4.0	7	2	1
*Wagner, Billy	2	2	2.57	12	0	70.0	49	36	77
*Waldron, Joe	1	2	3.71	28	2	51.0	57	11	39
*Walker, Jamie	4	2	4.50	50	2	58.0	59	24	38
Waring, Jim	1	4	8.01	17	2	51.2	77	15	27
White, Jim	6	3	5.09	38	0	70.2	71	24	45

Midland Angels (Angels) AA

BATTING	AVG	AB	R	H	2B	3B	HR	RBI	SB
Arias, George, 3B	.279	520	91	145	19	10	30	104	3
Boykin, Tyrone, OF	.271	210	34	57	11	3	7	25	2
Carpenter, Jerry, PH	.000	2	1	0	0	0	0	0	0
#Carvajal, Jovino, OF	.313	348	58	109	13	5	2	23	39
*Cohick, Emmitt, OF	.229	153	25	35	13	2	2	23	3
Daniels, Moe, OF	.202	84	9	17	5	0	1	4	2
#Diaz, Alfredo, SS	.240	25	3	6	3	0	0	4	0
*Glenn, Leon, 1B	.254	433	68	110	19	11	17	65	16
Gonzales, Rene, 2B	.176	17	1	3	0	0	0	2	0
Greene, Todd, C	.327	318	59	104	19	1	26	57	3
Guerrero, Pedro, DH	.302	252	40	76	13	0	7	40	0
#Harkrider, Timothy, SS	.291	460	66	134	22	4	2	39	3
Hosey, Steve, OF	.239	88	16	21	4	0	2	16	5
Monzon, Jose, C	.289	180	29	52	11	1	1	19	0
#Munoz, Orlando, 2B	.314	309	39	97	19	4	1	44	9
Ortiz, Bo, OF	.275	360	48	99	10	3	8	56	12
Ramirez, J.D., 2B	.271	251	34	68	16	1	10	36	1
Raven, Luis, OF	.267	86	9	23	2	1	5	15	1
Redington, Tom, 1B	.250	32	5	8	2	0	0	3	0
*Takayoshi, Todd, C	.278	18	2	5	0	1	0	0	1
Tejero, Fausto, C	.226	53	7	12	3	0	1	11	0
Urso, Joe, 2B	.324	37	6	12	3	0	0	4	0
Wolff, Mike, OF	.303	445	76	135	28	3	14	70	10

PITCHING	W	L	ERA	G	SV	IP	H	BB	SO
Akerfelds, Darrel	3	1	3.44	29	0	55.0	46	26	16
Blyleven, Todd	3	1	5.02	8	0	14.1	13	3	8
Bonanno, Rob	1	1	9.45	3	0	13.1	24	6	6
Brown, Willard	9	10	5.18	27	0	147.2	188	47	81
*Butler, Mike	1	1	4.50	19	0	24.0	24	9	14
Chavez, Tony	0	1	8.00	7	2	9.0	13	1	4
Edsell, Geoff	2	3	5.91	5	0	32.0	39	16	19
Hancock, Ryan	12	9	4.56	28	0	175.2	222	45	79
*Harris, Bryan	6	5	4.94	39	0	78.1	105	32	60
Holdridge, David	1	0	1.78	14	1	25.1	20	8	23

PITCHING	W	L	ERA	G	SV	IP	H	BB	SO
Keling, Korey	8	5	3.46	29	1	122.1	113	52	101
Mack, Tony	0	0	0.00	3	0	5.2	3	1	5
Nieves, Ernesto	0	1	4.05	6	0	13.1	15	10	3
Pricher, John	0	0	4.50	8	1	10.0	16	6	7
Ratekin, Mark	0	0	5.94	11	0	16.2	19	3	11
Renko, Steve	3	5	4.81	22	1	76.2	100	28	44
Schmidt, Jeff	4	12	5.83	20	0	100.1	127	48	46
Schooler, Mike	3	3	1.79	54	20	65.1	49	19	55
Sebach, Kyle	1	2	10.31	5	0	18.1	31	12	7
Snyder, John	8	9	5.74	21	0	133.1	158	48	81
Thibert, John	0	0	4.18	12	2	23.2	19	17	15
*VanRyn, Ben	1	1	2.78	19	1	32.1	33	12	24
Watson, Ron	0	0	4.91	3	0	3.2	2	6	3

San Antonio Missions (Dodgers) AA

BATTING	AVG	AB	R	H	2B	3B	HR	RBI	SB
Blanco, Henry, 3B	.255	302	37	77	18	4	12	48	1
#Butterfield, Chris, DH	.000	6	0	0	0	0	0	0	0
Cairo, Miguel, 2B	.278	435	53	121	20	1	1	41	33
Dandridge, Brad, C	.417	12	1	5	0	0	0	1	0
Guerrero, Wilton, SS	.348	382	53	133	13	6	0	26	21
Jaime, Angel, SS	.364	22	5	8	0	0	1	2	2
Landrum, Tito, OF	.238	260	42	62	13	1	8	25	5
#Latham, Chris, OF	.299	214	38	64	14	5	9	37	11
Loduca, Paul, C	.246	199	27	49	8	0	1	8	5
Luzinski, Ryan, C	.229	144	18	33	5	0	1	9	1
Maness, Dwight, OF	.223	179	29	40	2	3	5	24	4
*Marrero, Oreste, DH	.258	445	60	115	25	3	21	86	5
*Martin, Jim, OF	.235	327	43	77	20	3	4	36	18
*Melendez, Dan, 1B	.261	464	46	121	28	1	7	59	0
#Metcalfe, Mike, SS	.244	41	10	10	1	0	0	2	1
Otanez, Willis, 3B	.240	100	8	24	4	1	1	7	0
*Puchales, Javier, OF	.228	57	4	13	1	0	0	1	0
Rios, Eddie, 2B	.285	365	43	104	22	4	5	53	2
Romero, Willie, OF	.266	376	46	100	20	1	7	44	10
Steed, Dave, C	.252	123	13	31	10	1	3	16	0
*Yard, Bruce, SS	.359	39	7	14	3	0	0	4	0

PITCHING	W	L	ERA	G	SV	IP	H	BB	SO
*Brosnan, Jason	1	0	3.57	19	2	22.2	24	4	21
*Brunson, William	4	5	4.95	14	0	80.0	105	22	44
Camacho, Dan	1	1	1.59	11	2	11.1	9	8	8
Castro, Nelson	5	7	5.20	48	3	81.1	98	30	51
Correa, Ramser	1	4	4.53	42	17	49.2	54	21	34
*Cummings, John	0	2	3.95	6	0	27.1	28	7	13
Garcia, Jose	2	6	4.03	38	2	58.0	50	24	36
Herges, Matt	0	3	4.88	19	8	27.2	34	16	18
Hubbs, Dan	2	1	3.54	31	0	61.0	58	16	52
*Martinez, Jesus	6	9	3.54	24	0	139.2	129	71	83
*Oropesa, Eddie	1	1	3.12	16	1	17.1	22	12	16
Prado, Jose	7	11	3.48	28	1	144.2	126	64	93
*Pyc, Dave	12	6	3.38	26	0	157.0	170	49	78
*Rath, Gary	13	3	2.77	18	0	117.0	96	48	81
Troutman, Keith	1	2	3.15	38	2	65.2	64	18	50
Weaver, Eric	8	11	4.07	27	0	141.2	147	72	105

Shreveport Captains (Giants) AA

BATTING	AVG	AB	R	H	2B	3B	HR	RBI	SB
*Alguacil, Jose, SS	.250	4	1	1	0	0	0	1	1
Aurilia, Rich, SS	.327	226	29	74	17	1	4	42	10
Canizaro, Jay, 2B	.293	440	83	129	25	7	12	60	16
*Cruz, Jacob, OF	.297	458	88	136	33	1	13	77	9
Ehmann, Kurt, SS	.231	130	24	30	5	0	1	17	1
Florez, Tim, 3B	.268	295	37	79	11	2	9	46	4
Jenkins, Bernie, OF	.167	12	1	2	0	0	1	1	0
#Jensen, Marcus, C	.283	321	55	91	22	8	4	45	0
*Mayes, Craig, C	.222	9	0	2	1	0	0	3	0
*McFarlin, Jason, OF	.337	252	39	85	13	2	6	37	8
Miller, Roger, OF	.274	62	11	17	6	0	2	10	0
Mirabelli, Doug, C	.302	126	14	38	13	0	0	16	1
*Morrow, Chris, OF	.246	240	31	59	17	0	7	35	1
#Mueller, Bill, 3B	.309	330	56	102	16	2	1	39	6

Baseball Weekly's Top 10 Minor League Players

Here are the top 10 runners-up for 1995 Minor League Player of the Year in alphabetical order:

Bartolo Colon, SP
Cleveland Indians

Bartolo Colon, 20, was Carolina League Pitcher of the Year after missing the last few weeks and still finishing just one win short of the league leader. He was 13-3 with a 1.96 ERA and led the loop with 152 strikeouts in 129 innings. He signed with the Indians as a free agent in June 1993 from the Dominican Republic. In two years, opponents have hit just .198 against him.

Entire AAA outfield
Colorado Rockies

Yes, all three. Quinton McCracken, 25, hit .359 between New Haven and Colorado Springs, stealing 43 bases. The Duke grad and leadoff-hitter-in-training moved into the two-hole for the SkySox behind the league's top run-scorer, outfielder Trenidad Hubbard, 29, who hit .340, scored 102 runs and stole 37 bases before being promoted to the big club. Harvey Pulliam, 27, vied for the Triple Crown, leading the league with 25 homers and 91 RBI and finishing fourth in the batting race at .327.

Rocky Coppinger, SP
Baltimore Orioles

Rocky Coppinger, 21, was shuttled among the Orioles' farm teams at Class A Frederick, AA Bowie and AAA Rochester, combining for a 16-3 record, 1.97 ERA and 172 strikeouts in 187 innings. He was a 19th-round draft choice in 1993 and made his pro debut in 1994 at short-season Bluefield, where he posted a 2.45 ERA in 14 games.

BATTING	AVG	AB	R	H	2B	3B	HR	RBI	SB
Murray, Calvin, OF	.236	441	77	104	17	3	2	29	26
Reid, Derek, PH	.143	14	2	2	0	1	0	1	0
Simonton, Benji, OF	.306	108	18	33	9	3	4	30	3
Williams, Keith, OF	.305	275	39	84	20	1	9	55	5
*Wilson, Desi, 1B	.286	482	77	138	27	3	5	72	11
Witkowski, Matt, 1B	.289	38	7	11	1	0	0	5	0
Woods, Kenny, OF	.254	209	30	53	11	0	3	23	4

PITCHING	W	L	ERA	G	SV	IP	H	BB	SO
Bourgeois, Steve	12	3	2.85	22	0	145.1	140	53	91
Brannon, Cliff	0	0	5.40	3	0	10.0	13	4	7
Brewington, Jamie	8	3	3.06	16	0	88.1	72	55	74
Castillo, Mariano	3	1	3.13	22	0	37.1	38	13	31
Corps, Edwin	13	6	3.86	27	0	165.2	195	41	53
*Estes, Shawn	2	0	2.01	4	0	22.1	14	10	18
Frontera, Chad	3	5	4.17	20	1	82.0	88	39	52
Hyde, Rich	5	1	3.89	33	7	44.0	48	10	24
McLain, Mike	2	1	3.12	11	1	17.1	13	3	11
*Peterson, Mark	4	3	1.27	37	2	64.0	51	6	38
*Pickett, Ricky	2	0	1.71	14	3	21.0	9	9	23
Pote, Lou	2	2	5.33	28	3	50.2	53	26	30
Purdy, Shawn	6	3	3.75	52	21	62.1	61	18	33
Richey, Jeff	1	2	2.45	8	1	22.0	20	8	11
Soderstrom, Steve	9	5	3.41	22	0	116.0	106	51	91
Taulbee, Andy	4	5	3.95	14	0	86.2	107	27	38
Valdez, Carlos	3	2	1.27	22	5	64.0	40	14	51
Vanderweele, Doug	5	2	2.52	13	0	64.1	61	13	22
*Wanke, Chuck	2	3	4.35	43	0	41.1	35	22	40
*Whitaker, Steve	2	0	3.86	4	0	16.1	17	10	10

Baseball Weekly's Top 10 Minor League Players

(Cont'd from previous page)

Johnny Damon, OF
Kansas City Royals

The latest chapter in Johnny Damon's meteoric rise is the fact he's already lost his rookie eligibility for 1996 since being promoted to the big club in August '95. His success at the major league level was no surprise; he was outstanding in the minors. He hit .343 at AA Wichita in '95 for a .318 career average and was Texas League Player of the Year. The 21-year-old has the speed and talent to be a serious threat in the majors.

Derrick Gibson, OF
Colorado Rockies

Just 20 years old, Derrick Gibson (6-2, 230 pounds) led the South Atlantic League with 32 homers and led the minors with 115 RBI, finishing 10th in the batting race at .292. He added 16 doubles and 10 triples, and with 31 steals became the first player to hit 30 homers and steal 30 bases for one club in the minors since 1987.

Raul Ibanez, C
Seattle Mariners

Raul Ibanez didn't become a full-time catcher until 1995, but it clearly didn't hurt his offense. The 23-year-old was primarily a DH his first few years. He has always hit for average, but '95 was his breakthrough year in the power department—.332 with 20 homers and 108 RBI, 23 doubles, nine triples and a league-best .612 slugging percentage. He achieved this feat despite not starting his season until May and playing his home games at Riverside one of the toughest hitters' parks in the California League.

372

Tulsa Drillers (Rangers) AA

BATTING	AVG	AB	R	H	2B	3B	HR	RBI	SB
Charles, Frank, 1B	.253	479	51	121	24	3	13	72	1
Clinton, Jim, OF	.193	57	6	11	2	0	1	7	2
Edwards, Mike, 3B	.216	111	11	24	3	1	3	13	0
Estrada, Osmani, 3B	.266	410	44	109	23	3	3	43	0
#Frias, Hanley, SS	.281	360	44	101	18	4	0	27	14
Kennedy, Darryl, C	.251	195	26	49	9	1	3	26	0
#Mercedes, Guillermo, SS	.119	42	4	5	1	0	0	1	0
#Monell, Johnny, DH	.306	434	55	133	18	1	12	64	0
#Nunez, Rogelio, C	.224	263	27	59	4	0	2	17	0
#Parra, Franklin, OF	.245	261	27	64	9	2	2	26	7
*Sagmoen, Marc, OF	.231	242	36	56	8	5	6	22	5
#Sims, Wesley, SS	.233	43	4	10	1	1	0	5	0
Smith, Mike, 2B	.257	499	65	128	22	3	16	64	11
Texidor, Jose, OF	.269	494	55	133	33	1	5	64	1
*Thomas, Brian, OF	.269	458	61	123	24	9	4	35	8
Turco, Frank, OF	.208	149	23	31	3	1	1	12	4
Voigt, Jack, OF	.188	16	1	3	0	0	1	3	1

PITCHING	W	L	ERA	G	SV	IP	H	BB	SO
Castillo, Felipe	2	2	3.82	14	0	33.0	42	11	16
Cather, Mike	0	2	3.32	18	0	21.2	20	7	15
Davidson, Jackie	0	2	21.86	2	0	7.0	21	1	5
Davis, Jeff	1	0	0.00	1	0	7.0	2	1	4
Dreyer, Steve	2	4	2.89	10	0	62.1	56	19	48
Duncan, Chip	2	1	3.00	17	1	36.0	34	17	31
*Escamilla, Jaime	0	0	1.80	4	0	5.0	6	2	5
Geeve, Dave	3	8	5.17	15	0	94.0	108	20	38
Heredia, Wilson	4	2	3.18	8	1	45.1	42	21	34
Keusch, Joseph	0	0	0.00	2	0	2.2	1	0	0
*Kimel, Jack	2	2	7.32	17	0	35.2	52	23	10
*Knox, Kerry	2	2	3.41	5	0	29.0	28	9	14
Lacy, Kerry	2	7	4.28	28	9	82.0	94	39	49
Martin, Jerry	3	7	5.18	22	0	88.2	100	51	46
*Martinez, Ramiro	0	5	5.17	13	0	47.0	53	34	37
*Moody, Ritchie	0	1	6.97	11	0	20.2	24	18	9
Morvay, Joe	5	8	5.21	37	8	65.2	82	28	30
Patterson, Danny	2	2	6.19	26	5	36.1	45	13	24
Perez, David	3	2	5.24	8	0	46.1	49	18	25
Powell, John	1	4	3.89	7	0	39.1	45	16	27
Santana, Julio	6	4	3.23	15	0	103.0	91	52	71
Smith, Scotty	5	8	6.11	29	0	101.2	144	31	38
Wheeler, Earl	1	1	5.40	5	0	8.1	14	2	6
Wiley, Chad	6	9	3.89	26	0	159.2	165	52	69

Wichita Wranglers (Padres) AA

BATTING	AVG	AB	R	H	2B	3B	HR	RBI	SB
#Burton, Darren, OF	.239	163	13	39	9	1	1	20	6
*Damon, Johnny, OF	.343	423	83	145	15	9	16	54	26
Diaz, Lino, 3B	.350	226	40	79	15	3	6	43	0
Fasano, Sal, C	.290	317	60	92	18	2	20	66	3
Gonzalez, Raul, OF	.291	79	14	23	3	2	2	11	4
Jennings, Lance, C	.182	44	2	8	0	0	0	3	0
*Long, Kevin, OF	.292	250	38	73	14	1	1	26	9
Long, Ryan, 3B	.231	342	36	79	26	0	5	34	4
Marshall, Jason, SS	.226	146	14	33	1	1	0	9	0
#Martinez, Felix, SS	.263	426	53	112	15	3	3	30	44
Martinez, Ramon, 2B	.275	393	58	108	20	2	3	51	11
Medrano, Anthony, 2B	.000	5	0	0	0	0	0	0	0
*Murphy, Steve, OF	.333	39	9	13	2	0	0	4	0
*Myers, Rod, OF	.307	499	71	153	22	6	7	62	29
#Romero, Mandy, DH	.302	440	73	133	32	1	21	82	1
Sisco, Steve, 2B	.301	209	29	63	12	1	3	23	3
*Smiley, Rueben, OF	.240	104	16	25	3	1	2	13	1
Stewart, Andy, 1B	.259	216	28	56	18	0	3	32	1
Strickland, Chad, C	.224	183	16	41	7	0	1	21	0
*Sutton, Larry, 1B	.269	197	31	53	11	1	5	32	1

PITCHING	W	L	ERA	G	SV	IP	H	BB	SO
*Atkinson, Neil	3	0	4.80	40	1	50.2	52	21	32
Bevil, Brian	5	7	5.84	15	0	74.0	85	35	57
Bluma, Jaime	4	3	3.09	42	22	55.1	38	9	31
Bovee, Mike	8	6	4.18	20	0	114.0	118	43	72
Brewer, Nevin	3	2	3.96	19	0	50.0	54	21	21
*Browning, Tom	1	0	7.50	1	0	6.0	10	1	5
*Connolly, Chris	1	0	5.68	13	0	12.2	18	11	2
Dorlarque, Aaron	1	1	1.15	20	0	47.0	37	10	32
*Eddy, Chris	1	0	4.00	9	1	9.0	8	3	10
Evans, Bart	0	4	10.48	7	0	22.1	22	45	13
Fyhrie, Mike	3	2	3.04	17	1	74.0	76	23	41
*Granger, Jeff	4	7	5.93	18	0	95.2	122	40	81
Grundy, Phil	1	1	8.31	6	0	17.1	16	7	11
Harrison, Brian	1	1	4.73	15	2	26.2	35	7	11
*McDill, Allen	1	0	2.11	12	1	21.1	16	5	20
Morones, Geno	3	6	4.10	17	0	79.0	85	39	32
Paskievitch, Tom	1	1	5.06	5	0	5.1	6	2	3
Ralston, Kris	9	4	3.56	18	0	93.2	85	28	84
*Rawitzer, Kevin	6	4	5.25	28	1	48.0	48	19	42
Ray, Ken	4	5	5.97	14	0	75.1	83	46	53
Sheehan, Chris	0	2	5.51	31	2	50.2	51	16	31
Strange, Don	0	1	1.50	24	8	36.0	28	7	36
Toth, Robert	8	4	2.17	21	0	103.2	95	27	77
Wallace, Derek	4	3	4.40	26	6	43.0	51	13	24

(Cont'd from previous page)

Jesus Ibarra, 1B
San Francisco Giants

Jesus Ibarra, 23, tormented Midwest League pitchers, hitting .330 with 34 homers (second in the minors) and 100 RBI before being promoted to San Jose for the California League playoffs. One of just three players in the minors to win his organization's Triple Crown, Ibarra outhomered the entire rival team at Clinton. Though he had a slugging percentage of .725 at his hitter-friendly home park in Burlington, his power is real and his plate discipline excellent.

Andruw Jones, OF
Atlanta Braves

This 18-year-old from Curaçao could be the best pure prospect in the minors. The Braves' front office and opposing managers rave about him. Jones batted .279 with 25 homers, 100 RBI and 56 steals, becoming the first 20/100/50 player since Jose Cardenal in 1961. He led the South Atlantic League in steals and was the MVP despite not ranking in the top 10 in hitting.

Adam Riggs, 2B
Los Angeles Dodgers

Adam Riggs, 22, was a hitting machine for San Bernadino in 1995, starting hot and staying there for a .362 average, 24 homers, 106 RBI and 31 steals. His 196 hits were the most in a minor league season since 1987. In a prospect-studded league, Riggs was not only unanimously voted MVP but was also the California League's best batting prospect and most dangerous hitter.

(Cont'd from previous page)

Donne Wall, SP
Houston Astros

In a league in which hitters rule, Donne Wall became the first pitcher to win a PCL Triple Crown (leading the league in wins, ERA, and strikeouts) since 1942. At 17-6, with a 3.30 ERA, 119 strikeouts and just 32 walks in 177 innings, Wall, 28, was named MVP.

Honorable mention

George Arias, 3B, Midland (30 HR, 104 RBI); **Jay Payton**, OF, Binghamton/Norfolk (.307, 18-84-27); **Karim Garcia**, OF, Albuquerque (.319, 20-90); **Paul Wilson**, SP, Binghamton/ Norfolk (11-6, 2.41, 194 K in 187 IP); **Glendon Rusch**, SP, Wilmington (14-6, 1.74, 147 K in 166 IP, 110 H); **Matt Drews**, SP, Tampa (15-7, 2.27); **Angel Echevarria**, OF, New Haven (21-100); **David Kennedy**, 1B, New Haven (.306, 22-96); **Billy McMillon**, OF, Portland (.313, 14-93, league MVP); **Ron Wright**, 1B, Macon (32-104); **Jose Valentin**, C, Fort Wayne (.324, 19-65); **Derrek Lee**, 1B, Rancho Cucamonga (23-96); **Steve Cox**, 1B, Modesto (30-110); **Richie Sexson**, 1B, Kinston (.306, 22-85, league MVP); **Demond Smith**, OF, Cedar Rapids/West Michigan (.338, 40 SB); **Wendell Magee**, OF, Clearwater/Reading (.338, 9-67); **Tony Mounce**, SP, Quad City (16-8, 2.43); **Larry Wimberley**, SP, Piedmont (10-3, 2.67); **Derek Hacopian**, OF, Beloit (.324, 23-92); **Butch Huskey**, 3B, Norfolk (28-87); **Jason Kendall**, C, Carolina (.326, 8-71, Southern League MVP); **Nilson Robledo**, 1B, South Bend (20 HR, 108 RBI); **Luis Andujar**, SP, Birmingham (14-8, 2.85, league Pitcher of the Year); **Riccardo Ingram**, OF, Salt Lake (.348, 12-85).

Donnie Scott, Rookie
Billings Mustangs (Reds)

No one in the Cincinnati Reds organization would argue with their big winner on the farm: Give Donnie Scott players and he'll turn them into champions. With his track record the past four years (1992-95), he makes managing look easy.

Scott led his 1995 Billings Mustangs to a 49-20 record, winning both halves of the Pioneer League's Northern Division races before being upset in the playoffs by Medicine Hat. The Mustangs thus fell short of "four-peating" for the league championship.

"I think handling rookie players in their first year is probably the toughest managing job in baseball, and he's done an excellent job in discipline and teaching," said Chief Bender, the Reds' director of player development. "He's also an excellent baseball man when it comes to running a game."

Scott's 201-91 record for 1992-95 suggests the wisdom of a veteran, but he has only been managing for those four years, and is just 34 years old. He was catcher for the Rangers in 1983-84, the Mariners in 1985 and the Reds in 1991.

Scott has found room for both development and winning, and he loves working with the Reds' bright young prospects.

And Donnie Scott has gotten the attention of the Reds' brass.

"I wouldn't hesitate to move him to Double A or Triple A," Bender said.

Marc Bombard, AAA
Indianapolis Indians (Reds)

In his third year as Indianapolis manager, Bombard led his team to the best record in AAA at 88-56, though the team fell short of defending its American Association championship, losing to Louisville in the first round of playoffs.

Bombard, 45, has spent most of his career, both playing and managing, with the Cincinnati organization—21 years in all. He pitched in the minor league system 1971-76, including a stint as player/coach 1974-76. He was the Reds' minor league roving pitching instructor for the next five years before starting his managerial tenure.

Dave Trembley, Class A
Daytona Cubs (Cubs)

Trembley led the Daytona Cubs to an 87-48 record in 1995, winning both halves of the Florida State League's Eastern Division and beating Fort Myers in five games for the league title. It was his 12th year in the minors, all as either coach or manager.

Trembley, 43, has never played pro baseball. After serving as head baseball coach for Antelope Valley Junior College in New York State, he moved to Virginia to join the Cubs' organization as coach of their rookie Appalachian League team in 1985. He worked for the Pirates for a decade (1983-1993), then returned to the Cubs in 1994.

Ron Wotus, AA
Shreveport Captains
(Giants)

In his third season as Shreveport manager, Wotus took the team to the Texas League playoffs for its 10th year in a row with an 88-47 record, the best in the minors. The Captains won both halves of the league's Eastern Division, and easily won their third Texas League title in six years.

Originally a 16th-round draft pick for the Pirates as an outfielder, Wotus played professionally for 11 years, including two years with Pittsburgh.

Youth leagues

- ▶ Taiwan beats Spring, Texas, for 16th Little League championship title
- ▶ Championship scores
- ▶ Youth leagues taken to court
- ▶ Plus : How to find a team

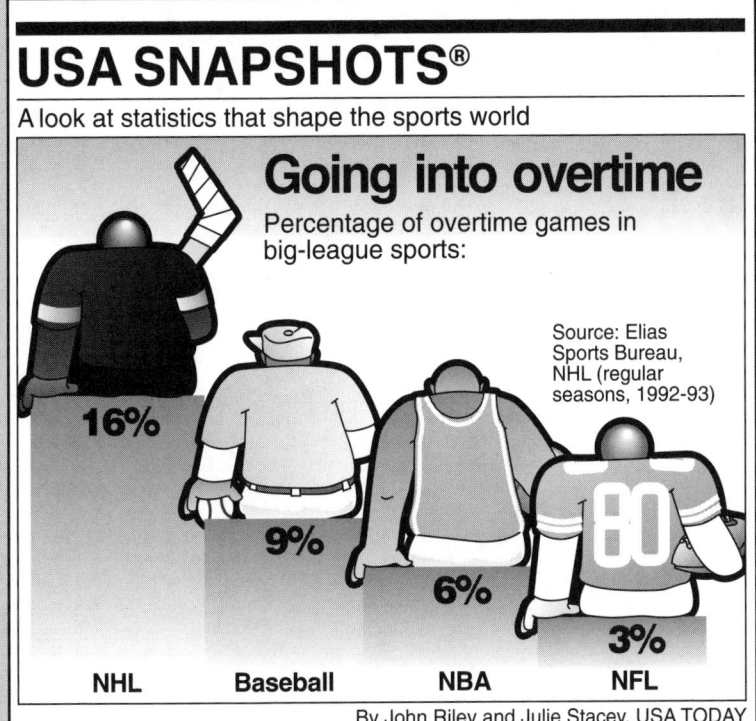

USA SNAPSHOTS®

A look at statistics that shape the sports world

Going into overtime

Percentage of overtime games in big-league sports:

Source: Elias Sports Bureau, NHL (regular seasons, 1992-93)

16% NHL

9% Baseball

6% NBA

3% NFL

By John Riley and Julie Stacey, USA TODAY

Little League championship: Taiwan tromps Spring, Texas, 17-3

After a three-year slump, Taiwan turned heads again at the 1995 Little League World Series. The team won its 16th title—but first since 1991—with a 17-3 victory over Spring, Texas. The game was called after four innings because of the 10-run mercy rule.

"No matter where we put the ball, they hit it," said Spring second baseman Daniel Grotte. "They are just such an awesome team."

"We were the best in the United States; what more could you ask for?" said losing pitcher Wardell Starling.

The winners came from Tainan, a city of about 200,000. They outscored their tournament opponents 47-6 and improved Taiwan's record to 16-2 in Little League finals.

"I can't explain why the international teams are so dominant," said Spring manager Don Turley. "Taiwan is well disciplined, and I've heard they play year-round. That's going to give you a tremendous advantage."

At least Spring scored. Its three fourth-inning runs—two on Starling's 250-foot home run—were the most scored against Taiwan since its national tournament.

Taiwan has undergone a rebuilding since its last title in '91. The Philippines won in '92 but forfeited that crown for using ineligible players. After that, Little League installed stricter rules regarding age and the pool players are chosen from.

In '93, Taiwan and three other countries were banned because of ineligible players. Last year, a sloppy Taiwan team went 1-2.

The game drew 42,000 fans, the most for a World Series championship game.

Taiwan put the pressure on early. Leadoff hitter Chia Ming Cheng hit a home run to left. Two batters later, pitcher Chih Hsiang Lin hit the first of his two home runs, giving him a record six for the series. The 5-foot-6 right-hander struck out 11.

"We heard that he would be throwing in the 60s," first baseman Mike Cepeda said. "When the game started, he brought it at 73 mph. We thought we'd get around on him; it just didn't happen."

Spring was the first Texas team to reach the final since Westbury American from Houston defeated West New York, N.J., 8-2 in 1966.

—by Pete Coe

Lawyers join the lineup: Lawsuits eclipse playoffs

Ronnie Auceda, 12, just wanted to pound his mitt and play his way into the Little League World Series. Instead, his team went to court and was disqualified early in the playoffs in a flap about eligibility.

"I'll watch it on TV to see who wins, but I'm real disappointed," said the outfielder for the Vaquero All-Stars of Glendale, Calif.

It was championship month in youth baseball and softball, but every year disputes put lawyers in the lineup, and some scores are settled with lawsuits.

"You'll find cases all across the board," said James Gray, assistant director of the National Sports Law Institute at Marquette University. "Some reflect issues we're going through as a society. The question of gender is part of the political landscape. As far as injuries, we want people to do what is 'reasonable' to provide a safe environment."

But, he adds, "It's evident some parents get caught up in winning and losing." And some sue over players left off all-star teams, banned because of where they live or disqualified for other reasons.

But the folks filing suit say they stand on principle.

"My overwhelming experience is these are tremendous organizations, but in our case we had no recourse," said lawyer John Giardinelli, who sued when a boy was barred from a league in a residency dispute.

Lawyer Phillip Marrone represented two California teams, the Vaquero and Verdugo all-stars. They were banned from the Little League tournament, initially for participating in charity games. Little League said such games are not allowed so no team gains an edge in preparation. The teams sued and were reinstated by a judge. After Vaquero won two games, it was disqualified again for allegedly using two players from beyond league boundaries. Marrone was unable to get further court relief. Vaquero was ousted last month.

Said Little League spokesman Dennis Sullivan: "When you charter with Little League, you say, 'I will subscribe to these rules.' What's difficult is when the court system even sees fit to hear these complaints."

Some suits have far-reaching impact. After girls sued, Little League changed its federal charter in 1974 to admit them. Injury cases focus attention on equipment and rules.

PONY Baseball consultant and past president Roy Gillespie worries about the impact of suits over rules and eligibility. "When the child sees this, I don't know

377

Championship scores: NABF

▶**Freshman (12 and under):** Bartlett, Tenn. 2, Livonia, Mich. 1

▶**Sophomore (14 and under):** Renton, Wash. 10, Baltimore 2

▶**Junior (16 and under):** Long Island, N.Y. 4, Lexington, Ky. 2

▶**Senior (18 and under):** Springfield, Ohio 4, Marietta, Ohio 0

▶**High School:** Suffolk County, N.Y. 3, Apopka, Fla. 2

▶**College:** Washington, D.C. 4, Fairfield, Ohio 3

▶**Major (unlimited):** Westchester, N.Y. 9, Louisville 5

YOUTH LEAGUES

1995 American Legion World Series

Aiea, Hawaii 2, Bellevue, Wash. 0

Championship scores: Babe Ruth

▶**Bambino (11-12):** Abbeville, La. 9, Kokomo, Ind. 4

▶**13 year olds:** Longwood, Fla. 7, Trumbull, Conn. 4

▶**13-15 year olds:** Glendale, Ariz. 9, South Shore, N.Y. 6

▶**16 year olds:** Columbia Basin, Wash. 3, Iron Area, N.J. 0

▶**16-18 year olds:** Vancouver, Wash. 9, San Luis Obispo, Calif. 1

Championship scores: AABC

▶**Roberto Clemente (8 and under):** Park Valley, Calif. 14, Dallas 9

▶**Willie Mays (10 and under):** Punado, Calif. 5, Dallas 2

▶**Pee Wee Reese (12 and under):** Puerto Rico Gigantes 15, Levittown, P.R. 6

▶**Sandy Koufax (14 and under):** Dallas 12, West Covina, Calif. 3

▶**Mickey Mantle (16 and under):** Baltimore 7, Memphis 4

▶**Connie Mack (18 and under):** Dallas 6, Cincinnati 3

▶**Stan Musial (unlimited):** Sacramento 5, Bridgeview, Ill. 1

whether they ever believe there is a rule that you can't get around," he said.

Ronnie Auceda still frets about his Vaquero team's finish. "They probably didn't want us to participate. They came up with all these rules to kick us out," he said. But with the resilience of a 12-year-old, he adds, "I had a lot of fun this season, and I still feel like we are champions."

Little League not shy about defending turf

Lawyers for Little League Inc., the world's largest youth baseball and softball organization, are throwing curves at its rivals with a half-dozen lawsuits. At issue: Little League says local chapters switching to other affiliations are commandeering its assets. It illustrates Little League's depth—3 million players worldwide— and other groups' desires to tap into the market.

"We have no objections to teams leaving and affiliating with another organization," said David Baron, Little League's lawyer in its suit against five California teams. "But they can't take over Little League's equipment, uniforms, bank accounts."

Little League is being unreasonable, said PONY lawyer Alan Wilion. "If you have local volunteers buying a charter and raising funds, that money belongs to the team," Wilion said. "I don't think Little League is entitled to a bucket of spit."

Little League won't discuss its ongoing litigation. Most of its suits have been against PONY, one of the largest youth baseball organizations, with 400,000 players. In 1994, Little League sued five Southern California chapters that switched to PONY. A settlement was reached in March, 1995.

"We are ecstatic," PONY lawyer Rob Schelling said about the settlement. But he contends the suit was Little League's way of saying it's tired of losing franchises. Said Schelling: "[Little League] doesn't give a rip about some used bats and baseballs."

In its unresolved suit against Toluca Baseball Inc. of Toluca Lakes, Calif., Little League is suing PONY and parents and supporters on the Toluca board of directors. More than 400 youngsters played PONY ball there last summer. Little League wants assets amounting to $30,000. Toluca said it has $4,000 in assets and nearly $15,000 in debts. Toluca President Frank Miceli said 80% of Toluca wanted to play PONY ball because Little League is ability-based while PONY is age-based and "gives us a better chance to develop our players."

Little League's Baron thinks there's more to it.

"PONY convinced Toluca's board of directors to defect. Little League is ending up funding the competition."

Babe Ruth Commissioner Ron Tellefson thinks competition is good. "If one of our teams changes . . . it's a message that we didn't do a good enough job for that community."

Said American Legion Commissioner Jim Quinlan: "Losing teams happens to all of us. You learn from your mistakes and go on."

Small players, big trouble

Some lawsuits involving baseball and softball:

▶**Access:** In a federal suit in Connecticut, Valerie and Ronald Suhanosky of Milford are suing Little League under the Americans with Disabilities Act in behalf of their daughter, Lauren, who has a neurological condition. In 1990, Little League began its Challenger Division for disabled children. Lawyer Lawrence Berliner said the family does not want Challenger play abolished, but "they are seeking more opportunities for a comparable game of baseball." Berliner noted that when the family coached in Challenger, they were told practice games against regular teams would violate the league charter and insurance provisions. Little League has argued that it is not covered by the disabilities act.

▶**Boundary dispute:** Doug Reinhardt, 10, was barred in 1995 from the Temecula (Calif.) Valley National Little League on grounds he did not live within boundaries. Said lawyer John Giardinelli: "His mom and dad separated. The league wouldn't accept proof he lived in Temecula. He spent time between his mom and dad. His mom lived in Murieta." A judge issued a temporary order against the ban, but the youth wound up in PONY League. "It became a matter of dollar and cents, and [the father] had made his point," said Giardinelli.

▶**Firing flap:** John Thomas sued in 1993 when dismissed as coach of an all-star team in the Kearney (Neb.) Little League. A district judge dismissed the suit. In June 1995, the Court of Appeals of Nebraska ruled that Thomas could sue the league. The coach, seeking $1,200 damages, was dismissed on the eve of the tournament after having coached for a month.

▶**Hardball:** In an antitrust suit set for trial in Novemebr 1995, the Amateur Softball Association sued Dixie Softball over its refusal to let players compete for Dixie as well as other softball organizations. The ASA sued after Dixie disqualified a team from its Virginia tournament for having competed in an ASA tournament.

Championship scores: Dixie

▶**Youth (11-12):** Ville Platte, La. 2, Pensacola, Fla. 1

▶**Dixie Boys (13-14):** Valdosta, Ga. 5, Yazoo City, Miss. 1

▶**Pre-majors (15-16):** Daphne, Ala. 6, Columbia County, Ga. 4

▶**Majors (15-18):** Lake Charles, La. 13, Columbia County, Ga. 12

379

▶**9 and under:** Valencia, Calif. 11, Germantown, Tenn. 10

▶**10 and under:** Broken Arrow, Okla. 4, Des Moines 3

▶**11 and under:** San Juan, P.R. 6, Omaha 2

▶**12 and under:** Honolulu 18, Kansas City, Mo. 2

▶**13 and under:** Encinitas, Calif. 9, Kansas City, Mo. 2

▶**14 and under:** Encinitas, Calif. 6, Seattle 0

▶**15 and under:** Cucamonga, Calif. 5, Brunswick, Ohio 0

▶**16 and under:** Springfield, Ill. 2, Cedar Rapids, Iowa 1

▶**High school:** Brooklyn 4, Miami 1

▶**18 and under:** Baltimore 23, Wichita, Kan. 10

Who's playing the field

▶**Little League Baseball Inc.:** Founded in 1939. 196,000 teams, 2.7 million participants in the USA, 3 million worldwide. Ages: 5-18.

▶**Dixie Baseball Inc. (includes Dixie Softball):** Founded in 1956. 24,241 baseball teams, 363,615 players; 4,369 softball teams, 65,535 players (total 429,150 players, 11 states). Ages: 4-18

▶**American Legion Baseball:** Founded in 1925. 4,680 teams, 84,000 players. Ages: 16-18.

▶**National Police Athletic League Baseball:** Founded in 1960. 200,000 players in regional and national tournaments. Ages: 14-16.

▶**PONY Baseball/Softball Inc.:** Founded in 1951. 28,500 teams, nearly 400,000 athletes in 45 states and 12 foreign countries. 2,000 softball teams. Ages: 5-18

▶**Babe Ruth League Inc.:** Founded in 1951. 5,800 leagues, 41,000 teams, 815,000 players in baseball; 3,500 teams, 70,000 participants in softball. Ages: 5-18

▶**American Amateur Baseball Congress:** Founded in 1935. 12,895 teams, 257,900 players. Ages: 8-up

▶**National Amateur Baseball Federation:** Founded in 1914. 5,000 teams, 110,000 players (who advance into tournament competition). Ages: 12-up (including 30-and-over leagues).

How to find a team

To find a team in your area, contact the national headquarters listed below for a regional reference.

▶**American Amateur Baseball Congress:** 118-19 Redfield Plaza, P.O. Box 467, Marshall, MI 49068; (616) 781-2002.

▶**American Legion:** P.O. Box 1055, Indianapolis, IN 46206; (317) 630-1213.

▶**Babe Ruth League:** 1771 Brunswick Ave., P.O. Box 5000, Trenton, NJ; (609) 695-1434.

▶**Continental Amateur Baseball Association:** 82 University St., Westerville, Ohio 43081; (614) 882-2103

▶**Dixie Baseball:** P.O. Box 222, Lookout Mountain, TN 37350; (615) 821-6811.

▶**Little League:** P.O. Box 3485, Williamsport, PA 17701; (717) 326-1921.

▶**National Amateur Baseball Federation:** P.O. Box 705, Bowie, MD 20718; (301) 262-5005.

▶**National Police Athletic League:** 614 U.S. Hwy. 1, Ste. 20, North Palm Beach, FL 33408; (407) 844-1823

▶**PONY Baseball/Softball:** P.O. Box 225, Washington, PA 15301-0225; (412) 225-1060.

High school & college baseball

▶ 1995 Super 25 high schools

▶ All-USA high school teams

▶ 1995 Top 25 coaches' poll

▶ 1996 college preview

▶ 1995 College World Series

▶ *and more ...*

USA SNAPSHOTS®

A look at statistics that shape the sports world

Olympic All-Stars

Olympic baseball debuted in 1984 and gained medal status in 1992. Can you name the four major leaguers on 1995's All-Star rosters who played in the Olympics?

Answer: Mark McGwire, Athletics (1984); Barry Larkin, Reds (1984), Mickey Morandini, Phillies (1988); Hideo Nomo, Dodgers (1988, for Japan)

Source: USA Baseball, Baseball Weekly

By Scott Boeck and Bob Laird, USA TODAY

USA TODAY Super 25:
Final 1995 high school rankings

▶1. Germantown, Tenn. (38-0)

Highlight: Won second Class 3A state title.

Top players: Jay Hood (.436, 44 RBI, 45 runs, 5-0 as pitcher); Chris Lotterhos (.484, 34 RBI, 52 runs); Matt Hale (10-0, 1.95 ERA).

▶2. Elkins, Missouri City, Texas (32-2)

Highlight: Won first Class 5A state title in second varsity season.

Top players: Steven Truitt (.423, 12 HR, 42 RBI); Ivan Heredia (12-0, 0.41 ERA); Jason Gray (.372, 25 RBI, 14-for-14 SB).

▶3. Fountain Valley, Calif. (26-3-1)

Highlight: Won second consecutive Southern Section Division I title.

Top players: Greg Hanoian (.436, 36 RBI); Dan Keller (.381, 7-0, 1.42 ERA); Chris Ponchak (.333, 30 runs, 5-1, 1.45 ERA).

▶4. Key West, Fla. (35-2)

Highlight: Won Class 4A state title.

Top players: Adrian Merkey (.448, 21 RBI); Craig Lariz (.444, 5 HR, 42 RBI).

▶5. Mission Bay, San Diego (30-2)

Highlight: Won fourth San Diego Section Division II title in 10 years.

Top players: Kevin Reese (405, 28 RBI, 10-0, 1.82 ERA); Josh Glassey (.385, 7 HR, 40 RBI); Justin Spencer (.402, 6 HR, 39 RBI).

▶6. St. Thomas Aquinas, Fort Lauderdale, Fla. (27-4)

Highlight: Won first Class 5A state title.

Top players: Billy Brown (.425, 41 runs, 11 HR, 27 RBI); Chad Whitaker (.425, 7 HR, 33 RBI, 32 walks); Tim Burton (10-0, 0.23 ERA, 60 innings).

▶7. Lyman, Longwood, Fla. (31-3)

Highlight: Won first Class 6A state title.

Top players: Teddy Koller (.409, 23 RBI); Jason Shipley (.355, 28 RBI, 19 SB); Tommy Dixon (7-2, 1.36 ERA).

▶8. Glen Oak, Canton, Ohio (28-2)

Highlight: Won first Division I state title.

Top players: Mike Muzi (10-0, 0.66 ERA): Alan Gilhousen (.382, 23 RBI, 37 runs); Greg McClellan (.381, 30 RBI, 35 runs).

▶9. Delran, N.J. (25-1)

Highlight: Won second Group II state title.

Top players: Jim Hansen (11-0, 4 saves, 1.07 ERA); Pat Poehls (8-0, 3 saves, 0.91 ERA); Scott Gutulieus (.416, 32 RBI).

▶10. Green Run, Virginia Beach, Va. (26-2)

Highlight: Won first Class 3A state title.

Top players: Chris Elmore (11-0, 0.55 ERA, 106 SO, 69 innings); David Abbott (.491, 5 HR, 44 RBI, 16 doubles); John Defere (.405, 7 HR, 38 RBI).

▶11. Morris, Ill. (38-4)

Highlight: Won first Class 2A state title.

Top players: Jon Overton (.463, 30 RBI, 32 SB, no errors in CF); Quinn Schafer (13-0, 1.10 ERA)

▶12. Harrison, West Lafayette, Ind. (34-2)

Highlight: Won first state title.

Top players: Eric Martin (6-0); Jason Hettinger (13-0).

▶13. Providence, Charlotte, N.C. (27-4)

Highlight: Won Class 4A state title.

Top players: Josh Gibbons (.415, 22 RBI, 30 SB); Travis Thompson (.333, 7 HR, 35 RBI); Jeremy Schumacher (14-2, ERA, 137 SO).

▶14. Calvert Hall, Towson, Md. (28-2)

Highlight: Won Maryland Inter-scholastic Athletic Association A Conference title.

Top players: Kevin Olkowski (.440, 39 RBI, 31 runs); Joe Miller (.374, 40 runs); Andy Bair (9-0, 0.11 ERA, 104 SO, 63 innings).

▶15. Tottenville, Staten Island, N.Y. (37-2)

Highlight: Won fourth Public School Athletic League A Division title.

Top players: Tom Gregorio (.481, 11 HR, 52 RBI); Paul Stabile (.425, 13-0, 0.44 ERA); Jason Marquis (11-0, 1.26 ERA).

▶16. Norman, Okla. (34-5)

Highlight: Won Class 5A state title.

Top players: Rick Park (.379, 10 HR, 36 RBI, 9-1, 1.63 ERA); Tyler Bodin (.409, 35 RBI, 18 doubles).

▶17. Columbus, Ga. (27-5)

Highlight: Won fifth Class 3A state title.

Top players: Jason Simmons (.443, 32 RBI, 10-1, 1.93 ERA); Derek Mann (.433, 35 runs, .530 on-base percentage); Brent Schoening (12-0, 0.34 ERA, 123 SO, 81 innings).

▶18. Mount Carmel, San Diego (30-5)

Highlight: Won fifth San Diego Section Division I title.

Top players: Eric Chavez (.537, 49 runs, 51 SB, 11-1, 1.31 ERA); Eric Munson (.510, 6 HR, 39 RBI, 31 runs): Dave Uris (13-1, 0.61 ERA, 5 SHO).

▶19. Grand Prairie, Texas (33-4)

Highlight: Won Class 5A state semi-finals.

Top players: Kerry Wood (14-0, 0.77 ERA, 159 SO); Jeff Dover (.441, 38 RBI, 15 doubles); Kevin Walker (12-3, 0.86 ERA, 145 SO, 98 innings).

▶20. Vestavia Hills, Birmingham, Ala. (32-4)

Highlight: Won fourth Class 6A state title in five years.

Top players: Josh Hancock (10-0, 0.92 ERA, 137 SO, 72 innings); Lance Ruble (.416, 41 RBI).

▶21. Petal, Miss. (29-1)

Highlight: Won third Class 4A state title.

Top players: Nate Rolison (.548, 55 RBI, .675 on-base percentage, 1.012 slugging percentage, 1 error at first base); Cliff Wren (.471, 11 HR, 8-1, 1.40 ERA) Jay Lewis (9-0, 1.33 ERA).

▶22. Pleasure Ridge Park, Louisville (39-3)

Highlight: Won second consecutive state title.

Top players: Andre Montgomery (.410, 13 HR, 43 RBI); Eric Bishop (12-0, 0.52 ERA); Eric Burdon (.407, 23 RBI, 30 SB).

▶23. Antioch, Calif. (23-2)

Highlight: Won third North Coast Section Division I–3A title.

Top players: Aaron Miles (.543, 33 RBI, 34 runs); Brian Oliver (.378, 32 runs); Manuel Bermudez (11-1, 1.44 ERA, school career record 35 wins and 304 SO).

▶24. Horizon, Scottsdale, Ariz. (27-6)

Highlight: Won first Class 5A state title.

Top players: Ryan Mills (13-0, 0.87 ERA); Chip Gosewisch (.509, 47 runs, 40 RBI, Class 5A state record 59 hits).

▶25. Seneca Valley, Harmony, Pa. (20-7)

Highlight: Won first Class 3A state title.

Top players: Brent Ruby (8-3, 1.03 ERA, .380, 18 RBI); Todd Raithel (6-0, 0.89 ERA).

—*ranked by Dave Krider, USA TODAY*

two or three runners on steal attempts.

Catcher Ben Davis (Malvern Prep, Pa.) signed with the San Diego Padres for a $1.3 million bonus.

Player of the year: Catcher Ben Davis

School: Malvern (Pa.) Prep
Ht.: 6-3   **Wt.:** 195
Bats: R-L   **Throws:** R
Statistics: Made no errors in last two years. Threw out eight of 13 on steal attempts this year. Batting average went from .396 to .514 in junior year, home runs from two to six and RBI from 17 to 37. Also had four doubles, seven triples, 21 walks (10 intentional) and 28 runs. Had .646 on-base percentage. Drafted No. 2 overall by San Diego Padres. Signed day of draft ($1.3 million signing bonus).
Personal profile: Word that best describes me: Aggressive. Favorite book: Joseph Heller's *Catch-22*. Worst habit: Playing the radio too loud. Perfect happiness is: Going 5-for-5 and throwing out

Coach of the year: Phil Clark

Home: Germantown, Tenn.
Age: 38 **Family:** Wife, Donna, 37; children, Zach, 8, and Ryne, 5
College: Memphis State, 1979
1995 record: 38-0
Career record: 378-132 in 16 years. Coached Class 1A state champs at Skyview Academy (Memphis) in 1981 and 1986 while placing second in 1983 and 1984. Won Class AAA state title at Germantown in 1995 while placing second in 1992 and 1993.
Personal profile: Word that best describes me: Bald—I let my players shave my head after we won the state title. Favorite book: John Grisham's *The Firm*. Greatest fear: That I'd have to give up coaching. Hardest decision I've made: Making team cuts each year.

Team roster

P Chad Hutchinson

School: Torrey Pines (San Diego)
Ht.: 6-6   **Wt.:** 230
Bats: R   **Throws:** R
Statistics: 11-0, 1.20 ERA (116 strikeouts in 67 innings). School records: 16-strikeout game, 25 career victories. Batted .345 with 30 RBI. Gatorade Circle of Champions national player of year. Signed with Stanford for football and baseball. Drafted No. 26 overall by Atlanta Braves.

P Kerry Wood

School: Grand Prairie, Texas
Ht.: 6-4   **Wt.:** 185
Bats: R   **Throws:** R

Statistics: 14-0, 0.77 ERA (school-record 157 strikeouts in 81⅓ innings). Has 94-mph fastball. Signed with McLennan Junior College (Texas). Drafted No. 4 overall by Chicago Cubs.

IF Michael Barrett
School: Pace Academy (Atlanta)
Ht.: 6-2　　　Wt.: 185
Bats: R　　　Throws: R
Statistics: Led 27-8 team to Class 1A state title. School records: .624 batting average (.566 career), 58 RBI, 67 runs. Stole 24 bases in 28 tries. Signed with Clemson. Drafted No. 28 overall by Montreal Expos.

IF Chad Hermansen
School: Green Valley (Henderson, Nev.)
Ht.: 6-2　　　Wt.: 185
Bats: R　　　Throws: R
Statistics: Led team to 31-4 record and third consecutive Class 3A state title. Batted .473, 68 RBI, 69 runs. Signed with Miami (Fla.). Drafted No. 10 overall by Pittsburgh Pirates, signed and reported to Bradenton, Fla., for rookie league.

IF Jay Hood
School: Germantown, Tenn.
Ht.: 6-1　　　Wt.: 175
Bats: R　　　Throws: R
Statistics: Led team to 38-0 record, Class 3A state title and No. 1 in USA TODAY Super 25 rankings. Batted .436, 44 RBI, 45 runs, on 48 hits. Made four errors in 101 chances. Had 5-0 pitching record (35 strikeouts in 35⅓ innings). Signed with Georgia Tech. Drafted in fourth round by Minnesota Twins.

IF Nate Rolison
School: Petal, Miss.
Ht.: 6-5　　　Wt.: 225
Bats: L　　　Throws: R
Statistics: Led team to 29-1 record and Class 4A state title. School records: .548 batting average, 55 RBI, .675 on-base percentage, and 1.012 slugging percent-

age. Made one error at first base. Signed with Miami (Fla.). Drafted in second round by Florida Marlins.

OF Jaime Jones
School: Rancho Bernardo (San Diego)
Ht.: 6-4　　　Wt.: 190
Bats: L　　　Throws: L
Statistics: San Diego Section CIF career records: 150 hits, 139 runs, 32 HR. School record: 81 stolen bases. Batted .448, 34 RBI, 48 runs. Had 4-0 pitching record (0.00 ERA in 22⅔ innings). Signed with Long Beach State. Drafted No. 6 overall by Florida Marlins.

OF Reggie Taylor
School: Newberry, S.C.
Ht.: 6-1　　　Wt.: 175
Bats: L　　　Throws: R
Statistics: Batted .464, four HR, 22 RBI. Used 6.5 speed in 60-yard dash to steal 28 bases in 28 attempts. Struck out just six times. Has major league arm and outstanding bat speed. Drafted No. 14 overall and signed with the Philadelphia Phillies.

OF Eric Valent
School: Canyon (Anaheim, Calif.)
Ht.: 5-11　　　Wt.: 185
Bats: L　　　Throws: L
Statistics: Broke Rob Deer's school record with 10 consecutive hits. Batted .506, nine HR, 44 runs, 32 RBI in 89 at-bats. Made no errors. Signed with UCLA. Drafted in 19th round by Detroit Tigers.

1995 Baseball Weekly/ABCA Top 25 coaches' poll (college baseball)

1. Cal State Fullerton (57-9) Poll points: 825 (33 No. 1 votes). Postseason results: Won national championship; undefeated in College World Series (4-0); undefeated in South Regional; won Big West tournament.

2. Southern Cal (49-21) Poll points: 781. College World Series runner-up (4-2); West Regional champion; Pac-10 champion.

3. Miami (Fla.) (48-17) Poll points: 754. Tied for third place in College World Series (2-2); won Atlantic II Regional.

4. Florida State (53-16) Poll points: 702. Tied for fifth place in College World Series (1-2); won Atlantic I Regional and Atlantic Coast Conference.

5. Tennessee (54-16) Poll points: 699. Tied for third place in College World Series (2-2); won Mideast Regional; won Southeastern Conference.

6. Stanford (40-25) Poll points: 643. Tied for fifth place in College World Series (1-2); won Midwest I Regional; second in Pac-10 South.

7. Clemson (54-14) Poll points: 634. Tied for seventh place in College World Series (0-2); won East Regional; second in Atlantic Coast Conference.

8. Oklahoma (42-16) Poll points: 617. Tied for seventh place in College World Series (0-2); won Midwest II Regional.

9. Texas Tech (51-14) Poll points: 543. Second in Midwest I Regional; won Southwest Conference.

10. Auburn (50-13) Poll points: 521. Second in Midwest II Regional; won Southeastern Conference Western Division.

11. Oklahoma State (46-19) Poll points: 455. Second in Mideast Regional; won Big Eight.

12. Rice (43-19) Poll points: 395. Third in South Regional; fourth in Southwest Conference.

13. Texas A&M (44-22) Poll points: 388. Second in Atlantic II Regional; second in Southwest Conference.

14. Louisiana State (47-18) Poll points: 368. Third in South Regional; second in SEC Western Division.

15. Alabama (42-23) Poll points: 321. Second in East Regional; won SEC Western Division.

16. Wichita State (53-17) Poll points: 319. Fourth in Midwest I Regional; fifth in Missouri Valley Conference.

17. Long Beach State (39-25) Poll points: 311. Second in West Regional; second in Big West.

18. Texas (44-19) Poll points: 260. Third in Midwest II Regional; third in Southwest Conference.

19. Mississippi (40-22) Poll points: 233. Second in Atlantic I Regional; fifth (tied) in SEC West.

20. Central Florida (49-13) Poll points: 189. Fourth in Atlantic I Regional; won Trans-America Conference.

21. Florida International (50-11) Poll points: 153. Fourth in Atlantic II Regional; fourth in Trans-America Conference.

22. Pepperdine (36-19) Poll points: 117. Fourth in West Regional; won West Coast Conference.

23. Fresno State (41-22) Poll points: 116. Tied for fifth in West Regional; won Western Athletic Conference.

24. North Carolina (39-23) Poll points: 62. Third in Atlantic II Regional; third (tied) in Atlantic Coast Conference.

25. South Alabama (41-17) Poll points: 52. Tied for fifth in Atlantic I Regional; second in Sun Belt Conference tournament.

The Baseball Weekly/*American Baseball Coaches Association poll is voted on by 33 Division I head coaches, representing all areas of the USA.*

1996 college preview:
Top schools and players

Here's a look at the top contenders for the 1996 college season:

▶ **Cal State Fullerton (57-9):** The Titans are talking dynasty after their tremendous national championship run in '95. **Mark Kotsay**, arguably the best college player in the nation, returns for his junior year. He hit .422 with 22 homers and 90 RBI, and recorded 11 saves as the team's closer, allowing just one run all season. **Brian Loyd** (.360, 10 HR, 73 RBI) and **Jeremy Giambi** (.349) are also back.

▶ **Florida State (53-16):** The Seminoles lost their two top pitchers, but five everyday starters are back to try to bring FSU its first national championship after 14 CWS trips. **J.D. Drew** (.308, 14 HR) will lead the 'Noles offense, along with **Scott Zech** (.333).

▶ **Florida (32-24):** Pitcher **John Kaufman** is back after missing nearly the entire year with elbow surgery. **John Tamargo** (.316) is also back after missing a bit of the season, while **Chuck Hazzard** (.347, 7 HR) and **Brandon Marsters** (.278) are expected to continue to blossom.

▶ **Pepperdine (36-19):** Southpaw **Randy Wolf** (9-1, 2.16 ERA), RHP **Eric Brubaker** (10-2, 1.25 ERA), and a pair of junior starters—**Greg Gregory** and **Jason LeBlanc**—are all back. The heart of their offense is gone, but second baseman **Justin Hodgdon** (.345) will be counted on.

▶ **Arizona State (34-21):** ASU is hoping to leave nothing to chance this season behind right-hander **Kaipo Spenser** (8-5, 3.06)—a top candidate for the Olympic team. **Cody McKay** (son of A's coach Dave McKay) is also back after a standout summer for the Canadian national team.

▶ **Stanford (40-25):** While the everyday lineup will have some holes to fill, the return of catcher **A.J. Hinch** for his senior season helps. Hinch turned down the Minnesota Twins, who made him their third-round pick, to play in the Olympics. **Kyle Peterson** returns as the staff ace after a tremendous freshman season (14-1, 2.96 ERA). He'll be helped by junior **Brendan Sullivan**.

▶ **Louisiana State (47-18):** The Tigers are regulars in the NCAA regionals, and '96 should be little different. **Warren Morris** (.369, 8 HR) will be counted on to lead the team after a great summer with the U.S. national team; he's joined by **Eddy Furniss** (.326, 9 HR as a freshman) and **Nathan Dunn**. Coach Skip Bertman—who will lead the U.S. Olympic team in Atlanta—lost his top two starters at LSU, but left-hander **Eddie Yarnall** (5-0) is back.

▶ **California (32-25):** Some key players return to lead Cal to a possible CWS trip. Sophomores **Dan Cey** (.293, and yes, Ron's son) and **Ivan Lewis** (.317, 42 SB) will key the offense, but pitching will carry the Bears. **Ryan Drese** (5-5, 4.95) had a tremendous summer for the U.S. national team; he's joined by junior **Keith Evans** (7-6, 4.58) and sophomore **Jim Vorhis** (3-5, 4.32).

▶ **Texas (44-19):** Coach Cliff Gustafson is college baseball's all-time winningest coach, so a fine team should be no surprise, despite a two-year streak of failing to reach Omaha. The double-play combination of **Wylie Campbell** and **Kip Harkrider** returns—one of the finest in the nation—as does defending Southwest Conference batting champion **MacGregor Byers** (.380).

▶ **Oklahoma State (46-19):** The Cowboys are still looking for coach Gary Ward's first national crown. **Wyley Steelmon** is back after hitting .309 with 11 homers as a sophomore, as is catcher **Ryan Folmer** (.308). **Greg Dean** (9-1) leads the pitching staff.

—by Rick Lawes

Kotsay top of the class

With the pair of College World Series that Cal State Fullerton's Mark Kotsay has had, you have to wonder what he could possibly do as an encore. The sophomore has played in two series in two years with the Titans, he's already the CWS all-time leader in batting average and slugging percentage, and he's the only player ever to hit two grand slams in the CWS.

Perhaps what he can do is take more credit.

"I couldn't have accomplished anything I accomplished here without my teammates. They led the way for me, they guided me, they pushed me," Kotsay, 19, said after the Titans won the CWS, defeating the University of Southern California.

Said Fullerton associate coach George

Horton: "What Mark did here is the same thing he's been doing all year ... and he did it against the best college competition in the country."

Kotsay ended the season with a .422 average, 21 homers and 90 RBI. Also the Titans closer, he was 2-1 with 11 saves and a 0.31 ERA—allowing just one run all year in 21 outings (29 innings).

"If I'm a scout and I don't draft Mark Kotsay in the first round, then I'm making a big mistake," Horton said. "You can write this down: He will play in the big leagues."

Records tumble in power-packed series

In the 1995 College World Series, 22 records were broken, among them:
▸**Double plays in entire series:** 43.
▸**Home runs in entire series:** 48.
▸**Batting average for entire series:** .303
▸**Total bases for series:** 26, Geoff Jenkins, Southern Cal.
▸**Home runs in single game:** 3, J.D. Drew, Florida State vs. Southern Cal, June 6.
▸**Team batting average for series:** .372, Cal State Fullerton.
▸**Team home runs for series:** 14, Southern Cal.
▸**Team RBI for series:** 50, Southern Cal.
▸**Team total bases for series:** 131, Southern Cal.
▸**Team slugging percentage in series:** .648, Cal State Fullerton.
▸**Hits allowed by team for series:** 73, Southern Cal.
▸**Sacrifice bunts, both teams, championship game:** 5, Cal State Fullerton (4) vs. Southern Cal (1).
▸**Series attendance:** 182,759.

Cal State Fullerton teammates piled up on Mark Kotsay (bottom right) after he pitched the final out to win the College World Series. Cal State defeated Southern Cal by a score of 11–5.

Marketplace

- ▷ **Baseball-tie junkie**
- ▷ **On-line baseball**
- ▷ **DNA pen–The Club for sports cards**

- ▷ **Joe Carter's pine tar alternative**
- ▷ **Green baseball wear**
- ▷ *and more...*

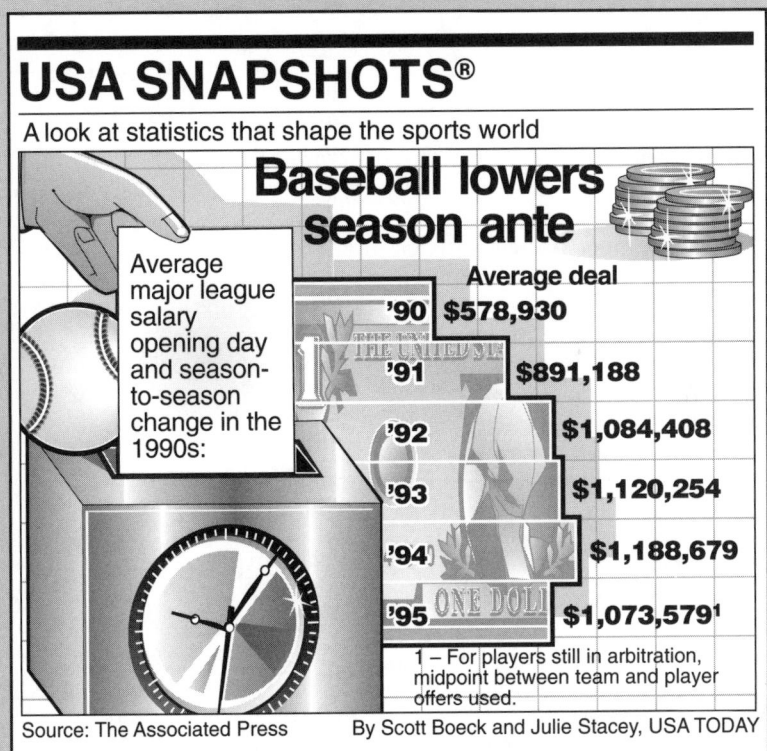

USA SNAPSHOTS®

A look at statistics that shape the sports world

Baseball lowers season ante

Average major league salary opening day and season-to-season change in the 1990s:

	Average deal
'90	$578,930
'91	$891,188
'92	$1,084,408
'93	$1,120,254
'94	$1,188,679
'95	$1,073,579[1]

1 – For players still in arbitration, midpoint between team and player offers used.

Source: The Associated Press   By Scott Boeck and Julie Stacey, USA TODAY

Baltimore Orioles' telecaster Mel Proctor says he has a "sickness" for buying baseball ties wherever he goes.

Who says there are no ties in baseball?

If you can tell a lot about a man by the way he dresses, what does it say about Orioles' telecaster Mel Proctor, whose obsession with baseball neckwear grows with each passing road trip?

"I need to see a psychiatrist," says the Prince of Ties, who owns nearly five dozen baseball ties. "I'm a junkie. I go into a store and I should have on handcuffs. It's awful. It's a sickness."

Proctor is not alone. Collecting ties with a baseball pattern has become a fashion statement among front-office employees, the media, fans and players. "In baseball, you don't want to get too formal," says Cubs president Andy MacPhail, who wore the popular Nicole Miller "Fly Ball" tie to the news conference announcing his hiring last winter. "When you wear a suit, you want to express the game's informality. The tie's a vehicle to do that."

"You go to the park and see other people wearing them, or you see somebody who has one you don't have, and it becomes a nice conversation piece," says Luis Mayoral, Latin American liaison for the Rangers and owner of more than two dozen baseball ties.

The baseball tie craze ignited in 1990, when Orioles' radio announcer and ESPN play-by-play man Jon Miller debuted Sunday Night Baseball telecasts by wearing a Nicole Miller print featuring colorful World Series ticket stubs.

"I started getting letters," Jon Miller says. "People actually starting sending me some ties in the mail....I became a tie junkie."

Many players and team officials spend their afternoons shopping. Says Proctor, "It gives me something to do on the road. My wife goes crazy every time I come back from a road trip because she knows I probably bought three, four, five ties."

Insiders say Minneapolis' Mall of America, the nation's largest mall, is the best place to find baseball ties. Stores in Boston, Kansas City, Atlanta, Anaheim and, of course, New York City are also favored.

At $60 each, the clever, hand-made silk Nicole Miller ties are not only expensive, but collectibles. There are never more than 1,200 made of each print. "If you've got money, you can find a Nicole Miller," Proctor says, who figures he has spent more than $2,000 on baseball ties. "But for me, it has become a challenge to find baseball ties in out-of-the-way places, the little stores."

—by Dennis Tuttle, a free-lance writer from Alexandria, Va.

Click: You're hooked! Fantasy goes on-line

Steve Pearson and the other 11 owners in the Federal League will finish their three-week fantasy draft this week without ever meeting face-to-face or talking on the telephone.

Fielding teams as far apart as Seattle and Gainesville, Fla., the league conducts all business over the computer network known as the Internet. By using personal computers with modems, phone lines and software, the Federal League has a reach rivaling any scouting system.

With baseball's work stoppage and subsequent late start this season, Internet-working kept alive the league Pearson participates in, says the 32-year-old computer programmer from Santa Maria, Calif.

"It would have been very, very difficult otherwise," says Pearson, who is in his second year with this league and is a competitor in another. "When it looked like the strike was about to be over, we had to verify that all the previous owners were going to participate. We had to find two [new] owners fairly quickly."

Creating a reliable and secure communications system was part of the reason the U.S. Department of Defense, along with universities and laboratories, joined to build the Internet more than two decades ago.

But for the baseball fan, today's Internet is much more than a glorified messaging system. Fans can trade comments about their favorite teams in bulletin-board-like Usenet news groups that have names such as alt.sport.baseball.redsox. They can chat about, or bemoan, labor negotiations in rec.sport.baseball and act like Bill James in rec.sport.baseball.analysis.

Bill Hayward, 35, of Chicago says he gets up-to-the-minute information on the Net. "In addition, it provides the opportunity to have meaningful discussions [electronically] with others who follow baseball closely, which is a great deal of fun."

Need to learn how to run a fantasy league, or perhaps just a formula for assessing performance? Check the files from baseball archives kept on computers at Swarthmore College in Pennsylvania, Washington University in St. Louis and the University of California–Berkeley.

Other files list rosters, Rotisserie player values, games by position, team and individual stats for previous years, even every box score.

"With a little determination and an eye for good solid information, you can arm yourself very well for any league," says Bill Lalor, owner of Fantasy Sports Northwest in Seattle. After operating other sports leagues on the Internet, Fantasy Sports Northwest is trying its first Internet baseball season.

Lalor expects the Internet to be a hit with baseball fans. Once a baseball fan checks out the World Wide Web, they'll be hooked, he says. The Web is a section of the Internet that allows on-screen display of headlines, text, photos, graphics, even video clips and sounds. This mix of media, hence its labeling as "multimedia," is organized in "pages" and can be looked at easily by pointing and clicking your computer "mouse."

"Every day there are more and more locations popping up, especially on the World Wide Web, that provide a wealth of baseball information," Lalor says. "Maybe that was one advantage of the strike—it allowed the true baseball junkie time to develop information centers."

The first baseball team to officially hit the Web is the Seattle Mariners. In its Mariners Home Plate site it mixes short video clips, photos of Ken Griffey Jr. and other players, and official Mariners press releases with ticket information and official Mariners jackets, jerseys, shirts and caps that you can order by phone.

Sports fans can click to reach the *Raleigh* (N.C.) *News & Observer's* Nando.net Sports Server, the first sports news service created for the Web.

All sports are covered, but each baseball team has its own "page" packed with up-to-date statistics and stories from the Associated Press and other sources, free for the reading (just register the first time you use it).

Two media franchises known for their exhaustive national sports coverage, ESPN and USA TODAY, hit the Web recently, too. Their on-line services, though run differently, seek to become the stopping place for sports fans.

ESPN teamed with Starwave, a company founded by Microsoft co-founder Paul Allen, to create ESPNet SportsZone, which became operational in early April. The site covers all sports, with insight from ESPN personalities.

When the baseball season starts, users can call up interactive baseball cards for each player. For now, the service is free; after a few months, ESPN and Starwave will review its success and decide on a pricing strategy.

USA TODAY's on-line service includes news, business, entertainment and weather information, but plans to focus on sports. Special software lets you dial into the service and, once logged in, you can cruise other Web sites.

The service costs $14.95 per month for three hours and $3.95 each additional hour. For an additional $49.95, you can add the USA TODAY Baseball Manager, which uses stats from the Elias Sports Bureau and can be customized to run your fantasy league.

Even Internet veterans admit fantasy leaguers aren't likely to toss away their newspapers and magazines or click off the TV soon. "It's an additional source," Lalor says.

But on the Net, adds Pearson, "I find intelligent individuals that discuss their hometown teams with in-depth coverage that I can get nowhere else."

—by Mike Snider, USA TODAY

Vehicles to get you on the electronic highway

Whether you play in fantasy leagues

or not, you can cover a lot of territory by roaming the Internet. Here's what it takes:

▶Equipment: A personal computer, preferably an IBM-compatible PC powered by a 486 microprocessor or a fast Macintosh with at least a 14,400-bit-per-second modem, some communications software and a telephone connection. This lineup is more power than what you need to "play" on the Internet, but will make for faster display of graphics.

▶How to get access: Many universities and workplaces have direct connections; talk to the computer systems people. Or buy an all-in-one package such as Spry's Internet in a Box (about $99, not including phone charges) with dial-up access and required software, at software retailers. Or find a local provider in the Yellow Pages, newspaper classifieds or a computer or Internet magazine.

All major on-line services—CompuServe (800-848-8199), Prodigy (800-776-3449) or America Online (800-827-6364)—have varying, and growing, degrees of Internet access—designed to make getting around on the Internet easier. If you've never been on-line, one of these might be your best bet. Plus, each has areas dedicated to sports information and chatting.

What's out there?

▶Electronic mail: Just as many offices have e-mail through internal computer systems, the Internet sends mail messages worldwide. You can also subscribe to electronic mailing lists. For example, you could send a message to the address listserv:majordomo@world.std.com that says simply "subscribe bosox" followed by your name to get on a list for Boston Red Sox fans. If this scares you, try one of the already mentioned on-line services or an all-in-one Internet package; they make these functions easy.

▶Internet USENET groups: Imagine some 10,000 electronic bulletin boards out there; naturally some deal with baseball. The USENET group name gives a hint about what might be discussed: rec.sport.baseball, rec.sport.baseball. analysis, rec.sport.baseball.fantasy, alt.sports.baseball.atlantabraves.

▶File Transfer Protocol (FTP): This lets you get files from other computers. For instance, Ken Emery's Internet Baseball Archive at Swarthmore College (http://ftp.baseball.org/pub/baseball/) and the University of California–Berkeley archive (ftp://ftp.baseball.org/pub/baseball/) are like clearinghouses of roster lists, Rotisserie values, games by position and stats.

Browsing the Web

▶The World Wide Web: This section of the Internet has been "upgraded" to allow the posting of photos, video, graphics and sounds. Web sites, actually computers called servers, let you call in and access information organized into "pages" using Web browsing software.

On the pages, some of the text will have hyperlinks (words like this are usually blue and underlined) that can zap you to another page at that location or to another page at another Web site.

Your browsing software may already have a search list. If not, try http://www.yahoo.com/entertainment/sports/baseball. That will give you a list of links including those listed in this story and many more.

The Seattle Mariners Home Plate is found at http://www.mariners.org.

Raleigh (N.C.) *News and Observer*'s Nando.net Sports Server is found at http://www.nando.net/sptsserv.html.

ESPNet's SportsZone is found at http://espnet.sportszone.com.

The Society of American Baseball Research (Halsey Hall chapter) Web site (http://www.skypoint.com/subscribers/ashbury/hhhomepage.html.) lists numerous links in addition to telling about how the organization works.

Web-savvy fans have already posted their own Web pages. Jason Kint (http://pear.wustl.edu/jekint/baseball.html) has a page dedicated to baseball in general, while Kevin Mahoney's is dedicated solely to the Cleveland Indians (http://oucsace.cs.ohio.edu/personal/kmahoney/Indians/ indians.html).

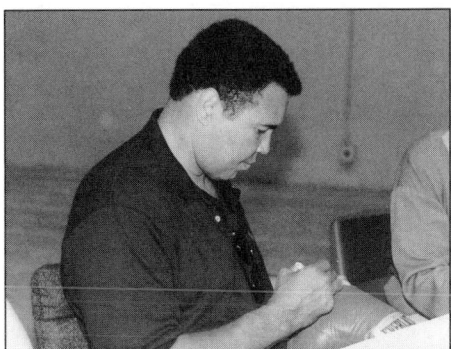

Like many other sports stars, Muhammad Ali uses the new DNA pen to sign forgery-proof autographs

By Ross Forman

DNA pen will limit autograph forgeries

The answer to stopping counterfeit autographs is DNA. Harlan J. Werner, president of Sports Placement Service of Malibu, Calif., unveiled the first Sports DNA Pen at the 16th annual National Sports Collectors Convention in St. Louis last July.

More than 40,000 collectors attended the four-day show and more than 50,000 free autographs were signed, although only Muhammad Ali autographs were signed with the DNA Pen.

How does it work? Some hair is snipped from the celebrity, then sent to a laboratory where fragments of DNA are isolated and diffused into ink to be used by a special pen.

Each signature will then automatically include the celebrity's actual DNA and, to further the anticounterfeiting process, the item is prestamped with a special thumb print, the date of the signatures, and the number of the signature with that particular pen.

"I see the Sports DNA Pen on par with The Club [used to stop car theft]," Werner said. "Sure, we're looking to capitalize on the fear of the collector and the insecurity of the business, but this is a guarantee that the autograph is authentic."

The pens are not for sale—only the process itself is being hawked at select card shows.

—by Ross Forman

Carter's new tack helps batters get a grip

Besides being one of the all-time sluggers, Joe Carter might leave another legacy to the game: cleanliness.

For years, most ballplayers have attained greater grips on their bats by applying a rag soaked with a thick, smelly substance called pine tar. Carter is not a fan of this baseball ritual.

"I've never liked pine tar because it's never been sticky enough," he said. "It would build up and it was a mess. It's a mess to carry around."

So Carter and his longtime friend and business partner, Bill Hildenbrand, went looking for an alternative. They found their answer at the University of Akron.

After a year of development by the school's Applied Polymer Research Laboratory, Joe Carter Enterprises perfected a product that "not only gives the batter a better grip, it's nowhere near the mess."

Called Tack Tube, it resembles a foam tube that's sliced open on one side. On the inside of the tube is a tacky polymer, which can be cleanly applied to a bat by wrapping the tube around the handle.

"I like it because it applies in cold weather; a lot of things we have would not really work in cold weather," said Carter, who began testing the invention last April when he set a major league mark with 31 RBI in the month. "You can put it in your back pocket, take it wherever you want to go and you don't have to worry about that buildup.... You can put your hands on the bat with this on, take your hands off, and it won't be on your hands."

Carter test-marketed the product using fellow major leaguers.

"I brought it out to the All-Star Game, and guys like Wade Boggs really liked it," he said. "And you know as picky a hitter as he is, that's something else."

Hildenbrand has the Georgia Tech team sold on the product. Ultimately, it's the aluminum bat market and its millions of Little Leaguers and softball players that Joe Carter Enterprises is after.

"When I was in college, we didn't have anything," Carter said. "We'd put the adhesive tape on backwards for a better grip."

Franklin has signed on as the exclusive distributor in the USA; Carlos Baerga is the company's representative in Puerto Rico. Suggested retail price: $6.95-$7.95.

Eco-friendly MLB sportswear maker recycles cotton

Fifteen years ago, it's safe to say, Bret Llewellyn wasn't the most politically correct of college students. "We threw our beer cans out the window and thought it was cool," he says. Now, the Alfred State College graduate is an environmentally friendly entrepreneur.

The raw material for his Underground Activewear, licensed by MLB Properties, is recycled goods. Llewellyn manufactures T-shirts, sweatshirts and hats using an innovative process that reclaims the cotton fibers wasted during normal textile production.

Eventually, Llewellyn expects to do $500,000 in business from his baseball line.

"We feel in two, three, four years, you'll see everyone recycling [in the apparel industry]," he says. "I went through all the major trade publications last month and they all had at least 10 stories or advertisements talking about recycled products. Fashion designers in Europe are using recycled stuff. This generation, they're all being brought up environmentally. We weren't."

Nostalgia

▶ **Luke Easter—gentle giant**

▶ **The true story of Wally Pipp**

▶ **Hall of Fame fighters**

▶ **Mulcahy: Great losing pitcher**

USA SNAPSHOTS®

A look at statistics that shape the sports world

Dressed for success

The New York Yankees have retired more uniform numbers than any team: 13. Most commonly retired numbers by all major league baseball teams[1]:

Number	Total retired
4	7
1/3/5	6
6/8/9/14/19/20/32/44	4

1 – Four players and a manager have had their numbers retired by two teams.

Source: Major League Baseball   By Aaron Cullers and Nick Galifianakis, USA TODAY

Luke Easter, the Indians' Gentle Giant, hit the longest homer ever (477 feet) at Cleveland Municipal Stadium.

Indians' Gentle Giant had late, great start

Name a player who became a major league star in his mid-30s after only a few years of organized ball. Michael Jordan tried, but Luke Easter succeeded.

Easter had just turned 34 when he broke in with the Cleveland Indians in 1949, but he told the Indians he was 28.

Easter, like Jordan, was an outsized performer, standing 6-4½ and weighing 240 pounds. He used his size to launch home runs that became instant legends, inspiring newspaper photos the next day with dotted lines showing where Big Luke's drive was last seen leaving the stadium. Bob Feller put him on par with Mickey Mantle and added, "The only man I ever saw with more power was the Babe."

Easter first attracted attention in the 1930s playing for semipro teams in the St. Louis area. But a professional contract eluded him, perhaps due to spotty fielding. After barnstorming with a team of black ballplayers called the Cincinnati Crescents, he won a contract in 1947 with the Homestead Grays—the New York Yankees of black baseball—just as integration of the majors sounded the death knell for the Negro leagues.

Easter was in that first wave of players to break the color line. Bill Veeck bought Easter's contract from the Grays in 1949 and sent the overage rookie to San Diego in the Pacific Coast League. He was an immediate sensation, batting .363, belting 25 home runs and driving in 92 runs in 80 games before going out with a busted kneecap at the end of June. Sportswriters freely compared him to Joe DiMaggio and Ted Williams.

Easter won the starting job as the Indians' first baseman in 1950. Over the next three seasons, he hit 86 homers and drove in 307 runs with a respectable .270 average. Along the way, he belted what was regarded as the longest home run ever hit in cavernous Cleveland Municipal Stadium— a 477-foot shot on June 23, 1950, into the upper right-field stands. In the fourth game of the 1953 season, Easter was struck by a pitch that broke a bone in his left foot and ended his major league career. But he continued his legend in the minors. In 1957 he became the first man to hit a ball over the 60-foot-high center-field scoreboard—400 feet from home plate—at Buffalo's Offermann Stadium. In 1959, he moved to the Rochester Red Wings, where he played until 1964. One sportswriter who came of age in Rochester during that time said, "I was convinced Luke Easter was the greatest man alive."

—by John G. Leyden, a free-lance writer from Davidsonville, Md.

Wally Pipp: The man Gehrig replaced

Lost among 70 years of blurred memories and distortions, the truth exists about how Lou Gehrig's 2,130 consecutive game streak began.

But since Wally Pipp, the man whom Gehrig replaced at first base for the New York Yankees in 1925, never revealed exactly why Gehrig replaced him, we are left to sort through the rumors and myth.

There will be no such distortion or questions for Cal Ripken—his every move has been chronicled. But when Gehrig broke Everett Scott's then-record of 1,307 consecutive games in 1933, it was little more than a footnote.

Pipp, who died in 1965, expounded several reasons why manager Miller Huggins didn't have his name in the line-up on June 2, 1925 (Gehrig's streak started the game before, as a pinch-hitter).

The most famous reason, and the most cited, is that Pipp had a headache from getting beaned in a previous game. It made good copy, but it wasn't totally accurate. (The beaning incident actually occurred on July 2 in batting practice, a month after Gehrig replaced Pipp.) Pipp might have had a headache. More likely, though, he was given a day off because he and the Yankees were struggling.

Meanwhile, Gehrig produced three hits in his second start and cracked 20 home runs that year, and was on his way to the Hall of Fame. But Pipp crafted a solid 15-year career that is often overlooked. He had a lifetime .281 average, 1,941 hits, and American League home run titles in 1916 and 1917, and he drove in more than 100 runs twice. But because of Gehrig's streak, Pipp became the brunt of jokes whenever a player took a day off.

Gehrig, on the other hand, became a legend. In addition to his ironman streak, he hit more than 40 homers in a season five times, produced more than 150 RBI seven times, and had a .340 career batting average with 493 home runs and 1,995 RBI. He was the first major leaguer to have his number retired. Once Pipp left New York and retired after the 1928 season, all people remembered was his alleged headache. But his family remembers a warm, fun-loving father who never took the slights seriously.

"My dad was more than just a guy who Lou Gehrig replaced," says Tom Pipp, 66, President and CEO of Pipp Mobile Storage Systems in Grand Rapids, Mich. "I think he was a better ballplayer than people make him out to be. Then he got this Lou Gehrig thing hung on him by every sportswriter in the country and it stuck. Don't get Pipped. Don't quit for a day. I bet it will become a word in the dictionary one day."

Tom Pipp said he never heard his father say he merited Hall of Fame recognition. But the records speak well, placing him among the top 15 in most Yankee offensive categories.

Noted baseball analyst and author Bill James concurs: "[Pipp] was a very good player. But in the game's history there are too many guys like that for him to be considered a Hall of Famer."

An interesting sidelight to the story occurred early in the 1924 season, when Boston thought Phil Todt was worth keeping rather than accepting the Yankees' offer of Gehrig—then Pipp's backup.

Todt? He batted .258 in eight seasons with 57 home runs, lending credence to the theory that some of the best trades are the ones you never make.

—by Joel Poiley, a sports editor with the Tampa Tribune

Wally Pipp's career stats

Career	G	AB	R	H
15 yrs.	1872	6914	974	1941

Avg.	HR	RBI	SB	Fld.%
.281	90	996	125	.992

During World War II, Army Sergeant Joe DiMaggio (far left) and Navy Chief Specialist Pee Wee Reese (third from left) signed baseballs for the big brass before an Army–Navy championship game. The Navy won 5–4.

War games: Hall of Fame exhibit tells of those who fought instead of playing

Bob Feller enlisted in the Navy two days after Japan bombed Pearl Harbor. He was the best pitcher in the majors, yet Feller gave no thought to his career when it came time to fight for his country.

"We were losing big in the Pacific and just as big in Europe," the Hall of Famer said from his home near Cleveland, where he pitched 18 seasons for the Indians and missed most of four others to World War II. "There happened to be more important things than playing baseball."

Thousands from the major, minor and Negro leagues traded their baseball uni-

forms for military uniforms. Their experience, and that of baseball on the home front, was told in "Baseball Enlists," an exhibit that opened last Memorial Day at the National Baseball Hall of Fame to commemorate the 50th anniversary of the end of the war.

Some of baseball's biggest stars went into the military. Joe DiMaggio joined the Army. Ted Williams flew planes for the Marines. Another two dozen players enshrined in the Hall of Fame also served in World War II, including Yogi Berra, Hank Greenberg, Ralph Kiner, Stan Musial, Jackie Robinson, Duke

Snider, and Warren Spahn.

The exhibit, which will run through the end of 1996, chronicles their contribution. It includes a seven-part video, along with wartime photos, mementos, equipment, scorecards and other 1940s artifacts. Some of the items:

▶ President Franklin D. Roosevelt's 1942 "green light" letter, telling commissioner Kenesaw Mountain Landis that baseball should continue during the war as a morale booster on the home front.

▶ Photographs of Manila's Rizal Stadium, where the diamond became a field of death in the savage fighting between American and Japanese troops during the battle for the Philippine capital.

▶ A 1940s St. Louis Cardinals cap with a Marine Corps insignia stuck on its bill. Pilots in the Pacific wore baseball caps when they weren't flying, a fashion statement that caught on with youngsters back home.

The exhibit also examines the era's social changes, with women getting more recognition on the diamond and the majors edging closer to integration.

—by Chris Carola

hitter going into the eighth inning at old Baker Bowl [in Philadelphia] when Vince DiMaggio [of the Boston Braves] hit a single. Tony Cuccinello got a double off me in the ninth. And I had another no-hitter going into the eighth the next year against Cincinnati at old Crosley Field when Ernie Lombardi hit a single." He won both games by shutouts.

Of greater joy than the two near no-hitters to Mulcahy are the two wins against Carl Hubbell, his hero: "To me he was the greatest man in the world besides my dad, and I never dreamed I'd ever meet him, much less beat him," Mulcahy told a Philadelphia sportswriter in 1946. He beat the Giants' Hall of Famer 3-2 at the Polo Grounds in 1940, and earlier that year, in what he calls the greatest thrill of his career, shut out Hubbell and the Giants, 7-0.

Mulcahy joined the Phillies in 1935, and by mid-1939 he was averaging more than 250 innings a year. In March 1941, he was the first major leaguer to be drafted into the war.

—by Robert Jackson, a free-lance
writer from New Castle, Pa.

The 'Phutile Phils': Mulcahy wasn't as bad as he looked

Hall of Fame pitcher Burleigh Grimes once told a scout, "If your winning percentage is as good or better than that of your team, you are a pretty good pitcher." By that benchmark, Hugh Mulcahy was a pretty good pitcher. In a four-year tenure (1937-40) with the Phillies, he was the losingest pitcher in baseball—40-76, a winning percentage of .344. But the "Phutile" Phillies' winning percentage was just .331. Any question about Mulcahy's ability under those circumstances was settled when he was selected for the NL All-Star team in 1940.

Still, Mulcahy has fond memories of those days. His best games: "I had a no-